Lecture Notes in Computer Science 12736

More information about this subseries at http://www.springer.com/series/7409

Xingming Sun · Xiaorui Zhang ·
Zhihua Xia · Elisa Bertino (Eds.)

Artificial Intelligence and Security

7th International Conference, ICAIS 2021
Dublin, Ireland, July 19–23, 2021
Proceedings, Part I

Editors
Xingming Sun
Nanjing University of Information Science and Technology
Nanjing, China

Xiaorui Zhang
Nanjing University of Information Science and Technology
Nanjing, China

Zhihua Xia
Jinan University
Guangzhou, China

Elisa Bertino
Purdue University
West Lafayette, IN, USA

ISSN 0302-9743 ISSN 1611-3349 (electronic)
Lecture Notes in Computer Science
ISBN 978-3-030-78608-3 ISBN 978-3-030-78609-0 (eBook)
https://doi.org/10.1007/978-3-030-78609-0

LNCS Sublibrary: SL3 – Information Systems and Applications, incl. Internet/Web, and HCI

This Springer imprint is published by the registered company Springer Nature Switzerland AG
The registered company address is: Gewerbestrasse 11, 6330 Cham, Switzerland

Preface

The 7th International Conference on Artificial Intelligence and Security (ICAIS 2021), formerly called the International Conference on Cloud Computing and Security (ICCCS), was held during July 16–19, 2021, in Dublin, Ireland. Over the past six years, ICAIS has become a leading conference for researchers and engineers to share their latest results of research, development, and applications in the fields of artificial intelligence and information security.

We used the Microsoft Conference Management Toolkits (CMT) system to manage the submission and review processes of ICAIS 2021. We received 1013 submissions from authors in 20 countries and regions, including the USA, Canada, the UK, Italy, Ireland, Japan, Russia, France, Australia, South Korea, South Africa, Iraq, Kazakhstan, Indonesia, Vietnam, Ghana, China, Taiwan, and Macao, etc. The submissions covered the areas of artificial intelligence, big data, cloud computing and security, information hiding, IoT security, multimedia forensics, encryption and cybersecurity, and so on. We thank our Technical Program Committee (TPC) members and external reviewers for their efforts in reviewing the papers and providing valuable comments to the authors. From the total of 1013 submissions, and based on at least three reviews per submission, the Program Chairs decided to accept 122 papers to be published in two Lecture Notes in Computer Science (LNCS) volumes and 183 papers to be published in three Communications in Computer and Information Science (CCIS) volumes, yielding an acceptance rate of 30%. This volume of the conference proceedings contains all the regular, poster, and workshop papers.

The conference program was enriched by a series of keynote presentations, and the keynote speakers included Michael Scott, MIRACL Labs, Ireland, and Sakir Sezer, Queen's University of Belfast, UK. We enjoyed their wonderful speeches.

There were 49 workshops organized as part of ICAIS 2021 which covered all the hot topics in artificial intelligence and security. We would like to take this moment to express our sincere appreciation for the contribution of all the workshop chairs and their participants. We would like to extend our sincere thanks to all authors who submitted papers to ICAIS 2021 and to all TPC members. It was a truly great experience to work with such talented and hard-working researchers. We also appreciate the external reviewers for assisting the TPC members in their particular areas of expertise. Moreover, we want to thank our sponsors: Association for Computing Machinery; Nanjing University of Information Science and Technology; Dublin City University; New York University; Michigan State University; University of Central Arkansas; Université Bretagne Sud; National Nature Science Foundation of China; Tech Science Press; Nanjing Normal University; Northeastern State University; Engineering Research Center of Digital Forensics, Ministry of Education, China; and ACM SIGWEB China.

April 2021

Xingming Sun
Xiaorui Zhang
Zhihua Xia
Elisa Bertino

Organization

General Chairs

Martin Collier	Dublin City University, Ireland
Xingming Sun	Nanjing University of Information Science and Technology, China
Yun Q. Shi	New Jersey Institute of Technology, USA
Mauro Barni	University of Siena, Italy
Elisa Bertino	Purdue University, USA

Technical Program Chairs

Noel Murphy	Dublin City University, Ireland
Aniello Castiglione	University of Salerno, Italy
Yunbiao Guo	China Information Technology Security Evaluation Center, China
Suzanne K. McIntosh	New York University, USA
Xiaorui Zhang	Engineering Research Center of Digital Forensics, Ministry of Education, China
Q. M. Jonathan Wu	University of Windsor, Canada

Publication Chairs

Zhihua Xia	Nanjing University of Information Science and Technology, China
Zhaoqing Pan	Nanjing University of Information Science and Technology, China

Workshop Chair

Baowei Wang	Nanjing University of Information Science and Technology, China

Organization Chairs

Xiaojun Wang	Dublin City University, Ireland
Genlin Ji	Nanjing Normal University, China
Zhangjie Fu	Nanjing University of Information Science and Technology, China

Technical Program Committee Members

Saeed Arif	University of Algeria, Algeria
Anthony Ayodele	University of Maryland, USA
Zhifeng Bao	Royal Melbourne Institute of Technology, Australia
Zhiping Cai	National University of Defense Technology, China
Ning Cao	Qingdao Binhai University, China
Paolina Centonze	Iona College, USA
Chin-chen Chang	Feng Chia University, Taiwan, China
Han-Chieh Chao	Taiwan Dong Hwa University, Taiwan, China
Bing Chen	Nanjing University of Aeronautics and Astronautics, China
Hanhua Chen	Huazhong University of Science and Technology, China
Xiaofeng Chen	Xidian University, China
Jieren Cheng	Hainan University, China
Lianhua Chi	IBM Research Center, Australia
Kim-Kwang Raymond Choo	University of Texas at San Antonio, USA
Ilyong Chung	Chosun University, South Korea
Robert H. Deng	Singapore Management University, Singapore
Jintai Ding	University of Cincinnati, USA
Xinwen Fu	University of Central Florida, USA
Zhangjie Fu	Nanjing University of Information Science and Technology, China
Moncef Gabbouj	Tampere University of Technology, Finland
Ruili Geng	Spectral MD, USA
Song Guo	Hong Kong Polytechnic University, Hong Kong
Mohammad Mehedi Hassan	King Saud University, Saudi Arabia
Russell Higgs	University College Dublin, Ireland
Dinh Thai Hoang	University of Technology Sydney, Australia
Wien Hong	Nanfang College of Sun Yat-sen University, China
Chih-Hsien Hsia	National Ilan University, Taiwan, China
Robert Hsu	Chung Hua University, Taiwan, China
Xinyi Huang	Fujian Normal University, China
Yongfeng Huang	Tsinghua University, China
Zhiqiu Huang	Nanjing University of Aeronautics and Astronautics, China
Patrick C. K. Hung	University of Ontario Institute of Technology, Canada
Farookh Hussain	University of Technology Sydney, Australia
Genlin Ji	Nanjing Normal University, China
Hai Jin	Huazhong University of Science and Technology, China
Sam Tak Wu Kwong	City University of Hong Kong, China
Chin-Feng Lai	Taiwan Cheng Kung University, Taiwan, China
Loukas Lazos	University of Arizona, USA

Sungyoung Lee	Kyung Hee University, South Korea
Chengcheng Li	University of Cincinnati, USA
Feifei Li	Utah State University, USA
Jin Li	Guangzhou University, China
Jing Li	Rutgers University, USA
Kuan-Ching Li	Providence University, Taiwan, China
Peng Li	University of Aizu, Japan
Yangming Li	University of Washington, USA
Luming Liang	Uber Technology, USA
Haixiang Lin	Leiden University, Netherlands
Xiaodong Lin	University of Ontario Institute of Technology, Canada
Zhenyi Lin	Verizon Wireless, USA
Alex Liu	Michigan State University, USA
Guangchi Liu	Stratifyd Inc., USA
Guohua Liu	Donghua University, China
Joseph Liu	Monash University, Australia
Quansheng Liu	University of South Brittany, France
Xiaodong Liu	Edinburgh Napier University, UK
Yuling Liu	Hunan University, China
Zhe Liu	University of Waterloo, Canada
Daniel Xiapu Luo	Hong Kong Polytechnic University, Hong Kong
Xiangyang Luo	Zhengzhou Science and Technology Institute, China
Tom Masino	TradeWeb LLC, USA
Suzanne K. McIntosh	New York University, USA
Nasir Memon	New York University, USA
Sangman Moh	Chosun University, South Korea
Yi Mu	University of Wollongong, Australia
Elie Naufal	Applied Deep Learning LLC, USA
Jiangqun Ni	Sun Yat-sen University, China
Rafal Niemiec	University of Information Technology and Management, Poland
Zemin Ning	Wellcome Trust Sanger Institute, UK
Shaozhang Niu	Beijing University of Posts and Telecommunications, China
Srikant Ojha	Sharda University, India
Jeff Z. Pan	University of Aberdeen, UK
Wei Pang	University of Aberdeen, UK
Chen Qian	University of California, Santa Cruz, USA
Zhenxing Qian	Fudan University, China
Chuan Qin	University of Shanghai for Science and Technology, China
Jiaohua Qin	Central South University of Forestry and Technology, China
Yanzhen Qu	Colorado Technical University, USA
Zhiguo Qu	Nanjing University of Information Science and Technology, China

Yongjun Ren	Nanjing University of Information Science and Technology, China
Arun Kumar Sangaiah	VIT University, India
Di Shang	Long Island University, USA
Victor S. Sheng	University of Central Arkansas, USA
Zheng-guo Sheng	University of Sussex, UK
Robert Simon Sherratt	University of Reading, UK
Yun Q. Shi	New Jersey Institute of Technology, USA
Frank Y. Shih	New Jersey Institute of Technology, USA
Biao Song	King Saud University, Saudi Arabia
Guang Sun	Hunan University of Finance and Economics, China
Jianguo Sun	Harbin University of Engineering, China
Krzysztof Szczypiorski	Warsaw University of Technology, Poland
Tsuyoshi Takagi	Kyushu University, Japan
Shanyu Tang	University of West London, UK
Jing Tian	National University of Singapore, Singapore
Yoshito Tobe	Aoyang University, Japan
Cezhong Tong	Washington University in St. Louis, USA
Pengjun Wan	Illinois Institute of Technology, USA
Cai-Zhuang Wang	Ames Laboratory, USA
Ding Wang	Peking University, China
Guiling Wang	New Jersey Institute of Technology, USA
Honggang Wang	University of Massachusetts Dartmouth, USA
Jian Wang	Nanjing University of Aeronautics and Astronautics, China
Jie Wang	University of Massachusetts Lowell, USA
Jin Wang	Changsha University of Science and Technology, China
Liangmin Wang	Jiangsu University, China
Ruili Wang	Massey University, New Zealand
Xiaojun Wang	Dublin City University, Ireland
Xiaokang Wang	St. Francis Xavier University, Canada
Zhaoxia Wang	A-Star, Singapore
Sheng Wen	Swinburne University of Technology, Australia
Jian Weng	Jinan University, China
Edward Wong	New York University, USA
Eric Wong	University of Texas at Dallas, USA
Shaoen Wu	Ball State University, USA
Shuangkui Xia	Beijing Institute of Electronics Technology and Application, China
Lingyun Xiang	Changsha University of Science and Technology, China
Yang Xiang	Deakin University, Australia
Yang Xiao	University of Alabama, USA
Haoran Xie	The Education University of Hong Kong, China
Naixue Xiong	Northeastern State University, USA

Wei Qi Yan	Auckland University of Technology, New Zealand
Aimin Yang	Guangdong University of Foreign Studies, China
Ching-Nung Yang	Taiwan Dong Hwa University, Taiwan, China
Chunfang Yang	Zhengzhou Science and Technology Institute, China
Fan Yang	University of Maryland, USA
Guomin Yang	University of Wollongong, Australia
Qing Yang	University of North Texas, USA
Yimin Yang	Lakehead University, Canada
Ming Yin	Purdue University, USA
Shaodi You	Australian National University, Australia
Kun-Ming Yu	Chung Hua University, Taiwan, China
Weiming Zhang	University of Science and Technology of China, China
Xinpeng Zhang	Fudan University, China
Yan Zhang	Simula Research Laboratory, Norway
Yanchun Zhang	Victoria University, Australia
Yao Zhao	Beijing Jiaotong University, China

Organization Committee Members

Xianyi Chen	Nanjing University of Information Science and Technology, China
Zilong Jin	Nanjing University of Information Science and Technology, China
Yiwei Li	Columbia University, USA
Yuling Liu	Hunan University, China
Zhiguo Qu	Nanjing University of Information Science and Technology, China
Huiyu Sun	New York University, USA
Le Sun	Nanjing University of Information Science and Technology, China
Jian Su	Nanjing University of Information Science and Technology, China
Qing Tian	Nanjing University of Information Science and Technology, China
Yuan Tian	King Saud University, Saudi Arabia
Qi Wang	Nanjing University of Information Science and Technology, China
Lingyun Xiang	Changsha University of Science and Technology, China
Zhihua Xia	Nanjing University of Information Science and Technology, China
Lizhi Xiong	Nanjing University of Information Science and Technology, China
Leiming Yan	Nanjing University of Information Science and Technology, China

Li Yu	Nanjing University of Information Science and Technology, China
Zhili Zhou	Nanjing University of Information Science and Technology, China

Contents – Part I

Artificial Intelligence

Big Data

Contents – Part II

Big Data

Cloud Computing and Security

Information Hiding

IoT Security

Multimedia Forensics

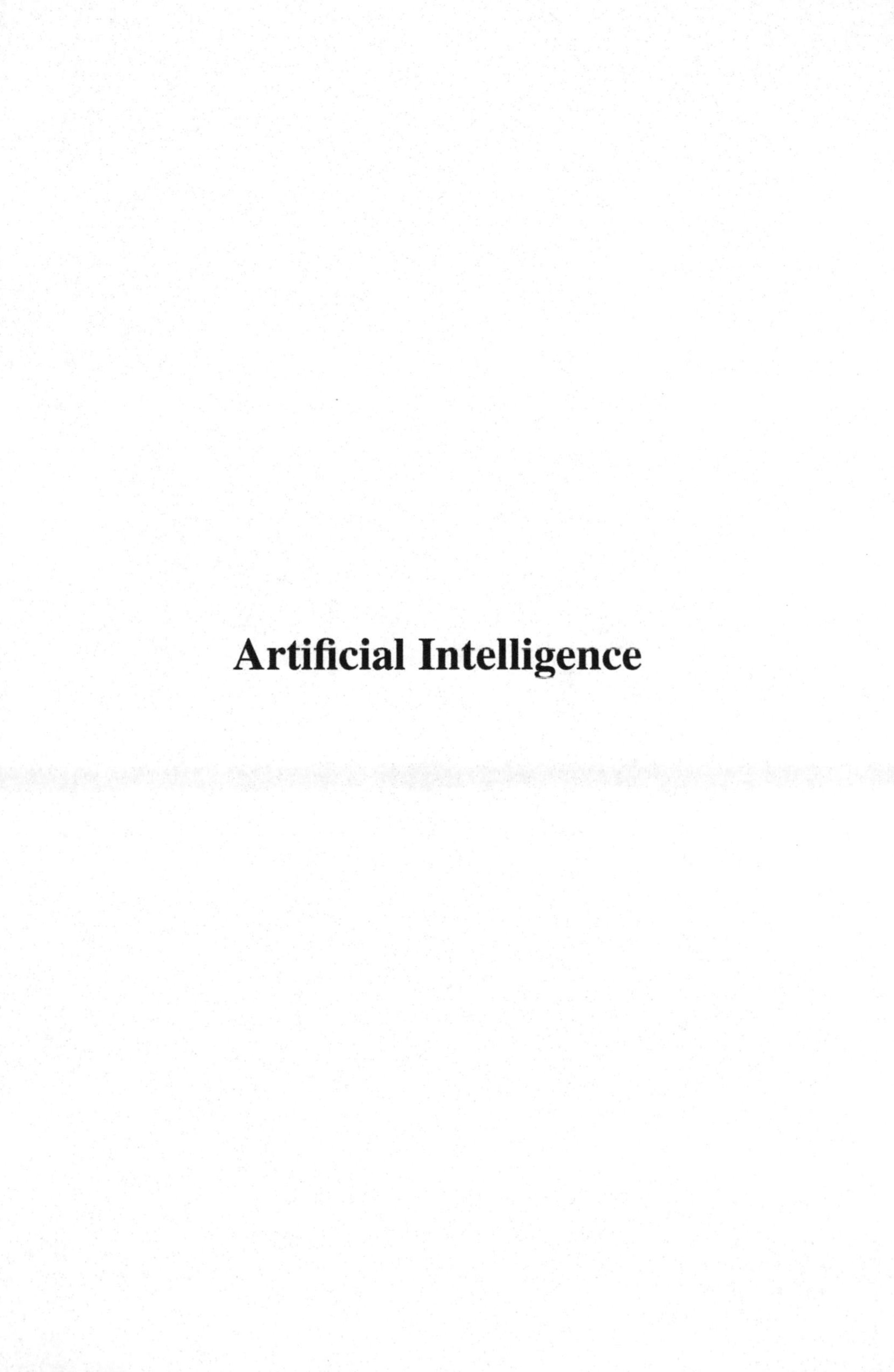

Artificial Intelligence

Research on Spoofing Jamming of Integrated Navigation System on UAV

Zeying Wang[1(✉)], Haiquan Wang[1], and Ning Cao[2]

[1] College of Software, Beihang University, Beijing 100191, China
[2] College of Information Engineering, Sanming University, Sanming 365004, China

Abstract. In order to conduct trajectory spoofing on Unmanned Aerial Vehicle (UAV) effectively, based on the analysis of the GPS spoofing jamming principle, combined with the control characteristics of the GPS/INS integrated navigation system to carry out the UAV spoofing trajectory planning. Firstly, according to the characteristics of UAV flight, the initial mobility constraint model of UAV is established. Secondly, the spoofing trajectory of UAV is planned under this constraint condition. Two trajectory planning algorithms for extension line and tangent line are proposed. Finally, simulation verification and analysis are conducted according to the proposed algorithms. The results show that both planning methods can deflect the UAV flight path, however, the planning method set by tangent is more strongly biased than the planning method set by the extension line, and the final spoofing effect is better.

Keywords: UAV · GPS/INS integrated navigation · Flight path · Spoofing jamming · Mobility constraint

1 Introduction

Since the advent of UAVs, which are widely used in various fields because of their strong mission capability, low manufacturing cost and low requirements for flight environment. While enjoying the technological innovation brought by drones, we should not lose sight of the problems brought by them. Although UAVs can improve the efficiency and save costs for users, many of them are illegal operations, which results in the "difficult management" of UAVs. It is of great value and significance to control UAVs by means of jamming method to eliminate various security accidents caused by the black flight of UAVs. Among them, spoofing jamming is more advantageous than the common type of suppressed jamming realized by power advantage. Spoofing jamming allows the UAV's receiver to successfully lock onto a spurious signal similar to the original satellite signal, thereby locating the wrong location [6, 7]. Ideally, the UAV is not aware that it has been disturbed and is finally induced to complete the task set by the fraudster. However, in reality, the UAV may detect that it has deviated from its flight path by detecting its flight status through INS. In this case, how to complete the spoofing of the UAV flight path more effectively is an urgent problem to be solved. There are differences in the types and technical routes of existing anti UAV means in various countries of the world. At

X. Sun et al. (Eds.): ICAIS 2021, LNCS 12736, pp. 3–13, 2021.
https://doi.org/10.1007/978-3-030-78609-0_1

present, the main technologies used are destruction capture [8], interference blocking [9], detection control [10], etc.

In order to effectively control the illegal activities of UAV, the wind is taken as deception signal in reference 11, and the kinematic model of UAV is redefined. A path tracking recognition algorithm is proposed. Through this algorithm, the relationship between deception signal and UAV heading angle is determined [11]. According to the characteristics of repeater deception jamming and generative deception jamming, the GPS receiver is used to obtain the current approximate position of the target, and then the observation and deception coordinates are sent into the space-time parameter model to obtain the deception signal parameters in Literature [12]. Reference [13] presents the implementation scheme of GPS repeater deception jamming system. Combined with the control characteristics of UAV GPS/INS integrated navigation system, position deception is completed by changing the calculation of each satellite signal propagation delay by the other GPS receiver [13]. Aiming at the problem of black flying UAV threatening airspace security, combined with the normalized innovation square detection of GPS/INS system and the principle of GPS deception, the influence of deception distance and GPS positioning accuracy on trapping UAV is analyzed, so that the UAV can be lured to the designated position without being detected by UAV [14, 15].

According to the principle of interference realization, it can be divided into generating spoofing jamming and forwarding spoofing jamming [16]. Generating spoofing jamming is based on the characteristics of satellite signals, which can independently highly imitate or fabricate satellite signals to generate spoofing signals and then impose spoofing [17]. However, forwarding spoofing jamming is to add a certain time delay on the basis of the original satellite signal to generate spoofing signal, and make the receiver track the spoofing signal through power advantage and other strategies, so as to get the wrong location to impose spoofing [18]. Up to now, many researchers still continue to study spoofing in depth, and most of them focus on forwarding spoofing, while the research on generative spoofing is less. In this paper, based on the research of spoofing principle, the forwarding spoofing jamming is carried out.

The simple GPS spoofing only focuses on the change of UAV's positioning position, without considering the role of INS in the navigation system [19]. From the perspective of integrated navigation, aiming at the constraint conditions that need to be satisfied in the course planning of UAV, this paper establishes a preliminary maneuverability constraint model and designs a deception trajectory planning method for UAV. Firstly, based on the research of the principle of forwarding spoofing jamming, this paper analyzes the work principle of integrated navigation. Secondly, according to the characteristics of the UAV navigation system, it studies the spoofing process and establishes a mobility constraint model. Then, under the constraint condition, the fraud trajectory of the UAV is planned, and two planning methods are proposed, the detailed derivation process is given. Finally, the simulation analysis and verification of the proposed planning methods are carried out.

In order to solve the aforementioned the trajectory spoofing on Unmanned Aerial Vehicle (UAV) problem, two trajectory planning algorithms for extension line and tangent line are proposed. Compared with the previous relevant results, the main contributions can be divided into the following two aspects. First, based on the related content of the GPS spoofing jamming principle, using the control characteristics of GPS/INS integrated navigation system, the trajectory planning of UAV spoofing is carried out. Second, two trajectory planning algorithms for extension line and tangent line are proposed to solve the problem of the UAV flight path, and the final spoofing effect of the planning method of tangent is better.

2 Forwarding Spoofing Jamming

The GPS receiver needs at least 4 satellite signals to achieve positioning. By tracking and demodulating the satellite signals, the satellite position and the pseudo-range to the receiver are calculated. According to the principle of pseudo-range positioning, the simultaneous equations are solved, and then according to Newton iteration and least squares method, the receiver position and clock difference information are calculated to realize the positioning and timing function.

Based on the above pseudo-range positioning principle, the forwarding spoofing jamming is that the other information of the satellite signal has not changed, but the propagation delay is increased, so that the pseudo-range observed by the receiver is changed, thereby achieving the purpose of interference [20]. The jammer receives the original satellite signal and then calculates the required delay according to the spoofing position. The original satellite signal is delayed and power is amplified to generate a spoofing signal, which is transmitted by the jammer, so that the receiver is deceived to receive the spoofing signal in a certain area, and then obtains the false pseudo-range, lead to get the wrong positioning, and achieves the purpose of fraud [13]. The principle of forwarding spoofing jamming is shown in Fig. 1.

In Fig. 1, J is a spoofing device, R is the receiver on UAV, and F is the spoofing position. After receiving the real satellite signal, J calculates the delays required for each satellite signal according to each position information, then spoofing device J changes the power of the adjusted satellite signal and forwards it to receiver R to locate the position F. Let the location of the spoofing device is (x_J, y_J, z_J), the position of the target receiver R is (x_R, y_R, z_R), the coordinate of the spoofing position F is (xF, yF, zF), and the coordinates of the i-th satellite are (xi, yi, zi), then the pseudo-range of the i-th satellite to the jamming source J is expressed as:

$$\begin{cases} \rho_i^J = P_{S_iJ} + c\left(\delta t_u - \delta t^{(i)}\right) + T_i + I_i + e_i \\ P_{S_iJ} = \sqrt{(x_i - x_J)^2 + (y_i - y_J)^2 + (z_i - z_J)^2} \end{cases} \quad (1)$$

In this formula (1), where P_{S_iJ} is the actual distance from the jammer to the satellite; $\delta t^{(i)}$ is the clock offset of the satellite; δt_u is the clock drift of the spoofing device; T_i is the tropospheric delay; I_i is the ionospheric delay; e_i is the pseudo-range observation error.

Similarly, the pseudo-range of the i-th satellite to R and the expected spoofing location F can also be expressed as:

$$\begin{cases} \rho_i^R = P_{S_iR} + c\left(\delta t_u - \delta t^{(i)}\right) + T_i + I_i + e_i \\ P_{S_iR} = \sqrt{(x_i - x_R)^2 + (y_i - y_R)^2 + (z_i - z_R)^2} \end{cases} \quad (2)$$

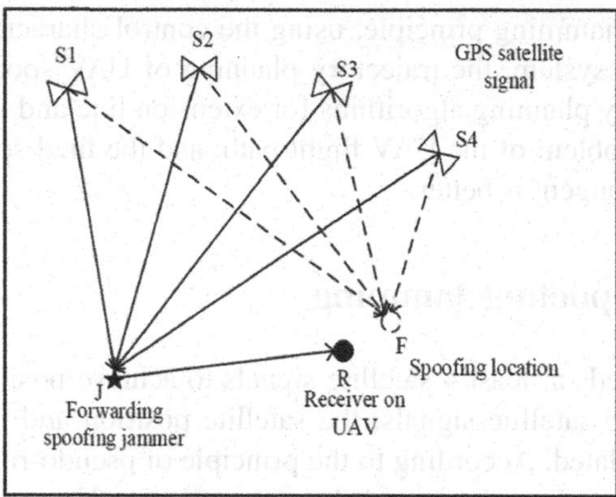

Fig. 1. Schematic diagram of forwarding spoofing jamming

$$\begin{cases} \rho_i^F = P_{S_iF} + c\left(\delta t_u - \delta t^{(i)}\right) + T_i + I_i + e_i \\ P_{S_iF} = \sqrt{(x_i - x_F)^2 + (y_i - y_F)^2 + (z_i - z_F)^2} \end{cases} \tag{3}$$

According to the GPS pseudo-range positioning principle, the key to the forwarding spoofing jamming is to calculate the delay value of each channel signal. If F is position that want to deceive, the delay required to forward each satellite signal via J is:

$$\Delta t_i = \left(\rho_i^F - \rho_i^J - P_{JR}\right) \Big/ c = \left(P_{S_iF} - P_{S_iJ} - P_{JR}\right) / c \tag{4}$$

P_{JR} is the distance between the jamming source J and the receiver R. In the case of calculating these delays, there may be an unreasonable deployment of the initial spoofing point location or the location of the jamming source, and thus the final forwarding delay may be negative. However, it is impossible to generate a negative delay in the actual engineering implementation, so delay correction is required.

Take $t_p = \min(\Delta t_i)$, the actual signal delay sent to R via J is:

$$\Delta \mathrm{t}_i = \Delta \mathrm{t}_i - t_p \tag{5}$$

It can be seen that it is possible to eliminate the existence of a negative value by delay correction, and not to change the preset spoofing position.

3 GPS/INS Integrated Navigation System Spoofing

3.1 GPS/INS Integrated Navigation

The inertial navigation system uses two kinds of inertial sensors, the gyroscope and the accelerometer, to measure the acceleration and other information of the UAV, and then calculates the navigation parameters such as the position, velocity and posture angle of the vehicle through integration algorithm. At work, the INS isolates the outside world and relies on the UAV's own equipment to complete the navigation task, which is characterized by concealment, independence and anti-jamming. However, the independence of the INS also makes the cumulative error gradually larger, and the navigation is biased.

GPS utilizes multiple navigation satellite signals that operate around the earth to provide users with continuous, real-time, and all-round high-precision navigation services. Users can obtain the current position or speed information at any time. However, because satellite signals travel to the ground over long distances, they are highly susceptible to be interfered through attenuation, occlusion, or multipath effects.

As can be seen from the above introduction, although both navigation methods are commonly used at present, they have their own advantages and disadvantages, which cannot meet the requirements of the advanced UAV navigation system. As shown in Fig. 2, as a "golden combination" navigation system, GPS/INS integrated navigation achieves high-precision and reliable navigation and positioning through complementing advantages and disadvantages of the two systems.

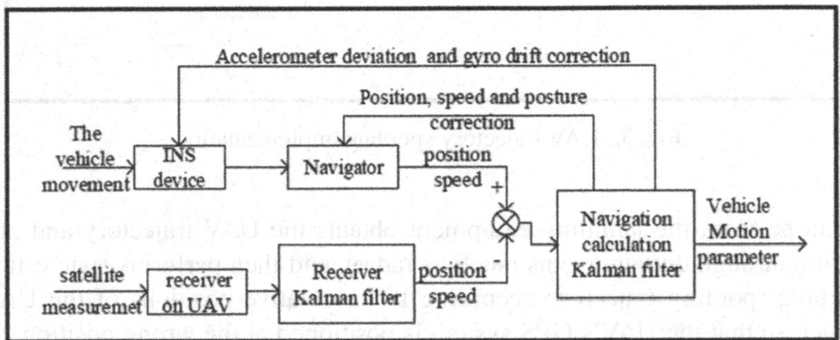

Fig. 2. GPS/INS integrated navigation system block diagram

The inertial navigation system provides the current posture and speed information of the UAV to the GPS navigation system to improve the antenna orientation accuracy. The GPS navigation system corrects the inertial navigation system's accumulated error over time through its accurate positioning function.

3.2 Spoofing Control of Integrated Navigation

Ideally, the deceptive jammer will cause the receiver to locate the preset error location by transmitting a spurious signal. During this time, the deceived device is often unaware of the jamming and is eventually induced to complete the task set by the deceiver. However, in reality, the UAV has its own navigation device, and the flight path is adjusted by detecting its own flight posture or flight condition. Based on the state described above, when spoofing jamming is performed, the UAV is not likely to operate directly according to the preset spoofing trajectory. Instead, it adjusts its own trajectory according to the original trajectory and the detected spoofing position. Therefore the final running trajectory is different from both the original trajectory and the spoofing trajectory.

Forwarding spoofing jamming deceives the receiver's location, which is the first step in UAV trajectory spoofing. In the integrated navigation system, the GPS measurement value is used to correct the cumulative error of the INS, and the positioning result of the INS also affects the final positioning result of the integrated navigation. Therefore, it is necessary to consider the role of INS in spoofing when conducting integrated navigation spoofing. The overall UAV navigation spoofing control process is shown in Fig. 3.

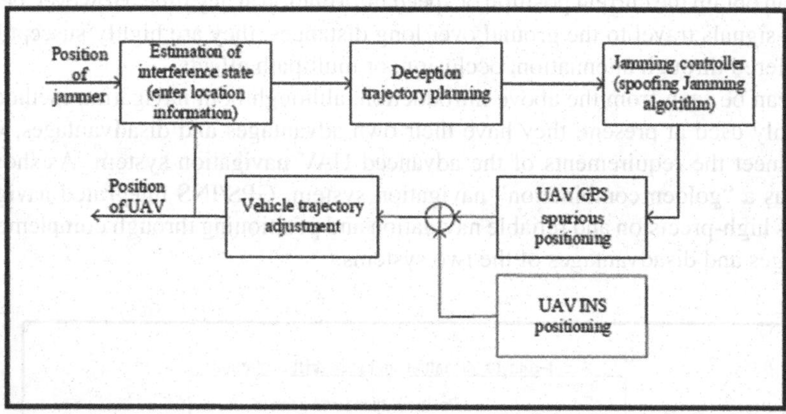

Fig. 3. UAV trajectory spoofing implementation

As can be seen, the jamming equipment obtains the UAV trajectory and position information through certain means (such as radar), and then performs state estimation and planning spoofing trajectory according to the relative positions of the UAV and the jammer, so that the UAV's GPS system is positioned at the wrong position. At this time, the UAV inertial navigation system adjusts the UAV's own flight path by providing wrong positioning information, so as to achieve the purpose of trajectory spoofing [21].

In the whole process of spoofing, the most core technology is the planning of spoofing trajectory. In this paper, the requirement of the UAV inertial navigation system is taken as a constraint condition to be satisfied in the flight path planning, and a preliminary mobility constraint model is established [22, 23]. The model mainly considers the two factors of UAV flight speed and posture control, that is, assuming that the UAV flies towards a certain position at a constant speed, the flight trajectory will be adjusted towards the target point at this speed no matter where the UAV is positioned. This paper proposes the following two spoofing trajectory planning schemes.

4 Spoofing Trajectory Planning

Initialize maneuver constraint conditions: in the two-dimensional coordinate system, the UAV's uniform flight speed v, jamming source position A(xA, yA), target position of UAV B(xB, yB) and UAV position P0 (xP_O, yP_O) are known. Then, the circle with UAV position as the center and v as the radius is all possible positions that UAV can reach.

4.1 Extension Line

As shown in Fig. 4, the actual position of the UAV is P0, and the next moment it reaches the circle with radius R = v. The jamming source is at A, and the UAV spoofing trajectory is planned as the extension line of the AP0. Due to the speed constraint, the distance between different spoofing points is R. The specific implementation process is as follows:

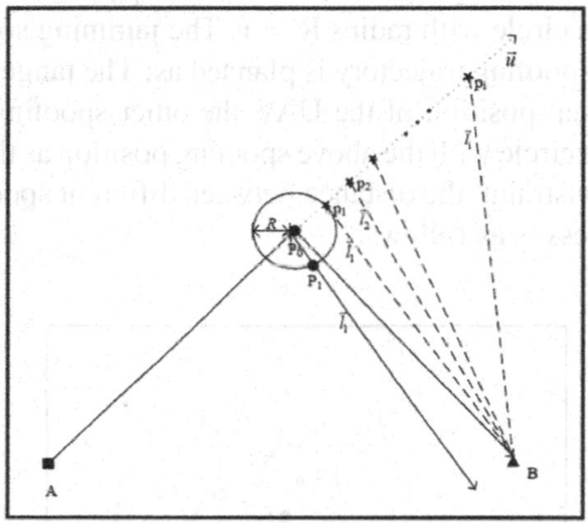

Fig. 4. Extension line planning method

$$\vec{u} = \left[\frac{x_A - x_{P_0}}{|AP_0|}, \frac{y_A - y_{P_0}}{|AP_0|} \right] \tag{6}$$

$$|AP_0| = \sqrt{(x_A - x_{P_0})^2 + (y_A - y_{P_0})^2} \tag{7}$$

1) Obtain the AP_0 direction vector $\vec{u}$:
2) According to this vector, the spurious signal from the jamming source causes the UAV to be positioned at a series of spoofing positions $p_i(x_{p_i}, y_{p_i})$.
3) At the point p1 of the first spoofing position, due to the existence of inertial navigation and other constraints, the UAV is still flying toward the point B, as indicated by the dotted line in the Fig. 4, thereby obtaining the flight direction vector $\vec{l_1}$ in p_1B direction:

$$\vec{l_1} = \left[\frac{x_{p_1} - x_B}{|p_1B|}, \frac{y_{p_1} - y_B}{|p_1B|} \right] \tag{8}$$

$$|p_1B| = \sqrt{(x_{p_1} - x_B)^2 + (y_{p_1} - y_B)^2} \tag{9}$$

4) The actual situation is that the UAV flies in the direction represented by this vector at point P_0, and there is a speed constraint, so that it will fly to the $P_1(x_{P_1}, y_{P_1})$ point at the next moment.

$$[x_{P_1}, y_{P_1}] = R\vec{l_1} + [x_{P_0}, y_{P_0}] \tag{10}$$

The next moment takes p_2 as the spoofing position and continue to deceive according to this spoofing process. Loop through this spoofing process and finally realize the setting of the spoofing trajectory.

4.2 Tangent Line

As shown in Fig. 5, the actual position of the UAV is p_0 point, and the next time the position is reached on a circle with radius $R = v$. The jamming source is at the A point position, and the UAV spoofing trajectory is planned as: The tangent to the circle whose center is the initial actual position of the UAV, the other spoofing position is B to the intersection point of the circle with the above spoofing position as the center of the circle, and due to the speed constraint, the distance between different spoofing points is R. The specific operation process is as follows:

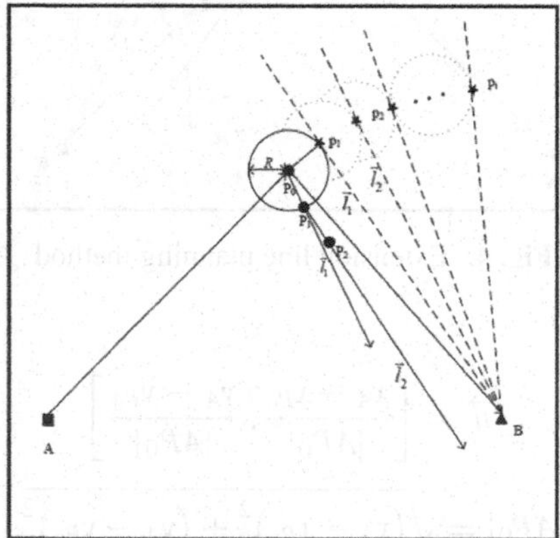

Fig. 5. Tangent planning method

In the triangle $\Delta P_0 p_1 B$, three conditions of P_0 coordinate, B coordinate, and $\angle P_0 p_1 B = 90°$ are know, $|P_0 B| = \sqrt{(x_{P_0} - x_B)^2 + (y_{P_0} - y_B)^2}$, $|P_0 p_1| = R$, $|p_1 B| = \sqrt{|P_0 B|^2 - |P_0 p_1|^2}$, list the equations shown in (11):

$$\begin{cases} \sqrt{(x_{p_1} - x_B)^2 + (y_{p_1} - y_B)^2} = |p_1 B| \\ \sqrt{(x_{p_1} - x_{P_0})^2 + (y_{p_1} - y_{P_0})^2} = |P_0 p_1| \end{cases} \tag{11}$$

Solving the equation to obtain the coordinates of the two groups of tangent lines at the spoofing position $p_1(x_{p_1}, y_{p_1})$, round off the tangent point closer to the distance, and keep the far tangent point.

At this spoofing location, the spurious signal from the jamming source causes the UAV to be positioned at the first spoofing position p_1. Due to the existence of inertial navigation and other constraints, the UAV still flies towards the point B, as shown in the dotted line in the Fig. 5, and the flight direction vector $\overrightarrow{l_1}$ is obtained.

$$\overrightarrow{l_1} = \left[\frac{x_{p1} - x_B}{|p_1B|}, \frac{y_{p1} - y_B}{|p_1B|}\right] \tag{12}$$

$$|p_1B| = \sqrt{\left(x_{p_1} - x_B\right)^2 + \left(y_{p_1} - y_B\right)^2} \tag{13}$$

The actual situation is that the UAV is flying in the direction of $\overrightarrow{l_1}$ vector at point P_0, and its arrival distance is at the point $P_1\left(x_{P_1}, y_{P_1}\right)$ position of R.

$$\left[x_{P_1}, y_{P_1}\right] = \overrightarrow{l_1} \times R + \left[x_{P_0}, y_{P_0}\right] \tag{14}$$

In the next moment, with p_1 as the center of the circle, $\Delta p_1 p_2 B$ triangle is obtained. According to the process of 1), 2), 3), the equation is set to calculate the intersection point p_2 of B to the tangent line, and set the location of the cheat position at this moment to obtain the new flight direction vector $\overrightarrow{l_2}$. And then the next actual flight position is obtained.

Finally, this process loops and finally completes the planning of the spoofing trajectory.

5 Simulation Analysis

According to the methods proposed in the previous section, using Matlab as the implementation tool, the theoretical knowledge was simulated and modeled to verify the accuracy and reliability of the scheme. The initial setting was carried out according to the constraint conditions proposed in the planning. Writing the code according to the formulas and the final simulation results are shown in Fig. 6.

In the simulation experiment, the position of the jamming source is marked by the asterisk; the position of the target point is marked by the triangle; and the position of the UAV is marked by the circle in the Fig. 6. The curves formed by each hexagonal shape are the planned deceived trajectory, while the curves formed by square shape are the actual flight trajectory of the UAV. Because the whole process is carried out in a cycle, so the cycle ending condition set in the simulation is as follows: the distance between the actual flight position of the UAV and the jamming source can be obtained in real time; when the actual distance between the UAV and the jamming source is gradually approached and then removed, the spoofing will be stopped.

By comparing a) and b) in the Fig. 6, it can be seen that both methods can pull the UAV to a certain angle, but the planning method with tangent line is more powerful than the planning method with extension line, resulting in better spoofing effect.

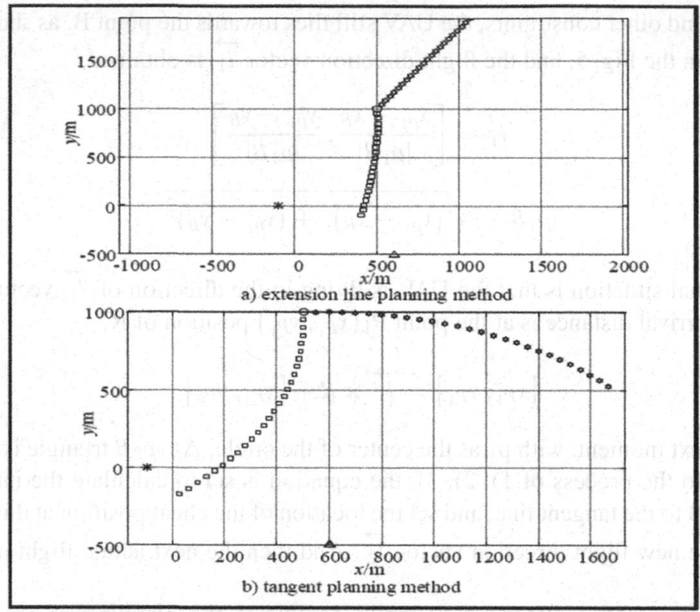

Fig. 6. Simulation diagram of cheat trajectory planning

6 Conclusion

In this paper, the problem of conducting trajectory spoofing on Unmanned Aerial Vehicle (UAV) effectively is studied. UAV GPS/INS integrated navigation is regarded as the interfered object. Based on the research of spoofing principle, the forwarding spoofing jamming is carried out. According to the characteristics of integrated navigation, two spoofing trajectory planning methods are proposed and verified by MATLAB simulation. The simulation process is based on the theory, and the simulation results verify the correctness of the theory to a certain extent, and provide guidance for the engineering implementation of jamming.

Acknowledgement. The authors received no specific funding for this study.

Conflicts of Interest. The authors declare that they have no conflicts of interest to report regarding the present study.

References

1. Lin, R.Z.: Research on integrated navigation of UAV based on inertial/GPS/optical flow. Ph.D. dissertation, Xian University (2018)
2. Qu, Y.J.: Research on INS/GNSS/VISUAL integrated navigation technology for small UAVS. Ph.D. dissertation, Harbin Institute of Technology (2020)

3. Tang, J.J., Hu, W., Liu, X.S., et al.: Unmanned aerial vehicle integrated navigation system based on SINS/ADS/MCP. J. Chin. Inertial Technol. **26**(01), 33–38 (2018)
4. Dong, W.: Research on attitude estimation and path planning algorithm for multi-UAV based on GPS/INS combination. Ph.D. dissertation, Yanshan University (2017)
5. Liu, M.: UAV integrated navigation system under GPS failure. J. Univ. Jinan (Sci. Tech.) **29**(02), 129–132 (2015)
6. Jeong, S., Sin, C.S.: GNSS interference signal generation scenario for GNSS interference verification platform. In: International Conference on Control, Automation and Systems, pp. 1363–1365 (2015)
7. Jeong, S., Kim, T., Kim, J.: Spoofing detection test of GPS signal interference mitigation equipment. In: International Conference on ICT Convergence, pp. 625–651 (2014)
8. Zhang, J., Li, R.W., Cui, K.T.: Analysis on the influence of UAV control means and UAV radio countermeasure equipment on air traffic control operation of Civil Aviation. China Radio **08**, 16–18 (2019)
9. Kerns, A.J., Shepa, D.P., Bhatti, J.A., et al.: Unmanned aircraft capture and control via GPS Spoofing. J. Field Robot. **31**(04), 617–636 (2014)
10. Zhao, Y.: Research on jamming countermeasure technology of civil small UAV. Technol. Manag. (12), 55 (2018)
11. Ma, C., Yang, J., Chen, J.Y., et al.: Path following identification of unmanned aerial vehicles for navigation spoofing and its application. ISA Transactions (2020). https://doi.org/10.1016/j.isatra
12. Liao, Q., Hao, J.M., Zheng, N.E., et al.: Research on GPS navigation interference method based on trajectory deception. J. Inf. Eng. Univ. **21**(02), 141–145 (2020)
13. Li, C.: Research on GPS deception jamming in UAV navigation system. Ph.D. dissertation, Nanjing University of Aeronautics and Astronautics (2017)
14. Wang, W.Y., Chen, C.: Method of trapping UAV equipped with GPS/INS integrated navigation system. J. Ordnance Equipment Eng. **41**(11), 212–217 (2020)
15. Fan, Y., Quan, C.: Combined application of GPS and inertial navigation system. Manuf. Autom. **34**(03), 68–69 (2012)
16. Cheng, X., Cao, K., Xu, J., et al.: Analysis on forgery patterns for GPS civil spoofing signals. In: 2009 Fourth International Conference on Computer Sciences and Convergence Information Technology, Seoul (2009)
17. He, L., Li, W., Guo, C.J.: Generative spoofing research. Comput. Appl. Res. **33**(08), 2405–2408 (2016)
18. Larcom, J.A., Liu, H.: Modeling and characterization of GPS spoofing. In: 2013 IEEE International Conference on Technologies for Homeland Security, Waltham, MA (2013)
19. Li, C., Wang, X.D.: Jamming technology of unmanned aerial vehicle GPS/INS composite navigation system based on trajectory deception. J. Nanjing Univ. Aeronaut. Astronaut. **49**(03), 420–427 (2017)
20. Huang, L., Lü, Z.C., Wang, F.X.: Spoofing pattern research on GNSS receivers. J. Astronaut. **7** (2012)
21. Xu, F.X.: Design and implementation of vector tracking loop for satellite navigation receiver. Ph.D. dissertation, Harbin Engineering University, Harbin (2017)
22. Yuan, C.: Research on anti-jamming technology applied on the GPS software. Ph.D. dissertation, Nanjing University of Aeronautics and Astronautics (2014)
23. Wang, H.Y., Yao, Z.C., Fan, Z.L., Zheng, T.: Experiment study of spoofing jamming on GPS receiver. Fire Command Control (07), 44–50 (2016)

Multi-penalty Functions GANs via Multi-task Learning

Hongyou Chen, Hongjie He(✉), and Fan Chen

Key Lab of Signal and Information Processing, Sichuan Province, Southwest Jiaotong University, Chengdu 611756, China

hjhe@home.swjtu.edu.cn

Abstract. Adversarial learning stability is one of the difficulties of generative adversarial networks (GANs), which is closely related to networks convergence and generated images quality. For improving the stability, the multi-penalty functions GANs (MPF-GANs) is proposed. In this novel GANs, penalty function method is used to transform unconstrained GANs model into constrained model to improve adversarial learning stability and generated images quality. In optimization divergence tasks, two penalty divergences (Wassertein distance and Jensen-Shannon divergence) are added in addition to the main optimization divergence (reverse Kullback-Leibler divergence). In network structure, in order to realize the multi-divergence optimization tasks, the generator and discriminator are multi-task networks. Every generator subtask corresponds to a discriminator subtask to optimize the corresponding divergence. In CELEBA and CIFAR10 data sets, the experimental results show that although the number of parameters is increased, the adversarial learning stability and generated images quality are significantly improved. The performance of the novel GANs is better than most GANs models, close to state-of-the-art models, SAGANs and SNGANs.

Keywords: Deep learning · Generative adversarial networks (GANs) · Adversarial learning stability · Multi-penalty functions · Multi-task learning

1 Introduction

Generative adversarial networks (GANs) is a popular and important generation model, it was invented by Goodfellow I J, et al. [1]. Adversarial learning stability is a classic and difficult problem in GANs [2, 3], it is directly related to the training convergence and generated images quality. In recent years, many GANs models have been proposed to improve the adversarial learning stability [2, 3], such as DCGANs [4], WGANs [5] and its variant models [6–9] etc. Although DCGANs [4] uses convolutional neural network (CNN) to replace the multi-layer perceptron (MLP) [1], but the design of the network is very skilled. Generally, improving the adversarial learning stability can be considered from the optimization objective function.

Different optimal divergence represents different objective function, some divergences are better than Jensen-Shannon (JS) divergence. WGANs successfully uses

X. Sun et al. (Eds.): ICAIS 2021, LNCS 12736, pp. 14–26, 2021.
https://doi.org/10.1007/978-3-030-78609-0_2

Wasserstein distance as objective function [5], compared with JS divergence, Wasserstein distance is more stable during training. It requires the discriminator to satisfy the 1-Lipschitz condition. WGANs-GP [6], WGANs-LP [7] use gradient penalty and Lp-norm normalization respectively to make the discriminator satisfy the 1-Lipschitz condition, gradient penalty and Lp-norm normalization replace the weight clipping of WGANs. BEGANs [8] uses the boundary balance strategy to optimize the Wasserstein distance, the generated images have some noise points. Some GANs models try to get rid of the 1-Lipschitz constraint, such as WGANs-div [9], GANs-QP [10] and designing GANs approach [11], usually increases the difficulty of the loss function design. LSGANs [12] uses Pearson divergence, D2GANs [13] uses mixed divergence (KL and reverse KL divergence), its objective functions are more complex. SNGANs [14] optimizes reverse KL divergence and uses spectral normalization to optimize the network parameters.

From the above, many divergences of GANs optimization are convex functions, such as WGANs [5], LSGANs [12], D2GANs [13], SNGANs [14], etc. Due to the strategy diversity in zero-sum game and the possibility of neural network falling into local optimal solution, the optimization problem of GANs can still be regarded as non-convex optimization problem [2, 3]. In addition, the above GANs models only optimize their divergences without any additional constraint, they belong to unconstrained optimization problems. Non-convex and unconstrained optimization weaken the adversarial learning stability. Fortunately, in order to obtain better and more stable solutions to these situations, penalty function method is widely used.

In this work, in order to improve the stability, training effects of GANs and reach better local optimal solution, a multi-penalty functions GANs (MPF-GANs) is proposed. Its main optimization divergence is reverse KL divergence, and its constrained optimization divergences are W distance and JS divergence. In generator structure, it is a multi-task network with three outputs. In discriminator structure, it is a multi-task residual network with three outputs. A generator subtask and a discriminator subtask optimize a divergence. The main contributions are as follows.

A. The unconstrained optimization problem of GANs is transformed into a constrained optimization problem, and its optimization objective functions are designed by penalty function method. Find a group of divergence combination which can effectively improve the adversarial learning stability and training effect, select the reverse KL divergence as the main optimization function, W distance and JS divergence as the penalty functions (*See* Sects. 4.1*and* 4.2 *for details*).
B. In order to facilitate the implementation of the MPF-GANs, the generator and discriminator are designed as a multi-task convolution network and a multi-task residual network, respectively. Every multi-task network consists of three branch networks, one learning reverse KL divergence and the other two learning W distance and JS divergence, respectively. Multi-task network can share the shallow layers and middle layers, so that the tasks can not only constrain each other, but also not affect the main optimization function too much (*See* Sect. 4.2 *for details*).
C. Many experiments are done to test the performance of MPF-GANs, and the experimental results are compared with most GANs. It can effectively improve the stability adversarial learning and generated images quality. Its training effects are better than

most GANs and close to the state-of-the-art models, SAGANs and SNGANs (*See* Sect. 5 *for details*).

2 Related Work

2.1 Adversarial Learning Stability

Adversarial learning stability is always a difficulty [2, 3] during training GANs. Usually, improving the stability can be considered from the aspects of optimization objective function, balance of generator and discriminator and so on.

A. *Objective function.* Optimizing JS divergence is more likely to lead to instability, W distance can be used to replace JS divergence, such as WGANs [5], WGANsGP [6], WGANsLP [7]. These GANs models need discriminator to satisfy 1-Lipschitz condition. BEGANs [8] optimizes the Wasserstein distance via boundary balance strategy. WGANs-div [9], GANs-QP [10] and designing GANs approach [11] may not consider the 1-Lipschitz condition. Pearson, mixed divergence and reverse KL divergence can also be used to replace JS divergence also, such as LSGANs [12], D2GANs [13] and SNGANs [14], respectively.
B. *Balance of generator and discriminator*. The balance between generator and discriminator will affect the adversarial learning stability. Turing GANs [15], Relativistic GANs [16] and VDB-GANs [17] improve the adversarial learning stability by increasing the difficulty of discriminator classification task. These GANs models achieve this goal through Turing test condition, relativistic discriminator and variational bottleneck layer in discriminator, respectively.
C. *Some other models.* In addition to the above methods, some other methods can also improve the stability. LP-GANs [18], PG-GANs [19] and MSG-GANs [20] are progressive growing strategy GANs models. These GANs can also reduce the convergence difficulty. Constructing GANs that satisfy some strict mathematical properties, such as function smoothness, can also improve the stability [21]. SAGANs [22] integrates self-attention mechanism. SSGANs [23] integrates self-supervised learning method. Realness GANs [24] uses two anchor distributions replace the expected labels of discriminator output.

From the above, almost all GANs models are optimized for single divergence, the generator is a single task network. Multi-divergence optimization based on multi-penalty functions method is not widely used in GANs adversarial learning.

2.2 Penalty Function Method

In order to obtain more stable and accurate solutions, penalty function method is widely used in many optimization problems. Folding concave penalty combined with local linear approximation algorithm can increase the accuracy of local optimal solution [25]. Dual optimization combined with penalty function method, such as Lagrange method, can be used to deal with nonlinear optimization problems [26]. By introducing smooth and exact L1 penalty function, it can make the approximate solution closer to the theoretical optimal solution [27]. In multi-dimensional PDE control optimization problem and high-dimensional linear regression problem, the penalty function method is still effective [28, 29].

The effectiveness of the penalty function method is verified in many optimization problems. It can make the original optimization problem obtain more stable and accurate local optimal solution.

3 Generative Adversarial Networks

GANs uses the principle of two-player zero-sum game, generator and discriminator are two game players [1–3]. The generator G simulates the implicit distribution of training images via different random vectors, the discriminator D classifies the training images and generated images. Remember that random vector set is Z, training set is X. z and x are their samples, respectively. $G(Z)$ is the generated images set, and its probability density is $f_G(x)$. The probability density function of X is $f_X(x)$. Then the loss functions of G and D are [1],

$$loss_D = \frac{1}{m}\left[\sum_{i=1}^{m} \log D(x_i) + \sum_{i=1}^{m} \log(1 - D(G(z_i)))\right] \tag{1}$$

$$loss_G = \frac{1}{m}\sum_{i=1}^{m} \log(1 - D(G(z_i))) \tag{2}$$

Where m is batch size. According to the above equations, the minimax two-player zero-sum game of GANs is [1],

$$\min_G \max_D V(G, D) = E_{x \sim f_X(x)}[\log D(x)] + E_{z \sim f_Z(z)}[\log(1 - D(G(z)))] \tag{3}$$

In Eq. (3), if and only if $f_G(x) = f_X(x)$, the theoretical optimal solution is achieved. From Eqs. (1)–(3), its optimized divergence is $\mathrm{JS}(f_X(x) \parallel f_G(x))$ [1]. Different optimization objective functions represent different optimization divergences. From the perspective of optimization problems, it can be expressed as the following unconstrained optimization problem, adversarial learning is only the method to realize this optimization problem.

$$\min JS(f_X(x) \,||\, f_G(x)) \tag{4}$$

It is obvious that different GANs objective functions only need to replace the optimization divergence in Eq. (4), such as WGANs [5] is minimize $\mathrm{W}(f_X(x), f_G(x))$, LSGANs [12] is minimize $\mathrm{Pearson}(f_X(x) \parallel f_G(x))$.

4 MPF-GANs

In this section, firstly, it introduces the transformation of unconstrained GANs model into constrained GANs model via multi-penalty functions method. Secondly, it introduces the network structure of novel GANs model and its specific objective functions. Finally, it explains the training method of the proposed GANs model.

4.1 Multi-penalty Functions Method in GANs

In unconstrained optimization problem, penalty function method is widely used to improve the accuracy and stable of the original optimization problem, such as references [25–27]. If div($f_X(x) \parallel f_G(x)$) represents a divergence, such as JS, KL, Pearson or others. Comparison Eq. (4), the objective functions of multi-penalty functions GANs can be expressed as,

$$\begin{cases} \min \; div(f_X(x)\,||f_G(x)) \\ s.t \; div_i(f_X(x)\,||f_G(x)) = 0, i = 1, 2, \ldots, k \end{cases} \tag{5}$$

Where, div($f_X(x) \parallel f_G(x)$) is main optimization function, div$_i$($f_X(x) \parallel f_G(x)$) is one of penalty functions. Thus, this GANs optimization problem is transformed into a constrained GANs model.

Considering the performance of reverse KL divergence in practice, such as state-of-the-art SNGANs [14], reverse KL divergence is selected as the main optimized divergence. In penalty functions, W distance and JS divergence are selected. JS divergence is usually more unstable than other divergence [5], using it as a penalty function can make the main optimization function jump out of some local optimal solutions. The similar method is likes simulated annealing. W distance can avoid gradient vanishing [5–7], it can narrow the search range of feasible solutions, stabilize the adversarial learning. Then, the unconstrained optimization is transformed into constrained optimization,

$$\begin{cases} \min \; div(f_X(x)\,||f_G(x)) \\ s.t \; W(f_X(x), f_G(x)) = 0, JS(f_X(x)\,||f_G(x)) = 0 \end{cases} \tag{6}$$

Obviously, W distance and KL divergence are 0 if and only if $f_X(x) = f_G(x)$, and the minimum value is 0, which is obviously in line with the optimization purpose of GANs. Thus, through multi-penalty functions method, its new objective function is,

$$\min F(x, \lambda_1, \lambda_2) = reverse\,KL + \lambda_1 W + \lambda_2 JS \tag{7}$$

Where $F(\cdot)$ is new objective function. λ_1 and λ_2 are penalty factors, which can usually set the same positive real number.

4.2 Network Structure and Its Objective Functions

The multi-task learning technique [30, 31] facilitates the use of a neural network to optimize multiple different tasks, the shallow and middle layers of multi-task sharing can make each task restrict each other, but not affect the main task too much. In MPF-GANs, the generator is designed as a multi-task learning network with one input and three outputs to optimize reverse KL divergence, W distance, and JS divergence. In the classification network, the residual network [32, 33] can make reasonable use of the shallow features to improve the classification accuracy and reduce the vanishing gradient. The multi-task discriminator is designed as a binary classification model with shallow residual blocks.

As shown in Fig. 1, MPF-GANs contains a multi-task convolution network generator and a multi-task residual network discriminator. $G(z)$ and D are to optimize the main task, reverse KL($f_X(x) \| f_G(x)$). $G_1(z)$ and x are to optimize the W($f_X(x), f_G(x)$). $G_2(z)$ and D_2 are to optimize the JS($f_X(x) \| f_G(x)$). $G(z)$, $G_1(z)$, $G_2(z)$ are generator subtasks. D, D_1, D_2 are discriminator subtasks, *Resblock3* and *Resblock4* don't share the parameters, just *Resblock1* and *Resblock2* share parameters (Fig. 2).

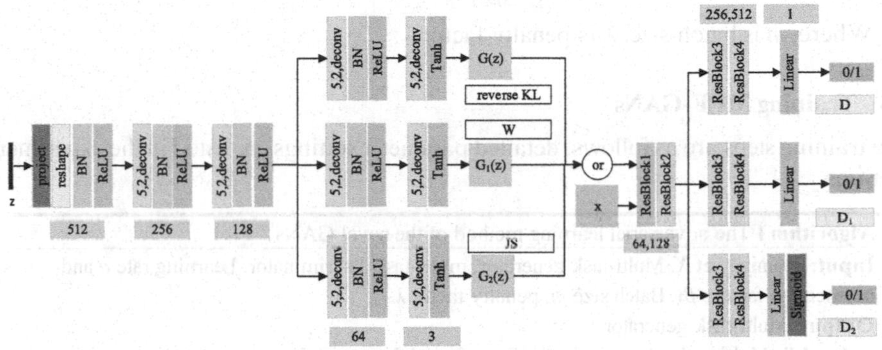

Fig. 1. Network structure of MPF-GANs. In *deconv block*, 5 is convolution kernel size, 2 is convolution stride size. *Resblock* is shallow residual block. The feature map channels are marked, such as 512, 256, 128, etc.

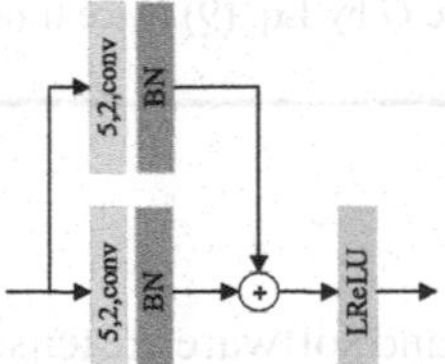

Fig. 2. Shallow residual block. In *conv block*, 5 is convolution kernel size, 2 is convolution stride size. '+' represents feature maps addition operation. In Fig. 1, *Resblock1* without BN operation, *Resblock2* to *Resblock4* contain BN operation.

In Fig. 1, reverse KL divergence via hinge loss function [14], W distance via WGANs loss functions [5], JS divergence via cross entropy loss function [1]. All loss functions as follows.

$$loss_D = \frac{1}{m}\left[\sum_{i=1}^{m} \min(0, -1 + D(x_i)) + \sum_{i=1}^{m} \min(0, -1 - D(G(z_i)))\right] \tag{8}$$

$$loss_G = -\frac{1}{m}\sum_{i=1}^{m} D(G(z_i)) \tag{9}$$

$$loss_{D_1} = \frac{1}{m}\left[\sum_{i=1}^{m} D_1(x_i) - \sum_{i=1}^{m} D_1(G_1(z_i))\right] \tag{10}$$

$$loss_{G_1} = -\lambda\frac{1}{m}\sum_{i=1}^{m} D_1(G_1(z_i)) \tag{11}$$

$$loss_{D_2} = \frac{1}{m}\left[\sum_{i=1}^{m} \log D_2(x_i) + \sum_{i=1}^{m} \log(1 - D_2(G_2(z_i)))\right] \quad (12)$$

$$loss_{G_2} = \lambda \frac{1}{m} \sum_{i=1}^{m} \log(1 - D_2(G_2(z_i))) \quad (13)$$

Where, m is batch size, λ is penalty factor.

4.3 Training MPF-GANs

The training steps are as follows, detailed parameter settings are listed in the experiment sections.

Algorithm 1 The adversarial learning method of the novel GANs

Input: Training set X. Multi-task generator, multi-task discriminator. Learning rate α and momentum factors β_1. Batch size m, penalty factor λ.

Output: Multi-task generator

1: **while** Multi-task generator has not converged **do**
2: Sample $\{x_i\}_{i=1}^{m} \sim f_X(x)$ a batch of training samples. Sample $\{z_i\}_{i=1}^{m} \sim f_Z(z)$ a batch of random vectors.
3: Update D_1 by Eq. (10), weight clipping once time. Update G_1 by Eq. (11). Adam.
4: Update D_2 by Eq. (12). Update G_2 by Eq. (13). Adam.
5: Update D by Eq. (8). Update G by Eq. (9) twice times. Adam.
6: **end while**

5 Experiments

In this section, the main hardware and software are tensorflow 1.13.1, pytorch 1.2.0 GPU version, CUDA 10.0 SDK, cudnn 7.6, opencv 3.4. GPUs include NVIDIA gtx1080, gtx1080ti, rtx2080ti. The other parts are as follows.

5.1 Evaluation Metrics and Data Sets

Two of the most commonly used indices are selected to evaluate the generated image quality, which are Inception Score (IS) [14, 22], Frechet Inception Distance (FID) [14, 22]. IS is the higher the better, FID is the lower the better. In Training data set, two most commonly used open data sets are selected, which are CELEBA and CIFAR10. In the CELEBA, the first 50,000 image are selected, and these images are cut out 64×64 pixel size as training set. CIFAR10 training set contains 50,000 color images, every image is 32×32 pixels.

5.2 Penalty Factor λ of MPF-GANs

Table 1 shows the experiment results via different penalty factor λ. Every experiment generated 50,000 images. From Table 1, it can be seen that penalty factor λ has influence on training effects. When λ is 1.0e−3, it can reach the best FID, and well IS in CELEBA and CIFAR10, that is to say, it can simulate training set distribution better and diversity expression.

Table 1. Results in CELEBA and CIFAR10 via different penalty factor λ

Image source	Epoch	λ	IS ($\sigma \times 0.01$)	IS ($\sigma \times 0.1$)	FID	
			CELEBA	CIFAR10	CELEBA	CIFAR10
Training set	–	–	2.71 ± 2.48	10.70 ± 1.47	0.00	0.00
Generated images	23	1.0e−2	2.07 ± 4.65	5.93 ± 0.62	28.14	51.27
	23	1.0e−3	2.05 ± 4.88	**6.13** ± 0.55	**24.33**	**42.13**
	23	1.0e−4	**2.09** ± 5.51	5.83 ± 0.42	33.30	52.50

5.3 Experiments of MPF-GANs

In this section, reverse KL divergence GANs and MPF-GANs are tested. Reverse KL divergence via hinge loss function [14] and its neural network is the same as DCGANs [4]. MPF-GANs tested that the discriminators are CNN and ResNet, respectively. The reverse KL divergence basic settings are RMSProp, learning rate is 0.0002, momentum factor is 0.9, batch size is 64. In MPF-GANs, the basic settings are Adam, 0.0002, 0.5, batch size is 64, penalty factor λ is 1.0e−3. All experimental results come from the same computer, it has a rtx2080ti GPU. Every experiment generated 50,000 images.

In CELEBA Table 2, when the network is CNN, hinge loss effects are worse than the MPF-GANs. At the same time, in MPF-GANs (CNN and ResNet), ResNet discriminator effects are better than the CNN discriminator. The MPF-GANs (ResNet) performs best in IS and FID, MPF-GANs (ResNet) can best simulate the training set distribution. Because MPF-GANs needs training multiple divergences, and ResNet network parameter complexity is larger than CNN, the training time of hinge loss (single task) is the least, followed by MPF-GANs (CNN), and MPF-GANs (ResNet) is the most. In Table 3, it has similar effects in CIFAR10.

Table 2. Convergence effects in CELEBA

GANs	Parms/M	Epoch	Time/s	IS ($\sigma \times 0.01$)	FID
Training set	–	–	–	2.71 ± 2.48	0.00
Hinge GANs (CNN)	9.45	23	**2547.22**	1.97 ± 5.40	39.17
Ours (CNN)	18.08	23	3885.04	2.02 ± 4.15	28.01
Ours (ResNet)	30.59	23	5879.48	**2.05** ± 4.88	**24.33**

5.4 Experiments of Different GANs

To verify the performance of the proposed GANs, many GANs are tested. Table 4 and Table 5 show the final training effects in CELEBA and CIFAR10. LSGANs, WGANs, Realness GANs, RGANs have the same or basically same as DCGANs network structure. SNGANs and SAGANs are two state-of-the-art models.

Table 3. Convergence effects in CIFAR10

GANs	Parameters/M	Epoch	Time/s	IS ($\sigma \times 0.1$)	FID
Training set	–	–	–	10.70 ± 1.47	0.00
Hinge GANs (CNN)	8.83	23	**1574.09**	5.73 ± 0.32	52.17
Ours (CNN)	17.45	23	2377.54	5.97 ± 0.64	48.58
Ours (ResNet)	29.95	23	3431.35	**6.13** ± 0.55	**42.13**

Table 4. Results in CELEBA with different GANs.

GANs	Parms/M	Epoch	Divergence	IS ($\sigma \times 0.01$)	FID
Training set	–	–	–	2.71 ± 2.48	0.00
BEGANs [8]	4.47	35	W	1.76 ± 1.18	48.65
DCGANs [4]	9.45	25	JS	1.92 ± 1.13	49.69
LSGANs [12]	9.45	35	Pearson	1.96 ± 2.17	39.85
WGANs [5]	9.45	35	W	2.01 ± 2.25	42.42
Realness GANs [24]	9.45	**20**	KL	1.94 ± 5.61	38.37
RGANs [16]	9.45	25	Based on JS	1.83 ± 3.68	40.96
Turing GANs [15]	9.74	25	Based on JS	1.97± 4.40	46.59
SNGANs (CNN) [14]	6.60	30	KL*	1.87 ± 3.42	26.70
SNGANs (ResNet) [14]	2.46	30	KL*	1.90 ± 4.17	**20.51**
SAGANs [22]	10.98	30	W	2.01 ± 4.99	22.25
Ours (ResNet)	30.59	23	KL* + λ(W + JS)	**2.05** ± 4.88	24.33

The basic settings are as follows, batch size is 64 in all GANs. *(i)* BEGANs selects Adam, and learning rate, momentum factor are 0.0002, 0.5, respectively. *(ii)* DCGANs, Realness GANs, RGANs, and Turning GANs select Adam, the other parameters are 0.0002, 0.5, respectively. *(iii)* LSGANs, WGANs select RMSProp, the other parameters are 0.0002, 0.9, respectively. *(iv)* SNGANs and SAGANs select Adam, other parameters are the same original papers. In SNGANs, training 3 times discriminator per training 1 time generator. In Realness GANs [24], KL represents KL divergence between discriminator output distributions and anchor distributions. KL* represents reverse KL divergence. Every experiment generated 50,000 images.

From the data in Table 4 and Table 5, the effects of the proposed GANs and the classical effective GANs are compared first. Then, the proposed GANs and state-of-the-art GANs are compared.

Table 5. Results in CIFAR10 with different GANs.

GANs	Parms/M	Epoch	Divergence	IS ($\sigma \times 0.1$)	FID
Training set	–	–	–	10.70 ± 1.47	0.00
BEGANs [8]	3.67	35	W	5.01 ± 0.23	117.11
DCGANs [4]	8.83	25	JS	5.11 ± 0.63	54.24
LSGANs [12]	8.83	35	Pearson	5.26 ± 0.20	49.13
WGANs [5]	8.83	35	W	5.23 ± 0.39	55.44
Realness GANs [24]	8.83	25	KL	5.31 ± 0.35	55.63
RGANs [16]	8.83	25	Based on JS	5.52 ± 0.25	53.37
Turing GANs [15]	1.87	25	Based on JS	4.69 ± 0.42	71.06
SNGANs (CNN) [14]	6.53	30	KL*	5.33 ± 0.38	48.36
SNGANs (ResNet) [14]	2.16	30	KL*	**6.14** ± 0.44	**38.27**
SAGANs [22]	8.57	30	W	5.87 ± 0.24	44.51
Ours (ResNet)	29.95	**23**	KL* + λ(W + JS)	6.13 ± 0.55	42.13

(a) *The proposed GANs and classical GANs*

The effects of the following GANs models are compared, BEGANs, DCGANs, LSGANs, WGANs, Realness GANs, RGANs, Turing GANs and the proposed GANs. In terms of IS index from Table 4, the proposed GANs has obvious advantages, it shows that the proposed GANs has better diversity expression and image quality. In terms of FID, it has better advantages, it shows that the proposed GANs can simulate the training set distribution better than other GANs models. From Table 5, there is a similar experiment effects. From the above, the proposed GANs has better training results.

(b) *The proposed GANs and state-of-the-art GANs*

Firstly, in Table 4 and Table 5, compared with SNGANs (CNN) and SNGANs (ResNet). SNGANs (ResNet) has better IS and FID values, which shows that using ResNet to build GANs has better effects.

Compared with SNGANs (ResNet), SAGANs, and the proposed GANs, it can be seen that the proposed GANs has better diversity expression via IS values. SNGANs (ResNet) has the best strongest ability to simulate training data distribution via FID values. The proposed GANs is close to them.

From the above, the proposed GANs is better than classical GANs and close to state-of-the-art GANs models.

Figure 3 shows the convergence curves. All the GANs models can be iterate stably, which shows that they can carry out stable adversarial learning. Relatively, it can be seen that WGANs, RGANs, SNGANs and the proposed GANs have relatively smoother and more stable adversarial learning. Combined with the final convergence effects, the convergence of SNGANs is stable, and the local optimal solution is the best. The convergence process of the proposed GANs is closest to SNGANs. From the above, in convergence process, the proposed GANs can close to state-of-the-art GANs, SNGANs (Figs. 3 and 4).

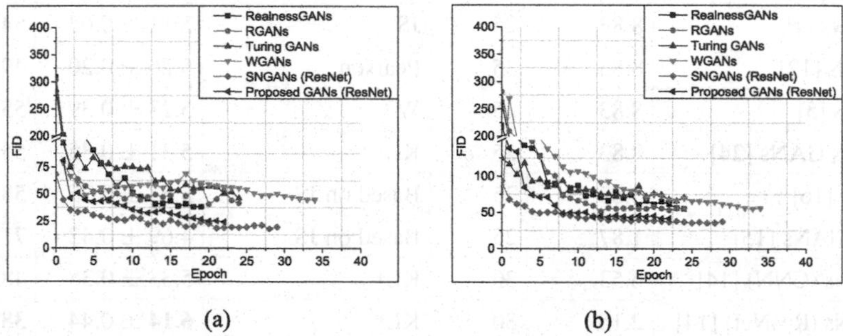

Fig. 3. Convergence processes are shown. Figures (a) and (b) show FID curves in CELEBA and CIFAR10 data sets, respectively. 5,000 generated images per epoch.

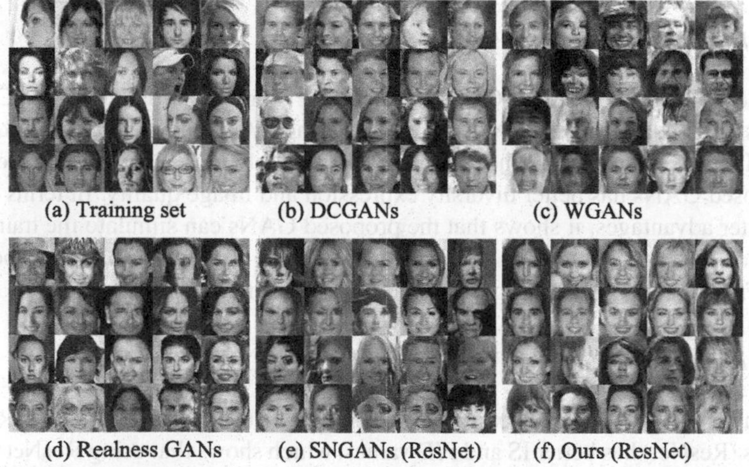

Fig. 4. Some generated image samples in CELEBA. From these pictures, it can be seen that the generated images are human faces. Usually, it is difficult to directly observe the generated images quality by human eyes. The effects comparison is evaluated by IS and FID metrics. See Table 4 and Table 5 for details.

6 Conclusion

In conclusion, a novel GANs MPF-GANs is proposed. It can improve adversarial learning stability and generated images quality. Based on the multi-penalty functions method, the reverse KL divergence is selected as the main optimization function, W distance and

JS divergence are selected as the penalty functions. In generator, a multi-task network is designed, in discriminator, a shallow multi-task residual network is designed. Multi-task generator and discriminator are used to optimize these divergence functions, respectively. From the experimental data, although the parameters are increased, it improves adversarial learning stability and generated images quality. Its performance is better than classical GANs, such as DCGANs, BEGANs and LSGANs, etc., closes to state-of-the-art GANs, SAGANs and SNGANs.

Acknowledgments. This work is supported by National Natural Science Foundation of China (Grant Nos. U1936113 and 61872303).

References

1. Goodfellow, I.J., Pouget-Abadie, J., Mirza, M., et al.: Generative adversarial nets. In: International Conference on Neural Information Processing Systems, pp. 2672–2680 (2014)
2. Gui, J., Sun, Z.N., Wen, Y.G., et al.: A review on generative adversarial networks: algorithms, theory, and applications. arXiv:2001.06937v1 (2020)
3. Hong, Y.J., Hwang, U., Yoo, J., et al.: How generative adversarial networks and their variants work: an overview. ACM Comput. Surv. **52**(1), Article 10, 1–43 (2019)
4. Radford, A., Metz, L., Chintala, S.: Unsupervised representation learning with deep convolutional generative adversarial networks. In: International Conference on Learning Representations (2016)
5. Arjovsky, M., Chintala, S., Bottou, L.: Wasserstein GAN. arXiv:1701.07875v3 (2017)
6. Gulrajani, I., Ahmed, F., Arjovsky, M., et al.: Improved training of Wasserstein GANs. In: International Conference on Neural Information Processing Systems, pp. 5769–5779 (2017)
7. Zhou, C.S., Zhang, J.S., Liu, J.M.: Lp-WGAN: using Lp-norm normalization to stabilize wasserstein generative adversarial networks. Knowl.-Based Syst. **161**(2018), 415–424 (2018)
8. Berthelot, D., Schumm, T., Metz, L.: BEGAN: boundary equilibrium generative adversarial networks. arXiv:1703.10717v4 (2017)
9. Wu, J.Q., Huang, Z.W., Thoma, J., et al.: Wasserstein divergence for GANs. arXiv:1712.01026v4 (2018)
10. Su, J.L.: GAN-QP: a novel GAN framework without gradient vanishing and Lipschitz constraint. arXiv:1811.07296v2 (2018)
11. Basioti, K., Moustakides, G.V.: Designing GANs: a likelihood ratio approach. arXiv:2002.00865v2 (2020)
12. Mao, X.D., Li, Q., Xie, H.R., et al.: Least squares generative adversarial networks. In: IEEE International Conference on Computer Vision, pp. 2813–2821 (2017)
13. Nguyen, T.D., Le, T., Vu, H., et al.: Dual discriminator generative adversarial nets. In: International Conference on Neural Information Processing Systems (2017)
14. Miyato, T., Kataoka, T., Koyama, M., et al.: Spectral normalization for generative adversarial networks. In: International Conference on Learning Representations (2018)
15. Su, J.L.: Training generative adversarial networks via turing test. arXiv:1810.10948v2 (2018)
16. Jolicoeur-Martineau, A.: The relativistic discriminator: a key element missing from standard GAN. In: International Conference on Learning Representations (2019)
17. Peng, X.B., Kanazawa, A., Toyer, S., et al.: Variational discriminator bottleneck improving imitation learning, inverse RL, and GANs by constraining information flow. In: International Conference on Learning Representations (2019)

18. Denton, E., Chintala, S., Szlam, A., et al.: Deep generative image using a laplacian pyramid of adversarial networks. In: International Conference on Neural Information Processing Systems, pp. 1486–1494 (2015)
19. Karras, T., Aila, T., Laine, S., et al.: Progressive growing of GANs for improved quality, stability, and variation. In: International Conference on Learning Representations (2018)
20. Karnewar, A., Wang, O.: MSG-GAN: multi-scale gradients for generative adversarial networks. In: International Conference on Computer Vision and Pattern Recognition, pp. 7799–7808 (2020)
21. Chu, C., Minami, K., Fukumizu, K.: Smoothness and stability in GANs. In: International Conference on Learning Representations (2020)
22. Zhang, H., Goodfellow, I., Metaxas, D., et al.: Self-attention generative adversarial networks. In: International Conference on Machine Learning (2019)
23. Chen, T., Zhai, X.H., Ritter, M., et al.: Self-supervised GANs via auxiliary rotation loss. In: IEEE Conference on Computer Vision and Pattern Recognition (2019)
24. Xiangli, Y.B., Deng, Y.B., Dai, B., et al.: Real or not real, that is the question. In: International Conference on Learning Representations (2020)
25. Fan, J.Q., Xue, L.Z., Zou, H.: Strong oracle optimality of folded concave penalized estimation. Ann. Stat. **42**(3), 819–849 (2014)
26. Armand, P., Omheni, R.: A mixed logarithmic barrier-augmented lagrangian method for nonlinear optimization. J. Optim. Theory Appl. **173**(2), 523–547 (2017)
27. Xu, X.S., Dang, C.Y., Chan, F.T.S., et al.: On smoothing L1 exact penalty function for constrained optimization problems. Numer. Funct. Anal. Optim. **40**(1), 1–18 (2019)
28. Jayswal, A., Preeti: An exact L1 penalty function method for multi-dimensional first-order PDE constrained control optimization problem. Eur. J. Control **52**(2020), 34–41 (2020)
29. Li, N., Yang, H.: Nonnegative estimation and variable selection under minimax concave penalty for sparse high-dimensional linear regression models. Stat. Pap. **62**(2), 661–680 (2019). https://doi.org/10.1007/s00362-019-01107-w
30. Ruder, S.: An overview of multi-task learning in deep neural networks. arXiv:1706.05098v1 (2017)
31. Vandenhende, S., Georgoulis, S., Proesmans, M., et al.: Revisiting multi-task learning in the deep learning era. arXiv:2004.13379v1 (2020)
32. He, K.M., Zhang, X.Y., Ren, S.Q., et al.: Deep residual learning for image recognition. In: International Conference on Computer Vision and Pattern Recognition, pp. 770–778 (2016)
33. He, K., Zhang, X., Ren, S., Sun, J.: Identity mappings in deep residual networks. In: Leibe, B., Matas, J., Sebe, N., Welling, M. (eds.) ECCV 2016. LNCS, vol. 9908, pp. 630–645. Springer, Cham (2016). https://doi.org/10.1007/978-3-319-46493-0_38

Community Detection Model Based on Graph Representation and Self-supervised Learning

Feng Qiao[1], Chenxi Huang[2], Song Xu[2], and Jin Qi[2](✉)

[1] School of Automation, Nanjing University of Posts and Telecommunications, Nanjing 210023, China
[2] School of Internet of Things, Nanjing University of Posts and Telecommunications, Nanjing 210003, China
qijin@njupt.edu.cn

Abstract. Community detection is an important issue of social network analysis, which is used to find the potential connections between individuals. At present, the mainstream community detection methods consider using neural network to establish the nonlinear model of nodes and edges to overcome the shortcomings of the traditional linear model. However, the design of such models does not fully consider the characteristics of the graph structure data, requiring sophisticated design skills, and the model does not have the ability to continuously optimize the results of community detection. Fully considering characteristics of community network, this paper proposes an end-to-end Deep Graph Clustering (DGC) model. This model introduces the Graph Neural Network (GNN) to represent the community network, and also introduces the idea of self-supervised learning to continuously optimize the results. At the same time, the optimization scheme and training tricks are proposed to improve its performance. The experimental results show that the DGC model can gradually improve the community detection results through self-supervised learning, and finally surpass existing models.

Keywords: Graph neural network · Community detection · Self-supervised learning · Clustering algorithm

1 Introduction

With the continuous expansion of the Internet, more and more diversified data have become its subsidiary products, such as comments, social network data, multiple spatio-temporal data, etc., which have influenced every aspect of human life. Therefore, the analysis of these data is becoming a hot topic for researchers in various fields. In the study of social media or online data, one of the challenges is to discover the underlying structures that have group effects, known as community structures. Such identification of communities of similar and closely related individuals is of great significance and has been widely used in many fields, including sociology, biology and computer science [1].

For community detection tasks, some researchers turn it into graph clustering problem, and put forward some transformation methods. For example, in Normalized Cut

X. Sun et al. (Eds.): ICAIS 2021, LNCS 12736, pp. 27–40, 2021.
https://doi.org/10.1007/978-3-030-78609-0_3

(N-cut) [2], the processing of Laplace matrix is the main topic. Other researchers turn it into spectral clustering problems, for example, the modular maximization model [3] first constructs a graph based on eigenvectors, and then solves the top k eigenvectors as the representation vectors for clustering. However, they are often unable to combine nodes and edges to obtain the deeper community structure information. Therefore, how to effectively combine this two information to better solve the community detection problem is very important [4].

When topology information and node contents are both considered, it can be chosen to combine the two objective functions directly in a linear form. However, some classical graph embedding methods, such as Local Linear Embedding (LLE) [5], indicate that relationships between nodes in the realistic network are not necessarily linear. Therefore, these kind of applications in the real networks are still limited.

In recent years, Deep Learning (DL) has been widely applied in many fields [6]. Some researchers have designed special convolutional networks to fuse the graph topology and node information in a nonlinear way [7]. However, with the proposal of the GNN [8], it is possible to train end-to-end on a graph dataset. Moreover, such networks need much fewer artificial design. Its excellent performance in graph classification proves its strong ability to represent graph structure data [9]. Therefore, this paper uses the derived model of GNN to learn and represent graph structure data.

However, unlike the graph classification problem focused on by the GNN, community detection is an unsupervised clustering problem. In the field of computer vision, many studies have shown that it is feasible to apply such unsupervised methods to the DL model [10], which can enable the model to obtain universal representational features. Similarly, in the representation of graph data, the idea of unsupervised learning should have great potential, and the experimental results also verify this.

In order to make full use of graph network's advantages in graph representation and better complete community detection tasks, this paper proposes a community detection model based on GNN and self-supervised learning. This model adopts Graph Attention Network (GATs) [11] to jointly represent individual information and graph topology information in community data to generate representation vectors. Then, the idea of self-supervised learning is adopted to improve the traditional clustering algorithm. This paper also puts forward the design, optimization and training tricks for this kind of self-supervised learning model, and proves that these skills can play the corresponding effect.

The remaining sections of this paper are arranged as follows: Sect. 2 introduces the related work of DL combined with community detection and background technologies used in this model. Section 3 introduces the community detection model proposed in this paper; Sect. 4 verifies the effectiveness and advancement of the new community detection model proposed in this paper through experiments and analysis. Section 5 summarizes the work of this paper and puts forward the prospect.

2 Related Work

At present, researches on community detection are mainly categorized into three categories, which are (1) community detection only considering the graph topology, (2) only considering node information and (3) detection combining both above information. Most recent studies have combined them to achieve improvements, as shown in research [12, 13]. However, they did not consider the nonlinear combination of them and needed to manually adjust the weights, which limited the effectiveness of community detection tasks.

In recent years, DL model has achieved great success in many applications. This is because Deep Neural Network (DNN) can use a huge nonlinear space to describe a complex object and has better generalization capability. Some community detection studies using DL methods, such as the research work described in [14], have improved the representational ability of community networks through DNN and achieved better results in community detection. However, they only considered the graph topology or node content information. Therefore, some scholars use Deep Auto Encoder (DAE) in [15] to fuse graph topology and node information, and achieve excellent performance. However, neither of them fully considered the graph structure data, nor provided an end-to-end neural network training mode, so the model could not continuously iterate and optimize the performance of community detection.

3 Model and Method

3.1 Preliminaries

The essence of community detection is the clustering problem, but different from traditional clustering problems, community data is usually graph structured. In this paper, the topological and individual characteristics of the community network are fully considered by means of the GNN to simplify and represent the graph structure data to generate representation vectors. Based on these vectors, the traditional clustering ideology is used to cluster the individuals. Therefore, the key point of the problem is how to train the GNN in the context of unsupervised learning so that it can represent the community network reasonably.

Assume that f_θ is the mapping function of the GNN, where θ is its corresponding learnable parameter. The node feature in the community network after f_θ mapping is recorded as the characteristic feature. Given the training set with N nodes $G_{train} = (V_{train}, E_g)$, where $V_{train} = \{x_1, x_2, \ldots, x_N\}$ is the node in the training set, and E_g is the edge set; It is expected to find a set of parameters θ^* that allow f_{θ^*} to fuse edges and nodes to generate good characteristic features.

In supervised learning, due to the existence of the ground truth, each node is bound to the label y_n in $\{0, 1\}^k$, where k is the number of categories. A typical context of use is the graph classification, to be specific, $f_\theta(x_n, E_g)$ is used to generate the characteristic vector of x_n, denoted as r_n, and a parameterized classifier g_W is used to predict the community to which x_n belongs based on r_n, where W is the parameter of the classifier. The parameters θ and W can be optimized by the following formula:

$$\min_{\theta,W}\frac{1}{N}\sum\nolimits_{n=1}^{N} l\left(g_W\left(f_\theta\left(x_n, E_g\right)\right), y_n\right) \quad (1)$$

Where, l is a polynomial of classification error.

The difficulty is, as for unsupervised learning scenario described here, there is no ground truth, which makes it very difficult to optimize the parameter θ. Assuming that θ is artificially distributed as a Gaussian in the absence of learning, in this case f_θ does not produce a good characteristic feature. However, the performance of this random feature in the classification task is still far better than the random classification [16]. Therefore, inspired by [17], this paper tries to use this advantage to guide the identification ability of the GNN, so that it can generate fine representation vectors for clustering, and finally complete the community detection task.

3.2 Models

Graph Attention Network. GATs [11] are novel neural network architectures that operate on graph-structured data. Given a graph $G = (V, E)$ with M nodes, where node $V = \{x_1, x_2, \ldots, x_M\}, x_m \in \mathbb{R}^F, F$ is the feature dimension of the node, E is the edge set; after processing by GATs, the new node $V^{'} = \left\{x_1^{'}, x_2^{'}, \ldots, x_M^{'}\right\}, x_m^{'} \in \mathbb{R}^{F^{'}}$ with the dimension of $F^{'}$ is generated. In order to obtain sufficient representational capability, at least one learnable linear transformation W is required, which is used to calculate the attention coefficient e_{ij}:

$$e_{ij} = a(Wx_i, Wx_j) \tag{2}$$

Where: $W \in \mathbb{R}^{F^{'} \times F}$ is the weight matrix used for training, a is the $\mathbb{R}^{F'} \times \mathbb{R}^{F'} \rightarrow \mathbb{R}$ attention mechanism. The e_{ij} indicates the importance of the j-th to the i-th node. In order to make the attention coefficient easier to calculate, the author introduced *softmax* function to regularize all adjacent nodes of i:

$$\alpha_{ij} = \frac{\exp(LeakyReLU\,(e_{ij}))}{\sum_{k \in \mathcal{N}_i} \exp(LeakyReLU\,(e_{ik}))} \tag{3}$$

Where: $\mathcal{N}_i$ is all adjacent nodes of node i, which are obtained by edge set E, and *LeakyReLU* is the activation function. The attention coefficient between different nodes after regularization is obtained, which can be used to calculate the final representation vector of each node:

$$x_i^{'} = \sigma(\frac{1}{K}\sum\nolimits_{k=1}^{K}\sum\nolimits_{j \in \mathcal{N}_i} \alpha_{ij}^k W^k x_j) \tag{4}$$

Where: σ is a nonlinear mapping function, and K is the number of attention heads.

Self-supervised Learning. Self-supervised learning is a popular topic in the field of unsupervised learning [18]. The use of pretext tasks simplifies the solution of the original task, avoids manual marking of samples, and realizes unsupervised feature extraction. Self-supervising is proposed to break the limitation of such hand-crafted labels, aiming to train the network efficiently without manual labeling. The core problem of self-supervising is how to generate Pseudo-label, which does not involve manual works. In this paper, the idea of self-supervised learning is introduced into the community detection task to optimize its performance.

Deep Graph Clustering Model. Referring to the idea of self-supervised learning, this paper proposes a novel graph clustering method, which can be used to train the GNN in an end-to-end fashion. The framework of the method is shown in Fig. 1. This framework alternately completes three tasks, including: generating the representation vector set R of community data through GATs, generating pseudo-label through clustering results based on R, and optimizing formula 1 through training of GATs using these pseudo-labels. Each iteration is denoted by *Episode*, and this kind of iteration progressively optimizes performance of community detection.

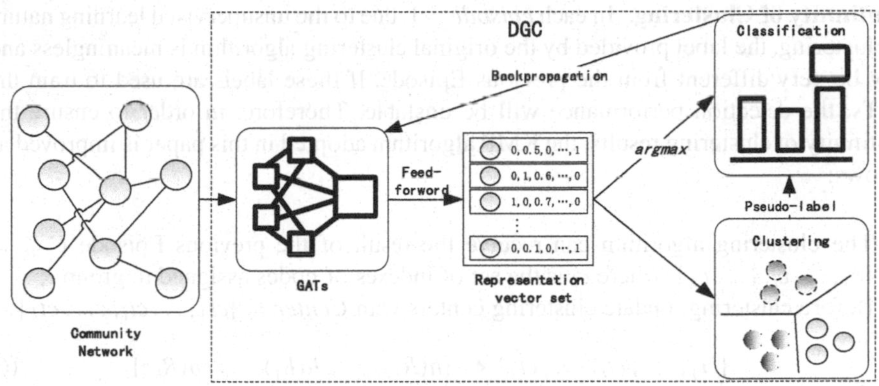

Fig. 1. The structure of the DGC

This paper mainly studies k-means++ (KMP), but other clustering methods can also be used. Since, as long as the clustering algorithm is appropriately modified to adapt to the DGC framework, the outcomes won't differ much. Set representation vectors $R = \{r_1, r_2, \ldots, r_N\}$ generated by GATs as the input of KMP, then divide these nodes into k groups according to the geometric criterion. More precisely, the model optimizes the $d \times k$ centroid matrix C and the community class y_n of individual x_n by following formula:

$$\min_{C \in \mathbb{R}^{d \times k}} \frac{1}{N} \sum\nolimits_{n=1}^{N} \min_{y_n \in \{0,1\}^k} \left\| GAT_W\left(x_n, E_g\right) - Cy_n \right\|_2^2, \quad y_n^T 1_k = 1 \tag{5}$$

Where: d is the dimension of the representation vector output by GATs. Note that y_n here is given by the clustering algorithm and is not the ground truth. Solve formula 5, and a set of optimal allocation $(y_n^*)_{n \leq N}$ and a centroid matrix C^* are obtained, where y_n^* is used to determine the pseudo-label of each node.

3.3 Model Optimization

Warmup Training. According to the principle of inductive bias [19], some preliminary information can be used to change the preference of GATs, so that the model can get better clustering results quickly. Therefore, in the first *Episode* of optimization, the model is warmed up. The method is designed as follows:

1. Instead of using $GAT_W(x_n, E_g)$ to generate the representation vector set R, the node feature x_n is used to avoid loss of data integrity.
2. Using the representation vector set R as the input, the preliminary clustering is carried out on the nodes, and the pseudo-label is generated for the first time.
3. Use pseudo-label to warm up the training of GATs, and the number of warm-up iterations is determined by *warmupEpochs*.

It is worth noting that the optimal *warmupEpochs* values varies from different datasets, but the overall impact of *warmupEpochs* is traceable.

Continuity of Clustering. In each *episode* >1, due to the unsupervised learning nature of clustering, the label provided by the original clustering algorithm is meaningless and may be very different from the previous Episode. If these labels are used to train the GATs, the detection performance will be unstable. Therefore, in order to ensure the continuity of clustering results, the KMP algorithm adopted in this paper is improved as follows:

1. The clustering algorithm can receive the result of the previous Episode $C_{out} = \{c_1, \ldots c_i, \ldots, c_k\}$, where c_i is the set of indexes of nodes assigned to group i;
2. Before clustering, update clustering centers with $Center = \{ct_1, \ldots ct_i, \ldots, ct_k\}$:

$$\{ct_1, \ldots, ct_i, \ldots, ct_k\} \Leftarrow \{h(R_1), \ldots, h(R_i), \ldots, h(R_k)\} \quad (6)$$

   Where: ct_i is the cluster center of c_i, h is the centralized function, and R_i is the set of all representation vectors r_n with the index in c_i;
3. The updated center set *Center* is used for clustering and generate the result C_{out}.

This design ensures the continuity of the cluster centers, and the change of the center is only related to GATs training, but has nothing to do with the clustering algorithm itself. GATs training is a continuous process, so there is no drastic change in the cluster centers and the pseudo-label do not change significantly. Therefore, the continuity of clustering can be guaranteed and the algorithm can converge.

Incremental Training. For each *episode* >1, the training required in each Episode varies. At the early stage of training, it is hoped that the model can maximize the advantages of random exploration, so the training steps should be reduced accordingly, so as to avoid the model losing its ability to explore other better schemes. However, in the later stage of training, it is hoped that the model can continuously optimize for this result to obtain accurate representation vectors. Then, the training steps of GATs should be increased correspondingly to make the neural network fully trained. Therefore, the incremental training scheme is adopted in this paper. The number of training cycles experienced by GATs in each *Episode* is denoted by *Epoch* and its increment is *inc*. The upper and lower thresholds of the *Epoch* are *epochMin* and *epochMax* respectively, and the training step of GATs in each *Episode* is:

$$epoch = \begin{cases} ceil(epochMin + inc \times episode), & epoch < epochMax \\ epochMax, & epoch \geq epochMax \end{cases} \quad (7)$$

Where: *episode* is the current iteration, and *ceil* is the ceiling function.

4 Experiments

We compare the performance of DGC and some of the most advanced community detection algorithms on non-overlapping real community networks. Some baselines for comparing the effects of community detection, social network data sets, and experimental parameter settings are also described in detail.

4.1 Datasets

In this paper, the performance of DGC was tested on four open datasets, which are citation networks Citeseer and Cora, diabetes dataset PubMed [8] and ego-network Facebook107 (FB107) [20]. Their detailed information and key specifications are given in Table 1:

Table 1. Specifications of each dataset

Dataset	Nodes	Edges	Dimension	Communities
Citeseer	3312	4732	3703	6
Cora	2708	5429	1703	7
PubMed	19729	44338	500	3
Facebook107	1045	26749	576	9

4.2 Baselines and Metrics for Comparison

The baselines can be divided into three types: (1) make use of network structural information alone, (2) consider node contents alone, and (3) utilize both those two types of information [7].

In the first class, CNM and Louvain, which adopt the same greedy optimization as did by modularity maximization model, are used to partition network structure. Besides, AE-link based on auto encoder also be adopted.

In the second class, we chose four methods which have their own characteristics, i.e., Affinity Propagation (AP) and DP are state-of-the-art non-parameter algorithms, LDA is a well-known topic model for data clustering algorithm, and AE-Content is an approach based on auto encoder.

The third class of methods uses both network structure and node contents. There are three non-overlapping algorithms which are PCL-DC, Block-LDA, and auto encoder based DAECD.

This paper focuses on community detection with the predefined number of communities. Given that there are k communities, the community detection results can be evaluated by measuring the degree of consistency between the ground truth and community labels detected by the algorithm. Therefore, the Normalized Mutual Information (NMI) and Fowlkes-Mallows Index (FMI) [21] are used as metrics.

4.3 Parameters Setting

Parameters of GATs. In this paper, four different datasets are selected, each of which has an independent GATs parameter setting, as shown in Table 2:

Table 2. GATs parameters settings for different datasets

Parameter	Dataset			
	Cora	Citeseer	PubMed	Facebook107
Training set	140	120	60	45
Cross-validation set	500	500	500	110
Patience	100	100	100	100
Learning rate	0.005	0.005	0.005	0.005
Hidden units	8	8	8	8
Attention head input	8	8	8	8
Attention head output	1	1	8	1
L_2 regularization	0.0005	0.0005	0.001	0.0005
Dropout rate	0.6	0.6	0.6	0.6

All parameters are based on the settings in the original GATs paper [11] and have been modified in a small range. Among them, the training set should include all community types with the same number of samples for each type. The cross-validation set is used for early stopping with a patient value to prevent potential overfitting. The test set is not adopted, because it's meaningless to the clustering problem.

Parameters of DGC. The parameters of DGC mainly include the *warmupEpochs* and the increment of training steps *inc*. Figure 2 shows the change of NMI when *warmupEpochs* is taken at different values on the Cora dataset.

In Fig. 2, the initial NMI and the optimal NMI are the average NMI of the first 10 episodes and the last 10 episodes, respectively. It can be seen from the figure that when only introduce inductive bias with no warmup, the model achieves its best, because GATs can maximum the possibility of exploration. However, the initial NMI this time is the lowest, the number of episodes needed to achieve the same clustering result will increase accordingly. With the increase of warmup iterations, the optimal NMI in the figure decreases. But at this time, the model can find a relatively good clustering scheme more quickly. In addition, when the number of warmup iterations is greater than 10, the initial NMI starts to decline, because the over-fitting of GATs on inductive bias causes the model to fall into this "local optimal", but the NMI value of this "local optimal" is not ideal. In conclusion, the *warmupEpochs* is set according to the actual needs of users. In this paper, it is hoped to improve the efficiency of model learning without sacrificing performance as much as possible, so the value of *warmupEpochs* for the Cora dataset is 6. Similarly, you can set the corresponding parameter values for the other three datasets based on this rule.

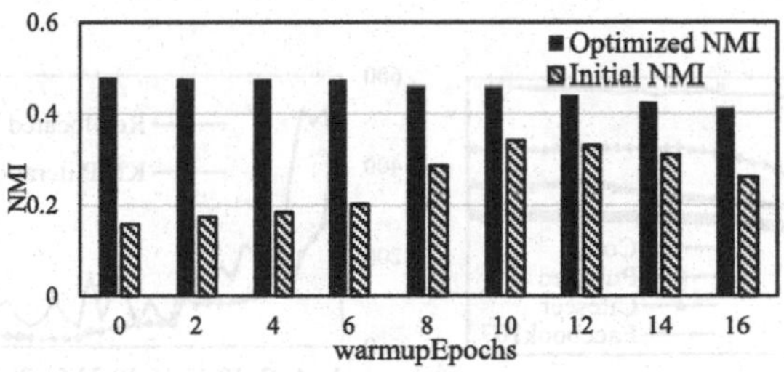

Fig. 2. The clustering results varies with *warmupEpochs*

For increment of training step *inc*, we hope that the model can explore the best clustering scheme, so it needs to be set as small as possible. However, considering the different complexity of datasets, the simpler the dataset, the faster the training, the smaller the *inc* needs to be set; on the contrary, the larger the *inc* needs to be set for the complex dataset, so as to achieve the balance between accuracy and efficiency. Table 3 shows the parameters of the DGC model determined in this paper:

Table 3. DGC parameters settings for different datasets

Parameter	Dataset			
	Cora	Citeseer	PubMed	Facebook107
warmupEpochs	6	20	1	3
inc	0.2	1	0.1	0.2

4.4 Preliminary Study of DGC

This paper explores the iterative process of clustering results of the model, convergence iteration step of KMP and the change of category reallocation individuals, in order to understand the working pattern and clustering process of DGC. In addition, the effect of inductive bias on the model is also presented.

Figure 3 shows the training trajectory of the DGC and describes the changes of various indicators and parameters in the model during the iteration process of community detection. The left shows the variation of NMI on each dataset, which measures the model's ability to predict the category information. The results show that with the increase of clustering iteration, the performance of the model on each dataset becomes better and more stable. For Facebook107 and PubMed, which are smaller datasets, the initial growth rate of the model is relatively fast, so GATs can train more quickly. For the Citeseer dataset, the warmup level of the model is higher, Therefore, a better result is achieved at the beginning, but the increase of the NMI in the subsequent training was not as obvious as that of other datasets. The complexity of Cora dataset is between the above two, and its NMI growth curve is relatively flat.

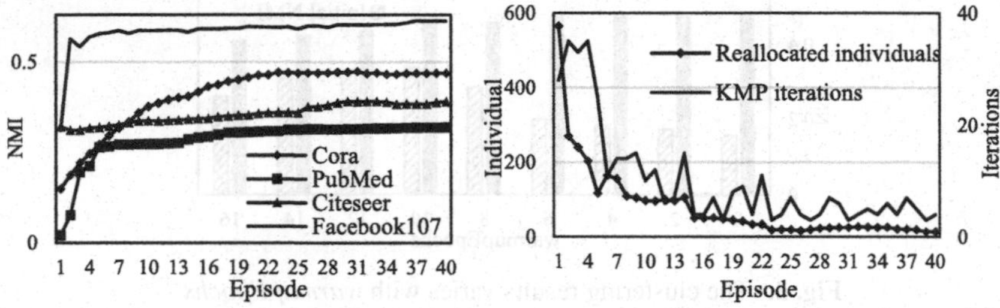

Fig. 3. Training trajectory of the DGC

The right shows the number of reallocated individuals and the change of KMP iteration step with the clustering episode on the Cora dataset. These two indicators show the change level of network parameter θ of GATs. When the level of change is large, the output representation vector r_n changes greatly, leading to the reallocation of more individuals, and the iteration step of KMP also increase correspondingly. As can be seen from the figure, the overall trend of both shows a consistent downward trend, indicating that with the increase of clustering episode, GATs training gradually becomes sufficient. Finally, the number of reallocated individuals tends to be stable, indicating that the model has approached the limitation of optimization, and the difference between the clustering results obtained at this time is slight.

Table 4. The effect of inductive bias on DGC

Dataset	NMI		
	Cora	Citeseer	PubMed
Cora	0.4552	0.4735	≈4%
Citeseer	0.3231	0.394	≈22%
PubMed	0.3073	0.323	≈5%
Facebook107	0.5971	0.6046	≈1.2%

Table 4 shows the impact of the inductive bias on the community detection results. The results show that the inductive bias had different degrees of improvement on the model, and the Citeseer data set had the greatest improvement, up to 22%, while the Facebook107 data set had the least improvement, only 1.2%. Since the latter is a relatively simple data set, the efficiency and representational capacity of DGC are high enough, while for the former, due to its complexity, the dependence on inductive bias is relatively high.

4.5 Experimental Results

We compared the performance of DGC and the ten methods mentioned above on NMI and FMI, and the results are shown in Table 5 and 6. The bold item is the optimal method, and the item with superscript * is the suboptimal method. It proves that the DGC framework proposed in this paper achieved the optimal performance on the Cora, Citeseer and Facebook107 data sets, and the overall performance is also optimal. DGC performs slightly less well on PubMed, but it still achieves a promising performance. This figure also shows that the two community detection methods based on DL are superior to other methods, which indicates the potential of DL in the field of community detection, and this potential needs to be further developed.

Table 5. Comparison of DGC and other algorithms on NMI

Methods		Dataset				Avg.
		Cora	Citeseer	PubMed	FB107	
Link	Louvain	0.3976	0.3474	0.1766	0.5582*	0.3700
	CNM	0.4709*	0.3406	0.2184	0.3884	0.3546
Content	AP	0.3234	0.3169	0.1380	0.2624	0.2602
	DP	0.0146	0.0197	0.0136	0.1834	0.0578
	LDA	0.0272	0.0257	0.0265	0.1357	0.0538
Link + Content	PCL-DC	0.1950	0.0295	0.2684	0.4265	0.2299
	Block-LDA	0.0158	0.0058	0.0079	0.0563	0.0215
Autoencoder	AE-link	0.3544	0.3043	**0.3421**	0.4587	0.3649
	AE-content	0.2422	0.2220	0.2184	0.2743	0.2392
Deep Learning	DAECD	0.4177	0.3642*	0.3192	0.5096	0.4305*
	DGC (ours)	**0.4735**	**0.3940**	0.3230*	**0.6046**	**0.4488**

In addition, traditional algorithms based on edges or edges and nodes also do remarkable jobs in some datasets. For example, CNM's performance on Cora dataset and Louvain's performance on FB107 are both suboptimal. Compared with algorithms based on DL, these traditional algorithms have considerable advantages in time complexity. This reminds researchers not to overlook the power of classical algorithms.

Table 6. Comparison of DGC and other algorithms on FMI

Methods		Dataset				Avg.
		Cora	Citeseer	PubMed	FB107	
Link	Louvain	0.0857	0.0453	0.0634	0.3530	0.1368
	CNM	0.3286	0.1411	0.2818	0.2216	0.2432
Content	AP	0.0105	0.0089	0.0022	0.0811	0.0257
	DP	0.1245	0.1251	0.1445	0.0895	0.1209
	LDA	0.1397	0.1347	0.1628	0.1525	0.1474
Link + Content	PCL-DC	0.3891	0.2474	0.6305*	0.2933	0.3900
	Block-LDA	0.1550	0.1476	0.0147	0.0960	0.1033
Autoencoder	AE-link	0.3055	0.2866	0.0360	0.2634	0.2228
	AE-content	0.2864	0.3267	0.5633	0.0230	0.2998
Deep Learning	DAECD	0.4526*	0.3933*	**0.6621**	0.4633*	0.4928*
	DGC (ours)	**0.4619**	**0.4869**	0.5729	**0.7157**	**0.5593**

It can be concluded that, in most cases, the DGC algorithm has significant advantages over other algorithms in community detection tasks. And the overall result of the algorithm is also optimal. Therefore, the method proposed in this paper, which combines the node and edge information through the DNN to carry out nonlinear representation of individuals, and uses self-supervised learning to gradually optimize the clustering results, is conducive to improving the accuracy of community detection.

5 Conclusion

This paper proposes a new end-to-end community detection model, DGC, which combines the advantages of graph representational and self-supervised learning. First, GATs is used to represent the community network and generate the representation vector set. Then the nodes are clustered based on the representation vector set and the clustering results are used to generate pseudo labels. Then, the idea of self-supervised learning is introduced to train and optimize GATs with pseudo label. Finally, the above process is iterated to achieve excellent community detection results. The experiment shows that the DGC model in this paper is superior to most of the models used for comparison in terms of the effect, and reaches the optimal overall performance, indicating its excellent community detection ability. At the same time, the model in this paper provides more possibilities for the research of community detection through the mode of continuous optimization through self-supervised learning.

References

1. Liu, F., et al.: Deep learning for community detection: progress, challenges and opportunities. In: Proceedings of the Twenty-Ninth International Joint Conference on Artificial Intelligence, pp. 4981–4987. International Joint Conferences on Artificial Intelligence Organization, Yokohama, Japan (2020)
2. Shi, J., Malik, J.: Normalized cuts and image segmentation. IEEE Trans. Pattern Anal. Mach. Intell. **22**, 888–905 (2000)
3. Newman, M.E.J.: Modularity and community structure in networks. Proc. Natl. Acad. Sci. **103**(23), 8577–8582 (2006). https://doi.org/10.1073/pnas.0601602103
4. Ganesh, J., Ganguly, S., Gupta, M., Varma, V., Pudi, V.: Author2Vec: learning author representations by combining content and link information. In: Proceedings of the 25th International Conference Companion on World Wide Web, pp. 49–50. International World Wide Web Conferences Steering Committee, Republic and Canton of Geneva, CHE (2016)
5. Roweis, S.T., Saul, L.K.: Nonlinear dimensionality reduction by locally linear embedding. Science **290**, 2323–2326 (2000)
6. Shao, L., Cai, Z., Liu, L., Lu, K.: Performance evaluation of deep feature learning for RGB-D image/video classification. Inf. Sci. **385–386**, 266–283 (2017)
7. Cao, J., Jin, D., Yang, L., Dang, J.: Incorporating network structure with node contents for community detection on large networks using deep learning. Neurocomputing **297**, 71–81 (2018)
8. Kipf, T.N., Welling, M.: Semi-Supervised Classification with Graph Convolutional Networks. arXiv:1609.02907 [cs, stat] (2016)
9. Xu, K., Hu, W., Leskovec, J., Jegelka, S.: How Powerful are Graph Neural Networks? arXiv: 1810.00826 [cs, stat] (2018)
10. Goodfellow, I., et al.: Generative adversarial nets. In: Ghahramani, Z., Welling, M., Cortes, C., Lawrence, N.D., Weinberger, K.Q. (eds.) Advances in Neural Information Processing Systems 27, pp. 2672–2680. Curran Associates, Inc. (2014)
11. Veličković, P., Cucurull, G., Casanova, A., Romero, A., Liò, P., Bengio, Y.: Graph Attention Networks. arXiv:1710.10903 [cs, stat] (2017)
12. He, D., Feng, Z., Jin, D., Wang, X., Zhang, W.: Joint identification of network communities and semantics via integrative modeling of network topologies and node contents, p. 9 (2017)
13. Zhang, Y., Levina, E., Zhu, J.: Community detection in networks with node features. Electron. J. Stat. **10**(2), 3153–3178 (2016). https://doi.org/10.1214/16-EJS1206
14. Yang, L., Cao, X., He, D., Wang, C., Wang, X., Zhang, W.: Modularity based community detection with deep learning, p. 7 (2016)
15. Zhang, T., Xiong, Y., Zhang, J., Zhang, Y., Jiao, Y., Zhu, Y.: CommDGI: community detection oriented deep graph Infomax. In: Proceedings of the 29th ACM International Conference on Information & Knowledge Management, pp. 1843–1852. Association for Computing Machinery, New York (2020)
16. Noroozi, M., Favaro, P.: Unsupervised Learning of Visual Representations by Solving Jigsaw Puzzles. arXiv:1603.09246 [cs] (2017)
17. Caron, M., Bojanowski, P., Joulin, A., Douze, M.: Deep Clustering for Unsupervised Learning of Visual Features. arXiv:1807.05520 [cs] (2018)
18. de Sa, V.R.: Learning classification with unlabeled data. In: Cowan, J.D., Tesauro, G., Alspector, J. (eds.) Advances in Neural Information Processing Systems, vol. 6, pp. 112–119. Morgan-Kaufmann (1994)
19. Battaglia, P.W., et al.: Relational inductive biases, deep learning, and graph networks. arXiv: 1806.01261 [cs, stat] (2018)

20. McAuley, J., Leskovec, J.: Learning to discover social circles in ego networks. In: Proceedings of the 25th International Conference on Neural Information Processing Systems, vol. 1, pp. 539–547. Curran Associates Inc., Red Hook (2012)
21. Tharwat, A.: Classification assessment methods. ACI. ahead-of-print (2020)

Efficient Distributed Stochastic Gradient Descent Through Gaussian Averaging

Kaifan Hu(✉), Chengkun Wu, and En Zhu

School of Computer, National University of Defense Technology, Changsha 410073, Hunan, China
{kaifan_hu,chengkun_wu,enzhu}@nudt.edu.cn

Abstract. Training of large-scale machine learning models presents a hefty communication challenge to the Stochastic Gradient Descent (SGD) algorithm. In a distributed computing environment, frequent exchanges of gradient parameters between computational nodes are inevitable in model training, which introduces enormous communication overhead. To improve communication efficiency, a gradient compression technique represented by gradient sparseness and gradient quantization is proposed. Base on that, we proposed a novel approach named *Gaussian Averaging SGD* (GASGD), which transmits 32 bits between nodes in one iteration and achieves a communication complexity of $\mathcal{O}(1)$. A theoretical analysis demonstrates that GASGD has a similar convergence performance compared with other distributed algorithms with a significantly smaller communication cost. Our experiments validate the theoretical conclusion and demonstrate that GASGD significantly reduces the communication traffic per worker.

Keywords: Communication-efficient · Distributed optimization · Parallel computing

1 Introduction

Deep learning is widely used in various fields. Recently, more complex and lager models with over millions and even billions of parameters have appeared. i.e., BERT [7] (1.1B). A simple way to train such a model effectively is to use a distributed SGD algorithm. It can be formulated as below, where w_t represents the parameters of the model in iteration t, η_t is the learning rate, or the step size. And $g^p(x)$ is the gradient on a data batch $x \in \mathcal{X}_p$, in which the $\mathcal{X}_p$ is a subset of dataset $\mathcal{X}$ computed by the local computing worker p.

$$w_{t+1} = w_t - \eta_t \frac{1}{P} \sum_{p=1}^{P} g^p(x)$$

Supported by the Open Fund from the State Key Laboratory of High Performance Computing (No. 201901-11).

X. Sun et al. (Eds.): ICAIS 2021, LNCS 12736, pp. 41–52, 2021.
https://doi.org/10.1007/978-3-030-78609-0_4

Traditional distributed SGD algorithms need to transfer all local gradients to relevant workers, which results in some communication overhead. As the model becomes larger, the communication overhead might be overwhelming in terms of training time. Many studies have proposed to address this issue. Two typical types include sparsification and quantization. Sparsification methods select a portion of gradients for transmission among them all and achieve a higher compression ratio. Differently, quantization methods use a low precision representation for the gradient. i.e., TernGrad [19] uses three values (-1, 0 and 1) and 1BitSGD [13] only uses 1 bit. The quantization could achieve a compression ratio of up to 32 at most, assuming the gradients are *Float*32 values.

In this paper, we proposed a novel algorithm named *Gaussian Averaging SGD* (GASGD), which is different from sparsification and quantization. Our algorithm GASGD only needs to transfer one 32-bit value for each worker and minimize the communication complexity. The key idea is based on an approximately Gaussian distribution of gradients, we maintain an average of the gradient distribution rather than all gradients from each worker. Our theoretical analysis shows that the GASGD can converge as other distributed algorithms do. Our empirical results also validate the analysis and that our algorithm has better performance than others. Respectively, GASGD has achieved 2.6× and 1.3× speedup on execution time per iteration compared to the QSGD and Top-K in training the LSTM-PTB model (which has nearly 66 million parameters).

Our Contributions as follows:

- By examining the scalability challenge of gradient synchronization in distributed SGD and analyzing its computation and communication complexities, we have proposed a Gaussian distribution averaging algorithm (GASGD) for distributed workers to exchange only one mean value globally.
- We give a theoretical analysis of the convergence of GASGD and demonstrated that our algorithm achieves an overall improvement compared to other sparsification and quantization algorithms with a lower computation complexity.

To the best of our knowledge, GASGD is the first attempt that can reduce the communication down to 32 bits per iteration for distributed SGDs.

2 Related Work

Quantization. 1-bit SGD [13] is to quantize the gradients into 1 bit to transfer, and the experiment in which it used the 1-bit SGD to train a speech model achieved a higher speedup. After 1-bit SGD, 8-bit quantization [6] has been proposed. It maps each *Float*32 gradient to 8 bit: 1 bit for sign,3 bit for the exponent, and the other 4 bit for the mantissa. Quantized SGD (QSGD) [2] proposed another method which used stochastic rounding to estimate the gradients and could quantize the gradients into 4 or 8 bit. Similar to QSGD, there is another approach named TernGrad, which uses 3-level values (-1, 0 and 1) to represent a gradient, could quantize the gradients into 2 bit. QSGD and TernGrad also give a theoretical analysis to demonstrate the convergence of their quantization algorithm. Moreover, both of them also do lots of experiments to demonstrate that their algorithm works a lot. SignSGD [3] transmits the sign of gradient elements by quantizing the harmful components to -1 and the others to 1. There are also some attempts to apply the quantization method to the entire model, not only the gradients to transfer, but also the parameters in the model. The DoReFa-Net [22] used 1-bit to represent the parameters in the model and 2-bit for gradients. Furthermore, LPC-SVRG [21] also applies that quantization method to another classical optimization algorithm - SVRG [9], which gives a code-based approach that combines gradient clipping with quantization.

Sparsification. Sparsifing the whole gradients to a part of them is another way to solve the communication bottleneck. Threshold-v [17] selects the elements by giving a threshold v that whose absolute values are larger than a fixed defined threshold value, which is difficult to choose in practice and uses zeros to represent the other elements. Unlike the threshold-v, Top-K [1] selects the k largest gradient values in absolute value, and there is also a random version named Random-K [16]. To further realize a lower loss on the accuracy, DGC [12] apply a local update inspired by the momentum SGD, and a warm-up step for the selection of hyperparameter K. After finding that the gradient variance affects the convergence rate, Wangni et al. [18] proposed an unbiased sparse coding to maximize sparsity and control the variance to ensure the convergence rate. Concurrently, Adacomp [5] has been proposed to automatically modify the compression rate depending on the local gradient activity, which realizes a 200× higher compression ratio for the fully-connected layer in deep learning model and 40× for the convolutional neural layer with a sightly loss in top-1 accuracy on the ImageNet.

3 Distributed SGD with Guassian Distribution Averaging

As mentioned in Sect. 1, since all workers are required to exchange their gradients, gradient synchronization poses a fundamental scalability challenge for data-parallel distributed SGDs. Although sparsity and quantization methods are significant to reduce the communication complexity of gradient synchronization, the computational efficiency of sparsity and quantization could be critical to gradient synchronization's scalability. Shi et al. pointed out that although the Top-K algorithm could reduce communication traffic for each worker, its computational overhead can offset communication reduction, which results in even higher execution time for each iteration. As we have observed in the experimental evaluation on distributed systems with a bandwidth of 100-Gbps bandwidth network, the high computational cost of the top-K algorithms can overshadow its benefits in communication efficiency. The same problem occurs with quantization algorithms, i.e., QSGD [2] and TernGrad [19]. Shi et al. [14] proposed a simple way to avoid expensive sorting and selecting the first K elements on all gradient values. They assume a Gaussian distribution of gradients and estimates a statistical threshold to select the gradient value. It has proved the importance of low computation complexity for compression. All these studies above could reduce the computational cost of gradient decent while proving the model's ability to converge. However, they all require computing workers to exchange at least a not-so-small portion of gradients.

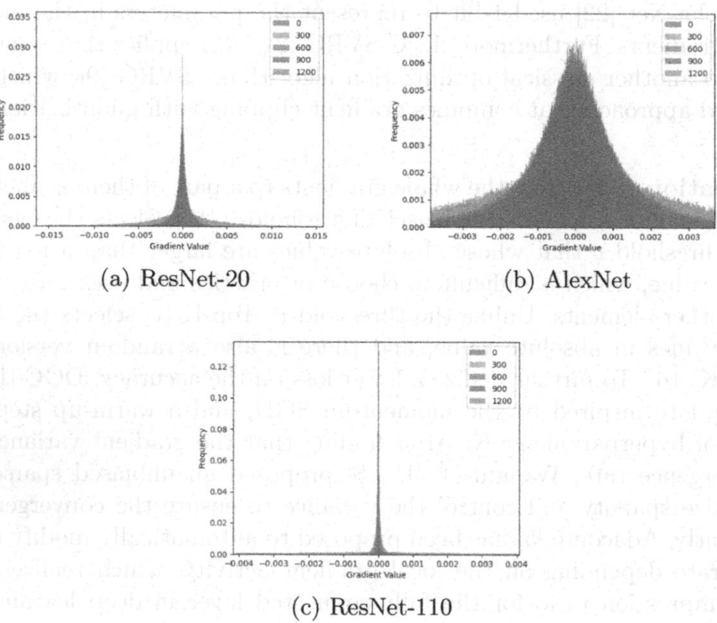

(a) ResNet-20 (b) AlexNet

(c) ResNet-110

Fig. 1. Progression of gradient distribution during training.

Based on previous studies, we proposed a novel approach to optimize the communication process. We assume that gradients computed per iteration obey a Gaussian distribution, and we could locally estimate standard deviation. Instead of selecting top gradient elements, we can exchange the standard deviation across the distributed workers and get a mean of these standard deviation values. A global mean of standard deviation could be used for gradient synchronization in all workers. We refer to our algorithm as *Gaussian Average* (GASGD). It effectively reduces the communication cost per iteration down to one values (32 bits), achieving a communication complexity of $\mathcal{O}(1)$. To further maintain the information, we also compute the mean of the gradient vector locally and adapt it to the decoding process.

3.1 Gradient Distribution

Shi et al. [14] have carried out many experiments to discuss the gradient distribution in deep learning models. Moreover, it assumed the Gaussian distribution of gradient values and proposed the Gaussian-K sparsification algorithm. Figure 1 shows the frequency distribution of gradient values with a single machine for three representative models: ResNet-20 [8], AlexNet [11], and ResNet-110. We could find that most of the values are close on either side of zero, following a normal distribution. Besides, as the models finish more iterations of the training, more gradient values converge to the center around zero (a lower standard deviation than before). In our algorithm, we also give an assumption that the gradient obey a Gaussian distribution.

3.2 Details of GASGD

As we assume a Gaussian disrtibution of gradient values ($g \sim N(\mu, \sigma^2)$), for a gradient vector $\mathbf{g} = \{g_1, g_2, \ldots, g_n\} \in \mathbb{R}^n$, we could estimate two key parameters from all gradient values as follows,

$$\overline{\mu} = \mu(\mathbf{g}) = \frac{1}{n}\sum_{i=1}^{n} g_i, \quad \overline{\sigma} = \sigma(\mathbf{g}) = \sqrt{\frac{1}{n-1}\sum_{i=1}^{i}(g_i - \overline{\mu})^2)}$$

Algorithm 1. Parallel GASGD algorithm on node k

Require: dataset $\mathcal{X}$
Require: minibatch size b per node
Require: the number of node N
Require: optimization function SGD
Require: init parameters ω_0, η_0
1: **for** $t = 0, 1, \ldots, T$ **do**
2:   **for** $i = 1, \ldots, b$ **do**
3:     Sample data x from the dataset $\mathcal{X}$
4:     $g_t^t \leftarrow \frac{1}{b}\nabla f(x; w_t)$
5:   **end for**
6:   $\mu_k^t \leftarrow \mu(g_k^t)$ and $\sigma_k^t \leftarrow \sigma(g_k^t)$
7:   $g_{normal}^t \leftarrow (g_k^t - \mu_k^t)/\sigma_k^t$
8:   $\overline{\sigma}^t \leftarrow$ **Allreduce**(σ_k^t, **average**)
9:   $g_k^t \leftarrow g_{normal}^t \cdot \overline{\sigma}^t + \mu_k^t$
10:   $\omega_{t+1} \leftarrow SGD(\eta_t, g_k^t)$
11: **end for**
12: $k_b \leftarrow Argmin(loss_k)$
13: $\omega^k \leftarrow Broadcast(\omega, k_b)$

The GASGD algorithm is described in details above. As shown in Algorithm 1, node k starts training with a learning rate of η_0 and an initial parameter ω_0. In an iteration t, node k compute its stochastic gradients g_k^t with a mini-batch form dataset $\mathcal{X}$ (Line 2 to 5). After obtaining local gradients, it then estimates the mean and standard deviation in Gaussian distribution through the equation above (Line 6). Before all nodes call the Allreduce operation to exchange their local standard deviation and get back the global mean of standard deviations (Line 8), It would map their gradient value to a standard normal distribution (Line 7). Then the local gradient would be decode by using the global standard deviation (Line 9). Finally, the model's parameters are updated using the new gradient and the specific learning rate η_t with an optimization function SGD at Line 10. At the end of the training process, one more operation, for synchronizing the model across all nodes, is to find the node which has a minimal loss and broadcast the model parameters to the others.

3.3 Convergence Analysis

Distributed Optimization (specifically SGD) can be considered as an online learning system to be analyzed in its framework. The convergence analysis is based on the convergence proof of GOGA (General Online Gradient Algorithm) by Bottou [4], similarly as the previous works [19]. We adopt two assumptions and one lemma to our analysis.

Assumption 1. *$L(\omega)$ has a single minimum ω^* and gradient $-\nabla_\omega L(\omega)$ always points to ω^*.*

$$\forall \epsilon > 0, \quad \inf_{||\omega-\omega^*||>\epsilon} \quad (\omega - \omega^*)^T \nabla_\omega L(\omega) > 0$$

Assumption 2. *Learning rate η_t is positive and constrained as follow,*

$$\begin{cases} \sum \eta_t^2 < +\infty \\ \sum \eta_t = +\infty \end{cases}$$

The constraints about learning rate η_t ensure that η_t could change at a appropriate speed. We defined the square of distance between the current weight w and the minimun weight ω^* we want to get below:

$$h_t \triangleq ||\omega - \omega^*||^2$$

where $||\cdot||$ is l_2-norm. We also define the set of all random variables before step t as follows:

$$D_t \triangleq (z_{1...t-1}, b_{1...t-1})$$

Under the Assumption 1 and 2 above, using Lyapunov process and Quasi-Martingales convergence theorem, Bottou proved the Lemma 1 below.

Lemma 1. *If $\exists \mathcal{A}, \mathcal{B} > 0$ s.t.*

$$\mathbb{E}\{(h_{t+1} - (1 + \eta_t^2 \mathcal{B}) h_t) | D_t\} \leq -2\eta_t (w - w^*)^T \nabla_\omega C(\omega_t) + \eta_t^2 \mathcal{A}$$

then $L(z, \omega)$ converges ***almost surely*** *toward the minimum ω^*. i.e. $P(\lim_{t \to +\infty} \omega_t = \omega^*) = 1$*

To further give a proof to our algorithm, we make another assumption that the gradients have a bound as follows. We also denote that $g_t + \nabla G$ as the net gain. As $\mathbb{E}(\nabla G) = 0$, we would have $\nabla_\omega C(\omega_t) = \mathbb{E}(g_t + \nabla G)$.

Assumption 3 (Gradient Bound)

$$\mathbb{E}||g_t + \nabla G|| \leq \mathbb{A} + \mathbb{B}||\omega - \omega^*||^2$$

Theorem 1. *When the learning system is updated as follow equation,*

$$\omega_{t+1} = \omega_t - \eta_t(g_t + \nabla G)$$

then, it would ***converges almost surely*** *towards minimum* ω^*. *i.e.* $P(\lim_{t\to+\infty} \omega_t = \omega^*) = 1$

Proof.

$$h_{t+1} - h_t = -2\eta_t(\omega_t - \omega^*)^T(g_t + \nabla G) + \eta_t^2(g_t + \nabla G)^2$$

Taking the expectation of the equation above based on the condition D_t, we have

$$\mathbb{E}\{h_{t+1} - h_t|D_t\} = -2\eta_t(\omega_t - \omega^*)^T\mathbb{E}\{g_t + \nabla G|D_t\} + \eta_t^2\mathbb{E}\{||g_t + \nabla G||^2|D_t\}$$

By using the following condition: $\nabla_\omega C(\omega_t) = g_t + \nabla G$, then

$$\mathbb{E}\{h_{t+1} - h_t|D_t\} = -2\eta_t(\omega_t - \omega^*)^T\nabla_\omega C(\omega_t) + \eta_t^2\mathbb{E}\{||g_t + \nabla G||^2|D_t\}$$
$$\rightarrow \mathbb{E}\{h_{t+1} - h_t|D_t\} + 2\eta_t(\omega_t - \omega^*)^T\nabla_\omega C(\omega_t) = \eta_t^2\mathbb{E}\{||g_t + \nabla G||^2|D_t\}$$

From the Gradient Bound (Assumption 3), we can further have:

$$\mathbb{E}\{h_{t+1} - h_t|D_t\} + 2\eta_t(\omega_t - \omega^*)^T\nabla_\omega C(\omega_t) \leq \mathcal{A}\eta_t^2 + \mathcal{B}\eta_t^2||\omega - \omega^*||^2 = \mathcal{A}\eta_t^2 + \mathcal{B}\eta_t^2 h_t$$

$$\mathbb{E}\{(h_{t+1} - (1 + \eta_t^2\mathcal{B})h_t)|D_t\} \leq -2\eta_t(w - w^*)^T\nabla_\omega C(\omega_t) + \eta_t^2\mathcal{A}$$

The equation above satisfies the condition of Lemma 1, which is proved by Bottou, and could proves the Theorem 1.

4 Experiments and Results

In this section, we first describe our experimental setup and then present our evaluation results to validate the convergence of GASGD. Besides, we compare its performance with Dense SGD (without compression), one sparsification techniques Top-K [1] and one quantization technique QSGD [2].

Table 1. System parameters of each computation node.

HW/SW module	Description
CPU	Intel(R) Xeon(R)Gold 6132 14-core multi-core × 2
GPU	NVIDIA Tesla V100 SXM2 × 4
OS	CentOS Linux release 7.6.1810
Memory	256 GB(shared by 2 CPUs)
Development Environment	CUDA 10.0, PyTorch 1.3.0, Horovod 0.18.2
Network Between Nodes	100-Gbps InfiniBand

4.1 Experiment Setup

We performed all experiments on a GPU-V100 cluster. The main system parameters of each node in GPU-V100 are listed in the Table 1 above.

We have implemented GASGD on top of PyTorch [41] v1.3.0 with CUDA [44] v10.1 and utilized Horovod [45] v0.18.2 for data-parallel implementation of different models. Top-K and QSGD implementation are adapted from a Github repository (GRACE) [20], which is a gradient compression framework for distributed deep learning. Both implementations use the PyTorch Tensor API.

In our tests, we have employed two different DNN models, including (1) three types of Convolutional Neural Networks (CNNs), i.e., VGG-16 [15], ResNet-110 and AlexNet using CIFAR-10 [10] or CIFAR-100 dataset; and (2) RNN which consists of the recurrent neuron, i.e., the 2-layers Long Short Term Memory (LSTM) neural network model which has 1500 hidden units per layer using Penn Treebank corpus (PTB) dataset. We train the CNNs using the momentum SGD with learning rate decay and use vanilla SGD with learning rate decay for RNN.

Table 2. Experimental setup for neural network models

Type	Net	# Params	Dataset	Batch size	Base learning rate
CNN	AlexNet	23,272,266	CIFAR-10	128	0.01
	ResNet-110	1,727,962	CIFAR-10	128	0.01
	VGG-16	14,728,266	CIFAR-100	128	0.01
RNN	LSTM-PTB	66,034,000	PTB	20	22

4.2 Convergence Accuracy

To validate the convergence of the GASGD algorithm, we train all four deep learning models, with 140 epochs for AlexNet, ResNet-110, and VGG-16, 90 epochs for LSTM-PTB with four workers. We measure the top-1 accuracy for the first three models and the perplexity score for LSTM-PTB. The details are shown in Table 2.

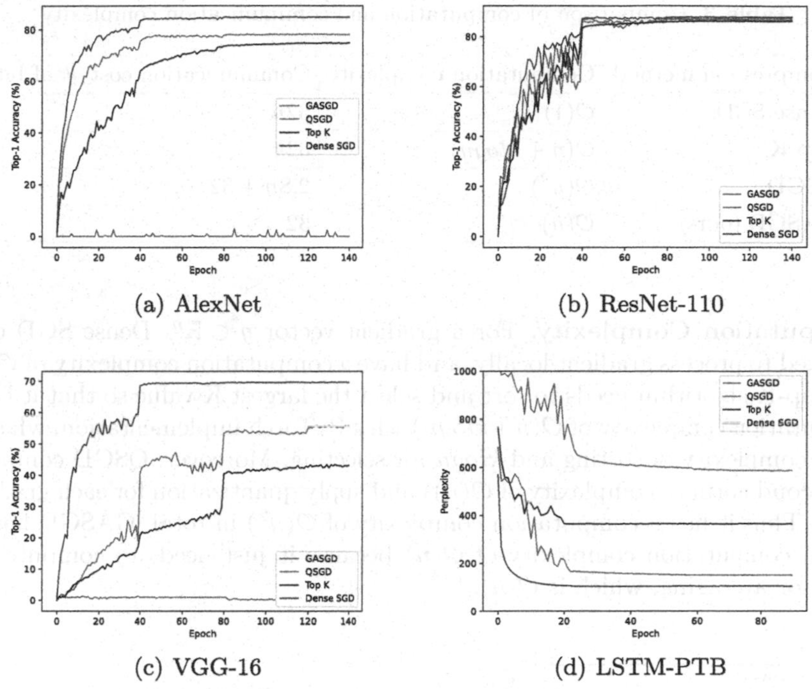

(a) AlexNet

(b) ResNet-110

(c) VGG-16

(d) LSTM-PTB

Fig. 2. Comparison of convergence accuracy with 4 workers.

Figure 2 shows that the convergence performance of different models with four workers. These results demonstrate that GASGD could converge and achieve a closer top-1 accuracy to Dense SGD within the same number of epochs among these three algorithms. GASGD achieves 78.27%, 87.60%, 56.46% top-1 accuracy for AlexNet, ResNet-110, VGG-16 and 150.51 perplexity for LSTM-PTB (Dense SGD: 84.61%, 87.99%, 69.71% top-1 accuracy and 104.83 perplexity). Furthermore, GASGD has a better performance than the other two algorithms for AlexNet, VGG-16, and LSTM-PTB.

4.3 Computation and Communication Complexity

GASGD algorithm is designed to improve gradient synchronization with reduced communication traffic without costly additional computation to process the local gradients. To obtain an insight view on its impact to computation and communication in gradient synchronization, we have characterized the asymptotic computation complexity and the amount of communication traffic (number of bits) per worker for GASGD, in comparison with the dense SGD, QSGD, and Top-K. In data-parallel distributed SGD, each worker hosts a full copy of the model and the gradients after each training iteration. We assume a model with n parameters, therefore n gradients as well (Table 3).

Table 3. Comparison of computation and communication complexity

Compression method	Computation complexity	Communication cost # of bit
Dense SGD	$\mathcal{O}(1)$	$32n$
Top K	$\mathcal{O}(n + klogn)$	$32k$
QSGD	$\mathcal{O}(n^2)$	$2.8n + 32$
GASGD (ours)	$\mathcal{O}(n)$	32

Computation Complexity. For a gradient vector $g \in \mathbb{R}^n$, Dense SGD does not need to process gradient locally, and have a computation complexity of $\mathcal{O}(1)$. The top-K algorithm needs to sort and select the largest K value so that it has a computation complexity of $\mathcal{O}(n+klogn)$ with PyTorch implementation, where n is the complexity of sorting and $klogn$ for selecting. Moreover, QSGD computes the second norm (a complexity of $\mathcal{O}(n)$) and apply quantization for each gradient value. Thus it has a computation complexity of $\mathcal{O}(n^2)$ in total. GASGD has an overall computation complexity of $\mathcal{O}(n)$ because it just needs to compute one value for averaging, which is $\mathcal{O}(n)$.

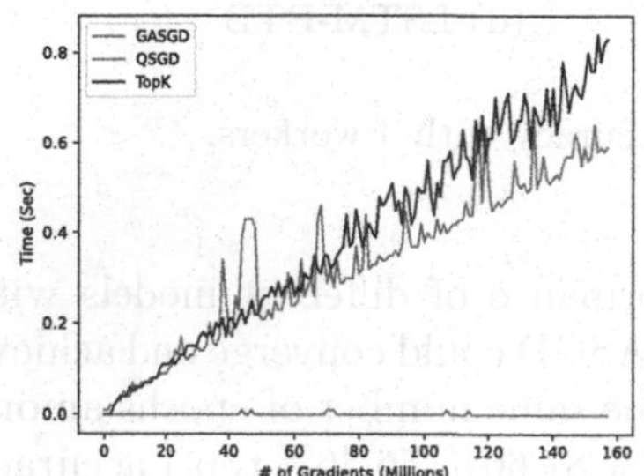

(a) Comparison of GASGD computation time with other algorithm

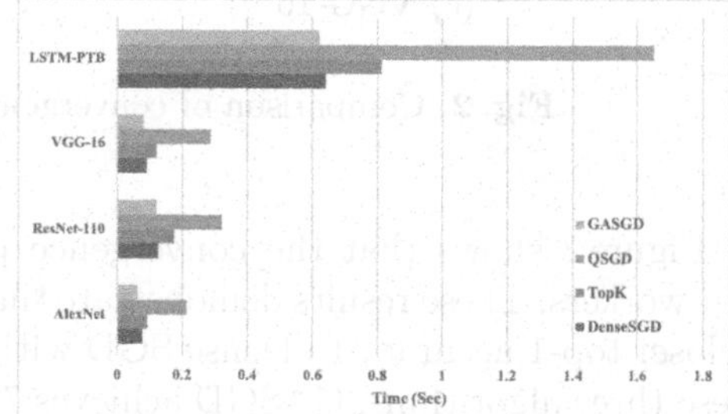

(b) Comparison of Average Iteration Time with 4 Workers

Fig. 3. The performance of GASGD on computation and communication cost.

Communication Complexity. Obviously, Dense SGD transfers all the gradients for each worker with no information loss. Thus its cost is $32n$ bits. Top-K selects the k gradients for transferring, i.e., $32k$ bits. QSGD transfers $2.8n + 32$ bits, as the author reported. GASGD transfer one value for averaging (32 bits) and achieve a communication complexity of $\mathcal{O}(1)$ for each worker.

Based on the analysis above, we also have designed some experiments to validate our results. Figure 3(a) shows that GASGD has a much lower computation complexity than the Top-K and QSGD algorithm. As shown in Fig. 3(b), GASGD has a minimum average iteration time among all four algorithms. Besides, the execution time per iteration is always the longest for the QSGD algorithm. Compare to the others, the main reason is that the overhead from its high computation complexity mitigates the benefit from the communication reduction on the 100-Gbps bandwidth InfiniBand network. These validation results demonstrate that GASGD has a better performance on convergence accuracy, computation complexity, and execution time with the other distributed algorithms. Furthermore, we could give a layer-wise implementation to improve algorithm performance over the initial implementation in which we stitch together the gradients of each layer.

5 Conclusion

In this paper, we proposed a novel compression GASGD method in distributed SGD based on the gradient distribution assumption, which just transfers one value for averaging and achieves a communication complexity of $\mathcal{O}(1)$ for each worker. We have theoretically analyzed the convergence of GASGD and also given the experimental results to validate our analysis. The GASGD has an overall improvement compared to the other algorithms. In the future, we would give a further optimization on both implementation and algorithm itself.

References

1. Aji, K.A.F., Heafield, K.: Sparse communication for distributed gradient descent. In: Proceedings of the 2017 Conference on Empirical Methods in Natural Language Processing, Copenhagen, Denmark, pp. 440–445 (2017). https://doi.org/10.18653/v1/d17-1045
2. Alistarh, D., Grubic, D., Li, J., Tomioka, R., Vojnovic, M.: QSGD: communication-efficient SGD via gradient quantization and encoding. In: Advances in Neural Information Processing Systems 30, pp. 1709–1720 (2017)
3. Bernstein, J., Wang, Y.X., Azizzadenesheli, K., Anandkumar, A.: signSGD: compressed optimisation for non-convex problems. In: Dy, J., Krause, A. (eds.) Proceedings of the 35th International Conference on Machine Learning, vol. 80, pp. 560–569. Stockholmsmässan, Stockholm, 10–15 July 2018
4. Bottou, L.: Online learning and stochastic approximations (1998)
5. Chen, C., Choi, J., Brand, D., Agrawal, A., Zhang, W., Gopalakrishnan, K.: AdaComp: adaptive residual gradient compression for data-parallel distributed training. In: 32nd AAAI Conference on Artificial Intelligence, AAAI 2018, pp. 2827–2835, January 2018
6. Dettmers, T.: 8-bit approximations for parallelism in deep learning. In: International Conference on Learning Representations (2016)
7. Devlin, J., Chang, M.W., Lee, K., Toutanova, K.: Bert: pre-training of deep bidirectional transformers for language understanding (2018)
8. He, K., Zhang, X., Ren, S., Sun, J.: Deep residual learning for image recognition. In: IEEE Conference on Computer Vision and Pattern Recognition, pp. 770–778 (2016). https://doi.org/10.1109/cvpr.2016.90
9. Johnson, R., Zhang, T.: Accelerating stochastic gradient descent using predictive variance reduction. In: Advances in Neural Information Processing Systems 26, pp. 315–323 (2013)

10. Krizhevsky, A.: Learning Multiple Layers of Features from Tiny Images. University of Toronto, May 2012
11. Krizhevsky, A., Sutskever, I., Hinton, G.E.: ImageNet classification with deep convolutional neural networks. In: Pereira, F., Burges, C.J.C., Bottou, L., Weinberger, K.Q. (eds.) Advances in Neural Information Processing Systems 25, pp. 1097–1105 (2012)
12. Lin, Y., Han, S., Mao, H., Wang, Y., Dally, W.J.: Deep gradient compression: reducing the communication bandwidth for distributed training. In: International Conference on Learning Representations, May 2018
13. Seide, F., Fu, H., Droppo, J., Li, G., Yu, D.: 1-bit stochastic gradient descent and application to data-parallel distributed training of speech DNNs. In: Interspeech 2014 (2014)
14. Shi, S., Chu, X., Cheung, K.C., See, S.: Understanding top-k sparsification in distributed deep learning. In: International Conference on Learning Representations (2020)
15. Simonyan, K., Zisserman, A.: Very deep convolutional networks for large-scale image recognition. In: International Conference on Learning Representations, May 2015
16. Stich, S.U., Cordonnier, J.B., Jaggi, M.: Sparsified SGD with memory. In: Advances in Neural Information Processing Systems 31, pp. 4447–4458 (2018)
17. Strom, N.: Scalable distributed DNN training using commodity GPU cloud computing. In: INTERSPEECH, pp. 1488–1492 (2015)
18. Wangni, J., Wang, J., Liu, J., Zhang, T.: Gradient sparsification for communication-efficient distributed optimization. In: Advances in Neural Information Processing Systems 31, pp. 1299–1309 (2018)
19. Wen, W., et al.: TernGrad: ternary gradients to reduce communication in distributed deep learning. In: Advances in Neural Information Processing Systems 30, pp. 1509–1519 (2017)
20. Xu, H., et al.: Compressed communication for distributed deep learning: survey and quantitative evaluation. Technical report, KAUST, April 2020
21. Yu, Y., Wu, J., Huang, J.: Exploring fast and communication-efficient algorithms in large-scale distributed networks. In: Proceedings of Machine Learning Research, vol. 89, pp. 674–683 (2019)
22. Zhou, S., Ni, Z., Zhou, X., Wen, H., Wu, Y., Zou, Y.: DoReFa-Net: training low bitwidth convolutional neural networks with low bitwidth gradients. In: IEEE Conference on Computer Vision and Pattern Recognition (2016)

Application Research of Improved Particle Swarm Optimization Algorithm Used on Job Shop Scheduling Problem

Guangzhi Xu[1(✉)] and Tong Wu[2]

[1] China Academy of Electronics and Information Technology, National Engineering Laboratory for Risk Perception and Prevention (NEL-RPP), Beijing 100041, China

[2] Department of Intelligent Manufacturing, Beijing Institute of Computer Technology and Application, Beijing 100854, China

Abstract. Aiming at the needs of the job shop to arrange production scheduling reasonably in the actual industry, an improved particle swarm optimization method is proposed to solve the job shop scheduling problem (JSSP). By analyzing the scheduling characteristics of the job shop and according to various resource constraints, a process-based coding and activity scheduling decoding mechanism suitable for particle swarm optimization is designed. Use the proportional mutation strategy and the ring topology structure to improve the traditional particle swarm optimization algorithm, and combine the elite selection learning strategy to retain excellent individual information which accelerate the convergence speed. The improved particle swarm optimization algorithm is used to solve standard instance problems of different scales, and the effectiveness of the algorithm is verified by comparing with other methods.

Keywords: Particle swarm optimization · Large-scale optimization · Job shop scheduling problem

1 Introduction

The job shop scheduling problem is one of the most representative and core scheduling problems, and has important practical significance for the advanced manufacturing industry. In recent years, it has attracted a large number of researchers to conduct in-depth research on this problem. Many effective optimization algorithms are proposed for the NP-hard problem of job shop scheduling. A distributed particle swarm optimization algorithm is proposed in Literature [1], using coding and decoding technology method to solve job shop scheduling problem, through simulation examples to verify the effectiveness of this algorithm, and then extended this method to other actual assembly systems. An ant colony algorithm with a local search mechanism is proposed to solve the dual-objective job shop scheduling problem, the purpose of seeking a balance between the two objectives [2]. An improved artificial bee colony algorithm is proposed to solve the more complex job shop scheduling problem [3]. Literature [4] mixed genetic algorithm and

X. Sun et al. (Eds.): ICAIS 2021, LNCS 12736, pp. 53–65, 2021.
https://doi.org/10.1007/978-3-030-78609-0_5

particle swarm optimization algorithm with Cauchy distribution to obtain an improved algorithm with better performance to solve flexible job shop scheduling problem. Literature [5] applied tabu search as a local search method, and combined with particle swarm optimization algorithm to establish an algorithm framework for solving job shop scheduling problems. A particle swarm optimization algorithm based on neighborhood structure is proposed which performs a meticulous search through critical path analysis technique. This algorithm is more effective for complex job-shop problems [6].

In this paper, an improved particle swarm optimization algorithm is proposed which is based on the ring topology, combined with the variable ratio mutation strategy and the elite learning strategy, according to a coding and decoding technology to solve job shop scheduling problem. So as to provide a new way for the research of job shop scheduling problem.

2 Mathematical Model of Job Shop Scheduling Problem

A typical job shop scheduling problem is described as follows: a scheduling system has n sets of workpieces to be processed J = {1, 2, ..., n}, which can be set on m machines M = {1, 2, ..., m} to complete the processing task. Each workpiece has m processing steps, named separately $O_{1m}, \ldots, O_{2m}, \ldots, O_{nm}$, where O_{11} represents the first step of workpiece 1, O_{1m} represents the mth step of workpiece 1, and so on to the mth step of workpiece n. Each workpiece has a predetermined processing route, and the processing operation time of the process of each workpiece on the corresponding machine is defined. The purpose of scheduling is how to reasonably arrange the processing order of all workpieces on each machine tool to satisfy the optimization constraints [7]. Workshop scheduling problems generally have two general constraints, which named order constraints and resource constraints. In the process of processing, in addition to satisfying the constraints, the following ideal conditions are usually assumed:

(1) The processing of the next process can be started only after the processing of the previous process of each workpiece is completed, and no process has the priority of preemptive processing;
(2) At the same time, a certain process of a workpiece can only be processed on one machine, and a lathe cannot process two processes at the same time;
(3) The processing time of each workpiece includes its preparation time and processing setting time, and the processing time remains unchanged;
(4) During the entire processing process, once the process is performed, it cannot be interrupted, and each lathe is fault-free and effective;
(5) Each workpiece cannot be processed multiple times on the same lathe, and all lathes handle different types of processes;
(6) Without special regulations, the processing time of the workpiece remains unchanged.

In a typical job shop scheduling problem, conditions 1 and 2 are the sequence constraints and resource constraints of the processing process, and the other conditions are the ideal processing conditions designed to construct a fault-free processing process [8].

In order to establish an ideal mathematical model, J = {1, 2, …, n} represents the workpiece set, M = {1, 2, …, m} represents the machine set, each workpiece has the same process, The process set is O = {1, 2, …, m}, and the workpiece Ji has O_{ij} processes, then the set of all processes is $I = \sum_{i=1}^{n}\sum_{j=1}^{m} O_{ij}$, where each process meets the sequence constraints. Set T_{ij} represent the processing time of step O_{ij}, F_{ij} is the completion time of step O_{ij}, and A(t) represents the set of steps being processed at time t. If the operation O_{ij} is to be processed on the machine M_k, it is expressed as $E_{ijk} = 1$, otherwise it is $E_{ijk} = 0$. Using minimized maximum completion time as the optimization goal, the mathematical model can be described as follows,

$$S = \min\left(\max_{i \in n}(\max_{k \in m} X_{ik})\right) \tag{1}$$

The constraints are

$$F_{ik} \leq F_{ij} - T_{ij},\ \mathrm{k} \in P_{ij};\ \ i = 1, 2, \ldots, n;\ j = 1, 2, \ldots, m \tag{2}$$

$$\sum\nolimits_{j \in A(t)} E_{ijk} \leq 1,\ \ k \in m;\ \ t \geq 0 \tag{3}$$

$$F_{ij} \geq 0,\ i = 1, 2, \ldots,\ n;\ \ j = 1, 2, \ldots, m \tag{4}$$

where X_{ik} is the completion time of the workpiece i on the machine k. Formula (1) is the minimized the maximum workpiece completion time, which is makespan performance index. Equation (2) is used to guarantee sequence constraints between processes, and Eq. (3) indicates that each lathe can only process one process at the same time. Equation (4) ensures that all processes are completed.

A typical example is shown in Table 1, including 3 workpieces, 2 processes, and 2 machines in job shop scheduling problem.

Table 1. Processing timetable for job shop scheduling problem

Workpieces	Process	Machine and processing time	
		M1	M2
J1	O_{11}		2
	O_{12}	2	
J2	O_{21}	3	
	O_{22}		2
J3	O_{31}	1	
	O_{32}		1

Disjunctive graph models are generally used to describe job shop scheduling problems. For the job shop scheduling problem of n workpieces and m machines, the corresponding disjunctive graph model is represented by $G = (N, A, E)$, where N is the set of points composed of all the processing steps, including virtual operations 0 and n * m + 1 (respectively representing start processing and end processing); *A* represents a set of arcs connected by a sequence of prescribed constraints in the same workpiece. The connected arc is also called a directed arc and is represented by a solid line. The dotted line connects the extraction arcs between all processes on the same machine, and the extraction arcs of all machines form the set *E*.

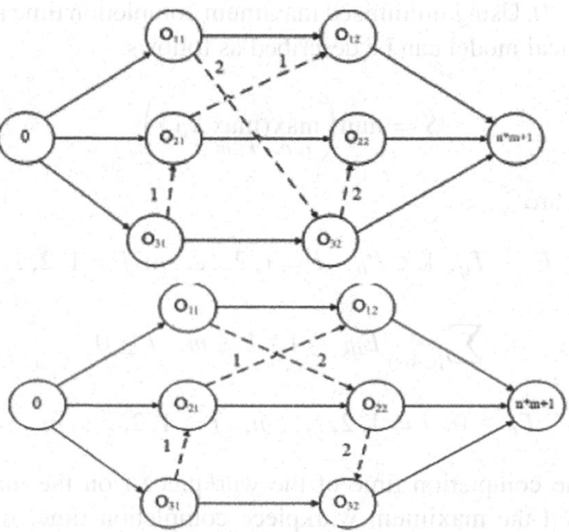

Fig. 1. The feasible disjunction diagram in Table 1

Figure 1 is an example of the JSSP problem extraction graph shown in Table 1, which represents two different feasible solutions. In the Fig. 1, the arc set 1 constitutes E1 which represents the sequence of processes on the machine 1, and the arc set 2 constitutes E2 which corresponds to the sequence of workpieces processed on the machine 2. It can be analyzed that the ultimate goal of scheduling is to find a solution that traverses all processes and satisfies the shortest path in set E. Optimizing the maximum completion time in the scheduling scheme is to make the longest path shorter in set E. As shown in the example, the longest path of the extraction graph b is 7 unit times in set E2 corresponding to machine 2, which is more unit time than E1 corresponding to machine 1. In order to reduce the spent time in set E2, find a new solution through the optimization scheme, such as inserting the original process O_{32} into the idle machine 2, which change the processing sequence on the machine 2. Shortening the longest path makes it possible to find an optimized solution in a shorter time.

Compared with the traveling salesman problem, the job shop scheduling problem has a more complicated situation, which is caused by the following reasons [9]:

1) The scope of the solution space is obviously increased. Assuming that there are n work pieces and m machines, which can combine $(n!)^m$ solutions. For example, a scheduling problem with a scale of 10 * 10, the solution space is expanded to 3.96 * 1065, if it traverses all the values in the solution space, it need to use

a computer that operates 100 million times per second to continuously work for 1.26 * 1050 years.

2) Due to the various constraints of the problem, the difficulty of encoding and decoding is increased, especially for the optimization algorithm for solving continuity problems, appropriate processing is required.
3) When solving hypersurface optimization problems, there are often more irregularly distributed suboptimal solutions. Due to the lack of prior information of the problem, it is more difficult to find the optimal solution to the problem.

3 Job Shop Scheduling Algorithm Based on Improved Particle Swarm Optimization

This paper proposes an improved particle swarm optimization algorithm for the job shop scheduling problem. First step, the process of the workpiece is coded. Next step, the discrete scheduling problem is converted into a continuous problem that can be solved by the particle swarm optimization algorithm. Then, the target area is searched according to an improved particle swarm optimization algorithm. Finally, the optimal solution obtained by the algorithm is activated decoding. Determine the processing sequence of the workpiece, and select the optimal processing procedure of the job shop scheduling problem according to the minimum completion time.

3.1 Encoding Operation

Encoding operation is an important process link of particle swarm optimization algorithm applied to workshop production scheduling problems. Without encoding operation, particle swarm optimization algorithm cannot be used to solve discrete scheduling problems. Therefore, this chapter uses a process-based coding technique to make continuous optimization algorithms for solving discrete problems. Through coding, each particle contains all the workpiece processes, which represents a feasible solution to the corresponding scheduling problem. Different discrete values are used to represent different workpieces, and the number of occurrences of the values indicates different processing procedures for each workpiece. For example, if a processing workshop needs m machines to process n workpieces, each particle is composed of n × m variable dimensions, and the variable dimensions in the particles represent the sequence-constrained process. After decoding operations, the machine pair can be obtained. The processing sequence of the workpiece process forming a feasible solution to the job shop scheduling problem.

For example, a 3 × 3 workshop scheduling problem consisting of 3 machines and 3 workpieces. After the encoding operation, one of the particles is [1 2 2 3 3 2 1 1 3], and the values 1, 2, and 3 represent different workpieces. One of the workpieces has 3 different processing steps, so each number is appearing 3 times. Use O_{ij} to represent the j-th processing step of the i-th workpiece, then the operation step indicated by the corresponding particle is $[O_{11}\ O_{21}\ O_{22}\ O_{31}\ O_{32}\ O_{23}\ O_{12}\ O_{13}\ O_{33}]$.

Owing to the particle swarm optimization algorithm is an optimization algorithm for solving continuity problems, it is necessary to convert continuous real numbers into discrete codes to use the particle swarm optimization algorithm. First, sort the particles in ascending order, take the corresponding position index to form a matrix of the same size, divide all the elements in the matrix by the number of operations and take an integer, and then determine the dimensional order of the process of each workpiece in the particle, use a continuous series of ascending numbers indicate the process of the workpiece. The starting data of different workpieces is associated with the corresponding workpiece number, and a continuous code is formed according to the sequence of the processes. For example, a particle's process-based code is [1 2 2 3 3 2 1 1 3], and it becomes [1 4 5 7 8 6 2 3 9] by the above conversion method, where the value 1 indicates the first of the 1 workpiece. In the process, the value 2 represents the second process of 1 workpiece, the value 4 represents the first process of 2 workpiece, and so on, and the value 9 represents the third process of 3 workpiece. The values 1, 2, and 3 are used to represent the sequence constraints of 1 workpiece process, respectively, to avoid repeated occurrence of the values. The above method provides a way to solve discrete optimization problems using continuous intelligent optimization methods.

3.2 Particle Swarm Initialized

The initialized particle swarm should be widely distributed and cover most of the search space. Therefore, in this chapter, the initial population is generated by random distribution, then the initial population is normalized by coding technology, so that each initial particle meets the constraints of the actual problem, ensuring the feasibility and rationality of each particle. Randomly perturb of 20% particles and select the same number of particles to form the initial population. Expand the distribution of the initial population through the above methods [10].

3.3 Improved Particle Swarm Algorithm

In this part, the improved particle swarm algorithm based on the ring topology and proportional variation of the elite learning strategy is used to solve the scheduling optimization problem of the job shop.

Niching Methods with Ring Topology. Most existing niching methods usually suffer from the niching parameters adjustment, such as the species distance in species conserving genetic algorithm and the species radius in the speciation-based PSO. The niching radius should be set to neither too large nor too small. If it set too large, which would be very hard to capture the global optima exactly. On the other hand, if the niche radius set too small, these niches tend to prematurely converge. Relying on the niching radius is a main disadvantage for niching methods.

In this paper, it will prove that a PSO with ring topology can urge stable niching behavior and maintain diverse population without any niching parameters. In particular, one key advantage of this type of PSO algorithms is that there is no need to specify any niching parameters, which are usually required in existing traditional niching methods. In reducing the premature convergence of PSO, more ring communication topologies (two neighborhood members and one interacting member) have been shown to be very effective.

The appropriate PSO algorithm with a ring topology uses the local memory of particles to form a stable network. It reserves the best positions it has found so far and maintains solutions diverse through elitist learning strategy instead of one particle *p*best only. A ring topology is described as follows. One particle interacts with two neighboring particles to form an ecological niche. The first particle is the neighbor of the last one and vice versa. The neighborhood of the *i*-th particle returns the best-fit personal best solution $nbest_i$ in its neighborhood, which represents the neighborhood best for the *i*-th particle.

Different particles residing on the ring are possible to have different *nbests*. So it is possible to converge to different optima for different particles over time.

$$v_{ij}^{k+1} = wv_{ij}^{k} + c_1 r_1 (pbest_{ij}^{k} - x_{ij}^{k}) + c_2 r_2 (nbest_{ij}^{k} - x_{ij}^{k}) \quad (5)$$

The ring topology neighborhood structure not only provides an opportunity to decelerate the rapid information propagation from the super individuals, but also makes different neighborhood bests to exist together (rather than becoming homogeneous) over time. The reason is that a particle's *nbest* will be updated only when there exists a better personal best around [11].

Elitist Select and Learning Strategy. It is obvious that PSO with ring topological structure supplies the opportunity for each particle to learn from its local niche best and the *p*best solutions. Correspondingly, the possibility of being trapped by local optimum will be decrease. However, owing to the natural difficulties of multimodal functions it is also liable to be trapped by local optima. Furthermore, particle's *p*best is used as the learning source of other PSOs. The promising particles are adopted used as the potentially exemplars to guide the particle flying. In traditional PSO algorithm, each particle will abandon its current *p*best solution if even better solution is existing. However, the abandoned solutions may also have better character and include the hopeful information about the global optimal solution. So as to make use of the useful historical information, one elitist set is constructed as an exemplar guidance pool.

The elitist set is composed by a history *p*best and other satisfactory suboptimal individuals with 10 individuals. The sub-optimal solutions record some abandoned individuals; however, the location is opposite to the *p*best solutions. After one iteration, the worst solution in elitist set is updated by the current particle or the *p*best with better function value. Each particle learns information from the elitist set (*eset*) randomly, which is described as (6).

$$v_{ij}^{k+1} = wv_{ij}^{k} + c_1 r_1 (eset_{ij}^{k} - x_{ij}^{k}) + c_2 r_2 (nbest_{ij}^{k} - x_{ij}^{k}) \quad (6)$$

Mutation Strategy. A new hybrid mutation strategy is proposed which intends to maintaining the diversity and avoiding premature convergence. The proposed mutation strategy balances between exploration and exploitation by means of combining the mutation operation of differential evolution (DE) with the global search ability of PSO.

In traditional algorithms, large search space usually means higher risk for divergence, so it is an adventure to make particles have larger search space. Therefore, how to enlarge the exploitation areas of particles is an important improving direction for PSO. However, too large exploitation areas will mismatch the inherent need of algorithm to decrease the quality of particles. Mutation operation can preserve information through crossover operation in differential evolution. If a random number is larger than the crossover probability the component of the original position of the particle will be copied to the new individual. So, it is natural to combine both sides to utilize their advantages simultaneously. Conservatism and adventurism principle mutation, i.e., scaling mutation strategy, is defined as follows

$$l_j = \begin{cases} 0 \; if \quad s_j < -1 \\ 1 \; else \end{cases} \tag{7}$$

$$v_{ij}^{k+1} = wv_{ij}^k + c_1r_1(\text{eset}_{ij}^k - x_{ij}^k) + c_2r_2(lbest_{ij}^k - x_{ij}^k) \tag{8}$$

$$x_{ij}^{k+1} = x_{ij}^k + |s_j| \cdot l_j v_{ij}^{k+1} \tag{9}$$

where Gaussian random number s˜ N (0, 1), lj ∈ {0, 1}. If sj < −1, lj = 0, xk + 1ij = xkij. At this current conservatism principle procedure, the corresponding j-th component of the i-th particle will preserve the initial information from the previous position.

If sj ≥ −1, lj = 1. Currently, it becomes the adventurism principle, in which particles are possible to move to new positions with different coefficients. So, the search space is possible to be scaled by this mutation strategy according to the above analysis.

$$v_{ij}^{k+1} = wv_{ij}^k + c_1r_1(eset_{ij}^k - x_{ij}^k) + c_2r_2(nbest_{ij}^k - x_{ij}^k) \tag{10}$$

$$x_{ij}^{k+1} = x_{ij}^k + |s_j| \cdot l_j v_{ij}^{k+1} \tag{11}$$

3.4 Decoding Operations

The optimal solution for the job shop scheduling problem must be active scheduling, so this chapter uses active decoding operations to calculate the minimum maximum completion time by calculating the processing time of the process on each machine. The activity decoding operation flow is: first, determine the machine number of the workpiece process represented by each particle; then, calculate the start processing time and completion processing time of the workpiece process; then, according to the sequence constraints and resource constraints, the workpiece process is the corresponding machine starts processing at the earliest allowable processing time. After finishing all the workpiece processes, calculate the total processing time of each machine one by one, and select the longest time as the adaptation value.

This chapter uses the most commonly minimum maximum completion time as the optimization goal of the job shop scheduling problem, that is makespan. Through the decoding operation, the corresponding makespan value can be obtained.

4 Process Steps of JSSP-SERPSO Algorithm

Steps of the algorithm are as follows:

Step 1: Initialize the population and define control parameters of the elite library.
Step 2: Encode the generated particles, calculate the fitness value of each particle, and record the optimal value. Establish an elite library using the best 10 particles in the population.
Step 3: Construct a ring topology structure, use the left (right) particles of the current particle to form a niche neighborhood, and record the optimal particles in the neighborhood.
Step 4: Update each particle in the population according to formula (10) and (11), replace the current individual optimal particle with a random particle in the elite library, replace the global optimal particle with the optimal particle in the neighborhood, and mutate the dimension of the current particle using normal distribution.
Step 5: Calculate the optimal solution through decoding. If the iteration termination criterion is met, stop the iteration and output the optimal solution. If not, return to Step 2.

In Step 4, the replacement operation represents that the particles obtain update information from better elite particles and neighborhood particles in the population, while the mutation operation improves the diversity of the population and provide more effective and feasible solutions.

5 Experiments and Results Analysis

In order to verify the performance of the proposed JSSP-SERPSO algorithm, several experiments are developed using the standard JSSP test, including a total of 10 scheduling problems in LA (LA01, LA02, LA06, LA07, LA11, LA12, LA18, LA23, LA26, LA31). The goal is to minimize the maximum completion time of workpieces. The designed experiments compare the results of the proposed JSSP-SERPSO algorithm with other algorithms that are GA, LSGA, GRASP, PGA. Parameters of the JSSP-SERPSO algorithm are set as follows: the population size is set to n = 100; the size of elite library is 10; the maximum number of iterations is MaxIter = 10000. For the large-scale problems after LA18, the maximum number of iterations MaxIter = 30000. For each test problem, the experiment runs 20 times continuously. The parameter settings of the comparison algorithms are designed according to the original pattern.

Table 2 gives the optimization results of JSSP-SERPSO and some other algorithms in the literature. Best is for JSSP - SERPSO algorithm to get the optimal solution, "–" indicates no corresponding data. In order to try to eliminate the random factor, algorithms run independently 20 times, selecting average value as an indicator of algorithm, which is to make the algorithm more stable and effective. As Table 2 shows, JSSP-SERPSO can basically obtain the optimal solution for small-scale simples about LA01, LA02, LA06, LA07, LA11 and LA12 problems. Its average value can also reach the optimal solution, which has good stability. For the larger and more difficult problem of LA18, JSSP-SERPSO also achieves excellent results and achieves an optimal value. In the LA23 with a size of 15 $\times$ 10, JSSP-SERPSO may obtain the optimal solution, but its mean value cannot obtain the value of the optimal solution. JSSP-SERPSO in scale for LA26 problem, not to find the optimal value to solve the problem, according to the average index, the lack of certain algorithm local search ability which need to design a kind of auxiliary local search algorithm to improve the local search ability of the algorithm. In LA31 problem, JSSP-SERPSO can obtain the optimal value of the problem every time, which shows the effectiveness of the algorithm in dealing with larger scale scheduling problems.

Table 2. Comparison results between JSSP-SERPSO and other algorithms

Instance	Size	BKS	SERPSO		GA	LSGA	GRASP	PGA
			Best	Mean				
LA01	10 × 5	666	666	666	666	—	666	666
LA02	10 × 5	655	655	655	666	—	655	681
LA06	15 × 5	926	926	926	926	—	926	926
LA07	15 × 5	890	890	890	890	—	890	890
LA11	20 × 5	1222	1222	1222	1222	—	1222	1222
LA12	20 × 5	1039	1039	1039	1039	—	1039	1039
LA18	10 × 10	848	848	851	848	857	848	916
LA23	15 × 10	1032	1032	1039	1032	1047	1032	1072
LA26	20 × 10	1218	1246	1251	1231	1307	1271	1278
LA31	30 × 10	1784	1784	1784	1784	1784	1784	—

It can also be seen from the table that JSSP-SERPSO compares with other algorithms. Because the basic structure and operational mode design of GA algorithm are more suitable for the optimization of discrete problems, JSSP-SERPSO usually shows certain advantages in solving discrete problems. PSO algorithm is an optimization method for solving continuous problems, so coding and decoding are needed to facilitate. Therefore, PSO algorithm has certain disadvantages compared with GA in algorithm construction. However, this does not hinder the diversity of problem solving, so PSO optimization algorithm can be explored and applied in a broader field. GA algorithm solves scheduling optimization problems, whether for small scale problems or large scale problems, shows better optimization performance and strong stability, with excellent overall performance. Compared with GA, JSSP-SERPSO is only slightly superior to GA algorithm in LA02.

Table 2 gives the comparative results of JSSP-SERPSO, LSGA, GRASP and PGA. According to the average value of JSSP-SERPSO algorithm, LA18, LA23, and LA26 problems, JSSP-SERPSO has a superior optimization effect and achieves a smaller maximum completion time, while LSGA only obtains the same optimization performance in

LA31 problems. For GRASP algorithm, the optimal value obtained on problem LA26 is slightly lower than the average value obtained by JSSP-SERPSO algorithm, which basically achieves the same performance on other problems. However, the optimal value obtained by PGA on the small scale LA02 problem and the large scale LA18, LA23 and LA26 problem is not as good as the average value obtained by JSSP-SERPSO algorithm.

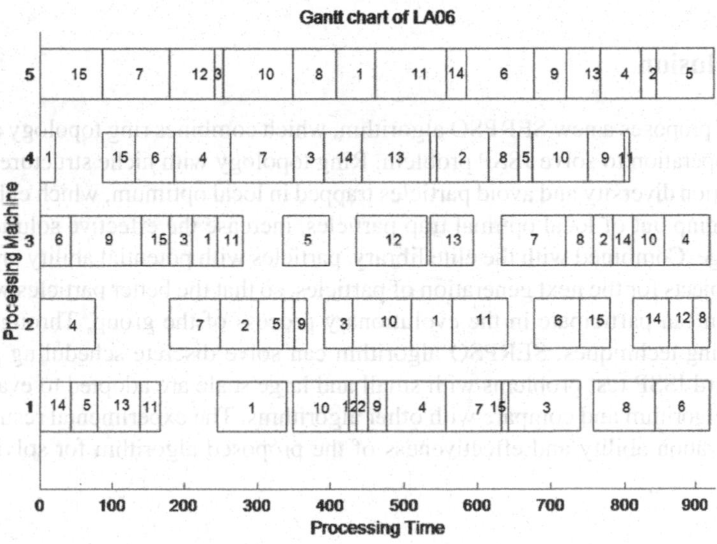

Fig. 2. Gantt chart of problem LA06

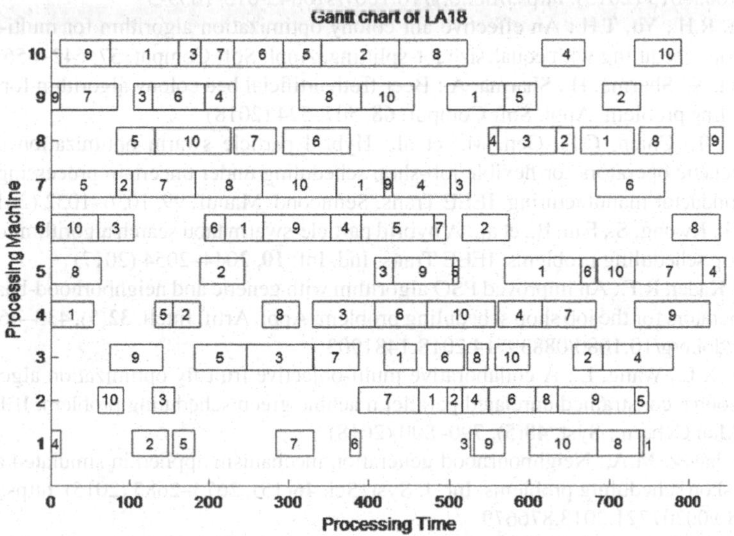

Fig. 3. Gantt chart of problem LA18

Figures 2, 3 give the JSSP-SERPSO Gantt chart for problems of LA06, LA18. As can be seen from the figure, the minimum maximum completion time was obtained in the whole processing process due to the adoption of the active decoding strategy.

The experimental results show that the JSSP-SERPSO algorithm proposed in this chapter achieves good results in solving job shop scheduling problem and provides an effective way for solving JSSP problem.

6 Conclusion

This paper proposes a new SERPSO algorithm, which combines ring topology and scale mutation operation to solve JSSP problem. Ring topology with niche structure increase the population diversity and avoid particles trapped in local optimum, which enhance the ability to jump out of local optimal trap particles, increase the effective solution of the search range. Combined with the elite library, particles with potential ability are used as learning objects for the next generation of particles, so that the better particles with good information can participate in the evolutionary process of the group. Through coding and decoding techniques, SERPSO algorithm can solve discrete scheduling problem. Ten standard JSSP test problems with small and large scale are adopted to evaluate the proposed algorithm and compare with other algorithms. The experimental results verify the optimization ability and effectiveness of the proposed algorithm for solving JSSP problems.

References

1. Nouiri, M., Bekrar, A., Jemai, A., Niar, S., Ammari, A.C.: An effective and distributed particle swarm optimization algorithm for flexible job-shop scheduling problem. J. Intell. Manuf. **29**(3), 603–615 (2015). https://doi.org/10.1007/s10845-015-1039-3
2. Huang, R.H., Yu, T.H.: An effective ant colony optimization algorithm for multi-objective job-shop scheduling with equal-size lot-splitting. Appl. Soft Comput. **57**, 642–656 (2017)
3. Sharma, N., Sharma, H., Sharma, A.: Beer froth artificial bee colony algorithm for job-shop scheduling problem. Appl. Soft Comput. **68**, 507–524 (2018)
4. Jamrus, T., Chien, C.F., Gen, M., et al.: Hybrid particle swarm optimization combined with genetic operators for flexible job-shop scheduling under uncertain processing time for semiconductor manufacturing. IEEE Trans. Semicond. Manuf. **99**, 1036–1052 (2017)
5. Hao, G., Kwong, S., Fan, B., et al.: A hybrid particle-swarm tabu search algorithm for solving job shop scheduling problems. IEEE Trans. Ind. Inf. **10**, 2044–2054 (2017)
6. Abdel-Kader, R.F.: An improved PSO algorithm with genetic and neighborhood-based diversity operators for the job shop scheduling problem. Appl. Artif. Intell. **32**(5), 433–462 (2018). https://doi.org/10.1080/08839514.2018.1481903
7. Zheng, X.L., Wang, L.: A collaborative multi-objective fruit fly optimization algorithm for the resource constrained unrelated parallel machine green scheduling problem. IEEE Trans. Syst. Man Cybern.: Syst. **48**(5), 790–800 (2018)
8. Cruz-Chávez, M.A.: Neighbourhood generation mechanism applied in simulated annealing to job shop scheduling problems. Int. J. Syst. Sci. **46**(15), 2673–2685 (2015). https://doi.org/10.1080/00207721.2013.876679
9. Spanos, A.C., Ponis, S.T., Tatsiopoulos, I.P., et al.: A new hybrid parallel genetic algorithm for the job-shop scheduling problem. Int. Trans. Oper. Res. **21**(3), 479–499 (2014)

10. Li, Y., et al.: Intelligent prediction of private information diffusion in social networks. Electronics **9**(5), 719 (2020)
11. Zhang, L., Li, Y., Liao, Y., Kong, R., Wu, W.: An empirical exploration of intelligence system based big data. J. CAEIT **11**(6), 608–613 (2016)

Artificial Intelligence Chronic Disease Management System Based on Medical Resource Perception

Yuntao Ma[1], Genxin Chen[2], Wenqing Yan[3], Bin Xu[3], and Jin Qi[1,3](✉)

[1] NanJing Pharmaceutical Co., Ltd., Nanjing 21000, China
qijin@njupt.edu.cn
[2] School of Automation, Nanjing University of Posts and Telecommunications, Nanjing 21000, China
[3] School of Internet of Things, Nanjing University of Posts and Telecommunications, Nanjing 21000, China

Abstract. Chronic diseases have the characteristics of high morbidity, low awareness, and high disability and fatalities, which have a huge impact on human health. How to optimize chronic disease management through existing technologies is a worthy research direction. This article takes chronic disease management as the research object, and designs an artificial intelligence chronic disease management system based on medical resource perception by combining technologies such as Artificial Intelligence (AI), user portrait, and Knowledge Graph (KG). Supported by multi-dimensional medical big data, through multi-party linkage, the functions of patient-oriented risk assessment, hierarchical diagnosis and treatment, and diagnosis and treatment decision assistance for medical workers and follow-up planning assistance are realized. The project achieved 60,243 patient-time management of chronic disease patients through cooperation with a tertiary grade A hospital in Nanjing, and the drug compliance of chronic disease patients was 94.5%. Practice results demonstrate that the system can promote the efficient and orderly operation of the chronic disease management ecology.

Keywords: Chronic diseases · Artificial intelligence · User portrait · Knowledge graph · Medical big data

1 Introduction

With the development of society and economy, the change of people's lifestyles and the intensification of population aging, Non-communicable Chronic Diseases (NCDS) are becoming increasingly an important public health problem for sustainable social and economic development at home and abroad [1]. NCDS are characterized by high morbidity, low awareness, and high disability and fatalities [2]. The "Progress in Disease Control and Prevention in China (2015)" report shows that 86.6% of Chinese residents died of NCDS, and the burden of NCDS accounted for more than 70% of the total disease burden [3]. NCDS have become a major public health problem affecting China's

X. Sun et al. (Eds.): ICAIS 2021, LNCS 12736, pp. 66–77, 2021.
https://doi.org/10.1007/978-3-030-78609-0_6

economic and social development [4]. The World Health Organization (WHO) pointed out that through effective health management of patients with NCDS, as well as the discovery and elimination of chronic disease-related risk factors, timely assessment of the patient's health status and provision of targeted health guidance can improve patients health awareness, reduce the incidence of diseases and medical expenses, to achieve the goal of improving the health of the population and improving the quality of life of the population [5].

At present, chronic disease management generally has the following problems. First, the cost of NCDS patients' health management is relatively high. Many studies have shown [6–8] that the results of per capita management costs of community interventions such as dyslipidemia, hypertension and diabetes are similar, and health management costs account for about 23.9%–26.4% of the total cost. In addition, the distribution of medical resources is unbalanced, the long-term shortage of community health service personnel, and the uneven quality of personnel have led to the flow of community residents who need NCDS management services to large hospitals, which aggravated the uneven distribution of resources [9]. Under the conditions of increasing demand for medical services, patients may not be able to obtain satisfactory and reasonable medical services, so how to optimize the allocation of medical resources has become an urgent social problem to be solved. Finally, the traditional disease-centered medical and health services in the past cannot meet the differentiated needs of chronically ill patients for long-term and continuous health management. Studies have shown that in terms of empathy for the quality of community NCDS management, among patients with different educational levels, the higher the educational level, the greater the gap between perception and expectations [10].

In recent years, the world's medical and health expenditure has increased year by year. However, with the increasing demand for medical services, medical resources are still in short supply [11], and not all diseases or all patients can obtain satisfactory and reasonable medical services. How to improve the efficiency of medical ecological operation by optimizing the allocation of medical resources, so as to expand the welfare of all beneficiaries, is a research point worth entering at present.

To sum up, an efficient NCDS management plan needs to use a variety of AI, big data, "Internet +" and other technologies to achieve real-time, full-process management of patients from multiple aspects such as monitoring, intervention, and effect evaluation. Adopt intelligent means to provide patients with timely feedback, quickly screen key intervention targets, and improve the efficiency of graded management services for patients with NCDS. This article proposes a NCDS management system based on AI, and conducts pilot verification in a medical complex, and achieves good results.

2 Related Work

With the rapid development of mobile communication technology and the popularization of intelligent electronic devices, such as smart phones, tablets, smart bracelets, etc., mobile medical technology has gradually attracted the attention of experts. Since Robert first proposed the concept of mobile health in 2005 [12], Internet + chronic disease management has been widely used in patient health information testing, intelligent health education, remote diagnosis and consultation, network platform information sharing, community mutual assistance and self-management Waiting for the scene [13–17]. These studies show that "Internet +" as an efficient and fast chronic disease management method has opened up new ways for NCDS diagnosis and personalized treatment, so that patients can fully understand their own NCDS conditions and improve their self-management capabilities.

In order to promote the management efficiency and quality of NCDS, some researchers focus on big data processing and analysis of NCDS of AI, using technologies such as cloud computing and data mining, provide risk assessment for patients at high risk of NCDS early warning, early disease prediction, lifestyle intervention, customized auxiliary treatment and follow-up, doctor-patient interaction and other services [18–21]. In addition, some researchers have paid attention to the cognitive research on the integration of medical resources. For example, based on the social welfare function [22], a mixed integer programming model that weighs utilitarianism and fairness is established to solve the problem of medical resource allocation among different levels of hospitals. There are also researchers who use hospital medical resources in conjunction with other medical resources from the perspective of game theory [23] to achieve the problem of maximizing benefits for this resource. In addition, the work [24] use fuzzy analytic hierarchy process to propose an evaluation model based on a multi-level evaluation index system to evaluate the effectiveness of medical resource allocation.

However, there are few researches on the allocation of medical resources from the perspective of collaborative cognition of resources. The purpose of this paper is to build a cognitive computational medicine engine for the prevention and management of NCDS in the whole population. With the clinical pathway as the core, it provides comprehensive, continuous and active management for NCDS patients through resource optimization, scientific coordination of interactions among professional doctors, family doctors, pharmacists, nursing staff and patients' families and other measures.

3 Artificial Intelligence Management System Based on Resource Cognition

This paper designs and constructs a set of artificial intelligence chronic non-communicable disease health management platform based on medical complex and hierarchical diagnosis and treatment. By linking the resources of different medical institutions and different participants of health management, data from multiple dimensions, such as portrait of patients, diagnosis clinical path and medication history, were collected to assist and support the development of NCDS management, and good results were achieved.

First of all, the platform will collect, clean, organize and integrate massive health big data of medical institutions. Through patient portraits, national NCDS health guide, KG, etc., it will study the establishment of NCDS management tools such as special disease knowledge base, clinical decision support system, and intelligent health consultation service. The data analysis model is used to manage patients' conditions at different levels, optimize medical resources, and provide services for patients at different levels.

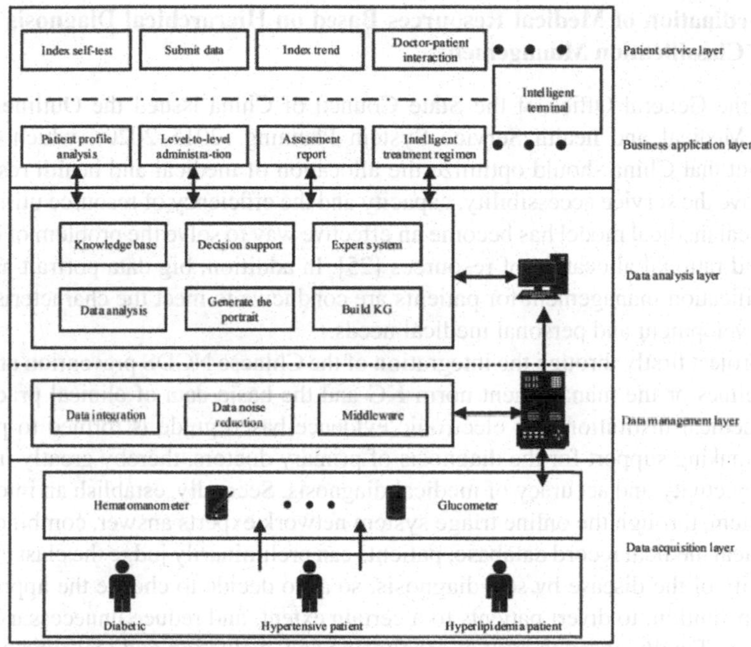

Fig. 1. Management framework of NCDS patients based on resource awareness

3.1 System Architecture

The artificial intelligence chronic non-communicable disease management service platform is divided into data collection layer, data management layer, business application layer and patient service layer, as shown in Fig. 1. The data collection layer collects patient health data through IoT devices, and the data management layer classifies and aggregates the data of NCDS such as diabetes and hypertension to form a special disease database; the business application layer builds NCDS patients on the basis of the NCDS big data center Specialized disease files, NCDS intelligent knowledge base based on KGs, data analysis models for risk prediction and early warning, and personalized patient health portraits to better support the patient service layer of the platform. The patient service layer is connected with the information system of medical institutions to provide online medical treatment, medicine delivery home, patient consultation and other services in Internet hospitals, and to build a closed-loop service system of outpatient, inpatient, general practitioner and home-based integration for disease prevention, diagnosis and intervention. Through the system's computer application terminal, doctors and patients' mobile phone application terminal service collaboration, a comprehensive health service is formed.

3.2 Coordination of Medical Resources Based on Hierarchical Diagnosis and Classification Management

In 2015, the General Office of the State Council of China issued the Outline of the National Medical and health Service System Planning (2015–2020), which clearly pointed out that China should optimize the allocation of medical and health resources and improve the service accessibility, capacity and the efficiency of resource utilization. Hierarchical medical model has become an effective way to solve the problem of collaborative and rational allocation of resources [25]. In addition, big data portrait analysis and classification management for patients are conducive to meet the characteristics of NCDS development and personal medical needs.

The project firstly through the integration of the Chinese NCDS prevention and control guidelines or the management norm KG and the basic data of clinical practice in various medical institutions, an electronic evidence-based guide is formed to provide decision-making support for the diagnosis of primary doctors, thereby greatly improving the objectivity and accuracy of medical diagnosis. Secondly, establish an intelligent triage system, through the online triage system network experts answer, combined with the historical medical record database, patients can preliminarily judge the classification and severity of the disease by self-diagnosis, so as to decide to choose the appropriate medical institution, to divert patients to a certain extent, and reduce unnecessary waste of resources. Finally, through system monitoring and evaluation and real-time analysis of big data in the background, personalized reports can be formed for different patients, assist doctors in risk prediction and early warning, automatically issue early warning prompts for different health problems, and indicate color code icons for different management levels. Provide personalized health guidance for patients with NCDS to improve the scientific management and service efficiency of NCDS.

3.3 Big Data Analysis of NCDS Based on Multi-dimensional Data Fusion

There are many data sources related to NCDS, and it is necessary to collect, transmit, synthesize, filter and synthesize data from various sources. In this project, a set of direct reporting interface for NCDS data has been developed. Each medical institution reports diagnosed patients with different types of NCDS (such as hypertension, diabetes, etc.) through the interface. The content of the interface includes basic patient information, diagnosis code, type of disease, etc. The interface is connected with clinical business systems such as Hospital Information System (HIS), electronic medical records, and medical record systems of medical institutions.

The system establishes a consistent data structure for NCDS health data from different sources in different business domains, and then aggregates it uniformly to form a NCDS big data center. The NCDS Big Data Center collects, connects and integrates personal health files, basic public health data, health examination data, clinical diagnosis and treatment data, disease monitoring data, patient health management data, in real time along the time dimension of the individual's life course. The key businesses include physical examination data, hospital medical data, NCDS management data of primary medical and health institutions, etc. The big data center has formed a complete big data center business logic through data collection, data management, business application and service coordination. Through structural transformation based on the standards of each disease data set, it performs comparison conversion and unified storage.

The big data application production area is divided in the big data center, which is used to deploy the application software system such as data mining, modeling and analysis. Based on the entities and relationships of the graph database in the knowledge graph, the system uses semantic search to segregate data. According to the research needs of different NCDS, extract the data subsets corresponding to different diseases to the district for development and utilization, forming disease big data labels and key population research cohorts. In the light of the analysis model and index of NCDS type and risk factor monitoring data, combined with Logistic regression classification algorithm, the independent risk factor model of NCDS was established with disease type as dependent variable and age, body mass index, smoking status, dyslipidemia and hypertension as independent variables. Combining random forest classification algorithm, K-Means clustering algorithm, and decision tree classification algorithm to analyze NCDS related symptoms, drugs, health risk factors, risk of complications, and treatment effects, so as to support the prevention and intervention of NCDS. Through the above data analysis, the risk assessment system for all kinds of NCDS can be completely constructed, the awareness rate of NCDS can be improved, and a healthy defense line can be built, as shown in Fig. 2.

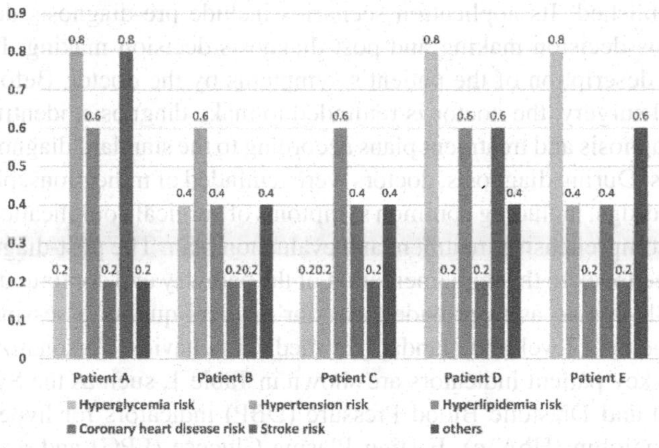

Fig. 2. Example of NCDS risk assessment in patients

3.4 NCDS Decision Support System Based on Clinical Pathway

The clinical pathway is to establish a set of standardized treatment modes and procedures for a certain disease. Through the control and adjustment of the clinical pathway's key points the functions of mutation screening and interception can be realized, which can regulate the behavior of medical staff and help patients accepted the treatment items of refinement, standardization, sequencing, reducing the differences of diagnosis and treatment, to achieve "one disease, one treatment".

Table 1. Customized treatment objectives for a diabetic patient

Index	Current	Normal	Target
SBP	110	<120	<140
DBP	77	<80	<80
HbA1c	6.0	<6.5	<6.5
FPG	5.2	<6.1	<7.0
RBG	6.3	<8.0	<8.0
TC	6.2	<5.2	<4.1
LDL	3.5	<3.38	<2.6
HDL	1.06	>1.04	>1.04
TG	1.61	<1.7	<1.7
BMI	25.3	18–24	18–24

This project establishes a NCDS decision system consisting of KG, reasoning machine and man-machine communication. In view of clinical knowledge base, information is collected, sorted, classified, filtered, processed and logically related knowledge points are established. Its application scenarios include pre-diagnosis decision making, in-diagnosis decision making and post-diagnosis decision making. Pre-diagnosis decision is the description of the patient's symptoms by the doctor. Before diagnosis, medication and surgery, the doctor is reminded to make diagnosis, identify key points and relevant diagnosis and treatment plans according to the standard diagnosis and treatment guidelines. During diagnosis, doctors were reminded of indications, pharmacology and efficacy of drugs, including common symptoms of surgical complications, as well as postoperative comprehensive treatment and evaluation plan. The post-diagnosis evaluation provides feedback to the implementation of the pathway and continuously improves the clinical pathway, so as to provide basis for medical quality assessment, improve hospital management level and standardize medical behavior. Personalized treatment goals based on key patient indicators are shown in Table 1, such as the Systolic Blood Pressure (SBP) and Diastolic Blood Pressure (DBP) indicators for hypertension, the Glycated Hemoglobin (HbA1c), Fasting Plasma Glucose (FPG) and Random Blood Glucose (RBG) indicators for diabetes, the Serum Total Cholesterol (TC), Low Density Lipoprotein (LDL), High Density Lipoprotein (HDL) and Triglyceride (TG) indicators for hyperlipidemia, and the common indicator Body Mass Index (BMI).

The system builds a KG of disease diagnosis based on authoritative medical guidelines, medical literature, and expert clinical paths, and establishes the relationship information between different concepts and data. The logical reasoning layer description extracts high-level semantic information from abstract concepts and by defining related reasoning relationships between concepts, it can infer new knowledge content from a large amount of metadata. At the same time, the system using intelligent question and answer to create a one-stop closed-loop application platform for NCDS patient guidance, post-diagnosis intelligent inquiry, intelligent knowledge push, and intelligent follow-up.

By establishing an online patient interactive communication platform to enhance the relationship between grassroots family doctors and pharmacies and patients, assist doctors and pharmacists to reduce the time for patients to consult and improve patients' satisfaction with diagnosis and treatment, as shown in Fig. 3.

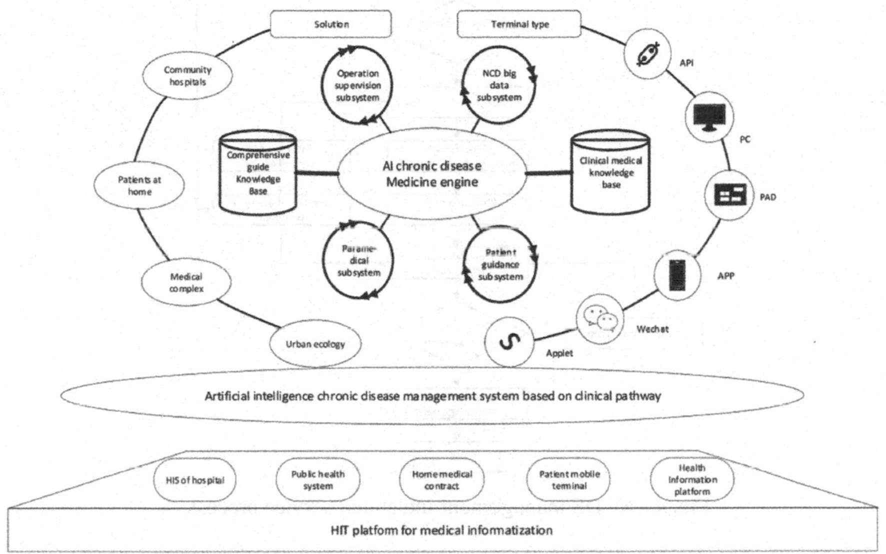

Fig. 3. Artificial intelligence chronic disease management system based on clinical pathway

3.5 NCDS Management Service Integration

On the basis of the integration of health data and intelligent analysis and diagnosis, the platform establishes a series of NCDS management services such as auxiliary diagnosis of NCDS, integrated management of NCDS, prescription outsourcing of medicines, intelligent follow-up of patients, online consultations, and patient education, Most of which can be invoked by the service interface for the business systems of various medical institutions, and can also be integrated into the NCDS management platform for patients to use directly, as shown in Fig. 4.

The auxiliary diagnosis service can remind the doctor that the patient is a NCDS patient when the patient seeks medical treatment, and provide reference to the doctor according to the medication history, examination records and electronic medical records. When doctors handle consultations, enter diagnoses, enter prescriptions or medical orders, and register for hospitalization, the AI analysis program sends them to the intelligent reminder service center, which queries each related application one by one and returns the prompt results to the client for presentation.

The integrated management system of NCDS collects and stores patient information at the first consultation, evaluates the patient's condition, self-management ability according to professional questionnaires and standards, grades and stratifies, automatically generates an assessment summary, and based on the patient's condition to carry

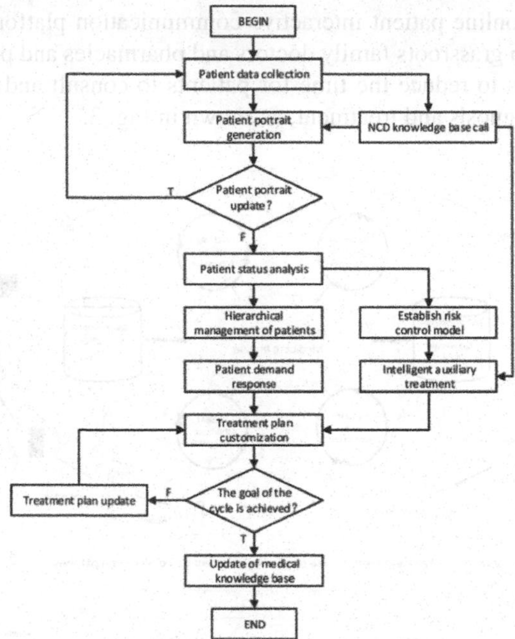

Fig. 4. NCDS management integrated service process

out personalized follow-up intervention, analyzes patients' self-behavior management issues, combine patient's data for comprehensive assessment, intelligently generate control goals, blood glucose monitoring plans, diet treatment plans, exercise treatment plans, knowledge learning plans, and the compliance rate of patient intervention cycle treatment is shown in Fig. 5.

The intelligent follow-up service supports medical staff to open NCDS education clinics, provides patients with first-diagnosis assessment, personalized self-management prescriptions, and for patients to use timed, fixed-point, quantitative three fixed drug rules for the whole intelligent reminder service, supports primary health care institutions to carry out individualized NCDS health education services to improve the ability and efficiency of NCDS education and management of grassroots medical staff.

4 Practice Result

The project cooperates with tertiary grade A hospital in Nanjing to form a medical consortium with a regional primary medical institution, combined with the type 2 diabetes big data clinical application demonstration center recognized by the Jiangsu Provincial Health Commission, and is closely integrated with "Internet + medical services", to provide patients with integrated services online and offline, inside and outside hospitals, and hospital communities, implement standardized diagnosis and treatment, and establish a multi-dimensional collaboration mechanism. NCDS data mainly summarized the online management of 12,415 diabetic patients in 2019, with a total of 121,061 follow-ups, and the overall glycation standard reached 63.1%. It managed 17,999 patients with hypertension online, completed 198 diagnosis in the medical consortium community, with a blood pressure control compliance rate of 73%, and provided 738 remote community holter examinations. The platform applies different integrated services to large medical institutions and primary medical and health institutions, with 60,243 diagnosis and NCDS patients drug compliance 94.5%.

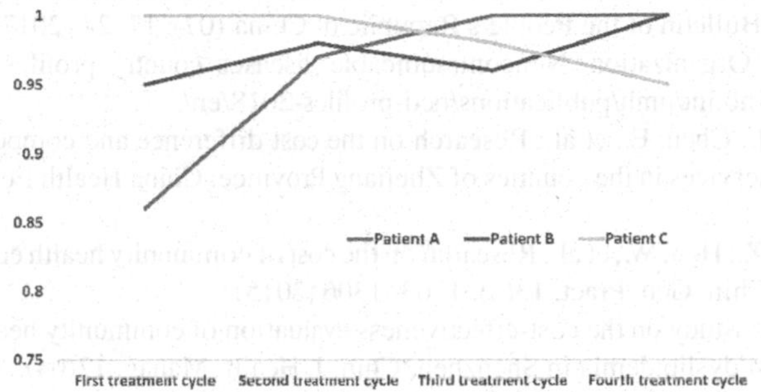

Fig. 5. Example of compliance rate of patients' periodic treatment plan

5 Conclusion

Based on the design, construction and implementation of AI NCDS management platform, this paper summarizes and organizes the NCDS related data of medical and health institutions, and on this basis, relying on big data, AI and other technologies, the establishment of NCDS auxiliary diagnosis and NCDS a series of integrated services related to NCDS management such as an integrated management system and intelligent follow-up of patients. The integrated services are open to all levels of medical and health institutions in the medical complex, and exercise, diet, and medication are implemented for patients through doctors and patient apps to achieve multi-dimensional long-term health management. The construction of the platform has improved the utilization efficiency of medical and health data, established related data models, provided full-course health services for patients with NCDS, and created data research value for subsequent research based on big data.

Acknowledgment. This paper was supported by the National Natural Science Foundation of China (61802208 and 61772286), Project funded by China Postdoctoral Science Foundation (2019M651923 and 2020M671552), Natural Science Foundation of Jiangsu Province of China (BK20191381), Primary Research & Development Plan of Jiangsu Province Grant (BE2019742), the Opening Project of Jiangsu Key Laboratory of Data Science and Smart Software (No. 2020DS301).

References

1. World Health Organization. World Health Statistics 2018: Monitoring health for the SDGs. World Health Organization, Geneva (2018)

2. Rutledge, G.E., Kimberly, L., Caitlin, M., et al.: Coordinated approaches to strengthen state and local public health actions to prevent obesity, diabetes, and heart disease and stroke. Prev. Chronic Dis. **15**, 170493 (2018)
3. Progress in disease prevention and control in China. Capital Public Health **9**(03), 97–101 (2015)
4. Notice of the General Office of the State Council on Printing and Distributing China's Medium and Long-term Plan for the Prevention and Treatment of Chronic Diseases (2017–2025). The State Council Bulletin of the People's Republic of China (07), 17–24 (2017)
5. World Health Organization. Noncommunicable diseases country profiles 2018 [EB/OL]. https://www.who.int/nmh/publications/ncd-profiles-2018/en/
6. Xiu, L., He, H., Chen, E., et al.: Research on the cost difference and compensation of basic public health services in the counties of Zhejiang Province. China Health Econ. **31**(9), 53–55 (2012)
7. Xia, T., Zhao, Z., Hou, W., et al.: Research on the cost of community health education services in Shenzhen. Chin. Gen. Pract. **13**(8), 1303–1306 (2015)
8. Zhuo, Z., et al.: Study on the cost-effectiveness evaluation of community health management for people with dyslipidemia in Shenzhen. Chin. J. Health Manag. **12**(04), 313–318 (2018)
9. Chen, K., Zhang, A., Ye, J.: Research on the equilibrium of my country's medical and health resources allocation based on the degree of agglomeration. Chin. Med. Manag. Sci. **10**(05), 5–10 (2020)
10. Yang, L., Gao, Y., Wu, S., Li, H.: Research on influencing factors of community chronic disease management based on service quality gap model. Soft Sci. Health **34**(07), 60–65 (2020)
11. Zhang, M., Xiao, Y., Yuan, J., Li, X.: Study on the status quo of community health management of chronic diseases in my country. J. Chengdu Med. Coll. **14**(05), 650–653+657 (2019)
12. Istepanian, R., Laxminarayan, S., Pattichis, C.S.: M-Health: Emergin Mobile Health Systems. Springer, London (2010)
13. MacKinnon, G., Brittain, E.: Mobile health technologies in cardiopulmonary disease. Chest **157**(3), 654–664 (2020). https://doi.org/10.1016/j.chest.2019.10.015
14. Wang, H.: Establishment and evaluation of internet-based community hypertension self-management intervention model. Jinan University (2017)
15. Chen, J.: Application research of remote ECG monitoring in out-of-hospital management of patients with chronic heart failure. Kunming Medical University (2017)
16. Wang, D., Ding, M.: Impact of network-based continuous follow-up nursing on postoperative rehabilitation and quality of life of patients with cardiac pacemaker implantation. Gen. Nurs. **16**(04), 499–501 (2018)
17. Luo, H., Zhang, F., Qi, R., Lin, Y.: Construction of "Internet +" health education program for cancer patients. Chin. J. Nurs. **52**(12), 1482–1485 (2017)
18. Huang, X., et al.: Discussion on the implementation path of precision diagnosis and treatment based on big data of health care. Chin. J. Hosp. Manag. **33**(05), 369–372 (2017)
19. Guo, C., Chen, J.: Big data analytics in healthcare: data-driven methods for typical treatment pattern mining. J. Syst. Sci. Syst. Eng. **28**(6), 694–714 (2019). https://doi.org/10.1007/s11518-019-5437-5
20. Bahri, S., Zoghlami, N., Abed, M., Tavares, J.M.R.S.: Big data for healthcare: a survey. IEEE Access **7**, 7397–7408 (2019). https://doi.org/10.1109/ACCESS.2018.2889180
21. Xu, T., Yu, G.: Application scenarios and value analysis of big data sharing in health care. China Digit. Med. **15**(07), 1–3 (2020)
22. Wu, Q., Miao, R., Song, Y., Cheng, Y., Jiang, Z.: Research on medical resource allocation decision-making for hierarchical diagnosis and treatment. Ind. Eng. Manag. **23**(03), 150–156 (2018)

23. Sfar, A.R., Challal, Y., Moyal, P., et al.: A game theoretic approach for privacy preserving model in IoT-based transportation. IEEE Trans. Intell. Transp. Syst. **99**, 1–10 (2019)
24. Wen, T., Zhang, Z., Qiu, M., Qingfeng, W., Li, C.: A multi-objective optimization method for emergency medical resources allocation. J. Med. Imaging Health Inform. **7**(2), 393–399 (2017). https://doi.org/10.1166/jmihi.2017.2027
25. Zhou, Y.: Thinking about the allocation of medical resources under the background of hierarchical diagnosis and treatment. New **14**(04), 27–36 (2020)

Research on Deep Learning Denoising Method in an Ultra-Fast All-Optical Solid-State Framing Camera

Jian Zhou[1], Zhuping Wang[2], Tao Wang[3], Qing Yang[4], Keyao Wen[3], Xin Yan[3], Kai He[3], Guilong Gao[3], Dong Yao[3], and Fei Yin[3,4](✉)

[1] Xi'an Modern Control Technology Research Institute, Xi'an 710065, China
[2] Xi'an Institute of Electromechanical Information Technology, Xi'an 710065, China
[3] Key Laboratory of Ultra-Fast Photoelectric Diagnostics Technology, Xi'an Institute of Optics and Precision Mechanics, Chinese Academy of Sciences, Xi'an 710119, China
yinfei@opt.ac.cn
[4] School of Mechanical Engineering, Xi'an Jiaotong University, Xi'an 710049, Shaanxi, China

Abstract. The ultra-fast all-optical solid-state framing camera (UASFC) is a new type of X-ray ultra-fast diagnostic technology. It uses X-ray excitation to change the refractive index distribution of the ultra-fast detection chip, and time-tuned multi-wavelength probe light for ultra-fast detection on the order of picoseconds or less. Due to the uneven intensity of the probe light wavelength and spatial diffraction, the noise of the detection image is too high, which directly affects the spatial and temporal resolution of the system. To improve the detection performance of the UASFC system, we adopted NLM image optimization technology based on a convolutional neural network, using 50 shots of the reticle image as the learning set and iterating the weight of the NLM image optimization filter. The CCD image obtained by the four-channel wavelength spectroscopy system is noise-reduced and optimized, which greatly improves the image contrast and edge definition, reduces image noise, and further improves the time and space resolution of the UASFC system.

Keywords: Ultra-fast all-optical solid-state framing camera · Convolutional neural network · Non-local mean filtering · Spatial resolution · X-ray

1 Introduction

The ultra-fast all-optical solid-state framing camera is a new type of ultra-fast imaging technology based on the semiconductor photorefractive effect, which has become a research hotspot [1, 2]. This technology can achieve high-time-resolution detection of ultra-short X-ray radiation fields. In the diagnosis of inertial confinement fusion (ICF) and other extreme conditions, it can perform picosecond high-spatial-resolution imaging of targets [3, 4]. Although traditional fringe cameras and framing cameras based on vacuum technology can obtain better time resolution, they have their shortcomings. The streak camera can obtain a target time resolution of ~200 fs, but the obtained images are

X. Sun et al. (Eds.): ICAIS 2021, LNCS 12736, pp. 78–85, 2021.
https://doi.org/10.1007/978-3-030-78609-0_7

limited to 1D; the frame camera can obtain 2D ultra-fast imaging, but its time and space resolution are limited to 35 ps and 20 lp/mm, respectively [5–7]. UASFC technology abandons the vacuum system of image conversion and realizes ultra-fast detection on the order of picoseconds. In Switzerland, Bionta et al. (2014) used Si3N4 to achieve a single high-precision measurement of X-ray pulses with a time resolution of 50 fs. [8] The Xi'an Institute of Optics and Mechanics of the Chinese Academy of Sciences conducted research on all-optical solid-state ultra-fast diagnostic technology, and obtained 3 ps time resolution and 30lp/mm spatial resolution [9, 10].

In the UASFC, the quality of probe light diffraction imaging and the processing of the acquired target image are important means to improve a system's diagnostic capabilities. In the acquisition of a probe laser image, due to factors such as uneven laser intensity and spatial diffraction, the quality of the probe laser image is serious. To improve probe light imaging quality requires algorithmic processing on the probe laser image to reduce noise. There are many techniques to improve the quality of laser images, such as the Gaussian filter [11], bilateral filter [12], and non-local means (NLM) [13].

In view of the different characteristics of the target object captured by the UASFC, a targeted image processing method can be used to optimize the probe laser image. In the field of ICF radiation field detection, due to the similarities between images collected by the probe laser, those collected by multiple high-speed observations of the same phenomenon also have similarities, so deep learning can be used. NLM filtering performs noise reduction on the target image. In image processing, it takes advantage of the fast convergence speed of the convolutional neural network to increase the processing speed and optimize the image quality [14–17].

2 Theoretical Model

2.1 Principle of NLM Filtering Algorithm

The idea of the non-local mean filtering algorithm is that the collected image contains much redundant information, and there are many similar image blocks distributed on the entire image. These image blocks have different positions, but the gray level information is similar. Through the similarity analysis of multiple images, we can calculate the similarity between these blocks and the image block where the current noise is located, and process the target image by the weighted average.

Antoni Buades proposed the NLM filtering algorithm in 2005. This method successfully avoided the existing noise reduction algorithm based on the assumption of the regularity of the noise image and the loss of image structure information during noise reduction. The algorithm is widely used due to its excellence in maintaining edge and image structure information, and has become a research hotspot in the field of image processing.

The basic principle of the NLM algorithm is shown in Fig. 1, which contains pixels P, Y1, and Y2 and their respective neighborhoods. P and Y1 can be seen to have similar neighborhood structures, and the neighborhood similarity of P and Y2 is very small, so when P is filtered, the similarity weight of Y2 is larger than that of Y1. The final restoration result of pixel P can be obtained by searching all pixels in the image that have similar neighborhoods to P, and weighting and averaging them according to the obtained similarity.

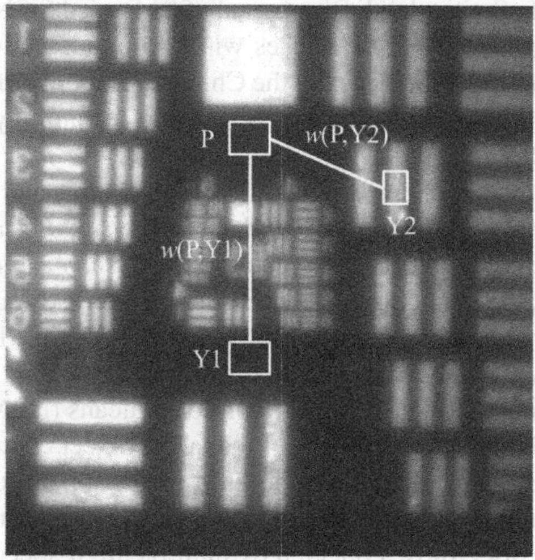

Fig. 1. Principle of NLM filtering algorithm

The NLM filtering algorithm for image denoising calculates the similarity of pixels in units of image blocks, which are square neighborhoods with a certain pixel at the center. Suppose the gray value of a polluted image at pixel i is $v(i)$, and the estimated gray value after filtering is $NL(v)(i)$. For any pixel i, the filtered $NL(v)(i)$ can be obtained by calculating the weighted average of pixels with similar neighborhoods in the entire noise image,

$$NL(v)(i) = \sum^{j \in I} \omega(i,j)v(j) \tag{1}$$

where I is the entire image space, and the weight coefficient is the degree of influence of pixel j on pixel i,

$$\omega(i,j) = \frac{1}{C(i)} e^{-\frac{\left\| v(N_i) - v(N_j) \right\|_{2,\alpha}^2}{h^2}} \tag{2}$$

where N_i is the reference block, or the image block of the pixel to be restored; N_j is the similar block, of the same size as N_i; $v(N_i)$ is the gray value of each pixel in the reference block; and $v(N_j)$ is similar The gray value of each pixel in the block; $\left\| v(N_i) - v(N_j) \right\|_{2,\alpha}^2$ is the Gaussian weighted Euclidean distance; α is the standard deviation of the Gaussian kernel; h is the attenuation parameter that controls the degree of filtering; and $C(i) = \sum^{j \in I} e^{-\frac{\left\| v(N_i) - v(N_j) \right\|_{2,\alpha}^2}{h^2}}$ is the normalized parameter. $\omega(i,j)$ satisfies $\omega(i,j) \in [0, 1]$ and $\sum^{j \in I} \omega(i,j) = 1$.

2.2 Principles of Convolutional Neural Networks

A convolutional neural network has the advantages of a traditional neural network and the characteristics of convergence speed. It has the functions of forward and backward propagation. During forward propagation, the upper layer output is used as the current layer input, and the activation function is introduced to transform the input to get the output of the current layer. The formula is

$$x^l = f\left(W^l x^{l-1} + b^l\right) \tag{3}$$

where l is the current number of layers of the convolutional neural network, W is the weight vector, b is the bias vector, and f is the activation function.

When the output error of the convolutional neural network is relatively large, the information must be backpropagated, for which the error must first be calculated as

$$E^N = \frac{1}{2}\sum_{n=1}^{N}(t_n - y_n)^2 \tag{4}$$

where N is the number of training samples, and t_k^n and y_k^n are the actual value of the nth sample and the network output value, respectively.

In the process of backpropagation, the convolutional layer is updated and can be expressed as

$$x_j^l = f\left(\sum_{i \in M_j} x_i^{l-1} k_{ij}^l + b_j^l\right) \tag{5}$$

where k is the convolution kernel, and M_j is the input feature.

Sampling processing can change the size of the feature map. The size of the sampling operator is $n \times n$. After sampling processing, the size of the feature map becomes the original $1/n$. The sampling method is

$$x_j^l = f\left(\beta_j^l down\left(x_i^{l-1}\right) + b_j^l\right) \tag{6}$$

where *down*() is the sampling function.

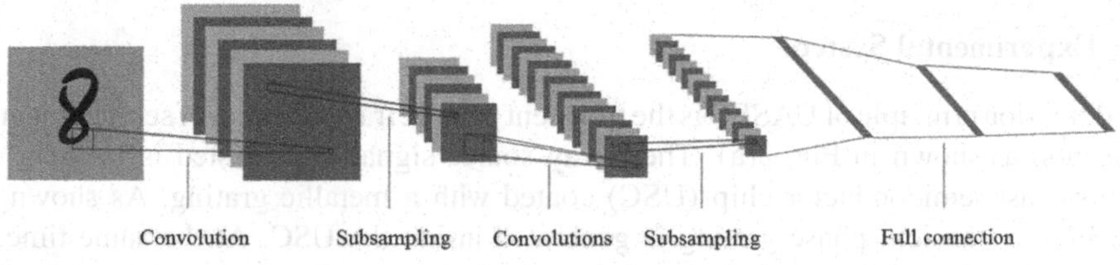

Fig. 2. Convolutional neural network structure

The convolutional neural network includes input, output, convolution, downsampling, and fully connected layers, as shown in Fig. 2. The feature map of the convolutional layer and the convolution of the feature map of the previous layer can establish a certain relationship,

$$X_j^l = f\left(\sum_{i \in M_j} X_i^{l-1} k_{ij}^l + b^l\right) \tag{7}$$

The downsampling layer performs convolution operations with the neurons in the previous layer through a convolution check to obtain a certain neuron in the feature map of the lth layer. The neuron X in the downsampling layer can be obtained as

$$X_j^l = f\left(\frac{1}{n} \sum_{i \in M_j} X_i^{l-1} + B^l\right) \tag{8}$$

where n is the size of the sampling window.

2.3 NLM Deep Learning Image Processing Method Based on Convolutional Neural Network

Since the UASFC is mainly used to capture the relatively simple and repeatable ultra-fast process of graphics, it fully excavates the information of similar image blocks in this type of image, and estimates the difference between pixels through the similarity between image blocks. Similarly, the correction value of the pixel to be evaluated is obtained through the weighted average and other methods. In the construction of a training set, the high-contrast reticle image is used as the input of the neural network, and the denoised image based on NLM noise suppression is used as the output of the network model. The weights of the network model are updated using the reverse conduction algorithm, and the functions between image blocks are learned into the newly created model through iterative learning, so as to realize the noise reduction and optimization processing of the image of the UASFC frame sampling system. Margins: set to 1.0" (2.54 cm) (top, bottom, left, and right).

3 Experiment and Analysis

3.1 Experimental System

The detection principle of UASFC is the transient photorefractive effect of semiconductor materials, as shown in Fig. 3(a). The X-ray source signal to be tested is incident on an ultra-fast semiconductor chip (USC) coated with a metallic grating. As shown in Fig. 3(b), a transient phase grating is generated inside the USC. At the same time, a sub-wavelength and time-coded ultra-fast probe beam enters and is modulated by the USC. Through the wavelength selective framing system, the images at different time points are spatially separated and directed to different positions on the CCD.

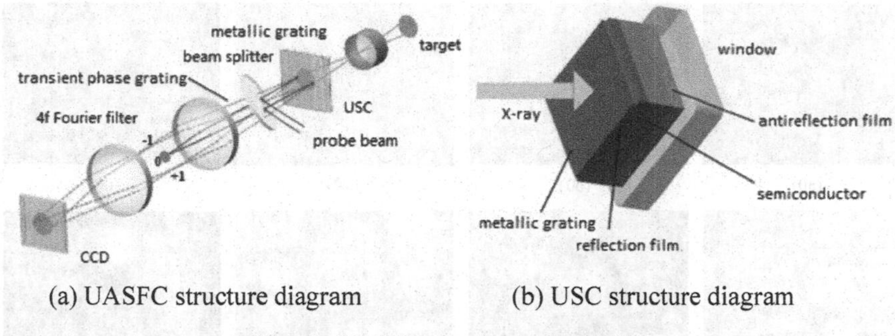

(a) UASFC structure diagram (b) USC structure diagram

Fig. 3. UASFC experimental principle

We used a Synergy FEMTO SOURCE femtosecond laser as the excitation pulse source. The main parameters of the pulse laser are a 200 fs pulse width, center wavelength 400 nm, repetition frequency 1 kHz, and single pulse energy of about 6.6 nJ. To verify the image processing capability of the NLM-based convolutional neural network and the noise reduction effect of the sampled image of the readout device, we adopted a four-channel wavelength splitting system to perform wavelength splitting and sampling of the UASFC probe light. The center wavelengths of the four channels were 770 nm, 780 nm, 785 nm, and 790 nm.

Using the reticle as the test pattern, the noise reduction process based on NLM technology was performed, and 50 sets of sample images were obtained through repeated experiments.

Through the learning of sample images, the images acquired by the four-framing spectroscopic acquisition system CCD were processed for noise reduction.

3.2 Image Processing

Taking the standard reticle optical image as the sample set input terminal, as shown in Fig. 4(a0)~(d0), we used the image processed by the NLM filter noise reduction algorithm as the sample set output terminal, as shown in Fig. 4(a1)~(d1), and completed a set of four-channel sample set operations. Through the learning of 50 sets of samples, the iteration and construction of the convolutional neural network were completed.

Through the deep learning of the filter function weight parameters, the noise filter optimization was completed. The CCD mixed image obtained by the four-channel spectroscopic system was used as the optimized filter function input image, as shown in Fig. 5(a), to obtain the noise optimized output image, as shown in Fig. 5(b). The image contrast, boundary definition, and noise were all optimized.

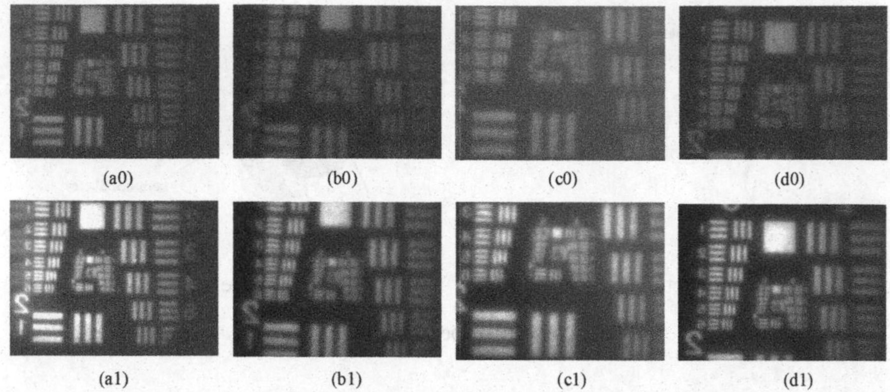

Fig. 4. NLM noise reduction processing sample set of reticle images

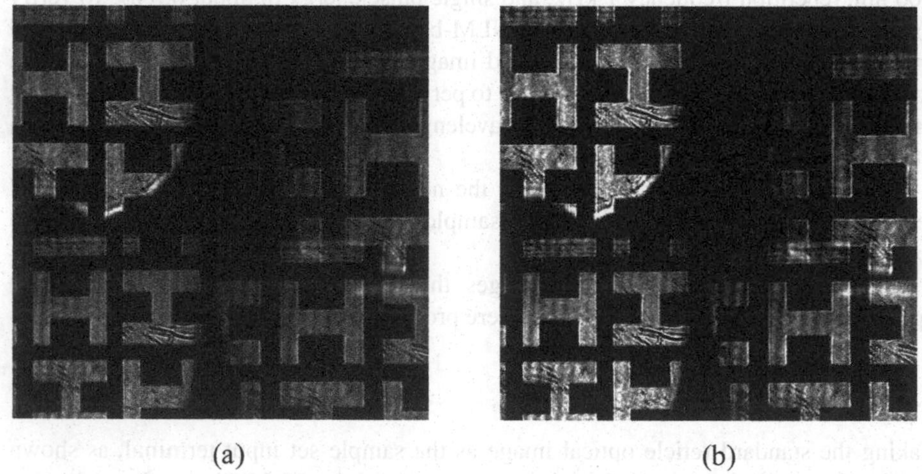

Fig. 5. Target image processing result

4 Conclusion

We used an image processing method based on non-local mean filtering using a convolutional neural network to optimize the image obtained by a four-framing wavelength spectroscopy system in an ultra-fast all-optical solid-state framing camera. Through demonstration and verification experiments on reticle images excited by a femtosecond pulse laser, we obtained the following conclusions. A convolutional neural network can greatly enrich the detailed information of UASFC images and improve the signal-to-noise ratio. By compressing the dynamic range of an unevenly illuminated image, the visual effect of the processed image was significantly better than that of the unprocessed image, which improved the detection accuracy and quality of UASFC.

References

1. Baker, K.L., Stewart, R.E., Steele, P.T., Vernon, S.P., Hsing, W.W.: Ultrafast semiconductor x-ray detector. Appl. Phys. Lett. **101**(3), 031107 (2012)
2. Vernon, S.P., et al.: X-ray bang-time and fusion reaction history at picosecond resolution using RadOptic detection. Rev. Sci. Instrum. **83**(10), 10d307 (2012)
3. Apruzese, J.P., Thornhill, J.W., Whitney, K.G., et al.: Comparative analysis of time-resolved and time-integrated x-ray data from long pulse Z-pinch implosions on Saturn. Phys. Plasmas **8**(8), 3799–3809 (2001)
4. Lazier, S.E., Barber, T.L., Derzon, M.S., et al.: Time and space resolved measurements of visible-light and soft x-ray emission from foam z-pinch plasmas and implosions. Rev. Sci. Instrum. **68**(1), 660–663 (1997)
5. Byrd, J.M., Feng, J., Huang, G., et al.: Progress on modeling of ultrafast x-ray streak cameras. In: IEEE Proceedings of Particle Accelerator Conference, pp. 3961–3963 (2007)
6. Oertel, J.A.: A large-format gated x-ray framing camera. In: Proceedings of SPIE - The International Society for Optical Engineering, vol. 5194, pp. 214–222 (2004)
7. Hilsabeck, T.J., Hares, J.D., Kilkenny, J.D., et al.: Pulse-dilation enhanced gated optical imager with 5 ps resolution. Rev. Sci. Instrum **81**(10), 10E317 (2010)
8. Bionta, M.R., Hartmann, N., Weaver, M., et al.: Spectral encoding method for measuring the relative arrival time between x-ray/optical pulses. Rev. Sci. Instrum. **85**(8), 083116 (2014)
9. Gao, G.L., He, K., Tian, J.S., Zhang, C.M., Zhang, J., Wang, T., et al.: Ultrafast all-optical solid-state framing camera with picosecond temporal resolution. Opt. Exp. **25**, 8721 (2017)
10. Gao, G.L., Tian, J.S., Wang, T., He, K., Zhang, C.M., et al.: Ultrafast all-optical imaging technique using low-temperature grown GaAs/AlxGa1-xAs multiple quantum well semiconductor. Phys. Lett. A **381**, 3594–3598 (2017)
11. Chen, P., Qian, H., Zhu, M.: Fast Gaussian particle filtering algorithm. J. Huazhong Univ. Sci. Technol. (2008)
12. Elad, M.: On the origin of the bilateral filter and ways to improve it. IEEE Trans. Image Process. **11**(10), 1141–1151 (2002)
13. Haichun, N.: Enhancement and binary representation of laser facula. J. Harbin Inst. Technol. **35**(8), 916–918 (2003)
14. Liu, J.B., Liu, B.Z.: Non-local mean image denoising method based on deep learning. Comput. Simul. **37**(8), 228–234 (2020)
15. Buades, A., Coll, B., Morel, J.M.: A non-local algorithm for image denoising. In: Computer Vision and Pattern Recognition, vol. 2, pp. 60–65 (2005)
16. Hu, J., Lu, H.L., Zhang, J.: Laser image enhancement based on convolutional neural network. Laser J. **41**(9), 147–150 (2020)
17. Dai, Z., Yang, Y.: Ultrasound image denoising based on deep learning. Inf. Technol. **9**, 57–60 (2020)

LSTM-XGBoost Application of the Model to the Prediction of Stock Price

Sun Yu[1], Liwei Tian[2(✉)], Yijun Liu[1], and Yuankai Guo[3]

[1] Guangdong University of Technology, Guangzhou 510006, China
[2] Guangdong University of Science and Technology, Dongguan 523083, China
[3] Ankang Vocational Technical College, Ankang 725000, China

Abstract. With the rapid rise of economic globalization and digital economics, the rapid development of the global economy has been promoted. As the most important part of the financial industry, the stock market has an important impact on economic fluctuations. How to improve the changing trend of stock market fluctuations has become a hot topic that many scholars and investors pay most attention to. This paper uses the XGBoost model to train the opening price, closing price, highest price, lowest price, trading volume, change, adjusted closing price, and converted time data information in the processed stock historical data set, and train it The results are saved. Then input each attribute into the LSTM model for prediction, and use the prediction result of each attribute as the test set of prediction after XGBoost training, and continuously adjust the parameters of each model, and finally get the optimal stock fluctuation prediction model, LSTM_XGBoost model. The LSTM_XGBoost model is applied to the five stocks ES = F, YM = F, AAPL, SI = F, and CL = F to predict the rise and fall of five stocks. The model is compared and verified by five evaluation indexes: the root mean square error RMSE, the average absolute error MAE, the coefficient of determination R2, the accuracy rate, and the f1-score. It is found that the LSTM-XGBoost model proposed in this paper has risen and fallen in stocks. There is a certain degree of stability and feasibility in the forecast.

Keywords: LSTM · XGBoost · RNN · Stock price forecast · Time series data

1 Introduction

With the continuous strengthening of economic globalization, financial trade and business exchanges between countries are increasing. The rise and fall of stock price is affected by both internal and external factors. Due to its nonlinearity and irregularity, stock time series prediction is usually considered as one of the most challenging tasks. Therefore, it has important theoretical value and practical significance to study the value of stock time series data and the prediction of its rise and fall trend.

As early as 1879, William Stanley Jevons had applied time series analysis to economic problems. In 1995, Arbabi and Mansur proposed a prediction system and method combining neural network with statistical prediction, which showed good prediction effect, and provided important reference for many scholars in the future research of

X. Sun et al. (Eds.): ICAIS 2021, LNCS 12736, pp. 86–98, 2021.
https://doi.org/10.1007/978-3-030-78609-0_8

neural network combination model. In 2000, Henrique S. Hippert proposed a hybrid prediction system, which combined linear model and multilayer neural network, and showed good performance in time series data prediction. In 2015, Kazuhiro Kohara used prior knowledge and neural network to improve the ability of multiple prediction [1]. The results show that the event knowledge and neural network are effective in stock forecasting. In 2018, Kim, Ha Young proposed a new hybrid long-term short-term memory (LSTM) model to predict stock price volatility. The model combines LSTM model with various generalized autoregressive conditional heteroscedasticity (GARCH) models. Through experimental comparison, it is found that GEW-LSTM hybrid model has better prediction performance [2–4]. Shaolong Sun proposed a hybrid ensemble learning method, which combines AdaBoost algorithm and LSTM network to predict financial time series. The empirical results show that this method is superior to some other single prediction models and ensemble learning methods, and it is a promising method for financial time series data forecasting [5]. Weiling Chen proposed a new RNN boost hybrid model to predict the volatility of China's stock market. The experimental results show that the model is superior to other popular methods and can achieve good prediction performance [6]. In 2019, Sidra Mehtab proposed a hybrid stock price forecasting method using machine learning, deep learning and natural language processing. The results show that the method is effective and practical in stock forecasting [7]. In 2020, the first mock exam of ARI-MA-LS-SVM stock was proposed by Chenglin Xiao. The experimental results show that the hybrid model is better than the single model in the prediction of stock price, and the prediction performance is better [8]. According to the research of the above scholars, it is not difficult to see that the combined model has incomparable advantages in time series prediction.

In this paper, the LSTM-XGBoost combination model is constructed by using the combination forecasting method of LSTM and XGBoost [9, 10].This paper uses the LSTM-XGBoost model to predict the stock price and compares it with the single LSTM network model and RNN network model, so as to verify that the LSTM XGBoost model proposed in this paper is stable and feasible in the stock price forecast.

2 Related Work

2.1 Long and Short-Term Memory Neural Network (LSTM)

LSTM (Long and Short-Term Memory) is the variant of Recurrent Neural Network (RNN). It is a general term for a series of neural networks that can process time series data [11]. There are input gate, forgetting gate and output gate in LSTM unit. When information enters the LSTM network, it can be selected by request. Only the information that meets the requirements of the algorithm will be left behind, while the information that does not meet the requirements will be forgotten through the forgetting gate. LSTM adds and removes neuron information through gating unit. In order to get the correct information, sigmoid neural network layer and multiplication operation are used to determine the information.

Although in theory, RNN can deal with any long-distance dependence problem, in fact, it is difficult to implement in solving long-range data training due to problems such as gradient disappearance and explosion [12]. In order to solve the problem of gradient vanishing and gradient explosion in the training of long sequence data, LSTM introduces "gate" mechanism and memory unit, that is to use LSTM unit to replace the hidden layer neural unit of RNN. The difference between LSTM structure and the main data transmission unit of ordinary RNN is shown in Fig. 1.

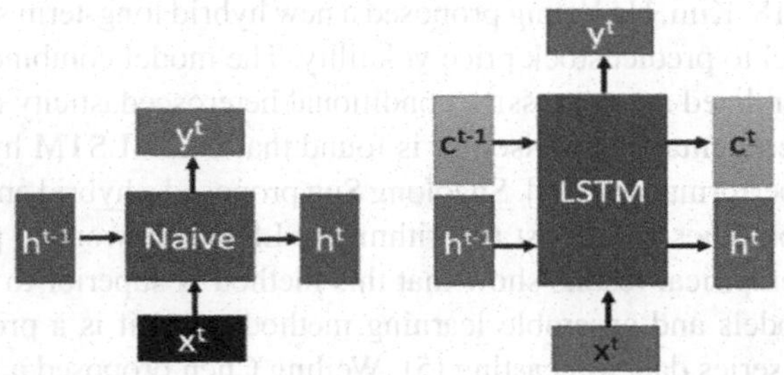

Fig. 1. Comparison of input and output between LSTM and RNN

It can be seen from Fig. 1 that there is only one transfer state ht in RNN unit, while there are two transmission states ht and ct in LSTM.Among them, ct is the unit state value of the current hidden layer, and ct-1 is the unit state value of the previous hidden layer. ht is the output of the hidden layer, and ht-1 is the output of the previous hidden layer.

2.2 XGBoost Model

XGBoost (eXtreme Gradient Boosting) is a machine learning system based on Gradient Boosting. It is an optimized distributed gradient enhancement library, which aims to achieve high efficiency, flexibility and portability. XGBoost provides parallel tree promotion, which can quickly and accurately solve many data science problems. Tree set model is used to treat trees as a set of classification and regression trees for basic learners, so it has good effect in retrospective prediction. XGBoost is an improved algorithm of GBDT, and the value of optimization objective function is the core of XGBoost. The specific process of objective function optimization is as follows.

The prediction model of XGBoost can be expressed as formula (1)

$$\hat{y}_i = \sum_{k=1}^{K} f_k(x_i) \tag{1}$$

K: Total number of trees, f_k: The k-th tree, $\hat{y}_i$: the prediction result of sample x_i.

The objective function is represented by formula (2)

$$obj(\theta) = \sum_{i=1}^{n} l(y_i, \hat{y}) + \sum_{k=1}^{K} \Omega(f_k) \tag{2}$$

$l(y_i, \hat{y})$: Training error of sample x_i, $\Omega(f_k)$: The regular term of the k-th tree.

$$\mathrm{obj}^{(t)} = \sum_{i=1}^{n} \mathrm{l}((\mathrm{y_i}, \hat{\mathrm{y}}^{(t-1)}) + \mathrm{f}(\mathrm{x_i})) + \Omega(\mathrm{f_t}) + \mathrm{C} \tag{3}$$

Taylor expansion is used to approximate the original objective function

$$obj^{(t)} \approx \sum_{i=1}^{n} l[(y_i, \hat{y}^{(t-1)}) + g_i f_t(x_i) + \frac{1}{2} h_i f_t^2(x_i)] + \Omega(f_t) + C \tag{4}$$

In model training, the objective function can be expressed by formula (5)

$$obj^{(t)} = \sum\nolimits_{j=1}^{t} [(\sum\nolimits_{i \in I_j} g_i) w_j + \frac{1}{2} (\sum\nolimits_{i \in I_j} h_i + \lambda) w_j^2] + \gamma T \tag{5}$$

Definition formula (6),

$$G_j = \sum\nolimits_{i \in I_j} g_i, H_j = \sum\nolimits_{i \in I_j} h_i \tag{6}$$

By introducing formula (6) into formula (5), Formula (7) is obtained,

$$\begin{aligned} obj^{(t)} &= \sum\nolimits_{j=1}^{t} [G_j w_j + \frac{1}{2} (H_j + \lambda) w_j^2] + \gamma T \\ &= -\frac{1}{2} \sum\nolimits_{j=1}^{T} \frac{G_j^2}{H_j + \lambda} + \gamma T \end{aligned} \tag{7}$$

According to the optimal results of formula (6) and formula (7), the optimal decision tree node is found, and then the calculation and prediction are carried out.

3 Model Construction

LSTM-XGBoost is constructed by combining LSTM and XGBoost. The specific flow chart is shown in Fig. 2. In order to prevent over fitting phenomenon in the training process of LSTM model, dropout layer is added and the forgetting rate is set to 0.2.

The construction process of LSTM-XGBoost model is as follows:

(1) Obtain the historical data of stock index and process the missing value;
(2) The "date" attribute in the dataset is decomposed into "year", "month" and "weekday", which are referred to as time component;
(3) Using the LSTM method of keras package, the LSTM model is implemented. The attributes of "open", "high", "low", "close", "volume" and "adj close" in the stock history data set are trained respectively, and the LSTM stock price prediction model is constructed, in which units = 128, batch in LSTM model_ size = 64;
(4) The LSTM stock price forecasting model is used to predict the attributes of "open", "high", "low", "close", "volume" and "adj close";
(5) The prediction results are recombined with the "time component" to construct the "text" test set.
(6) Using XGBRegressor method in sklearn package, XGBoost algorithm is implemented. The attributes of "Open", "High", "Low", "Close", "Volume", "Adj Close" in stock historical data set are trained to build XGBoost stock price prediction model;

(7) XGBoost stock price forecasting model is used to predict the reconstructed data set "text" after LSTM prediction. In order to compare with other models, XGBoost model uses default parameters;
(8) Compare the difference between the real value and the predicted value, and judge the performance of LSTM-XGBoost model in the stock price forecast.

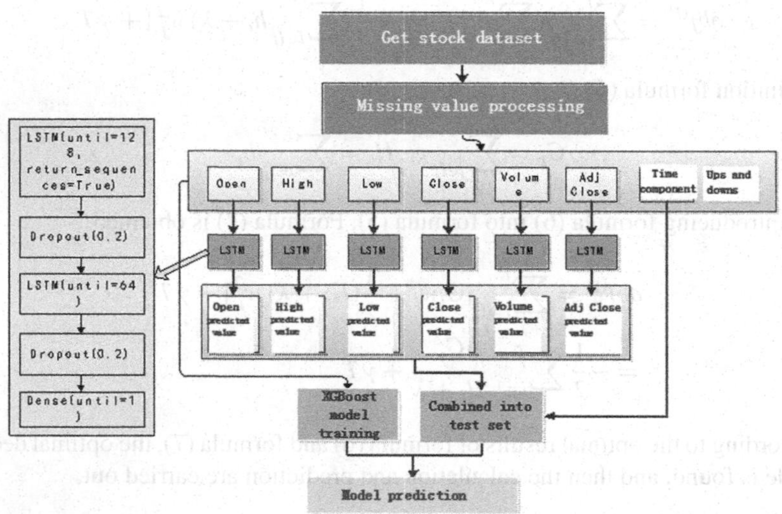

Fig. 2. LSTM-XGBoostModel building diagram

4 Simulation Experiment

In this paper, the experiment is carried out on Intel i7 3.1 ghz dual core four thread CPU and windows 8 operating system. The simulation platform is pycharm, and the python language is used for programming. Sklearn, pandas, numpy, keras and Matplotlib packages in Python are used respectively. The experimental data set was passed https://finance.yahoo.com Download, select the opening price, closing price, highest price, lowest price and trading volume of e-mini S & P500 (ES = F) from January 2002 to August 2020, with a total of 4725 data. Among them, 80% of ES = F stock data is used as training set, and 20% of data is used as test set. The changes of each attribute in ES = F stock data are shown in Table 1.

Table 1. ES = F Change chart of each attribute of stock data

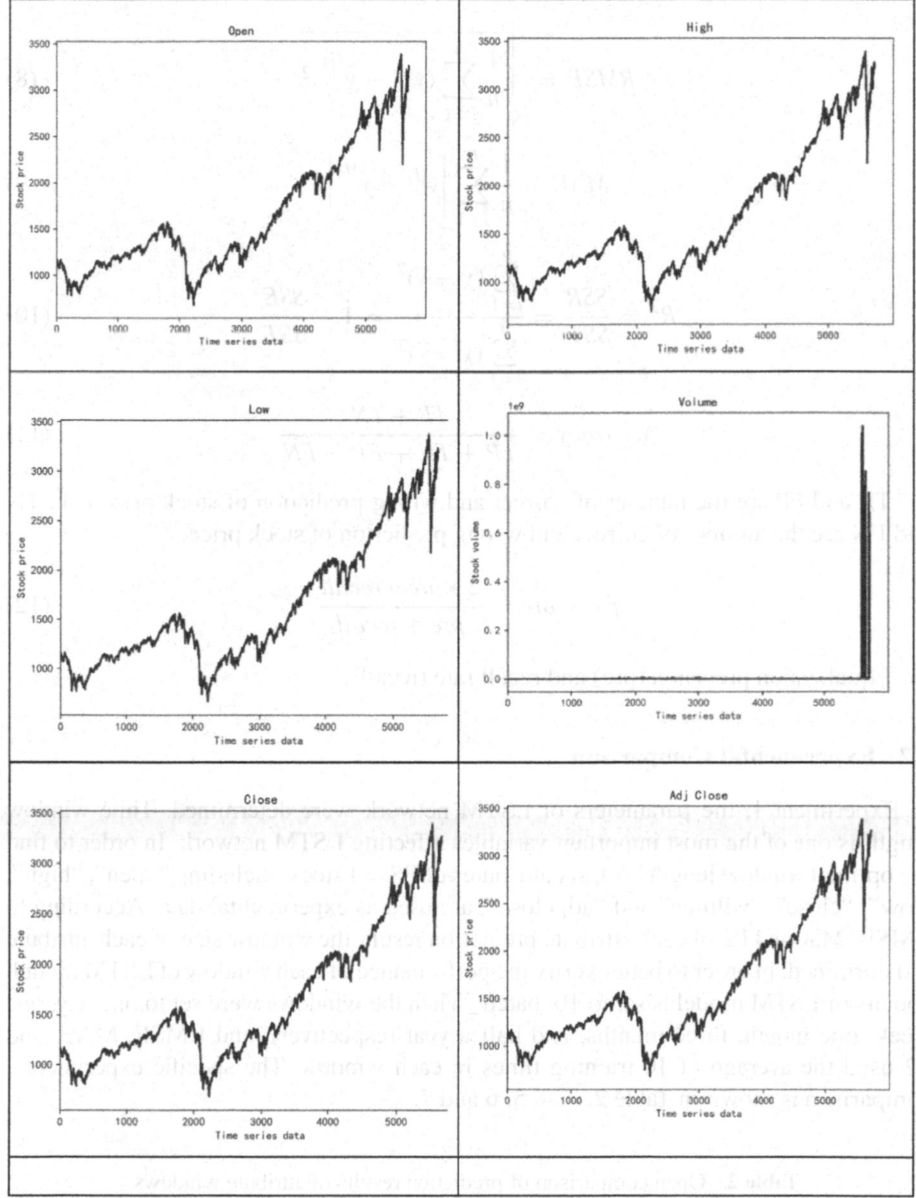

4.1 Evaluating Indicator

The performance evaluation indexes of stock forecasting model are root mean square error (RMSE), mean absolute error (RMSE), determination coefficient R2, accuracy and F1 score. RMSE and RMSE are used to measure the accuracy of the prediction model,

R2 is used to measure the fitting ability of the prediction model, and accuracy and F1 score are used to measure the accuracy of the prediction model.

$$RMSE = \sqrt{\frac{1}{n}\sum_{i=1}^{n}(y^{(i)} - \widehat{y}^{(i)})^2} \tag{8}$$

$$MAE = \frac{1}{n}\sum_{i=1}^{n}\left|y^{(i)} - \widehat{y}^{(i)}\right| \tag{9}$$

$$R^2 = \frac{SSR}{SST} = \frac{\sum_{i=1}^{n}(\widehat{y} - \overline{y})^2}{\sum_{i=1}^{n}(y - \overline{y})^2} = 1 - \frac{SSE}{SST} \tag{10}$$

$$Accuracy = \frac{TP + TN}{TP + TN + FP + FN} \tag{11}$$

TP and FP are the number of correct and wrong prediction of stock price rise, TN and FN are the number of correct and wrong prediction of stock price.

$$f1\_score = \frac{2 * pre * recall}{pre + recall} \tag{12}$$

Equalization precision (pre) and recall rate (recall).

4.2 Experimental Comparison

In Experiment 1, the parameters of LSTM network were determined. Time window length is one of the most important variables affecting LSTM network. In order to find the optimal window length (W), six attributes of ES = f stock, including “open”, “high”, “low”, “close”, “volume” and “adj close”, are used as experimental data. According to RMSE, Mae and P2 of each attribute prediction result, the window size of each attribute is determined. In order to better verify the performance of each window of LSTM model, epochs of LSTM model is set to 10, batch_ Then the windows were set to one day, one week, one month, three months, and half a year respectively, and RMSE, MAE, and P2 used the average of 10 training times in each window. The specific experimental comparison is shown in Table 2, 3, 4, 5, 6 and 7.

Table 2. Open comparison of prediction results of attribute windows

Window size	1	7	30	90	180
RMSE	**1270.98**	5002.03	8915.17	9669.21	9140.32
MAE	**24.3963**	41.3908	59.5100	68.6469	60.1048
R^2	**0.9821**	0.9295	0.8744	0.8638	0.8712

Table 3. High comparison of prediction results of attribute windows

Window size	1	7	30	90	180
RMSE	**768.74**	3636.71	7752.76	7962.88	7782.34
MAE	**17.6888**	38.0986	62.7833	50.9378	64.8920
R^2	**0.9892**	0.9491	0.8916	0.8886	0.8912

Table 4. Low comparison of prediction results of attribute windows

Window size	1	7	30	90	180
RMSE	**1066.91**	5245.60	9656.68	10757.64	9484.07
MAE	**20.7882**	44.4795	63.8474	57.8145	63.3581
R^2	**0.9848**	0.9253	0.8625	0.8469	0.8650

Table 5. Close comparison of prediction results of attribute windows

Window size	1	7	30	90	180
RMSE	**1273.77**	4476.19	8701.98	8342.23	8513.99
MAE	**22.3174**	43.6851	56.1627	61.6803	63.1581
R^2	**0.9820**	0.9367	0.8771	0.8821	0.8797

Table 6. Volume comparison of prediction results of attribute windows

Window size	1	7	30	90	180
RMSE	1.1000e+16	0.9678e+16	**0.9553e+16**	1.0021e+16	1.0057e+16
MAE	41285747.44	46530125.11	**38994040.05**	38822740.80	40332606.43
R^2	0.4713	0.5348	**0.5408**	0.5183	0.5166

Table 7. Adj CloseComparison of prediction results of attribute windows

Window size	1	7	30	90	180
RMSE	**1227.35**	4887.07	8398.61	8341.29	8202.48
MAE	**20.6443**	49.2456	60.9482	53.6753	53.2474
R^2	**0.9826**	0.9309	0.8813	0.8821	0.8841

According to Tables 2, 3, 4, 5, 6 and 7, when the window size is 1, the RMSE, MAE, and P2 of the "Open", "High", "Low", "Close" and "Adj Close" attributes are the best performance. When the sliding window is 30, the prediction performance of the "volume" attribute is the best compared with other window sizes. According to the comparison, the sliding window of "Open", "High", "Low", "Close" and "Adj Close" is set to 1, that is, the sliding window of "volume" attribute is set to 30. After determining the sliding window of each attribute, LSTM model is trained, and the prediction results are shown in Fig. 3. According to Fig. 3, it is obvious that the prediction fitting degree of each attribute of LSTM model is relatively good.

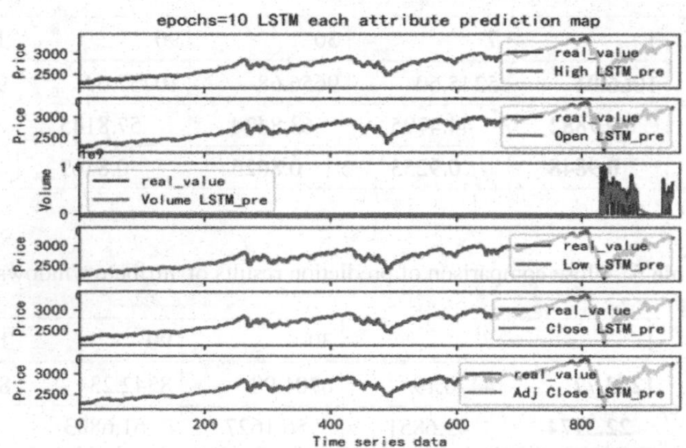

Fig. 3. LSTM prediction chart of each attribute of the model

In Experiment 2, after confirming the parameters of LSTM model, the XGBoost model was trained. The XGBoost parameters were the default parameters, and the training set was the first 80% data of ES = f stock. The XGBoost trained model was saved, and the prediction results of each attribute of LSTM model in Experiment 1 were integrated with time attributes to form a test training set. The XGBoost trained model is used to predict the new test set, and the final prediction results of ES = f stock are obtained. The comparative experimental data of LSTM-XGBoost model, LSTM and RNN models with epochs of 1, 10 and 30 are shown in Table 8, 9 and 10.

Table 8. Epochs = 1 Comparison of model prediction results

	LSTM-XGB	LSTM	RNN
RMSE	612.5332	613.0891	**611.2626**
MAE	**15.5**	15.7	15.6
Accuracy	**0.60**	0.59	0.58
$f1$_score	**0.7524**	0.7358	0.7248

Table 9. Epochs = 10 Comparison of model prediction results

	LSTM-XGB	LSTM	RNN
RMSE	612.6305	656.2361	**610.3129**
MAE	**15.5**	17.0039	**15.5**
Accuracy	**0.60**	0.39	0.57
$f1\_score$	**0.7524**	0.0238	0.1554

Table 10. Epochs = 30 Comparison of model prediction results

	LSTM-XGB	LSTM	RNN
RMSE	615.5513	**610.3231**	610.6260
MAE	**15.6**	**15.6**	**15.6**
Accuracy	**0.60**	**0.60**	**0.60**
$f1\_score$	**0.7524**	0.7524	0.7508

It can be seen from Table 8 that when epochs = 1, the prediction accuracy and fitting degree of LSTM-XGBoost model are better than those of LSTM and RNN models. According to Table 9, when epochs = 10, the prediction performance of LSTM-XGBoost model is significantly higher than that of LSTM-XGBoost model. Although RNN model is slightly better than LSTM-XGBoost model in fitting degree, the prediction accuracy of LSTM-XGBoost model is higher than that of RNN model. Table 10 shows the comparison results of each model when epochs = 30. Although the prediction performance of the models is relatively close, the LSTM-XGBoost model proposed in this paper has reached the prediction performance of LSTM and RNN models when epochs = 1 and epochs = 30. No matter what value epochs is used, the LSTM-XGBoost model shows good prediction performance, which indicates that LSTM-XGBoost model is more stable and practical.

For the first mock exam, we further verify the stability of LSTM-XGBoost model in the prediction of stock price fluctuation, and compare it with the single model LSTM, and compare with the RNN model which performs well in stock price prediction. In order to verify the generalization ability and prediction performance of the models, three models were applied to mini Dow Jones Indus. - $5 Sep 20 (YM = f), AAPL, silver Sep 20 (Si = f) and crude oil SEP, respectively 20 (CL = f), the data sets of four stocks are time series data of "open", "high", "low", "close", "volume" and "adj close" from February 2002 to mid August 2020, in which the first 80% of the data set is the training data set, and the remaining 20% is the test data set. After the model is trained and tested, the experimental results are compared and analyzed. The experimental results are shown in Tables 11, 12, 13 and 14.

From Tables 11, 12, 13 and 14, we can see that LSTM-XGBoost model has good prediction performance in the rise and fall forecast of the four stocks. According to

Table 11. "YM = F" Comparison of model prediction results

Model	Epochs = 1			Epochs = 10			Epochs = 30		
	LSTM-XGB	LSTM	RNN	LSTM-XGB	LSTM	RNN	LSTM-XGB	LSTM	RNN
RMSE	**58552**	70056	59087	**58522**	65292	85784	**59882**	71790	85134
MAE	**162**	197	168	**162**	185	234	**166**	202	233
Accuracy	**0.58**	0.41	0.42	**0.58**	0.41	0.41	**0.58**	0.41	0.41
$f1$_score	**0.74**	0.0	0.07	**0.74**	0.0	0.0	**0.74**	0.0	0.0

Table 12. "APPL" Comparison of model prediction results

Model	Epochs = 1			Epochs = 10			Epochs = 30		
	LSTM-XGB	LSTM	RNN	LSTM-XGB	LSTM	RNN	LSTM-XGB	LSTM	RNN
RMSE	**9.52**	10.8	15.24	**9.56**	14.06	13.15	**9.56**	13.39	13.91
MAE	**2.02**	2.30	3.03	**2.03**	2.88	2.74	**2.04**	2.76	2.85
Accuracy	**0.54**	0.45	0.45	**0.54**	0.45	0.45	**0.53**	0.45	0.45
$f1$_score	**0.71**	0.0	0.01	**0.70**	0.0	0.01	**0.69**	0.0	0.01

Table 13. "SI = F" Comparison of model prediction results

Model	Epochs = 1			Epochs = 10			Epochs = 30		
	LSTM-XGB	LSTM	RNN	LSTM-XGB	LSTM	RNN	LSTM-XGB	LSTM	RNN
RMSE	**0.04**	1.44	1.29	**0.04**	0.76	1.13	**0.04**	1.44	1.29
MAE	**0.13**	1.18	1.12	**0.12**	0.85	1.04	**0.13**	1.18	1.12
Accuracy	**0.59**	**0.59**	**0.59**	**0.59**	**0.59**	**0.59**	**0.59**	**0.59**	**0.59**
$f1$_score	**0.74**	**0.74**	**0.74**	**0.74**	**0.74**	**0.74**	**0.74**	**0.74**	**0.74**

Table 14. "CL = F" Comparison of model prediction results

Model	Epochs = 1			Epochs = 10			Epochs = 30		
	LSTM-XGB	LSTM	RNN	LSTM-XGB	LSTM	RNN	LSTM-XGB	LSTM	RNN
RMSE	**1.48**	22.74	54.81	**1.51**	36.14	66.74	**1.91**	56.05	62.35
MAE	**0.76**	4.63	7.32	**0.77**	5.91	8.10	**0.93**	7.41	7.82
Accuracy	**0.54**	0.46	0.46	**0.51**	0.46	0.46	**0.53**	0.46	0.46
$f1$_score	**0.63**	0.0	0.0	**0.64**	0.0	0.0	**0.69**	0.0	0.0

RMSE, MAE, accuracy and F1_ In the score evaluation index, it can be clearly seen that the lstm-xgboost model is significantly better than the LSTM model in the prediction of the rise and fall of the stock YM = F, APPL and Cl = F, and has a comparative advantage compared with the RNN model. The accuracy and F1 of the three models are shown in Table 13_ In RMSE and Mae, lstm-xgboost model is better than LSTM and RNN models. It further shows that the performance of LSTM xgboost model is stable and efficient.

5 Conclusion

This paper proposes a hybrid financial time series model based on LSTM and XGBoost, namely LSTM_XGBoost model. The XGBoost model is used to train the opening price, closing price, highest price, lowest price, trading volume, up and down range, adjusted closing price and converted time data information of the processed stock historical data set, and the training results are saved. Then the opening price, closing price, highest price, lowest price, trading volume and adjusted closing price are separately input into LSTM model for prediction. The prediction results of each attribute are used as the test set of XGBoost training prediction, and the parameters of each model are continuously adjusted to obtain the optimal stock rise and fall prediction model. The model is verified by the ups and downs of ES = F, YM = F, AAPL, SI = F and Cl = F. Through the evaluation indexes of root mean square error RMSE, mean absolute error MAE, prediction accuracy and F1_ LSTM was found by comparing score_ XGBoost model in the prediction of five stocks show stable and good prediction performance, that is, the LSTM XGBoost model proposed in this paper is stable and feasible in the stock price forecast. But the overall prediction performance needs to be further improved. In the later stage, we will consider the influence of network public opinion and the correlation between various attributes on the rise and fall of stocks to improve the performance of the model for stock price prediction. So as to bring more valuable reference for people to master the overall rise and fall of stock price.

Acknowledgement. The paper is funded by Dongguan social science and technology development (general) project (No. 2020507154645) in 2020 and the key platform construction leap up program project of Guangdong University of science and technology: network engineering application technology research center of Guangdong University of science and technology.This work is supported by Natural Science Foundation of Guangdong Province of China with No. 2020A1515010784.

References

1. Kohara, K., Ishikawa, T., Fukuhara, Y.: Stock price prediction using prior knowledge and neural networks. Intell. Syst. Account. Finan. Manag. **6**(1), 11–22 (2015)
2. Nelson D., Pereira A., Oliveira R.: Stock market's price movement prediction with LSTM neural networks. In: International Joint Conference on Neural Networks. IEEE (2017)
3. Kim, H.Y., Won, C.H.: Forecasting the volatility of stock price index: a hybrid model integrating LSTM with multiple GARCH-type models. Expert Syst. Appl. **103**(8), 25–37 (2018)
4. Althelaya K.A., El-Alfy E.S.M., Mohammed, S.: Stock market forecast using multivariate analysis with bidirectional and stacked (LSTM, GRU). In: 21st Saudi Computer Society National Computer Conference (2018)

5. Sun, S., Wei, Y., Wang, S.: AdaBoost-LSTM ensemble learning for financial time series forecasting. In: Shi, Y., et al. (eds.) ICCS 2018. LNCS, vol. 10862, pp. 590–597. Springer, Cham (2018). https://doi.org/10.1007/978-3-319-93713-7_55
6. Chen, W., Yeo, C.K., Lau, C.T.: Leveraging social media news to predict stock index movement using RNN-boost. Data Knowl. Eng. **118**(11), 14–24 (2018)
7. Mehtab S., Sen J.: A robust predictive model for stock price prediction using deep learning and natural language processing. Papers (2019)
8. Xiao, C., Xia, W., Jiang, J.: Stock price forecast based on combined model of ARI-MA-LS-SVM. Neural Comput. Appl. **32**(10), 5379–5388 (2020). https://doi.org/10.1007/s00521-019-04698-5
9. Greff, K., Srivastava, R.K., Jan, K.: LSTM: A Search Space Odyssey. IEEE Trans. Neural Netw. Learn. Syst. **28**(10), 2222–2232 (2016)
10. Chen T., Guestrin C.: XGBoost: a scalable tree boosting system. In: ACM SIGKDD International Conference on Knowledge Discovery & Data Mining (2016)
11. Sundermeyer, M., Schlüter, R., Ney H.: LSTM neural networks for language modelling. In: Interspeech, pp. 601–608 (2012)
12. Miao, Y., Gowayyed, M., Metze, F.: EESEN: end-to-end speech recognition using deep RNN models and WFST-based decoding (2016)

Test of Integrated Urban Rail Transit Vehicle-to-Ground Communication System Based on LTE-U Technology

Tong Gan[1](✉), Qiang Ma[1], Xin-Hua Shen[2], and Yi-Dong Jia[3]

[1] Beijing Metro Consultancy Corporation Ltd., Beijing 100071, China
[2] CALTTA Technologies Corporation Ltd., Beijing 100071, China
[3] School of Computer and Communication Engineering, University of Science and Technology Beijing, Beijing 100083, China

Abstract. With the continuous promotion of LTE in urban rail transit, the authorized spectrum resources of LTE-M system are limited, which limits LTE's ability to meet the data transmission requirements of urban rail transit. LTE-U, an emerging wireless technology which use an unauthorized spectrum to achieve LTE, can effectively alleviate the pressure of spectrum resource shortage. In this paper, we analyze the technical advantages of LTE-U in urban rail transit applications. By building an LTE-U test network and simulating the radio channel characteristics at the equipment work site in the laboratory, the LTE-U system is tested for its ability to carry services such as CBTC, CCTV/PIS, emergency text and train operation status information in urban rail transit. The test results show that LTE-U system can meet the demand of carrying urban rail transit services and is a feasible solution to the existing problems of urban rail transit.

Keywords: LTE-U · CBTC · CCTV · PIS

1 Introduction

With the continuous development of urbanization in China, urban rail transit has gradually become a fast and convenient mode of public transportation, playing an important role in solving urban traffic congestion and driving the development of intercity industries. In order to improve the quality of operation service and safety guarantee ability, Communication Based Train Control (CBTC) system, Passenger Information System (PIS) and Closed-circuit Television (CCTV) monitoring and control (CCTV) system are used. These systems become an important part of the urban rail transit system [1]. CBTC is a signalling system based on radio communication, which achieves precise closed-loop control of trains through two-way, real-time data transmission between on-board equipment and ground equipment. PIS and CCTV systems also require vehicle-to-ground communication for information exchange between trains and the ground, also PIS and CCTV services require high transmission rates. Therefore, the car-to-car communication system should comprehensively carry the urban rail transit service with CBTC signal

X. Sun et al. (Eds.): ICAIS 2021, LNCS 12736, pp. 99–108, 2021.
https://doi.org/10.1007/978-3-030-78609-0_9

system as the core, which can provide effective bandwidth for PIS and CCTV services while meeting the low delay, high reliability and priority transmission of CBTC service [2].

Long Term Evolution-Metro (LTE-M) is an LTE system based on Long Term Evolution (LTE) radio communication technology, customized to meet the service needs of urban rail transit. LTE-M system fully takes into account the requirements of urban rail transit service for reliability and real-time, which can realize the comprehensive bearing of single system for multiple services. LTE-M system has the ad-vantages of high communication rate, high spectrum utilization, mature multiservice priority scheduling mechanism and so on [3]. However, LTE-M technology works in the 1785–1805 MHz dedicated frequency band, in addition to urban rail, the frequency band has been widely used in airports, oil, power, heavy railways and other fields, these application areas may overlap with LTE-M system operating area, resulting in co-frequency interference. And with the significant increase in the demand for data transmission between trains and land, the current spectrum resources have restricted the network capacity of the urban rail transit wireless communication system. Not only a large number of data between trains and land cannot be timely up-loaded and downloaded, but also restrict the choice of urban rail transit wireless communication system construction plan. The introduction of LTE technology into the 5.8 GHz open band (LTE in Unlicensed spectrum, LTE-U) can alleviate or even solve the problem of insufficient frequency resources for urban rail communications and meet the demand for data transmission between trains and land with higher spectrum utilization on the basis of richer spectrum resources [4, 5].

As a complementary technology to LTE in licensed bands, LTE-U was first introduced by Qualcomm at the 3GPP RAN62 summit in December 2013, and 3GPP introduced it as a key technology in LTE R13 [6]. Cagri investigated the modes that affect the performance of downlink scheduling algorithm, and proposed a novel QoS-aware downlink-scheduling algorithm, which increased the QoS-aware fairness and overall throughput of the edge users [7]. Li investigated the effect of MU-MIMO enabled WiFi AP on the performance of traffic offloading in LTE-U, the paper suggested that adaptive utilization of antenna numbers on the MU-MIMO enabled AP based on SNR, and deciding CSI feedback length were critical to achieve high rate performance for traffic offloading in LTE-U [8]. Liu proposed a unified hybrid adaptive channel access scheme, which takes advantages of both the DCM and LBT mechanisms. It can adaptively adjust the important parameters, such as the back-off window size and the duty-cycle time fraction based on the WiFi traffic and the available licensed spectrum resource while guaranteeing the fair coexistence between the WiFi and LTE-U systems [9]. Manzoor investigated the problem of unlicensed spectrum sharing among WiFi and LTE-U systems, then they proposed a fair time-sharing model based on the ruin theory to share redundant spectral resources from the unlicensed band with LTE-U without jeopardizing the performance of the WiFi system [10].

LTE-U is basically the same as LTE-M in the network architecture, only the RF work unit of the frequency band is not the same. The network architecture includes Evolved Packet Core (EPC), Base Band Unit (BBU), Radio Remote Unit (RRU) and User Equipment (UE). LTE-U system has excellent mobility and switching performance, which can support high-speed (160 km/h above) environments such as urban rail fast lines, with small switching time delay and strong service continuity. It is conducive to the transmission of highly reliable service data such as urban rail CBTC and traffic dispatching. It also has the advantages of strong anti-interference ability, large coverage radius, strong maintainability, flexible deployment, good QoS guarantee and high network security [11].

This work tests the proposed LTE-U system based on LTE-U technology to verify the performance of the LTE-U system for carrying integrated urban rail transit services. While ensuring the high reliability of CBTC service transmission, it can meet the transmission requirements of emergency text dispatching and train operation status information services, and provide an effective transmission channel for CCTV and PIS services.

The structure of this paper is as follows: Sect. 1 introduces the research back-ground, network architecture and advantages of LTE-U technology; Sect 2 introduces the test objectives and test contents; Sect. 3 introduces the test environment; Sect. 4 draws the results of this system test; and Sect. 5 is a summary.

2 Test Objectives and Contents

2.1 Test Objectives

The purpose of this test is to simulate the field wireless channel characteristics in the laboratory environment, and to verify that the LTE-U system is capable of carrying CBTC services, CCTV/PIS services, emergency text and train operation status information in the urban rail transit environment (80 kmh, 120 kmh, 160 kmh, 200 kmh).

2.2 Test Contents

In order to verify the availability of LTE-U system for wireless communication in urban rail transit vehicles, the LTE-U communication system is tested. The test consists of the following four main parts:

- The capability of LTE-U system to carry CCTV/PIS services
- The capability of LTE-U system to carry CBTC services
- The capability of LTE-U system to comprehensively carry CBTC, CCTV/PIS, emergency text and train operation status information services
- Transmission performance testing of LTE-U systems

3 Test Environment

The core network ZXTS eTC500, the LTE baseband processing unit ZXSDR B8200, and the 5725–5850 MHz band Radio Remote Unit 8504-S5800 were used in this test to build the LTE network. The train access unit (TAU) is also required, as well as a client and server that can run CCTV and PIS service simulation software simultaneously. The ACE MX wireless channel simulator was used to simulate train speed and multipath, and the EUBUS tunable attenuator was used to support large scale switching channel simulation at 5.8 GHz.

The channel simulator is able to simulate the small-scale radio decay characteristics of LTE in the 5.8 GHz band, and support no less than 4 paths, the maximum delay of the path is not less than 1 μs, and the maximum speed of the supported Doppler frequency deviation of the train is not lower than 200 km/h.

Tunable attenuators are mainly used to simulate the ability to switch cells at certain speeds, and are capable of simulating large scales decay characteristics at 5.8 GHz LTE frequency.

The service performance test software is Ixchariotv6.7, which is installed on the service server and service client to test the basic LTE performance. The statistical interval for all test metrics is 1 s. For performance such as transmission delay, it is necessary to support timestamping on simulated service packets and to calculate latency by performing timestamp analysis on the end. Also, latency estimation is not allowed in the form of ping packages.

Figure 1 shows the connection performance test of the system.

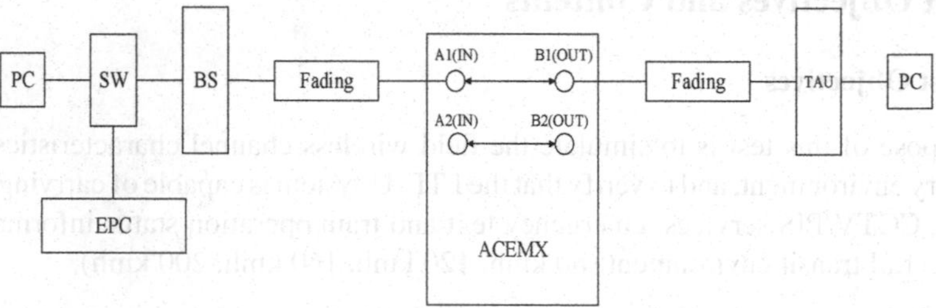

Fig. 1. Testing the connectivity performance of LTE-U system

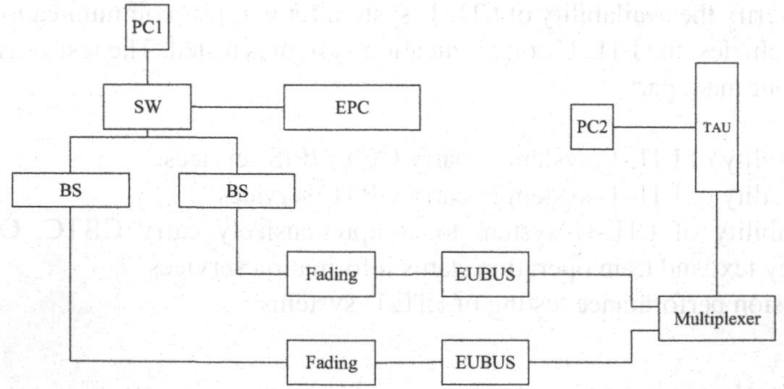

Fig. 2. Testing the switchover interrupt of LTE-U systems under static channel model.

3.1 Channel Environment

The channel model is simulated using a channel simulator, and the model should be able to represent the wireless decay characteristics in a typical urban rail transit scenario. The channel model is divided into a static model and a dynamic model, in which the static model includes three points; far, medium and near, and the default speed model is loaded at 200 km/h with the following power ranges for the far, medium and near points:

- far point: $[-85, -100)$ dBm;
- medium point: $[-75, -85)$ dBm;
- near point: > -75 dBm.

Figure 2 and Fig. 3 show the switchover interrupt test in static and dynamic mode respectively.

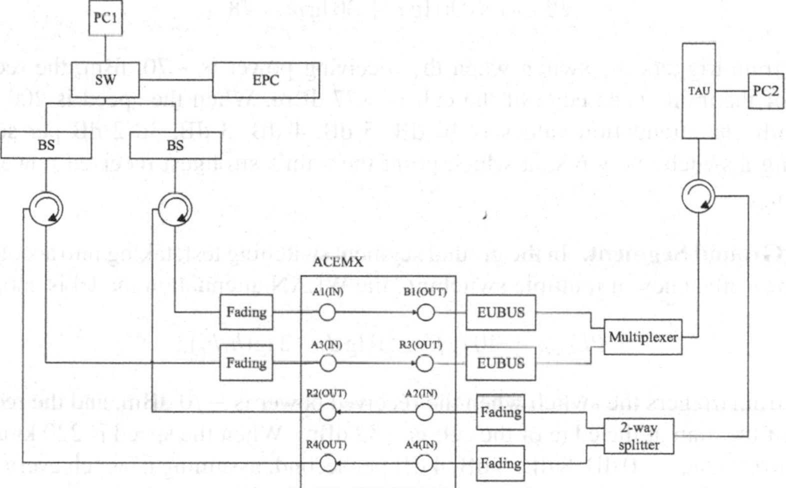

Fig. 3. Testing the switchover interrupt of LTE-U systems under dynamic channel model.

The switchover model includes underground tunnel segment as well as surface segment. Laboratory switching channel characteristics are simulated using programmable attenuators, while small-scale decay (e.g., multipath decay, Doppler frequency bias) is loaded using a channel simulator. Table 1 and Table 2 show the relative delay and relative decay of the tunnel and surface channel models, respectively.

Table 1. Tunnel channel model

Tap	Relative latency (ns)	Relative decline (dB)
1	0	0
2	90	−4
3	180	−8

Table 2. Ground channel model

Tap	Relative latency (ns)	Relative decline (dB)
1	0	0
2	180	–8

Underground Tunnel Segments In the underground tunnel segment switching test, taking into account the simulation efficiency of multiple switching, the ITU-R tunnel correction model is adopted:

$$PL_{total} = 20\lg f + 30\lg d - 28 \tag{1}$$

the train triggers the switch when the receiving power is −70 dBm, the received power of the train at the edge of the cell is −77 dBm. When the speed is 200 km/h, 220 km/h, the attenuation values is 10 dB, 5 dB, 4 dB, 3 dB, 3d 2 dB per second, assuming a switch every 6 s, at which point the train's strongest received power is – 50 dBm.

Above Ground Segment. In the ground segment switching test, taking into account the simulation efficiency of multiple switching, the WLAN attenuation model is adopted:

$$PL_{total} = 40\lg f + 50\lg d - 2\lg(h_r h_t) \tag{2}$$

the train triggers the switch when the received power is −70 dBm, and the received power of the train at the edge of the cell is −82 dBm. When the speed is 220 km/h, the attenuation value is 10 dB, 8 dB, 5 dB, 4 dB per second, assuming a switch every 4 s, at which point the train's strongest received power is −55 dBm.

3.2 Service Model

The CCTV system service is variable video surveillance analog data with uplink transmission rate of 4 Mps in 2 channels. The data packet adopts the RTP protocol and the data size is 1400 bytes.

The PIS service is a channel of video analog data with variable speed of 2–8 Mbps downlink. The data packet adopts RTP protocol with the size of 1400 bytes.

The distribution of loading services should be able to reflect the service requirements of the docked CBTC system. The data packets of each service flow adopt UDP or RTP (only used when testing the performance of packet loss) protocol with the size of 400 bytes, and the data rates of downlink and uplink are 256 kbps and 256 kbps, generating 4 service streams. The type of CBTC service is QCI1, GBR.

The type of train operation status information service is QCI 2, GBR with uplink rate of 100 kbps. The data packet adopts UDP protocol with the size of 400 bytes.

The type of emergency text service is QCI 2, GBR with downlink rate of 10 kbps. The data packet adopts UDP protocol and its size is 400 bytes.

4 Results

(1) The capability of LTE-U system to carry services

Projects	Index	Results
CCTV/PIS operational functionality testing	CCTV/PIS rate meets requirement	PASS
Transmission Latency Performance Test for CCTV and PIS Services	The maximum latency for CCTV and PIS services is less than 300 ms	PASS
Packet Loss Performance Test for CCTV and PIS Services	The rate of packet loss of CCTV and PIS services is less than 1%	PASS
Switching Latency Performance Test for CCTV and PIS Services	The maximum switching latency for CCTV and PIS services is less than 500 ms	PASS
Ultimate Performance Testing	The test results meet the RSRP boundary values and SINR values for service metrics	PASS

(2) The capability of LTE-U system to carry CBTC services

Projects	Index	Results
Transmission Latency Performance Test for CBTC Services	The maximum latency for CBTC services is less than 150 ms	PASS
Packet Loss Performance Test for CBTC Services	The rate of packet loss of CBTC services is less than 0.5%	PASS
Switching Latency Performance Test for CCTV and PIS Services	The maximum switching latency for CBTC services is less than 150ms	PASS
Switching Packet Loss Performance Test for CBTC Services	Switching packet loss rates meets the requirements	PASS
Probability of Transmission Outage Test for CBTC Services	The probability of transmission interruption which less than 2.4 s is 100%	PASS
Carrying CBTC Service Test in Congestion Scenarios	Under conditions of data saturation, it is able to meet the requirements of CBTC service and train status information service in priority	PASS
Carrying CBTC Service Test under Interference Environment	Latency and packet loss rate meet the requirements when SINR is reduced to –2 dB	PASS

(3) The capability of LTE-U system to comprehensively carry CBTC, CCTV/PIS, emergency text and train operation status information services

Projects	Index	Results
Average Performance Metrics Testing for Integrated Services	CBTC, train status, emergency text, CCTV/PIS service index meet the requirements	PASS
Performance Metrics Testing of Integrated Services in Switch Scenarios	The switching latency of each service meets the requirements	PASS
Carrying Integrated Service Test under Interference Environment	The latency and packet loss rate of CBTC, train status, emergency text, CCTV/PIS service meet the requirements	PASS
Carrying CBTC Service and CCTV Service Test in Congestion Scenarios	CBTC, train status, emergency text, CCTV/PIS service index meet the requirements	PASS
LTE-U Network Transmission Capability Testing Under Extreme Conditions	Loaded with 4-channel CBTC service, 1-channel train status information service, 1-channel emergency text service, 2-channel 2 Mbps CCTV service and 1-channel 6 Mbpss PIS service, the system's ultimate RSRP is −98 dBm and SINR is 18 dB	PASS

(4) Transmission performance testing of LTE-U systems

Projects	Index	Results
20 MHz Co-frequency Uplink Throughput Test	Co-frequency networking; With 80 km/h, 120 km/h, 160 km/h, 200 km/h channel simulator and switchover simulator;	PASS
20 MHz Co-frequency Downlink Throughput Test	Co-frequency networking; With 80 km/h,120 km/h, 160 km/h, 200 km/h channel simulator and switchover simulator;	PASS
20 MHz Inter-frequency Uplink Throughput Test	Inter-frequency networking; With 80 km/h, 120 km/h, 160 km/h, 200 km/h channel simulator	PASS
20 MHz Inter-frequency Downlink Throughput Test	Inter-frequency networking; With 80 km/h,120 km/h, 160 km/h, 200 km/h channel simulator and switchover simulator;	PASS

(*continued*)

(*continued*)

Projects	Index	Results
40 MHz Co-frequency Uplink Throughput Test	Co-frequency networking; With 80 km/h, 120 km/h,160 km/h, 200 km/h channel simulator and switchover simulator;	PASS
40 MHz Co-frequency Downlink Throughput Test	Co-frequency networking; With 80 km/h, 120 km/h,160 km/h, 200 km/h channel simulator and switchover simulator;	PASS
40 MHz Switching Uplink Throughput Test	Co-frequency networking; No Channel Simulator; With switch simulator; Simulation of leaky cable and waveguide scenarios with no Doppler effect	PASS
40 MHz Switching Downlink Throughput Test	Co-frequency networking; No Channel Simulator; With switch simulator; Simulation of leaky cable and waveguide scenarios with no Doppler effect	PASS
80 MHz Switching Uplink Throughput Test	Co-frequency networking; No Channel Simulator; With switch simulator; Simulation of leaky cable and waveguide scenarios with no Doppler effect	PASS
80 MHz Switching Downlink Throughput Test	Co-frequency networking; No Channel Simulator; With switch simulator; Simulation of leaky cable and waveguide scenarios with no Doppler effect	PASS

5 Conclusion

The LTE-U vehicle-to-ground communication system can meet the needs of urban rail transit comprehensive carrier CBTC, CCTV, PIS, emergency text and train operation status information services. In particular, the wide bandwidth and high throughput of the LTE-U system is a viable solution to meet the capacity requirements of PIS and CCTV in the future.

Acknowledgement. The authors thank the reviewers for their valuable suggestions, which greatly improved the quality of the paper.

Funding Statement. This paper is supported by the research on the application of LTE-U in rail transit.

Conflicts of Interest. The authors declare that they have no conflicts of interest to report regarding the present study.

References

1. Zhang, H.: Application research of LTE-U for urban rail transit integrated service bearing system. Railw. Locomotive Car **39**(4), 1–4 (2019)
2. Jung, Y., Kang, M., You, Y.: Complexity effective frequency and sidelink synchronization algorithm for LTE device-to-device communication systems. Comput. Mater. Continua **62**(1), 443–458 (2020)
3. Dawaliby, S., Bradai, A., Pousset, Y.: In depth performance evaluation of LTE-M for M2M communications. In: 12th International Conference on Wireless and Mobile Computing, Networking and Communications (WiMob), pp. 1–8. IEEE, New York (2016)
4. Zhang, R., Wang, M., Cai, L.X., et al.: LTE-unlicensed: the future of spectrum aggregation for cellular networks. IEEE Wirel. Commun. **22**(3), 150–159 (2015)
5. Chen, B., Chen, Z., Pappas, N., et al.: Bringing LTE to unlicensed spectrum: technical solutions and deployment considerations. In: IEEE 23rd International Workshop on Computer Aided Modeling and Design of Communication Links and Networks (CAMAD), pp. 1–7. IEEE, Barcelona (2018)
6. Jeon, J., Niu, H., Li, Q., et al.: LTE with listen-before-talk in unlicensed spectrum. In: IEEE International Conference on Communication Workshop (ICCW), pp. 2320–2324. IEEE, London (2015)
7. Gungor, V.C., Uyan, O.G.: QoS-aware downlink scheduling algorithm for LTE networks: a case study on edge users. In: 25th Signal Processing and Communications Applications Conference (SIU), pp. 1–4. IEEE, Antalya (2017)
8. Li, Z., Dong, C., Li, A., et al.: Performance analysis for traffic offloading with MU-MIMO enabled AP in LTE-U networks. In: IEEE Global Communications Conference, pp. 1–6. IEEE (2017)
9. Liu, S., Yin, R., Guanding, Y.: Hybrid adaptive channel access for LTE-U systems. IEEE Trans. Veh. Technol. **68**(10), 9820–9832 (2019)
10. Manzoor, A., Tran, N.H., Saad, W., et al.: Ruin theory for dynamic spectrum allocation in LTE-U networks. IEEE Commun. Lett. **23**(2), 366–369 (2018)
11. Uyan, O.G., Gungor, V.C.: QoS-aware LTE-a downlink scheduling algorithm: a case study on edge users. Int. J. Commun. Syst. **32**(15), 4066 (2019)

Research on Efficient Image Inpainting Algorithm Based on Deep Learning

Tao Qin[1], Juanjuan Liu[2(✉)], and Wenchao Xue[3]

[1] National Computer Network Emergency Response Technical Team/Coordination Center of China, Beijing 100020, China

[2] School of Computer and Communication Engineering, University of Science and Technology Beijing, Beijing 100083, China

[3] Engineering Agent Construction Management Office of Navy Logistics Department, Beijing 100036, China

Abstract. The rapid development of deep learning has brought a new development direction for image inpainting, changing the traditional image inpaiting algorithm, which can only repair the problem of small area damage based on the structure and texture of the damaged image. In recent years, image inpainting algorithm based on deep learning has received widespread attention from industry and academia so that it has made great progress. However, the current image inpainting algorithm based on deep learning still has the problem of consuming so much time. In order to solve the above problem, an end-to-end image inpainting algorithm suitable for real-time scene was proposed. The mask of the damaged image generated by D-linkNet network, the edge information of the damaged image, and damaged image were used to control the network input, which avoided the damage to the existing semantics of the image and retained the intact image outside the damaged. On this basis, in order to improve the performance of image inpainting, Convolutional Block Attention Module (CBAM) was used in the residual network. Experimental results show that, compared with edge information-based deep learning algorithm Edge Connect, the repair speed is twice as fast as Edge Connect while the repair results are similar.

Keywords: Deep learning · Image inpainting · D-LinkNet · CBAM attention

1 Introduction

Image inpainting belongs to a branch of computer vision, which is to repair the defect area in the image according to the existing information in the image. With the rapid development of deep learning, image inpainting has become a research hotspot and has been widely used in the fields of image redundant target removal, criminal investigation facial reconstruction, aerospace engineering and bioengineering. There are two traditional image inpainting methods, one is based on sample block [1, 2], and the other is based on sparse representation [3]. These two methods can only repair small and medium-sized defects in the image. With the rapid development of deep learning theory, this has

X. Sun et al. (Eds.): ICAIS 2021, LNCS 12736, pp. 109–120, 2021.
https://doi.org/10.1007/978-3-030-78609-0_10

brought new opportunities for image inpainting technology, and gradually evolved a new image inpainting method – image inpainting method based on deep learning [4].

Although image inpainting using deep learning has achieved good results, the model of deep learning algorithm takes too much time, and it is difficult to be applied to scenes with high time requirements such as criminal investigation and edge calculation. In 2019, the Edge Connect [5] method based on edge information has achieved great repair effect. Edge Connect algorithm constructs a two-stage image inpainting network. The first stage is responsible for repairing the edge of the image, and the second stage is for filling the image content. The algorithm needs to train two image inpainting networks, which takes too much time. At the same time, the repair effect of the first stage has a great impact on the second stage, which largely determines the repair effect of the second stage.

In view of shortcomings of Edge Connect method, this paper proposes an end-to-end generative adversarial network, through which faster and natural inpainting results can be obtained. Our paper makes the following contributions:

(1) This paper proposes an end-to-end image inpaiting method to improve the network repair speed;
(2) CBAM (Convolutional Block Attention Module) attention is added in the network to improve the inpainting effect;
(3) D-LinkNet network is used to generate the mask to avoid damage to the normal area.

The work arrangement of this paper is as follows: the second part mainly summarizes the related work of this paper and introduces the development of image inpainting algorithms based on deep learning. The third part mainly introduces the network module of this paper, including segmentation network, image inpainting network and attention module. The fourth part mainly analyzes the experimental results as well the advantages and disadvantages of this method. The fifth part is the conclusion, which summarizes the methods of this paper and puts forward the development direction.

2 Related Work

Most of the image inpainting methods based on deep learning use GAN (Generative Adversarial Networks), which is generated by the Ian J. Goodfellow et al. [6]. GAN is composed of the generative network and the discriminant network. The generative network is mainly responsible for generating data information, and the discriminant network is responsible for determining which data information is generated by the generative network, that is, false data. In the process of confrontation, the generated information is closer to the real data, so as to "cheat" the discriminant network. However, the ability of the discriminant network to identify real or false data is getting stronger and stronger. The generative network and the discriminant network game each other in this process, and reach a state of dynamic equilibrium. So that the discriminating network cannot distinguish between true and false, and obtain a better generator. Since GAN was put forward, a large number of scholars have started to apply it to image inpainting. Deepak Pathak et al. [7] firstly used GAN in image inpainting in 2016, they proposed a context-based adaptive encoder. The generative network adopts the structure of encoder and decoder, and the discriminant network adopts the structure of five-layer convolution to judge the generated or real image. This method can only deal with the damaged image of fixed damaged area, without adding texture details consistent with the real image, making people look particularly fuzzy. However, it is the first method of GAN network image inpainting and subsequent researchers have made improvements on the basis of this paper. Chao Yang et al. [8] proposed a new network structure in 2017, which added a texture generative network on the basis of the structure of encoder and decoder. They propose to divide the damaged area into fixed size patches and divide other parts of the image into patches of the same size. They then extract their texture information by the texture generation network and find the information of the closest two patches to match to ensure the visual consistency of the image. This method can process the damaged images of higher resolution, however, it can only repair the images of fixed areas and cannot meet people's needs for image inpainting. In the same year, Satoshi iizuka [9] et al. proposed a new network structure, which improved the discriminant network of the structure of encoder and decoder. They construct a global discriminant network and a local discriminant network. They then input the repaired complete image and repaired damaged areas into the discriminant network respectively. On the basis of keeping the original structure unchanged, the author added expansion convolution in the generative network to increase the sensor field. This method can produce fine texture details, but it cannot repair large areas of the image. Nvidia [10] proposed a brand new image inpainting method in 2018, in which they proposed the idea of partial convolution to repair the image with irregular holes. The author convolves the mask updated from the previous layer with the image in each layer and obtains great inpainting results. However, the author also pointed out in the paper that although this method can reconstruct the missing area of the image well, it cannot guarantee that the generated image is exactly the same as the real image.

Kamyar Nazeri et al. [5] proposed an image inpainting method combining edge information in 2019. The author constructs a two-stage image inpainting network in this paper. They firstly use the edge generative network to supplement the edge information of the damaged image. They then use the content generation network to carry out the semantic repair of the image information. Finally, the author verifies that this method can achieve good repair results through experiments. The work of our paper is based on the Edge Connect method proposed by Kamyar Nazeri et al. By simplifying the network structure and improving the training speed of the network, in order to achieve better repair results, by adding CBAM attention to the network, finally by using the split network to generate an image mask to avoid repairing other intact areas.

3 Image Inpainting Network Model

In this paper, shadow areas are generated randomly in the images of the Places2 dataset as the damaged image dataset. The network module of image inpainting is shown in Fig. 1: (1) Image segmentation network is necessary to produce a mask of the damaged image, which is used to limit the damaged area. (2) The Canny edge detector is useful to detect the edge information of the damaged image. (3) During the image inpainting, the damaged image, the mask of the damaged image generated by D-LinkNet [11] and the edge of the damaged image are input into the image inpainting network. CBAM attention module is added into the image inpainting network for accurate repair of the damaged image. In this section, the network module used in the paper is briefly introduced.

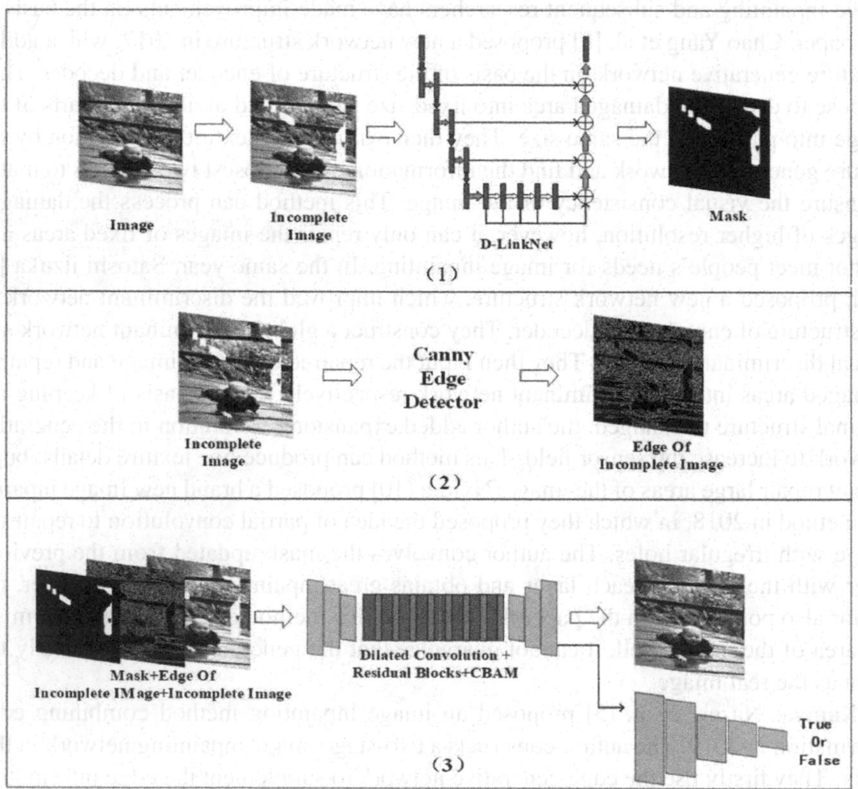

Fig. 1. Image inpainting network model

3.1 Segmentation Network

Image segmentation is an important part of image processing, which is widely used in medical diagnosis and treatment, image beautification and automatic driving. Image segmentation is to classify each pixel in the image into its own category, which is equivalent to a marking process. Each pixel is marked and then the pixels belonging to the same category are grouped together, so we can segment the image into different regions. For example, the nose, mouth, eyes and other parts can be segmented by using segmentation network in face image.

In this paper, while repairing the damaged area without changing the other intact part of the image, generating a mask is necessary to restrict the damaged region. The mask of the damaged image is that the part of the damaged is white, while the other part is black. The mask is added with the damaged part during the inpainting process, and the damaged image is restricted. For a damaged image, its mask is not obtained directly, so it is important to produce the mask. The process of mask generation is to separate the damaged area (the pixel point of the damaged area is different from the intact area, the pixel point is 255) from the image, which is similar to the image segmentation. Therefore, D-LinkNet segmentation network is used in this paper to produce the image mask.

D-LinkNet [11] is an improvement on the basis of LinkNet network. Encoder adopts ResNet structure, the middle part adds dilated convolution to increase the sensor field of the network, and the last part adds the results obtained from the first two parts for feature fusion. This network is first used for road segmentation in high-resolution satellite images, which is a very simple and efficient segmentation method. The damaged image is input into the segmentation network to obtain a clear mask image.

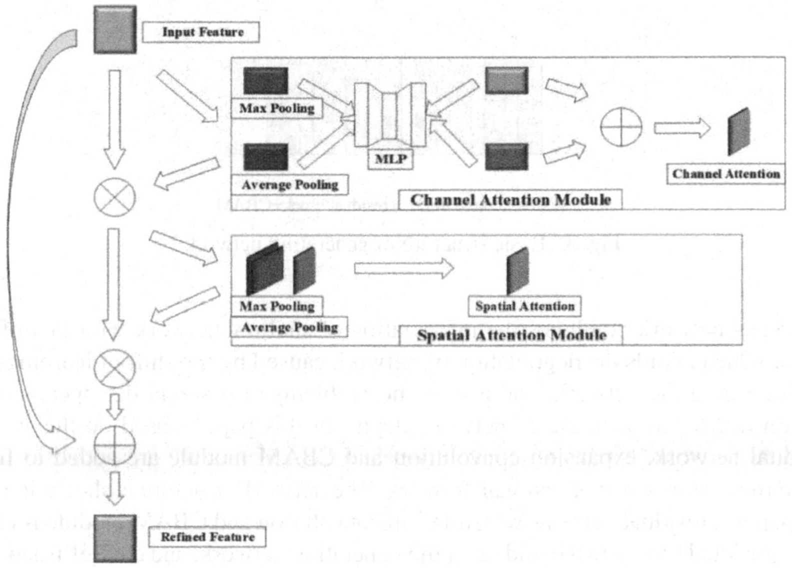

Fig. 2. CBAM attention mechanism

3.2 CBAM Attention Module

CBAM attention module is mainly used between the two feature layers of convolutional neural network [12]. Channel attention and spatial attention are mainly used. In the channel attention module, the main problem to be solved is which channel information is more important. There are two pooling methods used in the channel attention module: average pooling and maximum pooling. Three full connection layers are used and the two outputs are superimposed after two pooling methods. The spatial attention module mainly solves the problem of which position is more important in the two-dimensional plane. Two pooling methods are also used, and then the convolution layer is passed to obtain the convolution result. The operation process is shown in Fig. 2.

3.3 Improving Inpainting Network

The image inpainting network used in this paper is generated countermeasure network. The basic idea of generative antagonism is to reach an equilibrium state through the dynamic game of generating network and discriminating network. The generating network is responsible for generating some missing things in the new image to "cheat" the network, and the discriminating network is responsible for identifying the authenticity of the output of the generated network. In this paper, the structure of the generated network is that three-layer convolution is used for down sampling, then eight residual blocks of dilation convolution are connected, and finally three-layer convolution is used for up sampling, as shown in Fig. 3. Different from edge connect, this paper only uses one generated countermeasure network, which greatly shortens the repair time. Meanwhile, in order to ensure the effect of network, CBAM module is added to the residual block.

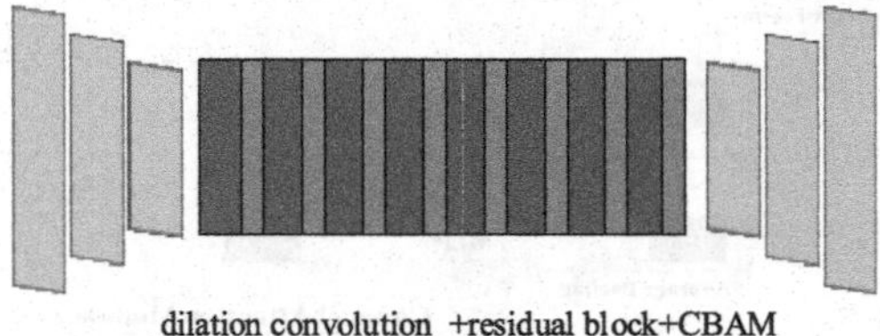

Fig. 3. Basic structure of generating network

Residual network combines the information of shallow network with that of deep network, which avoids the degradation of network caused by the shift of learning focus while deepening the network, and avoids the problems of gradient disappearance and explosion due to the increase of network depth. In this paper, based on the structure of residual network, expansion convolution and CBAM module are added to further improve the performance of residual network. The network structure is shown in Fig. 4. In this paper, a residual network with dilation convolution and CBAM module is used in the eight residual blocks in the middle of the generating network, and the ReLu activation function is not used in the latter layer of the residual block. Expanding convolution can increase the receptive field of the network and extract more features, while CBAM module gives more weight to the important features to obtain more important features. The combination of the two can obtain a wider range of effective features and improve the performance of the network.

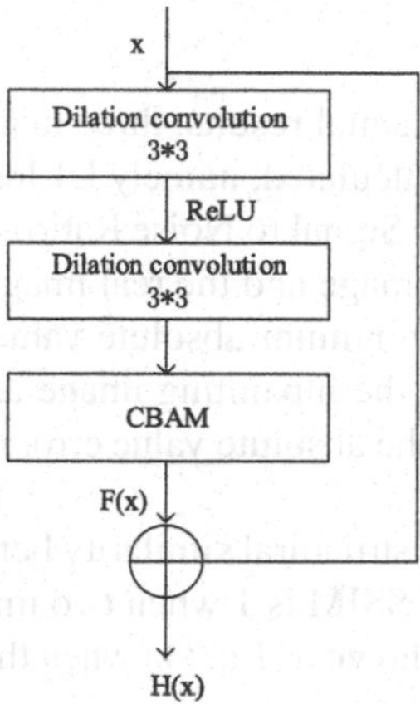

Fig. 4. Basic structure of residual block

4 Experiments

In this experiment, 5000 images are selected from the places2 [13] dataset for training and 2991 images are selected for testing. These images are images about the scene. In this paper, the official weight of Edge Connect is used for testing. The batchsize in the training process is 6, and the number of iterations is 300,000. The code is carried out in Pytorch.

4.1 Qualitative Analysis

This experiment is mainly compared with the current most advanced Edge Connect method. Comparison experiments of the two methods are performed on the same dataset for the reliability of the test. The experimental inpainting results are shown in Fig. 5 with the same configuration and the same number of iterations.

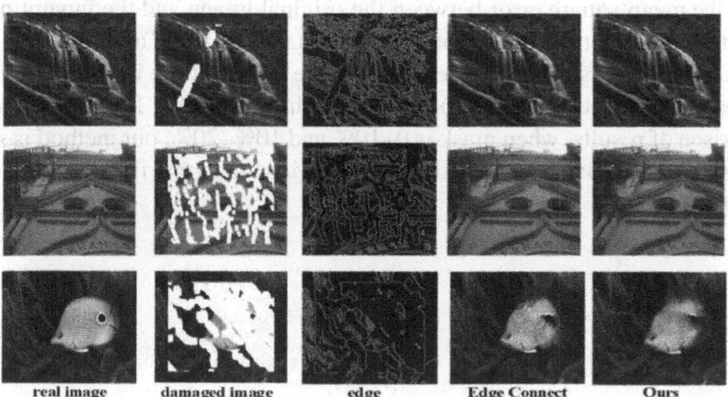

Fig. 5. Inpainting image effect contrast

4.2 Quantitative Analysis

For the objectivity of the experimental results, three indicators commonly used to evaluate the image quality are also calculated, namely L1 loss, SSIM (Structural Similarity Index Measure) and PSNR (Peak Signal to Noise Ratio), which are used to calculate the difference between the restored image and the real image.

L_1 loss, also known as the minimum absolute value error, represents the absolute value of the pixel error between the inpainting image and the real image. The smaller the value of L_1 loss, the smaller the absolute value error of the image when we calculate it.

SSIM calculate the degree of structural similarity between two images, and its value is between 0 and 1. The value of SSIM is 1 when two images are exactly the same. The calculation formula of SSIM is shown as Eq. (1) when the structural similarity of image x and y is calculated:

$$SSIM(x, y) = \frac{(2\mu_x\mu_y + c_1)(2\sigma_{xy} + c_2)}{(\mu_x^2 + \mu_y^2 + c_1)(\sigma_x^2 + \sigma_y^2 + c_2)} \tag{1}$$

In Eq. (1), μ_x and μ_y represent the average value of image x and y separately. σ_x^2 and σ_y^2 represent the variance of image x and y separately. σ_{xy} represents the mean variance of image x and y. c_1 and c_2 represent two different constants. We want the result as large as impossible when the SSIM between the inpainting image and the real image is calculated.

PSNR is an objective standard to evaluate an image. It is the signal-to-noise ratio of an image, whose unit is dB. The larger PSNR is, the smaller the image noise is and the less distortion is. The calculation formula of PSNR is shown in Eq. (2):

$$PSNR = 10 \times \log_{10}\left(\frac{(2^n - 1)^2}{MSE}\right) \tag{2}$$

In Eq. (2), all the calculations are based on the pixel points of the image. MSE represents the mean square error between the original image and the inpainting image, n represents the number of bits per pixel, and we take the value of n as 8. We want the result as large as impossible when we calculate the PSNR of the inpainting image.

The comparison results of the experiment are shown in Table 1. As can be seen from the comparison of results, when mask is 0–10% and 10%–20%, our method is similar to that in Edge Connect. But our method is slightly worse than that in Edge Connect when mask is 20%–60%.

Table 1. Comparison of experimental results

	Mask	Edge connect	Ours
L_1	0–10%	0.006	0.007
	10%–20%	0.016	0.017
	20%–30%	0.027	0.030
	30%–40%	0.040	0.043
	40%–50%	0.053	0.057
	50%–60%	0.079	0.084
SSIM	0–10%	0.979	0.978
	10%–20%	0.944	0.937
	20%–30%	0.892	0.878
	30%–40%	0.834	0.815
	40%–50%	0.762	0.737
	50%–60%	0.623	0.593
PSNR (dB)	0–10%	32.978	32.565
	10%–20%	27.602	26.982
	20%–30%	24.649	24.029
	30%–40%	22.589	22.047
	40%–50%	20.908	20.421
	50%–60%	18.448	17.998

4.3 Time Analysis

From the above data, we can see that our method is similar to the Edge Connect method. But from the network structure, we have improved our structure, so the time efficiency is higher than Edge Connect method.

The inpainting time of each image is calculated, and the results are shown in Table 2. Masks are not used directly in this paper because there are no masks in the natural damaged image. Our approach is closer to natural image inpainting than Edge Connect method.

Table 2. Time comparison of each image

	Edge connect	Ours
Time(s)	0.0230	0.0124

4.4 Comprehensive Evaluation Function

In order to synthesize each index, this paper constructs a weighted function P to comprehensively evaluate the performance of image inpainting. The larger the value of P, the better the quality of image inpainting. The function is represented as follows Eq. (3):

$$P = \frac{w_1 \times S_S + w_2 \times P_S}{w_3 \times L_1 + w_4 \times t} \tag{3}$$

Among them, S_S and w_1 represent the value and weight coefficient of SSIM, Ps and w_2 respectively represent the value and weight coefficient of PSNR, L_1 and w_3 respectively represent the value and weight coefficient of L_1, and t and w_4 represent the value and weight coefficient of inpainting time respectively.

From the experimental comparison in Table 1, it can be seen that other performance indicators are not significantly different, so we make w_1 take 0.3, w_2 take 0.01, w_3 take 2, observing the influence of time weight w_4 on image inpainting performance, and the results are shown in Fig. 6. The solid line depicts the algorithm we used in this paper, and the dotted line depicts the edge connect algorithm. It can be seen from the figure that when w_4 is about 0.70 (actually 0.69906, about 0.70), the comprehensive performance of the proposed algorithm is better than that of edge connect algorithm. The algorithm proposed in this paper is more suitable for scenes with larger time weight and smaller delay, such as the scene of edge computing.

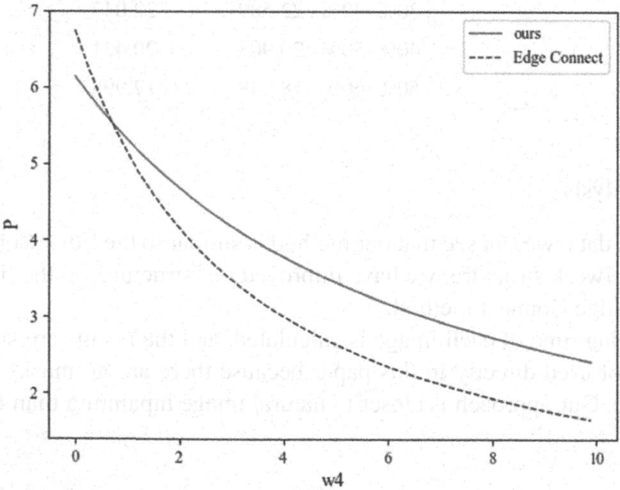

Fig. 6. w4 and P transformation curve

In order to further describe the influence of time on the comprehensive evaluation function, we take w_4 as 0.70 to draw the transformation curve between time t and comprehensive evaluation index P, as shown in Fig. 7. As can be seen from Fig. 7, when the effect P is the same, our algorithm consumes less time. In other words, under the same comprehensive performance, the speed of this algorithm is faster than that of Edge Connect algorithm.

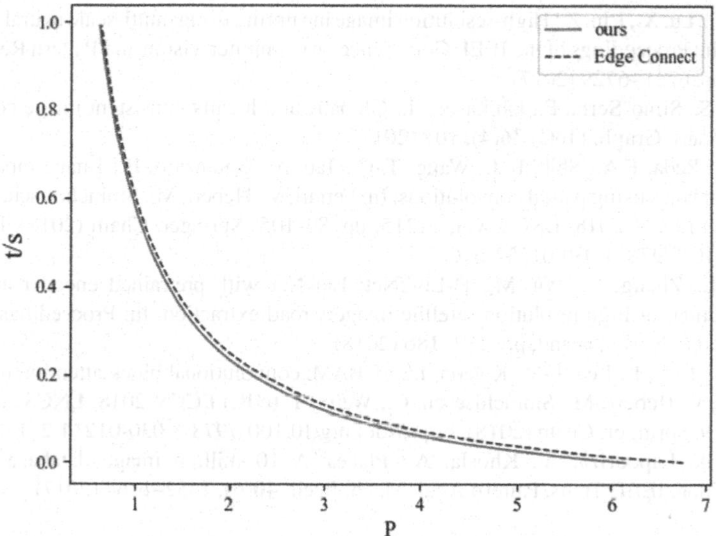

Fig. 7. Transformation curve of t and P

5 Conclusion

This paper proposes a one-stage image inpainting method based on the Edge Connect method. Our inpainting results are similar to Edge Connect network, but our approach has great potential in the future. Our approach is closer to the natural image inpainting and faster than Edge Connect method. Since the training resources are limited, we have not used all the training data. We believe that the next research work can bring about greater improvement.

References

1. Criminisi, A., Patrick, P., Kentaro, T.: Object removal by exemplar-based inpainting. In: Proceedings of IEEE Computer Society Conference on Computer Vision and Pattern Recognition, USA, vol. 2 (2003)
2. Xu, Z., Sun, J.: Image inpainting by patch propagation using patch sparsity. IEEE Trans. Image Process. **19**(5), 1153–1165 (2010)
3. Gao, C.Y., Xu, X.E., Luo, Y.M.: Object image restoration based on sparse representation. Chin. J. Comput. (9), 4 (2019)
4. Yu, J., Lin, Z., Yang, J.: Generative image inpainting with contextual attention. In: Proceedings of the IEEE Conference on Computer Vision and Pattern Recognition, New Zealand, pp. 5505–5514 (2018)
5. Nazeri, K., Ng, E., Joseph, T.: Edgeconnect: generative image inpainting with adversarial edge learning. arXiv preprint arXiv:1901.00212, 1901 (2019)
6. Goodfellow, I., Pouget-Abadie, J., Mirza, M.: Generative adversarial nets. In: Advances in Neural Information Processing Systems, pp. 2672–2680 (2014)
7. Pathak, D., Krahenbuhl, P., Donahue, J.: Context encoders: feature learning by inpainting. In: Proceedings of the IEEE Conference on Computer Vision and Pattern Recognition, USA, pp. 2536–2544 (2016)

8. Yang, C., Lu, X., Lin, Z.: High-resolution image inpainting using multi-scale neural patch synthesis. In: Proceedings of the IEEE Conference on Computer Vision and Pattern Recognition, USA, pp. 6721–6729 (2017)
9. Iizuka, S., Simo-Serra, E., Ishikawa, H.: Globally and locally consistent image completion. ACM Trans. Graph. (ToG) **36**(4), 107 (2017)
10. Liu, G., Reda, F.A., Shih, K.J., Wang, T.-C., Tao, A., Catanzaro, B.: Image inpainting for irregular holes using partial convolutions. In: Ferrari, V., Hebert, M., Sminchisescu, C., Weiss, Y. (eds.) ECCV 2018. LNCS, vol. 11215, pp. 89–105. Springer, Cham (2018). https://doi.org/10.1007/978-3-030-01252-6_6
11. Zhou, L., Zhang, C., Wu, M.: D-LinkNet: LinkNet with pretrained encoder and dilated convolution for high resolution satellite imagery road extraction. In: Proceedings of CVPR Workshops, New Zealand, pp. 182–186 (2018)
12. Woo, S., Park, J., Lee, J.-Y., Kweon, I.S.: CBAM: convolutional block attention module. In: Ferrari, V., Hebert, M., Sminchisescu, C., Weiss, Y. (eds.) ECCV 2018. LNCS, vol. 11211, pp. 3–19. Springer, Cham (2018). https://doi.org/10.1007/978-3-030-01234-2_1
13. Zhou, B., Lapedriza, A., Khosla, A.: Places: A 10 million image database for scene recognition. IEEE Trans. Pattern Anal. Mach. Intell. **40**(6), 1452–1464 (2017)

Subspace Classification of Attention Deficit Hyperactivity Disorder with Laplacian Regularization

Yuan Wang, Yuan Gao, Junping Jiang, Min Lin, and Yibin Tang(✉)

College of Internet of Things Engineering, Hohai University, Changzhou 213022, China
tangyb@hhuc.edu.cn

Abstract. Attention Deficit Hyperactivity Disorder (ADHD) is a common nerobehavioral disease in school-age children. Its accurate diagnostic methods have drawn widespread attention in recent years. Among them, neurobiological diagnosis methods are proved as a significant way to identify ADHD patients. By employing some neurobiological measures of ADHD, machine learning is treated as a useful tool for ADHD diagnosis (or classification). In this work, we develop a Laplacian regularization subspace learning model for ADHD classification. In detail, we use resting-state Functional Connectivities (FCs) of the brain as input neurobiological data and cast them into the subspace learning model which is carried out in an existing binary hypothesis testing framework. In this testing framework, under a hypothesis of the test subject (ADHD or healthy control subject), training data generates its corresponding feature set in the feature selection phase. Then, the feature set is turned to its projected features by the subspace model for each hypothesis. Here, a Laplacian regularization is employed to enhance the relationship of intra-class subjects. By comparing the subspace energies of projection features between two hypotheses, a label is finally predicted for the test subject. Experiments show, on the ADHD-200 database, the average accuracy is about 91.8% for ADHD classification, which outperforms most of the existing machine learning and deep learning methods.

Keywords: ADHD classification · Subspace learning · Laplacian regularization · Binary hypothesis

1 Introduction

Attention Deficit Hyperactivity Disorder (ADHD) is a common neurobehavioral disease in school-age children. It is characterized by inattention, excessive activity, and lack of self-control [1]. Many individuals who suffered from ADHD persist in the symptoms during their adulthood [2]. Current clinical diagnosis is with the direct observation of patients, which mainly depends on the subjective scores from various Hamilton scales [3]. Some questionnaires are taken for children to investigate their multiple performances in life, and then clinicians judge the disease status. However, such a diagnostic method is highly subjective and requires experienced clinicians. It frequently causes

X. Sun et al. (Eds.): ICAIS 2021, LNCS 12736, pp. 121–131, 2021.
https://doi.org/10.1007/978-3-030-78609-0_11

misdiagnosis for patients with mild symptoms. Therefore, the objective ADHD diagnosis becomes more attractive. Various objective methods have been proposed, wherein ADHD classification with Machine Learning (ML) and Deep Learning (DL) has made great developments in recent years.

Nowadays, well-developed imaging approaches, e.g., structural Magnetic Resonance Imaging (sMRI), functional Magnetic Resonance Imaging (fMRI), Positron Emission Computed Tomography (PET), and Electroencephalogram (EEG) [4, 5], provide plenty of objective data for diagnosis. Among these approaches, fMRI has more advantages in detecting psychological disorders. It monitors the Blood-Oxygen-Level-Dependence (BOLD) signals to discover the dynamic change in brain regions. With a series of data operations, more advanced biosignals can be extracted from the BOLD signals. Here, Functional Connectivity (FC) has received increasing attention by revealing the dysfunctions of the brain network [6]. Therefore, given a set of resting-state fMRI data, we focus on the FC analysis for ADHD classification.

Machine learning is an effective method to distinguish ADHD patients from healthy control subjects [7, 8]. The ML-based ADHD classification methods mainly include three phases, i.e., feature selection, feature extraction, and label decision. In feature selection, some recognizable biosignals are selected from a huge number of biosignals as their typical ones. Some feature selection algorithms are recommended such as Support Vector Machine Recursive Feature Elimination (SVM-RFE) [9], Least Absolute Shrinkage and Selection Operator (LASSO) [10], and Elastic Network [11]. Feature extraction contributes to the model design for capturing high-level features from selected features, where dimensionality reduction is a common and effective approach [12–14]. For example, a feature extraction framework is proposed with the forward-backward learning strategy to obtain low-dimension subspaces for FC data [15]. Label decision is another crucial phase to impact the classification performance. Many well-designed classifiers, e.g., logistic regression, random forest, and decision tree, are incorporated for ADHD classification. Most existing machine learning methods are carried out in a training-and-test framework. However, it may hinder the further promotion of classification accuracy. In practice, the features of test subjects often cannot be well included in the feature space of training data (a.k.a. training subjects) due to ADHD databases of small size. As a result, a binary hypothesis framework is presented to overcome this problem. For example, a binary hypothesis testing approach with dual subspace clustering is deployed and achieves a remarkable ADHD classification performance [16].

Besides, deep learning has been successfully applied in ADHD classification. Different from ML-based methods, the classification via deep learning integrates the aforementioned three phases as a whole. It flexibly learns the high-level features from various biosignal sets [17, 18]. As we know, a Convolutional Neural Network (CNN) is exploited to extract FC features through a fully connected network and then achieves an acceptable classification result [19]. Later, a three-dimensional CNN (3D-CNN) model [20] further uses various fMRI data to comprehensively analyze the local spatial abnormal patterns of ADHD patients. Moreover, another 3D-CNN variant is provided for the feature training, which adopts the linear discriminant analysis for classification [21].

Affected by recent research progress, we propose an ADHD classification method by Laplacian regularized subspace learning and binary hypothesis testing. The Laplacian approach enhances the relationship of intra-class subjects in the learned subspace. Under the binary hypothesis framework, the subspace energy is exploited as a measure for the label prediction of the test subject. Experiments show, on the ADHD-200 database, the average classification accuracy is about 91.8%, which outperforms most of the existing ML-based and DL-based methods.

2 Material and Method

2.1 Image Data Preprocessing

In our work, all resting-state fMRI data is from the ADHD-200 consortium (http://fcon_1 000.pro-jects.nitrc.org/indi/adhd200/). ADHD-200 database is an open-source database of fMRI scans and contains the corresponding clinical characteristics of ADHD and healthy control subjects. We use four datasets of the ADHD-200 database to investigate our ADHD classification method. These datasets are from New York University Medical Center (NYU), NeuroImage (NI), Kennedy Krieger Institute (KKI), and Peking University (PU), respectively. Their detailed information is given in Table 1.

In ADHD data processing, we obtain the time course value of BOLD signals from the connectome website (http://www.preprocessed-connectomes-project.org/adhd-200/). The preprocessing steps include removing of first four time points, slice time correction, motion correction (first image taken as the reference), registration on $4 \times 4 \times 4$ voxel resolution in Montreal Neurological Institute (MNI) space, filtration (bandpass filter with 0.009 Hz–0.08 Hz) and smoothing via 6mm FWHM Gaussian filter. According to the Automatic Anatomical Label-116 template, we select the first 90 brain regions as regions of interest to establish the FC network. FCs are generated from the Pearson correlation coefficients between regional BOLD signals. Later, a Fisher's r-to-z transform is utilized to transform the sampling distribution of correlation coefficients for normality.

Table 1. Information about used ADHD-200 datasets

Site	Age	Female	Male	Control	ADHD	Total
NYU	7–18	77	145	99	123	222
KKI	8–13	33	46	61	22	83
NI	11–22	17	31	23	25	48
PU	8–17	52	142	116	78	194
PU_1*	8–17	36	48	62	24	86

*PU_1 is the first sub-dataset of PU.

2.2 Binary Hypothesis Testing Framework

The core idea of binary hypothesis testing is to use the FCs of the test subject (without seeing its label) to affect the FC selection of training data. During the feature selection phase, the typical FCs of training data can be got under the true hypothesis of the test subject, while the obscure ones are under the false hypothesis. Sequentially, we adopt the Laplacian regularized subspace learning model in the feature extraction phase. It respectively provides their subspace energies under different hypotheses as a measure for the label prediction of the test subject. Finally, by comparing these two energies, the label of the test subject under the true hypothesis is effectively identified. Its ADHD classification framework is shown in Fig. 1.

We design a binary hypothesis framework still within three phases, i.e., feature selection, feature extraction, and label decision. At the very beginning, we employ the label hypothesis of the test subject as healthy control ($\mathcal{H}_0$) or ADHD patients ($\mathcal{H}_1$). In the feature selection, both FCs of training and test data is applied to calculate the reliability of FCs via SVM-RFE. By sorting all feature reliability values in descending order, two rank sets ($\boldsymbol{R}^{\mathcal{H}_0}, \boldsymbol{R}^{\mathcal{H}_1}$) are obtained under different hypotheses. Then, the first k-th FCs of training data is pruned to form the selected feature sets ($\boldsymbol{X}^{\mathcal{H}_0}, \boldsymbol{X}^{\mathcal{H}_1}$), which are correspondingly guided by ($\boldsymbol{R}^{\mathcal{H}_0}, \boldsymbol{R}^{\mathcal{H}_1}$). In the feature extraction, optimal subspace projection matrices ($\tilde{\boldsymbol{P}}^{\mathcal{H}_0}, \tilde{\boldsymbol{P}}^{\mathcal{H}_1}$) are achieved through our Laplace regularized subspace learning model. Thus the projected feature sets of ($\boldsymbol{X}^{\mathcal{H}_0}, \boldsymbol{X}^{\mathcal{H}_1}$) are provided as ($\tilde{\boldsymbol{X}}^{\mathcal{H}_0}, \tilde{\boldsymbol{X}}^{\mathcal{H}_1}$) with

$$\begin{cases} \tilde{\boldsymbol{X}}^{\mathcal{H}_0} = (\tilde{\boldsymbol{P}}^{\mathcal{H}_0})^T \boldsymbol{X}^{\mathcal{H}_0} \\ \tilde{\boldsymbol{X}}^{\mathcal{H}_1} = (\tilde{\boldsymbol{P}}^{\mathcal{H}_1})^T \boldsymbol{X}^{\mathcal{H}_1} \end{cases}, \tag{1}$$

We introduce an energy comparison strategy in the label decision. To avoid the energy fluctuation influence impacted by the input selected features, an energy normalization operation is performed as

$$E^{\mathcal{H}_i} = \frac{||\tilde{X}^{\mathcal{H}_i}||_F^2}{||X^{\mathcal{H}_i}||_F^2}, \quad i \in \{0,\ 1\}, \tag{2}$$

where $E^{\mathcal{H}_i}$ is the normalized energy. Thus, we get the label prediction of the test subject by

$$\tilde{\mathcal{H}}_{true} = \begin{matrix} \mathcal{H}_1,\ \Delta E < 0 \\ \mathcal{H}_0\ \ otherwise \end{matrix}, \tag{3}$$

where $\Delta E = E^{\mathcal{H}_1} - E^{\mathcal{H}_0}$ is the energy difference between two hypotheses. Since in practice, the mean value of selected features (a.k.a. selected FCs) that share the same label is approximately zero, the subspace energy can be viewed as a scatter measure for intra-class subjects. As a result, Eq. (3) is adopted to test the scatter measures between different hypotheses.

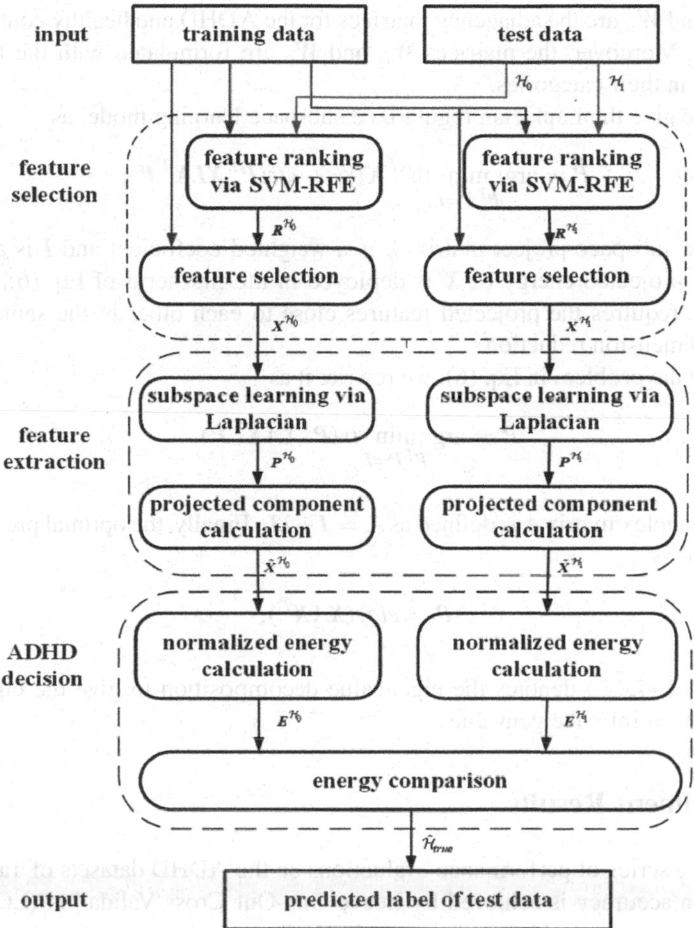

Fig. 1. Framework of proposed ADHD classification.

2.3 Laplacian Regularized Subspace Learning

Given the selected FCs as $\boldsymbol{X} = [\boldsymbol{X}_a\ ,\ \boldsymbol{X}_c]$, where $\boldsymbol{X}_a$ and $\boldsymbol{X}_c$ are the corresponding FCs of ADHD and healthy control subjects respectively, we firstly define the graph Laplacian matrix among the FCs. It is described as

$$\boldsymbol{L} = \boldsymbol{D} - \boldsymbol{W}, \tag{4}$$

where $\boldsymbol{W}$ is an adjacency matrix, $\boldsymbol{D}$ is a degree matrix with its diagonal elements as the row sum of $\boldsymbol{W}$ by $d_{ii} = \sum_j w_{ij}$. We set the adjacency matrix $\boldsymbol{W}$ as a block diagonal matrix with

$$\boldsymbol{W} = \begin{bmatrix} \boldsymbol{W}_a & \boldsymbol{0} \\ \boldsymbol{0} & \boldsymbol{W}_c \end{bmatrix}, \tag{5}$$

where $\boldsymbol{W}_a$ and $\boldsymbol{W}_c$ are the adjacency matrices for the ADHD and healthy control groups respectively. Moreover, the matrices $\boldsymbol{W}_a$ and $\boldsymbol{W}_c$ are formulated with the full binary conjunction in their categories.

Thus, we give the Laplacian regularized subspace learning model as

$$\tilde{\boldsymbol{P}} = \arg \min_{\boldsymbol{P}^T\boldsymbol{P}=\boldsymbol{I}} ||\boldsymbol{P}^T\boldsymbol{X}||_F^2 + \lambda tr(\boldsymbol{P}^T\boldsymbol{X}\boldsymbol{L}\boldsymbol{X}^T\boldsymbol{P}), \quad (6)$$

where $\boldsymbol{P}$ is a subspace project matrix, λ is a weighted coefficient and $\boldsymbol{I}$ is an identity matrix. The projected energy of $\boldsymbol{X}$ is deployed in the first term of Eq. (6), while the second term requires the projected features close to each other in the same category during the dimension reduction.

To solve the problem in Eq. (6), we rewrite it as

$$\tilde{\boldsymbol{P}} = \arg \min_{\boldsymbol{P}^T\boldsymbol{P}=\boldsymbol{I}} tr(\boldsymbol{P}^T\boldsymbol{X}\boldsymbol{A}\boldsymbol{X}^T\boldsymbol{P}), \quad (7)$$

where the complex matrix $\boldsymbol{A}$ is defined as $\boldsymbol{A} = \boldsymbol{I} + \lambda \boldsymbol{L}$. Finally, the optimal project matrix $\tilde{\boldsymbol{P}}$ is obtained as

$$\tilde{\boldsymbol{P}} = eig_r(\boldsymbol{X}\boldsymbol{A}\boldsymbol{X}^T), \quad (8)$$

where symbol $eig_r(.)$ denotes the eigenvalue decomposition to give the eigenvectors with the first r minimal eigenvalues.

3 Experiment Results

We conduct a series of performance evaluations on the ADHD datasets of Table 1. The classification accuracy is achieved by Leave-One-Out Cross Validation (LOOCV). In each test iteration, one subject is got from the database as the test subject, while the rest subjects are used as training data. As for the parameter setting, we choose the selected feature number $k = 110$ by SVM-RFE. The subspace dimension r is set as $r = 105$ for each dataset. Moreover, we further set $\lambda = 0.1$ to balance the term values in Eq. (6).

3.1 Subspace Dimension and Analysis

We first evaluate the accuracy performance with the subspace dimension variation in Fig. 2. It is observed that the highest accuracy is approximate with the subspace dimension $r = 105$. Meanwhile, the subspace dimension is not seriously reduced compared with the selected features of $k = 110$. The selected features now have limited redundant information. It also proves our selected feature number is fit for this subspace learning model. In this case, the task of subspace learning is to remove noise from input data rather than to reduce the feature number. As a result, this operation enhances feature discrimination to achieve remarkable accuracy.

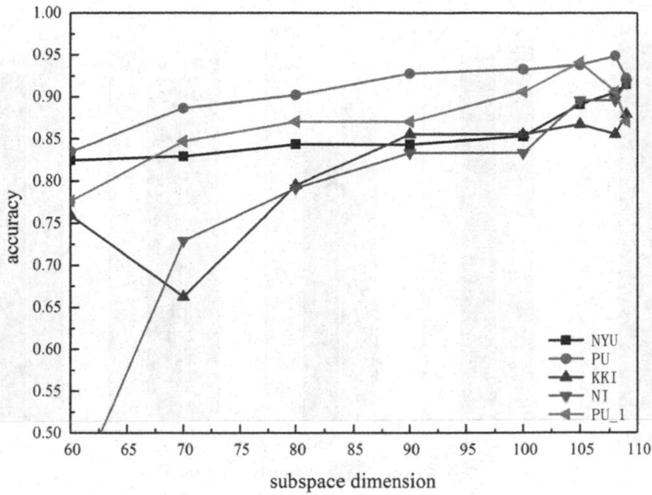

Fig. 2. Accuracy with subspace dimension

3.2 Classification Comparison

Various ADHD classification measures, including specificity, sensitivity, and accuracy, are given in Fig. 3. Our method reaches an average accuracy of 91.8%. In Fig. 3, the accuracy of KKI is the lowest. It is because of the subject imbalance problem, where the number of ADHD patients is seriously less than that of healthy controls. Conversely, NI's accuracy is acceptable for its balance subjects, though its dataset is of the smallest size. PU has the best classification performance. It benefits from its large dataset. With the subject number increasing, the subspace can be learned more effectively to contain reliable information about ADHD.

We further compare our method with other advanced ones in Table 2, including several ML- and DL-methods [19, 20, 22–25]. It shows our method outperforms these methods. Our method provides an alternative way to use binary hypothesis testing instead of the traditional training-and-test approach. With this strategy, the FCs of test data participate in the feature selection procedure. The subspace learning method then gives an effective scatter measure to make the sequential energy detection. Therefore, it can reliably deal with the classification task on different datasets, which significantly enhances the system robustness compared to the existing ML- and DL-based methods. Here, we also refer to a recent binary hypothesis method named dual-space learning with binary hypotheses (Dual-SP-BH) [25]. Since the dual spaces are employed for feature projection, it obtains an unsatisfied performance on NI. However, our method only learns one subspace to simplify the projection operation such that it brings better performance.

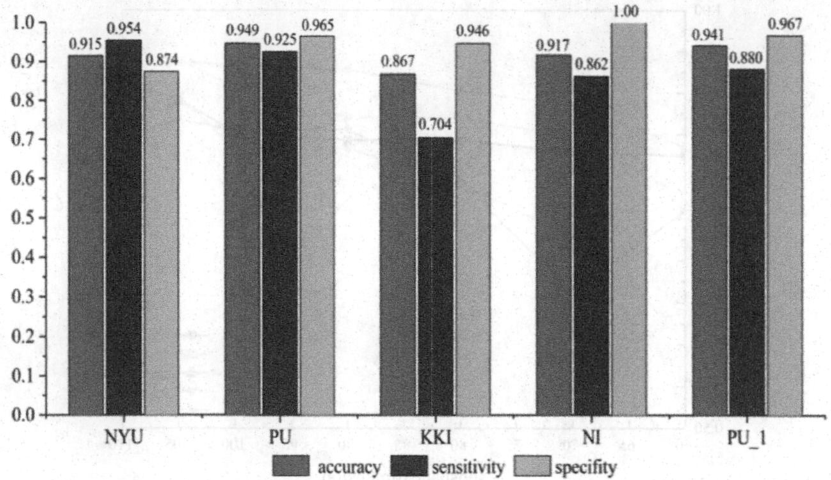

Fig. 3. Comparison of group classification on various datasets

Table 2. Accuracy comparison with various methods (%)

	NYU	PU	PU_1	KKI	NI	Average
Fusion fMRI [22]	52.7	–	85.8	86.7	72.9	–
FCNet [23]	58.5	–	62.7	–	60.0	–
3D-CNN [20]	70.5	63.0	–	72.8	–	–
Deep fMRI [19]	73.1	–	62.7	–	67.9	–
Deep Forest [24]	73.2	64.9	–	82.7	72.0	–
Dual-SP-BH [25]	**92.4**	92.3	89.4	85.5	81.2	88.2
Our method	91.5	**94.9**	**94.1**	**86.7**	**91.7**	**91.8**

3.3 ROC Analysis

We adopt Receiver Operating Characteristic (ROC) and Area Under Curve (AUC) to further evaluate our method. For the ROC measure, it is a balanced result for True Positive Rate (TPR) and False Positive Rate (FPR), describing a given confusion matrix. The indicators of TPR and FPR are computed as

$$\begin{cases} TPR = \dfrac{TP}{TP + FN} \\ FPR = \dfrac{FP}{FP + TN} \end{cases}, \tag{9}$$

where TP is the true positive, TN is the true negative, FP is the false positive, and FN is the false negative. Meanwhile, the value of AUC is defined as the area under the ROC curve. The higher the AUC is, the better classification performance our model is.

The ROC curves are depicted in Fig. 4 and Fig. 5 for the datasets of large and small sizes, respectively. In Fig. 4, NYU and PU datasets are tested. It is observed that their ROC values are rapidly converged to 1 with FPR increasing. Their AUC values are both above 0.9. It shows that the proposed classification method has a good performance on large datasets. As for the small datasets in Fig. 5, including KKI, NI, and PU_1, their ROC curves slowly increase compared with those in Fig. 4. Most of their AUC values are below 0.9 due to their small dataset size. Interestingly, the AUC on NI is even better than those on KKI and PU_1, though the size of NI is the smallest. We note that the data in KKI and PU_1 suffer from the subject imbalance problem. It seems such a factor seriously impacts the ADHD classification performance.

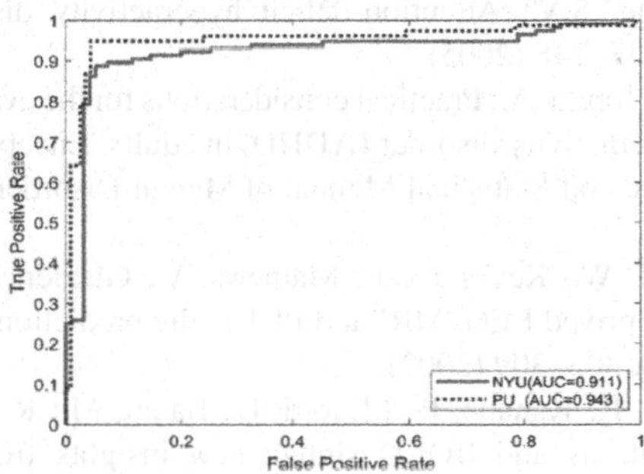

Fig. 4. ROC curves on large datasets

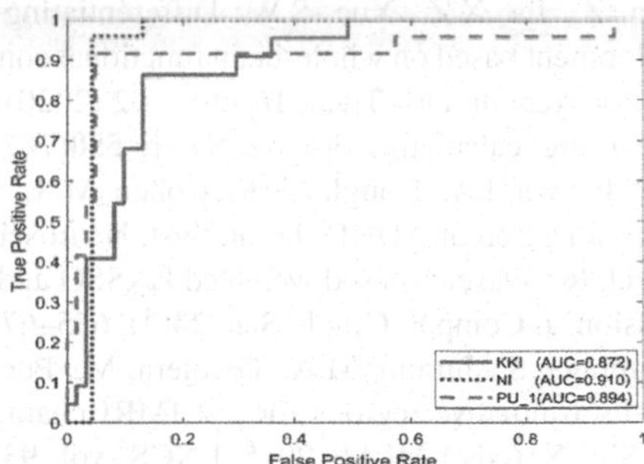

Fig. 5. ROC curves on small datasets

4 Conclusion

We propose an ADHD classification method by Laplacian regularized subspace learning and binary hypothesis testing. The binary hypothesis approach fully exploits the FC information on test data. Meanwhile, the Laplacian regularized subspace learning well obtains the subspace energies under different hypotheses and thus effectively gives the label prediction of test data. In our experiments, the average classification accuracy of ADHD is 91.8%. It outperforms most of the existing machine learning and deep learning methods.

Acknowledgements. This work is partly supported by Fundamental Research Funds for Central Universities, China, under Grant B200202217; Changzhou Science and Technology Program, China, under Grant CJ20200065 and CE20205043; Changzhou Science and Technology Program, China, under Grant CE20205043.

References

1. Biederman, J., Faraone, S.V.: Attention-deficit hyperactivity disorder. Lancet (London, England) **366**(9481), 237–248 (2005)
2. Weibel, S., Ménard, O., Ionita, A.: Practical considerations for the evaluation and management of attention deficit hyperactivity disorder (ADHD) in adults. Encephale **46**(1), 30–40 (2020)
3. Battle, D.E.: Diagnostic and Statistical Manual of Mental Disorders (DSM). CoDAS **25**(2), 191–192 (2013)
4. Dellabadia Jr., J., Bell, W., Keyes Jr., J., Mathews, V., Glazier, S.: Assessment and cost comparison of sleep-deprived EEG, MRI and PET in the prediction of surgical treatment for epilepsy. Seizure **11**(5), 303–309 (2002)
5. Lachaux, J.P., Fonlupt, P., Kahane, P., Minotti, L., Baciu, M.: Relationship between task-related gamma oscillations and BOLD signal: new insights from combined fMRI and intracranial EEG. Hum. Brain Mapp. **28**(12), 1368–1375 (2010)
6. Heuvel, M.P.V.D., Pol, H.E.H.: Exploring the brain network: a review on resting-state fMRI functional connectivity. J. Eur. College Neuropsychopharmacol. **20**(8), 519–534 (2010)
7. Sun, Y., Zhao, L., Lan, Z., Jia, X.Z., Xue, S.W.: Differentiating boys with ADHD from those with typical development based on whole-brain functional connections using a machine learning approach. Neuropsychiatr. Dis. Treat. **16**, 691–702 (2020)
8. Savage, N.: Machine learning: calculating disease. Nature **550**(7676), S115–S117 (2017)
9. Colby, J.B., Rudie, J.D., Brown, J.A., Douglas, P.K., Cohen, M.S., Shehzad, Z.: Insights into multimodal imaging classification of ADHD. Front. Syst. Neurosci. **6**, 59 (2012)
10. Zhao, Y., Chen, H., Todd, R.: Wavelet-based weighted LASSO and screening approaches in functional linear regression. J. Comput. Graph. Stat. **24**(3), 655–675 (2015)
11. Nuñez-Garcia, M., Simpraga, S., Jurado, M.A., Garolera, M., Pueyo, R., Igual, L.: FADR: functional-anatomical discriminative regions for rest fMRI characterization. In: Zhou, L., Wang, Li., Wang, Q., Shi, Y. (eds.) MLMI 2015. LNCS, vol. 9352, pp. 61–68. Springer, Cham (2015). https://doi.org/10.1007/978-3-319-24888-2_8
12. Soumyabrata, D., Ravishankar, R.A., Mubarak, S.: Exploiting the brain's network structure in identifying ADHD subjects. Front. Syst. Neurosci. **6**(75), 61–68 (2015)
13. Tabas, A., Balaguer-Ballester, E., Igual, L.: Spatial discriminant ICA for RS-fMRI characterization. In: 2014 4th International Workshop on Pattern Recognition in Neuroimaging, pp. 1–4. IEEE (2014)
14. Sidhu, G.S., Nasimeh, A., Russell, G., Brown, M.R.G.: Kernel principal component analysis for dimensionality reduction in fMRI-based diagnosis of ADHD. Front. Syst. Neurosci. **9**(6), 74 (2012)

15. Yao, D., Sun, H., Guo, X., Calhoun, V.D., Sui, J.: ADHD classification within and cross cohort using an ensembled feature selection framework. In: 2019 IEEE 16th International Symposium on Biomedical Imaging (ISBI). IEEE (2019)
16. Tang, Y., Wang, C., Chen, Y., Sun, N., Jiang, A., Wang, Z.: Identifying ADHD individuals from resting-state functional connectivity using subspace clustering and binary hypothesis testing. J. Atten. Disord. **25**(5), 736–748 (2019)
17. Mahmud, M., Kaiser, M.S., Hussain, A., Vassanelli, S.: Applications of deep learning and reinforcement learning to biological data. IEEE Trans. Neural Netw. Learn. Syst. **29**(6), 2063–2079 (2018)
18. Samek, W., Binder, A., Montavon, G., Lapuschkin, S., Müller, K.-R.: Evaluating the visualization of what a deep neural network has learned. IEEE Trans. Neural Netw. Learn. Syst. **28**(11), 2660–2673 (2016)
19. Riaz, A., Asad, M., Alonso, E., Slabaugh, G.: DeepFMRI: end-to-end deep learning for functional connectivity and classification of ADHD using fMRI. J. Neurosci. Methods **335**, 108506 (2020)
20. Zou, L., Zheng, J., Miao, C., Mckeown, M.J., Wang, Z.J.: 3D CNN based automatic diagnosis of attention deficit hyperactivity disorder using functional and structural MRI. IEEE Access **5**, 23626–23636 (2017)
21. Abdolmaleki, S., Abadeh, M.S.: Brain MR image classification for ADHD diagnosis using deep neural networks. In: 2020 International Conference on Machine Vision and Image Processing (MVIP), pp. 1–5. IEEE (2020)
22. Riaz, A., Asad, M., Alonso, E., Slabaugh, G.: Fusion of fMRI and non-imaging data for ADHD classification. Comput. Med. Imaging Graph. **65**, 115–128 (2018)
23. Riaz, A., et al.: FCNet: a convolutional neural network for calculating functional connectivity from functional MRI. In: Wu, G., Laurienti, P., Bonilha, L., Munsell, B.C. (eds.) CNI 2017. LNCS, vol. 10511, pp. 70–78. Springer, Cham (2017). https://doi.org/10.1007/978-3-319-67159-8_9
24. Shao, L., Zhang, D., Du, H., Fu, D.: Deep forest in ADHD data classification. IEEE Access **7**, 99 (2019)
25. Chen, Y., Tang, Y., Wang, C., Liu, X., Wang, Z.: ADHD classification by dual subspace learning using resting-state functional connectivity. Artif. Intell. Med. **103**, 101786 (2020)

Study the Quantum Transport Process: Machine Learning Simulates Quantum Conditional Master Equation

Yong Hu[1], Xiao-Yu Li[2], and Qin-Sheng Zhu[1](✉)

[1] School of Physics, University of Electronic Science and Technology of China, Chengdu 610054, People's Republic of China
zhuqinsheng@uestc.edu.cn

[2] School of Information and Software Engineering, University of Electronic Science and Technology of China, Chengdu 610054, People's Republic of China

Abstract. Quantum transport is a significant phenomenon in the mesoscopic system which is widely studied in recent years. In physical experiments, the fluctuation noise can reflect the microscopic properties of the quantum transport system easier than the transport current. In theory, the quantum conditional master equation (QCME) is a very effective method for studying quantum transport process of charge qubits. But, the QCME is an infinite recursive differential equation system that is difficult to solve theoretically. So, we try to solve this problem by combining the requirements of the solution and some advantages of the machine learning algorithms. Firstly, compared the calculation diagram of QCME and recurrent neural network (RNN), the relationship between them was found. Long Short-Term Memory (LSTM) has great advantages in processing time-series data as a typical network of RNN. Secondly, the behavior of parameters transfers from time t to $t + \Delta t$ in QCME is consistent with the behavior of parameter transfer in LSTM. Based on the above two reasons, the LSTM is used to simulate QCME. In the numerical experiment, an effective method is proposed to truncate QCME, and then the fluctuation noise spectrum data from a two-level quantum transport system is used to train the LSTM network and calculate the transition probability of electron with the parameters of LSTM.

Keywords: Quantum transport · Quantum master equation · Machine learning · LSTM

1 Introduction

As an important physical phenomenon in the mesoscopic system, quantum transport has been widely studied, for example, electrical transport [1], heat transport [2], and solid-state quantum information processors [3]. For traditional devices, the signal to noise ratio (SNR) can be improved by reducing the fluctuation noise, but in the quantum dot system, fluctuation noise will not be infinitely reduced. Actually, the quantum transport

X. Sun et al. (Eds.): ICAIS 2021, LNCS 12736, pp. 132–143, 2021.
https://doi.org/10.1007/978-3-030-78609-0_12

fluctuations of quantum devices are not necessarily harmful. These fine time-related fluctuations can sensitively reflect the specific dynamics of the transport process, the rich quantum transport characteristics, and the fine energy scale inside the device. Therefore, the systematic testing and analysis of quantum fluctuation noise have become an important theoretical tool and method to study the carrier transport characteristics in low-dimensional and mesoscopic nanodevices [4]. For theoretical calculation, we need to face an open system which consists of noise and quantum dot system and study its properties. There are many methods to study it, including the scattering matrix method developed by Buttiker and Beenakker et al. [5–7], and the non-equilibrium Green function method [8, 9], and the quantum master equation method [10–14].

For studying the dynamics of a charge qubit, the continuous measurement is required [7]. The master equation of quantum dot in this measurement process is obtained in some reasonable approximations when we integrate out the degrees of freedom of the noise from the von Neumann equation. Different from previous studies, S. A. Gurvitz and Ya. S. Prager [15] extend the "classical" master equation to the quantum master equation (QME) to describe general quantum transport problems starting with the many-body Schrödinger equation. Later, Xin-Qi Li et al. [16] follow Gurvitz's method to put forward the quantum conditional master equation (QCME) for studying the detailed process of electronic transport. Although the quantum conditional master equation can describe the electron transport process in detail, it is very difficult to further study the related physical quantities of this process because it is an infinite recursive differential equation system.

Recently, with the development of computer science and artificial intelligence, many effective machine learning algorithms have been proposed, such as neural networks, decision trees, Markov models, etc., and applied to successfully solve some quantum physics problems, such as quantum tomography [17, 18], quantum steganography[19, 20], quantum discord [21], and quantum multi-body problems [22] et al. The results of these studies show us that machine learning algorithms can become a new platform for solving quantum physics problems. In the study of quantum transport problems, especially studying some physical quantities, a large number of approximations in the process of solving a master equation need be made because the conditional quantum master equation is the infinite recursive differential equations. So, this solution process often leads to some simulation difficulties. Combining the requirements of this solution process and some advantages of the machine learning algorithms, it arouses the interest of this studying works.

In this paper, starting from the general QCME, a two-level quantum transport system is studied. Then, the transport current and the noise spectrum of the quantum transport system can be calculated from specific form of QCME. However, the QCME is an infinite recursive differential equation system that is difficult to solve theoretically. We found that QCME and recurrent neural network have many similarities. On the one hand, compared the calculation diagram of QCME and recurrent neural network (RNN), the relationship between them was found. As a typical network of RNN, Long Short-Term Memory (LSTM) has great advantages in processing time-series data. On the other hand, the behavior of parameters transfers from time t to $t + \Delta t$ in QCME is consistent with the behavior of parameter transfer in LSTM. In the numerical experiment, an effective method is firstly proposed to truncate QCME and then the fluctuation noise spectrum data from a two-level quantum transport system is used to train the LSTM network. From the convergence error curve of LSTM, a conclusion is reached that QCME is effective simulated by LSTM.

2 Quantum Conditional Master Equation

Here, we considered a quantum transport system as shown in Fig. 1. Electrons pass through a quantum dots system (S) from the left leader (L) to the right leader (R) under the excitation of an external bias voltage V.

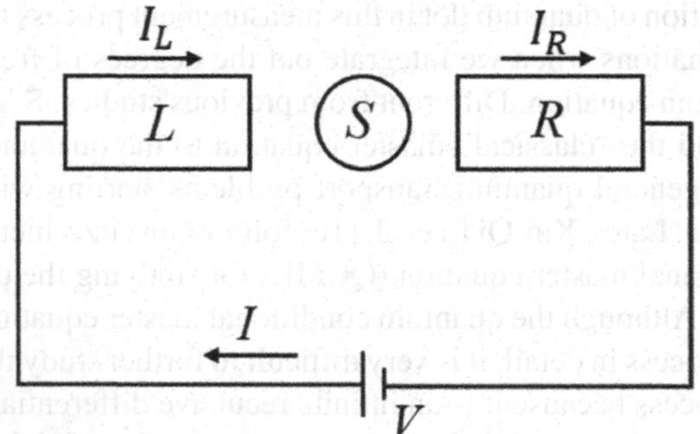

Fig. 1. Diagram of a general quantum transport system, L and R are the left and the right electrodes, S is the quantum dots system. I is the current from the right electrode to the left electrode along the wire. I_L is the current from the left electrode flow into the quantum system and I_R is the current from the quantum system flow into the right electrode. V is an external bias voltage.

The Hamiltonian of this composite system can be expressed as

$$H = H_s\left(a_\mu^\dagger, a_\mu\right) + H_E + H \tag{1}$$

$H_s\left(a_\mu^\dagger, a_\mu\right)$ is system (quantum dots) Hamiltonian. $a_\mu^\dagger\left(a_\mu\right)$ is creation (annihilation) operator, respectively. H_E is the Hamiltonian of the left and right electrodes and H' describes the interaction between the system and the electrodes. Then, regarding H' as a perturbation, a formal equation for the reduced density matrix can be obtained based on the second-order cumulant expansion [21].

$$\dot{\rho}(t) = -i\mathcal{L}\rho(t) - \int_0^t d\tau \mathcal{L}'(t)\mathcal{G}(t,\tau)\mathcal{L}'(\tau)\mathcal{G}^\dagger(t,\tau)\rho(t) \tag{2}$$

Here, the Liouvillian superoperators $\mathcal{L}$ are defined as $\mathcal{L}(\cdots) \triangleq [\mathrm{H_S}, (\cdots)]$, $\mathcal{L}'(\cdots) \triangleq \left[H', (\cdots)\right]$ and $\mathcal{G}(\mathrm{t}, \tau) \triangleq G(t,\tau) \times (\cdots)G^\dagger(t,\tau)$ with $\mathrm{G(t, \tau)}$ the usual propagator (Green's function) associated with the system Hamiltonian $H_s\left(a_\mu^\dagger, a_\mu\right)$. The reduced density matrix $\rho(\mathrm{t}) = \mathrm{Tr_E}[\rho_T(t)]$, $\langle \ldots \rangle = \mathrm{Tr_E}[(\cdots)\rho_\mathrm{E}]$ with ρ_E the density matrix of electrodes. The important assumption to obtain this reduced density matrix equation is that the interaction between system and environment is not strong enough.

The trace in Eq. (2) is the overall degrees of freedom for the electrodes, which does not reflect the detail of the transportation process. The Hilbert space of electrodes is classified as follows to record the electron numbers which are from the right electrode to the left electrode. The Hilbert space is introduced where no electron pass through the system as $E^{(0)}$, which is spanned by the product of all many-particle states of the two isolated electrodes, denoted as $E^{(0)} \triangleq span\{|\psi_L\rangle \otimes |\psi_R\rangle\}$. Then the Hilbert subspace $E^{(\mathrm{n})}(n = 1, 2, \cdots)$ are proposed, corresponding to n number electron passing through the system. The electrodes space in Eq. (2) is replaced by the Hilbert space $E = \oplus_n E^{(n)}$, leading to a conditional quantum master equation

$$\dot{\rho}^{(n)}(t) = -i\mathcal{L}\rho^{(n)}(t) - \int_0^t d\tau \mathrm{Tr}_{E^{(n)}}\left[\mathcal{L}'(t)\mathcal{G}(t,\tau)\mathcal{L}'(\tau)\mathcal{G}^{\dagger}(t,\tau)\rho_T(t)\right] \quad (3)$$

Here, $\rho^{(n)} = \mathrm{Tr}_{\mathrm{E}^{(n)}}[\rho_T(t)]$ is the reduced density matrix of n number electron passing through the system at time t.

The transport current and noise can be obtained by solving Eq. (3). Remarkably, $\rho(t) = \sum_n \rho^{(n)}(t)$, Eq. (2) can be expressed as Eq. (3) sums for n. The probability distribution function of the electron arrived at the left electrode is $P(n, t) \triangleq \mathrm{Tr}\left[\rho^{(\mathrm{n})}(t)\right]$. The current can be computed as below

$$I(\mathrm{t}) = e\frac{d\left[\sum_n nP(n,t)\right]}{dt} = e\sum\nolimits_n n\mathrm{Tr}\left[\dot{\rho}^{(n)}(t)\right] \quad (4)$$

The noise spectrum can be calculated using MacDonald's formula [4]

$$S(\omega) = 2\omega \int_0^{\omega} dt \sin(\omega t)\frac{d}{dt}[\langle \mathrm{n}^2(\mathrm{t})\rangle - (\bar{\mathrm{I}}\mathrm{t})^2] \quad (5)$$

3 Example: A Two-Level Quantum Transport System

As shown in Fig. 1, Consider quantum dots have only two energy levels involved in the transport process, the Hamiltonian of the quantum system can be expressed as

$$H_S = \sum\nolimits_{s=\uparrow,\downarrow}\left(\epsilon_1 a_{1s}^{\dagger}a_{1s} + _2 a_{2s}^{\dagger}a_{2s}\right) + \Omega(n_{1\uparrow}n_{1\downarrow} + n_{2\uparrow}n_{2\downarrow}) + C_E\left[\sum\nolimits_{s=\uparrow,\downarrow}(n_{1s} + n_{2s})\right]^2 \quad (6)$$

In Eq. (6), "s" represents the spin of electrons, "$\uparrow$" is spin up, "$\downarrow$" is spin down. ϵ_1 and ϵ_2 are the energy of two levels. $a_{j\uparrow}^{\dagger}(a_{j\uparrow})$ is creation (annihilation) operator in the jth $(j = 1, 2)$ energy level with spin up. Ω is Coulomb interaction energy when the same energy level is occupied by two electronics with different spin directions. $n_{1\uparrow}$ is the particle-number operator in the first energy level with spin up, $n_{1\uparrow} = a_{1\uparrow}^{\dagger}a_{1\uparrow}$. C_E is charge energy related to the number of electrons occupying the energy level. The Hamiltonian of the left electrode and the right electrode can be expressed as

$$H_E = \sum\nolimits_{ks}\left(\epsilon_{Lks}c_{Lks}^{\dagger}c_{Lks} + \epsilon_{Rks}c_{Rks}^{\dagger}c_{Rks}\right) \quad (7)$$

In Eq. (7), $\epsilon_{Lks}(\epsilon_{Rks})$ is the energy of the left (right) electrode. Considering that the electrons on the left and right electrodes are in a state of thermal statistical equilibrium, the electron distribution function can be expressed as

$$f(\epsilon) = \frac{1}{\exp[(\epsilon - \mu)/kT] + 1} \tag{8}$$

μ is Fermi energy. Because the external voltage V is symmetrically applied to the quantum system, the Fermi energy $\mu_L = eV/2$, $\mu_R = -eV/2$. The Hamiltonian of the quantum system coupled with electrodes can be expressed as

$$H' = \sum\nolimits_{\alpha kjs} \tau_{\alpha kj} c^{\dagger}_{\alpha ks} a_{js} + \text{h.c.} \tag{9}$$

In Eq. (9), $\alpha = L, R$; k is electronic momentum, $j = 1, 2$ represents the label of energy level, $s = \uparrow, \downarrow$ represents the spin of electronic. h.c. is hermitian conjugation.

Then we can obtain the Eq. (10) to describe the two-level transport system based on Eq. (3), Eq. (6), Eq. (7), Eq. (8), Eq. (9).

$$\begin{aligned} \dot{\rho}^{(n)}(t) = & -i\mathcal{L}\rho^{(\mathrm{n})}(\mathrm{t}) \\ & -\frac{1}{2}\sum\nolimits_{js}\left\{\left[A^{(-)}_{js}\rho^{(n)}a^{\dagger}_{js} + \rho^{(n)}A^{(+)}_{js}a^{\dagger}_{js} - A^{(-)}_{Ljs}\rho^{(n)}a^{\dagger}_{js} - a^{\dagger}_{js}\rho^{(n)}A^{(+)}_{Ljs} - A^{(-)}_{Ljs}\rho^{(n-1)}a^{\dagger}_{js} - a^{\dagger}_{js}\rho^{(n+1)}A^{(+)}_{Rjs}\right] + \text{h.c.}\right\} \end{aligned} \tag{10}$$

Where, $A^{(\pm)}_{js} = \sum_{\alpha=L,R} A^{(\pm)}_{\alpha js}$, $A^{(\pm)}_{\alpha js} = C^{(\pm)}_{\alpha js}(\gamma) a_{js}$, $C^{(\pm)}_{\alpha js}$ is the spectrum function of electronic in electrodes. The current value and noise spectrum can be calculated by Eq. (4) and Eq. (5). Then, we can better understand the two-level quantum transport system by the quantum conditional master equation Eq. (10).

4 Machine Learning Method Simulate Quantum Master Equation

4.1 Quantum Master Equation and LSTM Network

The current is only related to trace of density matrix ρ from Eq. (4), so we can use current data to construct $\mathrm{Tr}[\rho(t)]$. For an open quantum system, the relationship between $\rho(t)$ and $\rho(t + \Delta t)$ can be constructed with Kraus operators $\hat{K}$ in the case of Markovian approximation [24]

$$\rho(t + \Delta t) = \sum\nolimits_m \hat{K}_m \rho(t) \hat{K}^{\dagger}_m \tag{11}$$

$\hat{K}_m$ is a time-independent matrix and $\sum_m \hat{K}^{\dagger}_m \hat{K}_m = I$. We can get $\mathrm{Tr}[\rho(t + \Delta t)] = \mathrm{Tr}\left[\sum_m \hat{K}_m \rho(t) \hat{K}^{\dagger}_m\right] = \sum_m \mathrm{Tr}\left[\hat{K}_m \rho(t) \hat{K}^{\dagger}_m\right] = \mathrm{Tr}[\rho(t)]$ after tracing on Eq. (5), but under detail balance conditions $\rho(t) = \sum_n \rho^{(n)}(t)$, $\mathrm{Tr}[\rho(\mathrm{t} + \Delta\mathrm{t})] = \mathrm{Tr}[\sum_n \rho^{(n)}(t + \Delta t)] = \sum_n \mathrm{Tr}[\rho^{(n)}(t + \Delta t)] = \sum_n \sum_m \mathrm{Tr}\left[\hat{K}_m \rho^{(n)}(t) \hat{K}^{\dagger}_m\right]$. So, $\rho^{(i)}(t + \Delta t) = \varphi_i\left[\rho^{(0)}(t), \rho^{(1)}(t), \cdots, \rho^{(n)}(t)\right](i = 0, 1, 2, \cdots, n)$, our goal is to construct $\varphi_{\mathrm{i}}(i = 0, 1, 2, \cdots, n)$ with RNN based on current noise spectrum data.

An artificial neural network (ANN) is a powerful tool that can simulate arbitrary functions, the recurrent neural network (a kind of ANN) is used to construct the relationship between $\rho(t)$ and $\rho(t+\Delta t)$. Long-Short Term Memory network [25] (LSTM showed in Fig. 2) is a variant of RNN, which has a good effect on the time series problem. In the field of artificial intelligence, LSTM has achieved great success in unconstrained handwriting recognition [26], speech recognition [27, 28], generating captions for images [29–31], and machine translation [32]. I.A. Luchnikov and S. V. Vintskevich et al. point out RNN can be a new tool to simulate the Lindblad equation [33]. In an LSTM cell, the output can be obtained from the below equations

$$
\begin{aligned}
f_t &= \sigma\left(W_f \cdot \left[h_{t-1}, x_t\right] + b_f\right)\\
i_t &= \sigma\left(W_i \cdot \left[h_{t-1}, x_t\right] + b_i\right)\\
\tilde{C}_t &= \tanh\left(W_C \cdot \left[h_{t-1}, x_t\right] + b_C\right)\\
O_t &= \sigma\left(W_O \cdot \left[h_{t-1}, x_t\right] + b_O\right)\\
h_t &= O_t \times \tanh(C_t)
\end{aligned}
\tag{12}
$$

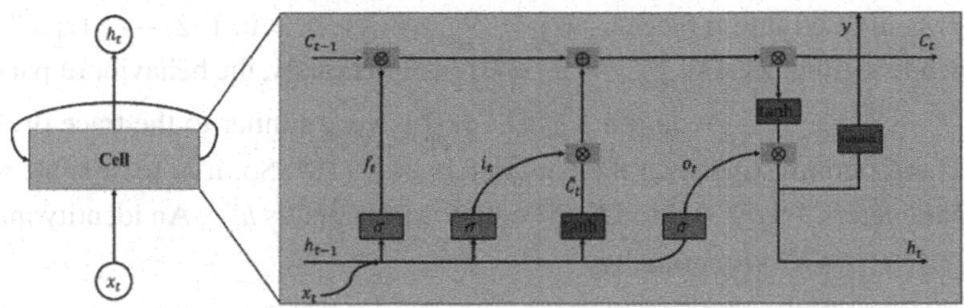

Fig. 2. A general diagram of the LSTM cell, x_t is input data, h_t is hidden state. σ, tanh, softmax are sigma function, tanh function, and softmax function, respectively. y is the target data. f_t is forgotten gate, output a number in [0,1] to C_{t-1}, "0" denotes the information at $t-1$ is discarded, "1" denotes the information at $t-1$ is completely reserved. i_t is input gate, it times $\tilde{C}_t$ to determine how much new information is added to the cell. O_t is an output gate to determine how much information to output. "↶" means **Cell** cycles in time.

The tanh function is defined as

$$
\tanh(x) = \frac{e^x - e^{-x}}{e^x + e^{-x}} \tag{13}
$$

The softmax function is defined as

$$
\mathrm{softmax}(x_i) = \frac{\exp(x_i)}{\sum_j \exp(x_j)} \tag{14}
$$

softmax function can map arbitrary number to one in the interval (0, 1]. The cost function is MSELoss with ℓ_1-norm item defined as

$$
\mathrm{MSELoss} = \sum_i \left(y_i - y_i'\right)^2 + \lambda \|\boldsymbol{W}\|_1 \tag{15}
$$

y_i and $y_i^{'}$ denote real value and the predicted value, λ is a positive number in the interval [0, 1]. We adjust the parameters $(\boldsymbol{W}, \boldsymbol{b})$ of the LSTM network to minimize the cost function MSELoss by using the back-propagation algorithm and stochastic gradient descent method (SGD).

Relationship Between the Quantum Master Equation and LSTM Network. The unfolding calculation diagram of Eq. (11) is shown in Fig. 3. Φ is a time-independent operator, defined as $\Phi(\cdot) = \sum_m \hat{K}_m(\cdot)\hat{K}_m^{\dagger}$. Firstly, compared Fig. 3 and the unfolding calculation diagram of RNN, the similarity between them is found.

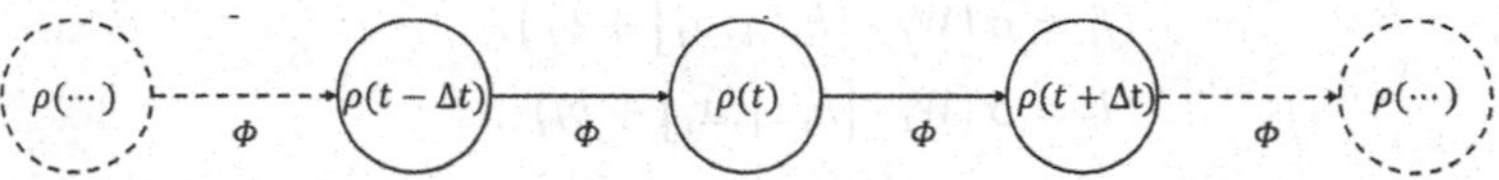

Fig. 3. The unfolding calculation diagram of Eq. (11), the right arrow represents density matrix evolves over time

Equation (4) reflects the relationship between the current and the trace of the density matrix. On the whole, the trace of density matrix $\mathrm{Tr}[\rho(t)] = 1$ is independent-time, but when $\rho(t)$ is divided into n pieces, $\rho(t) = \sum_n \rho^{(n)}(t)$, $n = 0, 1, 2, \cdots$, $\mathrm{Tr}\left[\rho^{(n)}(t)\right]$ is not independent-time because $\sum_n Tr\left[\rho^{(n)}(t)\right] = 1$. Secondly, the behavior of parameter $h_t = \left(h_t^{(0)}, h_t^{(1)}, h_t^{(2)}, \cdots\right)$ required $\sum_n h_t^{(n)} = 1$ is very similar to the trace of density matrix $\mathrm{Tr}[\rho(t)]$ contrasting with the parameters in LSTM. So, it is reasonable to map physics parameters $\mathrm{Tr}\left[\rho^{(n)}(t)\right]$ to LSTM network parameters $h_t^{(n)}$. An identity mapping from $\mathrm{Tr}\left[\rho^{(n)}(t)\right]$ to $h_t^{(n)}$ is defined as

$$h^{(n)}(t) \triangleq \mathrm{Tr}\left[\rho^{(n)}(t)\right] \tag{16}$$

For our study model—a two levels quantum transport system, the density matrix $\rho^{(n)}$ at time $t + \Delta t$ is related to three terms: $\rho^{(n)}(t)$, $\rho^{(n-1)}(t)$, $\rho^{(n+1)}(t)$ from Eq. (10). So, a time-independent map $\mathcal{F}$ can be constructed,

$$\mathcal{F} : \rho^{(n)}(t), \rho^{(n-1)}(t), \rho^{(n+1)}(t) \mapsto \rho^{(n)}(t + \Delta t) \tag{17}$$

but the current and noise spectrum only reflect the information on the diagonal of the density matrix. Obviously, it is unreasonable to use current data and noise spectrum to reconstruct the whole density matrix, but if we have some data (e.g. quantum coherence, quantum spin) related to off-diagonal elements, we can construct the map $\mathcal{F}$ by this method. Because we only have information about the trace of density, another time-independent map $\mathcal{P}$ is proposed

$$\mathcal{P} : \mathrm{Tr}\left[\rho^{(n)}(t)\right], \mathrm{Tr}\left[\rho^{(n-1)}(t)\right], \mathrm{Tr}\left[\rho^{(n+1)}(t)\right] \mapsto \mathrm{Tr}\left[\rho^{(n)}(t + \Delta t)\right] \tag{18}$$

Of cause, the mapping $\mathcal{P}$ can be generalized to a more general form $\mathcal{P}^{\diamond}$

$$\mathcal{P}^{\diamond} : \mathrm{Tr}\left[\rho^{(0)}(t)\right], \mathrm{Tr}\left[\rho^{(1)}(t)\right], \mathrm{Tr}\left[\rho^{(2)}(t)\right], \cdots, \mathrm{Tr}\left[\rho^{(\max\{n\})}(t)\right] \mapsto \mathrm{Tr}\left[\rho^{(n)}(t + \Delta t)\right] \tag{19}$$

From Eq. (12), the relationship between h_t and h_{t-1} can be constructed by the parameter $(\boldsymbol{W}, \boldsymbol{b})$ in LSTM networks. The task of machine learning is to learn parameters $(\boldsymbol{W}, \boldsymbol{b})$ based on data.

4.2 Experiment and Result Analysis

In our model, we use two layers of LSTM cell to build the network as shown in Fig. 4, the input dimension is 1, and the output dimension is $n+1$ in LSTM Cell**1**, the input dimension is $n+1$ and the output dimension is $n+1$ in LSTM Cell**2**. To correspond to the dimensions of our target data, we added a linsear layer (dimension is $(n+1)\times 1$) to output data after LSTM Cell**2**.

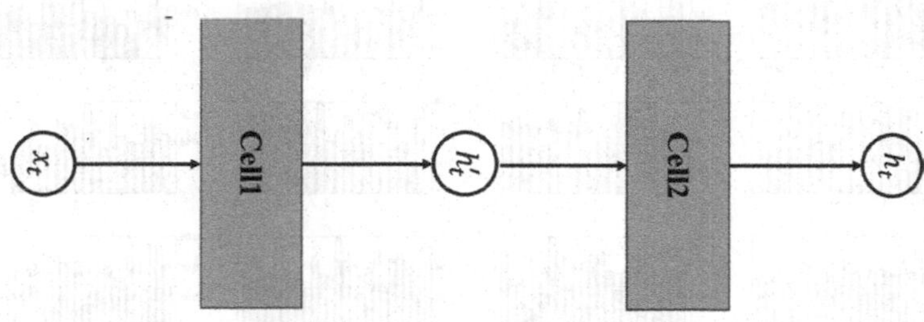

Fig. 4. Two spatially stack LSTM cells. x_t is input data, Cell**1** and Cell**2** are two different LSTM cell as shown in Fig. 2

Equation (3) can be obtained by summing Eq. (2) for all possible number of particles in theoretical analysis, but the particle number n is not from 0 to $+\infty$ in numerical calculations. So, we must make an effective truncation of the number of particles. The similarity between $\rho(t)$ and $\rho'(t) = \sum_{n=0}^{\max\{n\}} \rho^{(n)}(t)$ is used to decide how much the maximum value of n should be. The similarity value between ρ(t) and $\rho'(t)$ can be obtained from Eq. (20)

$$S\left[\rho(t), \rho'(t)\right] = \left|\mathrm{Tr}[\rho(t)] - \mathrm{Tr}\left[\rho'(t)\right]\right| \tag{20}$$

From Eq. (11), we can get $\mathrm{Tr}[\rho(t)] = 1$ at an arbitrary time and we map $\mathrm{Tr}\left[\rho^{(n)}(t)\right]$ to $h_t^{(n)}$, so $\mathrm{Tr}\left[\rho'(t)\right] = \sum_{n=0}^{M} h_t^{(n)}$ (M is the max value of n in numerical experiment). But we apply the softmax function to ensure similar behavior between $\rho'(t)$ and h_t, so $\mathrm{Tr}\left[\rho'(t)\right] = \sum_{n=0}^{M} \frac{\exp\left[h_t^{(n)}\right]}{\sum_j^M \exp\left[h_t^{(j)}\right]} = 1$. So $S\left[\rho(t), \rho'(t)\right] = 0$ at an arbitrary time under our calculation method and Eq. (20) is not an effective truncation method. Because $\mathrm{Tr}\left[\rho^{(n)}(t)\right]$ is a parameter that characterizes current, we can use the contribution of $\mathrm{Tr}\left[\rho^{(n)}(t)\right]$ to the total current to effectively truncate the number of particles. An evaluation function $E(M)$ is proposed

$$E(M) = \frac{MP_M}{\sum_{n=0}^{M-1} nP_n} \tag{21}$$

The numerator is the average value of M electrons passed at one time and the denominator is the weighted average of the number of electrons from 0 to $M-1$. To reflect the relationship between M and $E(M)$, we keep adjusting the value of M to calculate h_t at the last moment with $\sum_n h_t^{(n)} = 1$ and show histograms with probability n = 9~24 in Fig. 5. Figure 6 shows the relationship between $E(M)$ and M, and as the M increases $E(M)$ will gradually converge to a minimum. This means that Eq. (21) is an effective method can be applied to truncate the particle number n.

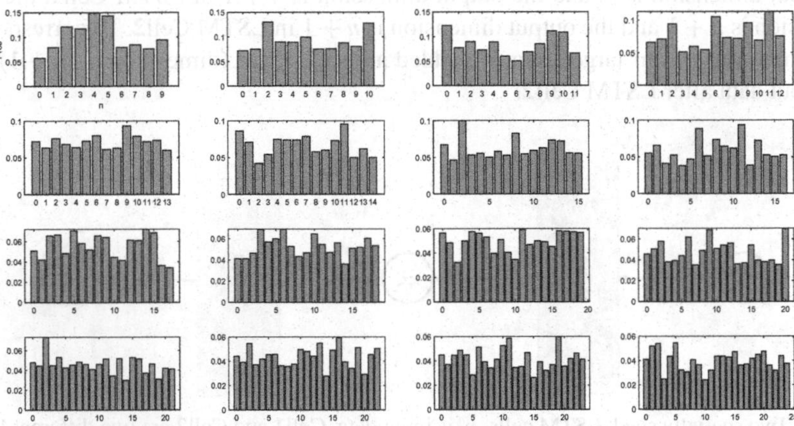

Fig. 5. Histograms with probability $M = 9 \sim 24$, the horizontal axis represents the number of particle n and the vertical axis represents probability P. In each subfigure, the total height of the green rectangle is 1

In a numerical experiment, we give a margin of error ϵ_m to decide M, that is $E(M) \leq \epsilon_m$. To save calculation time and meet accuracy requirements, we make $\epsilon_m = 0.04$ and then $M = 50$. In other words, Eq. (2) can be effectively equivalent to Eq. (3) to sum n from 0 to 50. So, in Fig. 4, the dimension of LSTM Cell **1** and LSTM Cell**2** are 1×51 and 51×51, respectively. The noise spectrum data (total number is 10000, 4/5 of them is the trained data set, the remaining is test data set) is used to train the network and error curve shown in Fig. 7.

As shown in Fig. 7(a), the training MSELoss declines rapidly in 0~30 epochs and after 30th epoch, MSELoss converges to a very small value, which means a good model is generated for training data set. But, in the machine learning process, overfitting always happens frequently and so the training step should be carefully designed to prevent overfitting. Adding l_1 -norm to MSELoss is a regularization technique to reduce overfitting in neural networks. As shown in Fig. 7(b), test MSELoss shows a rapid decline in 0~20 epochs, after the 20th epoch, MSELoss converges to a fixed value (very small). This means that a good relationship between $\mathrm{Tr}[\rho(t)]$ and $\mathrm{Tr}[\rho(t+\Delta t)]$ is constructed and overfitting does not occur based on our model.

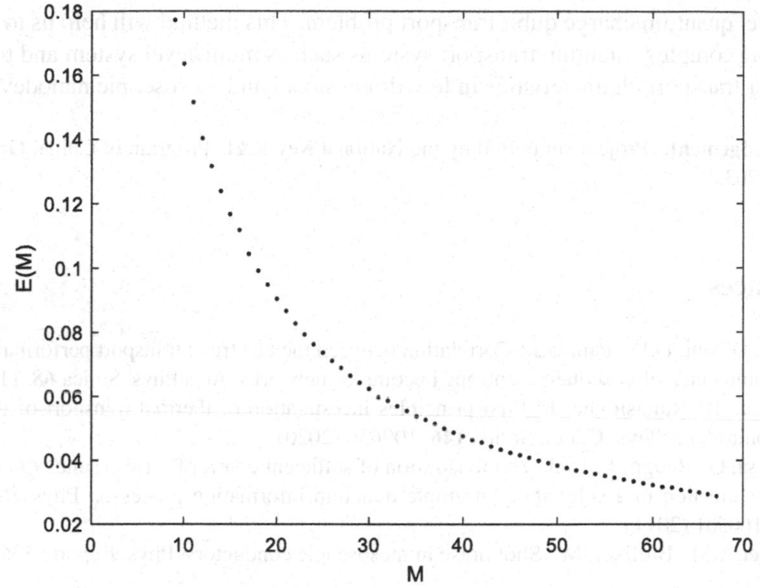

Fig. 6. The value of the point represents the value of evaluation function $E(M)$.

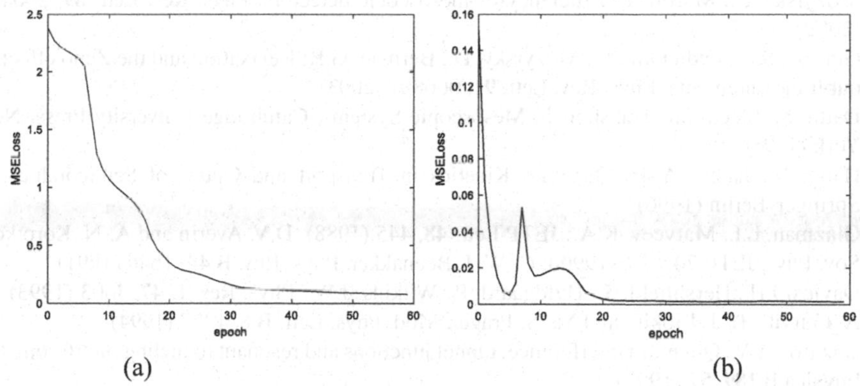

Fig. 7. The figure shows the mean-square error loss (MSELoss) which is equal to the expectations of cost change with epoch. (a) is training loss curve, (b) is testing loss curve.

5 Conclusion

In this paper, two main results about quantum master conditional equation are presented. One is that the QCME method is used to understand a quantum dots charge qubit transport problem, and the specific form of the QCME describing the two-level quantum dots system is obtained. The other is that the relationship between QCME and RNN is found, and the RNN is firstly applied to study QCME and successfully simulate the QCME of a two-level quantum charge qubit transport problem. This method will help us to understand more complex quantum transport systems such as multi-level system and to study the carrier transport characteristics in low-dimensional and mesoscopic nanodevices.

Acknowledgement. Project supported by the National Key R&D Program of China, Grant No. 2018YFĂ703.

References

1. Chen, D., Shi, D.D., Pan, G.J.: Correlation between the electrical transport performance and the communicability sequence entropy in complex networks. Acta Phys. Sinica **68**, 11 (2019)
2. Szpunar, B., Ranasinghe, J.: First-principles investigation of thermal transport of uranium mononitride. J. Phys. Chem. Solids **146**, 109636 (2020)
3. Moussa, O., Baugh, J., et al.: Demonstration of sufficient control for two rounds of quantum error correction in a solid-state ensemble quantum information processor. Phys. Rev. Lett **107**, 160501 (2011)
4. Blanter, Y.M., Buttiker, M.: Shot noise in mesoscopic conductors. Phys. Reports **336**, 1–166 (2000)
5. Gurvitz, S.A.: Measurements with a noninvasive detector and dephasing mechanism. Phys. Rev. B. **56**, 15215 (1997)
6. Mozyrsky, D., Martin, I.: Efficiency of mesoscopic detectors. Phys. Rev. Lett. **89**, 200401 (2002)
7. Gurvitz, S.A., Fedichkin, L., Mozyrsky, D., Berman, G.P.: Relaxation and the Zeno effect in qubit measurements. Phys. Rev. Lett. **91**, 066801 (2003)
8. Datta, S.: Electronic Transport in Mesoscopic Systems. Cambridge University Press, New York (1995)
9. Haug, H., Jauho, A.-P.: Quantum Kinetics in Transport and Optics of Semiconductors. Springer, Berlin (1996)
10. Glazman, L.I., Matveev, K.A.: JETP Lett. **48**, 445 (1988). D.V. Averin and A. N. Korotkov, Sov, Phys. JETP 70, 937 s1990d; C. W. J. Beenakker, Phys. Rev. B 44, 1646 (1991)
11. Davies, J.H., Hershfield, S., Hyldgaard, P., Wilkins, J.W.: Phys. Rev. B **47**, 4603 (1993). S. A. Gurvitz, H. J. Lipkin, and Ya. S. Prager, Mod. Phys. Lett. B 8, 1377 (1994)
12. Nazarov, Y.V.: Quantum interference, tunnel junctions and resonant tunneling interferometer. Physica B **189**, 57 (1993)
13. Gurvitz, S.A., Lipkin, H.J., Ya, S.P.: Interference effects in resonant tunneling and the Pauli principle. Phys. Lett. A **212**, 91 (1996)
14. Gurvitz, S.A., Prager, Y.S.: Microscopic derivation of rate equations for quantum transport. Phys. Rev. B **53**, 15932 (1996)
15. Gurvitz, S.A., Prager, Y.S.: Microscopic derivation of rate equations for quantum transport. Phys. Rev. B **53**, 23 (1995)
16. Xin-Qi, L., Jun, Y.L., Yong-Gang, Y.: Quantum master equation approach to quantum transport through mesoscopic systems. Phys. Rev. B **71**, 205304 (2005)
17. Torlai, G., Mazzola, G., Carrasquilla, J., et al.: Neural-network quantum state tomography. Nat. Phys. **14**, 447 (2018)
18. Zhang, Y., Kim, E.A.: Quantum loop topography for machine learning. Phys. Rev. Lett **188**, 21 (2017)
19. Qu, Z.G., Chen, S.Y., Wang, X.J.: A secure controlled quantum image steganography algorithm. Quantum Inf. Process. **19**(380), 1–25 (2020)

20. Qu, Z.G., Wu, S.Y., Liu, W.J., Wang, X.J.: Analysis and improvement of steganography protocol based on bell states in noise environment. Comput. Mater. Continua **59**(2), 607–624 (2019)
21. Li, X.-Y., Zhu, Q.-S., Zhu, M.-Z., Huang, Y.-M., Hao, W., Shao-Yi, W.: Machine learning study of the relationship between the geometric and entropy discord. EPL **127**, 20009 (2019)
22. Carleo, G., Troyer, M.: Solving the quantum many-body problem with artificial neural networks. Science **355**(6325), 602–605 (2017)
23. Yan, Y.J.: Quantum Fokker-Planck theory in a non-Gaussian-Markovian medium. Phys. Rev. A **58**, 2721 (1998)
24. Clark, L.A., Huang, W., Barlow, T.M., Beige, A.: Hidden quantum Markov models and open quantum systems with instantaneous feedback,arXiv:1406.5847v2 [quant-ph], 5 July 2014
25. Gers, F.A., Schmidhuber, J., Cummins, F.: Learning to forget: Continual prediction with LSTM. Neural Comput. **12**(10), 2451–2471 (2000)
26. Graves, A., Schmidhuber, J.: Offline handwriting recognition with multidimensional recurrent neural networks. In: Koller, D., Schuurmans, D., Bengio, Y., Bottou, L. (eds.) NIPS 2008, pp. 545–552 (2009)
27. Graves, A.: Generating sequences with recurrent neural networks, Technical report, arXiv: 1308.0850
28. Graves, A., Jaitly, N.: Towards end-to-end speech recognition with recurrent neural networks. In: ICML (2014)
29. Kiros, R., Salakhutdinov, R., Zemel, R.: Unifying visual-semantic embeddings with multimodal neural language models, arXiv: 1411.2539 (2014)
30. Vinyals, O., Kaiser, L., Koo, T., Petrov, S., Sutskever, I., Hinton, G.: Grammar as a foreign language, arXiv: 1411.4555 (2014)
31. Xu, K., Ba, J.L., Kiros, R., Cho, K., Courville, A., et al.: Show, attend and tell: Neural image caption generation with visual attention, arXiv: 1502.03044 (2015)
32. Sutskever, I., Vinyals, O., Le, Q.V.: Sequence to sequence learning with neural networks, arXiv: 1409.3215 (2014)
33. Luchnikov, I.A., Vintskevich, S.V., Grigoriev, D.A., Filippov, S.N.: Machine learning non-Markovian quantum dynamics. Phys. Rev. Lett **124**, 140502 (2020)

Neural Network Study Quantum Synchronization and Quantum Correlation Under Non-zero Temperature

Qing Yang[1], Qin-Sheng Zhu[1(✉)], Qing-Yu Meng[1], Yong Hu[1], and Xiao-Yu Li[2]

[1] School of Physics, University of Electronic Science and Technology of China, Chengdu 610054, People's Republic of China
zhuqinsheng@uestc.edu.cn

[2] School of Information and Software Engineering, University of Electronic Science and Technology of China, Chengdu 610054, People's Republic of China

Abstract. As an important part of quantum mechanics, quantum measurement can not only enable us to get the information of the quantum system, but also play an indispensable role in the control of the quantum system. The quantum synchronization phenomenon and the quantum correlation between the detector and the quantum system are very useful in quantum measurement process. However, there are still few studies on the nature of the quantum synchronization process and the realization of the classification of quantum synchronization. In this work, a two-qubit open system model which consists of a qubit system in a cavity and probing tool (another qubit) is proposed, the properties of quantum correlation are explored under non-zero temperature, and the characterizes of quantum synchronization also has been illustrated in different situation. It is shown the effect of different temperature for the quantum synchronization and the quantum correlation. Additionally, it is shown in the article that the process of synchronization under different parameter. Meanwhile, the artificial neural networks method is used to further study the classification of the quantum synchronization at non-zero temperature and it is shown an effective consequence. The results pave a way for subsequent research on the quantum synchronization and quantum correlation.

Keywords: Quantum synchronization · Quantum association · Artificial neural networks

1 Introduction

From classical physic to quantum physic, the measurement or detection is an essential part of physics. Different from the measurement of classical physics, the disturbance of the measurement or detection for the system is recognized because there exists the quantum correlation and quantum entanglement in the quantum system. The concept of the quantum measurement and related theory are put forward and applied in some quantum fields, such as quantum information [1–3], quantum engineering [4] which apply the principles of quantum mechanics to control quantum systems in order to

X. Sun et al. (Eds.): ICAIS 2021, LNCS 12736, pp. 144–154, 2021.
https://doi.org/10.1007/978-3-030-78609-0_13

better serve people's lives compared with the traditional method and quantum machine learning. Meanwhile, from a realistic point of view, when a quantum system is used to perform certain functions, how do we know if it is working as we designed it to? So, a reasonable measurement or detection method for this quantum system is particularly important. In the process of detection, the direct or indirect contact between the detection equipment and the system is required, and it arouses two interesting problems.

One is the quantum correlation [5, 6] which is shown the non-local interaction and mutual effect even though the system and the probe are separate. Studying it between the detector and the system will help us to understand the relationship between the measured values of the detector and the state of the quantum system. On the physical, it is shown that some special properties of the composite quantum system (the detector and the system) and stems from the superposition principle and the tonsorial structure of quantum states in quantum mechanics. Simultaneously, these properties cannot be presented by a classical system. In the past years, it had been regarded as true that entanglement is equivalent to quantum correlation until the concept of "quantum discord" was introduced by Ollivier and Zurek [7]. In fact, entanglement only represents a portion of the quantum correlations in realistic quantum systems. At present, the quantification method of quantum correlation fall into two categories, namely the entropy style discord (including quantum discord (QD) [8] and Rènyi discord [9] and the geometric discord (GD) [10, 11] (including Hilbert-Schmidt [12], Bures distance [13], trace-norm and Hellinger [14]), and these methods were introduced and have become a hot research topic in the past few years.

Another is the quantum synchronization which is an important property of quantum system. It provides convenience for quantum measurement and detection, and is widely used in the quantum information and quantum device design [15]. Especially, the quantum synchronization effect exerts a great advantage when studying systems that cannot be in direct contact with it, such as, the spin system is explored by quantum synchronization by establishing a connection between the system and the probe, and it is shown the quantum spin synchronization and anti- synchronization for the different dynamic parameters of the spin system [16]. Because there are many parameters that affect the quantum synchronization, it is difficult to identify whether the quantum synchronization occurs. Recently, machine learning has been used to assist in the study of the quantum synchronization [17]. They build the artificial neural network (ANN) model to learn the potential patterns of the quantum synchronization from previously given data sets, and make a decision or prediction for the quantum synchronization under the zero-temperature.

In this paper, the properties of an open system model which consist of the probing equipment (it is also a qubit system) and one qubit quantum system in the environment (cavity) is studied under the non-zero temperature. Firstly, the quantum correlation under different temperature is discussed, and the relationship of quantum synchronization and some strength has been explored by the machine learning under nonzero temperature. Simultaneously, the ANN method is further used to classify the learned data and recognize the new patterns according to the previous knowledge, and applied to distinguish the in-phase synchronization and out of synchronization.

2 Model

Considering a dissipative, isolated, and non-equilibrium spin-system with an immersive qubit q, which the system can hardly approached or measured (a similar system is described in Ref [16]). The quantum probe p is coupling with q, then reconstructs the dynamics feature rather than directly measure it (see Fig. 1). The microscopic Hamiltonian can be written as

$$H = \sum_{p}\left(\frac{\omega_p}{2}\sigma_p^z + \frac{\omega_q}{2}\sigma_q^z\right) + \lambda\sigma_p^x\sigma_q^x + \sum_k \Omega_k a_k^\dagger a_k + \sum_k g_k\left(a_k^\dagger + a_k\right) \quad (1)$$

Where the σ_p^i (i = x, y, z) being Pauli matrices, λ is coupling coefficient, Ω_k represent energies with bosonic eigenmodes a_k describing it, ω_i(I = q, p) is the frequency of probe and qubit (we always set $\hbar = 1$ in this paper).

By receiving the observable data of probe, which represented qubit can detect the properties of qubit. As the out of equilibrium qubit, interacting with environment can synchronize with another coupled qubit. The process of dissipation is depended on the changing of spectral density, which writes:

$$J(\omega) = \sum_k g_k \delta(\omega - \Omega_k) \quad (2)$$

Supposing weak dissipation in the model, then the dynamics features can be studied by in Born-Markov and secular approximate with Lindblad master equation:

$$\dot{\rho}(t) = -i[H_s + H_{LS}, \rho(t)] + \mathcal{D}[\rho(t)] \quad (3)$$

where the small Lamb shift H_{LS} commutes with H_s and $\mathcal{D}[\rho(t)]$ is the standard dissipater [17]. This master equation of this situation is also available for strong coupling strength on the condition that the system-bath coupling keep small. But when the temperature is varying with the decay rate fast, the properties of the quantum synchronization and quantum correlation will change.

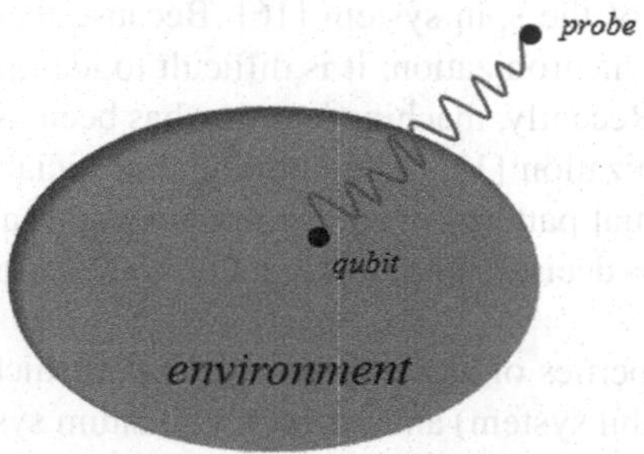

Fig. 1. Schematics of the model: a system ω_q interacting with its own environment, is connected with the probe which is out of the system. The shadowed area is the environment, the qubit q is immersed in it, and the coupling strength between qubit and probe is λ.

It is shown in Fig. 1 the model in this paper. The probe qubits are coupled with a probe by coupling coefficient λ, and synchronization will be reached though the corresponding conditions, then the information in system can be gained by the probe.

3 Quantum correlation

Based on the Bures distance (DBU), Cianciaruso et al. discussed the geometric measure of discord-type correlations, which is defined as follows:

$$D_{Br} = \inf_{\chi'} d_{Bu}^2(\rho, \chi') = \inf_{\chi'} 2\left(1 - Tr\left(\left[\sqrt{\chi'}\rho\sqrt{\chi'}\right]^{1/2}\right)\right) \tag{4}$$

With the set of classical-quantum states $' = \sum_i p_i i|i|^A \otimes \omega_i^B$, p_i is a probability distribution, $\{|i^A\}$ denotes an orthogonal basis for subsystem A, ω_i^B is an arbitrary ensemble of states for subsystem B, and $d_{Bu}(\rho, \chi')$ is the Bures distance.

Some numerical calculation methods were proposed in Ref [18]. However, it is difficult to obtain mathematically an analytic form for general models. We proposed a method to study D_{Br} based on the relation between quantum Fisher information and the Bures distance with the calculation method in [19]. The Bures distance can be written as:

$$\mathcal{P}^A = (\rho AB|\Gamma) = \frac{1}{4} {}^{min}_{H_A^\Gamma} F(\rho_{AB}; H_A^\Gamma) \tag{5}$$

Where F denotes the quantum Fisher information:

$$F(\rho_{AB}; H_A^\Gamma) = 4\sum_{i<k;q_i+q_k\neq 0} \frac{(q_i + q_k)^2}{q_i + q_k} |\langle\psi_i|(H_A^\Gamma \otimes \mathbb{I}_B)|\psi_k\rangle|2 \tag{6}$$

With q_i, $|\psi_i\rangle$ denoting respectively the eigenvalues and the eigenvectors of ρ_{AB}, and the minimum is taken over the set of all local Hamiltonians H_A^Γ.

And the density matrix is:

$$\rho(t) = \begin{bmatrix} \rho_{0000} & \rho_{0001} & \rho_{0011} & \rho_{0010} \\ \rho_{0100} & \rho_{0101} & \rho_{0111} & \rho_{0110} \\ \rho_{1100} & \rho_{1101} & \rho_{1111} & \rho_{1110} \\ \rho_{1000} & \rho_{1001} & \rho_{1011} & \rho_{1010} \end{bmatrix} \tag{7}$$

When $t = 0$, the initial state is $|\psi(0) = (|\uparrow> + |\downarrow>)(|\uparrow> + |\downarrow>)/2$. With the limit of Schrödinger, each analytical solution of the elements in the density matrix can be gain from Eq. [7].

$$\begin{cases} \frac{d\rho_{0000}}{dt} = \overset{\sim+}{\gamma}_2 \rho_{0101} + \overset{\sim+}{\gamma}_1 \rho_{1010} - \left(\overset{\sim-}{\gamma}_2 + \overset{\sim-}{\gamma}_1\right)\rho_{0000} \\ \frac{d\rho_{0101}}{dt} = \overset{\sim-}{\gamma}_2 \rho_{0000} + \overset{\sim+}{\gamma}_1 \rho_{1111} - \left(\overset{\sim+}{\gamma}_2 + \overset{\sim-}{\gamma}_1\right)\rho_{0101} \\ \frac{d\rho_{1010}}{dt} = \overset{\sim+}{\gamma}_2 \rho_{1111} + \overset{\sim-}{\gamma}_1 \rho_{0000} - \left(\overset{\sim-}{\gamma}_2 + \overset{\sim+}{\gamma}_1\right)\rho_{1010} \\ \frac{d\rho_{1111}}{dt} = \overset{\sim-}{\gamma}_2 \rho_{1010} + \overset{\sim-}{\gamma}_1 \rho_{0101} - \left(\overset{\sim+}{\gamma}_2 + \overset{\sim+}{\gamma}_1\right)\rho_{1111} \end{cases} \tag{8}$$

$$\begin{cases} \frac{d\rho_{0011}}{dt} = -\frac{1}{2}(\tilde{\gamma}_2^{+} + \tilde{\gamma}_1^{+} + \tilde{\gamma}_2^{-} + \tilde{\gamma}_1^{-})\rho_{0011} \\ \frac{d\rho_{1100}}{dt} = -\frac{1}{2}(\tilde{\gamma}_2^{+} + \tilde{\gamma}_1^{+} + \tilde{\gamma}_2^{-} + \tilde{\gamma}_1^{-})\rho_{1100} \\ \frac{d\rho_{1001}}{dt} = -\frac{1}{2}(\tilde{\gamma}_2^{+} + \tilde{\gamma}_1^{+} + \tilde{\gamma}_2^{-} + \tilde{\gamma}_1^{-})\rho_{1001} \\ \frac{d\rho_{0110}}{dt} = -\frac{1}{2}(\tilde{\gamma}_2^{+} + \tilde{\gamma}_1^{+} + \tilde{\gamma}_2^{-} + \tilde{\gamma}_1^{-})\rho_{1001} \end{cases} \quad (9)$$

Where $\gamma_1^{+} = cos^2(\theta_+ + \theta_-)J(E_1)[1 + \text{n}(E_1)]$, $\gamma_1^{-} = cos^2(\theta_+ + \theta_-)J(E_1)\text{n}(E_1)$ and $\gamma_2^{+} = sin^2(\theta_+ + \theta_-)J(E_2)[1 + \text{n}(E_2)]$, $\gamma_2^{-} = sin^2(\theta_+ + \theta_-)J(E_2)\text{n}(E_2)$.

The quantum correlation (especially the relationship of quantum discord in quantum correlation) for one temperature has been discussed a lot in previous work. Now we consider the quantum correlation under non-zero temperature. Studying the characters of QC under different temperatures.

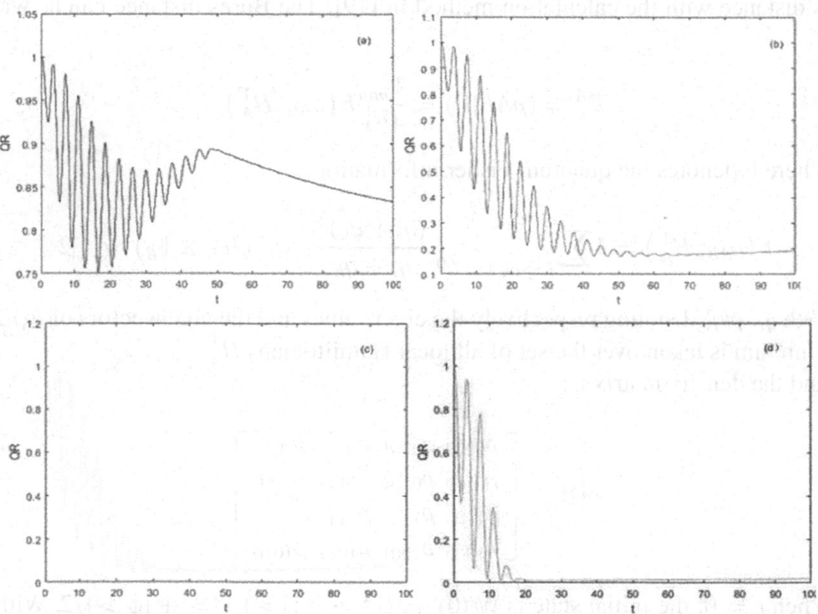

Fig. 2. A graph of quantum correlation over time at different temperatures in a spin-open system, (a) At a temperature of 0; (b) At a temperature of 1; (c) At a temperature of 3; (d) At a temperature of 5; both of them satisfy $\omega_q = 1.2$ and $\omega_p = 0.8\omega_q$, the coupling coefficient $\lambda = 0.2\omega_q$

As shown in Fig. 2, all the curves in the figure show a gradually attenuated oscillation, which tends to level off after a period of time, the trend of all curves behaves a good Markov characteristic. The quantum correlation constant always varying in 0–1. As Fig. 2 shows, the speed of the dissipation process increasing while the temperature rising. We infer that the faster the dissipation evolves as the temperature rises, the faster the equilibrium is reached. In addition, as the temperature rises, in the same time window, the final equilibrium state QR will be smaller and will eventually approach 0.

The curve change in Fig. 2(a) is different compared with other pictures. This result can be illustrated that when the temperature T = 0, the Hamiltonian:

$$H_{eff} = H_s + \partial \hat{\Theta} \tag{10}$$

Where the H_s is the system's Hamiltonian, and $\hat{\Theta}$ is a mechanical quantity operator while ∂ is a constant. And the energy is always at the lowest state, for $|\Psi = \sum_i |\psi_i \ (i = 1)$. That mean the Quantum noise of this system is disappeared, in other words, is inhabited under this situation. Put another qubit in the system, it will arouse a complex change, its status must be represented by the $|\Psi$ of the system at first, it is also the explanation of the risen period, then Markov process is taken place, finally it can become steady. With temperature rising, environmental status is not uniform, the consequence will appear Markov characteristics.

4 Quantum Synchronize Under Different Temperature

In previous work, dissipation-induced quantum synchronization had been studied in the bosons and nointeracting spins which in a common environment [20]. The quantum synchronization we discussed here is the system that qubit and the probe is predicted in spite of a common bath. The quantum synchronization is achieved when significant separation between the two maximum decay times describing the dynamics in case of competition between different oscillation modes. Until the relative phase about them are locked, local degrees of freedom are slowly decaying, they experience monochromatic oscillations and have the same frequency. Because of the principle of quantum entanglement, the properties and the state of the qubit in the system can be "detected" by the probe, it provides us a method to redrawn the qubit by the observed measurement of probe. In this work, $<\sigma_p^x(t)>$ is the observed measurement, and in the Heisenberg picture, the observable measurement O can be written to a general form:

$$\langle O(t) \rangle = \sum\nolimits_{k,\omega} < O_k(\omega) e^{-i\omega t} e^{-f_k(\omega)t} \tag{11}$$

Where the $O(\omega) = \sum_{\varepsilon} \prod(\varepsilon) O \prod(\varepsilon + \omega)$, ε in this function is the set of eigenvalues of H_s, and the f_k is the decaying rate. By diagonalizing the dynamical equations of motion within the degeneracy subspace, we can gain the observables dynamic characters of the probe and qubit. If the decaying rate f_k is not zero, they will achieve synchronization at a smaller decaying rate than f_k. We stress that interaction assist the phenomenon of quantum synchronization through two separate systems may obstruct quantum synchronization. With this condition, the system will reach a robust synchronization finally in this model. Actually, marked separation of decaying rate f_k formed in the system because of strong detuning, which favor the quantum synchronization.

Though monitoring the $<\sigma_p^x(t)>$ and $<\sigma_q^x(t)>$ in terms of fermionic quasiparticles in the dissipation system, we can find out the synchronization clearly. The expression of $<\sigma_p^x(t)>$ and $<\sigma_q^x(t)>$ is:

$$\begin{aligned}\left\langle\sigma_q^x(t)\right\rangle &= 2\cos(\theta_+ + \theta_-)e^{-\frac{(\tilde{\gamma}_1^- + \tilde{\gamma}_1^+)t}{2}} \times Re\left\{e^{iE_1t}\left[\rho_{01,11}(0) + \rho_{11,10}(0)\right]\right\} \\ &+2\sin(\theta_+ + \theta_-)e^{-(\tilde{\gamma}_2^- + \tilde{\gamma}_2^+)t/2} \times Re\left\{e^{iE_2t}\left[\rho_{01,11}(0) + \rho_{11,10}(0)\right]\right\}\end{aligned} \tag{12}$$

$$\begin{aligned}\left\langle\sigma_p^x(t)\right\rangle &= 2\frac{\sin(\theta_+ - \theta_-)}{\coth[E_2/(2T)]}e^{-\frac{(\tilde{\gamma}_1^- + \tilde{\gamma}_1^+)t}{2}} \times Re\left\{e^{iE_1t}\left[\rho_{01,11}(0) + \rho_{11,10}(0)\right]\right\} \\ &+2\frac{\cos(\theta_+ - \theta_-)}{\coth[E_1/(2T)]}e^{-(\tilde{\gamma}_2^- + \tilde{\gamma}_2^+)t/2} \times Re\left\{e^{iE_2t}\left[\rho_{01,11}(0) + \rho_{11,10}(0)\right]\right\}\end{aligned} \tag{13}$$

The E_1, E_2 can draw from $H_s = E_1\left(\eta_1^+\eta_1 - \frac{1}{2}\right) + E_2\left(\eta_2^+\eta_2 - \frac{1}{2}\right)$. Note that $0 \le \theta_+ \le \theta_- \le \frac{\pi}{4}$. And the operator η_i, $(i = 1, 2)$ stands for the Bose factor and the Lindblad super operator. As a result of such dynamical structure, in the long-time limit, synchronization take place if either $\gamma_1 \ll \gamma_2$ or $\gamma_1 \gg \gamma_2$. The frequency of such synchronous oscillations is $\omega_{sync} \simeq E_1$ for $\gamma_1 \gg \gamma_2$ which corresponding anti-synchronization and $\omega_{sync} \simeq E_2$ for $\gamma_1 \ll \gamma_2$ which corresponding synchronization. The cases where the two decaying rates are of the same order of magnitude are characterized by the absence of synchronization, that can be quantified using the so-called Pearson correlation coefficient.

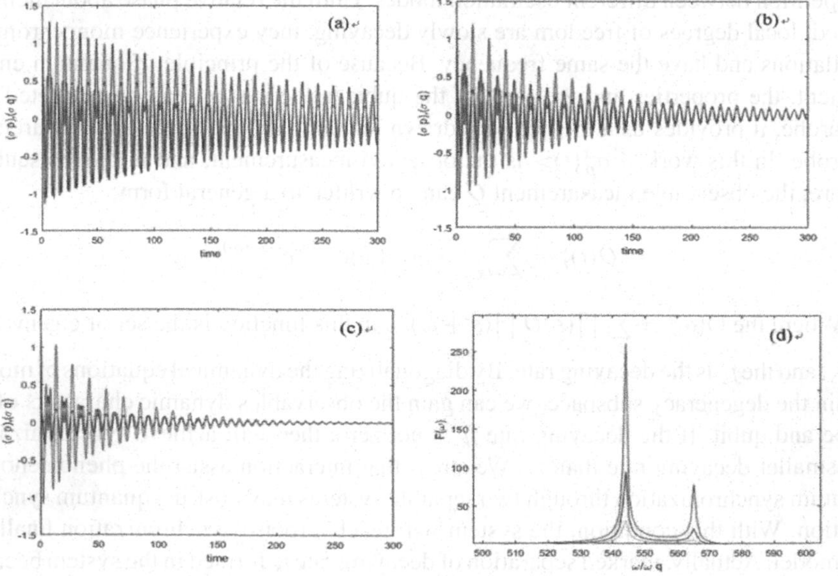

Fig. 3. The picture (a), (b), (c) is the dynamical synchronization of $<\sigma_p^x(t)>$ (the red line) and $<\sigma_q^x(t)>$ (the blue line), when $\omega_q = 1.2$, $s = 1$, $\omega_p = 2\omega_q$ and $\lambda = 0.2\omega_q$ for different temperature (a) T = 0; (b) T = 1; (c) T = 2. And figure (d) is absolutely transform $F(\omega)$ of $\sigma_p^x(t)$. (Color figure online)

Because of the energy of the system is connected with Boltzmann constant K_B,the definition of the temperature is $K_BT = 1$, it is available for many system under this magnitude. with the temperature raising, the frequency of the oscillation become faster than the zero and process of dissipation become faster, it induces quantum synchronization take place quickly.

Comparing (a), (b), (c) of Fig. 3, it found that when the temperature is higher, the corresponding oscillation is lower, and the corresponding synchronization phenomenon is correspondingly reached faster. It stems from: with the increasing of the temperature, the Markov feature which shows the decreasing behavior of the $<\sigma_p^x(t)>$ and $<\sigma_p^x(t)>$ is more obviously. So, it may be if synchronization is not reached, the oscillation phenomenon disappears. This is consistent with the characteristics we mentioned above in quantum correlation. The Fig. 3(d) is a Fourier variation graph. Its peak value depends on the values of ω_p, s, (where s = $log_{E_1/E_2} tan^2(\overline{\theta}_+ + \overline{\theta}_-)$), and temperature in the same time window. For fixed ω_p and s, the influence of temperature can been seen that when it rises, the smaller the peak value and the difference between the two peak values, This is also consistent with the phenomenon of dynamic oscillation attenuation.

As the complexity of the connection of qubit and probe, classical method is hard to find the relation between parameters and synchronization. But artificial neural network (ANN) can build a lot of units in each layer. Though the training and minimize the loss function, a useful ANN is able to approximate the synchronization and find the potential connection. We construct a feedforward neural, in which every neuron connects to every neuron in the next layer and feature only passes forward in each layer, namely, there is no loop in our network. Later, the application of ANN to explore the properties of them permits deeper understanding and clearer cognition.

The ANN can help identify the properties of the bath by measuring only the probe dynamics. Using the principle of supervised learning, we construct an artificial neural network (ANN) composed of three parts (input layer, hidden layer and output layer). Supervised learning first trains machine learning using samples (not including input samples) and then uses trained neural networks to make predictions. ANN has one or more hidden layers, we use a hidden layer. The functional relationship between the input layers, the hidden layer and the output layer are represented by the weight ω. Training task is to optimize the weight, as well as the possible parameters are used to determine activation function $\varphi(x)$ of each neuron, to minimize the classification of the training set error. Due to Principal Component Analysis (PCA), by transform F(ω) of $\sigma_p^x(t)$, ANN can learn to classify different dissipation.

In our model, the input layer has Q nodes, corresponding to the number of samples in the Fourier transform of the probe signal. Its hidden layer consists of 3 artificial neurons. The output layer gives the final result, it has a separate artificial neuron. Using the ANN must experience training, testing and result. The weight ω established a correlation between the input layer, hidden layer and the output layer. Optimize the weight of feature can be achieved by training progress with the method which called gradient descent.

The another thing is to determine the activation function $\varphi(x)$ of each neuron,then can minimize the error in the classification of training. The $\varphi(x)$ is defined as:

$$\varphi(x) = 1/(1 + e^{-x}) \tag{14}$$

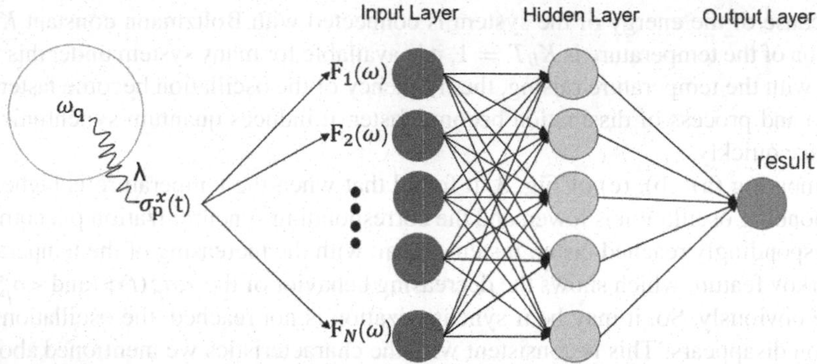

Fig. 4. The Fourier transform $F(\omega)$ of $<\sigma_p^x(t)>$ which is measured and used as the input data to optimize the hidden layer, then algorithm will learn to weight ω and come out the best result

It is shown in Fig. 4 that the visual image investigation scheme of volume ML, using neural network to explore the potential relationship between frequency ω and environment s.The input data in the input layer modulus is Fourier transform $\mathcal{F}(\omega)$ time domain function of $\sigma_p^x(t)$ time interval is divided into 101 points in [0,100], and the corresponding Fourier transform of the 101 points is used as the input data of the neural network. The neural network input layer is set to 101 the number of neurons, the number of neurons in hidden layer is also 101, including activation function $\varphi(x)$.In this scenario, the output layer has a neuron that contains our results.Connections between layers are considered feedforward, and the weights of these connections are optimized by back propagation. The probe frequency can be adjusted. Due to the change of ω_p, there is a corresponding $\sigma_p^x(t)$, as shown in Fig. 3. It is the task of the neural network to teach it how to distinguish the trajectories of the Fourier transform and to give the correct marks at the training level. When we give a new ω_p, the neural network predicts the value corresponding to the correct site training set is composed of N spectrum of three different labels, and the test set is composed of 0.3N spectrum of the other three different labels. By training these data, the neural network will learn how to divide the spectrum into three types of values corresponding to the s value. Distinguish the relative heights of the peaks in the Fourier diagram to distinguish between synchronous and asynchronous. ML needs more data to learn how to distinguish the subtle effects of the environment on the shape of the Fourier transform.

After a training, the ANN can classify the dissipation system by the Fourier transform of the σ_p^x varying by the time window. 71 sets of data of different temperature is applied to training the hidden layer for 20000 times. The loss function can be written as:

$$MSE = \frac{1}{n}\sum\nolimits_{i=1}^{m} (o - y)^2 \tag{15}$$

In this function, o is predicted output, and y is real data. The mean sum squared loss function is the sum, over all the data points, of the square of the difference between the predicted and actual target variables, divided by the number of data points. And the loss can be reduced by increasing the number of training set. This Data characteristic curve imply that we have found an available set of features and weight which avoided overfitting and underfitting. We draw out that the loss can reduce to $4.5*10^{-6}$ even smaller. In a controllable scale, by the temperature rising, the loss reduced more quickly and smaller. The relation of MSE and number of training data has been showed in Fig. 5.

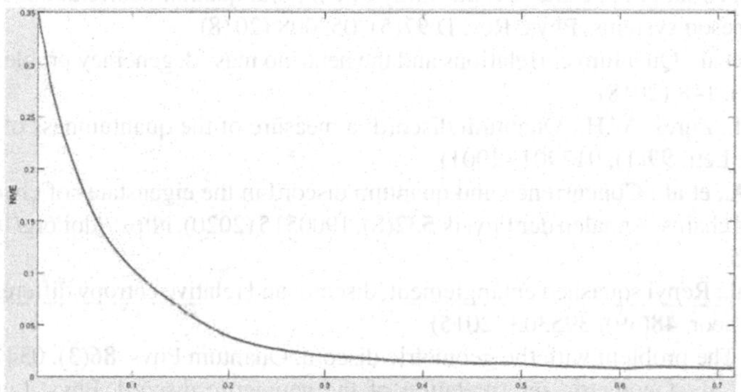

Fig. 5. The curve for training error of the training set by ANN when the temperature at 1.

There is 30 set of data and the ANN has been trained 20000 times. The MSE is dropped quickly before 2000 training sessions, and after training 4000 training sessions, the MSE is close to zero. This picture suggests that the method here is effective because of the curve is always convergent to a number which close to 0.

5 Conclusion

In this paper, the changing behaviors of quantum correlation and quantum synchronization has been studied for different parameters. With the increasing of the temperature, it is shown that the oscillation and Markov characteristics of the dynamical properties of quantum correlation and the quantum synchronization also presents decreasing behaviors. Simultaneously, the machine learning ANN method is further used to successfully determine the feature classification for quantum synchronous data under non-zero temperature based on a large number of generated data which come from the analyzing absolutely transform $F(\omega)$ of $\sigma_p^x(t)$, and the MSE can be reduced to 10^{-6}. The result shows that ANN is suitable for solving this kind of problem and the temperature is an important element to the synchronization process which provide an access for solving the synchronization problems.

Acknowledgement. Project supported by the National Key R&D Program of China, Grant No. 2018YFĂ703.

References

1. Bennett, C.H.: Quantum information and computation. Nature **48**, 24–30 (1995)
2. Bub, J.: Quantum information and computation. Philos. Phys. **404**(6775), 555–660 (2007)

3. Ziman, M., P., Bužek, V., et al.: Diluting quantum information: an analysis of information transfer in system-reservoir interactions. Phys. Rev. A **65**(1), 042105 (2002)
4. Rosencher, E., Fiore, A., Vinter, B., Berger, V., Bois, P., Nagle, J.: Quantum engineering of optical nonlinearities. Science **271**(5246), 168–173 (1996)
5. Naikoo, J., Alok, A.K., Banerjee, S.: Study of temporal quantum correlations in decohering B and K meson systems. Phys. Rev. D **97**(5), 053008 (2018)
6. Dixit, K., et al.: Quantum correlations and the neutrino mass degeneracy problem. Eur. Phys. J. C **78**(11), 1–8 (2018)
7. Ollivier, H., Zurek, W.H.: Quantum discord: a measure of the quantumness of correlations. Phys. Rev. Lett. **99**(1), 017901 (2001)
8. Ashouri, A., et al.: Concurrence and quantum discord in the eigenstates of chaotic and integrable spin chains. Annalen der Physik **532**(8), 1900515 (2020). https://doi.org/10.1002/andp.201900515
9. Wilde, et al.: Renyi squashed entanglement, discord, and relative entropy differences. J. Phys. A Math. Theor. **48**(39), 395303 (2015)
10. Piani, M.: The problem with the geometric discord. Quantum Phys. **86**(3), 034101 (2012)
11. Yao, Y., et al.: Geometric interpretation of the geometric discord. Phys. Lett. A **376**(4), 358–364 (2012)
12. Witte, C., Trucks, M.: A new entanglement measure induced by the Hilbert-Schmidt norm. Phys. Lett. A **257**(1–2), 14–20 (1999)
13. Spehner, D., Orszag, M.: Geometric quantum discord with Bures distance. New J. Phys. **15**(10), 603–610 (2013)
14. Gieres, F.: Mathematical surprises and Dirac's formalism in quantum mechanics. Reports Progress Phys. **63**(12)1893–1931(39) (2000)
15. Mari, A., et al.: Measures of quantum synchronization in continuous variable systems. Phys. Rev. Lett. **111**(10), 103605 (2013)
16. Giorgi, G.L., Galve, F., Zambrini, R.: Probing the spectral density of a dissipative qubit via quantum synchronization. Phys. Rev. A **94**(5), 52121–52121 (2016)
17. Garau Estarellas, G., et al.: Machine learning applied to quantum synchronization-assisted probing. Adv. Quantum Technol. **2**(7–8), 1800085 (2019)
18. Breuer, H.P., Petruccione, F.: The Theory of Open Quantum Systems. Oxford University Press (2007)
19. Hübner, M.: Explicit computation of the Bures distance for density matrices. Phys. Lett. A **163**(4), 239–242 (1992)
20. Liu, H.: Publisher's note: molecular-frame photoelectron angular distributions of strong-field tunneling from inner orbitals. Phys. Rev. A **88**, 069905 (2013)

Research on Intelligent Cloud Manufacturing Resource Adaptation Methodology Based on Reinforcement Learning

Zixuan Fang[1], Qiao Hu[2], Hairong Sun[3], Genxin Chen[4], and Jin Qi[1,5](✉)

[1] School of Internet of Things, Nanjing University of Posts and Telecommunications, Nanjing 210023, China
qijin@njupt.edu.cn
[2] School of Computer Science, Nanjing University of Posts and Telecommunications, Nanjing 210023, China
[3] China Mobile Online Service Company Limited, Nanjing 210029, China
[4] School of Automation, Nanjing University of Posts and Telecommunications, Nanjing 210023, China
[5] Nanjing Pharmaceutical Co., Ltd., Nanjing 21000, China

Abstract. In cloud manufacturing, an allocation platform integrates resources and assign tasks manufacturers. Improper allocation algorithm causes wasting of resources and budget. In this paper, a new bilateral adaptation algorithm based on Q-learning and improved Gale-Shapley algorithm is proposed for the manufacturer-dealer bilateral adaptation problem in the intelligent cloud manufacturing environment. The main idea of the algorithm is to first construct a manufacturer-to-dealer distance-based ordering model as well as a dealer-to-manufacturer Quality of Service based (QoS-based) ordering model, and then, a basic bilateral allocation result is obtained by the improved Gale-Shapley algorithm, which will allocate dealers and manufacturers into pairs depend on the overall cost and degree of satisfaction. At last, with the obtained pairing scheme, a more rational pairing approach can be obtained through the self-learning process in the Q-learning algorithm. Numerical experiment has been done and the proposed algorithm are compared with some traditional approaches. The experimental results show that the improved Gale-Shapley algorithm proposed in this paper obtains better results than other ways.

Keywords: Intelligent cloud manufacturing · Service resource adaptation · Gale-shapley · Reinforcement learning · Q-learning

1 Introduction

The concept of "cloud manufacturing" was proposed by academician Li Bohu and his team in 2009 and began the research and practice of "intelligent cloud manufacturing" in 2012 [1]. The so-called cloud manufacturing is a service-oriented, high-energy, low-consumption networked manufacturing new model, integrating cloud computing, Internet of Things, artificial intelligence, blockchain, edge computing and other technologies.

X. Sun et al. (Eds.): ICAIS 2021, LNCS 12736, pp. 155–166, 2021.
https://doi.org/10.1007/978-3-030-78609-0_14

Cloud manufacturing integrates manufacturing resources and service resources originally scattered around the world and control them through network platforms and other management tools. The production process of cloud manufacturing can be explained as the cloud manufacturing platform schedules the most appropriate manufacturing and service resources for the users (manufacturers, distributors and even users) through some kind of algorithm. Resource adaptation in the cloud manufacturing environment is a fairly important part of cloud manufacturing research. After receiving requests from various users in a certain period of time, the cloud manufacturing platform gives the best resource adaptation plan by considering the quality of service (QoS) resource, distance and various factors (time, cost, etc.).

In order to achieve the goal of service resource sharing, stable cooperation and rapid response to user needs in the intelligent cloud manufacturing environment, it is necessary to study the intelligent cloud manufacturing service resource adaptation method. For the study of stable allocation problem in the cloud manufacturing environment, Zhang Di builds a bilateral match multi-objective optimization model by transforming language preference information into bilateral match's satisfaction, introducing stable match constraints, and aiming at maximizing the match satisfaction of each party subject, to obtain bilateral match results [2]. In order to select stable partners for manufacturers and distributors in supply chain production and marketing, Shan et al. proposed a satisfaction evaluation method based on historical transaction information, introduced stable matching constraints, built a single-objective 0–1 integer planning model for maximizing overall satisfaction, and obtained bilateral matching results [3]. J. Wang et al. introduced a minimum QoS for task thresholds to guarantee the perceived quality of a single task, allowing the overall utility of QoS for multitasking to be optimized [4]. L. Pu proposed an ordered supply and demand side matching model on an online real-time platform, in which the demand side selects the supplier by maximizing the sum of the expectations of the service quality [5]. Y. Liu et al. transformed the supply and demand side matching problem into a travel agent problem, where the Suppliers are filtered by the traveler's least path indicator [6].

However, such researches are not fully considered, usually only one party's preferred demand or satisfaction is considered, and the satisfaction evaluation is not objective, which is not conducive to the development of long-term stable and win-win partnership; Therefore, in this thesis, multiple factors are fully considered in the construction of the manufacturer-distributor service resource adaptation model, the construction of the manufacturer-distributor choice model, and in order to improve the satisfaction of the cooperation between the two parties, the construction of the manufacturer-distributor bilateral adaptation model are based on the ordinal values according to the respective ranking of the two parties.

Research on solving stable fitness algorithms was first conducted by Roth and Shapley, American scholars who won the Nobel Prize in economics, who proposed the famous Gale-Shapley mechanism [7]. However, the Gale-Shapley algorithm is suitable for dealing with the bilateral fitness problem of dual-objective optimization and does not consider the situation of dealing with multi-objective optimization problems.

Currently, some scholars are also using machine learning for solving task scheduling problems, Bernd et al. introduced reinforcement learning to the assembly line in semiconductor factories, combining deep neural networks and reinforcement learning to solve the allocation problem during chip processing [8]. Chen et al. introduced reinforcement learning in multi-objective optimization to make factories in cloud manufacturing environment work more efficiently [9]. However, these articles using reinforcement learning do not consider the relationship between the user's own satisfaction and the fit between the service provider and the service responder. Therefore, in this paper, the Q-learning algorithm in reinforcement learning is used to train on the initial fit results provided by the GS algorithm.

In summary, this thesis addresses the adaptation problem of service resources for intelligent cloud manufacturing, divides the service resources into two levels of manufacturers and distributors according to the hierarchy, considers the factors such as massive multidimensional service resources, resource fragmentation, and poor collaborative interaction ability in intelligent cloud manufacturing, and establishes a manufacturer-dealer bilateral adaptation model based on geographic distance, QoS, and other factors. The model is solved by using the Gale-Shapley algorithm improved through Q-learning. The experimental results show that the improved Gale-Shapley algorithm proposed in this paper obtains better results than other traditional algorithms.

2 Description of the Problem

2.1 Stable Adaptation of Manufacturer-Distributor Service Resources

In the multi-level multi-subjects of the intelligent cloud manufacturing service resource supply chain, there are three subjects, namely, the source of the manufacturer, the middle of the distributor and the final customer, this paper mainly discusses the first two subjects, namely, the manufacturer - distributor, the first two subjects adaptation process between the manufacturer and the distributor is a kind of multi-to-many bilateral adaptation relationship. In this paper, according to the hierarchical relationship, if the manufacturer and the distributor cannot form a stable adaptation of the relationship, the situation will cause overall efficiency loss to the multi-level multi-subjects of intelligent cloud manufacturing service resources, so the stable adaptation of the first two layers is to feed the need of the multi-level multi-subjects of the inevitable requirements of sustainable operation.

Suppose there are i manufacturers, using the set $Z = \{z_1, z_2, \ldots z_i\}$ to denote; there are j dealers, using the set $X = \{x_1, x_2, \ldots x_j\}$ to denote, where the number of distributors j is less than the number of manufacturers i, i.e. $j \leq i$. Each manufacturer and distributor have a number of different attributes. x_j represent the features of the j th distributor. $x_j = (X_{LO_j}, X_{LA_j}, X_{RT_j}, X_{P_j})$ in which X_{LO_j}, X_{LA_j} represent, respectively, the longitude and latitude of the geographical location of the dealership, which can be defined by planar 2D coordinates. X_{RT_j} is the service response time of all manufacturers for the jth dealer, the shorter the service response time, the faster the manufacturer can get ready to respond to the dealer's needs. $X_{RT_j} = \{x_{rt_{i1}}, x_{rt_{i2}}, x_{rt_{i3}}, \ldots x_{rt_{ij}}\} \cdot x_{rt_{in}}$ means the service response time of the nth manufacture to the i th distributor. X_{P_j} Indicates the production per unit of time of each manufacturer for the manufacturing task proposed by the distributor. $Xp_j = \{xp_{i1}, xp_{i2}, xp_{i3}, \ldots xp_{ij},\} \cdot xp_{in}$ Indicates the unit time production of the nth manufacturer for the manufacturing task proposed by the i th distributor. Each z_i exists in manufacturer collection Z is represented by a tuple as follows, when $z_i \in Z$. $z_i = z_i = (Z_{LO_i}, Z_{LA_i})$ in which Z_{LO_i}, Z_{LA_i} They represent, respectively, the longitude and latitude of the geographic location of the manufacturer and can be defined by planar 2D coordinates.

Since both the manufacturer and the distributor have their own selection constraints, the manufacturer and the distributor that meet the selection criteria are represented by an ordered pair, the relationship Pair $\subseteq Z \cup X$. For each dealer x_j, both can select any manufacturer as their pair, denoted as $X(z_i) = \{(z_i \in Z, x_j \in X) : (z_i, x_j) \in \text{Pair}\}$. Similarly, for each manufacturer z_i, there exist a collection of selectable distributors $Z(x_j)$, which are indicated as follows, $Z(x_j) = \{(x_j \in X, z_i \in Z)(x_j, z_i) \in \text{Pair}\}$.

According to the above definitions and descriptions, any manufacture can find a distributor to be paired with. Due to $j \leq i$, the collection of dealers has $i - j$ individual subjects are not adapted. Specifically, from the first manufacturer z_1, the allocation will start with a collection of dealers $X = \{x_1, x_2, \ldots x_j\}$ and select a distributor to form an adapted subject pair with; in the case of the manufacturer z_1 after identifying a suitable dealer target, the whole process will be continued with the second manufacturer z_2 where the dealer selects one of the remaining $j - 1$ subjects in the set X to form an adaptation pair with it, and so on for the manufacturer.z_i, one of the remaining $j - i + 1$ subjects in the dealer set X can be selected to form a matching subject pair with it.

After the allocation, we will use the features we use such as the unit produce time and response time to evaluate the effect of the allocation.

2.2 Bilateral Matching Model Based on Manufacturer-Dealer Satisfaction

Manufacturers' Preference Sequence for Satisfaction with Distributors Based on Geographical Distance. The farther the distance is, the higher the logistics speed, time and cost of the manufacturing equipment required by the manufacturer to deliver its services will increase, thus indirectly affecting the quality of the manufacturer's products and services as well as the satisfaction of the distributors of the service demand. Therefore, the manufacturer ranks the distance from the distributor through longitude and latitude to establish the manufacturer's preference list.

The geographical locations of manufacturers and distributors are provided by GPS and their data can be obtained from the literature [11]. And the distance between each manufacturer and each distributor is calculated as follows.

$$D_{X \to Z} = 2 \times \cos^{-1} \sqrt{sin^2\frac{a}{2} + \cos(Lat1) \times \cos(Lat2) \times sin^2\frac{b}{2}} \times 6378.137 \quad (1)$$

$D_{X \to Z}$ represents the distance between manufacturer X and distributor Z, a refers to the Latitude difference and b refers to the Longitude difference, $Lat1$ represents the manufacturer's Latitude, $Lat2$ represents the distributor's Longitude.

The manufacturer's list of distributors is arranged in ascending order according to the relative distance size value of equation to form the manufacturer's preference list.

Dealers to The Manufacturer's QoS-Based Ranking Model. In this paper, we focus on the most commonly used service attribute indexes, reputation, time and reliability to assess manufacturer's capability. The QoS of dealer *i* for manufacturer *j* is calculated as follows.

$$Z_{i,j}^{\mathrm{QoS}} = h\left(Z_{i}^{time}\right) \times Z_{i,j}^{faith} \times Z_{i,j}^{production} \tag{2}$$

$h\left(Z_{i,j}^{time}\right)$ Indicate a decreasing function of the demand response time of an individual manufacturer to distributor *j*. As the manufacturer responds more quickly, the QoS will also decrease, so the decreasing function is used to represent the effect of response time on QoS. The formula is as follows.

$$h\left(Z_{i,j}^{time}\right) = 1 - \max\left(0, \min\left[log_{X_j^{time}}\left(Z_{i,j}^{time}\right), 1\right]\right) \tag{3}$$

X_j^{time} means the response time limits for services rendered on behalf of Dealer *j*. $Z_{i,j}^{time}$ will represent the response time of manufacturer *i* to a request from distributor *j*.

$Z_{i,j}^{faith}$ denote the reliability of the *j* th manufacturer for the *j* th distributor, based on the information the distributor knows, the higher manufacturer in the preference list, the better the reliability is.

$$Z_{i,j}^{faith} = \frac{1}{rank_j(i)} \tag{4}$$

$rank_j(i)$ is the ranking of manufacturer i in dealer *j*'s preference list.

$Z_{i,j}^{production}$ represents the output per unit of time of the i-th manufacturer's demand for the *j* th dealer's service, and the higher the output per unit of time, the higher the QoS rating.

Finally. $Z_{i,j}^{\mathrm{QoS}}$ need to be normalized. To standardize the treatment of indicators with different units and different ranges of values, this chapter uses the extreme difference transformation method to normalize the raw data values, mapping all the data on the interval [0, 1], which is calculated as follows.

$$sta\left(Z_i^{\mathrm{QoS}}\right) = \begin{cases} \dfrac{\max\left(Z_i^{\mathrm{QoS}}\right) - Z_i^{\mathrm{QoS}}}{\max\left(Z_i^{\mathrm{QoS}}\right) - \min\left(Z_i^{\mathrm{QoS}}\right)}, & \max\left(Z_i^{\mathrm{QoS}}\right) - \min\left(Z_i^{\mathrm{QoS}}\right) \neq 0 \\ 0, & \max\left(Z_i^{\mathrm{QoS}}\right) - \min\left(Z_i^{\mathrm{QoS}}\right) = 0 \end{cases} \tag{5}$$

Among them $Z_{i,j}^{\mathrm{QoS}}$ means the raw QoS attribute indicator values $sta\left(Z_{i,j}^{\mathrm{QoS}}\right)$ is the value of the standardized processed QoS attribute indicator.

3 Solving Algorithm Design

This chapter proposes allocation algorithms that combine the Gale-Shapley algorithm and the Q-learning algorithm to simultaneously achieve improved user experience and reduced service costs by improving manufacturer-distributor satisfaction with adaptation and reducing manufacturing time.

3.1 The Gale-Shapley Algorithm

The Gale-Shapley algorithm is often used to solve bilateral matching problems, and this algorithm has the advantages of easy implementation, efficient adaptation, and robustness.

There are various models of manufacturer and distributor production and distribution systems, with a strict one-to-one model where the number of manufacturers is equal to the number of distributors, which occurs in the process of adapting service resources for intelligent cloud manufacturing with multiple levels and entities in Japan, similar to the marriage matching problem.

Algorithm 1. Gale-Shapley Bilateral Adaptation Algorithm

```
input: attribute matrix with geographic location of manufacturer and distributor, production attributes;
output: Allocation results;

1:  calculate the two-dimensional distance between manufacturers and distributors by means of latitude and longitude data and formulas;
2:  construct a list of manufacturer's preferences for distributors by distance;
3:  calculate the distributor's list of preferences with manufacturers;
4:  for all distributors
5:      if all distributors are selected:
6:          skip to step 19
7:      else:
8:          select an unmatched distributor i from the list of distributors
9:          retrieve the manufacturer at position j from this distributor's preference list ;
10:          if the jth manufacturer has not been paired before:
11:              add pair(i,j) to allocation result
12:         else if the jth manufacturer already has a match:
13:             compare the previous distributor i' with the distributor inow doing the match;
14:                 if rank(i) > rank(i'):
15:                     add pair(i,j) to allocation result
16:                 else:
17:                     j = j + 1
18:                     jump to step 8;
19: at this time, all dealers have been adapted;
```

3.2 Q-learning Algorithm

Q-learning is a type of unsupervised learning in reinforcement learning, in which the learning process does not require external guidance, but rather changes or continues its direction through the results obtained by interacting with the environment during the learning process. q-learning has five components: subject, state, action, reward, and q-table. Prior to learning, the first state is initialized randomly, and for each step in the round, the first action a is selected from the Q-Table using a strategy based on the current state s (if the Q Table does not have that state, create rows s-a and initialize all to 0), then change the value of a, and continue the cycle to the end.

The formula for updating each value in the Q-learning algorithm for each value in the Q table is as follows.

$$Q_{t+1}(s,a) = Q_t(s,a) + \alpha\Big(r + \gamma \max_a Q(S_{t+1},a) - Q_t(s,a)\Big) \tag{6}$$

Among them $Q_t(s,a)$ denotes the value of Q before the update. $Q_{t+1}(s,a)$ denotes the value of Q after an update has been made $\alpha(0 < \alpha \leq 1)$ is the learning rate, which represents the importance that the learning subject attaches to future learning benefits during the learning process, the larger the learning rate, the more important the learning subject attaches to future benefits. r is the value of the gain after the operation has been performed. γ is the discount rate, the larger the discount rate, the more important the learning process places on the rewards that follow.

3.3 Bilateral Adaptation Algorithm Design Based on Gale-Shapley and Q-learning

To address the multi-objective problem of improving user satisfaction and manufacturing time spent in the bilateral adaptation problem, this paper divides the algorithm into two stages of Gale-Shapley ordering and Q-learning to find a better solution. The algorithm first obtains an allocation solution that takes into account both distance and QoS factors through the Gale-Shapley algorithm, but due to the many factors and optimization goals that the algorithm needs to consider, the Gale-Shapley algorithm may not always be able to obtain the best optimal solution. After that, in the reinforcement learning model, it will be more efficient to use the allocation solution that has already been derived by the Gale-Shapley algorithm as the initial state than when the zero state is used as the initial state. This is because the GS algorithm already yields a superior result.

In this paper, the Q-learning algorithm is used to improve the resulting ranking results by treating all manufacturer-distributor adaptations as states in Q-learning, treating replacing a manufacturer in an allocation as an action, replacing the currently specified manufacturer-distributor adaptation pair, and moving to the next adaptation pair can be viewed as moving from the current state to the next state. In the Q-learning process, however, since each state update replaces only one adaptation pair of an adaptation case, the reward value is set to the following.

$$r = rank_{now} - rank_{change} \tag{7}$$

Among them $rank_{now}$ is considered as the previous manufacturer's ranking in the dealership $rank_{change}$ is considered as the manufacturer's ranking in the dealership after the change. After the specified number of iterations, the Q-table will eventually converge to a fixed value nearby. After the iterations are completed for arranged times, for each state, i.e., dealer, the manufacturer that maximizes its Q value is selected until all dealers have completed the adaptation.

Algorithm 2. Improved Bilateral Adaptation Algorithm

input: GS algorithm allocation results
output: advanced results

1: calculation of reward value;
2. number of ***episode*** $= k$
3: **for** each ***episode***:
4: select the allocation result from the Gale-Shapley algorithm as the initial statet_{now};
5: **for** each distributor-manufacturer pair:
6: change the dealer's pair according to a custom selection strategy and get next status;
7: update Q-Table;
8: $t_{now} = t_{next}$;
9: jump to step 3;
10: after completing the cycle according to the set number of iterations, get the allocation result after training;
11: calculate satisfaction, time cost,
12: output results

4 Experimental Results and Analysis

All the experiments in this paper are based on data collected online by researchers at The Chinese University of Hong Kong [10, 11], and the dataset covers the latitude and longitude data at which each cloud manufacturing service provider and the user requesting the service are located, the response time of each manufacturer to the service provided by each distributor, and the unit time production of each manufacturer to the task proposed by each distributor. The GS algorithm is compared with two other algorithms (Table 1).

Table 1. Experimental parameter settings

Parameters	Values
Learning rate	0.9
Discount factor	0.5
Number of manufacturers	10, 15, 25, 30, 35, 40, 45, 50, 55
Number of distributors	10, 15, 25, 30, 35, 40, 45, 50, 55

The parameter settings in this paper are shown in the table below. Wherein, the learning rate and the discount factor are used to determine a good range of values through the experience gained from a large number of experiments. The final result is that the best bilateral fit is obtained when the learning rate is 0.9 and the discount factor is 0.5. To verify the robustness of the experimental results, different manufacturer and distributor number sizes were set up.

The evaluation metrics for the completed allocation use the sum of QoS quality, sum of satisfaction, and total reliability to compare the performance of the three algorithms: the stable matching algorithm, the greedy algorithm, and the random matching algorithm.

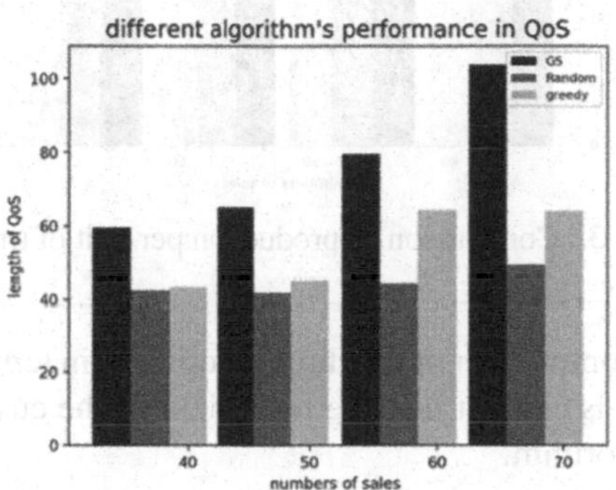

Fig. 1. Comparison of the three algorithms QoS

The Quality of Service Sum (QoS) depends on the manufacturer's reputation value, reliability and safety and the time required to complete the task. This paper sets up different numbers of dealers and manufacturers, and Fig. 1 shows that the improved GS and greedy algorithms proposed in this paper perform much better than random matching algorithms in terms of service quality summation.

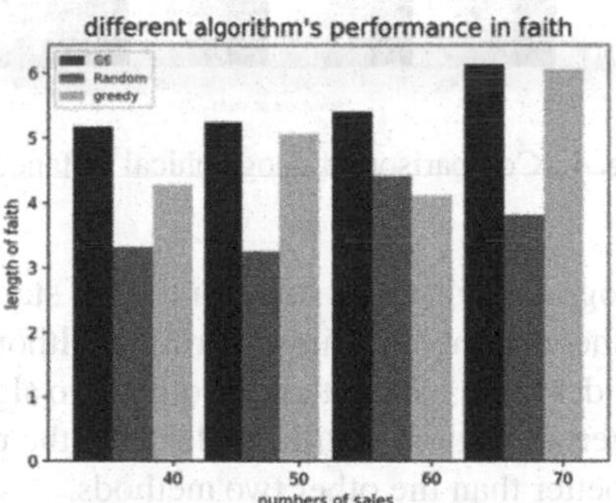

Fig. 2. Reliability comparison

Subsequently, Fig. 2 shows the comparison of the total user reliability between the stable adaptation algorithm and the greedy algorithm. It is clear that the total user reliability obtained by the improved GS stable fitting algorithm is always higher than the total user reliability obtained by the greedy algorithm. It can be seen that with the increase in the number of dealers. The lead of the stable fitting algorithm over the greedy algorithm is also increasing.

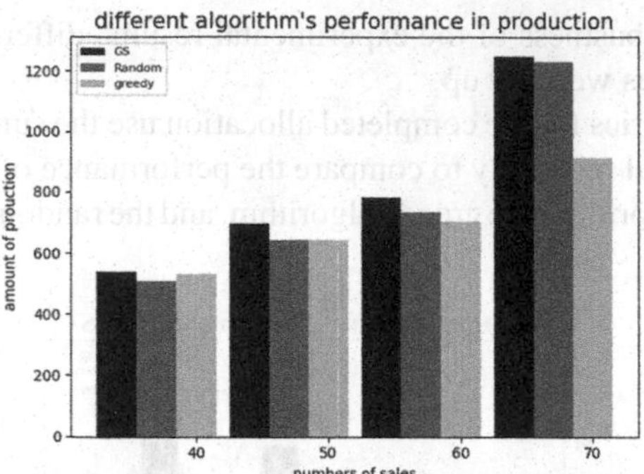

Fig. 3. Comparison of production per unit of time

Figure 3 shows the comparison of the three algorithms in terms of yield for different number of customers. It is evident that the total yield of the customers is increased by the stable adaptation algorithm.

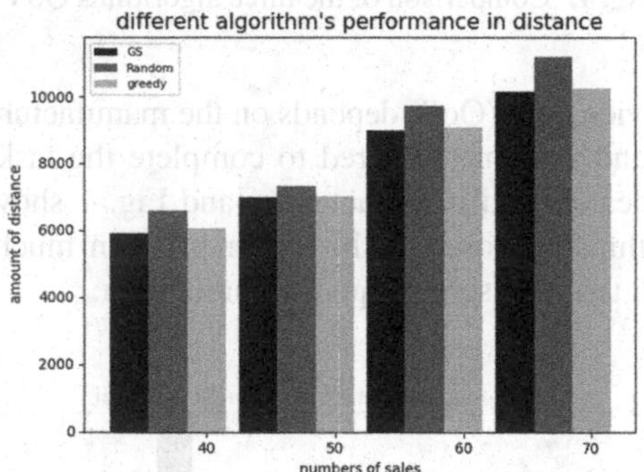

Fig. 4. Comparison of geographical distances

Figure 4 shows the geographic distance sums for the GS stable adaptation algorithm, the greedy algorithm and the random matching algorithm. Although the GS stable allocation algorithm has to consider more factors than the other two algorithms, the geographic distance sum obtained after allocation is still smaller than the other two algorithms, so the result is still slightly better than the other two methods.

Finally, this paper proposes a Gale-Shapley fitness game selection method (stable fitness method) improved by reinforcement learning that has addressed the problem of multi-manufacturer to multi-distributor resource allocation in intelligent cloud manufacturing. The proposed model can assign manufacturers to multiple distributors based on their preferences and distributor preferences. Simulations using simulated datasets have shown that the improved GS algorithm can achieve better reliability, QoS and user satisfaction. In general, the stable adaptation algorithm shows higher efficiency and scalability in different situations. The improved GS algorithm in this thesis is far superior to the random matching scheme and is also significantly superior to the greedy many-to-many adaptation algorithm, indicating that the Gale-Shapley algorithm improved in this thesis is relatively stable and efficient.

5 Conclusion

This paper focuses on manufacturing service resource management, the Q-learning-based Gale-Shapley algorithm is proposed for the problem of stable matching between manufacturers and distributors in manufacturing service resources. The algorithm firstly uses the Gale-Shapley algorithm to pair manufacturers and distributors to obtain a more stable pairing result, and then adopts the Q-learning algorithm on the basic result to achieve a better result. The experimental results show that the Q-learning-based Gale-Shapley algorithm has outstanding performance on the bilateral fitness problem, indicating that the algorithm is effective, and in future work, we will consider introducing deep reinforcement learning into the model and optimizing the model structure to make the model more realistic.

Acknowledgement. This paper was supported by the National Natural Science Foundation of China (61802208 and 61772286), Project funded by China Postdoctoral Science Foundation (2019M651923 and 2020M671552), Natural Science Foundation of Jiangsu Province of China (BK20191381), Primary Research & Development Plan of Jiangsu Province Grant (BE2019742), the Opening Project of Jiangsu Key Laboratory of Data Science and Smart Software (No. 2020DS301).

References

1. Li, B., et al.: Cloud manufacturing - a new model of service-oriented networked Manufacturing. Comput. Integrated Manuf. Syst. **16**(01), 1–7+16 (2010)
2. Di, Z., Tao, S., Ye, C., Liangqi, W.: A stable bilateral matching decision method based on language preference information. Oper. Manage. **28**(02), 60–66 (2019)
3. Shan, X., Wang, F., He, X., Jiang, G.: A study of supply chain production and marketing cooperation based on stable bilateral matching. Comput. Eng. Appl. **52**(23), 260–265+270 (2016)
4. Wang, J., et al.: Multi-task allocation in mobile crowd sensing with individual task quality assurance. IEEE Trans. Mob. Comput. **17**(9), 2101–2113 (2018)
5. Pu, L., Chen, X., Xu, J., Fu, X.: Crowd foraging: a qos-oriented self-organized mobile crowdsourcing framework over opportunistic networks. IEEE J. Sel. Areas Commun. **35**(4), 848–862 (2017)
6. Liu, Y., Guo, B., Wang, Y., et al.: TaskMe: Multi-task allocation in mobile crowd sensing. In: Proceedings of the 2016 ACM International Joint Conference on Pervasive and Ubiquitous Computing, pp. 403–414 (2016)
7. Wang, J., Huang, Q., Hu, W., et al.: Shapley value based customers voluntary demand response program: a stackelberg game approach. In: 2019 IEEE Innovative Smart Grid Technologies-Asia (ISGT Asia), pp. 3051–3056. IEEE (2019)
8. Waschneck, B., Reichstaller, A., Belzner, L., et al.: Optimization of global production scheduling with deep reinforcement learning. Proc. CIRP **72**(1), 1264–1269 (2018)

9. Chen, S., Fang, S., Tang, R.: A reinforcement learning based approach for multi-projects scheduling in cloud manufacturing. Int. J. Prod. Res. **57**(10), 3080–3098 (2019)
10. Zheng, Z., Zhang, Y., Lyu, M.R.: Investigating QoS of real-world web services. IEEE Trans. Serv. Comput. **7**(1), 32–39 (2014)
11. Zheng, Z., Zhang, Y., Lyu, M.R.: Distributed qos evaluation for real-world web services. In: 2010 IEEE International Conference on Web Services, pp. 83–90. IEEE (2010)

Automatic CT Lesion Detection Based on Feature Pyramid Inference with Multi-scale Response

Yangyang Tang[1], Zhe Liu[1](✉), Yuqing Song[1], Kai Han[1], Jun Su[1], Wenqiang Wang[1], Fan Hu[2], and Jiawen Zhang[3]

[1] School of Computer Science and Communications Engineering, Jiangsu University, Zhenjiang 212013, China
1000004088@ujs.edu.cn

[2] School of Financial Management, College of Mobile Telecommunications Chongqing, University of Posts and Telecom, Chongqing 401520, China

[3] Huashan Hospital, Fudan University, Department of Radiology, 12 Middle Wulumuqi Road, Shanghai 200040, China

Abstract. In modern medical applications, computed tomography image is used as one of the most useful tools for diagnosis and localization of lesions. It can provide patients with precise information about the location and size of their tumor lesions. Traditional medical diagnosis is not only very time consuming but also not very accurate. Nowadays, the automatic detection of lesions on computed tomography has become a research area of great interest, and researchers aim to use computer-aided diagnosis to assist in clinical medical diagnosis. However, for current detection algorithms, the accuracy of automatic lesion detection is still low, especially for small lesions. In this paper, to improve the accuracy of detection of small lesions, we propose a Multi-Scale Response Module (MSR) that incorporates global attention into Feature Pyramid Network (FPN) build on backbone. At each pyramid level, the proposed Aggregated Dilation Block (ADB) is used to capture the variations in the fine-grained scales. The response of the network to small lesion features is then reinforced by the Global Attention Block (GAB). We build a Feature Pyramid Network (FPN) based on the highly responsive output of the MSR module, with each layer of the FPN fusing high semantic information from low resolution layers. The experimental results show that our method has a higher detection accuracy with mAP value of 58.4 and a high sensitivity compared to the state-of-the-art methods.

Keywords: Deep lesion detection · Attention mechanism · Dilated convolution · RCNN

1 Introduction

According to the most recent statistics, we found that the diseases with the highest mortality rates in the world are malignant tumors, heart disease, pneumonia, and cerebrovascular diseases. In addition, the number of deaths caused by malignant tumors is

X. Sun et al. (Eds.): ICAIS 2021, LNCS 12736, pp. 167–179, 2021.
https://doi.org/10.1007/978-3-030-78609-0_15

increasing each year [1]. Therefore, accurate diagnosis is of great significance to the discovery and treatment of tumor disease. Diagnostic imaging is the most common method used to detect cancer, especially the rapid development of medical imaging technology in recent years has made it possible to obtain high-resolution CT and MRI datasets. At the same time, it also makes it possible to train high-resolution CT images to detect lesions.

In the diagnosis based on CT images, clinicians judge the presence of tumor based on their subjective medical knowledge and relevant laboratory report data, which is largely dependent on the experience of the doctor. However, with the rapid advancement of medical information systems in recent years, doctors now can easily access the medical image data of patients to facilitate the diagnosis of the disease, the massive task of analyzing lesions on computed tomography (CT) and magnetic resonance images (MRI) images is onerous for the physician. Therefore, we propose to automate the detection of tumors in computed tomography images by computer, aiming at alleviating the burden on doctors and expecting to achieve higher accuracy of analysis.

Currently, many laboratories and scholars in the field of computer vision and image recognition are attempting to introduce object detection techniques in the medical field. For example, [2–8] showcase some of the explorations that researchers have made in the field of medicine in recent years. However, the size of tumors varies greatly within a certain range. For example, in DeepLesion dataset, the size of the lesion area varies from 0.21 mm to 342.5 mm. As for the treatment of such large differences in spatial scale changes, the above methods failed to deal well with the low precision of detection of small lesions. Especially for small lesion regions detection, which is an important evidence to detect early lesions in the body, it is necessary to improve the detection accuracy for small lesions.

In this paper, we propose a fine-grained lesion detection method with a novel multi-scale global attention mechanism. For the samples of small lesions in dataset (DeepLesion), we improve the network structure based on the two-stage network of Faster RCNN and use ResNet101 network as backbone. First of all, we use dilation and erosion operations in a mathematical morphology approach to process the input CT images, which makes the diseased areas more visible. In order to fuse more semantic information when constructing the feature pyramid, we continue to deepen the network based on ResNet101 until the resolution of the feature map is 8×8. After up-sampling, the output of each layer residue block is fused with the high-resolution topographic map to preserve as much spatial and semantic information as possible at different scales. We then use multi-scale response (MSR) to facilitate lesion detection across fine-grained scales. Given a feature map with a specific resolution, the aggregated dilation block (ADB) in MSR is based on the split-transform merge principle, using the regional correlations in each pyramid feature generation block. As the dilation rate increases, new feature maps are generated from a wide range of contexts. Aggregated dilation blocks further increase the receptive fields of the top-down paths in the feature pyramid. The channel and spatial attention modules in the MSR then focus on the different lesion responses in feature maps. Finally, we re-sample the high-response features with the upper feature map and fuse it with the upper map again, which is then fed into the RPN to obtain the coordinates of the prediction score and the bounding box of the output category. The experiments show that the network using the MSR module has a significant improvement in accuracy compared to the original two-stage network.

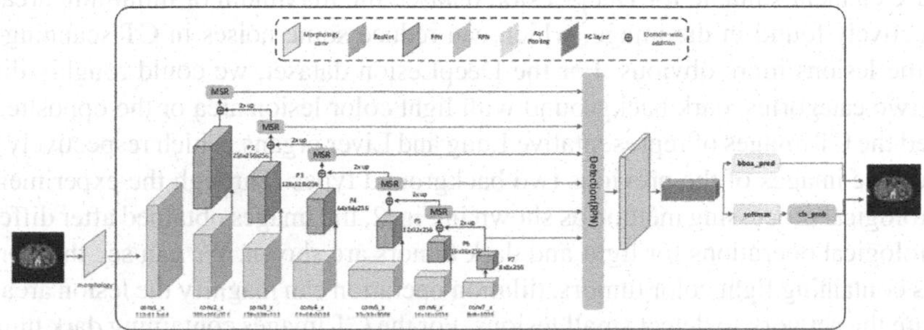

Fig. 1. The framework of the proposed lesion detection method

The main contributions of this work can be summarized as follows.

1) An Aggregated Dilation Block (ADB) is proposed. The block alleviates the shortcomings of the low-resolution feature layer in the network due to the large receptive field and the small target features are not obvious.
2) The Global Attention Block (GAB) is designed to reduce the influence of background noise and highlight the target features, which is effective for detecting obscure objects at different scales.

2 Proposed Method

The structure of framework we proposed is illustrated in Fig. 1. Firstly, we selected different morphological operations (dilation and erosion) for tumors with different colors in each organ as pre-processing, and then these feature-enhanced maps were fed into the network. We extracted features from the ResNet backbone (P2-P7) (Sect. 2.2). The extracted features are further processed by ADB (Sect. 2.3) and GAB (Sect. 2.4) in the MSR module. The output of the MSR is subsequently fed into the RPN while being up-sampled and summed with the output of the previous layer of high-resolution feature maps to create a feature pyramid network constructed from the output of the MSR module. Finally, the network undergoes Softmax loss (detection of classification probability) and Smooth L1 loss (detection of frame regression) to train classification probability and bounding box regression.

2.1 Mathematical Morphology Operations

Mathematical morphology image processing refers to a series of image processing techniques to enhance image shape features. The basic idea of morphology is feature enhancement by using a special structure element to measure or extract the corresponding shape or feature when given an input image. Common morphological processing methods include: erosion, dilation, opening and closing. Morphological operations rely on the correlation of pixel values rather than their absolute values, so they are very suitable for binary image processing. By constructing the corresponding mathematical morphology structure element suitable for DeepLesion dataset, the maximum or minimum area can be effectively found in the image, which can reduce some noises in CT scanning and make the lesions more obvious. For the DeepLesion dataset, we could roughly divide it into two categories, dark background with light color lesion area or the opposite. We selected the CT images of representative Lung and Liver organs, which respectively represented the images of the previous two background types. Through the experiment of morphological processing method as shown in Fig. 2, the images obtained after different morphological operations for light and dark tumors are shown. We can see that for CT images containing light color tumors, dilation operation can magnify the lesion area and facilitate the network to detect small lesions. For the CT images containing dark tumors, we can see that the tumor portion of the erosion manipulated images not only becomes larger, but also retains a lot of texture information. The formulas of dilation and erosion operations are shown as follows:

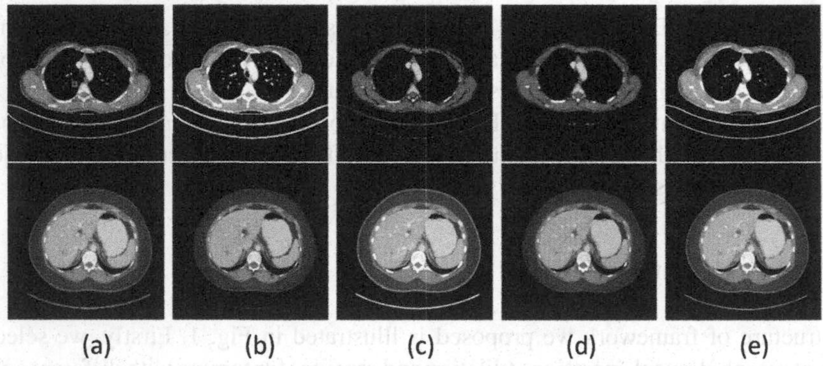

Fig. 2. The output of different colors tumors after morphological operations. Organs with representative light and dark colors of lesions in the dataset are shown. Where, (a)-(e) represent the labeled image, erosion, dilation, opening and closing respectively. First row is lung CT image and second row is liver CT image.

$$A \oplus B = \{x, y | (B)_{xy} \cap A \neq \varnothing\} \quad (1)$$

$$A \ominus B = \{x, y | (B)_{xy} \subseteq A\} \quad (2)$$

Where, $\oplus$ and $\ominus$ represent dilation and erosion respectively.

2.2 Feature Extraction Network

Faster-RCNN [9] is an object detection algorithm proposed by Kaiming He in 2015. Based on Fast-RCNN [10], this algorithm puts forward the RPN region proposal box

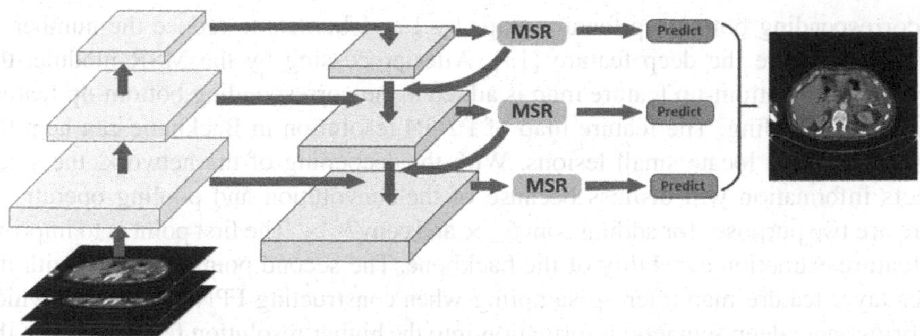

Fig. 3. The structure of FPN built based on the proposed MSR module

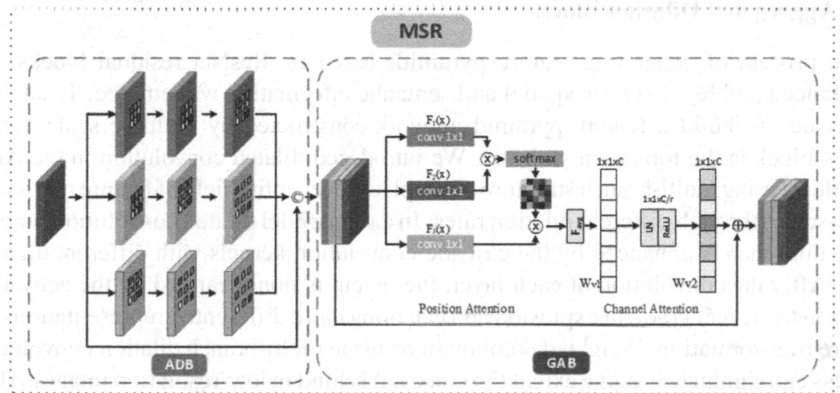

Fig. 4. The structure of MSR module. The detailed architecture of the Multi-Scale Response (MSR) module consists of two parts: Aggregated dilated block (ADB) in the blue dashed box on the left and Global attention Block (GAB) in the orange dashed box on the right. (Color figur online)

generation algorithm, which greatly improves object detection speed. The detection part is divided into four steps: The first step is to input the whole image into CNN for feature extraction. The second step is to generate the anchor box by RPN. In the third step, the RoI pooling layer makes each RoI generate a feature map with a fixed size. In the fourth step: Softmax Loss and Smooth L1 Loss are used for classification and Bounding box regression respectively.

We first modified the backbone of the model, the original backbone of Faster RCNN is VGG16 and we replaced it with ResNet101 [11]. The ResNet results on the ImageNet dataset [12] show that the performance of the residual structure is significantly better than the traditional convolution framework. Due to the down-sampling effect in traditional convolutional neural networks, small objects cannot acquire obvious features.

To address this issue. First of all, we deepened the backbone to continue to enhance the network's ability to extract deeper semantic information. conv2_ ×, conv3_ ×, conv4_ ×, conv5_ ×, conv6_ ×, and conv7_ × blocks are used to build the feature pyramid. P2, P3, P4, P5, P6 and P7 correspond to conv2_ × –conv7_ ×. We convolved the corresponding bottom-up feature maps by 1 × 1 kernels to reduce the number of channels and fuse the deep feature [13]. After processing by the MSR module, the corresponding bottom-up feature map is added to the corresponding bottom-up feature map by up-sampling. The feature map of P2–P4 resolution in Backbone can help the network find and locate small lesions. With the deepening of the network, the small objects information will dismiss because of the convolution and pooling operations. There are two purposes for adding conv6_ × and conv7_ ×. The first point is to improve the feature extraction capability of the backbone. The second point is to fuse with the upper layer feature map after up-sampling when constructing FPN, see Fig. 3, which can bring more deep semantic information into the higher resolution feature map in the upper layer.

2.3 Aggregated Dilation Block

In the process of generating feature pyramids based on ResNet residual blocks, the imbalanced problem between spatial and semantic information will emerge. To address this issue, we build a feature pyramid network constructed by multiple scale output of Res-block in the top-down pathway. We introduced dilated convolution in the ADB module by using multi-branch structure to adapt to the receptive field of feature maps with multi-scales through different dilation rates. In each parallel dilated convolution branch, the feature map is enhanced by the cascade convolution kernels with different dilation rates. After the convolution of each layer, the output is nonlinearized by the activation function to prevent gradient explosion and can bring more differential representations for feature transformation. Weighted combinations in the multi-branch dilation convolution process can eliminate to some extent the noise left behind in low-resolution images. Then we concatenate the output features of each branch with the original image to become an aggregated feature map. The feature map output by the ADB module has a larger receptive field.

In ADB module, $f \in R^{W \times D}$ is used to describe the architecture of ADB, where W and D are the width and depth of ADB respectively. The dilation rate of specific layer in ADB is expressed as f_{ij}, where $i = 1, 2, \ldots, W$ and $j = 1, 2, \ldots, D$ represent the index of width and depth respectively. The aggregated dilated operation is shown as follows:

$$\mathcal{F}(x) = \sum\nolimits_{i=1}^{W} \mathcal{T}_i(x|f_{i1}, f_{i2}, \ldots, f_{iD}) \tag{3}$$

where $T_i(x)$ represents the cascade-transformation.

As shown in Fig. 4, the parallel structure branch inside the ADB module is connected in series with convolution kernels with different dilation rates, and the output multi-scale feature map restores more detailed spatial information of the instance. It also provides more long-range context information for the construction of the feature pyramid. The receptive field of each layer is expressed as follows:

$$\mathcal{A}_{i0} = 1 \tag{4}$$

$$k_{ij} = k_{ij} + (k_{ij} - 1) \times (f_{ij} - 1) \tag{5}$$

$$\mathcal{A}_{ij} = r_{i,j-1} \times k_{ij} - \left(k_{ij} - 1\right) \times (\mathcal{A}_{i,j} - \prod_{k=1}^{j-1} s_k) \quad (6)$$

Where, $\mathcal{A}_{ij}$ denotes the receptive field, k_{ij} denotes the kernel size and s_k represents the stride.

From the formula, we can see that the size of the receptive field extracted by the convolution kernel with different dilation rates is also different. Usually in the feature extraction network, that is, in the backbone, the dilation convolution helps us identify the large object from the enlarged receptive field [14]. However, we added dilation convolution follows the output of the feature pyramid, expecting to provide more context spatial information to improve the detection accuracy of small lesions.

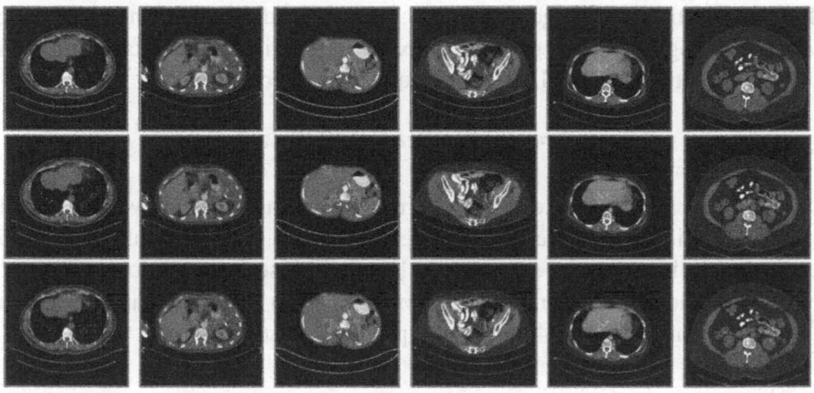

Fig. 5. Lesion detection results for sample CT images of various methods. Each row from top to bottom represents the label image, our proposed method, Faster R-CNN respectively

2.4 Global Attention Block

Inspired by the current popular attention mechanism, we propose a Global Attention Block (GAB). When the network's backbone extracts information from a large number of feature maps, the GAB allows the network to pay more attention to some vital information and improving the accuracy of detection. Each attention block consists of two parts: a spatial attention block and a channel attention block.

Object detection needs to be extremely sensitive to changes in spatial location, so we proposed spatial attention block which uses a self-attentive mechanism to model remote dependencies in order to enhance the network's global understanding of the visual scene. In addition, inspired by SENet [15], we proposed a channel attention block that aims to focus on the feature information we need.

We converted the input feature map x into three paths F_1, F_2 and F_3, where $F_1(x) = W_1x$ and $F_2(x) = W_2x$. Firstly, obtaining the attention map of the long-range correlation between each position in the feature map throughS_{ij}, where$S_{ij} = F_1(x_i)^T \otimes F_2(x_j)$.$S_{ij}$ is transformed into $A_{i,j}$ by *softmax*, where, $A_{ij} = softmax(s_{ij})$ represents the relationship between the position of i and the position of j in the feature map, and then A_{ij} and F_3 are multiplied to query the response relationship between pixels on the feature map.

$$z_i = \sum_{j=1}^{N} A_{i,j} \otimes F3(x_j), F_3(x) = W_3 x \tag{7}$$

Where i represent the index of query position. $N = H \times W$ and N represents number of feature locations. ⊗ denotes matrix multiplication.

After the spatial attention block, we compress the global information into channels through global average pooling, the main difference between the SE block and the block we proposed is the fusion module, which reflects the different goals of the two blocks. The SE module uses re-adjustment to re-calibrate the importance of the channel, but it does not fully simulate the long-range correlation. We captured the long-range correlation by using addition to aggregate the global context to all positions. The detailed architecture of the global attention block (GAB) is formulated as follows:

$$y_i = x_i + W_{v2} ReLU(LN(W_{v1} z)) \tag{8}$$

Where $W_{v1} \in R^{\frac{C}{r} \times C}$, $W_{v2} \in R^{C \times \frac{C}{r}}$. In order to obtain the lightweight attribute of the channel attention block, we reduced the parameters of the module from C to C/r. Where r is the bottleneck ratio, setting r too large will lose feature information and vice versa will consume a lot of computation, so we need to strike a balance between two costs, we found that when r = 4, the model performs best.

3 Experiments and Results

3.1 Datasets

The DeepLesion is the largest open dataset of multi-category, lesion-level labeled clinical medical CT images ever published by an NIH Clinical Center. By training deep neural networks on this dataset, it will be possible to obtain a large-scale universal lesion detector that can more accurately and automatically measure the size of all lesions in the patient's body, allowing initial assessment of cancer system-wide. The dataset contains 32,735 labeled lesion instances from 4,427 independent, anonymous patients. The dataset covers a wide range of lesions involving the lung, liver, mediastinum (mainly lymph nodes), kidney, pelvis, bone, abdomen and other soft tissues. We used 70% samples of the dataset for training, 15% for validation, and 15% for testing.

3.2 Training Schedule

We set training learning rate to 0.008 and training momentum to 0.9; after 10,000 iterations, the training weights decayed to 0.001; the training batch is 128, the mini_batch is 2; and the learning process is 12 epochs. The initialization weights for P1–P5 are from the ImageNet pre-trained model, and for the deepened network part.

Table 1. mAP and AP of each lesion type on the official split set of DeepLesion.

Methods	Total	BN	AB	ME	LV	LU	KD	ST	PV
Baseline	0.484	0.524	0.512	0.549	0.549	0.582	0.419	0.436	0.368
Baseline + (Res101)	0.512	0.526	0.515	0.553	0.557	0.591	0.436	0.447	0.414
Baseline + + ADB	0.545	0.527	0.521	0.557	0.569	0.604	0.487	0.452	0.465
Baseline + + MSR (ours)	**0.584**	**0.531**	**0.534**	**0.563**	**0.573**	**0.659**	**0.532**	**0.471**	**0.533**

Table 2. An ablation study with various configurations of the proposed modules. Lesion detection sensitivity is reported at different false positive (FP) rates on the DeepLesion test set.

Method	FPs per image				
	0.5	1	2	4	8
Baseline	0.560	0.677	0.763	0.832	0.867
Baseline + (Res101)	0.592	0.693	0.788	0.843	0.871
Baseline + + ADB	0.615	0.719	0.804	0.851	0.887
Baseline + + MSR (ours)	**0.658**	**0.752**	**0.827**	**0.881**	**0.891**

We initialize the parameters randomly. We resized the input image to 512×512 size. The optimization algorithm we used is stochastic gradient descent (SGD). The training time of our detector is about 60 h, compared to one-stage detector we have drawbacks in training cost and test speed, but speed is not very important in medical image detection scenario, compared to the need to accurately detect the focal area.

3.3 Hardware and Software Setup

Experiments were conducted on a Workstation with IntelCore i7, 2.7 GHz CPU, 8 GB RAM under Ubuntu 18.4, and a NVIDIA GTX 2080 video processing card with 11 GB memory. Faster RCNN was deployed in pytorch 1.5.1 framework and based on python3.7, cuda 10.1 and cudnn 7.6.3.

3.4 Evaluation

We quoted two evaluation metrics in our subsequent ablation experiments and comparisons. In our experiments, the object detection accuracy was measured by mean Average Precision (mAP) when IoUthres = 0.5. Another evaluation metric is the average sensitivity values at different false positives rates (FROC) of the whole test set.

3.5 Results

Ablation Study

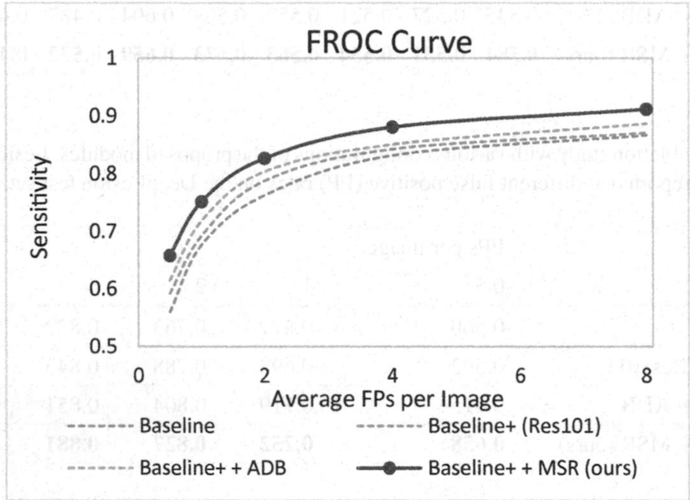

Fig. 6. Ablation FROC Curve on test set of official split test set of DeepLesion.

Table 3. mAP and AP of each lesion type of various methods on the official split test set of DeepLesion.

Methods	Total	BN	AB	ME	LV	LU	KD	ST	PV
YOLOv3 [16]	0.468	0.371	0.372	0.587	0.524	0.562	0.373	0.403	0.435
RetinaNet [17]	0.510	0.539	0.430	0.555	0.524	0.612	0.424	0.455	0.421
3DCE, 3 slices [5]	0.506	0.434	0.424	0.522	0.543	0.633	0.426	0.421	0.423
3DCE, 9 slices [5]	0.544	0.492	0.468	**0.577**	0.564	**0.663**	0.480	0.441	0.470
Ours	**0.584**	**0.531**	**0.534**	0.563	**0.573**	0.659	**0.532**	**0.471**	**0.533**

The proposed network consists of three main components: Faster R-CNN, ADB and GAB. In Table 1 and Table 2, Baseline denotes the original Faster R-CNN model, and Baseline + (Res101) denotes the method for deepening the backbone mentioned in Sect. 2.2. To assess the validity of each module, we performed ablation studies on the DeepLesion dataset. From Table 1, we can see that the original model was improved by our proposed method and the mAP values were improved to 10%. Based on the coarse lesion types provided by DeepLesion for each CT slice, we calculated the AP for each lesion type. Besides, the table shows that the AP values were increased by different magnitudes for different sites. The metrics assessed in Table 2 are the average sensitivity

Table 4. Comparison of the proposed method with state-of-the-art methods on the DeepLesion test set. Lesion detection sensitivity values are reported at different false positive (FP) rates.

Method	FPs per image				
	0.5	1	2	4	8
RetinaNet [17]	0.458	0.542	0.625	0.698	0.742
YOLOv3 [16]	0.520	0.626	0.719	0.795	0.843
Mask R-CNN [18]	0.398	0.527	0.656	0.777	0.852
ULDor [4]	0.529	0.648	0.748	0.844	0.861
3DCE, 3, slices [5]	0.569	0.673	0.756	0.816	0.858
3DCE, 9, slices [5]	0.593	0.707	0.791	0.843	0.878
3DCE, 27, slices [5]	0.625	0.733	0.807	0.857	**0.891**
Ours	**0.658**	**0.752**	**0.827**	**0.881**	**0.891**

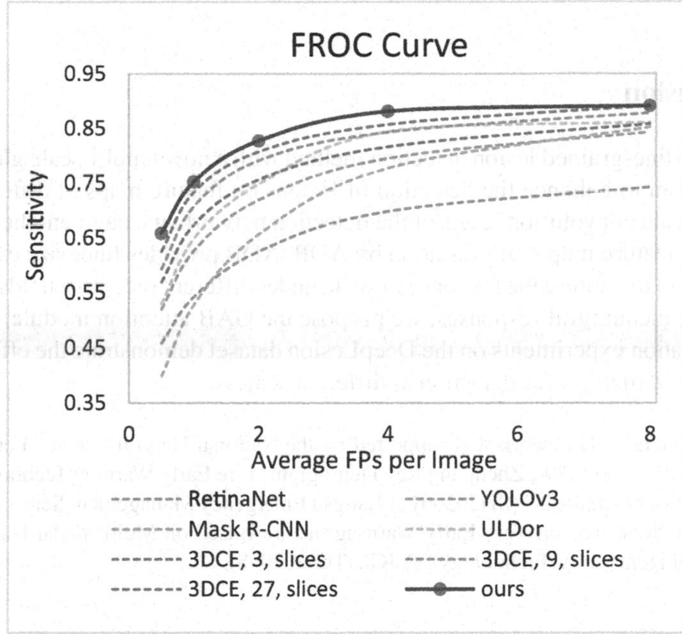

Fig. 7. FROC Curves of various methods.

values for the entire test set at different false positives rates. The comparison between different configurations shows that the proposed method achieves the highest sensitivity at different false positives rates. We plotted the FROC curves to make the results more intuitive, see Fig. 6. The detection results are also shown in Fig. 5.

Comparisons with State-of-the-Art. We compared our model with state-of-the-art methods. As can be seen from Table 2 and Table 4 we have chosen YOLOv3 [16], Reti-naNet [17], Mask R-CNN [18] and 3DCE [5] Yan et al. selected different numbers of slices and sent them to the detector. The detector generated 3D context information from different numbers of slices to help the detector make the final lesion prediction.From Table 3, we can see that the mAP value of our proposed detector is higher than other advanced detectors. Although it is slightly lower than 3DCE on the medi-astinum and lung organs, higher than other detectors on all other organs.

Table 4 shows the results of the evaluation, which indicates that our method is superior to the existing methods. We can see that the higher the number of CT slices that the detector selects as input for 3DCE, the higher sensitivity the detector has, due to the fact that the number of CT slices can provide more contextual information to the detector. However, in this paper, we obtained better results by selecting only a single CT slice as input. To make the comparison more straightforward, we plotted the FROC curves comparing the experimental results of several methods in Fig. 7.

In terms of the overall comparison results with state-of-the-art methods, our proposed method is superior in detection accuracy and sensitivity.

4 Conclusion

We propose a fine-grained lesion detection method with a novel multi-scale global attention mechanism to enhance the detection of lesions on feature maps of different sizes. In different scale convolution levels of the detection network, we augment the detector's awareness of feature map scale variation by ADB. ADB provides finer size estimates of the feature map to capture the response to scale under different receptive fields. To effectively choose meaningful responses, we propose the GAB attention module, where the results of ablation experiments on the DeepLesion dataset demonstrate the effectiveness of our proposed method for detection at different scales.

Acknowledgements. This work was supported by the National Natural Science Foundation of China (61976106, 61572239), Zhenjiang Key Deprogram "Fire Early Warning Technology Based on Multimodal Data Analysis" (SH2020011) Jiangsu Emergency Management Science and Technology Project "Research on Very Early Warning of Fire Based on Multi-modal Data Analysis and Multi-Intelligent Body Technology" (YJGL-TG-2020–8).

References

1. Contact Us|National Cancer Center Japan. https://www.ncc.go.jp/en/contact/index.html. Accessed 16 Sep. 16 2020
2. Lee, S.G., Bae, J.S., Kim, H., Kim, J.H., Yoon, S.: Liver lesion detection from weakly-labeled multi-phase CT volumes with a grouped single shot multibox detector. In International Conference on Medical Image Computing and Computer-Assisted Intervention, pp. 693–701. Springer, Cham, September 2018. https://doi.org/10.1007/978-3-030-00934-2_77

3. Yan, K., Wang, X., Lu, L., Summers, R.M.: Deeplesion: automated deep mining, categorization and detection of significant radiology image findings using large-scale clinical lesion annotations (2017). arXiv preprint arXiv:1710.01766
4. Tang, Y.B., Yan, K., Tang, Y.X., Liu, J., Xiao, J., Summers, R.M.: ULDor: a universal lesion detector for CT scans with pseudo masks and hard negative example mining. In: 2019 IEEE 16th International Symposium on Biomedical Imaging (ISBI 2019), pp. 833–836. IEEE, April 2019
5. Yan, K., Bagheri, M., Summers, R.M.: 3D context enhanced region-based convolutional neural network for end-to-end lesion detection. In: International Conference on Medical Image Computing and Computer-Assisted Intervention, pp. 511–519. Springer, Cham, September 2018. https://doi.org/10.1007/978-3-030-00928-1_58
6. Chiao, J.Y., Chen, K.Y., Liao, K.Y.K., Hsieh, P.H., Zhang, G., Huang, T.C.: Detection and classification the breast tumors using mask R-CNN on sonograms. Medicine **98**(19) (2019)
7. Ding, J., Li, A., Hu, Z., Wang, L.: Accurate pulmonary nodule detection in computed tomography images using deep convolutional neural networks. In: International Conference on Medical Image Computing and Computer-Assisted Intervention, pp. 559–567. Springer, Cham, September 2017. https://doi.org/10.1007/978-3-319-66179-7_64
8. Dou, Q., Chen, H., Yu, L., Qin, J., Heng, P.A.: Multilevel contextual 3-D CNNs for false positive reduction in pulmonary nodule detection. IEEE Trans. Biomed. Eng. **64**(7), 1558–1567 (2016)
9. Ren, S., He, K., Girshick, R., Sun, J.: Faster R-CNN: towards real-time object detection with region proposal networks. In: Advances in Neural Information Processing Systems, pp. 91–99 (2015)
10. Girshick, R.: Fast R-CNN. In: Proceedings of the IEEE International Conference on Computer Vision, pp. 1440–1448 (2015)
11. He, K., Zhang, X., Ren, S., Sun, J.: Deep residual learning for image recognition. In: Proceedings of the IEEE Conference on Computer Vision and Pattern Recognition, pp. 770–778 (2016)
12. Deng, J., Dong, W., Socher, R., Li, L.J., Li, K., Fei-Fei, L.: Imagenet: a large-scale hierarchical image database. In: 2009 IEEE Conference on Computer Vision and Pattern Recognition, pp. 248–255. IEEE, June 2009
13. Zhang, X., Lu, W., Li, F., et al.: Deep feature fusion model for sentence semantic matching. Comput. Mater. Continua **61**, 601–616 (2019)
14. Li, Z., Peng, C., Yu, G., Zhang, X., Deng, Y., Sun, J.: Detnet: a backbone network for object detection (2018). arXiv preprint arXiv:1804.06215.
15. Hu, J., Shen, L., Sun, G.: Squeeze-and-excitation networks. In: Proceedings of THE IEEE Conference on Computer Vision and Pattern Recognition, pp. 7132–7141 (2018)
16. Redmon, J., Farhadi, A.: Yolov3: an incremental improvement (2018). arXiv preprint arXiv: 1804.02767.
17. Lin, T.Y., Goyal, P., Girshick, R., He, K., Dollár, P.: Focal loss for dense object detection. In: Proceedings of the IEEE International Conference on Computer Vision, pp. 2980–2988 (2017)
18. He, K., Gkioxari, G., Dollár, P., Girshick, R.: Mask R-CNN. In: Proceedings of the IEEE International Conference on Computer Vision, pp. 2961–2969 (2017)

A Survey of Chinese Anaphora Resolution

Shengnan Li[1], Weiguang Qu[1,2](✉), Tingxin Wei[2,3], Junsheng Zhou[1], Yanhui Gu[1], and Bin Li[2]

[1] School of Computer and Electronic Information/School of Artificial Intelligence, Nanjing Normal University, Nanjing 210023, China
[2] School of Chinese Language and Literature, Nanjing Normal University, Nanjing 210097, China
[3] International College for Chinese Studies, Nanjing Normal University, Nanjing 210097, China

Abstract. Chinese anaphora resolution technology has been widely used in many natural language processing tasks, such as machine translation, information extraction and automatic text summarization. In this paper, we first introduce the resources for anaphora resolution, and then present the existing works on Chinese noun phrase resolution based on machine learning, deep learning and reinforcement learning techniques by analyzing the similarities and differences among them. Finally, we discuss the future development trend of Chinese anaphora resolution.

Keywords: Anaphora resolution · Chinese · Noun phrase

1 Introduction

Anaphora [1] is a substituted expression to refer to the denotation of a preceding word or phrase, which is a very common language phenomenon in language. There are several types of anaphora, pronoun anaphora, zero anaphora, and noun phrase anaphora. In many nlp tasks such as information extraction and machine translation, it is crucial to identify which word or phrase the anaphoric expression refer to for text understanding, therefore anaphora resolution is one of the fundamental tasks in natural language processing. Many researchers have put efforts on zero anaphora resolution and pronoun anaphora resolution, and have achieved outstanding improvements on these two subtasks. However, few studies focus on noun phrase resolution which is more complicated yet more urgent to be solved. In this paper, we present the development of noun phrase anaphora resolution from the perspectives of resource, method and feature attribute, especially on Chinese anaphora resolution. Finally, we give a brief discussion about the future trend of anaphora resolution.

2 Resources for Anaphora Resolution

For the task of anaphora resolution, three datasets are widely used to test and evaluate, which are MUC, ACE and OntoNotes. In this section, we give a detailed introduction to these datasets.

X. Sun et al. (Eds.): ICAIS 2021, LNCS 12736, pp. 180–192, 2021.
https://doi.org/10.1007/978-3-030-78609-0_16

2.1 MUC Dataset

The Message Understanding Conference (MUC) proposed two semantic evaluation tasks in 1995 and 1998—anaphora resolution and named entity disambiguation, and provided datasets for task evaluation, namely MUC-6 [2] and MUC-7 [3]. MUC-6 is composed of 25 articles from *The Wall Street Journal*, totaling approximately 30,000 words. It is the first corpus that can be used for the evaluation of anaphora resolution in a real sense. MUC-7 consists of a similar number of articles on aircraft crashes and rocket or missile launch. However, due to the emergence of some larger-scale datasets, MUC-6 and MUC-7 are no longer widely used. Despite of this, they have a profound impact on the study of anaphora resolution of the MUC corpus. Table 1 details the information of the MUC corpus.

Table 1. The statistics of the MUC corpus

Corpus	Language	Size of words			Size of files		
		Training	Dev&Test	Total	Training	Dev&Test	Total
MUC-6	English	12k	13k	25k	30	30	60
MUC-7	English	19k	21k	40k	30	37	67

2.2 ACE Dataset

Automatic Content Extraction (ACE) is an evaluation conference hosted by the National Institute of Standards and Technology. This event began since July 1997 and has been held for 7 sessions so far. The anaphora information in ACE is labeled in the form of an entity chain. The entity chain of each article is independently recorded in a corresponding XML file in the corpus. Therefore, the ACE corpus [4] replaces the MUC corpus as the new evaluation resource for anaphora resolution. The initial version of the ACE corpus only contains news. In the later versions, more types of articles, such as broadcast conversations, web logs and telephone conversations are added, which greatly increases the coverage of the evaluation. In 2003, ACE evaluation began to carry out the evaluation of anaphora resolution for the Chinese corpus. Table 2 details the information of the ACE corpus.

Table 2. The statistics of the ACE corpus

Corpus	Language	Training Size	Dev&Test Size	Total
ACE (2000–2004)	English	745k	215k	960k
	Chinese	455k	150k	615k
	Arabic	350k	150k	500k

2.3 OntoNotes Dataset

In 2011, the CoNLL conducted an evaluation of anaphora resolution for English [5]. In 2012, the evaluation for Chinese and Arabic was added [6] to study the differences of anaphora resolution in different languages. There are 5 released versions of the OntoNotes corpus. The latest two versions, OntoNotes 4.0 [7] and OntoNotes 5.0 [8] are used for the CoNLL-2011 shared task and CoNLL-2012 shared task respectively. OntoNotes collects a large number of articles on newswires, broadcast news and conversations, web texts and telephone conversations, and it integrates annotations in multiple levels, including part-of-speech tagging, component syntax analysis, named entity recognition and semantic role tagging, and so on. Its Chinese and English parts contain approximately 1 million and 1.6 million words respectively. At present, it is the largest anaphora resolution corpus. Table 3 details the information of OntoNotes.

Table 3. The statistics of the OntoNotes corpus

Corpus	Language	Size of words				Size of files			
		Train	Dev	Test	Total	Train	Dev	Test	Total
OntoNotes	English	1.3M	160k	170k	1.6M	1940	222	222	2384
	Chinese	750k	110k	90k	950k	1391	172	166	1729
	Arabic	240k	30k	30k	300k	359	44	44	447

3 Anaphora Resolution Methods

In this section, we present existing works on anaphora resolution implemented on the three datasets: MUC, ACE and OntoNotes. In general, the existing anaphora resolution methods can be categorized as rule-based, machine learning-based, deep learning-based and reinforcement learning-based methods. We will review these methods in English anaphora resolution and Chinese anaphora resolution respectively.

3.1 English Anaphora Resolution

The rule-based method [9–16] has been extensively studied. One of the advantages of the rule-based method is its simplicity for designing. However, this method has low flexibility. In the 1990s, the significant attention of anaphora resolution gradually evolved from the rule-based method to the machine learning method. This change was mainly due to the open access of the MUC-6 and MUC-7 datasets to the public. The machine learning method is classified into supervised and unsupervised methods [17–24]. The former requires lots of labeled training data, while the latter does not.

Recently, deep neural networks are used for anaphora resolution in many works [25–29]. One of the advantages of using deep neural networks is that it can extract useful features from the raw texts automatically without human intervention. In addition, these methods utilize word embedding to represent words and describe semantic relationships between them. However, these methods have many defects such as huge dimension size and inappropriate architecture. Hourali et al. [30] have tried addressing these issues by using contextual, semantic and syntactic information for a better representation of spans. They used the neural MCDM method for the accurate ranking of candidate antecedent to increase the detection rate of coreference mentions. Clark et al. [31] proposed a reinforcement learning method for anaphora resolution by only developing a co-reference chain model. Inspired by Clark, Fei et al. [32] proposed a method of anaphora resolution based on end-to-end deep reinforcement learning to avoid the cascading errors in the pipeline system. This method directly considers all text spans, and jointly recognizes entity mentions and performs clustering operating. Table 4 shows the performances of various methods in English anaphora resolution.

Table 4. Experiment results in English anaphora resolution with various methods

Method	Dataset	Model	F1%
Machine learning-based	MUC-6	Cardie et al. [23]	54
		Soon et al. [17]	62.60
		Ng and Cardie et al. [18]	66.30
		Yang et al. [19]	71.30
		Haghighi et al. [24]	70
		Yang et al. [21]	68.70
		Li et al. [22]	68.60
Rule-based		Raghunathan et al. [11]	77.70
	OntoNotes4.0	Lee et al. [12]	61.40
Reinforcement learning-based	OntoNotes5.0	Clark et al. [31]	65.73
		Fei et al. [32]	73.80
Deep learning-based		Lee et al. [26]	68.80
		Lee et al. [25]	73
		Zhang et al. [27]	76.50
		Kantor et al. [28]	76.61
		Joshi et al. [29]	76.90
		Hourali et al. [30]	80

3.2 Chinese Anaphora Resolution

In the task of anaphora resolution, there are many different types of anaphoric expression to be identified, such as common pronoun, demonstrative noun phrase, proper noun phrase, event anaphora and zero anaphora. In this section, we focus on the anaphora resolution of noun phrase in Chinese, which refer to pronouns, proper nouns, indicative noun phrases and common noun phrases. The existing methods of Chinese anaphora resolution can be categorized as rule-based methods and data-driven methods, which are detailed in the following parts of this section.

Rule-Based Methods for Chinese Anaphora Resolution. Due to the lack of fine labeled resources, the rule-based method is widely used in the early anaphora resolution system, which mainly focuses on the theoretical exploration and fusion of a large amount of domain knowledge and linguistic knowledge. These rule-based methods implement the anaphora resolution with some linguistic rules concluded by experts.

Zhang et al. [33] proposed a model using a rule-based filtering method for the CoNLL-2012 Shared Task (BCMI). They designed different filtering strategies for different situations. This method achieved an average F1 value of 51.83 in the experiment. Based on the model proposed by Zhang, Zhou et al. [34] added a semantic matching layer. This layer can properly overcome the defects in the Chinese semantic knowledge base by applying Web semantic knowledge. The experimental results on the ACE2005 Chinese corpus reached an average F1 value of 78.2.

In a word, the main idea of the rule-based hierarchical filtering model is to manually set a series of filtering rules for anaphora resolution, which requires a large amount of human labor with low system automation and poor portability. Although these rule bases cannot cover all language phenomena, these methods establish the foundation for future research.

Data-Driven Supervised Methods for Chinese Noun Phrase Resolution. In 2003, ACE initiated the evaluation on Chinese anaphora resolution, and some researchers started to apply the data-driven supervised method on Chinese anaphora resolution.

Hu et al. [35] designed a Chinese system based on a Maximum Entropy model. They extracted 12 features from raw texts to train a maximum entropy-based classifier, then had it tested on ACE news corpus, and achieved 78.87 on F1 value. Liu et al. [36] proposed a supervised correlation clustering algorithm for anaphora resolution. The learning algorithm based on gradient descent is proposed to make the feature parameters trained from the training set fit the objective of the correlation clustering better. With the feature set defined in [17], Liu defined and selected 10 features for Chinese anaphora resolution. Since anaphora resolution requires adequate information to identify the exact expression, and the existing features are still insufficient. Liu proposed a loss function based on minimizing decision errors and optimizing with a bottom-up clustering method [37]. The idea of this method is to use the information in the major opinion from the binary classification to correct wrong decisions, while at the same time, trying to avoid violating the decision made by the original binary classifier in general. The test result on the ACE Chinese corpus achieved 77.98 on F1 value. Li et al. [38] proposed a method based on feature ranking strategy for noun phrase resolution. This method processed personal pronouns and common noun phrases separately when selecting feature vectors, to take full use of the features of different noun phrases for anaphora resolution. The experimental results showed that the F1 value reached 80.72.

Tan et al. [39] proposed a Chinese noun phrases anaphora resolution method based on SVM. The method trained on the ACE2005 corpus of Chinese and resolved all general noun phrases with 13 selected feature vectors. Gao et al. [40] proposed a method based on SVM with 17 selected feature vectors and the experimental results on ACE 2005 achieved 71.59 on F1 value. Zhou et al. [41] considered that the traditional Laplacian support vector machine only uses Euclidean distance to calculate the distance between two samples, which may lead to the false high similarity between two samples from different categories. To address the issue of insufficient Chinese annotated corpus, a data-driven learning method of optimal distance measure is proposed. In this method, the similarity constraints between sample pairs are considered, and the Fisher discriminant criterion is introduced, which increases the similarity within the same category and highlights the discriminant features in the new metric space. Compared with the classical supervised methods on the ACE2005 Chinese corpus, the linear and kernel supervised methods achieve better results with fewer labeled samples. Zhou also proposed a Chinese anaphora resolution model based on an improved hierarchical filtering module [42]. Table 5 are the hierarchical filter modules used in this model.

Table 5. The sequence of filtering modules for Chinese anaphora resolution

Sequence	Data type	Features
1	Noun phrases	String matching
2	Noun phrases	Entity expression loose string I entity loose string matching
3	Noun phrases	Strict head word matching I loose head word matching
4	Noun phrases	Appositive I abbreviations
5	Noun phrases	HowNet semantic similarity calculation I Web Semantic Similarity Calculation
6	Pronoun	Singular and plural Identity; Gender Identity; Life degree; NER tag

Data-Driven Unsupervised Methods for Chinese Noun Phrase Resolution. The supervised machine learning method requires large scale of labeled training data. However, well-annotated corpus is not easily reachable since not only linguistic knowledge is needed, but also domain knowledge as well. Besides, word segmentation of Chinese also bring obstacles in understanding and annotation. Therefore, it is extremely labor-intensive and time-consuming to construct a large-scale anaphora resolution corpus. In the unsupervised learning model, there is no requirements for a large amount of labeled corpus, which can effectively save the time and cost of manual labeling. In this section, we mainly introduce the unsupervised method for Chinese noun phrase anaphora resolution.

Wang et al. [43] explored the reasons why the Chinese anaphora phenomenon is difficult to resolve and proved that English anaphora resolution technology can be extended to Chinese. It is the first work that attempts to use an unsupervised method to address Chinese noun phrases anaphora resolution.

According to Cardie [23] in English anaphora resolution, Zhou et al. [44] presented a new unsupervised clustering algorithm for noun phrase anaphora resolution. Different from Cardie, this approach firstly converted the issue of anaphora resolution into that of graph clustering, which did not make anaphora decisions for each pair of noun phrases in isolation but fully considered the correlation between items. Li et al. [45] proposed a Chinese anaphora resolution method based on association clustering, and then correlation clustering is used for automatic graph clustering. Compared with the traditional clustering methods such as link-first and link-best, the proposed algorithm takes full use of the relations among the noun phrases sufficiently. In addition, it does not need to specify the desired number of clusters and a distance threshold. It takes each item to be resolved in the test set as a vertex in the graph and regards the confidence value between the two items to be resolved as the weight corresponding to the edge connecting the two vertices, thus forming a graph G (V, E). Then, they use the associated clustering algorithm to automatically divide the graph G, so that the process of referencing resolution is transformed into the division process of the graph G.

However, one of the issues of traditional clustering methods is that it is difficult to judge when to stop. Besides, since it is difficult to obtain or estimate the total number of entities in text, the number of clusters cannot be predicted, which is an important parameter that influence the final performance on clustering. Most of the current methods are based on the experience gained from a large amount of data, without considering the characteristics of the task itself, which affects the performance of clustering in anaphora resolution. In addition, the clustering features used by the existing researches are directly manually selected, and the interference of the weaker distinguishing features on the clustering effect is not considered. To address these issues, Li et al. [46] proposed an unsupervised method (adaptive resonance theory, ART). This method makes full use of the characteristics of noun phrases and dynamically adjusts the number of clusters by changing network parameters. In addition, a feature selection method based on information gain ratio is adopted to reduce the interference of weaker features on cluster results. This method does not rely on manual annotation corpus under the premise of ensuring the correct recognition rate and can be directly applied to real texts cross domains.

Gao et al. [47] designed a Chinese noun phrase anaphora resolution system based on unsupervised clustering, including preprocessing, feature selection and clustering. In the preprocessing stage, the system obtains the feature information of noun phrases. With the feature information and a series of incompatible functions defined, a hierarchical clustering algorithm is used to cluster the noun phrases that may be in a co-reference chain.

Deep Learning-Based Methods for Chinese Noun Phrase Resolution. Most of the existing neural anaphora resolution models only focus on the linear features of text, ignoring the integration of structural information. Fu et al. [48] proposed two measures to address the issue with the constituency parse tree, which is based on the neural network model avoiding structural information loss. Considering the characteristics of Chinese, Fu et al. [49] proposed a Chinese anaphora resolution model with structural information involved. The constituency tree of all sentences in the document is compressed to obtain the leaf node depth. Structural information is vectorized by the Structural Embedding of Component Tree (SECT) method. In addition, the leaf node depth and the SECT information are used as three feature vectors in the model for Chinese anaphora resolution.

The specific process of the SECT method is as follows. (1) Define a syntactic sequence S(p) for word p which is the leaf node in the syntactic tree, save the path from the leaf node p to the root node of the syntactic tree. For example, for the "NR 李鹏(Li Peng)" node in Fig. 1, the corresponding S(p) is {NR, NP-PN, NP-SBJ, IP-HLN, TOP}. In the experiment, considering the performance and memory utilization, a window is set to limit the length of S(p). Due to the reason that the higher-level nodes in the syntactic tree are more ambiguous, with the help of window size limitation, the higher-level ambiguous nodes in the syntax tree will be removed. (2) A bidirectional LSTM is used to encode the variable-length syntax sequence S(p) into a fixed-length vector representation. Suppose x_t^p represents the t-th node of the word p in the syntactic sequence S(p), and v_t^p represents the hidden layer representation of x_t^p. The formula is as follows:

$$v_t^p = f_{BiLSTM}\left(v_{t-1}^p, x_t^p\right) \tag{1}$$

Then for a given word p, finally select $v_{BiLSTM}^p = v_T^p$ as the final vector representation for S(p).

```
Treebanked sentence:
--------------------
  李鹏 总理 同 阿卡耶夫 总统 举行 会谈
Premier Li Peng and President Akayev hold talks
Tree:
-----
    (TOP (IP-HLN (NP-SBJ (NP-PN (NR 李鹏(Li Peng))
                                (NN 总理(premier)))
                         (CC 同(and))
                         (NP-PN (NR 阿卡耶夫(Akayev))
                                (NN 总统(president))))
                 (VP (VV 举行(hold))
                     (NP-OBJ (NN 会谈(talk))))))
```

Fig. 1. Syntax tree example

Reinforcement Learning-Based Methods for Chinese Noun Phrase Resolution. The coreference resolution systems usually use a heuristic loss function for training, which needs to be adjusted carefully. Clark et al. [31] applied reinforcement learning to directly optimize the neural mention-ranking model used for coreference evaluation metrics, thus avoiding the selection of hyperparameters for each specific language, data set and evaluation metrics. The mention ranking model scores the possibility of mentioning, rather than comparing partial mention clusters. As a result, they operate in a simple environment in which coreference decisions are made independently. The experiments were conducted with two methods, enhanced strategy gradient algorithm and reward rescaling maximum profit target. The results showed that the latter method was more effective, which improved the performance of Chinese and English anaphora resolution respectively in CoNLL-2012 shared task.

3.3 Summary

In this section, we summarize the methods for noun phrase resolution based on machine learning, deep learning and reinforcement learning. Table 6 shows the performance of existing methods on Chinese datasets. It can be seen that the number of feature vectors has great impact on the final performance. Specifically, the performance of the same machine learning method with different number of feature vectors may be quite different. According to the language characteristics and background knowledge, choosing appropriate features can greatly improve the accuracy of the classification model. However, it does not mean that more features bring better performance. That is because with the increase of features, the possibility of data sparseness increases as well. Therefore, the efficiency of the classification model relies on the selection of powerful characteristic attributes.

Table 6. Experimental results on Chinese noun phrase anaphora resolution

Method	Dataset	Model	Feature	F1%
Supervised-based	ACE2005	Tan et al. [39]	13	63.30
		Hu et al. [35]	12	78.87
		Liu et al. [36]	10	78.01
		Zhou et al. [42]	11	77.10
	ACE2007	Li et al. [38]	10	80.72
	OntoNotes3.0 (news)	Gao et al. [40]	17	71.59
Unsupervised-based		Gao et al. [47]	14	59.43
	ACE2005	Zhou et al. [44]	9	62.05
		Li et al. [45]	9	76.45
		Li et al. [46]	8	70.20
Deep learning-based	OntoNotes5.0	Fu et al. [48]	3	62.35
		Fu et al. [49]	3	62.33
Reinforcement learning-based		Clark et al. [31]	—	63.88

4 Future Prospects

With an increasing probability of multiple languages in one text, the multilingual anaphora resolution becomes a hot topic. The main task of multilingual anaphora resolution is to directly apply the anaphora resolution method of a certain language to other languages. Due to the difference among languages in many perspectives, it is a big challenge for researchers to develop novel networks for it.

At present, another trend in anaphora resolution is to formalize and combine syntactic information, semantic knowledge and background knowledge in anaphora resolution.

Although papers based on the use of background knowledge, grammar and semantic knowledge for anaphora resolution have been published at top natural language processing conferences, the performance is still not very satisfactory, which is mainly caused by the following reasons: 1. the background knowledge extraction and the background knowledge formalization is very difficult. 2. It is difficult to automatically obtain grammatical and semantic knowledge and further formalize it into effective rules. Therefore, obtaining and using syntactic information, semantic knowledge, and background knowledge has been also a new hot topic in the development of anaphora resolution.

Acknowledgments. The authors thank the anonymous reviewers for their constructive suggestions which have resulted in improvement on the presentations. This research is supported by the National Science Foundation of China (grant 61772278, author: Qu, W.; grand number: 61472191, author: Zhou, J. http://www.nsfc.gov.cn/), the National Social Science Foundation of China (grant number: 18BYY127, author: Li B. http://www.cssn.cn) and Jiangsu Higher Institutions' Excellent Innovative Team for Philosophy and Social Science (grand number: 2017STD006, author: Qu, W. http://jyt.jiangsu.gov.cn).

References

1. Wang, H.: Survey: computation models and technologies in anaphora resolution. J. Chin. Inf. Process. **16**(6), 9–17 (2002). (In Chinese)
2. Vilain, M., Burger, J., Aberdeen, J., Connolly, D., Hirschman, L.: A model-theoretic coreference scoring scheme. In: Proceedings of the Sixth Message Understanding Conference (MUC-6), pp. 45–52. Morgan Kaufmann Publishers, San Francisco (1995)
3. Hirschman, L., Robinson, P., Burger, J., Vilain, M.: Automating coreference: the role of annotated training data. In: Proceedings of the AAAI Spring Symposium on Applying Machine Learning to Discourse Processing, pp. 118–121. AAAI, Rhode Island, USA (1997)
4. Doddington, G., Mitchell, A., Przybocki, M., Ramshaw, L., Strassel, S., Weischedel, R.: The automatic content extraction (ACE) program tasks, data, and evaluation. In: Proceedings of the Fourth International Conference on Language Resources and Evaluation, Lisbon, Portugal, pp. 837–840 (2004)
5. Pradhan, S., Ramshaw, L., Marcus, M., Palmer, M., Xue, N.: CoNLL-2011 shared task: modeling unrestricted coreference in ontonotes. In: Proceedings of the Fifteenth Conference on Computational Natural Language Learning: Shared Task, pp. 1–27, ACL, Portland, Oregon (2011)
6. Pradhan, S.S., Moschitti, A., Xue, N., Uryupina, O., Zhang, Y.: CoNLL-2012 shared task: modeling multilingual unrestricted coreference in OntoNotes. In: Joint Conference on Empirical Methods in Natural Language Processing and Computational Natural Language Learning Proceedings-Shared Task, pp. 1–40. ACL, Jeju Island (2012)
7. Weischedel, R., et al.: OntoNotes Release 4.0 LDC2011T03. Web Download. Philadelphia: Linguistic Data Consortium (2011)
8. Weischedel, R., Palmer, M., Marcus, M., Hovy, E., Pradhan, S., Ramshaw, L.: OntoNotes release 5.0 LDC2013T19. Web Download. Philadelphia: Linguistic Data Consortium (2013)
9. Harabagiu, S.: From lexical cohesion to textual coherence: a data driven perspective. Int. J. Pattern Recognit. Artif. Intell. **13**(2), 247–265 (1999)
10. Moosavi, N., Strube, M.: Lexical features in coreference resolution: to be used with caution. In: Proceedings of the 55th Annual Meeting of the Association for Computational Linguistics (Volume 2: Short Papers), pp. 14–19. ACL, Vancouver, Canada (2017)

11. Raghunathan, K., Lee, H., Rangarajan, S., Chambers, N., Manning, C.D.: A multipass sieve for coreference resolution. In: Conference on Empirical Methods in Natural Language Processing, pp. 492–501. DBLP, USA (2010)
12. Lee, H., Peirsman, Y., Chang, A., Chambers, N., Jurafsky, D.: Stanford's multi-pass sieve coreference resolution system at the CoNL-2011 shared task. In: Proceedings of the Fifteenth Conference on Computational Natural Language Learning: Shared Task, pp. 28–34. ACL, USA (2011)
13. Kibble, R.: A reformulation of rule 2 of centering theory. Comput. Linguist **27**(4), 579–587 (2001)
14. Zeldes, A., Zhang, S.: When annotation schemes change rules help: a configurable approach to coreference resolution beyond OntoNotes. In: Proceedings of the Workshop on Coreference Resolution Beyond OntoNotes, pp. 92–101. ACL, San Diego, California (2016)
15. Lee, H., Chang, A., Peirsman, Y., Chambers, N., Jurafsky, D.: Deterministic coreference resolution based on entity-centric, precision-ranked rules. Comput. Linguist. **39**(4), 885–916 (2013)
16. Haghighi, A., Klein, D.: Simple coreference resolution with rich syntactic and semantic features. In: Proceedings of 2009 Conference on Empirical Methods in Natural Language Processing, pp. 1152–1161. ACL, Singapore (2009)
17. Soon, W., Ng, H., Lim, D.: Machine learning approach to coreference resolution of noun phrases. Comput. Linguist. **27**(4), 521–544 (2001)
18. Ng, V., Cardie, C.: Improving machine learning approaches to coreference resolution. In: Proceedings of the 40th Annual Meeting of the Association for Computational Linguistics, pp. 104–111. ACL, Philadelphia, USA (2002)
19. Yang, X., Zhou, G., Su, J., Tan, C.: Coreference resolution using competition learning approach. In: Proceedings of the 41st Annual Meeting of the Association for Computational Linguistics, pp. 176–183. ACL, Sapporo, Japan (2003)
20. Qian, W., Guo, Y., Zhou, Y., Wu, L.: English noun phrase coreference resolution via a maximum entropy model. J. Comput. Res. Dev. **40**(9), 1337–1342 (2003). (In Chinese)
21. Yang, Y., Li, Y., Zhou, G., Zhu, Q.: Research on distance information for anaphora resolution. J. Chin. Inf. Process. **22**(5), 39–44 (2008). (In Chinese)
22. Li, Y., Yang, Y., Zhou, G., Zhu, Q.: Anaphora a resolution of noun phrase based on SVM. Comput. Eng. **35**(3), 199–204 (2009). (In Chinese)
23. Cardie, C., Wagstaff, K.: Noun phrase coreference as clustering. In: Proceedings of the Joint SIGDAT Conference on Empirical Methods in Natural Language Processing and Very Large Corpora, pp. 82–89 (1999)
24. Haghighi, A., Dan, K.: Unsupervised coreference resolution in a nonparametric Bayesian model. In: Proceedings of the 45th Annual Meeting of the Association of Computational Linguistics, pp. 848–855. ACL, Prague (2007)
25. Lee, K., He, L., Zettlemoyer, L.: Higher-order coreference resolution with coarse-to-fine inference. In: Proceedings of 2018 Conference of the North American Chapter of the Association for Computational Linguistics: Human Language Technologies, pp. 687–692. ACL, New Orleans, Louisiana (2018)
26. Lee, K., He, L., Lewis, M., Zettlemoyer, L.: End-to-end neural coreference resolution. In: Proceedings of 2017 Conference on Empirical Methods in Natural Language Processing, pp. 188–197. ACL, Copenhagen, Denmark (2017)
27. Zhang, R., Santos, C., Yasunaga, M., Xiang, B., Radev, D.: Neural coreference resolution with deep biaffine attention by joint mention detection and mention clustering. In: Proceedings of the 56th Annual Meeting of the Association for Computational Linguistics, pp. 102–107. ACL, Melbourne, Australia (2018)

28. Kantor, B., Globerson, A.: Coreference resolution with entity equalization. In: Proceedings of the 57th Conference of the Association for Computational Linguistics, pp. 673–677. ACL, Italy (2019)
29. Joshi, M., Levy, O., Weld, D.S., Zettlemoyer, L.: BERT for coreference resolution: baselines and analysis. In: Proceedings of 2019 Conference on Empirical Methods in Natural Language Processing and the 9th International Joint Conference on Natural Language Processing (EMNLP-IJCNLP), pp. 5802–5807. ACL, Hong Kong, China (2019)
30. Hourali, S., Zahedi, M., Fateh, M.: Coreference resolution using neural MCDM and fuzzy weighting technique. Int. J. Computat. Intell. Syst. **13**(1), 56–65 (2020)
31. Clark, K., Manning, C.: Deep reinforcement learning for mention-ranking coreference models. In: Proceedings of 2016 Conference on Empirical Methods in Natural Language Processing Texas, pp. 2256–2262. ACL, Austin, Texas (2016)
32. Fei, H., Li, X., Li, D., Li, P.: End-to-end deep reinforcement learning based coreference resolution. In: Proceedings of the 57th Conference of the Association for Computational Linguistics, pp. 660–665. ACL, Florence, Italy (2019)
33. Zhang, X., Wu, C., Zhao, H.: Chinese coreference resolution via ordered filtering. In: Joint Conference on Emnlp and Conll-shared Task, pp. 95–99. ACL, Jeju Island, Korea (2012)
34. Zhou, X., Liu, J., Luo, Y., Han, Y.: Comparison of Chinese anaphora resolution models. Comput. Sci. **43**(2), 31–34 (2016). (In Chinese)
35. Hu, N., Kong, F., Wang, H., Zhou, G., Zhu, Q.: Realization on Chinese coreference resolution system based on maximum entropy model. Appl. Res. Comput. **26**(8), 2948–2951 (2009). (In Chinese)
36. Liu, W., Zhou, J., Huang, S., Chen, J.: Coreference resolution with supervised correlation clustering. Comput. Sci. **36**(9), 182–185 (2009). (In Chinese)
37. Liu, W., Zhou, J., Huang, S.: global optimization based on clustering for coreference resolution. In: Frontier Progress of Chinese Computer Linguistics, pp. 295–301. CIPSC, China (2009). (In Chinese)
38. Li, Y., Gan, R., Yang, Y., Shi, S.: Chinese coreference resolution method based on feature respective selection strategy. Comput. Eng. **37**(18), 180–182 (2011). (In Chinese)
39. Tan, W., Kong, F., Wang, D., Zhou, G.: An SVM-based approach to chinese anaphora resolution. High-Performance Comput. Technol. 0(2), 30–36 (2010). (In Chinese)
40. Gao, J., Kong, F., Zhu, Q., Li, P.: Research of Chinese noun phrase anaphora resolution: an SVM-based approach. Comput. Sci. **39**(10), 231–234 (2012). (In Chinese)
41. Zhou, X., Liu, J., Shao, P., Xiao, L., Luo, F.: Chinese anaphora resolution based on metric-optimized Laplacian SVM. Acta Electron. Sin. **44**(12), 3064–3071 (2016). (In Chinese)
42. Zhou, X., Liu, J., Shao, P., Luo, F., Liu, Y.: Chinese anaphora resolution based on multi-pass sieve model. J. Jilin Univ. (Eng. Technol. Ed.) **46**(4), 1209–1215 (2016). (In Chinese)
43. Wang, C.S., Ngai, G.: A clustering approach for unsupervised Chinese coreference resolution. In: Proceedings of the 5th SIGHAN Workshop on Chinese Language Processing, pp. 40–47. ACL, Sydney, Australia (2006)
44. Zhou, J., Huang, S., Chen, J., Qu, W.: A new graph clustering algorithm for Chinese noun phrase coreference resolution. J. Chin. Inf. Process. **21**(2), 77–82 (2007). (In Chinese)
45. Li, Y., Zhou, J., Chen, J.: Applying correlation clustering to Chinese noun phrase coreference resolution. Comput. Sci. **34**(12), 216–218 (2007). (In Chinese)

46. Li, S., Zhao, T., Chen, C., Liu, P.: An unsupervised approach based on ART network for coreference resolution of Chinese. High-tech Commun. **19**(9), 926–932 (2009). (In Chinese)
47. Gao, J., Kong, F., Zhu, Q., Li, P., Hua, X.: Research of unsupervised Chinese noun phrase coreference resolution. Comput. Eng. **38**(17), 189–191 (2012). (In Chinese)
48. Fu, J., Kong, F.: Coreference resolution incorporating structural information. Comput. Sci. **47**(3), 231–236 (2020). (In Chinese)
49. Fu, J., Kong, F.: End to end Chinese coreference resolution with structural information. Comput. Eng. **46**(1), 45–51 (2020). (In Chinese)

Efficient 3D Pancreas Segmentation Using Two-Stage 3D Convolutional Neural Networks

Wenqiang Wang[1], Zhe Liu[1](✉), Yuqing Song[1], Jun Su[1], Yangyang Tang[1], Aihong Yu[1], and Xuesheng Liu[2]

[1] School of Computer Science and Communications Engineering, Jiangsu University, Zhenjiang 212013, China
1000004088@ujs.edu.cn

[2] Department of Anesthesiology, the First Affiliated Hospital of Anhui Medical University, Key Laboratory of Anesthesiology and Perioperative Medicine if Anhui Higher Education Institutes, Anhui Medical University, Hefei, China

Abstract. In recent years, 3D segmentation of the pancreas has received a lot of attention from researchers because of its importance for clinical diagnosis and treatment. However, there are many problems with 3D pancreatic segmentation: 1) because the shape of the pancreas is not regular enough compared to other organs in the abdomen, it has a relatively small shape and there is also an excessive background of interference, resulting in inaccurate segmentation results for the pancreas; 2) one of the main drawbacks of 3D convolutional neural networks for segmentation is the excessive memory occupation, which requires censoring of the network structure to fit a given memory budget. To address the above issues, this paper proposes a new coarse-to-fine method based on convolutional neural networks (CNNs). In the first stage, the segmentation is trained to obtain candidate regions. In the second stage, the approximate location of the pancreas is obtained after the first stage, and then the pancreas is finely segmented in this approximate location. The convolutional neural network used in this paper is a modified 3DUnet network, which is improved to require less memory and higher segmentation accuracy compared to the traditional 3DUnet network. This segmentation method requires a less demanding experimental environment than other algorithms, and can also improve accuracy by eliminating a large amount of irrelevant background interference. The combination of our proposed network structure and the two-stage segmentation method achieves advanced performance.

Keywords: Pancreas segmentation · Two-stage · Deep convolutional neural network · Computed tomography

1 Introduction

Pancreatic cancer is a very deadly malignancy. Automatic and accurate segmentation of the pancreas is an important prerequisite for computer-assisted clinicians to diagnose pancreatic cancer. In anatomy, the pancreas is an elongated gland with a length of about 14 cm –8 cm, a width of 3 cm –9 cm, and a thickness of 1.5 cm –5 cm. In addition,

X. Sun et al. (Eds.): ICAIS 2021, LNCS 12736, pp. 193–204, 2021.
https://doi.org/10.1007/978-3-030-78609-0_17

the pancreas is located in the upper abdomen area and the left quarter rib area, the back of the stomach and the retrospections space is approximately equal to the first lumbar vertebral body, lying on the posterior abdominal wall. The pancreas are divided into four parts: head, neck, body, and tail, and there is no obvious boundary between them. This paper focuses on the segmentation of the pancreas in a 3D computed tomography (CT) volume, which is more difficult than the segmentation of other abdominal organs such as the liver and kidney [1] because of its small size and excessive interference background. Pancreatic dataset used in this paper is the MSD (Medical Segmentation Decathlon) pancreatic dataset. The first place winner in the MSD competition, nn-Unet [2], had an accuracy of 80% for pancreatic segmentation dice.

With the rapid development of deep learning, methods based on convolutional neural networks (CNN) have excellent performance in the field of medical image segmentation, and 3D medical image segmentation has slowly entered the public view and shown good segmentation results [3]. Compared with 2D medical image segmentation [7], 3D medical image segmentation has the advantage of better access to image contextual information, which enables tighter correlation of segmentation results and thus optimises the segmentation results. The best approach is to use 3D neural networks such as V-Net [4] and 3D U-Net [5] directly. However, one of the main difficulties encountered with 3D convolution is that it requires a large amount of memory, which prevents 3D segmentation from being studied by the general public.

To solve the problem of excessive memory required for 3D convolution, the mainstream methods are to do 3D patch [5] or pseudo-3D convolution [6]. Although 3D patch does not require high computer performance, it ignores the global information, so the final recombination segmentation result will not be too satisfactory. In the traditional pseudo-3D convolutional operation [14], it still essentially uses 2D convolutional blocks to integrate contextual information, so it is still not as powerful as 3D convolution. Although majority voting [15] can enhance the pseudo-3D contextual information from different angles through 2D segmentation, it is still not as powerful as 3D convolution.

In addition, two-stage segmentation is increasingly used in the field of 3D segmentation [14]. For example, we were inspired by the automatic pancreatic segmentation proposed by Zhao et al. [7], but we still found that Zhao did not normalise the size of the training set in his experiments, and it did not work on computers with small memory. There is also the one proposed by Yu Q et al. [14], which is more efficient but actually uses 2D convolution to solve the 3D segmentation problem, while 3D convolution is more powerful, so this method is not desirable.

To address the above problems, this paper proposes a two-stage segmentation method and an improved 3DUnet, which not only solve the problem of excessive memory consumption, but also reduces excessive background interference, and also improves the dice accuracy. In this experiment, in the first stage of segmentation in this paper, the resolution size of the image is reduced to 1/4 of the original size, and then roughly determined to the location of the pancreas, and then in the second stage, the target region is finely segmented to obtain the final segmentation result.

In this paper, we evaluate the capabilities of U-Net, one of the most popular and successful deep learning models for biomedical image segmentation, while also identifying some potential areas for improvement after a closer look at the network architecture. We propose and hypothesise that the U-Net architecture may lack certain criteria and suggest some modifications based on current developments in deep computer vision. As a result, we have developed a new model called ResConv-3DUnet, which is an enhanced version of U-Net. In this paper, experiments are conducted using a public pancreas segmentation dataset, and the experimental results show that the method proposed in this paper can effectively solve the pancreas segmentation problem.

The contributions of this paper can be summarized as follows:

- The two-stage segmentation method proposed in this paper can greatly solve the problem of excessive memory requirement in 3D segmentation.
- ResConv-3DUnet, which we used in the experiment, not only consumes less computational memory resources, but also has a positive effect on the segmentation of small target pancreas.

2 Method

2.1 Segmentation Method Overview

Since the pancreas is relatively small in the whole CT image, there is a large amount of irrelevant background information that affects the segmentation results, so a better approach is to roughly locate the pancreas first, then remove the irrelevant background interference, and finally perform the segmentation.

The entire pancreas segmentation process can be roughly divided into two stages: the first stage is the coarse segmentation, which consists of down-sampling the 3D volumes and then initial localisation of the pancreas; the second stage is the fine segmentation stage, in which the approximate location of the pancreas is obtained in the first stage of segmentation, then the irrelevant background of the pancreas is removed, and finally the remaining regions of interest of the pancreas is finely segmented. The segmentation result is then obtained. The neural network used in the two-stage segmentation is the ResConv-3DUnet proposed in this paper.

2.2 Pre-processing

Because of the different number of slices of the pancreatic dataset used in this study, the z-axis spacing of the datasets varied, and they ranged from 0.7 mm to 7.5 mm. As showed in Fig. 1, this is a lateral view of the z-axis of the 3D CT scans of four patients who were not pre-treated. It can be seen that without processing, they are too different for segmentation, so our treatment is to interpolate in the z-axis so that their z-axis spacing is all specified as 1 mm. Because the number of z-axis slices increases after interpolation, the memory consumption requirement for training individual patients also increases, so training cannot be done directly. This paper addresses this problem by randomly selecting 48 consecutive slices for training in each epoch training.

Before training, the CT value is intercepted to [−100, 240] through HU constraints and normalized to [−1, 1]; Ground Truth only performs [0, 1] normalized. For 3D CT scans, the number of slices is not uniform which have more or fewer slices, which means that the size is not unified, so we cannot train together.

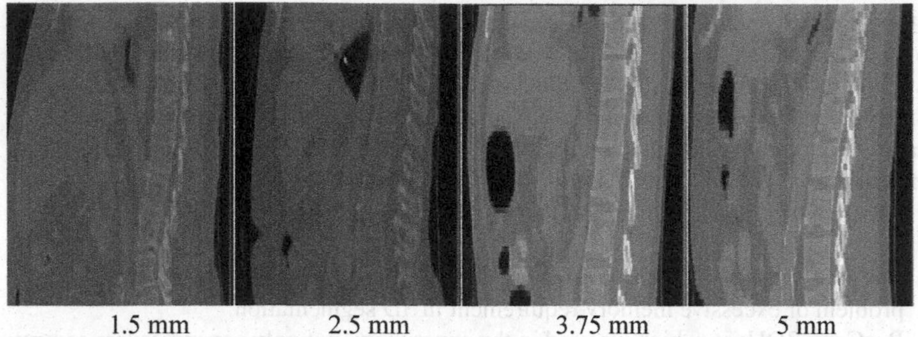

Fig. 1. The z-axis intervals of the four lateral views of CT data in the figure are 1.5mm, 2.5 mm, 3.75 mm and 5 mm respectively. It can be seen that with the increase of the interval, the CT volume becomes more and more blurry, which will not be conducive to our experiment if it is not processed.

In view of the above problems, the solutions given in this paper are as follows: 1) The z-axis interval between the CT volume and the label mask was interpolated to 1 mm, specifically by using cubic interpolations for the CT volume and the nearest interpolation for the label mask. 2) After the above interpolation process, the number of slices for a single patient was above 100 slices. In order to eliminate more slices that did not contain the pancreas, we used the label map to find slices that contained the pancreas. In order not to lose relevant information, we expanded 10 slices up and down in the pancreatic region, respectively, and then kept these slices, discarding all other CT slices, and labelled this preserved slice region as V0. 3) In the first stage of segmentation training, we interpolated the length and width of V0 to 128 × 128 and recorded it as V1. 4) Since the pancreas in the MSD pancreas dataset is less than 256 in length and 192 in width, we used labels to find the pancreas region in V0 and then expanded its length and width region outward to 256 × 192, recording this region as V2.

2.3 Training

The First Stage: Coarse Segmentation and Positioning. The length and width of each 3D CT scans decreased from 512 × 512 to 128 × 128, and sample down to a quarter of the original size. Since the number of slices varies and the size is not uniform, it is still necessary to randomly select 48 consecutive slices for training in each period. After many times of training, we obtained the final segmentation result, then obtained the approximate location of the pancreas, and obtained the minimum enclosing rectangle of the predicted area of the pancreas. Then we multiplied the obtained enclosing rectangle by 4 to obtain the minimum enclosing rectangle of the pancreas in the original 3D CT scans size.

The Second Stage: Fine Segmentation. In this pancreas datasets, the length of the pancreas is less than 256 and the width is less than 192. The label of the CT image was used to find the smallest external rectangular box of the pancreas, and then margins were added to extend the length and width to 256 and 192. And then each epoch training is randomly selected consecutively 48 slices, so when training after processing, the length, width and height of the data are unified to 256 × 192 × 48. Compared with the entire CT volume, the organs considered in this paper tend to occupy a relatively small area, so the final segmentation performance relies heavily on the coarse localization results. When we have this approximate region of pancreatic coordinates, we select this region and segment the pancreas only in this region. This has the advantage of not only reducing memory consumption but also removing a lot of background information that is not relevant to the pancreas.

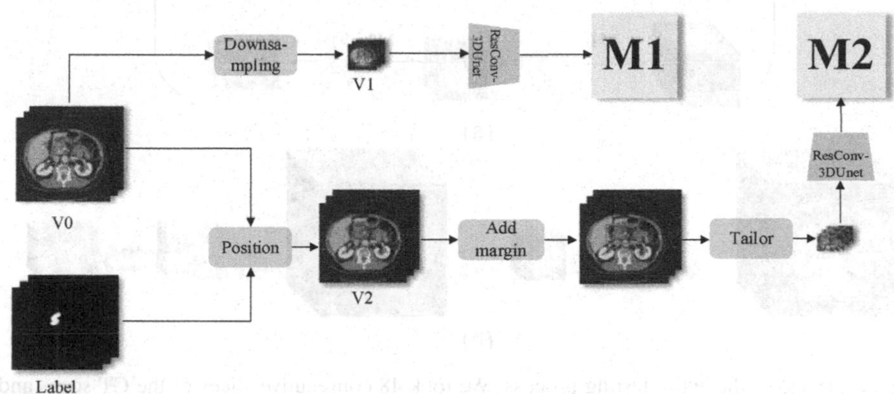

Fig. 2. 1) The pre-processed V0 is downsampled to V1; 2) We find the rectangular box with the smallest pancreas in V0 by the label of the pancreas, then expand the edges of the rectangular box, and finally mark this rectangular box region as V2 and perform segmentation. M1 and M2 are the segmentation models obtained after two training segmentation, respectively.

Training Details. In the first stage of training, we use the ResConv-3DUnet proposed in this paper to train V1. During training, 48 consecutive slices of the CT volume are randomly taken in each epoch, so its length, width and height are unified to 128 × 128 × 48. In this paper, the model obtained after training is denoted as M1. In the second stage of training, ResConv-3DUnet is also used to train V2, and 48 consecutive slices are randomly taken for training in each epoch, and its length, width and height are unified to 256 × 192 × 48. We denote the model obtained after training as M2. The overall flow of the segmentation is shown in Fig. 2. It can be seen that the volume of the CT image in the two experiments is not large, and it does not require much memory at all.

2.4 Testing

The test in this paper also requires two stages. In the first stage, we first reduced the 3D CT scans to a quarter of its original size, then we use M1 to simply locate the pancreas, and then the minimum boundary rectangle of the region is obtained and its

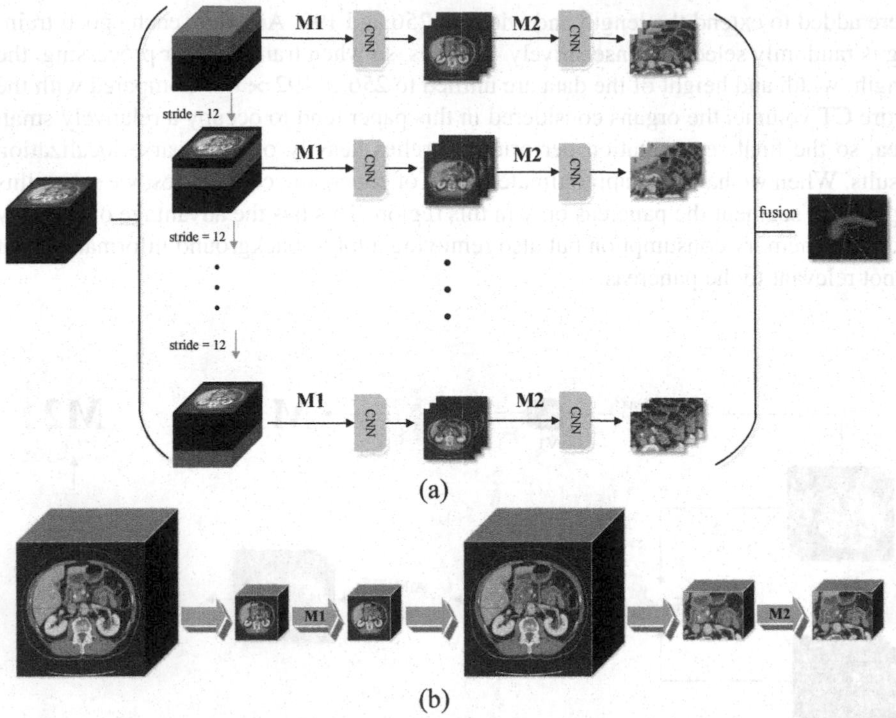

Fig. 3. (a) shows the entire testing process. We took 48 consecutive slices of the CT scans and tested them in 12 steps, then fused these test results to obtain the final segmentation results. M1 and M2 are the models obtained after two stages of training, respectively. (b) shows the detailed steps of the single test: 1) CT slices were reduced to 1/4 of the original image and then roughly segmented to simply locate the pancreas; 2) the segmented feature map was enlarged by 4 times to locate the approximate position of the pancreas in the original image; 3) the boundary of the target region was expanded to 256 × 192 and then it was cut; 4) the cut region was finely segmented to obtain the final segmentation result.

maximum and minimum length are recorded and record the position of the enclosing rectangular box, which is $x_{max}, x_{min}, y_{max}$ and y_{min} respectively, and then multiply them by 4 to predict the approximate pancreas position in the original 3D CT scans, which were called$X_{max} = 4 \times x_{max}, X_{min} = 4 \times x_{min}, Y_{max} = 4 \times y_{max}, Y_{min} = 4 \times y_{min}$. In the second stage, because the approximate position of the pancreas was obtained, so we can figure out its length and width:$X_{len} = X_{max} - X_{min}, Y_{len} = Y_{max} - Y_{min}$, then we extended its length and width to 256 × 192, which is a unified standard, and then cut out this area, and finally used M2 to accurately cut out the pancreas.

In two stages of testing a single patient CT image, we took 48 consecutive slices sequentially, with a step length of 12, and finally fused the test results together. The test flow is shown in Fig. 3. In addition, we still need to interpolate the z-axis interval of the data to 1mm before this test process, and then interpolate the z-axis of the prediction label finally obtained by the test to the original interval, and finally compare it with the ground truth to get the accuracy.

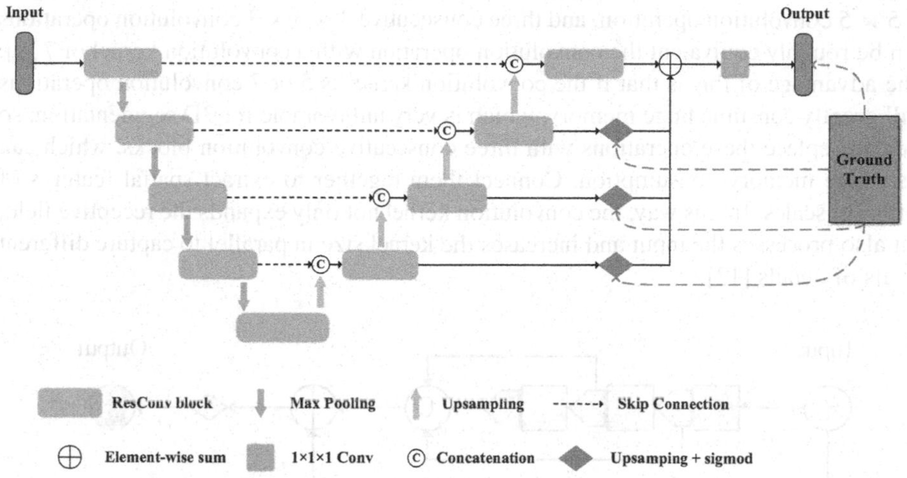

Fig. 4. The network architecture of our ResConv-3DUnet.

2.5 Network Architecture

Our network is based on the 3DUNet [5] architecture. Because the pancreas is small in the CT image, and some have tumors, so its shape and size are different, which is not conducive to segmentation. In response to the above problems, we have added the ResConv block to the encoder and decoder. In order to enhance the semantic expression ability of features at different scales. It also has four layers of encoders and four layers of decoders. For each layer of encoders, max pooling is used to decrease the resolution while increasing the feature map. At the same time, the function of the decoder is to increase the resolution while decreasing the feature map. In order to get more adequate training in the shallow layer and avoid the disappearance of the gradient, ResConv-3DUnet introduces a deep supervision mechanism [11]. The network architecture is shown in Fig. 4. Generally speaking, increasing the depth of a neural network can improve the representation ability of the network to a certain extent, but as the depth deepens, the neural network gradually appears difficult to train, including the gradient disappearance, gradient explosion and other phenomena. The deep supervision mechanism [11] can reduce gradient disappearance and promote network fusion when training deep neural networks, as well as to capture more meaningful features, and also to improve the directness and transparency of the hidden layer learning process. Deep supervision is the technique of adding a secondary classifier to some intermediate hidden layer of a deep neural network as a kind of network branch to supervise the backbone network. The deep supervision mechanism in this paper uses ground truth to supervise feature maps of different scales, which can conclude that the training speed of multi-scale convolution neural network model is faster and the convergence is more stable [19]. Finally, we use the concatenate operation to fuse the features of four scales and let them undergo 1 × 1 × 1 convolution to get the final output.

The ResConv block is composed of three consecutive 3 × 3 × 3 convolution blocks, show in Fig. 5. Two consecutive 3 × 3 × 3 convolution operations can be similar to a 5

× 5 × 5 convolution operation, and three consecutive 3 × 3 × 3 convolution operations can be roughly equivalent the convolution operation with a convolution kernel of 7 [9]. The advantage of this is that if the convolution kernel is 5 or 7 convolution operations will greatly consume huge memory, which is very unfavorable for 3D segmentation, so we can replace these operations with three consecutive convolution blocks, which can also save memory consumption. Connect them together to extract spatial features of different scales. In this way, the convolution kernel not only expands the receptive field, but also processes the input and increases the kernel size in parallel to capture different levels of details [13].

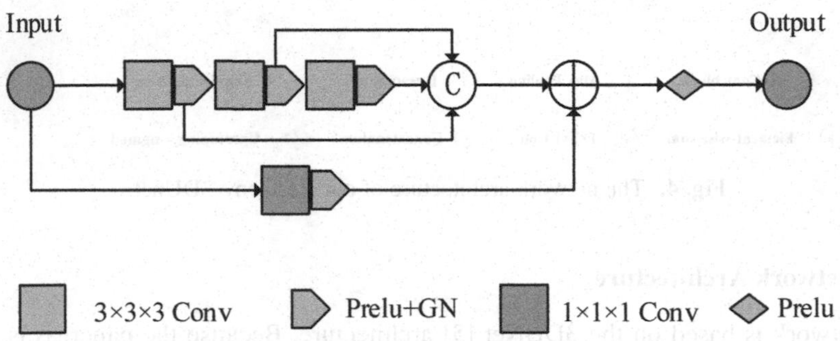

Fig. 5. ResConv block

We also add an additional residual connection, which adds a 1 × 1 × 1 convolutional layer, which allows us to get additional spatial information. After each convolution operation in this res block, there is a Prelu activation function and a Group Normalization.

Group Normalization [10] is proposed by He Kaiming's team. Group Normalization (GN) is an improved algorithm for the higher error rate of Batch Normalization (BN) when the batch size is small. Although the general GPU video memory in the classification algorithm can cover larger batch settings, the input image in 3D segmentation is large, and the memory requirement is huge, so the batch size is generally set relatively small, and the proposed GN has a significant improvement on this algorithm.

3 Experiments

3.1 Datasets

MSD (short for Medical Segmentation Decathlon challenge) provides 281 volumes of CT with labelled pancreas mask which have a spatial resolution of 512 x 512 and a slice count ranging from 37 to 751. We randomly split them into 201 volumes for training and 80 for testing.

3.2 Implementation Details

We adopted PyTorch 12 to implement all models. Our workstation was equipped with NVIDIA RTX 2080 Ti 11GB GPUs. And the viewable software for looking at 3D modeling is ITK-SNAP [18].

In the training network, the two-stage network is based on ResConv-3DUnet proposed in this paper. Moreover, the loss during training is dice loss [4]. During training, the batch size of the first stage is 3 and the batch size of the second stage is 1. Although the two network models are the same, the size of the input network image is different. In addition, the initial learning rate of the two experiments was lr = 1e4. Meanwhile, Adam was used as the optimizer, and the attenuation coefficient of deep supervision during the experiment was 0.33, which was attenuated once every 40 epoch. The training duration of the experiment was about 52 h.

3.3 Results

Our method has been successfully verified on MSD pancreas datasets, achieving state-of-the-art performance, and the dice accuracy can reach 84.6%, which is more accurate than the first place in the MSD competition. As the MSD competition is now closed and its submission entry has been closed, we are unable to submit the results to the official website for verification.

Table 1. Results of different algorithms on MSD pancreas

Method	Mean ± std	Min	Max	Params(M)
3D Unet-Patch [3]	79.98 ± 7.71	61.14	93.73	19
3D Unet-Full [16]	81.13 ± 8.20	61.84	93.49	13
2D FCN8s-A [17]	82.24 ± 6.88	62.99	92.61	130
2D RSTN-A [14]	83.29 ± 6.58	66.23	92.40	270
P3D FCN8s [15]	82.52 ± 7.00	61.75	92.86	400
P3D RSTN [14]	83.63 ± 6.65	64.21	93.02	810
Ours	84.68 ± 6.60	59.33	92.34	6

In order to demonstrate the effectiveness of our method, we compared it with state-of-the-art volumetric segmentation algorithms, in addition to comparing it with the accuracy of the pancreas segmentation that came first in the competition. The final comparison results are shown in Table 1. According to Table 1, it can be seen that our comparison experiments are roughly divided into the following categories: predicting segmentation results directly using 3D networks [3, 16]; segmenting 2D slices using a 2D model and then fusing the segmentation results into 3D results [17, 14]; and segmenting using a pseudo-3D (P3D) segmentation model [15, 14]. It can be easily seen from the table that our method outperforms them. Both the 2D segmentation and the P3D segmentation have a lower average DSC than ours. In addition, the standard deviation of the dice score in our method is also relatively small, suggesting that the method proposed in this paper would be more comprehensive in the segmentation of the experimental pancreas. More importantly, it can be seen from this comparison experiment that both 2D segmentation method and P3D segmentation method have reached a terrible number of parameters.

However, as our method uses the two-stage segmentation method proposed in this paper, the number of parameters is greatly reduced and the memory pressure is alleviated.

In order to further illustrate the effectiveness of our proposed network, we conducted ablation experiments under the two-stage method proposed in this paper. The initial baseline network was 3DUNet [5]. As the different modules are added, we record the accuracy of their dice separately so that they can be compared. Table 2 shows the final experimental comparison results. The evaluation metrics are the dice score and the number of parameters, respectively. The results show that the accuracy of our network is indeed higher than that of the baseline, and it can be seen from the number of parameters that our network is more efficient. It can be seen that the accuracy of 3D UNet improves with the addition of the ResConv block module. In addition, deep supervision also plays a role in improving the accuracy, although it is not as obvious as the former, but it can also be improved in practice.

Table 2. Results of different strategies on test set.

Strategies	Dice	Min	Max	Params
Baseline	75.99	2.60	91.86	16M
Baseline + DS	77.68	0.07	91.36	16M
Baseline + Rb	83.13	51.91	92.05	6M
ResConv3DUnet	84.68	59.33	92.34	6M

Figure 6 shows the test results of pancreas_088 and pancreas_299. The first row of the image shows a diseased pancreas, which is already severely diseased in the caudal part. From the figure, it can be seen that 3DUnet and baseline + DS can only roughly segment the diseased part of the pancreas, and the dice accuracy is not satisfactory. In contrast, the ResConv-3DUnet segmentation proposed in this paper was the best, and was able to segment the pancreas more completely, with a dice score of 77.47%. The shape of the pancreas in the second row was relatively normal, but the original baseline could only segment one point, and the accuracy was as low as 2.85%, while the ResConv-3DUnet segmentation had a more complete shape, which reflected the robustness of our network more. As can be seen from the figure, the segmentation result of the baseline + Rb (ResConv block) is relatively complete, but most importantly compared to the other three, the dice score obtained from our network architecture segmentation is the highest, indicating that the results of ResConv-3DUnet segmentation proposed in this paper are more consistent with the ground truth. Combined with Table 1, it can be seen that ResConv block can indeed increase the accuracy.

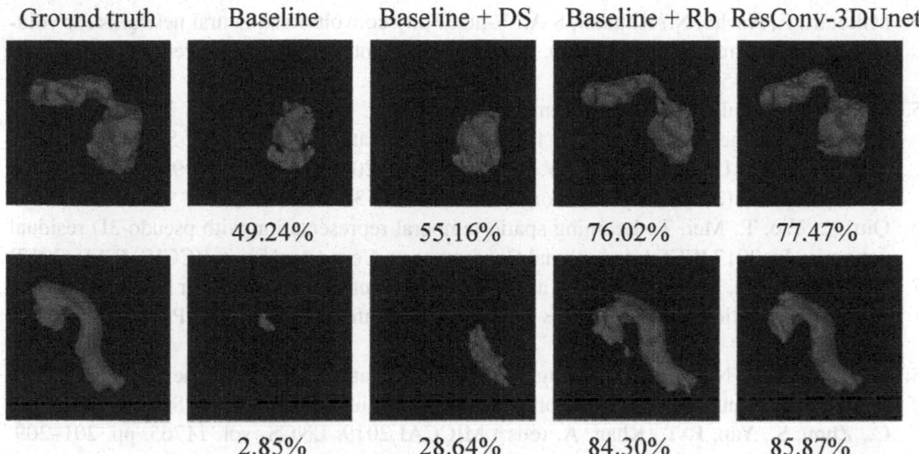

Fig. 6. The upper and lower rows of the above image show a severely diseased pancreas and a more normal shaped pancreas. The accuracy score is the dice score.

4 Conclusions

In this paper, we propose an end-to-end 3D segmentation method for the pancreas to reduce memory consumption, which includes both our proposed two-stage segmentation method and the ResConv-3DUnet presented in this paper. This experiment successfully completed the segmentation of MSD pancreas 3D datasets under the environment of 11G computer memory, and the accuracy of the proposed method outperformed those state-of-the-art volumetric segmentation algorithms, not only that, but also much higher than the score of winning the first place in the MSD competition. The experimental results show that this method can accomplish the pancreas segmentation task well and is expected to be applied in clinical practice.

Acknowledgment. This work was supported by Zhenjiang Key Deprogram "Fire Early Warning Technology Based on Multimodal Data Analysis" (SH2020011) Jiangsu Emergency Management Science and Technology Project "Research on Very Early Warning of Fire Based on Multi-modal Data Analysis and Multi-Intelligent Body Technology" (YJGL-TG-2020–8).

References

1. Roth, H.R., et al.: DeepOrgan: multi-level deep convolutional networks for automated pancreas segmentation. In: Navab, N., Hornegger, J., Wells, W.M., Frangi, A.F. (eds.) MICCAI 2015. LNCS, vol. 9349, pp. 556–564. Springer, Cham (2015). https://doi.org/10.1007/978-3-319-24553-9_68
2. Isensee, F., Petersen, J., Kohl, S.A.A, et al.: Nnu-net: breaking the spell on successful medical image segmentation (2019)
3. Roth, H.R., Oda, H., Zhou, X., et al.: An application of cascaded 3D fully convolutional networks for medical image segmentation. Comput. Med. Imaging Graph. Off. J. Comput. Med. Imaging Soc. **66**, 90 (2018)

4. Milletari, F., Navab, N., Ahmadi, S.A.: V-net: Fully convolutional neural networks for volumetric medical image segmentation. In: 2016 Fourth International Conference on 3D Vision (3DV), pp. 565–571 (2016)
5. Çiçek, Ö., Abdulkadir, A., Lienkamp, S.S., Brox, T., Ronneberger, O.: 3D U-Net: learning dense volumetric segmentation from sparse annotation. In: Ourselin, S., Joskowicz, L., Sabuncu, M.R., Unal, G., Wells, W. (eds.) MICCAI 2016. LNCS, vol. 9901, pp. 424–432. Springer, Cham (2016). https://doi.org/10.1007/978-3-319-46723-8_49
6. Qiu, Z., Yao, T., Mei, T.: Learning spatio-temporal representation with pseudo-3D residual networks. In: 2017 IEEE International Conference on Computer Vision (ICCV). IEEE (2017)
7. Wang, Z.H., Liu, Z., Song, Y.Q., et al.: Densely connected deep U-Net for abdominal multi-organ segmentation. In: 2019 IEEE International Conference on Image Processing (ICIP). IEEE (2019)
8. Zhao, N., Tong, N., Ruan, D., Sheng, K.: Fully automated pancreas segmentation with two-stage 3D convolutional neural networks. In: Shen, D., Liu, T., Peters, T.M., Staib, L.H., Essert, C., Zhou, S., Yap, P.-T., Khan, A. (eds.) MICCAI 2019. LNCS, vol. 11765, pp. 201–209. Springer, Cham (2019). https://doi.org/10.1007/978-3-030-32245-8_23
9. Szegedy, C., Vanhoucke, V., Ioffe, S., Shlens, J., Wojna, Z.: Rethinking the inception architecture for computer vision. In: Proceedings of the IEEE Conference on Computer Vision and Pattern Recognition, pp. 2818–2826.AWERTQ (2016)
10. Wu, Y., He, K.: Group normalization. Int. J. Comput. Vis. (2018)
11. Lee, C., Xie, S., Gallagher, P.W., et al.: Deeply-supervised nets. Int. Conf. Artif. Intell. Stat. 562–570 (2015)
12. https://pytorch.org/
13. Duta, I.C., Liu, L., Zhu, F., et al.: Pyramidal convolution: rethinking convolutional neural networks for visual recognition. arXiv preprint arXiv:2006.11538 (2020)
14. Yu, Q., Xie, L., Wang, Y., et al.: Recurrent Saliency Transformation Network: Incorporating Multi-Stage Visual Cues for Small Organ Segmentation. In: 2018 IEEE/CVF Conference on Computer Vision and Pattern Recognition. IEEE (2018)
15. Zhou, X., Ito, T., Takayama, R., Wang, S., Hara, T., Fujita, H.: Three-dimensional CT image segmentation by combining 2D fully convolutional network with 3D majority voting. In: Carneiro, G., Mateus, D., Peter, L., Bradley, A., Tavares, J.M.R.S., Belagiannis, V., Papa, J.P., Nascimento, J.C., Loog, M., Lu, Z., Cardoso, J.S., Cornebise, J. (eds.) LABELS/DLMIA -2016. LNCS, vol. 10008, pp. 111–120. Springer, Cham (2016). https://doi.org/10.1007/978-3-319-46976-8_12
16. Roth, H.R., et al.: Deep learning and its application to medical image segmentation. Med. Imaging Technol. **36**(2), 63–71 (2018)
17. Long, J., Evan, S., Trevor, D.: Fully convolutional networks for semantic segmentation. In: Proceedings of the IEEE Conference on Computer Vision and Pattern Recognition (2015)
18. Yushkevich, P.A., Piven, J., Hazlett, H.C., et al.: User-guided 3D active contour segmentation of anatomical structures: significantly improved efficiency and reliability. Neuroimage **31**(3), 1116–1128 (2006)
19. Cheng, J., Liu, Y., Tang, X., Sheng, V.S., Li, M., et al.: DDOS attack detection via multi-scale convolutional neural network. Comput. Mater. Continua **62**(3), 1317–1333 (2020)

Multi-UAV Task Allocation Method Based on Improved Bat Algorithm

Jiaqi Shi, Li Tan(✉), Xiaofeng Lian, Xinyue Lv, and Tianying Xu

College of Computer Science and Engineering, Beijing Technology and Business University, Beijing 100048, China
tanli@th.btbu.edu.cn

Abstract. At present, as a method of solving large-scale complex optimization problems, bionic algorithms are widely used in multi-UAV task allocation. Bat algorithm, as a kind of bionic algorithm, has problems such as long flying distance of UAV in the process of task allocation. In this paper, an improved bat algorithm for multi-UAV task allocation method is proposed. On the basis of the bat algorithm, the comparison of the number of drones and target points and the calculation of the flight distance of the drone are added. The experimental results show that the improved algorithm can reduce the calculation time and the flight time of the UAV, shorten the flight distance of the UAV, and improve the efficiency of the algorithm.

Keywords: Multi-UAVs · Task allocation · Bat algorithm · Flight distance · Calculation time

1 Introduction

1.1 Research Background

In recent years, multi-aircraft cooperative control has become a research hotspot in the field of unmanned aerial vehicles, and task allocation is the guarantee and basis for multi-aircraft cooperative control. Task allocation is to reasonably assign the tasks that need to be completed to the team members in the system according to the established goals, so as to achieve the purpose of performing tasks efficiently and optimizing the UAV system. Generally, multi-UAV mission planning can be divided into two parts: upper-level task allocation and lower-level path planning. Task allocation considers various constraints, takes the effective achievement of the overall task as the goal, assigns specific goals and action tasks to each aircraft, and each aircraft conducts specific combat path planning based on the assigned tasks. The function of path planning is to design or generate a path between a series of positions on the premise of satisfying self or external constraints such as maximum linear speed, maximum angular speed, operational safety, time and environmental variables. Path planning is the problem of determining the path of the UAV from the initial point to the target point. UAV path determination should avoid all collisions with surrounding obstacles. The main goal of the path planning algorithm is

X. Sun et al. (Eds.): ICAIS 2021, LNCS 12736, pp. 205–213, 2021.
https://doi.org/10.1007/978-3-030-78609-0_18

to find a collision-free path from the initial state to the target state in the configuration space of the UAV [1]. Path planning technology is very important for calculating the safe path to the final destination in the shortest time.

At present, scholars have done relevant research on task allocation models. The methods of task allocation can be divided into intelligent optimization algorithms and free market mechanism algorithms.

Bionic algorithms have been widely used in recent years. It achieves the purpose of optimization by simulating the behavior of natural creatures, and an optimization method that uses modern intelligent optimization algorithms to optimize the solution of task assignment problems. The difference between this method and the global search of the precise method is that its purpose is to find a satisfactory solution within an acceptable time range, and to adjust between the solution time and the solution quality. Its advantage is that it is easier to implement, and the calculation is not very complicated, and the quality of the solution is relatively high. Including genetic algorithm, particle swarm algorithm, ant colony algorithm, etc.

The contract network algorithm is derived from the contract mechanism that people use to manage goods and services in the business process [2]. The algorithm is to imitate the "manager-worker" mechanism of economic behavior to negotiate tasks and achieve task assignment. In the contract network algorithm, all subjects are divided into three roles: tenderer, bidder and bid winner. In the contract network algorithm of multi-UAV task allocation, the bidder is the task manager, responsible for the collection, release and management of task information [3]. The bidder is a drone, which evaluates the task based on its own information and resources, participates in bidding, and sends task requests to the tenderer. The winning bidder is the drone that has won the task and is responsible for completing the task.

1.2 Related Works

At present, scholars have done relevant research on task allocation models [4–7]. Literature [6] explored the cooperative task assignment of heterogeneous UAVs when the target types are different, and established a heterogeneous multi-UAV cooperative task assignment model. Literature [7] takes the heterogeneous multi-objective multi-UAV task assignment problem as a prototype, and designs a multi-UAV alliance group task assignment method based on time window to make the UAV task assignment effective and real-time It has been greatly improved. Literature [8] pointed out the task assignment problem faced by multiple UAVs under the condition of uncertain information on the actual battlefield. A task allocation model for multiple UAVs based on the interval information environment is established, and a random probability multi-attribute scheme ranking method is used to obtain a dynamic task allocation method for multiple UAVs in an uncertain environment. Literature [9] summarized and summarized the current research status of multi-UAV collaborative mission planning at home and abroad, focusing on the common models and algorithms of task allocation methods, discussed the advantages and disadvantages of various algorithms, and concluded that the multi-agent Market mechanism algorithms will have a wide range of applications in air combat.

As a method of solving large-scale and complex optimization problems, biomimetic algorithms have also been studied in the area of UAV task allocation. Sun Xiaolei et al.

[10] designed an overall control architecture that combines multi-UAV task allocation and trajectory planning, using an improved algorithm to find the shortest path between two track points, and treating this path as task allocation Process the input of the global objective function, and then use particle swarm optimization task allocation to iteratively optimize. Gao et al. [11] improved the multi-objective particle swarm optimization algorithm to solve the task assignment problem of multiple UAVs, and used two-stage SMC resampling to improve the shortcomings of the MOPSO algorithm. In the first stage, the re-sampling method is used to improve the problem of slow convergence of the particle swarm algorithm in the middle and late stages. In the second stage, resampling is used to expand the search range of the particle swarm optimization algorithm to prevent the algorithm from falling into a local optimal solution. Deng Ke et al. [12] proposed an adaptive inertial weight and quantum gate mutation operator based on the degree of particle convergence to solve the problem of poor adaptability of the standard quantum particle swarm algorithm to the discrete and narrow solution space in multi-UAV task allocation. The quantum particle swarm algorithm is improved. Wang et al. [13] proposed a task allocation method based on ant colony algorithm, which described in detail the robot alliance and high-level task allocation process. Du Jianjian et al. [14] aimed at the problem of multi-UAV cooperative reconnaissance planning, coding the scene and using the bat algorithm to solve it. N. Lin et al. [15] used an improved artificial potential field (APF) method to accelerate the convergence process of bat position update, and proposed an optimal success rate strategy to increase the adaptive inertia weight of the bat algorithm. In order to avoid falling into the local optimum, a third chaotic strategy is also proposed.

Aiming at the problem of multi-UAV task allocation, this paper improves on the bat algorithm, which reduces the time to complete the task and shortens the flight distance of the drone search task.

2 Improved Bat Algorithm

In order to reduce the complexity of the algorithm and shorten the flight distance of the UAV, this article improves on the bat algorithm, adding the comparison of the number of UAV and the target point and the comparison of the UAV flight distance calculation.

2.1 Bat Algorithm

Bats can fly freely and capture food accurately at night or in a very dim environment because they can send out ultrasonic pulse echoes to locate. Inspired by this, Yang proposed Bat Algorithm (BA) [16]. In the bat algorithm, in order to simulate the random search process of bats hunting prey and avoiding obstacles, the following three approximate idealized rule assumptions are made [17]:

(1) All bats in the population use echolocation to sense distance.
(2) The bat flies randomly at position x_i at speed v_i, has a fixed frequency $f_{\min}$, and has a wavelength λ and pulse loudness A that are automatically adjusted according to the distance between itself and its prey.

(3) Assuming that the change of impulse loudness is from a maximum value A_0 integer to a fixed minimum value $A_{\min}$, the change interval can be adjusted according to the problem.

Assuming that the bat search space is D-dimensional, the update rules of bat position x_i^t and velocity v_i^t in each generation are shown in formulas (1)–(3). Where $\beta \in [0, 1][0, 1]$ is a random variable. X_* is the current local optimal solution position of the group.

$$f_i = f_{\min} + (f_{\max} - f_{\min}) \times \beta \tag{1}$$

$$v_i^t = v_i^{t-1} + \left(x_i^t - X_*\right) \times f_i \tag{2}$$

$$x_i^t = x_i^{t-1} \times v_i^t \tag{3}$$

In the local search, the new local solution is generated by random walk method, as in formula (4). $\varepsilon \in [-1, 1]$ is a random number; A^t is the average loudness of the entire group in the same generation. During the search process, the bats will continuously reduce the loudness to a fixed value according to the distance from the target prey, and increase the frequency, narrow the range of the prey and prey. In this process, the sound wave loudness and frequency of each bat The degree update formulas are shown in (5) and (6), where α is the sonic loudness attenuation coefficient, and the value falls between 0 and 1 excluding 0 and 1; γ is the pulse frequency enhancement coefficient greater than 0; r_i^0 represents the bat Initial pulse frequency.

$$x_{new} = x_{dd} + \varepsilon \times A^t \tag{4}$$

$$A_i^t - 1 = \alpha \times A_t^i \tag{5}$$

$$r_i^t + 1 = r_i^0\left[1 - \exp(-\gamma \times t)\right] \tag{6}$$

2.2 Improved Bat Algorithm

The improved bat algorithm adds the comparison of the number of drones and target points and the calculation of the flight distance of the drone on the basis of the bat algorithm. The specific steps are:

(1) Obtain the size of the task area, the number of drones participating in the multi-drone task allocation, the number of targets that need to be searched, the initial position of the drone and the target, the speed of the drone, and the algorithm involved The number of groups and the number of iterations of the algorithm.
(2) Parameter initialization: bat population number m, iteration number N, objective function $f(x)$, bat position $X_i (i = 1, 2, 3, \ldots\ldots, m)$, velocity v_i and sound wave frequency f_i, sound wave loudness A_i and frequency r_i.

(3) Find the optimal position of the current population, and update the position and velocity according to formulas (2)–(4).
(4) Determine whether the number of drones is less than the number of target points. If the number of drones is less than the number of target points, the drone that is farthest from the target point stops working.
(5) Generate random number rand1 on [0,1], if rand1 > r_i, select an optimal solution in the solution set, generate a local solution around the selected optimal solution according to formula (4), otherwise update according to formula (4) Location of individual bats.
(6) Generate a random number rand2 on [0,1]. If rand2 < A_i and $f(x_i) < f(x_*)$, then accept the position, reduce A_i and increase r_i according to formulas (5) and (6).
(7) Sort the fitness values of all individuals in the population and find the current best X_*
(8) Compare the ant colony algorithm with the direct calculation of thc straight-line distance between two points, take the smaller one as the distance between the drone and the target position, and then compare to find the best task allocation strategy.
(9) Repeat steps (3) ~ (8) to determine whether the maximum number of iterations is met, and output the global optimal value.

3 Simulation and Result Analysis

3.1 Simulation

The experiment in this article is simulated in Matlab environment, the CPU model is Inter Core i7 6700T, and the area size is set to. Set five target points, up to three drones to complete the task, the initial position of the drone and the target point are given. The initial situation of the environment is shown in Fig. 1. The red × in the figure indicates

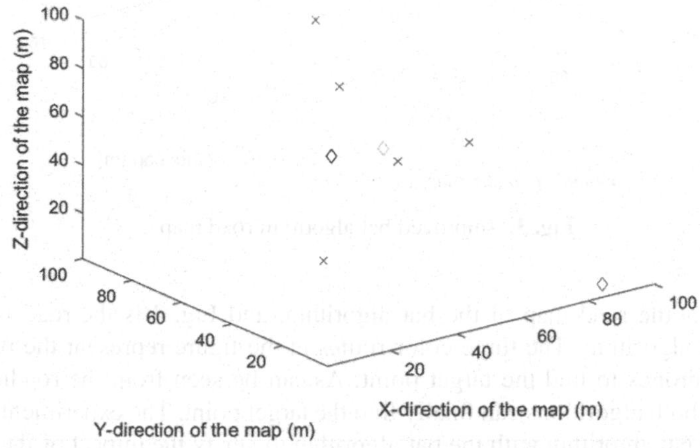

Fig. 1. Experimental initial environment

the position of the target point, and the three colors ◇ indicate the initial positions of the three UAVs.

In this experiment, the bat algorithm and the improved bat algorithm are implemented in the same scene. The experimental results of the two algorithms are shown in Figs. 2 and 3.

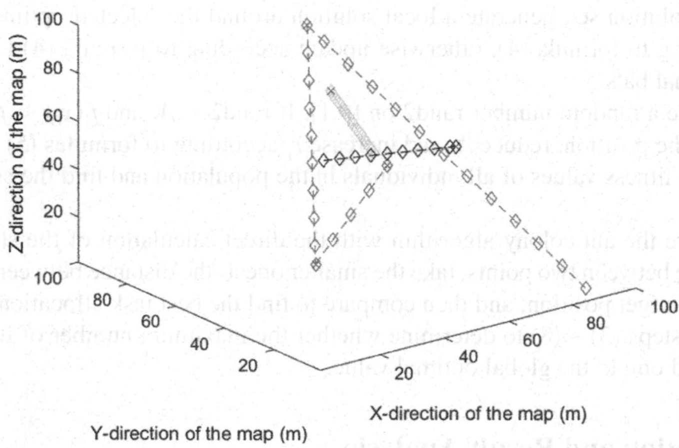

Fig. 2. Bat algorithm road map

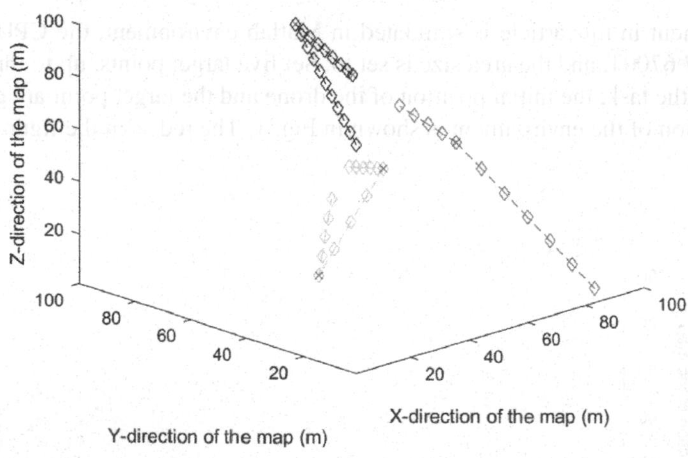

Fig. 3. Improved bat algorithm road map

Figure 2 is the road map of the bat algorithm, and Fig. 3 is the road map of the improved bat algorithm. The three color routes in the figure represent the paths taken by the three drones to find the target point. As can be seen from the roadmap in the above figure, both algorithms can finally find the target point. The experiment compares the improved bat algorithm with the bat algorithm to verify the impact of the improved algorithm.

3.2 Result Analysis

This paper mainly evaluates the performance of the proposed algorithm through the following three indicators:

Calculation time: It is an important indicator to evaluate the efficiency of the algorithm. It refers to the time required for the calculation of the algorithm, that is, the time required to calculate the flight path of the UAV. Calculation time = UAV start flight time-program start execution time.

UAV flying distance: refers to the total distance of all UAVs flying from the initial position to the final target, that is, the sum of the optimal distance for each step.

UAV flight time: refers to the time it takes for the UAV to fly from the beginning to when all the targets are found. Flight time = time when the last target was found-time when the drone started flying.

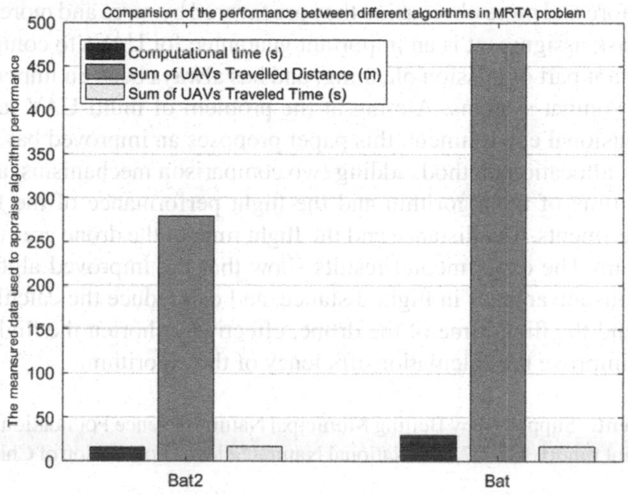

Fig. 4. Comparison of three indicators of two algorithms

Figure 4 is the overall comparison diagram of the three indicators of each algorithm. In the figure, Bat is the bat algorithm, and Bat2 is the improved bat algorithm. It can be seen from the figure that the revised algorithm has been improved in three aspects: calculation time, UAV flight distance and UAV flight time.

Table 1. Indicators of the two algorithms.

Heading level	Calculation time(s)	UAV flight distance(m)	UAV flight time(s)
Bat	29.5710	475.1572	17.6612
Bat2	15.7241	279.0111	16.7241

Table 1 shows the three index data of the two algorithms.

In terms of calculation time, the improved bat algorithm is approximately one-half of the original algorithm, indicating that the improved algorithm can effectively improve the efficiency of the algorithm and reduce the calculation time of the algorithm.

In terms of drone flight distance, the improved bat algorithm is about 200 m shorter than the original algorithm, indicating that the improved algorithm can effectively reduce the drone's flight distance.

In terms of UAV flight distance, the improved algorithm is slightly lower than the original algorithm, indicating that the improved algorithm can reduce UAV flight time.

4 Conclusions

With the continuous development of science and technology, the battlefield situation is becoming more and more severe, and the combat advantages of UAVs in modern warfare are becoming more and more obvious, so they are favored by more and more national military leaders. Task assignment is an important guarantee for UAVs to complete military tasks, an important part of mission planning, and has always been an important research topic for UAV combat systems. Aiming at the problem of multi-UAV task allocation in a three-dimensional environment, this paper proposes an improved bat algorithm for multi-UAV task allocation method, adding two comparison mechanisms, and analyzing the calculation time of the algorithm and the flight performance of the UAV through simulation experiments. The distance and the flight time of the drone are compared with the bat algorithm. The experimental results show that the improved algorithm in this paper has obvious advantages in flight distance, and can reduce the calculation time of the algorithm and the flight time of the drone, effectively shorten the flight distance of the drone, and improve the calculation efficiency of the algorithm.

Acknowledgement. Supported by Beijing Municipal Natural Science Foundation-Haidian original innovation joint fund(L182007); the National Natural Science Foundation of China(61702020).

References

1. Lin, Y., Saripalli, S.: Sampling-based path planning for UAV collision avoidance. IEEE Trans. Intell. Transp. Syst. **18**, 3179–3192 (2017)
2. Qian, Y., Xia, J., Liu, T.: Task assignment scheme based on contract net. J. Syst. Simul. **23**(8), 1672–1676 (2011)
3. Li, X., Zhai, J., Dai, Y.: A task allocation algorithm based on contract net protocol under the dynamic enviorment. Sci. Technol. Eng. **27**, 104–109 (2013)
4. Chen, X., Wan, Z., Wang, J.: A study of unmanned path planning based on a double-twin RBM-BP deep neural network. Intell. Autom. Soft Comput. **26**(6), 1531–1548 (2020)
5. Chen, X., Qiao, Y.: Summary of unmanned aerial vehicle task allocation. J. Shenyang Aerosp. Univ. **33**(6), 1–7 (2016)
6. Di, B., Zhou, R., Ding, Q.: Distributed coordinated heterogeneous task allocation for unmanned aerial vehicles. Control Decis. **28**(2), 274–278 (2013)
7. Wang, L.L.S.Q., Fanchun, S.Y.: Research on time window based coalition formation for Multi-UAVs task assignment. J. Electron. Inf. Technol. **35**(8), 1983–1988 (2013)

8. Chen, X., Tang, T.: Study on the dynamic task assignment of multi-ucav under dynamic uncertain environment. Fire Control Command Control **38**(1), 45–49 (2013)
9. Zhu, Y., Zhang, T., Cheng, N.: Research on cooperative mission planning of multiple UAVs. J. Syst. Simul. **20**, 194–199 (2009)
10. Xiaolei, S., Naiming, Q., Cheng, D., Weiran, Y.: Cooperative control algorithm of task assignment and path planning for multiple UAVs. Syst. Eng. Electronic. **37**(12), 2272–2276 (2015)
11. Gao, Y., Zhang, Y., Zhu, S., Sun, Y.: Multi-UAV task allocation based on improved algorithm of multi-objective particle swarm optimization. In: 2018 International Conference on Cyber-Enabled Distributed Computing and Knowledge Discovery, pp. 443–450. Institute of Electrical and Electronics Engineers Inc., United States. Zhengzhou (2018)
12. Deng, K., Lian, Z., Zhou, D., Li, X.: Task allocation of multi-unmanned aerial vehicle based on improved quantum particle swarm optimization. Command Control Simul. **40**(5), 32–36 (2018)
13. Wang, J., Yuesheng, G., Xiaomin, L.: Multi-robot task allocation based on ant colony algorithm. J. Comput. **7**(9), 2160–2167 (2012)
14. Du, J., Wan, X.: Multi-UAV cooperative reconnaissance mission planning based on bat algorithm. Election Meas. Technol. **42**(7), 40–43 (2019)
15. Lin, N., Tang, J., Li, X., Zhao, L.: A novel improved bat algorithm in uav path planning. Comput. Mater. Continua **61**(1), 323–344 (2019)
16. Yang, X.S.: A New Metaheuristic Bat-Inspired Algorithm. In: Nature Inspired Cooperative Strategies for Optimization (NISCO 2010), pp. 65–74, Springer-verlag, Berlin (2010). https://doi.org/10.1007/978-3-642-12538-6_6
17. Degang, X., Ping, Z.: Literature survey on research and application of bat algorithm. Comput. Eng. Appl. **55**(15), 1-12+13 (2019)

Deep Learning Models for Intelligent Healthcare: Implementation and Challenges

Sadaqat ur Rehman[1,2], Shanshan Tu[1(✉)], Zubair Shah[3], Jawad Ahmad[4], Muhammad Waqas[1], Obaid ur Rehman[5], Anis Kouba[6], and Qammer H. Abbasi[7]

[1] Engineering Research Center of Intelligent Perception and Autonomous Control, Faculty of Information Technology, Beijing University of Technology, Beijing 100124, China
sstu@bjut.edu.cn

[2] Department of Computer Science, Namal Institute, Mianwali 42250, Pakistan

[3] Department of Computer Science and Engineering, Hammad Bin Khalifa University, Doha, Qatar

[4] School of Computing, Edinburgh Napier University, Edinburgh, UK

[5] Department of Electrical Engineering, Sarhad University of Science and IT, Peshawar 25000, Pakistan

[6] Department of Computer Science, Prince Sultan University, Riyadh, Kingdom of Saudi Arabia

[7] James Watt School of Engineering, University of Glasgow, Glasgow G12 8QQ, UK

Abstract. The rapid developments of artificial intelligent (AI) is being transformed for its extensive use-cases, people-centered intelligent systems focusing on care delivery, research encounter complex problems related to improve the overall infrastructure and management of intelligent delivery service; for instance, bringing transformation in healthcare sector for monitoring patients with chronic disease. Most of these systems are driven by state-of-the-art learning algorithms i.e., Convolution Neural Network. The CNN algorithm is considered to be one of the most prominent architectures of DL. Recently, due to enormous growth in the amount of annotated data and the development of CNN hardware accelerator, further, boost the research on CNN and accomplished benchmark enactment on different applications. This paper presents cutting-edge applications of CNN for an intelligent healthcare system. We provide useful findings of different CNN features such as optimization, fast computation, design, activation function, and loss function. To our knowledge, this is the first comprehensive work to address the recent trends in the architecture of CNN, which offers insight to the underlying problems and provides the potential solutions for any given intelligent healthcare applications.

Keywords: Deep learning architecture · CNN application · Healthcare intelligence

1 Introduction

Recent developments in data analytics using wireless sensing systems for various applications, including remote healthcare, agriculture technologies, smart trackers, and augmented reality, positively transform lives. Data analysis is mostly driven by benchmark

X. Sun et al. (Eds.): ICAIS 2021, LNCS 12736, pp. 214–225, 2021.
https://doi.org/10.1007/978-3-030-78609-0_19

machine learning and deep learning algorithms. One of the most famous use cases these techniques in Convolution Neural Network (CNN) is a feed-forward artificial neural network. In this type of network, the interneuron pattern of connectivity is inspired by the neural connectivity, which in turn is initiated in the animal visual cortex. Distinct neurons in the visual cortex respond to stimuli merely from a constrained area of space, known as the receptive field. End to end connected neurons may have their receptive fields partially overlapping, encompassing the whole visual field. Earlier it was publicized that the reaction of distinct neurons to the stimuli within its receptive field can be estimated mathematically by a 3D convolution procedure widely used in CNNs [1].

By assembling several layers of distinct functions, CNN is designed to convert the input occurrence into a suitable output response (e.g., holding the class scores). Several diverse layers are generally used when establishing a CNN: pooling layer, convolutional layer, concatenation layer, adding a layer, non-linear layer, and fully connected (FC) layer.

Convolutional Network (ConvNet) in the areas of computer vision and big data analytics are massive and diverse [2–6], which involves plentiful computing resources. The ConvNet models [2, 7–11] also outclass the majority of the standard approaches in image processing. Dependency over data, high computation, and the need for great memory are the acute complications that refrain ConvNet from solving real-life problems.

Nevertheless, training fewer data-dependent, low computation power and memory needs is still an unresolved issue. In ConvNet architecture design, optimization of computation and speed, along with proficiency in processing, must be kept in mind. Considering that several researchers worked on the ConvNet data-flow behavior of the categorization stage and established a hardware platform to enhance the procedure for supervised learning. For instance, Graphical Processing Units (GPUs) [12], Field-Programmable Gate Array (FPGA) [13–17], and Application Specific Integrated Circuits (ASICs) [18–20]. Certainly, these hardware platforms are verified beneficial in enhancing the speed of the ConvNet categorization stage.

This work is focused on the latest improvements in the CNN model architecture for healthcare applications. Moreover, we also discuss challenges associated with DL models that hinder the performance in real-time healthcare applications. Our contributions are as follow:

1. Overview of the latest development in the CNN model for healthcare applications.
2. We highlight various conventional CNN models adaptation challenges over the latest CNN models.
3. We provide robust solutions for healthcare applications using the latest CNN model.
4. Highlight research gaps and direction in the adaptation of the CNN model in healthcare applications, which needs further investigation.

2 Application of CNN in Intelligent Healthcare

Neural Networks have been used in healthcare for several decades. They help to unveil the hidden pattern in healthcare data, helping doctors to diagnose the disease efficiently and effectively [21]. CNN is a type of deep learning algorithm which get popularity due its effectiveness in spatial feature extraction [22]. CNN has a range of application in natural language processing [23], face recognition [24] and computer vision [25]. Also, CNN is reshaping healthcare, some of the major healthcare applications are drug discovery, medicine, medical imaging and genome [26].

Some radiology applications are as follows:

- Lung cancer screening from CT scans
- Automatic tumor detection and characterization (mammography scans, MRI, or CT)
- Brain image analysis (both in health and disease)
- Gene expression profiling in several cancers (one molecular signature was found recently for hepatocellular carcinomas)
- Almost all CAD systems are trying to migrate into deep learning technologies including prostate, lung, and Multiple Sclerosis
- Segmentation of anatomical objects from medical scans (this varies a lot, from the prostate to brain substructures, and abdominal organs to the heart).

A big area for further transformation using deep learning in medicine is an automated microbiological analysis [27]. This is commonly performed by medical laboratory process, notwithstanding it has been partially automated, but requires human involvement to determine whether bacteria appear on a Petri dish and determine the type of bacteria.

Classical algorithms for image recognition in microbiology analysis aren't reliable enough [28]. Deep learning algorithms, in contrast, show significant results in this area. Talo [29] proposed a deep learning-based model for automatic classification of bacterial images. Furthermore, they also employed a transfer learning technique to boost up the training process of CNN.

Automating microbiological analysis with the help of deep learning is a big step forward, which will allow many patients to get their test result faster (medical labs working 24/7 is of high importance for people with urgent health needs), cheaper (without humans being involved, medical labs will be able to cut cost on the process), and expect more accuracy of their diagnoses (due to minimized risk of a human error happening in the lab) [30, 31]. Similar benefits apply to industrial microbiology labs. As healthcare is a vast field and covering all its sub-fields are beyond the scope of this article. Therefore, we cover specific applications of CNN in healthcare domain.

2.1 Applications of Deep Learning in Medicine

Deep learning algorithms play a vital role used in improving the field of medicine [32]. The drug discovery process is not only expensive but also very time-consuming and enormously complex. Recent data has shown that it costs up to 2.5 billion dollars and takes on average, nearly 12 years to ultimately develop a drug from scratch, and only about 1 in 10 of those making it past regulatory approval [33, 34]. Researchers are starting to integrate machine learning into the drug discovery process to make it more efficient, shorten the development time, and lower costs considerably [35, 36]. It also means a lot of time, resources, and money spent on conventional drug discovery strategies could be utilized in other areas for better return of investment, or new technologies.

One of the biggest obstacles in machine learning could be managing the enormous amount of biomedical information that is created daily with valuable data that must be extracted from the studies. The world's biomedical journals are producing up to ten thousand pieces of publishing content per day, a rate that is nearly impossible to manage effectively with current technologies [37]. Other companies are using machine learning to analyze data from patient samples in both healthy and diseased states to generate novel biomarkers and therapeutic agents. Machine learning allows researchers to make these potentially useful targets from the biological data and implement the first type of personalized medicine to date.

The integration of machine learning into the drug discovery process has created a variety of new startups that helped investigators decrease their research time and overall costs along the path to market a new drug [38]. Eventually, all of these new technologies will lead to a better understanding of each patient's molecular blueprint and will pave the path to personalized medicine.

Creating a drug discovery system using deep learning would be a very complicated endeavor, but the overall efficiency and savings in costs are entirely worth it in the long run. Drug discovery can be significantly accelerated with a deep-learning or AI model, which is something fundamental to consider when developing an early development system for novel compounds. The most crucial part of building a drug discovery system with deep learning is creating the custom algorithm for processing accurate prediction parameters for new and unexplored compounds [39].

These algorithms, powered by deep learning principles, will accurately predict the interaction between proteins and other drug compounds. They are entirely referenced from pre-existing data, such as from related experiments or simulations (see Fig. 1). By connecting all of these various references of parameters, it will be able to piece together and quickly predict whether or not a particular compound will be bio-active or not, at a fraction of the time it would take for traditional quantum mechanical calculations up to 99\% accuracy. This technology is equivalent to predicting, with nearly perfect accuracy, the activity of hundreds of compounds before actually formally testing them, with only a few dozen tests to perform. It is easy to see why so many pharmaceutical companies are adopting these tools for early research by accelerating the screening of candidate molecules over a thousand-fold faster than traditional calculations [40].

This new algorithmic approach has shown to be very successful in predicting the stability of organic molecules and managing the sub-structures relevant for microelectronic applications. Researchers will be able to precisely predict the behaviors and functions of novel molecules and proteins. With such high accuracy and computational effort, pharmaceutical companies are quickly acquiring fully integrated artificially-intelligent drug discovery platforms for future development.

The steady increase in demand for analyzing big data has encouraged the integration of machine algorithms like deep learning (DL) principles. DL is a class of machine learning algorithms that use artificial neural networks (ANNs) with multiple layers of nonlinear processing units for learning data representations. DL has already had a lot of success in other industries, such as computer games and speech recognition. But over the last ten years, deep learning has also had enormous success in the various research

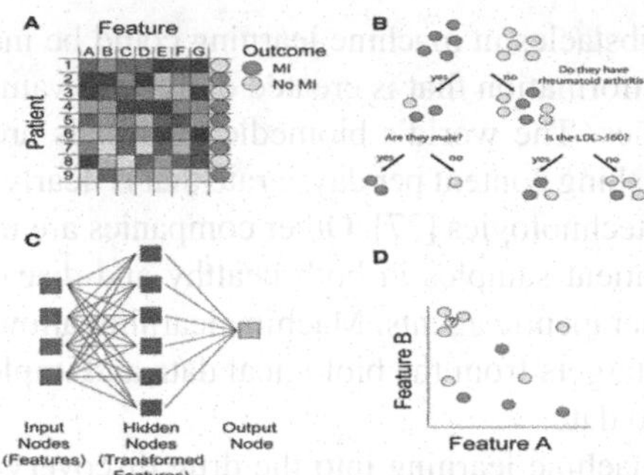

Fig. 1. An overview of drug discovery process using deep learning.

areas of artificial intelligence, especially in drug discovery [41, 42]. It is for sure that DL is completely changing the lives of everyone on a global scale.

Deep learning has evolved from the previous research on ANNs, and the technology has shown superior performance to other machine learning algorithms throughout multiple industries. Multiple applications of deep learning have applied in pharmaceutical research in recent years, starting to bear fruit, and its utility has gone beyond bio-activity predictions and into addressing the diverse number of issues in the drug discovery process. Some of the best examples are issues within bio-activity prediction, de novo molecular design, synthesis prediction routes, and biological imaging [43–49].

Synthesis predictions have a long history dating back to rule-based methods in the 1960s. Similar machine learning methods of ANN have been applied to compound activity prediction assessment for quite a long time [50]. DL methods are now usually being adopted to address specific activity issues from the beginning of the research study. In current times, some promising results were reported in reaction prediction using DL methods.

Over the past decade, there has been a remarkable increase in the amount of available compound activity and biomedical data owing to the emergence of new experimental techniques such as High Throughput Screening (HTS), parallel synthesis, among many others. The massive amount of data needing to be processed and increased automation technology has promoted further use of these advancements in deep learning. Even though it is still too early to compare, the results from DL indicate that it has the potential to achieve the same performance, or even superior to, the traditional rule-based methods of machine learning [51] (Fig. 2).

2.2 Deep Learning for Medical Imaging

Deep Learning can play a significant role in analyzing medical images quickly (faster than humans) and providing insights to the clinician to understand a complex clinical scenario better [52]. For example, currently, radiologists need ample time to give a report based on a radiology image (e.g., X-ray, MRI, CT, ultrasound). This increases the clinician's decision-making time significantly, which is unwanted when there is a critical clinical condition. A quick and timely decision is a must to administer a treatment plan to save a patient.

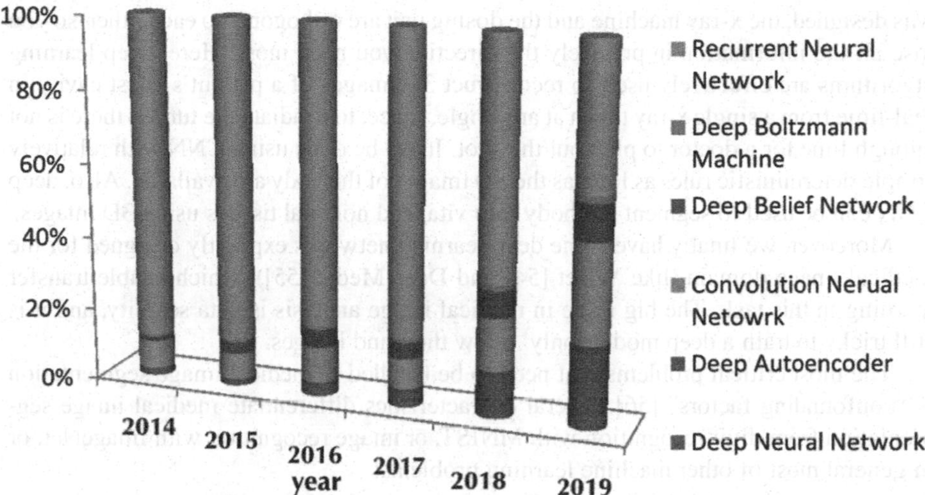

Fig. 2. Distribution of published papers that use deep learning in subareas of intelligent healthcare. These statistics are obtained from Google Scholar.

Deep learning can alleviate this problem by automatically learning essential features from the plenty of medical images available in the medical domain; then, suggesting the radiologist options to consider during report generation to speed up the clinical workflow. More or less, all medical imaging modalities can be benefited from this. Many researchers have already shown the effectiveness/applicability of various deep learning techniques on medical image processing/analyses [53].

Deep learning algorithms also play a major role in tumor detection from Computed Tomography (CT). For example, medical expert wants to treat tumor using radiation therapy, which means they want to shoot beams of radiation at it to kill the tumor while avoiding as much of your healthy tissue as possible, especially vital organs. However, the major problem here is the continuous movement of the lungs. The average person's breathing cycle (mileage may vary, particularly amongst lung cancer patients) is between 3 and 5 s. That means that after about 1.5 s, all the information is useless. It has changed too much, and in fact, it takes even less time. The major steps that are necessary to undertake in less than one second time span are:

1. Map out the entire chest cavity in 3D (somehow)
2. Detect the tumor and all the vital organs
3. Find the optimal (read: safest) direction from which to irradiate the tumor
4. Move the machine into position to irradiate the tumor from that angle
5. Irradiate the tumor
6. Repeat because the tumor and everything else in the body has now moved.

There is only time to take a single x-ray, but we need a 3D image. The x-ray projects 3D information into 2D, so we lose all the spatial information along the axis of the projection. Without that information, it's impossible to plan the shot angle. The device was designed, the x-ray machine and the dosing unit are orthogonal to each other, so you lose all the information in precisely the direction you need most! Here, deep learning algorithms are effectively used to reconstruct 3D images of a patient's chest cavity in real-time from a single x-ray taken at any angle. Since, to irradiate the tumor, there is not enough time for a doctor to plan out the shot. It can be done using CNN with relatively simple deterministic rules as long as the 3D images of the body are available. Also, deep CNN can be used to segment the body into vital and nonvital tissues using 3D images.

Moreover, we finally have some deep learning networks explicitly designed for the medical image domain (like V-Net [54] and Deep Medic [55]), which enable transfer learning in this task. The big issue in medical image analysis is data scarcity, and it is still tricky to train a deep model 'only' a few thousand images.

The most critical problems that need to be handled in medical image segmentation is "confounding factors" [56] Several characteristics differentiate medical image segmentation from digit recognition with MNIST, or image recognition with ImageNet, or in general most of other machine learning problems:

1). The data is collected in the real world, from a couple of data sources (i.e., hospitals). These data sources may use devices manufactured differently. Therefore, these images' qualities will be changed from different devices, and these differences serve as subtle confounding factors.
2). The medical application usually needs to answer the question about the underlying mechanism, instead of just predicting an answer for the label. Therefore, the correction of confounding factors is more critical than other machine learning applications.

Moreover, the confounding factor is a critical problem of fMRI segmentation, but not that important for CT-scan segmentation. A deep learning method is used to correct the confounding factor. Haohan et al. [57] proposed a selective-additive method that improved the generalizability of trained neural networks and corrected the confounding factors.

3 Limitations and Challenges of Deep Learning in Healthcare

Although deep learning techniques provide significant developments for different AI tasks in comparison to conventional approaches. Still, many researchers and developers have uncertainty for their use in medical applications [58]. This is due the strong mathematical theory characterizing the properties of deep learning algorithms and even simply why they work so well is still missing [59]. We summarized key issues associated with deep learning techniques in the context of healthcare as follows:

Most of the researchers in healthcare informatics use deep learning models as a Blackbox [60–63]. They even lack significant expertise and knowledge to select appropriate hyper-parameters, e.g., the kernel sizes of convolutional filters, the learning rate, and the number of layers. The internal dependencies of these hyper-parameters make them particularly costly for tuning.

1. Annotation of medical data requires medical experts, huge amount of time and is also costly [64]. Since, deep learning algorithms are highly reliable on the training data. Although it's hard to obtain disease specific data due to availability of healthcare data with many hospitals are kept under strict confidential. Therefore, these small datasets lead to overfitting in the training of deep learning models, which cause the system to memorize the training data instead of generalization. This leads to high error rate on the test data, although the error rate on the training dataset is very small. For this purpose, in order to avoid overfitting, regularization technique such as dropout [65] are introduced in the training phase to improve the generalization of the model.
2. It's easier to understand what lower-level layers are learning from the data because we can directly relate to the input space (e.g., images, audio, text). The deeper the layer, the more difficult this becomes. This doesn't mean that we have no clue what those layers are learning. Contributions exist for visualizing the weights in deep layers but there may still be more to discover about what knowledge is stored in these layers.
3. It has been shown by Moosavi et. al. [66] that CNN could give completely different predictions of two perceptually alike images. Similarly, Nguyen et. al. [67] also proved that CNN is easy to fool. They gave random noise or artificial images as an input to CNN, which predicted them into same object classes with high confidence.

In conclusion, we believe that helping in early, accurate and rapid diagnosis of life-threatening diseases, replacing basic Medicare processes, improving pathological results and treatment course standardization, and understanding genetics to predict future risks are some of the Deep Learning projects that have picked up speed in the Healthcare domain. The use of deep learning and neural networks are also mitigating health risks associated with re-admissions while bringing down the costs. Moreover, CNN is also being exceedingly used in clinical researches to find cures for un treatable diseases and replacing the lack of humongous datasets.

4 Conclusion and Future Work

This paper provided an in-depth review of current trends in the architecture of CNN. Understanding the mathematics behind CNN model is still challenging. Furthermore, CNN proficiently improve the accuracies of different applications in healthcare, helping doctors to easily diagnose the diseases. We hope that this research investigation and observations will help researchers and developers to gain better understanding of the recent advancements in CNN architecture with application to healthcare.

Acknowledgement. This work is supported in part by the Beijing Natural Science Foundation (No. 4212015), Natural Science Foundation of China (No. 61801008), China Ministry of Education - China Mobile Scientific Research Foundation (No. MCM20200102), China Postdoctoral Science Foundation (No. 2020M670074), Beijing Municipal Commission of Education Foundation (No. KM201910005025), China National Key Research and Development Program (No. 2018YFB0803600).

References

1. Rehman, S.U., et al.: Unsupervised pre-trained filter learning approach for efficient convolution neural network. Neurocomputing **365**, 171–190 (2019)
2. Krizhevsky, A., Sutskever, I., Hinton, G.E.: Imagenet classification with deep convolutional neural networks. Adv. Neural Inf. Process. Syst. 1097–1105 (2012)
3. Rehman, S.U., Shanshan, T., Yongfeng, H., Zhongliang, Y.: Face recognition: a novel unsupervised convolutional neural network method. In: 2016 IEEE International Conference of Online Analysis and Computing Science (ICOACS), pp. 139–144. IEEE (2016)
4. Rehman, O.U., Shiyou, Y., Shafiullah, K., Sadaqat, U.R.: A quantum particle swarm optimizer with enhanced strategy for global optimization of electromagnetic devices. IEEE Trans. Magn. **55**(8), 1–4 (2019)
5. Rehman, S.U., Shanshan, T., Yongfeng, H., Obaid, U.R.: A benchmark dataset and learning high-level semantic embeddings of multimedia for cross-media retrieval. IEEE Access **6**, 67176–67188 (2018)
6. Rehman, O.U., Sadaqat, U.R., Shanshan, T., Shafiullah, K., Muhammad, W., Shiyou, Y.: A quantum particle swarm optimization method with fitness selection methodology for electromagnetic inverse problems. IEEE Access **6**, 63155–63163 (2018)
7. Rehman, S.U., Tu, S., Yongfeng, H., Guojie, L.: CSFL: A novel unsupervised convolution neural network approach for visual pattern classification. AI Commun. **30**(5), 311–324 (2017)
8. Rehman, S.U., Tu, S., Rehman, O.U., Huang, Y., Magurawalage, C.M., Chang, C.C.: Optimization of CNN through novel training strategy for visual classification problems. Entropy **20**(4), 290 (2018)
9. Hui, L., Yu-jie, S.: Research on face recognition algorithm based on improved convolution neural network. 2018 13th IEEE Conference on Industrial Electronics and Applications (ICIEA), pp. 2802–2805 (2018). https://doi.org/10.1109/ICIEA.2018.8398186
10. Qin, Z., Zhang, Z., Zhang, S., Yu, H., Li, J., Peng, Y.: Merging and evolution: improving convolutional neural networks for mobile applications. Int. Joint Conf. Neural Netw. (IJCNN) **2018**, 1–8 (2018). https://doi.org/10.1109/IJCNN.2018.8489496
11. Rehman, O.U., Tu, S., Rehman, S.U., Khan, S., Yang, S.: Design optimization of electromagnetic devices using an improved quantum inspired particle swarm optimizer. Appl. Comput. Electromagnet. Soc. J. 1, **33**(9) (2018)
12. Koliousis, A., Watcharapichat, P., Weidlich, M., Mai, L., Costa, P., Pietzuch, P.: CROSSBOW: Scaling Deep Learning with Small Batch Sizes on Multi-GPU Servers. arXiv preprint arXiv: 1901.02244 (2019)
13. Tu, S., et al.: Optimisation-based training of evolutionary convolution neural network for visual classification applications. IET Comput. Vis. **14**(5), 259–267 (2020)
14. Rehman, S.U., et al.: Deep Learning Techniques for Future Intelligent Cross-Media Retrieval. arXiv preprint arXiv:2008.01191. (2020)
15. Karki, A., Keshava, C.P., Shivakumar, S.M., Skow, J., Hegde, G.M., Jeon, H.: Detailed characterization of deep neural networks on GPUs and FPGAs. In: Proceedings of the 12th Workshop on General Purpose Processing Using GPUs. ACM, pp. 12–21 (2019)
16. ur Rehman, S., Huang, Y., Tu, S., ur Rehman, O.: Facebook5k: a novel evaluation resource dataset for cross-media search. In: Sun, X., Pan, Z., Bertino, E. (eds.) ICCCS 2018. LNCS, vol. 11063, pp. 512–524. Springer, Cham (2018). https://doi.org/10.1007/978-3-030-00006-6_47
17. Rehman, S.U., Bilal, M., Ahmad, B., Yahya, K.M., Ullah, A., Rehman, O.U.: Comparison based analysis of different cryptographic and encryption techniques using message authentication code (mac) in wireless sensor networks (wsn). arXiv preprint arXiv:1203.3103. (2012)

18. Farabet, C., Martini, B., Akselrod, P., Talay, S., LeCun, Y., Culurciello, E.: Hardware accelerated convolutional neural networks for synthetic vision systems. Circuits and Systems (ISCAS), In: Proceedings of 2010 IEEE International Symposium on. IEEE, pp. 257–260 (2010)
19. Rehman, S.U., Huang, Y., Tu, S., Ahmad, B.: Learning a semantic space for modeling images, tags and feelings in cross-media search. In: U., L.H., Lauw, H.W. (eds.) PAKDD 2019. LNCS (LNAI), vol. 11607, pp. 65–76. Springer, Cham (2019). https://doi.org/10.1007/978-3-030-26142-9_7
20. Shah, S.A., Fan, D., Ren, A., Zhao, N., Yang, X., Tanoli, S.A.K.: Seizure episodes detection via smart medical sensing system. J. Ambient Intell. Humanized Comput. **11**(11), 4363–4375 (2018). https://doi.org/10.1007/s12652-018-1142-3
21. Lin, Q., Tu, S., Waqas, M., ur Rehman, S., Chang, C.C.: Tracking areas planning based on spectral clustering in small cell networks. IET Commun. **13**, 1921–1927 (2019)
22. Tu, S., et al.: Security in fog computing: A novel technique to tackle an impersonation attack. IEEE Access **6**, 74993–75001 (2018)
23. Wu, H., Shen, G., Lin, X., Li, M., Zhang, B., Li, C.Z.: Screening patents of ICT in construction using deep learning and NLP techniques. Engineering, Construction and Architectural Management (2020)
24. Han, W., et al. ContextNet: Improving convolutional neural networks for automatic speech recognition with global context. arXiv preprint arXiv:2005.03191 (2020)
25. Ling, H., Wu, J., Huang, J., Chen, J., Li, P.: Attention-based convolutional neural network for deep face recognition. Multimedia Tools Appl. **79**(9–10), 5595–5616 (2019). https://doi.org/10.1007/s11042-019-08422-2
26. Baskin, I.I.: The power of deep learning to ligand-based novel drug discovery. Expert Opinion on Drug Discovery, pp. 1–10 (2020)
27. Tu, S., et al.: ModPSO-CNN: an evolutionary convolution neural network with application to visual recognition. Soft Comput. **4**, 1–2 (2020)
28. Yang, Z., Zhang, Y.-J., Rehman, S., Huang, Y.: Image captioning with object detection and localization. In: Zhao, Y., Kong, X., Taubman, D. (eds.) ICIG 2017. LNCS, vol. 10667, pp. 109–118. Springer, Cham (2017). https://doi.org/10.1007/978-3-319-71589-6_10
29. Talo, M.: An Automated Deep Learning Approach for Bacterial Image Classification. arXiv preprint arXiv:1912.08765 (2019)
30. Brown, C., et al.: An Automated, Cost-Effective Optical System for Accelerated Antimicrobial Susceptibility Testing (AST) using Deep Learning. arXiv preprint arXiv:2005.11454 (2020)
31. Hakim, Z., Ierasts, T., Hakim, I., D'Penha, A., Smith, K.P., Caesar, M.C.: Connecting data to insight: a pan-canadian study on AI in healthcare. Healthc. Q. (Toronto, Ont.), 23, 13–19 (2020)
32. Porumb, M., Stranges, S., Pescapè, A., Pecchia, L.: Precision medicine and artificial intelligence: a pilot study on deep learning for hypoglycemic events detection based on ECG. Sci. Rep. **10**, 1–16 (2020)
33. Latif, J., Xiao, C., Tu, S., Rehman, S.U., Imran, A., Bilal, A.: Implementation and use of disease diagnosis systems for electronic medical records based on machine learning: a complete review. IEEE Access. **8**, 150489–150513 (2020)
34. Monshi, M.M.A., Poon, J., Chung, V.: Deep learning in generating radiology reports: a survey. Artif. Intell. Med. p. 101878 (2020)
35. Zhavoronkov, A., Vanhaelen, Q., Oprea, T.I.: Will artificial intelligence for drug discovery impact clinical pharmacology? Clin. Pharmacol. Ther. **107**, 780–785 (2020)
36. Sarode, K.D.: Applications of deep learning in drug discovery. In: Vyas, R. (ed.) Advances in Bioengineering, pp. 73–91. Springer, Singapore (2020). https://doi.org/10.1007/978-981-15-2063-1_4

37. Cukier, S., et al.: Checklists to detect potential predatory biomedical journals: a systematic review. BMC Med. **18**, 1–20 (2020)
38. Bagherian, M., Sabeti, E., Wang, K., Sartor, M.A., Nikolovska-Coleska, Z., Najarian, K.: Machine learning approaches and databases for prediction of drug–target interaction: a survey paper. Briefings Bioinform. (2020)
39. Lee, C.Y., Chen, Y.P.P.: Prediction of drug adverse events using deep learning in pharmaceutical discovery. Briefings Bioinform. **22**(2), 1884–1901 (2020)
40. Réda, C., Kaufmann, E., Delahaye-Duriez, A.: Machine learning applications in drug development. Comput. Struct. Biotechnol. J. **18**, 241–252 (2020)
41. Zhu, H.: Big data and artificial intelligence modeling for drug discovery. Annu. Rev. Pharmacol. Toxicol. **60**, 573–589 (2020)
42. Zhang, H., Saravanan, K.M., Yang, Y., Hossain, M.T., Li, J., Ren, X., Pan, Y., Wei, Y.: Deep learning based drug screening for Novel Coronavirus 2019-nCov. Interdisc. Sci. Comput. Life Sci. **12**(3), 368–376 (2020). https://doi.org/10.1007/s12539-020-00376-6
43. Robinson, M.C., Glen, R.C., Lee, A.A.: Validating the validation: reanalyzing a large-scale comparison of deep learning and machine learning models for bioactivity prediction. J. Comput.-Aided Mol. Des. **34**(7), 717–730 (2020). https://doi.org/10.1007/s10822-019-00274-0
44. Withnall, M., Lindelöf, E., Engkvist, O., Chen, H.: Building attention and edge message passing neural networks for bioactivity and physical–chemical property prediction. J. Cheminformatics **12**(1), 1–18 (2020). https://doi.org/10.1186/s13321-019-0407-y
45. Kotsias, P.C., Arús-Pous, J., Chen, H., Engkvist, O., Tyrchan, C., Bjerrum, E.J.: Direct steering of de novo molecular generation with descriptor conditional recurrent neural networks. Nature Mach. Intell. **2**, 254–265 (2020)
46. Sturm, N., et al.: Others. Industry-scale application and evaluation of deep learning for drug target prediction. J. Cheminformatics, **12**, 1–13 (2020). https://doi.org/10.1186/s13321-020-00428-5
47. Nehme, E., et al. DeepSTORM3D: dense 3D localization microscopy and PSF design by deep learning. Nature Methods, pp. 1–7 (2020)
48. Mahmud, M., Kaiser, M.S., Hussain, A.: Deep learning in mining biological data. arXiv preprint arXiv:2003.00108 (2020)
49. Kim, E., et al.: Inorganic materials synthesis planning with literature-trained neural networks. J. Chem. Inf. Model. **60**(3), 1194–1201 (2020)
50. Minovski, N., Župerl, Š, Drgan, V., Novič, M.: Assessment of applicability domain for multivariate counter-propagation artificial neural network predictive models by minimum Euclidean distance space analysis: a case study. Anal. Chim. Acta **759**, 28–42 (2013)
51. Gehrmann, S., et al.: Others. Comparing rule-based and deep learning models for patient phenotyping. arXiv preprint arXiv:1703.08705 (2017)
52. Haskins, G., Kruger, U., Yan, P.: Deep learning in medical image registration: a survey. Mach. Vis. Appl. **31**(1–2), 1–18 (2020). https://doi.org/10.1007/s00138-020-01060-x
53. Ma, X., et al.: Understanding adversarial attacks on deep learning based medical image analysis systems. Pattern Recognit. **110**, 107332 (2020)
54. Li, F., Tan, C., Dong, F., Jia, J.: V-Net deep imaging method for electrical resistance tomography. IEEE Sens. J. **20**, 6460–6469 (2020)
55. Singh, S.P.; Wang, L., Gupta, S., Goli, H., Padmanabhan, P., Gulyás, B.: 3D Deep Learning on Medical Images: A Review. arXiv preprint arXiv:2004.00218 (2020)
56. Sinha, A., Dolz, J.: Multi-scale self-guided attention for medical image segmentation. IEEE J. Bio. Health Inf. (2020)
57. Wang, H., Meghawat, A., Morency, L.P., Xing, E.P.: Select-additive learning: Improving generalization in multimodal sentiment analysis. In: 2017 IEEE International Conference on Multimedia and Expo (ICME). IEEE, pp. 949–954 (2017)

58. Doraiswamy, P.M., Blease, C., Bodner, K.: Artificial intelligence and the future of psychiatry: insights from a global physician survey. Artif. Intell. Med. **102**, 101753 (2020)
59. Irfanullah, K., Sattar, Q., Sadaqat-ur Rehman, A.: An efficient approach for sky detection. IJCSI Int. J. Comput. Sci. (2013)
60. Ahmad, B., Kiani, A.K., Rehman, S.U., Huang, Y., Yang, Z.: Multicast multipath TCP for reliable communication in wireless scenarios. In: 2019 IEEE 21st International Conference on High Performance Computing and Communications; IEEE 17th International Conference on Smart City; IEEE 5th International Conference on Data Science and Systems (HPCC/SmartCity/DSS), pp. 2212–2217. IEEE (2019)
61. Esteva, A., et al.: A guide to deep learning in healthcare. Nat. Med. **25**, 24–29 (2019)
62. Shickel, B., Tighe, P.J., Bihorac, A., Rashidi, P.: Deep EHR: a survey of recent advances in deep learning techniques for electronic health record (EHR) analysis. IEEE J. Biomed. Health Inform. **22**, 1589–1604 (2017)
63. Meyer, P., Noblet, V., Mazzara, C., Lallement, A.: Survey on deep learning for radiotherapy. Comput. Biol. Med. **98**, 126–146 (2018)
64. Tajbakhsh, N., Jeyaseelan, L., Li, Q., Chiang, J.N., Wu, Z., Ding, X.: Embracing imperfect datasets: a review of deep learning solutions for medical image segmentation. Med. Image Anal. **63**, 101693 (2020)
65. Adhikari, B.: DEEPCON: protein contact prediction using dilated convolutional neural networks with dropout. Bioinformatics **36**, 470–477 (2020)
66. Moosavi-Dezfooli, S.M., Fawzi, A., Frossard, P.: Deepfool: a simple and accurate method to fool deep neural networks. In: Proceedings of the IEEE conference on computer vision and pattern recognition, pp. 2574–2582 (2016)
67. Nguyen, A., Yosinski, J., Clune, J.: Deep neural networks are easily fooled: high confidence predictions for unrecognizable images. In: Proceedings of the IEEE conference on computer vision and pattern recognition, pp. 427–436 (2015)

An Improved YOLOv3 Algorithm Combined with Attention Mechanism for Flame and Smoke Detection

Hao Zhang[1], Zhiqiang Wang[1], Man Chen[1], Yumin Peng[1], Yanming Gao[1], and Junhuang Zhou[2](✉)

[1] CSG Power Generation Co., Ltd., Guangzhou 510630, China
[2] Guangzhou Power Electrical Technology Co., Ltd., Guangzhou 510700, China

Abstract. Traditional flame and smoke detection mostly rely on temperature and smoke sensor, but the detection of temperature detector and smoke detector has a certain lag. In order to solve this problem of hysteresis and low accuracy, we propose an improved YOLOV3 algorithm combined with attention mechanism for flame and smoke detection. Firstly, a multi-scene large-scale flame and smoke image dataset is built. The localization and classification of the flame and smoke areas in the image are annotated precisely. The suspected areas of the flame and smoke in the image are obtained by color analysis, so that the suspected areas of the flame and smoke objects are concerned. Then combined with the feature extraction ability of deep network, the problem of flame and smoke detection is transformed into multi-classification and coordinate regression. Finally, the detection model of flame and smoke in multi-scene is obtained. Our experiments show the effectiveness of the improved YOLOv3 algorithm combined with attention mechanism in flame and smoke detection. Our proposed method achieves outstanding performance in the dataset of flame and smoke image. The detection speed also meets the need of real-time detection.

Keywords: Flame and smoke detection · Attention mechanisms · YOLOv3 · Deep learning

1 Introduction

Understanding the content of a video or image has always been an important task in computer vision, such as flame and smoke detection. Different from the single object detection, the smoke object and the flame object in the image need to be paid attention to. The early fire detection based on computer vision divided the task into two tasks: flame recognition and smoke recognition. The main method is to use the color [1], texture [2], shape [3], and dynamic and static information [4, 5] of flame and smoke as the basis of flame and smoke detection. Finally, the flame and smoke objects in the image are identified. Most of these flame and smoke detection algorithms are based on hand-crafted features. It is difficult to achieve low false positive rate without reducing the detection rate. And most of the methods of flame and smoke recognition are based

X. Sun et al. (Eds.): ICAIS 2021, LNCS 12736, pp. 226–238, 2021.
https://doi.org/10.1007/978-3-030-78609-0_20

on the fixed scene or single fire type. If the fire type, the color and the scene change, it will decline the algorithm accuracy rate, these methods are not suitable for the actual application demand.

With the advent of the large image classification dataset ImageNet and the success of the convolutional neural network in image classification tasks, the researchers introduced convolutional neural network to the flame and smoke detection tasks. The method [6] designed a 12-layers convolutional neural network for forest fire recognition by using the ImageNet Dataset to pre-train the network. Then the self-built dataset (500 training sets and 100 test sets) is used for training test. In the training process, the hidden layer of the network is dropped out to reduce the probability of over-fitting, and the result is good on the self-built dataset. However, there are only 600 images in its self-built dataset, so it is possible to train the network by overfitting. It only has a single dataset scenario, which is not robust in general scenarios. In addition, the final output only contains the probability of flame and no flame, and does not contain the information of flame and smoke objects. Method [7] uses the classic convolutional neural network, combining convolution and maximum pooling, with the goal of determining whether the image contains flame or smoke objects. By movement of the 12×12 sliding window in the feature map, the detection speed is improved. Compared with method [6], method [7] trains more datasets and covers a wider range of scenarios. Its network is lighter and faster. But there are only three categories (flame, smoke and (no flame/smoke)), and they are not friendly to scenes with both smoke and flames. In addition, the final output does not contain the localization information of the flame and smoke objects, so it can not detect the flame state more accurately. In method [8], the precision of classification is further improved by the global and local fire detection of the images. But it only do a flame test and do not identify the smoke. In the scene of flame partly blocked by smoke, the effect is greatly affected. Besides, it is only classified, and does not include the localization information of flame and smoke object.

The flame and smoke detection algorithm mentioned above has achieved good results in the flame and smoke detection task, but there are some limitations. In order to alleviate these limitations, we build a large scale multi-scene flame and smoke dataset, and label the location and category of the flame and smoke objects. Secondly, we propose an improved YOLOV3 algorithm with attention mechanism for flame and smoke detection. Our model first analyzes the color information of smoke and flame before the image is input to the detection network. The suspected areas of flame and smoke objects are focused to distinguish the different contributions of different areas to the detection results. Next, we extract multi-scale features of flame and smoke to capture more abundant information of flame and smoke objects. The idea for this paper is shown in Fig. 1.

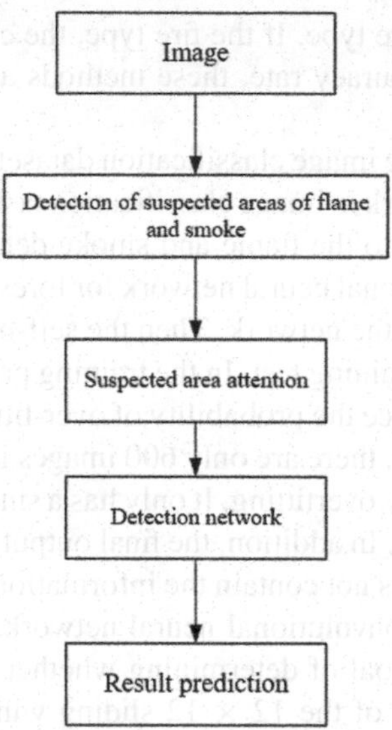

Fig. 1. The idea of our method

Overall, the paper has the following contributions:

(1) A large-scale multi-scene flame and smoke dataset is constructed, and the locations of the flame and smoke objects are precisely labeled.
(2) An improved YOLOv3 algorithm with attention mechanism for flame and smoke detection is proposed. With attention to the key regions of the image, the multiscale features of the flame and smoke are extracted using YOLOv3. The feasibility of deep learning in flame and smoke detection is verified by realizing the detection of flame and smoke objects.

Our method achieves excellent results over the multi-scene flame and smoke datasets that we have constructed, demonstrating the effectiveness of our work.

2 Related Work

Fire has always been the world's major threats and disasters. Early prevention and rapid detection of fire is one of the important means to reduce the occurrence of fire and spread of serious harm. Therefore, it is very important to be able to give timely and accurate warning of fire. Fire detection tasks can be divided into flame and smoke detection tasks. In the beginning, the way of detecting fire is to use temperature detector and smoke detector, but the result has a certain lag, which can not reach the aim of early prediction of fire. And it is not robust enough to the change of environment and is prone to the false alarm caused by electromagnetic interference. In recent years, fire detection based on computer vision has made significant progress, there are some outstanding performance of flame detection algorithms and smoke detection algorithms.

2.1 Flame Detection Algorithm

The early flame detection algorithm [11] mainly used artificial extraction of flame features, and then used a manually designed program to define a feature threshold to determine or train a machine learning classifier to determine. The manually extracted features include flame texture, flicker frequency, circularity, area change, the number of flame sharp corners, and the unique color of the flame in different color spaces. For example, the method [12] proposed a multi-feature The fusion flame detection algorithm first uses the improved Gaussian mixture model algorithm to extract foreground objects, filters the foreground area to obtain the suspected flame area, and finally detects the flame through the flame flicker recognition algorithm of statistical frequency counting. There are also some methods [13, 14] to separate the suspected flame object and the background in the color space of RGB, YUV, YCbCr and HIS, and then use other characteristics of the flame to distinguish the suspected flame object, so as to achieve the flame detection object. In addition, there are some methods [15] after separating the suspected flame object and background in the image, and then extracting the circularity of the flame, the area change rate and the number of flame sharp corners, and then using the trained support vector machine model to analyze these Features are processed to achieve the purpose of detecting flame.

The features used in the early flame detection algorithms and the judgment conditions and threshold rules are all hand-crafted, which cannot contain all the characteristics of the flame, so that the optimal effect is not achieved, although some methods use machine learning classification in the final detection step The algorithm performs classification, which improves a certain detection accuracy and increases the intelligence of detection, but still cannot avoid the shortcomings of manual design features, and the final output is the classification result of the flame, which does not contain the position information of the flame.

With the geometric growth of image data and the rapid development of deep learning models, automatic extraction of flame features has been achieved. The flame detection method based on deep learning uses a convolutional neural network to automatically extract flame features to achieve end-to-end flame detection, thereby improving the efficiency of flame detection. Work [16] uses the Faster-RCNN model to achieve end-to-end flame detection, and maintains a high flame detection rate in a variety of complex environments and the detection speed is not slow. Work [17] uses real flame image data combined with the data generated by the generated confrontation network to train the network, and achieves a higher detection rate and a lower false alarm rate.

2.2 Smoke Detection Algorithm

Early smoke detection algorithms are mostly based on three-stage method preprocessing, feature extraction and classification. They first segment the motion area or smoke suspected area from the object video image through preprocessing; then use wavelet analysis [18–20] and Various feature descriptors and other methods extract hand-crafted smoke features, such as texture, motion, space-time, optical flow vector and edge direction histogram and other features; finally use convexity, growth rate and support vector machine (SVM) [21] Wait to recognize smoke. Although smoke detection algorithms based on image processing have achieved good results [22], most of them are based on hand-crafted features, but the color, texture, and shape of the smoke are quite different and unstable, which leads to a low detection success rate. In addition, most of its methods are proposed for fixed scenes or single fire types. If the scene and fire type change, the accuracy of the algorithm will decrease.

With the outstanding performance of deep learning technology in computer vision, some methods [23] use deep learning models to extract useful features in fire video image sequences or single-frame images, and then use the extracted features for classification, although based on deep learning Compared with most traditional smoke detection algorithms, the method has achieved better classification performance, but most smoke detection algorithms based on deep learning [24] directly use the original image as the input of the neural network, which reduces the robustness of the network model. Due to the variability of smoke characteristics, it is still very challenging to detect smoke in videos and images.

In general, fire detection based on deep learning, with the explosion of data, the increase in computer computing power, and the development of deep network models, avoids the complexity of manual feature engineering. The use of computers to automatically extract features can achieve end-to-end real-time output, and can ensure detection accuracy and generalization ability. Therefore, the speed, accuracy, and robustness of flame and smoke detection based on deep learning are realistic requirements. For example, the method [6–8] uses convolutional neural networks to achieve the common detection of flame and smoke, and has achieved good results., But there are some limitations. As the attention mechanism [25–27] has achieved outstanding results in deep learning [28–30], this paper proposes an improved YOLOv3 algorithm combined with the attention mechanism for flame and smoke detection.

3 Method

In the visible image, the color of flame and smoke has obvious contrast characteristics with the surrounding environment, and the color of flame and smoke in the actual scene is affected by many environmental factors, such as temperature, combustion adequacy of burning material, burning material material, etc., making flame and smoke It has a special color distribution law. The color of the smoke produced by the smoke at the beginning of the fire is mostly grayish white or light blue. As time progresses, the color will change from gray to black, and most of the flame in the video image appears as Prominent and bright red and yellow, the color characteristics of these flame and smoke play an extremely important role in fire detection. However, the deep network cannot make full use of the rich color information displayed by these flame and smoke. In order to fully capture the color information of the object, an attention module is designed. First, the image is detected for suspected areas of flame and smoke, and the deep network is detected at the input The model pays attention to the suspected areas of flame and smoke before, and finally obtains the detection results from the detection network.

3.1 Suspected Area Detection

Detection of Suspected Flame Area. Use the color pattern shown by the flame to filter the image. According to the color characteristics of the flame, set the color filter range in the RGB color space, set the pixel value of the pixel that is not in the color range to 0, and keep the pixel value in the range unchanged, so as to get the RGB color space filter flame image. Its filtering range in RGB color space is as formula (1):

$$\begin{cases} R \geq R_0 \\ R \geq B, G \geq B \\ |G - B| + |R - B| \geq T_0 \end{cases} \tag{1}$$

Among them, R_0 is the threshold of the R component of the pixel, and T_0 is the threshold of |G-B|+|R-B|.

The image area that satisfies the formula (1) in the image is marked as R_{FLAME}, which is the flame suspected area.

Detection of Suspected Smoke Area. Use the color pattern shown by the smoke to filter the image. The difference between the U and V components of the smoke area in the YUV color space is much larger than that of other non-smoke areas. The pixel value range of the non-smoke area is compressed, so the image is filtered by the pixel filter rule of the YUV color space. The color law is as formula (2):

$$I_{color}(x, y) = \begin{cases} I_{rgb}(x, y) \text{ if } T_{max} > |U(x, y) - V(x, y)| > T_{min} \\ 0 \quad\quad otherwise \end{cases} \tag{2}$$

Where U(x, y) and V (x, y) are the values of the U and V components of the pixel at (x, y) in the YUV color space; $I_{rgb}(x, y)$ is at (x, y) The pixel value of the pixel in the RGB color space; T_{max} and T_{min} are thresholds.

The image area that satisfies the formula (2) in the image is marked as R_{SMOKE}, which is the suspected smoke area.

Suspected Area of Flame and Smoke. After color filtering, the suspected smoke area R_{SMOKE} and the flame suspected area R_{FLAME} are combined to obtain the flame and smoke suspected area R_{Color} after color analysis. The calculation method is as follows: Formula (3).

$$R_{Color} = R_{SMOKE} \cup R_{FIRE} \tag{3}$$

3.2 Attention Suspected Areas of Flame and Smoke

Using the suspected areas of flame and smoke obtained in Sect. 3.1, the key areas of the input feature extraction network are obtained, and the attention mechanism of the key areas is calculated as formula (4):

$$I_{i-attention} = w_i I_i \tag{4}$$

Among them, $I_{i\text{-}attention}$ represents the value of pixel i after the attention mechanism, I_i represents the value of pixel$i$ in the original image, and w_i represents the weight parameter.

3.3 Detection Network

The YOLOv3 algorithm is the most widely used algorithm in the YOLO series. YOLOv3 uses the idea of residual network to build the Darknet-53 network as a feature extraction network, and uses three different size feature maps to perform multi-scale prediction on the object image, thereby further improving the detection performance of the model. Our detection network is based on YOLOv3, and the network structure is shown in Fig. 2:

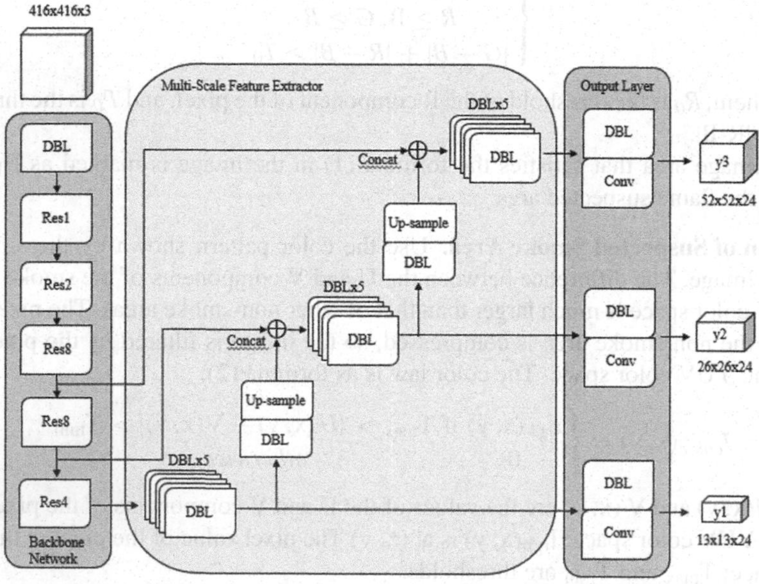

Fig. 2. The structure of the detection network

Our detection network uses the K-means clustering algorithm to initialize the anchor box to predict the coordinates of the bounding box. K-means clustering uses the Euclidean distance formula, and the accuracy of the detection result will be affected by the size of the anchor frame. The IOU distance represents the intersection ratio between the predicted box and the actual bounding box. In order to eliminate the influence caused by using the Euclidean distance formula, this article uses the IOU distance formula instead of the Euclidean distance formula. The distance measurement formula is:

$$d(\text{box}, \text{centroid}) = 1 - \text{IOU}(\text{box}, \text{centroid}) \quad (5)$$

Among them, box is the actual bounding box information, centroid is the clustering center, and IOU is the intersection ratio of the predicted box and the actual bounding box. YOLOv3 has 3 anchor boxes for each scale feature map. The larger the scale, the smaller the anchor frame is used to obtain more object edge information. The original anchor frame parameter values are generated by clustering on a public dataset. There are many types of public datasets. The determined anchor frame parameter values are universal, but they are not applicable to the flame and smoke dataset made by this article. Before training, it is necessary to design a new anchor box size and ratio to improve the detection rate of the bounding box. According to the number of object categories to be detected set in this article, the number of calculation channels is $3 \times (4 + 1 + 3) = 24$, where "4, 1, 3" in the brackets represent the 4 predictions of the center point coordinates, One confidence level and three object category scores, the final output of the three scale feature maps are $13 \times 13 \times 24$, $26 \times 26 \times 24$, $52 \times 52 \times 24$.

4 Experiments

4.1 Dataset

At present, there is no open source standard dataset for flame and smoke detection tasks. We use open source flame and smoke videos and images collected on the Internet and combine ourselves to shoot flame and smoke videos and images of specific scenes, and then decompose the video into frames After that, we obtained a total of 50,000 images containing flame and smoke. After screening, 5,000 flame and smoke images that fit the real scene were obtained, which were used as datasets for training and testing of our method. Figure 3 is an example of part of our dataset.

Fig. 3. Examples of flame and smoke images

We have performed fine manual annotation on the filtered flame and smoke images. The content of the annotation includes the category and location information of the flame and smoke objects, and is processed and stored in the xml file format, and then all the images are according to 4: Randomly divide the ratio of 1, in which the training set is 4000 images, and the test set is 1000 images (Fig. 4).

Fig. 4. Annotated sample example

4.2 Experimental Details

The data source mainly comes from open source flame and smoke images collected on the Internet and images taken by myself, a total of 5,000. In the hyperparameter setting, the input image size is fixed at 416 × 416. In the detection of suspected flame area, R_0 is set to 135 and T_0 is set to 20; in the detection of suspected smoke area, T_{min} is set to 63, and T_{max} is set to Set it to 178; the attention parameter for the key area is set to $w_i = 1.5$, that is, the pixel i belongs to the suspected area of flame and smoke, then $w_i = 1.5$, otherwise $w_i = 1$; in the detection network, the learning rate is 0.001, btach size Set to 64. The experimental equipment uses the NVIDIA 1080Ti GPU computing platform, and uses the Darknet deep learning framework to build the YOLOv3 object detection model under the UBUNTU 18.04 operating system.

4.3 Evaluation Index

The mAP (mean Average Precision) is a commonly used indicator to measure detection accuracy in object detection. It refers to the average of the average accuracy of multiple categories. AP refers to the average accuracy of a single category, which measures the model in a certain category. To identify the quality of the effect, the AP used in this article is AP_{50} by default, that is, the average accuracy of a single category under the premise that the IOU of the prediction box and ground truth is greater than 50%, and mAP is the average of all APs, and the value of mAP is higher. Large means that the overall recognition accuracy of the model is higher. In this article, mAP is used to judge the effect of the detection model.

4.4 Experimental Results

We divide the dataset into 4000 images as the training set and 1000 images as the test set. The loss and mAP value during model training and testing are shown in Fig. 5 and Fig. 6.

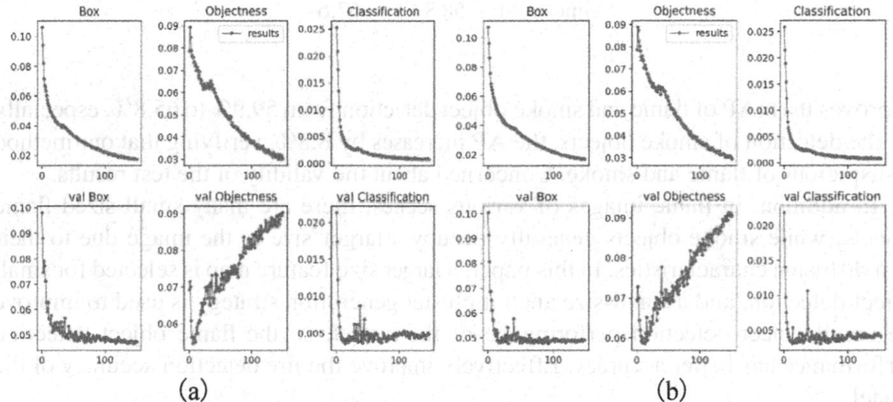

Fig. 5. Model training process and test process loss diagram, where Fig. 5(a) represents the traditional YOLOv3 algorithm, Fig. 5(b) represents our method

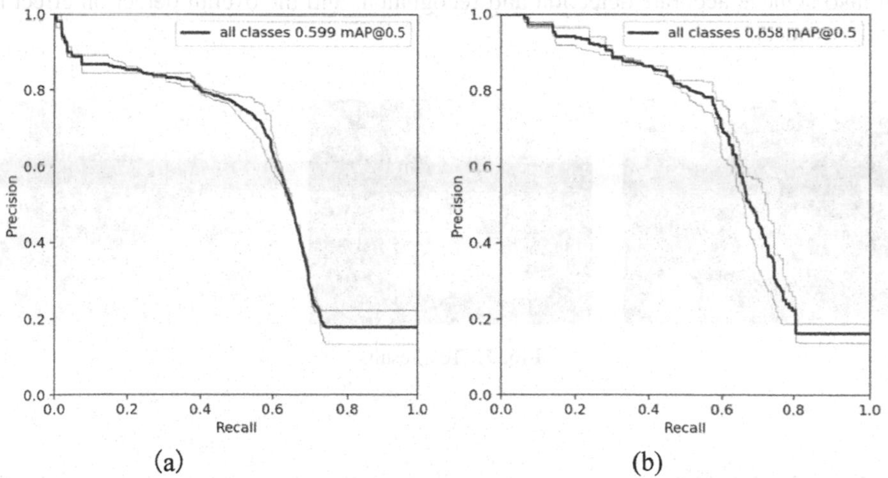

Fig. 6. The AP curve of each network during the test. Figure 6(a) represents the traditional YOLOv3 algorithm, and Fig. 6(b) represents our method

We use the classic YOLOv3 and our method to test on the dataset, respectively calculate the average accuracy of various objects, and calculate the average accuracy (mAP) of the flame and smoke objects. The test results are shown in Table 1.

The experimental results show that our method performs well on both flame and smoke detection tasks. Compared with the classic YOLOv3 network, our method

Table 1. Test set results (%)

Method	YOLOv3	Ours
mAP	59.9	65.8
Flame AP	61.3	64.1
Smoke AP	58.8	67.6

improves the mAP of flame and smoke object detection from 59.9% to 65.8%, especially for the detection of smoke objects, the AP increases by 8.8%, verifying that our method is suspicious of flame and smoke. Concerned about the validity of the test results.

In addition, in flame images of various scenes, there are many small-sized flame objects, while smoke objects generally occupy a larger size in the image due to their own diffusion characteristics. In this paper, a larger size feature map is selected for small object detection, and a small-size anchor cluster generation strategy is used to improve the small object detection performance of the model, so the flame object detection performance has better accuracy. Effectively improve the fire detection accuracy of the model.

The test results are shown in Fig. 7. It can be seen that our method can accurately detect the thinner smoke, which shows that our method is effective in paying attention to the suspected smoke area. Secondly, there are small objects in the image. Our method can also achieve accurate detection and recognition, and the overall detection effect is relatively ideal.

Fig. 7. Test results

5 Conclusion

This paper proposes an improved YOLOv3 algorithm combined with attention mechanism for flame and smoke detection. Our method first analyzes the color information of smoke and flame. Before the image is sent to the detection network, the suspected flame and smoke object Focus on regions, distinguish the different contributions of different regions of the image to the detection results. Secondly, we extract the multi-scale features of flame and smoke to capture more abundant flame and smoke object information. Our experiments verify the improvement of YOLOv3 combined with the attention mechanism The algorithm is effective in detecting flame and smoke objects, and at the same time, it has achieved better performance on the flame and smoke image dataset we constructed, especially in the detection of small objects, and it also meets real-time detection speed. Testing needs. However, due to the inherent characteristics of flame and smoke that are not fixed in shape, it is difficult to obtain a high-precision object detection frame by using a fixed anchor point to achieve coordinate regression. Therefore, in future research, we will focus on improving the anchor point method in the detection of flame and smoke objects to obtain higher detection accuracy.

Acknowledgement. This work was supported by the science and technology program of CSG Power Generation Co., LTD.(Research and Application of Intelligent Perception Technology in Power Plant Production Area Based on Machine Vision 020000KK52190017).

References

1. Li, Z., Mihaylova, L.S., Isupova, O., Rossi, L.: Autonomous flame detection in videos with a dirichlet process Gaussian mixture color model. IEEE Trans. Ind. Inf. **14**(3), 1146–1154 (2017)
2. Prema, C.E., Vinsley, S.S., Suresh, S.: Efficient flame detection based on static and dynamic texture analysis in forest fire detection. Fire Technol. **54**(1), 255–288 (2018)
3. Foggia, P., Saggese, A., Vento, M.: Real-time fire detection for video-surveillance applications using a combination of experts based on color, shape, and motion. IEEE Trans. Circ. Syst. Video Technol. **25**(9), 1545–1556 (2015)
4. Han, X.-F., Jin, J.S., Wang, M.-J., Jiang, W., Gao, L., Xiao, L.-P.: Video fire detection based on Gaussian mixture model and multi-color features. SIViP **11**(8), 1419–1425 (2017). https://doi.org/10.1007/s11760-017-1102-y
5. Jian, W.L.: Research on Fire Detection Method Based on Video Smoke Motion Detection. Master's thesis, Nanchang Hangkong University (2018)
6. Fu, T.J., Zheng, C.E., Tian, Y., Qiu, Q.M., Lin, S.J.: Forest fire recognition based on deep convolutional neural network under complex background. Comput. Modernization **3**, 52–57 (2016)
7. Frizzi, S., Kaabi, R., Bouchouicha, M., Ginoux, J M., Moreau, E., Fnaiech, F.: Convolutional neural network for video fire and smoke detection. In: IECON 2016–42nd Annual Conference of the IEEE Industrial Electronics Society, pp. 877–882. IEEE (2016)
8. Zhang, Q., Xu, J., Xu, L., Guo, H.: Deep convolutional neural networks for forest fire detection. In: 2016 International Forum on Management, Education and Information Technology Application. Atlantis Press (2016)
9. Xiang, X.B.: Research on smoke detection algorithm based on video. Zhejiang University, Hangzhou (2017)
10. Xiao, X., Kong, F.Z., Liu, J.H.: Dynamic and static feature based surveillance video fire detection algorithm. Comput. Sci. **46**(z1), 284–286 (2019)
11. Chen, T.H., Wu, P.H., Chiou, Y.C.: An early fire-detection method based on image processing. In: 2004 International Conference on Image Processing, 2004. ICIP 2004, vol. 3, pp. 1707–1710. IEEE (2004)
12. Chen, J., He, Y., Wang, J.: Multi-feature fusion based fast video flame detection. Build. Environ. **45**(5), 1113–1122 (2010)
13. Celik, T., Demirel, H., Ozkaramanli, H.: Automatic fire detection in video sequences. In: 2006 14th European Signal Processing Conference, pp. 1–5. IEEE (2006)

14. Celik, T., Demirel, H.: Fire detection in video sequences using a generic color model. Fire Saf. J. **44**(2), 147–158 (2009)
15. Chi, R., Lu, Z.M., Ji, Q.G.: Real-time multi-feature based fire flame detection in video. IET Image Proc. **11**(1), 31–37 (2016)
16. Yan, Y.Y., Zhu, X.Y., Liu, Y., Gao, S.B.: Flame detection based on the faster R-CNN model. J. Nanjing Normal Univ. (Nat. Sci. Ed.) **2018**(03), 1–5 (2018)
17. Aslan, S., Güdükbay, U., Töreyin, B.U., Çetin, A.E.: Deep convolutional generative adversarial networks based flame detection in video. arXiv preprint arXiv:1902.01824 (2019)
18. Dimitropoulos, K., Barmpoutis, P., Grammalidis, N.: Higher order linear dynamical systems for smoke detection in video surveillance applications. IEEE Trans. Circ. Syst. Video Technol. **27**(5), 1143–1154 (2016)
19. Appana, D.K., Islam, R., Khan, S.A., Kim, J.M.: A video-based smoke detection using smoke flow pattern and spatial-temporal energy analyses for alarm systems. Inf. Sci. **418**, 91–101 (2017)
20. Barmpoutis, P., Dimitropoulos, K., Grammalidis, N.: Smoke detection using spatio-temporal analysis, motion modeling and dynamic texture recognition. In: 2014 22nd European Signal Processing Conference (EUSIPCO), pp. 1078–1082. IEEE (2014)
21. Wen, Z.B., Kang, Y., Cao, Y., Wei, M., Song, W.G.: Video smoke detection based on random forest feature selection. J. Univ. Sci. Technol. China **47**(8), 653–664 (2017)
22. Wang, S., He, Y., Yang, H., Wang, K., Wang, J.: Video smoke detection using shape, color and dynamic features. J. Intell. Fuzzy Syst. **33**(1), 305–313 (2017)
23. Luo, Y., Zhao, L., Liu, P., Huang, D.: Fire smoke detection algorithm based on motion characteristic and convolutional neural networks. Multimed. Tools Appl. **77**(12), 15075–15092 (2017). https://doi.org/10.1007/s11042-017-5090-2
24. Mao, W., Wang, W., Dou, Z., Li, Y.: Fire recognition based on multi-channel convolutional neural network. Fire Technol. **54**(2), 531–554 (2018)
25. Pan, Y., Yao, T., Li, Y., Mei, T.: X-Linear attention networks for image captioning. In: Proceedings of the IEEE/CVF Conference on Computer Vision and Pattern Recognition, pp. 10971–10980 (2020)
26. Chen, R., Zeng, G., Wang, K., Luo, L., Cai, Z.: A real time vision-based smoking detection framework on edge. J. Internet Things **2**(2), 55–64 (2020)
27. Zhou, S., Chen, L., Sugumaran, V.: Hidden two-stream collaborative learning network for action recognition. Comput. Mater. Continua **63**(3), 1545–1561 (2020)
28. Hu, B., Wang, J.: Deep learning for distinguishing computer generated images and natural images: a survey. J. Inf. Hiding Priv. Prot. **2**(2), 37–47 (2020)
29. Zhou, S., Wu, J., Zhang, F., Sehdev, P.: Depth occlusion perception feature analysis for person re-identification. Pattern Recogn. Lett. **138**, 617–623 (2020)
30. Xiang, L., Guo, G., Li, Q., Zhu, C., Chen, J.: Spam detection in reviews using LSTM-based multi-entity temporal features. Intell. Autom. Soft Comput. **26**(6), 1375–1390 (2020)

The Evaluation Method of Safety Classification for Electric Energy Measurement Based on Dynamic Double Fuzzy Reasoning

Tao Liu[2], Shaocheng Wu[2], Tong Peng[1(✉)], Sijian Li[2], Jie Zhao[2], and Xiaohong Cao[2]

[1] School of Cyberspace Security, Beijing University of Posts and Telecommunications, Beijing 100876, China
pengtong@bupt.edu.cn

[2] Shenzhen Power Supply Bureau Co. Ltd., Shenzhen 518001, Guangdong, China

Abstract. With the continuous improvement of the automation level of the electric energy metering system, the measurement security threats it facing increased contrast. Aiming at the fuzzy and dynamic characteristics of the information safety grade of the electric energy metering system, a multi-level and multi-factor security comprehensive evaluation model based on dynamic fuzzy theory which proposes a safety classification evaluation method based on dynamic double fuzzy reasoning, was established based on the study of the security static evaluation model. In this paper, the information security evaluation index system is established by analyzing the related factors of confidentiality, integrity and availability of electric energy measurement information security. The dynamic fuzzy probability vector of the safety grade is calculated based on the ameliorated D-S evidential theory, then the static weight determined by FAHP based on triangular fuzzy number and the time weight determined by the information entropy weight method based on time degree are integrated to calculate the dynamic weight vector of the index, and finally combines examples to analyze and verify the resulting data. This paper provided new solutions for the information security classification evaluation of the electric energy metering automation system.

Keywords: Measurement automation · Safety index · Fuzzy theory · Time weight · Dynamic assessment

1 Introduction

Over the last few years, with the rapid improvement of my country's economic level, the continuous development of automation technology, and the continuous expansion of the scale of the power grid have greatly promoted the progress of the electric energy metering system, and fully realized the automatic operation and management of the metering system [1]. Electric energy metering is a key part of an electric energy automation system. With the increasing demand for power grid energy measurement in production and life, the metering automation system relies more and more on the information system, and the information security threats and vulnerabilities faced have also increased [2]. Information

X. Sun et al. (Eds.): ICAIS 2021, LNCS 12736, pp. 239–252, 2021.
https://doi.org/10.1007/978-3-030-78609-0_21

security is the basic target of building an electric energy metering automation system. How to accurately analyze the safety status of the electric energy metering automation system and adopt corresponding safety protection measures in real time is a difficult point to be solved urgently [3].

Security level evaluation is an important part of information security. We can use this method to judge the security level of the current system and take corresponding security protection measures to improve the security of the metering system and lay the foundation for the reliable and high-quality development of the power grid [4]. Since the quality of information security is affected by many factors, and these factors have the characteristics of ambiguity, randomness and relevance, so it is difficult to measure accurately by simple qualitative or quantitative static evaluation. For this reason, researchers have transformed from static analysis assessment to dynamic analysis assessment [5]. However, the security level measurement method applied to the electric energy metering system has many limitations, and the security evaluation mechanism is still very imperfect in terms of comprehensiveness, timeliness and effectiveness [6]. How to integrate evaluation set and allocate index weight scientifically and reasonably is a key issue in the safety evaluation of the measurement system. In view of this, this article studies the security dynamic assessment technology of the measurement automation system, and a 5-layer indicator system for the measurement security evaluation is established. Considering the judgment bias between experts and the dynamic changes of index weights at different times, a classification measurement method for energy metering security based on dynamic double fuzzy reasoning is proposed to realize the hierarchical evaluation of information security to ensure the information security of the metering automation system.

The main contributions are as follows:

1) The safety index system of measurement automation system is established, the whole process of system safety evaluation is described and the evaluation level is defined.
2) The dynamic evaluation model of system security indexes is constructed, and the calculation process of index evaluation set based on dynamic fuzzy theory, static weight based on triangular fuzzy number, time weight based on time degree and comprehensive dynamic fuzzy evaluation level are described.
3) The evaluation model is verified by experimental analysis.

The remainder of this paper is organized as follows: Sect. 2 summarizes the existing related work; Energy metering safety index system is established in Sect. 3; Sect. 4, we build a dynamic security evaluation model of electric energy metering system; Sect. 5, the model is verified by the analysis of actual data and the results are discussed. Finally, some brief conclusions are presented in Sect. 6.

2 Related Work

From the current research, safety assessment methods can be divided into three categories: quantitative assessment, qualitative assessment, and comprehensive assessment [7]. Scholars at home and abroad have formulated information security assessment schemes based on various theories. Such as fuzzy analytic hierarchy process (FAHP) [8], Bayesian network [9], attack graph [10], fault tree [11] and grey theory [12], etc.

2.1 Method of Calculating Weight Set

At present, most of the studies for obtaining index weight sets are focused on the Delphi method, Expert Weighting method and Analytic Hierarchy Process (AHP) based on 1–9 scale or 3-scale. Deng et al. [13] proposed an urban power grid security assessment method based on fuzzy theory. The model determines the weight of the importance of each index based on the experience of experts, which fully reflects the experience and knowledge of experts, but is highly subjective. Qian et al. [14] proposed a smart microgrid security risk assessment method based on fuzzy set theory. The index weight is determined by the AHP method, but there are problems in that the consistency test process is complicated and the consistency standard lacks scientific basis. In order to solve the above problems, Liu et al. [15] adopted FAHP to determine the weight of each index, and transformed qualitative analysis into quantitative analysis. By using fuzzy theory to fuzzy the qualitative indexes in the hierarchical structure model to improve the accuracy of judgment. On this basis, Qian et al. [8] considered the combination of multi-source situational awareness technology and fuzzy reasoning to apply the network security risk perception of metering automation systems. This method comprehensively considers a variety of related indicators and analyzes and evaluates the safety quality of the system from multiple angles. However, the distribution of indicator weights not only depends to a large extent on the experts' own experience and professional knowledge, but also has certain subjective factors.

2.2 Method of Calculating Evaluation Set

At present, many scholars have carried out related research work on calculating membership degree. In the evaluation process based on fuzzy theory, the methods of calculating membership degree include Delphi method, D-S evidence theory method, gray theory etc. Liu et al. [16] introduced a balance function based on the variable weight principle. The variable weight balance function can determine the degree of membership more objectively, making the evaluation set obtained more objective. In [15], the improved D-S evidence theory is used to fusion and calibration of the metric values judged by all experts to obtain the safety performance level of each factor, which reduces the subjectivity and blindness of the evaluation. Xia et al. [12] proposed a safety assessment method based on AHP and grey fuzzy theory. Based on the evaluation weight of the expert group, this method uses gray fuzzy theory to construct the membership grade matrix, which effectively avoids the subjective influence of expert scoring. Later, Liu et al. [6] proposed a security situation assessment method based on Grey multi-attribute theory. This method combines the qualitative data, quantitative data, fuzzy value and precise value of the security situation to obtain the overall information security performance of the power dispatch automation software.

Obviously, in the traditional system security level measurement methods, too much attention is paid to the evaluation methods, and the selection and construction process of measurement safety evaluation indexes are ignored. Considering the subjective attitude of experts in the index evaluation process, the use of data fusion effectively reduces the deviation between different experts. However, it ignores the performance of the information security system in different time periods and lacks dynamic evaluation.

3 Energy Metering Safety Indexes

3.1 Safety Index System Modeling

In the process of information security level evaluation, the construction of scientific and reasonable index measurement system is the basis of security evaluation. In the automatic energy metering system, changes of any safety factor may lead to changes in the safety performance of the system. According to the safety requirements of the electric energy metering automation system, detailed analysis of the components and functional associations of the electric energy metering automation system, and the safety evaluation of the metering system is carried out. Generally, the confidentiality, integrity and availability of information affect the quality of information security, namely the degree of information security breaches is mainly reflected in these three aspects [17].

Therefore, the safety indicators are divided into multiple levels, and the overall safety quality level of the system is obtained by bottom-up evaluation. The security criteria layer can be divided into three types of characteristics: confidentiality, integrity, and availability, as a first-order indexes, then the factor level is divided into four categories: network communication, information, software, and hardware, as a secondary indexes, finally referring to the standard ISO/IEC 17799:2005 [18], a 4-layer information security level system including multiple sub-factors is established. The specific indicators of safety evaluation are shown in Fig. 1.

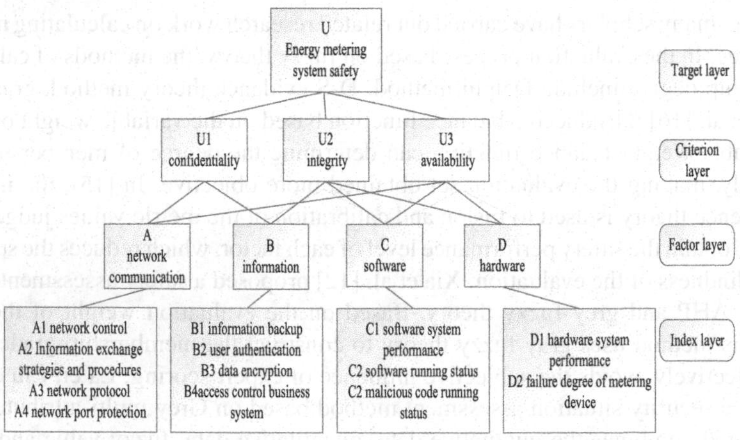

Fig. 1. Safety index system of electric energy measurement

3.2 Specific Evaluation Process

In this paper, the comprehensive dynamic evaluation is carried out according to the influence degree of each index on the safety of electric energy metering automation system. The safety evaluation process of the electric energy metering automation system is as Fig. 2.

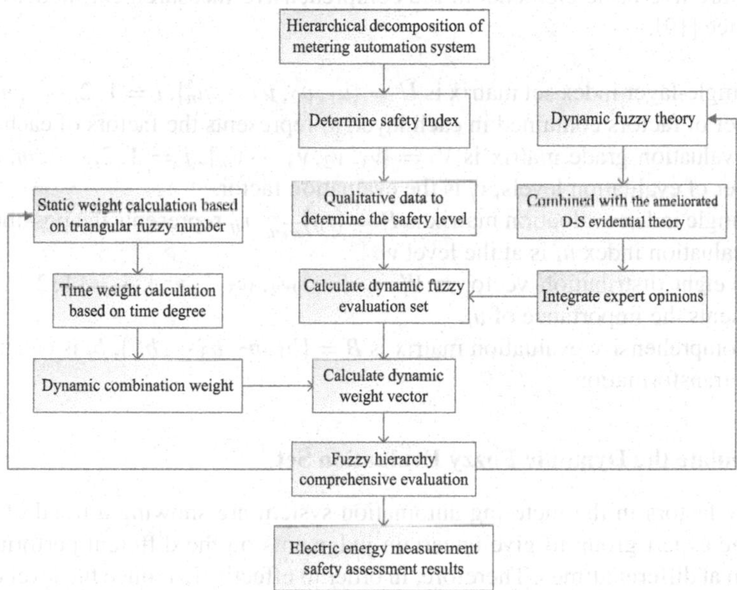

Fig. 2. Safety evaluation process

3.3 Index Security Classification

After the information security index is determined, set the measurement automation system security measurement level. Refer to the current classification of information security indicators at home and abroad, it is divided into seven levels, and the corresponding qualitative data are 1, 2, 3, 4 and 5. The higher the security level, the stronger the security performance of the system. The evaluation criteria corresponding to specific grades are shown in Table 1 below.

Table 1. Security rating

Grade	1	2	3	4	5
Evaluation level	Lower	Low	Middle	High	Higher
Score	[0,1)	[1,2)	[2,3)	[3,4)	[4,5]

4 Safety Performance Dynamic Evaluation Model

When measuring the information security level, the degree descriptors used are usually vague and inaccurate words, such as high, medium, and low. Besides the weight of each safety factor changes dynamically. Therefore, it is necessary to make a comprehensive assessment of these fuzzy safety indexes.

There are five basic elements in the comprehensive measurement model of safety performance [19].

1) The single-layer index set matrix is $U = \{u_1, u_2, u_3 \cdots u_n\}, i = 1, 2, \cdots, n$, n is the number of factors contained in each layer, u_i represents the factors of each layer.
2) The evaluation grade matrix is $V = \{v_1, v_2, v_3 \cdots v_m\}, j = 1, 2, \cdots, m$, m is the number of evaluation levels, v_j is the evaluation factor.
3) The single index evaluation matrix is $P = (r_{ij})_{n*m}$, r_{ij} represents the possibility that the evaluation index u_i is at the level v_j.
4) The weight distribution vector is $W = \{w_1, w_2, w_3 \cdots w_n\}$, $i = 1, 2, \cdots, n$, w_i represents the importance of u_i.
5) The comprehensive evaluation matrix is $B = \{b_1, b_2, b_3 \cdots b_m\}$, b_i is calculated by fuzzy transformation.

4.1 Calculate the Dynamic Fuzzy Evaluation Set

The safety factors in the metering automation system are showing a trend of change, leading the expert group to give uncertain judgments on the different performance of the system at different times. Therefore, in order to effectively reduce the level conflicts judged by experts and realize the dynamic fuzzy reasoning of security level assessment, a fuzzy evaluation method combining dynamic fuzzy theory [20] and improved D-S evidence theory [21] is introduced to construct dynamic membership.

Assuming that h experts are invited as the judging panel, the weight ratio of experts is $\lambda = [\lambda_1, \lambda_2, \cdots, \lambda_h]$, the higher the value of λ_h, the higher the credibility of the expert. According to the classification of index safety level, the probability vector of dynamic fuzziness of the ith expert to the jth index is

$$P_{ij} = \left\{ \left(\overleftarrow{p}_{ij1}, \vec{p}_{ij1} \right), \left(\overleftarrow{p}_{ij2}, \vec{p}_{ij2} \right), \cdots \left(\overleftarrow{p}_{ijm}, \vec{p}_{ijm} \right) \right\} \tag{1}$$

where $\overleftarrow{p}_{ijm}$ represents the improvement trend of the jth index judged by the ith expert at level m, $\vec{p}_{ijm}$ represents the variation trend of the jth index judged by the ith expert on level m.The two values are not taken at the same time, but only represent the change of the grade trend, such as $\overleftarrow{p}_{ijm} = \overleftarrow{0.3}$ 时, $\vec{p}_{ijm} = 0$.

Similarly, the dynamic ranking matrix $M = (m_{ik})_{h\times m}$ of h experts to index j is

$$M = \begin{bmatrix} M_1 \\ M_2 \\ \vdots \\ M_h \end{bmatrix} = \begin{bmatrix} m_{11} & m_{12} & \cdots & m_{1m} \\ m_{21} & m_{22} & \cdots & m_{2m} \\ \vdots & \vdots & \ddots & \vdots \\ m_{h1} & m_{h2} & \cdots & m_{hm} \end{bmatrix} \tag{2}$$

m_{hm} is the measurement of the jth index by the hth expert on grade m, and $M_i = P_{ij}$.

Then according to the weight distribution of the improved D-S evidence theory [21], the expert judgment results are fused, and the fusion method is as follows:

$$k = \sum_{j=1}^{m} \prod_{\substack{1 \le i \le h \\ \cap A_j = \emptyset}} m_i(A_j) = 1 - \sum_{j=1}^{m} \prod_{\substack{1 \le i \le h \\ \cap A_j = A}} m_i(A_j)$$

$$f(A) = \sum_{1 \le i \le h} \lambda_i m_i(A_j) \tag{3}$$

$$m(A) = \begin{cases} 0 & A = \emptyset \\ \prod_{\substack{1 \le i \le h \\ \cap A_j = A}} m_i(A_j) + kf(A) & A \neq \emptyset \end{cases}$$

where k indicates the degree of conflict between experts, $f(A)$ represents the weighted degree of support for index A by all experts. That is, the multiplication of the two means that the weight of k is assigned to the index A. In the calculation process, the dynamic change trend is consistent with the probability of the large value.

Thus, the probability distribution of the security level of indicator A is obtained through data fusion as:

$$P_j = \left\{ \left(\overleftarrow{p}_{j1}, \overrightarrow{p}_{j1} \right), \left(\overleftarrow{p}_{j2}, \overrightarrow{p}_{j2} \right), \cdots \left(\overleftarrow{p}_{jm}, \overrightarrow{p}_{jm} \right) \right\} \tag{4}$$

where $\sum_{i=1}^{m} \overleftarrow{p_i} + \sum_{i=1}^{m} \overrightarrow{p_i} = 1$.Then according to the probabilities assigned by each level and the corresponding qualitative data multiplied and summed to get the safety status level value of the indicator, the expression satisfies

$$p = p_{j1} \times 1 + p_{j2} \times 2 + p_{j3} \times 3 + p_{j4} \times 4 + p_{j5} \times 5 \tag{5}$$

The criterion for judging the dynamic trend is, if $\sum_{i=1}^{m} \overleftarrow{p_i} > \sum_{i=1}^{m} \overrightarrow{p_i}$, the dynamic trend is getting better, otherwise the opposite is true.

Similarly, after the above data processing, a dynamic evaluation set matrix $P_{n \times m}$ of all indexes can be obtained as follows:

$$P = \begin{bmatrix} P_1 \\ P_2 \\ \vdots \\ P_n \end{bmatrix} = \begin{bmatrix} (\overleftarrow{p}_{11}, \overrightarrow{p}_{12}) & (\overleftarrow{p}_{12}, \overrightarrow{p}_{12}) & \cdots & (\overleftarrow{p}_{1m}, \overrightarrow{p}_{1m}) \\ (\overleftarrow{p}_{21}, \overrightarrow{p}_{21}) & (\overleftarrow{p}_{22}, \overrightarrow{p}_{22}) & \cdots & (\overleftarrow{p}_{2m}, \overrightarrow{p}_{2m}) \\ \vdots & \vdots & \ddots & \vdots \\ (\overleftarrow{p}_{n1}, \overrightarrow{p}_{n1}) & (\overleftarrow{p}_{n2}, \overrightarrow{p}_{n2}) & \cdots & (\overleftarrow{p}_{nm}, \overrightarrow{p}_{nm}) \end{bmatrix} \tag{6}$$

4.2 Dynamic Weight of Safety Factors

When the traditional expert judgment method is adopted, the weight determination of the indicator depends on the subjective judgment of the expert, so this evaluation model has ambiguity and subjectivity, causing evaluation bias. In addition, because index weights may have different proportions at different times, a reasonable allocation of index weights is the key to comprehensive evaluation of safety performance. This paper combines static weight and time weight to effectively obtain the dynamic weight set of indicators.

1) Calculate the weight of static

Based on the analytic hierarchy process of 1–9 scale method, the process is complicated when the consistency test is performed and the number of iterations is large when adjusting the weight vector. On this basis, this paper improves it by using fuzzy FAHP based on triangular fuzzy number. Through pairwise comparison of each index in the system, simplify the calculation process, and refer to the literature [22] for details.

Suppose that at time t_j, h experts will judge each index, and the judgment criteria are shown in Table 2.

Table 2. Importance scale

Qualitative comparison of indexes	0.1–0.9 scale
a is absolutely more important than b	0.9
a is obviously more important than b	0.8
a is more important than b	0.7
a is slightly more important than b	0.6
A and B are equally important	0.5
b is slightly more important than a	0.4
b is more important than a	0.3
b is obviously more important than a	0.2
b is absolutely more important than a	0.1

Let $x_i = (l_i, m_i, u_i)$ be the triangular fuzzy value of index i, l_i is the lower limit of the scale, m_i is Middle value, u_i is upper limit. Establish the triangular fuzzy number judgment matrix $D = \left(d_{ij}\right)_{n*n}$ as follows:

$$D = \begin{bmatrix} d_{11}\ d_{12} & \cdots & d_{1n} \\ d_{21}\ d_{22} & & d_{2n} \\ \vdots & \ddots & \vdots \\ d_{n1}\ d_{n2} & \cdots & d_{nn} \end{bmatrix} \tag{7}$$

d_{ij} represents the scale value obtained by combining all expert groups, and the expression is

$$d_{ij} = \lambda_1 d_{ij}^1 + \lambda_2 d_{ij}^2 + \cdots \lambda_h d_{ij}^h \tag{8}$$

where λ_h is the proportion of the hth expert rating weight, d_{ij}^h is the judgment of the hth expert on the comparison of the importance of indicators i and j. Then the comprehensive evaluation value X_i of the triangular fuzzy number of the ith index is as follows:

$$X_i = \left(\frac{\sum_{j=1}^{n} l_{ij}}{\sum u_{ij}}, \frac{\sum_{j=1}^{n} m_{ij}}{\sum m_{ij}}, \frac{\sum_{j=1}^{n} u_{ij}}{\sum l_{ij}} \right) \tag{9}$$

According to the formula $m_i' = (l_i + 2m_i + u_i)/4$, the final evaluation value can be obtained by comprehensively calculating the triangular fuzzy number, and the evaluation index weight at time t_j can be obtained as:

$$w_i^j = \frac{m_i'}{\sum_{i=1}^{n} m_i'} \tag{10}$$

Similarly, the weight w_i at different times is

$$w_i = \left[w_i^1, w_i^2, \cdots w_i^s\right] \tag{11}$$

2) Calculate the weight of time

To ensure that the evaluation level is more reliable, the dynamic changes of system safety indicators over time should be considered. Therefore, it is necessary to solve the time weights at different moments. Assuming that the proportion of the assessment moment is $a = [a(t_1), a(t_2), \cdots a(t_s)]$, $\sum_{j=1}^{s} a(t_j) = 1, j = 1, 2, \cdots s$.

In order to integrate the preference degree of experts for each time, so the time degree $\theta = \sum_{j=1}^{s} \frac{s-j}{s-1} a(t_j)$ is introduced [23]. The higher the value of θ, the more biased the expert's judgment to the current moment. Reference [24], a function of time weight $f(a(t_j)) = -\sum_{j=1}^{s} a(t_j) \ln a(t_j)$ is established. Thus, the nonlinear model is established by using the principle of information entropy maximization.

$$\begin{cases} max\, f(a(t_j)) = -\sum_{i=1}^{s} a(t_j)\ ln\ a(t_j) \\ s.t.\ \theta = \sum_{j=1}^{s} \frac{s-j}{s-1} a(t_j) \\ \sum_{j=1}^{s} a(t_j) = 1 \end{cases} \tag{12}$$

3) Calculate the weight dynamic

Combining the index weights in the above two cases, the comprehensive weight distribution vector can be obtained as follows:

$$W = [w_1, w_2, w_3, \ldots, w_n] \tag{13}$$

According to Eq. (11) and Eq. (12), the static weight and time weight are combined as:

$$\begin{aligned} W_i &= a \times w_i^T \\ &= [a(t_1), a(t_2), \cdots, a(t_s)] \times \begin{bmatrix} w_i^1 \\ w_i^2 \\ \vdots \\ w_i^s \end{bmatrix} \end{aligned} \tag{14}$$

4.3 Calculate the Dynamic Comprehensive Evaluation Set

According to the constructed safety index system, the first-level index set is $U = \{u_1, u_2, u_3 \cdots u_n\}$, $i = 1, 2, \cdots, n$, The set of secondary indicators for the ith primary indicator is $U_i = \{u_{i1}, u_{i2}, \cdots, u_{ia}\}$, $j = 1, 2, \cdots, a$, a is the number of corresponding secondary indexes, the factor set corresponding to the jth secondary index is $U_{ij} = \{u_{ij1}, u_{ij2}, \cdots, u_{ijd}\}$, $k = 1, 2, \cdots, d$, d is the number of corresponding safety factors. From the above, the corresponding weights are $W = [w_1, w_2, \ldots, w_n]$, $W_i = [w_{i1}, w_{i2}, \ldots, w_{ia}]$, $W_{ij} = [w_{ij1}, w_{ij2}, \ldots, w_{ijd}]$.

In the process of obtaining the final security level of the system, the above process needs to be iterated many times. Firstly, the security level evaluation vector and the corresponding dynamic weight vector of each factor on the lowest sub-criteria level are obtained. After fuzzy transformation, the security level evaluation vector corresponding to the indicators on the criterion level can be obtained.

That is, according to Eq. (6) and Eq. (13) to fuzzy transform the parameters of the elements of the sub-factor layer, the dynamic fuzzy evaluation vector corresponding to the index of the upper layer can be obtained as follows:

$$
\begin{aligned}
X_{ij} &= W_{1\times d} \times P_{d\times m} \\
&= [w_{ij1}, w_{ij2}, \ldots w_{ijd}] \times \begin{bmatrix} \left(\overleftarrow{P}_{ij11}, \overrightarrow{P}_{ij11}\right) & \left(\overleftarrow{P}_{ij12}, \overrightarrow{P}_{ij12}\right) & \cdots & \left(\overleftarrow{P}_{ij1m}, \overrightarrow{P}_{ij1m}\right) \\ \left(\overleftarrow{P}_{ij21}, \overrightarrow{P}_{ij21}\right) & \left(\overleftarrow{P}_{ij22}, \overrightarrow{P}_{ij22}\right) & \cdots & \left(\overleftarrow{P}_{ij2m}, \overrightarrow{P}_{ij2m}\right) \\ \vdots & \vdots & \ddots & \vdots \\ \left(\overleftarrow{P}_{ijd1}, \overrightarrow{P}_{n1}\right) & \left(\overleftarrow{P}_{ijd2}, \overrightarrow{P}_{ijd2}\right) & \cdots & \left(\overleftarrow{P}_{ijdm}, \overrightarrow{P}_{ijdm}\right) \end{bmatrix} \\
&= \left[\left(\overleftarrow{P}_{ij1}, \overrightarrow{P}_{ij1}\right) \left(\overleftarrow{P}_{ij2}, \overrightarrow{P}_{ij2}\right) \cdots \left(\overleftarrow{P}_{ijm}, \overrightarrow{P}_{ijm}\right)\right]
\end{aligned} \tag{15}
$$

all the rest are determined in the same way, finally the security level of the entire system can be obtained.

5 Experiment and Analysis

In this example, 3 experts evaluated the information security performance of the metering system. Among them, the proportion of expert weight is 0.5, 0.3 and 0.2 respectively. According to the safety index system constructed in Sect. 3.1, the software index C is taken as an example to illustrate.

According to the safety rating table, three experts judge the grade of index C1 at first, as shown in Table 3.

According to Eq. (1), the data fusion of the first two experts can obtain the level probability distribution.

$$
C1 = \left[\left(\overleftarrow{0}, \overrightarrow{0.038}\right) \left(\overleftarrow{0}, \overrightarrow{0.366}\right) \left(\overleftarrow{0}, \overrightarrow{0.038}\right) \left(\overleftarrow{0}, \overrightarrow{0.424}\right) \left(\overleftarrow{0.134}, \overrightarrow{0}\right)\right] \tag{16}
$$

Table 3. Security level weight distribution

M_1	$(\overleftarrow{0}, \overrightarrow{0})$	$(\overleftarrow{0}, \overrightarrow{0.5})$	$(\overleftarrow{0}, \overrightarrow{0.1})$	$(\overleftarrow{0.2}, \overrightarrow{0})$	$(\overleftarrow{0.2}, \overrightarrow{0})$
M_2	$(\overleftarrow{0}, \overrightarrow{0.1})$	$(\overleftarrow{0.2}, \overrightarrow{0})$	$(\overleftarrow{0}, \overrightarrow{0})$	$(\overleftarrow{0}, \overrightarrow{0.6})$	$(\overleftarrow{0.1}, \overrightarrow{0})$
M_3	$(\overleftarrow{0.1}, \overrightarrow{0})$	$(\overleftarrow{0}, \overrightarrow{0.2})$	$(\overleftarrow{0}, \overrightarrow{0.2})$	$(\overleftarrow{0}, \overrightarrow{0})$	$(\overleftarrow{0.5}, \overrightarrow{0})$

Then, data fusion with the third expert, the security level of index C1 can be obtained as follows:

$$C1 = \left[\left(\overleftarrow{0}, \overrightarrow{0.0623}\right) \left(\overleftarrow{0}, \overrightarrow{0.3133}\right) \left(\overleftarrow{0}, \overrightarrow{0.1086}\right) \left(\overleftarrow{0}, \overrightarrow{0.1799}\right) \left(\overleftarrow{0.3359}, \overrightarrow{0}\right) \right] \tag{17}$$

According to Eq. (2), the value of the safety state level of index C1 can be obtained as 3.4138, which is most likely to be "High" safety level. According to the dynamic trend judgment standard, it is concluded that the dynamic change trend is getting better and better. Similarly, the security level judgment vectors of indicators C2 and C3 can be obtained.

When calculating the dynamic weight of the three indicators, first calculate the static weight of each indicator at different moments. Through the digital scaling method, the triangular fuzzy number judgment matrix is obtained by comparing pairwise, and then the judgment matrix of all experts is weighted according to Eq. (8) to obtain the comprehensive judgment matrix D.

$$D_1 = \begin{bmatrix} (0.500, 0.500, 0.500) & (0.200, 0.300, 0.400) & (0.150, 0.250, 0.350) \\ (0.600, 0.700, 0.800) & (0.500, 0.500, 0.500) & (0.250, 0.350, 0.450) \\ (0.650, 0.750, 0.850) & (0.550, 0.650, 0.750) & (0.500, 0.500, 0.500) \end{bmatrix} \tag{18}$$

According to Eq. (9), the comprehensive evaluation result of triangular fuzzy number can be determined as:

$$X_1 = \begin{bmatrix} 0.167 & 0.263 & 0.321 \\ 0.265 & 0.388 & 0.449 \\ 0.333 & 0.422 & 0.538 \end{bmatrix} \tag{19}$$

From Eq. (10), calculate the static weight of the evaluation index at t_1 time. $W_1^1 = [0.243, 0.332, 0.425]$. Similarly, we can get the static weight of the evaluation index C1 at t_2, t_3, t_4 time. Next, calculate the time weights at different moments. The time weight of index C1 is obtained by the established nonlinear model as $a = [0.159, 0.160, 0.231, 0.450]$. Therefore, according to Eq. (14), the dynamic weight of the safety index of C1 can be calculated as:

$$W_1 = [0.159, 0.160, 0.231, 0.450] \times \begin{bmatrix} 0.243, \ 0.332, \ 0.425 \\ 0.212, \ 0.369, \ 0.419 \\ 0.180, \ 0.421, \ 0.399 \\ 0.258, \ 0.315, \ 0.427 \end{bmatrix}$$
$$= [0.2302, 0.3508, 0.4189] \quad (20)$$

Similarly, the dynamic weight of the safety indicators of C2 and C3 can be calculated. Take the calculated 9 time weight values of index C1 as an example to more clearly describe the weight change of the index at different times. It can be seen from the simulation results in Fig. 3 that the influence of index C1 on indicator C fluctuates over time, and expert preference for time is more inclined to recent moments.

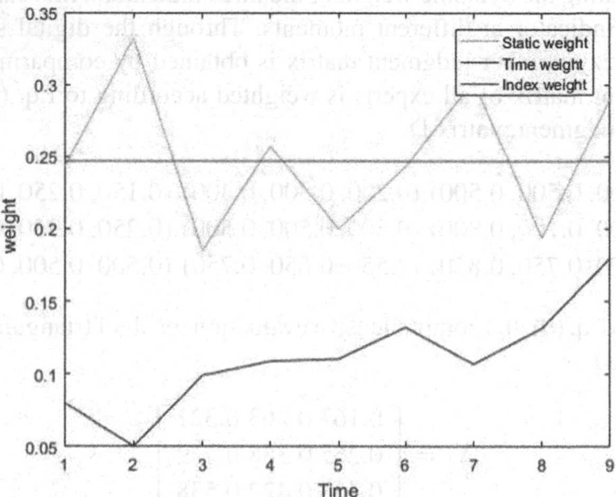

Fig. 3. Weight comparison

Finally, according to Eq. (15), the dynamic fuzzy comprehensive evaluation value of index C can be obtained as:

$$C = W \times \begin{bmatrix} C1 \\ C2 \\ C3 \end{bmatrix}$$
$$= \left[\left(\overleftarrow{0.232}, \vec{0}\right) \left(\overleftarrow{0}, \overrightarrow{0.3470}\right) \left(\overleftarrow{0.1434}, \vec{0}\right) \left(\overleftarrow{0}, \overrightarrow{0.1099}\right) \left(\overleftarrow{0.1667}, \vec{0}\right) \right] \quad (21)$$

Therefore, the value of the security status level of index C is 2.6305, which is most likely to be "Low" security level. According to the dynamic trend judgment standard, it is concluded that the dynamic change trend is getting worse and worse, so it is necessary to adopt safety protection measures for the metering system.

6 Conclusion

This paper proposes the evaluation method of safety classification for energy metering based on dynamic double fuzzy reasoning. The information security evaluation index system is established by analyzing the relevant factors of the confidentiality, integrity and availability of the associated energy metering security, and the model is modeled by fuzzy theory. Firstly, combine dynamic fuzzy reasoning and D-S evidence theory to solve the dynamic probability vector of index level. Secondly, the FAHP method based on triangular fuzzy numbers solves the static weight of index at different moments and the information entropy weight method based on time degree solves the time weights at different moments, then combines the two results to obtain a dynamic weight set of safety indicators according to a certain ratio. Finally, the security level of the entire system is evaluated through multiple iterations of fuzzy transformation. In the entire evaluation process, this method uses expert reliability and experience to perform data fusion on the expert decision value, which effectively reduces the deviation of the measurement value caused by the subjectivity of experts. In addition, under the dual dynamics of dynamic fuzzy reasoning and time weights, the dynamic evaluation of the safety level during the operation of the electric energy metering automation system is completed.

References

1. Gao, H., Dei, X., Liu, L.: Evaluation of communication security of integrated automation system in substation. Telecommun. Electr. Power Syst. **33**(232), 1–4 (2012)
2. Yu, J., Wang, X., Zhang, D., et al.: Innovation demonstration area construction of Tianjin eco-city smart grid facing multi energy interconnection. Electr. Power Constr. **36**(11), 58–61 (2015)
3. State Grid Corporation of China, Production Safety Accident Report of SGCC in 2014, pp. 10–18. China Power Press, Beijing (2014)
4. Zhang, R., Hu, X., Gao, J., et al.: Principle and Operation of Integrated Automation in Substation. China Power Press, Beijing (2008)
5. Guo, L., Dong, W., Sun, X., et al: A method of dynamic risk analysis and assessment for metro power supply system based on fuzzy reasoning. In: 2019 CAA Symposium on Fault Detection, Supervision and Safety for Technical Processes (SAFEPROCESS), Xiamen, China, pp. 555–561 (2019)
6. Liu, Y., Tang, Y., Zhang, Q., et al.: Power dispatch software security situation assessment method. Netinfo Secur. **19**(8), 15–21 (2019)
7. Feng, D., Zhang, Y., Zhang, Y.: Survey of information security risk assessment. J. Commun. **25**(7), 10–18 (2004)
8. Qian, B., Cai, X., Yong, X., et al.: Fuzzy inference based cyber security situation awareness of advanced metering system. Southern Power Syst. Technol. **13**(2) (2019)
9. Liu, Y., Man, H.: Network vulnerability assessment using Bayesian networks. In: Proceedings of the SPIE, vol. 5812, pp. 61–71 (2005)

10. Poolsappasit, N., Dewri, R., Ray, I.: Dynamic security risk management using Bayesian attack graphs. IEEE Trans. Dependable Secure Comput. **9**(1), 61–74 (2012)
11. Chen, J., Sun, T.: Study on quality risk assessment for power transformer based on fault tree analysis. In: 2016 China International Conference on Electricity Distribution (2016)
12. Xia, J., Fan, K., Lin, L.: Evaluation method of information security protection capability of industrial control system based on AHP and grey fuzzy theory. Network Security Technology or Application (2019)
13. Deng, C., et al.: A fuzzy comprehensive evaluation for metropolitan power grid risk assessment. In: 2016 International Conference on Smart Grid and Clean Energy Technologies (ICSGCE). IEEE (2016)
14. Qian, S., Yang, T.: Research on security risk assessment of smart microgrid based on fuzzy set theory. Energy Conserv. **39**, **449**(02), 12–15 (2020)
15. Liu, W., Zhang, L.: Formation security levels evaluation of distribution automation system based on FAHP and improved D-S. East China Electr. Power **38**(001), 67–71 (2010)
16. Liu, H., Sun, Y.: The safety assessment of thermal control system in power plant. In: ICCASM 2010, Taiyuan, pp. V10-581–V10-584 (2010)
17. Gao, J., Cui, Y., Luo, S., et al.: Research on controllability evaluation of information system. Netinfo Secur. (08), 67–75 (2015)
18. Zhuo, Y., Zhang, Q., Gong, Z.: Network situation assessment based on RST. In: Workshop on Computational Intelligence & Industrial Application. IEEE (2009)
19. Zeke, L., Zewen, C., Chunyan, W., Zhiguang, X., Ye, L.: Research on security evaluation technology of wireless access of electric power monitoring system based on fuzzy. In: 2020 IEEE 3rd International Conference on Computer and Communication Engineering Technology (CCET), Beijing, China, pp. 318–321 (2020)
20. Chen, S.: Theory and Application of Fuzzy Sets. Beijing Science Press (2005)
21. Guan, X., Guo, J., Wang, X.: Double fuzzy information security evaluation algorithm based on improved D-S theory. Comput. Eng. Appl. **53**(2), 112–117 (2017)
22. Gao, H., Zhang, B.: Research on transportation safety evaluation of railway dangerous goods handling station based on dynamic fuzzy theory. Railway Freight **037**(001), 55–60 (2019)
23. Xu, Z., Yager, R.: Dynamic intuitionistic fuzzy multi-attribute decision making. Int. J. Approximate Reasoning **48**, 246–262 (2008)
24. Jin, L., Mesiar, R., Qian, G.: Weighting models to generate weights and capacities in multicriteria group decision making. IEEE Trans. Fuzzy Syst. **26**(4), 2225–2236 (2018)

Offline Writer Identification Using Convolutional Neural Network and VLAD Descriptors

Dawei Liang[1,2], Meng Wu[2(✉)], and Yan Hu[3]

[1] Department of Computer Information and Cyber Security, Jiangsu Police Institute, Nanjing 210031, China

[2] College of Computer, Nanjing University of Posts and Telecommunications, Nanjing 210023, China
wum@njupt.edu.cn

[3] JinCheng College, Nanjing University of Aeronautics and Astronautics, Nanjing 211156, China

Abstract. This paper proposes a method for writer identification and retrieval. The focus of these two tasks is to extract discriminative features from handwriting documents. Traditional artificial features require researchers' experience and professional knowledge in language and handwriting, while the automatic features are extracted from large data handwriting samples. The proposed method uses local features and has better performance. We extract features via the convolutional neural network, subsequently aggregating to obtain the global feature vector. During the process, the system first enhances and preprocesses the handwriting samples and then feeds the patches into the ResNet50 that pretrained on ImageNet. Finally, the local features, i.e., the output of ResNet50, are aggregated into a global feature vector by the VLAD method. The evaluation is employed on the ICDAR2013 and CVL data sets. Experiments show this approach is close to the state-of-the-art methods, and it has good stability and robustness.

Keywords: Writer identification · Convolutional neural network · Data augmentation · Feature extraction · Vector of locally aggregated descriptors

1 Introduction

Same as facial structure [1] or speech [2], handwritten text is considered as a biometric identification. The application is that the authenticity of documents plays an important role in courts. While in the field of historical document analysis [3, 4], the identification and verification of the author's identity through text has also recently received attention. Through a set of known writers, the writer identification system attempts to identify the writer or the most similar one.

According to the handwritten text files to be recognized, the writer identification system can be divided into online and offline. The former determines the writer based on spatial coordinate information such as the writing speed, stroke order, and stroke strength

X. Sun et al. (Eds.): ICAIS 2021, LNCS 12736, pp. 253–264, 2021.
https://doi.org/10.1007/978-3-030-78609-0_22

of the handwritten text. The latter mainly deals with the structure, strokes, trace thickness, and other information in the image information. At present, the data content required for online recognition is large and more difficult to collect, in contrast, the images processed for offline recognition are easier to obtain, offline writer identification has attracted more attention from researchers. For offline recognition, according to whether the content of the text file to be processed is designated, offline handwriting recognition can be divided into text content dependency and text content independence. The former requires the handwritten text to be the specified content, in specific, the written content of all authors in the comparison database is consistent, and the text content independently does not require the written content.

For offline author recognition, the text image to be recognized contains relatively few writer biometrics, which makes it a challenge to identify writers. Simultaneously, the existence of other influencing factors, such as the change of authors' age, external writing environment, and tools used, etc. Therefore, researchers are committed to extracting distinguishing features from handwriting text images to identify writers. Common methods can be divided into two types [5], one is to use the global statistical information to analyze, such as the uniform direction of the word or word spacing [3, 5, 6], and the other is to analyze the information block at the letter level to extract features [5–9].

The methods are designed to extract distinguishable features from text. While the artificial features require expertise in text analysis. Researchers extracted handwritten features from handwritten text images and then encoded the handwritten features into global feature vectors by using the bag-of-words model or other feature representation methods. For example, global feature information can be extracted by Gabor filter [10] and local binary pattern (LBP) [11]. And local feature extraction is adopted by edge direction features, microstructure features, allograph-based histogram features, SIFT-based features [12], SURF-based features, etc. With the development of artificial intelligence technology in recent years, deep learning methods have shown powerful feature extraction capabilities, making researchers turn their attention to the application of deep learning in writer recognition [13]. This method directly extracts the writer's biometrics from the original image and does not require expert experience in language or mode.

Convolutional neural network (CNN) has amazing performance in deep learning [14], employing backpropagation to update the parameters in nonlinear networks. More recently, more and more CNN architectures derived in artificial intelligence, computer vision, machine translation, pattern recognition, speech recognition, natural language processing, and other fields, including AlexNet, GoogleNet, ResNet, VGG, etc.

Subsequently, the process of computing a single representation per image from many local feature descriptors is executed, denoted as encoding. Generally, the encoding consists of two steps: (1) an embedding step, in which a possible nonlinear function is applied to the local feature vectors, creating a high dimensional representation, and (2) an aggregation step, in which the embedded local descriptors are pooled into a fixed-length global descriptor. Some of the better coding methods are Fisher Vectors, the vector of locally aggregated descriptors (VLAD) [15], Gaussian mixture model (GMM) [12], etc.

This paper presents a method for offline handwriting recognition using convolutional neural networks. First, we employ a convolutional neural network, extracting discriminative features, subsequently, we enhance insufficient handwriting data by transfer learning. Transfer learning trains a neural network on large data sets and then applies the learned parameters and features to the target data set. For image data, the pretrained features learned are general, and then through fine-tuning the features can achieve better performance. Subsequently, the VLAD method encodes the local features to form a global feature representing the writer's biological characteristics. Finally, we classify different writers by comparing the distance between the global features of handwriting samples.

The rest of the paper is organized as follows: Sect. 2 brief reports the closely related work for writer identification. Section 3 describes the proposed pipeline. The experiments and results are presented in Sect. 4. Finally, a conclusion is given in Sect. 5.

2 Related Work

The advantage of textural methods is their interpretability in comparison to allograph-based methods. Furthermore, textural methods are typically faster to compute as the allograph-based methods train dictionary. He and Schomaker [17] presented a textural approach with the Δ-n Hinge feature, which is a generalization of the Hinge feature [5]. The method achieved state-of-the-art results on the ICDAR13 English and Greek subsets. Fiel and Sablatnig [7] proposed to use solely SIFT descriptors as the local descriptor, subsequently GMM was computed from SIFT descriptors of the training set. The similarity between handwritten documents was computed using the cosine distance between the corresponding Fisher vectors. They showed state-of-the-art results on the ICDAR 2011 and CVL dataset.

In the field of artificial features, researchers have adopted various methods based on experience. With the development of deep learning technology, automatic feature recognition has achieved better results. In 2015, Fiel and Sablatnig used CaffeNet to recognize writers. The processing included data augmentation, feature extracting, global feature calculate, and classification. On the ICDAR2011 and CVL datasets, using hard criterion evaluation methods, they achieved the highest recognition rate of 98.6% and 97.6%, respectively. At the same time, the recognition rate on the ICDAR2013 dataset was 40.5%. Two problems exist in the application: One is the character cutting error caused by data enhancement, and the other is the lack of Greek data during neural network training. In the same year, Christlein et al. first extracted lots of local CNN-based features from local image patches centered on the contour of the handwriting image. Then these local features are aggregated to form one global descriptor by using GMM for writer identification. The estimated hard criterion TOP-1 was 0.989 and 0.994 on ICDAR2013 and CVL data sets, respectively.

Researchers have adopted a variety of deeper neural network architectures and other image processing methods to obtain better feature representation and higher accuracy. In [18], Xing and Qiao introduced a data augmentation method to enhance the proposed method called DeepWriter. The DeepWriter utilized a multistream parallel CNN architecture to extract the spatial features between adjacent image patches. However, these data augmentation methods led to an overfitting situation and limitation of feature learning in CNNs. Cilia et al. [19] conducted experiments on the Avila Bible with 870 two-column pages from scribal hands. They used row detection to generate image data, tested five kinds of CNNs (VGG19, ResNet50, InceptionV3, InceptionResNetV2, and NASNetLarge) to find the best classification effects. Similarly, the representation between different levels was discussed in the same neural network architecture. Rehman et al. [17] studied the fine-tuning number of layers in the network architecture with transfer learning and obtained an accuracy rate of 88.11% on the QUWI dataset through AlexNet.

Compared with the above work, we adopt a pipeline based on the residual network while preprocessing the data through a variety of data processing methods. We assume that the feature learning method effectively avoids overfitting, improves the feature learning ability, and stabilize the accuracy of recognition.

3 Writer Identification Pipeline

The proposed Writer Identification pipeline (see Fig. 1) consists of three main steps: preprocessing and data augmentation; feature extraction from image patches using a pretrained ResNet50; encoding local features of every test document as global feature vectors using VLAD.

3.1 Dataset

We conduct experiments and evaluations on the CVL [20] and ICDAR2013 [21] datasets. There are 310 writers in the CVL dataset, and every writer has contributed at least five pages of content in English and German. The ICDAR2013 standard data set contains a divided training set and test set, with handwritten materials provided by 100 and 250 writers, respectively. Everyone contributes two pages of content in English and German. For the above two data sets, CVL provides row segmentation images, and ICDAR2013 does not. To enhance the universality of the system, we all use page-scanned documents for training and evaluation.

3.2 Preprocessing

In the proposed pipeline, pre-processing is the first step. In this process, the page images are processed into an appropriate format and fed into subsequent processing for parameter training or feature vector generation.

Patch Segmentation. For full-page handwritten documents, block segmentation needs to be applied to obtain appropriate data. First, we employ the OSTU method for binarization. Then we remove the extra content in the document while maintaining the aspect ratio of the image. For the text processed, we use the sliding window technique to intercept the appropriate patch, and the size of the sliding window is 128×128. The image slides from left to right and from top to bottom in the sliding window. For the training set, the slide size is smaller than the window size to ensure that few handwritten features are

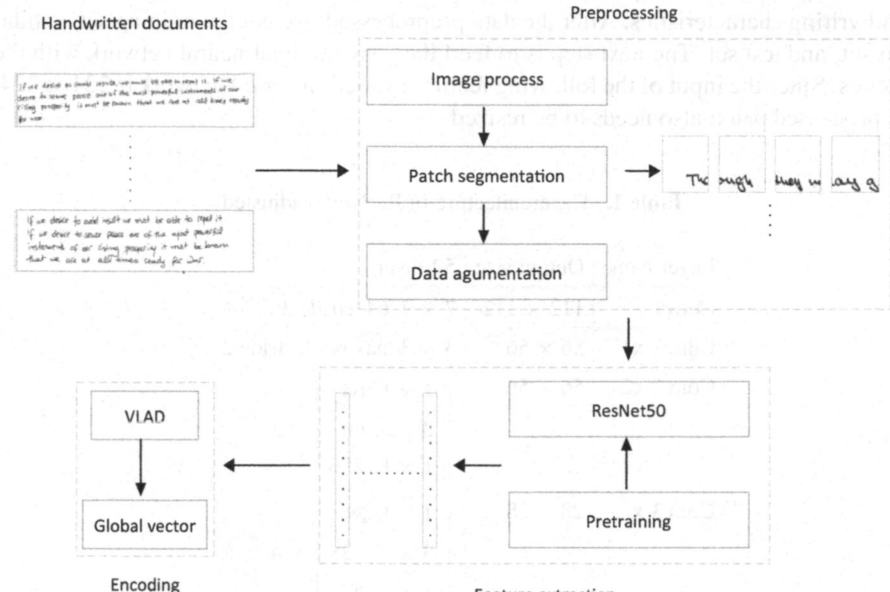

Fig. 1. The pipeline of handwritten feature learning, which consists of three parts: preprocessing (upper right dotted box), feature learning (bottom right dotted box), and encoding (bottom left dotted box). For writer recognition, the system compares the distance between the global vectors of the text.

lost. Simultaneously, the sliding step size is equal to the window size for the validation set. Since the blanks on the edges of the image, we remove blank patches and patches with fewer handwriting features. For one example, see Fig. 2 below. Finally, the training set and the validation set are divided, standardized, and normalized.

Fig. 2. Sample patches segmented from ICDAR2013 dataset (left) and CVL dataset (right).

Data Augmentation. The amount of data in the training set affects the performance of the neural network. In this manner, we use data augmentation technology to expand the training set, while paying attention to overfitting. Ordinarily, the image data enhancement techniques used include rotation, inversion, mirroring, partial enlargement, etc. To reduce image feature loss and avoid overfitting, we use contour, sharpening and inversion methods. The methods do not cause the increase, decrease, and deformation of handwriting characteristics. After the data preprocessed, we get the training set, validation set, and test set. The next step is to feed the convolutional neural network with the patches. Since the input of the following feature extraction neural network is 224 × 224, the processed patch also needs to be resized.

Table 1. The architecture of ResNet50 adjusted

Layer name	Output size	50-layer
Conv1	112 × 112	7 × 7, 64, stride 2
Conv2-x1	56 × 56	3 × 3 max pool, stride 2
Conv2-x2	56 × 56	$\begin{bmatrix} 1 \times 1, 64 \\ 3 \times 3, 64 \\ 1 \times 1, 256 \end{bmatrix} \times 3$
Conv3-x	28 × 28	$\begin{bmatrix} 1 \times 1, 28 \\ 3 \times 3, 128 \\ 1 \times 1, 52 \end{bmatrix} \times 4$
Conv4-x	14 × 14	$\begin{bmatrix} 1 \times 1, 256 \\ 3 \times 3, 256 \\ 1 \times 1, 1024 \end{bmatrix} \times 6$
Conv4-x	7 × 7	$\begin{bmatrix} 1 \times 1, 512 \\ 3 \times 3, 512 \\ 1 \times 1, 2048 \end{bmatrix} \times 3$
	1 × 1	Global pooling Full collect Drop out Softmax (100 or 50 output)

3.3 Feature Extraction

In the field of deep learning, researchers have constructed many classic architectures. He et al. first proposed ResNet in image classification and achieved exciting results. In ILSVRC and COCO2015, the ResNet achieved the first place, proving that it has a powerful feature learning ability. The main reason is that the residual unit added to the network solves the degradation problem and drives a deeper structure. In this work, we use resnet50 to extract handwritten features and make certain adjustments (see Table 1). We replace the second last pooling layer with a global average pooling layer, after that, adjust the output results of the last fully connected layer according to the classification results. In the training process, we use 100 and 50 multi-result classification methods on the ICDAR2013 data set and CVL data set, respectively.

Due to the lack of training data, the results obtained by straight CNN training will not fit well. For this reason, the method of transfer learning improves the performance of the system. Transfer learning is a system that recognizes and applies the knowledge and skills learned in previous tasks to new tasks. The principle is that the data features are similar, and the basic features can be pretrained on the basic data set. Then fine-tune the target data to extract advanced features. In this paper, we have used the pretrained parameters of the ResNet50 general architecture on the ImageNet data set, and then feed the parameters generated in the preprocessing step to the ResNet50, and continue to use the backpropagation algorithm for fine-tuning.

When the training converges, we obtain the ResNet50 parameters for handwriting recognition. The difference is that in the final feature acquisition phase, we use the parameters optimized by the cost function to calculate the output of the fully connected layer, which is the local feature of the input handwriting patch.

3.4 Encoding

Encoding refers to the process of constructing a single global feature descriptor from multiple local descriptors. A widely used coding method is called a bag of (visual) words (BoW). VLAD coding is a standard encoding method, similar to constructing a BoW histogram, and is used widely in writer identification and other information retrieval tasks [22]. In this paper, we calculate the vocabulary using the k-means algorithm with k centroids first. Subsequently, all local features of each handwritten image are assigned to the nearest cluster centroid. After that, all residuals between the cluster center and the specified local features are accumulated to each cluster [23]. See Eq. (1).

$$v_k = \sum_{f_S : NN(f_S) = c_k} (f_S - c_k) \tag{1}$$

Where $NN(f_s)$ refers to the nearest neighbor of f_s in dictionary D. All vk are concatenated as a global feature vector of one handwritten page v.

$$v = (v_1^T, v_2^T, \ldots, v_K^T)^T \tag{2}$$

3.5 Writer Identification

The CNN architecture used in the writer identification process is slightly different from its training process. In the training process, the last layer is the Softmax. We add global pooling before the penultimate fully connected layer set drops out, and the parameter is 0.5. Throughout training, the initial learning rate is 0.001, the momentum parameter is 0.9. The input is 224 × 224, and the number of classifications varies according to the data set. It is 50 for CVL and 100 for ICDAR2013.

In the writer identification process, we remove the last layer of ResNet50, utilize the penultimate fully connected layer to extract the local features of the preprocessed patch, and then apply VLAD to aggregate them to achieve the global feature. Subsequently, the system compares the L2 distances between the query global feature and the vocabulary to determine its writer.

4 Experiments and Results

We perform experiments on ICDAR2013 and CVL data set according to the above pipeline. In the following chapters, we describe the evaluation indicators and evaluation results based on our proposed method. Besides, we compare and analyze the mean with others.

4.1 Evaluation Metrics

TOP-N index is used in image information retrieval tasks, evaluating the generalization and recognition of the model. First, we obtain a vector by comparing the query sample and the vocabulary. Subsequently, we arrange the vector according to the distance. The smaller the distance, the closer it is to the classification. At this time, there are two criteria to evaluate the system's performance. For soft standards, as long as one of the N samples and the test sample come from the same writer, the identification is correct. For the hard standard, the identification is correct only when the prior N samples and test samples are from the same writer. This paper employs soft TOP1, TOP5, and TOP10 to test the system, while due to the number of pages provided by each writer in the data set is different, we use hard TOP2 and TOP3 standards.

With the standard evaluation protocol, we also employ mean average precision (mAP) to evaluate the approach. As mentioned above, we get a ranked list reflecting the distance between the query and the vocabulary. Assume that in the query there are N samples, we calculate the average precision AP (i) of the ith ($1 \leq i \leq N$) query document. See Eq. (3).

$$AP(i) = \frac{\sum_{k=1}^{n} P(k)r(k)}{R} \tag{3}$$

Where k is the rank in the list, n is the number of documents in the vocabulary, P(k) is the precision at rank k in the ranked list, R is the number of relevant documents, r(k) is an indicator function equaling the value 1 if the item at rank k is a relevant document, zero otherwise. The mAP is the mean value of the average precision of all query documents. See Eq. (4).

$$mAP = \frac{\sum_{i=1}^{N} AP(i)}{N} \tag{4}$$

4.2 Results and Analysis

The test results of the criterion and the comparison with other methods are listed in Table 2, which shows that the model proposed by Tang et al. has better performance. And the model we proposed is only 0.7%, 0.5%, and 0.4% worse on the soft TOP1, TOP5, and TOP10 standards. On mAP indicators, our method is 0.6% better than Christlein's. There are three reasons for this result. First, in the preprocessing, randomly segmenting of the patch causes loss of features. Increasing the number of iterations or improving the patch segmentation method can solve the problem, while it may cause overfitting. Secondly, we could reform ResNet50 by adding depth or using other architectures. Finally, the aggregation local feature could be further explored.

Table 2. Comparison of the performance with the other methods on the CVL data set (in %)

Models	S-TOP1	S-TOP5	S-TOP10	H-TOP2	H-TOP3	mAP
CS-UMD [20]	97.9	99.1	99.4	90.9	71.2	N/A
TEBESSA-C [20]	97.6	98.3	98.5	94.3	88.2	N/A
TSINGHUA [20]	97.7	99.0	99.1	95.3	94.5	N/A
Tang [24]	99.7	99.8	100	99.0	97.9	N/A
Christlein [12]	98.8	99.2	N/A	97.8	95.3	96.4
Proposed method	99.0	99.3	99.6	98.2	96.1	97.0

The ICDAR2013 data set is a mixture of English and Greek handwriting, while it poses a challenge to the generalization of the model. Table 3 shows the test results. In the results, the soft criterion is better, and the hard one is unsatisfactory. Compared with other models, the proposed model is relatively stable, and the gap with the optimal model is not much. The optimal solution differences of the soft TOP1, soft TOP5, and soft TOP10 indicators are 2.1%, 0.7%, and 0.2%, respectively. The reason is that appropriate image enhancement methods enable better training of CNN parameters and better system fitting effect. Simultaneously, there is still a little gap between state-of-the-art and the proposed method on the mAP criterion. We find that Christlein [12] adopted Exemplar SVM to classify the global vector while we accept L2 distance in this paper.

Table 3. Comparison of the performance with the other methods on the ICDAR 2013 data set (in %)

Models	S-TOP1	S-TOP5	S-TOP10	H-TOP2	H-TOP3	mAP
CS-UMD-a [21]	95.1	98.6	99.1	19.6	7.1	N/A
CS-UMD-b [21]	95.0	98.6	**99.2**	20.2	8.4	N/A
HIT-ICG [21]	94.8	98.0	98.3	**63.2**	36.5	N/A
Fie [25]	88.5	96.0	98.3	40.5	5.8	N/A
Christlein [12]	**97.1**	**98.8**	99.1	42.8	23.8	**67.7**
Proposed method	95.0	98.1	99.0	45.2	**36.9**	65.0

5 Conclusion

In this paper, we proposed a new pipeline for writer identification on two benchmark data sets. For better data preprocessing and proper data enhancement, we employed ResNet50 that has been pretrained and optimized in ImageNet. Subsequently, the VLAD algorithm aggregated local features into global features, and writer identification was performed. Evaluation showed that the model had good stability and robustness on the ICDAR2013 and CVL standard data sets.

In future work, efficient extraction of local features will be the focus, including the segmentation of handwritten data, which will improve the accuracy of writer recognition. Simultaneously, the current recognition accuracy also requires the scale of data sets, which relies on better data enhancement technology to provide more training data. Besides, local features are encoded more efficiently to obtain global features, thereby improving the recognition standard.

Funding Statement. This work was supported in part by the Postgraduate Research & Practice Innovation Program of Jiangsu Province under Grant KYCX 20_0758, in part by the Scientific Research Innovation Team of Jiangsu Police Institute under Grant 2018SJYTD15, in part by the Science and Technology Research Project of Jiangsu Public Security Department under Grant 2020KX005 and in part by the 13th Five-Year Plan for Jiangsu Education Science under Grant D/2020/01/22.

Conflicts of Interest. The authors declare that they have no conflicts of interest to report regarding the present study.

References

1. Uchôa, V., Aires, K., Veras, R., Paiva, A., Britto, L.: Data augmentation for face recognition with CNN transfer learning. In: 2020 International Conference on Systems, Signals and Image Processing (IWSSIP), Niterói, Brazil, pp. 143–148 (2020)
2. Huang, Z., Ng, T., Liu, L., Mason, H., Zhuang, X., Liu, D.: SNDCNN: self-normalizing deep cnns with scaled exponential linear units for speech recognition. In: ICASSP 2020 - 2020 IEEE International Conference on Acoustics, Speech and Signal Processing (ICASSP), Barcelona, Spain, pp. 6854–6858 (2020)
3. Brink, A., Smit, J., Bulacu, M., Schomaker, L.: Writer identification using directional ink-trace width measurements. Pattern Recogn. **45**(1), 162–171 (2012)
4. Bulacu, M., Schomaker, L.: Automatic handwriting identification on medieval documents. In: 14th International Conference on Image Analysis and Processing (ICIAP 2007), Modena, Italy, pp. 279–284 (2007)
5. Bulacu, M., Schomaker, L.: Text-independent writer identification and verification using textural and allographic features. IEEE Trans. Pattern Anal. Mach. Intell. **29**(4), 701–717 (2007)
6. Siddiqi, I., Vincent, N.: Text independent writer recognition using redundant writing patterns with contour-based orientation and curvature features. Pattern Recogn. **43**(11), 3853–3865 (2010)
7. Fiel, S., Sablatnig, R.: Writer identification and writer retrieval using the fisher vector on visual vocabularies. In: 12th International Conference on Document Analysis and Recognition (ICDAR), Washington DC, NY, pp. 545–549 (2013)

8. Jain, R., Doermann, D.: Writer identifification using an alphabet of contour gradient descriptors. In: 12th International Conference on Document Analysis and Recognition (ICDAR), Washington DC, NY, pp. 550–554 (2013)
9. Schomaker, L., Bulacu, M.: Automatic writer identification using connected-component contours and edge-based features of uppercase western script. IEEE Trans. Pattern Anal. Mach. Intell. **26**(6), 787–798 (2004)
10. Helli, B., Moghaddam, M.E.: A text-independent Persian writer identification based on feature relation graph (FRG). Pattern Recogn. **43**(6), 2199–2209 (2010)
11. Nicolaou, A., Bagdanov, A.D., Liwicki, M., Karatzas, D.: Sparse radial sampling LBP for writer identification. In: Proceedings of International Conference on Document Analysis and Recognition, pp. 716–720 (2015)
12. Christlein, V., Bernecker, D., Hönig, F., Maier, A., Angelopoulou, E.: Writer identification using GMM supervectors and exemplar-SVMs. Pattern Recogn. **63**, 258–267 (2017)
13. Christlein, V., Bernecker, D., Maier, A., Angelopoulou, E.: Offline writer identification using convolutional neural network activation features. In: Gall, J., Gehler, P., Leibe, B. (eds.) GCPR 2015. LNCS, vol. 9358, pp. 540–552. Springer, Cham (2015). https://doi.org/10.1007/978-3-319-24947-6_45
14. Rehman, A., Naz, S., Razzak, M.I., Hameed, I.A.: Automatic visual features for writer identification: a deep learning approach. IEEE Access **7**, 17149–17157 (2019)
15. Christlein, V., Gropp, M., Fiel, S., Maier, A.: Unsupervised feature learning for writer identification and writer retrieval. In: 14th IAPR International Conference on Document Analysis and Recognition (ICDAR), Kyoto, Japan, pp. 991–997 (2017)
16. Dawei, L., Wu, M.: A multi-patch deep learning system for text-independent writer identification. In: Wang, G., Chen, B., Li, W., Di Pietro, R., Yan, X., Han, H. (eds.) Security, Privacy and Anonymity in Computation, Communication and Storage. LNCS, vol. 12383, pp. 409–419. Springer, Cham (2020). https://doi.org/10.1007/978-3-030-68884-4_34
17. He, S., Schomaker, L.: Delta-n hinge: rotation-invariant features for writer identifification. In: 22nd International Conference Pattern Recognition (ICPR), Stockholm, Sweden, pp. 2023–2028 (2014)
18. Xing, L., Qiao, Y.: DeepWriter: a multi-stream deep CNN for text independent writer identification. In: 15th International Conference on Frontiers in Handwriting Recognition (ICFHR), Shenzhen, China, pp. 584–589 (2016)
19. Cilia, N.D., De Stefano, C., Fontanella, F., Marrocco, C., Molinara, M., Scotto di Freca, A.: A page-based reject option for writer identification in medieval books. In: Cristani, M., Prati, A., Lanz, O., Messelodi, S., Sebe, N. (eds.) ICIAP 2019. LNCS, vol. 11808, pp. 187–197. Springer, Cham (2019). https://doi.org/10.1007/978-3-030-30754-7_19
20. Kleber, F., et al.: CVL-database: an off-line database for writer retrieval, writer identification and word spotting. In: 12th International Conference on Document Analysis and Recognition (ICDAR), Washington DC, NY, pp. 560–564 (2013)
21. Louloudis, G., et al.: ICDAR 2013 competition on writer identification. In: 12th International Conference on Document Analysis and Recognition (ICDAR), Washington DC, NY, pp. 1397–1401 (2013)
22. Paulin, M., Mairal, J., Douze, M., Harchaoui, Z., Perronnin, F., Schmid, C.: Convolutional patch representations for image retrieval: an unsupervised approach. Int. J. Comput. Vis. **121**(1), 1–20 (2016)
23. Chen, S., Wang, Y., Lin, C., Ding, W., Cao, Z.: Semi-supervised feature learning for improving writer identification. Inf. Sci **482**, 156–170 (2019)

24. Tang, Y., Wu, X.: Text-independent writer identifification via CNN features and joint Bayesian. In: 15th International Conference on Frontiers in Handwriting Recognition(ICFHR), Shenzhen, China, pp. 566–571 (2016)
25. Fiel, S., Sablatnig, R.: Writer identification and retrieval using a convolutional neural network. In: Azzopardi, G., Petkov, N. (eds.) CAIP 2015. LNCS, vol. 9257, pp. 26–37. Springer, Cham (2015). https://doi.org/10.1007/978-3-319-23117-4_3

A Light-Weight Prediction Model for Aero-Engine Surge Based on Seq2Seq

Yu Peng[1], Xiaoyu Li[1](✉), Chao Lu[2], Xiaolan Tang[3], and Bin Lin[4]

[1] School of Information and Software Engineering, University of Electronic Science and Technology of China, Chengdu 610054, China
xiaoyuuestc@uestc.edu.cn

[2] Science and Technology on Altitude Simulation Laboratory, Sichuan Gas Turbine Establishment Aero Engine Corporation of China, Mianyang 621000, China

[3] School of Computer Science, Southwest Petroleum University, Chengdu 610500, China

[4] School of Engineering, Sichuan Normal University, Chengdu 610066, China

Abstract. Surge is an abnormal fault caused by compressor in the process of aero-engine flight, which will reduce the performance of aero-engines. When the surge gets serious, it will even cause engine damage, endanger flight safety, and cause a huge loss of personnel and property. Therefore, it is of great significance to predict the aero-engine surge timely and accurately. At present, little research have been done on the prediction task of aero-engine surge, and there are problems of low prediction accuracy and long calculation time. In order to solve these problems, a light-weight prediction model for aero-engine surge based on Seq2Seq (sequence to sequence) is proposed, which is called Ligh4S. Ligh4S uses the one-dimensional convolution neural network instead of the LSTM (long short-term memory network) structure in tradition-al Seq2Seq, which allows the model to compute in parallel, thus greatly improving computational efficiency and reducing prediction time. Experiments on the experimental data of an aero-engine show that the model achieves the performances of 94.3%, 92.1%, 93.2% respectively on precision rate, recall rate and F1 score under the condition of significantly reducing the size of model and the amount of calculation. What's more, the model takes only 2ms to make a single prediction, which increases the prediction speed by about 98% compared with the LSTM-based Seq2Seq model.

Keywords: Aero-engine surge · Fault prediction · Light-weight · seq2seq

1 Introduction

As the main power device of aircraft, aero-engine works in the environment of high temperature, high pressure, high speed, strong vibration and so on for a long time, which increases the risk of mechanical failure and even system collapse. Aero engine surge is one of the main faults that affect the performance and safety of aircraft. It not only affects the working state of the engine, but also causes serious safety accidents. Therefore, in the early stage of engine surge or about to surge, timely and accurate

X. Sun et al. (Eds.): ICAIS 2021, LNCS 12736, pp. 265–277, 2021.
https://doi.org/10.1007/978-3-030-78609-0_23

identification of surge fault and appropriate measures to eliminate surge can avoid the occurrence of serious accidents caused by surge fault.

Surge prediction is actually one kind of fault prediction. The existing fault prediction technologies can be roughly divided into three categories [1], which are model-based method [2–5], knowledge-based method [6–8] and data-based method [9, 10]. The model-based method is difficult to model complex systems, and is easily affected by the uncertainty of model; while the knowledge-based method has the shortage of knowledge acquisition bottleneck and poor universality; the diagnosis effect of data-based method depends on the quantity, quality and processing method of raw data [11].

The data-based fault prediction method does not need to define an accurate mathematical model. It uses the data mining technology and machine learning method to analyze and process the hidden information in the raw data, and finally diagnose the fault. With the rapid development of artificial intelligence technology, deep learning has made outstanding achievements in many fields, such as machine reading comprehension [12], image recognition [13], recommendation system [14], intrusion detection [15]. And more and more researchers have begun to apply deep learning to fault diagnosis tasks. For example, Liu et al. [16] proposed an aeroengine fault fusion diagnosis model based on the combination of deep confidence network and decision fusion algorithm. The accuracy rate of fault diagnosis on HP JT9D engine can reach 99%. Yuan et al. [17] used LSTM for fault diagnosis and residual life prediction of aero-engine. Li et al. [18] used one-dimensional convolution network for fault prediction of industrial processes, which solved the problem of low recognition rate when BP network was used for fault detection. Chen et al. [19] proposed a hybrid depth calculation model (HDC) based on CNN, DNN and LSTM. The accuracy rate of this model in Aeroengine gas path fault diagnosis can reach 83%.

These researches only diagnose the faults of aeroengine, but not predict them. Different from the simple diagnosis task, prediction requires timely diagnosis before the fault occurs, so it is necessary to predict the future time, and the time each prediction consumes should not be too long. In this paper, we proposed a light-weight prediction model based on Seq2Seq for the prediction task of aero-engine surge fault (Ligh4S). The one-dimensional convolutional neural network is used to replace the LSTM in the traditional Seq2Seq structure, which enables Ligh4S to obtain the ability of parallel computing in training and prediction. The new structure significantly reduces the size of model and the amount of calculation, and makes the model achieve substantial performance in various metrics. Meanwhile, the time single prediction consumes is only 2 ms, which is about 98% faster than the LSTM-based Seq2Seq model. Ligh4s is composed of convolution network [20] and optimized Seq2Seq [21]. The optimized Seq2Seq uses one-dimensional convolutional neural network instead of LSTM as its new encoder and decoder, which improves the parallel computing ability of the model and realizes the prediction of future data. Finally, the CNN structure will classify and diagnose the surge fault of the output sequence from the Seq2Seq structure. In conclusion, Ligh4S completed the prediction task of aero-engine surge by predicting time-series data first and then classifying it.

2 Preliminary

2.1 CNN

A traditional convolutional neural network (CNN) consists of several convolutional layers (Conv), pooling layers (Polling), and fully connected layers (FC), which can be used to build different CNNs. CNN can perform convolution operation and extract features from local input blocks, so it performs well on computer vision problems. CNN is especially good at spatial problems because of its characteristics. But time problems can actually be regarded as a special type of spatial problems, just like the height and width of two-dimensional image, which does not contain RGB channels, and is called one-dimensional convolutional neural network. A one-dimensional convolutional network can recognize local patterns in a sequence and extract local subsequences from the sequence (shown in Fig. 1), but it is not sensitive to the overall time steps (the overall time steps refers to the steps far longer than the subsequence time steps).

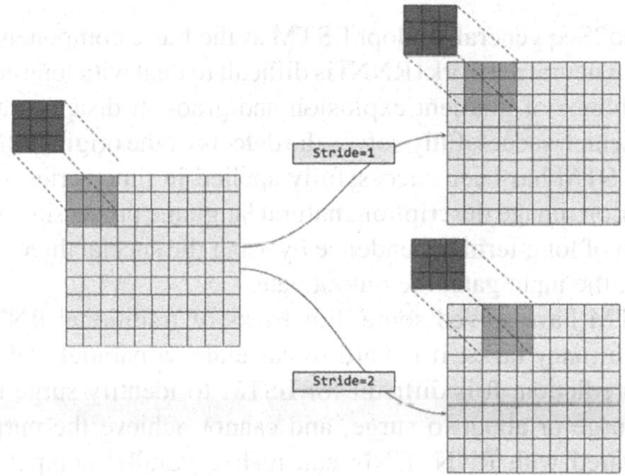

Fig. 1. A convolutional network uses convolution operations to process sequences

For simple tasks such as text classification and time series prediction, CNN can achieve the similar performance RNN in effect, and the computational cost is much lower. Compared with RNN, the parallel computing ability of CNN greatly improves the computational efficiency of Ligh4S. Therefore, using one-dimensional CNN can not only reduce the complexity of the model, but also improve the computational speed.

2.2 Seq2Seq

Seq2Seq is a model which is generally used in machine translation, man-machine dialogue, chat robot and other tasks in natural language processing. Seq2Seq is a kind of Encoder-Decoder structure. Encoder is used to compress the input sequence into a context vector of a fixed length, which can be the semantic presentation of the input sequence. In Fig. 2, symbol C is the context vector, and vector C comes from the last hidden state of the Encoder directly. Decoder is used to generate the corresponding output sequence according to the context vector. The way in Fig. 2 is to input the context vector directly into Decoder as the initial state to predict the output sequence, and the context vector can also be regarded as the input of each step.

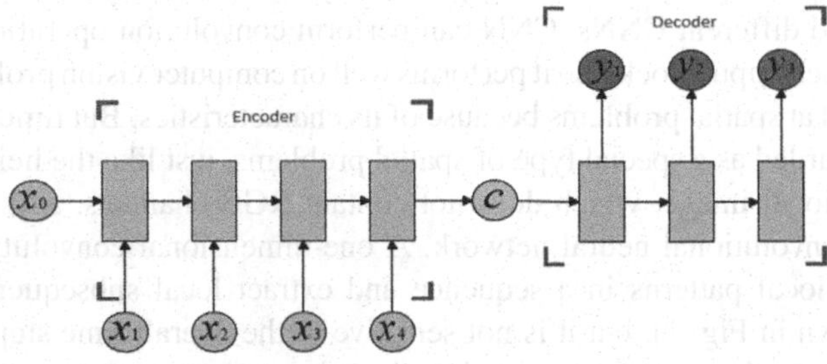

Fig. 2. The structure of Seq2Seq.

Traditional Seq2Seq generally adopt LSTM as the basic component of Encoder and Decoder. Recurrent neural network (RNN) is difficult to deal with long-term dependence, and there are problems of gradient explosion and gradient disappearance. LSTM is a variant of RNNs, which successfully solves the defects of the original RNN and becomes a popular RNN. LSTM has been successfully applied in time-series related tasks such as speech recognition, image description, natural language processing and so on. LSTM solves the problem of long-term dependence by using the special three "gate" structures: the forgotten gate; the input gate; the output gate.

Although LSTM have solved some drawbacks of traditional RNNs and achieved excellent results in many tasks, it is hard to calculate in parallel and time-consuming for training and prediction. It is difficult for LSTM to identify surge fault in the early stage of engine surge or about to surge, and cannot achieve the purpose of advance prediction. Compared with RNN, CNN can realize parallel computation with much lower computational cost, and one-dimensional convolution can also be used to solve time-series problems. Therefore, one-dimensional convolution network is used to replace the LSTM structure in the traditional Seq2Seq. Thus, the size of the prediction model is reduced and the calculation speed is improved, so as to predict the surge fault in advance.

3 Main Work

3.1 Conv1D

In order to simplify structure and optimize calculation speed of the model, we adopt the convolutional network structure, which as shown in the Fig. 3.·And we use Conv1D to represent such convolutional network structure in this paper.

Compared with the traditional CNN, Conv1D of this paper only adopts the convolution operation with stride s. After many experiments, the results showed that Conv1D performs better in surge prediction task compared with the traditional structure. The reason is that the information about original data can be retained without pooling operation.

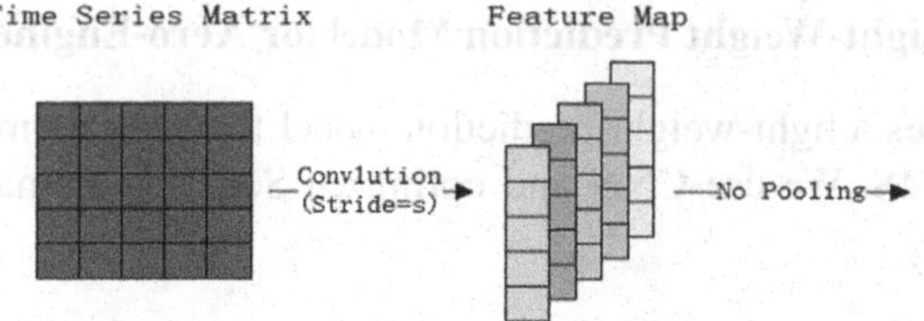

Fig. 3. The structure of Conv1D.

Meanwhile, Conv1D reduces the complexity of the model and the amount of calculation, thus improving the calculation speed.

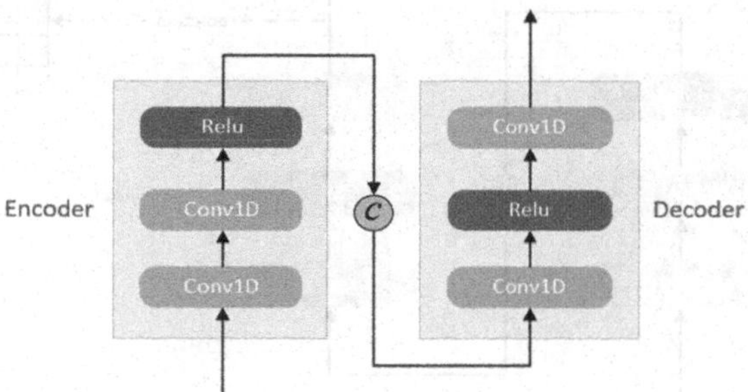

Fig. 4. Optimized Seq2Seq base on Conv1D.

3.2 Conv1D-Based Seq2Seq

This paper uses Conv1D structure to improve the traditional LSTM-based Seq2Seq model. The optimized Seq2Seq model is shown in the Fig. 4. In optimized Seq2Seq, Encoder and Decoder give up LSTM and choose Conv1D, and symbol *C* represents the context vector processed by Encoder. Conv1D is much less computational than LSTM, and because of the parallel computing of convolutional network, the computing speed of Conv1D is much faster. So that, Ligh4S can predict aero-engine surge fault in a shorter time.

Function *Relu* is used to process the output of the previous layer in appropriate positions of optimized Seq2Seq. The function is defined as Eq. (1).

$$Relu(x) = Max(0, x) \tag{1}$$

Function *Relu* can do gradient descent and backpropagation operations more efficiently. To some extent, it avoids gradient explosion and gradient disappearance problems. In addition, *Relu* simplifies the calculation process without the influence of complex operations such as exponential operation, which is common in other activation functions.

3.3 Ligh4S: A Light-Weight Prediction Model for Aero-Engine Surge

This paper proposes a light-weight prediction model for aero-engine surge fault based on Seq2Seq: Ligh4S. We use CNN and optimized Seq2Seq as main substructures to build Ligh4S.

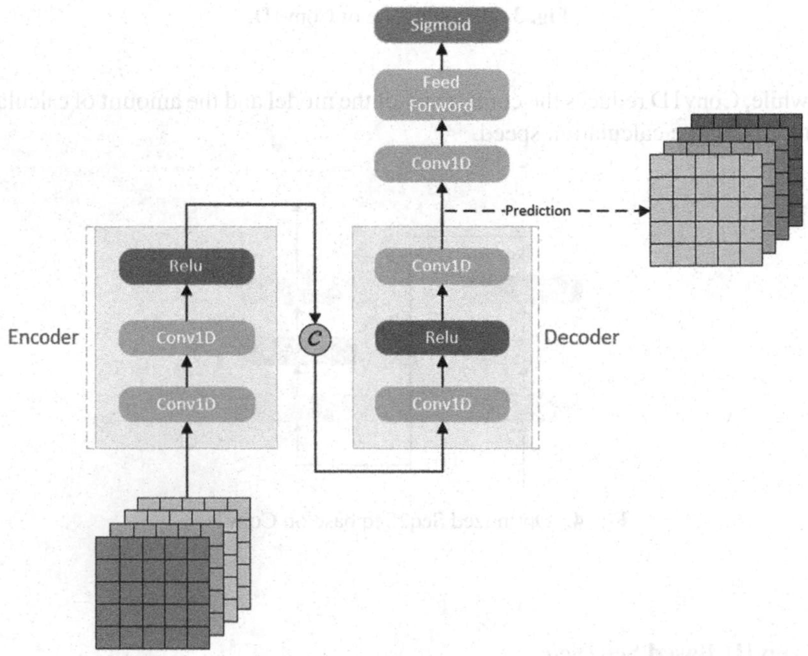

Fig. 5. The architecture of Ligh4S.

The CNN structure in this model is Conv1D, which is a one-dimensional convolutional network without pooling layer. Convolutional neural network can not only deal with spatial problems, but also be applied to some time-series problems. Conv1D can recognize local patterns in time series and extract local subsequences from sequences. Compared with RNN, Conv1D can realize parallel computing and spend much lower computational cost. Optimized Seq2Seq structure is also mainly based on Conv1D to improve its speed of calculation.

The overall architecture of Ligh4S is shown in Fig. 5. Since the traditional Seq2Seq is mainly used for natural language processing, it is necessary to do word embedding operation. In this paper, the input data of the model is the time-series data of sensors after pre-processing. Without passing through an embedding layer, the model will directly calculate the pre-processed data. Traditional Seq2seq is proposed to solve the problem of generating indefinite length sequences, and the role of optimized Seq2Seq in this paper is to predict the future data of sensors, and to provide the ability to compute in parallel by utilizing Conv1D. Ligh4S speeds up training and prediction. The final output of the optimized Seq2Seq is sequence data, and Conv1D will analyze the predicted time-series data, mine the potential information, and diagnosis whether the surge fault happens. Finally, the data goes through a full connection layer with activation function *Sigmoid*, and then Ligh4S converts the diagnosis result to a decimal between 0 and 1. Equation (2) is the definition of the activation function *Sigmoid*.

$$Sigmoid(x) = \frac{1}{1 + e^{-x}} \tag{2}$$

If the value processed by function *Sigmoid* is greater than or equal to 0.5, it will be judged as a surge fault.

In conclusion, Ligh4S simplifies its structure by introducing Conv1D and *Relu* function, thus reducing the amount of calculation. Conv1d can be used for parallel computing, which can greatly improve the computational efficiency compared with the sequential computation of RNN. In addition, the output of optimized Seq2Seq structure in Ligh4S can be used as an additional product, which represents a prediction result of the optimized seq2seq structure for the future time steps.

4 Experiment

4.1 Dataset

In this paper, we select some historical experimental data from one aero-engine as the dataset to train and evaluate our model. The experimental data are composed of numerical data collected from multiple sensors in different situations, including core engine stall, thrust increase, inertial starting oil cutting, starting stall, deflagration at high or low temperature, compressor distortion and so on. And we select the sensors closely related to aero-engine surge fault from all the sensors, such as engine compressor (high pressure rotor) outlet total pressure (Pt3), engine compressor high pressure rotor speed (N2), engine throttle rod (PLA). The moments of surge fault are marked manually by experts according to the corresponding rules and experiences. For example, if the numerical curve of the sensor PLA tends to be stable, once the sensor Pt3 appears to rise, drop or shake violently until return to stability, surge occurs at every moment in this interval. After manual labeled, the ratio of normal moments to surge moments in dataset is about 95:15.

The dataset is then shuffled and split into three subsets: training dataset, validation dataset, test dataset. We train the model on the training dataset, evaluate the model during training on the validation dataset, and do the final evaluation on the test dataset once the best parameters are learned.

Defining $X = \{x_1, x_2, \ldots, x_n\}$ to represent the training dataset with n moments in total. Defining $x_i = \{s_i^1, s_i^2, \ldots, s_i^m\}$, where x_i is the experimental data at moment i. Defining s_i^j to present the value of the jth sensor at moment i, and there are m sensors in total. Defining $L = \{0, 1\}$ to represent the 2 labels, where 0 means normal (negative sample) and 1 means surge (positive sample).

4.2 Missing Data Disposal

Sometimes there are missing values in the experimental data, and we should fill the missing data by some ways. The filling method in this paper is to use the average value of several moments before and after the missing data. This method is used to fill the missing data in all the three datasets.

4.3 Data Standardization

Different sensors have different range of their values. In order to eliminate the interference brought by dimension, each sensor needs to be standardized separately. So that its mean value could be 0 and its standard deviation could be 1.

Defining $X_{mean} = \{x^1_{mean}, x^2_{mean}, \ldots, x^m_{mean}\}$, and the symbol x^i_{mean} in Eq. (3) represents the average value of the *ith* sensor in time dimension.

$$x^i_{mean} = \frac{1}{n}\sum_{k=1}^{n} s^i_k \quad (3)$$

Defining $X_{std} = \{x^1_{std}, x^2_{std}, \ldots, x^m_{std}\}$, and the symbol x^i_{std} in Eq. (4) represents the standard deviation of the *ith* sensor in time dimension.

$$x^i_{std} = \frac{1}{n-1}\sum_{k=1}^{n} (s^i_k - x^i_{mean})^2 \quad (4)$$

Finally, the following 2 formulas are adopted to standardize the data on the time dimension. In Eq. (5) and Eq. (6), subtraction and division are all carried out on the time dimension.

$$X - = X_{mean} \quad (5)$$

$$X \div = X_{std} \quad (6)$$

The average value and standard deviation for standardization on validation dataset and test dataset are all calculated from training dataset, which are X_{mean} and X_{std} respectively.

4.4 Intercept Data with Sliding Window

As shown in Fig. 6 below, the time-series data is intercepted by the sliding window to generate the input data of Ligh4S. The specific method is to process the data collected by each sensor with a sliding window, which slides according to a fixed stride. The size of the sliding window is also fixed. Using *window_size* to represent the size of the sliding window and *window stride* to represent the sliding stride, both are the hyperparameters of Ligh4S.

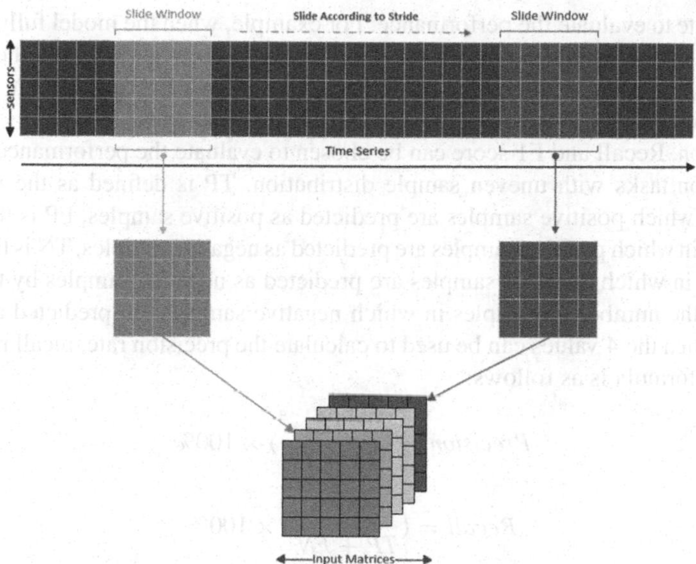

Fig. 6. Ligh4S uses a sliding window to intercept data.

Data extraction in the form of sliding window can increase the number of samples in raw dataset and provide more data for the training of Ligh4S. While the experimental data is too little, more samples can be obtained by a small sliding stride. What's more, the sliding window will have overlapping parts while sampling, which will make it easier for the model to learn the characteristics of aero-engine surge. Thus, the size of the sliding window is the time step of a single training sample.

4.5 Loss Function

The task involved in this paper is a binary classification problem, so the binary cross entropy function can be used as the loss function of Ligh4S. The loss function is defined in Eq. (6).

$$L(\theta) = \frac{1}{n}\sum_{i=1}^{n} -[y_i log(p_i) + (1 - y_i) log(1 - p_i)] \quad (7)$$

In Eq. (6), p_i represents the probability that the model predicts a sample as a positive sample (in this paper, the positive sample refers to the surge sample). y_i represents the real label of this sample, and if the sample is a positive example, the value is 1, otherwise the value is 0.

4.6 Evaluation Metrics

The ratio of normal moments to surge moments in dataset is about 95:15, therefore prediction for surge is an unbalanced classification problem. It is unreasonable to use accuracy rate to evaluate the performance. For example, when the model fully identifies the normal moments but judges all surge moments as normal moments, the accuracy rate can also achieve 95%. But the mode has no ability to identify the surge fault now. So it is necessary to choose other metrics to evaluate the model.

Precision, Recall and F1 score can be chosen to evaluate the performance of binary classification tasks with uneven sample distribution. TP is defined as the number of samples in which positive samples are predicted as positive samples, FP is the number of samples in which positive samples are predicted as negative samples, TN is the number of samples in which negative samples are predicted as negative samples by the model, and FN is the number of samples in which negative samples are predicted as positive samples. Then the 4 values can be used to calculate the precision rate, recall rate and F1 score. The formula is as follows:

$$Precision = (\frac{TP}{TP + FP}) \times 100\% \tag{8}$$

$$Recall = (\frac{TP}{TP + FN}) \times 100\% \tag{9}$$

$$F_1 = (\frac{2 \times Precision \times Recall}{Precision + Recall}) \times 100\% \tag{10}$$

Precision rate and recall rate are a pair of contradictory measures. F1 score is a balance between precision rate and recall rate, so it can evaluate the performance of the model as a whole.

5 Result and Discussion

5.1 Experiment Result and Analysis

The trend of precision rate, recall rate and F1 score with the training process is shown in Fig. 7. After the end of the 12th training, the variation of each metric on the training dataset is no longer obvious, while the precision rate, recall rate and F1 score on the test dataset began to decline. It means that the model starts to overfit. The best precision rate, recall rate and F1 score on the test dataset which Ligh4S achieved were respectively 94.3%,92.1%, and 93.2%.

To compare the performance of Ligh4S with other models, this paper also uses RNN, CNN, LSTM and the Seq2Seq base on LSTM to train on the same experimental data. The results are shown in Table 1. As can be seen from Table 1, Ligh4S outperformed the other three simple models in every metric, especially when it came to recall rate. However, with significantly reducing computation, the metrics of Ligh4S were only slightly lower than those of Seq2Seq (LSTM). The comparative results indicate that it is correct to fuse Seq2Seq with Conv1D.

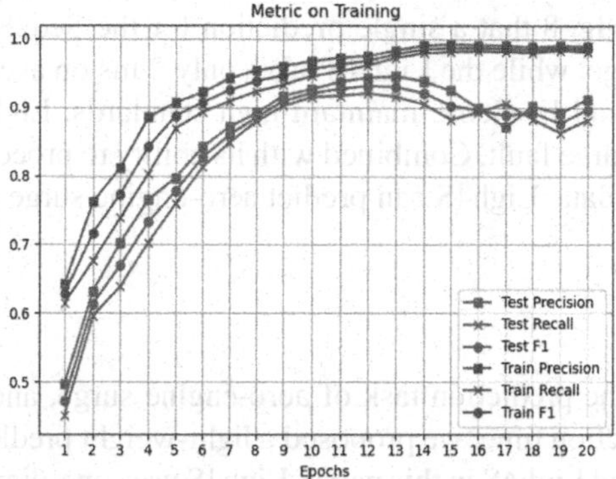

Fig. 7. The trend of evaluation metrics.

Table 1. Comparative results of models.

Model	Precision	Recall	F1 Score
Ligh4S	**94.3%**	**92.1%**	**93.2%**
Seq2Seq(LSTM)	95.7%	93.6%	94.7%
LSTM	92.5%	86.2%	89.2%
CNN	94.1%	84.2%	88.1%
RNN	86.3%	79.4%	82.7%

5.2 The Time Ligh4S and Seq2Seq (LSTM) Consume

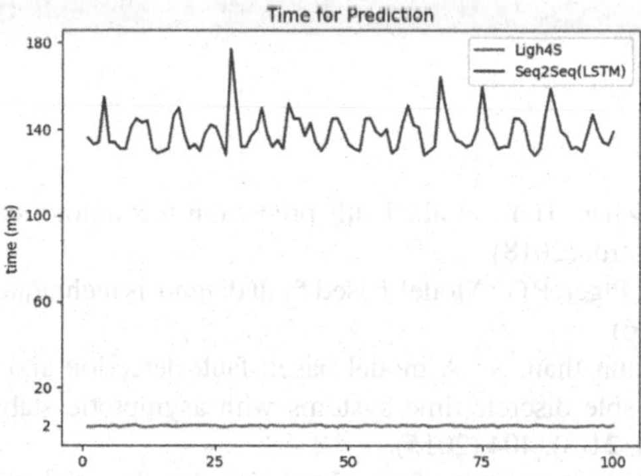

Fig. 8. The time Ligh4S and Seq2Seq (LSTM) consume.

Ligh4S was originally designed to predict aero-engine surge, so the model should not spend too much time to make a single prediction. We do prediction tasks for 100 times on Seq2Seq(LSTM) and Ligh4S respectively, and the time both model consume was shown in the Fig. 8.

We can see from Fig. 8 that a single prediction for the Seq2Seq (LSTM) can take up to 140 ms on average, while the Ligh4S takes only 2 ms on average. While ensuring that precision, recall and F1 Score maintain high standards, Ligh4S also takes much fewer time to predict surge fault. Combined with its ability to process long sequence and prediction time-series data, Ligh4S can predict aero-engine surge in advance.

6 Conclusion

In order to complete the prediction task of aero-engine surge, and ensure high performance and short prediction time, we proposed a light-weight prediction model based on Seq2Seq which is called Ligh4S in this paper. Ligh4S uses one-dimensional convolution network instead of LSTM in traditional seq2seq structure, which enables the model to obtain the ability of parallel computing in training and prediction. So that Ligh4S can predict time-series data in parallel, and significantly reducing the computation. What is more important is that Ligh4S can maintain good performance in each metric, and a single prediction takes only 2 ms. Ligh4S has improved the prediction speed of about 98% compared with Seq2Seq (LSTM). Due to light-weight and high performance of Ligh4S, it can be considered that deploy Ligh4S on edge devices to monitor and warn the aero-engine surge in real time. The method in this paper is mainly aimed at the prediction of aero-engine surge fault, but it also has the potential value on other similar time-series datasets of multi sensors. Especially when the number of sensors is large, the Seq2Seq structure in Ligh4S will performs better theoretically.

Acknowledgement. This work is supported by Sichuan Science and Technology Program, Grant No. 2019YFG0424. We would like to thank Sichuan Gas Turbine Establishment Aero Engine Corporation of China Mianyang for providing aero-engine surge dataset, and all the staff of this project for their effort.

References

1. Wu, L.J., Xia, R., Zhan, H.Y., et al.: Fault prediction technology based on deep learning. Comput. Meas. Control (2018)
2. Kuestenmacher, A., Plger, P.G.: Model-based fault diagnosis techniques. IFAC PapersOnLine **49**(15), 50–56 (2016)
3. Thumati, B.T., Jagannathan, S.: A model-based fault-detection and prediction scheme for nonlinear multivariable discrete-time systems with asymptotic stability guarantees. IEEE Trans. Neural Netw. **21**(3), 404 (2015)
4. Zhang, P., Huang, J.Q.: Aeroengine fault diagnosis using dual Kalman filtering technique. J. Aerosp. Power (2008)
5. Chao, Y., Kong, X.X., Wang, X.: Model-based fault diagnosis for performance degradations of turbofan gas path via optimal robust residuals. In: Asme Turbo Expo: Turbomachinery Technical Conference & Exposition (2016)
6. Dibowski, H., Holub, O., Rojícek, J.: Knowledge-based fault propagation in building automation systems. In: 16 International Conference on Systems Informatics, Modelling and Simulation (SIMS), pp. 124–132. IEEE (2016)

7. Steinegger, M., Melik-Merkumians, M., Zajc, J., et al.: A framework for automatic knowledge-based fault detection in industrial conveyor systems. In: 2017 22nd IEEE International Conference on Emerging Technologies and Factory Automation (ETFA). IEEE. (2018)
8. Liu, Y., Sun, R., Lu, Y., Zhang, S.: A knowledge-based online fault detection method of the assembly process considering the relative poses of components. Int. J. Precis. Eng. Manuf. **20**(10), 1705–1720 (2019). https://doi.org/10.1007/s12541-019-00218-6
9. Yin, K., Jiang, G., et al.: Fault analysis and diagnosis of aeroengine fuel metering device. DEStech Trans. Eng. Technol. Res. (2016)
10. Zhao, Z., Zhang, J., et al.: Sensor fault diagnosis of aero-engine based on divided flight status. Rev. Sci. Instrum. **88**(11), 115007 (2017)
11. Nor, N.M., Hassan, C.R.C., Hussain, M.A.: A review of data-driven fault detection and diagnosis methods: applications in chemical process systems. Rev. Chem. Eng. (2019)
12. Cui, Y., Che, W., et al.: Cross-lingual machine reading comprehension. arXiv preprint arXiv: 1909.00361 (2019)
13. Zheng, D., Ran, Z., Liu, Z., et al.: An efficient bar code image recognition algorithm for sorting system. CMC-Comput. Mater. Continua **64**(3), 1885–1895 (2020)
14. Zhou, G., Zhu, X., Song, C., et al.: Deep interest network for click-through rate prediction. In: Proceedings of the 24th ACM SIGKDD International Conference on Knowledge Discovery & Data Mining, pp. 1059–1068 (2018)
15. Ran, Z., Zheng, D., Lai, Y., Tian, L.: Applying stack bidirectional LSTM model to intrusion detection. CMC-Comput. Mater. Continua **65**(1), 309–320 (2020)
16. Che, C.C., Wang, H., et al.: Fault fusion diagnosis of aero-engine based on deep learning. J. Beijing Univ. Aeronaut. Astronaut. **4**(3), 621 (2020)
17. Yuan, M., Wu, Y., Lin, L.: Fault diagnosis and remaining useful life estimation of aero engine using LSTM neural network. In: 2016 IEEE International Conference on Aircraft Utility Systems (AUS), pp 135–140 (2016)
18. Li, Y., Feng, C.C.: Fault detection of industrial process based on deep learning of one-dimensional convolution neural network. Meas. Control Technol. (2019)
19. Chen, Z., Yuan, X., Sun, M.: A hybrid deep computation model for feature learning on aero-engine data-applications to fault detection. Appl. Math. Model. **83**, 487–496 (2020)
20. Krizhevsky, A., Sutskever, I., Hinton, G.E.: Imagenet classification with deep convolutional neural networks. In: Advances in Neural Information Processing Systems, pp. 1097–1105 (2012)
21. Sutskever, I., Vinyals, O., Le, Q.V.: Sequence to sequence learning with neural networks. In: Advances in Neural Information Processing Systems, pp. 3104–3112 (2014)

Simulation Analysis of PLC/WLC Hybrid Communication with Traffic Model

Zhixiong Chen[1](✉), Leixin Zhi[1], Peiru Chen[1], and Lei Zhang[2]

[1] School of Electronic and Communication Engineering, North China Electric Power University, Baoding 071003, China
chenzx1983@sohu.com

[2] Shandong Electric Power Research Institute, State Grid Corporation of China, Jinan 250002, China

Abstract. With the development of the Internet of Things and Smart Grids, a single communication model cannot satisfy with all Internet scenarios. Power line communication and wireless communication can complement each other, and the hybrid communication can save the construction costs and improve the robustness of the system. In this paper, we compared the differences between the IEEE 1901 and IEEE 802.11 protocols, and proposed two hybrid Medium Access Control layer protocol schemes. In this scheme, all stations have power line and wireless dual interfaces and can compete for the two channels. In order to make the scene more reasonable, the Poisson traffic model was introduced. Finally, the performance of throughput, collision probability, and time delay of different networking schemes was compared. The results show that the proposed hybrid communication can make full use of the resources of the two channels, improve the system throughput, and reduce the transmission delay. And it can be seen that this algorithm can improve the reliability and effectiveness of the network.

Keywords: Hybrid communication · MAC layer · Reuse-selected scheme · Traffic model

1 Introduction

With the development of the Internet of Things (IoT) technology, the application scenarios of IoT are becoming more and more abundant and the devices connected to the Internet will increase rapidly. In the future, the business traffic of the IoT will occupy a large proportion, and the growth of access terminals and traffic will put forward higher requirements and challenges for the existing network structure. However, wireless communication is easily blocked by obstructions, has fewer spectrum resources [1] and exists the problems that cannot be fully covered, which makes it impossible to meet the requirements of the IoT alone. The power line does not need to be re-wired, which is a useful supplement for wireless communication. Therefore, the PLC and WLC networking can complement each other, save construction costs and improve system performance.

X. Sun et al. (Eds.): ICAIS 2021, LNCS 12736, pp. 278–289, 2021.
https://doi.org/10.1007/978-3-030-78609-0_24

With the popularity of the ubiquitous power IoT, the networking of WLC and PLC also has become a research hot spot. The power system has realized important data connections in China, but there is still a large amount of user-side data and edge data that have not been collected and applied [2]. V. Fernandes studied the achievable data rate of the model of incomplete hybrid network of power line and wireless communication in single relay channel (HSRC) in [3]. In [4], the author proposed a relay scheme for wireless and power line hybrid communication networks and analyzed the network performance. Aiming to improve performance (date-rate and reliability) at the PHY layer, M. Sayed et al. [5] proposed a hybrid data communication system involving PLC and wireless channels. Through the above references, we found that the hybrid communications can improve the reliability and robustness of the system. However, the existing research mainly focuses on the physical layer and rarely involves the Medium Access Control layer (MAC). The research on MAC layer can realize resource sharing, reduce conflicts, hunger and other unfair phenomena, so the study of the MAC layer of hybrid communication has important significance. In IoT applications, the higher requirements on MAC layer in hybrid networking are put forward because of the increasing number of stations, especially the use of two different carrier sense multiple access (CSMA/CA) protocols with collision avoidance increases the difficulty of the theoretical research. In the MAC layer of the hybrid protocol, we discussed the selective CSMA/CA algorithm [6] of the power line and wireless in the first idle first use mode and established a system model of MAC layer using non-linear equations to calculate system performance. But the details of dual-channels coupling and fairness was not considered in this algorithm. Therefore, in this paper, a further algorithm of the hybrid communication MAC layer is proposed and this reuse-selected scheme can make full use of the resources of two channels to improve system performance.

In this paper, we proposed a reuse-selected scheme and compared with the PLC, WLC, and parallel schemes performance. In order to make the scene more reasonable, we introduce Poisson traffic model, because the arrival of the data packets obeys Poisson distribution. The different performance indicators can be obtained in different networking schemes. Therefore, the stations need to consider many factors when communicating.

The rest of this paper is as follows: Sect. 2 introduces the comparison between IEEE 1901 and IEEE 802.11 CSMA/CA protocols, and the explanation of MAC layer protocol in hybrid communication. Section 3 analyzes the system performance. Section 4 verifies the simulation. Finally, the work is summarized in Sect. 5

2 The Hybrid Communication Schemes

In this section, the differences between the IEEE 802.11, IEEE 1901 protocol, and the MAC protocol of hybrid communication are discussed. As shown in Fig. 1, a network topology with N nodes and a coordinator are considered. The stations have powerline-wireless dual interfaces, which can compete for PLC and WLC channels at the same time. The CSMA/CA protocol is used in both PLC and WLC channels. We assume that all stations are at the same priority and use the same parameter settings. And when a station competes for one channel, it will communication with the coordinator firstly.

In order to remove the influence of the physical layer, we regardless of packets loss or error by physical layer fading or noise, transmission failure is only related to collisions in the MAC layer. These assumptions suggest that the backoff process of a station is independent of the remaining $N - 1$ stations.

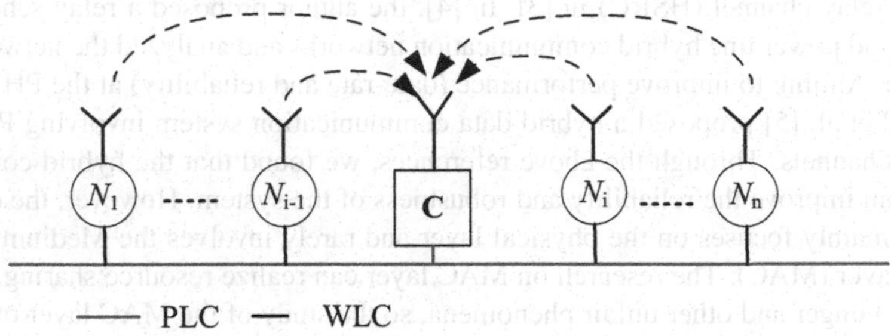

Fig. 1. The hybrid communication system model

2.1 The CSMA/CA Protocols of IEEE 1901 and 802.11

Although the IEEE 1901 and IEEE 802.11 protocols both use the CSMA/CA protocol in the MAC layer, but there are some differences between them. The CSMA/CA protocol in IEEE 802.11 has two counters: backoff procedure counter (BPC) and backoff counter (BC), where the value of BC is randomly selected in the contention window (CW), the CSMA/CA protocol in IEEE 1901 has three counters, BPC, BC, and deferral counter (DC). Because of the introduction of DC, the CSMA/CA protocol of the IEEE 1901 protocol becomes complicated. For the convenience of presentation, we use BPC1, BC1 and DC to represent the backoff procedure counter, the backoff counter and the deferral counter in IEEE 1901, and use BPC2 and BC2 to represent the backoff procedure counter and the backoff counter in IEEE 802.11 in this paper. Here are the differences between the two protocols.

Table 1. The value CW and DC in the different backoff stage in IEEE 1901.

	Priority CA0/CA1		*Priority CA2/CA3*	
Backoff stage i	**CW_{1i}**	**dc_i**	**CW_{1i}**	**dc_i**
0	**8**	**0**	**8**	**0**
1	**16**	**1**	**16**	**1**
2	**32**	**3**	**16**	**3**
3	**64**	**15**	**32**	**15**

In the CSMA/CA protocol of IEEE 1901, when a station has packets to send, the station will perform the backoff process, the initial value of DC is set to dc_0 and BC1 is randomly selected in $\{0, \ldots, CW_{10}\}$, where CW_{10} denote the contention window value of backoff stage 0 in the PLC channel. In this protocol, if the station detects the channel idle, then the DC value is unchanged, and BC1 decremented one; if the channel is busy, BC1 is frozen and DC decremented one. And if the power line channel becomes idle again, BC1 will decremented one again. This is the different from the IEEE 802.11 CSMA/CA protocol. Similar to the 802.11 protocol, when the BC1 is reduced to 0, the station will try to transmit the packets. If a collision happens, the station enters the next backoff stage, and draws BC1 uniformly at random in $\{0, \ldots, CW_{1i}\}$, where CW_{1i} denote the contention window value of backoff Stage i in the PLC channel. For the IEEE 1901 protocol, the value of CW_{1i} is related to the priority of the station. As shown in Table 1, the stations have four backoff stages and two priorities (CA0/CA1 and CA2/CA3). For the IEEE 802.11 protocol, $CW_{2i} = 2^i CW_{20}$, where CW_{2i} denote the contention window value of backoff stage i in the wireless channel (Fig. 2).

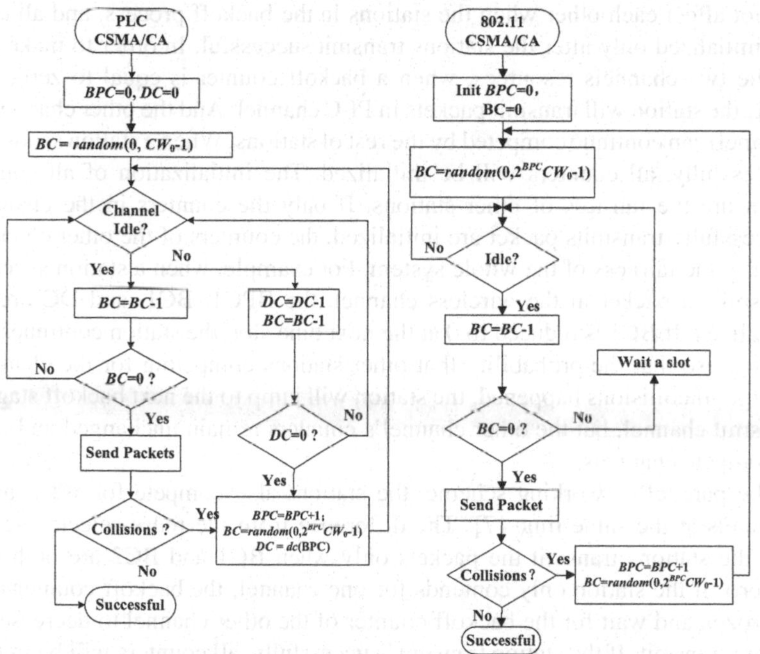

Fig. 2. The CSMA/CA protocol of IEEE 1901 and IEEE 802.11

The DC value in each backoff stage i is dci and decreased only when the PLC medium is busy. The DC remains unchanged when the channel is idle. If the DC is equal to 0 and the channel become busy again, the station enters to the next backoff stage (if the station is in the maximum backdoor stage, then re-enters the last backoff stage) and re-draws the value of BC1 without attempting a transmission. Because of DC in IEEE 1901 protocol, the value of the contention window is small, and at the same time it can provide better performance for the station and reduce collision probability. Because when the stations detect a congested channel, the DC can react in advance to make the station enter a higher backoff stage, thereby reducing collisions.

2.2 The MAC Layer Schemes of Hybrid Communication

In this section, two hybrid networking schemes are compared, which are reuse-selected network scheme and parallel network scheme. The reuse-selected algorithm is proposed in this paper. In this system, the stations have a power line-wireless dual interface so that the station can compete for two channels at the same time. When stations compete in two channels at the same time, the total 5 counters are required: BPC1, BPC2, BC1, BC2 and DC. The following describes the differences between the two networking schemes.

1) In the reuse-selected networking scheme, when the stations have packets to transmit, the counters are initialized and the backoff process is performed. The two channels do not affect each other when the stations in the backoff process, and all counters are initialized only after the stations transmit successful. In order to make full use of the two channels resources, when a backoff counter is equal to zero, such as BC1, the station will transmit packets in PLC channel. And the other channel (WLC channel) can continue competed by the rest of stations. When a station sends packets successfully, all counters will be initialized. The initialization of all counters is to ensure the fairness of other stations. If only the counters in the channel that successfully transmits packet are initialized, the counters of the other channel will destroy the fairness of the whole system. For example, when a station successfully transmits a packet in the wireless channel, the BPC1, BC1, and DC are not be initialized. If BC1 is reduced to 0 at the next time slot, the station continues to send packets, so that the probability that other stations competing for the channel will change. If collisions happened, the station will jump to the next backoff stage in the transmit channel, but the other channel's counters remain unchanged and continue to compete channels.
2) In the parallel networking scheme, the stations also compete for WLC and PLC channels at the same time [7]. The difference from the reuse-selected scheme is that the stations transmit the packets only when BC1 and BC2 are both reduced to zero. If the station only contends for one channel, the backoff counter needs to be frozen and wait for the backoff counter of the other channel to decrease to zero before transmit. If the station transmits successfully, all counters will be initialized; if collisions happened, the station will jump to the next backoff stage. In order to obtain higher reliability, we make the stations use two channels at the same time in the process of sending packets, so the power line channel and the wireless channel are in the same state. Therefore, we treat the two channels as a whole when analysis the system performance.

2.3 Traffic Model

In this section, we introduction a traffic model for stations. Because the generation of the data packets of the stations conforms to the Poisson distribution. We assume that the packet arrival rate of the station is subject to a Poisson process with the parameter of λ. In this system, each station has a packet buffer, and the maximum number of packets that are stored in the buffer of station n for transmission is denoted by $B_{n,max}$, the packets are arranged in the order of arrival and transmitted in the first-in-first-out (FIFO) order at the beginning of the next superframe [8], therefore the station obeys the M/M/1 queuing model. Among them, the stations can send at most N_{Buff} packets each time, and the excess packets will be discarded.

The $X_{n,\Gamma}$ denotes the packets generated by node n at an inter-arrival time Γ and the arrival of the packets obey the Poisson distribution of parameter λ. So $X_{n,\Gamma}$ follows the compound Poisson distribution. By analyzing the model of the packet arrival rate and Poisson process of the stations, we can get the characteristic function of $X_{n,\Gamma}$ is $\varphi^{X}_{n,\Gamma}(\tau)$

$$\begin{aligned}\varphi^{X}_{n,\Gamma}(\tau) &= \mathrm{E}(e(i\tau X_{n,\Gamma})) \\ &= \sum_{k=0}^{\infty} \exp(i\tau X_{n,\Gamma}) \cdot \exp(-\lambda) \cdot (\lambda^{k}/k!) \\ &= \exp(\lambda(\exp(i\tau) - 1))\end{aligned} \tag{1}$$

In a system with a total of N stations. If a station does not generate packets during a time interval Γ, the station will not compete for channel in the next superframe. Through the characteristic function, we can get the average number of stations $N(\lambda)$ competing in the channel.

$$N(\lambda) = N \sum\nolimits_{k=1} \frac{\lambda^{k}}{k!} e^{-\lambda} = N(1 - e^{-\lambda}) \tag{2}$$

3 Performance Analysis

In this section, the transmission probability of the stations in the two channels is analyzed, then the performance of two different hybrid networking schemes is analyzed.

3.1 The Transmission Probability in WLC/PLC Channel

Although the stations use the CSMA/CA algorithm in the PLC and WLC channels, the collision probability, throughput calculation methods and the results are not the same. Here, we discuss the transmission probability τ_1, τ_2 and the collision probability p_1, p_2 of the station in the independent PLC and WLC channels by analyzing the Markov process. The τ_1 and p_1 denote the probability parameters in PLC, and τ_2 and p_2 denote the probability parameters in WLC

$$
\begin{cases}
\tau_1 = \dfrac{\sum\limits_{i=0}^{m_1-2} t_i \prod\limits_{j=0}^{i-1}(1-s_j) + \prod\limits_{i=0}^{m_1-2}(1-s_j)\frac{t_{m_1-1}}{s_{m_1-1}}}{\sum\limits_{i=0}^{m_1-2} bc_i \prod\limits_{j=0}^{i-1}(1-s_j) + \prod\limits_{i=0}^{m_1-2}(1-s_j)\frac{bc_{m_1-1}}{s_{m_1-1}}} \\
\tau_2 = \dfrac{2(1-2p_2)}{(1-2p_2)(CW_{2\min}+1) + pCW_{2\min}(1-(2p)^{m2})}
\end{cases}
\tag{3}
$$

$$
\begin{cases}
p_1 = 1-(1-\tau_1)^{N(\lambda)-1} \\
p_2 = 1-(1-\tau_2)^{N(\lambda)-1}
\end{cases}
\tag{4}
$$

Since DC is introduced in IEEE 1901, the transmission probability τ_1 cannot be calculated directly like τ_2 [9], which can be calculated using the update-bonus function [10, 11]. The numerator of the equation of τ_1 denotes the number of the attempts to transmit before the stations successfully transmits packets, and the denominator denotes the total number of time slots spent before the packets are successfully transmitted. And t_i denotes the probability that the stations will attempt to transmit during the backoff stage *i*, and $s_i$represents the probability that the station sends packets successfully, bc_i represents the number of time slots spent. As for the expression of τ_2, $CW_{2\min}$ represents the minimum contention window value in the WLC channel, and m_1, m_2 represent the maximum number of backoff phase in the PLC and WLC respectively.

3.2 Performance of the Network Schemes

In hybrid communication, the calculation and analysis of the MAC layer will be more complicated. Here we assume that each station is independent of each other. The counter is initialized only after the station has successfully sent a packet, so the two channels are independent from each other during the backoff process.

In the reuse-selected scheme, when a station has a backoff counter reduced to zero, the station attempts to transmit in the corresponding channels, so the two channels have different transmission probabilities. In the parallel scheme, the stations attempt to transmit packets when both BC1 and BC2 are reduced to 0. Because the transmission probability of both protocols is related to the transmission probability of both channels, it can be represented uniformly as $\tau = f(\tau_1, \tau_2)$. After obtaining indicators such as the transmission probability of the station in the channel, the throughput and other performance of the system can be calculated. The system is analyzed as follows.

3.3 System Analysis

In this model, the station uses *Basic* mode to access the channel, but the frame structure of the station is different between the two channels. By referring to the standard [10, 12], we can get the successfully transmitted time T_{s1}, T_{s2} and the collision time T_{c1}, T_{c2} in PLC and WLC channel respectively.

$$
\begin{cases}
T_{s1} = \mathrm{PHY}_{hdr} + \mathrm{MAC}_{hdr} + E[P] + \mathrm{SIFS} + \delta + ACK + \mathrm{DIFS} + \delta \\
T_{c1} = \mathrm{PHY}_{hdr} + \mathrm{MAC}_{hdr} + E[P*] + \mathrm{DIFS} + \delta
\end{cases}
\tag{5}
$$

$$\begin{cases} T_{s2} = 2\text{PRS} + \textit{Preamble } P + E[P] + \text{RIFS} + ACK + \text{CIFS} \\ T_{c2} = \text{EIFS} \end{cases} \tag{6}$$

Where E[P*] is the average length of the longest packet payload when stations have collision in WLC channel, E[P] is the average length of the packets, and the EIFS denotes the length of the time slots when the station collision in a PLC channel. The PHYhdr and MAChdr denote the header data in WLC frame format, SIFS and DIFS are the short frame intervals and long frame intervals, respectively. PRS is the header data in the PLC, and RIFS and CIFS are the corresponding short frame and long frame intervals.

Although the frame structure of the station is different between the two channels, the average transmission time slot T_s and the average collisions time slot T_c can be calculated based on the probability of the station transmission in both channels. So, we can calculate the throughput S of the system

$$\begin{cases} p = 1 - (1-\tau)^{N(\lambda)-1} \\ P_{tr} = 1 - (1-\tau)^{N(\lambda)} \\ P_s = \dfrac{1 - (1-\tau)^{N(\lambda)-1}}{P_{tr}} \\ S = \dfrac{P_s P_{tr} E[p]}{P_{tr} P_s T_s + P_{tr}(1 - P_s)T_c + (1 - P_s)\sigma} \end{cases} \tag{7}$$

The P_{tr} denotes the probability that at least one station transmission in the channel, and P_s is the probability of successful transmission. T_s is the average time the channel is sensed busy because of a successful transmission, and T_c is the average time the channel is sensed busy by each station during a collision. $\sigma$is the duration of an empty slot time.

4 Performance Evaluation

In this section, we simulate the throughput, collision probability and MAC layer transmission delay of the proposed hybrid communication system. The throughput is normalized, assuming that the station does not drop packets at the physical layer and the collision occurs because more than one station send packet at the same time. In the system model, the station has the same priority CA0/CA1, the maximum backoff stage is 3 in both channels, and the minimum contention window value ($CW_{\min}$) is 8. The total simulation time is 10^9 μs, because the simulation results will be not smooth if the simulation time is too small, and each packet size is 4092bits. The system parameter settings are shown in the Table 2.

In Fig. 3 and Fig. 4, we compared the throughput and collision probability of different schemes. In Fig. 3, it can be observed that the WLC has the lowest throughput, followed by the PLC and the parallel scheme, and the highest is the reuse-selected scheme. In Fig. 4, it can be observed that the WLC has the highest probability of collision, followed by the reuse-selected scheme, the collision probability of power lines, and the lowest is the parallel network scheme. The reason that the WLC throughput here is lower than the power line is that the DC is introduced in IEEE 1901, so that the stations can be in

Table 2. Simulation parameter settings

Parameter	Size
Packet payload	4092 bits
MAChdr	272 bits
PHYhdr	128 bits
ACK	240 bits
Channel rate	1 Mbit/s
Slot time	50 μs
SIFS	28 μs
DIFS	128 μs
PRS	59 μs
Preamble P, ACK	240 μs
RIFS, CIFS	80μs/120μs
EIFS	8713 μs
Propagation Delay(δ)	1 μs

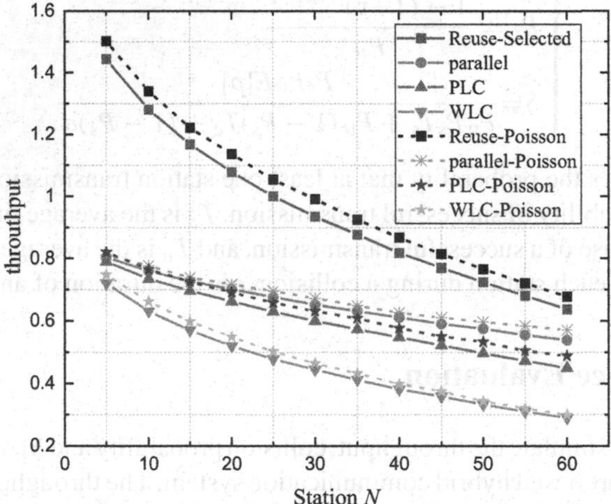

Fig. 3. The probability of transmission between different schemes

a reasonable backoff stage according to the degree of the congestion of channel, thus reducing the collision probability in the channel, and the throughput of the PLC channel is higher than the WLC channel. Only after the stations get the two channels, the packets can be sent in parallel scheme, so the probability of collision is lowest, and the throughput will be lower when the number of stations is fewer. As the number of stations increases, the congestion of the channel is reduced in parallel communication protocol, and the throughput decreases slowly, so this parallel scheme ensures the reliability of the system.

In the reuse-selected scheme, it can be observed that the throughput is much higher than other schemes. Because this scheme makes full use of the resources of both channels, and packets can be sent when one station's backoff counter reduced to zero, while the

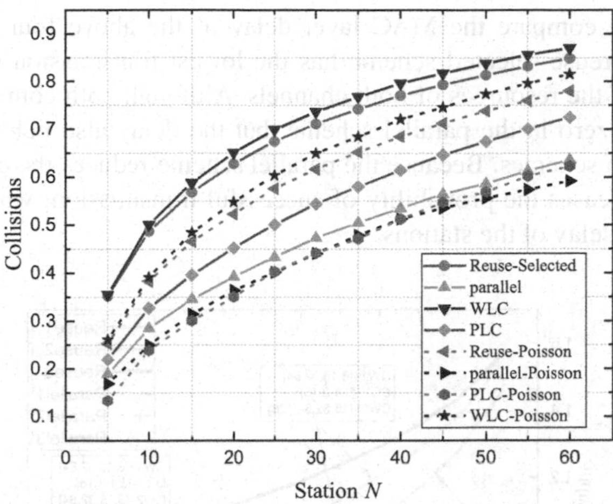

Fig. 4. The probability of collision between different schemes

other channel can still compete by the rest of the stations. However, as the number of stations increases, the throughput decreases significantly. In this scheme, when the station competes for a channel, it will attempts to transmis packets in the next slot and give up compete for the other channel, it will make other $N(\lambda)$-1 stations more likely to compete for the other channel, so the probability of collision of reuse-selected scheme is slightly greater than the PLC model. When the Poisson traffic model is introduced, only the stations that generate packets compete for channels, thus reducing the channels congestion. Therefore, the collision probability after the introduction of Poisson traffic model is less than the saturated collision probability and the throughput is increased in Fig. 4.

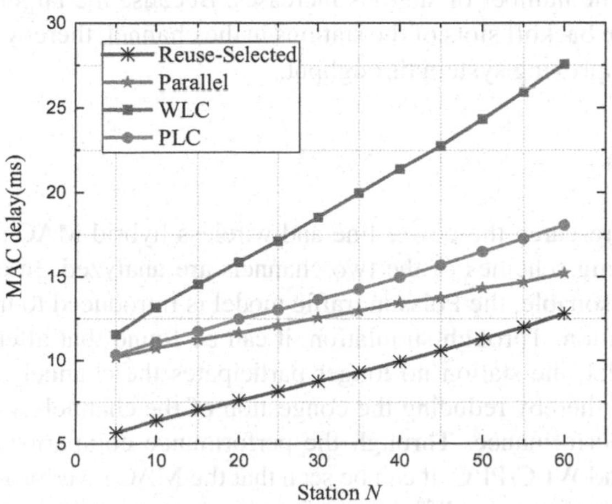

Fig. 5. Delay performance analysis of different schemes

In Fig. 5, we compare the MAC layer delay of the above four schemes. It can be seen that the reuse-selected scheme has the lowest transmission delay because it makes full use of the resources of both channels. Although both counters are required to be reduced to zero in the parallel scheme, but the delay also below the WLC and PLC transmission schemes. Because the parallel scheme reduces the congestion of the channel, and increases the probability of successful transmission, which also reduces the transmission delay of the stations.

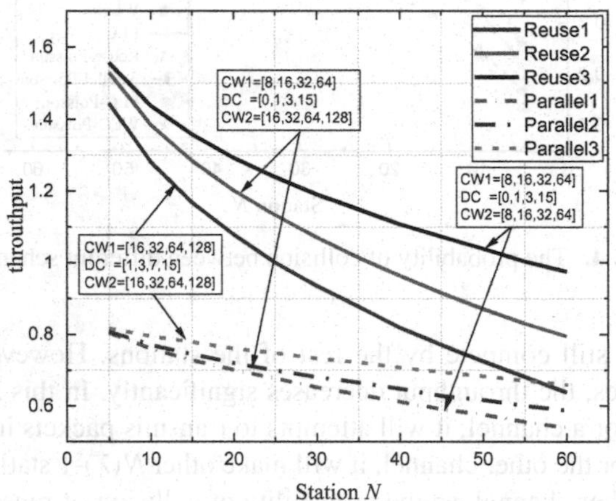

Fig. 6. Effect of *CW* values on performance of different schemes

In Fig. 6, we compare the throughput effects of different contention window values on reuse-selected and parallel schemes. It can be found that when the CW value is increased, the throughput of the stations increases significantly, and the change becomes more obvious as the number of stations increases. Because the larger backoff window values increase the backoff slots of the stations in the channel, thereby reducing channel congestion and improving system throughput.

5 Conclusion

In this paper, we research the power line and wireless hybrid MAC scheme. First, the different networking schemes of the two channels are analyzed. In order to make the research more reasonable, the Poisson traffic model is introduced to make the channels to the actual situation. Through simulation, it can be found that after the introduction of the traffic model, the station no longer participates the channel competition when no packets arrive, thereby reducing the congestion of the channels and improving part of the system's performance. Through the performance comparison between hybrid communication and WLC/PLC, it can be seen that the MAC layer protocols of different networking schemes focus on different performances. Among them, the reuse-selected communication scheme focuses on the utilization rate and transmission delay of the two channels, while the parallel scheme ensures the reliability of transmission and reduces the collision probability of stations in the channel. Compared to wireless channel or power line single channel, the above two schemes have improved the performance of the system.

Funding Statement. This work was supported by the Science and Technology Project of State Grid Corporation of China under Grant No. SGSDDK00KJJS1900405.

References

1. Li, L., Zhao, X.G., Geng, S.Y., et al.: An efficient partially overlapping channels assignment for smart grid IoT with differentiated QoS. IEEE Access **7**, 165207–165216 (2019)
2. Zhao, H.D., Wang, Z., Zhu, M.X., et al.: Application of 5G communication technology in ubiquitous power internet of things. In: 2020 Asia Energy and Electrical Engineering Symposium (AEEES) (2020)
3. Fernandes, V., Poor, H.V., Ribeiro, M.V.: Analyses of the incomplete low-bit-rate hybrid PLC-wireless single-relay channel. IEEE Internet Things J. **5**(2), 917–929 (2018)
4. Lee, J., Kim, Y.: Diversity relaying for parallel use of power-line and wireless communication networks. IEEE Trans. Power Deliv. **29**(3), 1301–1310 (2014)
5. Sayed, M., Tsiftsis, T.A., Al-Dhahir, N.: On the diversity of hybrid narrowband-PLC/wireless communications for smart grids. IEEE Trans. Wireless Commun. **16**(7), 4344–4360 (2017)
6. Chen, Z.X., Liu, Y.C., Liu, R., et al.: Improved CSMA/CA algorithm based on alternative channel of power line and wireless and first-time idle first acquisition. IEEE Access **7**, 41380–41394 (2019)
7. Liu, R., Yuan, J., Chen, Z., Liu, Y., Han, D., Guo, Y.: Research on the MAC layer performance of wireless and power line parallel communication. In: Liu, Q., Mısır, M., Wang, X., Liu, W. (eds.) CENet2018 2018. AISC, vol. 905, pp. 729–737. Springer, Cham (2020). https://doi.org/10.1007/978-3-030-14680-1_79
8. Shrestha, B., Hossain, E., Choi, K.W.: Distributed and CENTRALIZED Hybrid CSMA/CA-TDMA schemes for single-hop wireless networks. IEEE Trans. Wirel. Commun. **13**(7), 4050–4065 (2014)
9. Bianchi, G.: Performance analysis of the IEEE 802.11 distributed coordination function. IEEE J. Sel. Areas Commun. **18**(3), 535–547 (2000)
10. Christina, V., Albert, B., Junlien, H., Patrick, T.: How CSMA/CA with defferral affects performance and dynamics in power-line communications. IEEE/ACM Trans. Netw. **25**(1), 250–263 (2017)
11. Anurah, K., Eitan, A., Daniele, M., et al.: New Insights from a fixed-point analysis of single Cell IEEE 802.11 WLANs. IEEE/ACM Trans. Netw. **15**(3), 588–601 (2007)
12. IEEE Standard for Broadband over Power Line Networks: Medium Access Control and Physical Layer Specifications. IEEE Std 1901-2010 (2010)

A Study on the Influence of Economic Growth on Urban-Rural Income Gap in Five Northwest Provinces Based on Unit Root and Co-integration Test

Xidan Yao[1] and Dunhong Yao[2](✉)

[1] School of Economics, Qufu Normal University, Rizhao 276800, Shandong, China
[2] School of Computer and Engineering, Huaihua University, Huaihua 418000, Hunan, China
dh_yao@hhtc.edu.cn

Abstract. To provide better policy suggestion, and clarify the impact of economic growth on urban-rural income gap in the five provinces of northwest China, unit root test and Co-integration test were conducted on the data, which are from relevant contents of the National Bureau of Statistics of Gansu, Shaanxi, Qinghai, Ningxia Hui Autonomous Region and Xinjiang Uygur Autonomous Region, and a corrected error model was built to explore the impact of economic growth on urban-rural income gap. Results show that the absolute gap in the five northwestern provinces is widening, but the relative gap is narrowing. Thus we know that economic growth is negatively correlated with the gap between the rich and the poor in the five northwest provinces. The economic growth of the five northwest provinces is already in the third stage of the "inverted U" model, of which economic growth is conducive to help the northwest region out of poverty, promote social fairness, and accelerate the pace of build a well-off society in an all-round way.

Keywords: Five north-western provinces · Urban-rural income gap · Unit root and co-integration test · Corrected error model · Policy recommendations

1 Introduction

After the Third Plenary Session of the 11th CPC Central Committee, China began to implement a policy of internal reform and opening up to the outside world. Deng Xiaoping advocated that some regions and some people should be allowed to get rich firstly to drive and help other regions and people and finally achieve the goal of common prosperity. Since the reform and opening-up, China's economy has achieved rapid development and people's living standard has been greatly improved. China has made great efforts and achieved great results in reducing its absolute population: the number of urban residents in China has increased year by year; by the end of 2019, the proportion of urban residents in China was about 60.6%; China's rural poor population had decreased from 98.99 million at the end of 2012 to 5.51 million at the end of 2019; the cumulative reduction was 93.48 million. The poverty rate fell to 0.6% from 10.2% in 2012.

X. Sun et al. (Eds.): ICAIS 2021, LNCS 12736, pp. 290–302, 2021.
https://doi.org/10.1007/978-3-030-78609-0_25

It should be noted that while China's economy is growing rapidly, the people do not enjoy the fruits of development equally, and the gap between the rich and the poor in China is still at a high level. In 2019, China's economic GDP was nearly 100 trillion yuan, and the per capita GDP exceeded 10000 US dollars. According to incomplete statistics, China's middle class has grown rapidly from 109 million people in 2015 to more than 400 million, which ranked first globally. But at the same time, China has a population of 1.4 billion, and the proportion of middle-income people in the total population is not high. According to the 2015 annual wealth report released by Credit Suisse Research Institute, China's middle class has reached 109 million in absolute terms, which is the largest in the world. However, it only accounts for 11% of the national adult population, which is lower than 15.9% of the global average. At present, about 90% of China's population still lives below the middle-class level.

The income gap in China is mainly reflected in two aspects. First, the income gap between the east and the west of China is gradually widening along with economic development. It is due to the implementation of the strategy of giving priority to the development of the eastern coastal areas and then driving the economic development of the west. In addition, there are more talents, better geographical location, unique natural conditions, and a certain industrial base in the eastern region, which are conducive to the development of construction. On the contrary, due to the small population, poor natural environment, and poor transportation in the west of China, it is difficult to develop the region when the foundation is weak. The western region is relatively backward, with more poor people. It is the key place to building a moderately prosperous society in all respects of China. Secondly, with the economic development, the income gap between urban and rural residents has also widened. The main reason lies in the dual economic structure and the imbalance of industrial structure [1]. China has a long agricultural civilization, and the rural areas are engaged in traditional agricultural industries. The degree of agricultural mechanization is low, and the degree of industrial development needs to be improved. However, China's cities and towns are modern manufacturing, service, and information industries, with high labor productivity and relatively high incomes.

The year 2020 will be the last year for China to finish building a moderately prosperous society in all respects. The term "moderately prosperous" refers to the level of development, and "comprehensive" means comprehensive coverage. First, it requires comprehensive progress in political, cultural, social and ecological areas as well as economic development. Second, the coverage of the population should be comprehensive. A moderately prosperous life in an all-round way is a moderately prosperous life for all Chinese people, and it should benefit all Chinese people. Third, we need to cover all areas, not only urban prosperity, but also poor rural areas to achieve moderate prosperity. Because the two goals of well-off society and comprehensive society may sometimes conflict, the purpose of this paper is to clarify the relationship between them at this stage, so as to provide better policy suggestions, hoping to build an overall well-off society more efficiently. The western region is the top priority of poverty alleviation, so this paper takes the five provinces or autonomous regions in the northwest as the research scope. The main research is "whether the coverage area is comprehensive". Therefore, the gap between urban and rural income is taken as the research object to study whether promoting economic growth can narrow the income gap and whether it is consistent with the goal of building a moderately prosperous society in an all-round way. Firstly, by observing the relationship between absolute and relative income gap and between per capita GDP and Theil index in the chart, it is assumed that economic growth at the present stage is helpful to narrow the income gap between urban and rural areas in Northwest China. Then, the data was logarithmically processed and unit root test and co-integration test were carried out. After the variables passed the test, a modified error model was established, and the conclusion of the modified error model was consistent with the hypothesis.

2 Related Works

Since the reform and opening-up, China's economy has made remarkable achievements, but at the same time, the income gap has also been expanding. Although the Gini coefficient [2] has been in a downward trend since 2008, the overall level is still between 0.4 and 0.5, and the income gap is large. Therefore, the relationship between the two has attracted the attention and research of many scholars. The research of Li et al. [3] shows that there is a large income gap between urban and rural areas in China, and it makes a significant contribution to the income gap. Therefore, the following research on the income gap mainly focuses on the urban-rural income gap.

The relationship between economic growth and income gap has positive correlation, negative correlation and uncertainty. The most significant influence is Kuznets' "inverted U" hypothesis [4], which has been confirmed in developed countries. Kuznets believes that in the stage of economic underdevelopment, income distribution will tend to be unequal along with economic development. Subsequently, it experienced a period of temporary no big change in income distribution. In the end, when the economy is fully developed, income distribution tends to be equal. Scholars have different opinions on whether China's development conforms to the "inverted U" model.

Zhang et al. [5] believe that China's urban-rural income gap has entered the middle level of income. At the beginning of the third stage, when the relative gap is narrowed, the absolute income gap between urban and rural areas will reach a historical peak in the future. And then, gradually decrease and the trend of China's urban-rural income gap conform to the "inverted U" model. Liu et al. [6] found an "inverted U-shaped" relationship between China's urban-rural income gap and per capita GDP by using the data of 30 provinces and regions in China. Chen et al. [7] believe that economic development itself is not the reason for widening the urban-rural income gap and Kuznets "inverted U-shaped" curve is not established in China. Chen [8] believes that the research object and time of scholars may only be in the rising stage of Kuznets curve, therefore, the emergence and decline stage of "inverted U-shaped" inflection point has not been observed. Wang et al. [9] studied the panel data of China from 1979 to 2004. They found a heterogeneous panel Co-integration relationship between China's Theil index and economic growth: the relationship between urban-rural income gap and economic growth varies with different development stages and has regional differences. Cao Yu et al. [10] also put forward a similar point of view. Chen et al. [11] analyzed the panel data of 14 cities and prefectures in Hunan Province. They concluded that urbanization in the whole province is conducive to narrowing the urban-rural income gap. But from the perspective of different cities and prefectures, the improvement of urbanization in eastern Hunan, central Hunan, and Northern Hunan is conducive to narrowing the urban-rural income gap. At the same time, southern Hunan and Western Hunan will widen the urban-rural income gap. It can be seen that the relationship between the urban-rural income gap and economic growth is not the same in different provinces or even different cities.

The year 2020 is the end of the national campaign to fight poverty and build a moderately prosperous society in an all-round way. Building a well-off society in an all-around way requires higher requirements for various social and economic indicators and balanced development, that is, between urban and rural areas, between the eastern and western regions, and between individuals. The year 2020 is the decisive period for a well-off society in an all-round way. We should strengthen poverty alleviation and promote economic growth and narrow the gap between the rich and the poor. To clarify the relationship between economic growth and income gap is to clarify the relationship between efficiency and equity in this period. Both efficiency and fairness are the goals pursued by society. Sometimes they promote each other and sometimes contradict each other. Therefore, when formulating the national macroeconomic policies, the government must clarify the relationship between the two, analyze the specific problems, and suit the remedy to improve social welfare better and speed up building a well-off society in an all-around way.

In the key period of realizing the two centenary goals, by the end of 2019, there were 5.51 million rural poor people in China, including 3.23 million in the western region, which is the main battlefield for China to overcome poverty. And some scholars point out that the relationship between China's economic growth and urban-rural income gap is regional, and there may be different characteristics between economic growth and the urban-rural income gap in different provinces. To better study the relationship between efficiency and equity in poverty-stricken western areas, further realize poverty alleviation and build a well-off society in an all-around way. This paper focuses on analyzing the five northwest provinces' data to provide references and suggestions for policy implementation.

3 Theoretical Analysis and Hypothesis Testing

The development of the income gap between urban and rural residents in developed countries conforms to Kuznets' "inverted U" on the relationship between economic growth and income distribution. It goes through five stages: In the first stage, the income level is low and the relative gap is obvious; in the second stage, the income is in the middle and low level, the gap is widening rapidly; in the third stage, the income is in the middle level and the relative gap is narrowed; in the fourth stage, the income is in the middle and high level, and the absolute gap narrates synchronously; in the fifth stage, incomes are high and urban-rural integration is achieved. The income of urban and rural residents is basically equal, which is a stage of development from the post-industrial period to the stage of high-quality life [1]. This paper focuses on the relationship between economic growth and the urban-rural income gap in the five provinces or autonomous regions of northwest China. This paper aims to clarify the current stage of Kuznets' "inverted U" model and provides policy suggestions for poverty alleviation.

The income gap between urban and rural areas can be narrowed by the economic level improvement through many channels. For example, firstly, economic development and urbanization can create more employment opportunities for migrant workers and increase their income, thus narrowing the income gap between urban and rural areas. Secondly, economic growth enables the government to have more financial resources to support education. When farmers have more knowledge and culture, they will improve their competitiveness in the labor market and get higher income. In addition, as technology advances, farmers flood into secondary and tertiary industries, where they can earn higher wages. Finally, economic growth can reduce the surplus labor force in rural areas, increase farmers' per capita land capital, improve agricultural productivity and agricultural structure adjustment and improve farmers' per capita income. Therefore, this paper puts forward the following hypothesis: the current economic growth is conducive to narrowing the urban-rural income gap in northwest China.

In this paper, per capita GDP and urban-rural income gap from 2000 to 2019 are considered as the research objects. Co-integration test is carried out on the data and error correction model is established to explore the impact of economic growth on the urban-rural income gap so as to clarify the relationship between efficiency and fairness in the five provinces in the northwest, and then provide better policy suggestions and win the victory in building a moderately prosperous society in an all-round way.

4 Data Sources, Variable Selection and Descriptive Analysis

4.1 Data Sources

The data in this paper are from the relevant data of Gansu, Shaanxi, Qinghai, Ningxia Hui Autonomous Region and Xinjiang Uygur Autonomous Region of the National Bureau of Statistics. The data include the disposable income of urban residents, disposable income of rural residents (net income of rural residents before 2012), total provincial population, urban population and rural population. The data span from 2000 to 2019.

4.2 Variable Selection

This paper aims to study the impact of economic growth on the urban-rural income gap in the five provinces of Northwest China. Economic growth is generally measured by indicators such as gross domestic product (GDP), gross national product (GNP) and per capita gross domestic product (PGDP). Among these variables, GDP per capita can eliminates the effect of population size, reflects the extent of economic development and offsets some estimation errors. Therefore, this paper selects per capita GDP as a variable to measure economic growth and takes 2000 as the base period to adjust per capita GDP price. The indicators commonly used to measure income gap are absolute difference, relative difference, coefficient of variation, Gini coefficient and Theil index, etc. The Theil index [12] measures the income gap (or inequality) between individuals or regions. Since Northwest China's economic development is relatively backward and the income level is low, and Theil index is sensitive to the income changes of low-income groups, this paper will mainly use Theil index to measure the income gap between urban and rural areas. According to the known theory, the larger the index is, the larger the income gap is. After price adjustment, GDP per capita and Theil index are respectively represented by *RG* and *T*. The formula of the Theil index is as follows:

$$T_t = \sum_{i=1}^{2} \left(\frac{Y_{it}}{Y_t}\right) \log\left(\frac{Y_{it}/Y_t}{P_{it}/P_t}\right) \tag{1}$$

T represents Thiel index of urban and rural income, *Y* represents total household income, *P* represents the total population, and the subscript *t* represents the statistical period. The subscript *i* values 1 and 2, representing urban and rural areas respectively.

4.3 Descriptive Analysis

This paper selects the relevant data of Gansu Province, Shaanxi Province, Qinghai Province, Ningxia Hui Autonomous Region, and Xinjiang Uygur Autonomous Region on the official website of the National Bureau of statistics from 2000 to 2019, as shown in Table 1.

Table 1. Change in the relationship between urban and rural household income gap and per capita GDP in five northwest provinces from 2000 to 2019

Year	R (Yuan)	DR	RG (10000 Yuan)	T
2000	3604	3.41	0.54	0.1847
2001	4128	3.64	0.58	0.2037
2002	4714	3.82	0.64	0.2177
2003	5036	3.81	0.73	0.216
2004	5464	3.77	0.83	0.2116
2005	5987	3.78	0.94	0.2114
2006	6718	3.85	1.08	0.2146
2007	7767	3.87	1.29	0.2144
2008	8917	3.85	1.49	0.2108
2009	9719	3.83	1.59	0.2068
2010	10483	3.59	1.91	0.1858
2011	11898	3.48	2.21	0.1758
2012	13512	3.44	2.44	0.1694
2013	14501	3.12	2.65	0.1453
2014	15696	3.06	2.81	0.1381
2015	17241	3.07	2.80	0.1364
2016	18610	3.06	2.89	0.1338
2017	20095	3.05	3.11	0.13
2018	21594	3.03	3.33	0.1264
2019	22990	2.97	3.44	0.1204

Firstly, the weighted per capita GDP based on population of the five provinces is calculated by regional per capita GDP. Secondly, the urban per capita disposable income X_{1t} of the five northwest provinces is calculated through the disposable income of urban residents and urban population. Similarly, we can calculate the per capita disposable income of rural residents in the five northwest provinces. The absolute difference and relative difference are shown below respectively:

$$R = X_{1t} - X_{2t} \tag{2}$$

$$DR = \frac{X_{1t}}{X_{2t}} \tag{3}$$

The results are shown in Fig. 1:

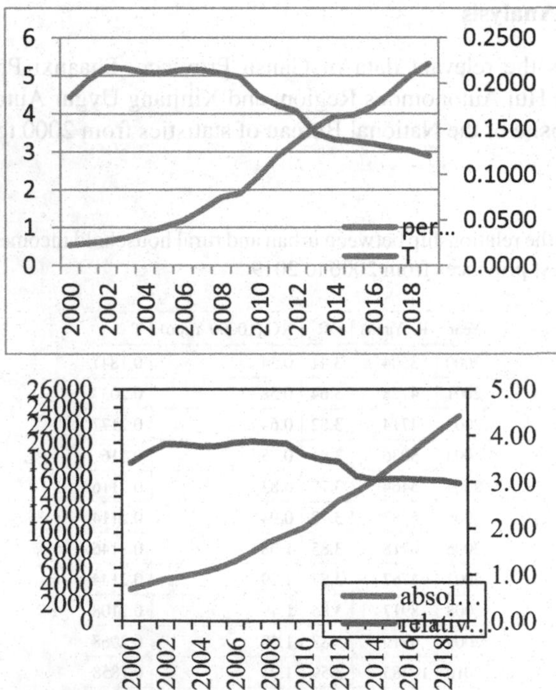

Fig. 1. Changes in the relationship between urban and rural household income gap and per capita GDP in five northwest provinces from 2000 to 2019

As seen from the above figures and tables, the absolute income gap R between urban and rural residents in the five northwest provinces or autonomous regions has continued to rise as a whole. In contrast, the relative income gap between urban and rural areas (DR) has a downward trend in the overall process. However, the value is still high, belonging to the category of great disparity. Generally speaking, the urban-rural income gap in the five western provinces or autonomous regions can be divided into two stages: from 2000 to 2010, the Theil index fluctuated around 0.2 in a stable stage, and from 2010 to 2019, the Theil index fell all the way. The income gap between urban and rural areas has been alleviated from 2010 to 2019, mainly because of the transformation of the second round of Western Development Strategy since 2010. The central government has paid more attention to supporting agriculture, rural areas and farmers, and also emphasized the coordinated development of urban and rural economies, which has improved the income level of rural residents While GDP per head has increased over time, Theil's index has dropped in fluctuations.

5 Results and Analysis

5.1 Stability Test

Most of the economic time series are non-stationary. If the non-stationary time series is directly treated as stationary time series for regression analysis, it will bring about pseudo-regression problem. The unit root test was carried out at the significance level of 5% and the variables were logarithmic, which were lnT and lnRG, respectively.

When the null hypothesis is rejected, there is no unit root which means that the sequence is stationary. The results in Table 2 and Table 3 show that both lnT and lnRG have unit roots, which disappear after the second-order difference. Therefore, the second-order difference sequence is stable. From this we can know that the two variables are second order integration, and there may be a co-integration relationship between them.

Table 2. Results of the unit root test for variable lnRG

Null Hypothesis: D (LNRG, 2) has a unit root			
Exogenous: Constant			
Lag Length: 1 (Automatic - based on SIC, maxlag = 4)			
		t-Statistic	Prob.*
Augmented Dickey-Fuller test statistic		−4.443254	0.0037
Test critical values	1% level	−3.920350	
	5% level	−3.065585	
	10% level	−2.673459	

*MacKinnon (1996) one-sided p-values.

5.2 Co-integration Test

lnRG and lnT are single integers of the same order, which satisfies the condition of Co-integration test. Taking lnRG as the explanatory variable and LNT as the explained variable, OLS regression was performed on it. Results are as follows:

$$\ln T_t = -0.285 \ln RG_t - 1.621 + \mu_t \quad (4)$$

Table 3. Unit root test results of lnT.

Null Hypothesis: D (LNT, 2) has a unit root			
Exogenous: Constant			
Lag Length: 1 (Automatic - based on SIC, maxlag = 4)			
		t-Statistic	Prob.*
Augmented Dickey-Fuller test statistic		−4.814216	0.0018
Test critical values	1% level	−3.920350	
	5% level	−3.065585	
	10% level	−2.673459	

*MacKinnon (1996) one-sided p-values

In the regression results, DW = 0.200736, there is a serious autocorrelation phenomenon. In model (4), according to the AIC criterion and SC criterion, after adding the appropriate lag term, the regression results of one lag period are finally selected.

$$\ln T_t = -0.253 \ln RG_t + 0.1431 \ln RG_{t-1} + 0.831 \ln T_{t-1} - 0.244 + \mu_t \quad (5)$$

After the correction, DW = 1.767229, the autocorrelation phenomenon of the model was significantly weakened, $R^2 = 0.980842$, the parameters significance was relatively high, and the regression fitting was good. The results are shown in Table 4.

Then, the stationarity test of the residual sequence is carried out. The results are shown in Table 5, and the t-statistic is −3.682980. At the 5% significance level, MacKinnon's critical value is $-3.6578 > t$. The residual sequence has no unit root and is a stationary sequence. Therefore, there is a Co-integration relationship between lnRG and lnT.

5.3 Estimation Results and Economic Significance of Error Correction Model

Both lnRG and lnT are **second order integrals**, and there is a Co-integration relationship between them, which means that the two variables have a long-term equilibrium relationship. The OLS estimation equation for the error correction model is as follows:

$$\begin{aligned}\Delta \ln T_t = & -0.347\Delta \ln RG_t + 0.458\Delta \ln RG_{t-1} - 0.202\Delta \ln RG_{t-2} \\ & + 0.740\Delta \ln T_{t-1} - 0.006 - 0.719e_{t-1} + \mu_t \end{aligned} \quad (6)$$

The above formula reflects the influence of the per capita GDP and Theil index on the urban-rural income gap and the impact of the previous period error on the current fluctuation. If the logarithm of per capita GDP increases by 1% point, the urban-rural income gap will be reduced by 0.347% points, suggesting that the overall effect is not significant. If the urban-rural income gap is 1% point higher than the equilibrium in the previous year, the urban-rural income gap would be decreased by an average of 0.719% points in the current year. In the recent 20 years, the per capita GDP of the five northwest provinces or autonomous regions is negatively correlated with the urban-rural income gap. It shows that accelerating economic construction and strengthening poverty

Table 4. Revised OLS regression results.

Dependent Variable: LNT				
Method: Least Squares				
Date: 06/30/20 Time: 10:48				
Sample (adjusted): 2001 2019				
Included observations: 19 after adjustments				
Variable	Coefficient	Std. Error	t-Statistic	Prob
C	−0.244393	0.180091	−1.357053	0.1948
LNRG	−0.253043	0.266724	−0.948706	0.3578
LNRG(-1)	0.143154	0.274469	0.521567	0.6096
LNT(-1)	0.831387	0.096572	8.609011	0.0000
R-squared	0.980842	Mean dependent var		−1.752789
Adjusted R-squared	0.977011	S.D. dependent var		0.222852
S.E. of regression	0.033789	Akaike info criterion		−3.752683
Sum squared resid	0.017126	Schwarz criterion		−3.553854
Log likelihood	39.65049	Hannan-Quinn criter		−3.719033
F-statistic	255.9906	Durbin-Watson stat		1.767229
Prob(F-statistic)	0.000000			

*MacKinnon (1996) one-sided p-values.

Table 5. Co-integration test results of lnRG and lnT

Null Hypothesis: RESID01 has a unit root			
Exogenous: None			
Lag Length: 0 (Automatic - based on SIC, maxlag = 3)			
		t-Statistic	Prob.*
Augmented Dickey-Fuller test statistic		−3.682980	0.0010
Test critical values	1% level	−2.699769	
	5% level	−1.961409	
	10% level	−1.606610	

*MacKinnon (1996) one-sided p-values.

alleviation can not only promote economic growth, but also narrow the gap between the rich and the poor. It is expected that the negative correlation between the two will be more obvious in the future and the five northwest provinces or autonomous regions are in the third stage of the "inverted U" model.

6 Conclusion and Discussion

6.1 Conclusion

According to the above model analysis, there is a co-integration relationship between per capita GDP and Thiel index in the five provinces or autonomous regions in Northwest China, so there is a long-term equilibrium relationship between the urban-rural income gap and economic growth. The absolute gap of per capita GDP is expanding, but the relative gap is decreasing. According to the established corrected error model, it is known that the economic growth of the five provinces or autonomous regions in Northwest China is negatively correlated with the gap between the rich and the poor. This region has been in the third stage of the "inverted U" model, that is, the middle level of income and the relative gap narrowing stage. The research hypothesis proposed above is consistent with this conclusion. Therefore, at this time, China's acceleration of economic construction in Northwest China can not only spur economic growth but also narrow the income gap. Moreover, it is expected to enter the fourth and fifth stages of the inverted U model after the economic development reaches a certain stage in the near future, so as to realize a virtuous cycle and finally realize the goal that the fruits of economic development are shared by the people.

6.2 Economic Significance

Because the western region has reached the third stage of Kuznets's inverted U model, policy makers can set their economic development strategies at their feet without worrying that growth will widen income inequality. At the present stage, China should strengthen the economic construction and poverty alleviation efforts in the western region, and actively implement various poverty alleviation policies, so as to improve the per capita disposable income of rural residents and the level of urbanization, and improve the material living standards of people in poor areas. As the poorest region in China, the western region can narrow the income gap between urban and rural areas while promoting economic growth, completing the last mile of building a moderately prosperous society in all respects.

The ultimate goal of economic development is to let all the people share the fruits. Completing the building of a moderately prosperous society in all respects is a phased goal and a key step in China's efforts to achieve national rejuvenation. China places this goal in a very important position. As the poorest region in China, the western region is already in the third stage of Kuznets inverted U model, indicating that the whole country has entered the third stage steadily. At this time, the acceleration of national economic construction will promote the development of China's economy to the fourth and fifth stages of Kuznets inverted U model. While stimulating high-quality economic development, we will further narrow the income gap, raise people's income and living standards, and set ourselves on a new journey toward building a modern socialist country.

In the context of the global pandemic of Covid-19 and the global economic downturn, China actively fulfilled its historical responsibility as a responsible major country and committed itself to injecting impetus into the global economic recovery while reviving its own economy. As China has entered the third stage of Kuznets' inverted U model, there is no need to worry about increasing income gap in order to realize economic recovery. While achieving high-quality economic development in China, it will not hinder the realization of a moderately prosperous society in all respects and will add impetus to global economic recovery.

6.3 Policy Suggestions

The government can reasonably guide and adjust the industrial structure, vigorously promote the supply-side structural reform, promote coordinated industrial development, transformation and upgrading, promote sustainable economic development, speed up the development of the tertiary industry, improve the infrastructure construction and social security system in the western region, promote residents' consumption, and narrow the income gap. At the same time, China needs to make progress while maintaining stability and promote high-quality economic development. China should step up efforts to develop strategic emerging industries such as "digital economy", "intelligent manufacturing", "life and health", and "new materials", and promote their further integration with traditional industries to improve quality and efficiency. Gradually narrow the income gap between urban and rural areas and bring it under control.

References

1. Liu, S., Xu, Y.: A study on the cause of the gap between urban and rural households' income and distribution and countermeasures. J. Financ. Econ. **5**, 93–103 (2004). https://doi.org/10.16538/j.cnki.jfc.2004.05.010
2. Chen, C.: Calculation of various gini coefficients from different regions in china and analysis using the nonparametric model. J. Quant. Tech. Econ. **1**, 133–142 (2007)
3. Li, S., Luo, C.: Re-estimating the income gap between urban and rural households in China. Proc. - Soc. Behav. Sci. **2**, 7151–7163 (2010). https://doi.org/10.1016/j.sbspro.2010.05.068
4. Thornton, J.: The Kuznets inverted-U hypothesis: panel data evidence from 96 countries. Appl. Econ. Lett. **8**, 15–16 (2001). https://doi.org/10.1080/135048501750041213
5. Zhang, J., Zhu, Y., Zhou, X.: The characteristic and tendency of per capita annual income between urban and rural households in China. Chin. J. Agric. Resour. Reg. Plan. **39**, 237–243 (2018). https://doi.org/10.7621/cjarrp.1005-9121.20181232
6. Liu, R., Ye, M.: Study on kuznets curve of urban-rural income difference in China. Inq. into Econ. Issues. **6**, 9–13 (2006)
7. Chen, B., Lin, Y.: Development strategy, urbanization and the rural-urban income disparity in China. Soc. Sci. China. **4**, 81–102 (2013)
8. Chen, Z.: Some methodological problems in the study of inverted U curve of income difference and polarization. Soc. Sci. China **5**, 78–83 (2002)
9. Wang, S., Ouyang, Z.: The rural-urban income disparity and its effects to economic growth in the case of China. Econ. Res. J. **42**, 44–55 (2007)
10. Cao, Y., Chen, X., Ma, Y.: Urbanization, urban-rural income gap and economic growth: an empirical research based on provincial panel data in China. Stat. Res. **27**, 29–36 (2010). https://doi.org/10.19343/j.cnki.11-1302/c.2010.03.005

11. Chen, N., Qu, H.: Relationship among urbanization, urban-rural income gap and economic growth in Hunan Province. J. Hunan Financ. Econ. Univ. **31**, 98–105 (2015). https://doi.org/10.16546/j.cnki.cn43-1510/f.2015.01.010
12. Song, H., Xu, P.: Analysis on the difference in economic development between Zhejiang and Shaanxi Provinces based on Theil index. In: Proceedings - 2020 International Conference Urban Engineering and Management Science, ICUEMS 2020, pp. 335–340 (2020). https://doi.org/10.1109/ICUEMS50872.2020.00080

Research on Intrusion Detection of Industrial Control System Based on FastICA-SVM Method

Haonan Chen[1], Xianda Liu[2(✉)], Tianyu Wang[3], and Xuejing Zhang[4]

[1] College of Information Science and Engineering, Northeastern University, Shenyang, China
[2] Shenyang Institute of Automation, Chinese Academy of Sciences, Beijing, China
liuxianda@sia.cn
[3] Key Laboratory of Networked Control Systems, Chinese Academy of Sciences, Beijing, China
[4] Institutes for Robotics and Intelligent Manufacturing, Chinese Academy of Sciences, Beijing, China

Abstract. As an important part of guard system, intrusion detection systems have great significance to the security of industrial control systems. Cause the industrial control systems of the on-site environment is often very complicated, the process data extracted on-site have a wide variety of features, and they always have complex associations and are not independent. The intrusion detection algorithms for traditional industrial control systems often do not solve this problem, which results in a decrease in the accuracy, precision and high false negative rate (FNR), false positives rate (FPR). Aiming at solving the current problems, this paper proposes an algorithm combining the Fast Independent Principal Component Analysis (FastICA) and Support Vector Machine (SVM). Finally compared with the SVM and PCA-SVM algorithms, the experimental results show that the accuracy rate has been significantly improved and slight FPR.

Keywords: Intrusion detection · FastICA · SVM

1 Introduction

Industrial control system is an part of modern manufacturing infrastructure which is the key point of the national economy. Thus maintaining the security of industrial system become very critical. The traditional view is that, in reality, the operating environment of the industrial control system is relatively isolated from the Internet, and the structure is simple and stable. It is considered a basically security structure. However, with the emergence of virus attacks against industrial control systems causing significant losses of personnel and property, such as Stuxnet [1] attack on Iranian nuclear power plants, people have gradually realized the importance of establishing a reliable defense system. Intrusion detection, as the second security barrier behind the firewall, plays a vital role in the smooth operation of the system.

In recent years, the research on the problem of industrial system intrusion detection is very active. Most of the research on industrial control network security issues focuses

X. Sun et al. (Eds.): ICAIS 2021, LNCS 12736, pp. 303–311, 2021.
https://doi.org/10.1007/978-3-030-78609-0_26

on state detection, fault diagnosis, intrusion detection, industrial control protocol analysis, and vulnerability mining, etc. In Ref [2], Ondrej Linda extracted from the feature information from the real network's data set, using neural network algorithm which has achieved good results. In Ref [3], Kim G proposed a hybrid intrusion detection method that combines the decision tree algorithm with the SVM algorithm and gets high accuracy under large sample conditions. In Ref [4], Shang merged with PSO and the OCSVM algorithm has greatly improved the accuracy compared to Grid-SVM.

The above literature used traditional machine learning methods. However, because the data generated by complex industrial sites often has high-dimensional characteristics, single traditional machine learning algorithm often leads to dimensionality disasters, so dimensionality reduction is necessary when processing data. But The traditional data dimensionality reduction algorithm principal component analysis (PCA) [5], only considers the weight of the data when selecting data features, and not consider the Internal relationship of data characteristics, which will not only affect the Robustness of the model, but also reduce the generalization ability of the model that will have an impact on the system detection accuracy. And traditional literature does not solve this problem. In this context, this paper proposes an intrusion detection system that integrates FastICA [6] and SVM, which better solves this problem. The method is applied to the process data of Secure Water Treatment (SWaT) Testbed of SUTD. Simulation experiments are performed on the experimental platform data, and the experimental results show that the algorithm has significantly improved the accuracy of intrusion detection compared to SVM and PCA-SVM.

2 Technology Analysis

2.1 Fast-ICA Principle

ICA is essentially a problem of finding the optimal solution, that is, how to make the separated independent signal approach the source signal to the greatest extent. Let us denote by $x = (x_1, x_2, \cdots, x_m)^T$ a zero-mean m-dimensional random variable that can be observed, and by $s = (s_1, s_2, \cdots, s_n)^T$ its n-dimensional transform [7]. Then the problem is to determine a constant matrix W so that the linear transformation of the observed variables.

$$s = Wx \tag{1}$$

In this paper, FastICA algorithm based on the maximization of negative entropy is used. First, through the centralization and whitening of the data, the correlation between the data features is removed, and we can get an unrelated data feature set is obtained $Z \in R^{n \times m}$. Then we need to estimate the independent features from the data set Z. Usually the whitening process is completed by PCA, and at the same time, features with low information entropy can be filtered out. Then we need to estimate the independent features from the data set Z. Then the independent components are estimated to the maximum extent from the uncorrelated data sets. FastICA uses the principle of maximum non-Gaussian estimation, and uses the maximization of negative entropy as a measure to solve the equation:

$$s = Bz = (s_1, s_2 \ldots s_n) \tag{2}$$

The core of the optimization algorithm for the negative entropy formula:

$$J(s) \propto [E\{G(s)\} - E\{G(v)\}]^2 \tag{3}$$

The optimization of this formula acquire the extreme value by Newton's method, gets the transition matrix B, and obtains each independent factors $s = (s_1, s_2, \cdots, s_n)^T$.

The steps of the ICA algorithm are as follows:

Input: whitening feature set $Z \in R^{n\times m}$, the number of independent components to be estimated d.

Process: initialize all $b_{i,0}(i=1,2,3,..d)$,assume each $b_{i,0}$ have unit norm $B_0 = (b_{1,0}, b_{2,0}, b_{3,0}, \ldots, b_{d,0})^T$,and k=0.

repeat

for i=1,2,3,…,d do

$$b_{i,k+1} = E\{zg(b_{i.k}{}^T z)\} - E\{g'(b_{i,k}{}^T z)\}b_{i,k}$$

And for

$$B_{k+1} = (b_{1,k+1}, b_{2,k+1}, b_{3,k+1}, \ldots, b_{d,k+1})^T$$

$$B_{k+1} = (B_k B_k{}^T)^{-1/2} B_k$$

$$k = k+1$$

Output: the conversion matrix obtained in the last iteration $B \in R^{d\times n}$.

After getting the conversion matrix, $B \in R^{d\times n}$, according to the formula (2),we can get a feature set which internal features are mutually independent.

2.2 SVM Principle

Use the main component after FastICA data reduction as SVM Input, support vector machine(SVM) was originally based on statistical Machine learning method and small sample data Building a model, and use the kernel function to achieve from low-dimensional space to high-dimensional feature space. The nonlinear mapping between spaces and the construction of the optimal super flat. Constructing and solving the optimal hyperplane problem can be transformed into Solve the problem of secondary regression [8]:

$$\min_{w,b,\varepsilon} \frac{1}{2}\|w\|^2 + C\sum_{i=1}^{m}\xi_i$$

$$s.t.y^i(w^T\Phi(x^{(i)}) + b) \geq 1 - \xi_i, i = 1, 2, \ldots m$$

$$\xi_i \geq 0, i = 1, \ldots, l \tag{4}$$

In the formula (4), C is the penalty factor, with the more larger of the C value the algorithm will more easy to Fall into overfitting. By using the Lagrange multiplier method, formula (5) Solve the quadratic programming problem by dividing it into the following dual programming:

$$\max W(\alpha) = \sum_{i=1}^{m} \alpha_i - \frac{1}{2}\sum_{i=1}^{m}\sum_{j=1}^{m} \alpha_i \alpha_j y^{(i)} y^{(j)} k(x^{(i)}, x^{(j)})$$

$$\text{s.t.} \sum_{i=1}^{m} \alpha_i y^{(i)} = 0$$

$$0 \le \alpha_i \le C, i = 1, 2, ..., m \tag{5}$$

The $k(x_i, x_j)$ is kernel function, $\alpha = (\alpha_1, \alpha_2, ..., \alpha_n)^T$ is the Lagrange multiplier corresponding to the inequality constraint in formula (5), if $\alpha_i > 0$ the corresponding sample is called support vector. According to functional theory, if the kernel function satisfies the Nercer clause, the data piece will corresponds to the inner product of a certain transformation space. A suitable kernel function can be Without increasing the computational complexity, turn the non-separable problem into Change to a separable question. In this paper, the kernel function selects the RBF [9] function:

$$k(x^i, x^j) = \exp(-\frac{\|x^i - x^j\|}{2\sigma^2}) \tag{6}$$

This function can realize the mapping from the original space to the infinite space. In the simulation experiment of this paper, the classification accuracy of the radial basis function is the highest, and the running time is the shortest.

When the data training sample is large, the quadratic programming problem will become very complicated, and the solution process will become very inefficient, so we need an algorithm to make the iterative process fast and efficient. This system uses the SMO [10] algorithm for parameter iteration. The basic idea is: first determine whether the problem meets the KTT conditions (Karush-Kuhn-Tucker conditions), if it is satisfied, you can directly find the solution to the optimization problem, otherwise choose two variables and fix the other Variables, construct a quadratic programming problem for these two variables. This makes each calculation easier and the calculation speed is greatly improved Can effectively improve the computational efficiency of the algorithm.

3 Structure Design of Intrusion Detection System

The intrusion detection system combine FastICA with SVM, collects field process data, undergoes FastICA dimensionality reduction processing, and then detects abnormal behaviors through SVM classification technology. It is mainly composed of data feature extraction, FastICA data dimensionality reduction, SVM model training, SVM model detection and on-site dynamic response. Its structure diagram is shown below:

The overall process can be roughly divided into four steps (Fig. 1):

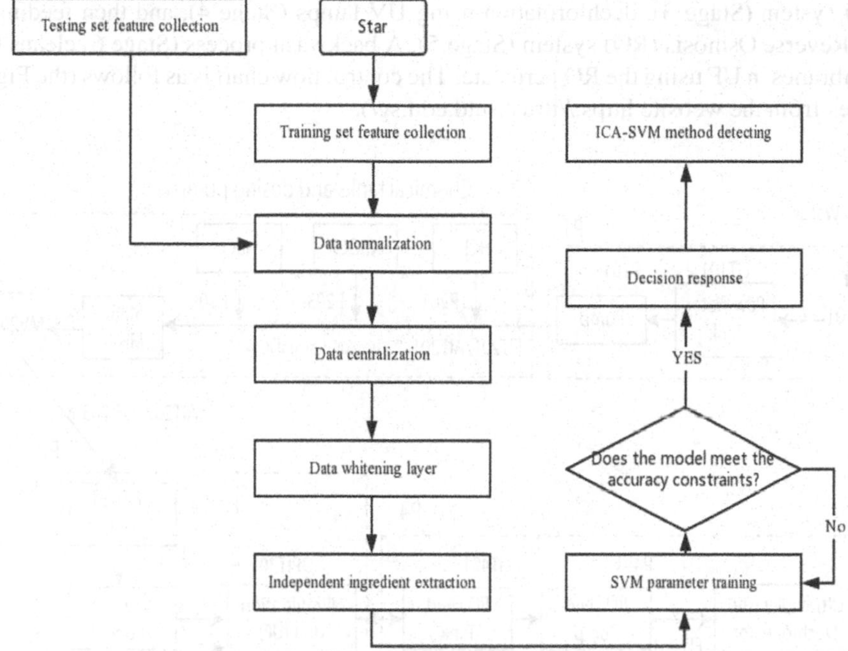

Fig. 1. Intrusion detection process diagram

(1) Data processing stage: Aiming at the large amount of process data in the industrial field, this article uses the FastICA algorithm to reduce the dimensionality of the training set and test set data. Accurately extract information principal elements, and ensure the independence between features, thereby revealing the process characteristics of the industrial control process more essentially, avoiding the "dimension disaster", and making the data structure more reasonable.
(2) SVM parameter iteration: the iterative algorithm adopts the SMO algorithm.
(3) Data training stage: After the data set is processed by dimensionality reduction, the obtained feature vector passes through the training module to obtain the models of the classifier.
(4) Data inspection stage: trained SVM classifier detect the test data set of data preprocessing, decision-making module Make appropriate decisions based on the results.

4 Experimental Data Description

The experimental data of this paper uses the Cyber-Physical System Platform (CPS.)—Secure Water Treatment (SWaT) from SUTD, which has been in operation since March 2015.

The testbed consists of a modern six-stage water treatment process that closely mimics a real world treatment plant. Stage 1 of the physical process begins by taking in raw water, followed by chemical dosing (Stage 2), filtering it through an Ultrafiltration

(UF) system (Stage 3), dechlorination using UV lamps (Stage 4), and then feeding it to a Reverse Osmosis (RO) system (Stage 5). A backwash process (Stage 6) cleans the membranes in UF using the RO permeate. The control flow chart is as follows (the Fig. 2 comes from the website https://itrust.sutd.edu.sg/):

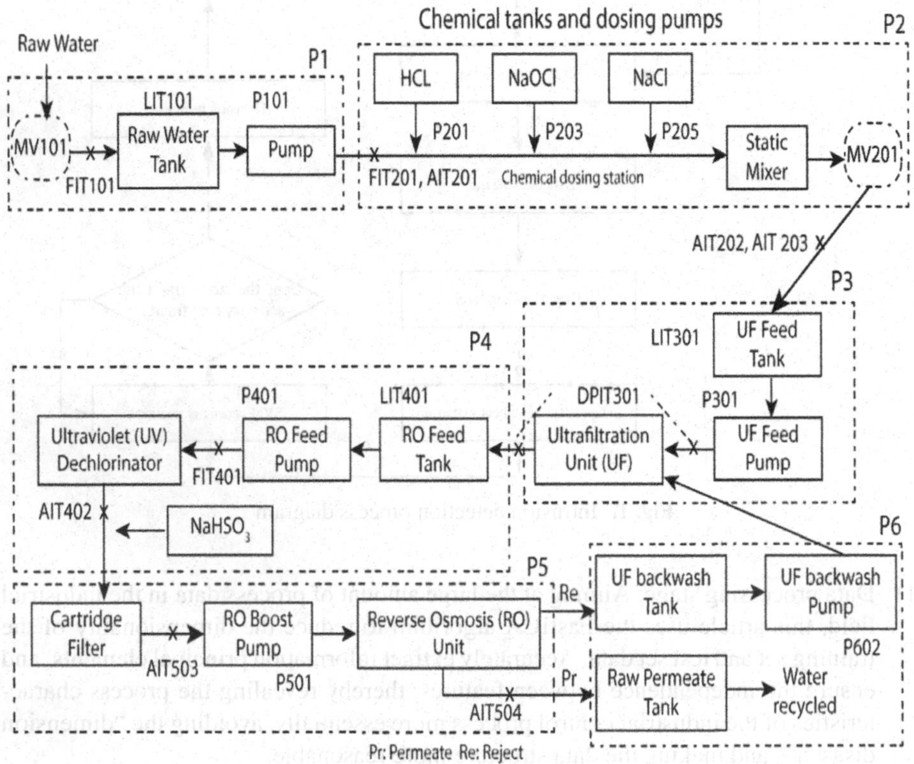

Fig. 2. SWaT's six-stage processes

The cyber portion of SWaT consists of a layered communications network, Allen-Bradley Programmable Logic Controllers (PLCs), Human Machine Interfaces (HMIs), Supervisory Control and Data Acquisition (SCADA) workstation, and a Historian. Data from sensors is available to the SCADA system and recorded by the Historian for subsequent analysis.

Our SWaT dataset consists of 11 days of continuous operation – of which 7 days' worth of data was collected under normal operation while 4 days' worth of data was collected with attack scenarios. During the data collection, all network traffic, sensor and actuator data were collected (Table 1).

Table 1. Experimental data information

Data information	
The number of information	34236
Data feature dimension	51
FastICA feature selection number	3
Number of abnormal data	4238
Number of normal data	29998
Proportion of number of training set and test set	2:8

5 Experiment Analysis

For the convenience of detection, this data is only divided into normal and abnormal. From the two kinds of data, 20% are randomly selected as the test set samples, and the remaining 80% is used to train the algorithm model. For the convenience of detection, this data is only divided into normal and abnormal. From the two kinds of data, 20% are randomly selected as the test set samples, and the remaining 80% is used to train the algorithm model. The algorithm model detects abnormal results using Precision, Recall, False Negative Rate, False Positives Rate, and Accuracy for evaluation. The result is shown in Fig. 3 (Table 2).

Table 2. Detection results of different attack types based on FastICA-SVM

Data set	FastICA-SVM detection results	
Text set	Accuracy	97.43%
	Precision	98.86%
	Recall	98.20%
	FNR	1.80%
	FPR	8.08%
Train set	Accuracy	97.29%
	Precision	98.79%
	Recall	98.10%
	FNR	1.90%
	FPR	8.45%

Cause the number of the data used in this article is small, the comparison of the algorithm results is not obvious, in order to highlight the difference in results between the algorithms. This paper only extracts 3 effective dimensions from 51 features. Use the training set to fit the parameters of the algorithms SVM, PCA-SVM, FastICA-SVM, and the test set is used for detection. The comparison of the experimental results is shown in Fig. 3.

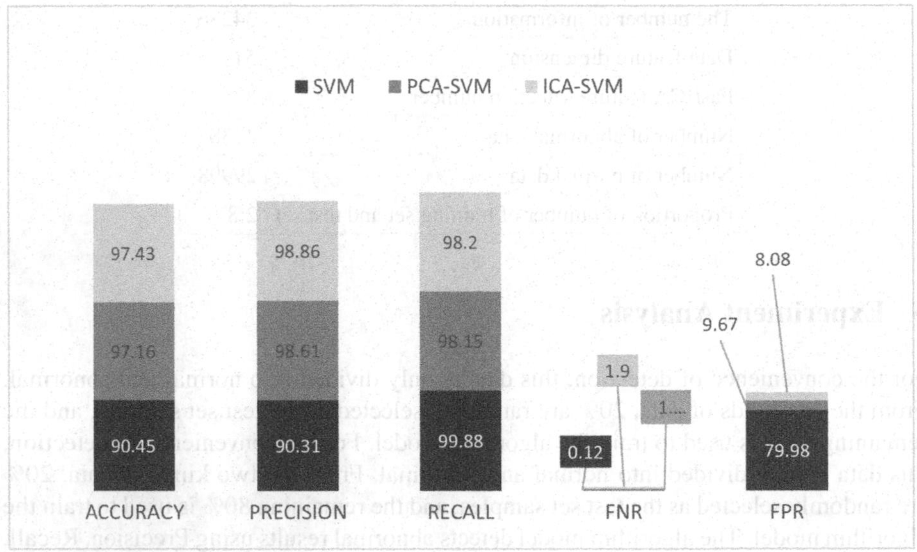

Fig. 3. SVM, PCA-SVM, FastICA-SVM algorithm test results comparison chart

Comparative experiment results show that the FastICA-SVM algorithm has the highest accuracy of 98.86%. And it is significantly higher than other algorithms in FNR and Precision.

6 Conclusion

In recent years, there have been more and more articles about anomaly detection in industrial control networks. However, in the past, many studies did not consider the complex correlation between the features of the data extracted on the spot when dealing with the process data. In this paper, based on the characteristics of FastICA algorithm, the data feature decoupling and dimensionality reduction are processed firstly. Secondly the data with independent features are obtained. Lastly the Swat data is processed in conjunction with the SVM classifier. The experimental results show that compared with the traditional intrusion detection algorithms SVM and PCA-SVM, the FastICA-SVM algorithm has higher accuracy and precision, and lower false negative rate. However, the content of this article still has some shortcomings. The algorithm only considers the conditions of medium-scale samples and does not conduct large-scale sample tests. It only pays attention to the accuracy of the algorithm test, and does not consider the real-time nature of the algorithm. Therefore, shortening the detection time as much as possible while ensuring the detection accuracy is next step of the research.

Funding Statement. This work is supported in part by "National Key R&D Program of China" (2019YFB2006300), Shenyang Science and Technology Development [2019] No. 66 (Z191001).

Conflicts of Interest. The authors declare that they have no conflicts of interest to report regarding the present study.

References

1. Shi, H., Shang, W., Chen, C., Zhao, J., Yin, L.: Key process Protection of High dimensional process data in complex production. Comput. Mater. Continua 645–658 (2019)
2. Jiang, J., Yasakethu, L.: Anomaly detection viaone class SVM for protection of SCADA systems. In: International Conference on Cyber-Enabled Distributed Computing and Knowledge Discovery, pp. 82–88 (2013).
3. Kim, G., Lee, S., Kim, S.: A novel hybrid intrusion detection method integrating anomaly detection with misuse detection. Expert Syst. Appl. **41**, 1690–1700 (2014)
4. Shang, W.L., Li, L., Wan, M.: Industrial communication intrusion detection algorithm based on improved one-class SVM. In: 2015World Congress on Industrial Control System Security, Londen, pp. 21–25 (2015)
5. Puyati, W., Walairacht, A.: Efficiency improvement for unconstrained face recognition by weightening probability values of modular PCA and wavelet PCA. In: 2008 10th International Conference on Advanced Communication Technology, Gangwon-Do, pp. 1449–1453 (2014)
6. Wei, T.: Asymptotic analysis of the generalized symmetric FastICA algorithm. In: 2014 IEEE Workshop on Statistical Signal Processing (SSP), Gold Coast, pp. 460–463 (2014)
7. Saideep, N., Kurup, D.G., Tripathi, S.: Detection of closely spaced sinusoids in noise using fastica algorithm. In: 2017 International Conference on Advances in Computing, Communications and Informatics (ICACCI), pp. 305–309 (2017)
8. Yang, Y., Wang, J., Yang, Y.: Industrial communication intrusion detection algorithm based on improved one-class SVM. In: 2015World Congress on Industrial Control System Security, pp. 21–25 (2015)
9. Puyati, W., Walairacht, A.: Improving SVM classifier with prior knowledge in microcalcification detection1. In: 2012 19th IEEE International Conference on Image Processing, pp. 2837–2840 (2012)
10. Peng, P., Ma, Q., Hong, L.: The research of the parallel SMO algorithm for solving SVM. In: 2009 International Conference on Machine Learning and Cybernetics, pp. 460–463 (2014)

KCFuzz: Directed Fuzzing Based on Keypoint Coverage

Shen Wang(✉), Xunzhi Jiang, Xiangzhan Yu, and Shuai Sun

School of Cyberspace Science, Harbin Institute of Technology, Harbin 150001, China
{shen.wang,jiangxunzhi,yuxiangzhan,sunshuai}@hit.edu.cn

Abstract. Directed fuzzing, as an efficient method to focus on a specific set of targets in the program, often works better than random fuzzing when combined with a researcher's empirical judgment. However, the current directed fuzzing work is not efficient enough. In previous studies, some have generated closer seed inputs by guiding the execution path through the distance from the target region, but the distance guided algorithm is less robust. Some studies used selective symbolic execution for directed testing to alleviate the path explosion problem, but it brings a higher false-positive rate. In this paper, we propose a keypoint coverage-based fuzzing (KCFuzz) method, which extracts the keypoint list using a control flow graph, obtains the keypoint list coverage information through runtime instrumentation, calculates the test priority of the seeds based on the overall coverage and keypoint coverage using an energy scheduling algorithm, and continuously generates test inputs closer to the target according to the specified mutation strategy. On this basis, a hybrid testing framework is implemented, using keypoint coverage directed fuzzing to generate a seed queue covering keypoints, using offspring generation strategies and hybrid execution technology, and further exploring the new state of the program according to changes in overall and keypoint coverage. The experimental results show that the KCFuzz method can efficiently induce the generation of seed queues to reach the target region, and at the same time, the depth and validity of the exploration paths are higher than those of the most advanced directed fuzzing methods such as AFLGo.

Keywords: Directed fuzzing · Keypoint coverage · Vulnerability mining

1 Introduction

In the field of vulnerability mining, fuzzing [8] has been the most concise and efficient testing solution, with the basic idea of providing a large number of randomly generated test cases to a program and monitoring for anomalous behavior (e.g., stack or buffer overflows, memory leaks, invalid reads and writes) [2]. The most important feature is that it does not require prior knowledge of the

X. Sun et al. (Eds.): ICAIS 2021, LNCS 12736, pp. 312–325, 2021.
https://doi.org/10.1007/978-3-030-78609-0_27

software and system to be tested and can be easily extended for functionality and applicability. Fuzzing is usually classified into white-box, gray-box, and black-box [5] based on the knowledge of the internal structure of the program. Gray-box fuzzing is more versatile [6] than white-box fuzzing because it does not depend on source code and is more accurate and intelligent than black-box fuzzing because it uses static or run-time information of the program, so gray-box testing is a more practical fuzzing technique. Specifically, AFL [11] and its variants [2,5–7,10] have attracted much attention.

Since gray-box fuzzing still relies on random mutations to generate test inputs, they are unable to focus on specific program states and test them adequately. The directed gray-box fuzzing solves this problem by generating test cases based on the code regions specified by the testers and driving the fuzzer through the corresponding methods and policies, so that the target program can execute to the specified code regions after running the test cases. Directed gray-box fuzzing is mainly applied to the recurrence of vulnerabilities based on patch comparison, the mining of vulnerabilities based on incomplete patches, the testing of vulnerabilities in suspicious regions, and the recurrence of crashes by vendors. Böhme et al. [1] recently proposed directed gray-box fuzzer AFLGo, based on the fuzzing framework AFL [11], calculating the distance from each basic block to many target locations utilizing Control Flow Graphs (CFGs) and Function Call Graphs (CG) derived from static analysis of the program. The distance between the execution path of the seed and the target region is used to determine whether this mutation is a more efficient seed, [4] which is then added to the seed pool and set to a high priority for further iterative testing. However, the feedback based on the path distance requires a complete construction of the entire program flow graph, and indirect calls and indirect judgment jumps in binary programs such as virtual table function pointers will cause the flow graph to be missing. Although some of the indirect call points can be recovered through pointer set value analysis or dynamic instrumentation, it is not universal.

To resolve the problem, we propose a novel directed gray-box fuzzing technique KCFuzz, which is based on the feedback algorithm of keypoint coverage to find a suitable set of keypoints, i.e., the parent nodes in the path to the target region. Using AFL as the basic framework, the program preprocessing and runtime coverage information acquisition is achieved through LLVM [10] instrumentation, and scripts are used to monitor the running state of the seed pool, extract the execution path of covered keypoints. Based on the overall coverage variation and keypoint coverage variation, seed priority and mutation strategies are set to generate seed queues that reach the target region. On this basis, the hybrid symbolic execution technology is combined to use the efficient test of coverage feedback fuzzing and symbolic execution to explore the deep code area, both of which share seed queues to achieve a balance of test diversity, exploration depth, and efficiency.

The main contributions of this paper are as follows.

- Proposed an energy scheduling algorithm based on keypoint coverage, which can effectively induce the generation of test cases that reach the target region in the absence of a complete call sequence. By capturing keypoint coverage information at runtime, seed priority and mutation strategies are set to generate seed queues that reach the target region based on the overall edge coverage variation and keypoint coverage variation.
- Proposed a directed fuzzing method based on hybrid execution, which explores the branches of the seed execution paths that have covered the keypoint locations by heuristic search algorithm. Actively guide the generation of test cases leading to the target area and realize deep exploration and path selection based on symbolic execution.
- Implemented KCFuzz, a directed fuzzing framework that uses keypoint coverage-based fuzzing tests to generate a seed queue covering a list of keypoints, feeding the seed queue to a hybrid symbolic execution engine that uses sub-generation strategies and hybrid execution techniques to bypass complex logic branches and deeply explore code regions of target points.
- The experimental results demonstrate that the depth and effectiveness of KCFuzz's exploration path are higher than the most advanced directional blur methods such as AFLGo.

2 Method

2.1 Keypoint Coverage Strategy Feedback

Store coverage information of all edges and keypoints at the same time. The LLVM pass in the Fuzzing phase is different from the previous LLVM pass that obtained CG and CFG, its main function is to obtain and store these two kinds of coverage information. The edge coverage is stored in bitmap_edge. Determine whether the current basic block is in the list according to the keypoint list obtained above, the keypoint coverage count is stored in bitmap_keypoint, and finally, the entire storage map is transferred to the shared memory. The Fuzzing program guides the seed selection and seed mutation process through an energy scheduling algorithm based on map changes.

The first stage is the initial fuzzing exploration stage. At this time, most of the keypoints in the definition list are not covered, and the AFL default edge coverage feedback method is used to guide the fuzzing process. Specifically, a random number is generated for each basic block to represent its location, the source address and target address of branch jump are recorded in the two-tuple, the XOR of the two is used as the key of the branch, and the execution times of each branch are stored at the same time, using 1 byte of storage as the value.

The second stage is when the key blocks in the list are covered, the second 64kb is used to store the count of the key basic blocks hit.

2.2 Energy Scheduling Algorithm Based on Keypoint Coverage

R. Padhye et al. [9] proposed a feedback model based on a specific domain. The target program under test collects runtime information according to the defined specific domain model and provides it to the main fuzzer process in the form of key-value pairs. A specified feedback method is implemented based on the reducer function to guide seed selection and generation. Based on this model, this paper implements an energy scheduling algorithm based on keypoint coverage.

The basic idea of the energy scheduling algorithm based on keypoint coverage is to find a series of parent nodes in the target code region. Based on the specified basic block, a complete CFG of keypoints is found through iteration and recursive reverse order. While also facing the problem of indirect calls, which can result in missing parent nodes. However, with the feedback based on the key basic block coverage, even if the coverage information is not available when the seed executes the path coverage to the missing parent node, but it can be sensed whenever a mutated seed executes to the parent node of the instrumentation, thus avoiding the complete ineffectiveness of the path distance directed algorithm due to the failure of path distance calculation.

Also, the algorithm does not need to calculate the distance from all basic blocks to the target point. And reverse recursion can locate the parent node of the uppermost indirect call. The context information is obtained by instrumentation analysis on the indirect call points located at the upper level, and then the set value analysis is used to further trace the upper parent node. In contrast, when AFLGo uses the shortest path distance calculation, it cannot judge whether it can reach the target position when encountering indirect calls.

The feedback method based on keypoints can be regarded as the mapping relationship: $kpf_i : K \rightarrow V$, where i is the program input, K is the set of keypoints, and V is the measurement information used for optimization. Define the key domain form as $d = (K, V, A, a_0, \triangleright)$, where A is the aggregate value set, a_0 is the initial aggregate value, $\triangleright : A \times V \rightarrow A$ is a reduction function. The energy scheduling algorithm is mainly used to update the kpf_i map obtained by the instrumentation when the program is running and the main fuzzing program to feedback the map.

For any $a \in A$, the reduction function of $v, v' \in V$ must satisfy the following properties:

$$a \triangleright v \triangleright v \tag{1}$$

$$a \triangleright v \triangleright v' = a \triangleright v' \triangleright v \tag{2}$$

For example, the keypoint is the code region allocated by memory, V and N are both natural numbers set N. The initial aggregate value a_0 is 0, and $\triangleright$ is the maximum value of natural numbers, so $d_{mem} = (L, N, N, 0, \max)$. Attribute 1 is satisfied: $\max(\max(a, v), v) = \max(a, v)$; attribute 2 is also satisfied $\max(\max(a, v), v') = \max(\max(a, v'), v)$. These two attributes ensure that every code region in the keypoint list can be fed back to the fuzzing process.

Define the decision function $is\_keypoint(i, S, D)$ as follows:

$$is\_keypoint(i, S, D) = \exists k \in K : p(S, k, d) \neq p(S \cup \{i\}, k, d) \quad \text{where } d = (K, V, A, a_0, \rhd) \tag{3}$$

which is used to save the seed input that causes the aggregated keypoint coverage information to change.

Algorithm 1. Energy scheduling algorithm based on keypoint coverage.

Input: instrumented program p, initial seed input S_0, key domain feedback D.
Output: Automatic generation of the corpus for input S.

$S \leftarrow S_0$
$totalCoverage \leftarrow \emptyset$
while given time budget not expires **do**
    for i in S **do**
        if sample fuzzprob(i) **then**
            $i' \leftarrow MUTATE(i)$
            $coverage, shf_{i'}^{1}, \ldots, shf_{i'}^{|D|} \leftarrow$ EXECUTE (p, i')
        if $coveragen \cap totalcoverage \neq \emptyset$ **then**
            $S \leftarrow S \cup \{i'\}$
            $totalCoverage \leftarrow totalCoverage \cup coverage$
        if $is\_keypoint\,(i', S, D)$ **then**
            $S \leftarrow S \cup \{i'\}$
return S

Algorithm 1 shows the fuzzing algorithm based on keypoint coverage feedback, which extends the traditional coverage-guided fuzzing algorithm. The gray area is part of the extended algorithm that differs from the standard coverage-based feedback algorithm. The fuzzing position collects not only the coverage information of the edges but also the hit information of a defined set of specific domains $shf_{i'}^{1}, \ldots, shf_{i'}^{|D|}$,these maps are passed to $is\_keypoint(i, S, D)$ to determine whether to treat input i as a high priority in the seed queue or to discard it.

In fact, in practice, a variety of specific domains can be combined for testing programs. Assuming that a specific domain set D is specified, corresponding to $d \in D$, $d = (K, V, A, a_0, \rhd)$ and the extension $is_keypoint$ is defined as follows:

$$is\_keypoint(i, S, D) = \forall_{d \in D} is\_keypoint(i, S, d) \tag{4}$$

For input i in S, $is\_keypoint(i, S, D)$ is true if it is true for any number of specific domains d in D. For example, given a set d_1, d_2, and d_3 containing three specific domains, which specify the number of loops of the base code, the code region of the specified sensitive memory operation, and the coverage information of the specified list of keypoints. The execution information of the seed file i changes the bucket corresponding to the coverage information of the list of keypoints, that is, $is\_keypoint(i, S, d_3)$ is satisfied, the seed file i is the keypoint; similarly, if the execution information of the seed file j does not change the number of loops in the execution region of d_1, nor does it change the override information of the list of key blocks executed by d_3, but changes the memory operation specified by d_2, then the seed j is also the keypoint.

2.3 Directed Fuzzing Technology Based on Hybrid Execution

Directed fuzzing technique based on the AFL framework for keypoint coverage, we study the directed fuzzing combined with the hybrid execution technology in symbolic execution. Based on the existing symbolic execution engine KLEE [3] for secondary development to achieve KLEE_cov.

KLEE belongs to the execution generation test in hybrid symbolic execution. General hybrid execution requires specific input to be executed simultaneously with the symbol execution, and execution generation test is to hybrid concrete values and symbolic values in the input.

Instead of the initial specific input, KLEE specifies a part of the symbol input or imposes limits on symbol value length or number of symbol files. Therefore, KLEE cannot directly utilize the seed files generated in the fuzzing for keypoint coverage. If the seed file in the fuzzing is used to perform analysis in KLEE, the seed file needs to be divided into two parts, one part as the concrete value and the other as the symbolic value. In this way, if the concrete value has a dependency on the symbolic value, it will not be possible to solve the resulting path constraint. To use KLEE, we need to change it from execution generation to hybrid execution.

The implementation method is as follows: enter the specific seed input into the bytecode file of the target program for concrete execution, maintain the symbolic state and concrete value, record the constraint conditions of the execution path, execute the symbolic value along the path guided by the concrete value at the branch, and finally solve the negative constraint to explore the new path. The method of hybrid execution is used to extract the complete execution path of the specific seed file and the constraint set of each conditional jump, and the inverse constraint solution can be selectively performed for some conditional branch jumps. For example, the reverse solution can be performed for the position judged as the turning point to generate the seed file closer to the target position. Through the combination of fuzzing and symbolic execution, the symbolic execution technique is used to quickly obtain the path constraints corresponding to the execution paths of these test seeds after the test seeds generated by the fuzzing based on keypoint coverage, and then selectively reverse the constraints to obtain new seeds for the next round of testing. The advantages of fast seed generation using fuzzing greatly save the memory and time consumption of KLEE using CopyOnWrite technology for symbol exploration and constraint solution. To avoid the influence of initial concrete value on symbol execution, partial bytes of input data can be modified to symbol variable for hybrid execution by traversing for a single specific input, avoiding repeated exploration of the same program state space.

2.4 Heuristic Search Algorithm

The latest version of KLEE includes a series of search algorithms including DFS, BFS, RandomState, and RandomPath. Modify the path search algorithm in KLEE, the modified version is called KLEE_cov, and add a new heuristic path selection algorithm to make the execution engine search for the target region more efficient. The new path search algorithm selects the path based on the depth of execution of the seed and the distance to the target region.

(1) Maintenance of execution information during specific execution.
Concrete execution is performed using test seeds generated from fuzzing based on keypoint coverage as the initial seeds of KLEE_cov. For example, concrete execution is performed using seed0 to obtain initial execution information including the number of instructions executed, edge count, basic block count, and overall coverage. This information is used as the initial baseline information.
(2) Maintenance of symbol state during symbol execution.
Get the paths covered by the concrete execution of seed0, the list of conditional branches, and the corresponding constraints, sort the symbolic run states according to the path depth, restore the symbolic run states of each conditional branch in turn, and store the constraint expressions for the unexplored children of each corresponding branch.
(3) Generation and representation of new constraints.
According to the symbol execution state obtained in (2) and sorted according to the path depth, extract the constraint set corresponding to the symbol status of each branch and the constraint expression of the unexplored branch in turn, merge the expressions, and then determine whether the constraints are solvable and wrong. If the solution fails to continue the path exploration of the next state, and finally get solvable constraints, the constraints are inverted to get a new set of constraints, and the solver is used to solve the problem to generate a new seed input seed0_i.
(4) Generation of offspring seeds.
The first-generation seed set seed0_i is implemented in sequence, and the concrete execution information ExePathProfile is obtained. Based on this information, the number of newly covered instructions, edge count, basic block count, etc. of each seed in seed0_i is calculated. What's more, we prioritize the first seed set and filter seed0_j as the initial stage of the second round of hybrid execution enter. The execution information obtained by the specific execution is used as feedback to select some seeds in the offspring for the next round of specific execution, which avoids the problem of path explosion and is more oriented.

The complete description of the process algorithm is shown in Algorithm 2.

2.5 KCFuzz Overview

The overall framework of KCFuzz is to generate seed queues that reach the target area through the energy scheduling algorithm covered by keypoints, so

Algorithm 2. Hybrid execution algorithm based on concrete execution coverage changes.

Input: instrumented program p, initial seed input S_0.
Output: Automatic generation of the corpus for input S.

```
ChildInput=S0
for i in ChildInput do
    InitialCoverage, ExecutionState* ← ConcreteExecution(i)
    SortByDepth(ExecutionState*)
    GenerateNewState(ExecutionState*,pendingExpr)
    for s in state do result=ResolvePendingState(s)
    if result==Failure then break
    if result==Unsat then continue
    fuzzbytes=GenerateChildFromState(s)
    ChildInput.append(fuzzbytes)
    for f in ChildInput do
        cov ← ConcreteExecution(f)
    ComputePriority(ChildInput)
while given time/memory bucket not expires do
    for f do in SortByPriority(ChildInput)
        S ← generationChildInput(f)
return S
```

that the mixed execution can quickly enter the parent node of the keypoints list, avoiding symbolic exploration in the early program state, but solving symbols at the turning point and the stop point, so as to achieve efficient mixed test. The overall structure of KCFuzz is shown in Fig. 1.

(1) Obtain a list of keypoints in the execution path to the target area through program preprocessing and analysis.
(2) The initial seed is input into the seed pool and passed to the input queue.
(3) The target program sequentially executes the test cases in the input queue, performs runtime analysis and monitors crash.
(4) Calculate the test priority of the seed according to the keypoint list coverage.
(5) Calculate the priority of the default AFL according to the seed size, execution time, execution times, etc.
(6) Comprehensive calculation of the final test priority.
(7) According to the priority, the seeds in the seed pool are mutated according to the mutation strategy and sent to the input queue
(8) When a list of keypoints is found to be covered, symbolic execution is introduced to induce the generation of closer seeds
(9) When it is found that it is impossible to explore a new path, symbolic execution is introduced, and the mutation generates the seed that makes the program enter a new state
(10) Neither mutation nor symbolic execution can make the test effective, track data correlation, and path the code.

(11) Seed pool cropping and minimizing seeds

Repeat (3)–(11)

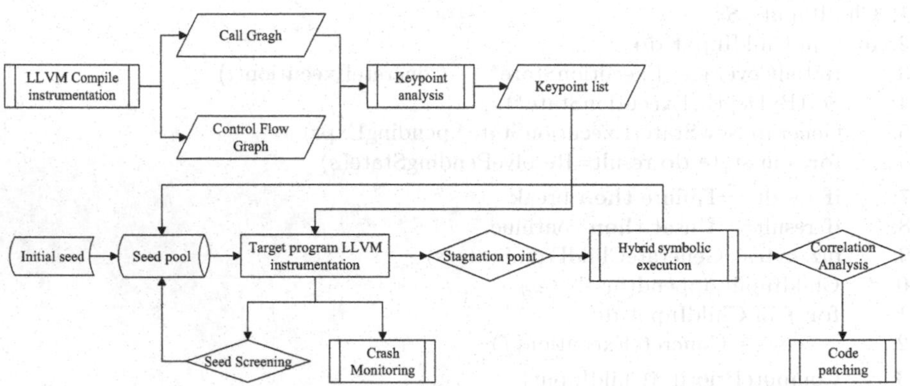

Fig. 1. Overall structure of KCFuzz

3 Experimental

3.1 KCFuzz Operational State Testing

In directed fuzzing, the overall program coverage remains an important fundamental metric for test efficiency and comprehensiveness. Higher overall coverage means that it can cover more running paths, reach deeper code regions, or execute branching paths that are difficult to trigger and are more likely to reach a given code region. On the other hand, KCFuzz's energy scheduling algorithm adopts a feedback method that integrates overall coverage and keypoint coverage. When none of the test queues in the seed pool covers the defined keypoints, the overall coverage feedback is used to drive the seed mutation and generation; when the execution path covers the keypoints, it switches to the basic block coverage feedback to guide the priority calculation of the seed queue and change the mutation generation of the seeds.

To test the overall coverage of KCFuzz, AFLGo, which is also a directed gray-box fuzzing framework, is selected for comparison testing, and KCFuzz is added to the vulnerability detection module Sanitizer for another set of control experiments. Here we select the libxml2 program for testing. libxml2 is a C language version of the XML parser and one of the programs in the Google fuzzer-test-suite[1] test benchmark. The same initial seed is used for the three frameworks, and the testing time for each framework is set to 12 h.

Where total_paths represents the total number of different execution states found (queued_paths), current_path represents the number of execution paths covered by the current fuzzing phase, pending_paths represents the number of

[1] https://github.com/google/fuzzer-test-suite.

inputs that have not yet been mutation tested, pending_favs represents the number of inputs waiting to enter fuzzing in the current queue cycle, and cycles_done represents the number of complete fuzzing cycles.

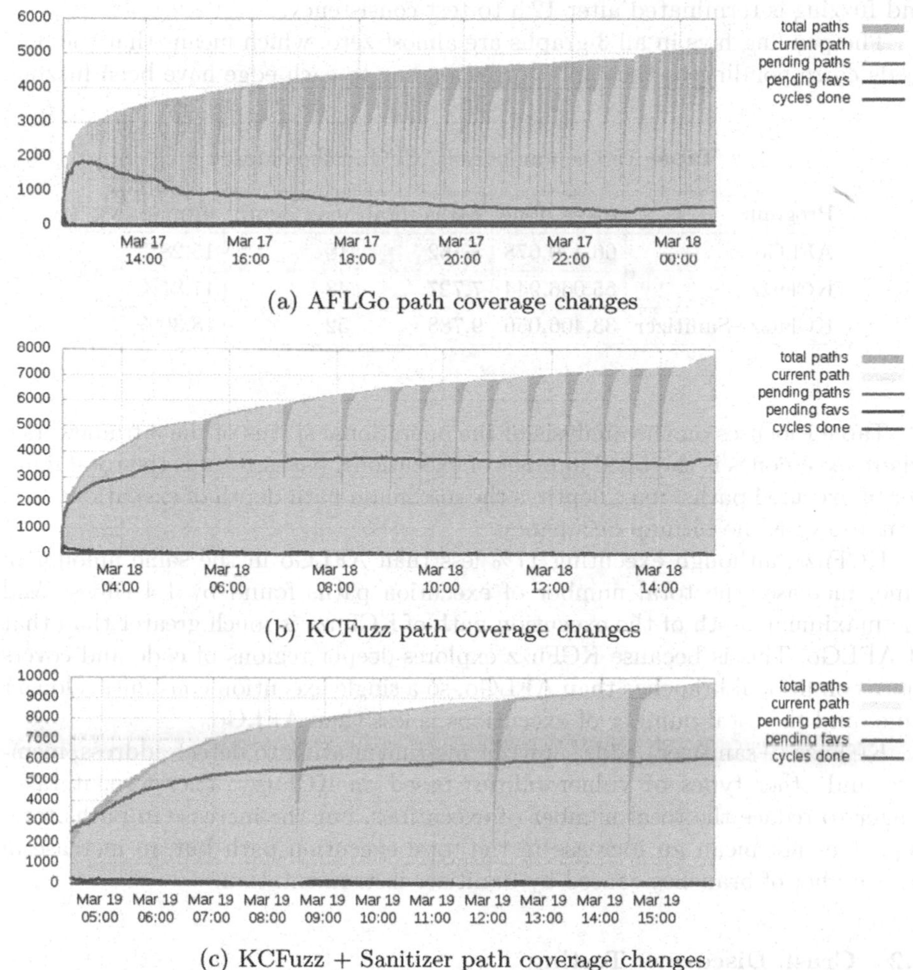

(a) AFLGo path coverage changes

(b) KCFuzz path coverage changes

(c) KCFuzz + Sanitizer path coverage changes

Fig. 2. Trend graph of the overall coverage of the 3 fuzzing frameworks AFLGo, KCFuzz and KCFuzz+Sanitizer

Figure 2(a) shows that the current_path changes dramatically, indicating that the seed mutations are highly variable. When the mutations destroy the legitimacy of the seed format, the program exits with a surface parsing error causing the coverage path to drop. Figure 2(b) and Fig. 2(c) show that the vast majority of KCFuzz does not exit early in the program.

The pending_paths in Fig. 2(a) drop rapidly after reaching their peak, indicating that the seeds in the queue that triggered the new path change are being fuzzed out, and the total_paths are not changing much, meaning that the likelihood of discovering new paths is low. Figure 2(b) and Fig. 2(c) show that the pending_paths are not decreasing, and the total_paths are increasing slowly, which means that new execution paths can be found if the test is continued, and fuzzing is terminated after 12 h to test consistency.

The pending_favs in all 3 graphs are almost zero, which means that the 'fav' seeds corresponding to the tuple corresponding to each edge have been fuzzing.

Table 1. The number of ACFG in the dataset

Program	execs_done	paths_total	max_depth	bitmap_cvg
AFLGo	66,440,678	5,162	18	15.28%
KCFuzz	55,066,944	7,727	48	11.87%
KCFuzz+Sanitizer	33,406,056	9,788	52	18.39%

Table 1 focuses on the analysis of the operational status of the 3 frameworks, where exec_dones is the total number of executions, paths_total is the total number of executed paths, max_depth is the maximum path depth of executions, and bitmap_cvg is the bitmap occupancy.

KCFuzz, although executing 17% less than AFLGo in the same amount of time, increases the total number of execution paths found by 1.4 times. And the maximum depth of the execution path of KCFuzz is much greater than that of AFLGo. This is because KCFuzz explores deeper regions of code and covers more conditional branches than AFLGo, so a single execution consumes a longer time, and the total number of executions is less than AFLGo.

KCFuzz (+sanitizer) adds sanitizer instrumentation to detect address, memory, and other types of vulnerabilities based on KCFuzz. Therefore, it takes longer to reduce the total number of executions, but the increase in paths_total here does not mean an increase in the total execution path but an increase in the number of branches caused by Sanitizer instrumentation.

3.2 Crash Discovery Testing

The ultimate goal of this paper is to test the ability of KCFuzz to discover and reproduce targeted crashes. In this experiment, the target point was set to a basic block in the xmlNewDocElementContent function (valid.c:952), which is a memory leak vulnerability and has the vulnerability number CVE-2015-8317. Figure 3(a) shows that over 12 h, AFLGo did not find the vulnerability in this location, and KCFuzz also did not find the expected crashes. It is worth noting that after KCFuzz added the Sanitizer when instrumenting the key blocks of libxml2, a large number of crashes were found. After further merging and analyzing these crashes, it is found that most of the crashes have the same cause and are classified into different uniq crashes due to the different backtrace,

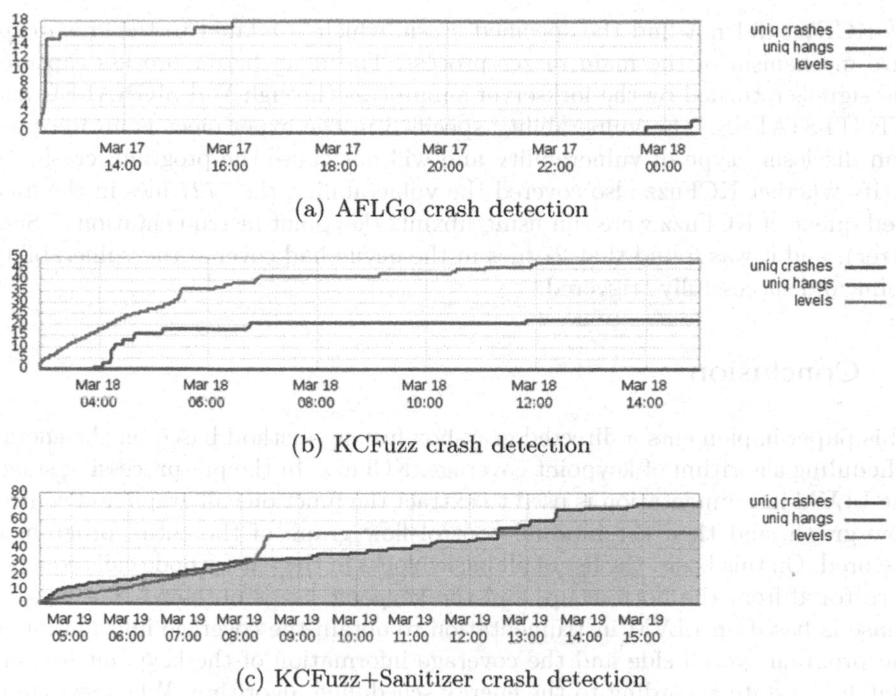

(a) AFLGo crash detection

(b) KCFuzz crash detection

(c) KCFuzz+Sanitizer crash detection

Fig. 3. Comparison of three fuzzy frameworks AFLGo, KCFuzz and KCFuzz+Sanitizer for crash detection

registers, and memory data of the crash site. Through the crash site analysis and judgment, it was finally judged as two crashes.

One of the crashes is a UAF type vulnerability, and the backtrace allows you to see part of the backtrace path, where some of the locations are in a predefined set of keypoints. The original allocation of the block was allocated by xmlmalloc in xmlDictLookup, and finally released in xmlDictFree in the xmlFreeParserCtxt function. However, the call to xmlDictComputeFastQKey in the xmlDictQLoookup function again uses this memory to cause the vulnerability. What's more, when the initial key block list is created, the xmlSAX2StartElementNs function encounters an indirect call problem for this vulnerability when backtracking to reach the xmlSAX2StartElementNs function cannot recursively find the parent node in reverse order, and the indirect call is caused by the function pointer. This will cause AFLGo's calculation based on path distance to fail and cannot induce seeds to generate seeds closer to the target. Whereas, KCFuzz's test case switches to keypoint coverage feedback once it runs to the topmost node xmlSAX2StartElementNs and gives high priority to the corresponding seeds, inducing seed mutation coverage to the child nodes closer to the target, which shows the effectiveness of the method in terms of path depth, keyblock coverage, and crash triggering.

KCFuzz did not find the specified crash, which is related to the crash capture mechanism of the main fuzzer process. The main fuzzer process captures the signals returned by the forkserver subprocess through WIFSIGNALED and WEXITSTATUS. The vulnerability specified in the experiment is an information disclosure type of vulnerability and will not cause the program. crash. To verify whether KCFuzz also covered the vulnerability, the 7727 files in the final seed queue of KCFuzz were run using libxml2 (keypoint instrumentation + Sanitizer), and it was found that 27 files in the queue had covered the vulnerability point and successfully triggered.

4 Conclusion

This paper implements a directed gray-box fuzzing method based on the energy scheduling algorithm of keypoint coverage: KCFuzz. In the pre-processing stage, the LLVM instrumentation is used to extract the function call graph and control flow graph, and then the internal control flow graph of the entire program is restored. On this basis, the list of all basic blocks in the parent node call sequence is restored from the bottom up, and the keypoint list is obtained. The fuzzing phase is based on LLVM instrumentation to obtain the coverage information of the program overall side and the coverage information of the keypoint list and switch the state according to the energy scheduling algorithm. When switching to the state based on the change of keypoint coverage, local small batch seed mutations are performed according to the specified mutation strategy to avoid deviating from the possible reachable calling sequence again. The experimental results show that the fuzzing based on keypoint coverage is robust and can effectively induce the generation of test cases that reach the target region in the absence of a complete call sequence.

Acknowledgment. The authors thanks the Information Countermeasure Technique Institute, Harbin Institute of Technology for the 1080Ti graphics card.

Funding Statement. This work is supported by the National Natural Science Foundation of China (Grant Number: 61471141, 61361166006, 61301099), Basic Research Project of Shenzhen, China (Grant Number: JCYJ20150513151706561), and National Defense Basic Scientific Research Program of China (Grant Number: JCKY2018603B006).

References

1. Böhme, M., Pham, V.T., Nguyen, M.D., Roychoudhury, A.: Directed greybox fuzzing. In: Proceedings of the 2017 ACM SIGSAC Conference on Computer and Communications Security, pp. 2329–2344 (2017)
2. Böhme, M., Pham, V.T., Roychoudhury, A.: Coverage-based greybox fuzzing as Markov chain. IEEE Trans. Software Eng. **45**(5), 489–506 (2017)

3. Cadar, C., Dunbar, D., Engler, D.R., et al.: KLEE: unassisted and automatic generation of high-coverage tests for complex systems programs. In: OSDI, vol. 8, pp. 209–224 (2008)
4. Chen, C., Cui, B., Ma, J., Wu, R., Guo, J., Liu, W.: A systematic review of fuzzing techniques. Comput. Secur. **75**, 118–137 (2018)
5. Chen, P., Chen, H.: Angora: efficient fuzzing by principled search. In: 2018 IEEE Symposium on Security and Privacy (SP), pp. 711–725. IEEE (2018)
6. Gan, S., et al.: CollAFL: path sensitive fuzzing. In: 2018 IEEE Symposium on Security and Privacy (SP), pp. 679–696. IEEE (2018)
7. Lemieux, C., Sen, K.: FairFuzz: targeting rare branches to rapidly increase greybox fuzz testing coverage. arXiv preprint arXiv:1709.07101 (2017)
8. Li, J., Zhao, B., Zhang, C.: Fuzzing: a survey. Cybersecurity **1**(1), 1–13 (2018). https://doi.org/10.1186/s42400-018-0002-y
9. Padhye, R., Lemieux, C., Sen, K., Simon, L., Vijayakumar, H.: FuzzFactory: domain-specific fuzzing with waypoints. Proc. ACM Program. Lang. **3**(OOPSLA), 1–29 (2019)
10. Wang, J., Chen, B., Wei, L., Liu, Y.: SkyFire: data-driven seed generation for fuzzing. In: 2017 IEEE Symposium on Security and Privacy (SP), pp. 579–594. IEEE (2017)
11. Zalewski, M.: American fuzzy lop (2017)

Deep Adversarial Learning Based Heterogeneous Defect Prediction

Ying Sun[1], Yanfei Sun[1,2(✉)], Fei Wu[1], and Xiao-Yuan Jing[1,3]

[1] Nanjing University of Posts and Telecommunications, Nanjing 210023, China
sunyanfei@njupt.edu.cn
[2] Jiangsu Engineering Research Center of HPC and Intelligent Processing, Nanjing 210003, China
[3] Wuhan University, Wuhan 430072, China

Abstract. Cross-project defect prediction (CPDP) is a hot study that predicts defects in the new project by utilizing the model trained on the data from other projects. However, existing CPDP methods usually assume that source and target projects have the same metrics. Heterogeneous defect prediction (HDP) is proposed and has attracted increasing attention, which refers to the metric sets from source and target projects are different in CPDP. HDP conducts prediction model using the instances with heterogeneous metrics from external projects and then use this model to predict defect-prone software instances in source project. However, building HDP methods is challenging including the distribution difference between source and target projects with heterogeneous metrics. In this paper, we propose a **D**eep adversarial learning based **HDP** (DHDP) approach. DHDP leverages deep neural network to learn nonlinear transformation for each project to obtain common feature represent, which the heterogeneous data from different projects can be compared directly. DHDP consists of two parts: a discriminator and a classifier that compete with each other. A classifier tries to minimize the similarity across classes and maximize the inter-class similarity. A discriminator tries to distinguish the source of instances that is source or target project on the common feature space. Expensive experiments are performed on 10 public projects from two datasets in terms of F-measure and G-measure. The experimental results show that DHDP gains superior prediction performance improvement compared to a range of competing methods.

Keywords: Adversarial learning · Metric learning · Heterogeneous defect prediction

1 Introduction

Software defect prediction (SDP) is an important step in software project development to improve software reliability and assure software quality, which has attracted increasing attention [1, 2]. SDP assists software developers in detecting potentially defective software instances before software release. Within-project defect prediction (WPDP) [3, 4] is a hot topic in prior works, which builds a prediction model by utilizing historical data

X. Sun et al. (Eds.): ICAIS 2021, LNCS 12736, pp. 326–337, 2021.
https://doi.org/10.1007/978-3-030-78609-0_28

of a project and then apply this model to judge the defect proneness of new instances within the same project. WPDP methods usually assume that we can obtain sufficient amount of historical data for model building. WPDP works well if the model is trained by sufficient data. In practice, sufficient and complete data is not always available. Collecting sufficient data from new project is difficult. Thus it is difficult to perform WPDP well without sufficient historical data. Therefore, cross-project defect prediction (CPDP) [6] has been proposed to build prediction model by using existing data from external projects and then predicting the labels of data from a new project.

The existing CPDP methods usually assume that the software metrics from different projects are same. In fact, the source project and target project may use heterogeneous metrics, i.e., the metrics we used and the number of the metrics are usually different. We call CPDP in heterogeneous scenario as heterogeneous defect prediction (HDP) [6, 7].

To address the problems of heterogeneous data from different projects, many methods have been proposed. Jing et al. [6] proposed a method named CCA+ which uses the unified metric representation to make the data from different projects can be compared, and uses canonical correlation analysis to maximize the correlation from different projects. Nam and Kim [7] used feature selection technique and feature match technique to reduce the remove irrelevant metrics and reduce the difference between source and target projects. These studies focused on feature selection technology. Recently, deep learning is used to extract features in many fields such as data mining and image processing, etc. Furthermore, these researches demonstrated that deep learning based methods can improve the performance of the model.

In this paper, we propose an approach called deep adversarial learning for heterogeneous defect prediction (DHDP). DHDP including feature mapping, discriminator and classifier. We adopt two fully-connected neural networks (FNNs) as feature mapping to transform the respective features to a common space, in this way the features of different projects can be directly compared. The discriminator maximizes the discrimination both in intra-projects and inter-project. The classifier is used to make the instances statistically indistinguishable by identifying the origin project of instance. These two parts are trained under the adversarial framework and compete with each other.

The rest of this paper is organized as follows. In Sect. 2, we discuss previous related works in SDP. In Sect. 3, we describe the details of the proposed DHDP approach. We give the experiment setting in Sect. 4. The experimental results are shown in Sect. 5. Finally, we make a conclusion in Sect. 6.

2 Related Works

2.1 Cross-Project Defect Prediction

To make full use of information from one or more projects, many cross-project defect prediction (CPDP) methods have been proposed in SDP studies [8–12]. Zimmermann et al. [13] first conducted CPDP model and only 3.4% of cross-project predictions had satisfactory experiment results. The experimental results showed that CPDP was a difficult challenge. Ma et al. [14] proposed transfer naïve bayes to reduce the distribution difference across projects. Xia et al. [9] proposed a hybrid method for CPDP. Herbold et al. [15] reproduced recent CPDP methods and then evaluated the prediction performance of the methods. They concluded that the method proposed by CamargoCruz and Ochimizu [16] always perform best for all datasets. Jing et al. [10] first introduce subclass discriminant analysis (SDA) in CPDP and unify it into both CPDP and WPDP. To solve class imbalance problem and semi-supervised learning problem, they improved SDA and proposed SSTCA + ISDA method. Wu et al. [17] proposed a method called CKSDL that considers the class imbalance problem and semi-supervised problem. They first applied semi-supervised dictionary learning technique for SDP. Zhou et al. [18] compared the performance between different CPDP methods in SDP and first used module size to build prediction models. These two unsupervised methods ManualDown and ManualUp have comparable prediction performance to most of the CPDP methods in this paper. Hosseini et al. [19] conducted systematic CPDP methods review with metrics, models, datasets and performance for providing guidelines for further studies.

2.2 Heterogeneous Defect Prediction

HDP refers to using data with heterogeneous metrics from different projects to build prediction models. To solve the heterogeneous problem, Jing et al. [6] proposed CCA + that utilized unified metric representation and CCA based transfer learning. Unified metric representation can make the data from different projects comparable, and CCA can maximize the correlation of the data across projects from different companies in the common space. Nam and Kim [7] proposed a HDP method, which applied metric selection and metric match technologies to make the metric similarity come closer. Then they built HDP model on the selected data. Li et al. [20] proposed CTKCCA that introduced cost-sensitive learning, kernel technique and CCA technology to address class imbalance problem and linearly inseparable problem in HDP.

2.3 Adversarial Learning

Adversarial learning is proposed in Generative adversarial network (GAN) by Goodfellow et al. [21] recently. The original GANs framework consist of two parts: a generative network G and a discriminative network D, which have opposite goals and compete with each other. G generates instances that D cannot distinguish the generated instances are real or fake during generation process; D distinguishes the real instances and fake instances during the discrimination process. The training goals of G and D are opposite and the objective function of GANs is defined as follows:

$$\min_{G}\max_{D} V(D,G) = E_{x\sim P_{data}(x)}\left[\log D(x)\right] + E_{x\sim P_{z}(z)}\left[\log(1 - D(G(z)))\right] \quad (1)$$

where x denotes the real input data, z denotes the noise input data. $P_{data}(x)$ is the distribution of data x, and $P_z(z)$ is the distribution of noise data z. G defines a probability generation distribution P_g as the distribution of the instances $G(z)$ obtained when $z \sim P(z)$, and this minimax game has a global optimum.

Adversarial learning has become the research hotspot gradually and has various applications in various fields, including visual tracking [22] and semantic segmentation [23], and improves the model performance. We introduce adversarial learning into

HDP for reducing the distribution difference between heterogeneous data from different projects.

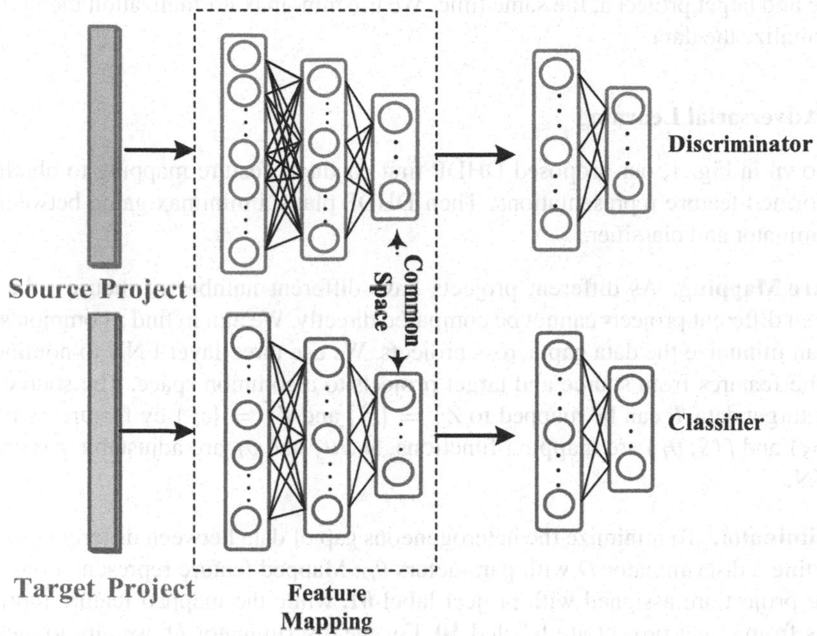

Fig. 1. The general architecture of DHDP consists of three major parts: feature mapping, discriminator and classifier

3 Proposed Approach

In this section, we describe the data preprocessing procedure and then describe the DHDP approach in detail. The conceptual illustration of DHDP is shown in Fig. 1.

3.1 Problem Formulation

Assume that $S = \{s_1, s_2, ..., s_m\} \in R^{d \times m}$ $T = \{t_1, t_2, ..., t_n\} \in R^{d \times n}$ separately denote the source and target project, where s_i denotes the ith instance in source project and t_i denotes the ith instance in target project. m and n represent the number of instances in source and target project. $Y^S = \{y_1^s, y_2^s, ..., y_m^s\} \in R^{m \times c}$ represents the label set of source data. $c = 2$ is the number of the class in SDP.

3.2 Data Preprocessing

We preprocess the data to improve the data quality by using the following preprocessing step:

Data Normalization: the metric values of different projects have different scales, which lead to obvious difference. The value magnitudes are scaled to appreciably low values by performing normalization. This normalization is applied to the data from both source and target project at the same time. We use min–max normalization method [24] to normalize the data.

3.3 Adversarial Learning

As shown in Fig. 1, our proposed DHDP first conducts feature mapping to obtain the transformed feature representations. Then DHDP plays a minimax game between the discriminator and classifier.

Feature Mapping. As different projects have different number of metrics, the data between different projects cannot be compared directly. We aim to find a common space that can minimize the data gap across projects. We use three-layer FNN to nonlinearly map the features from source and target projects to a common space. The source data S and target data T can be mapped to $Z^S = \{z_i^S\}$ and $Z^T = \{z_i^T\}$ by feature mapping. $f(S;\theta_S)$ and $f(S;\theta_T)$ are mapping functions, and θ_S and θ_T are adjustable parameters of FNN.

Discriminator. To minimize the heterogeneous gap of data between different projects, we define a discriminator D with parameters θ_D. Mapped feature representations from source project are assigned with project label **01,** while the mapped feature representations from target project are labeled **10**. For the discriminator D, we aim to increase the classification accuracy for an unknown instance. We use a two-layer FNN to implement the discriminator. In this step, a discrimination loss as adversarial loss L_D.based on cross-entropy function is defined as

$$L_D(\theta_D) = -\frac{1}{n_b}\sum_{i,j=1}^{n_b}\left(p_i\left(\log D\left(z_i^S;\theta_D\right)\right) + \log D\left(z_j^T;\theta_D\right)\right) \tag{2}$$

Each instance from different projects is assigned a project label p_i, which is expressed as one-hot vector. n_b is the number of instances in each batch. $D(.;\theta_D)$ is the generated project probability per project of an instance.

Classifier. To explore the discriminative information of intra-project data after feature mapping, a classifier is employed to predict the class (defective or defective-free) of an instance in the common space. We design a feed-forward network which uses softmax function on the last layer of neural network to predict the source data. The classifier takes the mapped data as input data in common space and generates a class probability $\hat{p}$ as output. The classifier loss L_C is defined as follows:

$$L_C(\theta_C) = -\frac{1}{m}\sum_{i}^{m} y_i^S \log \hat{p}_i(z_i^S) \tag{3}$$

where θ_C denotes the parameters of the classifier.

To further ensure that the instances from different classes are well separated and the instances from the same class are close, we design a pair-wise constraint. We design it based on the prior assumption of consistency, which means nearby instances are likely to belong to the same class, i.e., we consider that the instance has the same class with its nearby instance. Specifically, we expect the distance between an instance and another instance in the same class are closer than the distances between this instance and another instance from other class. For the given instances from source project and from target project, we compute the square distance $d(z_i^S, z_j^T)$. This can be formulated as the following equations:

$$\begin{aligned} d(z_i^S, z_j^T) \leq \gamma_1, \text{ if } \mathrm{I}_{ij} = 1 \\ d(z_i^S, z_j^T) \geq \gamma_2, \text{ if } \mathrm{I}_{ij} = -1 \end{aligned} \tag{4}$$

where $\mathrm{I}_{ij} = 1$ means that z_i^S and z_j^T are the nearby instances, and otherwise $\mathrm{I}_{ij} = -1$. γ_1 and γ_2 are small and large distance threshold values. The discriminative loss L_d between different projects is defined as:

$$L_d(\theta_C) = \sum_{i,j} \left\| z_i^S - z_j^T \right\|_2 + \sum_{i,j} f\left(1 - I\left(\gamma - d\left(z_i^S, z_j^T\right)\right)\right) \tag{5}$$

where $f(\cdot)$ is a logistic loss function, $\gamma_1 = \gamma - 1$ and $\gamma_2 = \gamma - 1$. The first term aims to reduce the difference for each similar training pairs. The second term exploits the discriminative information using the large margin criterion.

By combining the above losses, we can obtain the total function of the classifier loss L_{CL} as

$$L_{CL}(\theta_C) = L_C + \lambda L_d \tag{6}$$

3.4 Optimization

The optimal feature representations can be obtained by minimizing three loss terms in Eq. (2) and Eq. (6) together, which can be optimized through stochastic gradient descent algorithm. Considering that the optimization goals of discriminator and classifier are opposite, we employ the min-max game for optimization just as shown in the following sub-process:

$$\left(\hat{\theta}_S, \hat{\theta}_T, \hat{\theta}_D, \hat{\theta}_C\right) = \arg \min_{\theta_S, \theta_T, \theta_C} \left(L_C(\theta_S, \theta_T, \theta_C) - L_D\left(\hat{\theta}_D\right)\right) \tag{7}$$

$$\left(\hat{\theta}_D\right) = \arg \max_{\theta_D} \left(L_D\left(\hat{\theta}_S, \hat{\theta}_T, \hat{\theta}_C\right) - L_D(\theta_D)\right) \tag{8}$$

Table 1. An overview of projects used in experiment

Dataset	Project	Number of instances	Percentage of defective instances	Number of metrics
AEEEM	EQ	324	39.81	61
	JDT	997	20.66	61
	LC	691	9.26	61
	ML	1862	12.16	61
	PDE	1497	13.96	61
NASA	CM1	505	9.50	37
	MW1	403	7.69	37
	PC1	1107	6.97	37
	PC3	1563	10.24	37
	PC4	1458	12.21	37

4 Experimental Setup

4.1 Datasets

We perform experiments on publicly and available datasets from two datasets including AEEEM [25] and NASA [26] datasets. The details about these datasets are shown in Table 1.

AEEEM is collected by D'Ambros et al., and each project consists of 61 metrics including o-o metrics, previous defects, entropy code metrics, etc. NASA dataset is commonly used to build different defect prediction models. Each project dataset contains the class labels and various static code metrics.

Table 2. Confusion matrix

		Predicted	
		Positive	Negative
Actual	Positive	TP	FN
	Negative	FP	TN

Table 3. Formulation

Measure	Definition
Pd	$TP/(TP+FN)$
Pf	$FP/(FP+TN)$
Precision	$TP/(TP+FP)$
F-measure	$\frac{2*Pd*Precision}{Pd+Precision}$
G-measure	$\frac{2*Pd*(1-Pf)}{Pd+(1-Pf)}$

4.2 Evaluation Measures

We totally employ two widely used measures F-measure [20] and G-measure [18] to evaluate the performance of the prediction models. The measures can be defined by using False Positive (FP), True Positive (TP), False Negative (FN), and True Negative (TN) in the matrix in Table 2.

F-measure is a harmonic mean measure that balance *Pd* and *Precision*, which ranges from 0 to 1 (from worst to best). *Pd* denotes the ratio of the number of defective instances correctly predicted to the number of defective instances, and *Precision* denotes the ratio of the number of defective instances to the number of instances that are predicted correctly. *G-measure* is the harmonic mean of *Pd* and *Pf*, which is a good indicator of performance for SDP. *Pf* denotes the ratio of the number of defective-free instances wrongly predicted to the number of defective-free instances. Table 3 shows the formulations in this paper.

4.3 Baselines

We compare DHDP with two HDP methods: CCA + [6], HDP-KS [7] and two representative CPDP methods CKSDL [17] and ManualDown [18]. Specifically, we use the common metrics from different projects on CPDP methods.

4.4 Experiment Settings

We organize the HDP setting on the project from different datasets. For example, we select one project from the dataset as the target data, and separately use other projects from the other dataset as source data.

We conduct experiments with different parameters of the networks on different datasets. For feature mapping, we employ three-layer FNN to feature mapping. For project discriminator, we use a two-layer FNN and the classifier also uses a two-layer FNN. The batch size is set as 64 and the parameters λ is set as 0.1 empirically.

Table 4. Comparison results in F-measure for each target project

Projects	ManualDown	CKSDL	CTKCCA	HDP-KS	DHDP
EQ	0.65	0.27	0.35	0.53	**0.66**
JDT	0.41	0.28	0.35	0.64	**0.67**
LC	0.21	0.44	0.33	0.47	**0.68**
ML	0.25	0.26	0.35	0.53	**0.69**
PDE	0.33	0.28	0.35	0.57	**0.72**
CM1	0.34	0.48	0.33	0.34	**0.52**
MW1	0.29	0.28	0.33	0.28	**0.34**
PC1	0.29	0.25	0.35	0.48	**0.60**
PC3	0.32	0.29	0.45	0.35	**0.51**
PC4	0.31	0.16	0.45	0.53	**0.68**
Average	0.34	0.30	0.37	0.47	**0.61**

5 Experimental Results

Tables 4 and 5 report the values of F-measure and G-measure for DHDP versus baselines on AEEEM and NASA datasets. The values in bold denote the best performance. Compared with two CPDP methods, DHDP achieves the best performance of two measures on average prediction performance. Compared with two HDP methods, DHDP achieves the best values of F-measure and G-measure on average prediction and performs best on most of projects of G-measure.

We use a widely used statistical test called Scott-Knott effect size difference (ESD) test [28] to clarify whether DHDP statistically performs better than other baselines. Scott-Knott ESD test merges different treatment means into statistically different groups.

From Fig. 2, we can see the results of statistical test for DHDP and baselines on all the projects in F-measure and G-measure. X-axis and y-axis in Fig. 2 represent the methods and ranking values, respectively. Different colors represent different groups with statistical significance. From the figure, DHDP always has the lowest ranking and has the different groups with the baselines. It means DHDP significantly outperforms the related methods with statistical significance.

Table 5. Comparison results in G-measure for each target project

Project	ManualDown	CKSDL	CTKCCA	HDP-KS	DHDP
EQ	**0.70**	0.58	0.55	0.63	0.69
JDT	0.61	0.68	0.55	0.57	**0.70**
LC	0.56	0.52	0.53	0.67	**0.68**
ML	0.55	0.65	0.55	0.57	**0.69**
PDE	0.61	0.68	0.55	0.63	**0.68**
CM1	0.60	0.55	0.53	**0.66**	0.53
MW1	0.60	0.68	0.54	0.68	**0.68**
PC1	0.60	0.63	0.55	0.62	**0.66**
PC3	0.59	0.69	0.63	0.53	**0.72**
PC4	0.64	0.15	0.63	0.63	**0.68**
Average	0.61	0.58	0.56	0.62	**0.67**

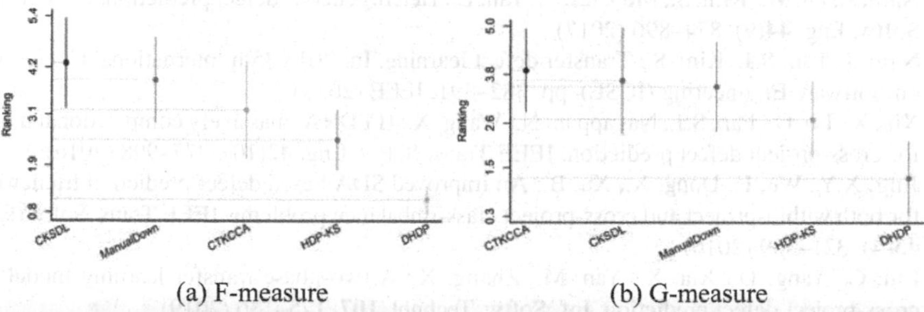

(a) F-measure (b) G-measure

Fig. 2. Statistical results with Scott-Knott ESD test in F-measure and G-measure across all projects for DHDP. The smaller ranking, the better performance.

6 Conclusions

In this paper, we propose a novel DHDP approach for HDP, which aims to learn discriminative representations in common space. DHDP uses adversarial learning into two processes: a discriminator tries to distinguish the project label of unknown feature representations to minimize the distribution gap between different projects; a classifier generates that enhance the discrimination of feature representations in common space. The experiment results on two widely used datasets have demonstrated that DHDP outperforms baselines.

Funding Statement. This paper was supported by the National Natural Science Foundation of China (61802208 and 61772286), China Postdoctoral Science Foundation Grant 2019M651923, and Natural Science Foundation of Jiangsu Province of China (BK0191381).

Conflicts of Interest. The authors declare that they have no conflicts of interest to report regarding the present study.

References

1. Catal, C.: A comparison of semi-supervised classification approaches for software defect prediction. J. Intell. Syst. **23**(1), 75–82 (2014)
2. Fu, W., Menzies, T.: Revisiting unsupervised learning for defect prediction. In: Proceedings of the 2017 11th Joint Meeting on Foundations of Software Engineering, pp. 72–83 (2017)
3. Arar, O.F., Ayan, K.: Software defect prediction using cost-sensitive neural network. Appl. Soft Comput. **33**, 263–277 (2015)
4. Li, J., He, P., Zhu, J., Lyu, M.R.: Software defect prediction via convolutional neural network. In: 2017 IEEE International Conference on Software Quality, Reliability and Security (QRS), pp. 318–328. IEEE (2017)
5. He, Z., Shu, F., Yang, Y., Li, M., Wang, Q.: An investigation on the feasibility of cross-project defect prediction. Autom. Softw. Eng. **19**(2), 167–199 (2012)
6. Jing, X., Wu, F., Dong, X., Qi, F., Xu, B.: Heterogeneous cross-company defect prediction by unified metric representation and CCA-based transfer learning. In: Proceedings of the 2015 10th Joint Meeting on Foundations of Software Engineering, pp. 496–507 (2015)
7. Nam, J., Fu, W., Kim, S., Menzies, T., Tan, L.: Heterogeneous defect prediction. IEEE Trans. Softw. Eng. **44**(9), 874–896 (2017)
8. Nam, J., Pan, S.J., Kim, S.: Transfer defect learning. In: 2013 35th International Conference on Software Engineering (ICSE), pp. 382–391. IEEE (2013)
9. Xia, X., Lo, D., Pan, S.J., Nagappan, N., Wang, X.: HYDRA: massively compositional model for cross-project defect prediction. IEEE Trans. Softw. Eng. **42**(10), 977–998 (2016)
10. Jing, X.Y., Wu, F., Dong, X., Xu, B.: An improved SDA based defect prediction framework for both within-project and cross-project class-imbalance problems. IEEE Trans. Softw. Eng. **43**(4), 321–339 (2016)
11. Liu, C., Yang, D., Xia, X., Yan, M., Zhang, X.: A two-phase transfer learning model for cross-project defect prediction. Inf. Softw. Technol. **107**, 125–136 (2019)
12. Zhu, K., Zhang, N., Ying, S., Zhu, D.: Within-project and cross-project just-in-time defect prediction based on denoising autoencoder and convolutional neural network. IET Softw. **14**(3), 185–195 (2020)
13. Zimmermann, T., Nagappan, N., Gall, H., Giger, E., Murphy, B.: Cross-project defect prediction: a large scale experiment on data vs. domain vs. process. In: Proceedings of the 7th Joint Meeting of the European Software Engineering Conference and the ACM SIGSOFT Symposium on the Foundations of Software Engineering, pp. 91–100 (2009)
14. Ma, Y., Luo, G., Zeng, X., Chen, A.: Transfer learning for cross-company software defect prediction. Inf. Softw. Technol. **54**(3), 248–256 (2012)
15. Herbold, S., Trautsch, A., Grabowski, J.: A comparative study to benchmark cross-project defect prediction approaches. IEEE Trans. Softw. Eng. **44**(9), 811–833 (2017)
16. Cruz, A.E.C., Ochimizu, K.: Towards logistic regression models for predicting fault-prone code across software projects. In: 2009 3rd International Symposium on Empirical Software Engineering and Measurement, pp. 460–463. IEEE (2009)
17. Wu, F., et al.: Cross-project and within-project semisupervised software defect prediction: a unified approach. IEEE Trans. Reliab. **67**(2), 581–597 (2018)
18. Zhou, Y., et al.: How far we have progressed in the journey? An examination of cross-project defect prediction. ACM Trans. Softw. Eng. Methodol. **27**(1), 1–51 (2018)
19. Hosseini, S., Turhan, B., Gunarathna, D.: A systematic literature review and meta-analysis on cross project defect prediction. IEEE Trans. Softw. Eng. **45**(2), 111–147 (2017)

20. Li, Z., Jing, X.Y., Wu, F., Zhu, X., Xu, B., Ying, S.: Cost-sensitive transfer kernel canonical correlation analysis for heterogeneous defect prediction. Autom. Softw. Eng. **25**(2), 201–245 (2018)
21. Goodfellow, I., et al.: Generative adversarial networks. In: Proceedings of the International Conference on Neural Information Processing Systems, pp. 2672–2680 (2014)
22. Song, Y., et al.: VITAL: visual tracking via adversarial learning. In: Proceedings of the IEEE Conference on Computer Vision and Pattern Recognition, pp. 8990–8999 (2018)
23. Hung, W.C., Tsai, Y.H., Liou, Y.T., Lin, Y.Y., Yang, M.H.: Adversarial learning for semi-supervised semantic segmentation. arXiv preprint arXiv:1802.07934 (2018)
24. Kotsiantis, S.B., Kanellopoulos, D., Pintelas, P.E.: Data preprocessing for supervised leaning. Int. J. Comput. Sci. **1**(2), 111–117 (2006)
25. D'Ambros, M., Lanza, M., Robbes, R.: An extensive comparison of bug prediction approaches. In: 2010 7th IEEE Working Conference on Mining Software Repositories, pp. 31–41. IEEE (2010)
26. Menzies, T., Greenwald, J., Frank, A.: Data mining static code attributes to learn defect predictors. IEEE Trans. Softw. Eng. **33**(1), 2–13 (2006)
27. Jureczko, M., Madeyski, L.: Towards identifying software project clusters with regard to defect prediction. In: Proceedings of the 6th International Conference on Predictive Models in Software Engineering, pp. 1–10 (2010)
28. Tantithamthavorn, C., McIntosh, S., Hassan, A.E., Matsumoto, K.: An empirical comparison of model validation techniques for defect prediction models. IEEE Trans. Softw. Eng. **43**(1), 1–18 (2016)

Smart Grid Data Anomaly Detection Method Based on Cloud Computing Platform

Jiahua Liu[1,2], Shang Wu[3], Wanwan Cao[3](✉), Yang Guo[3], and Shuai Gong[3]

[1] NARI Group Corporation/State Grid Electric Power Research Institute, Nanjing 211000, People's Republic of China

[2] Nari Information Communication Technology Co., Ltd., Nanjing 210003, People's Republic of China

[3] Information and Communication Branch of State Grid Anhui Electric Power Co., Ltd., Hefei 230009, People's Republic of China

Abstract. Aiming at the problem of untimely fault detection caused by the large number and wide distribution of power grid equipment, this paper designs a cloud computing platform-based smart grid data anomaly detection method. This method uses cloud computing architecture to design a grid smart cloud platform, and realizes the aggregation and storage of large amounts of data in the cloud platform. After that, the STL decomposition method is used to decompose the electricity meter data on the cloud platform, and then the decomposed residual data is used for abnormal analysis to complete the detection of abnormal data in the smart grid. And the accuracy of the method is verified through experiments.

Keywords: Smart grid · Cloud computing · Decomposition · Abnormal detection

1 Introduction

As the scale of power construction continues to expand, the scope of smart grid coverage continues to increase, and various power operation data in the grid system also increase [1]. When there are problems in the grid system, such as substation equipment failure, electric meter fuse, transmission line interruption, etc. [2], the meter data in the smart grid will subsequently be abnormal. Therefore, real-time monitoring and abnormal detection of meter data in the power grid can detect abnormalities or accidents in the power grid in time, and avoid more serious power loss and equipment damage caused by failure to handle failures in time [3]. Anomaly detection on data in the smart grid has great economic and safety value for the smart grid.

Anomaly detection has always been a hot field in data analysis. According to different detection methods, traditional anomaly detection methods are generally divided into statistics-based, density-based, cluster-based, classification-based, and spectral decomposition-based. However, the power grid equipment data is time-series data with temporal correlation, so the anomaly of the time series must be judged according to the context information [4], the traditional anomaly detection method is not applicable.

X. Sun et al. (Eds.): ICAIS 2021, LNCS 12736, pp. 338–345, 2021.
https://doi.org/10.1007/978-3-030-78609-0_29

The current anomaly detection algorithm for time series can be divided into time series decomposition method, classification and regression tree [5], ARIMA [6], exponential smoothing [7] and neural network [8]. Compared with the following methods, the time series decomposition method has a simpler algorithm and shorter time required for the algorithm to run. Therefore, it is more suitable for applications where the amount of data is large and the timeliness requirements are relatively high. However, there are numerous and widely distributed power grid equipment. If an abnormality detection model is installed in each substation, a large amount of human and financial resources will be consumed. If the regional substation equipment data is collected and processed, the single-node algorithm model cannot meet the huge data volume requirements in the power grid, which will result in failure to detect abnormalities in time. Therefore, this paper designs a power grid cloud platform that collects and summarizes equipment data and other functions. At the same time, the STL (Seasonal and Trend decomposition using Loess) decomposition method is run on the cloud platform, and the powerful computing power of the cloud platform and the MapReduce structure decomposition task are used to realize the rapid analysis and abnormal detection of huge data, and complete the detection of abnormal data in the smart grid.

2 Preparation

2.1 Cloud Computing Architecture

Cloud computing is an Internet-based computing method that provides individual users or corporate users with on-demand computing through heterogeneous network interconnection and autonomy [10]. Cloud computing is an emerging IT service delivery method, which has the characteristics of ultra-large scale, versatility, high scalability, low cost, high reliability, and on-demand services [11]. Therefore, it can provide users with a more convenient and efficient experience and a lower service cost. The application scenarios of cloud computing have also increased, and IDC cloud, enterprise cloud, cloud storage system, development and test cloud, collaboration cloud, etc. have been widely used [12].

Cloud computing architecture is usually divided into two parts: service and management [13]. The service part provides users with various cloud-based services, including software services, platform services and infrastructure services. The management part is based on the management layer, which can timely and effectively manage the cloud computing center to ensure the stability and safety of the entire cloud computing center.

2.2 STL Decomposition Method

A Seasonal-Trend Decomposition Procedure Based on Loess proposed by Robert B Cleveland, that is, STL is a decomposition algorithm specifically used to process time series data. Its principle is to use robust local weighted regression as a smoothing method to decompose a certain time series $Y = (T, X)$ into three components, namely trend component Q, periodic component C and residual component R.

$$Y_i = Q_i + C_i + R_i \tag{1}$$

The trend component can show the rate of change of low frequency in the time series, the periodic component can show the periodic change of frequency, and the residual component, as the name suggests, is the component of the time series after removing the trend component and the periodic component.

STL time series decomposition algorithm is mainly divided into two parts, namely inner loop and outer loop. In the inner cycle stage, Loess smoothing of the time series Y is required to obtain the trend component Q and the period component C. In the outer loop part, the residual component is obtained.

The smoothing process is as follows. For a point (t_i, x_i) in the time series, the interval size is determined to be s_c, and the weight value w_j^i of a time point t_j in the interval is as follows

$$w_j^i = \left(1 - (\frac{|x_j - x_i|}{x_{\text{Farthest}} - x_i})^3\right)^3 \tag{2}$$

Where x_{Farthest} represents the point farthest from x_i in the interval. Perform linear regression on x_i through x_j to obtain a smooth straight line $y' = a + bt$, then the smooth value at time point t_i is y_i',For the time series Y, after the interval size is determined as s_c, the subsequence can be obtained. By smoothing the subsequence, the periodic subsequence C′ can be obtained, and low-pass filtering is performed on it to obtain the low frequency component L, then the periodic component C = C′ − L. then:

$$Q' = Y - C \tag{3}$$

Smooth Q′ with an interval size of s_q to obtain the trend component Q. Then the residual component R = Y − Q − C.

3 Model Building

3.1 Smart Grid Cloud Computing Architecture

Figure 1 shows the overall framework of the smart grid cloud computing platform proposed in this paper. It is divided into display cloud layer, computing cloud layer, data cloud layer, infrastructure cloud layer and management cloud layer. Among them, the display cloud layer provides software services, through which users can issue commands and obtain feedback. Calculation cloud layer and data cloud layer provide platform services, and huge computing tasks are completed in this layer. The infrastructure cloud layer provides infrastructure services, which provide hardware and software support for cloud computing. The management cloud layer provides management of accounts, security, operation and maintenance, services, billing, etc., and efficiently manages the entire smart grid cloud computing platform to ensure the stable operation of the entire platform.

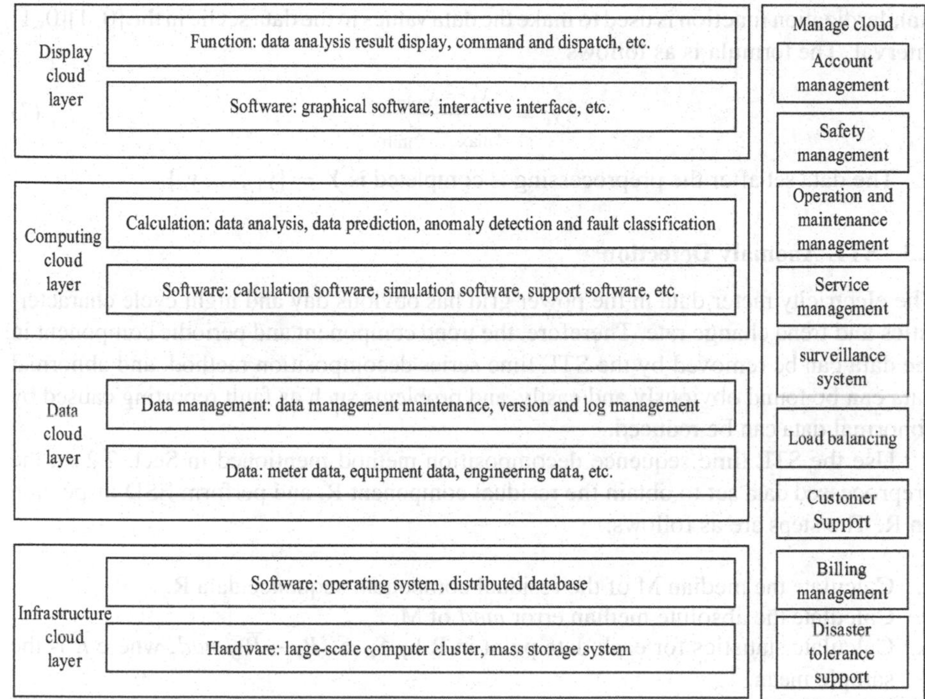

Fig. 1. The overall framework of the smart grid cloud computing platform.

3.2 Data Preprocessing

Since the electricity meter data in the smart grid has a wide range of sources and has been transmitted for a long time, there will be problems with missing data and inconsistent formats. Therefore, before data decomposition, the data needs to be preprocessed. This paper uses Newton interpolation to complete the missing data, and then uses the min – max standardization function to standardize all data with inconsistent formats.

Suppose the original data set corresponding to time series $T = \{t_1, ..., t_n\}$ is $X = \{x_1, ..., x_n\} = \{f(t_1), ..., f(t_n)\}$, if the (t_i, x_i) data is missing, then

$$\begin{aligned} P(t_i) &= f(t_1) + (t_i - t_1)f[t_2, t_1] + (t_i - t_1)(t_i - t_2)f[t_3, t_2, t_1] + ... \\ &+ (t_i - t_1)(t_i - t_2)...(t_i - t_{n-1})f[t_{n-1}, ..., t_2, t_1] \end{aligned} \tag{4}$$

$$R(t_i) = (t_i - t_1)(t_i - t_2)...(t_i - t_n)f[t_{n-1}, ..., t_2, t_1] \tag{5}$$

$$x_i = f(t_i) = P(t_i) + R(t_i) \tag{6}$$

Among them, $i = 1, ..., t$, and $f[t_i, t_j]$ is the first-order difference quotient of $f(t)$ at points t_i and t_j, $P(t_i)$ is the Newton interpolation approximation function, and $R(t_i)$ is the remainder function.

Suppose the data set that completes the missing value completion is $X' = \{x'_1, ..., x'_n\}$, where the largest data value is x'_{max}, and the smallest data value is x'_{min}, and the min – max standardization function is used to make the data values in the data set lie in the [0, 1][0, 1] interval. The formula is as follows

$$y_i = \frac{x'_i - x'_{\min}}{x'_{\max} - x'_{\min}} \quad (7)$$

The data set after the preprocessing is completed is $Y = \{y_{1,}, \ldots, y_n\}$.

3.3 STL Anomaly Detection

The electricity meter data in the power grid has obvious day and night cycle characteristics and trend change rate. Therefore, the trend component and periodic component in the data can be removed by the STL time series decomposition method, and abnormal data can be found obviously and easily, and problems such as fault reporting caused by abnormal data can be reduced.

Use the STL time sequence decomposition method mentioned in Sect. 2.2 on the preprocessed data set to obtain the residual component R, and perform ESD inspection on R. The steps are as follows:

1. Calculate the median M of the residual component sequence data R.
2. Calculate the absolute median error *mad* of M.
3. Calculate statistics for each data point in R by $S_i = (R_i - \overline{R})/mad$, where $\overline{R}$ is the sample mean.
4. Count the largest number in S. If the number is greater than the threshold σ, it will be regarded as an abnormal point and will be removed from the time series data set.
5. Iteratively execute steps 1–4.

4 Experiment Analysis

The experimental data in this paper is selected from the 2020 transformer data collected by a substation of the State Grid Jiangsu. 70% of the data is used as the training set and the remaining 30% is used as the test set. In order to verify the feasibility of the algorithm, the following Figs. 2 and 3 show the detection accuracy of changing the parameters s_c, s_q and observing the algorithm respectively.

In order to verify the performance of the algorithm, as shown in Fig. 4, by comparing the algorithm in this paper with ARIMA and regression tree, the accuracy and recall rate are used to measure the superiority of the algorithm in this paper.The accuracy formula is:

$$ACC = \frac{TP + TN}{TP + FP + FN + TN} \quad (9)$$

The recall formula is:

$$REC = \frac{TP}{TP + FN} \quad (10)$$

Among them, TP means that the true outliers are distinguished, FP means that non-outliers are classified as outliers, FN means that true outliers are not distinguished, and TN means that non-outliers are not classified as outliers.

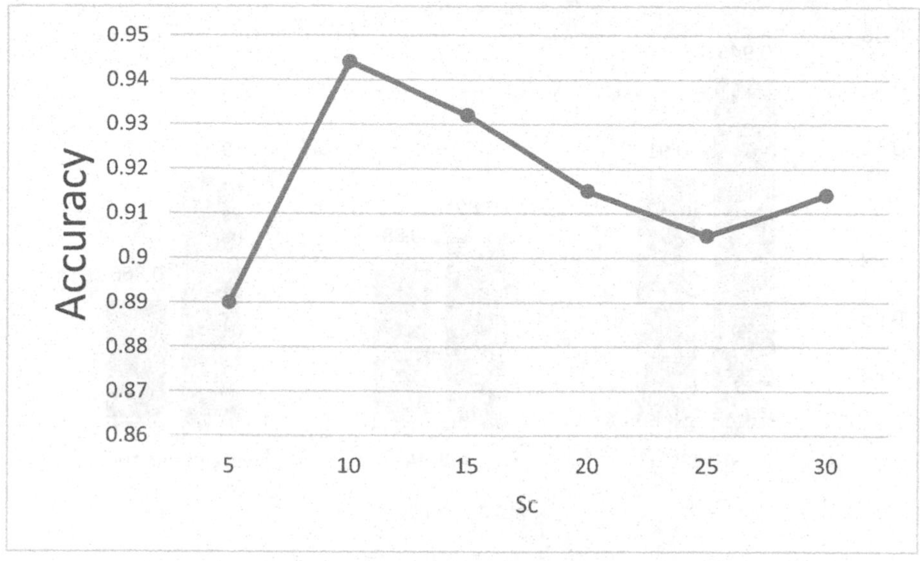

Fig. 2. The influence of parameter on the accuracy of the algorithm.

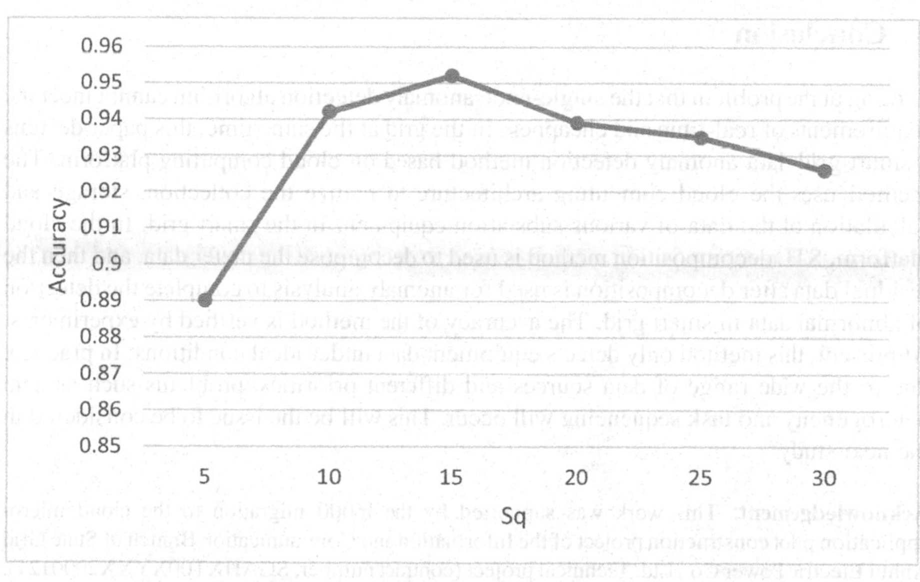

Fig. 3. The influence of parameter on the accuracy of the algorithm

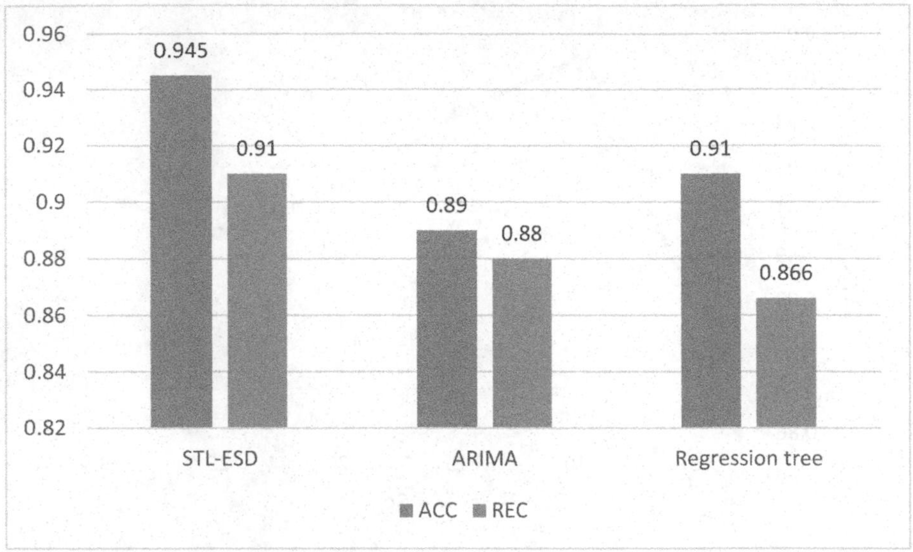

Fig. 4. 3 algorithm evaluation indicators

5 Conclusion

Aiming at the problem that the single-node anomaly detection algorithm cannot meet the requirements of real-time and cheapness in the grid at the same time, this paper designs a smart grid data anomaly detection method based on cloud computing platform. The method uses the cloud computing architecture to realize the collection, storage and calculation of the data of various substation equipment in the smart grid. In the cloud platform, STL decomposition method is used to decompose the meter data, and then the residual data after decomposition is used for anomaly analysis to complete the detection of abnormal data in smart grid. The accuracy of the method is verified by experiments. At present, this method only detects equipment data under ideal conditions. In practice, due to the wide range of data sources and different priorities, problems such as data heterogeneity and task sequencing will occur. This will be the issue to be considered in the next study.

Acknowledgement. This work was supported by the I6000 migration to the cloud micro-application pilot construction project of the Information and Communication Branch of State Grid Anhui Electric Power Co., Ltd. Technical project (contract number: SGAHXT00XYXX2000121).

References

1. Zhang, L., Shen, X., Zhang, F., Ren, M., Ge, B., Li, B.: Anomaly detection for power grid based on time series model. In: 2019 IEEE International Conference on Computational Science and Engineering (CSE) and IEEE International Conference on Embedded and Ubiquitous Computing (EUC), New York, NY, USA, pp. 188–192 (2019)

2. Jian, Z., Guo, J., Xu, X., Wang, B., Yi, Y., Ye, H.: Risk analysis of wild fire on electric grid transmission lines considering cascading failure. In: 2019 IEEE 3rd Conference on Energy Internet and Energy System Integration (EI2), Changsha, China, pp. 872–876 (2019)
3. Jianfeng, D., Jian, Q., Jing, W., Xuesong, W.: A vulnerability assessment method of cyber physical power system considering power-grid infrastructures failure. In: 2019 IEEE Sustainable Power and Energy Conference (iSPEC), Beijing, China, pp. 1492–1496 (2019)
4. Qin, Y., Lou, Y.: Hydrological time series anomaly pattern detection based on isolation forest. In: 2019 IEEE 3rd Information Technology, Networking, Electronic and Automation Control Conference (ITNEC), Chengdu, China, pp. 1706–1710 (2019)
5. Chen, J., Chen, M., Wei, X., Chen, B.: Matrix differential decomposition-based anomaly detection and localization in NFV networks. IEEE Access **7**, 29320–29331 (2019)
6. Radoglou-Grammatikis, P.I., Sarigiannidis, P.G.: An anomaly-based intrusion detection system for the smart grid based on CART decision tree. In: 2018 Global Information Infrastructure and Networking Symposium (GIIS), Thessaloniki, Greece, pp. 1–5 (2018)
7. Dinh, P.T., Lee, T., Canh, T.N., Dang, S.P., Chul Noh, S., Park, M.: Abnormal SDN switches detection based on chaotic analysis of network traffic. In: 2019 25th Asia-Pacific Conference on Communications (APCC), Ho Chi Minh City, Vietnam, pp. 250–255 (2019)
8. Andryukhin, E.V., Veligura, A.N.: Industrial network anomaly behavior detection via exponential smoothing model. In: 2018 IEEE Conference of Russian Young Researchers in Electrical and Electronic Engineering (EIConRus), Moscow, pp. 1458–1462 (2018)
9. Wang, X., Zhao, T., Liu, H., He, R.: Power consumption predicting and anomaly detection based on long short-term memory neural network. In: 2019 IEEE 4th International Conference on Cloud Computing and Big Data Analysis (ICCCBDA), Chengdu, China, pp. 487–491 (2019)
10. Jia, R., Yang, Y., Grundy, J., Keung, J., Li, H.: A highly efficient data locality aware task scheduler for cloud-based systems. In: 2019 IEEE 12th International Conference on Cloud Computing (CLOUD), Milan, Italy, pp. 496–498 (2019)
11. De Donno, M., Tange, K., Dragoni, N.: Foundations and evolution of modern computing paradigms: cloud, IoT, edge, and fog. IEEE Access **7**, 150936–150948 (2019)
12. Fowley, F., Pahl, C., Jamshidi, P., Fang, D., Liu, X.: A classification and comparison framework for cloud service brokerage architectures. IEEE Trans. Cloud Comput. **6**(2), 358–371 (2018)
13. Gill, S.S., Buyya, R.: Failure management for reliable cloud computing: a taxonomy, model, and future directions. Comput. Sci. Eng. **22**(3), 52–63 (2020)

A Flexible Planning Approach Using Label Member

Li Xu, Wohuan Jia, Yueqi Li, and Linshan Shen(✉)

College of Computer Science and Technology, Harbin Engineering University, Harbin 150001, China
shenlinshan@hrbeu.edu.cn

Abstract. In this paper, we present a novel approach to flexible planning based on a two-stage paradigm of label member generation and solution extraction. The approach provides a new perspective on the flexible planning problem and speeds up the process of the problem solving in the artificial intelligence system plan. On the basis, we propose a novel algorithm based on label member by thoroughly exploring the structure of flexible planning graph, and apply the memorization strategy and heuristic information to prune the search space. The algorithm is provably sound, complete and polynomial-time and polynomial-space of label member generation. And the problems handled by the algorithm are more complex than the classical ones and much closer to the real world, which makes the solution plan safer. Else, because of wide application of intelligent planning, our research is very helpful to the development of artificial intelligent, robotology, intelligent agent, machine learning and so on.

Keywords: Intelligent planning · Flexible graphplan · Label member

1 Introduction

Intelligent planning is an intersectional subject which deals with knowledge representation, data mining, human-machine interaction, intelligent security, cognitive science and so on [1–6]. Not only is its development of importance in artificial intelligence, but it also will fundamentally change the traditional way the human operates a computer. Its research started in the 1950's. The problem solving system QA3 designed by Green in 1969 is considered as the first intelligent planning system. The STRIPS planner, designed by Fike and Nilsson in 1971, have historical significance in intelligent planning, in which knowledge representation and reasoning methods deeply affect later planning systems. But confined to objective conditions, the field was under the conservative state at one time. It was not until the end of 1980's that the planning field was improved greatly. Over the last few years we have seen a significant improvement of the efficiency of planning systems. This is mainly due to several new approaches in plan generation. One of approaches was Graphplan proposed by Blum and Furst. In their seminal paper on the Graphplan system, they described a new plan generation algorithm based on planning graph, which was much faster than any other algorithms known at that time. Graphplan caused revolutionary progress in intelligent planning, and it started a whole series

X. Sun et al. (Eds.): ICAIS 2021, LNCS 12736, pp. 346–357, 2021.
https://doi.org/10.1007/978-3-030-78609-0_30

of research efforts [7–10] that refined this approach by making it even more efficient and by extending it to improve the quality of plan. However, planning problems under Graphplan framework are cast in terms of imperative constraints that are either wholly satisfied or wholly violated. It is argued that this framework is too rigid to capture the full subtlety of many real problems. Hence, a new flexible planning problem is defined, which supports the soft constraints often found in reality. This paper just discusses this kind of complicated problems - flexible planning problems [11–13].

Flexible planning method, introduced by Miguel in 2000, has considered AI planning problems in terms of both the techniques to improve the efficiency of plan synthesis and the extension of the classical domain definition to support soft constraints. Some flexible problems in theory and in practice are international puzzles, but a lot of famous scholars home and abroad still devote themselves to the research. Many highly efficient flexible planning methods have been developed. The most remarkable approach in them was flexible Graphplan. This paper just introduces a novel flexible planning algorithm based on label field by thoroughly exploring the structure of flexible planning graph, which extends and improves the flexible Graphplan in several ways. The memory occupied by the approach is much less than flexible Graphplan's and the speed is faster. Therefore, the algorithm has good performance in terms of time and space.

2 The Limitation of Graphplan

In the real world, there exists a case that the users need a safe, satisfactory, high-quality plan beyond caring about the complexity of plan. Namely, they care how well the goal is arrived, not how to arrive. In order to deal with this case, the planning algorithm must capture the detail of problems and some ideas of users, but the classical valid plan was weighed by the length, which don't take into account the user's requirement and taste. Furthermore, the practice also proves that it has become increasingly clear that classical AI planning is insufficient to capture the full subtlety of many real world problems.

This paper discusses the problems in *STRIPS-like* domains. The section will analyze the reasons why the classical planning method exists some shortages. An illustrative example follows, derived from the logistics domain (see Fig. 1).

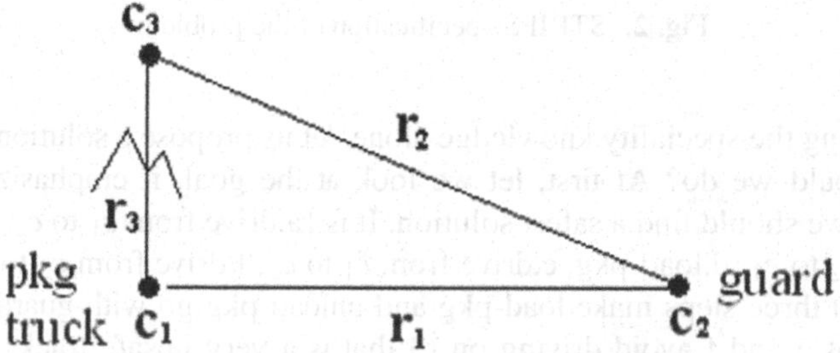

Fig. 1. An example of flexible planning problem

In Fig. 1, c_i represent city, r_i represent road. The single goal of this problem is to transport pkg to c_3. There are three possible actions: load, drive, and unload. Load-object requires object and truck are at the same place. Unload-object has precondition "on object truck".

This problem has a valid plan apparently, that is {*load-pkg, drive from* c_1 *to* c_3*, unload-pkg*}. But now the problem becomes more complex. The problem is added much detail: firstly, we know the package is quite valuable; secondly, r_1 and r_2 are major roads and r_3 is a very unsafe track through the hills; Last, the goal of this problem is to transport pkg to c_3 safely, that is, we emphasize safety based on the original goal (Fig. 2).

Initial Conditions: (and(at truck C_1)(at pkg C_1)(at guard C_2)(connects r_1 C_1 C_2)
(connects r_2 C_2 C_3)(connects r_3 C_1 C_3))

Goal: (at pkg C_3)

operator:

load

params: (?t truck)(?o pkg)(? o guard)(?c city)
: precondition(at ? t ? c)(at ? o ? c)
: effect(on ? o ? t)

drive

params: (?t truck)(? c city)(? d city)(? r road)
: precondition(at ? t ? c)(connects ?r ? c ? d)
: effect(at ? t ? d)

unload

params: (?t truck)(? o pkg)(? o guard)(? c city)
: precondition(at ? t ?c) (on ? o ? t)
: effect(at ? o ? c)

Fig. 2. STRIPS specification of the problem

Now, leaving the speciality knowledge alone, let us propose a solution for the problem. How should we do? At first, let we look at the goal, it emphasizes safety not efficiency, so we should find a safest solution. It is {a.drive from c_1 to c_2, b.load-guard, c.drive from c_2 to c_1, d.load-pkg, e.drive from c_1 to c_2, f.drive from c_2 to c_3, g.unload-pkg}. The first three steps make load-pkg and unload-pkg go with guard's protection, while the steps e and f avoid driving on r3 that is a very unsafe track. This solution includes seven steps, four steps more than the classical one, but it considers the detail of the problem and safety that is what goal emphasizes.

Graphplan can not acquire the 7-step solution, because it will end when it acquire a 3-step plan. This is owing to it is insufficient to capture the total detail of the planning problem. The classical Graphplan is helpless to the large and complex real world problems, so a means of expressing priorities and preferences via flexible constraints is required. Flexible planning method emerges as the times require.

3 Flexible Planning

We can see from the example above, that flexible planning method can synthesize the detail of problems and user's taste. It trades the compromise between plan length and satisfaction degree, and it pays more attention to the quality of plan.

3.1 Important Definitions

Definition 1: Satisfaction degree

L is composed of a finite number of membership degrees, $l_{\perp}, l_1, l_2, \cdots, l_{\mathrm{T}}$. The endpoints, $l_{\perp} \in L$ and $l_{\mathrm{T}} \in L$ respectively denote a complete lack of satisfaction and a complete satisfaction. The no-op action is a special case which has a satisfaction of l_{T}. Satisfaction degrees are used to express how satisfactory people are when to carry out an action under the given preconditions.

Definition 2: Subjective degree of truth

K is composed of a finite number of membership degrees, $k_{\perp}, k_1, k_2, \cdots, k_{\mathrm{T}}$. Boolean propositions are captured at the endpoints of K, with $k_{\perp} \in K$ and $k_{\mathrm{T}} \in K$ indicating total falsehood and total truth respectively.

The set of the example is defined as $k_{\perp}, k_1, k_2, k_{\mathrm{T}}$. Here, it is very natural and reasonable to apply membership function in fuzzy mathematics to evaluate subjective degree of truth of the flexible propositions.

Definition 3: Flexible propositions

A flexible proposition is described by a fuzzy relation, R, which is defined by a membership function $\mu_R(\cdot) : \phi_1 \times \phi_2 \times \Lambda \times \phi_j \to K$, where $\phi_1 \times \phi_2 \times \Lambda \times \phi_j$ is the Cartesian product of the subsets of Φ (the set of plan objects).

Flexible propositions are assigned subjective truth degrees. The flexible operators map from the space of flexible preconditions to a set of flexible effects and a satisfaction degree. Therefore, subjective knowledge can be utilized to entail inferences over preferred combinations of actions. For example, "valuable package k_2" is a flexible proposition. The content of the proposition is subjective, which is the detail of the problem. We assume the package value 100 dollars. Some think it is valuable, others think not. Whether the package is valuable or not lies on subjective consciousness. If we add the flexible proposition "valuable package k_2" in initial conditions, it can express the user thinks the package valuable comparatively. Flexible propositions are very important because we can add the detail of problems and the subjective consciousness into them.

Definition 4: Label field

A totally ordered set which is composed of a finite number of label member.

Definition 5: Label member

A positive integer, an element of label field. For each proposition or action, the label member is the number of the layer at which it appears in the graph for the first time. For each mutex, the label member is the number of the layer at which it appears in the graph for the last time.

3.2 Flexible Planning Problem

```
(operator load
  (params(?t truck)(?p pkg)(?l location)(?g guard))
    {when
      (preconds(at ?t ?l)(at ?p ?l)(valuable ?p≤k1))
      (effects(on ?p ?t)(at ?p ?l))
      (satisfaction lT)}
    {when (preconds(at ?t ?l)(at ?p ?l)(on ?g ?t) (valuable ?p≥k2))
          (effects(on ?p ?t)(at ?p ?l))
          (satisfaction lT)}
    {when (preconds(at ?t ?l)(at ?p ?l) (not(on ?g ?t)) (valuable ?p≥k2))
          (effects(on ?p ?t)(at ?p ?l))
          (satisfaction l2)})
(operator drive
  (params(?v vehicle)(?o location)(?d location)  (?r1 major-road)(?r2 track))
  {when (preconds(at ?v ?o)(connects ?r1 ?o ?d))
    (effects (not (at ?v ?o)(at ?v ?d))
    (satisfaction lT)}
  {when (preconds(at ?v ?o)(connects ?r2 ?o ?d))
        (effects (not (at ?v ?o)(at ?v ?d))
        (satisfaction l1)})
```

Fig. 3. The flexible operators-load and drive

A flexible planning problem consists of 4-tuple, <Φ, O, I, Γ>, denoting the sets of plan objects, flexible operators, initial conditions consisting of flexible propositions, and flexible goal conditions respectively.

(1) The set of plan objects is the same with classical ones.
(2) A flexible operator, $o \in$ O, must recognize how well its preconditions are satisfied. Flexible operators are described by fuzzy relations which map from the precondition space to a totally ordered satisfaction scale, L and a set of flexible effect propositions. A flexible operator (see Fig. 3) consists of a set of disjoint conditional clauses, Σ. Each $\sigma \in \sum$ is a triple $<\Theta, E, k_i>$ respectively denoting a conjunction of flexible preconditions, a conjunction of flexible effect propositions and the satisfaction degree of this operator given these preconditions. Each σ_i maps a subset of the space of preconditions to a particular set of effects and a satisfaction degree in L.
(3) Initial conditions include flexible propositions which will affect the valid plan and its satisfaction degree.
(4) A flexible plan goal $r \in \Gamma$ maps from the space of flexible propositions to L. Each goal is defined using a number of clauses, as shown in Fig. 4. In it, θ is a flexible proposition and l is satisfaction degree.

```
(goad r
        {when θ_i (satisfaction l_i )}
          {when θ_j (satisfaction l_j )})
```

Fig. 4. General formats of flexible goals

Because of the particularity of flexible planning, the participation of man in planning is necessary. The fuzzy characteristic of man's own determines the fuzzy characteristic of flexible planning. So it is reasonable to exploit fuzzy theory to flexible planning algorithm. And the introduction to flexible planning problem is given above.

4 Flexible Graphplan

Below, in order to shed light on the sources of strength of flexible Graphplan, we introduce flexible Graphplan algorithm.

4.1 Satisfaction Degree Propagation

In flexible Graphplan, expanding the flexible planning graph needs to propagate satisfaction degrees of propositions and actions. As is well known, the approach of satisfaction degree propagation has a notable impact on the efficiency of the flexible Graphplan algorithm, and it is recognized as the emphasis and the difficulty in the flexible Graphplan algorithm. We pay enough attention to the problem in this paper as well.

(1) The satisfaction degrees of propositions
Label proposition nodes with highest satisfaction degree of those attached to all actions that assert it as an effect.
(2) The satisfaction degrees of actions
The satisfaction degrees of actions equal to the lowest satisfaction degree among its own and the satisfaction degrees attached to each precondition.
(3) The satisfaction degree of flexible plan
We can acquire the satisfaction degree of flexible plan by the satisfaction degree of actions and propositions. The satisfaction degree of a flexible plan is defined as the conjunctive combination of the satisfaction degrees of each action and each goal used in the plan. The quality of a plan is its satisfaction degree combined with its length, where the shorter of two plans with equivalent satisfaction degree is better.

4.2 Description of the Algorithm

Flexible Graphplan algorithm is composed of two phases: construction of flexible planning graph and flexible plan extraction. The algorithm begins with explicitly constructing flexible planning graph, which offers a means of organizing and maintaining search information. Flexible solution extraction involves searching for a sequence of actions and solving the flexible planning problem, which can be done by a backward search over the flexible planning graph structure. The two parts will be carried out alternately.

In the phase of construction of flexible planning graph, initial conditions are placed in the first proposition level of the graph at first. A generic action level is generated as follows. Each clause of each flexible operator is instantiated in all possible ways to propositions of the previous level. Provided that all preconditions are not mutex, an action instance with the associated satisfaction is inserted to the flexible planning graph for each such instantiation. Also insert all the no-ops and the precondition edges. Then check the action nodes for mutexes and memorize these mutexes. To create a generic proposition level, simply place all the add effects of the actions (including no-ops) of the previous level in the proposition level, connecting them via the appropriate add and delete edges. Mark two propositions as mutex if all ways of generating the first are mutex of all ways of generating the second, and infer the satisfaction degree for each proposition.

Flexible plan extraction from a flexible planning graph may be viewed as solving a CSP. Propositions are regarded as CSP variables whose domain elements are the actions which produce the associated proposition as an effect. In addition, unary preference constraints are constructed from the satisfaction degrees associated with each action, specifying a preference degree for each potential assignment. Boolean binary constraints are generated from the mutexes in the flexible planning graph. Each variable instantiation represents the choice of an action node to support the proposition node represented by the variable. The preconditions of each chosen action must also be supported. Continue the process above until it either succeeds or has proven that the goal set is not reachable.

4.3 Analyzing the Structure of Flexible Planning Graph

From the introduction above, we can see flexible Graphplan algorithm is based on constructing and analyzing a flexible planning graph.

By exploiting the following observations concerning monotonicity in the flexible planning graph, we can draw a conclusion that one can avoid duplicated work during expanding a flexible planning graph.

Propositions are monotonically increasing: if proposition p is present at level i, it will appear at level $i + 1$ and at all subsequent proposition levels.

Actions are monotonically increasing: if action a is present at level i, it will appear at level $i + 1$ and at all subsequent action levels.

Mutexes are monotonically decreasing: if mutex m between actions a and b is present at level i, then m is present at all previous action levels in which both a and b appear. The same is true for mutexes between propositions.

Nogoods are monotonically decreasing: if subgoals p, q and r are unachievable at level i, then they are unachievable at all previous proposition levels.

These observations suggest one can discard a multi-level flexible planning graph. Instead, all one needs is memorizing a set of label members. Action, proposition, mutex, and nogood are all annotated with an integer label member: for proposition and action nodes, this integer denotes the first flexible planning graph level at which the proposition or action appears; for mutex and nogood nodes, the label member marks the last level at which the relation holds. One may interleave forward expansion and backward extraction to search a solution plan by adding an additional label member. By this scheme, the costs of time and space during expansion phase are vastly decreased. The idea is shown in the following algorithm.

5 The Flexible Planning Algorithm Based on Label Field

In the following part, we first describe the algorithm, then apply memorization and prune strategy to improve its performance, and prove that the time and space complexity of the generation of label member is polynomial.

5.1 Description of the Algorithm

Our algorithm is composed of two parts: generation of label member and flexible plan extraction. The two parts will be carried out alternately.

*Part*1. Generation of label member for each proposition, action and mutex.
*Step*1. The label members of all propositions are initialized to ∞.
*Step*2. The construction of the proposition set with label member "1".
All the initial conditions are set to label member "1".
*Step*3. The construction of the action set with label member "1".
For each clause of each operator, there is a counter, which is initialized to 0. If a precondition of the clause appears in the proposition set with label member "1", get its counter incremented. As soon as the counter for a clause reaches the total number of its preconditions, the clause can be instantiated. All the clauses initialized come into being the action set with label member "1" (not including no-ops).
The satisfaction degrees of the actions equal to the satisfaction degrees of associated clauses given these preconditions and the values vary with the generation of label member.

*Step*4. The construction of the action-action mutex set with label member "1".
Examine action-action mutexes in the actions with label member "1" and the no-ops that maintain the propositions with label member "1" according to the definition of mutex stated above. If exist, set the label member of these mutexes to "1". The mutex set varies with the generation of label member.
*Step*5. The construction of the proposition set with label member "*i*".
The effects of actions with label member "$i-1$", if not present in the proposition set with label member lower than or equal to $i-1$, just have label member "*i*".
Infer the satisfaction degrees of the propositions with label member lower than and equal to *i* according to the approach stated above.
*Step*6. The construction of the proposition-proposition mutex with label member "*i*".
Examine proposition-proposition mutexes in the propositions with label member lower than or equal to *i* by using the definition of mutex stated above. If the proposition-proposition mutexes with label member "$i-1$" still exist, change their label members to "*i*", and set the label members of new proposition-proposition mutexes to "*i*". The mutex set varies with the generation of label member.
*Step*7. Exit.
If each goal has a label member lower than ∞, and no pairwise propositions of the goal set is in the proposition-proposition mutex set with label member "*i*", then the algorithm is over and turn to search a valid plan.
Else, if no propositions are labeled "*i*" in *Step*5, and the proposition-proposition mutex set with label member "$i-1$" is empty after Step6, then it shows no valid plan exists (this is equivalent with planning graph has been level off from time step $i-1$ on[1]). The algorithm is over.
*Step*8. The construction of the action set with label member "*i*".
For each clause of each operator, there is a counter, which is initialized to 0. If a precondition of the clause appears in the proposition set with label member lower than or equal to *i*, get its counter incremented. As soon as the counter for a clause reaches the total number of its preconditions and the label members of the proposition-proposition mutexes concerning any two of these preconditions are lower than *i*, the clause can be instantiated into action. These actions (not including no-ops), if not present in the action set with label member lower than or equal to $i-1$, just have label member "*i*".
Infer the satisfaction degrees of the actions with label member lower than and equal to *i* according to the approach stated above.

---

[1] *Proof.* No propositions are labeled "*i*" in *Step*5, which is equal to that there are no new propositions generated in level *i* of the flexible planning graph, namely, the propositions in level*i* are the same as those in level $i-1$. In addition, just because the propositions in level *i* and in level $i-1$ are the same and mutexes are monotonically decreasing, proposition-proposition mutex relations can not increase in level *i*, which accordingly implies the actions that can be applied to the two levels are the same. Else, since proposition-proposition mutex set with label member "$i-1$" is empty after *Step*6, the mutex relations do not decrease either, that is to say, the mutexes in level *i* are not changed. To sum up, the propositions, the mutexes and the actions of level *i* are identical with those of level $i-1$. In fact, it is not hard to see that once two adjacent levels $i-1$, *i* are identical, all future levels will be identical to $i-1$ as well, so we can say the graph has been level off from level $i-1$ on.

*Step*9. The construction of the action-action mutex with label member "i".
Examine action-action mutexes in the actions with label member lower than or equal to i and the no-ops that maintain the propositions with label member lower than or equal to i. If the action-action mutexes with label member "$i-1$" still exist, change their label member to "i", and set the label members of new action-action mutexes to "i". The mutex set varied with the generation of label member.
*Part*2. Flexible solution extraction.
In the flexible planning problem, a main task is solution extraction. The paper adopts the approach of backward-chaining strategy. Every time executing *Step*7 of the above algorithm, we examine whether at this time all the propositions in the goal set appear and none of them are mutex, if not, continue to generate label members. If it is true, we will begin to search a valid plan.
The basic idea of flexible solution extraction is: above all, judge whether there exists a valid plan, if not, the algorithm over, otherwise, the valid plan extraction. We will follow up the way of searching the plan backward-chaining on the basis of the label members of propositions, actions and mutexes. Firstly the goals are viewed as a proposition set. Then we begin searching the valid plan, until finding it. ★ Choose a proposition in the set. Look for an action, action1, which satisfies the following requirements: firstly, the action is a no-op or in the action set with label member lower than or equal to $i-1$; secondly, the effects of the action include the proposition; last, if there are many such actions meeting the first two requirements, we should choose the one with highest satisfaction degree. Then, choose another proposition in the set. Look for an action, action2, which satisfies the following requirements: firstly, the action is a no-op or in the action set with label member lower than or equal to i – 1; secondly, the effects of the action include the proposition; thirdly, action1 and action2 must be guaranteed not in the action-action mutex set with label member "$i-1$"; last, if there are many such actions meeting the first three requirements, we should choose the one with highest satisfaction degree. If such action does not exist, the algorithm backtracks at once. Go on with the job in this way, until we have found such actions for each proposition in the set and any pair of these actions is not in action-action mutex set with label member "$i-1$". Let $i = i - 1$ and the preconditions of these actions comprise a proposition set. Carry out ★ until the proposition set is the subset of initial conditions.
Calculate the satisfaction degree of the flexible plan according to the approach stated above. If the value is less than l_T, the algorithm will go on to generate label member to look for the valid plan with higher satisfaction degree. Else, the algorithm is over.

5.2 Optimizations

Our algorithm is sound and complete: any plan the algorithm finds is a legal plan, and only if there exists a legal plan then the algorithm will find one. Below, we describe some optimizations to the algorithm.

One additional aspect of flexible solution extraction is that before backtracking in the recursion it memorizes what it has learned, storing nogoods and the time step t. When the algorithm creates a subgoal set at some time step lower than or equal to t, first see if the set is a nogood before searching it. If so, then the algorithm backtracks right away without searching further (since nogoods are monotonically decreasing). This memorization step is used to speed up search.

The cost of generation of label member can be reduced as follows. Consider the case where a plan with satisfaction degree l_i has been found. If $l_i < l_T$, the algorithm searches onwards in order to look for a plan with a higher satisfaction degree. However, there is no point in instantiating flexible operator clauses with a satisfaction degree less than or equal to l_i: a plan with this satisfaction degree l_i has been found already - a longer plan with the same satisfaction degree is deemed to be of a lower quality. The conjunctive combination rule implemented via the min operator ensures that no plan of satisfaction degree l_j can contain an action of satisfaction degree l_i, where $l_i < l_j$. Hence, the completeness of the search is not affected by omitting such actions in future generation of label member. Flexible solution extraction can be ameliorated using a similar basis to that for generation of label member. Once a plan of satisfaction degree l_i has been found, all search paths that necessarily lead to a plan with satisfaction degree lower than or equal to l_i can be pruned. Hence, the flexible solution extraction needs only extend to l_j, such that $l_j > l_i$, guaranteed by the use of the min operator.

5.3 Time and Space Complexity of the Generation of Label Member

As we demonstrate in the following theorem, the space and the time taken by our algorithm to generate label members is polynomial in the length of the problem's description and the number of time steps.

Theorem 1. Consider a flexible planning problem with n objects, p propositions in the initial conditions, and m flexible operators each having a constant number of formal parameters. Let r be the largest number of the clauses of any flexible operator and l be the largest number of the effects of any clause. Then, the space of t-label member generated by our algorithm, and the time needed to generate the label member for each proposition, action and mutex, are polynomial in n, m, p, r, l and t.

Proof. Let K be the largest number of formal parameters in any flexible operator. Since operators cannot create new objects, the number of different propositions that can be created by instantiating an flexible operator is $O(rln^{\mathrm{K}})$. So, the maximum number of propositions with the same label member is $\max(p, O(mrln^{\mathrm{K}}))$ and the maximum number of proposition-proposition mutexes with the same label member is $C^2_{\max(p,O(mr\ln^{\mathrm{K}}))}$. Since any operator can be instantiated in at most $O(n^{\mathrm{K}})$ distinct ways and consists of r clauses at most, the maximum number of the actions with the same label member is $O(mrn^{\mathrm{K}})$ and the maximum number of action-action mutexes with the same label member is $C^2_{O(mrn^{\mathrm{K}})}$. Thus the total number of label members is polynomial in n, m, p, r, l and t, since K is constant.

The time needed to generate a new label member for actions, propositions and mutexs can be broken down into (a) the time to determine mutexes between propositions, (b) the time to instantiate the operators in all possible ways to preconditions with label member lower than or equal to the new one, (c) the time to determine mutexes between actions, and (d) the time to infer the satisfaction degrees of propositions and actions. It is clear that the time is polynomial in the number of actions and propositions with label member lower than or equal to the new one.

6 Conclusion

In this paper, we intensively analyze the structure of flexible planning graph at first and introduce a novel flexible planning algorithm based on label member in the following. The algorithm can automatically find a range of plans given a flexible planning problem using a single run. It maintains the strength of flexible Graphplan, possesses some preeminent properties, and the solution plan has higher performance in terms of safety.

Acknowledgement. This work described in this paper is partially supported by the Fundamental Research Funds for the Central Universities (3072020CFQ0602, 3072020CF0604, 3072020CFP0601) and 2019 Industrial Internet Innovation and Development Engineering (KY10600200021, KY10600200034).

References

1. Zhang, Y.C., Zhou, T.Y., Zhu, J.H., Wang, Q.X.: Domain-independent intelligent planning technology and its application to automated penetration testing oriented attack path discovery. J. Electron. Inf. Technol. **42**(9), 2095–2107 (2020)
2. Kim, J., Hong, T., Hastak, M., Jeong, K.: Intelligent planning unit for the artificial intelligent based built environment focusing on human-building interaction. J. Asian Archit. Build. Eng. (2020)
3. Li, C., Ouyang, D.T., Wang, X.Y., Wei, W.: An intelligent planning-based modeling method for diagnosis and repair 2020. Wirel. Commun. Mob. Comput. (2020)
4. Yang, H.J., Chen, J.W., Wang, C., Cui, J.J., Wei, W.S.: Intelligent planning of product assembly sequences based on spatio-temporal semantic knowledge. Assem. Autom. **40**(5), 755–768 (2020)
5. Rybina, G.V., Blokhin, Y.M.: Methods and software implementation of intelligent planning for integrated expert system design. Sci. Tech. Inf. Process. **46**(6), 434–445 (2019)
6. Panteleev, M.G.: Advanced iterative action planning for intelligent real-time agents. In: Proceedings of INTELS, St. Petersburg, Russia, pp. 244–252 (2019)
7. Zhu, M., Fan, G.D., Li, J., Wang, F.Y.: A service composition approach based on overall QoS and modified graphplan. Int. J. Web Grid Serv. **15**(4), 319–339 (2019)
8. Deng, S.Y., Du, Y.Y., Qi, L.: A web service composition approach based on planning graph and propositional logic. J. Organiz. End User Comput. **31**(3), 1–16 (2019)
9. Akila, T.H., Siriweera, S., Paik, I., Kumara, B.T.G.S.: Constraint-driven dynamic workflow for automation of big data analytics based on Graphplan. In: Proceedings of the ICWS, Honolulu, HI, pp. 357–364 (2017)
10. Bryce, D., Cushing, W., Kambhampati, S.: State agnostic planning graphs: deterministic, non-deterministic, and probabilistic planning. Artif. Intell. **175**(3–4), 848–889 (2011)
11. Miguel, I., Jarvis, P., Shen, Q.: Flexible Graphplan. In: Proceedings of the ECAI, Prague, The Czech Republic, pp. 506–510 (2000)
12. Miguel, I., Shen, Q.: Fuzzy rrDFGP and planning. Artif. Intell. **148**, 11–52 (2003)
13. Miguel, I.: Dynamic flexible constraint satisfaction and its application to AI planning. Distinguished Dissertations, Ph.D. dissertation, University of Edinburgh, UK (2004)

A Survey and Future Perspectives of Hybrid Deep Learning Models for Text Classification

Samuel K. Akpatsa(✉), Xiaoyu Li, and Hang Lei

School of Information and Software Engineering, University of Electronic Science and Technology of China, Chengdu, China

hlei@uestc.edu.cn

Abstract. The advances in deep learning (DL) models have proven to achieve outstanding results in text classification tasks. This success is due to DL models' potential to reach high accuracy with less need for engineered features. Despite their popularity, DL models have their strengths and weaknesses in their learning capacity, depending on the task. Researchers in the recent past have proposed various hybrid models to compensate for these weaknesses. This study presents a performance analysis of hybrid DL models compared to stand-alone DL models on various text classification tasks. Various research articles published between 2015 and 2020 on text classification using hybrid DL models were selected from leading computer science and engineering journals and analyzed. The findings suggest that hybrid DL models can better capture a syntactic representation of text, extract multiple feature maps, and effectively improve text classification results. The study also presents an improved awareness of different hybrid DL architectures in the field of text classification.

Keywords: Text classification · Capsule network · Deep learning · Natural language processing · Sentiment analysis

1 Introduction

Many studies have been done in the field of text classification in recent years. Deep Learning (DL) methods, along with the success of Machine Learning (ML) techniques in many application domains, have emerged as a powerful technique that can classify the massive amount of unstructured text generated daily into different categories for further use. Moreover, the quest for better text classification accuracy has led to the introduction of hybrid DL models to develop a novel technique with a more robust architecture for text classification tasks. This approach has been gaining popularity in recent years due to its potential to outperform stand-alone DL models. Although some recent surveys have shown the effectiveness of DL models on text classification tasks [1–5], most of them lost sight of the enormous potential of hybrid frameworks and their high-quality performance in this research area [6]. This paper presents a comprehensive overview and a performance analysis of different hybrid DL models and compares their performances to conventional stand-alone DL models on various text classification tasks. The paper

X. Sun et al. (Eds.): ICAIS 2021, LNCS 12736, pp. 358–369, 2021.
https://doi.org/10.1007/978-3-030-78609-0_31

also highlights the new trends and prospects of hybrid DL models for text classification research.

The rest of the paper is structured as follows; Sect. 2 presents an overview of text classification and its applications; Sect. 3 describes state of the art and the current research trend in text classification; Sect. 4 presents a review of hybrid DL models for text classification at document, sentence, and aspect levels. The discussions section highlights the importance of hybrid DL and suggestions for future directions in this research area. The final section presents a summary of the findings.

2 Overview of Text Classification and Its Applications

Text classification is the process of organizing natural language text into some predefined classes. It forms a fundamental part of Natural Language Processing (NLP) as it offers a useful framework for the understanding of textual data processing. Text classification has been extensively studied in a number of real applications over the years [7–12]. Text classification can be binary, multi-class, or multi-label. **Binary text classifiers** assign one of two possible labels to each text sample, which is the standard approach for most sentiment analysis. **Multi-class text classifiers** assign each sample a unique label for each text sample from a set of more than two classes. **Multi-label text classifiers** assign one or more labels from a set of more than one class to each text sample. Text classification has attracted significant attention from the research community and industry because of its broad applications (Table 1).

Table 1. Applications of text classification

Text classification task	Applications
Sentiment analysis	*Market research, social media monitoring, customer feedback*
Topic modeling	*Recommender systems, bio-informatics, document annotation*
Intent detection	*Spam detection, email classification, product analysis*
Language detection	*Document classification, speech recognition, email filtering*

Textual data is all around us, from web pages, surveys, emails, social media, to user review comments. This massive text data contains a vast amount of valuable information that needs to be regularized and classified into different categories for further use. Conventional approaches of text classification, in general, consist of a feature extraction stage, where some sparse lexical features, such as n-grams, are extracted to represent a text document. This is followed by a classification stage, where the features are sent to a linear classifier for further processing. Prior literature suggests that two of the most common conventional approaches to feature selection are bag-of-words (BoW) and Term Frequency - Inverse Document Frequency (TF-IDF) [2]. These models have achieved excellent results in the past. However, when there are many labels with different topical granularities, BoW representation may not be sufficient. It overlooks local orderings of words, and consequently, unable to grasp local semantic information.

ML algorithms have performed better on most text classification tasks. The most representative supervised classification learning methods used for text classification are Logistic Regression, Decision Tree, Support Vector Machine, K Nearest Neighbors, and Naive Bayes [13]. Even though these ML techniques achieve considerable success on text classification tasks, they ignore word order in texts and have data sparsity, which eventually influences their overall performance.

3 State of the Art Text Classification Techniques

3.1 Deep Learning Techniques for Text Classification

The current state-of-the-art for text classification uses DL models to capture complex linguistic information from texts. The advances in DL models on text classification have gained significant attention by overcoming conventional model challenges. According to this study [14], DL allows computational models of multiple processing layers to learn data representations with different abstraction levels. Besides, the non-linearity of DL methods and their ability to easily integrate pre-trained word embeddings often result in superior classification accuracy compared to classical linear classifiers [15]. Consequently, DL models have achieved state-of-the-art performances on several text classification tasks, such as sentiment analysis, topic modeling, question answering, and intent detection, [6, 8, 9, 16, 17].

Over the years, different DL architectures such as Recurrent Neural Network (RNN), Convolutional Neural Network (CNN), Capsule Networks, and Transformers have demonstrated incredible success in supervised and unsupervised learning tasks. RNN is considered as one of the fundamental DL architectures used by many researchers for text classification tasks [2, 7, 18]. Even though the standard RNN is susceptible to vanishing gradient problems, various variants have been proposed to compensate for its weakness. These models LSTM [19, 20], GRU [21, 22], and BRNN [8, 23, 24] have proven to be more effective than the standard RNN in many tasks. The use of CNN for NLP tasks was pioneered by these studies [16, 25, 26], resulting in considerable growth of CNN-based networks in the succeeding literature in recent years [24, 27–30]. Besides, Capsule Networks has a higher potential for better representation and understanding of a given NLP task through its dynamic routing-by-agreement algorithms [31]. Even though studies confirming the efficiency of Capsule Networks on text classification are rare, several works provide further evidence that Capsule Networks possess several advantages over CNN [6, 9, 32–35].

Most text classification datasets are somewhat small, making it challenging to train DL models as they tend to overfit and not generalize well in practice. The concept of transfer learning is to overcome this challenge [36]. Transfer learning refers to pre-trained language representations trained on an extensive collection of text that contains a considerable amount of world-knowledge [13]. This approach is considered one of the critical breakthroughs for DL methods' impressive performance on many NLP tasks. There are two main types of pre-trained language representations in NLP: feature-based (word embeddings) and fine-tuning models [37]. Word embeddings are widely used to initialize the first layers of text classification neural network-based deep learning models. The three most symbolic word embedding architectures successfully used for DL are

Word2vec, Global Vectors (GloVe), and Embeddings from Language Models (ELMo). These word representations capture semantic and syntactic information of words that help improve text classification tasks [38–40].

However, recent years have seen the proliferation of multiple fine-tuning pre-trained language models for text classification. Amongst the lot, Bidirectional Encoder Representations from Transformers (BERT) remain the most popular and widely used NLP pre-trained model for text classification. It is a context-informed word embedding technique for NLP pre-training developed by Google [37]. BERT's key technical innovation is applying the bidirectional training of Transformer architecture [41] and an attention framework that learns contextual relations between words in a text [37]. BERT offers an advantage over context-free models such as Word2vec or GloVe since it considers word order to produce more accurate feature representations that are dynamically informed by the words around them, which results in better model performance. By fine-tuning BERT pre-trained model, practitioners can achieve state-of-the-art results on downstream tasks. Various successful examples of using BERT have been proposed for text classification [42–44].

3.2 Hybrid Deep Learning Models for Text Classification

It is widely acknowledged that DL models have achieved remarkable success in text classification and other NLP tasks. Nevertheless, the current trend suggests a rise in hybrid models because existing conventional DL models cannot entirely meet task requirements. Hybrid DL models focus on establishing a new model that can obtain even better classification results. Besides, the research community has an apparent desire to improve text analysis accuracy from other perspectives other than merely enhancing a single DL model's performance. Hybrid DL models are consistently yielding better results on text classification tasks. This section presents a representative summary of these models applied to different text classification tasks. We grouped hybrid DL models adopted for text classification into three categories based on their architectural designs:

- CNN-RNNs based hybrid models.
- Capsule-RNNs based hybrid models.
- Attention-based hybrid models.

CNN-RNNs Hybrid Models. The CNN-RNNs-based hybrid models use the CNN layer to utilize its max-pooling operations to capture key features of the input text. On the other hand, the RNN layers are used to learn long-term dependency between the text sentences. This paper [17] presents a novel neural network framework that combines asymmetric CNN with BLSTM (AC-BLSTM) to model sentences and documents. The model also applied multiple asymmetric convolution operations to deepen its dept and enhance high feature representation. The model achieves state-of-the-art performance on standard sentiment classification and document classification tasks.

Capsule-RNNs Hybrid Models. The Capsule-RNNs based hybrid models use RNN to encode input instances (e.g., sentence, paragraphs) and outputs the hidden vectors. The Capsule Networks uses its dynamic routing by agreement algorithm to enhance the text sequence's representation for a better classification result. This study [9] demonstrates the use of such a framework, a Capsule model based on RNN (RNN-Capsule) for text classification. The model achieves state-of-the-art sentiment classification accuracy on a Movie Review Dataset (Table 3). Additionally, the experimental result indicates that the RNN-Capsule model can output words that best reflect sentiment categories of a dataset's domain specificity.

Attention-Based Hybrid Models. The attention-based hybrid frameworks utilize the attention layer to add weights to the context information captured by CNNs, RNNs layers and assign higher values to words that contribute more to the text classification. For example, this paper [24] builds a hybrid framework, BRCAN, that reserves the merits of BLSTM, CNN with attention mechanism, and word2vec models to address the challenging issues with multi-class text classification fine-grained sentiment analysis. The experimental results show that BRCAN has better performance than stand-alone CNN, RNN, and several other baseline methods widely used for text classification tasks.

4 Literature Survey

Generally, text classification can be performed at three different levels; document-level, sentence-level, and aspect-level [12]. This section presents a review of hybrid DL models used on different text classification tasks.

4.1 Document-Level Text Classification

Text classification at the document-level considers the whole document as the primary classification unit to determine its overall opinion [45]. Most hybrid DL models' robustness means that they are beneficial on document-level datasets, consisting of many words and different topics. Several authors have used different hybrid DL frameworks to augment text representation and improve classification performance. This paper [7] introduced a hybrid DL model, 'Recurrent Convolutional Neural Networks' (RCNN), to text classification that outperforms a stand-alone CNN model on benchmark document level datasets (Table 2). The model's key element was using a bi-directional recurrent structure to capture contextual information from neighboring words in both directions. The output of the recurrent layer is fed into CNN, where the max pool operation captures the key features for the softmax layer that classifies the text provided. Similarly, the authors in [20] explore 2D max-pooling operations and 2D convolution to integrate the time-step dimension and feature vector dimension of information in a novel framework (BLSTM-2DCNN). The model achieves state-of-the-art on sentence-level classification datasets and outperforms CNN, BLSTM, and RCNN proposed in this study [7] on the 20Newsgroup dataset (Table 2).

In a related study, this paper [28] proposed a hybrid parallel CNN-RNN framework, CNN-RNN attention-based neural network (CRAN), to model the local patterns and long-distance dependency patterns in text simultaneously. The attention layer combines the CNN and RNN layers' output to enable a return vector to pick relevant local features from sequences generated by the RNN. The experimental result shows that the

Table 2. Performance analysis of deep learning models on 20NewsGroup Dataset.

DL model	20NG
CNN [7]	94.79
BLSTM [20]	94.0
RCNN [7]	96.49
BLSTM-2DCNN [20]	**96.5**

attention mechanism is an efficient framework that can unify CNN and RNN. Also, the CRAN model, with fewer parameters, achieves state-of-the-art performance on several document-level datasets. Moreover, evidence from research suggests that many traditional ML and DL methods perform poorly on multi-label text classification tasks. To address this challenge, this study [46] developed an ensemble application of CNN-RNN architecture to capture the global and local semantic information of texts and model a high-order label correlation to overcome the challenges associated with multi-label text classification. The experimental result suggests that the model suffers over-fitting when trained against smaller datasets but achieves state-of-the-art performance on large-scale datasets.

One major issue of text classification is how to represent text documents to make them mathematically computable. Various strategies, such as Word2vec and Glove, have been proposed to enhance text representation for different applications effectively. However, these models are not suitable for long-text document representation compared with Doc2vec embeddings. The underlying intuition about Doc2Vec is that the document representation should be good enough to predict the document's words. This study [47] demonstrates the use of Doc2vec embedding as a pre-trained model to initialize five different DL models, namely CNN, LSTM, BiLSTM, CNN-LSTM, and CNN-BiLSTM, with different configurations for document-level sentiment analysis. The models were trained on a dataset that contains 2003 French online articles scrapped from national and international newspapers. Each article contains an average of 4000 words. Experimental results show that the CNN-BiLSTM model achieved the best accuracy on the dataset. However, document-level text classification has proven to be limited in providing enough information, as it does not consider individual sentences or different aspects that a document might contain.

4.2 Sentence-Level Text Classification

This text classification scope obtains the relevant categories of a single sentence by classifying whether a sentence is positive, neutral, or negative. In the recent past, DL models such as RNNs, CNN, Capsule Networks have achieved outstanding results on sentence-level datasets such as Movie Reviews (**MR**) with one sentence per review and Stanford Sentiment Treebank (**SST-1** and **SST-2**). Nevertheless, many researchers have proposed different hybrid DL models for text classification tasks at this scope with significant success. For instance, a study proposed a novel and unified model that combines the strengths of CNN and LSTM to capture local features of phrases and learn a global semantic representation of sentences [11]. The proposed architecture produced better results than stand-alone CNN and RNN on sentiment classification and question type classification tasks. Another study demonstrated the empirical effectiveness of hybrid DL models [48]. The authors presented a generic inference hybrid framework, conv-RNN, which seamlessly integrates CNN and RNN in extracting different aspects of linguistic information from text. The conv-RNN model shows its effectiveness on semantic understanding and outperforms the state-of-the-art on several benchmark datasets on sentence classification.

Table 3. Deep learning models for sentence-level classification tasks.

Model	SST-1	SST-2	MR
CNN [16]	48.0	87.2	81.5
LSTM [19]	46.4	84.9	–
BLSTM [20]	49.1	87.6	80.0
RNN-Capsule [9]	49.3	–	**83.8**
C-LSTM [11]	49.2	87.8	–
AC-BLSTM [17]	**52.9**	**91.1**	83.1
BLSTM-2DCNN [20]	52.4	89.5	82.3
BGRU-CNN [21]	51.2	–	83.7
BLSTM-C [23]	50.2	89.5	–
Conv-RNN [48]	51.67	88.91	81.99
CNN-BRNN [49]	48.9	89.6	–
CNN-LSTM [50]	51.50	89.56	83.1

A related study, a novel capsule-based hybrid DL model (BGRU-Capsule), was introduced to demonstrate Capsule Networks' efficiency in extracting richer textual information for text classification tasks [51]. The model obtains implicit semantic information effectively within less training time. A similar approach combined BGRU, CNN, and Attention mechanism to improve text classification results [52]. The model demonstrates a deeper level of feature representation and beats a single CNN model on a text classification dataset. Several other researchers have used similar approaches to perform text classification tasks and showed some performance gain compared to using a stand-alone DL model [49, 50, 53–58] (Table 3).

However, the sentence-level text classification has the same issue as the document-level text classification as it does not have adequate detail because a sentence can contain numerous entities with different aspects. As a result, a feature-based opinion mining and summarization methodology has been added, which considers the different facets of the sentence and its sentimental polarity.

4.3 Aspect-Level Text Classification

Aspect-level text classification obtains the relevant categories of sub-expressions within a sentence (also known as opinion units). Sentiment classification at this level is commonly referred to as aspect-based sentiment analysis [12]. Aspect level text classification is challenging since modeling the semantic relatedness of a target word with its surrounding context words is difficult [4]. However, the overall effectiveness of hybrid models offers researchers the opportunity to explore further the difficulty of modeling the semantics of sub-expressions. One paper introduces the Attention-based Aspect-level Recurrent Convolutional Neural Network (AARCNN) to analyze the aspect-based sentiment analysis task [59]. The model integrates attention mechanisms and target information analysis, enabling it to concentrate on the essential parts of the sentence and fully use the target information. The model was tested on multi-language datasets and demonstrated better performance over other conventional DL methods (Table 4).

Table 4. A summary of reviewed publications on different text classification scopes

Scope	Studies using hybrid DL models
Document-level	[7, 17, 20, 24, 28, 46, 47]
Sentence-level	[8, 9, 11, 21–23, 48–56, 58]
Aspect-level	[59]

5 Discussion

Though the mainstream DL architectures such as CNN, RNNs, and Capsule Net-works adopt different ways of understanding natural languages, they have achieved great success in text classification tasks over the years. However, existing models of text classification tasks still need improvement to enhance the accuracy of results. Several hybrid models have been proposed in the recent past to compensate for the shortcomings in stand-alone DL models' learning capacities. These works have prov-en that hybrid DL models are more effective at the semantic representation of texts within less training time, extract text content dependencies better, suffer less from the data sparsity problems, and optimize the text classification performance. Besides, most hybrid DL models' robustness means that they generally overfit when trained on a smaller dataset but benefit from many training data. Hybrid DL models have also demonstrated a deeper level of feature representation and better performances with significantly fewer parameters. As the hybrid DL approach for text classification research grows, we expect to see this trend continue with even better model designs. However, some unresolved issues need to be addressed to improve the performance of existing models.

5.1 Open Issues and Research Opportunities

There is an imbalance in the implementation of hybrid DL models on other text classification application domains such as intent detection and topic modeling. Due to these frameworks' considerable efficiency on sentiment classification tasks, there is a need to test their efficacy on other text classification tasks. Additionally, it remains unclear whether the ordering of models in the hybrid approach affects how well the final model performs. For example, in a CNN-RNN model, the initial convolutional layer may lose some of the text sequence information. As a result, the full potential of the subsequent RNN layer cannot be entirely harnessed. A better understanding of the ordering sequence of models can help future researchers develop better hybrid models to solve different text analysis scenarios. Besides, the accuracy of hybrid DL models on smaller datasets is far from satisfactory as they are prone to overfitting. To pursue better classification performance, the extent of overfitting on text classification must be well studied and quantified. Finally, the overall effectiveness of hybrid DL models offers researchers the opportunity to explore further the difficulty of modeling the semantics of sub-expressions.

5.2 Suggestions for Future Directions

Recent empirical improvement on text classification results has demonstrated that rich unsupervised pre-trained models are an integral part of DL methods for text classification. While word embedding architectures such as word2vec and GloVe are still relevant for DL models, there are limitations to what these models can capture as they do not take context into account. Researchers should focus on using context-informed pre-trained models such as ELMo and BERT to initialize the first layers of hybrid DL frameworks. The learned representation of these pre-trained models can result in more accurate feature representation, which will enhance the performance of the final model. Moreover, Capsule networks have a unique architecture that automatically learns the part-whole relationships within data in a more robust representation than other deep neural networks. The dynamic routing-by-agreement algorithms of capsule networks have a higher potential for better representation and understanding of a given NLP task. The complexity of its algorithms allows for better modeling of semantics in multidimensional data and addresses the representation limitations of CNNs and RNNs. While studies have proven the effectiveness of capsule networks in image classification tasks, future works should fully explore their validity in the text classification domain.

Finally, the attention mechanism has also shown its efficacy by assigning different weights to individual words in sentences according to their importance to the classification task. These frameworks have achieved better performance in challenging text classification tasks. A combination of these models in a novel hybrid framework could enhance the instance representation of text and effectively improve classification results.

6 Conclusion

Hybrid DL models have shown to be a promising solution to many complex tasks, such as multi-label text classification. This paper examines the relative performance of hybrid DL models over stand-alone DL models. Although most of these frame-works have been evaluated on different datasets, empirical results suggest that hybrid DL models generally perform better than individual DL models on most text classifi-cation tasks. However, this survey was limited to hybrid DL models for text classifi-cation tasks in

NLP, focusing on sentiment analysis. Future works should consider extending the study to other NLP tasks and measuring their efficiency on similar datasets.

Acknowledgment. This study was supported by the National Key R\&D Program of China, Grant No. 2018YFĂ703.

Conflicts of Interest. The authors declare no conflicts of interest.

References

1. Habimana, O., Li, Y., Li, R., Gu, X., Yu, G.: Sentiment analysis using deep learning approaches: an overview. Sci. China Inf. Sci. **63**(1), 1–36 (2019). https://doi.org/10.1007/s11432-018-9941-6
2. Kowsari, K., Jafari Meimandi, K., Heidarysafa, M., Mendu, S., Barnes, L., Brown, D.: Text classification algorithms: a survey. Information **10**(4), 150 (2019)
3. Minaee, S., Kalchbrenner, N., Cambria, E., Nikzad, N., Chenaghlu, M., Gao, J.: Deep Learning Based Text Classification: A Comprehensive Review. arXiv Prepr. arXiv:2004.03705 (2020)
4. Zhang, L., Wang, S., Liu, B.: Deep learning for sentiment analysis: a survey. Wiley Interdisc. Rev. Data Min. Knowl. Discov. **8**(4), e1253 (2018)
5. Zhou, Y.: A review of text classification based on deep learning. In: Proceedings of the 2020 3rd International Conference on Geoinformatics and Data Analysis, pp. 132–136 (2020)
6. Katarya, R., Arora, Y.: Study on text classification using capsule networks. In: 2019 5th International Conference on Advanced Computing & Communication Systems (ICACCS), pp. 501–505 (2019)
7. Lai, S., Xu, L., Liu, K., Zhao, J.: Recurrent convolutional neural networks for text classification (2015)
8. Minaee, S., Azimi, E., Abdolrashidi, A.: Deep-Sentiment: Sentiment Analysis Using Ensemble of CNN and Bi LSTM Models. arXiv Prepr. arXiv:1904.04206 (2019)
9. Wang, Y., Sun, A., Han, J., Liu, Y., Zhu, X.: Sentiment analysis by capsules. In: Proceedings of the 2018 World Wide Web Conference, pp. 1165–1174 (2018)
10. Zheng, D., Ran, Z., Liu, Z., Li, L., Tian, L.: An efficient bar code image recognition algorithm for sorting system. Comput. Mater. Contin. **64**, 1885–1895 (2020)
11. Zhou, C., Sun, C., Liu, Z., Lau, F.: A C-LSTM neural network for text classification. arXiv Prepr. arXiv:1511.08630 (2015)
12. Liu, B.: Sentiment Analysis: Mining Opinions, Sentiments, and Emotions. Cambridge University Press, Cambridge (2015)
13. Rodríguez Medina, S.: Multi-Label Text Classification with Transfer Learning for Policy Documents: The Case of the Sustainable Development Goals (2019)
14. LeCun, Y., Bengio, Y., Hinton, G.: Deep learning. Nature **521**(7553), 436–444 (2015)
15. Goldberg, Y.: A primer on neural network models for natural language processing. J. Artif. Intell. Res. **57**, 345–420 (2016)
16. Kim, Y.: Convolutional neural networks for sentence classification. arXiv Prepr. arXiv:1408.5882 (2014)
17. Liang, D., Zhang, Y.: AC-BLSTM: asymmetric convolutional bidirectional LSTM networks for text classification. arXiv Prepr. arXiv:1611.01884 (2016)
18. Lan, Y., Hao, Y., Xia, K., Qian, B., Li, C.: Stacked residual recurrent neural networks with cross-layer attention for text classification. IEEE Access **8**, 70401–70410 (2020)

19. Tai, K.S., Socher, R., Manning, C.D.: Improved semantic representations from tree-structured long short-term memory networks. arXiv Prepr. arXiv:1503.00075 (2015)
20. Zhou, P., Qi, Z., Zheng, S., Xu, J., Bao, H., Xu, B.: Text classification improved by integrating bidirectional LSTM with two-dimensional max pooling. arXiv Prepr. arXiv:1611.06639 (2016)
21. Li, W., Liu, P., Zhang, Q., Liu, W.: An improved approach for text sentiment classification based on a deep neural network via a sentiment attention mechanism. Future Internet **11**(4), 96 (2019)
22. Rathnayaka, P., Abeysinghe, S., Samarajeewa, C., Manchanayake, I., Walpola, M.: Sentylic at IEST 2018: gated recurrent neural network and capsule network based approach for implicit emotion detection. arXiv Prepr. arXiv:1809.01452 (2018)
23. Li, Y., Wang, X., Xu, P.: Chinese text classification model based on deep learning. Future Internet **10**(11), 113 (2018)
24. Zheng, J., Zheng, L.: A hybrid bidirectional recurrent convolutional neural network attention-based model for text classification. IEEE Access **7**, 106673–106685 (2019)
25. Collobert, R., Weston, J., Bottou, L., Karlen, M., Kavukcuoglu, K., Kuksa, P.: Natural language processing (almost) from scratch. J. Mach. Learn. Res. **12**(Aug), 2493–2537 (2011)
26. Kalchbrenner, N., Grefenstette, E., Blunsom, P.: A convolutional neural network for modelling sentences. arXiv Prepr. arXiv:1404.2188 (2014)
27. Conneau, A., Schwenk, H., Barrault, L., Lecun, Y.: Very deep convolutional networks for text classification. arXiv Prepr. arXiv:1606.01781 (2016)
28. Guo, L., Zhang, D., Wang, L., Wang, H., Cui, B.: CRAN: a hybrid CNN-RNN attention-based model for text classification. In: Trujillo, J.C., Davis, K.C., Du, X., Li, Z., Ling, T.W., Li, G., Lee, M.L. (eds.) ER 2018. LNCS, vol. 11157, pp. 571–585. Springer, Cham (2018). https://doi.org/10.1007/978-3-030-00847-5_42
29. Kim, H., Jeong, Y.-S.: Sentiment classification using convolutional neural networks. Appl. Sci. **9**(11), 2347 (2019)
30. Young, T., Hazarika, D., Poria, S., Cambria, E.: Recent trends in deep learning based natural language processing. IEEE Comput. Intell. Mag. **13**(3), 55–75 (2018)
31. Sabour, S., Frosst, N., Hinton, G.E.: Dynamic routing between capsules. In: Advances in Neural Information Processing Systems, pp. 3856–3866 (2017)
32. Fentaw, H.W., Kim, T.-H.: Design and investigation of capsule networks for sentence classification. Appl. Sci. **9**(11), 2200 (2019)
33. Kim, J., Jang, S., Park, E., Choi, S.: Text classification using capsules. Neurocomputing **376**, 214–221 (2020)
34. Xiao, L., Zhang, H., Chen, W., Wang, Y., Jin, Y.: MCapsNet: capsule network for text with multi-task learning. In: Proceedings of the 2018 Conference on Empirical Methods in Natural Language Processing, pp. 4565–4574 (2018)
35. Zhao, W., Ye, J., Yang, M., Lei, Z., Zhang, S., Zhao, Z.: Investigating capsule networks with dynamic routing for text classification. arXiv Prepr. arXiv:1804.00538 (2018)
36. Howard, J., Ruder, S.: Universal language model fine-tuning for text classification. arXiv Prepr. arXiv:1801.06146 (2018)
37. Devlin, J., Chang, M.-W., Lee, K., Toutanova, K.: BERT: pre-training of deep bidirectional transformers for language understanding. arXiv Prepr. arXiv:1810.04805 (2018)
38. Aubaid, A.M., Mishra, A.: Text classification using word embedding in rule-based methodologies: a systematic mapping. TEM J.-Technol. Educ. Manag. Inform. **7**(4), 902–914 (2018)
39. Kant, N., Puri, R., Yakovenko, N., Catanzaro, B.: Practical Text Classification With Large Pre-Trained Language Models. arXiv Prepr. arXiv:1812.01207 (2018)
40. Lenc, L., Král, P.: Word embeddings for multi-label document classification. In: RANLP, pp. 431–437 (2017)

41. Vaswani, A., et al.: Attention is all you need. In: Advances in Neural Information Processing Systems, pp. 5998–6008 (2017)
42. Adhikari, A., Ram, A., Tang, R., Lin, J.: DocBERT: BERT for Document Classification. arXiv Prepr. arXiv:1904.08398 (2019)
43. González-Carvajal, S., Garrido-Merchán, E.C.: Comparing BERT against traditional machine learning text classification. arXiv Prepr. arXiv:2005.13012 (2020)
44. Sun, C., Qiu, X., Xu, Y., Huang, X.: How to Fine-Tune BERT for Text Classification? arXiv Prepr. arXiv:1905.05583 (2019)
45. Behdenna, S., Barigou, F., Belalem, G.: Document level sentiment analysis: a survey. EAI Endorsed Trans. Context. Syst. Appl. **4**(13), 1–8 (2018)
46. Chen, G., Ye, D., Xing, Z., Chen, J., Cambria, E.: Ensemble application of convolutional and recurrent neural networks for multi-label text categorization. In: 2017 International Joint Conference on Neural Networks (IJCNN), pp. 2377–2383 (2017)
47. Rhanoui, M., Mikram, M., Yousfi, S., Barzali, S.: A CNN-BiLSTM model for document-level sentiment analysis. Mach. Learn. Knowl. Extr. **1**(3), 832–847 (2019)
48. Wang, C., Jiang, F., Yang, H.: A hybrid framework for text modeling with convolutional RNN. In: Proceedings of the 23rd ACM SIGKDD International Conference on Knowledge Discovery and Data Mining, pp. 2061–2069 (2017)
49. Hassan, A., Mahmood, A.: Efficient deep learning model for text classification based on recurrent and convolutional layers. In: 2017 16th IEEE International Conference on Machine Learning and Applications (ICMLA), pp. 1108–1113 (2017)
50. Wang, X., Jiang, W., Luo, Z.: Combination of convolutional and recurrent neural network for sentiment analysis of short texts. In: Proceedings of COLING 2016, the 26th International Conference on Computational Linguistics: Technical Papers, pp. 2428–2437 (2016)
51. Du, Y., Zhao, X., He, M., Guo, W.: A novel capsule based hybrid neural network for sentiment classification. IEEE Access **7**, 39321–39328 (2019)
52. Chen, X., Ouyang, C., Liu, Y., Luo, L., Yang, X.: A hybrid deep learning model for text classification. In: 2018 14th International Conference on Semantics, Knowledge and Grids (SKG), pp. 46–52 (2018)
53. Ali, N.M., El Hamid, A., Mostafa, M., Youssif, A.: Sentiment analysis for movies reviews dataset using deep learning models. In: ALIAA, Sentiment Analysis for Movies Reviews Dataset Using Deep Learning Models, 14 June 2019 (2019)
54. Gangwar, A.K., Ravi, V.: A Novel BGCapsule Network for Text Classification. arXiv Prepr. arXiv:2007.04302 (2020)
55. Guo, Y., Jin, C., Li, W., Ji, C., Fang, Y., Duan, Y.: A novel method of text representation on hybrid neural networks. In: 2017 10th International Congress on Image and Signal Processing, BioMedical Engineering and Informatics (CISP-BMEI), pp. 1–6 (2017)
56. Ingole, P., Bhoir, S., Vidhate, A.V.: Hybrid model for text classification. In: 2018 Second International Conference on Electronics, Communication and Aerospace Technology (ICECA), pp. 7–15 (2018)
57. Salur, M.U., Aydin, I.: A novel hybrid deep learning model for sentiment classification. IEEE Access **8**, 58080–58093 (2020)
58. Yenter, A., Verma, A.: Deep CNN-LSTM with combined kernels from multiple branches for IMDB review sentiment analysis. In: 2017 IEEE 8th Annual Ubiquitous Computing, Electronics and Mobile Communication Conference (UEMCON), pp. 540–546 (2017)
59. Zhu, Y., Gao, X., Zhang, W., Liu, S., Zhang, Y.: A bi-directional LSTM-CNN model with attention for aspect-level text classification. Future Internet **10**(12), 116 (2018)

Non-contact Heart Rate Measurement Based on Fusion Technology

Jiancheng Zou, Yingyan Li(✉), and Bo Zhang

College of Science, North China University of Technology, Beijing 100144, China
zjc@ncut.edu.cn

Abstract. Among the various physiological indicators of human health, the heart rate occupies an important position, which can directly reflect the health of the human body. Therefore, it is particularly necessary to monitor human heart rate. At present, heart rate monitoring is mainly measured by a single infrared camera or optical camera, which extracts the heart rate based on subtle changes in temperature or skin color. Low resolution of the infrared image is prone to distortion. Optical image is easy to lose details when the illumination is not enough. Limited by the imaging principles of infrared and optical images, its measurement accuracy needs to be improved. In response to the above problems, we propose a heart rate measurement method based on data fusion. According to the human heart rate data measured by the infrared camera and the optical camera, the accuracy of heart rate monitoring is improved through multi-feature data fusion and analysis. The fusion model is constructed by using the least square method and neural network, and the optimal fusion mode is selected. Experimental results show that the fusion model based on neural network has a higher accuracy compared with other measurement methods.

Keywords: Heart rate measurement · Data fusion · Optical camera · Infrared camera

1 Introduction

Heart rate is a physiological indicator reflecting the state of human health. Abnormal heart rate often indicates certain diseases of the body [1]. Data show that the risk index of cardiovascular disease death increases with increasing heart rate [2, 3]. The earliest measurement method of heart rate is taking the pulse in traditional Chinese medicine [4], and then a wider range of measuring equipment appeared. It can be divided into contact detection and non-contact detection [5]. The non-contact measurement method will not bring physiological burden to the human body, and has the advantages of non-invasive and low price, which has attracted wide attention. With the development of image processing technology [6], the method of heart rate detection based on face video tends to be mature, including visible light method and near-infrared method. However, due to the imaging principle, the universality and measurement accuracy still need to be improved.

X. Sun et al. (Eds.): ICAIS 2021, LNCS 12736, pp. 370–382, 2021.
https://doi.org/10.1007/978-3-030-78609-0_32

In 1938, Hertzman [7] first proposed Photo Plethysmo Graph (PPG) [8], which converted the light intensity change signal into electrical signal. Due to the single point contact of PPG technology and the rapid development of image processing technology, Hu S [9] proposed the Imaging PhotoPlethysmo Graph (IPPG) in 2008, which uses cameras and other electronic imaging devices to photograph the skin on the human body surface, and extracts the human body parameter information by sensing the changes of reflected light. In 2010, Poh Mingzher [10] adopted blind source separation technology to realize heart rate detection based on common color camera in visible light environment.

As the heart contracts and relaxes at a certain frequency, the blood flow shows a pulsating change, which leads to changes in skin temperature throughout the body. In 1999, Zhang Dong [11] summarized the relationship between skin temperature and blood flow through infrared thermal imaging, and proved the feasibility of measuring heart rate with infrared image. In 2007, Marc garbey [12], a professor at the University of Houston in the United States, first proposed to use thermal infrared images for heart rate detection, and to realize the measurement of human heart rate through adaptive filtering and fast fourier transform.

2 Heart Rate Measurement Based on Optical Image

The non-contact human heart rate detection based on visible light video mainly includes three key steps: (1) Face detection, tracking and locating of region of interest (ROI); (2) Heart rate signal extraction from image frame; (3) Filter the extracted signal.

2.1 Face Detection and ROI Location

The video image of human face contains a lot of interference information, such as complex background, occlusion and other non-human parts. In this paper, Adaboost algorithm [13] and Kanade-Lucas-Tomasi(KLT) [14] feature point tracking algorithm are used for face detection and continuous tracking. The haar feature structure is similar to a window traversing the image with step size 1. After one traversal, the width/length is scaled up and repeated sliding. When sliding to a position, the difference between the total pixel value corresponding to the white position and the black position in the area covered by the window is the Haar eigenvalue. Since human faces contain many features, this paper uses Adaboost training algorithm to find the key features from a large number of feature sets and generate training classifiers. Then, a series of strong classifiers are established to build cascade classifiers to obtain correct face images. After determining the face coordinates of the first frame, the face position of the continuous video is then determined by looking for the KLT feature points of other image frames.

With the beating of the heart, there will be changes in skin color. However, compared with other parts of the body, the face has more arterial blood vessels, and the periodic changes in skin color are more obvious. In 2008, Verkruysse W [15] extracted different parts of the face as regions of interest, and respectively used IPPG technology to extract pulse waves. Experimental results show that the pulse wave extracted from forehead is more pure and less affected by environment.

2.2 Signal Extraction

Using the normal ambient light as the experimental light source, each frame image is separated by three channels, and the average value is calculated in ROI region (see Eq. (1)–(3)):

$$R = \text{mean}(\text{sum}(\text{img}(:, :, 0))) \tag{1}$$

$$G = \text{mean}(\text{sum}(\text{img}(:, :, 1))) \tag{2}$$

$$B = \text{mean}(\text{sum}(\text{img}(:, :, 2))) \tag{3}$$

Since the oxygen-containing hemoglobin has the highest absorption rate of green light, and the light can penetrate the skin to reach the micro artery layer which can reflect the pulse wave, so this paper selected G channel signals to extract the heart rate information.

2.3 Signal Filtering

In addition to the heart rate information, there are a series of other clutter superimposed in the green channel. In this paper, the fast Fourier transform algorithm (see Eq. (4)) is selected to transform the signal from the time domain to the frequency domain. According to the human heart rate range, we select the band-pass frequency of [0.45 Hz–5 Hz] to remove high-frequency signals and study the signal spectral structure. Then the inverse Fourier transform of the filtered signal is carried out (see Eq. (5)). After processing, the heart rate signal shows more obvious periodicity (Fig. 1).

$$F(W) = \int_{-\infty}^{+\infty} f(t)e^{-j\omega t}dt \tag{4}$$

$$f(t) = \frac{1}{2\pi}\int_{-\infty}^{+\infty} F(w)e^{i\omega t}dw \tag{5}$$

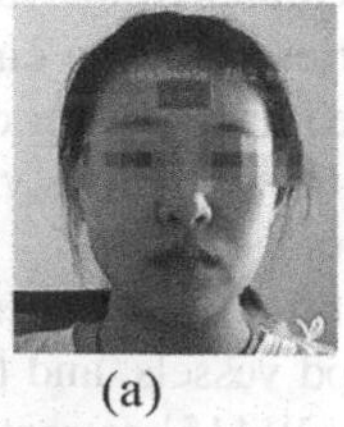

(a)

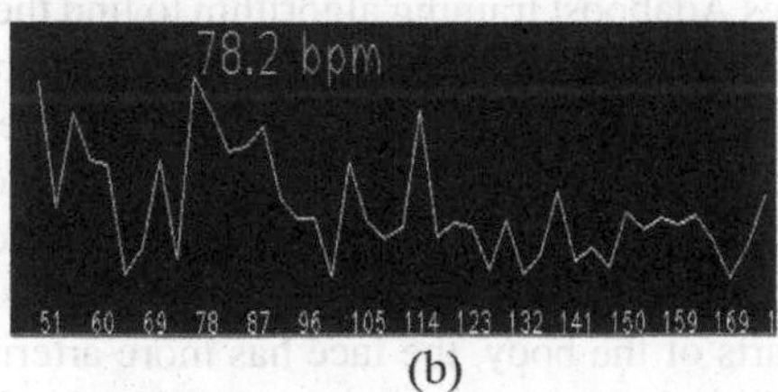

(b)

Fig. 1. Optical images measure heart rate. (a) ROI positioning; (b) real-time heart rate signal.

3 Heart Rate Measurement Based on Infrared Images

The non-contact human heart rate measurement based on infrared video mainly includes three key steps: (1) The time series signal is obtained by the center of gravity method; (2) The first-order differential and low-pass filtering are applied to the obtained time series signals; (3) AR power spectrum analysis.

3.1 Extraction of Time Series Signals

In this paper, 850 nm infrared emission tube is used to collect the image of the part containing human face. The facial feature point tracking algorithm is used to extract the face region, and the region of interest for heart rate detection is obtained according to the physiological proportional relationship. In this paper, the concave part of the upper lip with dense blood vessels is selected as the detection area, which is a high-quality detection sample.

There is a significant correlation between skin temperature and blood flow, and heart activity directly determines the speed of blood flow. Therefore, the skin temperature will change with the beating of the heart periodically, which makes the gray value of infrared image have obvious periodicity.

In this paper, the gray barycenter method [16] is used to calculate the barycenter coordinates of each frame, and the upper left endpoint of the region of interest is taken as the reference point. Measure the distance between the center of gravity and the reference point in each frame to form a time series signal [17]. The center of gravity $p(x_0, y_0)$ of the image is obtained by weighted sum of pixel position coordinates and corresponding gray values. For the M * N infrared image f, the center of gravity is processed for the image whose gray value exceed the threshold T (see Eq. (6)–(8)).

$$x_0 = \frac{\sum_{i=1}^{m}\sum_{j=1}^{n} x_i f_{ij}}{\sum_{i=1}^{m}\sum_{j=1}^{n} f_{ij}} \tag{6}$$

$$y_0 = \frac{\sum_{i=1}^{m}\sum_{j=1}^{n} y_j f_{ij}}{\sum_{i=1}^{m}\sum_{j=1}^{n} f_{ij}} \tag{7}$$

$$f_{ij} = \begin{cases} 0, \text{Pixel gray value} < T \\ f_{ij}, \text{Pixel gray value} \geq T \end{cases} \tag{8}$$

3.2 Process Time Series Signals

First order differential processing is used to eliminate the random trend and improve the data stability. Considering that the normal heart rate ranges from 1 Hz to 1.6 Hz, a low-pass filter with a cut-off frequency of 2 Hz is selected, which will block the high-frequency signal exceeding the set threshold. The setting of low-pass filter eliminates the influence of high-frequency components in the differential signal.

3.3 AR Power Spectrum Analysis

Finally, the AR model power spectrum analysis of the filtered signal is carried out [18, 19]. Power spectrum estimation is divided into non-parametric method and parametric method. The parameter calculation of AR model mainly uses linear equation, which is relatively simple and widely used.

Any random signal with power spectral density can be regarded as a physical network excited by white noise:

$$x(n) = -\sum_{k=1}^{p} a_k x(n-k) + \omega(n) \tag{9}$$

The transfer function of the AR model can be obtained by z-transformed:

$$H(z) = \frac{X(z)}{W(z)} = \frac{1}{1 + \sum_{k=1}^{p} a_k z^{-k}} \tag{10}$$

When using an auto-regressive model, the expression of power spectral density is expressed as follows:

$$P_{xx}(\omega) = \frac{\sigma_\omega^2}{\left|1 + \sum_{k=1}^{p} a_k e^{-j\&k}\right|^2} \tag{11}$$

Where: σ_ω^2 is power spectral density of white noise. Therefore, as long as the values of σ_ω^2 and all a_k are solved, the power spectrum of the random signal $x(n)$ can be obtained. This paper uses Brug algorithm [20, 21] to estimate AR model parameters (Fig. 2).

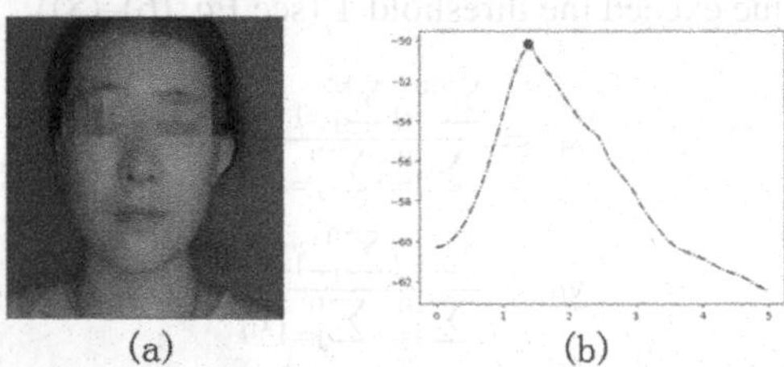

Fig. 2. Infrared images measure heart rate. (a) target area positioning; (b) AR power spectrum curve.

4 Heart Rate Measurement Based on Data Fusion

Considering the shortcomings of infrared camera or optical camera using single feature to measure human heart rate, this paper proposes a multi-feature measurement method based on data fusion. The data obtained by the above measurement methods are fused to correct the inherent defects of single camera. In this way, the measurement accuracy can be improved by reducing the requirements of the measurement environment and improving the robustness of the measurement method.

For the fitting of two-dimensional discrete data, a smooth curve or straight line can be used to interpolate or approximate a series of irregular data points. Similarly, for the discrete data fitting in three-dimensional space, the surface or plane fitting is performed on discrete data. This paper studies the fitting problem of small sample data in three-dimensional space. There are many ways to deal with this problem. The paper focuses on the following two methods: least squares method (LS) [22] and neural network (NN) [23]. The above-mentioned methods are used to fuse the measurement data respectively, and the optimal measurement method is selected based on the principle of optimal measurement accuracy.

4.1 Experimental Setup

This paper uses infrared acquisition system, optical camera and wrist instrument to measure human heart rate at the same time (see Fig. 3). During the measurement, the tester sits at a distance of 1m from the camera and keeps his body as still as possible to avoid measurement errors caused by shaking.

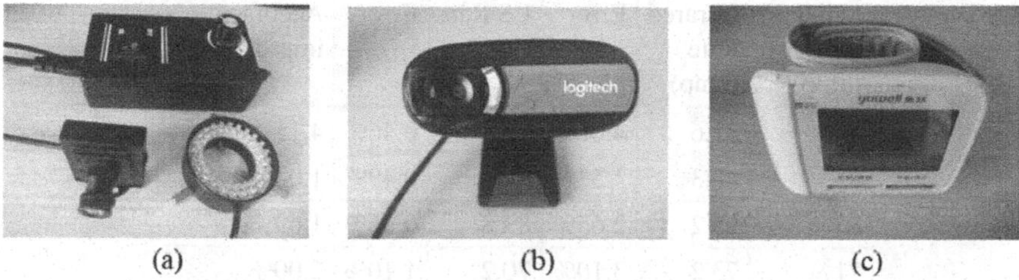

(a) (b) (c)

Fig. 3. Experimental device. (a) infrared camera; (b) optical camera; (c) Wrist heart rate device.

4.2 Data Fusion Based on Least Squares

Construction Regression Model. The least square method finds the best function of matching data by minimizing the sum of squares of errors. The general expression of the multiple linear regression model using the least square method is:

$$Y = \beta_0 + \beta_1 x_1 + \beta_2 x_2 + \varepsilon \tag{12}$$

Where: $\beta_j (j = 0, 1, 2)$ is regression parameters; x_1, x_2 are explanatory variable; Y is explained variable; ε is random error term. Expressed in matrix form as:

$$Y = \begin{bmatrix} y_1 \\ y_2 \\ \vdots \\ y_m \end{bmatrix}, X = \begin{bmatrix} 1 & x_{11} & x_{12} \\ 1 & x_{21} & x_{22} \\ \vdots & \vdots & \vdots \\ 1 & x_{m1} & x_{m2} \end{bmatrix}, \beta = \begin{bmatrix} \beta_0 \\ \beta_1 \\ \beta_2 \end{bmatrix}, \varepsilon = \begin{bmatrix} \varepsilon_1 \\ \varepsilon_2 \\ \vdots \\ \varepsilon_m \end{bmatrix}$$

The model can also be expressed as: $Y = X\beta + \varepsilon$. Which m represents the sample observation. In order to prevent the interference caused by negative numbers, the least square method uses the residual sum of squares to measure the effect of data fitting. The expression of the residual sum of squares is:

$$Q(\beta_0, \beta_1, \beta_2) = \sum_{i=1}^{m} (y_i - (\beta_0 + \beta_1 x_{i1} + \beta_2 x_{i2}))^2 = \sum_{i=1}^{m} \hat{\varepsilon}_i^2 = \hat{\varepsilon}_i^T \hat{\varepsilon}_i \quad (13)$$

The residual sum of squares is deriving from $\hat{\beta}$, and make its derivative equal to zero. At this time, the regression coefficient $\hat{\beta}_0, \hat{\beta}_1, \hat{\beta}_2$ that minimizes the residual sum of squares is obtained. The$\hat{\beta}$ expression is as follows:

$$\hat{\beta} = (X^T X)^{-1} X^T Y \quad (14)$$

Experimental Results. The following table shows the 6 sets of measurement results. Table 1 and Table 2 are the measurement results based on infrared camera, the optical camera, and the least squares data fusion. The relative errors of the three measurement results and the standard heart rate value are calculated.

Table 1. Comparison of infrared image and least square fusion measurement results.

Standard Rate (bmp)	Infrared Rate (bmp)	Error	LS Rate (bmp)	Error	Accuracy improvement
78	81.6	4.62%	78.4	0.46%	4.15%
85	86.3	1.53%	84.6	0.49%	1.04%
83	85.2	2.65%	83.8	0.96%	1.69%
71	73.2	3.10%	70.2	1.10%	2.00%
74	76.2	2.97%	73.2	1.08%	1.89%
95	92.3	2.84%	94.7	0.31%	2.53%

Table 2. Comparison of optical image and least square fusion measurement results.

Standard Rate (bmp)	Optical Rate (bmp)	Error	LS Rate (bmp)	Error	Accuracy improvement
78	76.3	2.18%	78.4	0.46%	1.72%
85	84.1	1.06%	84.6	0.49%	0.57%
83	86.6	4.34%	83.8	0.96%	3.38%
71	68.3	3.80%	70.2	1.10%	2.71%
74	71.3	3.65%	73.2	1.08%	2.57%

The experimental results show that the measurement based on least squares is more accurate compared with the measurement based on a single optical camera or infrared camera.

4.3 Data Fusion Based on Neural Network

Construction of Neural Network. In this paper, Pytorch, a third-party library for machine learning, was used to establish a two-layer neural network. The training set and test set are randomly divided in proportion accounting for 80% and 20% respectively. The multiple linear regression model is defined as:

$$\hat{y} = \omega_1 x_1 + \omega_2 x_2 + \text{bias} \tag{15}$$

The neural network algorithm for multi-sample vectorization is as follows:

$$y^{[1]} = w^{[1]}X + b^{[1]} \tag{16}$$

$$a^{[1]} = \mathrm{Re\,LU}(y)^{[1]} \tag{17}$$

$$\hat{y} = y^{[2]} = w^{[2]}a^{[1]} + b^{[2]} \tag{18}$$

Where $w^{[i]}$, $b^{[i]}(i = 1, 2)$ are the weight matrix and bias matrix of the i-th layer network, respectively;

$X = \begin{bmatrix} x_1^{(1)} & x_1^{(2)} & x_1^{(3)} & \cdots & x_1^{(m)} \\ x_2^{(1)} & x_2^{(2)} & x_2^{(3)} & \cdots & x_2^{(m)} \end{bmatrix}$, m represents the number of samples, and each sample has two features;

$w^{[1]} = \begin{bmatrix} w_1^{(1)} & w_2^{(1)} \\ w_1^{(2)} & w_2^{(2)} \\ w_1^{(3)} & w_2^{(3)} \\ \vdots & \vdots \\ w_1^{(n)} & w_2^{(n)} \end{bmatrix}$, $w^{[2]} = \begin{bmatrix} w_1 & w_2 & w_3 & \cdots & w_n \end{bmatrix}$, $b^{[1]} = \begin{bmatrix} b_1 \\ b_2 \\ b_3 \\ \vdots \\ b_n \end{bmatrix}$, $b^{[2]}$ is a real number, n is the number of neurons.

This paper uses mean squared error (MSE) as the cost function of the model, and the expression is:

$$\cos\,t\_func = \frac{1}{m}\sum_{i=1}^{m}(y - \hat{y})^2 \tag{19}$$

Where:y is actual value,$\hat{y}$ is predicted value. Then through back-propagation, the gradient of the loss is automatically calculated according to the weight and bias. In this paper, the stochastic gradient descent algorithm is used to adjust the weights and biases, moving toward the global minimum. The expression is:

$$w^{[i]} = w^{[i]} - \alpha d(w^{[i]})(i = 1, 2) \tag{20}$$

$$b^{[i]} = b^{[i]} - \alpha d(b^{[i]})(i = 1, 2) \tag{21}$$

Where: $d(w^{[i]})$, $d(b^{[i]})$ are the partial derivatives of the loss function with respect to weights and biases, respectively; α is learning rate to control the step length of each gradient descent.

Experimental Results. Table 3 and Table 4 are given the measurement results of different method. The improvement of accuracy is calculated separately.

Table 3. Comparison of infrared image and neural network fusion measurement results.

Standard Rate (bmp)	Infrared Rate (bmp)	Error	NN Rate (bmp)	Error	Accuracy improvement
96	94.9	1.15%	96.2	0.21%	0.94%
76	81.1	6.71%	78.6	3.42%	3.29%
71	72.6	2.25%	70.4	0.85%	1.40%
87	85.2	2.07%	86.1	1.03%	1.04%
69	75.1	8.84%	68.4	0.87%	7.97%
70	72.7	3.86%	68.9	1.56%	2.30%

Table 4. Comparison of optical image and neural network fusion measurement results.

Standard Rate (bmp)	Optical Rate (bmp)	Error	NN Rate (bmp)	Error	Accuracy improvement
96	98.5	2.62%	96.2	0.21%	2.41%
76	79.6	4.73%	78.6	3.42%	1.31%
71	69.5	2.11%	70.4	0.85%	1.26%
87	88.1	1.26%	86.1	1.03%	0.23%
69	64	7.25%	68.4	0.87%	6.38%
70	66.8	4.57%	68.9	1.56%	3.01%

5 Results Analysis

This paper uses infrared camera, optical camera and wrist device to measure the heart rate at the same time. Part of the training data is shown in the table below (Table 5).

Table 5. Experimental data.

Groups	1	2	3	4	5	6	7	8	9	10
Standard Rate	58	67	62	85	77	75	89	80	92	106
Infrared Rate	57.1	70.8	64.8	82.8	81.6	78.6	86.4	82	94.2	103.2
Optical Rate	61.9	62.2	65	78.2	74.3	73.5	92.2	80.3	89.1	108.2

Scatter plots are used to give experimental results based on least squares and neural network sample training set and test set. The training set prediction results are shown in Fig. 4, and the sample prediction set prediction results are shown in Fig. 5. By observing the distribution of Fig. 4 and Fig. 5, it can be concluded that the least squares performance on the prediction set is poor; and the heart rate measurement method with neural network, whether it is the test set or the training set, tends to a straight line y = x for most samples, which proves that the model has a strong generalization ability without over-fitting.

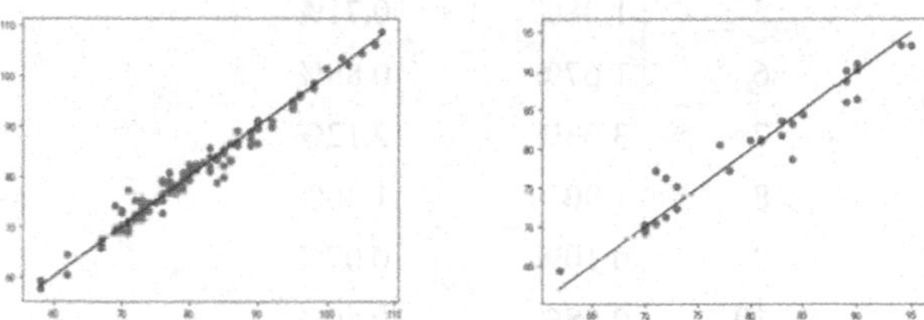

Fig. 4. The prediction results of training set and test set based on least squares.

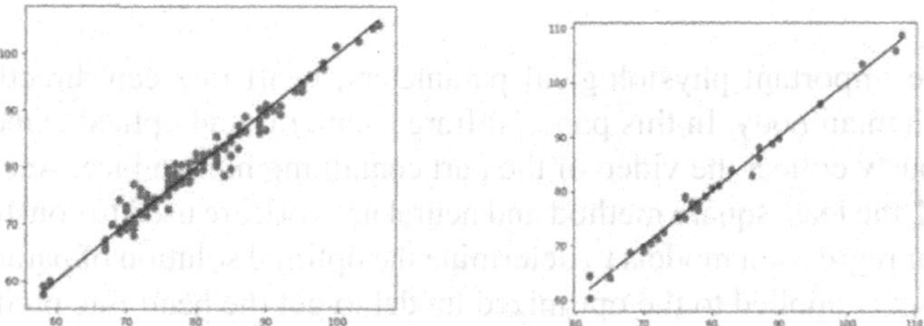

Fig. 5. The prediction results of training set and test set based on neural network.

For the determination of regression parameters, the least square method and neural network method are different. The least square method directly derivates the objective function to find the global minimum. The gradient descent method is an iterative method, given a learning rate to adjust the parameters in the direction of the fastest gradient descent. Compared with the least squares data fusion method, the method based on neural network has a more obvious improvement in accuracy. The following table shows the error rates of two different fusion methods. It can be seen from the following table that the method based on neural network fusion measurement has a lower error rate (Table 6).

Table 6. Comparison of error rates of different fitting methods.

Groups	LS Error Rate	NN Error Rate
1	0.47%	0.22%
2	1.34%	1.17%
3	3.05%	1.86%
4	1.11%	0.60%
5	1.08%	0.71%
6	1.67%	0.88%
7	3.63%	2.12%
8	1.90%	1.40%
9	0.10%	0.07%
10	0.58%	0.60%

6 Conclusion

As one of the important physiological parameters, heart rate can directly reflect the health of the human body. In this paper, infrared cameras and optical cameras are used to simultaneously collect the video of the part containing human face. According to the data collected, the least square method and neural network are used to construct different multiple linear regression models to determine the optimal solution of parameters. After that, the test set is applied to the optimized model to get the heart rate prediction value, and the correlation coefficient between the predicted value and the real value of the heart rate is calculated by the model. The model was repeated for 5 times, and the mean of the correlation coefficient between the real heart rate and the predicted value was taken as the result of the prediction accuracy. The experimental results show that the measurement method of data fusion can obtain more accurate heart rate than the traditional method, and has stronger robustness to the small shaking of human body. In the above methods, the data fusion method based on neural network shows stronger stability in test set and training set.

In addition, this paper uses linear regression to build the prediction model, and the application effect in the complex scene with occlusion remains to be discussed, so it puts forward higher requirements for the construction of the model.

References

1. Krstacic, G., Krstacic, A., Martinis, M.: Non-linear analysis of heart rate variability in patients with coronary heart disease. In: Proceedings on Computers in Cardiology, pp. 673–675. IEEE, Memphis (2002)
2. Krstacic, G., Krstacic, A., Martinis, M.: Dynamic non-linear changes in heart rate variability in patients with coronary heart disease and arterial hypertension treated by Amlodipine Besylate. In: Proceedings on Computers in Cardiology, pp. 485–488. IEEE, Thessaloniki (2003)

3. Plaza-Florido, A., Alcantara, J.M.A., Migueles, J.H.: Inter- and intra-researcher reproducibility of heart rate variability parameters in three human cohorts. Sci. Rep. **10**(1), 1–11 (2020)
4. Cheng, M.Y., Xia, Y.Q., Lan, S.: Human pulse wave signal detection system. Beijing Biomed. Eng. **25**(5), 520–523 (2006)
5. Matsunaga, D., Izumi, S., Kawaguchi, H.: Non-contact instantaneous heart rate monitoring using microwave Doppler sensor and time-frequency domain analysis. In: 2016 16th International Conference on Bioinformatics and Bioengineering, pp. 172–175. IEEE, Taichung (2016)
6. Liu, J., Ma, L., He, J., Zhang, Q., Chen, H., Pan, L.: A comparative study of assessment methods for medical image quality. In: 2012 5th International Conference on BioMedical Engineering and Informatics, pp. 131–134. IEEE, Chongqing (2012)
7. Hertzman, A.B.: The blood supply of various skin areas as estimated by the photoelectric plethysmograph. Am. J. Physiol. Legacy Content **124**(2), 328–340 (1938)
8. Hertzman, A.B., Spealman, C.: Observations on the finger volume pulse recorded photoelectrically. Am. J. Physiol.-Legacy Content **119**, 334–335 (1937)
9. Zheng, J., Hu, S., Chouliaras V. and Summers, R.: Feasibility of imaging photoplethysmography. In: 2008 International Conference on BioMedical Engineering and Informatics, pp. 72–75, IEEE, Sanya (2008)
10. Poh, M.Z., Mcduff, D.J., Picard, R.W.: Non-contact, automated cardiac pulse measurements using video imaging and blind source separation. Opt. Express **18**(10), 10762–10774 (2010)
11. Zhang, D., Xue, L.G.: Comparison of facial skin temperature and facial blood flow. J. Biomed. Eng. **16**(1), 81–85 (1999)
12. Garbey, M., Sun, N., Merla, A., Pavlidis, I.: Contact-free measurement of cardiac pulse based on the analysis of thermal imagery. IEEE Trans. Biomed. Eng. **54**(8), 1418–1426 (2007)
13. Viola, P., Jones, M.: Fast and robust classification using asymmetric adaboost and a detector cascade. Adv. Neural Inf. Process. Syst. **14**, 1311–1318 (2001)
14. Tomasi, C., Kanade, T.: Detection and tracking of point features. Tech. Rep. Kansai Univ. **9**(9), 9795–9802 (1991)
15. Verkruysse, W., Svaasand, L.O., Nelson, J.S.: Remote plethysmographic imaging using ambient light. Opt. Express **16**(26), 21434–21445 (2008)
16. Ou-Yang, M., Chen, Y.T.: A gray level weighting method to reduce optical aberration effect in holographic data storage system. IEEE Trans. Magn. **47**(3), 546–550 (2011)
17. Mao, X.G., Shang, P.J.: Multivariate singular spectrum analysis for traffic time series. Stat. Mech. Appl. **526**, 121063 (2019)
18. Song, X., Liu, Z., Sun, Y.: Fault diagnosis and analysis of ball mill jars based on wavelet denoising and AR model power spectrum. In: 2020 IEEE International Conference on Artificial Intelligence and Computer Applications, Dalian, Liaoning, pp. 414–419 (2020)
19. Dowla, F., Lim, J.: Relationship between maximum-likelihood-method and autoregressive modeling in multidimensional power spectrum estimation. In: IEEE International Conference on Acoustics, Speech, and Signal Processing, pp. 193–196. IEEE, San Diego (1984)
20. Wei, H.: Vehicle audio signal estimation of AR model and power spectrum estimation based on artificial neural network. In: 2013 Chinese Automation Congress, pp. 876–881. IEEE, Changsha (2013)
21. Thorvaldsen, T.: A comparison of the least squares method and the Burg method for autoregressive spectral analysis. IEEE Trans. Antennas Propag. **29**(4), 675–679 (1981)
22. Chen, J., Yin, Y.: Filter design based on a novel non-iterative least square method with adjustable parameter. In: IEEE International Conference on Signal Processing, Communications and Computing, pp. 1–3. IEEE, Qingdao (2018)

23. Kayri, M., Kayri, I., Gencoglu, M.T.: The performance comparison of Multiple Linear Regression, Random Forest and Artificial Neural Network by using photovoltaic and atmospheric data. In: 14th International Conference on Engineering of Modern Electric Systems, pp. 1–4. IEEE, Oradea (2017)
24. Alhussain, A., Kurdi, H., Altoaimy, L.: A neural network-based trust management system for edge devices in peer-to-peer networks. Comput. Mater. Continua **59**(3), 805–815 (2019)

Research on Cotton Impurity Detection Algorithm Based on Image Segmentation

Haolong Yang[1], Chunqiang Hu[1], and Qi Diao[2](✉)

[1] ChongQing University, ChongQing 400044, China
[2] Zhejiang Dongfang Polytechinc College, Wenzhou 325000, China

Abstract. With the widespread application of computer and multimedia technology in the agricultural field, problems such as complex workloads have been effectively resolved, contributing to the promotion of agricultural information, modernization, industrialization, and intelligence. The impurity content of cotton seriously affects its quality and price. Thus, how to effectively detect the impurity rate has become a difficult problem for the cotton processing industry. From the perspective of computer image segmentation, this paper performs color segmentation, maximum entropy segmentation, and level set segmentation on the image library, and compares the performance of the algorithms. Experiments demonstrate that the image segmentation algorithm is more accurate and robust compared with manual detection.

Keywords: Color segmentation · Maximum entropy segmentation · Level set segmentation

1 Introduction

In the past, due to the limitations of technology, the detection of products often relied on traditional manual recognition. However, in actual operation, traditional manual detection has apparent defects, mostly relied on human visual recognition. But human eye recognition has excellent limitations, such as intense subjectivity which is susceptible to external interference, and even weather, noise, and mood affect inspection. Various problems appeared (such as a decline in detect accuracy when worker's eye feel very fatigued) when long-term work of the human eye. For some defects, it is difficult to distinguish with an inconspicuous colour difference, and may result in misjudgment [1]. According to research when the scale of the defect is less than 0.5mm, it is difficult for the human eye to detect the defect; When the moving speed is faster than 180 m per minute, it will be tough to capture the surface defects of the aluminium profile. Quality of the product can have a very negative impact [2]. Traditional manual test also takes up of the product can have a very negative impact [2]. Traditional manual test also takes up manpower and increases corporate expenses. The manufacturer was trying to find an efficient detection method to improve the accuracy and shorten the time during the detection. The manufacturer was committed to improving economic efficiency and reducing the cost of production. With the development of artificial intelligence, the detection method based

X. Sun et al. (Eds.): ICAIS 2021, LNCS 12736, pp. 383–394, 2021.
https://doi.org/10.1007/978-3-030-78609-0_33

on deep learning has been applied in production and has achieved excellent achievement. Most image segmentation methods based on clustering algorithms use single-objective function to implement image segmentation. To avoid the defect, this paper proposes a new image segmentation method based on a multi-objective particle swarm optimization (PSO) clustering algorithm. This unsupervised algorithm not only offers a new similarity computing approach based on electromagnetic forces, but also obtains the proper number of clusters which is determined by scale-space theory [3].

Artificial intelligence(AI) can be considered as an algorithm that automatically adjusts its parameters through deep learning to gradually improve its performance, and ultimately achieves the process of the human evolution. With the rapid development of the artificial intelligence, our lives have undergone tremendous changes, and the relationship between humans and machines has been redefined. Artificial intelligence can be applied in many different ways [4]. AI has already entered our lives. In 2016, a popular game Prisma was AI. Many people grab their own phones to catch the elves, and others take Prisma's own photos in photoshop. In the same year, Toyota Motor developed the AI technology for auto-driving. It can temporarily control the AI technology in an emergency. When the driver encounters an emergency during driving, it can temporarily control the car to avoid. An accident occurred in a panic situation. When we are overwhelmed by unexpected situations, it has used our own careful logic to help us avoid possible accidents.

Artificial intelligence has a significant impact on human society and can create substantial economic benefits for people not tired. The quality of economic development directly determines the status quo of the social development. When the economic situation develops well, other aspects of society will also be improved. In the past two decades, artificial intelligence has penetrated into almost all fields, such as economics, computer design, manufacturing, etc. Artificial intelligence plays a role in various fields and also creates huge economic benefits in practical applications. The achievement of artificial intelligence research also show that, in some respects, computers are far superior to humans in dealing with problems. The core of AI is to better combine human intelligence with machine intelligence, which can be an essential issue with which artificial intelligence has always faced. The impact of artificial intelligence on human beings is also reflected in the cultural aspect. Artificial intelligence promotes the improvement of human knowledge, improves people's quality of cultural life, and promotes the improvement of human language. Artificial intelligence can lead to earlier health diagnoses and more accurate predictions of natural disasters such as typhoons and earthquakes. All of this shows that artificial intelligence brings many benefits to people's lives. While artificial intelligence has brought many positive effects to people, it has also brought many negative voices. At the beginning of the 21st century, a technologist Bill Joycy had expressed concern about publishing articles on the technologist's [5]. Many people who like chess should remember the direct game between Bobby Fischer and the IBM supercomputer Deep Blue in 1997. Deep Blue finally won. John McCarthy, one of the founding pioneers of artificial intelligence, expressed concern that he felt that Deep Blue's victory was due to his computing power, not to the understanding of chess itself, which made him very disappointed [5]. There are two main models of deep learning, and one is the machine learning model that needs human supervision, which is the convolutional neural network model (CNN) applied in this project. The other unsupervised machine learning model is Deep Brief Network (DBN) [6].

The process of artificial intelligence research can be described as a process from bold guessing to knowledge to learning [7]. Machine learning is an important branch of artificial intelligence and a way to implement AI [8]. Machine learning is the use of machines to learn from previous experiences. Unlike traditional programming, developers need to predict and program every potential condition, and a machine learning solution can effectively adapt the output based on the data. In the past thirty years, the development of machine learning involved many disciplines, such as probability theory [9], statistics [10], programming. Researchers hope to solve problems in artificial intelligence by means of machine learning. In theory, machine learning mainly designs and analyzes some algorithms, and then "learns" through computers. The good news is that after years of research, this "learning" has evolved into automatic "learning". Machine learning analyzes and rules from a series of data to make predictions. A machine learning algorithm builds a computer model of the real world and then trains the model through the data [7]. Machine learning has been widely used in many fields, such as data mining, natural language processing, and biometrics.

Image recognition technology is an important field of artificial intelligence [11]. Combined with the development of machine learning technology in recent years, it has great researches value and commercial value. As a matter of fact, a single recognition function can no longer meet people's needs, and accurate image prediction is the trend that people pursue [12]. In the process of picking, transportation, purchase and processing of cotton, it is very easy to mix impurities. If these impurities are not treated in time, they will not only affect the quality of raw cotton, but also reduce the quality of cotton fabric. Therefore, the rapid detection of impurity content in raw cotton is of great significance for the purchase and smooth circulation of cotton and the quality assurance of cotton textile products.

As the main agricultural economic crop in XinJiang, cotton is not only high in yield but also of good quality due to the advantageous growth environment. However, the impurity content directly affects the grade of cotton in the process of cotton processing. Thus, effective detection of impurity content has become a key method to improve cotton quality.

Whether picking cotton by hand or by machine, impurities will be mixed in. Effectively eliminating cotton impurities is the key to effectively improve the quality of cotton spinning industry. In recent years, machine vision system, photoelectric induction system and ultrasonic detection system have been applied in cotton impurity detection field. The machine vision system based on image processing and pattern recognition has the advantages of fast and accurate information acquisition, mature feature extraction and processing methods, and can effectively combine with pattern classification methods. Compared with other methods, machine vision system is more suitable for cotton impurity detection due to cost, accuracy and speed. With the rapid development of computer and multimedia technology, its technology is widely used in the agricultural field, and many detection methods have emerged. Researchers worldwide start from the physics of cotton impurities and the spectral characteristics of the functional groups of the composition, using some detection technologies such as visible light machine vision, infrared band spectral images, and tomographic X-ray photography and digital image processing and chemometric analysis methods to identify and classify raw cotton impurities [13].

As a powerful mathematical analysis and simulation tool, Python is widely used in mathematical analysis, signal and image processing, and neural networks, providing various processing functions. Based on Python software, this paper adopts different image segmentation algorithms to detect cotton impurities and compare their performances.

2 Algorithm Description

Meanwhile, the used CNN model is robust and improves the security of information transmission. An image may have multiple object areas, if we choose enough object areas to represent the information, the capacity is considerable. However, not all areas are suitable for information hiding, the object areas should be filtered based on the requirements to construct a database that can meet most of the requirements of information transmission [23]. Instead of using the whole image, we extract the need object areas based on bounding box by Mask RCNN to represent information. These areas have chances to avoid geometric attacks on the image, which improved the robustness.

Image segmentation is a classic problem in computer vision research in recent years, which has attracted much attention in the image field. During image segmentation, the meaningful features or regions in the image are extracted. These features can be the original features of the image such as color, texture, and shape, or the spatial frequency spectrum such as histogram features. Segmentation methods are roughly divided into methods based on histogram thresholds, methods based on clustering, methods based on edge detection, methods based on regions, and methods based on graphs.

Image segmentation refers to the separation of different regions with special meaning in the image, making these regions do not intersect each other, and each region should meet the consistency condition of a specific region [14].

For an image g(x, y), segmentation is to divide the image into sub-regions gi(x, y), i = 1,2,…N that meet the following N conditions:

$\cup$ gi (x, y) = g(x, y) indicates that all sub-regions make up the whole picture;

gi (x, y) denotes connected areas. Connectivity refers to the existence of a path connecting any two points in the area.

gi (x, y) $\cap$ gj(x, y) = Ø(i, j = 1, 2 . . . , N; i $\neq$ j) indicates that there are no common elements in any two sub regions.

The area gi(x, y) satisfies a certain uniformity condition. Uniformity (or similarity) refers to a certain similarity criterion for features such as grayscale, texture, and color that no pixels in a region meet.

2.1 Color Segmentation

Color is a visual characteristic of the surface of an object. Every object has its own unique color characteristics. Objects of the same type often have similar color characteristics. Therefore, objects can be distinguished based on color characteristics [15]. The color feature is a significant visual feature of every object and is very robust to image quality and size changes, rotation, and the noise.

To segment a color image, an appropriate color space is first selected, and then an appropriate segmentation method is selected. There are many factors influencing the effect of color image segmentation, among which the essential factor is the change of light. The color of the image changes due to the influence of light. If only the color information is considered and the brightness information is not considered, the segmentation will be inaccurate. Therefore, general color image segmentation usually combines color information and brightness information. In reference [15], the RGB model is used to realize the detection of cotton impurities with good results.

In RGB color space, the correlation among R (red), G (green) and B (blue) is relatively high. For the same color attribute, under different illumination conditions, the values of R (red), G (green), B (blue) are easy to diverge, and it is difficult to determine a specific color threshold and its distribution in the color space. The HSV (Hue, Saturation, Value) color space is a separable luminance component, but the calculation of conversion from RGB color space to HSV color space is large, and when the brightness value and saturation are low, the calculation amount of using HIS (Hue, Intensity, Saturation) or HSV color space is large, and the H component calculated by HIS or HSV color space is not reliable when the brightness value and saturation are low.

RGB is the most basic and uneven color space model. The color distance of the pixel has a large gap with the perception of the human eye making it suitable for display systems but not suitable for image segmentation. The HSV color space model is more in line with human visual characteristics than that of the RGB. In the HSV color space, hue H and saturation S contain color information while brightness I has nothing to do with color. In this experiment, the HSV space model is selected, and the conversion function provided by Python software is used directly for the convenience of the experiment [16]. The function method is used to threshold the H, S, and V3 components. In image enhancement technology, the existing multi-scale algorithm processes RGB three channels independently, which solves the color shift problem, at the same time, breaks the relationships among RGB three channels. This will cause problems as halo, underexposure and over exposure. The paper use an adaptive multi-scale algorithm based on HSV color space. The traditional RGB space multi-scale algorithm is mapped to the HSV color space. The saturation component is adjusted adaptively according to the correlation coefficient while the brightness component is enhanced. And the RGB space is converted to obtain the enhanced image. Experiments with the algorithm is applied to the low light images and back lighting images. This experiment selects saturation segmentation, which is simple to use and convenient to determine the threshold [17].

2.2 Maximum Entropy Segmentation Algorithm

In the information theory, entropy is a measure of the uncertainty of the probability of the occurrence of events. In the image, it is a manifestation of the statistical characteristics of the image, reflecting the amount of information contained in the image.

The principle of maximum entropy was proposed by E. T. Jaynes in 1957, applying the concept of information entropy to image segmentation. The basic idea is to use the gray distribution density function of the image to define the information entropy of the image and determine the optimal threshold by maximizing the total entropy of the target and background after segmentation [18, 19]. According to the concept of Shannon entropy, the entropy for an image with a gray range of (0, 1,..., l-1) is defined as:

$$\mathrm{Ht} = -\sum\nolimits_{i=0}^{l-1} Pi \log pi \quad (1)$$

where pi denotes the probability of the i-th gray level. The threshold t divides the image into two categories: background and target. The probability distributions of the two categories are:

$$\frac{p0}{pt}, \frac{p1}{pt}, \ldots, \frac{pt}{pt} \quad (2)$$

$$\frac{pt+1}{1-pt}, \frac{pt+2}{1-pt}, \ldots, \frac{pl-1}{1-pt} \quad (3)$$

The entropy related to the two types of probability distributions are:

$$\mathrm{H_O}(t) = \sum\nolimits_{i=0}^{t} \frac{pi}{pt} \log \frac{pi}{pt} = \log pt + \frac{Ht}{Pt} \quad (4)$$

$$\mathrm{H_O}(t) = \sum\nolimits_{i=0}^{t} \frac{pi}{pt} \log \frac{pi}{pt} = \log pt + \frac{Ht}{Pt} \quad (5)$$

The total entropy of the image H(t) is the sum of Ho(t) and HB(t), namely,

$$\mathrm{H}(t) = \log(1-pt) + \frac{Ht}{pt} + \frac{HT-Ht}{1-pt} \quad (6)$$

The threshold when the total entropy is maximized is the optimal threshold.

2.3 Level Set Segmentation Algorithm

Sethian conducted a lot of research on the evolution of curves in the early stage. He and Osher first proposed the time-dependent level set description of the moving interface in 1988 and constructed a high-precision and stable numerical solution of the level set equation. Afterward, the level set method was perfected. The level set method converts the evolution of n-dimensional surfaces into an implicit way of the evolution of level set functions in n + 1 dimensional space, mainly including three elements: the data representation of the hypersurface, a series of PDEs (partial differential equations) that control the evolution of the surface, and the corresponding numerical solutions. All information related to surface motion and the situation of the motion surface itself are reflected in the level set function [20]. The definition of the level set is as:

The differentiable function f : Rn → R corresponding to the real number c is the real point set, and {(x1, x2,..., xn) | f(x1, x2,..., xn) = c} is a level set function of the differentiable function f.

Different from traditional image segmentation methods, Active Contour Model (ACM, also known as Snakes) initializes a parameterized closed curve with an energy function around the target to be segmented; under the combined action of the inherent internal force of the curve (the force that controls the bending and stretching of the curve) and the external force of the image, it finally converges to the boundary contour of the target. It surpasses traditional image segmentation methods in segmentation accuracy, noise resistance, stability, and robustness. The mathematical description of the Snake model is to find a continuous closed curve to minimize the objective function of equation [22]:

$$E_{Snake} = \int_0^1 [\text{Eint}(BV(s) + Eext(Vs))]ds \tag{7}$$

Where, Vs(x(s), y(s)), s is arc length; V(s) is the contour curve; Eint(V(s)) = w1(s)|Vs|2 + w2(s)|Vss|2 denotes internal energy; Vs and Vss represent the first and second partial derivatives of S, respectively; Vs controls the contour line as short as possible; Vss controls the contour line as smooth as possible. The first-order differential derivative w1 is used to control the elastic energy contribution affected by the interval, and the second-order differential weight w2 is used to control the curvature energy contribution affected by the point change. Eext(V(s)) is an external energy function and mostly uses the gradient of the image. It is the contraction limiting force of the dynamic contour line and is adopted to control the contour line as close as possible to the area with high gradient change. The steps to realize the Snake model are: 1) initializing the contour; 2) making the contour evolve and converge to a suitable shape and position by minimizing the energy function [21, 22].

3 Experiment Analysis

3.1 The Programming Language -python

Python is used as the programming language in this project. In the beginning, the C++ language and Matlab were considered as the main programming languages, but after a few days of trials, Python was finally chosen as the programming language for the project. Python was developed by Guido van Rossum in 1989. Rossum's initial idea was very simple, and he hoped that Python would be easier to read. The name of Python comes from the BBC TV series Monty Python's Flying Circus. Guido is also a programmer himself. He has been involved in the design of a teaching language called ABC, designed for non-professional programmers. However, the ABC language has not been successful. The reason is that Guido believes that it is not open (the relatively closed development language, scalability, and promotion are relatively unsuccessful). Guido wants to avoid this error in Python. At the same time, he wants to achieve something that has flashed in ABC but has not been realized. Python is a high-level interpretive, compulsive, interactive, and object-oriented scripting language. As an interpreted language, the code written in Python is readable and easy to learn due to its simple syntax and indentation space. The Python language is a simple and powerful programming language. Compared with other programming languages, it focuses on the syntax and structure of programming languages. Python is more concerned with the programming language itself, but how to solve problems with Python. According to TIOBE's programming language rankings released in 2018, Python ranks in the top three, known as the 2018 annual programming language. Python ranked first in the annual interactive rankings of the five top programming languages released by IEEE Spectrum in 2017. As a programming language, Python has many advantages. It is very use-friends to beginners and easy to learn. Compared to other programming languages, Python has a huge advantage. It has a very rich library and is compatible with different operating systems. For developers, source code written in Python is easy to maintain, which is a significant advantage. This project uses deep learning to identify the surface defects of aluminium profiles. Since Python can refer to numpy, scipy lights, convenient mathematical operations, third-party libraries, in the visualization can call matplotlib, for various vertical fields (such as the image, voice, and text preprocessing phases are all available to the library).

The TensorFlow framework was developed by Google's Google Brain team and of ficially released at the end of 2015. The TensorFlow framework is a basic system that can be applied in many areas. Since Google has played an important role in promoting deep learning, TensorFlow has gained great popularity and popularity from deep learning enthusiasts since its inception. The TensorFlow framework is primarily used for machine learning and deep neural network research. The TensorFlow framework and the Theano framework have many common developments and therefore have many things in common. They have similar design concepts and are based on computational graphs to implement an automatic calculus system. The TensorFlow programming interface supports Python and C ++. As the version continues to update, the alpha versions of the Java, R, and Haskell APIs are also supported. In addition, TensorFlow also supports Window7, Windows10 and Windows Server2016 systems, as well as AWS. In model training, the TensorFlow framework does not require a separate python interpreter or danced model decoder to train models on a variety of servers and mobile devices. As one of the current popular deep learning frameworks, TensorFlow has received a lot of criticism while gaining many supporters. Critics believe that the interface of TensorFlow is iteratively fast, but the compatibility issue has not been resolved, which has led to many open-source codes not running on the new version of TensorFlow and has led to problems with many third-party frameworks based on TensorFlow. The design of TensorFlow's interface is not friendly to deep learning users. Its interface is complex and difficult to understand. There are many abstract concepts that make it difficult for deep learning enthusiasts who are new to TensorFlow to understand. Many developers have tried to build a more optimized interface based on TensorFlow, but it has not been implemented so far. TensorFlow still does not have a user-friendly unified interface.

OpenCV is a cross platform computer vision and machine learning software library based on BSD license (open source), which can run on Linux, windows, Android and Mac OS operating systems. Besides, it provides a series of high-efficiency computer interface, such as C ++ and python. OpenCV provides a wealth of visual processing algorithms, and it is partly written in C language, coupled with its open source features, properly handled, without the need to add new external support can also complete the compilation link to generate executor.

3.2 Implementation

An image may have multiple object areas, if we choose enough object areas to represent the information, the capacity is considerable. However, not all areas are suitable for information hiding, the object areas should be filtered based on the requirements to construct a database that can meet most of the requirements of information transmission [23].

In this paper, Cotton Impurity Detection Algorithm Based on Image Segmentation is the subject of research. In the project, I've considered many programming languages and frameworks and try to use them into the project. Finally, I decide to use Python as a programming language. And the Pytroch is the framework of the project. The main objectives of the project are to improve the accuracy and speed of Cotton Impurity Detection, improve the Cotton Impurity Detection efficiency, and further improve the economic efficiency of manufacturers.

Some raw cotton was randomly selected and spread to a thickness of 1cm. In this experiment, a Panasonic (DMC-FX01) camera was used to take pictures under dark light, normal light, and light (flash) conditions. Besides, one of the three situations was selected as the research object; the photo is presented in Fig. 1:

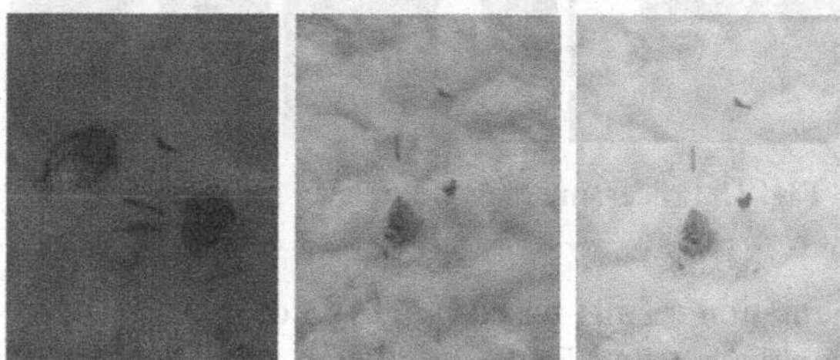

Fig. 1. Three cases of the original figure

In this experiment, The pictures under dark light, normal light, and light (flash) conditions. The segmentation results based on HSV color space method. The maximum entropy segmentation method and The segmentation effect based on the level set method was used to write code and deal with the research object.

The segmentation results based on HSV color space are illustrated in Fig. 2.

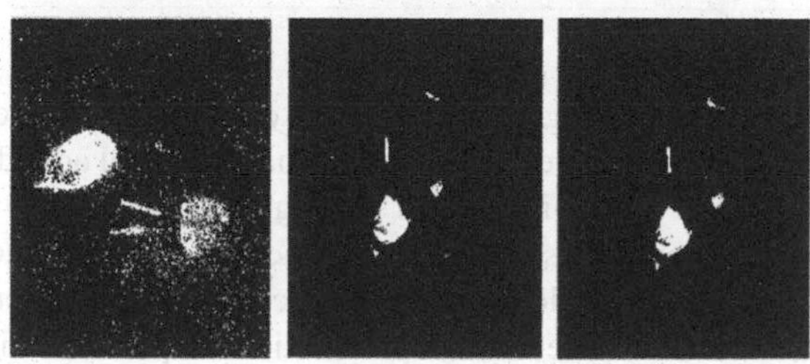

Fig. 2. The processing of color segmentation

The maximum entropy segmentation effect is exhibited in Fig. 3.

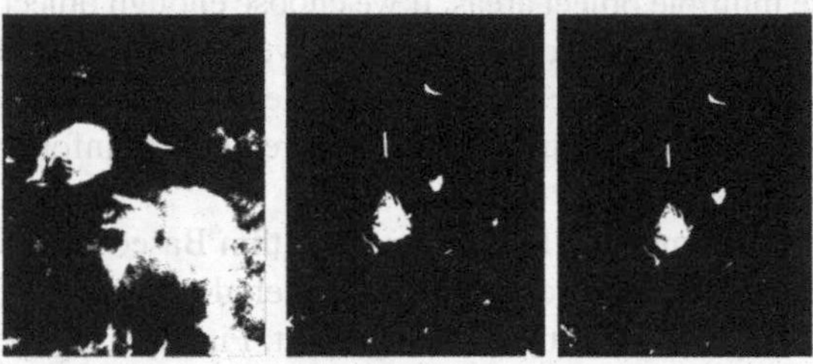

Fig. 3. The maximum entropy segmentation processing figure

The segmentation effect based on the level set is displayed in Fig. 4.

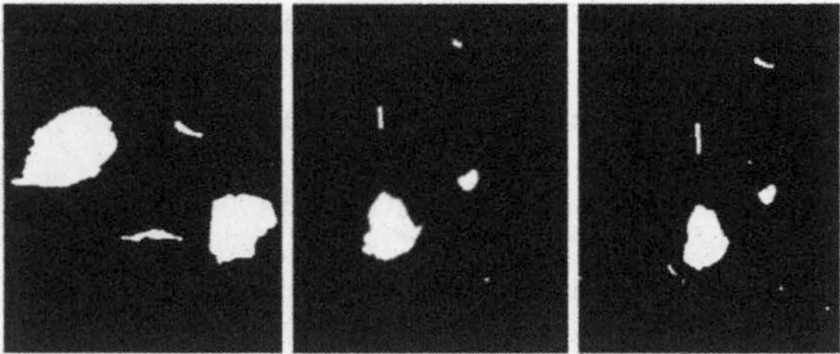

Fig. 4. Processing diagram of level set segmentation

After the segmentation results based on HSV color space method. The maximum entropy segmentation method and The segmentation effect based on the level set method calculation, the impurity content in the three cases is displayed in Table 1.

Table 1. Impurity content

Algorithm	Impurity content (%)
Space division	10.16
Maximum entropy segmentation	3.26
Segmentation based on level set	2.77

It can be observed from the segmentation effect diagram that there is not much difference between the segmentation effect under normal light and added light conditions. The segmentation effect is quite different in low light. According to the color characteristics, the HSV space completes the image segmentation better and accurately. The segmentation effect is affected in low light. Specifically, maximum entropy segmentation is most affected, followed by level set segmentation. Experiments indicate that color segmentation has a better segmentation effect while it is not universal. After calculation, the impurity content in the three cases is 10.16%, 3.26%, and 2.77%, respectively.

4 Conclusion

In this paper, Cotton Impurity Detection detection is the subject of research. In the project, I have considered many programming languages and frameworks and try to use them into the project. Finally, I decide to use Python as a programming language because of its advantage. The main objectives of the project are to improve the further improve the economic efficiency of manufacturers.

Under different light intensities, three different algorithms are used for image segmentation. Both can complete the segmentation effect and can basically detect cotton impurities, providing the foundation for the next step of the cotton detection device. However, segmentation still has certain difficulties for images with complex backgrounds. In specific problems, it is necessary to select a suitable segmentation algorithm according to the actual situation and improve it to obtain a better segmentation effect, so as to improve the accuracy and robustness of the segmentation.

Funding Statement. The authors received no specific funding for this study.

Conflicts of Interest. The authors declare that they have no conflicts of interest to report regarding the present study.

References

1. Zhang, H.: "Research on surface defect detection method based on deep learning", Ph.D. dissertation, Soochow University, China (2018)
2. Wu, G., Xu, K.: On-line monitoring technology for steel plate surface quality. Beijing Science Press (2010)
3. Liu, Z., Xiang, B., Song, Y., Lu, H., Liu, Q.: An improved unsupervised image segmentation method based on multi-objective particle swarm optimization clustering algorithm. Comput. Mater. Continua **58**(2), 451–461 (2019)
4. Roper, B.: "How artificial intelligence will change the world".
5. Vardi, M.Y.: Artificial intelligence: past and future. Commun. ACM (2012). https://doi.org/10.1145/2063176.2063177
6. Bingtao, H., Wang, J.: Deep learning for distinguishing computer generated images and natural images: a survey. J. Inf. Hiding Priv. Prot. **2**(2), 37–47 (2020)
7. Oliva, D., Cuevas, E.: An Introduction to Machine Learning. Springer Publishing Company, Incorporated (2015) https://doi.org/10.1007/978-3-319-20010-1
8. Hossain, B., Morooka, T., Okuno, M., Nii, M., Yoshiya, S., et al.: Surgical outcome prediction in total knee arthroplasty using machine learning. Intell. Autom. Soft Comput. **25**(1), 105–115 (2019)
9. Indira, B., Valarmathi, K.: A perspective of the machine learning approach for the packet classification in the software defined network. Intell. Autom. Soft Comput. **26**(4), 795–805 (2020)
10. Gumaei, A., Al-Rakhami, M., AlSalman, H.: Dl-har: deep learning-based human activity recognition framework for edge computing. Comput. Mater. Continua **65**(2), 1033–1057 (2020)
11. Renugambal, A., Bhuvaneswari, K.S.: Image segmentation of brain mr images using OTSU's based hybrid WCMFO algorithm. Comput. Mater. Continua **64**(2), 681–700 (2020)

12. Fang, W., Zhang, F., Ding, Y., Sheng, J.: A new sequential image prediction method based on LSTM and DCGAN. Comput. Mater. Continua **64**(1), 217–231 (2020)
13. Diao, Q.: An improved image classification approach of sparse coding. Intell. Comput. Appl. **9**(05), 50–53 (2019)
14. Zhang, C., Yang, W.Z., Liu, Z.H.: Color image segmentation method based on HSV comprehensive saliency. Comput. Eng. Des. **34**(11), 3944–3947 (2013)
15. Li, X.Y., Zhuang, Y.T., Pan, Y.H.: Content-based image retrieval technology and system. Comput. Res. Dev. **38**(3), 344–352 (2001)
16. Zhang, G.Q.: Research on color image segmentation in HSV space. Comput. Eng. Appl. **46**(26), 179–181 (2010)
17. Wei, J.D.: Research on cotton image segmentation strategy in natural scene based on HSV color model. Cotton Sci. **20**(1), 34–38 (2008)
18. Long, J.W., Shen, X.J., Chen, P.H.: Adaptive minimum error threshold segmentation algorithm. Acta Autom. Sinica **38**(7), 1135–1136 (2012)
19. He, W.X., Yang, H., Zhao, G., et al.: A quantile-based SORA method using maximum entropy method with fractional moments. J. Mech. Des. **143**(4), 1–40 (2021)
20. Mao, X., Cai, J.H., Zhang, S.L.: An image segmentation method based on weighted Chebyshev distance. J. Taiyuan Univ. Sci. Technol. **41**(06), 449–455 (2020)
21. Wang, J.W., Liu, H.: Calculation method of plant leaf area based on Snake model. Comput. Eng. **39**(1), 234–238 (2013)
22. Fang, W., Pang, L., Yi, W.N.: Survey on the application of deep reinforcement learning in image processing. J. Artif. Intell. **2**(1), 39–58 (2020)
23. Luo, Y.J., Qin, J., Xiang, X., et al.: Coverless image steganography based on image segmentation. Comput. Mater. Continua **64**(2), 1281–1295 (2020)

Improving Text Matching with Semantic Dependency Graph via Message Passing Neural Network

Yongkang Song[1,2], Dianqing Liu[1,2], Dazhan Mao[1,2], and Yanqiu Shao[1,2](✉)

[1] School of Information Science, Beijing Language and Culture University, Beijing 100083, China

[2] National Language Resources Monitoring and Research Center (CNLR) Print Media Language Branch, Wuhan, China

Abstract. Text matching is a core natural language processing research problem. Deep semantic alignment and comparison between two text sequences lie in the core of text matching. While the attention-based model achieves high accuracy through word-level or char-lever alignment, they ignore the deep semantic relations between words and have poor generalization performance. This paper presents a neural approach to leveraging the Chinese Semantic Dependency Graph for text matching. This model uses Message Passing neural network to encode the semantic relation between word and use these semantic associations to assist semantic alignment and comparison. Experimental results demonstrate that our method substantially achieves state-of-the-art performance compare to the strong baseline model. The further discussion shows that our model can improve the text alignment process and have better robustness and comprehensibility.

Keywords: Text matching · Chinese semantic dependency graph · Message passing neural network

1 Introduction

Text semantic matching is an essential and core problem in natural language processing. It can be applied to many NLP tasks, such as dialog systems, natural language inference, paraphrase identification, and answer selection. The study of text matching is of great significance for natural language understanding and has a wide range of realistic application scenarios.

Figure 1 In the text matching tasks, a model takes two text sequences as input and predicts a category or scala value indicating their relationship. Nowadays, deep neural networks are the most popular choices for text matching. There are two main types of text matching models, representation-based model, and the interaction-based model. Representation-based models ([1, 2]) encode sentences into fixed-size vectors and use similarity measures such as cosine distance and Manhattan distance to measure semantic relationships. They choose different encoders, such as CNN, MLP, BILSTM, Transformer, etc. to get the distributed representation of sentences. However, Expressing the

X. Sun et al. (Eds.): ICAIS 2021, LNCS 12736, pp. 395–406, 2021.
https://doi.org/10.1007/978-3-030-78609-0_34

text as a fixed-size vector will lose a certain amount of information and ignore the fine-grained interactive relation between texts. Recently, some studies [3–5] incorporate tree structure into the encoding process to learn improved sentence representations. [6] enrich interaction features between two sentences by comparing their subtree structures. Other work [7] introduces external knowledge, such as synonyms, antonyms, synonyms, and other features to assist the alignment process in text matching. However, there are few studies on using semantic structure information to improve the text matching process. Text matching is a task that requires an in-depth understanding of text semantics. Compared with shallow information such as syntactic structure, synonyms, and antonyms, We believe that the semantic dependency graph is more suitable for the text matching task's requirements.

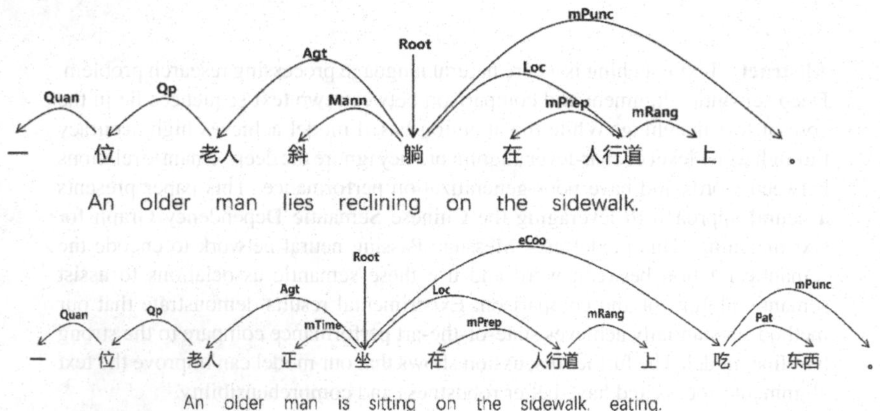

Fig. 1. The Chinese Semantic Dependency Graph for two sentences. The sentence pair is randomly selected from our training data.

Figure 1 shows that the Chinese Semantic Dependency Graph [8] can provide some in-depth semantic information beyond plain text. For example, we can see the relationship between '老人' and '躺' is 'Agt.' And the relationship between '老人' and '坐' is 'Agt' also. In the first sentence, older man is the agent of lying, while in the second sentence, older man is the agent of sitting. We can also see that the words pointed to by the two sentences' 'Root' tags are different. This information cannot be reflected in plain text. It is not clear to what extent the word vector contains this information, so we think it is meaningful to study whether the semantic structure information of the text is helpful for text matching.

An intuitive way to use semantic dependency graphs is to calculate the matching degree of the two graphs' subgraphs, manually customize rules to assign weights to different types of matching edges, and finally get the matching score. Such manual rules are cumbersome and do not have the generalization ability to migrate to other tasks. Nowadays, the most popular text matching model is based on the attention mechanism, which mainly uses the attention mechanism to align two sentences word by word and uses the alignment information to calculate the matching score. Based on this idea of attention alignment, another intuitive approach is to calculate the attention matrix of the edge between two graphs and mix it with the attention matrix between words, hoping to get a more reasonable attention distribution. However, this approach breaks the connection between the semantic dependency edge and the word. To more fully combine word meaning and semantic relations, we propose a novel text-matching approach to leverage the Chinese semantic dependency graph for semantic alignment and comparison. Specifically, we still use the idea of interactive text matching. The difference is that it enables the model to use the text's semantic structure information when computing interactive attention, and we use a message-passing mechanism to allow the model to focus on semantic association and word information at the same time.

The contributions of this paper are as follows:

We integrate the semantic dependency graph into the deep learning model to get better semantic alignment and comparison of text matching.
We explored the impact of different ways of encoding semantic dependency graphs on text matching.
We explored the reasons why using graph structures can bring improvements.

2 Related Work

2.1 Neural Text Matching Model

Text matching is a widely used NLP technology that aims to model the semantic relation between two texts. Early work on text matching used traditional text matching algorithms such as TFIDF, latent semantic analysis (LSA) [9], and latent Dirichlet allocation(LDA) [10], BM25, Jaccard, SimHash. These traditional methods mainly solve the matching problem at the linguistic level or the similarity problem at the lexical level and cannot reflect the match at the semantic level.

In recent years, deep learning methods have become the mainstream of many NLP tasks, such as convolutional neural networks(CNNs), recurrent neural networks(RNNS), and Long Short-Term Memory architectures(LSTM). Accordingly, many text matching applications take these models as text encoders in their matching processes. DSSM ([11]) is the earliest research effort to apply a deep neural network model on text matching. In DSSM, each piece of text is vectorized through a 5-layer neural network, and then a matching score for a text pair is calculated as the cosine similarity between their representations. Reference [13] ranks short text pairs using CNN to preserving local information in the text representation. Unlike the traditional Siamese network [12] that uses Euclidean distance or cosine distance to calculate the similarity between two sentences directly and predict the results, the system uses a similarity matrix to calculate similarity. Reference [14] also uses the Siamese structure. The difference is that they use a shared RNN to encode two sentences and use Manhattan distance to measure similarity. Moreover, [5] uses tree-LSTM to get better sentence pair representation and have improved on text matching tasks.

However, these models fail to learn fine-grained interaction features and can hardly model complex relations. Latter works adopt the matching aggregation framework to match two sequences. Reference [15] uses a simple form of attention for alignment and aggregate aligned representations with feed-forward networks. Reference [4] integrates the syntax tree to enhance the alignment process. It consists of two parts: one uses the sequence model to collect the context information of words, and the other uses the tree model to encode the text's syntactic structure information. It increases the accuracy of the SNLI to above 88%. Some other researchers are working to improve the calculation method of attention. [18] designed multiple attention functions to compare word vectors of two sentences. They combine four attention mechanisms to model different angles of matching. Reference [7] uses external knowledge, such as synonyms and antonyms, to improve the word alignment process. Recently, some researchers have begun to use semantic information for text matching. Reference [17] has shown that the joint training of Bert and semantic role labeling can improve text matching, making us more convinced that using in-depth semantic analysis such as semantic dependency graph is helpful for text matching.

Most of the previous researchers only used the sentence's surface information, such as syntactic structure, synonyms and antonyms, semantic roles, and so on. We believe that semantic dependency analysis can better reflect the text's deep semantics as an in-depth semantic analysis. In this paper, we explore the use of the Chinese semantic dependency graph as a graph structure representation method to assist text matching.

2.2 Chinese Semantic Dependency Graph

As an extension of the syntactic dependency tree, the semantic dependency graph's structure representation belongs to the Directed Acyclic Graph, which was first proposed by open [19]. Chinese semantic dependency parsing [19] is a sentence-level semantic analysis of natural language. In the traditional syntactic analysis, a sentence's linear structure needs to be transformed into a dependency tree. Each word in the penalty can be regarded as a node, and the core word of the entire sentence depends on a virtual root node (ROOT). The semantic dependency graph parsing allows the use of graph structure to express the information of a sentence. A word can be the argument of multiple predicates(non-local), and the dependency arcs may cross each other(non-projection), which leads to more resonant capture semantic information. The final structure representation of Chinese semantic dependency graph parsing is a single-root directed acyclic graph-only one root node is allowed in the entire sentence, and each word requires at least one parent node. In semantic relationship categories, the Chinese semantic dependency graph parsing task defines 170 relationships, comprehensively covering Chinese semantic phenomena.

In recent years, graph-based methods [21, 22] and transition-based methods [23] have been applied to dependency parsing tasks. Significantly, the Biaffine network, which belongs to the graph-based methods, has proved to be one of the states of the art methods in dependency parsing tasks. However, the current Chinese semantic dependency parser's performance has not yet reached the practical application standard. We choose to use manually labeled data for experiments to verify the semantic dependency graph's effectiveness for text matching tasks.

3 Methodology

As shown in Fig. 2, our model consists of four components: 1) sequence encoder, which converts the sentence to vector representation, and applies BiLSTM to get context embedding. 2) graph encoder, which uses a message-passing neural network to build interaction between the word in sentences. 3) matching and aggregation layer, which obtains the interactive information of two sentences through the attention mechanism and use operations such as dot products and differences to calculate similarity and dissimilarity. 4) pooling layer, our matching model converts the resulting vectors obtained above to a fixed-length vector with pooling and feeds it to the final classifier to determine the overall inference relationship.

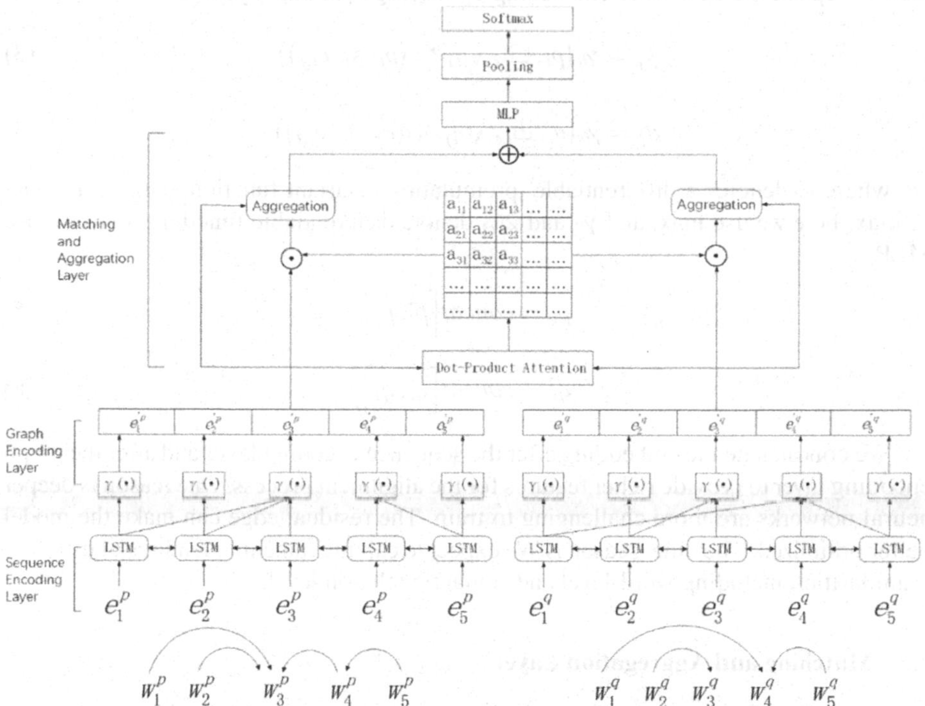

Fig. 2. A high-level view of our neural matching networks

3.1 Sequence Encoding Layer

The purpose of the sequence encoding layer is to encode the two texts, respectively. Commonly used sequence encoders include MLP, CNN, BILSTM, etc. Here we use BILSTM to obtain the contextual representation of each word. To bookkeep the notations for later use, we use write as $\overline{p_i}$ the hidden state generated by the BiLSTM at time i over the sequence p, the same is applied to $\overline{q_i}$.

$$\overline{p_i} = BiLSTM\,(p, i), \forall i \in \left[1, \ldots, l_p\right] \tag{1}$$

$$\overline{q_i} = BiLSTM\,(q, i), \forall i \in \left[1, \ldots, l_q\right] \tag{2}$$

3.2 Graph Encoding Layer

The graph coding layer integrates the semantic association and structure information of the sentence into the word representation. We use the Message Passing Neural Network [25] to encode the Chinese Semantic dependency graph. As is shown in Fig. 2, the corresponding Chinese semantic dependency graph, let $\left\{p_1^k, p_2^k, p_3^k, \ldots, p_{\ell_p}^k\right\}$ be the hidden states of input nodes in k-th layer.the dependency relation between p_i^k, p_j^k is $e_{i,j}$, then we update the new word embedding by message passing layer:

$$p_i^{'} = \gamma_\theta\left(p_i, \boxdot_{j \in N(i)} \varnothing_\Theta\left(p_i, p_j, e_{i,j}\right)\right) \tag{3}$$

$$q_i^{'} = \gamma_\theta\left(q_i, \boxdot_{j \in \mathcal{N}(i)} \varnothing_\Theta\left(q_i, q_j, e_{i,j}\right)\right) \tag{4}$$

where $\boxdot$ denotes a differentiable, premutation invariant function, e.g., sum, mean or max, here we use max, and γ_θ and $\varnothing_\Theta$ denote differentiable functions, here we use MLP.

$$p_i = concat\left[\overline{p_i}, p_i^{'}\right] \tag{5}$$

$$q_i = concat\left[\overline{q_i}, q_i^{'}\right] \tag{6}$$

We concatenate the embedding after the sequence encoding layer and after the graph encoding layer to provide richer features for the alignment process. One reason is deeper neural networks are more challenging to train. The residual edge can make the model better optimized. The other reason is We expect to capture matching features of different granularities, including word-level and semantic relation level.

3.3 Matching and Aggregation Layer

The matching and aggregation layer obtains the interactive information of two sentences by calculating attention word by word. A simple form of alignment based on the attention mechanism is used following [21]. As shown in Fig. 3, it takes features from the two sequences as input and computes the alignment representations as output. Information from the first sequence of length ℓ_p and the second sequence is denoted as length ℓ_q. The similarity score $a_{i,j}$ calculated as the dot product of the projected vectors:

$$a_{i,j} = p_i^T q_j \tag{7}$$

$$\tilde{p}_i = \sum_{j=1}^{l_p} \frac{exp(a_{ij})}{\sum_{k=1}^{l_q} exp(a_{ik})} q_j, \forall i \in \left[1, \ldots, l_p\right] \tag{8}$$

$$\tilde{q}_i = \sum_{j=1}^{l_p} \frac{exp(a_{ij})}{\sum_{k=1}^{l_p} exp(a_{ik})} p_i, \forall i \in [1, \ldots, \ell_q] \tag{9}$$

Where $\tilde{p}_i$ is a weighted summation of $\{q_j\}_{j=1}^{l_q}$, Intuitively, the content in $\{q_j\}_{j=1}^{l_q}$ is relevant to p_i will be selected and represented as $\tilde{p}_i$.The same is performed for each word in other sentence. Then we aggregate the features obtained by the features of the encoding layer. The aggregation layer includes concatenation, subtraction and multiplication, aim to get the results of the comparison between the sentences and their attention weights. A perceptron network layer G forwards the aggregation of each sentence. The outputs of G are the weight vectors As shown in Eqs. (10) and (11).

$$m_p = G[p_i, \tilde{p}_i, p_i - \tilde{p}_i, p_i \odot \tilde{p}_i] \tag{10}$$

$$m_q = G[q_i, \tilde{q}_i, q_i - \tilde{q}_i, q_i \odot \tilde{q}_i] \tag{11}$$

3.4 Pooling Layer

The pooling layer is to extract further the features obtained by the aggregation layer. We consider that summation could be sensitive to the sequence length and hence less robust. We instead suggest the following strategy: compute both average and max pooling, and concatenate all these vectors to form the final fixed length vector $\boldsymbol{m}$. Our experiments show that this leads to significantly better results than summation. The final fixed length vector $\boldsymbol{m}$ is calculated as follows:

$$m_{p,ave} = \sum_{i=1}^{l_p} \frac{m_{p,i}}{l_p}, m_{p,max} = \max_{1 \leq i \leq l_p} m_{p,i} \tag{12}$$

$$m_{q,ave} = \sum_{i=1}^{l_p} \frac{m_{q,i}}{l_q}, m_{q,max} = \max_{1 \leq i \leq l_q} m_{q,i} \tag{13}$$

$$\boldsymbol{m} = [m_{p,ave}, m_{p,max}, m_{q,ave}, m_{q,max}] \tag{14}$$

We then put $\boldsymbol{m}$ into a final multilayer perceptron classifier. The MLP has a hidden layer with ReLU activation and softmax output layer in our experiments.

4 Experiments and Analysis

4.1 Datasets

Since the accuracy of the current semantic dependency analysis technology is not up to the practical application standard, the automatically annotated semantic dependency graph is noisy. We manually annotated the semantic dependency graph on the 10006 Chinese text inference sentence pair. The sentence pair are selected manually and annotated from the CCL2018 Chinese Natural Language Inference dataset. There are three types of label in this dataset: neutral, entailment, contradiction. A pair of labeled examples can be seen in Fig. 1. The number of the training set is 8006, the validation set is 1000, and the test set is 1000. Three categories are balance in each dataset (Table 1).

Table 1. Category statistics of datasets

	Neutral	Entailment	Contradiction	Total
Train	2770	2734	2502	8006
Test	337	364	299	1000
Dev	337	351	351	1000

4.2 Implementation Details

Chinese word embedding is trained from the People's Daily and other corpora by the method proposed by Li et al. [24]. The word embedding dimension is 300. The experiment uses the pytorch and torch geometric deep learning framework. The batch size is 32. The LSTM hidden layer dim is set to 300. The learning rate is 0.0003, and the dropout rate is 0.5. We use the Adam function as an optimization function. The first moment is set to be 0.9 and the second 0.999. We use the cross-entropy function as a loss function. Besides, early stopping is used to prevent over-fitting. We removed all periods in the experiment. The evaluation uses accuracy, which calculated as Eq. (15).

$$Acc = \frac{\tilde{l}_{correct}}{l} \tag{15}$$

Where $\tilde{l}_{correct}$ represents the number of labels that are correctly classified; l is the number of true labels of raw dataset.

4.3 Experimental Results

Table 2 shows the results of different models. The first group of models is based on sentence encoding. The model of Bowman [25] encodes the two texts with different LSTM. The approach proposed by [26] presents a memory augmented neural network, the neural semantic encoder(NSE), to encode sentences. The next group of methods in the table is the inter-sentence attention-based model. [15] proposed a decomposable attention model without relying on any word-order information. The ESIM [4] model is a very classic and effective text matching model. And we also compared with pre-trained language models such as Roberta. Unfortunately, the accuracy of pre-trained language models still exceeds a lot.

4.4 Ablation Analysis

We further analyze the significant components that are of importance to help us achieve good performance. We first remove the graph encoder layer from the best model to explore how the non-semantic dependent graph's information will affect the results. Secondly, we no longer splice the sequence encoder's output and the graph encoder but only use the graph encoder's output. We also explored the impact of the graph encoding method on the results.

Table 2. Accuracies of different models on our dataset

Model	Acc
BiLSTM [25]	61.12%
NSE [20]	62.36%
ESIM [4]	66.89%
Decomp Att [15]	66.32%
Roberta	73.74%
Our Model	68.51%

Table 3. Ablation study results

Model	Acc
– no graph encoder	66.83%
– no sequence encoder	63.41%
– no concatenate	66.12%
– default	68.51%
– Mean	67.13%
– Undirected graph	67.24%

As shown in Table 3, the first group verifies the necessity of the graph encoder and sequence encoder. We first remove the graph encoder in our model, and the correct rate of the whole model drops by 1.68%, which proves that the semantic dependency graph is useful for this task. In the second additional experiment, we removed the sequence encoder. The results showed that the effect was reduced by 5.1% without the sequence encoder, which shows that the sequence encoder is still necessary for text matching tasks. The second group tried different semantic dependency graph encoding methods. And when using undirected graphs or using the mean function to aggregate graph information, there is an inevitable loss of accuracy.

Figure 3 shows an example where the traditional model is classified incorrectly, and our model is categorized correctly. We can see that due to the graph structure's pooling effect's information dissemination, the attention distribution shows a trend of being homogenized. One possible reason is the pooling effect of the spread of graph structure information, which prevents the model from paying too much attention to local matching. And weak local matching signal may also lead to good matching, which coincides with the conclusion drawn in [16]. Another possible reason is that the semantic dependency graph's edges can provide useful information to help alignment.

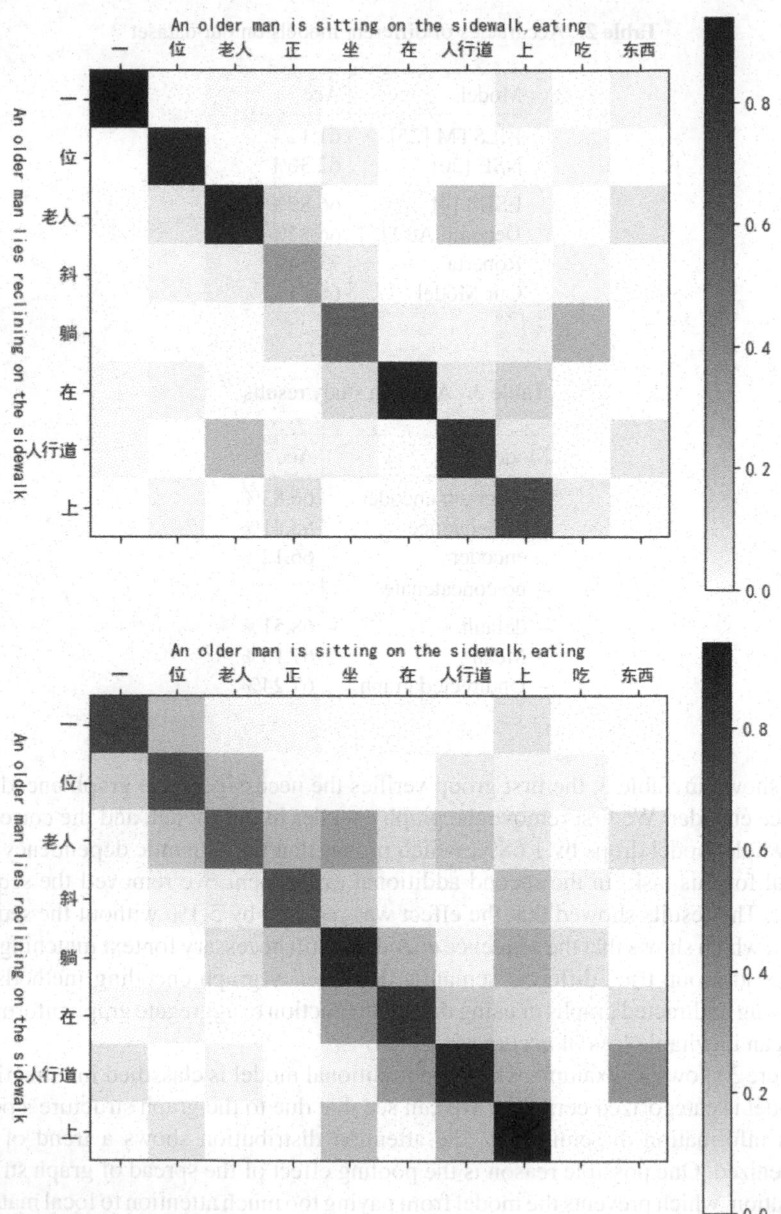

Fig. 3. Attention weights of different models. The above is the attention weight from ESIM, and the bottom is the attention of our model.

4.5 Conclusion and Future Work

We present a neural network model to incorporate the Chinese semantic dependency graph for text matching. We verify the effectiveness of the semantic dependency graph for this task on the manually annotated textual data. Our work's main contribution is to use the semantic relation between words to improve word alignment and semantic comparison. Benefit from the pooling function of the graph structure, our model can avoid some misclassification caused by local matching. When external knowledge is not easy to obtain, it is feasible to use the semantic relationship between words to improve text matching.

Further work interesting to us includes exploring the different ways of encoding semantic dependency graph in text-matching and combining semantic dependency graph with common sense knowledge. Another point worthy of research is how to improve the accuracy of the text matching while not suffering a significant loss in speed.

Acknowledgements. This research project is supported by the National Natural Science Foundation of China (61872402), the Humanities and Social Science Project of the Ministry of Education (17YJAZH068), Science Foundation of Beijing Language and Culture University (supported by "the Fundamental Research Funds for the Central Universities") (18ZDJ03), the Open Project Program of the National Laboratory of Pattern Recognition (NLPR), the Fundamental Research Funds for the Central Universities, and the Research Funds of Beijing Language and Culture University (20YCX147). In addition, I would also like to thank my teacher Shao Yanqiu. Without her careful guidance and encouragement, this paper would not have been completed.

Conflicts of Interest. We declare that we do not have any commercial or associative interest that represents a conflict of interest in connection with the work submitted.

References

1. Hu, B., et al.: Convolutional neural network architectures for matching natural language sentences. In: Ghahramani, Z., et al. (eds.) Advances in Neural Information Processing Systems, pp. 2042–2050. Curran Associates, Inc. (2014)
2. Qiu, X., Huang, X.: Convolutional neural tensor network architecture for community-based question answering. In: Proceedings of the 24th International Conference on Artificial Intelligence, pp. 1305–1311. AAAI Press (2015)
3. Williams, A., et al.: A broad-coverage challenge corpus for sentence understanding through inference. Presented at the (2018). https://doi.org/10.18653/v1/N18-1101
4. Chen, Q., Zhu, X., Ling, Z., Wei, S., Jiang, H., Inkpen, D.: Enhanced LSTM for natural language inference. In: Proceedings of the 55th Annual Meeting of the Association for Computational Linguistics (vol. 1: Long Papers), pp. 1657–1668 (2017). https://doi.org/10.18653/v1/P17-1152
5. Tai, K., et al.: Improved Semantic Representations From Tree-Structured Long Short-Term Memory Networks. 1, (2015). https://doi.org/10.3115/v1/P15-1150
6. Liu, Y., et al.: Structured Alignment Networks for Matching Sentences. Presented at the (2018). https://doi.org/10.18653/v1/D18-1184
7. Chen, Q., et al.: Neural Natural Language Inference Models Enhanced with External Knowledge. Presented at the (2018). https://doi.org/10.18653/v1/P18-1224
8. Ding, Y., Shao, Y., Che, W., Liu, T.: Dependency graph based chinese semantic parsing. In: Sun, M., Liu, Y., Zhao, J. (eds.) CCL/NLP-NABD -2014. LNCS (LNAI), vol. 8801, pp. 58–69. Springer, Cham (2014). https://doi.org/10.1007/978-3-319-12277-9_6
9. Deerwester, S., et al.: Indexing by latent semantic analysis. J. Am. Soc. Inf. Sci. **41**, 391–407 (1990). https://doi.org/10.1002/(SICI)1097-4571(199009)41:6%3c391::AID-ASI1%3e3.0.CO;2-9

10. Blei, D., et al.: Latent dirichlet allocation. J. Mach. Learn. Res. **3**, 993 (2013)
11. Huang, P.-S., et al.: Learning deep structured semantic models for web search using clickthrough data. Presented at the (2013) https://doi.org/10.1145/2505515.2505665
12. Chopra, S. et al.: Learning a similarity metric discriminatively, with application to face verification. In: Proceedings of the Computer Vision and Pattern Recognition, pp. 539–546, vol. 1 (2005). https://doi.org/10.1109/CVPR.2005.202
13. Severyn, A., Moschitti, A.: Learning to Rank Short Text Pairs with Convolutional Deep Neural Networks. Presented at the (2015). https://doi.org/10.1145/2766462.2767738
14. Mueller, J., Thyagarajan, A.: Siamese recurrent architectures for learning sentence similarity. In: Proceedings of the Thirtieth AAAI Conference on Artificial Intelligence, pp. 2786–2792. AAAI Press (2016)
15. Parikh, A., et al.: A Decomposable Attention Model for Natural Language Inference (2016)
16. Chen, H., et al.: MIX: multi-channel information crossing for text matching. In: Proceedings of the 24th ACM SIGKDD International Conference on Knowledge Discovery & Data Mining, pp. 110–119 ACM, London United Kingdom (2018). https://doi.org/10.1145/3219819.3219928
17. Zhang, Z., et al.: Explicit Contextual Semantics for Text Comprehension. arXiv:1809.02794 [cs]. (2019)
18. Tan, C., et al.: Multiway Attention Networks for Modeling Sentence Pairs. Presented at the (2018). https://doi.org/10.24963/ijcai.2018/613
19. Oepen, S., et al.: SemEval 2014 Task 8. Broad-Coverage Semantic Dependency Parsing. In: Proceedings of the 8th., Dublin, Ireland, pp. 63–72 (2014)
20. Munkhdalai, T., Yu, H.: Neural Semantic Encoders. Presented at the (2017). https://doi.org/10.18653/v1/E17-1038
21. Wang, W., Chang, B.: Graph-based dependency parsing with bidirectional LSTM. In: Proceedings of the 54th Annual Meeting of the Association for Computational Linguistics (vol. 1: Long Papers), pp. 2306–2315. Association for Computational Linguistics, Berlin, Germany (2016). https://doi.org/10.18653/v1/P16-1218
22. Dozat, T., Manning, C.: Deep Biaffine Attention for Neural Dependency Parsing (2016)
23. Yu, J., et al.: Domain adaptation for dependency parsing via self-training. In: Proceedings of the 14th International Conference on Parsing Technologies, pp. 1–10. Association for Computational Linguistics, Bilbao, Spain (2015). https://doi.org/10.18653/v1/W15-2201
24. Li, S., Zhao, Z., Hu, R., Li, W., Liu, T., Du, X.: Analogical Reasoning on Chinese Morph ological and Semantic Re-lations. arXiv preprint arXiv:1805.06504 (2018)
25. Gilmer, J., Schoenholz, S.S., Riley, P.F., Vinyals, O., Dahl, G.E.: Neural message passing for quantum chemistry. In: Proceedings of the 34th International Conference on Machine Learning - Volume 70, Sydney, NSW, Australia, pp. 1263–1272 (2017)

Demonstration of Low Power and Low Cost Wireless Sensor Network with Edge Computing

Sikong Han[1], Zhiyi Li[1,2], Lu Gao[1], Jian Xu[1(✉)], and Wu Zeng[1,2]

[1] Wuhan Polytechnic University, Wuhan 430023, Hubei, China
[2] Nanjing Crystal Technology, Co., Ltd., Nanjing 210039, Jiangsu, China

Abstract. With development of Internet of Things (IOT), wireless sensor networks (WSNs) have been widely used for many applications. Due to the advantage of automatic information collection and analysis, WSNs received a lot of attention in structural health monitoring. Integrating the sensor technology, embedded technology, information processing technology and wireless communication technology, the monitoring for the structural health condition could be done by real-time. Meanwhile, some precaution can be made by connecting the WSN to the cloud and using big data analysis technology. However, for one board system, the more information processing, the more power consumption there would be. On the other side, the power is the most important parameter for WSNs. In this paper, we proposed a new WSN node with low cost and low power by using an ARM Cortex-M4® microcontroller and an BLE-4.0 module and/or RF transceiver module for wireless connection. Moreover, a new strategy based on the edge computing technology is also embedded in the system. When nodes operate, it would analyze the event first that upload the processing task to the master node or just execute this task locally. Other than this event, the node goes to sleep mode and only wakes up by sensing and processing. Test results show that this method is more feasible and adaptive than other methods.

Keywords: Wireless sensor networks · Structural healthy monitoring · Hardware design

1 Introduction

With development of Internet of Things (IOT) and wireless communication technologies, Wireless sensor networks (WSNs) are widely used in many applications, such as the environmental monitoring and industrial on-site monitoring [1–4]. In general, WSNs are made up of many nodes, which are master nodes and slave nodes. There would be one master node with several slave nodes or several master nodes with more slave nodes. The topology is decided by the specific application. And, the longevity of WSNs depends on the power consumption of the node.

Usually, every node has one central processing unit (CPU), several sensors, some data interfaces and communication modules [5, 6]. Therefore, low power design of the node is the main method to extend the reliable working hours of WSNs. However, the parts

X. Sun et al. (Eds.): ICAIS 2021, LNCS 12736, pp. 407–416, 2021.
https://doi.org/10.1007/978-3-030-78609-0_35

given above are necessary for one node. Moreover, there must be some data processing on board to have low latency [7] to give decision of the actuator. Hence, some strategy must be applied to reduce the power consumption.

This paper proposes a low power consumption and low cost design for the node of WSNs. And a low power operation strategy is also proposed to apply to this node. For the design, an ARM Cortex-M4® microcontroller as the CPU, the nRF24L01 and BLE102 module for the wireless communication and some sensors. The strategy for the low power operation is setting the node go to sleep while no event to process. A case study of a WSNs node is examined to demonstrate the design.

2 Low Power Design for the WSNs Node

Generally, a WSNs node would connect many sensors and/or actuators to collect information and/or execute corresponding control. When the control needed, some data analysis and/or computation should be done. Sometimes, the final decision may involve the user. Therefore, the node must have the module for the communication between the user and the node. Before the smartphone popularized, the communication is often between the node and the computer [8-9], which requires the master node have the internet connection. Nowadays, smartphone is almost everywhere as well as Apps. More generally, the mobile terminals have been the most used device for the communication, which means the node with connection with user's smartphone would be the ultimate solution for the WSNs. Figure 1 gives the two topology of the WSNs. The left one is the traditional design for the node. In this design, only the slave node is used for the information collection and the operation execution. The master node is for the communication between the slave node and itself and the computer and itself as well as some data analysis. The right one is for the design in this paper. In this design, the slave node and the master node almost have the same function. Each one can be set to either slave or master. Moreover, both of them are able to communicate with the smartphone.

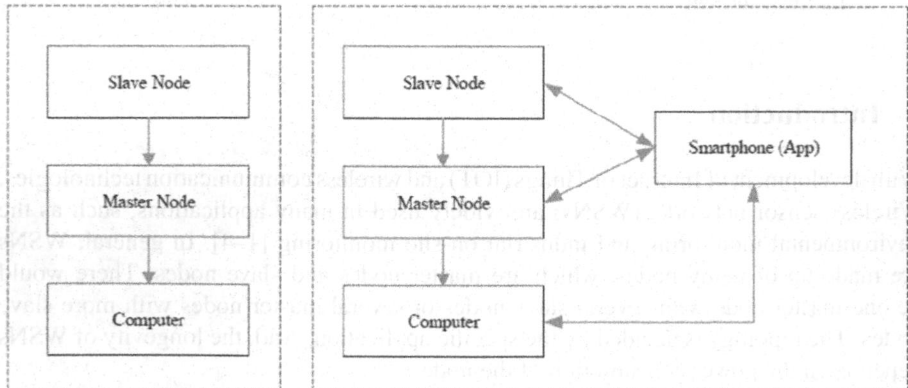

Fig. 1. Two topology of WSNs: left for one chain communication, right for multi-chain communication.

2.1 System Design of the WSN Node

In order to realize the node with low power, all the electronics with low power are under consideration. Due to the smartphone involved in the WSNs operation, the node should have some ability to process the data analysis. Meanwhile, in order to lower the power consumption while the node operates, some operating strategies are applied.

Figure 2 gives the block diagram of the WSNs node. In this design, an ARM Cortex-M4® low power microcontroller STM32F407 is used as the CPU to control all the other modules. With the independent FPU, this microcontroller could do some data processing at the same time. Sensor unit consists several sensors on the node board. For the industrial IoT applications, a temperature sensor (ADT7320), a humidity sensor (HTU21D) and a 3-axis acceleration sensor (LIS3DH) are employed in the design for demonstration. Actually, some GPIOs are reserved for connecting other sensors, such as the strain sensor, the pressure sensor, the tilt sensor and the magnetic field sensor et al. through the IIC or SPI protocol. For wireless modules, a low power RF transceiver nRF24L01 and a low power Bluetooth module BLE102 are employed. The former one is used for the remote communication, the letter one is used for the near field communication. Besides, an Ethernet circuitry, a USB port and a CAN port are reserved in this design, which will be applied when this board is assigned to the master node. Moreover, a TF Card port is also embedded for the data reservation. Figure 3 gives the schematic of the design.

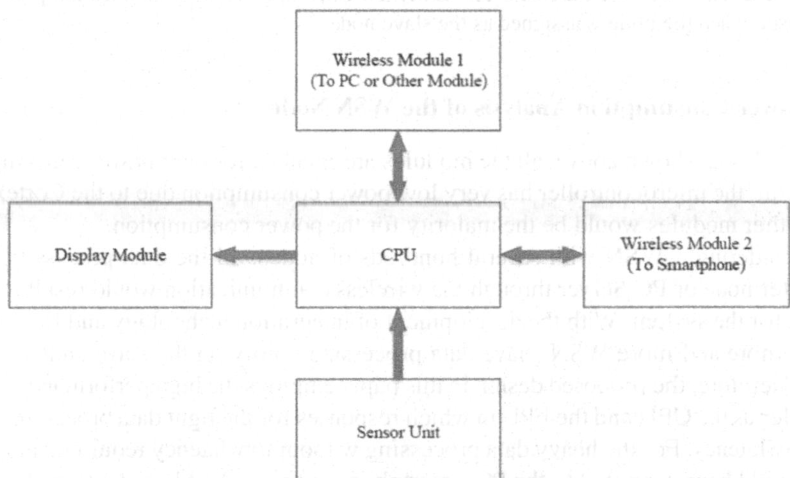

Fig. 2. Block diagram of the design of the node.

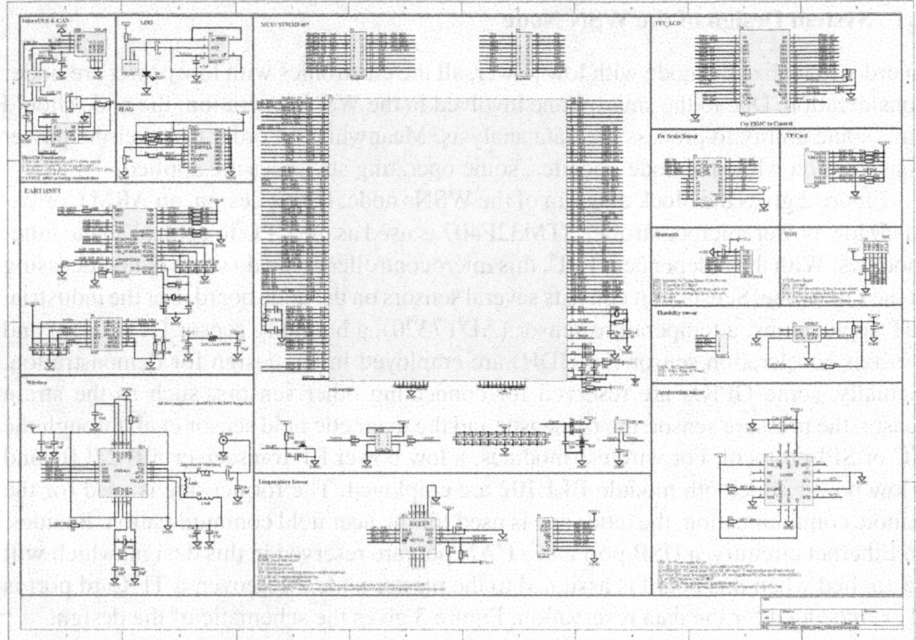

Fig. 3. Schematic deign of the node. The Ethernet, USB and CAN communication port would not be used when the node is assigned as the slave node.

2.2 Power Consumption Analysis of the WSN Node

With the design shown above, all the modules are checked for their power consumption. In general, the microcontroller has very low power consumption due to the Cortex-M® core. Other modules would be the majority for the power consumption.

Considering a WSN with several hundreds of nodes, all the data processing done by master node or PC Server through the wireless communication would result to large latency for the system. With the development of integration technology and Edge Computing, more and more WSNs have data processing ability on the slave and/or master node. Therefore, the proposed design in this paper employs the high performance microcontroller as the CPU and the FPU in which responses for the light data processing tasks with low latency. For the heavy data processing without low latency requirements, these tasks would be transmitted to the PC, smartphone or sever. And in order to make nodes to a network, the 2.4 GHz transceiver nRF24L01 is employed. For the data exchange between the node and the smartphone, the low power Bluetooth module BLE102 is used. Moreover, the USB port and the Ethernet port are also reserved in our design for a master node which responses for the communication between the PC or server and the node. Figure 4. gives the current drawn of all the components of a node in our design and all the power consumption is shown in Table 1 in detail. Apparently, the CPU and the wireless modules mainly contribute the power consumption. However, in practical operation, the CPU does not work all the time and the sensors and other components are not always under control. This would greatly reduce its power consumption. Meanwhile, the power consumption of all modules are shown in Fig. 4. and Table 1. In fact, only one wireless module would be used for the WSN. Therefore, the whole power consumption for one node with data processing is around 100 mW, which means a 1000 mAh battery can makes the node work over 36 h.

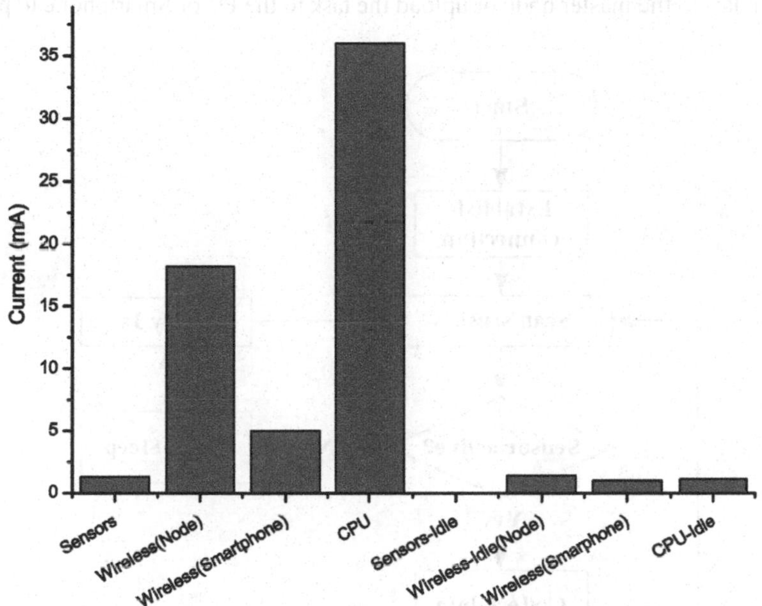

Fig. 4. Current drawn of all the modules of the node.

Table 1. Power consumption of proposed design.

Module name	Current drawn (mA)	Power consumption (mW)
Sensors	1.3	4.3
Wireless(Node)	18.2	60
Wireless(Smartphone)	5	16.5
CPU-All Enabled	36	118.8
Sensors-Idle	0.003	0.01
Wireless-Idle(Node)	1.4	4.63
Wireless(Smartphone)	1	3.3
CPU-Idle	1.1	3.63

To realize the WSN node and further reduce the power consumption, the control strategy for the microcontroller and other modules is critical. In this paper, a sleep-wake up process is proposed and applied to the hardware. Firstly, specifying the working intervals of the sensor unit. Then setting the program of the microcontroller to get the data only at the end of time interval. Then, drive the controller to the sleep mode to wait the next wake up operation. Considering there may be some data processing requirement, the microcontroller must decide if the task need to be done locally. If so, the microcontroller will do the data processing in the sleeping time. Otherwise, the node will transfer this task with data to the master node or upload the task to the PC or Smartphone to process.

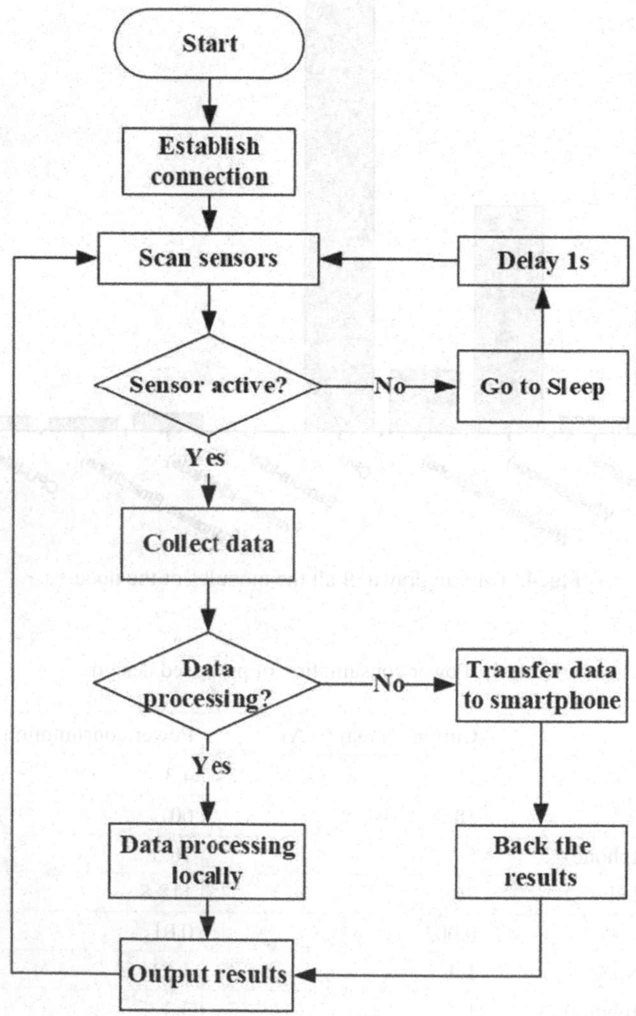

Fig. 5. Workflow for a WSN node.

Obviously, when operate, the majority of power consumption is the CPU. However, when it goes to sleep-wake up mode, the power consumption is almost least. Therefore, in this paper, we make a strategy to reduce the power consumption of the node as following: in general, the node is in sleep mode and monitoring all the transceiver port of the CPU with collecting the data from the sensor unit by waking up itself about 1s interval. Once there is data coming, the CPU wakes up to identify if it is the local task to process whatever the CPU is doing. With this method, the power consumption is dramatically reduced. Figure 5 shows the workflow for the process of the node.

3 Hardware Realization of the WSN Node

With the design consideration above, some node boards are made. Figure 6 shows the board for one node. The microcontroller STM32F407ZTG is as the CPU for the control and light data processing. The nRF24L01 module is used for the wireless connection between the nodes. The USB port is for the data exchange between the node and the PC, which is also for the power supply port. The BLE102 module is connected on the board for the wireless connection between the nodes and the smartphones. JTAG port is for programming and debugging. Display port is for the on-site display of information by the node.

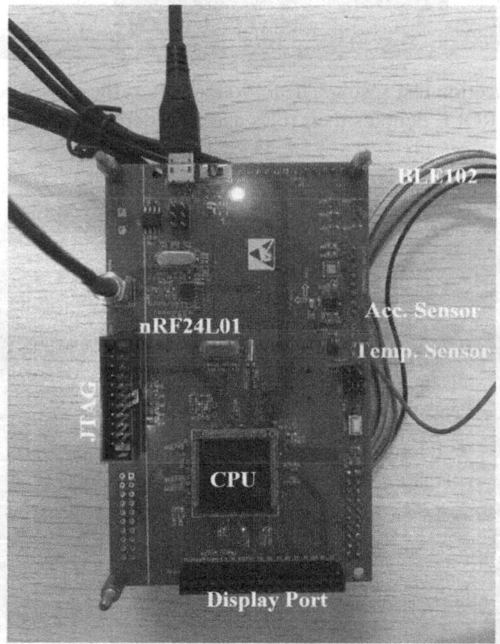

Fig. 6. Front side of the PCB of one WSNs Node.

With the made boards, two nodes are tested. Figure 7 shows the connection test results through the Bluetooth module BLE102. As shown, a touch screen is used for the control and user interface. There are two buttons set on the screen to let the user choose one as the slave node or the master node. As seen, the ROLE denotes the left node is assigned as the slave node and the right one is assigned as the master node. And STA is set for display the connection status. Obviously, the two nodes are connected through the bluetooth modules and the ambient temperature and humidity are successfully detected and displayed at both nodes.

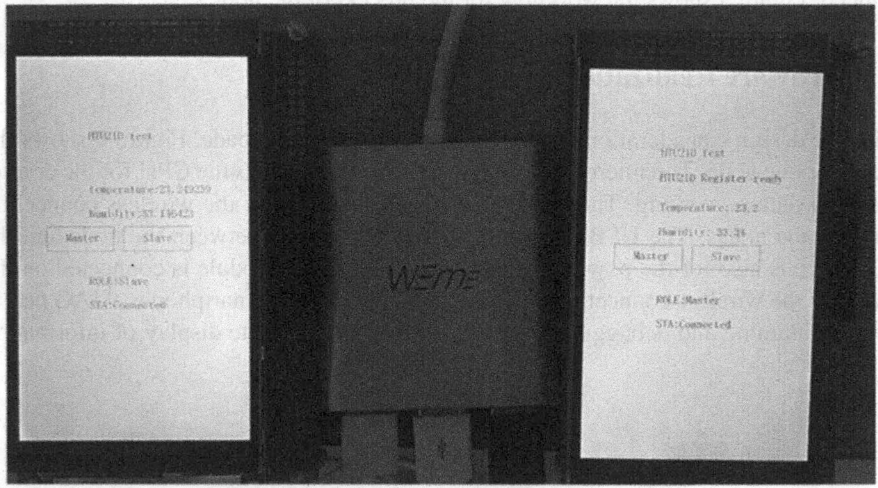

Fig. 7. Bluetooth connection test result. The left one is set as the slave node and the right one is set as the master node. ROLE denotes their roles and STA denotes the connection status.

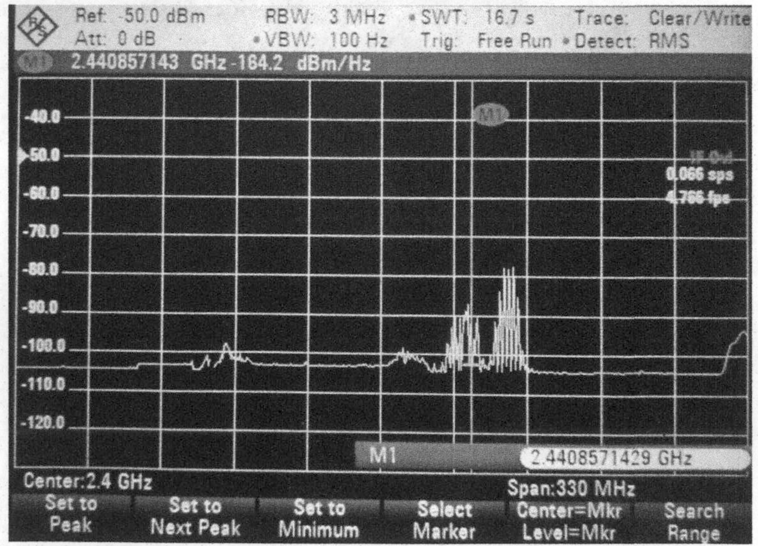

Fig. 8. Frequency spectrum of the node using RF connection.

After bluetooth connection test, the RF connection with the 2.4 GHz transceiver nRF24L01 is also tested. With antennas, the nodes can connect each other very quick and the connection is stable. However, we found that, without the antenna, the nodes can also connect each other within 10 cm. Therefore, we test the frequency spectrum of the note when it operates without the antenna. Figure 8 shows the test results. Obviously, the node can work as the radiate power as low as −80 dBm. As shown in Fig. 9, the RF connection can be succeed without the antenna. The left one is the node with a tach screen and the right one is the other node without display. As seen on the screen, there are two buttons set for the connection selection. When select the right one, the text displayed under buttons gives the current status. Apparently, the left node is set as the master node for collecting the data from other nodes. And the ambient temperature and humidity are also detected by the other node and transmitted to this master node with its status is RX_Mode. The last text is used for denoting if the data received. In Fig. 9, the data is received successfully.

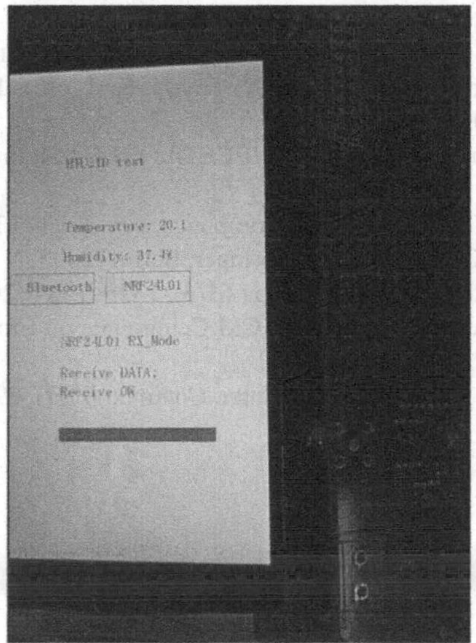

Fig. 9. RF connection test for the node.

4 Conclusion

This paper gives a demonstration of a low power and low cost design for the WSNs for industrial IoT applications. Based on the embedded technologies and the edge computing theories, a design with ARM Cortex-M microcontroller with FPU is proposed and realized. Power consumption is investigated and the current drawn of all the modules are plotted. CPU and wireless modules are the main contributors. Considering sensors and wireless modules not operate all the time in practical, a strategy for the control is also proposed. With this strategy, the power consumption could be reduced as low as 100 mW, which makes the design suitable for the remote operation by a battery or a solar panel. For the demonstration, the design is realized and two nodes are made. One temperature sensor and one humidity sensor are employed and integrated on board. Sensors test is done through two kinds of wireless connections. By the self-made user interface, the role of the node can be assigned by the user and the status of the node can be also shown on screen. In addition, the connection between nodes can be done through the bluetooth module or the RF module. Field test results shows that the connection is stable and reliable either through the bluetooth or the RF module with antenna respectively. However, even there is no antenna, the nodes can be connected with each other within 10 cm.

References

1. Akyildiz, I.F., Su, W., Sankarasubramaniam, Y., Cayirci, E.: IEEE Communication Magazines (2002)
2. Culler, D., Estrin, D.: Computer, pp. 41–49 (2004)
3. Guevara, J., Barrero, F., Vargas, E., Becerra, J., Toral, S.: Environmental wireless sensor network for road traffic applications. IET Intell. Transp. Syst. **6**(2), 177 (2012). https://doi.org/10.1049/iet-its.2010.0205
4. Lu, K., Qian, Y., Rodriguez, D., Rivera, W.: IEEE GLOBECOM. Proceeding **2007**, 1108–1112 (2007)
5. Tseng, Y.C., Pan, M.S., Tsai, Y.Y.: IEEE Computers, vol. 39, No. 7, pp. 55-62, July 2006
6. Basten T, Geilen M, de Groot H. (Eds.), Springer, Berlin (2003)
7. Hu, B., Sun, Z.: Computers. Mater. Continua **61**(3), 1323–1344 (2019)
8. Van Dam, T., Langendoen, K.: The First ACM Conference on Embedded Networked Sensor Systems, Los Angeles CA, November 2003
9. Janarthanan, A., Kumar, D.: Computers. Mater. Continua **60**(3), 895–912 (2019)

Analysis on Spatial Pattern Evolution of Cultivated Land in Urban Area Based on Spatial Autocorrelation Analysis – A Case Study of Luoyang City

Huang Wei[1], Wang Mengyu[1(✉)], and Chen Xueye[2]

[1] School of Computer and Communication Engineering, Zhengzhou University of Light Industry, Zhengzhou 450002, China

[2] Key Laboratory of Urban Land Resources Monitoring and Simulation, Ministry of Natural Resources, Shenzhen 518034, China

Abstract. Cultivated land is the basis of human survival and security. Taking cultivated land of Luoyang as the research object, based on GIS technology, using landscape pattern index method, kernel density analysis and spatial autocorrelation analysis, this paper analyzes the characteristics and change trend of cultivated land spatial pattern of Luoyang from 2010 to 2018. The research results show that: (1) The spatial fragmentation of cultivated land are enhanced. In addition, cultivated land dominates the whole landscape of Luoyang city. (2) During the study period, most of the areas outside the municipal district in the northeast and some areas in Luanchuan County in the southwest have high kernel density, while the rest areas surrounding Luanchuan County are relatively sparse. The areas with high and very high kernel density of cultivated land showed the characteristics of expansion first and then contraction, while the areas with low kernel density expanded from 2014 to 2018. (3) The amount of cultivated land in Luoyang has a high spatial autocorrelation. In the local spatial autocorrelation, the "high-high" typology is concentrated and distributed in the border zone of the north and northeast of Luoyang city. "Low-low" typology is concentrated in Luanchuan county and Songxian County as well as the district of Luoyang City, which is heavily influenced by topography and urbanization. The expansion during the study period occurred in the jurisdiction area of Luoyang city, and most of it was transferred from "high-low" type area.

Keywords: Cultivated land · The least cultivated areas · Landscape pattern · Kernel density · Spatial autocorrelation

1 Introduction

Cultivated land resources are the material basis for human life and production, and the control of their quantity can not only guarantee the safety of food production, but also affect the regional sustainable development [1]. The current situation of cultivated land resources in China, such as acreage decreasing year by year, poor quality and

X. Sun et al. (Eds.): ICAIS 2021, LNCS 12736, pp. 417–428, 2021.
https://doi.org/10.1007/978-3-030-78609-0_36

uneven spatial distribution, still exists [2]. In recent years, China has successively put forward policies such as the red line of 1.8 million mu of farmland, basic farmland protection, and the balance of farmland occupation and compensation to ensure food security [3]. With the rapid development of social economy and city, the structure of land use has changed, and the spatial pattern of cultivated land has been significantly affected. Therefore, in addition to earnestly carrying out the existing farmland protection system and implementing the system of farmland occupation and compensation balance in each region, we also need to accurately reflect the change of farmland spatial pattern through scientific research.

At present, landscape index analysis method is widely used by scholars. Based on the characteristics of landscape pattern index analysis, it extends the comparative analysis of landscape pattern index at different granularity [4, 5] and landscape index screening at different scales [6]. Geostatistics analysis is a spatial statistical analysis method based on the theory of regional variables, which was first applied in mining industry and later developed and penetrated into more and more fields such as geography [7]. Some scholars used this method to analyze the spatiotemporal variation characteristics of cultivated land quality or soil nutrients. Quadrature analysis, kernel density estimation and spatial clustering analysis are commonly used to analyze the spatial distribution characteristics of geographical objects [8, 9]. These methods can determine the concentration degree of the specific type of blocks in the study area, the overall and local orientation aggregation characteristics, etc.

Therefore, with the support of GIS platform, this paper takes Luoyang city in Henan Province as the research area and each administrative region as the basic unit. The current data of land use in 2010, 2014 and 2018 are mainly selected. Landscape pattern index analysis, kernel density estimation and spatial autocorrelation analysis were used for the analysis. By comparing the spatial distribution pattern of cultivated land in different periods, this paper analyzes the dynamic change rule of the spatial distribution pattern of cultivated land in Luoyang, in order to find out the key factors that affect its evolution, and then point out the direction for restoring cultivated land area and fertility and rationally allocating land resources.

2 Data and Research Methodology

2.1 Overview of the Study Area

The research area of this study is luoyang, a prefecture-level city in Henan Province in central China, which is located in western Henan province. The geographical range of luoyang is 112°16′-112°37′ east longitude and 34°32′-34°45′ north latitude, with the total area of the city reaching 15230 km^2. Luoyang city is rich in water resources, mineral resources and tourism resources.The topographical composition is diverse, mainly mountains, hills and plains, with mountains accounting for 45.51%, hills 40.73% and plains 13.8%. Mountains are mainly distributed in Luanchuan county, Songxian County and Luoning County in the southwest. The plains are mainly distributed in luoyang city, Yanshi City and Mengjin County in the northeast of the study area.The hills are in the middle of the transition zone. Location diagram of Luoyang is shown in Fig. 1.

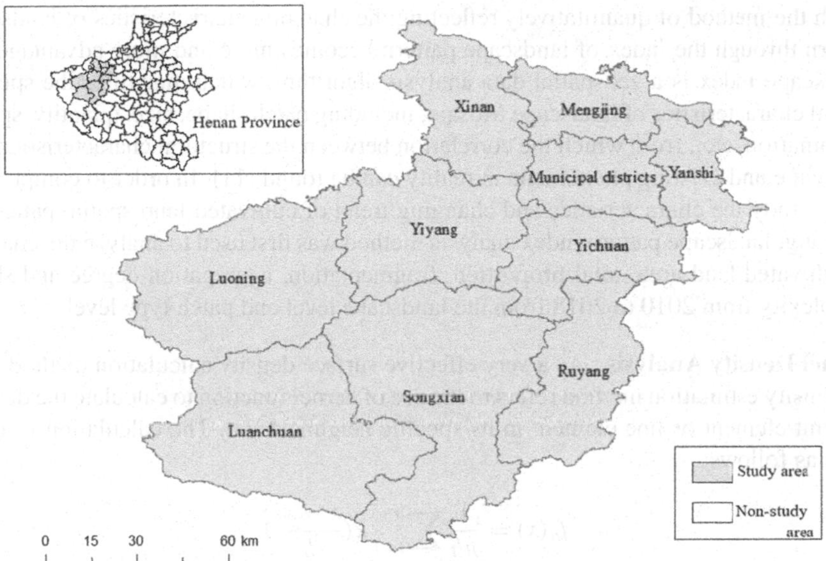

Fig. 1. Location diagram of Luoyang city

2.2 Data Sources and Processing

The subject data used for the study were obtained from three land survey databases in 2010, 2014 and 2018 respectively. The database contains the original land use data and administrative division data of each county and district of Luoyang city. The data of landscape pattern index calculation, kernel density analysis and farmland transfer matrix are extracted from the land survey database.

Before all kinds of analysis, the data needed in this study should be integrated from the land survey database. Since the original data in the database is stored in each independent administrative region, it is necessary to import the land map spot data of Luoyang in the same year in ArcGIS, integrate them into a factor class by using tools, and then extract the cultivated land map spot. The data of cultivated land map spot elements in the third period obtained through operation in 2010, 2014 and 2018 respectively, then it will be used in landscape pattern index calculation and kernel density analysis. In addition, since the land classes in the database are classified according to the second-class standard of "Land Use Status Classification" (GB/T 21010-2007) [10], in order to facilitate the production of the subsequent farmland transfer matrix, it is necessary to add a first-level field for the ground class spot data of these three phases, so as to facilitate the fusion according to this field. After that, the data of each district in each year is extracted from the land survey database and used as the basis for making the nuclear density map.

2.3 Research Methodology

Landscape Pattern Index Analysis. In landscape ecology, there are many ways to study the changing characteristics of landscape pattern in the process of evolution, among which the method of quantitatively reflecting the changing characteristics of landscape pattern through the index of landscape pattern becomes more and more advantageous. Landscape index is a geospatial data analysis algorithm, which quantifies the specific spatial characteristics of landscape Mosaic, including patch shape, size, quantity, spatial combination, etc., from which the correlation between the structural characteristics of a landscape and existing phenomena in reality can be found [11]. In order to comprehensively study the characteristics and changing trend of cultivated land spatial pattern in Luoyang, landscape pattern index analysis method was first used to analyze the changes of cultivated land area, total proportion, fragmentation, aggregation degree and shape complexity from 2010 to 2018 from the landscape level and patch type level.

Kernel Density Analysis. As a very effective surface density calculation method, kernel density estimation method refers to the use of kernel function to calculate the density of point element or line element in its specific neighborhood. The calculation formula (1) is as follows:

$$f_n(x) = \frac{1}{nh}\sum\nolimits_{i=1}^{n} k(\frac{x - x_i}{h}) \tag{1}$$

Where, $fn(x)$ represents the estimated kernel density at the point x to be estimated, h is the bandwidth, n is the number of sample points in the circle with the radius of bandwidth, k is the kernel density function, and x-x_i is the distance between the point to be estimated and the i-th sample point. In order to reflect more detailed luoyang gathering for the spatial distribution characteristics of cultivated land and space, this study adopted the spatial analysis of kernel density method, making the research of kernel density figure, find the cultivated land spatial distribution of bearing characteristics of density in the study area, the density characteristics and evolution of dynamic migration trend.

Spatial Autocorrelation Analysis. Spatial autocorrelation is an important index reflecting the degree of correlation between a geographic phenomenon or an attribute value on a regional unit and the same phenomenon or attribute value on adjacent regional units [12]. It is also a measure of the degree of aggregation of values in the spatial domain. It has global spatial autocorrelation and local spatial autocorrelation, which is a quantitative and objective method used to quantify the degree of aggregation of similar features of geographical objects and where such aggregation occurs. There are many ways to detect spatial correlation, and this paper used the most commonly used global Moran's I. Moran's I is the Moran index, which can measure global or local spatial correlation. Moran's I's calculation formula (2) is:

$$I = \frac{n\sum\limits_{i=1}^{n}\sum\limits_{j=1}^{n} wij(Xi - \overline{X})(Xj - \overline{X})}{\sum\limits_{i=1}^{n}\sum\limits_{j=1}^{n} wij \sum\limits_{i=1}^{n} (Xi - \overline{X})^2} \tag{2}$$

Where n represents the total number of spatially observed objects in the target area; Xi and Xj are the observations of the i-th and j-th objects in the spatial location respectively, $\overline{X}$ is the average observation of all the objects; and Wij is the spatial weight matrix, and the value of *Wij* indicates the adjacency between the *i*-th and *j*-th objects in the spatial location. The value of *Wij* is the spatial weight matrix, and the value of *Wij* indicates the neighborhood between *i* and *j*. The value of Global Moran's I ranges from ± 1, and if $I > 0$, it indicates a positive spatial correlation; when $I < 0$, it indicates a negative spatial correlation. The positive spatial correlation indicates that the objects are spatially aggregated, while the negative spatial correlation indicates that the objects are spatially discrete. If $I = 0$, it means random distribution of research objects.

Local spatial autocorrelation analysis focuses on the spatial correlation between specific units and adjacent units and can effectively reflect the spatial differences caused by spatial autocorrelation between different towns. Therefore, this study will take towns as a unit to calculate the least cultivated areas of each town in Luoyang city, and then analyze the spatial autocorrelation and spatial aggregation characteristics of the least cultivated areas from both global and local aspects with the help of Geoda software platform. The calculation formula is shown in Eq. (3), and the meaning of each variable in the equation is the same as that in Eq. (2).

$$I = \frac{\sum_{j=1, j \neq i}^{n} w_{ij}(x_i - \overline{x})(x_j - \overline{x})}{\sum_{i=1}^{n} (x_i - \overline{x})^2} \quad (3)$$

3 Results and Analysis

3.1 Landscape Pattern Index Analysis

This study will select several landscape indexes with good independence and high sensitivity for analysis and try to cover all aspects of the characteristics of cultivated land. Detailed information of each landscape pattern index is shown in Table 1.

Now rasterize the basic vector farmland map spot data obtained above, and then select the appropriate particle size according to the research situation (The topography of the study area is composed of mountain, hill and plain, and the former two are relatively large, making the landscape index more sensitive to granularity change [12]),Then import the resulting raster data into Fragstats, select the corresponding Landscape metrics and Class metrics for calculation, and the results are shown in Table 2.

Combining Table 1 and Table 2, we can analyze that the cultivated land area (TA) of Luoyang did not change strongly from 2010 to 2018, but still showed a trend of first decreasing and then increasing, and generally increased. The proportion of landscape area occupied by plaques (PLAND) showed similar changes as TA, provided that the total landscape area in the study area remained unchanged. It can be inferred that the arable land was reduced in the early period by the expansion of other land types and recovered in the later period by a series of cultivated land protection policies. At the same time, the PLAND index maintained values around 30% during the study period, indicating that cultivated land in Luoyang is still dominant across the landscape and that agricultural production is still not neglected.

Table 1. Details of the selected landscape pattern index.

Index name	Application scales involved in this study	Values	Unit	Characterization of meaning
Landscape area (TA)	Landscape level	TA > 0	Hectares (hm^2)	Equals the total area of a given landscape and is the basis for studying other indicators
Number of plaques (NP)	Landscape level	NP ≥ 1	pcs	Equal to the total number of all patches in the landscape, indirectly representing the degree of fragmentation of the landscape
Mean Plaque Shape Index(MSI)	Landscape level	MSI > 1	None	Shows the appearance and edge features of the plaques, measuring the complexity of the landscape shape relative to a standard shape of the same size
Agglomeration Index (AI)	Landscape level	0 ≤ AI ≤ 100	%	shows the degree of aggregation of the patches
Percentage of landscape area occupied by patches (PLAND)	Landscape level	0 < PLAND ≤ 100	%	Equals the percentage of the total area of a given patch type over the entire landscape, reflecting the proportion and dominance of the patch type in the landscape

The value of cultivated land fragmentation (NP/TA) has been increasing during the study period, and due to natural disturbances and human activities, the large cultivated land patches are fragmented into small scattered patches, the spatial fragmentation of cultivated land is increasing, and the spatial heterogeneity is increasing. The mean plaque shape index (MSI) of cultivated land maintained a high value and at the same time

Table 2. Cultivated land landscape class and type class indices in Luoyang, 2010–2018

Year	Landscape class					Type class
	Landscape area (hm^2)	Number of plaques (pcs)	Mean Plaque Shape Index	Agglomeration Index (%)	Landscape fragmentation (NP/TA)	Percentage of landscape area occupied by patches (%)
2010	434069.87	41322	1.7085	90.9792	0.0952	29.7645
2014	432076.61	43136	1.6937	90.8539	0.0998	29.6318
2018	435430.68	45257	1.6796	90.6948	0.1039	29.8704

showed a decreasing trend, indicating that the appearance shape and edges of cultivated land plaques are more complex and cultivated land continues to be modified by human activities, causing it to move towards a regular appearance. The Agglomeration Index (AI) of cropland continued to decrease while maintaining high values, suggesting that cropland is generally aggregated, but that aggregation dynamics decreased during the study years. In addition to the fact that the patches of a scattered landscape are scattered, they are also interspersed with other land types, thus indicating that the cultivated land in the study area is occupied by the increase of urban expansion, human production activities and other phenomena, thus breaking up into smaller patches, which is consistent with the variation in the number of patches (NP).

3.2 Kernel Density Analysis

After data preprocessing, the cultivated land surface elements of each year's vector data are obtained. The surface elements need to be converted into point elements first, and then the kernel density analysis tool is used for measurement. After the calculation, the kernel density area of the study area was cut out by using ExtractByMask tool. The kernel density map of cultivated land distribution in Luoyang city was obtained. To facilitate observation, the density value is divided into 6 levels by natural breakpoint classification method. The generated kernel density map reflecting the spatial evolution of cultivated land in Luoyang from 2010 to 2018 is shown in the Fig. 2.

The results show that the overall pattern of the sparse distribution of cultivated land in Luoyang in the three years 2010, 2014 and 2018 is consistent, showing high density in most of the northeast and parts of the southwest, and low density in the northwest and southeast. Overall, during the period 2010–2018, the spatial distribution of high and low value areas of cultivated land density in Luoyang was very concentrated, clearly influenced by topographic conditions and long-term human activities. The areas of significant cultivated land evolution are mainly distributed in Xin'an County, Yiyang County, Yichuan County, Luoning County and Luanchuan County, and the evolution of high-value areas is stronger than that of low-value areas, especially as most of the very high value areas show a significant shrinkage. The net increase in density was mainly in

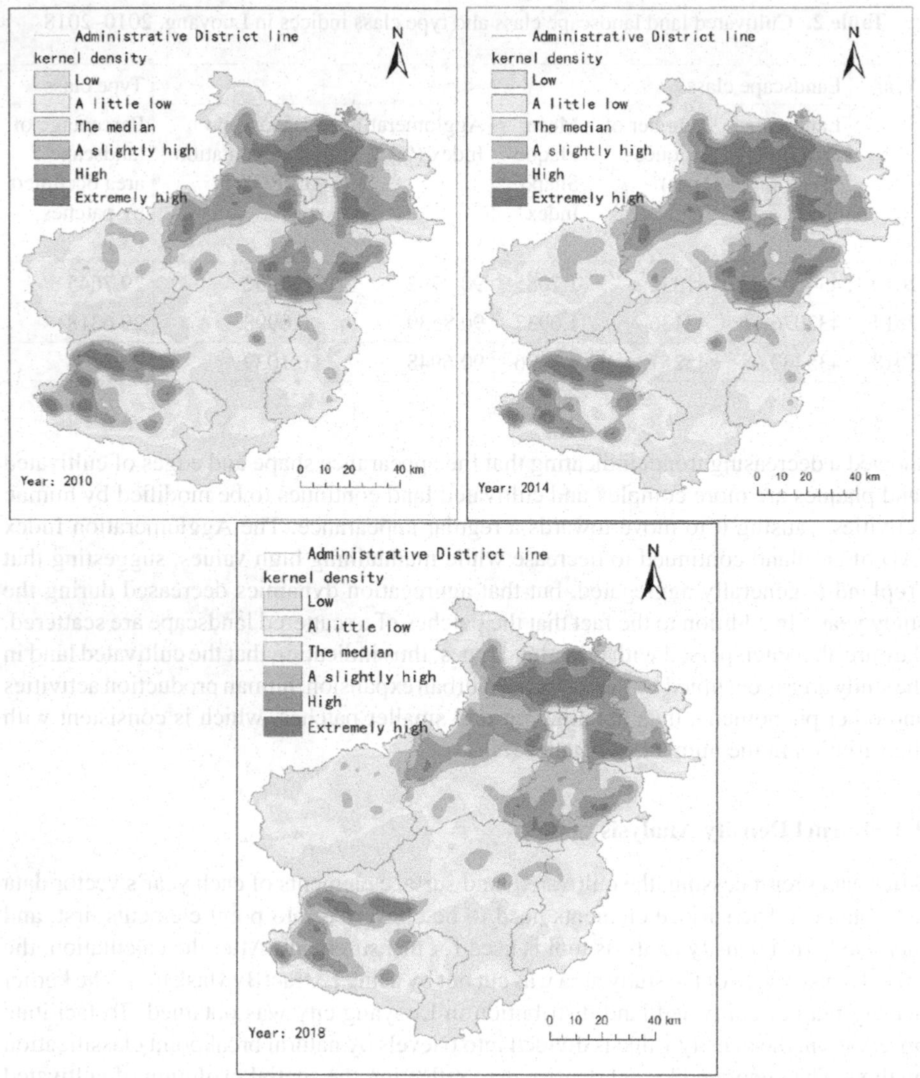

Fig. 2. Distribution diagram of kernel density value of cultivated land in Luoyang in 2010, 2014 and 2018

the northeastern part of Song County and Crescent City, with scattered distribution in other areas.

3.3 Spatial Autocorrelation Analysis

Global Spatial Autocorrelation Analysis. This study takes township as a unit and statistics the spatial autocorrelation of the least cultivated areas in 2010, 2014 and 2018. A field calculator is used in ArcGIS to calculate the ratio of the cropland area of the township to the total area of the township, and then a Rook spatial weight matrix is created in Geoda. Calculate the global Moran index for each year, and check the significance of the index values, as shown in Table 3.

Table 3. Global Moran's I and test for the least cultivated areas in Luoyang City

Year	Moran's I	z-value	p-value	Threshold ($\alpha = 0.01$)
2010	0.6695	14.3689	0.0001	2.58
2014	0.6756	14.4509	0.0001	2.58
2018	0.7007	15.0804	0.0001	2.58

Table 3 shows that the Moran's I for the least cultivated areas in the city of Luoyang was 0.6695, 0.6756 and 0.7007 in 2010, 2014 and 2018, respectively, all greater than 0 and closer to 1. All the z-values are greater than the critical value of 2.58 and pass the significance test of $\alpha = 0.01$, which indicates that there is an obvious positive spatial correlation of the least cultivated areas in Luoyang City in these three years, i.e., the townships in the study area show clustering of high or low values of the least cultivated areas in the spatial distribution.

In addition, the global Moran's I increases year by year from 2010 to 2018, which can indicate that the clustering of high or low values of the least cultivated areas in the townships of Luoyang City is becoming stronger and stronger.

Local Spatial Autocorrelation Analysis. In Geoda, three LISA aggregation plots were calculated for 2010, 2014 and 2018 data, with each township assigned a colour, where "insignificant" means that its spatial autocorrelation is insignificant. The "high-high" type indicates that the township has a high value of the least cultivated areas not only for itself, but also for the surrounding townships. The "low-low" type indicates that the township has a low value of the least cultivated areas not only for itself, but also for the surrounding townships. The "low-high" type indicates that the township has a low value of the least cultivated areas, while its neighboring township have a high value of the least cultivated areas. The "high-low" type indicates that the township has a high value of the least cultivated areas and a low value of the land tenure of its neighbours. As shown in Fig. 3.

(1) "High-high" type districts, accounting for about 24% of the city, approximately present the phenomenon of distribution around the jurisdiction of Luoyang City. There are changes in some of the townships, but no significant changes overall. From 2010 to 2014, the "high-high" type dynamics were balanced, with type changes occurring in Yanshi City and Ichuan County, but no change in the total number of types. From 2014 to 2018, the number of townships in the "High-High" type zone increased by two, namely, Fudian Township in the south of Yanshi City and Tianhu Township in the north of Song County. Overall, cultivated land is increasing in the border area between Songxian and Yichuan counties; Yanshi City has experienced more frequent changes in cultivated land use during this period.

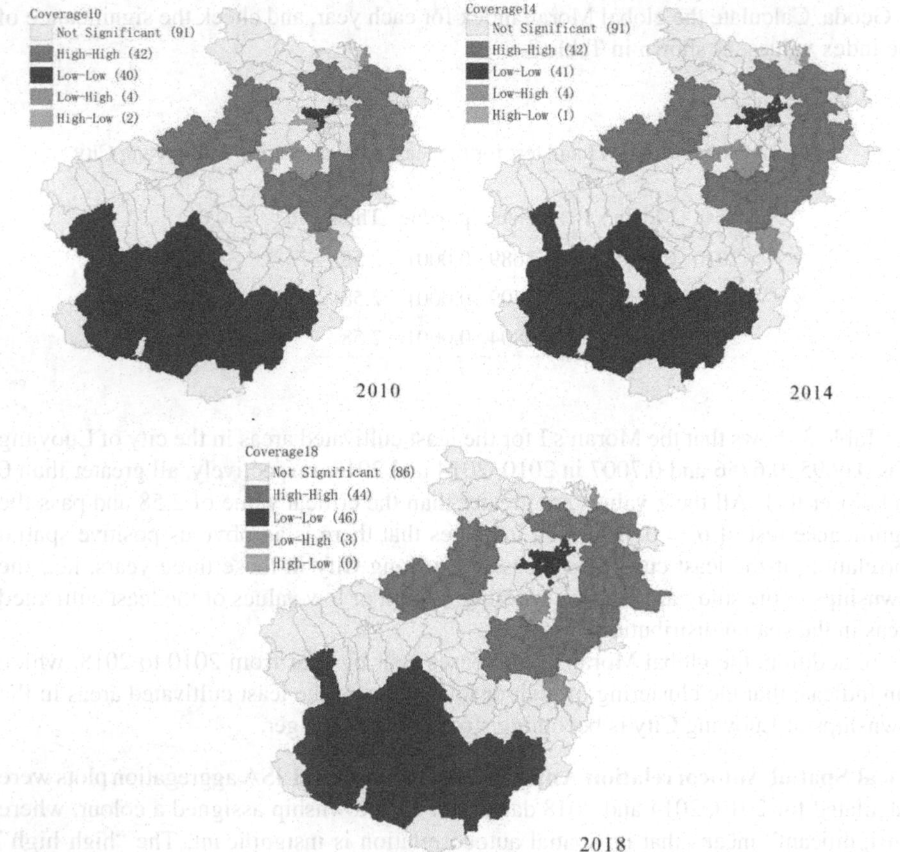

Fig. 3. LISA agglomeration diagram of the least cultivated areas in Luoyang in 2010, 2014 and 2018

(2) The distribution of "low-low" type areas is very concentrated, mostly concentrated in the southwestern part of Luoyang, mainly in Luanchuan County and Song County, as well as in the jurisdiction of Luoyang City, accounting for about 24% of the city. The southwestern part of Luoyang is mountainous and has complex topography, and the least cultivated areas in townships is generally low. The modernization of the city center is booming, and many areas have zero cultivated land, so they are characterized as "low-low". From 2010 to 2018, the "low-low" type of areas showed an increasing trend, with the most significant changes in the jurisdiction of Luoyang City. From 2010 to 2014, the Xujaying Street Office, Anle Town and Dongguan Street Office in the periphery of downtown area changed from the previous "insignificant" type or "high-low" type to "low-low" type, which shows that the downtown area is expanding and building outward.

(3) "Low-high" type area. The local Moran index of the townships is less than zero, and There is a significant negative spatial correlation between the least cultivated areas of this type of township, with large local spatial differences. It is obvious from the figure

that the number of townships belonging to this type is very small, from 2010 to 2014, this type of geographical area including Ichuan County Chengguan Township Street Office, Yiyang County Jinping Township, Ruyang County Chengguan Township and Jili District Kangle Street Office, the overall no change. In 2018, the type of Yiyang County Jinping Township shifted to the "not significant" type. In general, the "low-high" type townships are mostly the economic and political centers of a county or district, and the scale of urbanization is relatively larger than that of the surrounding townships, thus creating the phenomenon of high values encircling low values.

(4) "high-low" type area. The local Moran index of the township is less than 0, and the spatial relationship also presents negative correlation. However, the specific characteristics are opposite to the "low-high" type. This type is only concentrated in the jurisdiction of Luoyang City. In 2010, Xujiaying Street office and Hongshan Street Office, both located in the handover zone between the urban area and the surrounding county, had an obvious advantage over the urban area in the least cultivated areas. In the following years, with the development and expansion of the city, they gradually turned into a "low-low" type.

4 Discussion and Conclusions

(1) According to the analysis results of the landscape pattern index, the cultivated land area of Luoyang city decreased first and then increased from 2010 to 2018, which was regarded as an increase of 0.43% in 2018 compared with 2010. The spatial fragmentation and spatial heterogeneity of cultivated land are enhanced, indicating that the appearance of cultivated land patches is gradually regularized under the continuous transformation of human activities, and the cultivated land is characterized by high aggregation, although its value decreases during the study period. In addition, cultivated land dominates the whole landscape of Luoyang city.

(2) From the calculation results of nuclear density, during the study period, most of the areas outside the municipal district in the northeast and some areas in Luanchuan County in the southwest had high nuclear density, while the rest areas, mainly around Luanchuan County, were relatively sparse. The areas with high and very high core density of cultivated land showed the characteristics of expansion first and then contraction, while the areas with low core density expanded from 2014 to 2018.

(3) Finally, through the global spatial autocorrelation analysis of the cultivated land holdings, we verified that the cultivated land holdings in Luoyang had a high spatial autocorrelation. At the same time, in the analysis of local spatial autocorrelation, the LISA cluster map of cultivated land holdings in Luoyang in the three years of 2010, 2014 and 2018 shows that "high-high" and "low-low" dominate, with little spatial difference. "High-high" agglomeration areas are distributed in the border areas of the north and northeast of Luoyang city, the north of Yiyang County, the southwest of Xin 'an County, the south of Mengjin County, Yanshi City and most of Yichuan County. By comparing LISA diagram of the third phase, it is not difficult to find that the "high-high" type in Yanshi city and Yichuan County

has a slight expansion. "Low-low" areas are concentrated in Luanchuan county, Songxian County and luoyang City, which are heavily affected by topography and urbanization. During the study period, the "low-low" expansion occurred in the jurisdiction area of Luoyang city, and most of them were transferred from the "high-low" type. Present around the low density decline type of development.

Funding. The research was Supported by the Open Fund of Key Laboratory of Urban Land Resources Monitoring and Simulation, Ministry of Natural Resources, Grant No. (KF-2019-04-038). This research was also funded by Key scientific and technological projects in Henan Province, Grant No. (212102210105).

References

1. Zhu, L., Yang, A.M., Xia, X.X., Wu, H.Q.: Spatial distribution pattern and change characteristics analysis of cultivated land in the Manas River Basin from 1975 to 2015. Chinese J. Eco-Agric. **28**(6), 887–899 (2020)
2. Zhao, Q.G., Zhou, S.L., Wu, S.H., Ren, K.: The change of Cultivated land resources in China and its Sustainable utilization and protection countermeasures. ACTA Pedol. Sinica **43**(4), 662–672 (2006)
3. Shangguan, C.X., Zheng, G.Q., Zhang, W., Zhang, Y.: High-quality development mode and policy demand of china's grain industry under the background of rural revitalization strategy -- a case study of Henan province, a major grain-producing area. Agric. Econo **04**, 3–5 (2020)
4. Wang, X.B.: Study on scale characteristics of Human influence landscape based on terrain difference. Central China Normal University, China (2011)
5. Zhang, Q., Chen, C.L., Wang, J.Z., et al.: The spatial granularity effect, changing landscape patterns, and suitable landscape metrics. In: the Three Gorges Reservoir Area, 1995–2015. Ecological Indicators (114) (2020)
6. Li, P.L., Liu, Y.F., Li, Q.L., Wei, X.J.: Selecting landscape metrics based on spatial heterogeneity at different scales in the Jianghan plain of Hubei, the southern hills of Hunan and the Guizhou plateau. Ecol. Sci. **35**(6), 53–61 (2016)
7. Sun, Y.J., Wang, J.F., Bai, Y.C.: Progress in geostatistical methods. Adv. Earth Sci. **19**(2), 268–274 (2004)
8. Zhu, Q.: Temporal and spatial evolution of cultivated land landscape pattern and its influencing factors in Yangzhou city. Yangzhou University, China (2019)
9. Chen, Y.L., Zhu, Q., Chen, X.M.: Study on the chracteristics of distribution of Hakka place-names based on spatial clustering in Shicheng County. J. N.W. Norm. Univ. (Nat. Sci.) **56**(1) 98–106 (2020)
10. "Land Use Status Classification" (GB/T 21010-2007)
11. Chen, W.B., Xiao, D.N., Li, X.Z.: Classification, application, and creation of landscape indices. Chin. J. Appl. Ecol. **01** 121–125 (2002)
12. Zeng, Y.Q., Pan, H.Y., Zhou, J.M., Ma, W.L.: Research on spatial-temporal pattern change of per capita cultivated land area based on spatial autocorrelation – a case study of Sichuan province. Jiangsu Agric. Sci. **43**(9), 388–391 (2015)
13. Zhu, K.Q.: Analysis of landscape granularity effect and landscape pattern in land consolidation project area. Nanjing University, China (2011)

Research of Spatial Pattern for Cultivated Land Quality in Henan Province Based on Spatial Autocorrelation

Wang Hua[1], Zhu Yuxin[1], Wang Mengyu[1](✉), Wang Yifan[1], and Chen Xueye[2]

[1] School of Computer and Communication Engineering, Zhengzhou University of Light Industry, Zhengzhou 450002, China

[2] Key Laboratory of Urban Land Resources Monitoring and Simulation, Ministry of Natural Resources, Shenzhen 518034, China

Abstract. The quality of cultivated land determines the productivity and level of regional development, and it also directly affects the country's food security and ecological security. In order to improve the quality of cultivated land and the efficiency of cultivated land zoning protection, this reserch starts from the perspective of spatial pattern, uses the spatial correlation analysis method to study the county scale space gathered characteristics and difference of cultivated land quality in Henan province and put forward more effective zoning protection measures accordingly. The results show that the spatial distribution of cultivated land quality in Henan province has an obvious aggregation law. Positive correlation type (high - high and low - low) take the form of "group", more strong clustering; the negative correlation type has no obvious concentrated region and shows a discrete state. Then according to the results of local spatial autocorrelation of cultivated land quality, the cultivated land protection is divided into four types in this paper. The conservation measures proposed in this research has comprehensively considered natural quality, economic conditions, utilization level and the effects of spatial attributes of cultivated land, and provide a more scientific reference for refined cultivated land management in Henan Province.

Keywords: Cultivated land quality · Spatial distribution characteristics · Spatial autocorrelation · Henan province · Zoning protection

1 Introduction

Cultivated land is the material basis for human survival and development. And the quality of cultivated land is related to the level of regional utilization and productivity of cultivated land, which has a direct impact on food security and ecological security [1]. The quality of cultivated land varies greatly across regions due to demographic, economic and natural factors [2], but it is not only influenced by ecological environment, soil nutrients and its combination, but also closely related to the uniformity and complexity of spatial distribution [3]. Therefore, studying the spatial aggregation characteristics and regularity of cultivated land quality can not only grasp the current situation of cultivated

X. Sun et al. (Eds.): ICAIS 2021, LNCS 12736, pp. 429–442, 2021.
https://doi.org/10.1007/978-3-030-78609-0_37

land utilization in the region [4], but also carry out the work of cultivated land protection, so as to improve the quality of cultivated land and ensure the rational use of resources [5].

In recent years, the research on the spatial pattern of cultivated land quality has gradually attracted the attention and exploration of many scholars at home and abroad [6, 7]. In terms of research methods, most scholars currently have chosen to use spatial autocorrelation analysis, kriging interpolation and landscape ecology [8] and other technical means to study the spatial pattern of cultivated land [9]. Among them, Kriging interpolation is mainly used to describe and model the spatial pattern of cultivated land quality [10], and landscape ecology is often used to study the change trend of spatial pattern of cultivated land [11]. Both of these ignore the impact of spatial heterogeneity on the quality of cultivated land. Spatial autocorrelation technology has comprehensively considereds the differences in the spatial distribution of cultivated land quality, and can visualize spatial data while analyzing the spatial aggregation law of cultivated land quality. Therefore, it has been widely used in spatial research in recent years [12]. In terms of research objects, there are relatively few studies on the spatial characteristics of cultivated land quality [13]. And most of the existing studies consider prefecture-level cities or counties as the target area for analysis. Although smaller research areas are more conducive to describing the spatial aggregation of cultivated land quality [14], it does not fully grasp the spatial distribution characteristics of cultivated land quality in the macro area, which is not conducive to the proposaling more scientific and reasonable measures for cultivated land utilization and protection [15]. Therefore, this paper chooses Henan Province, the most important agricultural, livestock and food production base in China, as the study area to analyze the spatial differences and distribution rule of cultivated land quality in this area, which not only provides a guarantee for national food security, but also ensures the sustainable development of the region. In the research process, this paper starts from the perspective of spatial correlation, and uses methods such as spatial autocorrelation to comprehensively analyze the spatial aggregation characteristics and differences of cultivated land quality in Henan Province at the county scale. Based on this, the corresponding zoning protection scheme for cultivated land is put forward.

2 Overview of the Study Area and Research Methodology

2.1 Overview of the Study Area

Henan province is located in the central region of China, with the boundary between 31°23′-36°22′ north latitude and 110°21′-116°39′ east longitude. It is named because its jurisdiction is mostly located south of the Yellow River. It is an important transportation hub and one of the largest grain bases in China. In 2018, Henan Province's total grain production of about 66.49 million tons, ranking second in the country. Henan Province spans the four major water systems of Haihe, Huanghe, Huaihe and Yangtze River, with more abundant runoff resources, and the terrain is high in the west and low in the east. It west adjacent shaanxi, so more hilly; connected with Anhui and Shandong to the east therefore consists of the basin and the plain, the north adjacent shanxi and hebei, south hubei, with a total area of about 16700000 hm^2, accounting for 1.73% of the nation's total. Among them, mountains account for about 26%, hills account for about 18%, and plains account for about 56%. The cultivated land area of The whole province is about 1,268,340 hm^2, ranking the third in China, and the per capita cultivated land area is about 0.0127 hm^2, including 5354, 200 hm^2 of irrigated land, which accounts for 66% of the cultivated land area of the whole province, and 1379500 hm^2 of paddy field, which accounts for 17% of the total cultivated land area of the whole province (Fig. 1).

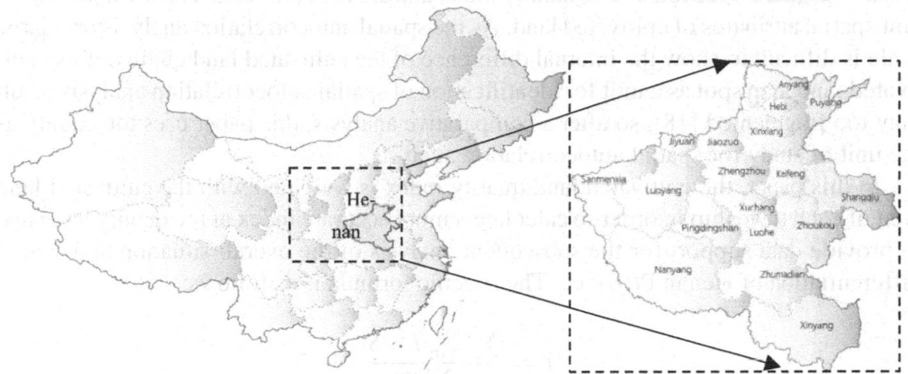

Fig. 1. Location map of Henan Province

2.2 Research Methodology

Data Preprocessing. In this paper, the cultivated land quality of 159 urban areas in Henan Province in 2018 is the object of the study. The basic data comes from the 2018 Cultivated Land Quality Grade Update Project of Henan Province, the Henan Provincial Bureau of Land and Resources, the Bureau of Agriculture, and the county statistical yearbook., and the data mainly include the update results of cultivated land quality, traffic and water conservancy planning, land economic conditions and utilization status data, soil map data and so on.

Data pre-processing consists of two main modules, namely the conversion of information files into standardized geographic information and the processing of map data. Use Arcgis10.2 to unify the coordinate system of all the above data and graph data, so as to ensure the similarity of the internal attributes of the research unit [16], and then the standardized map data of more than 23.7 million cultivated land equally divided units with townships in Henan Province as the unit are processed. To avoid to cultivated land map spot as a unit for identification of spatial autocorrelation analysis result is too fragmented, degree is low, this research by the area weighted average method, the in the villages and towns as the calculating unit of cultivated land quality index is transformed to the county as the unit, and then calculate the 159 counties of henan province separate cultivated land quality grade. Spatial autocorrelation analysis of the above results was then performed using Geoda, start by creating the Weight file using the Weight tool in GeoDa. The determination of the spatial weight is the basis of the spatial autocorrelation analysis [17]. According to the different spatial position relations, the spatial adjacency relationship can be divided into 3 categories: Rook (common edge adjacent), Queen (common edge or corner adjacent) and nearest K Point relationship. Through the spatial statistical analysis of the adjacency of cultivated land patches in the study area, this paper choosed to use the Queen's adjacency principle to determine the spatial weights and then construct the spatial weight matrix.

Area-Weighted Methods. The quality index and area of cultivated land are both important spatial attributes of cultivated land. As the spatial autocorrelation analysis on a large scale is difficult to show the internal difference of the cultivated land quality, if use cultivated land map spot as a unit for identification of spatial autocorrelation analysis result may too fragmented [18], so after a comparative analysis, this paper uses the county as the unit of study for spatial autocorrelation analysis.

In this paper, the cultivated land quality index is weighted with the cultivated land area of each township in order to calculate a more accurate index at the county level and to provide data support for the subsequent analysis of the overall situation and spatial differentiation of Henan Province. The specific formula is as follows:

$$Y = \frac{\sum_{i\,\min}^{i\,\max} i \times Si}{\sum S} \tag{1}$$

where Y denotes the average farmland quality of the target county, i denotes the farmland quality index of the corresponding township, S_i represents the corresponding farmland area of township i, and the denominator is the sum of the farmland areas of all the townships under the study, that the total farmland area of the county.

Spatial Autocorrelation. The first law of geography proposed by Tobler has been the theoretical basis for spatial autocorrelation analysis, and cultivated land as continuous space also satisfies this law [19] that there is spatial correlation or similarity. Detecting the presence of spatial autocorrelation between things and measuring the degree of correlation depend on the global spatial autocorrelation and local spatial autocorrelation indices, respectively.

Global spatial autocorrelation summarizes the degree of spatial dependence within an overarching spatial context and is a measure of similarity between neighboring regions. There are many ways to detect spatial correlation, and this paper used the most commonly used global Moran's I to measure the spatial dependence of farmland quality indices in each county in Henan Province, calculated as follows:

$$I = \frac{n \sum_{i=1}^{n} \sum_{j=1}^{n} wij\left(Xi - \overline{X}\right)\left(Xj - \overline{X}\right)}{\sum_{i=1}^{n} \sum_{j=1}^{n} wij \sum_{i=1}^{n} \left(Xi - \overline{X}\right)^2} \tag{2}$$

Where n represents the total number of spatially observed objects in the target area; Xi and Xj are the observations of the i-th and j-th objects in the spatial location respectively, $\overline{X}$ is the average observation of all the objects; and Wij is the spatial weight matrix, and the value of Wij indicates the adjacency between the i-th and j-th objects in the spatial location. The value of *Wij* is the spatial weight matrix, and the value of *Wij* indicates the neighborhood between *i* and *j*. When $Wij = 1$, *i* is adjacent to *j*, and when $Wij = 0$,*i* is not adjacent to *j*. The value of Global Moran's I ranges from ±1, and if $I > 0$, it indicates a positive spatial correlation; when $I < 0$, it indicates a negative spatial correlation. The positive spatial correlation indicates that the objects are spatially aggregated, while the negative spatial correlation indicates that the objects are spatially discrete. If $I = 0$, it means random distribution of research objects.

Although global spatial autocorrelation analysis can reflect whether the research objects are clustered in space, it cannot further show the location and characteristics of spatial clustering. Local spatial autocorrelation analysis can more intuitively show the spatial agglomeration of cultivated land quality in the study area. so combining global spatial autocorrelation and local spatial autocorrelation thus reveals the spatial correlation of cultivated land quality and the character of their spatial aggregation at the the same time. In this paper, the local spatial autocorrelation is performed for each county in Henan Province, and the LISA clustering map is used to analyze the spatial location of clustering or dispersion of farmland quality in Henan Province. The calculation formula is as formula (3), the meaning of the variables in the formula is the same as formula (2).

$$I = \frac{\sum_{j=1, j \neq i}^{n} wij(xi - \overline{x})(xj - \overline{x})}{\sum_{i=1}^{n} (xi - \overline{x})^2} \tag{3}$$

3 Results and Analysis

3.1 Characteristics of the Spatial Distribution of Cultivated Land Quality

The cultivated land area of Henan Province is about 81.123 million square kilometers, accounting for 48.58% of the total area of the province. In order to further observe and analyze the spatial distribution of cultivated quality, this paper uses the natural breakpoint method in ArcGIS to classify cultivated land quality into five levels, which ensures that not only the nature of the internal elements of each group is similar, but also the number and scope of subjects are similar between groups. In ArcGIS, the cultivated land quality index obtained after data preprocessing and its corresponding grades are output as a map, and the spatial distribution map of the three types of cultivated land quality shown in Fig. 2 is obtained. It can be seen from the figure that the level of cultivated land quality in Henan Province has obvious aggregation characteristics in spatial distribution.

Due to the diversity of landforms and climatic differences in different regions of the province, the natural quality of cultivated land in various regions is also different. It can be seen from the figure that the natural quality grades of cultivated land in Henan Province are mainly concentrated in 12–13. There are 55 counties with natural grades between 12–13, covering an area of 38,505 km^2, accounting for 47.46% of the province's cultivated land area. The cultivated land with higher score is mainly concentrated in the northern and central plains of Henan Province, where the cultivated land has superior natural conditions and high productivity. The cultivated land with low score is mainly concentrated in the western hilly area, which is affected by soil and terrain, etc., and the cultivated land in this area has poor natural conditions.

The utilization grade of cultivated land quality in Henan Province is predominantly grade 10–11, mainly concentrated in 42 counties belonging to Kaifeng, Zhumadian, Zhoukou and Xinyang cities, with a total area of 26,883 km^2, accounting for 33.14% of the total cultivated land area of the province. The utilization level of cultivated land is also spatially distributed in the form of agglomeration. The cultivated land with higher utilization level is concentrated in the northern and central-eastern plains, while the low-scoring cultivated land is mostly distributed in the western hilly areas with poor farmland infrastructure. The spatial distribution of the economic and utilization categories is similar, with high scores concentrated in the northern part of Henan Province and the Middle East, mainly in the 7–8 region, with an area of 31,909 km^2, accounting for 39.33% of the total cultivated land, which is due to the convenience of transportation in the region and the better development of specialty products circulation and tourism, especially in cities such as Puyang, Xinxiang, Jiaozuo and Zhengzhou. Constrained by topography and transportation, the economic conditions in the western hills are more backward.

In general, the quality of cultivated land in Henan Province has obvious characteristics of agglomeration in spatial distribution, which is higher in the north than in the middle than in the west. It is because the central and northern plains are conducive to urban expansion and the construction of transportation routes, which drives economic development; the developed economy makes farmland infrastructure more perfect, and due to climatic reasons, there is sufficient rainfall and heat, and abundant groundwater resources, and the quality of cultivated land in Henan Province is higher than in the west. Soils are generally fertile and the productivity of cultivated land is high, resulting in a high level of cultivated land use and natural quality in the north-central region.

3.2 Analysis of Results of Global Spatial Autocorrelation of Cultivated Land Quality

This paper uses 159 counties in Henan Province to calculate Global Moran's I values for farmland quality in Henan Province using Geoda and Arcgis 10.2 tools for spatial autocorrelation analysis, yields the Moran's scatter plot as shown in Fig. 3. From the magnitude of Moran's I value, the quality of cultivated land in Henan Province all show more obvious positive spatial correlation [20]. The natural quality of cultivated land (Moran's I $\approx$ 0.9414) showed the strongest positive spatial correlation, while the utilization level (Moran's I $\approx$ 0.7705) and economic level (Moran's I $\approx$ 0.5524) in turn showed a weaker Relevance.

In this paper, we work out the global Moran index for different cultivated land quality classes and combined it with the spatial distribution map to reveal the differences in the spatial distribution of the natural quality, economic conditions and utilization level of Henan Province's cultivated land. The research results show that the natural quality of cultivated land in Henan Province is highly spatially related. Combined with the spatial distribution map (Fig. 2), it can be seen that the spatial pattern of natural grades is clustered and the more uniform in spatial distribution. The spatial autocorrelation of the utilization level is second to that of the natural level, which indicates that the cultivated land with similar utilization level is more spatially clustered in the region. Combined

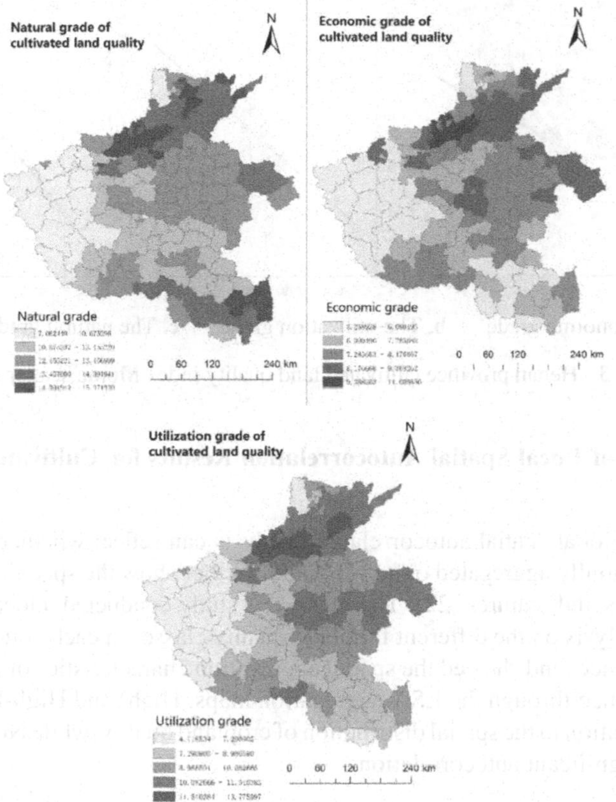

Fig. 2. Spatial distribution of cultivated land quality in Henan Province

with Fig. 2, it is clear that the lower utilization levels are clustered in the western part of the province, others are slightly scattered. The spatial autocorrelation of economic grades is the weakest of the three. It can be clearly seen from Fig. 3 that compared with natural quality and utilization level, the spatial pattern of economic grades is the most scattered. Although it still has a certain degree of aggregation, The economic level between counties and districts in the Central Plains is quite different.

In general, the quality of cultivated land in Henan Province is relatively uniform in spatial distribution, cultivated land with similar quality grades are basically distributed in the form of aggregation, especially the natural quality is the most concentrated, which is very conducive to land reclamation management according to local conditions. And protection plan should comprehensively consider the economic development status and utilization level in the region, and coordinate the three to realize the fine management of the cultivated land quality [21].

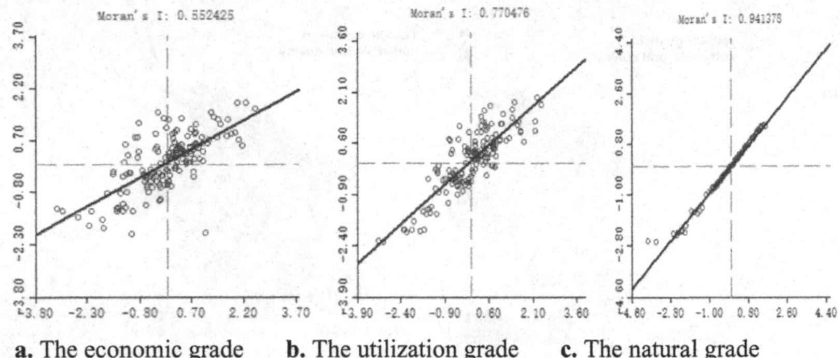

a. The economic grade **b.** The utilization grade **c.** The natural grade

Fig. 3. Henan province cultivated land quality index Moran scatter plot

3.3 Analysis of Local Spatial Autocorrelation Results for Cultivated Land Quality

Although the global spatial autocorrelation analysis can reflect whether the quality of farmland is spatially aggregated or not, it cannot further show the specific spatial aggregation locations and features [22]. Therefore, this study conducted a local spatial autocorrelation analysis on the different farmland quality classes in each county and district of Henan province, and showed the spatial aggregation characteristics of farmland quality in the province through the LSA aggregation maps. High) and High-Low indicate a negative correlation in the spatial distribution of cropland quality, while Not-Significance indicates no significant autocorrelation.

Analysis of Results of Local Spatial Autocorrelation of Natural Quality of Cultivated Land. Combined with the LISA aggregation plot A and Table 1 show that there are 32 and 22 counties and districts of the HH and LL types with positive correlation spatial, accounting for 20.13% and 13.84% of the total number of counties and districts in the province respectively. There were 1 and 0 counties and districts of LH and HL types respectively, accounting for 0.63% of the total; 104 counties and districts showed non-significant spatial autocorrelation, accounting for 65.41% of the total number of counties and districts in the province. Spatial distribution of HH type cultivated land is mainly concentrated in the northern part of Henan Province, such as Jiaozuo City, northern Zhengzhou City, Hebi City, and the line of Huijia, Hongqi District, Yanjin County, Shuixian County, Puyang County; while LL type cultivated land is concentrated in the western part of Henan Province, such as Sanmenxia City, Luoyang City and Nanyang City. Combined with the actual conditions, we can see that most of the cultivated land in the northern part of Henan Province is located in the plains, flat terrain, fertile soil, natural conditions are more favorable; while in the western part of the country, cultivated land is located in the mountainous area, limited drainage and irrigation conditions, uneven terrain and cultivated land is weak, so the natural conditions of cultivated land are poorer.

Analysis of Results of Local Spatial Autocorrelation of Economic Conditions of Cultivated Land. Combined with the economic LISA aggregation plot B and Table 1 show that HH and LL types with spatially positive correlation have 22 and 25 counties each, accounting for 13.84% and 15.72% of the total number of counties and districts in the province, respectively; the number of counties and districts of the HL type among the spatial autocorrelation types is zero, and there is only one county of the LH type, accounting for 0.63% of the total. 111 counties and districts showed non-significant on spatial correlation, accounting for 69.81% of the total number of counties and districts in the province. Spatially, the HH type is mainly concentrated in the northern part of Henan Province in the line of Wenzhi County, Wuzhi County, Huijia County, Hongqi District, Yanjin County, Shuixian County, and Puyang County; the LL type is concentrated in groups in the area of Lingbao City-Xichuan County, Luoning County-Nanzhao County, and Yiyang County-Lushan County in the west, and in the area of Pingqiao, Zhengyang, Luoshan, Xincai, Xixian, Guangshan, Xin County, and Hengchuan County in Xinyang City. In reality, the cultivated land in the northern part of Henan Province is more powerful, and the natural quality is relatively high, so the crop yield is larger, while the terrain is flat and convenient for transportation of products, so the economic conditions are developed.

Analysis of Local Spatial Autocorrelation Results for Cultivated Land Quality. The results of LISA cluster plot C and Table 1 show that there each 24 and 25 counties of the HH and LL types, accounting for 15.09% and 15.72% of the total number of counties in the province, respectively; the LH and HL type counties in the spatial autocorrelation are both zero; there are 110 counties with non-significant spatial autocorrelation, accounting for the total number of 69.18% counties in the province. The spatial distribution of the utilization level is similar to that of the economy. The HH type is mainly concentrated in Wen County, Wuzhi County, Huojia County, Hongqi District, Yanjin County, Hua County, Puyang County, Hui County and Yuanyang County in northern Henan Province. And Zhengzhou City, Huiji, Xingyang, Jinshui, Zhongyuan District, etc. Type LL is also concentrated in Sanmenxia City-Luoyang City and the western counties and districts of Nanyang City, as well as the area of Zhengyang, Xixian, Luoshan and Guangshan counties in Xinyang City. In practice, the cultivated land in the northern part of Henan Province has fertile soil, high natural quality, suitable climate for crop growth, and developed economic conditions, better infrastructure, which is conducive to farming, and generally higher utilization levels; while the mountainous areas in the western part of the province have poor natural conditions and cultivated land The number is relatively small and the cultivation is limited, so the utilization level is low (Fig. 4).

In general, the quality of cultivated land in Henan Province is spatially distributed in the form of gathered, and the positive correlation between HH and LL types of cultivated land is particularly obvious. HH-type cultivated land is concentrated in the northern part of Henan Province and tends to be distributed along the river. This is due to the flat terrain, convenient transportation and abundant groundwater resources in the northern plains, making the cultivated land in this area not only high in natural quality, but also economically developed in the region, The farmland infrastructure is complete, so the input and output benefits are high. Affected by factors such as topography and soil quality, LL-type cultivated land is concentrated in the western hilly areas in the form of clusters. This area is generally inconvenient for transportation and relatively backward economic. The LH and HL types of cultivated land with negative correlations only

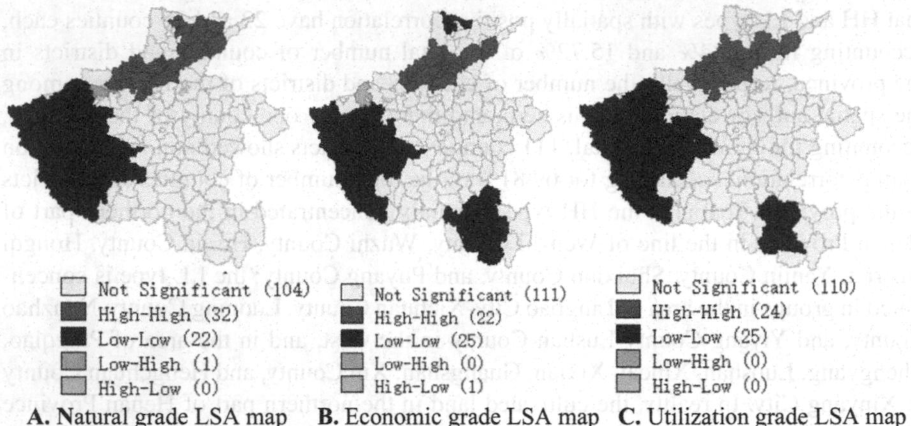

A. Natural grade LSA map **B.** Economic grade LSA map **C.** Utilization grade LSA map

Fig. 4. Cultivated land quality local spatial correlation gathered figure in Henan province

Table 1. Types of local spatial autocorrelation and statistical summary of county in Henan province

Autocorrelation types	Cultivated land quality index		Cultivated land use index		Cultivated land economic index	
	Number	Ratio/%	Number	Ratio/%	Number	Ratio/%
High-High	32	20.13	24	15.09	22	13.84
High-Low	0	0	0	0	1	0
Low-High (LH)	1	0.63	0	0	0	0
Low-Low (LL)	22	13.84	25	15.72	25	15.72
non-significant	104	65.41	110	69.18	111	69.81
aggregate	159	100.00	159	100.00	159	100.00

exist in the natural and economic levels, namely Mengjin County in Luoyang City and Mianchi County in Sanmenxia City. Therefore, the positive correlation type dominates the cultivated land with spatial correlation in Henan Province status.

3.4 Conservation Zoning of Cropland Based on Local Spatial Autocorrelation

Based on the natural quality of cultivated land, comprehensive utilization level and economic development, and taking into account spatial polarization and diffusion effects, this paper classifies the protection of cultivated land in Henan Province into four categories: restricted construction areas, reserve control areas, key improvement areas and comprehensive improvement areas. Among them, the cultivated land of HH types has higher comprehensive quality and obvious aggregation effect, which is geographically advantageous, mostly located in cities with convenient transportation and developed economy, easy to manage centrally, and the soil in this area of high natural quality, which is conducive to land reform, so it should be classified as restricted construction zone, strictly prohibit non-agricultural construction to protect cultivated land and food security.

On the contrary, LL type cultivated land should be classified asreserve control zone to protect cultivated land and food security. Because of this type of cultivated land is mostly concentrated in the western mountainous areas, where the quality of cultivated land, transportation conditions and economic development are relatively poor, making land remediation more difficult, so it should be included in the reserve control area, and remediation should be targeted based on the basic situation of each county and region, and the investment for remediation should be increased or farming should be reduced according to local conditions. Local spatial correlation is High-Low types means the higher-quality cultivated land is surrounded by lower-quality cultivated land in this region, which is similar to a "convex land" in terms of space [23].

Due to spatial polarization, the central unit is susceptible to the driving influence of the surrounding units [23], so the higher-quality cultivated land in this region is susceptible to the negative influence of the lower-quality region. Then assimilated into the LL type, land reform will be more difficult at that time. So the improvement of the time sequence should be backward, should be classified as a comprehensive improvement of the area. The cultivated land of LH types is the opposite, high-quality cultivated land surrounds low-quality land, the same by the influence of spatial polarization, low-quality land is easily assimilated by the high-quality land around it, so the region's cultivated land reform potential is large, should focus on the improveing the low quality land to transform the whole conversion to HH, and therefore this area is classified as a priority improvement area.

This paper also integrates the quality of utilization and economic quality, respectively, from the level of utilization of cultivated land and regional economic efficiency of two perspectives, divides the cultivated land of Henan province into corresponding output-efficient and output-inefficient areas, the results of the division are detailed in Table 2. From the table it can be seen that the northern region of Henan Province, such as Jiaozuo City, northern Zhengzhou City, Hebi City, as well as Huojia, Hongqi District, Yanjin County, slip County and so on, the cultivated land in these areas has well standardization and continuous, which is conducive to large-scale mechanized operations and centralized management, and mostly located in the agricultural and economically developed areas, good location conditions, and cultivated land natural quality level is high, land reclamation is less difficult. In addition, these areas's soil is fertile, low and flat terrain, and convenient transportation. Therefore, they should prohibit non-farm construction to ensure food security.

Table 2. Zoning of cultivated land protection based on local spatial autocorrelation in Henan province

Cultivated Land quality	Autocorrelation types	Regional name	Typical district	Protection measures	Advice
Natural	High-High	Restricted construction	Jiaozuo City, northern Zhengzhou City, Hebi City to Yanjin County, Puyang County and so on	Safeguarding the quality and quantity of currently cultivated land	Prohibiting non-agricultural construction
	Low-Low	Reserve control	Sanmenxia city to Luoyang city, and Nanyang city surrounding counties	Selective rectification according to local conditions	Encourage non-agricultural construction
	Low-High	Key Improvement	Mengjin County and its surrounding counties	Focus on rectifying low-scoring areas	Avoid non-agricultural land development
Economic	High-High	Output efficiency	North Of Henan Province Wen County, Wuzhi County, Hongqi District, to Puyang County area	Maintain the current level of input and output	Prohibiting non-agricultural construction
	Low-Low	Output inefficient	From Luoning County to Nanzhao County in western Henan Province, from Yiyang County to Lushan County, and Pingqiao County, Xinyang City and so on	Appropriately reduce the input of rectification	Encourage non-agricultural construction
	High-Low	Comprehensive Improvement	Xin'an County and its surrounding areas	Prioritize protection of high-score areas	Proper conduct non-agricultural construction
Utilization	High-High	Output efficiency	Huojia County to Puyang County, Qinyang county to Hui County first line, Yuanyang County and Zhengzhou City Huiji, Jinshui Districts	Improve the current farmland infrastructure and promote further development of the utilization level	Prohibiting non-agricultural construction
	Low-Low	Output inefficient	Sanmenxia to Luoyang, and most counties in Nanyang City	Reduce rectification investment	Encourage non-agricultural construction

4 Discussion and Conclusions

From the perspective of spatial pattern analysis, this paper adopts the spatial autocorrelation analysis method and uses Arcgis and Geoda to study the spatial aggregation characteristics and differences in the quality of cultivated land in Henan Province at the county scale, and then proposes corresponding fine zoning protection measures based on this analysis. The research conclusions are as follows:

(1) In Henan Province, the quality of cultivated land is spatially distributed with obvious aggregation characteristics, with natural grades showing a decreasing pattern from northeast to southwest counties, and economic grades and utilization grades similar in spatial distribution, with high grades mainly concentrated in the northern part of the province in Jiaozuo City, northern Zhengzhou City, Hebi City, and Hongqi District, Yanjin County, Shuixian County, while the quality in the western mountains are generally lower.

(2) The global autocorrelation analysis on the quality of cultivated land in Henan Province shows that the quality of cultivated land in the province is spatially distributed in an aggregated form. From the value of Global Moran's I, the natural quality index > utilization index > economic level index. It indicates that the natural conditions of Henan's cultivated land have the strongest spatial correlation, followed by the utilization level, and the economic conditions have the weakest correlation.

(3) From the results of the local spatial autocorrelation study on the quality of cultivated land at the county level, it can be seen that among the counties with spatially correlation, HH and LL land of positive correlation type dominate, and they aredistributed in aggregate form in space. The results of the local spatial autocorrelation analysis classify Henan's cultivated land into four categories: restricted construction zones, reserve control zones, key improvement zones and comprehensive improvement zones. At the same time, combined with the actual situation of each area, the corresponding protection or rectification Suggestions are proposed, provide scientific reference and technical support for Henan's targeted cultivated land protection and refined cultivated land management.

Funding. The research was Supported by the Open Fund of Key Laboratory of Urban Land Resources Monitoring and Simulation, Ministry of Natural Resources, Grant No. (KF-2019–04-038). This research was also funded by Key scientific and technological projects in Henan Province, Grant No. (212102210105).

References

1. Qian, F.K., Zhang, J.Y., Wang, Q.B.: Spatial Correlation Analysis and Driving Mechanism of Cultivated Land Quality in Donggang. Chin. J. Soil Sci. **49**(05), 1048–1053 (2018)
2. Gao, J.G., Huang, R.: Protection zoning of cultivated land based on cultivated land quality index and spatial autocorrelation on southern area of Jiangsu Province. Res. Soil Water Conserv. **26**(03), 213–218 (2019)
3. Sun, C.K., Xu, J.L., Yu, D., Zhou, W., Wang, J.P., Liang, Z.B.: Spatial distribution of cultivated land quality at different scales in Chongyi County. Chin. J. Eco-Agric. **27**(04), 601–612 (2019)
4. Fang, Y., Chen, Y.: Research on spatial pattern of cultivated land quality in Hubei province. Hubei Agric. Sci. **55**(17), 4533–4537 (2016)
5. Wei, S.C., Xiong, C.S., Luan, Q.L., et al.: Protection zoning of cultivated land quality index based on local spatial autocorrelation. Trans. Chin. Soc. Agric. Eng. (Trans. CSAE) **30**(18), 249–256 (2014)
6. Zhao, J.J., Zhang, H.Y., et al.: Research on the quality evaluation of cultivated land in provincial area based on AHP and GIS: a case study in Jilin province. Chin. J. Soil Sci. **43**(01), 70–75 (2012)
7. Shi, Y.Q., Li, T.S.: Analysis of spatial variation of cultivated land quality in Wugong county. Chin. J. Soil Sci. **48**(02), 257–262 (2017)
8. Yang, Y.X., Sun, T., Zhang, L.H., et al.: Fractal mechanism of spatial distribution of cultivated land quality in Beijing-Tianjin-Hebei region. Trans. Chin. Soc. Agric. Eng. **48**(02), 165–171 (2017)
9. Yang, L.Y.: Analysis for the characteristics of spatial difference of cultivated land quality in Fujian province. Chin. J. Agric. Resour. Reg. Plan. **39**(11), 52–58 (2018)

10. Lin, C., et al.: Prediction of Spatial Distribution of Topsoil Organic matter content in cultivated land using Kriging methods. Arid Zone Res. **34**(04), 798–805 (2017)
11. Duan, Z.S., et al.: Spatial pattern of cultivated land quality in Guangxi based on landscape index and Gini coefficient. J. South. Agric. **46**(01), 175–180 (2015)
12. Zhang, H., Zhao, X.M., Ouyang, Z.C., et al.: Spatial disparity features and protection zoning of cultivated land quality based on spatial autocorrelation—a case study of Shanggao County, Jiang province. Res. Soil Water Conserv. **25**(01), 304–312 (2018)
13. Yu, H.M., Yang, X.P., Guo, X.: The Research on the spatial characteristics of the newly increased cultivated land quality in hilly regions of South China* -a case study of Yichun City in Jiangxi province. Chin. J. Agric. Resour. Reg. Plan.**40**(01), 110–117 (2019)
14. Liu, M., Zhao, C.W., Shi, M.H.: Spatial autocorrelationanalysis of multi-scale land use change at mountainous areas in Guizhou province. Trans. Chin. Soc. Agric. Eng. (Trans. CSAE) **28**(20), 239–246 (2012)
15. Yang, J.Y., Du, Z.R., Du, Z.B., et al.: Well-facilitied capital farmland assignment based on land quality evaluation and LISA. Trans. Chin. Soc. Agric. Mach. **48**(06), 109–115 (2017)
16. Ma, R.H., Li, Q., B. Li, X., et al.: Comparison plotting methods of appraising subregion in farmland Grading of county. Geo Gr. Territorial Res. **18**(02), 93–95 (2002)
17. Yang, K.Z., Feng, D.T., Shen, T.Y.: Recent advances in the study of spatial econometrics. Res. Dev. **2**, 7–12 (2009)
18. Zhang, H., et al.: Multi-scale spatial autocorrelation analysis of cultivated land quality in China's southern hillside areas: a case study of Lichuan county, Jiangxi province. Chin. J. Eco-Agric. **26**(02), 263–273 (2018)
19. Tobler, W.R.: A computer movie simulating urban growth in the detroit region. Econ. Geogr. **46**(02), 234–240 (1970)
20. Anselin, L.: Local indicators of spatial association—LISA. Geogr. Anal. **27**(02), 93–115 (1995)
21. Zhang, Z., Wei, C.F., Li, P., et al.: Effect of household behaviors on cultivated land quality in hilly areas of Sichuan basin, China. Trans. CSAE **25**(04), 230–236 (2009)
22. Xiao, J.Y., Tan, S.H.: Regularity of the spatial variation of grain yield at provincial scale in China. China Land Sci. **27**(08), 26–32 (2013)
23. Zhu, Y.M., Yao, S.M.: Overview of studies of regional linkages in foreign countries. World Reg. Stud. **10**(02), 16–24 (2001)

Preamble Selection and Allocation Algorithm Based on Q Learning

Weibo Yuan[1(✉)], Yun Zang[1], and Lei Zhang[2]

[1] North China Electric Power University, Baoding 071003, China
[2] Shandong Electric Power Research Institute, State Grid Corporation of China, Ji'nan 250002, China

Abstract. Machine-type Communication (MTC) is one of the three typical scenarios of 5G cellular communication network and is supposed to support connection density of 1 million devices per square kilometer. Random access initiated by such a large amount of devices may lead to congestion, conflicts and packet loss. This work designed a Q-learning-based dynamic preamble allocation scheme to solve the overload problem caused by large-scale MTC devices. The core enhancement considered in this work is Early Data Transmission (EDT) mechanism. MTC devices were divided into two groups of delay-sensitive and delay-tolerant according to the maximum delay tolerance of the services. Some of the preamble resources were pre-reserved for Delay-Sensitive Devices (DSD). Each DSD selected a preamble randomly from the pre-reserved set and performed EDT. Each Delay-Tolerant Device (DTD) selected a preamble randomly from the rest of the preambles and performed normal 4-step random access procedure. The number of elements in the pre-reserved set was dynamically adjusted using Q-learning algorithm according to the successful access proportion of the two types of devices. And then the base station would update and broadcast the service types which were permitted to use EDT. Simulation results show that the scheme proposed in this work improves the successful access proportion and meet the delay requirement of DSDs, and guarantees the throughput of the system at the same time.

Keywords: MTC · Random access · EDT · Dynamic preamble allocation

1 Background

One of the main challenges of Machine-Type Communication (MTC) is that the current Random Access (RA) protocol cannot support large-scale short packet transmission [1]. In recent years, the number of MTC devices has been increasing rapidly [2, 3] and makes it more challenging to optimize the operation of cellular network in dynamic wireless environment [4, 5]. It is estimated that by the end of 2020, there will be about 50 billion MTC devices [6, 7]. This on one hand exacerbates the shortage of limited spectrum resources, and on the other hand, using traditional RA mechanism will inevitably lead to congestion and confliction when a large number of MTC devices are activate and require

X. Sun et al. (Eds.): ICAIS 2021, LNCS 12736, pp. 443–454, 2021.
https://doi.org/10.1007/978-3-030-78609-0_38

to connected to the base station simultaneously as the available preamble resources are limited. In addition, to reduce costs, MTC devices usually have poor computing ability and memory and make it challenging to realize complex machine learning algorithms in MTC devices [8].

In June 2018, the 3rd Generation Partnership Project (3GPP) announced that the first phase of fully functional standardization of 5G has completed [9]. The 3GPP recommends dynamic allocation of Random Access Channel (RACH) resources to solve the RAN congestion problem [10]. Literature [11] proposed an adaptive algorithm to determine the number of preambles without knowing the number of devices and access probability, which can maximize the RACH throughput. Literature [12] proposed a dynamic preamble grouping strategy based on delay sensitivity, which fully considered the Quality of Service (QoS) requirements of Delay-Sensitive Devices (DSDs) and divided the preambles into two groups. In the case of severe congestion, Delay-Tolerant Devices (DTDs) performed strict Access Class Barring (ACB) backoff mechanism to guarantee the successful access of DSDs. Reference [13] considered different communication requirements between DSDs and DTDs and proposed a Q-learning-based algorithm to allocate dedicated orthogonal resources to DSDs. Hoglund, et al. [14] provided some initial results on Early Data Transmission (EDT) performance which show that it exhibits gains in battery life improvement by up to 46% and reduction of message latency by 85 ms at the cell edge.

In order to support massive MTC (mMTC) scenarios, 3GPP has conducted a lot of research on improving access ability, transmission efficiency, power consumption, flexibility and other performance, and random access enhancement is one of the key technologies. In December 2018, 3GPP R15 formally established a project for 2-step random access (2-step RA) [15]. For contention-based random access, enhanced design was made in terms of channel structure and access procedures, and related standardization work was completed in June 2020 in R16. In 2-step RA, the two uplink (UL) messages in the traditional 4-step random access, Msg1 and Msg3, are combined into a new MsgA, and the two downlink (DL) messages, Msg2 and Msg4, are combined into a new MsgB. The 2-step RACH can significantly reduce the delay, signaling cost, and power consumption during random access.

The objective of this work is to design a dynamic preamble allocation algorithm to achieve short packet transmission of MTC devices with less signaling overhead, thereby improving information transmission efficiency, increasing the access success rate of DSDs, and reducing average access delay.

The remainder of this article is organized as follows. Early Data Transmission mechanism is described briefly in Sect. 2. Section 3 sets up the system model and analyze the success access probability of MTC devices. A preamble selection and allocation algorithm based on Q-learning is proposed in Sect. 4 and simulation results and analysis are given in Sect. 5. Section 6 ends the article with conclusions and recommendations.

2 Early Data Transmission

2.1 Overhead Analysis of RRC-Related Signaling

The RRC protocol defined by 3GPP R15 mainly covers the following functions:

System Information. Handle system information broadcast including NAS public information. Some of the system information is only available when the UE is in RRC_IDLE state, and other information is available when the UE is in RRC_CONNECTED state.

RRC Connection Setup Control. Contains all procedures related to RRC connection establishment, modification and release, including paging, initial security activation, setup of SRB and DRB, handover within LTE (including sending UE context messages), configuration of underlying protocols, ACB, and wireless link failure.

Inter-RAT (Radio Access Technology) Mobility. Includes secure activation and UE context information transmission in addition to the mobility process.

Measurement, configuration and reporting. Measurement, configuration and reporting of inter-band, inter-frequency and inter-RAT mobility.

Other Functions. Includes dedicated NAS information transmission and UE wireless access capability information transmission.

Table 1 shows the contents and sizes of typical signaling messages involved in the RRC connection establishment/release progress. It is assumed that all messages are successfully transmitted, without re-transmission occurring and no user movement or handover.

2.2 Overview of Early Data Transmission Mechanisms

EDT was proposed by 3GPP in [16] to reduce access delay. EDT is one of the most attractive technologies to reduce signaling overhead and end-to-end transmission delay. In EDT, the uplink authorization of the data is broadcast in advance, allowing the data transmission to be held by the RACH.

The core idea of EDT is to enable uplink and downlink data transmission in Message 3(Msg3) and Message4(Msg4). If the entire data transfer is completed in Msg3, the network can move the UE to radio resource control idle (RRC_IDLE) mode. This cuts down the signaling in RRC release process, shortens the total transmission time, and thus improves the battery life of the device and reduces the message latency [17]. If the resource allocation of data in EDT Msg 1 uses uplink shared channel (USCH), the parameters including 'EDT-TBS' are pre-configured by gNB in SIB2 before the EDT process starts [18]. If the size of data in Msg1 is less than or equal to the maximum value broadcasting in 'EDT-TBS', the device will initiate a RA process using EDT, otherwise, use traditional 4-step RA.

Table 1. Overhead of the signaling involved in RRC connection establishment and release.

Uplink/downlink	Signaling content	Size (Bytes)
RRC connection setup		
Uplink	Preamble	139
Downlink	Random access response	7
Uplink	RRC connection requests	7
Downlink	RRC connection setup + UE contention resolution identity MAC CE	38
Uplink	Buffer status report	2
Uplink	RRC connection setup complete	20
Downlink	RLC status report	3
Downlink	Security mode command	11
Downlink	RRC connection reconfiguration	118
Uplink	Buffer status report	2
Uplink	Security mode complete	13
Uplink	RRC connection reconfiguration complete	10
Downlink	RLC status report	3
Uplink	Buffer status report	2
Uplink	Uplink information transfer	13
Downlink	RLC status report	3
RRC connection release		
Downlink	RRC connection release	10
Uplink	RLC status report	3

The working progress of EDT is generally as follows:

UE receives system information required by EDT procedure, such as (N)PRACH preamble configured for EDT, maximum TBS for EDT.

UE randomly selects a (N)PRACH preamble from the preamble set dedicated for EDT and sends it to inform gNB that data will be sent via EDT.

gNB receives the EDT preamble and responds with the appropriate TBS based on random access messages (including uplink Msg3).

UE transmits the necessary information (UE identity, continuing identity, PPC messages) and user data in Msg3.

gNB receives Msg3 and keeps UE in RRC_IDLE or moves UE to RRC_CONNECTED if further data is available.

If the UE receives instructions from Msg4 that it can move to RRC_IDLE, the EDT process and data transmission are completed, and the UE goes on with its idle mode. Otherwise, UE moves to RRC_CONNECTED and informs gNB that it has completed the state transition.

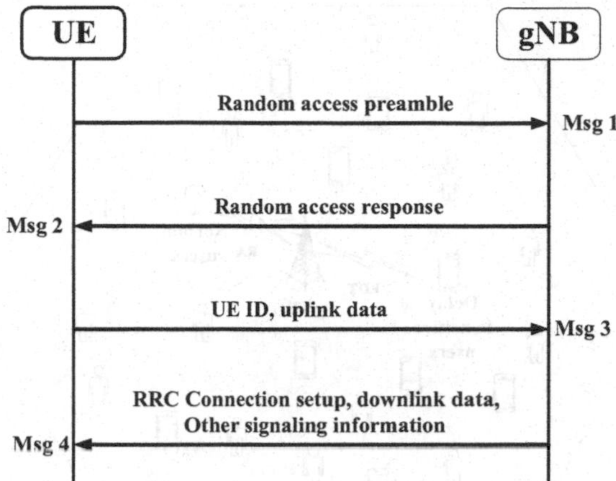

Fig. 1. Early data transmission signaling diagram

As can be seen from Fig. 1, if the device selects EDT for information transmission, then when the device completes the access, the data packets have been successfully transmitted. Compared with the signaling overhead in the random access process introduced in Table 1, the signaling overhead required by the EDT process will be greatly reduced, thus effectively increasing the system payload and reducing the transmission delay.

3 System Model

3.1 System Model

As shown in Fig. 2, this work considers the scenario in which multiple MTC devices are densely deployed within the coverage of a single base station. There is a macro station with a coverage radius of 500 m in the center of the area. Let the total number of user devices be N, and these users are randomly distributed. Assume that the MTC devices have different types of application.

According to the categories and characteristics of data services commonly used in mobile Internet and Internet of Things as pointed out in Literature [19], and combined with the system model in this paper, different services are classified according to the time delay and packet size (see Table 2 for details). DSDs use EDT to perform their random access procedure, and the remaining DTDs use traditional random access to connect to the base station. As preamble resources and bandwidth of the cellular system are both limited, collisions will inevitably occur when multiple users engage in random access.

In order to solve this problem, in this work we divide the preamble resources into two sub-sets: one is pre-reserved for DSDs to initiate EDT and enable the base station to recognize an EDT attempt; The other for the remaining DTDs to initiate random access procedure. The base station broadcast in advance the service category allowed to use EDT. When the terminal is included in this category, the pre-reserved preamble can be selected to start an EDT process when needed.

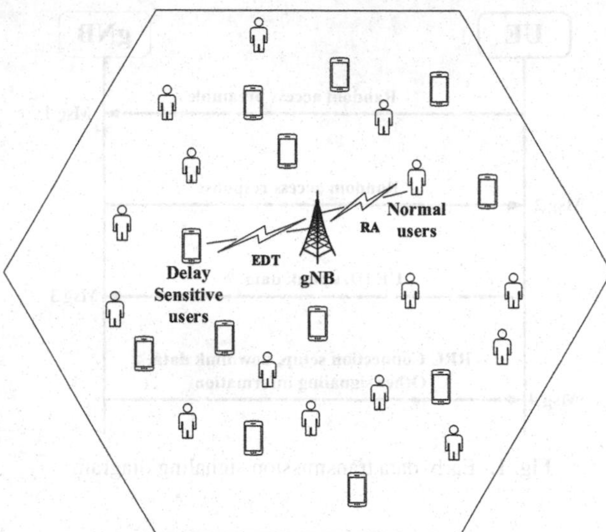

Fig. 2. System model

Table 2. Type of services

Description	Example	Feature
Instant message	WeChat	Burst small data,delay sensitive
VoIP	Tango,FaceTime	Periodic small data,delay sensitive
Streaming	YouTube	Periodic large data,delay sensitive
SNS	Facebook,Twitter	Burst small data
Web Browsing	Chrome	Burst large data,delay sensitive
Cloud	Siri,iCloud	Large data
Email	G-mail	Burst large data
File Transfer	APP store	Periodic large data
Gaming	Steam	Burst large data
M2M	Mobile payment	Small data,delay sensitive

When it initiates the access process, the user randomly selects a preamble in the preamble set and sends an access request to the base station. If the preamble is sent successfully, the user transmits the packet; If there is no preamble resource to choose from, it will enter the random retreat state, and after the retreat time, it will issue the access request to the base station again until the maximum number of retransmission of preamble is reached. Thus, access time delay t can be expressed as $t = T + m(T + B)$; T is the random access time interval, B is the average number of time slots in each retreat stage, and m is the number of retransmission of the preamble in a random access process.

3.2 Probability Analysis of Success Access

In the time slot *i*, the number of devices initiating access is $N_i = n$, among *n* devices, the number of Delay-Sensitive-Devices is *X*, the remaining equipment number is $Y = n\text{-}X$. The number of reserved preamble is *L*, the remaining preamble number is 64-*L*. When the Delay-Sensitive user initiates access, UE randomly selects one of the L preamble resources reserved by the base station broadcast for transmission, and the probability of randomly selecting one preamble is equal for all devices. Then the probability of choosing preamble *l* for any Delay-Sensitive Device is 1/*L*. Let P_0, P_1 and P_2 represent the idle, successful transmission, and collision probability of the preamble *l*, respectively.

The probability of preamble *l* being idle is:

$$P_0 = \left(1 - \frac{1}{L}\right)^X \tag{1}$$

The probability of preamble *l* successful transmission is:

$$P_1 = C_X^1 \frac{1}{L}\left(1 - \frac{1}{L}\right)^{X-1} \tag{2}$$

The probability of collision of the preamble *l* is:

$$P_2 = 1 - \left(1 - \frac{1}{L}\right)^X - C_X^1 \frac{1}{L}\left(1 - \frac{1}{L}\right)^{X-1} \tag{3}$$

Let L_0, L_1 and L_2 be the number of leading preamble that are idle, successfully transmitted and collided in slot *i*, respectively. When the current preamble collides, the base station will randomly select a device to allocate the preamble, so the number of preambles that is finally successfully connected is $L_1 + L_2$.

Then the number of devices successfully connected in time slot *i*, namely the number of preamble successfully transmitted is:

$$L_x = L_1 + L_2 = X(P_1 + P_2) = X * \left[1 - \left(1 - \frac{1}{L}\right)^X\right] \tag{4}$$

Then the success probability of EDT is $P_X = L_X/X$.

The successful probability of random access initiated by the remaining DTDs is similarly obtained $P_Y = K_Y/Y$.

4 Preamble Selection and Allocation Algorithm Based on Q-learning

In this section, we use Q-learning algorithm to optimize the allocation of preambles. In the time slot *i*, the status of the system is defined as $s_i = [X_i, L_i]$, where X_i is the number of active DSDs which require to connect to the base station and L_i is the number of pre-reserved preambles in slot *i*.

The objective of this work is to improve the access success rate of DSDs and shorten average access delay of MTC devices. When the access success rate of DSDs is below the threshold, the base station will increase the number of pre-reserved preambles to ensure successful access of DSDs, and at the same time update the category of services allowed to use EDT. When the access success rate of DSDs is above the threshold, some pre-reserved preambles may be wasted and causes congestion of DTDs in traditional random access procedure. In this case, the base station will gradually reduce the number of pre-reserved preambles and update the service type category to improve system capacity and the access success rate of the remaining DTDs on the premise of making the success rate of DSDs stable.

The action set under state S_i is defined as $a_{s_i} = [L_i - 2; L_i - 1 : L_i + 1 : L_i + 2]$. The reason for setting the action set in such a way is that when the access success rate of the DSDs is low, the base station can increase the pre-reserved preamble to improve the access success rate and shorten the system delay of the DSDs. Under the condition of maintaining a certain number of reserved preamble and ensuring the access success rate of DSDs, the number of pre-reserved preamble should be appropriately reduced, so as to improve the system capacity and ensure the access of more devices.

The reward function *R(s,a)* is a function of state *s* and action *a*. It represents the reward or punishment of action *a* in state *s*. When the algorithm converges, it will always select the action with best rewards under given state *s*. In the proposed preamble allocation algorithm, the success rate of access of DSDs and the remaining DTDs are both considered. The reward function is given in Eq. (5), where ω_1, ω_2 and p_{x}, p_{y} are the weighted coefficients and access success rate of DSD and DTD users.

$$R(s, a) = \omega_1 p_X + \omega_2 p_Y \tag{5}$$

Since this article gives priority to ensuring the access success rate of delay-sensitive devices, so $\omega_1 > \omega_2$. After the agent's state space, action space and reward function are set up, the agent can learn and interact with the environment. In the exploring stage, the action selected under state *s* is in accordance with the *ε-greedy* selection rules, and select probability P_g decreases gradually with the increase of number of training, and specific P_g calculation is given by:

$$p_g = p_{start} - (p_{start} - p_{end}) \cdot time\big/times \tag{6}$$

Where p_{start}, p_{end}, *time, times* are starting period exploring probability, late period exploring probability, the current learning times and total learning times, respectively. At the beginning of learning, the agent is not clear which actions are beneficial. P_g is set to be a large value to let the agent have more opportunity to randomly selected an action to explore better rewards.

With the increase of learning times, the agent will make relatively accurate judgment on the quality of each action, and be able to distinguish which action will bring more benefits, so the value of P_g becomes smaller and smaller. This will reduce the exploration opportunities of the agent and make it have more chance to select the action with the highest *Q* value to improve the benefits of the system. After the action is executed, the *Q* value will be updated according to the Eq. (7):

$$Q(s, a) = (1 - \alpha)Q(s, a) + \alpha(R(s, a) + \gamma \max(Q(\overline{s}, \sim))) \tag{7}$$

Where α is learning rate, which Indicates the ratio of current learning experience to total learning experience. The larger the value of α, the easier it is to forget the previous learning experience. In contrast, the smaller the value of α, the less the agent can gain from the new learning. γ is discount factor. After selecting an action, the agent will move to a new state. Part of the maximum Q value under new state will also be returned, and the discount factor represents its percentage in the Q value to be updated.

5 Simulation Results and Analysis

This section presents and analyzes the simulation results of the algorithm, and the specific simulation parameters are shown in Table 3 and Table 4.

Table 3. System related parameters

Simulation parameters	Value
Number of base stations	1
Coverage radius of the base station	500
Total number of new arrival devices	Poisson distribution ($\lambda = 16$)
Number of new arrival DSDs	Poisson distribution ($\lambda = 2 + \lfloor p_x + 0.5 \rfloor$)
Total number of preambles	64
Initial number of reserved preambles	16
Random access time interval /ms	10
Random access retreat time set	[0, T, 2T, 3T, 4T, 5T, 6T, 7T, 8T, 9T]

Table 4. Q-learning parameters

Simulation parameters	Value
ω_1	0.7
ω_2	0.3
P_max	0.5
P_min	0.05
α	0.2
γ	0.8

In the simulation process, Q tables were recorded for each study, and 1×10^6 groups of Q tables were finally obtained. In this paper, Q table is an array of $64 \times 25 \times 4$, $Q = [q_{i,j,l}], 1 \leq i \leq 64,\ 1 \leq j \leq 25,\ 1 \leq l \leq 4$. In this article, the convergence of Q table is described by the sum of squares of each element of the difference between adjacent Q tables (defined as QL). Figure 3 describes the convergence of Q table during simulation. We can see that after about 4×10^5 times learning, the Q table tends to converge.

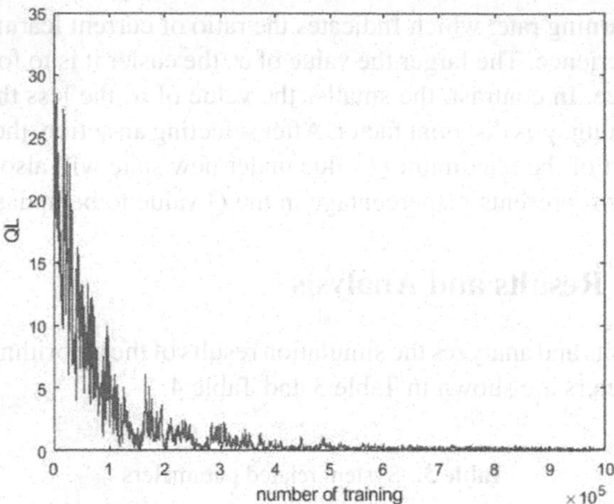

Fig. 3. The relationship between the sum of squares of each element of adjacent Q table difference and the number of training times

Figure 4 demonstrates the average access delay after learning. Compared with random access and the dynamic preamble grouping strategy based on delay sensitivity characteristic proposed by literature [12], the average access delay of total devices is reduced, especially when the new arrival number of devices increases in each slot, thus improves the overall latency performance of the system.

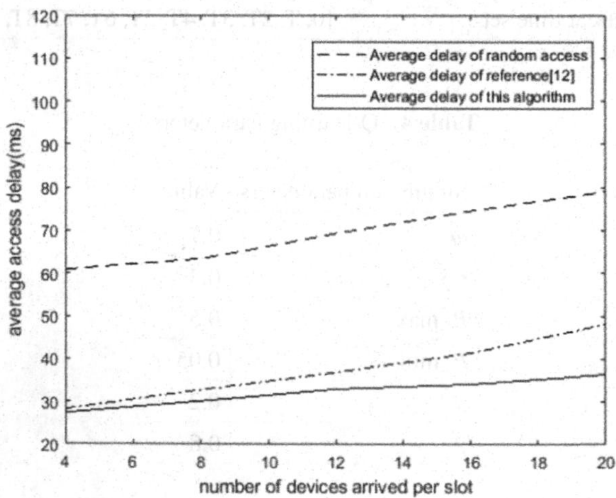

Fig. 4. Average transmission delay vs number of devices arrived per slot

Figure 5 shows the average access success rate of delay-sensitive devices. Since this work gives priority to ensuring access to delay-sensitive devices, the access success rate of DSDs is improved when the algorithm converges. Since EDT enables uplink and downlink data transmission in Msg3 and Msg4, the signaling overhead of the preamble allocation algorithm is lower than the comparison algorithm, thus increasing the throughput.

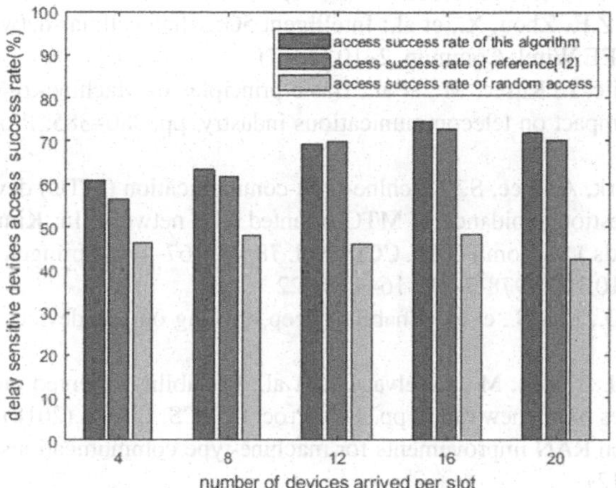

Fig. 5. Average access success rate of DSDs vs number of devices arrived in each slot

6 Conclusion

This article studies the preamble allocation scheme in random access with the coexistence of large-scale delay-sensitive devices and delay-tolerant devices in massive MTC scenario which are often suffered from congestion. Part of the preambles is pre-reserved for delay-sensitive devices to access using EDT, which fully guarantees the latency requirements of delay-sensitive-devices. At the same time, the access success rate of the remaining devices can be guaranteed as far as possible without sacrificing the access success rate of delay-sensitive devices. Simulation results show the feasibility and effectiveness of the scheme. The dynamic preamble allocation strategy improves the access success probability of delay-sensitive devices and shorten the average access latency of all types of devices.

Funding Statement. This work was supported by the Science and Technology Project of State Grid Corporation of China under Grant No. SGSDDK00KJJS1900405.

References

1. Ghavimi, F., Che, H.H.: M2M communications in 3GPP LTE/LTE-A networks: architectures, service requirements, challenges, and applications. IEEE Commun. Surv. Tutorials **17**(2), 525–549 (2015)
2. Pocovi, G., Shariatmadari, H., Berardinelli, G., et al.: Achieving ultra-reliable low-latency communications: challenges and envisioned system enhancements. IEEE Netw. **32**(2), 8–15 (2018)

3. 3GPP, "Study on Small Cell Enhancements for E-UTRA and EUTRAN: higher layer aspects," 3rd Generation Partnership Project (3GPP), TR 36.842, December 2013. http://www.3gpp.org/ftp/Specs/archive/36-series/36.842/
4. Imran, A., Zoha, A., Dayya, A.: Challenges in 5G: how to empower SON with big data for enabling 5G. IEEE Netw. **28**(6), 27–33 (2014)
5. Li, R.P., Zhao, Z.F., Zhou, X., et al.: Intelligent 5G: when cellular networks meet artificial intelligence. IEEE Wirel. Commun. 2–10 (2017)
6. Galetic, V., Bojic, I., Kusec, M., et al.: Basic principles of Machine-to-Machine communication and its impact on telecommunications industry, pp. 380–385. Proc. MIPRO, Opatija (2011)
7. Jung, K.-R., Park, A., Lee, S.: Machine-type-communication (MTC) device grouping algorithm for congestion avoidance of MTC oriented LTE network. In: Kim, T.-H., Stoica, A., Chang, R.-S. (eds.) SUComS 2010. CCIS, vol. 78, pp. 167–178. Springer, Heidelberg (2010). https://doi.org/10.1007/978-3-642-16444-6_22
8. Tang, J., Sun, D., Liu, S., et al.: Enabling deep learning on IoT devices. Computer **50**(10), 92–96 (2017)
9. Mahmood, N.H., Lopez, M., Laselva, D., et al.: Reliability oriented dual connectivity for URLLC services in 5G new radio, pp. 1–6. Proc. ISWCS, Lisbon (2018)
10. 3GPP, "Study on RAN improvements for machine-type communications," Technical report, TR 37.868 (2012)
11. Choi, J.: On the adaptive determination of the number of preambles in RACH for MTC. IEEE Commun. Lett. **20**(7), 1385–1388 (2016)
12. Zhao, X., Wang, C., Wang, W.: Dynamic preamble grouping and access control scheme in machine-to-machine communication. In: Proceedings of WCSP, Xi'an, China, pp.1–6 (2019)
13. Hussain, F., Anpalagan, A., Khwaja, A.S., Naeem, M.: Resource allocation and congestion control in clustered M2M communication using Q-learning. Trans. Emerg. Telecommun. Technol. **28**(4), 1–12 (2017)
14. Hoglund, A., Van, D.P., Tirronen, T., Liberg, O., Sui, Y., Yavuz, E.A.: 3GPP release 15 early data transmission. IEEE Commun. Standards Mag. **2**(2), 90–96 (2018)
15. 3GPP RP-171043. Revision of study on 5G non-orthogonal multiple access, ZTE Corporation
16. Sony, "Discussions on 2 Steps RACH Procedure," 3rd Generation Partnership Project(3GPP),TRR1–1700668, January 2017. https://portal.3gpp.org/ngppapp/CreateTdoc.aspx?mode=view&contributionId=755711
17. Thota, J., Aijaz, A.: On performance evaluation of random access enhancements for 5G uRLLC. In: IEEE Wireless Communications and Networking Conference (WCNC), pp. 1–7. Marrakesh, Morocco (2019)
18. Raftopoulou, M., Jorguseski, L., Litjens, R.: Design and assessment of low-latency random access procedures in 5G networks. In: European Conference on Networks and Communications (EuCNC), Valencia, Spain, pp. 406–411 (2019)
19. HUAWEI. Mobile Broadband Review 2014H1[R] (2014)

An Improved Object Detection Algorithm Based on CenterNet

Jiancheng Zou, Bailin Ge(✉), and Bo Zhang

North China University of Technology, Beijing 100144, China

Abstract. CenterNet (Object as Points) is a recently popular single-stage anchor free object detection algorithm. First, this article adds a new attention module in which the mean and maximum values of the channel are used, it also introduces variance information to better express the feature distribution of each layer from different aspects. Second, we improved the loss function and replaced the original L1 loss function with the IoU loss function, so that the loss function of the borders and the center point regression has the scale invariance, which is consistent with the final standard IoU judgment, and will not increase the model inference time. Finally, multi-scale images are used for training. By enriching the number of samples of different sizes, the problem of model overfitting due to less data is effectively reduced. This paper compares the improved CenterNet algorithm with the original algorithm on the Pascal VOC data set for training and testing. The final model increases the mAP by 3.5% under the unaugmented test and 3.03% mAP for using horizontal flipping augmented test. In terms of time overhead, there is only a small expenditure, it can still maintain the detection speed of 12 ms per frame.

Keywords: Object detection · CenterNet · Lightweight attention mechanism

1 Introduction

Object detection is one of the basic tasks in computer vision. There are many applications in reality, and it is a more commonly used and very popular direction. Common object detection algorithms are generally divided into two types according to the composition of the network: single-stage object detection algorithms and two-stage object detection algorithms.

The two-stage object detection algorithm is to split the entire process of object detection into two steps for calculation. First, it recommends candidate regions and generates frames that may contain objects. For example, from the earliest R-CNN [1], Fast R-CNN [2] first used the Selective Search algorithm to obtain the region of interest, and later Faster R-CNN [3] used RPN (Region Proposal Networks) to obtain the prediction box, and used the convolutional neural network to generate the prediction box. Then infer the category and location of the target. Until the proposal of Faster R-CNN, the use of RPN to generate the prediction box, and the generation of the prediction box is added to the network model, the two-stage object detection algorithm can achieve end-to-end.

X. Sun et al. (Eds.): ICAIS 2021, LNCS 12736, pp. 455–467, 2021.
https://doi.org/10.1007/978-3-030-78609-0_39

The single-stage object detection algorithm, as the name suggests, is to directly apply the algorithm to the input image to output the detection result, without splitting the task into different sub-tasks, such as YOLO series [4–7], SSD algorithm [8], RetinaNet algorithm [9] and so on.

In the past two years, the research on anchor free single-stage object detection algorithms based on key points has become more and more popular. The original intention of anchor free design is to get rid of the anchor, because the use of the anchor will cause the following problems.

1) The use of anchor boxes causes a serious imbalance in the number of samples, which is why Focal loss can significantly improve the accuracy of single-stage object detection.
2) The size and proportion of the anchor need to be manually specified, and the parameters are set subjectively. In this process, hyperparameters are introduced. The more hyperparameters, the more difficult it is to tune the model.

After abandoning the anchor box, how to express an object has become the core issue. CornerNet [10] converts the detection frame to detect the upper left corner and the lower right corner, and then matches the two corners. Usually single-stage object detection algorithms will have the problem of insufficient perception of the information inside the object, so enhancing the use of the object center area information is one of the directions for improvement. CenterNet [11] adds a center point prediction object based on CornerNet For branch, a part of the central area is generated by predicting the upper left and lower right points, and then checking whether the central point is in the area, this idea can better reduce the probability of false detection. ExtremeNet [12] uses another description method, describing an object by using four points up, down, left and right of the target, and judging the authenticity by the center point. The Object as Points [13] method uses the center point to predict the objectcategory, width, height, and center offset, and then detects the object. Since only the center point is detected, there is less content to predict, and the center point is highly symmetric Features, achieve higher accuracy and faster speed in detection. Object as Points become one of the main representative algorithms of anchor free.

The work in this paper is mainly to optimize the Object as Points, which mainly includes three parts: preprocessing, network backbone and loss function to improve the accuracy of the detection algorithm. We add attention modules to make the network more targeted to learn related features. In addition to using the mean feature information of each layer in the attention module, we also add the maximum feature information and the mean square error information of each layer to reduce the attention module. The multiple of downsampling allows the attention module to learn more. We add a channel attention mechanism to the high-level part of the network based on the principle of shallow learning of low-level semantic features of convolutional neural networks and deep learning of high-level semantic features. At the same time, the loss function is improved, and the IoU loss function [14] is used to approximate the width and height and the center point position offset. Because the IoU loss function has the characteristics of scale invariance, it can make the position of medium and small objects more accurate.

Adding multi-scale images for training as image enhancement in the preprocessing stage can reduce the lack of data samples and has certain reference value.

2 Related Work

2.1 Channel Attention Module

One of the basic architectures used by the CenterNet model is the ResNet [15] network architecture. We optimize the ResNet backbone network and add an attention mechanism to the backbone network so that the network has a contrast between channels after convolution. By comparing the features between different channels, learn which channel features are more important, and the output weight is greater. Which channel features are less important, and the output weight is smaller. The maximum weight is 1 and the minimum weight is 0. Usually sigmoid is used as the final activation function to map features to this range.

In the SE module [16], first select the global average pooling feature of each feature map as the representative of the current layer, and then fully connect with a certain number of neurons for dimensionality reduction. In the paper, the number of input channels is divided by a reduction factor. Then the number of neurons is compressed by the reduction factor. The down-sampling learning feature is performed like the bottleneck layer in Resnet and then mapped back. In the original text, reduce used 16. Then use the ReLU activation function to activate, the non-linear activation function can improve the expressive ability of the network, and the squeeze operation is completed. Then perform the expansion operation, expand the number of neurons from the current number of neurons to the same number of neurons as the input channel through full connection, and obtain the weights of different channels. Finally, multiply the learned weight of each channel by each position of the input feature map to obtain the final feature map. The attention mechanism between channels can make the network pay more attention to channels with large features and contribute more to the correct output, and suppress those channels that do not help the correct output (Fig. 1).

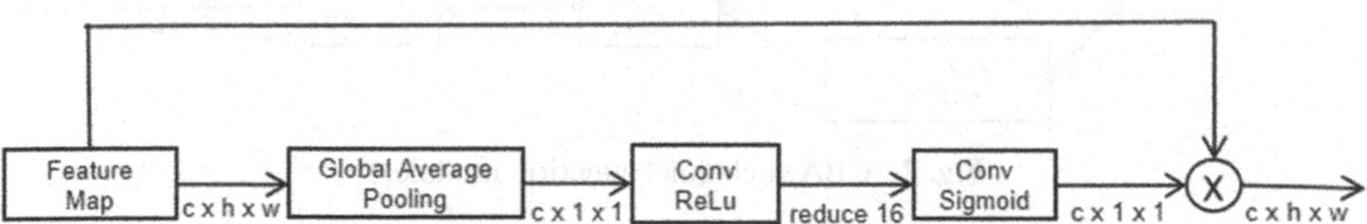

Fig. 1. SENet channel attention module.

We have added an optimized attention module to the basic network Resnet18. We did not add attention modules to all stages, because adding too many modules will not only cause convergence difficulties for the network, but also cause a decrease in accuracy if used improperly. Through the analysis of the network architecture, the deeper the level represents the higher the semantics and the more abstract the content. So we added attention modules to the Conv4 and Conv5 layers in ResNet. Then adjusted the number of neurons used in the modules. Through comparative experiments, we found that the degree of dimensionality reduction of the attention channel has a great impact on the function of the attention module. If the number of channels is reduced more dimensionality, the model performance is not good enough. So we choose reduce to 4 for dimensionality reduction learning features.

In order to obtain the weights between different channels, the attention module generally uses the Sigmoid function as the activation function, because the Sigmoid activation function is a saturated nonlinear activation function. For arbitrarily large and arbitrarily small features, the activation function can map it to 0 to Within 1 interval. There are two sections in the attention model, but the first section uses the ReLU activation function. If the first activation function is changed to the Sigmoid function, the range of features input in the second stage will be smaller, which is convenient for the second stage to learn more information between levels. Because the basic architecture is ResNet18, a module with a residual structure, and each layer has only two residual blocks, there is no need to worry about the disappearance of the gradient. In front of the activation function, we also added a batch normalization layer. During the training process, backpropagation will cause the parameters of each layer to be continuously updated. The input of each layer will also change constantly, and the data distribution is also different. Add Batch normalization can solve the problem of continuous changes in the data distribution of the middle layer during the training process, which leads to changes in the input characteristics of the subsequent layers and learning difficulties.

We also borrowed ideas from the CBAM module [17]. In the channel attention mechanism, SENet only uses the mean value of each channel of the feature map as input, while CBAM uses the mean and maximum value of each channel as input. The two channels share a set of fully connected parameters for training. Here we find that it is better to calculate the two channels separately (Fig. 2).

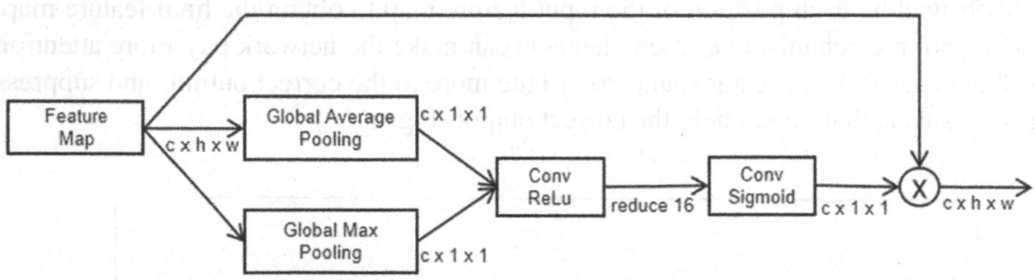

Fig. 2. CBAM channel attention module.

Global average pooling uses the average value of the features in each layer as the feature, and global maximum pooling uses the largest feature in the current feature map as the input feature. More information can be obtained through the combination of the two. Think about it, there is actually more information that can be used. In normal times, when we talk about the distribution of data, we usually use the mean and variance to express the distribution of the data. So we add the variance information of each layer to the attention network. Variance information can express the distribution of eigenvalues of the current layer, whether all eigenvalues are large, or part of the data is relatively large, and the rest of the data is relatively small. The addition of variance information can make the attention network more powerful and improve the detection effect. So far we have proposed a new type of attention module with the following structure (Fig. 3):

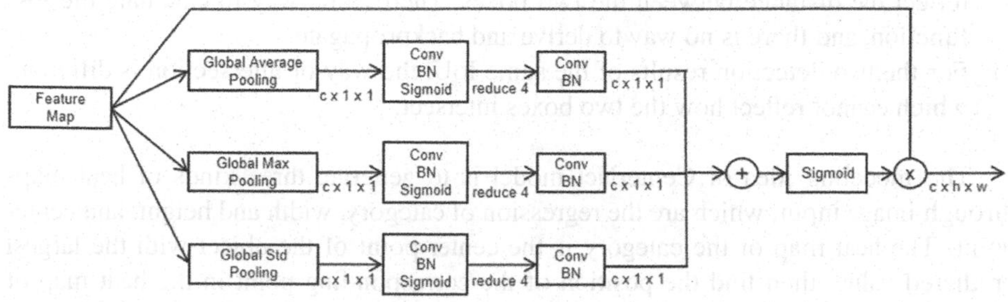

Fig. 3. Our attention module.

2.2 IoU Loss Function

In the prediction module of the original model, not only the center point must be predicted, but also the width and height of the object and the offset of the center point must be predicted. For this regression prediction, the original algorithm uses the L1 loss function for approximation. The L1 loss function uses the length and width of the object and the offset of the center position to subtract the length and width of the predicted object and the offset of the center position respectively. Then the sum is The loss function can be obtained. However, this loss function does not have scale invariance. For small objects, the calculated loss function will be very small. For some targets that account for a larger proportion of the picture, the calculated loss function will be larger. As a result, the detector's effect on object detection of different scales is not balanced enough.

At present, the improvement ideas are basically the same for the return of the frame. From L1 loss function, L2 loss function, Smooth L1 loss function, IoU loss function, GIoU loss function [18], DIoU loss function [19] and CIoU loss function [20], the main improvement idea is through the value of IoU The calculation of the loss function, or adding a correction term to limit the position of the frame, helps the network to better regression prediction of the frame.

The IoU loss function makes up for the lack of scale invariance of the L1 loss function, and combines it with the final evaluation standard IoU to solve the problem of inconsistency between the loss function and the final evaluation standard. There is a certain improvement in the performance of the detector without increasing the inference time. We use the most commonly used IoU expression for calculation, the expression is as follows:

$$IoU\ loss = 1 - \frac{Intersection(box1, box2)}{Union(box1, box2)} \tag{1}$$

The two disadvantages of IoU are:

1) When the prediction box and the real box do not intersect, IoU is 0, which cannot reflect the distance between the two boxes. There is no way to calculate the loss function, and there is no way to derive and backpropagate.
2) For the two detection results of the same IoU, the way of intersection is different, which cannot reflect how the two boxes intersect.

The modeling idea of CenterNet model is to generate three kinds of heat maps through image input, which are the regression of category, width and height, and center point. The heat map of the category is the center point of the object with the largest predicted value, then find the position of the corresponding point in the heat map of width and height, and extract the values of width and height. This modeling idea has determined that the predicted point is the center point of the target, and based on a known information, the width and height regression is performed on the center point. So we use the IoU loss function for correction. In contrast, the GIoU, DIoU, and CIoU loss functions are improved versions of the IoU loss function, but there will be some redundant calculations for the current algorithm. The current algorithm does not require correction items to adjust the position of the box, because the current algorithm returns to the frame. The known information of is the return of the frame at the position of the center point. The modeling idea of the model just avoids the appearance of these two shortcomings. Finally, the improved loss function based on the CenterNet model proposed in this paper is:

$$L_{\text{det}} = L_k + \lambda_{IoU} L_{IoU}, \quad \lambda_{IoU} = 3 \tag{2}$$

2.3 Multi-scale Image Training

The preprocessing of the input image can make the model converge faster, prevent the network from over-fitting, and make the model more reliable and robust against more complex environment detection results. The pre-processing methods used in this article mainly include: subtracting the mean, dividing by variance, random horizontal flipping, random cropping, random color enhancement methods, and also adding multi-scale image training.

Our model does not limit the scale of the input. For different scales of network input, the parameters and structure of the model will not change, so we can input multi-scale images into the model. Multi-scale image training is performed by randomly selecting an image size when inputting each batch, and converting the entire batch to the current random size for training. In the read image, some objects may be small in size, and some objects may be large in size, not all of them are the same size. By looking at the detection results, we know that object detection detectors generally have the best detection results for moderate targets, but are not very effective for small and large objects. The receptive field of the model has a great influence on the detection effect. Corresponding to the depth of the current network, the object that matches the size of the receptive field generally has a better detection effect. Through multi-scale image training, some object sizes are reduced and the number of small targets is increased, so that the detector can detect small targets better. Randomly to a large size, enlarge the image, increase the data of large-size targets, and make the detector adapt to the detection of large targets. The advantage of multi-scale image training is to use image enhancement methods to increase the number of samples in samples of different sizes, so that the model can learn more and the effect of model detection is better.

In the experiment of this article, the image training size we selected ranges from 128 * 128 pixels to 640 * 640 pixels. Because the model is down-sampled by 32 times, the step size for multi-scale training is an integer multiple of 32. We choose The step size is 64 pixels. In the process of training the model, the size of each training sample is the same, and one is randomly selected from the array as the current input size.

3 Experiments and Analysis

The experiment uses Intel Core i7 8700 CPU, NVIDIA TITAN Xp graphics card, 12 GB video memory, and the operating system uses Ubuntu 16.04. We use the same open source environment as the original text, the inference framework is pytorch, and the version is 0.4.1.

3.1 Experimental Data

The experiment done in this article is based on the Pascal VOC data set, which is a commonly used object detection data set. We use the training validation sets of VOC2007 and VOC2012 for training, and the training samples have a total of 16,551 samples. Tested on the test set of VOC2007, the test set contains a total of 4952 pictures. In the test, the horizontal flip was also used as an enhancement test. During the test, we used a picture with a size of 384 * 384 pixels for input into the network.

3.2 Experimental Process

This experiment uses the pre-trained model trained on ImageNet for initialization, and the Adam optimization algorithm [21] is trained for a total of 150 epochs. The initial learning rate is the same as the original and set to 0.000125. The learning rate is divided by the 60th and 110th iterations 10. Reduce the learning rate to make the model converge. At the same time, we conduct ablation studies through comparative experiments to see the impact of different changes on the accuracy of the model.

3.3 Experimental Results

We compare the models from the following points:

1) The number of parameters and the number of floating point operations of the original model and the improved model.
2) Comparison of the test results of the original model and the improved model on the test set.

3) In the process of improving the model, a comparison of the accuracy of different component models is added.

We compare the improved model with the original model in terms of parameters and the number of floating point operations. The model parameters are how many parameters the current model has to learn. The full name of FLOPS is floating point operations per second, which is the number of floating point operations per second and represents the computing performance of the hardware. FLOPs is the abbreviation of floating point operations, which represents the number of floating point operations that a model needs to calculate once, and to a certain extent also reflects the speed of model inference. It can be seen that our model has only increased by 0.49M in the amount of parameters and 0.71M FLOPs, so the components we added are extremely lightweight.

Comparing our final modified model with the original model on the PASCAL VOC2007 test set, we can see that the model's mAP has increased by 3.5% without data enhancement. Using horizontal flip for data enhancement testing, the model's mAP has increased by 3.03%. Our modification is extremely lightweight, but the effect is very cost-effective and has a good accuracy increase (Table 1).

Table 1. Comparison between the original model and the improved model.

Model	Params	FLOPs	mAP(%)
CenterNet	12.88M	8319.62M	70.37/72.56
Ours	13.37M	8320.33M	73.87/75.59

The following is a comparison of APs for each category in the non-enhanced test. We can see that our model's detection effect in each category has a certain improvement over the original detection effect. Our detection algorithm is difficult to detect bottles and potted plants. The increase in category is greater, and the effect of the detector is more balanced (Table 2).

In order to fully explain the effect of each step of our improvement, we use the controlled variable method to compare the results with the original model by changing only a part of it each time to judge whether the current changes are really helpful to the model. By analyzing the data in Table 3, we can get the following conclusions:

1) The effect of using the attention module we designed is better than the original model. The original model adds the SE module or the channel attention module in CBAM.
2) By improving the loss function and using the IoU loss function for training, the accuracy of the model is improved.
3) The use of multi-scale training can alleviate the problems caused by insufficient data, reduce the degree of overfitting of the model, and bring about an improvement in accuracy.

Table 2. Comparison of the test results of the originalmodel and the improved model in each category (mAP%).

Class	CenterNet	Ours
Aero	71.00	73.95
Bike	78.39	81.72
Bird	69.92	73.64
Boat	59.22	67.81
Bottle	43.17	49.21
Bus	77.22	80.29
Car	78.24	79.40
Cat	83.60	83.10
Chair	52.92	55.00
Cow	75.85	78.95
Table	68.34	71.41
Dog	78.59	82.66
Horse	82.09	84.34
mbike	80.31	84.77
Person	72.96	76.80
Plant	44.53	49.57
Sheep	72.36	76.69
Sofa	71.16	71.89
Train	79.47	81.98
Tv	68.03	74.31

Table 3. Comparison of test results with different attention mechanisms.

Model id	Model	mAP(%)
A	CenterNet	70.37/72.56
B	A + SE Module	71.10/72.97
C	A + CBAM Module	71.29/73.24
D	A + Our Attention Module	72.12/73.53
E	D + IoU Loss	72.46/73.91
F	E + Multi Scale Training	73.87/75.59

The following is a comparison between the improved detection algorithm and the original algorithm on the test set. The threshold is set to 0.3. In the following comparison picture, the left picture is the detection effect of the CenterNet model, and the right picture is the final detection effect of the improved model in this article. It can be seen that for small objects, our detection algorithm is more powerful, and both the recall rate and the accuracy of the frame have been improved. In addition, in the detection results of our model, due to the improvement of the model, the detection effect of the algorithm in this paper is less than that of the original model (Figs. 4, 5 and 6).

Fig. 4. Comparison of the detection effect of the original algorithm (left) and the improved algorithm (right) on small targets.

Fig. 5. Comparison of the detection effect of the original algorithm (left) and the improved algorithm (right) on small targets.

Fig. 6. Comparison of the detection effect of the original algorithm (left) and the improved algorithm (right) at the center point.

4 Conclusion

This article first introduces the types of object detection algorithms based on deep learning algorithms and the typical algorithms in each type. We propose an improved strategy for CenterNet. Our improvement is lightweight and only takes up very little inference time. Using multi-scale images for training can increase the number of targets of different sizes. Add an attention mechanism to the network, reduce the degree of dimensionality reduction of the attention mechanism, use more neurons for fitting, and add variance information to allow the network to use more information to learn the weight of each layer of the channel. Use the IoU loss function for training to better take care of medium and small targets and make the loss function scale-invariant. Perform training tests on the PASCAL VOC dataset, and study the impact of different changes on the model by using the controlled variable method for ablation. At the same time, among our changes to the network, only the attention model consumes a small amount of time in inference. It is a lightweight component that has minimal impact on the time of the model. Finally, at the input size of 384, the model does not use the enhancement test to increase the mAP by 3.5%. When the horizontal flip is used, the model increases by 3.03% mAP. It can be seen that each of our improvements has a significant effect on the performance of the model. The following will further improve the model, add the mixup enhancement algorithm, and replace the network backbone. So that the network can still maintain a good detection effect under the condition of lighter weight, and improve the performance of the algorithm.

References

1. Girshick, R., Donahue, J., Darrell, T., et al.: Rich feature hierarchies for accurate object detection and semantic segmentation. In: Proceedings of the IEEE Conference on Computer Vision and Pattern Recognition, pp. 580–587. IEEE, Columbus (2014)

2. Girshick, R.: Fast R-CNN. In: Proceedings of the IEEE International Conference on Computer Vision, pp. 1440–1448. IEEE, Santiago, CL (2015)
3. Ren, S., He, K., Girshick, R., et al.: Faster R-CNN: towards real-time object detection with region proposal networks. In: Advances in Neural Information Processing Systems, pp. 91–99. NIPS, Montreal, CA (2015)
4. Redmon, J., Divvala, S., Girshick, R., et al.: You only look once: unified, real-time object detection. In: Proceedings of the IEEE Conference on Computer Vision and Pattern Recognition, pp. 779–788. IEEE, Las Vegas (2016)
5. Redmon, J., Farhadi, A.: YOLO9000: better, faster, stronger. In: Proceedings of the IEEE Conference on Computer Vision and Pattern Recognition, pp. 7263–7271. IEEE, Honolulu (2017)
6. Redmon, J., Farhadi, A.: Yolov3: An incremental improvement. arXiv preprint arXiv:1804.02767 (2018)
7. Bochkovskiy, A., Wang, C.Y., Liao, H.Y.M.: YOLOv4: Optimal Speed and Accuracy of Object Detection. arXiv preprint arXiv:2004.10934 (2020)
8. Liu, W., et al.: SSD: single shot multibox detector. In: Leibe, B., Matas, J., Sebe, N., Welling, M. (eds.) ECCV 2016. LNCS, vol. 9905, pp. 21–37. Springer, Cham (2016). https://doi.org/10.1007/978-3-319-46448-0_2
9. Lin, T.Y., Goyal, P., Girshick, R., et al.: Focal loss for dense object detection. In: Proceedings of the IEEE International Conference on Computer Vision, pp. 2980–2988. IEEE, Venice (2017)
10. Law, H., Deng, J.: Cornernet: detecting objects as paired keypoints. In: Proceedings of the European Conference on Computer Vision, pp. 734–750. Munich, DE (2018)
11. Duan, K., Bai, S., Xie, L., et al.: Centernet: keypoint triplets for object detection. In: Proceedings of the IEEE International Conference on Computer Vision, pp. 6569–6578. IEEE, Seoul (2019)
12. Zhou, X., Zhuo, J., Krahenbuhl, P.: Bottom-up object detection by grouping extreme and center points. In: Proceedings of the IEEE Conference on Computer Vision and Pattern Recognition, pp. 850–859. IEEE, Long Beach (2019)
13. Zhou, X., Wang, D., Krähenbühl, P.: Objects as points. arXiv preprint arXiv:1904.07850 (2019)
14. Yu, J., Jiang, Y., Wang, Z., et al.: Unitbox: an advanced object detection network. In: Proceedings of the ACM International Conference on Multimedia, pp. 516–520. Amsterdam, NL (2016)
15. He, K., Zhang, X., Ren, S., et al.: Deep residual learning for image recognition. In: Proceedings of the IEEE Conference on Computer Vision and Pattern Recognition, pp. 770–778. IEEE, Las Vegas (2016)
16. Hu, J., Shen, L., Sun, G.: Squeeze-and-excitation networks. In: Proceedings of the IEEE Conference on Computer Vision and Pattern Recognition, pp. 7132–7141. IEEE, Salt Lake City (2018)
17. Woo, S., Park, J., Lee, J.-Y., Kweon, I.S.: Cbam: convolutional block attention module. In: Ferrari, V., Hebert, M., Sminchisescu, C., Weiss, Y. (eds.) ECCV 2018. LNCS, vol. 11211, pp. 3–19. Springer, Cham (2018). https://doi.org/10.1007/978-3-030-01234-2_1
18. Rezatofighi, H., Tsoi, N., Gwak, J.Y., et al.: Generalized intersection over union: a metric and a loss for bounding box regression. In: Proceedings of the IEEE Conference on Computer Vision and Pattern Recognition, pp. 658–666. IEEE, Long Beach (2019)
19. Zheng, Z., Wang, P., Liu, W., et al.: Distance-IoU loss: faster and better learning for bounding box regression. In: Proceedings of the AAAI Conference on Artificial Intelligence, pp. 12993–13000. AAAI, New York (2020)

20. Zheng, Z., Wang, P., Ren, D., et al.: Enhancing Geometric Factors in Model Learning and Inference for Object Detection and Instance Segmentation. arXiv preprint arXiv:2005.03572 (2020)
21. Kingma, D.P., Ba, J.: Adam: A method for stochastic optimization. arXiv preprint arXiv: 1412.6980 (2014)

Survey on Image Object Detection Algorithms Based on Deep Learning

Wei Fang[1,2(✉)], Liang Shen[1], and Yupeng Chen[1]

[1] School of Computer and Software, Engineering Research Center of Digital Forensics, Ministry of Education, Nanjing University of Information Science and Technology, Nanjing, China
Fangwei@nuist.edu.cn
[2] Provincial Key Laboratory for Computer Information Processing Technology, Soochow University, Suzhou, China

Abstract. With the development of image processing technology, computer vision is becoming more and more popular. In recent years, deep learning has flourished, significant progress has been made in object detection. Especially after the R-CNN framework was proposed, the object detection framework based on deep learning has gradually become the mainstream, which can be divided into two categories: region-based and regression-based. Taking these two types of frameworks as the main body, this paper summarizes the research background and then discusses the object detection algorithms based on candidate regions represented by Faster R-CNN and the algorithms based on regression represented by the YOLO series. According to the development history, this paper summarizes the framework proposed in recent years, compares and analyzes the performance of object detection algorithms on public datasets, and introduces the application scenarios of those algorithms. Finally, this paper discusses the current difficulties and challenges in object detection and looks forward to the future development direction.

Keywords: Deep learning · Object detection · Computer vision · CNN

1 Introduction

Object detection is a basic problem in the field of computer vision and image processing. It is a hot spot in theory and application research in recent years, and it is widely used [1]. The main task of object detection [2] is to locate the object of interest from the input image, and then accurately determine the category of each object of interest. At present, object detection technology has been widely used in daily life safety, robot navigation, intelligent video surveillance, traffic scene detection, aerospace, and other fields. At the same time, object detection is the basis for other advanced visual problems such as behavior understanding, scene classification, and video content retrieval. However, because there may be great differences between different instances of the same type of object, different types of objects may be very similar, and different imaging conditions and environmental factors will have a great impact on the appearance of the object [3], making object detection very challenging.

X. Sun et al. (Eds.): ICAIS 2021, LNCS 12736, pp. 468–480, 2021.
https://doi.org/10.1007/978-3-030-78609-0_40

The traditional object detection process is as follows: (1) Using sliding windows of different scales to select candidate regions at different positions in the image; (2) Using scale-invariant feature transformation (SITF [4]), directional gradient histogram (HOG [5]) And other algorithms to extract the characteristics of the image information of each window. (3) Use classifiers such as deformable component model (DPM [6]) and support vector machine (SVM [7]) to classify features. (4) Use NMS [8] algorithm to merge candidate boxes to achieve object detection. However, traditional algorithms rely on hand-designed features which is inefficient.

In recent years, with the continuous development and maturity of deep learning [9], deep convolutional neural networks have been increasingly used in the field of computer vision [10–13]. Object detection technology based on deep learning has gradually become a research hotspot, and certain results have been achieved. Object detection algorithms based on deep learning are divided into two categories: object detection algorithms based on candidate regions and object detection algorithms based on regression. The object detection algorithm based on the candidate region is also called the two-stage algorithm. The regression-based object detection algorithm has only one stage, which directly regresses the predicted target object to achieve object detection.

2 Object Detection Algorithms Based on Regions

This section will mainly introduce the object detection algorithms based on regions in recent years, analyze their respective characteristics, and their improvements and innovations compared to previous algorithms.

2.1 R-CNN

The R-CNN image object detection model was proposed by Girshick et al. [14] in 2014. It is the pioneering work of the candidate region and convolutional neural network framework, and it is also the first that can be truly applied to industrial-grade image object detection. The solution laid the foundation for the development of object detection based on CNN. The detection accuracy of the R-CNN algorithm on the PASCAL VOC2007 [15] dataset has reached 58.5%, which is a leap forward compared with the traditional algorithm. The network structure is shown in Fig. 1.

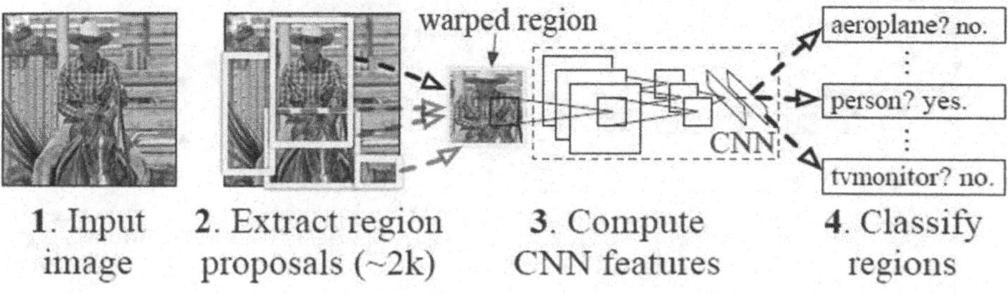

Fig. 1. The diagram of R-CNN network

R-CNN first uses the selective search algorithm [16] to extract 2000 candidate regions from the input image and uses clipping and deformation algorithms to fix the size of the candidate region to 277 × 277 to adapt to the input of the fully connected layer. Perform feature calculation for each candidate area through CNN forward propagation; then send the feature vector of each candidate area into a specific linear classifier for classification and predict the probability value; finally, use NMS(non-maximum suppression) algorithm eliminates redundant target boxes and finds the best-predicted position of the target. Although the mAP (mean average precision) of the R-CNN model reaches 58.5% and 53.3% on the VOC2007 and VOC2012 data sets. Compared with the traditional object detection algorithm, this model has made leapfrog progress. However, there is still a lot of room for improvement. For example, the 2000 candidate regions extracted from a single image need to be input into the CNN one by one, resulting in a huge computational overhead, which affects the detection speed.

2.2 Faster R-CNN

Ren et al. [17] proposed the Faster R-CNN network in 2016, using Region proposal networks (RPN) replace the selective search algorithm, making the whole process of candidate region generation, candidate region feature extraction, classification and regression in one go, and truly realize the end-to-end training of the network.

The structure of Faster R-CNN is shown in Fig. 2. It includes the following 4 parts: (1) Convolutional layer, which is used to extract feature information; (2) RPN network (region proposal networks, RPN) is used to recommend candidate regions; (3) ROI pooling layer, which is used to convert input images of different sizes into fixed-length output; (4) Classification and regression, which is used to output the category and the precise positions of the candidate boxes. Among them, the RPN network's introduction is the key to Faster R-CNN to reduce the time-consuming in the candidate area, and it is also the most important part different from Fast R-CNN.

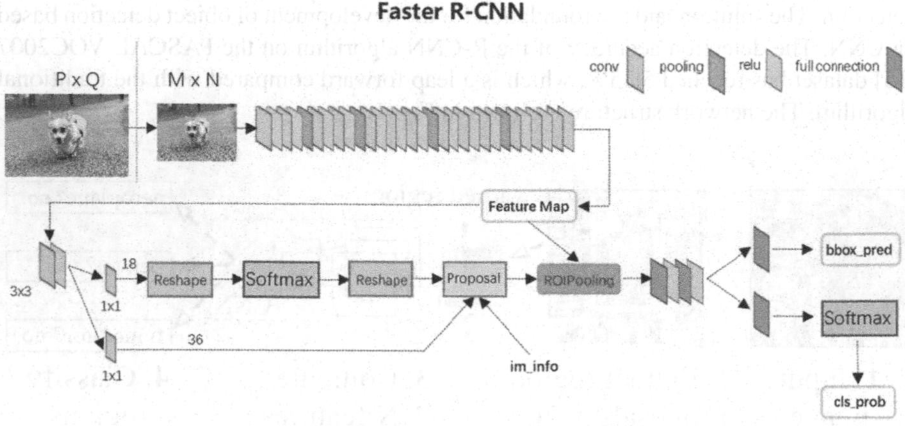

Fig. 2. The diagram of Faster R-CNN network

Since the network structure of Faster R-CNN is mainly composed of two networks, that is, the candidate region generation network RPN and Fast R-CNN, these two networks must be trained separately during training, so the loss function is mainly divided into RPN loss and Fast R-CNN loss, and both parts of the loss include classification loss and regression loss. The entire loss function includes four small loss functions, which are the two loss functions of the RPN layer and the two loss functions of the Fast R-CNN fully connected layer. Therefore, the loss function of Faster R-CNN is a multi-task loss function. The overall calculation formula is as follows:

$$\mathrm{L}(\{p_i\}, \{t_i\}) = \frac{1}{N_{cls}} \sum\nolimits_i L_{cls}\left(p_i, p_i^*\right) + \lambda \frac{1}{N_{reg}} \sum\nolimits_i p_i^* L_{reg}(t_i, t_i^*) \tag{1}$$

Fast R-CNN uses RPN to improve the detection speed and, at the same time, improve the detection accuracy. However, Fast R-CNN has lost the object's detailed information after multiple downsampling, and the detection effect of small objects is still not good. Besides, in generating candidate regions by the RPN network, the object size may be variable, and the receptive field may be inconsistent when mapped to the original image due to the use of anchors of different scales.

2.3 Mask R-CNN

Although Faster R-CNN uses ROI Pooling to obtain uniform-dimensional candidate regions, the pixel deviation caused by the rounding and zeroing operation of ROI Pooling on the feature map during the pooling process will have a certain impact on the positioning of the bounding box. The Mask R-CNN [18] proposed by He et al. uses ROI Align and adopts bilinear interpolation to obtain the feature map's pixel value, thereby obtaining more accurate pixel information. In addition to outputting the bounding box's position information and the object types' confidence, Mask R-CNN also adds an object mask output branch and uses a fully convolutional network to predict the segmentation mask for each candidate area. Make the output of the object accurate to the pixel level. Mask R-CNN has good results in human body keypoint detection and instance segmentation tasks.

2.4 TridentNet

In 2019, Li et al. constructed a three-branch network TridentNet [19] using dilated convolution, which better solved the multi-scale detection problem than the previous algorithm. TridentNet verified the influence of different sizes of receptive fields on the detection results for the first time; that is, Large receptive fields are more conducive to detecting large objects, and small receptive fields are more conducive to detecting small objects. Figure 3 shows the structure of TridentNet. TridentNet uses ResNet as the basic network. The first three stages follow the original structure. In the fourth stage, three different receptive field networks are parallelized. The three branches use hole convolutions with different numbers of holes. Their receptive fields from small to large. Objects of different sizes are detected separately, which better realizes multi-scale object detection. The three branches share weights, which enables the network to learn

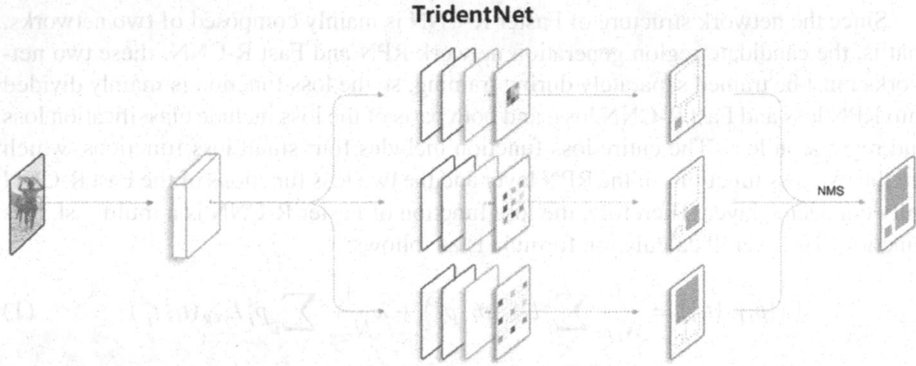

Fig. 3. The diagram of TridentNet network

essential object detection information and reduces the number of parameters and the risk of overfitting.

TridentNet's detection of multi-scale objects has a significant improvement in accuracy compared to previous algorithms, and its accuracy on the COCO data set has reached 48.4%. However, the increase in the network model scale increases the amount of calculation, resulting in a low detection speed of the network, making it difficult to perform real-time detection.

2.5 Summary of Detection Algorithms Based on Candidate Regions

The object detection network structures introduced in this section are all object detection algorithms based on candidate regions, all two-stage detection algorithms. From the R-CNN network to the Mask R-CNN network, these algorithms all adopt the basic idea of "candidate region + convolutional neural network + classification regression" and continuously improve the detection accuracy and speed. However, overall, these networks' real-time performance is poor, and it is not easy to meet actual needs. Table 1 summarizes these Two-stage object detection networks' performance on the VOC2007 and COCO data sets, "–" means no relevant data.

Table 1. Comparison of object detection algorithms based on candidate regions

Model	VOC2007	VOC2012	COCO	FPS
R-CNN	58.5	53.3	–	0.02
Faster R-CNN	78.8	75.9	21.9	5
Mask R-CNN	79.7	81.4	37.1	5
TridentNet	–	–	48.4	–

3 Object Detection Algorithms Based on Regression

The regression-based object detection algorithm is called the One-Stage model. Compared with the candidate region-based object detection algorithm, this type of algorithm omits the candidate region generation step and directly extracts the features. object classification and object regression are implemented in the same convolutional neural network. The object detection process is simplified into an end-to-end regression problem, which greatly improves the speed of the object detection algorithm based on deep learning. Representatives of such algorithms are YOLO series and SSD series [20–25]. This chapter selects the YOLO series for a detailed introduction.

3.1 YOLO v1

Detection accuracy and detection speed are important criteria for judging the quality of the image object detection model. Although the detection accuracy of the image object detection model based on the candidate region is high, its low efficiency in detecting images is its main drawback.

YOLO (You Only Look Once) [26] is an end-to-end object detection algorithm using a regression strategy. The algorithm discards the suggestion box generation and only needs to "look once" to get the regression location information and category information. The structure of the YOLO model mainly includes 18 convolutional layers, 2 fully connected layers and 6 pooling layers. The function of the convolutional layer is to extract the characteristic information of the input image. The fully connected layer's function is to calculate the probability value of the object position and category, and the pooling layer is to reduce the pixel value of the original image. The YOLO model uses regression analysis to calculate the position and confidence of multiple sliding windows. The principle of YOLO is: Suppose an image is divided into S × S grids. If the center of the object falls on the grid, the grid needs to estimate the specific location of the detection object. Each grid needs to predict N bounding boxes, and the output result is the position coordinates (x, y, w, h) and confidence of each bounding box. The calculation formula of Confidence is defined as follows:

$$Confidence = \Pr(Object) \times IOU_{pred}^{truth} \tag{2}$$

When the detection object falls in the divided grid, Pr(Object) = 1; otherwise, it is 0. The second item is the IOU value between the predicted box and the actual box. Assuming that each grid needs to predict a category of information, denoted as M category, the final output tensor of the network is S × S × (5 × N + M). Take the PASCAL VOC data set as an example; the image input is 448 × 448, S = 7, B = 2, there are 20 categories (C = 20), and the output tensor is 7 × 7 × 30. The disadvantages of YOLO are: (1) When the distance between the detected object objects is close, and the objects are small, the detection effect is poor; (2) If the target object is deformed or other conditions, the generalization ability of the model is weak.

3.2 YOLO v2 and YOLO 9000

In order to obtain faster and more accurate detection results, YOLO v2 [27] made many improvements on the basis of YOLO: (1) After each layer of convolutional layer, a BN

[28] layer was added to speed up the convergence speed of the entire network. (2) Use high-resolution images to train the network model. At present, many object detection algorithms use the pre-trained model obtained on the ImageNet data set as the basic feature extraction network, but the input image size of many pre-trained models is less than 256 × 256. For example, YOLO uses 224 × 224 images to train the classification network but uses 448 × 448 images for detection, which causes the model to adapt to changes in resolution. YOLO v2 uses 224 × 224 images to pre-train the classification network, and then uses 448 × 448 images to fine-tune the network model, and finally uses 448 × 448 images for detection so that the network does not need to spend time adapting to different resolutions. Besides, YOLO v2 also uses the K-means [29] clustering algorithm to determine the size of the anchor and uses Darknet-19 as the basic feature extraction network. YOLO9000 is a framework that can detect more than 9000 categories based on YOLO v2. For the detection data set, it can be used to learn the bounding box and confidence of the predicted object and to classify the object. For the classification data set, it can only be used to learn the classification, which greatly expands the types of objects that the model can detect.

3.3 YOLO v3

YOLO v3 [30] made the following improvements on the basis of YOLO 9000: (1) Use the ideas of Faster R-CNN for reference. The prediction of "objectness" is added to each candidate frame, and the probability of it belonging to the foreground or background is judged. The difference is that YOLOv3 only assigns a bounding box to each real frame. (2) Multi-scale fusion prediction is adopted. YOLOv3 draws on the idea of FPN and uses multi-scale feature maps to extract fine-grained features and increase the detection effect of small objects. (3) Adopt Darknet-53 as the backbone network. Darknet-53 combines the advantages of Darknet-19 and ResNet, the backbone network of YOLOv2. The accuracy of Top-5 on ImageNet is comparable to ResNet-152 while reducing the amount of calculation and further improving the speed. Although YOLOv3 has improved the detection effect of small objects compared with YOLO9000, the detection effect of large objects has decreased slightly.

3.4 YOLO v4

In 2020, Bochkovskiy et al. proposed YOLOv4 [31]. This model uses CSPDarknet53 with a larger receptive field and larger parameters as the backbone network. SPP is added to CSPDarknet53 as an additional module of Neck to increase the receptive field. Use PANet (Path Aggregation Network) to replace FPN in YOLOv3 for multi-channel feature fusion, and use YOLOv3 as Head. These constitute the model framework of YOLOv4. The YOLOv4 object detection algorithm is more complicated than YOLOv3 in network structure, and it uses many training techniques to improve the accuracy of the neural network. By introducing the Mosaic data enhancement algorithm and using the GA algorithm to select the optimal hyperparameters, YOLOv4 improves the existing algorithm so that it has a lower training threshold and can obtain better results under the condition of limited GPU resources. Among them, the Mosaic data enhancement algorithm randomly reads four pictures at a time and performs operations such as flipping and zooming the four pictures, respectively. This algorithm of combining four pictures into one picture can enrich the background of the detected object. CSPDarknet53 adds CSPNet (Cross Stage Partial Network) to each residual block of Darknet53 and integrates it into the feature map through gradient changes. The feature map is divided into two parts, one for convolution operation, and the other with the previous the convolution results are combined. In the object detection problem, CSP can effectively improve the learning ability of CNN while reducing the amount of calculation. In YOLOv4, the fusion algorithm is changed from addition to multiplication so that the network can obtain more accurate object detection capabilities.

3.5 RetinaNet

In 2017, Lin et al. [32] proposed that the imbalance of sample categories is why the detection accuracy of single-stage object detection networks is generally lower than that of two-stage object detection networks. In response to this problem, the author uses Focal Loss instead of cross-entropy as the loss function to train the model. The Focal Loss function reduces the weights of easy-to-classify samples so the model focuses on difficult-to-classify samples during training. To prove the effectiveness of Focal Loss, the author designed RetinaNet, whose structure is shown in Fig. 4.

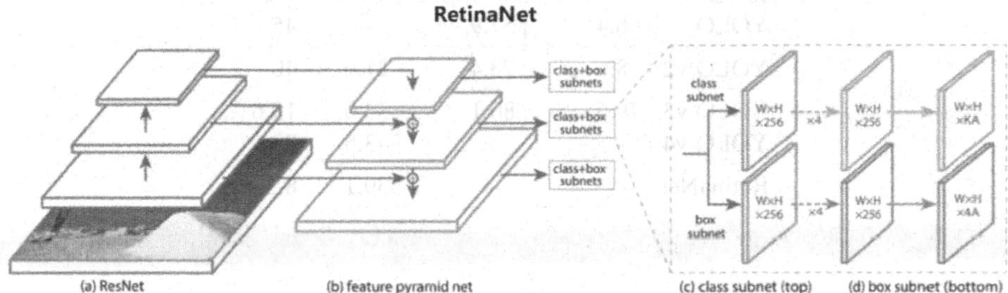

Fig. 4. The diagram of RetinaNet network

This network uses the structure of ResNet + FPN as the feature extraction network to obtain a feature map set that is more expressive and contains multi-scale target area information, and then uses two FCN sub-networks with the same structure but not sharing parameters on the set. The network structure of RetinaNet has not been significantly improved. Its biggest bright spot is the proposal of Focal Loss. Its formulas are as follows:

$$p_t = \begin{cases} p, & y = 1, \\ 1 - p, & other. \end{cases} \tag{3}$$

$$\alpha_t = \begin{cases} \alpha, & y = 1 \\ 1 - \alpha, & other. \end{cases} \tag{4}$$

$$FL(p_t) = -\alpha(1 - p_t)^{\gamma} \log(p_t) \tag{5}$$

Take binary classification as an example, where $p \in [0,1]$ is the probability that the model predicts a positive sample; $\alpha \in [0,1]$ is called a weighting factor, and the total loss of positive and negative samples is controlled by setting a suitable α value. $(1\text{-pt})\,\gamma$, $\gamma > 0$, called modulation factor, its purpose is to reduce the weight of easy-to-separate samples, so that the model can focus on training hard-to-separate samples.

As a one-stage object detection network, RetinaNet has reached the accuracy of a two-stage object detection network, and its accuracy on the COCO data set has increased to 40.8%. However, the improvement of RetinaNet detection accuracy is at the expense of detection speed. Compared with the previous one-stage detection network, the detection speed is significantly reduced, and it is difficult to achieve real-time detection.

3.6 Summary of Detection Algorithms Based on Regression

This section's detection models are regression-based object detection algorithms, which are all one-step detection models. Table 2 shows the performance of each network on the VOC2007, VOC2012 and COCO data sets. "–" means no relevant data.

Table 2. Comparison of object detection algorithms based on regression

Model	VOC2007	VOC2012	COCO	FPS
YOLO	66.4	57.9	–	45
YOLO v2	78.6	73.4	21.6	40
YOLO v3	79.6	80.1	33.0	19.6
YOLO v4	–	–	43.5	23
RetinaNet	–	–	39.1	8.2

4 Application Scenarios

4.1 Meteorological Satellite Cloud Image Detection

Meteorological satellites receive and measure radiation from various bands and generate cloud image products based on the radiation information. Due to the advantages of wide coverage, strong timeliness, and high resolution, meteorologists often use cloud images to monitor weather changes process. Meteorological staff must accurately analyze weather development trends, development speeds, the scope of influence etc. How to balance various things within a limited time is important. That is a huge test. Because of the large amount of satellite cloud image data in the aviation meteorological business and the timeliness requirements are high in the specific weather analysis process. Through the YOLO network, the function of detecting cumulus clouds in the entire meteorological satellite cloud image is realized. The detection results can be basically consistent with the manual judgment results. It satisfies business needs and solves the current problems of insufficient manual energy and low efficiency.

4.2 Medical Image Detection

Different from traditional natural image detection, medical image detection is to detect a certain type or a specific category (tumor, tuberculosis, etc.), which is characterized by detecting the fine-grained difference of target objects. The difficulty lies in: (1) the shape, size, and position of the target object vary greatly; (2) the shape of the target object varies in different periods and environments; (3) the shapes of the diseased tissue and the non-pathological tissue are small. The main process of medical image detection is: firstly segment the area where the target object is located, then extract the candidate area and complete the feature extraction, and finally perform the classification. Aiming at the problem of data distribution differences and poor domain adaptability in medical images, Li et al. proposed a CLU-CNN domain adaptation framework, which has no specific domain to adapt to training. It has good scalability and accurate positioning capabilities on small data sets.

5 Future Development Outlook

Object detection is a vital research field with a wide range of application prospects. Although the current object detection algorithm has been widely used in real life, there are still many challenges. The future object detection algorithm deserves further research in the following aspects:

5.1 Training Framework Under Small Data Set

Small-scale data training is a problem that needs attention in practical engineering applications, especially in industrialized scenarios. In many application fields, the number of training samples is much smaller than general data sets such as MS COCO. Currently, transfer learning is mainly used to initialize parameters for few samples. However, for special fields such as medical and military, there is no target data in the existing large data sets, and the effect of migration learning will be affected. He Kaiming et al. verified the importance of the object detection framework around pre-training and found that using the ImageNet pre-training model can speed up the early training stage's convergence speed. However, it may not necessarily bring the effect of regularization or ultimately improve the accuracy. The necessity and scope of application of future pre-training and fine-tuning algorithms are also worth exploring.

5.2 Optimization of the Loss Function

In the One-Stage detection network, the detection model is mainly trained by optimizing the classification loss and the positioning loss at the same time. Due to a large number of anchor boxes, the problem of imbalance between positive and negative samples is more serious. To solve this problem, many detection networks such as YOLO and RetinaNet have introduced new classification loss functions to solve the problem of sample imbalance by re-weighting the samples. However, the relationship between different samples has not been fully considered, and it cannot be well adapted to different types of data sets. Therefore, the design of the loss function still needs innovation. In 2019, Chen et al. [33] proposed replacing classification loss with sorting and solving the sorting problem through AP-loss (average-precision loss). He proposed an optimization algorithm that can cleverly combine the error-driven update mechanism and the backpropagation mechanism in the deep network in learning progress. This method can significantly improve the detection performance of the One-Stage network.

6 Conclusion

This paper first reviews the research background of object detection. Then, it summarizes the existing classic image object detection models in detail from the perspective of candidate regions and regression algorithms. It also summarizes each model's improvement strategies compared with the previous models, as well as its advantages and disadvantages. The future development and technology trends of image object detection are analyzed based on the current development situation. At present, the image object detection technology is relatively mature, and the detection accuracy and detection speed in the experiment has reached a high level, but the detection results in the real scene still have some gaps compared with the experimental data. Therefore, image object detection still has challenges in the future, especially in the applicability of different scenarios, small sample training models, and loss function optimization. There is still much room for improvement and development potential. There is still much room for improvement and development potential.

Acknowledgement. This work was supported by the National Natural Science Foundation of China (Grant No.42075007), the Open Project of Provincial Key Laboratory for Computer Information Processing Technology under Grant KJS1935, Soochow University,and the Priority Academic Program Development of Jiangsu Higher Education Institutions.

References

1. Fang, W., Pang, L., Yi, W.: Survey on the application of deep reinforcement learning in image processing, J. Artif. Intell. **2**(1), 39–58 (2020)
2. Szeliski, R.: Computer vision: Algorithms and Applications. Springer, Berlin (2010). https://doi.org/10.1007/978-1-84882-935-0
3. Zhu, D., Luo, Y., Dai, L., et al.: Salient object detection via a local and global method based on deep residual network. J. Vis. Commun. Image Representation **54**, 1–9 (2018)
4. Lowe, D.G.: Distinctive image features from scale-invariant keypoints. Int. J. Comput. Vis. **60**(2), 91–110 (2004)
5. Dalal, N., Triggs, B.: Histograms of oriented gradients for human detection. In: IEEE Conference on Computer Vision and Pattern Recognition, CVPR, vol. 1, pp. 886–893 (2005)
6. Felzenszwalb, P.F., Girshick, R.B., McAllester, D., et al.: Object detection with discriminatively trained part-based models. IEEE Trans. Pattern Anal. Mach. Intell. **32**(9), 1627–1645 (2009)
7. Cristianini, N., Shawe-Taylor, J.: An Introduction to Support Vector Machines and Other Kernel-Based Learning Methods. Cambridge University Press, Cambridge (2000)

8. Neubeck, A., Van Gool, L.: Efficient non-maximum suppression. In: International Conference on Pattern Recognition, ICPR, pp. 850–855 (2006)
9. LeCun, Y., Bengio, Y., Hinton, G.: Deep learning. Nature **521**(7553), 436–444 (2015)
10. Krizhevsky, A., Sutskever, I., Hinton, G.E.: Imagenet classification with deep convolutional neural networks. In: Advances in Neural Information Processing Systems, pp. 1097–1105 (2012)
11. Szegedy, C., Liu, W., Jia, Y., et al.: Going deeper with convolutions. In: Proceedings of the IEEE Conference on Computer Vision and Pattern Recognition, pp. 1–9 (2015)
12. He, K., Zhang, X., et al.: Deep residual learning for image recognition. In: Proceedings of the IEEE Conference on Computer Vision and Pattern Recognition, pp. 770–778 (2016)
13. Fang, W., Zhang, F., Ding, Y., Sheng, J.: A new sequential image prediction method based on LSTM and DCGAN. Comput. Mater. Continua **64**(1), 217–231 (2020)
14. Girshick, R., Donahue, J., Darrell, T., et al.: Rich feature hierarchies for accurate object detection and semantic segmentation. In: Proceedings of the IEEE Conference on Computer Vision and Pattern Recognition, pp. 580–587 (2014)
15. Everingham, M., Van Gool, L., et al.: The pascal visual object classes (VOC) challenge. Int. J. Comput. Vis. **88**(2), 303–338 (2010)
16. Uijlings, J.R.R., Van De Sande, K.E., Gevers, T., et al.: Selective search for object recognition. Int. J. Comput. Vis. **104**(2), 154–171 (2013)
17. Ren, S., He, K., et al.: Faster R-CNN: towards real-time object detection with region proposal networks. In: Advances in Neural Information Processing Systems, pp. 91–99 (2015)
18. He, K., Gkioxari, G., Dollár, P., et al.: Mask R-CNN. In: Proceedings of the IEEE International Conference on Computer Vision, pp. 2961–2969 (2017)
19. Li, Y., Chen, Y., et al.: Scale-aware trident networks for object detection. In: Proceedings of the IEEE International Conference on Computer Vision, pp. 6054–6063 (2019).
20. Liu, W., et al.: SSD: single shot multibox detector. In: Leibe, B., Matas, J., Sebe, N., Welling, M. (eds.) ECCV 2016. LNCS, vol. 9905, pp. 21–37. Springer, Cham (2016). https://doi.org/10.1007/978-3-319-46448-0_2
21. Fu, C.Y., Liu, W., Ranga, A., Tyagi, A., et al.: DSSD: Deconvolutional single shot detector. arXiv preprint arXiv:1701.06659 (2017)
22. Jeong, J., Park, H., Kwak, N.: Enhancement of SSD by concatenating feature maps for object detection. arXiv preprint arXiv:1705.09587 (2017)
23. Li, Z., Zhou, F.: Feature fusion single shot multibox detector. arXiv preprint arXiv:1712.00960 (2017)
24. Yi, J., Wu, P., Metaxas, D.N.: ASSD: attentive single shot multibox detector. Computer Vision and Image Understanding, vol. 189, p. 102827 (2019)
25. Hu, J., Shen, L., Sun, G.: Squeeze-and-excitation networks. In: Proceedings of the IEEE Conference on Computer Vision and Pattern Recognition, pp. 7132–7141 (2018)
26. Redmon, J., Divvala, S., Girshick, R., et al.: You only look once: unified, real-time object detection. In: Proceedings of the IEEE Conference on Computer Vision and Pattern Recognition, pp. 779–788 (2016)
27. Redmon, J., Farhadi, A.: YOLO9000: better, faster, stronge. In: Proceedings of the IEEE Conference on Computer Vision and Pattern Recognition, pp. 7263–7271 (2017)
28. Ioffe, S., Szegedy, C.: Batch normalization: Accelerating deep network training by reducing internal covariate shift. arXiv preprint arXiv:1502.03167 (2015)
29. Hartigan, J.A., Wong, M.A.: Algorithm AS 136: a k-means clustering algorithm. J. Royal Stat. Soc. **28**(1), 100–108 (1979)
30. Redmon, J., Farhadi, A.: Yolov3: An incremental improvement. arXiv preprint arXiv:1804.02767 (2018)
31. Bochkovskiy, A., Wang, C.Y., Liao, H.Y.M.: YOLOv4: Optimal Speed and Accuracy of Object Detection. arXiv preprint arXiv:2004.10934 (2020)

32. Lin, T.Y., Goyal, P., Girshick, R., et al.: Focal loss for dense object detection. In: Proceedings of the IEEE International Conference on Computer Vision, pp. 2980–2988 (2017)
33. Chen, K., Li, J., Lin, W., et al.: Towards accurate one-stage object detection with ap-loss. In: Proceedings of the IEEE Conference on Computer Vision and Pattern Recognition, pp. 5119–5127 (2019)

Autocoder Guide Multi-category Topic Clustering for Keywords Matching

Yang Ying(✉), Yaru Sun(✉), Xihai Deng, and Du Wenjia

The Third Research Institute of Ministry of Public Security, Shanghai 201204, China
yangying@mcst.org.cn

Abstract. In the task of multi-category keyword extraction, how to make effective use of text topic information is a very challenging research problem. In order to solve the problems such as weak cluster center information representation and noise influence of non-topic word feature in unlabeled topic clustering, we proposed a keyword extraction model of multi-category topic clustering based on autocoder. The modeling was carried out respectively from the aspects of node representation and topic cluster division to effectively alleviate the influence of high-dimensional noise features on the establishment of cluster centers. In the evaluation, the Gini impurity was used as an index to measure the fitting degree between the clustering effect of the method and the artificial clustering, and the cluster center was used to measure the topic similarity of the words in the clustering results. The results on the THUCNews and short text datasets show that the model can obtain information beneficial for keyword extraction tasks, and achieve better performances on various evaluation indexes.

Keywords: Keyword extraction · Topic clustering · Multi-topic matching · Automatic code

1 Introduction

Keywords are compact representations of the document's content, consisting of one or more words. The richness of the subject information is used as a criterion for evaluating keywords. It is a challenging task in datamining to extract keywords and match topics in text with multiple topics. When extracting keywords from multiple categories, it is also a challenge in the task of keyword extraction to automatically encode and generate classified keywords. It is very important to solve this kind of problem for document retrieval and data mining.

Traditional statistical learning methods usually use eigenvalue quantization to get keywords from the candidate sets constructed after preprocessing. For example, TF-IDF model based on frequency features, LDA and HMM model mining hidden information of words and sentences [1]. These models may be limited by the data domain, have poor portability performance, and some disturbance problems may occur when the sample data size is large. On the one hand, when the text length is too long and short, the feature vectors are sparse and the coincidence rate between words is low. On the other

X. Sun et al. (Eds.): ICAIS 2021, LNCS 12736, pp. 481–493, 2021.
https://doi.org/10.1007/978-3-030-78609-0_41

hand, the method of eigenvalue quantization does not consider the complete structural information in the text. To alleviate these problems, most existing models [2–5] utilize an end-to-end framework to accomplish this task. The end-to-end model can compensate for the lack of feature semantics by considering the multi-dimensional features of text. The model first maps the word nodes to the high-dimensional space, then calculates the distance between the points, and then clusters the close ones into a cluster, the center of which becomes the cluster center. Reference [6] has been proved effective by some natural language inference methods to extract and integrate text information. To classify words is to ensure that words of the same class are grouped into a cluster, and the distance between different clusters of different classes is far enough. The cluster points are updated by iterating the data, the groups of different categories are divided, and the cluster centers are calculated by the distance between the cluster points. However, due to the influence of node feature representation, some problems may arise. This method does not guarantee that the average cluster center can represent the topic information of the cluster, has limitations and cannot be well applied to the new data. The presence of words that are not keywords in the text will also increase the noise effect on the performance of the model.

To solve the above problems, this paper proposes a relationship extraction model that Automatic Coder Guide Multi-Category Topic Clustering for Keywords Extraction (ACGTC). The automatic encoder layer is constructed based on the basic features to encode the word features containing the topic information to improve the quality of the basic features. The encoder use the Graph Convolutional Neural Network (GCN) combined with the attention mechanism. The Graph Neural Network (GNN) [7] is an effective method to encode the information features of text nodes. It represents the words in the sentence as nodes in the graph, and node representation depends on its adjacent nodes. The application of neural network to graph structure can directly obtain node-dependent information, so as to highlight the topic features and alleviate the influence of noisy words. The attention mechanism not only enables the model to capture the rich semantic information in the text, but also enables the model to learn the correlation strength between nodes, so as to make better use of the sentence topic information. The information of topic features of keywords is strengthened, while the information of theme features of noise words is weakened. It provides the clustering layer with better word information with obvious topic features. Therefore, for the keyword extraction task of multi-topic classification, we adopt the method of combining the GNN with the attention mechanism. The model includes an auto-encoder layer and a topic cluster layer. The model is modeled from the aspects of node representation and topic cluster classification to effectively mitigate the influence of high-dimensional noise features on cluster center establishment. In the model evaluation part, we consider the fitting degree of model effect and artificial clustering, and use Gini impurity as the index to measure. The experimental results show that the model achieves satisfactory results in THUCNews and short text datasets.

Our contributions are summarized as follows.

- In this paper, we propose a new multi-topic clustering model, which uses the GNN to capture a wide range of context-dependent information and improve the feature representation capability of key nodes.

- We also propose an auto-encoder layer to learn the correlation of feature space. By encoding the dependency information between nodes into the feature of nodes, we enhance the dependency between nodes and effectively capture the topic dependency information.
- ACGTC has achieved better performance on THUCNews and short text datasets.

2 Related Work

2.1 Graph Neural Networks

The application of GNN in graph structure data modeling has attracted more and more attention, including social network prediction system with clear relationship structure [8–10], recommendation system [11], knowledge graph [12], etc., as well as unstructured scenes with unclear relationship structure: image classification [13], text processing [14–20], etc. In this paper, we use GNN to model unstructured text data.

Some recent studies have focused on the application of GNNs to text classification tasks, which involves modeling text as graphs. Reference [15] proposed to convert documents into word co-occurrence graphs, and then use them as the input of the convolutional layer to capture the discontinuous and long distance semantics effectively by taking advantage of the graphical representation. Reference [16] represents the text in the form of concept graph. The matching signals are summarized through the GCN, and the sentences containing the same concept vertex are compared to match a pair of texts. Reference [17] constructs a text graph tensor to learn intra-graph propagation and inter-graph propagation from the three perspectives of semantic, syntactic and contextual information of the text, which is used to coordinate and integrate heterogeneous information between graphs. We draw inspiration from the above work, but it is designed for classification tasks, and there is a difference between classification tasks and generating tasks.

Some research is based on GCN to do generation tasks. Reference [18, 19] proposed a Graph2Seq neural network model based on graph sequences. Combining the attention mechanism and following the traditional encoder method, it constructed a graph encoder and a sequence encoder, and encoded SQL query in SQL-to-text task based on the attributes between graph neural network learning nodes. Reference [20] proposed to solve the problem of AMR-to-text based on the GNN. Although these efforts use GNNs as encoders, they all leverage information in the form of graphs that already exist, such as SQL queries, Abstract Meaning Representation graphs (ARM graphs), and dependency graphs. The text input for these tasks is relatively long, and our work with shorter texts is more challenging.

2.2 Keyword Extraction

Keywords extraction is conducive to information retrieval, automatic index, automatic classification, automatic clustering, automatic filtering and other applications. The topic in the text is not unique, if only focus on text corpus, it may lead to the bottleneck and misunderstanding of knowledge acquisition. Current methods focus on how to extract keywords or phrases that express text topics. Reference [21] proposed a method to extract key concepts of topics from public classification by using topic model. It ranks tags according to their importance relative to a topic and uses the top tags as key concepts to extract a topic. Reference [22] proposed a keywords extraction algorithm that represented document by graph, document word by node and relationship between document words by edge. Degree and proximity center were used to measure topic keywords. Reference [23] proposed a keywords extraction method using three main factors, which are the time, topic relevance and participants of the previous topic, which are different from other keywords. The current speaker should be considered more important than what the other participants say. Inspired by the above work, this paper combines text topic and graph representation sequence model to generate short text topic keywords.

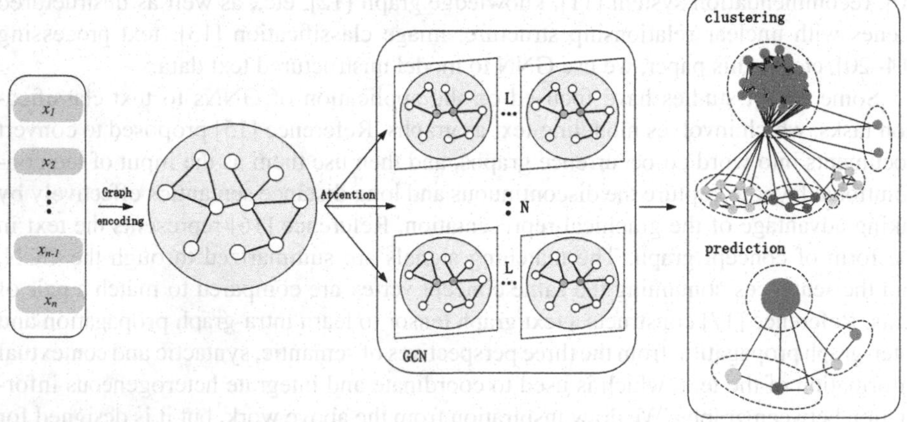

Fig. 1. The framework of ACGTC model.

3 ACGTC

3.1 Overview

The goal of the model is to cluster the topic information for the keywords in the sentence and output the keywords with text topic information. The framework of ACGTC model is shown in Fig. 1, mainly including the autocoder layer and the topic clustering layer.

The autocoder can encode the word information. The text is divided into sentence units and the sentences are coded as the input of the model. Then N attention matrices are constructed by using multi-head attention mechanisms. The GCN at the L layer represents the node information through N attention matrices. The topic clustering layer divides the keyword categories according to the feature information of the output of the auto-encoder. At last, the new words are judged and predicted by the clustering cluster.

3.2 Autocoder Layer

The autocoder layer can gather more comprehensive information from the sentence into node features, facilitating the model to understand the internal structure of the text and the relationship between topics. Its purpose is to make the feature information of the words containing the topic information in the sentence more prominent.

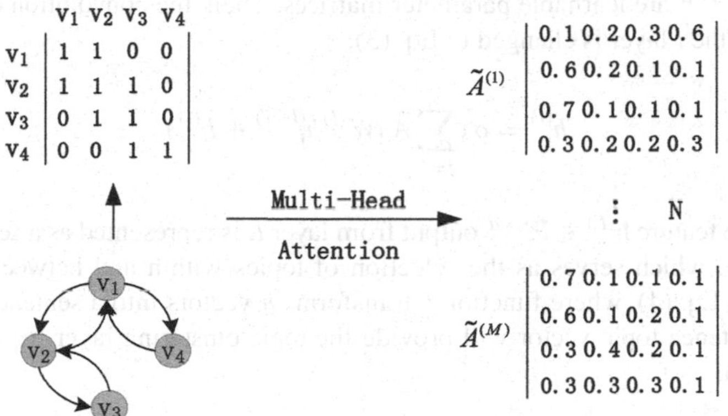

Fig. 2. Attention guidance graph.

Construct the graph of sentence X with N words, according to word embedding and adjacency matrix A. The x_i represents the word embedding of the i-th word in the sentence, and the word represents the node in the graph. A_{ij} represents the relationship or edge between the i-th node and the j-th node. Initially, if node i is associated with node j, then $A_{ij} = 1$; otherwise, $A_{ij} = 0$, $A_{ij} = A_{ij}$. In the process of general graph convolution, the input of convolution calculation for node i at the l layer is $h^{(l-1)}$, and the output is $h_i^{(l)}$ after Eq. (1). Where, $W^{(l)}$ is a weight matrix for linear transformation, $b^{(l)}$ is a deviation vector, and σ represents the activation function. The initial input to $h_i^{(0)}$ is x_i, $x_i \in \mathbb{R}^{d\times 1}$, d is the dimension of the feature.

$$h_i^{(l)} = \sigma(\sum_{j=1}^{n} A_{ij} W^{(l)} h_j^{(l-1)} + b^{(l)}) \tag{1}$$

The node contains sentence structure and topic information which have great influence on word classification. How to make the key nodes contain richer information is the key to solve the problem. The attention mechanism can assist the model to query and correlate closely node features effectively to obtain useful information. In this paper, multi-head attention is used to guide the transformation of adjacency matrix into attention matrix $\tilde{A}_{ij}$, as shown in Fig. 2. Multi-head attention can pay attention to the information of different subspaces, and each element in the matrix corresponds to the weight of edges between corresponding nodes, so as to capture the relationship density between nodes in the topic area. The calculation of the t-head attention matrix in the l layer includes a query and a set of key-value pairs, as shown in Eq. (2),

$$\tilde{A}^n = soft\max\left(\frac{QW_i^Q \times (KW_i^K)^T}{1/\sqrt[2]{d}}\right)V \tag{2}$$

where Q and K are representations of the $l-1$ layer of the model, and $W^Q \in \mathbb{R}^{d\times d}$ and $W^K \in \mathbb{R}^{d\times d}$ are learnable parameter matrices. Then, the convolution computation for node i at the l layer is changed to Eq. (3),

$$h_i^{(l)} = \sigma(\sum_{j=1}^{n} \tilde{A}_{ij} W^{(l)} h_j^{(l-1)} + b^{(l)}) \tag{3}$$

The node feature $\mathrm{h}^{(L)} \in \mathbb{R}^{n\times d}$ output from layer L is represented as a sentence topic feature h_{topic}, which serves as the selection of topics within and between sentences. As shown in Eq. (4), where function f transforms n vectors into a sentence topic vector. This sentence topic vector will provide the topic clustering layer for further topic classification.

$$h_{topic} = f(\mathrm{h}^{(L)}) = f(GCN(\mathrm{h}^{(0)})) \tag{4}$$

3.3 Topic Clustering Layer

The topic clustering layer can filter and classify the sample data based on the words and topic features output by the autocoder. In the process, the top-down method is selected to filter the samples, which facilitates the removal of part of the noise data and reduces the workload of iteration on the sample data.

It is necessary to feedback the features of the autocoder output during the clustering operation. It evaluates whether the topic vector belongs to the topic feature domain. Cross-validation is adopted here to make the distance between the same category as small as possible and the distance between different categories as large as possible, as shown in Eq. (5).

$$L = \sum_{i=1}^{n} \min_k \left\| x^{(i)} - \mu_k \right\|^2 \tag{5}$$

Under the condition that m topics are determined, m topic features are generated by sentence training of seeded themes $T = \{T_1, T_2 \ldots T_m\}$, treatment of predictive word features are divided into thematic seed library $V_T = \{V_{T1} \ldots V_{Tk} \ldots\}$ and the noise phrase $O = \{O_1 \ldots, O_i \ldots\}$, where $V_{Ti} = \{v_1^{Ti} \ldots, v_i^{Ti}, \ldots\}$, v_i^{Ti} represents the key words in the topic T_i. Firstly, the topic at the sentence level is filtered, and the topic vector related to the topic is reserved into the topic seed bank. Then, the words in the sentence are filtered by calculating the words and topic feature vectors, the words related to the topic are retained to the topic phrase, and unrelated to the topic are removed to the noisy set.

Algorithm 1: Topic clustering

Input: established thematic features $T=\{T_1, T_2..., T_m\}$, thematic seed bank $V_T=\{V_{T1},..., V_{Tk}...\}$, the noise phrase $O=\{O_1, ..., O_i...\}$.

Output: expanded keyword set $V_{Ti}=\{ v_1^{Ti} ,..., v_i^{Ti} ,...\}$

```
for(k=1;k<=m;k++):
    B = similar(V_Ti, T_k);
    The topic takes the T_k with the highest value in B set as the topic;
    for(i=1;i<=len(V_Ti);i++);
        C = similar(V_Ti, V_i^Ti);
        Add top n words from C set to keyword set;
end for
```

4 Experiments

4.1 Data

The experiment is trained and tested on the THUCNews data set, which is 830,000 news documents extracted from Sina News and can be used as a large-scale datasets. The text of the datasets is in UTF-8 format and consists of 14 categories, namely *finance, lottery, real estate, stocks, household, education, technology, society, fashion, politics, sports, constellation, games* and *entertainment*. The text format is divided into title and text. The title of the datasets was separately extracted and used as a small short text datasets to test the model. The short text datasets was named Sma-THUCNews. The 80% of the data in the datasets is used as the training set and 20% as the test set. The description of the datasets is shown in Table 1.

Table 1. Description of THUCNews and Sma-THUCNews datasets.

Datasets	Samples
Training set	676,074
Testing set	160,000
Validation set	160,000

4.2 Setup

The test on the validation set shows that the number of heads of multi-head attention is selected from $N = \{1, 2, 3, 4\}$, and the number of layers from the autocoder is selected from $L = \{2, 3, 4, 5\}$. Through the preliminary experiments on the validation set, it is found that the combination setting of ($N = 2, L = 3, d = 330$) achieves the best effect on the THUCNews data set. In the case that the number of vertices is relatively small, the reduction of L value will alleviate the problem of excessive smoothing of the model. The combination of ($N = 3, L = 2, d = 300$) was set on the Sma-THUCNews data set to get the best results. The model is CUDA9.0 training under NVIDIA GeForce GTX 1650. The training cycle is 100, and every 10 cycles takes about 240 s. The dictionary has a size of 100,000. The dropout rate is set to 0.1 and the Adam optimizer is used for training parameters. The initial learning rate was 0.01, the value of epoch was 10, and the learning rate per epoch was reduced to half of the original.

4.3 Baseline

The Baseline is selected as TF-IDF, Kmeans, LDA, RNN [24], CopyRNN [24], and CovRNN [25] to compare unsupervised model and supervised model. Tf-idf, Kmeans and LDA belong to the unsupervised model, while RNN, CopyRNN and CovRNN are supervised models. Tf-idf, Kmeans and LDA are statistics-based methods, which are mainly based on the number of candidate keywords as their importance to the text. This can not reflect the semantic information contained in the text and can not better express the topic features. RNN, CopyRNN and CovRNN can capture text context information from the perspective of text sentence structure.

4.4 Evaluation Index

In this paper, the average clustering center distance and Gini impurity were used to evaluate the model results. Average clustering center distance is used to measure the concentration degree in different types of samples. The lower this index is, the closer the word features in the clustering results are. The average cluster center distance is calculated as shown in Eq. (6), where x_j is the sample vector belonging to category C_i, c_i is the center vector of the category, and n is the size of the category.

$$\overline{D}_i = \frac{1}{n} \sum_{x_j \subset C_i} \left\| x_j - \overline{c}_i \right\| \tag{6}$$

The Gini impurity derived from the classification and regression tree, which measures the proportion of noise nodes in the category, is an approximation of entropy. It's a measure of clutter, or impurity. In this paper, the similarity between clustering results and manual annotation is reflected. Gini impurity calculation is shown in Eq. (7). Where y_j is the category of a sample, k is the category label in the original data set, and J is the total number of samples in class C_i.

$$I(C_i) = 1 - \max_{1 \le k \le K} \frac{\sum_{j=1}^{J} y_j = k?}{J} \tag{7}$$

Table 2. The words most similar under each topic.

Topicl	Similar words	Similar value	Topic	Similar words	Similar value
Finance	Fast Xuntong	0.6810	Society	Economics	0.6901
	Blue Ants	0.6352		Stratum	0.6586
	Reputation	0.6333		Public opinion	0.6498
Lottery	Sports lottery	0.6822	Fashion	Vogue	0.7092
	Bet	0.6456		Fashionable dress	0.6704
	Welfare Lottery	0.6291		Simplicity	0.6587
Real estate	Landed estate	0.7690	Politics	Current affairs	0.7413
	House property	0.6934		Top-rated news	0.5951
	Invest	0.6822		Hot points	0.5933
Stocks	Stock market	0.7440	Sports	Athletics	0.6523
	Speculate	0.6911		European message	0.6275
	A-share	0.6817		Basketball	0.6247
Household	Furniture	0.7468	Constellation	Fortune	0.7067
	Furniture store	0.7114		Sagittarius	0.6730
	Design	0.7057		Aries	0.6595
Education	Educators	0.6400	Games	Stand-alone	0.6969
	Moral education	0.6393		Arcade	0.6892
	Preschool	0.6184		Player	0.6725
Technology	High-tech	0.6363	Entertainment	Cultural recreation	0.6820
	Hi-tech	0.5659		Casino	0.6536
	Innovate	0.5610		Arder	0.6226

4.5 Result

The word vectors were evaluated and matched with the words most similar to each topic. The cosine distance was used to calculate the similarity of the word vectors, and the results were shown in Table 2. It can be seen that the generated word vectors have a higher matching degree with the word vectors with similar meanings. This shows that the model can better capture topic information. But for some similar topics, the matching word vectors are controversial. For example, in social and political topics, "hot spots" would be more appropriate under social topic. Although the value of the two keywords and their topic is low, this show that the model still has the problem of semantic differentiation. The results included some entities, such as Blue Ants (organization) and Fast Xuntong (tool). This indicates that the model focuses more on the representation of the subject in the training process.

Table 3. Gini impurity coefficient and cluster center distance evaluation results of each model in THUCNews dataset.

Model	Gini impurity (average value)	Gini impurity (standard deviation)	Cluster center distance
Tf-idf	0.533	0.252	2.416
Kmeans	0.459	0.224	2.295
LDA	0.464	0.212	2.275
RNN	0.421	0.196	2.283
CopyRNN	0.392	0.182	1.392
CovRNN	0.383	0.173	1.385
ACGTC	**0.325**	**0.097**	**0.645**

Gini impurity and cluster center distance were used to evaluate the clustering results, as shown in Table 3. It can be seen from the results that the ACGTC model has low Gini impurity and cluster center distance, which indicates that the model can accurately classify the subject categories of words. CopyRNN and CovRNN perform equally well. In the text data with complex categories, the neural network model can better identify the topic of the word than the statistical model.

It is found that the distribution of long text (news content) is roughly the same as that of short text (news title). As shown in Fig. 3, the text topics captured by the model are consistent for both short and long texts.

4.6 Analysis and Discussion

Ablation Study. The attentional layer and the graph neural network layer of the model were analyzed by ablation. In order to make the display of data results clear, we selected large, medium and small topic data for visualization, technology (162,928 samples), society (50,848 samples) and constellation (3577 samples). We have removed some distant outliers from the presentation of the results.

As shown in Fig. 4, (a) shows the data visualization of the ACGTC model for the three topics. (b) shows the visualization of the data of the three topics after removing the attention layer of the ACGTC model. (c) shows the visualized figure of ACGTC model with the GCN layer removed and only one layer of feedforward neural network and attention layer output. (d) is the visualized image processed by only one layer of feedforward neural network after removing the attention layer and GCN layer. We found that the distribution of data was relatively dispersed after removing the attention layer and the graph neural network layer. This shows that these two layers has an important impact on the performance of the model. However, after removing the attention layer only, there is no obvious data dispersion, only the phenomenon of individual data outliers. The data distribution between different topics is clearer. However, after only removing the graph attention layer, the data showed significant dispersion. We suspect that this is related to the representation of the topic feature information by the graph neural network. The GCN layer is important compared to the attention layer. This also shows another reason, the representation of data information is particularly important.

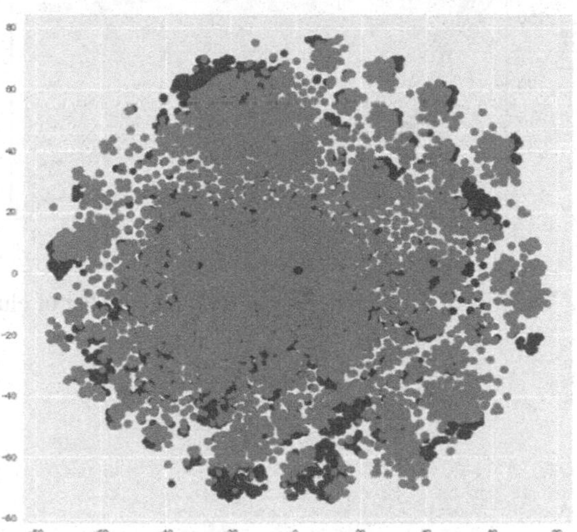

Fig. 3. A data distribution of title and text content.

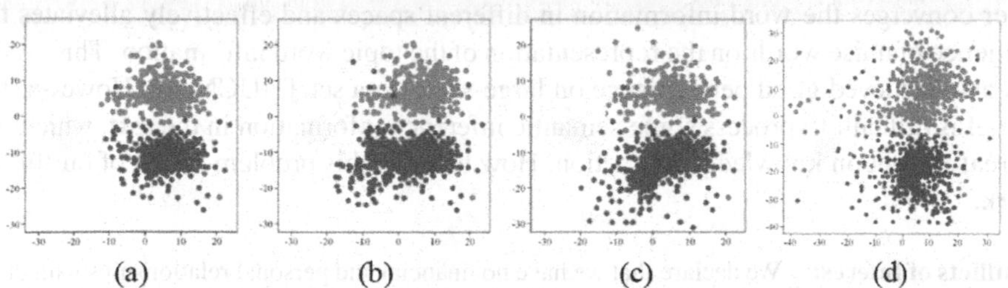

Fig. 4. Ablation analysis graph.

The Influence Analysis of the Number of Clusters. Equation (7) is used as the loss function to observe how each model changes with the number of clusters under the data of three topics, as shown in Fig. 5. We find that the loss of each model decreases gradually with the increase of the number of clusters. When the number of clusters is 2–3, the variation degree of loss value of each model becomes slower. Therefore, there may be an optimal value between 2 and 3. The neural network model is better than the model of eigenvalue quantization in the case of large amount of data. This proves that the representation of text topic information is conducive to topic clustering. With the increase of the number of clusters, the gap between models decreases, but the impact on the loss also decreases. ACGTC can capture the topic features of words sensitively in the text and is optimal in each model.

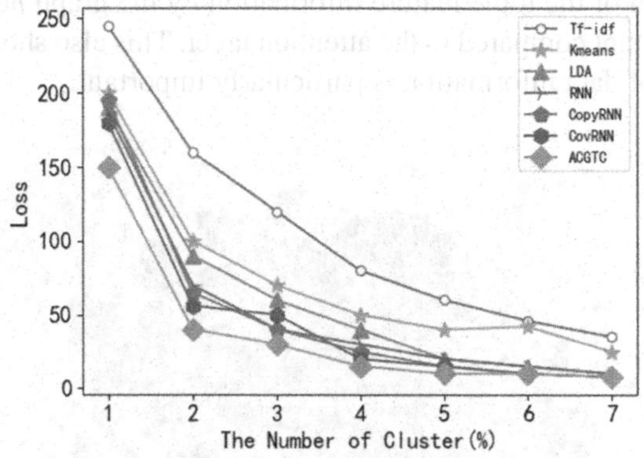

Fig. 5. The loss of each model varies with the number of clusters.

5 Conclusion

In this paper, a new multi-topic clustering model, called ACGTC, is proposed to construct a self-encoder by combining the graph neural network with the attention mechanism to effectively capture the semantic information of topics in words. The topic clustering layer converges the word information in different spaces and effectively alleviates the influence of noise words on the representation of the topic word information. This model has also achieved good performance on large-scale data set THUCNews. However, the model is difficult to process some semantic inference information in the text, which has a great impact on knowledge extraction. How to solve this problem is one of our future work.

Conflicts of Interest. We declare that we have no financial and personal relationships with other people or organizations that can inappropriately influence our work. There is no professional or other personal interest of any nature or kind in any product, service and/or company that could be construed as influencing the position presented in, or the review of, the manuscript entitled.

References

1. Liu, Y.W., Wei, Y.: Analysis of emotion based on LDA thematic model. Electron. Sci. Technol. **7**, 12–16 (2019)
2. Boudin, F.: A comparison of centrality measures for graph-based keyphrase extraction. In: Proceedings of IJCNLP, pp. 834–838. Nagoya, Japan (2013)

3. Palshikar, G.K.: Keyword extraction from a single document using centrality measures. Pattern Recogn. Mach. Intell. **4851**, 503–510 (2007)
4. Bulgarov, F., Caragea, C.: A comparison of supervised keyphrase extraction models. In: Proceedings of WWW, pp. 13–14. Florence, Italy (2015)
5. Mothe, J., Ramiandrisoa, F., Rasolomanana, M.: Automatic keyphrase extraction using graph-based methods. In: Proceedings of SAC, pp. 728–730. Sanya, China (2018)
6. Chen, Q., Zhu, X.D., Ling, Z.H., et al.: Enhanced LSTM for natural language inference. In: Proceedings of ACL, Vancouver, Canada, pp. 1657–1668 (2017)
7. Liu, P., Ren, H., Shi, X., et al.: MoTransFrame: model transfer framework for CNNs on low-resource edge computing node. CMC-Comput. Mater. Continua **65**(3), 2321–2334 (2020)
8. Hamilton, W.L., Ying, Z., Leskovec, J.: Inductive representation learning on large graphs. In: Proceedings of NIPS, pp. 1024–1034 (2017)
9. Li, Y., Jin, H., Yu, X., et al.: Intelligent prediction of private information diffusion in social networks. Electronics **9**(5), 719 (2020)
10. Sun, W., Cai, Z., Li, Y., et al.: Data processing and text mining technologies on electronic medical records: a review. J. Healthcare Eng. **2018**, 1–8 (2018)
11. Ying, R., He, R., Chen, K., et al.: Graph convolutional neural networks for web-scale recommender systems. In: Proceedings of the KDD, pp. 974–983 (2018)
12. Hamaguchi, T., Oiwa, H., Shimbo, M., et al.: Knowledge transfer for out-of-knowledge-base entities: a graph neural network approach. In: Proceedings of IJCAI, pp. 1802–1808 (2017)
13. Kampffmeyer, M., Chen, Y., Liang, X., et al.: Rethinking knowledge graph propagation for zero-shot learning. In: Proceedings of CVPR, pp. 11487–11496 (2019)
14. Li, Z., Sun, Y., Zhu, J., Tang, S., Zhang, C., Ma, H.: Improve relation extraction with dual attention-guided graph convolutional networks. Neural Comput. Appl. **33**(6), 1773–1784 (2020). https://doi.org/10.1007/s00521-020-05087-z
15. Peng, H., Li, J.X., He, Y., et al.: Large-scale hierarchical text classification with recursively regularized deep graph-CNN. In: Proceedings of WWW, pp. 1063–1072 (2018)
16. Liu, B., Niu, D., Wei, H., et al.: Matching article pairs with graphical decomposition and convolutions. In: Proceedings of ACL, pp. 6284–6294 (2019)
17. Liu, X., You, X., Zhang, X., et al.: Tensor graph convolutional networks for text classification. In: Proceedings of AAAI, pp. 8409–8416 (2020)
18. Xu, K., Wu, L.F., Wang, Z.G., et al.: Graph2Seq: graph to sequence learning with attention-based neural networks, arXiv preprint arXiv:1804.00823 (2018)
19. Xu, K., Wu, L., Wang, Z., et al.: SQL-to-text generation with graph-to-sequence model. In: Proceedings of EMNLP, pp. 931–936 (2018)
20. Beck, D., Haffari, G., Cohn, T.: Graph-to-sequence learning using gated graph neural networks. In: Proceedings of ACL, pp. 273–283 (2018)
21. Xue, H., Qin, B., Liu, T.: Topical key concept extraction from folksonomy through graph-based ranking. Multimedia Tools Appl. **75**(15), 8875–8893 (2014). https://doi.org/10.1007/s11042-014-2303-9
22. Nagarajan, R., Nair, A.H.S., Aruna, P.: Keyword extraction using graph based approach. Int. J. Adv. Res. Comput. Sci. Softw. Eng. **6**, 25–29 (2016)
23. Song, H.-J., Go, J., Park, S.-B., Park, S.-Y., Kim, K.Y.: A just-in-time keyword extraction from meeting transcripts using temporal and participant information. J. Intell. Inf. Syst. **48**(1), 117–140 (2016). https://doi.org/10.1007/s10844-015-0391-2
24. Meng, R., Zhao, S., Han, S., et al.: Deep keyphrase generation. In: Proceedings of ACL, pp. 582–592 (2017)
25. Zhang, Y., Xiao, W.: Keyphrase generation based on deep seq2seq model. IEEE Access **6**, 46047–46057 (2018)

Adversarial Defense Networks via Gaussian Noise and RBF

Jingjie Li[1], Jiaquan Gao[1](✉), Qi Jiang[1], and Guixia He[2]

[1] School of Computer and Electronic Information, Nanjing Normal University, Nanjing 210023, China

[2] Zhijiang College, Zhejiang University of Technology, Hangzhou 310024, China

Abstract. Convolutional Neural Networks (CNNs) have excellent representative power and are state-of-the-art classifiers on many tasks. However, CNNs are vulnerable to adversarial examples, which are samples with imperceptible perturbations while dramatically misleading the CNNs. It has been found that, in past studies, Radial Basis Function (RBF) network can effectively reduce the linearization of the neural networks model, and Gaussian noise injection can prevent the network from overfitting, all of which are conducive for defending against adversarial examples. In this paper, we propose an incorporated defense method with Gaussian noise injection and RBF network, and analytically investigate the robustness mechanism of incorporated defense method. For our proposed method, it has the following two advantages: (1) it has significant classification accuracy, and (2) it can resist to various adversarial attacks effectively. The experimental results show the proposed method achieves the performance of about 79.25% accuracy on MNIST dataset and 43.87% accuracy on Fashion-MNIST dataset, even in the full white-box attack where attackers can craft malicious adversarial examples from defense models.

Keywords: Adversarial examples · RBF · Gaussian noise

1 Introduction

CNNs have recently outperformed machine learning methods in various tasks, such as image classification [1–3], object detection [4–6], and speech recognition [7–9]. However, like many classification machine learning algorithms, deep learning methods can be easily fooled by small imperceptible perturbations in the input [10]. The main reason may be that the linear classifier is used at the last layer of deep learning methods. Although linear classifiers are very effective for the linear classification, they force the model to assign high confidence to these regions far from the decision boundary. Thus the adversarial attack can easily

The research has been supported by the Natural Science Foundation of China under grant number 61872422, and the Natural Science Foundation of Zhejiang Province, China under great number LY19F020028.

X. Sun et al. (Eds.): ICAIS 2021, LNCS 12736, pp. 494–504, 2021.
https://doi.org/10.1007/978-3-030-78609-0_42

make some changes in multiple dimensions of the input image, which makes the perturbed images cross the classification boundary. The perturbed images are misclassified by the network in the end.

In order to mitigate the effect of adversarial attacks, the following two kinds of defense techniques are proposed: data-level method and algorithmic-level method. The former includes adversarial training [11,12], pre-processing methods using basis functions [13] and noise removal [14]. The later can be seen in literatures [15–20], and the deep model is modified or the algorithm is trained by reducing the magnitude of gradients [17], or masking gradient [18]. However, these approaches are not completely effective against several different white-box and black-box attacks [14]. Similar to the methods based on pre-processing, they may decrease accuracy to defense some attacks. Generally, most of these defense strategies make the classification accuracy descend on clean data.

As mentioned above, successful adversarial attacks are mainly due to that fact that the models are linearly high in high dimension. This greatly decreases the flexibility of the models and makes the decision boundary close to the manifolds of the training data. In order to improve the nonlinearity of the model, Goodfellow et al. [11] have explored a variety of methods, including shallow and deep RBF networks. They used the shallow RBF network to achieve good performance against adversarial perturbations. However, they found that it was difficult to train the deep RBF network.

In this paper, we explore the incorporated network model with the deep neural network and RBF network, which not only ensures that the network model can effectively resist perturbations, but also makes the network model be trained easily. Meanwhile, small noise is added before the network input, which improves the robustness of the network attack and resists the white-box and black-box attack effectively.

2 Related Work

2.1 Adversarial Examples

The adversarial examples were first introduced by Szegedy et al. [12]. Szegedy et al. show that the prediction of the network can be changed arbitrarily by applying imperceptible non-random perturbations to the input image. The malicious input is $X' = X + \alpha$ and α is a lightly perturbation with $\|\alpha\| < \epsilon$, where ϵ is so small that it makes no visual difference between X and X' for human being but deep neural networks will be fooled.

In addition, Szegedy et al. point out that the adversarial examples are relatively robust and can be generalized in neural networks with different depths and activation functions. In other words, if we use one neural network to generate the adversarial examples, another neural network also misclassifies these examples even when it is trained with different hyper-parameters, or when it is trained on different subset of a dataset. This phenomenon makes the black-box attacks feasible.

Finally, Szegedy et al. also state that it is linear transformation of high-dimensional space of the model that leads to the phenomenon of adversarial examples, and proposes the Fast Gradient Sign Method (FGSM) for crafting adversarial examples. FGSM is an untargeted attack method and uses the same attack strength at every dimension:

$$X_{FGSM} = X + \varepsilon sign\left(\bigtriangledown_X J\left(X, y\right)\right). \tag{1}$$

In this equation, the adversarial examples are obtained by adding a transformed gradient to the input X, where ε is small enough to be undetectable.

2.2 Gaussian Noise

In the space domain and frequency domain, Gaussian noise (also known as normal noise) is commonly used. The probability density function of the Gaussian random variable Z is given by the following formula:

$$p\left(Z\right) = \frac{1}{\sqrt{2\pi}\sigma} e^{-\frac{(Z-\bar{Z})^2}{2\sigma^2}}, \tag{2}$$

where Z is the gray value, and its mean and deviation are $\bar{Z}$ and σ, respectively.

The perturbation is extremely small in general in order to get a normal example. In [21], Gu and Rigazio consider an alternative strategy by adding Gaussian noise damage into the adversarial examples. The aim of this additional noise strategy is to remove the adversarial examples "blind spot" areas of the classification space through adding extra "larger" interference noise to the input. Moreover, adding the ordinary tiny perturbation does not have a impact on the performance of the neural network. Experimental results show that the Gaussian noise injection can defend against samples to some extent.

2.3 RBF

RBF networks [22–24] are neural networks with one hidden layer of RBF units and a linear output layer. An RBF unit is a neuron with multiple real input $X = (X_1, \cdots, X_n)$ and one output y. Each unit is determined by n-dimensional vector C and the parameter $\beta > 0$. The output y is computed as:

$$y = \varphi\left(\xi\right); \xi = \beta \left\|X - C\right\|^2, \tag{3}$$

where $\varphi : \mathbf{R} \rightarrow \mathbf{R}$ is the suitable activation function. Typically, Gaussian $\varphi\left(Z\right) = e^{-z^2}$. Thus the network computes the following function $f : \mathbf{R}^n \rightarrow \mathbf{R}^n$:

$$f_s\left(X\right) = \sum_{j=1}^{h} \omega_{ij} \varphi\left(\beta_j \left\|X - C_j\right\|\right), \tag{4}$$

where $\omega_{ij} \in \mathbf{R}$ and f_s is the output of the sth output unit.

Compared with normal networks, RBF networks use radial basis function units at the last layer. Unlike the linear unit, RBF unit is activated in a well-defined region of its input space [25]. In this case, the goal of the feature extractor network is to map the data to a new representation, where each kind of data forms a cluster. Experimental results show that when RBF is combined with CNN, it can effectively resist the disturbance.

3 Method

3.1 Model

Inspired by the defense methods in [21,25], we combine the data-level defense method with the algorithm-level defense method, and propose an incorporated model with Gaussian noise injection and RBF network on neural networks. Noth that the network can be any CNN (see Fig. 1).

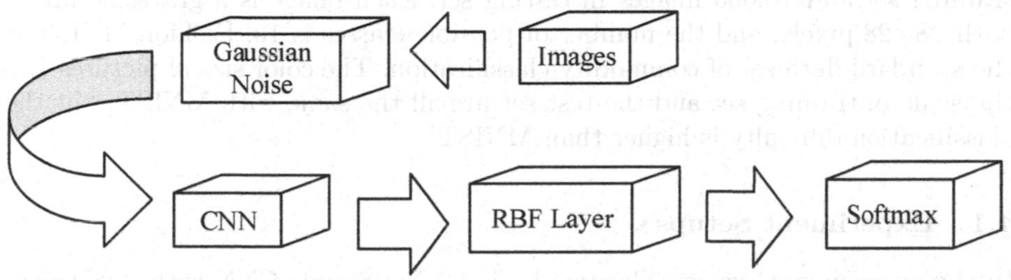

Fig. 1. The incorporated network model.

Here we take the classic Lenet-5 [26] network as the example to demonstrate the proposed model (see Fig. 2). In this figure, the LeNet-5 network structure is in the dashed box, and before the image input into the LeNet-5 network, the tiny Gaussian noise is added to the image. After the feature extraction and the classification through LeNet-5 network, the output of LeNet-5 is set as the input into the RBF network. The RBF output is the final classification result of our proposed model.

3.2 Loss Function

When training the proposed model, we calculate the loss of the final output and use the cross-entropy loss function, the loss is computed as:

$$Loss = loss\left(\hat{y}, y\right) \tag{5}$$

$$loss = -\sum_{i=1}^{N} y_i log\left(\hat{y_i}\right) + \left(1 - y_i\right) log\left(1 - \hat{y_i}\right), \tag{6}$$

where $\hat{y}$ is the final output of the proposed model and y is the true label.

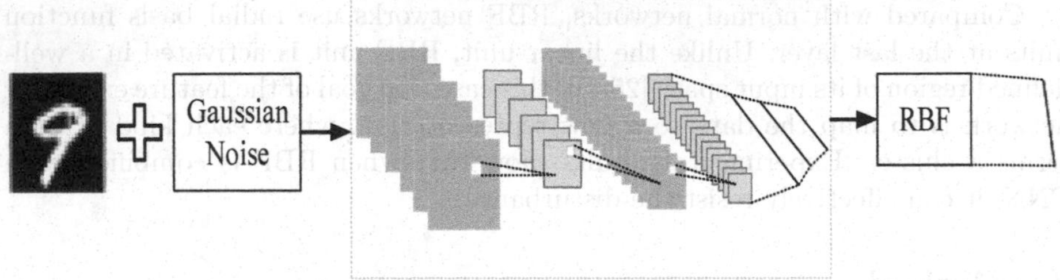

Fig. 2. The incorporated network model based on LeNet-5.

4 Experiments

These experiments in this paper are based on two benchmark datasets: MNIST [26] and Fashion-MNIST [27]. MNIST contains 60,000 images in the training set and 10,000 images in testing set. Each image is a grayscale image with 28×28 pixels, and the number of possible classes is 10. Fashion-MNIST is the standard data set of commodity classification. The color size of pictures and the scale of training set and the test set are all the same with MNIST, but the classification difficulty is higher than MNIST.

4.1 Experiment Setups

In the experiments, we consider two basic CNNs: Simple-CNN with two convolutional layers (S-CNN) and LeNet-5. The activation function in each network is RELU and loss function is the cross-entropy function. The detailed model structure and the parameter information are shown in Table 1, and Table 2 contains the chosen training hyper-parameters for all models.

In order to verify the superiority of the proposed model, the following three defense methods are chosen: the basic CNN model, the CNN model combined with RBF network (CNN_RBF) [25] and the centers are set as 300 in RBF network, and a CNN model incorporating Gaussian noise (Gauss_CNN) [21] with standard deviation $\sigma = 0.3$ on MNIST and Fashion-MNIST.

Moreover, five test sets are set in the defense experiments. For the network based on S-CNN, we first set the 10,000 clean test set images of the MNIST dataset as Test Set I. We then generate adversarial examples test sets by attacking four models(S-CNN, S-CNN_RBF, Gauss_S-CNN, the proposed model), which are set as Test Sets from II to V. For the network based on LeNet-5, two benchmark datasets, MNIST and Fashion-MNIST, are chosen. For each dataset, the same numbers of the clean test set images are set in Test Set I. Finally, we generate adversarial examples test sets by attacking four models (LeNet-5, LeNet-5_RBF, Gauss_LeNet-5, the proposed model), which are set as Test Sets from II to V.

Table 1. Network model parameters.

LeNet-5	Parameters	S-CNN	Parameters
Conv.	32, 5 × 5	Conv.	32, 3 × 3
Max Pooling	2 × 2	Max Pooling	2 × 2
Conv.	64, 5 × 5	Conv.	64, 3 × 3
Max Pooling	2 × 2	Max Pooling	2 × 2
Full Connection	1024	Full Connection	128
Softmax	10	Softmax	10

Table 2. Overview of training parameters.

	S-CNN	LeNet-5
Learning Rate	0.01	0.01
Optimizer	Adam	Adam
Batch Size	128	128
Epochs	20	20

4.2 Experiment Results

In this section, we report the results of several experiments for the task of classification. We first start with S-CNN model on MNIST. Next, the proposed method is applicable to another classical model LeNet-5 on MNIST and Fashion-MNIST. A series of adversarial examples of each test set are generated by FGSM attack, as shown in Fig. 3.

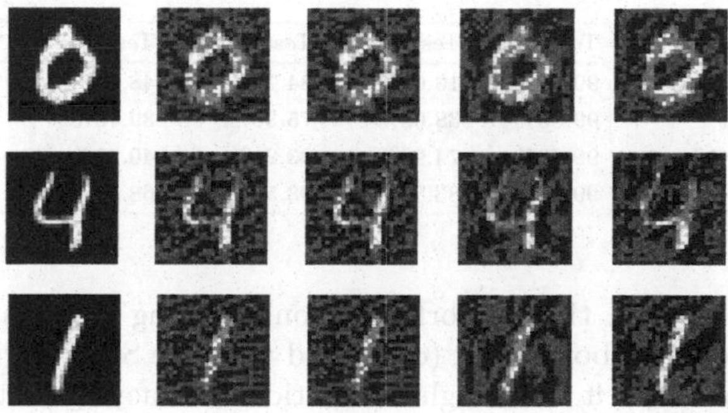

Fig. 3. An illustration of each test set. In this figure, the leftmost column displays the original images, and the next four columns show adversarial examples corresponding to Test Set II, III, IV and V from left to right.

S-CNN. In this section, we compare the recognition accuracy of the four network models in each dataset and the experimental results are shown in Table 3.

Observing the data of the first column (Test Set I) in Table 3, the proposed network model does not drop the accuracy significantly on clean images. That is, Gaussian noise can prevent the network model from overfitting, and the interference of Gaussian noise is equivalent to the data augmentation of the original dataset. From Test Set II to Test Set V, the diagonal data indicate the recognition accuracy of each network model under the white-box attack. Compared with these diagonal data, the performance of S-CNN_RBF and Gauss_S-CNN against white-box attack are improved, especially the improvement effect of S-CNN_RBF is obvious, which is more than 65% higher than S-CNN. Therefore, adding the RBF network after the softmax layer of basic network can greatly improve its robustness. This is due to that fact that the strong local approximation ability of RBF network successfully makes the basic model S-CNN better fit the real decision boundary and compress the adversarial space, and thus the basic mode with RBF can be against the white-box attack effectively. Furthermore, the data in the Test Set II show that defensive performance of four models can be against the black-box attack. Obviously, although S-CNN_RBF model has higher performance against the white-box attack, the defense performance against the black-box attack is still only about 30%. This is due to the fact that the adversarial examples of Test Set II are generated by the original model, and the adversarial examples have the ability to migrate across model. Therefore, utilizing RBF network can resist the white-box attack, though it cannot be against the migration attack effectively. The migration attack is defined as the attack that uses other network against vulnerabilities to generate adversarial examples of the space, and use its migration ability against unknown network.

Table 3. Experimental results based on S-CNN model on MNIST dataset.

	Test Set I	Test Set II	Test Set III	Test Set IV	Test Set V
S-CNN	99.14%	10.69%	84.70%	48.80%	79.16%
S-CNN+RBF	99.00%	38.08%	75.36%	39.70%	75.58%
Gauss+S-CNN	99.20%	74.90%	93.21%	40.23%	84.31%
Gauss+S-CNN+RBF	99.13%	83.80%	93.55%	68.77%	79.25%

In addition, though the network with only adding Gaussian noise is not ideal against the white-box attack (compared with the S-CNN, there is only an increase of about 30%), it has a high recognition accuracy against the black-box attack, which increases by more than 70%. This is because the perturbations are extremely small, and there is a "blind spot" area in the input space of the image. Using extra noise to images can undermine the dominance against perturbations. In this way, adversarial examples can be removed from the "blind spot" to obtain correct classification. Meanwhile, the extra noise will have less impact on the performance of neural network. From the last line in the Table 3, we can observe that the incorporated model with Gaussian noise and RBF network can promote each other. Compared with other defense model against the white-box attack and the black-box attack, the defense performance of the proposed model has improved effectively. From the Test Set I to Test Set V, the proposed model almost keeps the superiority. In conclusion, the proposed network structure has better robustness against the white-box and black-box attacks.

LeNet-5. Another classic network model, Lenet-5, is used in this section, and experiments are carried out on two datasets: MNIST and Fashion-MNIST datasets. The detailed defense performance on the MNIST and Fashion-MNIST is reported in Table 4 and Table 5, respectively.

Table 4. Experimental results based on LeNet-5 model on MNIST dataset.

	Test Set I	Test Set II	Test Set III	Test Set IV	Test Set V
LeNet-5	99.19%	16.86%	59.28%	33.67%	57.37%
LeNet-5+RBF	98.82%	34.57%	42.90%	31.37%	53.40%
Gauss+LeNet-5	98.67%	86.38%	92.23%	36.34%	83.16%
Gauss+LeNet-5+RBF	99.08%	82.25%	92.12%	69.03%	71.16%

Observing the data reported in Table 4, the same conclusions as in S-CNN are obtained. The diagonal data from Test Set II to Test Set V represent those defense models performance against the white-box attack. In addition, the data from Test Set II to Test Set V except diagonal are the performance of each defense model against the black-box attack. Though data analysis, LeNet-5_RBF has a better defense performance against the white-box attack, while Gauss_LeNet-5 has better performance against the black-box attack. The proposed model incorporated the merits of them has better defense performance both in two aspect of against white-box and black-box attacks. Obviously, the proposed model based on LeNet-5 has a recognition accuracy of over 70% on each adversarial examples test set.

Table 5. Experimental results based on LeNet-5 model on Fashion-MNIST dataset.

	Test Set I	Test Set II	Test Set III	Test Set IV	Test Set V
LeNet-5	91.43%	11.18%	31.90%	12.86%	28.46%
LeNet-5+RBF	90.72%	32.43%	30.20%	15.72%	33.98%
Gauss+LeNet-5	89.31%	57.88%	72.81%	8.94%	56.28%
Gauss+LeNet-5+RBF	88.96%	58.03%	73.07%	20.18%	43.87%

Observing data in Table 5, the improvement is not so obvious in the Fashion-MNIST dataset compared with the MNIST dataset, but the improvement trend in each defense model is consistent with MNIST dataset. Like LeNet-5_RBF, it is helpful to enhance the robustness of the model and the defense ability against the white-box attack. The average defensive performance of the Gauss_LeNet-5 against black-box attack is about 60%. And the proposed incorporated model on MNIST dataset is slightly better than it on Fashion-MNIST dataset. However, Gauss_LeNet-5 and the proposed model defense accuracy have a drop in the clean test set. This phenomenon is due to that fact that Fashion-MNIST dataset is more complicated than MNIST dataset. Adding Gaussian noise on Fashion-MNIST dataset has a impact on classification task. The recognition accuracy in the fourth column of the Table 5 on each network in the Test Set IV is less than 20%. The reason may be that images in Test Set I are generated by attacking the Gauss_LeNet-5 model, and the incorporated noise is larger compared to original image. Therefore these noises make the models have low accuracy in the classification task. However, the consistent trend of ascension on Test Set IV again indicates that the incorporated model structure is effective in defense adversarial examples.

In summary, compared the defense performance with other three models against white-box and black-box attacks, the proposed model can defend adversarial examples effectively on Fashion-MNIST.

5 Conclusion

In this paper, we propose an incorporated defense method with Gaussian noise and RBF network. The experimental results show that the proposed method can effectively be against the adversarial examples in the white-box and black-box attacks. Furthermore, compared with other methods, the proposed method effectively improves the classification accuracy on adversarial images, and does not drop the accuracy significantly on clean images.

References

1. He, K., Zhang, X., Ren, S., Sun, J.: Deep residual learning for image recognition. In: Proceeding of the IEEE Conference on Computer Vision and Pattern Recognition, pp. 770–778. IEEE, Las Vegas (2016)
2. Zoph, B., Vasudevan, V., Shlens J., Le, Q.V.: Learning transferable architectures for scalable image recognition. In: Proceeding of the IEEE Conference on Computer Vision and Pattern Recognition, pp. 8697–8710. IEEE, Salt Lake City (2018)
3. Cao, Y.Q., Tan, C., Ji, G.L.: A multi-label classification method for vehicle video. J. Big Data **2**(1), 19–31 (2020)
4. Ren, S., He, K., Girshick, R.B., Sun, J.: Faster R-CNN: towards real-time object detection with region proposal networks. Adv. Neural. Inf. Process. Syst. **39**(6), 1137–1149 (2017)
5. He, K., Gkioxari, G., Dollár, P., Girshick, R.B.: Mask R-CNN. In: Proceedings of the IEEE International Conference on Computer Vision, pp. 2980–2988. IEEE, Venice (2017)
6. Qayyum, A., Ahmad, I., Iftikhar, M., Mazher, M.: Object detection and fuzzy-based classification using UAV data. Intell. Autom. Soft Co. **26**(4), 693–702 (2020)

7. Bahdanau, D., Chorowski, J., Serdyuk, D., Brakel, P., Bengio, Y.: End-to-end attention-based large vocabulary speech recognition. In: IEEE International Conference on Acoustics, pp. 4945–4949. IEEE, Shanghai (2016)
8. Chiu, C.C., et al.: State-of-the-art speech recognition with sequence-to-sequence models. In: IEEE International Conference on Acoustics, Speech and Signal Processing (ICASSP), pp. 4774–4778. IEEE, Calgary (2018)
9. Park, J., Kim, S.: Noise cancellation based on voice activity detection using spectral variation for speech recognition in smart home devices. Intell. Autom. Soft Co. **26**(1), 149–159 (2020)
10. Nguyen, A.M., Yosinski, J., Clune, J.: Deep neural networks are easily fooled: high confidence predictions for unrecognizable images. In: IEEE Conference on Computer Vision and Pattern Recognition (CVPR), pp. 427–436. IEEE Computer Society, Boston (2015)
11. Goodfellow, I.J., Shlens, J., Szegedy, C.: Explaining and harnessing adversarial examples. In: 3rd International Conference on Learning Representations (ICLR). San Diego, CA, USA (2015) arXiv:1412.6572. Accessed 20 Mar 2015
12. Szegedy, C., et al.: Intriguing properties of neural networks. In: 2nd International Conference on Learning Representations (ICLR). Banff, AB, Canada (2014). arXiv:1312.6199. Accessed 19 Feb 2014
13. Xu, W., Evans, D., Qi, Y.: Feature squeezing: detecting adversarial examples in deep neural networks. In: 25th Annual Network and Distributed System Security Symposium (NDSS). The Internet Society, San Diego, California, USA (2017). arXiv:1704.01155. Accessed 5 Dec 2017
14. Meng, D., Chen, H.: MagNet: a two-pronged defense against adversarial examples. In: Proceeding of the 2017 ACM SIGSAC Conference on Computer and Communications Security, pp. 135–147. ACM, New York (2017)
15. Folz, J., Palacio, S., Hees, J., Dengel, A.: Adversarial defense based on structure-to-signal autoencoders. In: 2020 IEEE Winter Conference on Applications of Computer Vision (WACV), pp. 3568–3577. IEEE, Snowmass Village (2020)
16. Wong, E., Kolter, J.Z.: Provable Defenses against Adversarial Examples via the Convex Outer Adversarial Polytope. In: International Conference on Machine Learning (ICML), pp. 5283–5292. PMLR, Stockholmsmässan, Stockholm, Sweden (2018)
17. Papernot, N., McDaniel, P.D., Wu, X., Jha, S., Swami, A.: Distillation as a defense to adversarial perturbations against deep neural networks. In: 2016 IEEE Symposium on Security and Privacy (SP), pp. 582–597. IEEE Computer Society, San Jose (2018)
18. Buckman, J., Roy, A., Raffel, C., Goodfellow, I.J.: Thermometer encoding: one hot way to resist adversarial examples. In: 6th International Conference on Learning Representations (ICLR). OpenReview.net, Vancouver (2018). https://openreview.net/forum?id=rJUYGxbCW. Accessed 16 Feb 2018
19. Zhang, J., Wang, J.: A survey on adversarial example. J. Inf. Hiding Privacy Protect. **2**(1), 47–57 (2020)
20. Chen, H., Zhu, H.Q., Yan, L.M., Wang, J.W.: A survey on adversarial examples in deep learning. J. Big Data **2**(2), 71–84 (2020)
21. Gu, S., Rigazio, L.: Towards deep neural network architectures robust to adversarial examples. In: 3rd International Conference on Learning Representations (ICLR). San Diego, CA, USA (2015). arXiv:1412.5068. Accessed 9 Apr 2015
22. Peng, J.X., Li, K., Irwin, G.W.: A novel continuous forward algorithm for RBF neural modelling. IEEE T. Automat. Contr. **52**(1), 117–122 (2007)

23. Moody, J.E., Darken, C.J.: Fast learning in networks of locally-tuned processing units. Neural Comput. **1**(2), 281–294 (1989)
24. Broomhead, D.S., Lowe, D.: Multivariable functional interpolation and adaptive networks. Complex Syst. **2**(3), 321–355 (1988)
25. Vidnerová, P., Neruda, R.: Deep networks with RBF layers to prevent adversarial examples. In: Rutkowski, L., Scherer, R., Korytkowski, M., Pedrycz, W., Tadeusiewicz, R., Zurada, J.M. (eds.) ICAISC 2018. LNCS (LNAI), vol. 10841, pp. 257–266. Springer, Cham (2018). https://doi.org/10.1007/978-3-319-91253-0_25
26. LeCun, Y., Bottou, L., Bengio, Y., Haffner, P.: Gradient-based learning applied to document recognition. P. IEEE **86**(11), 2278–2324 (1998)
27. Han, X., Kashif, R., Roland, V.: Fashion-mnist: a novel image dataset for benchmarking machine learning algorithms. arXiv:1708.07747. Accessed 15 Sept 2017

Intelligent Detection and Early Warning System of Railway Track

Yunzuo Zhang(✉) and Wei Guo

Shijiazhuang Tiedao University, Shijiazhuang 050043, China
zhangyunzuo888@sina.com

Abstract. Rail trains are an indispensable part of the transportation, so technological innovations such as artificial intelligence will inevitably promote the overall development of unmanned driving technology in this field, how to ensure the safety of unmanned trains is related to intelligent rail detection technology is very important, such as the detection of foreign body intrusion on rails, turnouts, curved rails, etc. These technologies have become the basic technology of rail train automatic driving technology. This paper divides the key technology of rail intelligent detection into three parts, and conducts in-depth analysis and research from these three aspects: curved track detection and warning module, turnout detection and warning module, obstacle detection and warning module, and combined with the actual needs of each module, Continuously through experiments, choose more suitable and optimal algorithms to achieve and then integrate the module algorithms to achieve the synchronization of the work between each module without interfering with each other, and design and implement the intelligent rail detection and early warning system to enhance the interactive experience. According to the functional requirements of different modules of the system, this paper selects core algorithms such as curvature radius, Hough transforms and frame difference method to improve each module, and verifies the feasibility of the selected algorithm.

Keywords: Curvature radius · Hough probability transformation · Frame difference method

1 Introduction

The traditional railway system includes an intelligent flaw detection system of railway track, foreign matter intrusion detection system of railway train, etc. The obstacle recognition system of the train based on video image recognition technology can realize the automatic detection of obstacles in the track of the direction of the man-less driving [1–3]. For the railway intelligent detection and warning system, several aspects of the technology should be integrated, such as track bending detection, switch detection, obstacle detection, track tracking, and critical warning. This technique depends on the image recognition processing technology, the realization of synchronous detection and warning of train operation process, namely in the procession of the train, the system can

X. Sun et al. (Eds.): ICAIS 2021, LNCS 12736, pp. 505–515, 2021.
https://doi.org/10.1007/978-3-030-78609-0_43

real-time detect the status of the current train lines on the road ahead, if there are any curved rail line, the front rail or obstacles ahead, pay timely treatment and early warning system. Of course, this technology requires a fixed HD camera installed in front of the train to obtain real-time data. The image processing technology is targeted at the acquired image data set for batch processing to achieve fast and accurate results.

The intelligent railway detection and warning technology firstly capture the railway image of the road in front of the train, that is, the track where the train is located, through the high-definition camera in front of the train [4–7]. The captured images are transmitted to the system in real time, through the intelligent detection warning system tracks in recognition of the front rails in the captured image information and extract tracks, and then through the steel rail has been extracted from the point of equal extract, a fitting method for quadratic fitting after they conform to the curvature of the two tracks curve, and then use curvature radius calculation method to calculate two curve radius of curvature, within the scope of a value, not curved track, beyond count curved track; Based on the two curves, Hough transform method is used to detect all the lines outside a certain slope range, to judge whether there is a switch. For the detection of obstacles, the frame difference method is used to detect whether there is an obstacle contour, and the area ratio method is used to judge whether there is an obstacle.

The core modules are as follows:

(1) Curved track detection and warning module
This process is only given the current train tracks recognition, so the interested region is obtained by image segmentation image, through the perspective transformation image correction, after using Sobel gradient operator combination of adaptive threshold method in orbit, extraction pixel through sliding window technology, according to these pixels are quadratic fitting, finally calculate the radius of curvature of the fitted curve, according to the radius of curvature threshold relation judgment curved track, then the warning.
(2) Switch detection and warning module
The process is the switch testing process, because only need to consider the train's rail switch, so we want to is obtained by image segmentation of interested area, and then through the Hough way detection probability, transform interested area exists Hough line, calculation of the detected line slope, after many tests to get a range of slope, filtered according to the size of the slope, screening to within the range of straight line is the switch.
(3) Obstacle detection and warning module

First of all, the obstacles that a train can encounter are much less diverse than those that a car can encounter, and the probability of encountering them is also quite small. Therefore, the detection of obstacles in front of the train is not very difficult. With the development of video monitoring, the intelligent monitoring algorithm has been gradually improved [8]. The moving target detection algorithm is mainly used in intelligent monitoring. In the moving target detection algorithm, the traditional algorithm has disadvantages such as inaccurate detection results and low anti-interference performance [9]. Moving target detection is one of the emphases and difficulties in the field of computer vision and image processing. It is the foundation of moving target tracking and behavior recognition. Frame difference method, background difference method, and the optical flow method are several common methods for moving target detection [9]. In this module, the frame difference method, a commonly used and easy to use an algorithm, is used to detect the obstacle, and then the contour area of the obstacle in the image is calculated through contour detection, and then the ratio of the contour area to the image area is obtained. Based on this ratio, whether the existing obstacle will affect the train can be judged, and then an early warning is issued. The flow chart of railway intelligent detection and warning technology is shown in Fig. 1.

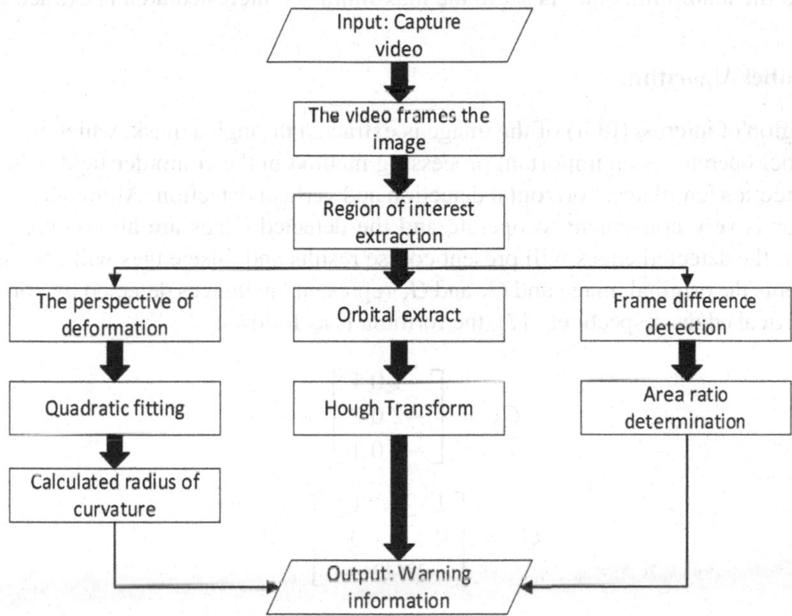

Fig. 1. Flow chart of railway intelligent detection and early warning technology

2 Intelligent Detection Technology

2.1 Perspective Transform

Perspective transformation is the process of projecting an image onto the original plane and mapping it to the desired visual plane. The principle of perspective transformation is to transform the three-dimensional model of an image in the three-dimensional space [10–13]. Because the train track to be tested in this paper is on the track plane, and the camera captured images in the three dimensional approximate horizontal and vertical plane, then on the research content of this article, for a rail line detection especially curved track rail will there is a certain error or mistake, so this article will need to track image perspective transformation, projection mapping to the camera to capture images of 3D plane, can be roughly understanding to the rail line formed in the form of a bird's eye view, thus processing rail have many conveniences.

2.2 Region of Interest Extraction

The region of interest (ROI) of the image is extracted through a mask, which is actually a binary image [14], with a maximum value of 255 and a minimum value of 0. In this paper, the mask value of the region of interest is set as the maximum value, and the mask value of the non-region of interest is set as the minimum value, then the region of interest is extracted. Define the interested region we usually adopt is to draw the rectangle, which we will in advance, we want to interested in the area of four coordinates, according to the coordinates at four, after the mask with matrix, surrounded by four coordinate areas is set to the minimum, other is set to the maximum, so interested area is extracted.

2.3 Sobel Algorithm

The region of interest (ROI) of the image is extracted through a mask, which is actually a b Sobel operator is an important processing method in the computer field, which has two detection templates: horizontal detection and vertical detection. Although the Sobel operator is very convenient to operate and the detected edges are all continuous and smooth, the detected edges will present coarse results and false edges will appear. If A represents the original image and G_x and G_y represent the images detected by horizontal and vertical edges respectively [7], the formula is as follows:

$$G_X = \begin{bmatrix} -1\,0\,1 \\ -2\,0\,2 \\ -1\,0\,1 \end{bmatrix} + A \tag{1}$$

$$G_Y = \begin{bmatrix} 1 & 2 & 1 \\ 0 & 0 & 0 \\ -1 & -2 & -1 \end{bmatrix} + A \tag{2}$$

The approximate value of the horizontal and vertical gradient of each pixel of the image is calculated as follows.

$$G = \sqrt{G_X^2 + G_Y^2} \tag{3}$$

Finally, the direction of the gradient is calculated.

$$\theta = \tan^{-1}\left(\frac{G_X}{G_Y}\right) \tag{4}$$

3 Bend Detection

3.1 Quadratic Fit

Curve fitting is essentially the dynamic approximation of data points, that is, the trajectory modeling of logarithmic data points. With this fitting function, future trend prediction and system performance analysis can be carried out on the data. Suppose the fitting equation is a quadratic curve: y = ax + bx + c, the data point (x_i, y_i) is known, I = 1,2…N. The mean square error of the approximate fitting curve is

$$Q(a,b,c) = \sum_{i=1}^{n} \left(ax_i^2 + bx_i + c - y_i\right)^2 \tag{5}$$

Take the derivative of the above equation and you get the coefficients of the quadratic fitting curve equation,

$$\begin{cases} a = \frac{D_a}{D} \\ b = \frac{D_b}{D} \\ c = \frac{D_c}{D} \end{cases} \tag{6}$$

When you figure out the coefficients of the quadratic function you get the quadratic function. In the above paper, the data set of orbital line points has been obtained. Then, the data can be fitted into a quadratic curve. Do the same for each frame, and you get a quadratic fitting of a continuous trajectory.

3.2 Calculate Radius of Curvature

Through the study of on-board video images, the track detection template is constructed, and the calculation of the curvature of the track is realized through regional growth and curve fitting, which can automatically detect the minimum radius of curvature of the track in front of the train and provide the driver with early warning function to ensure the safe operation of the train [15]. If we know the quadratic fitting equation y = $a*y*y+b*y+c$ of the orbital line, then at y meters away, the radius of curvature is calculated as follows:

$$R = \frac{\left(1+(x')^2\right)^{1.5}}{x''} = \frac{\left(1+(2ay+b)^2\right)^{1.5}}{2a} \tag{7}$$

4 Detect Fork in the Road

4.1 Hough Probability Transformation

Probabilistic Hough transformation is an updated version of Hoff linear transformation, which has good experimental results and is relatively simple to use [9]. Probabilistic Hough transform with past Hoff differed from the linear transformation, Hoff linear transformation will detect all lines in the image are extracted, no matter how long is the line, just as a straight line will reveal it, and there will be a threshold limit Hoff probability transformation, if detection lines will there be greater than the threshold line exists, so will the linear filter do not say, but only for those who are less than the threshold of the straight line segment is used to identify the corresponding logo, only record the start and endpoints of these segments. As long as the above steps are repeated in this article, all line segments that meet the requirements in an image can be identified.

5 Obstacle Detection

5.1 Frame Difference Method

The video stream captured by the camera must be continuous. If there is no moving target in a particular scene, then there will be very subtle changes between successive frames in the video stream. If there is a moving target, then the chances of successive frames in the video stream will be obvious. Frame difference method, namely the frame difference method, takes advantage of this feature and subtracts the pixels corresponding to different frames to obtain the absolute value of gray difference [16–18]. When this gray value is greater than the given threshold value, this paper can regard it as a moving target, so as to realize the function of detecting moving targets.

On the train track video sequence, this paper use of frame differential method, although the scene is a moment transformation rather than a fixed, because this article will extract the interested region video sequences, and for the tracks, change between consecutive frames is not very big, in this paper, by setting the threshold to filter out these changes, so when foreign invasion on the track, the algorithm can be detected quickly.

5.2 Set the Area Ratio T Threshold

Obstacle detection and the warning is ultimately to achieve the purpose of the warning. There should be no false alarms. Unlike the warning of curved rails and switches, the warning of obstacles means that there may be danger ahead, so false alarms should be avoided as far as possible. As mentioned above, in the process of detecting foreign bodies by frame difference method, there is slight noise caused by orbital changes. However, after setting a threshold value in this paper, these noises can be ignored without false positives.

6 Experiment

6.1 The Design of Experimental

According to the functional architecture requirements of the system, different modules of the system have strong independence. Except that the video frame conversion module is the basis of other modules, the remaining three modules can run independently without interference. According to this characteristic, this article uses the multi-threaded way of working. The system can be divided into four threads.

Since each module of the system has its own independence, the integrated system can not cause great conflicts between modules, and each module should be run at the same time. Therefore, it is necessary to establish a good thread relationship between each module of the system. The details are as follows:

(1) Storage and reading threads of files: including the access to intermediate processing results of programs such as curved rail detection, switch detection and obstacle detection, and the reading of image files generated and processed finally;
(2) Curved track detection thread: including sliding window detection, quadratic fitting, and calculation of the radius of curvature after track extraction;
(3) Switch detection thread: it includes the function of extracting the region of interest in the image frame and Hough probability transformation to detect the existence of line segments in the image frame.
(4) Obstacle detection thread: including the function of detecting the frame difference method of the continuous frame image extracted from the track and determining the obstacle by the area ratio of the detection results;

The multi-threaded workflow of the system is shown in Fig. 2.

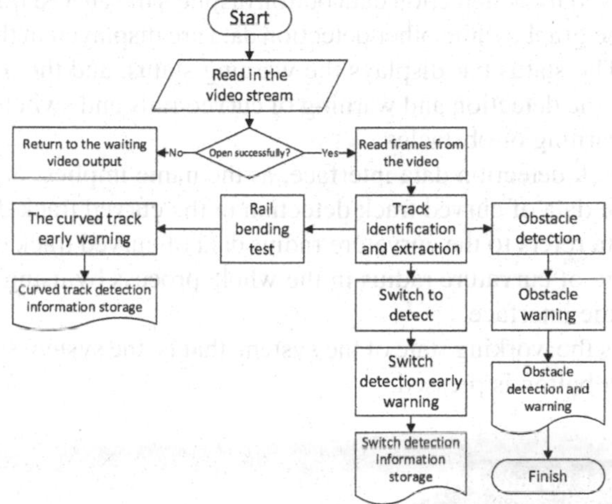

Fig. 2. The system flow chart

6.2 The Experimental Results and Analysis

In this paper, the research and experiment of intelligent railway identification and detection and early warning technology are carried out, and a detection and early warning system is designed through the research and experiment. According to the actual needs of system design and combining with the reality, the framework of railway intelligent detection technology is formulated, and appropriate methods and technologies are selected to realize the included functional modules, so as to achieve the expected effect as far as possible. The work described in this article is as follows:

(1) Intelligence advanced research analyzes the track key technology required for the detection of early warning as well as the basic framework, realizes the intelligent detection of the tracks, each module detailed research and analysis of methods and

techniques, including rail bending test, switch the key techniques and algorithms needed for the detection and obstacle detection, and through continuous experiments verify the feasibility of the algorithm.

(2) According to the specific requirements of railway intelligent detection and warning system design, the overall framework and modules of the system are designed linearly, and then the railway intelligent detection and warning system is implemented based on Python and PYQT to give users an intuitive experience.

In the main interface, through the button operating system-related functions, the start button operates the entire system to start operation, that is, to read in the image data captured by the camera, and the system curved track, turnout, obstacle detection function multi-threaded execution, real-time display; The stop button controls the entire system to stop working; The button of curved track detection data and other detection data is available only if the start button is pressed, otherwise, these two buttons are not available. The curved track detection data button displays the curved track detection data in the form of a line graph, while other detection data are displayed in the form of picture processing data. The status bar displays the warning status, and the light is on. Yellow lights are used for the detection and warning of curved rails and switches, and red lights are used for the warning of obstacles.

The curved track detection data interface, as the name implies, is to facilitate us to check all real-time data of curved track detection in the curved track detection module. Of course, this data refers to the curvature radius data of curved track detection. We can observe the change of curvature radius in the whole process by using the line graph of the upper part of the interface.

Figure 3 shows the working state of the system, that is, the system shows the working state after the start button is pressed.

Fig. 3. The system work

Under the working state of the system, the working conditions of each detection and warning module are as follows: track warning, switch warning and obstacle warning indicator light is displayed as shown in Fig. 4, 5, and 6.

Fig. 4. The curved track early warning

Fig. 5. The turnout detection early warning

Fig. 6. The obstacle detection early warning

7 Conclusion

In this paper, the intelligent identification and detection of railway track and the related technology of early warning are studied, and the detection of curved track, switch, and the obstacle is realized. In this method, the core algorithms such as radius of curvature, Hough transform, and frame difference method are selected to experiment with each module.

However, this method still has the following problems:

(1) In this paper, the method of Hough probability transformation is applied for the detection of the turnout. Although the identification and detection results after the region of interest are extracted and satisfactory, it is unavoidable to calculate some orbits with small curvature, which will produce errors and disturb the occurrence of early warning behavior. The obstacle detection algorithm still needs to be improved in the later stage, because the difficulty in collecting data sets brings great inconvenience and the experimental data is still few, so it is difficult to improve the robustness of the program.
(2) The experimental data used in the research process of this paper have some regularity. Because the system in this paper is track detection, the Angle of video stream acquisition is fixed. Therefore, when the system in this paper is applied to some other special scenes, its robustness will be very low.

The next research direction is to optimize the algorithm and apply the method to more complex scenes to improve the accuracy and reliability of the system.

Acknowledgement. This work was supported by the National Nature Science Foundation of China (Grant No. 61702347), Natural Science Foundation of Hebei Province (Grant No. F2017210161), Science and Technology Research Project of Higher Education in Hebei Province (Grant No. QN2017132).

References

1. Wang, W., Liang, R., Huang, T.: Design of video recognition system for subway train obstacle. Urban Mass Transit **22**(6), 166–169 (2019)
2. Zhang, X., Wang, B.: Research on intelligent detection method of railway intrusion based on multiple. Electron. Des. Eng. **27**(17), 89–92 (2019)
3. He, C.: Research on automobile autonomous driving system. Microcomput. Appl. **36**(9), 123–125 (2020)
4. Liu, F., Wu, Z., Ren, S., Zhu, C.: Improved checkerboard grid corner detection method under complex background. Comput. Eng. Des. **40**(12), 3474–3478 (2019)
5. Yu, H., Jiang, X., Yan, Z., Yan, X., Wang, C.: A rectification method of multi-projection 3D display system based on perspective transformation. Inf. Technol. Inf. **9**, 162–164 (2020)
6. Chu, K., Guo, J., Zhu, D.: Fast extraction method of lane lines in complex road environment. Res. Explor. Lab. **39**(7), 11–15 (2020)
7. He, Y.: Moving target detection based on improved frame difference method and background subtraction method. Yanshan University (2016)
8. Yin, Z.: Superelevation design method based on curve radius. Qinghai Traffic Sci. Technol. **1**, 51–55 (2018)
9. Zhang, L., Han, Y., Zhao, Y., Liu, J.: Hough transform and faster-RCNN method for detecting pedestrians on rails. J. Dalian Jiaotong Univ. **41**(2), 100–103
10. Tang, T., Liu, Y., Tang, C., Han, Z., Guo, Y.: Moving object detection and recognition based on computer vision. Electron. Technol. Softw. Eng. **4**,128–129 (2020)
11. Yan, B.: Improvement of the economic management system based on the publicity of railway transportation products. Intell. Autom. Soft Comput. **26**(3), 539–547 (2020)
12. Niu, H.W., Yao, J., Zhao, J., Wang, J.: SERVQUAL model based evaluation analysis of railway passenger transport service quality in china. J. Big Data **1**(1), 17–24 (2019)
13. Gao, J., Lin, X.: Mathematical interpolation and correction of three-dimensional modelling of high-speed railway. Intell. Autom. Soft Comput. **26**(5), 1023–1034 (2020)
14. He, J., Xing, Z., Hu, R., Qiu, J., Su, S., et al.: Directional antenna intelligent coverage method based on traversal optimization algorithm. Comput. Mater. Continua **60**(2), 527–544 (2019)
15. Aguilar, L., Nava-Díaz, S.W., Chavira, G.: Implementation of decision trees as an alternative for the support in the decisionmaking within an intelligent system in order to automatize the regulation of the VOCS in non-industrial inside environments. Comput. Syst. Sci. Eng. **34**(5), 297–303 (2019)
16. Yang, P., Liu, G., Li, X., Qin, L., Liu, X.: An intelligent tumors coding method based on drools. J. New Media **2**(3), 111–119 (2020)
17. Li, C.L., Sun, X.M., Cai, J.H.: Intelligent mobile drone system based on real-time object detection. J. Artif. Intell. **1**(1), 1–8 (2019)
18. Kim, D., Kim, S.: Network-aided intelligent traffic steering in 5G mobile networks. Comput. Mater. Continua **65**(1), 243–261 (2020)

Train Driver State Detection System Based on PCA and SVM

Yunzuo Zhang(✉) and Yaning Guo

Shijiazhuang Tiedao University, Shijiazhuang 050043, China
zhangyunzuo888@sina.com

Abstract. Train drivers play an important role in the process of train running and their driving state directly determines whether the train arrives safely and in time. Therefore, ensuring the good mental state of train drivers is related to the safety of train and passengers. Long-distance driving, short rest and high-intensity working environment may lead to a series of behaviors such as inattention, dozing or fatigue, which may cause serious safety accidents during the train driver driving. In order to realize the real-time monitoring of the train driver's state and reduce the safety accidents caused by the train driver's own driving behaviors, this paper designs and implements the train driver's state detection system based on PCA and SVM. First, the system processes the video captured by the train camera to extract the images of the train driver's head posture. Second, use these images as PCA technology training samples for feature extraction, and classify the driver's head postures through SVM technology. Third, the system recognizes the current driving state of the train driver and reminds the illegal operation behavior, ensuring the correctness of the driver's behavior to the greatest extent. Experimental results show that the driver state detection accuracy rate reaches 86.6667%.

Keywords: PCA · SVM · Driving state · Train safety

1 Introduction

Nowadays, there are more and more people taking trains, and the number of trains is constantly increasing. Long-distance trains are becoming more common and the workload of train drivers is increasing. Long distance driving and short-time rest can easily lead to the train drivers' inattention, dozing and physical fatigue. In addition, because the train belongs to the rail vehicle, only a limited number of adjustments of the direction during driving. So there is a high possibility that train drivers will relax their vigilance and leave the driver's seat. Once a train transportation safety accident occurs due to the lack of attention of the train driver during the running of the train, it will not only cause huge property losses, but also endanger the lives of passengers, and at the same time will have a bad impact on the society [1].

With the rapid development of science and technology, in order to effectively supervise the safe operation of the train, the corresponding video monitoring equipment has been installed inside the train and along the railway, which has played a certain role

X. Sun et al. (Eds.): ICAIS 2021, LNCS 12736, pp. 516–526, 2021.
https://doi.org/10.1007/978-3-030-78609-0_44

in promoting train safety. Through several investigations, it is learned that the current supervision of drivers is to watch the video recorded in the cab after the train runs to determine whether the driver has violated the regulations during the driving. This kind of manual monitoring mode is easy to cause the fatigue of the monitoring personnel, especially in the face of multi-channel monitoring video, it is easy to see the situation of misjudgment, and it is difficult to respond to the abnormal in time [2]. Therefore, there is an urgent need for intelligent video monitoring to assist the monitoring staff [3]. It is very necessary to study the driver's state detection system which meets the needs of modern life and promptly warn the train driver's unsafe driving behavior.

Feature extraction is to transform and analyze video frames containing human behaviors, and ultimately obtain the features that can effectively describe human behavior in the video. The difficulty is how to choose the feature extraction method which can cope with various transformations and has high robustness. The quality of the extracted features will directly affect the final recognition effect. The characteristics used to describe the target behavior can be divided into two categories: global characteristics and local characteristics. Global features are mainly used to describe the motion in the entire video frame, such as contour coefficient [4], boundary features [5], optical flow [6] and so on. Local features mainly describe the target in the local domain or region of interest of the video frame, such as Scale Invariant Feature Transform (SIFT) [7], Motion Scale Invariant Feature Transform, MoSIFT [8] etc. This paper designs and implements a train driver state detection system based on Principal Components Analysis (PCA) and Support Vector Machine (SVM). The PCA technology is used to complete the feature extraction of the various states of the driver, and the SVM technology is used to classify the driving state of the driver, so as to accurately and real-time judge the driving state of the train driver and issue a real-time warning of the bad driving state.

2 System Design

The overall flow chart of the train driver state detection system based on PCA and SVM is shown in Fig. 1 [9]. This system is based on PCA and SVM and its function is to detect the driving state of train drivers and give warning to their bad driving state. Firstly, the video is divided into frames and saved in pgm format. The skin color detection method is used to extract the driver's face area in the image. Then the PCA technology is used to complete the feature extraction of the train driver's driving state and the SVM method is used to classify. Finally, the task of identifying and judging the driving status of train drivers is completed.

A train driver is considered to be in good driving condition when facing forward and holding the operating lever. When the driver's head is tilted, it can be regarded as poor driving condition, and the system will give a warning to the driver. In individual cases, train drivers occasionally bow and turn their heads to meet the needs of their work, but these behaviors are a minority and do not affect the normal judgment of the system. Therefore, the occurrence of inaccurate judgment in special situations can be ignored.

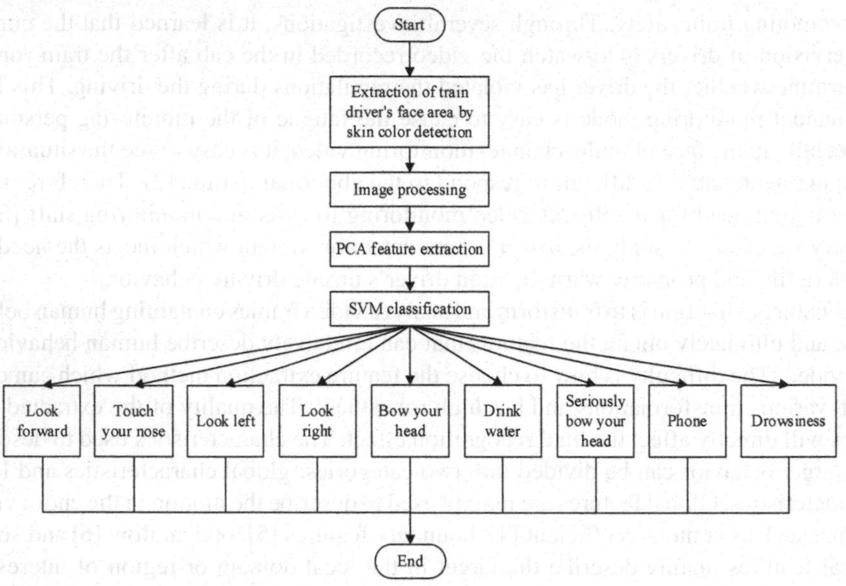

Fig. 1. Flow chart of the whole system.

3 Key Technologies

This part introduces the key technologies involved in system design and implementation.

3.1 Skin Color Detection

The computer stores and saves color pictures by the three-dimensional plane matrix data structure. Each dimensional plane matrix is composed of many small squares and each small square has a value, which is the pixel value, representing the average brightness of the small square. The corresponding arrangement and combination of the pixel values of the three plane matrices can make the image display a certain color. Human skin has the characteristic color that can be clearly distinguished from the external environment color. In the NTSC color space, the pixel values of the skin color in the second plane matrix are mostly concentrated in the range of 0.03–0.2. Therefore, the skin can be filtered out by turning the pixel values in the second plane matrix in the range of 0.03–0.2 into white and other areas into black [10].

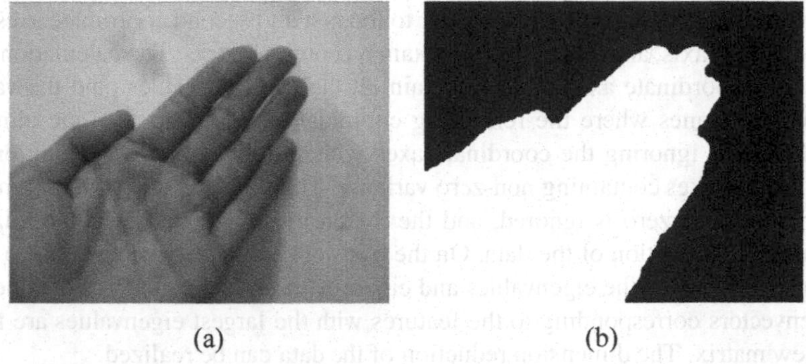

Fig. 2. Skin color detection: (a) Original image; and (b) Skin color detection effect chart.

3.2 PCA Technology

PCA [11] is the abbreviation of principal component analysis, which often reduces the data dimension through linear transformation, so that the original data can be transformed and linearly independent linear components in each dimension direction are obtained.

Suppose there are two-dimensional sample data with two feature attributes (feature 1 and feature 2), and the sample data points are randomly distributed within the blue ellipse in Fig. 3. Regarding the oblique 45° direction as the main linear component direction, then the dashed line perpendicular to this direction is the sub-linear component direction. The purpose of PCA dimensionality reduction can be achieved by discarding the data in the sub-linear component direction.

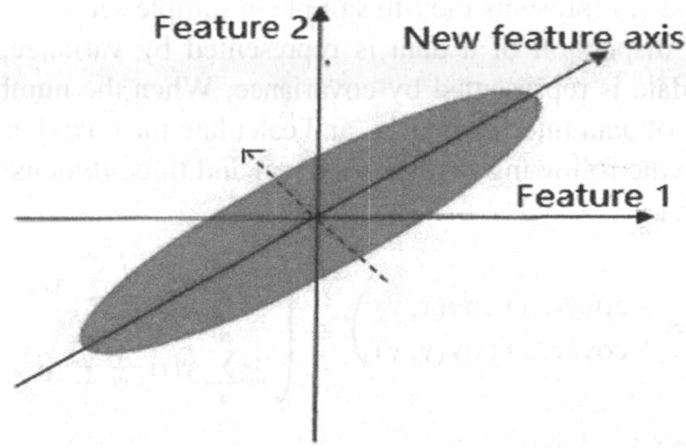

Fig. 3. PCA data dimension reduction diagram.

The main work of PCA is to reduce the dimensionality of the sample data and obtain the new orthogonal vector. In other words, it is to find a set of orthogonal coordinate axes (the choice of the new coordinate axis is closely related to the data value). Calculate the variance of the original data, and use the direction with the largest variance as the first coordinate axis, and the direction of the plane perpendicular to the first coordinate axis with the largest variance as the second coordinate axis. Taking the direction with the largest variance of the plane perpendicular to the first and second coordinate axes as the third coordinate axis, and so on, we can obtain n coordinate axes. The calculation shows that the first coordinate axes almost contain all the variance values, and the variance values of the planes where the remaining coordinate axes are located are almost all zero. Therefore, ignoring the coordinate axes with variance of zero, leaving only the first coordinate axes containing non-zero variance. That is to say, the feature dimension with a variance of zero is ignored, and the dimension is reduced, which realizes the dimensionality reduction of the data. On the basis of calculating the covariance matrix of the original matrix, the eigenvalues and eigenvectors of the matrix are obtained, and the eigenvectors corresponding to the features with the largest eigenvalues are formed into a new matrix. The dimension reduction of the data can be realized.

Sample mean:

$$\overline{x} = \frac{1}{n}\sum_{i=1}^{n} xi \tag{1}$$

Sample variance:

$$\operatorname{var}(X) = \frac{\sum_{i=1}^{n}(xi-\overline{x})(xi-\overline{x})}{n-1} \tag{2}$$

Covariance of sample X and sample Y:

$$\begin{aligned}\operatorname{cov}(X,Y) &= E[(X-E(X))(Y-E(Y))] \\ &= \frac{\sum_{i=1}^{n}(xi-\overline{x})(yi-\overline{y})}{n-1}\end{aligned} \tag{3}$$

Among them, n represents the total number of samples, xi represents the i-th sample in sample set X, and yi represents the i-th sample in sample set Y.

The degree of dispersion of a data is represented by variance, and the correlation between two data is represented by covariance. When the number of dimensions increases, put a lot of data into the matrix, and calculate the covariance of the pairwise data cyclically. See the following two-dimensional and three-dimensional examples.

Two-dimensional:

$$c = \begin{pmatrix} \operatorname{cov}(x,x) & \operatorname{cov}(x,y) \\ \operatorname{cov}(y,x) & \operatorname{cov}(y,y) \end{pmatrix} = \begin{pmatrix} \frac{1}{m}\sum_{i}^{m} xi^2 & \frac{1}{m}\sum_{i}^{m} xiyi \\ \frac{1}{m}\sum_{i}^{m} yixi & \frac{1}{m}\sum_{i}^{m} yi^2 \end{pmatrix} \tag{4}$$

Three-dimensional:

$$c = \begin{pmatrix} \operatorname{cov}(x,x) & \operatorname{cov}(x,y) & \operatorname{cov}(x,z) \\ \operatorname{cov}(y,x) & \operatorname{cov}(y,y) & \operatorname{cov}(y,z) \\ \operatorname{cov}(z,x) & \operatorname{cov}(z,y) & \operatorname{cov}(z,z) \end{pmatrix} \tag{5}$$

Perform eigenvalue decomposition on the covariance matrix to obtain eigenvalues and eigenvectors, where vector v is the eigenvector of matrix A and λ is the eigenvalue corresponding to eigenvector v.

$$Av = \lambda v \tag{6}$$

Unitize v orthogonally to obtain a set of orthogonal unit vectors. That is to decompose matrix A into the form of Eq. 7.

$$A = Q\Sigma Q^{-1} \tag{7}$$

Among them, Σ is a diagonal matrix, Q is a matrix composed of the eigenvectors of matrix A, and the elements on the diagonal of the diagonal matrix are the eigenvalues of the original matrix, so Σ is a known quantity.

Arrange the eigenvalues in descending order, select the first k eigenvalues, and form the eigenvector matrix P with their corresponding eigenvectors and P is the matrix after the data has been reduced in dimension.

3.3 SVM Technology

SVM [12] is the abbreviation of Support Vector Machine, which is a generalized linear classifier used to classify sample data. The basic SVM classifies binary samples through the obtained linear function. This linear function appears in the form of a point, a straight line, and a plane in one-dimensional space, two-dimensional space, and three-dimensional space, and so on. When the spatial dimension is ignored, the linear function has a name—hyperplane. The purpose of SVM is to find a hyperplane that can distinguish samples, and to make the distance between the hyperplane and the sample relatively farthest, that is, the maximum margin.

If two types of samples are separated by a linear function, this group of samples is linearly separable, otherwise, it is non-linearly separable (As shown in Fig. 4).

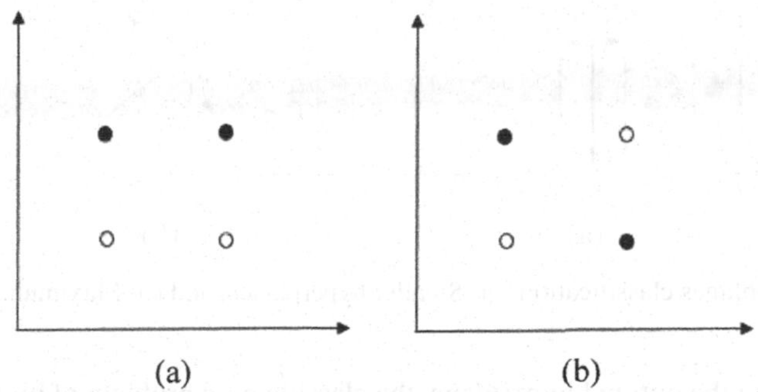

Fig. 4. Linear and nonlinear separability of samples: (a) Linear separable samples; and (b) Nonlinear separable samples.

In Fig. 5, there are three classification lines, H_1, H_2 and H_3. It can be seen from the figure that H_1 and H_2 can not distinguish the two types of samples. Therefore, H_1 and H_2 are not the classification lines meeting the classification conditions. H_3 can distinguish the two types of samples. Therefore, H_3 is the classification line meeting the classification conditions, that is, H_3 is the hyperplane that can distinguish the two types of samples.

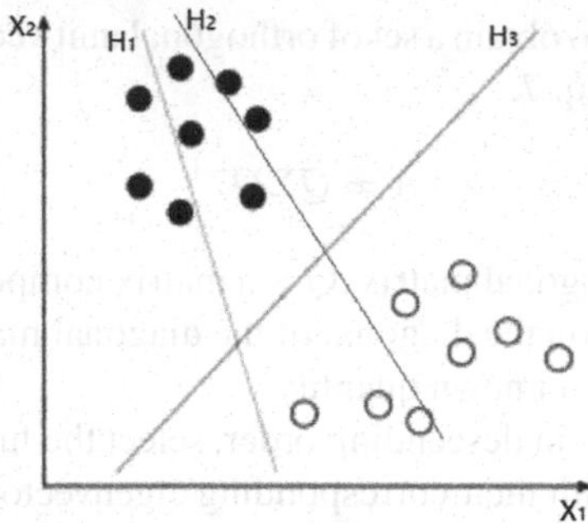

Fig. 5. Classification line.

For SVM, the sum of the vertical distances between the data points in the two sample sets and the hyperplane is the largest, that is, the maximum margin. In a two-dimensional space, it is expressed as the distance between the point and the classification line. Assuming that the line is $y = wx + b$, when the sum of the distances from the points on both sides of the line to the line takes the maximum value, this line is the optimal classification line, that is, the optimal hyperplane. The hyperplane in Fig. 6(a) is not the optimal hyperplane, and the hyperplane in Fig. 6(b) is the optimal hyperplane.

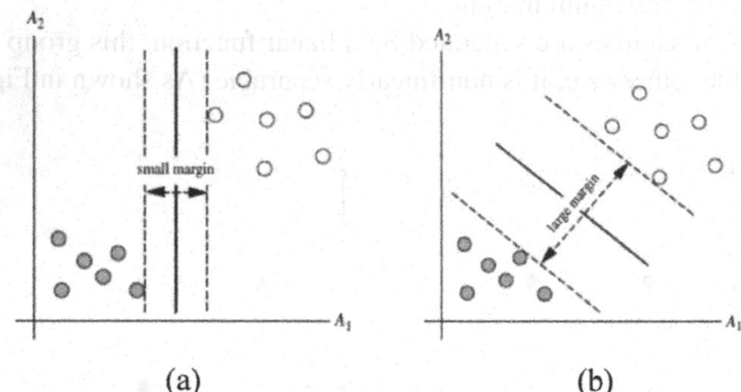

Fig. 6. Hyperplanes classification: (a) Smaller hyperplanes; and (b) Maximum hyperplanes.

By selecting the optimal hyperplane, the classification problem of binary samples is completed, and the SVM algorithm can be extended to solve the classification problem of multi-class samples by using the one-to-one voting strategy.

4 System Implementation and Results Display

This part introduces the implementation process of the train driver state detection system based on PCA and SVM, and shows the detection results of the system.

4.1 System Implementation

The hardware environment used in this experiment is: Inter(R) Core(TM) i7–4790 CPU @ 3.60 GHz 3.60 GHz, memory is 16.0 GB, operating system is Windows 10 Enterprise Edition 64-bit, using MATLAB R2016a as the experimental platform.

The train driver state detection system based on PCA and SVM [13] reads the train driver's driving video, saves the video in the form of frames in a folder, and uses the skin color detection method to find and intercept the train driver's head area from the video frame. Since the system has certain requirements for the pictures to be detected, the pictures are processed in order of illumination compensation, gray scale, interception of fixed size, and modification of the picture format.

The training of PCA [14] is carried out according to the process of reading training set image data, generating sample matrix, image feature reduction processing, and driver gesture recognition. The training process is shown in Fig. 7.

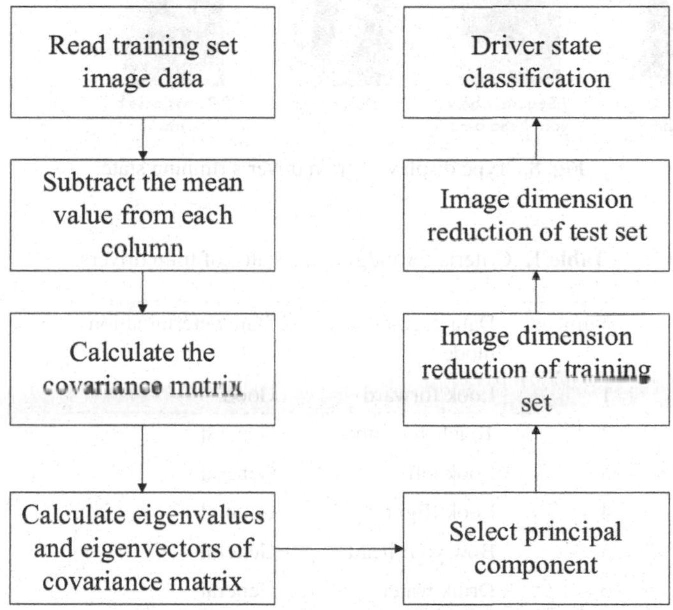

Fig. 7. PCA training process.

There are two purposes for the introduction of SVM [15–18] into the train driver state detection system. First, SVM can complete the classification and recognition of multiple types of samples through a one-to-one voting strategy [19–23]; Second, driver status detection is not a linear separable sample classification problem, and there must be indivisible situation, so the error cost coefficient of SVM should be used to identify the driver to be detected more accurately driving posture images.

4.2 Results Display

Train driver state detection system based on PCA and SVM adds various types of driving status to the template library according to all possible postures of the driver's upper body in the surveillance video (see Fig. 8), including looking forward, bowing head, Phoning, drinking water and so on. The number and degree are divided for each posture. The specific criteria are shown in Table 1.

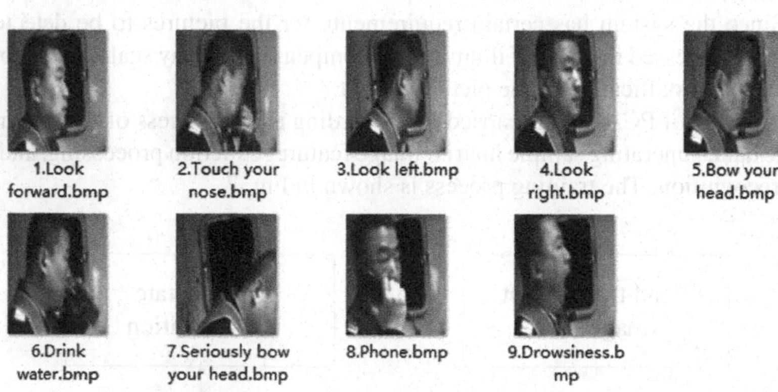

Fig. 8. Type display of train driver's running state.

Table 1. Criteria for judging the status of train drivers.

Number	Data augmentation mode	State determination
1	Look forward	Good
2	Touch your nose	General
3	Look left	General
4	Look Right	General
5	Bow your head	General
6	Drink water	General
7	Seriously bow your head	Bad
8	Phone	Bad
9	Drowsiness	Bad

Train driver state detection system based on PCA and SVM can identify and detect the driving status of train drivers in a video and issue real-time warnings. Part of the running process is shown in Fig. 9.

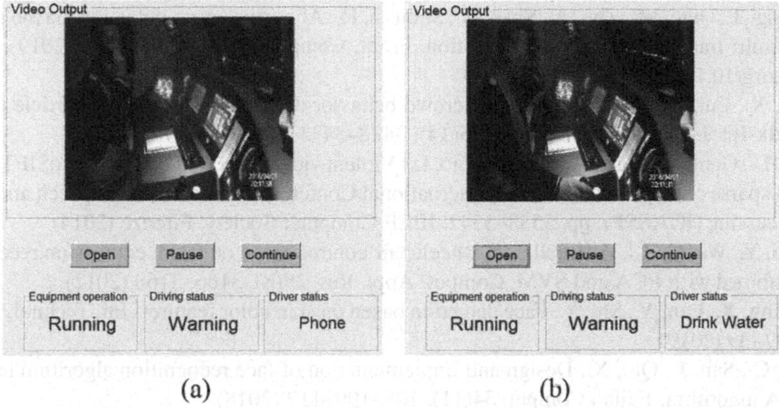

Fig. 9. Video detection results: (a) Bad driving conditions of railway drivers; and (b) System stop interface.

5 Conclusions

This paper designs and implements the train driver state detection system based on PCA and SVM. The system can process the video captured by the camera inside the train, and automatically collect the image of the railway driver's head posture from it. It can accurately identify the driver's various driving states and warn his bad driving state, which has certain application value. In addition, in the later work, as the amount of data increases, the classification of driving states will be more accurate, and the detection accuracy of the system will be further improved.

Acknowledgement. This work was supported by the National Nature Science Foundation of China (Grant No. 61702347), Natural Science Foundation of Hebei Province (Grant No. F2017210161), Science and Technology Research Project of Higher Education in Hebei Province (Grant No. QN2017132).

References

1. Zhou, R.: Research on locomotive driver fatigue detection system based on video signal. Harbin Institute of Technology, Chinese (2013)
2. Shen, Z.: CTCS-2+ATO system technology status and development prospects. Railway Standard Des. **9**, 136–141 (2017)
3. Huang, K., Chen, X., Kang, Y.: Overview of intelligent video surveillance technology. Chinese J. Comput. **20**(6), 1093–1118 (2015)
4. Gouiaa, R., Meunier, J.: Human posture recognition by combining silhouette and infrared cast shadows. In: International Conference on Image Processing Theory, pp. 49–54. IEEE Computer Society, Paris (2016)
5. Cheema, S., Eweiwi, A.: THURAU C. action recognition by learning discriminative key poses. In: IEEE International Conference on Computer Vision Workshops, pp. 1302–1309. IEEE Computer Society, Barcelona (2011)

6. Wang, T., Qiao, M., Zhu, A., Shan, G., Snoussi, H.: Abnormal event detection via the analysis of multi-frame optical flow information. Front. Comp. Sci. **14**(2), 304–313 (2019). https://doi.org/10.1007/s11704-018-7407-3
7. Gu, X., Cui, J., Zhu, Q.: Abnormal crowd behavior detection by using the particle entropy. Optik-Int. J. Light Electron Opt. **125**(14), 3428–3433 (2014)
8. Xu, L., Gong, C., Yang, J., Wu, Q., Yao, L.: Violent video detection based on MoSIFT feature and sparse coding. In: 2014 IEEE International Conference on Acoustics, Speech and Signal Processing (ICASSP), pp. 3538–3542. IEEE Computer Society, Firenze (2014)
9. Luo, Y., Wu, C., Li, Z.: Intelligent wheelchair control based on facial expression recognition combined with PCA and SVM. Comput. Appl. Res. **29**(8), 3166–3168 (2012)
10. Zhang, X., Lan, Y., Shi, Y.: Face detection based on skin color features. Inf. Technol. Inform. **4**, 37–39 (2019)
11. Jin, C., Sun, J., Qiu, X.: Design and implementation of face recognition algorithm based on PCA algorithm. Fujian Comput. **34**(11), 108–109+117 (2018)
12. Li, R.: Research on Face Recognition Algorithm Based on PCA Improvement Combined with SVM. Kunming University of Science and Technology, Chinese (2018)
13. Hu, M.: Face Recognition System Based on PCA and SVM. Computer Age (12), 60–63+67 (2017)
14. Yuan, J.: Design and research of face recognition system based on PCA. Hebei University of Science and Technology, Chinese (2019)
15. Dong, C.: Face recognition based on PCA and SVM algorithm. Radio TV Inf. **10**, 107–110 (2018)
16. Wang, Z., Jiao, R., Jiang, H.: Emotion recognition using wt-svm in human-computer interaction. J. New Media **2**(3), 121–130 (2020)
17. Zhang, T.: Research and Integration of Facial Expression Recognition. Chongqing University of Posts and Telecommunications, Chinese (2016)
18. Li, R., Liu, Y., Qiao, Y., Ma, T., Wang, B., et al.: Street-level landmarks acquisition based on SVM classifiers. Comput. Mater. Continua **59**(2), 591–606 (2019)
19. Zhang, Y., Tao, R., Wang, Y.: Motion-state-adaptive video summarization via spatiotemporal analysis. IEEE Trans. Circuits Syst. Video Technol. **27**(6), 1340–1352 (2017)
20. Xu, Z.: Applications and techniques in cyber intelligence. Comput. Syst. Sci. Eng. **34**(4), 169–170 (2019)
21. Zhang, Y., Tao, R., Zhang, F.: Key frame extraction based on spatiotemporal motion trajectory. Opt. Eng. **54**(5), 1–3 (2015)
22. Chen, R., Pan, L., Zhou, Y., Lei, Q.: Image retrieval based on deep feature extraction and reduction with improved CNN and PCA. J. Inf. Hiding Privacy Protection **2**(2), 9–18 (2020)
23. Yuan, S., Wang, G.Z., Chen, J.B., Guo, W.: Assessing the forecasting of comprehensive loss incurred by typhoons: a combined PCA and BP neural network model. J. Artif. Intell. **1**(2), 69–88 (2019)

The Offset-Image Recognition Based on Dense Coding

Junxiao Cao[1], Ziyu Yao[2], Jinjin Chen[3], Yuanyuan Zhang[3], Xingze Tai[1], Tian Zhang[2], and Jiaquan Gao[2(✉)]

[1] Honors College, Nanjing Normal University, Nanjing 210023, China
[2] School of Computer and Electronic Information, Nanjing Normal University, Nanjing 210023, China
[3] School of Mathematical Sciences, Nanjing Normal University, Nanjing 210023, China

Abstract. In this paper, the influence of dense coding on the recognition of offset-image is explored by improving the feature extraction ability of network model. By the experimental results, we find that adding the PCANet convolution layer to obtain more filters cannot effectively improve the network recognition ability of the offset-image recognition. Based on this background, we propose a new dense network framework on the basis of the FPH framework. Experimental results on the AR dataset and MNIST variations show that the proposed network framework is effective and improves significantly the ability of the offset-image recognition.

Keywords: PCANet · Dense coding · Offset-image

1 Introduction

As we know, the deep learning method represented by CNN performs very well in the image recognition problem where the training set is consistent with the test set. However, when there is a large distribution difference between the training set and the test set, which is called offset-image in this paper, the recognition ability of convolutional neural network is greatly reduced. For example, the large-scale trained neural networks DeepID [1], VGG [2] and LightCNN [3] have poor performance in face recognition and number recognition with offset [4]. However, the spectral histogram features extracted from FPH framework perform surprisingly well in the problem of image recognition with offset. For example, in 2015, Chen et al. [5] combined CNN with LBP-like feature extraction framework (called FPH framework in this paper) to design PCANet network. Without considering prior information such as illumination and other offset information,

This work was funded by the Natural Science Foundation of China under grant number 61872422, and the Natural Science Foundation of Zhejiang Province, China under great number LY19F020028.

X. Sun et al. (Eds.): ICAIS 2021, LNCS 12736, pp. 527–539, 2021.
https://doi.org/10.1007/978-3-030-78609-0_45

it shows a recognition rate beyond the neural network and traditional recognition methods. Through the analysis, we can see that in PCANet network, the image has been decomposed all the time. From the generation of feature graph, the coding of pattern map to the calculation of histogram, the feature dimension has been rising, and at the same time, the noise has been further diluted. Improving the filtering ability of the offset information and enhancing the feature redundancy can make the obtained features more robust.

In fact, deepening the depth and breadth of the network to improve the feature extraction ability of the model is the "consensus" in the field of deep learning. For example, in the visual competition ILSVRC in the development of deep learning, the network depth rising up from the initial 8 layers (AlexNet) to 19 layers (VGG) and 152 layers (ResNet), the network recognition rate is also increasing. To explore its root, improving the ability of feature extraction can make the feature more robust. We know that in the PCANet network, the feature map of the layer is convoluted with the corresponding filter operator to obtain the new feature map as the input of the next layer, which can effectively extract the local features of the image. However, if the double-layer convolution layer is extended to three or five layers or even more, the local receptive field will be greatly improved, which will make the occlusion information diffuses in the process of image decomposition.

In PCANet, the generation method of pattern map is relatively simple, which is not enough to capture all the features of feature map, which is not conducive to the recognition of offset-image. Therefore, we propose a dense coding method, which greatly enriches the generated pattern graph. The recognition results on AR, LFW and MNIST variables show the effectiveness of the proposed network framework.

2 Offset-Image Recognition Network Based on FPH Framework

The network structure diagram is shown in Fig. 1. First, the image set is input into the network from the input layer, and then the image filtering operation is carried out by using the extended filter bank to extract the rich information of the image such as contour, edge, texture, etc., and at the same time, the offset information that affects the classification is filtered out. Then, in order to solve the consumption problem of huge time and space brought by the rich feature map, the network adopts the reversible operation of hash binarization, which is reversible, to code the feature maps. Pattern graph coding compacts graphical feature representation, reduces feature dimension, and enriches features. Second, the network concatenates hash binary coding graph and segments the histogram feature extraction operation. The block operation is conducive to retain the local features of the image, and the generation of high-dimensional histogram further reduces the impact of offset information on the features. At the end of the network, the histogram features are put into the classifier of the network.

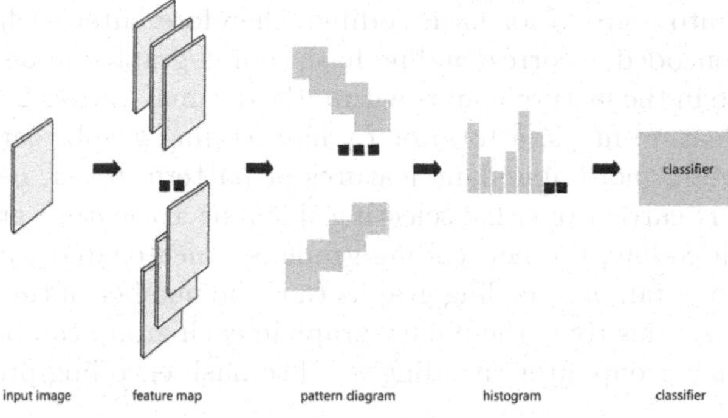

Fig. 1. Image recognition based on FPH frame

For the classification network of identifying offset-images, the ability of image feature extraction and noise filtering largely determines the recognition accuracy. In order to meet this requirement, the network filter needs to meet the characteristics of rich scale and direction information, enough quantity and easy calculation. Therefore, the complex filter bank $o = \{o_{PCA-PCA}, o_{PCA-Gabor}, o_{PCA-ICA}, o_{PCA-DCT}\}$ is used as the filter to extract image features, which avoids complex parameter training process while extracting features and filtering noise.

The network uses hash binary operation to compress the feature map and encode it. Based on the Heaviside step function, the binary operation of the feature graph is carried out. The coefficient greater than 1 is coded as 1 and the coefficient less than 1 is coded as 0. Binary coding introduces robustness to network identification. As in the above formula $\zeta = I * o$ (which I represents the input image and o represents the transform basis function), the result ζ reflects the response degree of both. When the operation result ζ is greater than 0, it means that the pixel value in the neighborhood filter is positively correlated with the filter operator, and the value is positively correlated with the correlation degree; when the operation result ζ is less than 0, the pixel value in the neighborhood filter is negatively correlated with the filter operator, and the absolute value of the value is positively correlated with the correlation degree. This binarization makes the network robust to illumination offset. It is assumed that the image x_1 contaminated by illumination offset information is composed of clean image x and additive illumination noise x_0, that is $x_1 = x + x_0$, after convolution by filter, the result is as follows: $\zeta_1 = h * x_1 = h * x + h * x_0$. Then when the correlation of input increment sum x_0 and h caused by illumination is consistent with that of sum x and h, ζ_1 and ζ has the same sign positive and negative. Thus, the binary operation makes the network have certain illumination robustness.

Secondly, hash coding is needed to compress feature space, fuse feature information and reduce network computation. If the input image is obtained by convolution, all the feature images are binarized, and then each L_2 feature images

$O^{l'}$ is divided into a group for hash coding. Therefore, after each group of feature maps are encoded, a corresponding hash coding graph will be obtained, and each pixel value in the feature map is within the decimal integer 2^L. After coding all the image feature maps, a total of L_1 hash coding graphs can be obtained. In order to obtain more abundant features of pattern graph, dense coding of pattern graph is carried out. By selecting different L_2 feature graphs from L_1 groups for hash coding, the new coding graph is concatenated with the original coding graph to obtain nL_1 coding graphs (n is the number of times of extended coding plus 1). At this time, the binary graph in each group can be set as l', and the result of each group after encoding is . The hash encoding process is shown in Eq. (1)

$$Hash^p = \sum_{L'}^{L_2} 2^{l'-1} H(O^{l'}) \tag{1}$$

Finally, histogram features are extracted. In general image recognition problems, the global histogram of image feature map can reflect its statistical information well. However, it is easy to lose the local information of the image, which is not conducive to the recognition of the offset-image. Locality is one of the criteria for robust feature extraction. Therefore, this paper chooses the block histogram: firstly, according to the specific size of the image, the hash coding image is divided into small blocks, and the histogram features in each block are extracted block by block. Finally, all histogram features are cascaded as the histogram features of the whole image. In addition to not losing the local features of the image, block extraction of histogram features can bring some occlusion robustness to the network. Assuming that the network input image is affected by scarves, glasses and other occlusions, the filter used in this paper has strong ability to extract texture and edge information and filter noise information, which makes the extracted features reduce the impact of offset information. The offset information results in a large difference between the histogram of the occluded image block and the original image block, but the histogram of the other image blocks that are not occluded is consistent with the original image. Therefore, the block histogram extraction makes the network have a certain occlusion robustness [6].

After getting p groups coding feature maps after hashing binarization, each feature map is divided into B blocks according to the type of image, so each block histogram is represented as follows: $Hist^p_B$, where $b = 1, 2, ..., B$. Next, concatenate the histogram of all blocks in the hash coding feature graph to get the block histogram feature of the feature graph: $Hist^p = [Hist^p_1, Hist^p_2, ..., Hist^p_B]$.

Then cascading all the block histogram features of the p groups hash coding graph to obtain the histogram features $Hist$ of the input image p: $Hist = [Hist^1, Hist^2, ..., Hist^B]$.

Finally, the nearest neighbor method based on Chi square or L2 distance and SVM method are selected for classification. For face images, the nearest neighbor method is selected for classification. Firstly, the chi square or L2 distance between the feature vectors of all images in the test set and the eigenvectors of all images in the training set is calculated, and then the category of the training set with the highest similarity (i.e. the minimum distance) of the test image is taken as the sample prediction result. The specific selection of the distance formula to measure the characteristic distance will be introduced in Sect. 4. For the classification of digital images, support vector machine (SVM) is selected to find the hyperplane that can separate all the samples, which satisfies the shortest distance of all data in the training set to this hyperplane.

3 Dense Coding Method Based on Pattern Graph Features

3.1 Reason Analysis of Dense Coding in Offsct-Image Recognition

After the image is filtered by the filter, the feature information which is conducive to classification is extracted, and the discriminative feature map is obtained. In the FPH framework, after extracting the image feature map, the pattern map is encoded.

In the analysis of PCANet feature extraction, the pattern map coding method in network is similar to LBP method [7]. First, each pixel value in the feature map is compared with the eigenvalues in the surrounding neighborhood (such as LBP [7], LXP [8], etc.), or the binary code is generated by quantifying the eigenvalue (such as QBC [9]), and then the binary code is converted into decimal code according to certain rules. It can be seen that the histogram coding is mainly divided into two processes: binarization of the feature image, that is, converting a single pixel value into a binary string according to a certain method; and then reversible compression of the binarized image. Using the Heaviside step function (if the pixel value is greater than 0, the code is 1; otherwise, the code is 0). The pixels at the same position in every 8 feature maps are compressed to 1, that is, 64 pattern maps in the network are reduced to 8.

However, we can find that line coding is adopted in PCANet, that is, 8 decomposed feature images of an image in one main direction are converted into decimal system. Such a single coding method ignores the relationship between the feature images in different main directions. In Fig. 2, when the information of the first image column (d) is not rich enough, the image recognition rate will not be affected as shown in Fig. 2.

3.2 Dense Coding

According to the above descriptions, we propose to connect the coding values of an image in different main directions through different coding schemes after the binarization feature map and before the decimal coding process, and then convert the binary to decimal system, and connect the newly added coding map with the previously generated code map in series. This transformation scheme greatly enriches the pattern diagram generated by the network.

Figure 2 shows the generation process of PCANet feature map and pattern map: firstly, the input image is decomposed in eight main directions obtained by

PCA algorithm to obtain the first layer convolution layer result. Then, each feature graph in Fig. 2(b) is further decomposed, and each graph is further divided into 8 feature graphs. Finally, 64 feature graphs in Fig. 2(c) can be obtained. According to the pattern map coding method in PCANet, eight characteristic graphs in each row in Fig. 2(c) are coded into a pattern map, and the first column picture in Fig. 2(d) can be obtained. In order to enrich the pattern diagram, select to use the characteristic graph of each column in Fig. 2(c) to generate a pattern diagram. The generated pattern graph in this example is shown in the second column of Fig. 2(d). Not only can the pattern graph be calculated by column, but also 8 random number arrays can be generated from numbers 1 to 64 by random number algorithm, and pattern graphs can be generated by grouping according to the characteristic graphs corresponding to each group of random numbers, as shown in the fourth column of the third column in Fig. 2(d). It can be seen that compared with the original single coding strategy, after adding different coding strategies, 64 feature graphs generate more abundant pattern graphs, which makes them more discriminative. The dense feature map coding can be obtained by concatenating the pattern graphs generated by the proposed coding strategy to the original schema.

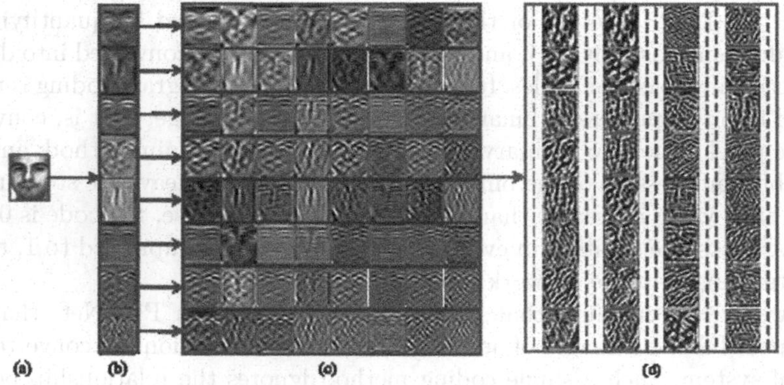

Fig. 2. The formation process of dense coding in PCANet network

4 Related Experiments and Results Analysis

In order to verify whether the dense coding method of pattern map can effectively improve the recognition rate of offset-image, experiments are carried out in this paper. The experimental environment is MATLAB r2018b, and the experimental platform is 2.6 GHz CPU and 8 GB RBM.

4.1 Data Set Description

AR data set [10] is widely recognized and widely used offset face databases. In addition to the typical face data set, this paper also selects the offset digital image data set MNIST variations [5]. Compared with the more typical MNIST data set, the digital image of MNIST variations contains the offset information such as rotation, random noise and random background. The specific information of the two datasets are shown in Figs. 3 and 4, respectively.

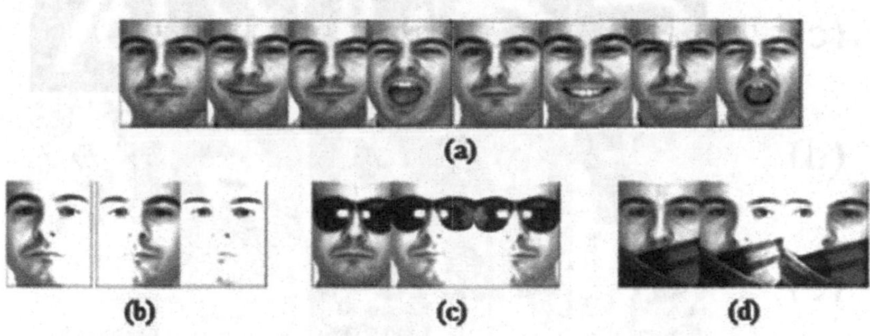

Fig. 3. Training data and test data samples of AR database.

The AR face dataset contains 126 images of people, with an average of 23 images per person, with a total of 3276 images. The data set contains a variety of occlusion offset information (such as lighting, scarf, sunglasses, etc.). 119 subjects (65 males and 54 females) are selected for the experiment. Among them, 952 (119 individuals, 8 per person) frontal face images without any offset information are selected from the training set, as shown in Fig. 3 (a); 357 (119 individuals, 3 per person) images in test set I are selected, including three illumination conditions of left, right and front, as shown in Fig. 3 (b); Test set II has 357 (119 people, 3 pieces per person), including three kinds of illumination conditions: Sunglasses occlusion and normal light, right and left strong light, as shown in Fig. 3 (c); Test set III has 357 (119 people, 3 pieces per person), including three kinds of light conditions, including scarf shielding and normal light, and left strong light and right strong light, as shown in Fig. 3 (d). All images are first cropped and aligned to a pixel matrix of 112×92. In the experiment, 2 times, 4 times and 8 times down sampling of the data sets are performed, and the corresponding dimensions are $56 \times 46 = 2576, 28 \times 23 = 644$ and $14 \times 11 = 154$, respectively.

The MNIST variations are the result of introducing controlled migration information such as rotation, random noise and background noise into the MNIST data set and combining the above two kinds of migration information. Consistent with the MNIST dataset, the MNIST variations contain 10 handwritten digits (0–9, 10 digits in total), with an average of 21000 images per digit (including 1000 training sets and 5000 test sets), with a total of 210000 images, and the image size is 28×28. According to the difference of offset information,

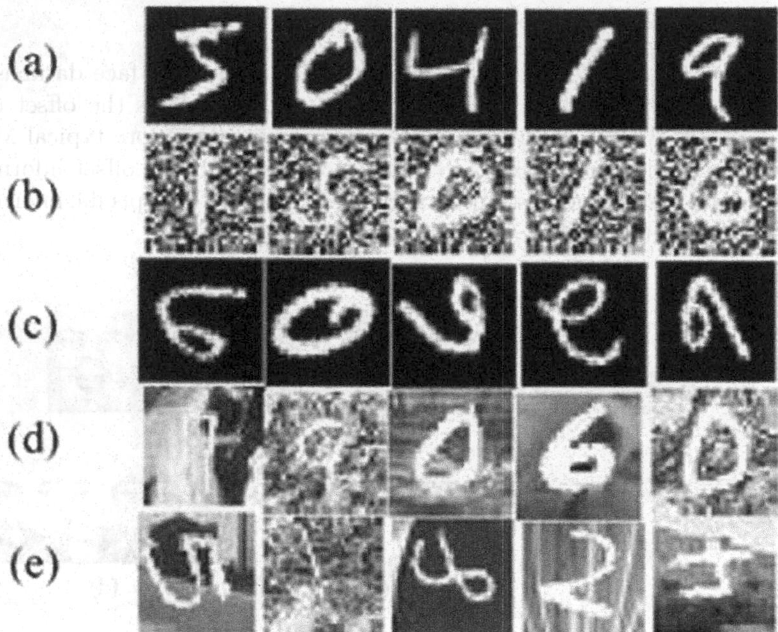

Fig. 4. Training data and test data samples of MNIST variations

the dataset is divided into five sub datasets. As shown in Fig. 4 (a), a total of 10000 pieces is selected as the training data from the MNIST variations. It can be seen from the figure that the training set is consistent with the MNIST dataset, and there is no offset information such as rotation and background noise. The test set mainly includes four test sets: (1) Test set I: random noise is added after handwritten digits on the MNIST dataset, and the dataset is divided into five sub datasets, as shown in Fig. 4 (b); and (2) Test Set II: rotate MNIST handwritten digits, and the dataset is divided into five sub datasets, as shown in Fig. 4 (c); and (3) Test set III: add random background image noise after handwritten digits on the MNIST dataset, and the dataset is divided into five sub datasets, as shown in Fig. 4(d); and (4) Test set IV: rotate handwritten digits on MNIST dataset randomly and add background noise, and the dataset is divided into five sub datasets, as shown in Fig. 4 (e).

4.2 Analysis of Experimental Results of Pattern Map Dense Coding

This section mainly verifies whether the dense coding method proposed in this paper can effectively improve the recognition ability of the network for offset-images. This paper mainly sets up experiments from the following aspects: using PCANet algorithm to classify offset-images (referred to as R coding scheme), enriching pattern maps by column coding, and enriching pattern graphs by column coding and diagonal coding are used for classification (R + C + D for short);

pattern graph is enriched by column, diagonal and random coding methods to classify (R + C + D + G for short).

Experiments are carried out on the datasets introduced in the previous section. For the proposed dense coding scheme, only the pattern map coding method is changed, and other parameters follow the original PCANet.

Table 1. Experimental results of pattern graph dense coding scheme on AR test sets.

	Test set I			Test set II			Test set III		
Pixel dimension	154	644	2576	154	644	2576	154	644	2576
R	68.63	76.48	90.2	56.3	72.88	87.68	7.79	80.11	92.72
R+C	70.87	78.43	92.44	58.26	74.52	87.98	73.39	84.31	93.56
R+C+D	70.87	79.27	92.68	59.38	75.08	88.08	75.07	84.59	93.28
R+C+D+G	70.59	77.87	91.23	58.26	74.96	88.24	73.39	84.3	92.44

According to the results in Table 1, when the dimension of input image is from 154 to 644 and then to 2576, the recognition accuracy is gradually improved. On AR data set, for test sets I, II and III, the feature dimension will gradually increase with the increasing density of coding, and the recognition performance will be improved to a certain extent (except that the recognition rate of coding scheme R + C and R + C + D is consistent on test set I). However, when the feature dimension is too high, it will lead to dimension disaster to a great extent. For example, from R + C + D to R + C + D + G, the recognition performance of R + C + D + G decreases slightly. The only exception is that the recognition performance of case R + C + D + G above test set II is slightly improved under 2576 pixel dimension.

Table 2. Experimental results of pattern graph dense coding scheme on MNIST variations.

Coding method/data set	Test set I	Test Set II	Test set III	Test set IV
R	81.50	39.80	81.90	30.00
R+C	81.00	39.90	81.90	28.80
R+C+D	80.40	40.50	82.10	29.00
R+C+D+G	83.10	39.80	81.90	29.10

As can be seen from the results in Table 2, it is obvious that the dense coding scheme has little effect on the MNIST variations. For test sets I and IV, the improvement of feature dimension reduces the recognition rate. For test set III, the feature recognition rate after dense coding is only consistent with that of

PCANet method. Test sets I, III and IV contain noisy background offset information, which makes the increase of pattern map, and will not have a favorable impact on the recognition effect.

For test set II without noisy background offset information, dense coding to a certain extent, such as from R to R + C and then to R + C + D, can slightly improve the recognition rate, but when the coding scheme increases to R + C + D + G, the dimension disaster causes the performance degradation.

Therefore, when the dense coding scheme is used to enrich the feature pattern map, it can improve the recognition rate. However, causing dimension explosion is a problem to be considered and solved, which needs to be determined according to the specific image type and pixel dimension.

4.3 Comparison Between Offset-Image Recognition Network and Other Methods

This section mainly verifies whether the migration image recognition network based on dense coding can effectively improve the recognition ability of offset-image. The encoding mode is R + C + D + G. The two networks are called DensePPNet and DensePGNet.

First of all, we will discuss the comparison of DensePPNet, DensePGNet and the single algorithm of network, such as filter expansion mode P-P, P-G, coding mode R + C + D + G. The experimental data are shown in Table 3. From Table 3, we can see that the recognition rate of the two algorithms is higher than that of single filter generation or coding. This verifies the effectiveness of the offset recognition network generated by the two algorithms.

Table 3. Experimental results of offset-image recognition network and single algorithm on each test set of AR.

	Test set I		Test set II		Test set III	
Pixel dimension	644	2576	644	2576	644	2576
P	80.11	89.92	88.52	87.68	83.19	91.60
P-P	85.99	89.80	90.89	92.72	87.27	94.12
P-G	88.52	91.88	91.95	94.40	86.55	94.84
R+C+D+G	77.87	91.23	74.96	88.24	84.30	92.44
DensePPNet	86.5	92.3	91.2	92.7	87.5	95.3
DensePGNet	87.4	92.8	92.5	94.5	88.2	95.9

Second, three kinds of spectral histogram features, namely POEM, PCANet and MBC, and two deep convolution neural networks, LCNN and VGG face, are selected for comparison. The digital images with offset, PCANet and DCTNet are selected as spectral histogram features, and LeNet-5 is selected as the convolution neural network. The parameters used in all networks are the same as those in the original paper.

Experiments are carried out on AR face dataset and MNIST variations introduced in Sect. 4.1. The results are shown in Figs. 5 and 6.

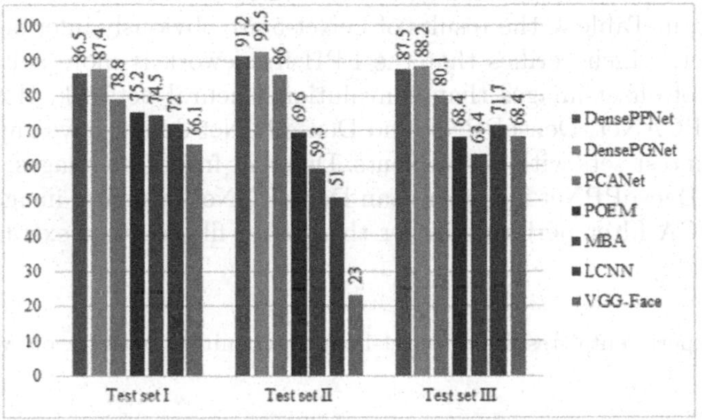

Fig. 5. Experimental results of each network on AR test sets (picture dimension is 644)

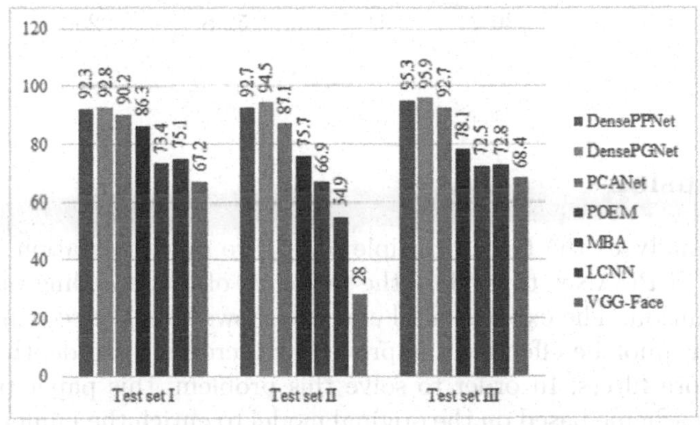

Fig. 6. Experimental results of each network on AR test sets (image dimension 2576)

From Figs. 5 and 6, it can be concluded that spectrum histogram features are better than convolution neural network in the problem of offset-image recognition, and higher recognition rate can be obtained. Among the features of several spectral histogram, PCANet is also prominent. However, the performance of the proposed network is better than that of PCANet. And from the results, DensePGNet has a higher recognition rate than DensePPNet. This is because PCA filter and Gabor filter are convoluted to obtain more abundant filters than PCA filter self convolution, "singularity" decomposition direction is more diverse, and more discriminative features are obtained. According to the results in Tables 1, 2 and 3, we can see that the recognition rate of the new network results on test sets II and III increases more than that on test set I. This verifies the ability of the filter expansion and dense coding to filter the offset information.

However, in Table 4, the results of LeNet-5 are obviously inferior to PCANet and DCTNet, which verifies that the FPH framework is more suitable for the recognition of offset-images than convolutional neural network. However, compared with PCANet, DensePPNet and DensePGNet do not have any advantage, especially on test sets with rot elements. Different from face images, the recognition rate of DensePPNet is higher than DensePGNet in digital images. It can be seen that PCA filter performs better than other filters when extracting digital information.

Table 4. Experimental results of offset-image recognition network on MNIST variations

Method/data set	Test set I	Test Set II	Test set III	Test set IV
DensePPNet	84.5	36.5	82.4	29.3
DensePGNet	80.8	35.4	80.4	28.5
PCANet	81.5	39.8	81.9	30.0
DCTNet	81.9	39.8	81.5	29.8
LeNet-5	36.2	41.5	52.8	23.2

5 Conclusion

This paper analyzes the basic principle of feature map generation and pattern map coding in PCANet to explore the influence of dense coding on the offset-image recognition. The experimental analysis shows that the recognition ability of the filter cannot be effectively improved by increasing the depth of PCANet to obtain more filters. In order to solve this problem, this paper proposes the dense coding scheme based on the original model to enrich the number of pattern graphs in the network and improve the ability of network offset recognition. The experimental results show the effectiveness of the proposed method.

References

1. Sun, Y., Wang, X., Tang, X.: Deeply learned face representations are sparse, selective, and robust. In: 2015 IEEE Conference on Computer Vision and Pattern Recognition (CVPR), pp. 2892–2900. IEEE, Boston (2015)
2. Lui, Y.M., Bolme, D., Phillips, P.J., et al.: Preliminary studies on the good, the bad, and the ugly face recognition challenge problem. In: 2012 IEEE Computer Society Conference on Computer Vision and Pattern Recognition Workshops, pp. 9–16. IEEE, Providence (2012)

3. Wu, X., He, R., Sun, Z.: A lightened CNN for deep face representation. https://arxiv.org/abs/1511.02683. Accessed 15 Nov 2015
4. Li, X., Liang, R.: A survey of occluded face recognition: from subspace regression to deep learning. Acta Sinica Sinica **41**(1), 1–28 (2017)
5. Chan, T.H., Jia, K., Gao, S., et al.: PCANet: a simple deep learning baseline for image classification? IEEE T. Image Process. **24**(12), 5017–5032 (2015)
6. Wright, J., Ma, Y.: Dense error correction via l1-minimization. IEEE T. Inform. Theory **56**(7), 3540–3560 (2010)
7. Ojala, T., Pietikainen, M.: Multiresolution gray-scale and rotation invariant texture classification with local binary patterns. IEEE T. Pattern Anal. **24**(7), 971–987 (2002)
8. Zhang, B., Shan, S., Chen, X., et al.: Histogram of gabor phase patterns (HGPP): a novel object representation approach for face recognition. IEEE T. Image Process. **16**(1), 57–68 (2007)
9. Daugman, J.G.: High confidence visual recognition of persons by a test of statistical independence. IEEE T. Pattern Anal. **15**(11), 1148–1161 (1993)
10. Martinez, A., Benavente, R.: The AR face database. Technical report, Purdue University West Lafayette (1998)
11. Huang, G.B., Mattar, M., Berg, T., et al.: Labeled faces in the wild: a database for studying face recognition in unconstrained environments. Technical report, University of Massschusetts (2008)
12. Huang, G.B., Mattar, M., Lee, H., et al.: Learning to align from scratch. In: Proceedings of the Advances in Neural Information Processing Systems, pp. 773–781. Springer, Heidelberg (2012)

Self-supervision Adversarial Learning Network for Liver Lesion Classification

Cong Ma[1], Zhe Liu[1(✉)], Yuqing Song[1], Chengjian Qiu[1], Aihong Yu[1], and Jiawen Zhang[2]

[1] School of Computer Science and Communications Engineering, Jiangsu University, Zhenjiang 212013, China
1000004088@ujs.edu.cn

[2] Huashan Hospital, Department of Radiology, Fudan University, 12 Middle Wulumuqi Road, Shanghai 200040, China

Abstract. The lack of training samples is one of the main factors affecting the development of deep learning methods. Deep learning models often fail to learn useful features and have serious over-fitting problems when lacking of training data. In this work, we exploit two popular unsupervised learning techniques: adversarial learning and self-supervised learning, which is aimed at mine more useful representations and relieve over-fitting problems. Our training scheme is mainly divided into three steps. Firstly, we train a self-supervision network with unsupervised learning to extract obvious features from our liver lesion samples and these features will be transferred to next step. Secondly, we use the final output feature map generated by self-supervision network to train a discriminator by adversarial learning. Finally, the backbone network is trained under the constraint of discriminator and classifier. Our main idea is to train a discriminator with adversarial learning and self-supervised learning. Then, we use the discriminator to constrain the backbone network, which is aimed to reduce the backbone network solution search space. In particular, Different from generating data with GAN, we use GAN to feature adversarial learning for feature augmentation. Our experiments on liver lesion classification in CT show an average accuracy as 92.51% compared with the baseline training scheme, which demonstrates our proposed method can mime useful features and relieve over-fitting problem. It can assist physicians in the early detection and treatment of liver lesions.

Keywords: Self-supervised learning · Adversarial learning · Liver lesions

1 Introduction

The world Health Organization survey shows that the incidence of liver cancer and mortality Ranked 4th and 2nd in the world [1]. Medical image analysis plays a great important role in early diagnosis and treatment of liver tumor. Computed tomography (CT), Magnetic Resonance Imaging (MRI) and Liver Biopsy (LB) are the main methods for clinical analysis and diagnosis of liver tumor. Compared with the latter two methods, CT is often used to assist liver tumor diagnosis because of its robustness, high resolution

X. Sun et al. (Eds.): ICAIS 2021, LNCS 12736, pp. 540–552, 2021.
https://doi.org/10.1007/978-3-030-78609-0_46

and convenience. Focal liver lesion detection and classification are common medical problems, which determines the type of liver lesion. Hepatocellular carcinoma (HCC), hemangiomas (HEM) and metastasis (MET) are common liver lesion types [2].

With the increase in the number of patients, there will be a lot of medical CT images. However, the current number of professional physicians is very small. Traditional manual analysis often requires repeated comparison of CT slices in different periods, which is time-consuming and laborious and relies heavily on the judgment of professional physicians. So that doctors have a heavy workload, which inevitably leads to some misdiagnosis and missed diagnosis. Therefore, it is of great significance to develop computer-aided diagnosis systems which can assist physicians in the early detection and treatment of liver lesions.

In recent years, deep convolutions neural networks (DCNN) have achieved good results in the field of computer vision and also in the medical domain [3]. DCNN can mine the high-level feature representations, which has been proven to be superior to hand-crafted low-level features and mid-level features [4]. In most medical imaging tasks, medical data annotation is usually made by professional physicians and it takes a lot of time and effort, which is the key bottleneck for deep learning methods in medical domain. Researchers attempt to overcome this challenge by using data augmentation schemes, such as translation, rotation, flip and scale. Using such data augmentation schemes to improve the training process of network has become a standard procedure in computer vision tasks [2]. However, little additional information can be gained from small modifications to the images (e.g. the translation of the image a few pixels to the right) [5]. Therefore, how to improve the model performance under limited data remains to be solved.

The conventional approach to deal with this problem is to augment existing data by using data augmentation schemes. In addition to data augmentation, the extracting effective and discriminant features is related to improve model performance [6]. In this research we proposed a self-supervision adversarial learning network to feature extracting within our dataset to improve performance for liver lesion classification. The dataset used includes 4 categories: Hepatocellular carcinoma, cyst, metastasis, hemangioma and healthy liver parenchyma. Our experiments show that the proposed feature augmentation method improves the baseline results in classification accuracy.

Contribution. Our work is the first attempt to combine self-supervised learning [7] with adversarial learning [8] in the medical images, which can help to mine more useful representations for our classification. When we have small medical training samples, our model can avoid complex knowledge transfer and avoid relieve over-fitting. Our experiment show that our model can obviously improve the performance of liver lesion classification in limited medical data compared to baseline (we employ resnet34 [9] as our baseline).

2 Related Work

In recent years, people are focused on the development of computer-aided diagnostic tool, because it can help radiologists to classify different types of lesions [3, 10]. At the same time, due to deep learning has prominent effects compared with traditional methods on the ImageNet competition [11], which makes deep learning techniques to become more and more popular on medical imaging filed [12].

Recently, a number of approaches have been proposed to address the classification of liver tumors. For example, in [13], the author used synthetic new medical images by employing Generative Adversarial Networks (GAN) and arrived the results about sensitivity and specificity that had increased to 85.7% and 92.4% respectively. Avi Ben-Cohen et al. had synthesis new data by mixing the class specified and unspecified representation of different factors in the training data. They yielded an average improvement of 7.4% in accuracy over the baseline training scheme [14]. Their work showed that synthetic medical images could effectively improve the model performance. However, in the method above the synthesis new data based on existing data to improve the classification performance of liver lesion. K. Yasaka et al. proposed a convolution neural network to achieve the classification based on 1068 lesion CT images and conducted the testing with the models preserved in different processes which yielded an overall accuracy of 84% [3]. Besides, [15] combined patches of lesion region feature with whole-lesion region information, their method obtains an overall accuracy of 87.23% on the dataset which contains 480 CT liver slice images. Although to some extent, the above methods can alleviate few-sample problem, there are still the following problems: (1) The training fluctuates greatly and new synthesized unknown lesions need to be labeled again by the physician. (2) It is difficult for the network to learn the classification characteristics of different lesions.

In [16], the authors employed end-to-end deep learning approach to discriminate liver metastases from colorectal cancer and benign cysts in abdominal CT images of the liver, obtaining an accuracy of 96% and F1-score of 0.92 based on an in-house clinical biobank with 230 liver lesions originating from 63 patients. However, the method only can use pre-trained model on others large dataset, which needs computed intensively. [17] propose a multi-view knowledge-based collaborative (MV-KBC) deep model to separate malignant from benign nodules using limited chest CT data, this method above learns 3-D lung nodule characteristics by decomposing a 3-D nodule into nine fixed views. The method achieved an accuracy of 91.60% for lung nodule classification with an AUC of 95.70% on the benchmark LIDC-IDRI data set. But the method fails to extract fine features.

In order to develop an effective way for liver lesion classification, we focus on extracting features about rich contextual semantic information with multiple approaches in our dataset. We design a self-supervision adversarial learning network. Our main idea is to train a discriminator with adversarial learning and self-supervised learning. Then, we use the discriminator to constrain the backbone network, which is similar to the function of regularization and imposes soft constraints on the backbone network parameters.

3 Methods and Materials

In this section, we provide the details of our system model under small medical training data. We first introduce our learning framework and its training strategy in Sect. 3.1. Then, self-supervised learning is discussed in Sect. 3.2. Finally, we discuss adversarial learning in Sect. 3.3.

3.1 Overall Structure

In this study, we propose a self-supervision adversarial learning network (see Fig. 1). Figure 1 is the overall structure of our model. Our network includes three mainly steps. First of all, we train a SSNet (self-supervised network) (see Fig. 2) using a cross-entropy loss and SSNet will be as a part of step two. The second step we train an adversarial learning model (see Fig. 3) by using adversarial loss. In our adversarial learning model, the self-supervised network as a feature extractor to extract global features and fix the parameters of the self-supervised network. At the same time, the final output feature generated by SSNet and generator are used as true samples and fake samples respectively and generate adversarial training improve the performance of our model in liver lesion classification. The third step we train a generator (see Fig. 4) using a classification loss under the constraint of the discriminator which is fixed parameters in the step two. In order to improve generator liver lesion classification accuracy, we use hyperparameter λ to balance the influence of discriminator to generator (which is used to classify).

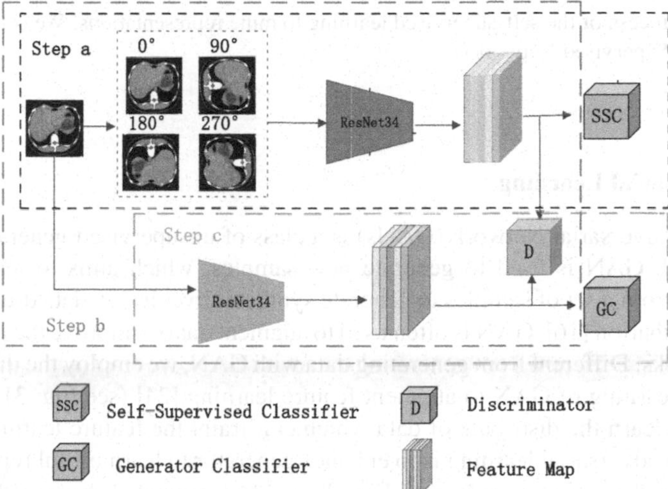

Fig. 1. Our Network structure. In this structure we will perform Self-supervised learning and adversarial learning. Step (a) (b) and (c) perform the self-supervised learning (black dotted box), adversarial learning (blue dotted box) and classification, respectively. (Color figure online)

3.2 Self-supervised Learning

Self-supervised learning (see Fig. 2), which learns by constructing artificial labels given only the input signals, has recently gained considerable attention for learning representations with unlabeled datasets [18], i.e., Gidaris et al. [19] proposed to rotate the image and predict the rotation angle. It has been widely used in the video domain [20], the robotics domain [21] and the image domain [22]. We focused on the medical image domain in this paper. This surrogate task mines useful representations for downstream image classification tasks. There are many other surrogate tasks besides rotating classification. For example, the network can be trained to solve the context prediction problem, like the relative location of disjoint patches [7]. To predict such transformations, a model should distinguish between what is semantically natural or not. Consequently, it learns high-level semantic representations of inputs [19]. Other surrogate tasks include predicting the unsupervised clustering classes [22], image in-painting [23] and so on.

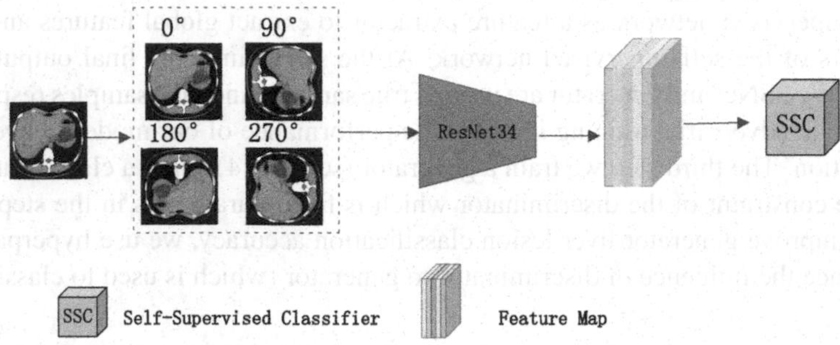

Fig. 2. The process of the self-supervised learning to mine representations. We call the network as SSN (Self-Supervised Network)

3.3 Adversarial Learning

Generative Adversarial Network (GANs) is a class of unsupervised generative models [13]. In [15], GAN is used to generate new samples, which aims to learn the data distribution from a set of samples to generate synthesis liver lesion data drawn from the learned distribution [16]. GAN is often used to augment data to improve the performance of special tasks. Different from generating data with GAN, we employ the thought of the adversarial learning of GAN to augment feature learning [24] (see Fig. 3). The ability of GAN can learn the distribute of data which constraint the feature learning. The key idea of using adversarial learning is to enhance generator to learn useful representation.

In our third training step (see in Fig. 3), we use generate adversarial training to promote the generator for classification task. The feature maps generated by SSNet and generator are viewed as true samples and false samples respectively, and then generate adversarial training for both to improve of generator in liver lesion classification. Using generate adversarial training, we do not need to designed complex cost function and training method to classification task. Our network can learn more better representations from using generate adversarial training. The experiment is shown in Sect. 4.

When we train our model, there are three mainly loss functions including Self-supervised loss, adversarial loss and classifier loss. The adversarial loss is similar to GAN. In GAN, discriminator as D and generator as G, playing the following two-player minimax game, which denotes loss optimization of the generative adversarial model in below [21]:

$$\underset{G}{min}\,\underset{D}{max}\; \mathrm{E}_{x\sim \mathrm{P}_{data}}[\log D(x)] + \mathrm{E}_{x\sim \mathrm{P}_{z}}[\log(1 - D(G(z)))] \quad (1)$$

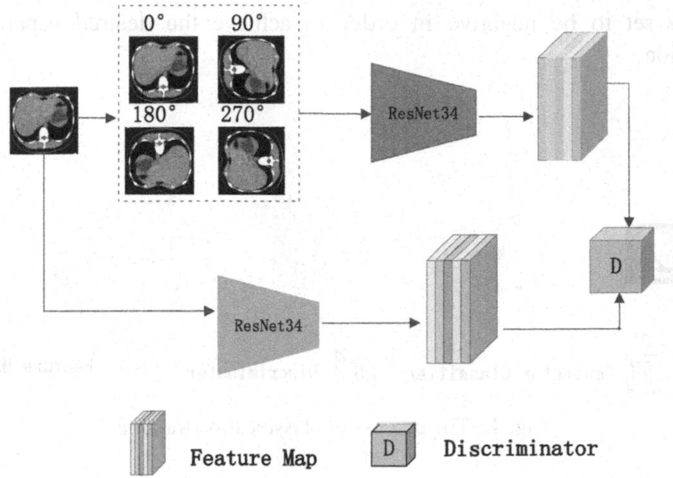

Fig. 3. The process of adversarial learning

where E denotes expectation, x and z are samples drawn from P_{data} and P_z respectively. The discriminator D is trained to maximized D(x) for images x with $x \sim P_{data}$ and to minimize D(G(z)) for images G(z) with $x \sim P_z$. G(z) which denotes the features generated is adopted to fool D during training. Therefore, the generator is trained to maximize D(G(z)).

In our model, when we train the first step, the classifier of SSNet is cross entropy classification loss L_{SSC} is as follows:

$$L_{SSC} = -\frac{1}{N}\sum\nolimits_{i=1}^{N}[y^{(i)}\log\hat{y}^{(i)} + (1 - y^{(i)})\log\left(1 - \hat{y}^{(i)}\right)] \quad (2)$$

When train the second step, we were inspired by [19], the adversarial loss can be divided into discriminator loss L_D and generator loss L_G.they are as follows:

$$L_D = \max_D \frac{1}{N}\sum\nolimits_{i=1}^{N}[\log(D(E(x^{(i)}))) + \log(1 - D(G(x^{(i)})))] \quad (3)$$

$$L_G = \max_D \frac{1}{N}\sum\nolimits_{i=1}^{N}\log(1 - D(G(x^{(i)}))) \quad (4)$$

where N is the batch size, x^i represents the i-th sample (i = 1, 2, …, N). E $(x^{(i)})$ represents the i-th sample output feature maps form SSNet. G $(x^{(i)})$ represents the i-th sample output feature maps from generator.

In the third step (see Fig. 4), the classifier of generator is Cross entropy classification loss L_{GC} (see formula 5)

$$L_{GC} = -\frac{1}{N}\sum\nolimits_{i=1}^{N}[y^{(i)}\log\hat{y}^{(i)} + (1 - y^{(i)})\log\left(1 - \hat{y}^{(i)}\right)] \quad (5)$$

In particular, in order to carry out the efficiency liver lesion classification, we use hyperparameter λ to balance the feature earned. So that the third step loss L is as follows:

$$L = \lambda L_D + L_{GC} \quad (6)$$

where λ is set to be negative in order to achieve the desired separation of the representation.

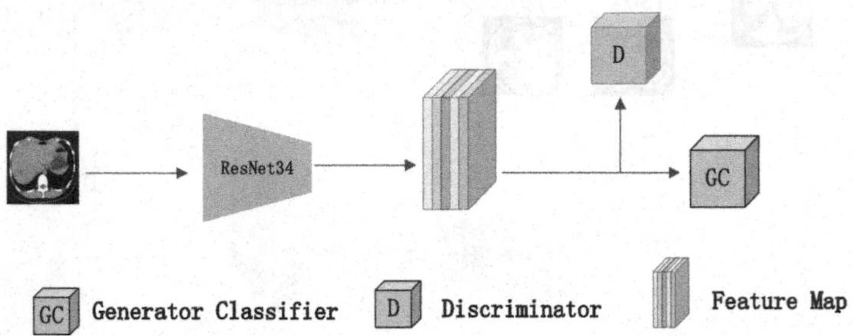

Fig. 4. The process of classification training

4 Experiments and Results

4.1 Dataset and Implementation

In this work, experimental data was obtained from the Affiliated Hospital of Jiangsu University, the CT scans were acquired with a slice collimation of 5–7 mm, a matrix of 512 × 512 pixels, and an inplane resolution of 0.57−0.89. The dataset comprises four types of 430 portal CT scans from 120 patients: 163 metastases (MET), 83 hemangiomas (HEM) and 184 Hepatocellular carcinoma (HCC). In order to increase the diversity of data, 84 samples were taken from the non-marked liver location Image of Healthy, so our final classification dataset have 514 images. Figure 5 shows a set of data samples from the different categories. The lesion sample in the picture is the lesion area taken according to the doctor's mark. The image input to the classification network is a region of interest captured based on the annotations of radiologists. In order to remove irrelevant information about other organs and tissues in the CT scans for liver lesion classification, we cut the image intensity values of all CT scans to the range of [−100, 400] HU [24]. After all CT scan HU values were truncated, we normalized all slice intensities into the range [0, 1] with min-max normalization.

We set batch size is 64 and the learning rate is 0.001 for 50 epochs. In each epoch, our training is divided into three steps, when train the first step, we perform 20 epochs, after that we perform adversarial learning with 25 epochs. In the third step, we train classification model 10 epochs. The input to our classification system is 64 × 64 image from the region of interests by random cropping. All training processes were performed using a NVIDIA GeForce GTX 1080 Ti GPU.

4.2 Evaluation

We use 5-fold cross validation to evaluate the classification performance with and without our proposed method, our training perform on the dataset which is included in Sect. 4.1. Healthy tissues are used to enhance the diversity of training data and make the model have the judgment ability on lesions and non-lesions. The results are presented in Table 1. By using this training strategy, we achieved an improvement of 10.2% on average accuracy.

Table 1. Results with and without K-fold cross-validation were compared in the final epoch.

Fold	Baseline [ACC.%]	Proposed [ACC.%]
1	83.68	88.81
2	79.53	90.09
3	82.16	94.60
4	83.32	92.46
5	81.23	95.44
Avg	82.01 ± 2.2	92.28 ± 3.1

Classification confusion matrix with and without our proposed strategy are presented (see Fig. 5 and Fig. 6). From the results, we can see that our proposed method was able to improve the overall classification accuracy along all classes. However, there are some mistakes between MET, HEM, Normal. Figure 7 shows the comparison in baseline and our proposed method with ROC curves. Our proposed method improves AUC along all classes.

In order to explore the impact of different strategies on liver lesion classification, we compared baseline, baseline with adversarial learning, baseline with self-supervision and our proposed method. Table 2 has showed the performance comparison of models with different strategies. We can find self-supervision can achieve better result than using the adversarial learning.

However, there was a serious over-fitting problem when we trained baseline with self-supervision. In order to alleviate over-fitting problem in our dataset, we use generate adversarial training to promote model self-supervision to relieve over-fitting problem. We did an experiment to compare feature learning based on adversarial constraint. It can be found that the baseline with feature adversarial constraint and self-supervision has better performance than baseline with self-supervision.

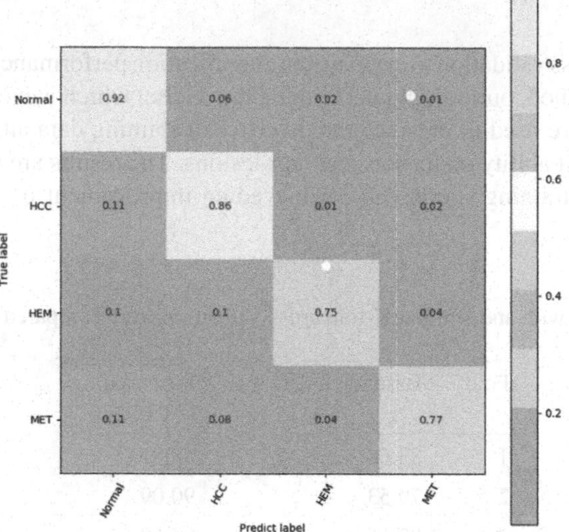

Fig. 5. Mixed matrix for the baseline

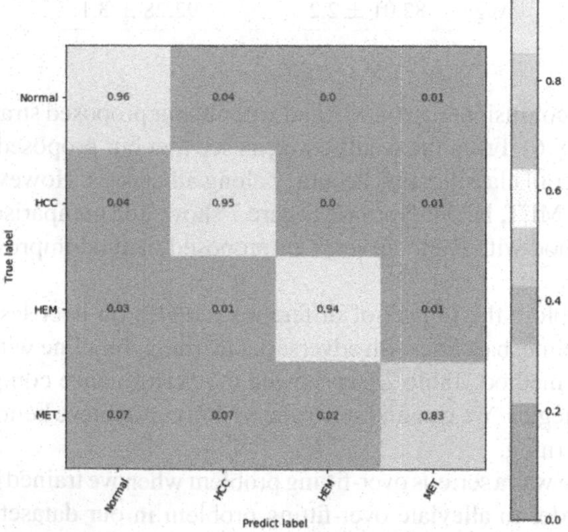

Fig. 6. Mixed matrix for our proposed method

Previous studies have proven that deep learning based on methods are superior to traditional methods, people more tend to use deep learning for liver lesions classification [3, 4, 15]. Due to the limited number of openly available liver lesion dataset with confirmed presence of malignant tumors, direct comparative with other published results is difficult. However, we comparative results reported in this study show the improvement with regards to state of art methods, including classic network. The results are presented

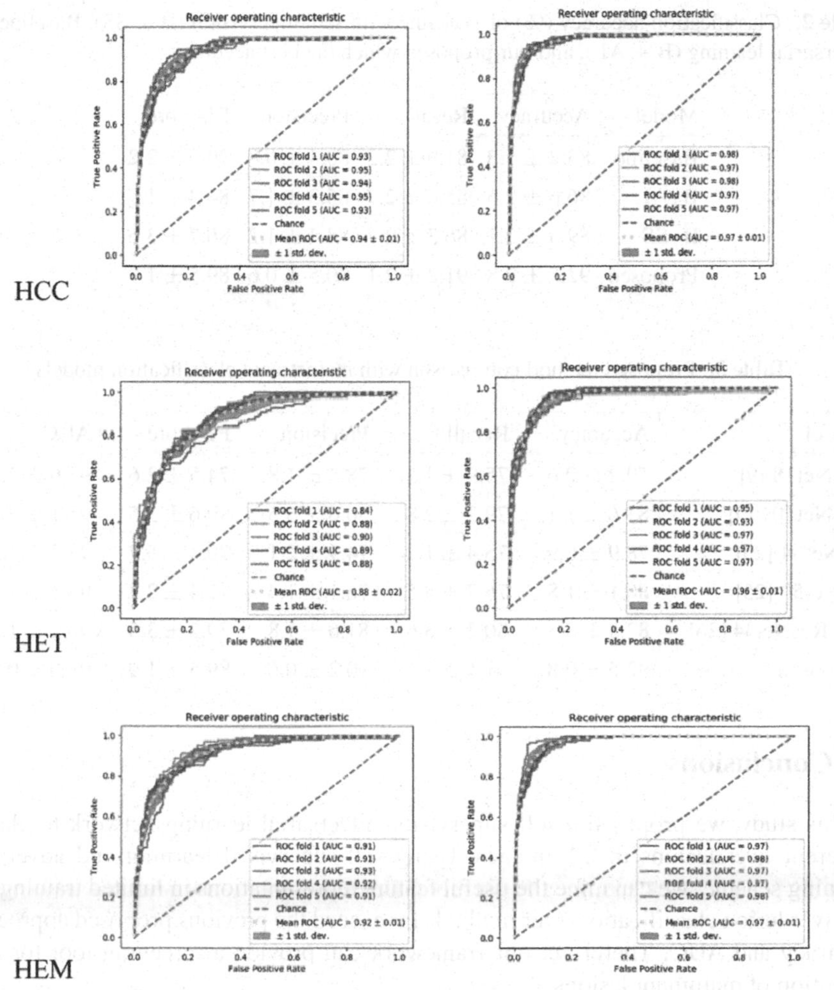

Fig. 7. Comparison in baseline and our proposed method with ROC curves. Left column show the results of baseline and Right column show the results of our method. Our method improves AUC along all classes.

in Table 3. It shows the proposed method, which surpasses the previous classic network model.

Table 2. Classification accuracy (%) of Baseline with self-supervision (B + SS), Baseline with adversarial learning (B + AL), and our proposed which the best accuracy.

Model	Accuracy	Recall	Precision	F1-score
Baseline	83.2 ± 1.3	81.9 ± 2.2	80.4 ± 0.8	79.6 ± 2.2
B+AL	86.6 ± 2.5	85.6 ± 2.7	85.3 ± 1.7	84.3 ± 1.9
B+SS	89.5 ± 3.1	86.3 ± 2.7	88.4 ± 1.2	86.7 ± 3.6
Proposed	92.5 ± 2.8	91.2 ± 2.1	90.5 ± 0.6	89.5 ± 1.9

Table 3. Proposed method comparison with mainstream classification models

Model	Accuracy	Recall	Precision	F1-score	AUC
ResNet18 [9]	79.2 ± 0.6	75.9 ± 1.5	78.3 ± 1.8	74.5 ± 2.6	93.6 ± 2.2
ResNet101 [9]	81.6 ± 1.1	79.2 ± 2.8	80.6 ± 3.5	80.6 ± 3.5	95.1 ± 3.1
SENet34 [25]	78.9 ± 0.9	75.4 ± 1.2	74.9 ± 2.1	70.4 ± 5.7	93.5 ± 1.5
SENet50 [25]	80.1 ± 1.8	76.7 ± 3.5	76.1 ± 1.4	77.4 ± 2.2	94.1 ± 1.75
SE_ResNet34 [26]	83.5 ± 3.3	80.3 ± 3.6	81.6 ± 1.8	79.2 ± 3.5	96.7 ± 1.9
Proposed	92.5 ± 0.8	91.1 ± 2.1	90.2 ± 0.6	89.5 ± 1.9	98.0 ± 0.1

5 Conclusions

In this study, we proposed a self-supervision adversarial learning network to classify different liver lesions in CT images. Using self-supervised learning and adversarial learning scheme, we can mine the useful feature representations in limited training data for liver lesion classification. Our methods far exceed the previous proposed approaches accuracy and AUC. Therefore, our framework can provide a screening tool for early detection of malignant lesions.

Acknowledgements. This work was supported by the National Natural Science Foundation of China (61976106, 61572239), Zhenjiang Key Deprogram "Fire Early Warning Technology Based on Multimodal Data Analysis" (SH2020011) Jiangsu Emergency Management Science and Technology Project "Research on Very Early Warning of Fire Based on Multi-modal Data Analysis and Multi-Intelligent Body Technology" (YJGL-TG-2020-8).

References

1. Bray, F., Ferlay, J., Soerjomataram, I., et al.: Global cancer statistics 2018: GLOBOCAN estimates of incidence and mortality worldwide for 36 cancers in 185 countries. CA: Cancer J. Clin. **68**(6), 394–424 (2018)
2. Greenspan, H., Van Ginneken, B., Summers, R.M.: Guest editorial deep learning in medical imaging: overview and future promise of an exciting new technique. IEEE Trans. Med. Imaging **35**(5), 1153–1159 (2016)

3. Yasaka, K., Akai, H., Abe, O., et al.: Deep learning with convolutional neural network for differentiation of liver masses at dynamic contrast-enhanced CT: a preliminary study. Radiology **286**(3), 887–896 (2018)
4. Setio, A.A.A., Ciompi, F., Litjens, G., et al.: Pulmonary nodule detection in CT images: false positive reduction using multi-view convolutional networks. IEEE Trans. Med. Imaging **35**(5), 1160–1169 (2016)
5. Frid-Adar, M., Diamant, I., Klang, E., et al.: GAN-based synthetic medical image augmentation for increased CNN performance in liver lesion classification. Neurocomputing **321**, 321–331 (2018)
6. Luo, L., Xiong, Y., Liu, Y., et al.: Adaptive gradient methods with dynamic bound of learning rate. arXiv preprint arXiv:1902.09843 (2019)
7. Doersch, C., Gupta, A., Efros, A.A.: Unsupervised visual representation learning by context prediction. In: Proceedings of the IEEE International Conference on Computer Vision, pp. 1422–1430 (2015)
8. Goodfellow, I., Pouget-Abadie, J., Mirza, M., et al.: Generative adversarial nets. In: Advances in Neural Information Processing Systems, pp. 2672–2680 (2014)
9. He, K., Zhang, X., Ren, S., et al.: Deep residual learning for image recognition. In: Proceedings of the IEEE Conference on Computer Vision and Pattern Recognition, pp. 770–778 (2016)
10. Adcock, A., Rubin, D., Carlsson, G.: Classification of hepatic lesions using the matching metric. Comput. Vis. Image Underst. **121**, 36–42 (2014)
11. Deng, J., Dong, W., Socher, R., et al. ImageNet: a large-scale hierarchical image database. In: 2009 IEEE Conference on Computer Vision and Pattern Recognition. IEEE, pp. 248–255 (2009)
12. Litjens, G., Kooi, T., Bejnordi, B.E., et al.: A survey on deep learning in medical image analysis. Med. Image Anal. **42**, 60–88 (2017)
13. Frid-Adar, M., Klang, E., Amitai, M., et al.: Synthetic data augmentation using GAN for improved liver lesion classification. In: 2018 IEEE 15th International Symposium on Biomedical Imaging (ISBI 2018), pp. 289–293. IEEE (2018)
14. Ben-Cohen, A., Mechrez, R., Yedidia, N., et al.: Improving CNN training using disentanglement for liver lesion classification in CT. In: 2019 41st Annual International Conference of the IEEE Engineering in Medicine and Biology Society (EMBC), pp. 886–889. IEEE (2019)
15. Liang, D., et al.: Residual convolutional neural networks with global and local pathways for classification of focal liver lesions. In: Geng, X., Kang, B.-H. (eds.) PRICAI 2018: Trends in Artificial Intelligence: 15th Pacific Rim International Conference on Artificial Intelligence, Nanjing, China, August 28–31, 2018, Proceedings, Part I, pp. 617–628. Springer, Cham (2018). https://doi.org/10.1007/978-3-319-97304-3_47
16. Romero, F.P., Diler, A., Bisson-Gregoire, G., et al.: End-to-end discriminative deep network for liver lesion classification. In: 2019 IEEE 16th International Symposium on Biomedical Imaging (ISBI 2019), pp. 1243–1246. IEEE (2019)
17. Xie, Y., Xia, Y., Zhang, J., et al.: Knowledge-based collaborative deep learning for benign-malignant lung nodule classification on chest CT. IEEE Trans. Med. Imaging **38**(4), 991–1004 (2018)
18. Lee, H., Hwang, S.J., Shin, J.: Self-supervised label augmentation via input transformations. In: International Conference on Machine Learning, PMLR, pp. 5714–5724 (2020)
19. Gidaris, S., Singh, P., Komodakis, N.: Unsupervised representation learning by predicting image rotations. arXiv preprint arXiv:1803.07728 (2018)
20. Lee, H.Y., Huang, J.B., Singh, M., et al.: Unsupervised representation learning by sorting sequences. In: Proceedings of the IEEE International Conference on Computer Vision, pp. 667–676 (2017)
21. Jang, E., Devin, C., Vanhoucke, V., et al.: Grasp2vec: learning object representations from self-supervised grasping. arXiv preprint arXiv:1811.06964 (2018)

22. Caron, M., Bojanowski, P., Joulin, A., et al.: Deep clustering for unsupervised learning of visual features. In: Proceedings of the European Conference on Computer Vision (ECCV), pp. 132–149 (2018)
23. Pathak, D., Krahenbuhl, P., Donahue, J., et al.: Context encoders: feature learning by inpainting. In: Proceedings of the IEEE Conference on Computer Vision and Pattern Recognition, pp. 2536–2544 (2016)
24. Chen, P., Song, Y., Yuan, D., et al.: Feature fusion adversarial learning network for liver lesion classification. In: Proceedings of the ACM Multimedia Asia, pp. 1–7 (2019)
25. Hu, J., Shen, L., Sun, G.: Squeeze-and-excitation networks. In: Proceedings of the IEEE Conference on Computer Vision and Pattern Recognition, pp. 7132–7141 (2018)
26. Li, X., Wang, W., Hu, X., et al.: Selective kernel networks. In: Proceedings of the IEEE/CVF Conference on Computer Vision and Pattern Recognition, pp. 510–519 (2019)

Mining Consumer Brand Relationship from Social Media Data: A Natural Language Processing Approach

Di Shang[1(✉)], Zhenda Hu[2], and Zhaoxia Wang[3]

[1] University of North Florida, Jacksonville 32224, USA
d.shang@unf.edu

[2] Shanghai University of Finance and Economics, Shanghai 200433, China

[3] Singapore Management University, Singapore 178902, Singapore
zxwang@smu.edu.sg

Abstract. There is a rich collection of studies exploring different aspects of consumer brand relationship. Traditional approaches of questionnaires and analysis are based on measurements collected from a relatively small number of survey participants. With the advancements in natural language processing (NLP) techniques, opportunities exist for applying NLP techniques to discover consumer brand relationship from social media platforms that possess a large amount of data on consumer opinion and sentiment. In this study, we review consumer brand relationship analysis focusing on leveraging NLP and machine learning techniques to address some challenges associated with discovering customer brand relationship from social media data and propose a methodological framework for the approach. This study has implications for both academic research and practitioners as it presents an alternative way to investigate consumer brand relationship.

Keywords: NLP · Text mining · Consumer brand relationship · Machine learning

1 Introduction

The mass customization in many industries has caused increasing complexity of businesses operations in a global setting [1]. When a company operates over such a large geographical area, knowing consumer brand relationship is becoming more and more important for its business successes. Shimp and Madden were the first to introduce the concept of consumer brand relationship [2]. They defined consumer brand relationship (CBR) as "consumer forms a relation with consumption objects (products, brands, stores, etc.), which range from feelings of antipathy, to slight fondness, all the way up to the what would, in person-person relations, amounts to love." It is a relationship that consumers have with a product or a company which reflects how they think and feel about it. Aaker

X. Sun et al. (Eds.): ICAIS 2021, LNCS 12736, pp. 553–565, 2021.
https://doi.org/10.1007/978-3-030-78609-0_47

states that a business should think of a brand as a product, a person, an enterprise and a symbol to build the brand identity framework [3]. Most studies on consumer brand relationship rely on data collected from surveys in which participants directly report their perceptions in given dimensions. The survey studies often suffer from limited size of participants and prolonged time of preparing and conducting surveys.

With the advent of social media platforms, more and more consumers prefer to post their feedback, reviews and opinions of services and products online through social media platforms such as Twitter, Facebook and Google+ [4–6]. Such social media data provide a potentially rich source of information that can generate insights for better understanding consumer brand relationship. Collectively, such information may provide rich knowledge which may not be captured in traditional data collection methods such as administering a survey questionnaire. In addition, text mining technique and sentiment analysis based on social media data have been widely applied to brand authenticity, consumer brand relationship and engagement [7–9].

In this paper, we summarize the existing methods of applications of text mining and sentiment analysis to understand consumer brand relationship. Based on the previous research, we propose a methodological framework to assessing consumer brand relationship from social media as an alternative to traditional survey methods. Our framework allows researchers and practitioners to utilize existing survey items to develop training data for machine learning algorithms, incorporating large social media data by data augmentation and reducing the needs for direct survey inputs. We conduct a preliminary test of the approach with a secondary social media data set.

The rest of the paper is organized as follows: Sect. 2 discusses the existing consumer brand relationship research; Section 3 discussed related applications of data augmentation methods; Section 4 conducts a preliminary experiment on the proposed framework; finally, Sect. 5 concludes the paper by noting several limitations and suggesting potential improvements.

2 Related Work and Methods

2.1 Existing CBR Research Based on Surveys and Social Media

Previous studies have developed different dimensions that provide perspectives on consumer brand relationship and how relationships should be measured. Some suggest that the nature of brand relationship can be divided into three components: cognition, affection and conation [10], whereas Keller thought that brand relationships can be characterized in two dimensions of activity and intensity [11]. Barnes created a customer relationship index according to the interpersonal relationship measures [12]. Brand relationship index measures the relationship quality that a business has attained with consumers by 1) trust 2) commitment 3) awareness 4) attention 5) recognition and 6) interaction. The dimensions interact with each other, and sometimes are interchangeable. For instance, brand awareness establishes brand trust. Once consumers are bond to a brand, they are more likely to make repeat purchases, which then bridges the gap between trust and loyalty.

Social media has become a great way for businesses to engage with customers and build brands [13]. Social media platforms such as Facebook, LinkedIn, and Twitter give companies more ways to reach out to customers. More and more companies use Facebook Pages and Twitter handlers for brand communication and customer engagements [14]. Stephen and Galak describe two different types of social media involving a brand [15]. Earned social media is "referring to social media activity related to a brand that is not directly generated by the brand owner or its agents". In contrast, owned social media is "activity that is generated by the brand owner (or his/her agents) in social networking services that it can control". The applications of social media strategies help to increase such business values as raising brand awareness, boosting brand reputation, and enhancing brand loyalty [16]. Therefore, social media platforms should be used to create the illusion of a permanent brand presence in the informational environment of consumers. Brand loyalty level may be increased by an interactive, customized, and responsive way of social media use through networking and conversation with the consumers.

While the literature presents a rich collection of measurements of consumer brand relationship, all the studies rely on data collected from surveys. Consumers are asked to directly rate brand relationships on a numeric scale according to their perceptions in a given dimension. Some research suggests that rating brands via surveys can provide greater validity [17], and these are widely used in marketing practices. Though survey studies can obtain direct answers from customers or users, they suffer from some limitations. One limitation is its sample size. Researchers and industry practitioners have tried to increase sample sizes by sending surveys to hundreds and even thousands of customers, but they are still a small portion of the customer population. Another limitation is the time needed for conducting survey studies. Companies normally need to go through design, delivery, collection, and analysis processes, and it can easily take months for distributing and collecting surveys. Researchers have recognized the limitations of surveys such as the difficulty and expense in recruiting participants, collecting responses and ensuring truthful answers [18].

Social media and consumer review platforms have completely changed the way consumers communicate. Social media platforms help businesses gather richer, actionable insight about customer sentiment on their company, their brand, and specific products or services. Social media platforms have provided a valuable source for companies to collect information about a large number of customers in real-time. The abundant publicly available social media data and the advancements in NLP techniques motivate us to develop a flexible and automated means of estimating consumer brand relationship from social media data. The proliferation of social media use by both businesses and consumers offers a valuable data source to understand consumer perceptions. Text analysis of user-generated content (UGC) is a frequently used approach in the literature for mining consumer perceptions from social media data [19]. In marketing, researchers have employed text mining techniques on UGC to discover how product features or brands are perceptually clustered by consumers [20].

Many customer conversions on social media platforms reflect their opinions and attitude and thus can be used to measure consumer brand relationship. As shown in Table 1, well-established measurement items in survey studies can find their variants in social media data. The existing works, such as applications of NLP and text mining on social media [21–23] have laid a solid foundation for achieving the goals of this research. NLP and text mining have helped businesses and researchers to better know what is happening on the Internet, and it helps customer side as well.

Table 1. Examples of social media data related to brand relationship.

Dimension	Source	Example
Commitment	Survey Item	I would like to recommend [brand] to my friends
	Social Media Data	[brand] is my number one favorite treat I recommend these to anyone who wants to ...
Trust	Survey Item	This [brand] is reliable
	Social Media Data	I've been buying [brand] for 12 years and they never turn it down. Always a trustworthy company
Awareness	Survey Item	I know the product line of [brand]
	Social Media Data	[brand] just launched a new ... Compared with old models, ...

2.2 Customer Brand Sentiment Analysis Based on Social Media

More and more marketing researchers have paid attention to social media and consumer review platforms in studying branding issues. Many companies keep abreast of customer sentiments to promote brands. Based on it, customer ratings and sentiment analysis can be used to quantify the overall positive and negative sentiments expressed online about a product or a brand [24], serving the same functions as ratings of survey respondents.

Specifically, some research utilized NLP and text mining for consumer brand sentiments by constructing domain lexicon. Mostafa used a random sample of 3516 tweets and an expert-predefined lexicon including around 6800 seed adjectives to evaluate consumers' sentiment towards famous brands such as Nokia and IBM, and results indicated a generally positive consumer sentiment towards several well-known brands [25]. Filipa et al. applied sentiment analysis to Yelp reviews of restaurants and built a specific aggregated dictionary for brand authenticity, consumer brand engagement and related constructs. Their findings revealed that online reviews could be an essential source of information for exploring sentimental attachment toward a focal object in brand authenticity and consumer brand engagement [26]. Bilro et al. also created a customer engagement dictionary based on WordNet 2.1 using Yelp customers' online reviews including 15,000 unique reviews of restaurants, hotels and nightlife entertainment. The findings indicated that the engagement cognitive processing dimension and hedonic experience had a significant effect on customers' review endeavor and customers seemed to be more engaged in positively advocating a company/brand than the contrary [27].

There are also some existing research in which the topics of social media users' representations and sentiments are identified to explore the relationship between customers and brands. Francesca and Alessandro utilized Emotional Text Mining to extract meaningful information for customer profiling and brand management. Specifically, the paper conducted the experiments on Twitter customer messages of a well-known sportswear brand to discover product preferences, representations, and sentiments. They proposed a bottom-up approach to classify unstructured data for the identification of social media users' representations and sentiments about a topic [7]. Byeongki et al. proposed an opportunity mining approach to identify product opportunities based on topic modeling and sentiment analysis of social media data. In their approach, latent product topics discussed by customers were identified in social media using topic modeling, thereby quantifying the importance of each product topic. Next, the satisfaction level of each product topic was evaluated using sentiment analysis. Finally, the opportunity value and improvement direction of each product topic from a customer-centered view were identified by an opportunity algorithm based on product topics' importance and satisfaction [9].

As for predicting customer sentiments towards brands, besides unsupervised methods, some supervised machine learning algorithms have also been adapted. For example, Hamid et al. constructed a procedure of brand authenticity sentiment analysis based on social media. Specifically, they established a framework using latent semantic analysis (LSA) and support vector machine (SVM) to predict both the brand authenticity dimensions and their sentiment polarity [8].

3 Data Augmentation Methods by Leveraging NLP Technology

Although the literature has built a solid ground of measurement items of consumer brand relationship, most survey studies develop or implement collections of only 20 to 30 items. While the number of items is sufficient to survey studies in which respondents are asked to directly rate brand relationships, it will not be feasible for NLP and machine learning approaches. NLP requires large databases of common phrases and sentences in a given language to understand or translate in natural language based on machine learning. In addition, the data about user comments on social networking sites are not always all available - the administrators often only allow positive comments and hide negative comments, which makes the dataset imbalanced [28]. The quality of NLP outcomes significantly depends on the availability of large corpora in a target domain. One way to increase the size of items for machine learning purpose is through data augmentation, and previous studies have concluded that text augmentation helps to further improve NLP model results [29].

Many data augmentation methods have been demonstrated to be effective. Zhang et al. found that one useful way to do text augmentation is replacing words or phrases with their synonyms [30]. In addition to the use of thesaurus, classic word embeddings, such as word2vec, GloVe and Fasttext, can be applied to perform similarity search. Fadaee et al. concluded that using contextualized word embeddings to replace target word outperforms static word embeddings [31]. Some other simple approaches have also been proved to be effective. They include inserting a synonym into a random position in the sentence, randomly choosing two words in the sentence and swapping their positions, and randomly removing a word in a sentence[1]. Similarly, Wei and Zou proposed easy data augmentation techniques for boosting performance on text classification tasks. The method includes four simple but powerful operations: synonym replacement, random insertion, random swap, and random deletion, which used only 50% of the available training set but achieved the same accuracy [32]. We apply some data augmentation techniques using NLPAug library to expand items adopted from [33], and some results from the augmentation are listed in Table 2.

Table 2. Results of data augmentation methods.

Methods	Results
Synonym	I would like to **suggest** [brand] to my friends
Random insertion	**Post** I would like to recommend [brand] to my friends
Random swap	**my** would like to recommend [brand] to **I** friends
Random deletion	I would ~~like~~ to recommend [brand] to my friends
Original text	I would like to recommend [brand] to my friends

In addition, NLP requires context in order to better understand the conversations of customers in social media. Different forms of context, such as cultural, places and events, have different effects on language understanding [34]. Corpora for machine learning should be representative and balanced with respect to the language that customers speak in a specific context. Incorporating contextual variables in NLP studies has shown to improve classification performance of social media analysis in that linguistic variations can be extreme [35]. Annotation can bring contextual variables into corpora, and annotated corpora can be used to train ML algorithms more efficiently and effectively [36]. An annotation development cycle normally follows model, annotate, train test, evaluate, and revise phases [37]. In order to provide statistically useful results, labelled data

[1] E. Ma. NLP Augmentation. https://github.com/makcedward/nlpaug, 2019.

on a sufficiently large corpus must be obtained [37]. Some examples of human annotated social media data based on measurement items of brand relationship from the literature are listed in Table 3. Consumer-brand related reviews are labeled with 1, and non consumer-brand related are labeled with 0.

Table 3. Examples of human annotated data.

Text	Label
I have been buying [brand] for a few years and am very happy with it	1
This [brand] are my number one favorite treat. I recommend these to anyone who ...	1
This is a good product. My kids like them	0
Super fast shipping, will be purchasing them again!	0

4 A Methodological Framework and Preliminary Testing

4.1 A Methodological Framework

Based on the discussion above, we propose a methodological framework for assessing brand relationship from social media data. Researchers and practitioners can use the framework to utilize well established survey items to conduct studies to discover consumer insights from social media data. As shown in Fig. 1, human annotation is often used to develop context-specific corpus for machine learning algorithms. Researchers can experiment with different annotation techniques to discover whichever best suit their research. Traditional survey instruments are well-established in the literature but usually have small data size. NLP augmentation techniques can be applied to increase the data size without compromising the data quality. Because of the diversified words and terms appearing in social media, word embedding techniques transform text data and provide a numerical representation that better captures the word meaning. Word vectors is a potent approach for quantitatively capturing word meaning. Embeddings generally represent geometrical encodings of words based on how frequently they appear together in a text corpus. The main idea is that a model can be trained on the context on each word, so similar words will have similar numerical representations [38].

4.2 Preliminary Testing

We use Amazon Fine Food Review dataset to test the proposed method to investigate consumer brand relationship from social media data. The dataset consists of 568454 reviews of 74258 fine foods from Amazon [39]. To test the

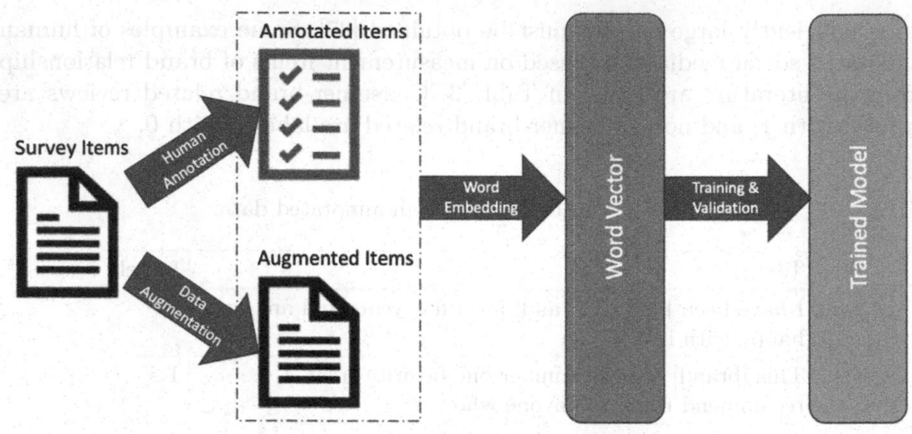

Fig. 1. Methodological framework.

generalizability of the proposed approach across brands, we retrieve five brands with the most reviews for our study, with a total of 3441 reviews. We adopt the well-established items from [33] (shown in Appendix) as the starting point to classify the review data. In this test, we focus on assessing consumer brand relationship in general, instead of examining individual dimensions.

Table 4. Summary of the deep learning model.

Layer	Output shape
InputLayer	(None, 120)
Embedding	(None, 120, 300)
Conv1D	(None, 118, 128)
Conv1D	(None, 118, 128)
MaxPooling1D	(None, 29, 128)
MaxPooling1D	(None, 23, 128)
Concatenate	(None, 52, 128)
GRU	(None, 52, 128)
LSTM	(None, 128)
Dense	(None, 32)
Dense	(None, 1)

NLP data augmentation is used to expand items using NLPaug library. Five graduate students worked as human annotators to mark a sample of 1000 reviews accordingly. The process resulted in 1000 labeled reviews, bringing up the training data to a total of 1480 labeled records. We applied FastText for word embedding because it uses n-gram characters as the smallest unit. In addition, FastText generates better word embeddings for rare words [40], which is very helpful for dealing with the rare words and typos which commonly appear in customer reviews. We used the data to train a deep network with an embedding layer (summarized in Table 4), and the model generated results with an average accuracy of 0.69, which show the feasibility of the proposed method.

5 Conclusions

In this paper, we summarize the existing methods of applications of text mining and sentiment analysis on consumer brand relationship and then introduce an approach for assessing consumer brand relationship from social media as an alternative to traditional survey methods. Our framework allows researchers and practitioners to utilize survey items to conduct consumer studies, incorporating large social media data and reducing the needs for direct survey inputs. In addition, using social media data, practitioners can monitor consumer brand relationship on social platforms and provide real-time recommendations to enhance the relationship.

The proposed method can be used to manage consumer relationships. Nowadays, customers expect to receive a customized and streamlined experience at all time. It is important to understand the preferences and purchasing habits of customers. The proposed method potentially benefits a business by making it simpler to track and investigate consumer relationship from social media. Businesses want to identify their customers quickly, address their main needs and also recommend extra services or products that may be of help to them. Understanding consumer relationship can help reduce the customer churn rate and identify which customers are most profitable.

We note several limitations with our experiment. First, our testing data is limited to brands of fine food. Future studies should examine a large range of brands. Second, consumers may express different opinions, concerns and sentiments across different social media platforms. Future studies should include other social media data, such as Twitter tweets, Yelp reviews and user forum threads. Furthermore, the noise and ambiguity of social media data present challenges to algorithmic solutions. Our proposed approach deserves further validation with a variety of social media data in different business contexts.

A Appendix

Consumer Brand Relationship Measurement Items adopted from [33]

1. I would like to recommend brand X to my friends.
2. Image of brand X is fit for my taste.
3. In product Y, no other brands can replace brand X in my heart.
4. Image of brand X fits my current lifestyle.
5. If I buy product Y next time, I would like to buy brand X again.

6. If brand X is out of stock, I will go to another store to look for it instead of buying other brands.
7. I think highly of the prospect of brand X.
8. Although the price of brand X is a little bit higher than other brands, I would like to choose it.
9. I will not regret for choosing brand X.
10. I would like to buy other products of brand X.
11. The product of brand X satisfies my request for category Y very well.
12. I am satisfied with this [brand].
13. The [brand] has come up to my expectations.
14. This brand is close to an ideal [brand].
15. I pay attention to the news about company X.
16. I would like to visit the website of company X.
17. I would like to join the brand X club to communicate with more customers of brand X.
18. I know the requirement of typical customers of brand X for product Y.
19. The communication with brand X customers makes me feel intimate.
20. I would like to help brand X clients rather than other brands clients.
21. I would like to make friends with brand X customers rather than other brands customers.
22. I know the differences of product attributes (such as function, appearance, capability) between brand X and other brands.
23. I know the product line of brand X.
24. I know the business scope of company X.
25. I know the current prices of main brand X products.
26. I know the development history of company X.
27. I think that company X is familiar with the customers requirement for product Y.
28. I think that company X will deal with the feedback from customers.
29. I believe that company X will respect the customers' benefit.
30. I think that company X commitment to customers is credible.
31. This [brand] is reliable.
32. This is an honest [brand].
33. I trust this [brand].
34. I can recognize brand X only through its logo or advertising.
35. I can associate its advertising or logo with brand X's name.
36. I feel that I understand this [brand].
37. The [brand] and I are meant for each other.
38. This [brand] reveals a lot about my personality.
39. This [brand] plays a decisive role in my life.
40. I believe that this [brand] provides sufficient options to get in touch with other consumers/users of this [brand].
41. It is interesting to share experiences with other consumers/users of this [brand].
42. I use or would like to use the option to discuss with other consumers/users of this [brand].

43. I am of the view that this [brand] provides sufficient options to get in touch with employees of this [brand].
44. It is important to me being able to contact employees of this [brand].
45. I use or would like to use the option to discuss about [brand] with employees of this [brand].
46. I think that this [brand] provides sufficient options to get in touch with the [brand] producer through interactive online applications.
47. It is important to me being able to get in touch with the [brand] producer through interactive online applications.
48. I use or would like to use the option to get in touch with the [brand] producer through interactive online applications.

References

1. Wang, Z., Joo, V., Tong, C., Xin, X., Chin, H.C.: Anomaly detection through enhanced sentiment analysis on social media data. In: 2014 IEEE 6th international conference on cloud computing technology and science, pp. 917–922. IEEE (2014)
2. Shimp, T.A., Madden, T.J.: Consumer-object relations: a conceptual framework based analogously on Sternberg's triangular theory of love. Adv. Consum. Res. **15**(1) (1988)
3. Aaker, D.A.: Building strong brands. Simon and Schuster, New York (2012)
4. Chou, W.Y.S., Hunt, Y.M., Beckjord, E.B., Moser, R.P., Hesse, B.W.: Social media use in the united states: implications for health communication. J. Med. Internet Res. **11**(4), e48 (2009)
5. Wang, Z., Chong, C.S., Lan, L., Yang, Y., Ho, S.B., Tong, J.C.: Fine-grained sentiment analysis of social media with emotion sensing. In: 2016 Future Technologies Conference (FTC), pp. 1361–1364. IEEE (2016)
6. Wang, Z., Ho, S.-B., Cambria, E.: A review of emotion sensing: categorization models and algorithms. Multimed. Tools Appl. **79**(47), 35553–35582 (2019). https://doi.org/10.1007/s11042-019-08328-z
7. Greco, F., Polli, A.: Emotional text mining: customer profiling in brand management. Int. J. Inf. Manag. **51**, 101934 (2020)
8. Shirdastian, H., Laroche, M., Richard, M.-O.: Using big data analytics to study brand authenticity sentiments: the case of starbucks on twitter. Int. J. Inf. Manag. **48**, 291–307 (2019)
9. Jeong, B., Yoon, J., Lee, J.-M.: Social media mining for product planning: a product opportunity mining approach based on topic modeling and sentiment analysis. Int. J. Inf. Manag. **48**, 280–290 (2019)
10. Reynolds, T.J., Gutman, J.: Laddering theory, method, analysis, and interpretation. J. Advert. Res. **28**(1), 11–31 (1988)
11. Keller, K.L.: Building customer-based brand equity. Mark. Manag. **10**(2), 14 (2001)
12. Fournier, S.: Secrets of customer relationship management: it's all about how you make them feel. J. Serv. Mark. **16**(7),700–703 (2002)
13. Liu, X., Shin, H., Burns, A.C.: Examining the impact of luxury brand's social media marketing on customer engagement: using big data analytics and natural language processing. J. Bus. Res. (2019)

14. Xie, K., Lee, Y.-J.: Social media and brand purchase: quantifying the effects of exposures to earned and owned social media activities in a two-stage decision making model. J. Manag. Inf. Syst. **32**(2), 204–238 (2015)
15. Stephen, A.T., Galak, J.: The effects of traditional and social earned media on sales: a study of a microlending marketplace. J. Mark. Res. **49**(5), 624–639 (2012)
16. Chierici, R., Del Bosco, B., Mazzucchelli, A., Chiacchierini, C.: Enhancing brand awareness, reputation and loyalty: the role of social media. Int. J. Bus. Manag. **14**, 153–160 (2019)
17. Bottomley, P.A., Doyle, J.R., Green, R.H.: Testing the reliability of weight elicitation methods: direct rating versus point allocation. J. Mark. Res. **37**(4), 508–513 (2000)
18. Steenkamp, J.-B., Van Trijp, H.: Attribute elicitation in marketing research: a comparison of three procedures. Mark. Lett. **8**(2), 153–165 (1997)
19. Fader, P.S., Winer, R.S.: Introduction to the special issue on the emergence and impact of user-generated content. Mark. Sci. **31**(3), 369–371 (2012)
20. Netzer, O., Feldman, R., Goldenberg, J., Fresko, M.: Mine your own business: market-structure surveillance through text mining. Mark. Sci. **31**(3), 521–543 (2012)
21. Coppersmith, G., Leary, R., Crutchley, P., Fine, A.: Natural language processing of social media as screening for suicide risk. Biomed. Inform. Insights **10**, 1178222618792860 (2018)
22. Press, V.G., Nyenhuis, S.M.: Do no harm: natural language processing of social media supports safety of aseptic allergen immunotherapy procedures. J.Allergy Clin. Immunol.**144**(1), 38–40 (2019)
23. Naaman, M.: Social multimedia: highlighting opportunities for search and mining of multimedia data in social media applications. Multimed. Tools Appl. **56**(1), 9–34 (2012)
24. Ludwig, S., et al.: More than words: the influence of affective content and linguistic style matches in online reviews on conversion rates. J. Mark. **77**(1), 87–103 (2013)
25. Mostafa, M.M.: More than words: social networks' text mining for consumer brand sentiments. Expert Syst. Appl. **40**(10), 4241–4251 (2013)
26. Rosado-Pinto, F., Loureiro, S.M.C., Bilro, R.G.: How brand authenticity and consumer brand engagement can be expressed in reviews: a text mining approach. J. Promot. Manag. **26**(4), 457–480 (2020)
27. Bilro, R.G., Loureiro, S.M.C., Guerreiro, J.: Exploring online customer engagement with hospitality products and its relationship with involvement, emotional states, experience and brand advocacy. J. Hosp. Mark. Manag. **28**(2), 147–171 (2019)
28. Luu, S.T., Van Nguyen, K., Nguyen, N.L.T.: Empirical study of text augmentation on social media text in vietnamese. arXiv preprint arXiv:2009.12319, 2020
29. Kobayashi, S.: Contextual augmentation: Data augmentation by words with paradigmatic relations. arXiv preprint arXiv:1805.06201, (2018)
30. Zhang, X., Zhao, J., Lecun, Y.: Character-level convolutional networks for text classification. Adv. Neural. Inf. Process. Syst. **649–657**, 2015 (2015)
31. Fadaee, M., Bisazza, A., Monz, C.: Data augmentation for low-resource neural machine translation. In: Proceedings of the 55th Annual Meeting of the Association for Computational Linguistics (vol. 2: Short Papers), pp. 567–573 (2017)
32. Wei, J., Zou, K.: Eda: easy data augmentation techniques for boosting performance on text classification tasks. In: Proceedings of the 2019 Conference on Empirical Methods in Natural Language Processing and the 9th International Joint Conference on Natural Language Processing (EMNLP-IJCNLP), pp. 6383–6389 (2019)

33. Zhou, Z.: How to measure brand relationship quality? Front. Bus. Res. China **1**(2), 300–318 (2007). https://doi.org/10.1007/s11782-007-0017-9
34. Garten, J., Kennedy, B., Sagae, K., Dehghani, M.: Measuring the importance of context when modeling language comprehension. Behav. Res. Methods **51**(2), 480–492 (2019). https://doi.org/10.3758/s13428-019-01200-w
35. Hovy, D., Søgaard, A.: Tagging performance correlates with author age. In: Proceedings of the 53rd annual meeting of the Association for Computational Linguistics and the 7th international joint conference on natural language processing (vol. 2: Short papers), pp. 483–488 (2015)
36. Neves, M., Ševa, J.: An extensive review of tools for manual annotation of documents. Briefings Bioinform. **22**(1), 146–163 (2021)
37. Saurı, R., Verhagen, M., Pustejovsky, J.: Annotating and recognizing event modality in text. In: Proceedings of 19th International FLAIRS Conference (2006)
38. Mikolov, T., Chen, K., Corrado, G., Dean, J.: Efficient estimation of word representations in vector space. arXiv preprint arXiv:1301.3781 (2013)
39. McAuley, J.J., Leskovec, J.: From amateurs to connoisseurs: modeling the evolution of user expertise through online reviews. In: Proceedings of the 22nd international conference on World Wide Web, pp. 897–908 (2013)
40. Bojanowski, P., Grave, E., Joulin, A., Mikolov, T.: Enriching word vectors with subword information. Trans. Assoc. Comput. Linguist. **5**, 135–146 (2017)

Weighted Hierarchy Mechanism over BERT for Long Text Classification

Yong Jin(✉), Qisi Zhu, Xuan Deng, and Linli Hu

Wuhan Yangtze Communications Industry Group Co., Ltd., Wuhan 430074, China
yongjin@fiberhome.com

Abstract. Text classification is a very significant task in natural language processing, especially for Chinese language processing task. Recently, huge progress has been obtained in text classification field except long text classification. Although BERT has outperformance in most NLP tasks, it still has obvious defect as it is very resource consuming and has limitation in dealing with long text. This paper focuses on long Chinese text classification. Based on BERT model, we adopt an innovative way to chunk long text into several segments and provide a weighted hierarchy mechanism for weighting these segments. We conduct several contrast experiments over BERT model including BERT+LSTM, BERT+CNN, and BERT+LSTM+CNN. Through optimizing models, the results show that the weighted hierarchy method can improve the accuracy of long Chinese text classification and different parameters of layers of neural networks added can also make some differences, especially the structure of LSTM or CNN over BERT, can improve the final effect based on weighted hierarchy mechanism. This paper provides a useful way for long Chinese text classification and comes up with a novel method on how to deal with long text to overcome the limitation of BERT in training long texts.

Keywords: Long text classification · BERT · Deep networks · Weighted hierarchy mechanism

1 Introduction

Text classification, a primary task in natural language processing (NLP) domain, has already attracted many researchers' attention in both academic and industrial fields. In recent years, for most text classification tasks, including sentiment classification, short texts (mostly shorter than 1000 characters) are applied for text classification task in research, and meanwhile short text classification task has reached significant results. However, the main challenge confronted now is long text classification problem because long text normally contains various information, and probably it illustrates different perspectives of different topics. This paper dedicates to long text classification, specifically, long Chinese text classification.

In this paper, it demonstrates that chunking long text into segments with different weights and then performing deep neural networks over BERT are helpful to overcome the limitation of traditional neural networks based on THUCnews public data set. This paper provides a new approach for long text classification.

X. Sun et al. (Eds.): ICAIS 2021, LNCS 12736, pp. 566–574, 2021.
https://doi.org/10.1007/978-3-030-78609-0_48

2 Related Work

Neural networks, especially deep network methods have been widely used in text classification field and proved to be valid methods. Some significant neural network models play an important role in industry as well as in academia. Gated Recurrent Unit(GRU) [1] (K. Cho et al. 2014), and Long Short-Term Memory (LSTM) [2] (Sundermeyer et al. 2012) are two methods derived from Recurrent Neural Network(RNN) model [3] (Mikolov et al. 2010), which takes the hidden state in the last step into training, solves the long-term dependency issue and provides a way for long text classification in the early times. Although some tricks including conditional computation [4] (Noam et al. 2017) and factorization [5] (Kuchaiev et al. 2017) has been applied to improve the computation efficiency, it is still difficult to accelerate RNN training due to structure constraint. Another model used quite frequently in text classification is Convolutional Neural Network (CNN) [6] (Yann et al. 1989). Compared with RNN models, it has an advantage over RNN model in training efficiency. However, CNN is also not a proper model for long text classification since it has long-term dependency issue. Specifically, CNN model is not able to capture all the information that a long sentence represents.

Bidirectional Encoder Representation from Transformers (BERT) [7] (J Devlin et al. 2018), based on attention mechanism [8] (Ashish et al. 2017), outperforms the earlier state-of-art model ever since it's released due to two innovative points. One is masked language model part, the other is next sentence prediction part. And outperformance of BERT in most NLP field proves robustness of this model.

However, BERT has its primary and fatal defect due to the model structure, which has already mentioned in A Lite BERT model (ALBERT) [9] (Zhezhong et al. 2020). Due to multi-head self-attention, which is a compulsory component in model, the time and RAM consumed is extremely high for long sentence. Thus BERT is mighty but still not a proper method to solve the long text classification problem.

Apart from models mentioned above that can be applied into classification tasks, many other models have been brought up by other researchers. One of them is hierarchy transformers [10] (Pappagari et al. 2019). A long sentence can be chunked into smaller segments. After that, time complexity for self-attention calculation is reduced from O(n^2) to O(nk), where n stands for the length of origin text and k stands for the number of segments. Although it conducts experiments on three different English data sets with RoBERT (Recurrence over BERT) and ToBERT (Transformer over BERT) fine-tuning, it only focuses on English data sets and it has no reformation of the model structure.

In this paper, we focus on Chinese corpus due to Chinese' special characteristics and propose a new approach of chunking called weighted hierarchy method. Besides, different neural networks are added to BERT to improve the effect for long Chinese text classification.

3 Methods

3.1 Weighted Hierarchy Method

In the paper, an innovative way named as the hierarchy method is applied in Chinese long text classification. Figure 1 is the explanation of chunking. In detail, a long sentence is chunked into several segments, where two adjacent segments share the same part. Segments and original labels are feed into BERT for fine-tuning. After that, new features of segments generated by BERT are concatenated for further training by various neural network models.

Chinese corpus has a distinguishing feature that some particular parts convey most valuable information in a sentence. Take the following text for example:

"新浪娱乐独家专访张译：孟烦了的前世今生(图)视频：新浪娱乐独家对话《团长》主演张译 新浪娱乐讯 张译(blog)是《我的团长我的团》中的"我"，就如《士兵突击()》(blog)中王宝强(听歌blog)扮演的许三多，……今天下午我们刚好拍孟烦了89岁走在腾冲街头的一场戏，很意识流。昨天我们开了临时会议,……,镜头里出现的是一个89岁的孟烦了，一个24岁的孟烦了。老头离去后我面对镜头思索，微笑，这是我们这部剧的结尾。我拍完看到导演出来是在强忍着泪水。

This text has totally 1145 Chinese characters with the corresponding label of "Entertainment". Figure 1 shows a typical example of Chinese texts with three segments where two ends of the sentences are closer to the theme label called *Entertainment*.

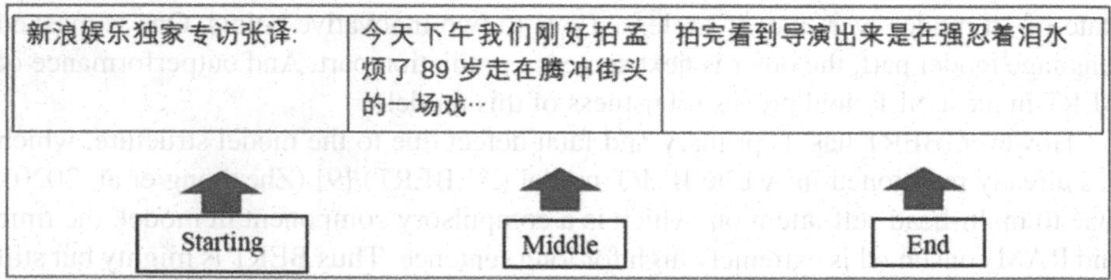

Fig. 1. Example of a Chinese text

According to the characteristic mentioned above, the segments are updated with different weights, Fig. 2 is the illustration of weighted hierarchy process. After weighting different segments of the total text, modified segments and corresponding labels are taken as the new input of the model for further training.

In the paper, based on the fact that the beginning and the end usually contain most information in the text, we propose a way of weighting to assign different importance to different segments. Referring to softmax function, for a segment contains L characters, the weights given to i-th character in segments is defined as follows:

$$w_i = \frac{e^{(l_i-0.5)^2}}{\sum_{i=0}^{L} e^{(l_i-0.5)^2}}, \text{ where } l_i = \frac{i}{L} \tag{1}$$

According to the formula (1), the weighting approach assigns higher weights to two ends of sentences instead of roughly giving every character equal weights.

In this way, it can not only overcome the limitation of BERT that only sentences with length smaller than 512 can be feed into BERT fine-tuning model [7], but also can reduce the time and resource cost of training. Different from BERT, which simply discards

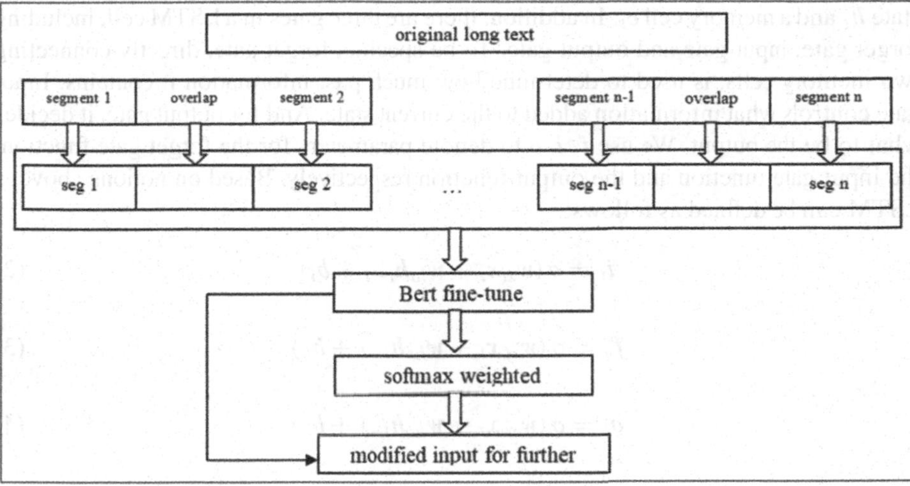

Fig. 2. Hierarchy method

information that exceeds 512 tokens, this method can explain almost all information that the sentences contain.

3.2 Deep Network Structure

In this paper, we add various layers of deep network models including LSTM and CNN on the output of BERT. Figure 3 shows how neural network layers are added into training and prediction, which includes BERT output layer, weighted hierarchy method layer, neural networks layer such as RNN and LSTM models, and finally the label prediction layer.

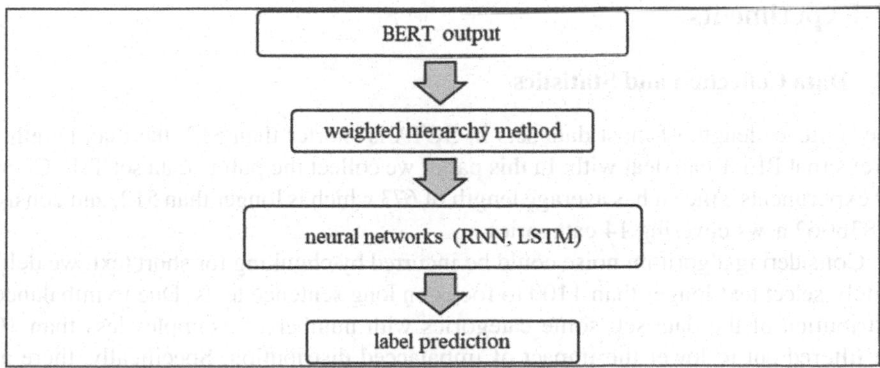

Fig. 3. Prediction process

LSTM, a sub-type of RNN model, are usually used in text classification because it well solves the vanishing gradient problem. In definition, LSTM introduce the hidden state $\boldsymbol{h}_t$ and a memory cell $\boldsymbol{c}_t$. In addition, there are three gates in a LSTM cell, including forget gate, input gate and output gate. To be specific, forget gate, directly connecting two memory cells, is used to determine how much past information it contains. Input gate controls what information added to the current state. And for output gate, it decides what to be the output. We use f, i, o to denote parameters for the forget gate function, the input gate function and the output function respectively. Based on notions above, a LSTM can be defined as follows:

$$\boldsymbol{i}_t = \sigma(\boldsymbol{w}_{xi}\boldsymbol{x}_t + \boldsymbol{w}_{hi}\boldsymbol{h}_{t-1} + \boldsymbol{b}_i) \tag{2}$$

$$\boldsymbol{f}_t = \sigma(\boldsymbol{w}_{xf}\boldsymbol{x}_t + \boldsymbol{w}_{hf}\boldsymbol{h}_{t-1} + \boldsymbol{b}_f) \tag{3}$$

$$\boldsymbol{o}_t = \sigma(\boldsymbol{w}_{xo}\boldsymbol{x}_t + \boldsymbol{w}_{ho}\boldsymbol{h}_{t-1} + \boldsymbol{b}_o) \tag{4}$$

$$\boldsymbol{g}_t = tahn(\boldsymbol{w}_{xg}\boldsymbol{x}_t + \boldsymbol{w}_{hg}\boldsymbol{h}_{t-1} + \boldsymbol{b}_g) \tag{5}$$

$$\boldsymbol{c}_t = \boldsymbol{f}_t \odot \boldsymbol{c}_{t-1} + \boldsymbol{i}_t \odot \boldsymbol{g}_t \tag{6}$$

$$\boldsymbol{h}_t = \boldsymbol{o}_t \odot \tanh(\boldsymbol{c}_i) \tag{7}$$

where $\sigma(\cdot)$ stands for the sigmoid function and $\odot$ represents the element-wise product.

CNN is a sophisticated model for classification. We add a layer of CNN into the model structure because it performs better than LSTM in observing local information.

Figure 4 depicts the model structure graph from raw inputs to BERT layer, to the layer of weighted and softmax, followed by the LSTM layer (or CNN layer, LSTM+CNN layer), and finally to the layer of label prediction.

4 Experiments

4.1 Data Collection and Statistics

The sentence length of most data sets in SOTA is shorter than 512, the max length of tokens that BERT can deal with. In this paper we collect the public data set THUCnews for experiments, since it has average length of 673 which is longer than 512, and consists of 836062 news covering 14 categories.

Considering algorithm noise could be incurred by chunking for short text, we deliberately select text longer than 1100 to focus on long sentence texts. Due to imbalanced distribution of the data set, some categories with number of examples less than 100 are filtered out to lower the impact of imbalanced distribution. Specifically, there are 14 labels of news in the data set including *Finance*, *Lottery*, *Real-estate*, *stock*, *Home*, *Education*, *Technology*, *City news*, *Fashion*, *Politics*, *Sports*, *Constellation*, *Game*, and *Entertainment*. After data selection, the news belongs to *Constellation* label is filtered out. Data statistics is shown in Table 1.

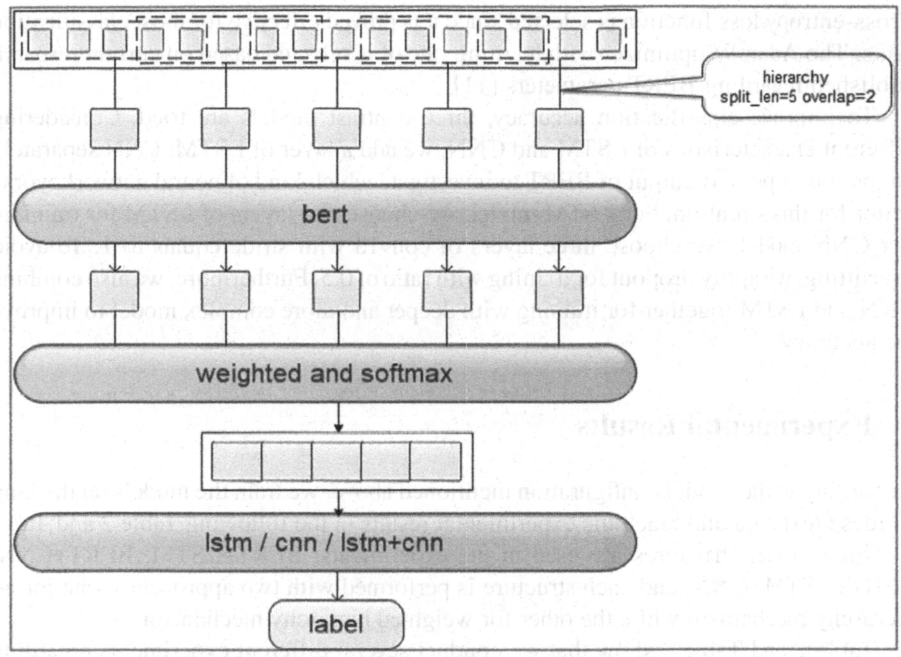

Fig. 4. Example of hierarchy model structure

Table 1. Data statistics

Counts	Label	Min length	Max length	Avg length
53441	13	1101	31698	1179.51

4.2 Training Process and Model Configuration

In this paper, we perform a set of experiments with different parameters and deep networks. THUCnews is separated into three parts with categories stratified: 80% of the data is used for training, the resting 20% data for validating and testing evenly. In addition, all long sentences are chunked into segments with origin labels relabeled. In the prediction phase, referring to the voting method, the most labels predicted by segments belonging to the same origin long text are selected as the final results.

All models are trained in GPU machines, with four GeForce GTX 1080 Nvidia GPUs in each machine.

As for BERT-only model, which is to obtain the BERT output illustrated in Fig. 3, we fine-tune BERT-base-Chinese pretrained model with max input sequence length equal to 200 to investigate how much valid information BERT model can get with partial limited information feed. As for comparation, the hierarchy part, max length for segment is 200 and the overlap length is 50 for the data set in which the text length is around 1109.

Cross-entropy loss function is selected since it is proved effective for most classification tasks. The AdamW optimizer with learning rate of is selected based on current research published regarding BERT parameters [11].

To improve classification accuracy, three contrast models are tried. Considering different characteristics of LSTM and CNN, we add a layer of LSTM, CNN separately on the top of pooled output of BERT to investigate which kind of neural network works better for this situation. For LSTM model, we choose two layers of LSTM for training. For CNN model, we choose three layers of conv1d with stride equals to 1. To avoid overfitting, we apply dropout for training with ratio of 0.5. Furthermore, we also combine CNN and LSTM together for training with deeper and more complex model to improve the accuracy.

5 Experimental Results

According to the model configuration mentioned above, we train the models on the long Chinese text data and reach the experimental results in the following Table 2 and Table 3. Three model structures are used in the experiments: BERT+LSTM, BERT+CNN, BERT+LSTM+CNN, and each structure is performed with two approaches: one for no hierarchy mechanism while the other for weighted hierarchy mechanism.

Table 2 and Table 3 show that we conduct several different experiments regarding long Chinese text classification with BERT where P stands for precision value, R stands for recall value, and F1 score indicates the whole measurement of both P and R values. Table 2 shows the results of the three models with no hierarchy mechanism, and Table 3 shows the results of weighted hierarchy mechanism.

Table 2. Experimental results for no hierarchy mechanism

Model	No hierarchy (weighted average)		
	F1	P	R
BERT+LSTM	0.737	0.72	0.764
BERT+CNN	0.723	0.739	0.732
BERT+LSTM+CNN	0.826	0.828	0.829

Through Table 2 and Table 3, we compare several pairs of experiments with the same model structure to check the robustness of weighted hierarchy model. According to the results, weighted hierarchy method works well for long Chinese text classification. And the parameters with max length equal to 200 and overlap length is 50 is the most appropriate parameters ever performed.

Base on the results shown above, even though BERT+LSTM+CNN network with weighted hierarchy mechanism works a little worse than no hierarchy mechanism, while for both BERT+LSTM and BERT+CNN networks, the evaluation scores including F1,

Table 3. Experimental results for weighted hierarchy mechanism

Model	Weighted hierarchy					
	Max length = 100, Overlap = 20			Max length = 200, Overlap = 50		
	F1	P	R	F1	P	R
BERT+LSTM	0.787	0.788	0.791	0.793	0.795	0.793
BERT+CNN	0.799	0.801	0.798	0.795	0.795	0.786
BERT+LSTM+CNN	0.810	0.814	0.807	0.813	0.811	0.816

P, and R of the weighted hierarchy mechanism are higher than those with no hierarchy, as shown in Fig. 5.

Also, the model BERT+CNN demonstrates better than BERT+LSTM, since the former one has F1 score of 0.799, compared to the latter one with 0.787, which to some extent illustrates that CNN capturing local information performs more important than LSTM since BERT has already captured sequence information.

Furthermore, different segment methods are also tried with max length and overlap parameters, while the results of the two configurations of weighted hierarchy approaches reveal that there is no significant difference between them.

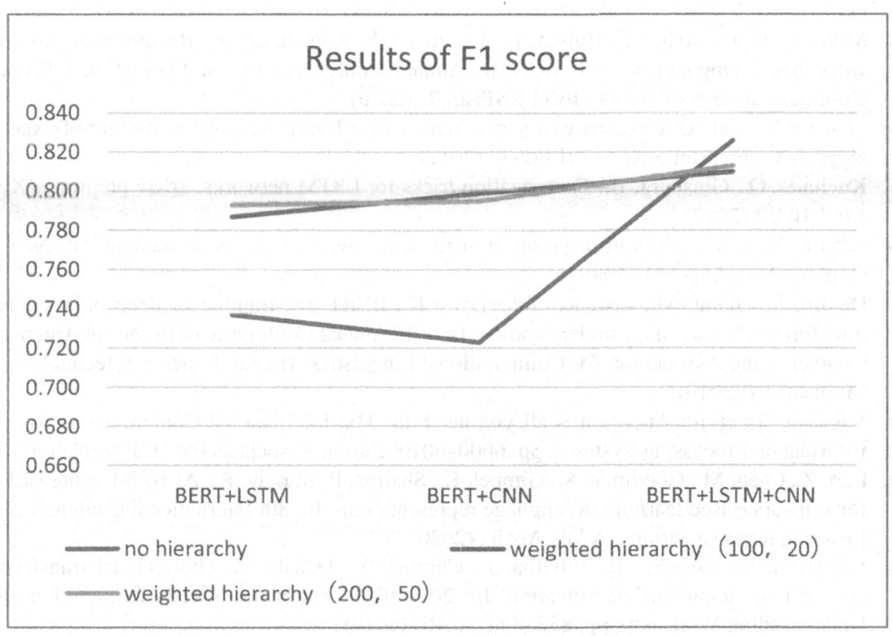

Fig. 5. Comparison of F1 scores

6 Conclusions and Future Work

In this paper, we perform several contrast experiments based on BERT model on long Chinese text data set: THUCnews. The results show that weighted hierarchy mechanism can improve the accuracy of long text classification. Specifically, the higher weights should be assigned to the starting and end parts. We also notice that with the combination with LSTM or CNN over BERT, it attains higher accuracy compared to the BERT baseline. Besides, for the parameters as we have tried so far, the parameters that max length equals to 200 and overlap length equals to 50 are the most appropriate in the experiments we conduct.

In future work, there are still several aspects that we can improve. Firstly, how to improve training efficiency is still a problem since it takes lots of time and resources to fine-tune BERT. Besides, other deep networks can be added to modify the current model structure to improve the accuracy. Finally, some other weighting metrics would also work better based on current network structure.

References

1. Cho, K., et al.: Learning phrase representations using RNN encoder-decoder for statistical machine translation. arXiv preprint arXiv:1406.1078 (2014)
2. Hochreiter, S., Schmidhuber, J.: Long short-term memory. Neural Comput. **9**(8), 1735–1780 (1997)
3. Mikolov, T., Karafiát, M., Burget, L., Černocký, J., Khudanpur, S.: Recurrent neural network based language model. In: 11th Annual Conference of the International Speech Communication Association, INTERSPEECH (2010)
4. Shazeer, N., et al.: Outrageously large neural networks: The sparsely-gated mixture-of-experts layer. arXiv preprint arXiv:1701.06538 (2017)
5. Kuchaiev, O., Ginsburg, B.: Factorization tricks for LSTM networks. arXiv preprint arXiv: 1703.10722 (2017)
6. LeCun, Y., et al.: Backpropagation applied to handwritten zip code recognition. Neural Comput. **1**(4), 541–551 (1989)
7. Devlin, J., Chang, M., Lee, K., Toutanova, K.: BERT: pre-training of deep bidirectional transformers for language understanding. In: 17th Annual Conference of the North American Chapter of the Association for Computational Linguistics: Human Language Technologies, Minneapolis (2019)
8. Vaswani, A., et al.: Attention is all you need. In: 31st International Conference on Neural Information Processing Systems, pp. 6000–6010. Curran Associates Inc., California (2017)
9. Lan, Z., Chen, M., Goodman, S., Gimpel, K., Sharma, P., Soricut, R.: ALBERT: a lite BERT for self-supervised learning of language representations. In: 8th International Conference on Learning Representations, Addis Ababa (2020)
10. Pappagari, R., Zelasko, P., Villalba, J., Carmiel, Y., Dehak, N.: Hierarchical transformers for long document classification. In: 2019 IEEE Automatic Speech Recognition and Understanding Workshop, pp. 838–844. ASRU (2019)
11. Sun, C., Qiu, X., Xu, Y., Huang, X.: How to Fine-Tune BERT for Text Classification? arXiv, abs/1905.05583 (2019)

Corrosion Detection in Transformers Based on Hierarchical Annotation

Yong Cao[1](✉), Yinian Zhou[2], Zhao Zhang[3,4], Wenjun Wu[1], Xihai Chen[3,4], Sha Yang[3,4], and Baili Zhang[1]

[1] School of Computer Science and Engineering, Southeast University, Nanjing, China
[2] School of Computer and Software, Nanjing University of Information Science and Technology, Nanjing, China
[3] State Key Laboratory of Smart Grid Protection and Control, Nanjing, China
[4] Nari Group Corporation, Nanjing, China

Abstract. Transformers are prone to metal corrosion due to long-term exposure in the external environment. It is necessary to detect corrosion in time to prolong their service life-time. Detecting metal corrosion based on deep learning is becoming a feasible method at present. However, because of the irregularity and detachability of metal corrosion, traditional annotation approach results in such problems as ambiguity and uncertainty in the annotating process. Thus, a novel hierarchical annotation approach is proposed in this paper. The rationale for this initiative is as follows: traditional annotation approach has been used to annotate a large area covering the range of corrosion, as long as the area is visually continuous and adjacent to the corrosion that cannot be clearly divided. The annotation result is recorded as training set A; secondly, in the annotating boxes from the first step, the areas with obvious and relatively independent features are re-annotated to form the second level of nested annotation. The annotation result is recorded as training set B. Finally, Faster R-CNN and YOLOv5 models were trained by A, B training sets respectively in the experiment. It can be concluded that the detection performance with hierarchical annotation approach proved better than traditional annotation approach for Faster R-CNN and YOLOv5 models.

Keywords: Deep learning · Faster R-CNN · YOLOv5 · Object detection · Hierarchical annotation

1 Introduction

Corrosion is considered as a destructive phenomenon that affects most transformers. It is the result of deterioration caused by metallic materials' surface and internal micro-structure reacting with corrosive environments [1, 2]. Due to long-term exposure in the external environment, corrosion has become a common defect to transformers. Corrosion can continuously impair the transformers' service life and cause economic losses before it is tackled promptly. Hence, it is necessary to regularly monitor their running condition.

Currently, non-destructive methods are usually applied in corrosion detection, such as X-ray [3], local wavenumber [4], infrared thermography [5, 6], magneto-optic imaging

X. Sun et al. (Eds.): ICAIS 2021, LNCS 12736, pp. 575–584, 2021.
https://doi.org/10.1007/978-3-030-78609-0_49

[7] and camera. Among them, X-ray detection technology has been proved inconvenient in practice, and it's also harmful to the surrounding environment. The detection technology that applies local wavenumbers with different frequencies is more complex in data collection. Using infrared thermography to collect and detect corrosion demands higher requirements for the collecting environment. Dudziak utilizes a neural-like algorithm to detect metal corrosion by magneto-optic imaging based upon Faraday rotation of polarized light, which is more technically demanding.

Compared with the above-mentioned detection methods, using Convolutional Neural Networks (CNN) [8] to perform corrosion detection with the RGB images collected by camera which can bring about such advantages as lower collecting cost, simpler operation and lower professional requirements. Following AlexNet [9], with the emergence of VGG [10], GoogleNet [11], ResNet [12] and other CNN models, object detection has achieved rapid development. One solution is recommended in literature [13] by utilizing sliding window to intercept regions, then to detect corrosion by CNN. However, this method costs more time-consuming. Fast R-CNN [14], Faster R-CNN [15], YOLO [16–18] and other object detection models based on region proposal can greatly shorten the detection time and ensure precision and recall remain unchanged. However, due to the irregular shape and detachability of corrosion, these object detection models cannot directly achieve satisfying results. Therefore, this paper proposes a novel hierarchical annotation approach: Firstly, traditional annotation approach has been applied to annotate a large area covering the range of corrosion, as long as the area is visually continuous and adjacent to the corrosion that cannot be clearly divided; then, in the annotating boxes from the first step, the areas with obvious and relatively independent features are re-annotated to form the second level of nested annotation.

In comparison experiment, two annotation approaches are respectively applied to annotate 1180 same pictures and be recorded as two different training sets. Besides, 206 pictures are annotated by traditional annotation approach as the test set; then are compared the detection results of Faster R-CNN and YOLOv5 trained by different training sets. The experimental findings indicate that the detection results of models trained by hierarchical annotation approach are better than those of models trained by traditional annotation approach. Besides, precision and recall of Faster R-CNN are better than those of YOLOv5.

In summary, our contributions in this work include:

1. A novel data annotation approach, hierarchical annotation approach, is proposed.
2. Minimum bounding box algorithm is applied for merging the intersecting boxes.
3. A novel formulation is proposed for recalculating precision in view of the features of corrosion.

2 Related Works

The shape and size of corrosion is irregular, which is caused by the size of equipment and the spread of corrosion. Simultaneously, the detachability of corrosion makes some components of transformers can be regarded as a whole piece of corrosion or as several individual corrosion.

Fig. 1. The results annotated by traditional approach

Figure 1 shows the results annotated by traditional approach. However, this approach has several drawbacks. Due to the detachability of corrosion, the screws as the parts of corrosion in Fig. 1(left), while other screws in another picture, Fig. 1(right), are annotated as independent corrosion; besides, in Fig. 1(left), the corrosive screw in the upper right corner and the non-corrosive screw in the lower right corner are both not annotated, which means the screws with different types have the same annotation results. These drawbacks indicate that using traditional annotation approach to annotate corrosion will generate ambiguity and uncertainty.

Fig. 2. The results annotated by hierarchical approach

Hence, to prevent the ambiguity and uncertainty in the process of annotation, one naive solution is presented: try to use small boxes instead of large boxes, as shown in Fig. 2(left). Therefore, after adopting this solution, the number of boxes with smaller size will increase, while the number of boxes with larger size will decrease to some extent. But this approach cannot solve this issue. In Fig. 2(left), the surrounding corrosion around boxes is omitted. Definitely, we can continue to refine the sizes of boxes to make it closer to corrosion. However, this operation will increase the workload of data annotation and the difficulty of problem solved.

Considering that Faster R-CNN and YOLO models based on region proposal utilize the predefined anchors with different sizes and shapes to detect objects with different sizes and shapes. Therefore, corrosion is detected mainly by the anchors with similar sizes. For the above reasons, this paper proposes a novel hierarchical annotation approach: Firstly, traditional annotation approach is used to annotate a large area within the range of corrosion, as long as it is visually continuous, adjacent to the corrosion that cannot be clearly divided. For example, in Fig. 2(right), we apply a large box, ground truth (GT)1, to annotate corrosion; Next, in the annotating box of the first step, the corrosion with obvious and relatively independent features is re-annotated to form the second level of nested annotation. As shown in Fig. 2(right), we apply the boxes, GT2 and GT3, to annotate the corrosion with obvious and relatively independent features.

Ambiguous problem generated by applying traditional approach to annotate corrosion can be solved by adopting hierarchical annotation approach, while being compatible with traditional annotation approach. Simultaneously, it obviously increases the number of GT and further achieves the effect of data enhancement.

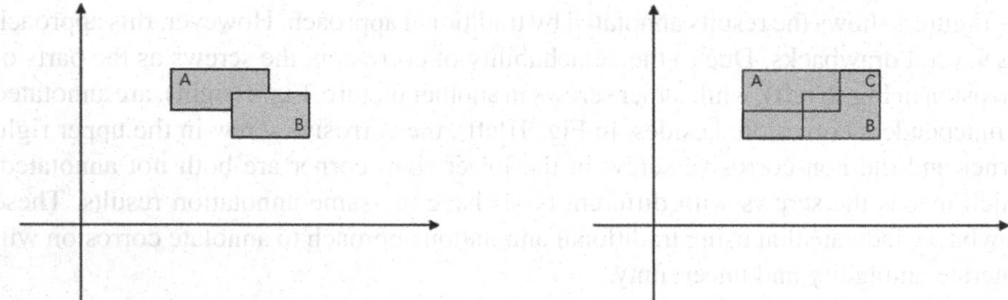

Fig. 3. Minimum bounding box algorithm

However, using hierarchical annotation approach results in lots of overlaps and nesting in the annotation results. Therefore, when using a model trained by hierarchical annotation approach to detect corrosion in transformers, the boxes in detecting result also have lots of overlaps and nesting. For this reason, this paper uses minimum bounding box algorithm to merge multiple intersecting boxes to one box, and the box is recorded as the final box.

For example, the boxes, A and B in Fig. 3(left), are generated by detection models; then, the orange box C in Fig. 3(right) is generated by minimum bounding box algorithm. Simultaneously, the box C is recorded as the final box instead of the boxes, A and B.

3 Experiment

In this Sects. 3.1 and 3.2 introduce the experimental environment and evaluating indicators; Sect. 3.3 uses traditional annotation approach to annotate the training set and test set, trains several object detection models, and calculates their precision and recall; Sect. 3.4 uses hierarchical annotation approach to re-annotate the training set while the test set remains unchanged, and repeats the above experimental process; Sect. 3.5 compares and analyzes experimental results.

3.1 Experiment Environment

The experimental software and hardware environment are shown in Table 1.

Table 1. Experimental software and hardware environment

CPU	I7-9800X/8@4.4 GHz
RAM	32 GB
GPU	Nvidia RTX2080Ti@11G
OS	Centos7
Deep learning framework	PyTorch
Object detection model	Faster R-CNN, YOLOv5
The volumes of training set, test set	1180, 206
Evaluating indicators	Precision, Recall, IoU

3.2 Evaluating Indicators

In this experiment, this paper uses model's precision and recall as evaluating indicators. The classification results can be divided into four categories according to the forecast results and the actual results. The confusion matrix for binary classification is shown in Table 2.

Table 2. Confusion matrix for binary classification

		Forecast result	
		Positive	Negative
Actual result	Positive	TP	FN
	Negative	FP	TN

We use GTs to represent the number of GT and PRs to represent the number of predicted boxes. Therefore, for one picture, the calculation formulations of precision (P) and recall (R) as follows:

$$GTs \neq 0, PRs \neq 0. P = \frac{TP}{TP + FP}, R = \frac{TP}{TP + FN} \tag{1}$$

$$GTs \neq 0, PRs = 0. P = 0, R = 0 \tag{2}$$

$$GTs = 0, PRs \neq 0. P = 0, R = 0 \tag{3}$$

$$GTs = 0, PRs = 0. P = 1, R = 1 \tag{4}$$

For multiple pictures:

$$P = \frac{p_1 + p_2 + \cdots + p_n}{N}, R = \frac{r_1 + r_2 + \cdots + r_n}{N} \tag{5}$$

Eventually, Intersection over Union (IoU) between the predicted box and the ground truth is applied to judge whether a predicted box is correct. IoU is an evaluation metric, which is used to measure how close an annotation or test output lines up with a ground truth. In this paper, the value of IoU greater than 0.5 indicates that one predicted box is correct. The calculation formulation is shown in Fig. 4.

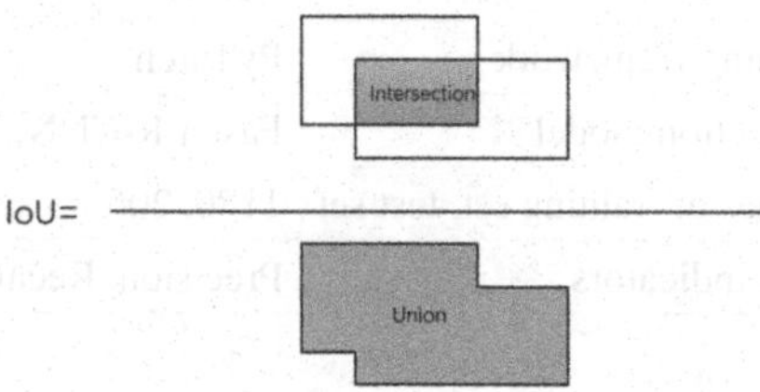

Fig. 4. IoU calculation formulation

In addition, the detachability of corrosion may result in one predicted box only is a part of GT. Although the box has correctness to some extent, it is judged as error because its IoU is less than 0.5. For example, the boxes in Fig. 5(left), PR1 and PR2, are the parts of GT with correctness to some extent, but their IoU are both less than 0.5, thus they are judged as errors.

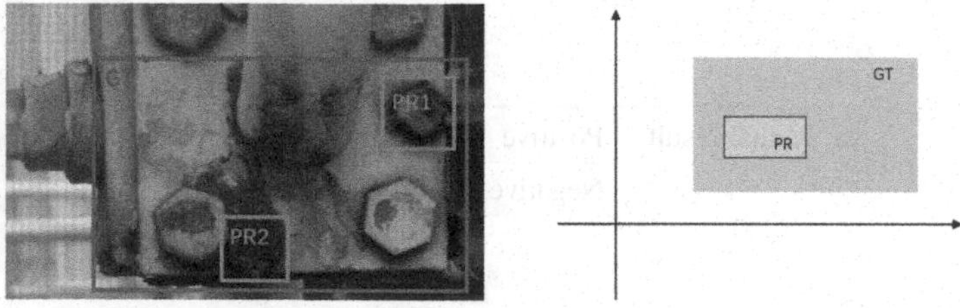

Fig. 5. The predicted boxes as the parts of GT

Thus, in order to weaken the impact of such conditions. According to the characteristics of corrosion, a novel calculation formulation is proposed. If one predicted box satisfies this condition, IoU $\leq 0.5\&\frac{GT\cap FR}{FR} > 0.98$, which is regarded as no forecast. After omitting such predicted boxes, the novel precision obtained is recorded as valid-P. Since those predicted boxes regarded as errors are omitted, the value of valid-P will be greater than the value of P.

3.3 Traditional Annotation Approach

Firstly, 1180 specimens were annotated by traditional annotation approach for training Faster R-CNN and YOLOv5 models. And this approach was also used to annotate 206 specimens as the test set. Then, VGG16 and Res101 respectively as backbone networks, momentum SGD [19] as optimizer were applied to train Faster R-CNN models;

DarkNet53 [17] as backbone network, momentum SGD as optimizer were applied to train YOLOv5 model. Finally, the above trained models were used to test and calculate the values of P, R and valid-P. The values of P, R and valid-P in the three models are shown in Table 3.

Table 3. The values of P, R and valid-P with traditional annotation approach

Model	P	R	valid-P
YOLOv5	33.23%	27.03%	35.78%
Faster R-CNN + VGG16	57.94%	52.60%	64.26%
Faster R-CNN + Res101	69.85%	68.51%	76.87%

3.4 Hierarchical Annotation Approach

Next, 1180 specimens were re-annotated by hierarchical annotation approach for training Faster R-CNN and YOLOv5 models, while the test set remain unchanged. Then, VGG16 and Res101 respectively as backbone networks, momentum SGD as optimizer were applied to retrain Faster R-CNN models; DarkNet53 as backbone network, momentum SGD as optimizer were applied to retrain YOLOv5 model. Finally, the above trained models were used to test.

After using minimum bounding box algorithm to merge the intersecting boxes of each picture, we calculate the values of P, R and valid-P. The values of P, R and valid-P in the three models are shown in Table 4.

Table 4. The values of P, R and valid-P with hierarchical annotation approach

Model	P	R	valid-P
YOLOv5	36.59%	35.38%	41.01%
FasterR-CNN + VGG16	58.87%	60.25%	66.52%
FasterR-CNN + Res101	82.45%	83.13%	95.74%

3.5 Major Findings and Discussion

In this experiment, the comparison results of each index between traditional annotation approach and hierarchical annotation approach are shown in Table 5.

Faster R-CNN + Res101 model has the best detection result, whose values of P, R are both higher than 80%. What's more, the value of valid-P even exceeds 95%. Besides, we have other experimental findings:

Table 5. The improvement of each index after adopting hierarchical annotation

Model	P↑	R↑	valid-P↑
YOLOv5	3.36%	8.35%	5.23%
FasterR-CNN + VGG16	0.93%	7.65%	2.26%
FasterR-CNN + Res101	12.60%	14.62%	18.87%

- The values of P, R and valid-P of Faster R-CNN model are greater than those of YOLOv5 model.
- In Faster R-CNN model, using Res101 as backbone network has greater values of P, R and valid-P than using VGG16.
- After training with hierarchical annotation approach, YOLOv5 and Faster R-CNN + VGG16 have a slight improvement in the values of P and valid-P and have a great improvement in the value of R; Besides, the values of P, R and valid-P of Faster R-CNN + Res101 have great escalation.

The reasons as follows:

- Faster R-CNN is two-stage, while YOLOv5 is single-stage. Faster R-CNN firstly filters out a large number of background regions through region proposal networks, so that subsequent classification can pay more attention to detecting corrosion, which contributes to the classification results. Therefore, the detection time in Faster R-CNN is longer, but the values of P, R and valid-P are greater than those of YOLOv5.
- The model structure of Res101 is more complicated than VGG16. Res101 has more convolution layers than VGG16, while its gradient can be better backpropagation by using batch normalization [20] and Rectified Linear Units [21]. Simultaneously, Res101 enables the model to be fully trained through the residual module [12]. Therefore, the values of P and R in Res101 are greater than those of VGG16 (Fig. 6).
- After using hierarchical annotation approach, the number of GT obviously increases in the training set, which is conducive to data enhancement; The object detection model detects objects with different sizes by predefined anchors with different sizes. Therefore, hierarchical annotation approach solves the ambiguity caused by traditional annotation while increasing the number of GT. In conclusion, the values of P, R and valid-P can be greatly improved.

Fig. 6. Outputs of Faster R-CNN + Res101 trained by hierarchical annotation approach

4 Conclusion

In this paper, Faster R-CNN and YOLOv5 models are applied to detect corrosion in transformers. Through preliminary experiments, it is found that precision and recall of models trained by traditional annotation approach are lower than expected. Hence, a novel hierarchical annotation approach is proposed by utilizing the characteristics of corrosion. Ultimately, according to experimental findings, the models' precision and recall have been greatly improved after adopting hierarchical annotation approach.

Acknowledgement. This work was partly supported by Open Research Fund from State Key Laboratory of Smart Grid Protection and Control, China, Rapid Support Project (61406190120) and the National Key R&D Program of China (2018YFC0830200).

References

1. Roberge, P.R.: Handbook of Corrosion Engineering. McGraw-Hill Education, New York (2019)
2. Roberge, P.R.: Corrosion Engineering. McGraw-Hill Education, New York (2008)
3. Dunn, W.L., Yacout, A.M.: Corrosion detection in aircraft by X-ray backscatter methods. Appl. Radiat. Isot. **53**(4–5), 625–632 (2000)
4. Gao, T., Sun, H., Hong, Y., et al.: Hidden corrosion detection using laser ultrasonic guided waves with multi-frequency local wavenumber estimation. Ultrasonics **108**, 106182 (2020)
5. Doshvarpassand, S., Wu, C., Wang, X.: An overview of corrosion defect characterization using active infrared thermography. Infrared Phys. Technol. **96**, 366–389 (2019)
6. Wicker, M., Alduse, B.P., Jung, S.: Detection of hidden corrosion in metal roofing shingles utilizing infrared thermography. J. Build. Eng. **20**, 201–207 (2018)
7. Dudziak, M.J., Chervonenkis, A.Y., Chinarov, V.: Nondestructive evaluation for crack, corrosion, and stress detection for metal assemblies and structures. In: Nondestructive Evaluation of Aging Aircraft, Airports, and Aerospace Hardware III. International Society for Optics and Photonics, vol. 3586, pp. 20–31 (1999)
8. LeCun, Y., Boser, B., Denker, J.S., et al.: Backpropagation applied to handwritten zip code recognition. Neural Comput. **1**(4), 541–551 (1989)
9. Krizhevsky, A., Sutskever, I., Hinton, G.E.: ImageNet classification with deep convolutional neural networks. In: Advances in Neural Information Processing Systems, vol. 25, pp. 1097–1105 (2012)
10. Simonyan, K., Zisserman, A.: Very deep convolutional networks for large-scale image recognition. arXiv preprint arXiv:1409.1556 (2014)
11. Szegedy, C., Liu, W., Jia, Y., et al.: Going deeper with convolutions. In: Proceedings of the IEEE conference on computer vision and pattern recognition, pp. 1–9 (2015)
12. He, K., Zhang, X., Ren, S., et al.: Deep residual learning for image recognition. In: Proceedings of the IEEE Conference on Computer Vision and Pattern Recognition, pp. 770–778 (2016)
13. Yao, Y., Yang, Y., Wang, Y., et al.: Artificial intelligence-based hull structural plate corrosion damage detection and recognition using convolutional neural network. Appl. Ocean Res. **90**, 101823 (2019)
14. Girshick, R.: Fast R-CNN. In: Proceedings of the IEEE International Conference on Computer Vision, pp. 1440–1448 (2015)
15. Ren, S., He, K., Girshick, R., et al.: Faster R-CNN: towards real-time object detection with region proposal networks. arXiv preprint arXiv:1506.01497 (2015)
16. Redmon, J., Divvala, S., Girshick, R., et al.: You only look once: unified, real-time object detection. In: Proceedings of the IEEE Conference on Computer Vision and Pattern Recognition, pp. 779–788 (2016)
17. Redmon, J., Farhadi, A.: Yolov3: an incremental improvement. arXiv preprint arXiv:1804.02767 (2018)
18. Jocher, G., Stoken, A., Borovec, J., et al.: ultralytics/yolov5: v3.1 - bug fixes and performance improvements (2020). https://doi.org/10.5281/zenodo.4154370
19. Sutskever, I., Martens, J., Dahl, G., et al.: On the importance of initialization and momentum in deep learning. In: International Conference on Machine Learning, pp. 1139–1147. PMLR (2013)
20. Ioffe, S., Szegedy, C.: Batch normalization: accelerating deep network training by reducing internal covariate shift. In: International Conference on Machine Learning, pp. 448–456. PMLR (2015)
21. Nair, V., Hinton, G.E.: Rectified linear units improve restricted Boltzmann machines. In: ICML (2010)

Fake Calligraphy Recognition Based on Deep Learning

Junjie Liu[1(✉)], Yaochang Liu[1], Peiren Wang[1], Ruotong Xu[1], Wenxuan Ma[1], Youzhou Zhu[2], and Baili Zhang[1,3]

[1] School of Computer Science and Engineering, Southeast University, Nanjing 211189, China
213182296@seu.edu.cn

[2] School of Fine Arts, Nanjing University of the Arts, Nanjing 210013, China

[3] Research Center for Judicial Big Data, Supreme Count of China, Nanjing 211189, China

Abstract. With the proliferation of fake calligraphy, how to effectively identify calligraphy works has attracted more and more experts. The current appraisal of fake calligraphy mainly relies on the subjective judgment of experienced experts, with large uncertainty and high appraisal costs. With the development of digital image technology and deep learning models, the use of computer technology to identify calligraphy fakes has become a feasible option. This paper proposes a calligraphic work recognition method based on deep learning. In view of the diversity of calligraphy works and the difficulty of sample collection, this article only selects some of the regular scripts by Yan Zhenqing, a famous calligraphy master, as the identification object at this stage. The research includes six aspects: the collection of genuine and counterfeit data sets, the selection of identification character sets, the preprocessing of calligraphy images, word segmentation, single word neural network training, and calligraphy authenticity identification. Finally, a complete scheme programs is provided to identify calligraphic works. The test results show that the scheme proposed in this paper can effectively extract the features of the Chinese character, and can correctly judge the authenticity of the work.

Keywords: Authenticity identification · Convolutional neural network model · Noise reduction processing

1 Introduction

At present, the identification of the calligraphy works mainly depends on the judgment of the experts, which is highly subjective. Thus, finding qualified senior experts becomes the key. But in many cases, this is either too expensive or difficult to find. As far as the intelligent recognition of calligraphy works is concerned, the diversity and variability of calligraphy works and the difficulty of sample collection have brought huge challenges and difficulties to calligraphy recognition. Aiming at the issue of calligraphy work recognition, this paper proposes a calligraphy work recognition scheme based on deep learning, which has been proved effective. The identification of the calligraphy works by means of deep learning can be explored in the following:

X. Sun et al. (Eds.): ICAIS 2021, LNCS 12736, pp. 585–596, 2021.
https://doi.org/10.1007/978-3-030-78609-0_50

In view of the diversity of calligraphy works, this paper select only Yan Zhenqing's regular script for research. It aims to explore six aspects including the acquisition of genuine and counterfeit data sets, selection of identification character sets, calligraphy image preprocessing, Chinese characters segmentation in calligraphic works, single character neural network training, and calligraphy authenticity identification. A complete implementation scheme is provided as follows.

First, the collection and acquisition of genuine and fake sets. Since the identification method in this thesis is based on the identification of a single Chinese character, in the process of obtaining the original and counterfeit collections, this article collected a large number of Yan Zhenqing regular scripts through a reliable calligraphy website (http://www.9610.com/), so as to form a positive sample set by chopping the target words in the regular script works. For the collection of negative samples, this article uses two methods to collect: one is to directly treat the target words in the regular script fake works of Yan Zhenqing in the previous dynasties; the other is to treat the target words in the regular script works of other famous calligraphers as a negative sample (such as Ouyang Xun).

The second step is to identify the choice of character set. In terms of distinguishing single character, this article takes a multi-angle evaluation of different Chinese characters. The evaluation criteria include the frequency of Chinese characters, the stability of Chinese characters, and whether they are commonly used characters. Finally, eight more ideal target recognition of Chinese characters are selected to train our neural network.

The third step is calligraphy image preprocessing. Due to the problems such as oxidation in the circulation of calligraphy works, the noise of calligraphy image is nonnegligible. In order to better extract the information conducive to the identification process of calligraphy works, the current research conducted binarization and median filtering processing on calligraphy works in advance to effectively suppress the noise in calligraphic works.

The fourth step is calligraphy word segmentation. The recognition object of a calligraphy work is the entire work, so it is necessary to segment the work, and then perform subsequent recognition and recognition operations after segmenting individual characters. A histogram segmentation algorithm is used to segment the original calligraphy works in view of the characteristics of conventional calligraphic works.

Finally, the fifth step and sixth step are single-character neural network training and calligraphy authenticity identification. This article uses GoogLeNet to train a word neural network. In the process of identifying calligraphy, first identify the target word through CnOcr, and then the target word are sent to the designated neural network for identification. And then based on the similarity between each word judge the possibility of the entire work being identified as true. A conclusion can be drawn by experiment that the authenticity of calligraphic works can be judged if it is fake by this scheme. Experimental results show that this method can better identify Yan Zhenqing's regular script works.

2 Preparation Stage

2.1 Collection and Acquisition of Authentic Collections and Fakes

We searched on the Internet and selected the scanned pictures of Yan Zhenqing's regular script works as the authentic collection. Some of the selected calligraphy works are from rubbings and some are from paper media, aiming to give our model the ability to recognize both of these two kinds of works. The list of selected calligraphy works is as follows:

"The Epitaph of Wang Lin", "The Epitaph of Guo Xuji", "Duo Pagoda Tablet", "Dongfang Shuo Painting Praise", "Guo Family Temple Stele", "The Story of Magu Immortal Altar", "Zang Huai Ke Stele", "Li Xuanjing Stele", "Self-information Post", "Yan Qinli Stele" and "Zhushantang Lianju"

At the same time, we searched in many ways to find similar fake pictures, such as copy works and other calligraphers' works as fake collections.

2.2 Determination of Commonly Used Character Sets

Word Frequency Statistics. In order to find out the commonly used characters in ancient Chinese, we conducted a character frequency statistics for Guwenguanzhi. At the same time, we also performed the same statistics on some of Yan Zhenqing's regular script works.

The following tables are the result of the frequency statistics of some commonly used characters in Guwenguanzhi (Table 1) or Yan's works (Table 2).

Table 1. Word frequency statistics of Guwenguanzhi.

Frequency rank	Characters	Frequency
1	之	5.1843%
2	而	2.5491%
3	其	2.2046%
4	以	2.1185%
5	不	1.9290%
6	也	1.9118%
7	者	1.8601%
8	于	1.4468%
9	有	1.3262%
10	为	1.0851%

Our data shows Guwenguanzhi and Yan Zhenqing's calligraphy works have the same 8 characters in the top 10 commonly used characters, accounting for 7.825% of the total character frequency of Yan Zhenqing's calligraphy works. The total sample size is sufficient.

Table 2. Word frequency statistics of Yan Zhenqing's regular script works.

Frequency rank	Characters	Frequency
1	之	2.0889%
2	而	0.9434%
3	其	0.9013%
4	以	0.8255%
5	不	0.8086%
6	也	0.7834%
7	者	0.7749%
8	于	0.6991%
9	有	0.6065%
10	为	0.5644%

The Characteristics of Common Words as Samples. The selection of commonly used words as samples is the result of comprehensive consideration of multiple factors.

First, the frequency of frequently used words should be high enough and the number should be relatively stable. Taking "Guwen Guanzhi" as a sample, the top ten frequently used characters account for 21.62%. If we take Yan Zhenqing's calligraphy as a sample (including a certain amount of poetry text with a small amount of commonly used characters), the top ten commonly used characters account for 8.996% of the frequency. According to the frequency statistics of those commonly adopted Chinese characters written by different calligraphers, the number of the top ten commonly used characters is about 40, and the total number of the top ten commonly used characters is about 500. Counting a single work, a small-scale text of about 100 characters basically guarantees that there are more than 5 commonly used characters. A medium-sized text of about 300 characters is basically guaranteed to have more than 20 commonly used characters. The larger the text size, the more stable the proportion of commonly used characters.

Second, the shape of the commonly used characters are stable, easy to form personal style, and have obvious characteristics. Referring to the Kangxi dictionary and the actual calligraphy works, a large number of traditional Chinese characters and variant characters have been produced in the historical evolution of Chinese characters, which is not easy to identify. However, the commonly used characters and characters selected from "Guwen Guanzhi" and calligraphy works have not changed basically, and they are basically consistent with modern Chinese. Due to the simples' structure and high frequency of writing, calligraphers are more likely to form a fixed format and obvious personal style. The common characters in different works of calligraphers have better consistency and more obvious characteristics, and the quality of the samples is higher.

Third, the shape of commonly used characters is simple, and the recognition accuracy is higher than that of unusual characters.

Commonly used glyphs need to be easily recognized by the computer. Certain single characters with extremely high frequency, such as "之", have a scattered font structure in ancient Chinese writing. The existing character recognition programs are difficult to recognize, so they cannot be used as samples for the construct of this model. It will be considered to be added to the set of commonly used characters after a breakthrough in the relevant technology. This means that we can not choose our characters set just according to the frequency simply.

Taking into account factors such as character frequency and character recognition, we finally choose "公", "而" "及", "于", "乃", "太", "也", and "子" to form the common characters set.

Selection of Reference Character Set. After determining the common used characters, the requirements of recognition algorithm are significantly reduced. At the same time, because the soft pen calligraphy image is closer to the picture than to the line, and there is a certain universal requirement for the algorithm, so the open source CnOcr is selected as the reference character set in the experiment.

3 Training Stage

3.1 Conception

We plan to construct several binary classifiers at this stage to realize the authenticity classification of each character in the common character set.

3.2 Design and Training of Single Character Neural Network

Model Selection. We use convolutional neural networks to construct these two classifiers. Among many well-known convolutional neural network models, GoogLenet has the characteristics of good performance, high accuracy and mature technology. In our test, the training effect is better than other common networks, so we use GoogLenet as the model to train.

Training Collection Acquisition. In order to ensure that the obtained training set is reliable, we used manual-screenshotting to cut out all the determined words in the common character set from the "authentic set" and "fake set" obtained in the preparation phase, and saved them separately as a model training set.

Model Training

Image Preprocessing. The single-character pictures segmented from the previous process have the characteristics of inconsistent image length and width and uneven distribution of RGB values, which may interfere with the training of the model. We enforced scaling and standardization of each input single-word image to solve this problem. The length and width after scaling are 224 pixels, the standardized mean is 0, and the standard deviation std is 0.5.

Training. Model training uses python 3.6.6 language environment, pytorch framework, GoogLeNet model, loss function selects the Cross-Entropy loss function commonly used by classifiers, optimizer selects Adam optimizer, learning rate selects 0.0001, and the number of training rounds is 20 epochs. During the training, the genuine pictures and fake pictures of each word are regarded as category 0 and category 1 respectively.

The calculation method of the cross entropy loss function is written below. In the function, y represents the labels of our training samples, and $\hat{y}$ represents the output of our network.

$$loss = -[ylog\hat{y} + (1 - y)\log(1 - \hat{y})] \tag{1}$$

Training Result. We can find that the loss is gradually decreasing. After 20 epochs of training, the last round of the loss function value for each word is much smaller. The following figure uses the word "也" as an example to depict the change process of the Cross-Entropy loss function (Fig. 1).

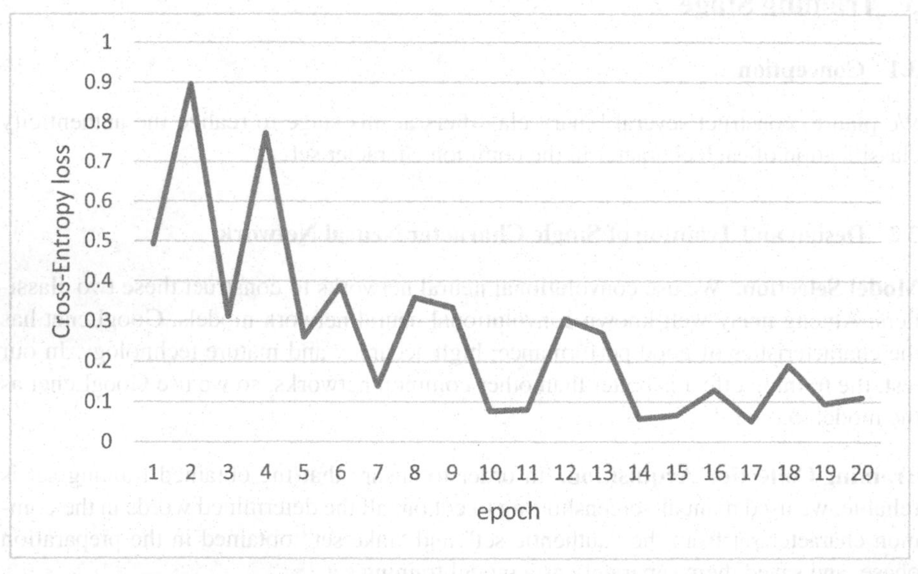

Fig. 1. Change process of the cross-entropy loss function.

4 Identification Stage

4.1 Preprocessing of the Image of the Sample to Be Identified

Before the calligraphy image recognition, certain digital image processing should be done on the calligraphy works to facilitate the subsequent segmentation and recognition operations.

First, we read the unprocessed calligraphy works through the imread() function in the Opencv library, and turn it into a two-dimensional matrix to facilitate further image processing. After the image is successfully read, the image is binarized, taking lowerb = (0, 0, 116), upperb = (255, 255, 255), using the inRange() to binarize the image according to the hsv threshold. Next, perform a circular kernel corrosion operation with a kernel of (3, 3) on the binarized graphics, thereby enhancing the text in the image and facilitating the subsequent image processing. Finally, we perform median filtering on the image to suppress the noise in the image and make the image smoother.

We can find the effect before and after image processing in following figures (Fig. 2, Fig. 3, and Fig. 4.).

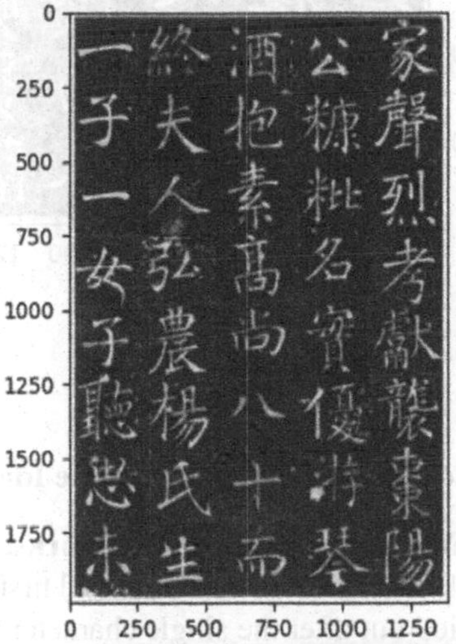

Fig. 2. Original graph.

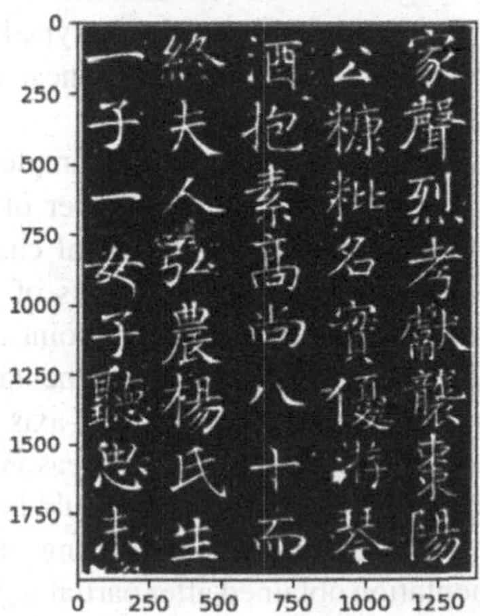

Fig. 3. Graph after circular kernel corrosion operation.

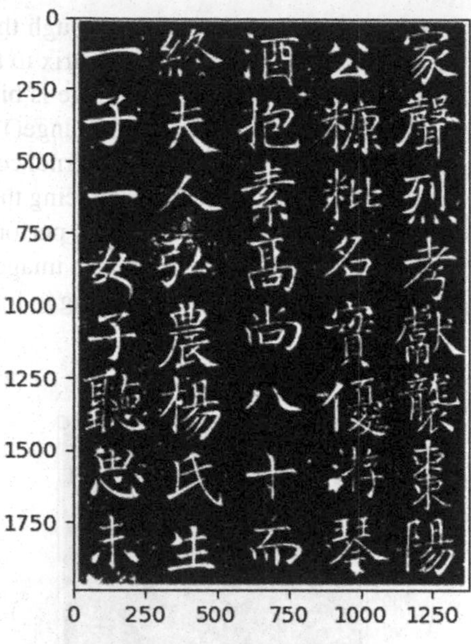

Fig. 4. Final graph.

4.2 Extraction of Common Words in Samples to Be Identified

Character Segmentation Method of Calligraphy Works. Before the recognition of calligraphy works, the whole work should be segmented firstly, and then the recognition of the next step can be carried out after the single character is separated.

The segmentation algorithms of the whole calligraphy works are currently the drip algorithm and the histogram segmentation method. The drip algorithm is easy to segment the complicated and even glued Chinese characters, while the columnar statistical graph segmentation method is more suitable for neatly typed Chinese characters. As the format of regular script calligraphy works is relatively neat, this project uses histogram segmentation method to segment calligraphy works.

Taking the calligraphy works in Fig. 4 as an example, in the column statistical graph segmentation method, we first count the number of non-zero pixels in the y-axis direction to generate the first columnar statistical chart (Fig. 5). The x-axis of the statistical chart represents the pixels on the x-axis of the image, and the y-axis represents the number of non-zero pixels at the pixel points. Then, the x-axis direction is segmented according to the statistical chart. The segmentation basis is that the x-axis coordinate which is less than a certain value in the x-axis coordinate is taken as the splitting point of the x-axis. It is found that 50 is more reasonable in the segmentation of calligraphy works. In the segmentation process, it should be noted that there are often multiple segmentation points at the vertical line spacing of regular script calligraphy works (Fig. 6), and the segmentation obtained after partial segmentation may not contain any characters. Therefore, we filter the segments whose X-axis width is less than 75 pixels after image segmentation, and then obtain the ideal X-axis segmentation. After this step, save the segments and proceed to the next step.

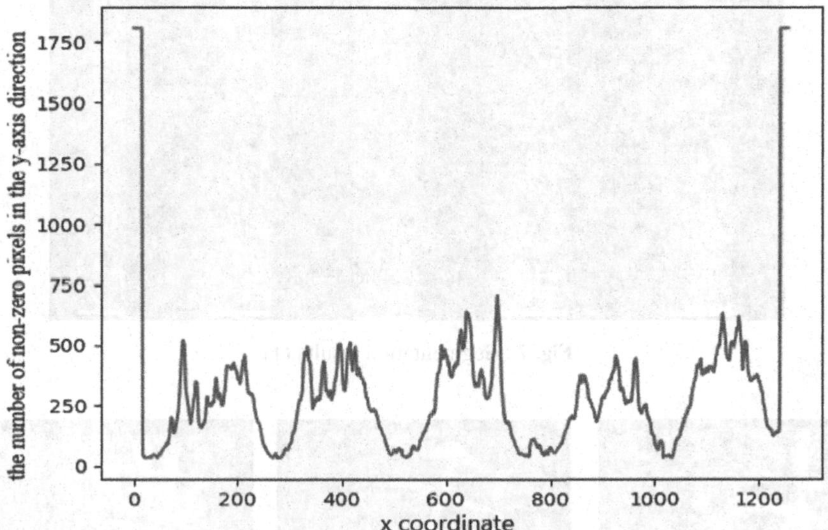

Fig. 5. The number of non-zero pixels in the y-axis direction in Fig. 3.

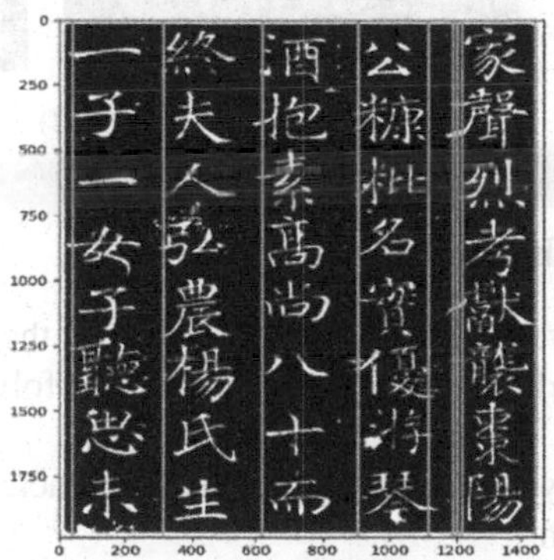

Fig. 6. Multiple segmentation points.

After the above segmentation, the segmentation results are as shown in Fig. 7.

Next, perform the same statistical segmentation processing on the y axis. Since the image object obtained after the previous segmentation is already a single vertical line image, a single text object can be obtained after the y axis is segmented again.

We can get the results like Fig. 8.

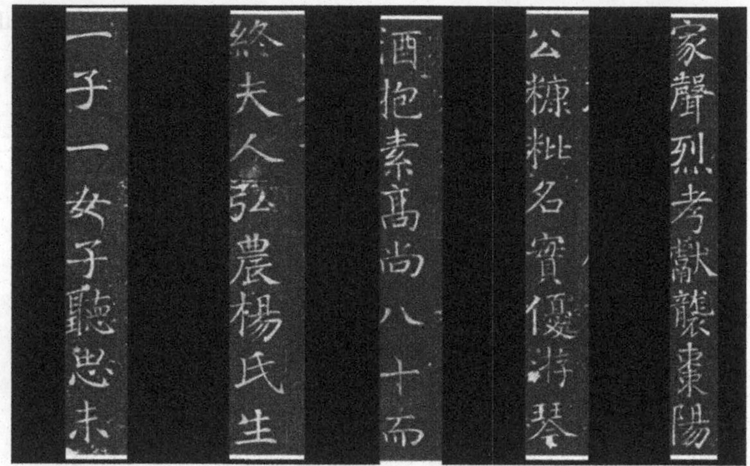

Fig. 7. Segmentation results (1).

Fig. 8. Segmentation results (2)

4.3 Identification of Authenticity

On the basis of the above work, the authenticity of the calligraphy works to be authenticated can be judged. The judgment method is as follows:

1) Divide the calligraphy work into individual characters through the histogram segmentation algorithm.
2) For each segmented word i, judge whether it is a word in the trained classifier by calling the API provided by the open source CnOcr. If so, put it into the convolutional neural network model for binary classifications, obtain the authentic probability p_i of the word, and count the number of all words that are found in all the trained models.
3) Calculate the probability of authenticity of the entire work. The preliminary calculation method is weighted average, and the calculation formula is:

$$P = \sum_{i=0}^{n} \frac{p_i}{n} \tag{2}$$

5 Experimental Results

Below, take a page of representative calligraphy work (Fig. 9) as an example to briefly describe the authenticity recognition effect of the model.

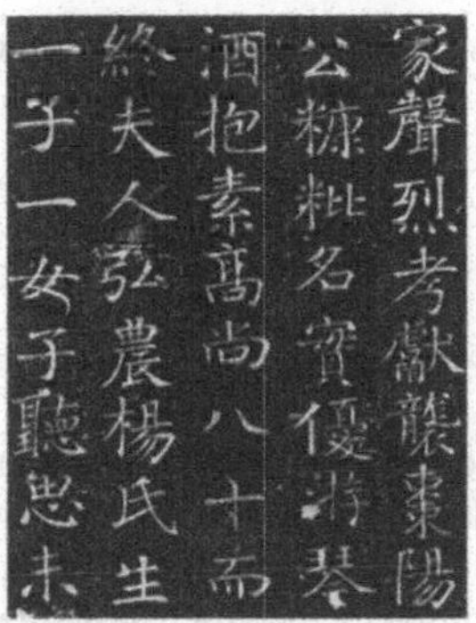

Fig. 9. A representative calligraphy work.

This picture is from "The Epitaph of Wang Lin". It contains common words such as "子" and "而". Putting it into the model can get the following (Fig. 10) running results:

```
model loading...
model loaded successfully!
cutting image...
image cutted!
而 was found
The possibility of single word:
0.9829310774803162
子 was found
The possibility of single word:
0.9966804385185242
amount of common used words:  2
seems like true: 2
The possibility that this calligraphy is authentic: 0.9898057579994202
```

Fig. 10. Program running results.

It can be seen that the model has a high recognition for Yan Zhenqing's regular script works. For other pages in Wang Lin's epitaph, this model can also achieve similar results. For forgeries, the model can also identify common characters, but the probability of authenticity of common words is less than 0.1. In addition, we have conducted 5 sets of experiments, and each group contained 5 positive samples and 5 negative samples. Finally, the total accuracy of the model is 92.455%. The number of characters in the commonly used character set is limited in the current. Hopefully, new authentic and fake sets can be obtained to the model in the future.

Funding Statement. This work was partly supported by Rapid Support Project (61406190120), the National Key R&D Program of China (2018YFC0830200) and Open Research Fund from Key Laboratory of Computer Network and Information Integration in Southeast University, Ministry of Education, China.

Conflicts of Interest. The authors declare that they have no conflicts of interest to report regarding the present study.

References

1. Qu, Y.: Study on calligraphy recognition of chinese characters based on deep learning. Electron. Test. **24**, 44–46 (2019)
2. Wang, Q.: Technical analysis of calligraphy style recognition. Arts **12**, 214–215 (2016)
3. Wang, P., Yao, H., Shen, J.: Identification of stone carving calligraphy character based on convolutional neural network. Comput. Eng. Des. **39**(03), 867–872 (2018)
4. Chen, R.: A calligraphy recognition method for handwritten chinese characters based on deep learning. Electron. World, 33–34 (2019)
5. Deng, X., Ma, X.: Weed recognition at seedling stage of rice field based on convolutional neural net-work and transfer learning. Agric. Mech. Res. **10**, 43–44 (2021)
6. Zhou, Z.: Machine Learning. Tsinghua University Press, Nanjing (2016)
7. Sidorov, O.: Artificial color constancy via GoogLeNet with angular loss function. Appl. Artif. Intell. **34**(9), 643–655 (2020)
8. Mohammed Aarif, K.O., Poruran, S.: OCR-Nets: variants of pre-trained CNN for Urdu handwritten character recognition via transfer learning. Procedia Comput. Sci. **171**, 2294–2301 (2020)
9. Zheng, H.: Research on Yan Zhenqing's calligraphy aesthetics. Beauty Times **4**, 73–75 (2020)
10. Ling, M., Li, J., Xiao, S.: Research on lane line recognition system based on gray image. Light Ind. Technol. **37**(01), 67–70 (2021)
11. Suriya, S., Dhivya, S., Balaji, M.: Intelligent character recognition system using convolutional neural network. EAI Endorsed Trans. Cloud Syst. **6**(19), 44–48 (2020)
12. Afef, M., Yu, M., McGee Rebecca, J.: Generalized linear model with elastic net regularization and convolutional neural network for evaluating aphanomyces root rot severity in lentil. Plant Phenom. 12–17 (2020)
13. Space of Calligraphy. http://www.9610.com/. Accessed 23 Sept 2020
14. Fu, F.: Research on scene character recognition algorithm. Fujian Comput. **36**(04), 38–42 (2020)
15. Zhang, J.: The practical application of optical character recognition (OCR) technology in internal audit. Taxation, 19–34 (2020)

A Top-k QoS-Optimal Service Composition Approach Under Dynamic Environment

Cheng Tian[1](✉), Zhao Zhang[2,3], Sha Yang[2,3], Shuxin Huang[2,3], Han Sun[2,3], Jing Wang[2,3], and Baili Zhang[1]

[1] School of Computer Science and Engineering, Southeast University, Nanjing 211189, China
220181734@seu.edu.cn

[2] State Key Laboratory of Smart Grid Protection and Control, Nanjing 211106, China

[3] Nari Group Corporation, Nanjing 211106, China

Abstract. To deal with low efficiency of existing Web service composition algorithms under dynamic environment, this paper proposes a Top-k QoS-optimal service composition algorithm based on QWSC-K static algorithm. The algorithm first considers the influence of dynamic environment on the existing service composition and service dependency graph, and classifies the changed services in dynamic environment. Moreover, different strategies are adopted to obtain the intermediate results of service composition for different categories of services. The influence of different service categories on the service dependency graph is analyzed to realize the updating of the service dependency graph. Finally, based on the updated service dependency graph and the intermediate results of the service composition, the adaptive incremental update can be applied to change the original service composition results, avoiding the time-consuming re-query process. Experiments show that the algorithm is efficient and accurate in dynamic environment.

Keywords: Dynamic environment · Service composition · Intermediate results · Dependency graph · Incremental updating · Adaptive

1 Introduction

Due to the limited functions of single Web service, how to combine exiting Web services to meet complex business requirements has become a research focus [1, 2]. The existing Top-k QoS-optimal service composition schemes have been utilized to provide users with multiple service compositions to meet their requirements [3–6]. However, most of these service composition methods are based on the static environment with fixed services. Faced with the dynamic changing service environment, it is often necessary to recalculate the built composite services, which is very inefficient. Therefore, many researchers propose their own solutions to the service composition problem in dynamic environment.

Literature [7, 8] proposes that artificial intelligence planning method can be used to process dynamic services and update composite services accordingly. However, because

X. Sun et al. (Eds.): ICAIS 2021, LNCS 12736, pp. 597–609, 2021.
https://doi.org/10.1007/978-3-030-78609-0_51

QoS of services is not taken into account in the process of service composition update, these methods usually cannot guarantee that the updated composite services still meet the non-functional requirements.

Literature [9] proposed a service composition method oriented to dynamic service environment. It is based on the shortest path graph search algorithm to search for chain-like composite services. However, this method cannot search for non-chain composite services that actually exist, such as composite services that can be modeled as Directed Acyclic Graph (DAG).

Literature [10, 11] respectively gives the methods of automatic service composition oriented to dynamic environment. However, these methods only focus on the changes of services functional factors (such as the change of service interface), and do not consider the influence of non-functional factors (such as service QoS). Thus, it is difficult to recommend a service composition under constrains of user QoS. Contrary to the above two works, literatures [12, 13] focus on improving the quality of service according to the change of QoS of atomic services.

Literature [14] proposes a composite service adaptive algorithm to deal with the dynamically changing service environment. However, this method only performs adaptive updating for a single optimal service composition, and does not solve the adaptive updating problem of the first k optimal service composition.

Therefore, this paper proposes a Top-k QoS-optimal service composition algorithm DQWSC-K in dynamic environment. The algorithm is based on the updated service dependency graph and uses an incremental adaptive algorithm to partly update the affected service state, avoiding time-consuming re-composition process.

The second section introduces the knowledge related to the proposed algorithm. The third section describes the service composition algorithm in dynamic environment. Section 4 gives the experimental results. The last part is the summary and prospect of the paper.

2 Related Knowledge

2.1 Service Dependency Graph Model

In order to accurately express the association relationship of Web services in the Web services set and their QoS information, this paper uses the service dependency graph *G* = *(V, E)* to model the Web services set.

In *G*, the node set *V* represents a set of services. Each service W_i is represented as a node in *G*. The directed edge set *E* represents the set of service matches. The set satisfies: $\forall e_k \in E$, $e_k = (v_n, v_m, tag_k)$, in which v_n and v_m respectively represent the service nodes corresponding to the start and the end of the edge. The tag_k satisfies the following relationship:

1. $tag_k \subseteq v_n.O$
2. $tag_k \subseteq v_m.I$

It is necessary to point out that when there is a service request R, the entrance service node Start and the exit service node End are dynamically generated in the graph. The two service nodes satisfy the following relationship:

Table 1. Service node.

Service name	Input parameters	Output parameters	QoS value
v_1	*A, B, C*	*D*	900
v_2	*A, B*	*E, F*	100
v_3	*C, E*	*H*	200
v_4	*C, F*	*G*	500
v_5	*L, J*	*D*	600
v_6	*K*	*H*	500
v_7	*H*	*D*	200
v_8	*G*	*H*	500

1. $Start.I = \varnothing; Start.O = R.I$
2. $End.I = R.O; End.O = \varnothing$

According to the above definition, if the service set is the service described in Table 1, the service request is R = <I, O>, in which the request input parameter is I = {A, B, C} and the request output parameter is O = {D}. The service dependency graph constructed is shown in Fig. 1.

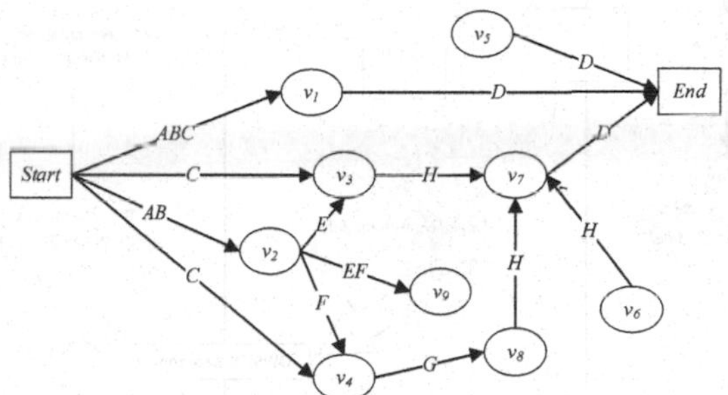

Fig. 1. Service dependency graph.

2.2 QWSC-K Algorithm Structure and Process

The Top-k QoS-optimal service composition algorithm QWSC-K [15] under static environment mainly includes three modules: the service filtering module, the obtaining the combined path sequence module and the combined path sequence conversion module. Firstly, in the service filtering module, an effective hierarchy filtering algorithm is adopted to filter the initial service set. The search space of the graph and the time complexity of the entire algorithm can be reduced greatly. Secondly, in the obtaining the combined path sequence module, the filtered service candidate set is used to construct a service dependency graph. Then traverse the service dependency graph. In the traversal process, the Top-k composition path information sequences associated with each service node are calculated and saved. The sequences are sorted according to global QoS values. Finally, in the combined path sequence conversion module, the Top-k composition path information sequences at the exit service node End are converted into the solution of the final Top-k service composition.

3 DQWSC-K Algorithm Description

The DQWSC-K algorithm mainly include four modules: dynamic service acquisition and classification module, service composition intermediate result acquisition module, service dependency graph updating module and incremental adaptive updating module. The algorithm framework is shown in Fig. 2.

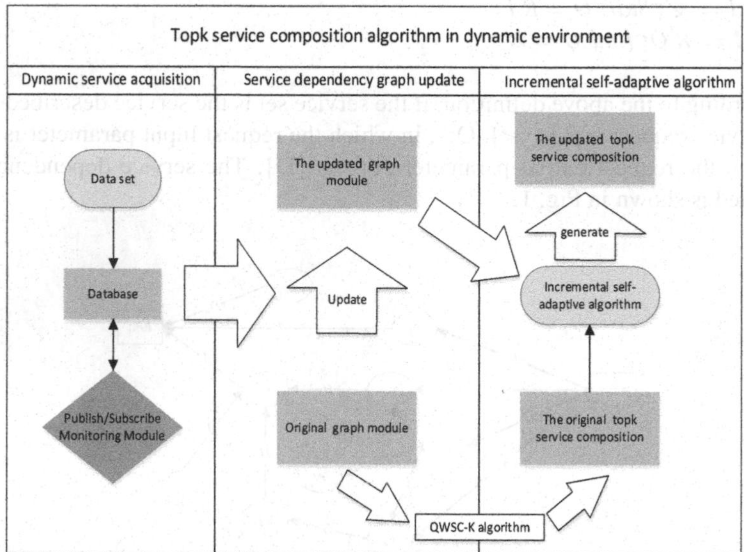

Fig. 2. Top-k service composition algorithm framework in dynamic environment.

3.1 Dynamic Service Acquisition and Classification Module

In accordance with the method described in literature [16], this paper receives events related to dynamic services from the publish/subscribe network, and uses soapUI to monitor and obtain Web services and their QoS. For the received dynamic services, this paper divides them into four categories according to different processing strategies: (1) new services: the services newly added to the service set; (2) failed services: the services that need to be deleted in the service set; (3) interface change services: the services existing in the original service set, but their input and output parameter set changes; (4) the services with changed QoS. As shown in Table 2, compared with Fig. 1, v10 in Table 2 (1) is a new service, v3 in Table 2 (2) is a failed service, v3 in Table 2 (3) is an interface change service, and v3 in Table 2 (4) is a service with changed QoS value from 200 to 1000.

Table 2. Dynamic services.

Dynamic services	Example
(1)New services	
(2)Failed services	
(3)Interface change services	
(4)Services with changed QoS	

3.2 Service Composition Intermediate Result Acquisition Module

In the process of running the QWSC-K algorithm, the effective service candidate set was obtained by using the hierarchical filtering algorithm. Then, according to the effective service candidate set, the combined path traversal algorithm is used to obtain the parameter source table and the combined path sequence information source table generated during the traversal process. These two tables are the intermediate result of service combination.

However, the intermediate state results obtained by the QWSC-K algorithm may be incomplete for new services and interface change services. The reason is that the new service and the interface change service could lead to a previously inaccessible service node becoming accessible, which may eventually lead to generating a new service composition. So when traversing the graph, the state of every reachable service node need to be recorded in order to check whether the original unreachable node becomes reachable due to the appearance of the new services or interface change services. However, in reality, the QWSC-K algorithm will directly filter out the previously unreachable nodes during the filtering phase, so new service combinations cannot be generated. Therefore, for the new services and the interface change services, the QWSC-K algorithm needs to be improved to remove the filtering stage, so that the intermediate states of all reachable service can be obtained.

The improved QWSC-K algorithm (IQWSC-K) is similar to the QWSC-K algorithm. After the filtering phase is removed, the parameter source table is obtained through the entire service set instead of the original valid service list. At the same time, the service dependency graph is directly constructed from the original service set.

For the failed services and the services with changed QoS, the emergence of these two types of dynamic services will not lead to the original unreachable service node reachable. Therefore, the QWSC-K algorithm can be directly used to filter and calculate the intermediate state result.

3.3 Service Dependency Graph Update Module

It can be seen from Sect. 3.1 that four types of dynamic services will have an impact on the structure or attributes of the service dependency graph. According to the type of dynamic service, the following strategies are used to update the service dependency graph respectively. First of all, for the new service, the corresponding node is added in the service dependency graph. And according to the matching relationship between this node and other nodes, the corresponding edge is added in the service dependency graph. Then, the precursor service node of the new service node is obtained according to the saved parameter source table. And the Top-k composite path sequence associated with the new node is obtained from the precursor service node and saved to the composite path information source table. Secondly, for the failed service, the corresponding node and its associated edges are removed from the service dependency graph. And the table items associated with the node are removed from the composite path information source table and parameter source table. Thirdly, for the service with changed QoS, the QoS values of the corresponding nodes in the service dependency graph are updated. And the Top-k composite path sequence associated with this node is found from the composite path information source table to update its global QoS value. Finally, for the interface change service, it is handled in two steps: (1) Delete the original service in the service dependency graph; (2) Handle the service as a new service. Thus, in the manner described above, we have transformed the four dynamic services into the three dynamic services for processing.

3.4 Incremental Adaptive Update Module

At present, for Top-k service composition algorithm, when dynamic services arrive, the service composition engine reruns the service composition process and generates a new Top-k service composition scheme. However, this approach is less efficient in a dynamic environment with real-time change. Through the analysis of the existing QWSC-K algorithm, it is found that in the process of generating service composition, each service node saves the composite path sequence from the starting node to the service node. This also shows that for each service node, only the change of service state in the precursor service set will have a direct impact on it. Thus, the generation of each dynamic service can only affect its associated subsequent services, while the state of its precursor services does not change. So, in the process of service composition, the service nodes affected by the dynamic service are updated in turn according to the state of the dynamic service and the intermediate results of the saved service nodes. After that, a new Top-k service composition scheme can be obtained.

When the dynamic service is received, according to specific categories of dynamic service, incremental adaptive algorithm (IA_Alg) takes the corresponding processing strategy and generates new Top-k service composition. The specific steps of IA_Alg algorithm are as follows:

(1) Analyze the impact of dynamic services and judge whether dynamic services may cause changes in the intermediate state of other services. Specifically, for failed services, interface change services and services with changed QoS, determine whether this dynamic service exists in the saved composite path information list. If it exists, it indicates that the new service may affect the state of the subsequent service nodes. If it does not exist, then the dynamic service will not affect other service nodes. For a new service, determine whether it can trigger a new service node. If so, it means that the service may generate a new service combination. It needs to continue to consider the influence of subsequent nodes. If not, it means that there is no influence.

(2) Update the status of the affected service. First, the priority queue PQ is used to store the dynamic services identified in the first step that may affect the state of other services. Then the services in PQ are popped up by loop and processed accordingly. In PQ, service nodes are saved in order from small to large according to their global QoS value in order to avoid repeated update of service state.
For different dynamic service types, the specific process of updating the service state is different. For the new service or the interface change service, it can make the original unreachable service become the reachable service. Therefore, on the one hand, for each service popped up from the PQ, it is necessary to determine whether it enables other service nodes to change from the unreachable state to the reachable state based on its output parameters. That is, each output parameter of the dynamic service need to be traversed to see if it can trigger a new service node. If it can trigger a new service node, the new service node needs to be added to PQ. On the other hand, it is necessary to determine whether these dynamic services have an impact on the Top-k composite path sequence stored in the subsequent service. Then update the state of their subsequent service nodes and add the affected subsequent

services to the PQ. For the failed service or the service with changed QoS, it is only necessary to determine whether they have an impact on the Top-k combined path sequence stored in subsequent services. If so, directly update the status of the subsequent service nodes and add the affected subsequent services to PQ.

(3) After all the services in the priority queue PQ are processed, determine whether the composite path sequence of the terminating service node End is updated. If the sequence is updated, the path sequence transformation algorithm will convert the new Top-k composite path sequence into the solution of the final service combination. If not, the original solution of the Top-k service composition is returned.

4 Experiment

4.1 Experimental Procedure

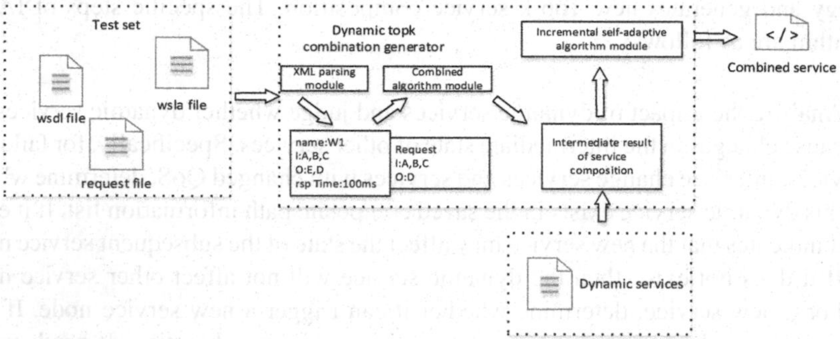

Fig. 3. Dynamic environment experiment system.

The experimental test set uses the data set generated by the WSBen tool, which contains 5 test sets with different number of services (200–10000). In the experiment, we also generate dynamic services in a random way for each test set. There are three types of files on each test set: the WSDL file describes the input and output parameters of the service; the WSLA file describes QoS information of the service; the request file describes the user's request. The whole experimental system is shown in Fig. 3.

This paper mainly selects QWSC-K algorithm based on re-execution as the comparison object of DQWSC-K algorithm. This paper mainly adopts the following two evaluation indexes: query response time and accuracy.

4.2 Query Response Time Evaluation

Because the intermediate results of the service composition obtained are different for the different dynamic service types in the DQWSC-K algorithm, the intermediate results of the service composition obtained for new services and interface change services are different from those for failed services and services with changed QoS. Therefore it is necessary to conduct experimental verification for these two situations. In order to verify the time performance of the algorithm, this paper conducts two sets of experiments: the same k value, the same number of dynamic services, and different service set sizes; the same k value, the same service set size, and different numbers of dynamic service. The specific experimental conditions are as follows:

Experiment 1: The influence of the same k value, the same service set size and different dynamic service quantity on the algorithm.

Figure 4 shows that when the dynamic service is a new service or an interface change service, k value is 5 and service size n = 1000, different dynamic service quantity has an impact on the execution time of DQWSC-K algorithm and QWSC-K algorithm. Figure 5 shows the impact of dynamic service as a failed service or a service with changes QoS on the execution time of DQWSC-K algorithm and QWSC-K algorithm under the same condition. It can be seen from Fig. 4 and Fig. 5 that the execution time of both DQWSC-K algorithm and QWSC-K algorithm increases with the increase of the number of dynamic services. But the execution time of QWSC-K algorithm increases with large amplitude, while that of DQWSC-K algorithm is smaller. This is because for QWSC-K algorithm, each addition of a dynamic service means an increase in the time to search the entire service space, the time consumption increases with large amplitude. In contrast, DQWSC-K algorithm can avoid re-search and consume less time, so the increase amplitude is lower.

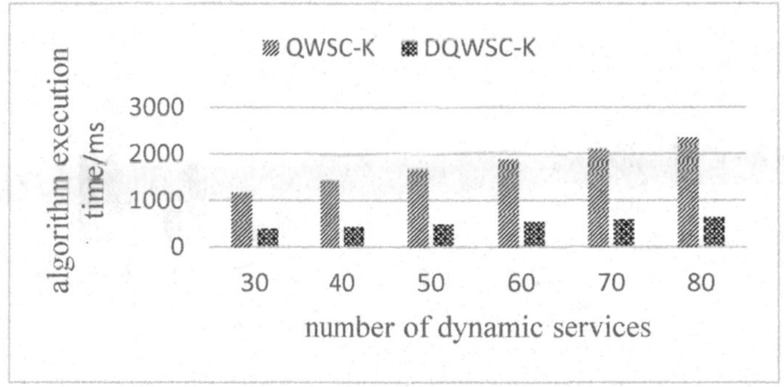

Fig. 4. Dynamic service is the new service or interface change service.

Experiment 2: The influence of the same k value, the same number of dynamic services, and different service set sizes on the algorithm.

Figure 6 shows that when the dynamic service is a new service or an interface change service, the value of k is 5 and the number of dynamic services is 10, different service set sizes have an impact on the execution time of DQWSC-K algorithm and QWSC-K algorithm. Figure 7 shows the impact of dynamic service as a failed service or a service with changed QoS on the execution time of DQWSC-K algorithm and QWSC-K algorithm under the same condition. As can be seen from Fig. 6 and Fig. 7, the execution time of the QWSC-K algorithm obviously depends on the size of the Web service set.

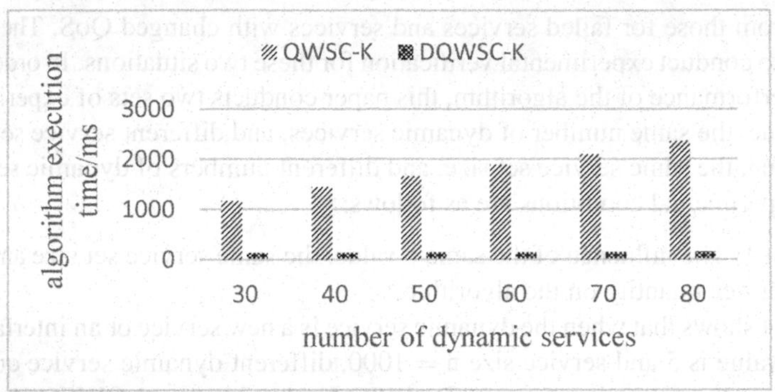

Fig. 5. Dynamic service is the failure service or service with changed QoS.

The more services there are, the longer the query execution time will be. This is because each time a dynamic service is generated, the QWSC-K algorithm needs to re-execute the query and search the entire service space, the execution time depends mainly on the number of services. But for the DQWSC-K algorithm, because the incremental adaption only needs to update the service state partially affected by the dynamic service, the execution time is lower than that of QWSC-K algorithm.

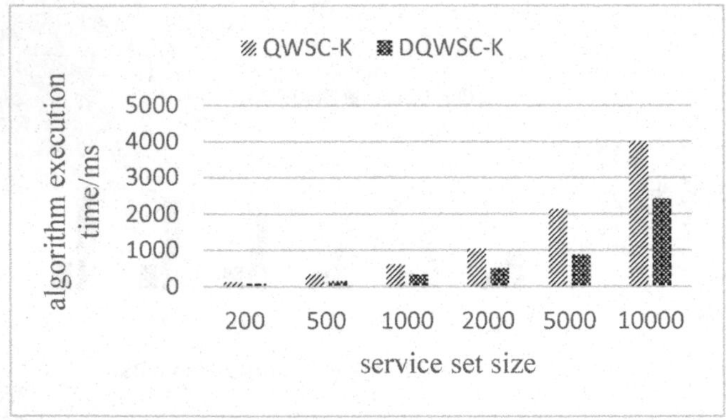

Fig. 6. Dynamic service is the new service or interface change service.

4.3 Accuracy Assessment

This section evaluates the accuracy of the two algorithms. It refers to whether the Top-k service combination returned by the two algorithms satisfies the query request and guarantees global QoS optimization. Because the QWSC-K algorithm has been proved theoretically and experimentally that the service composition it returns is globally optimal, by comparing whether the global QoS returned by QWSC-K algorithm is equal to the global QoS returned by DQWSC-K algorithm, we can determine whether the

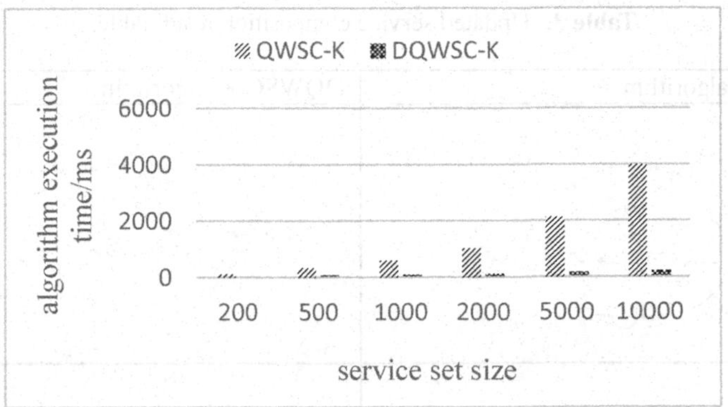

Fig. 7. Dynamic service is the failure service or service with changed QoS.

service combination returned by DQWSC-K algorithm is the global optimal QoS result. We respectively use two algorithms to conduct experiments based on the service dependency graph in Fig. 8: take the dynamic service as w_4, its QoS value changes from 10 to 30, and k is 3. The final experimental result is shown in Table 3.

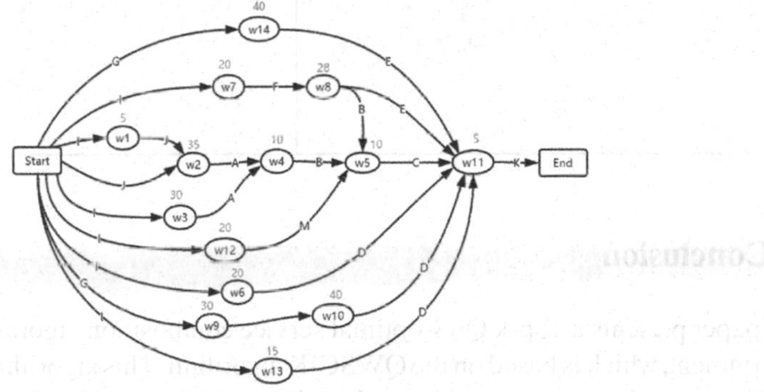

Fig. 8. Service dependency graph.

The result shows that the Top-k service combination results returned by QWSC-K algorithm and DQWSC-K algorithm are consistent and can be executed correctly. And the associated global QoS is also the same. This shows that the DQWSC-K algorithm can deal with the dynamic changing service environment and automatically update the service combination as required to ensure that the updated results still meet the query request and the global QoS is optimal.

Table 3. Updated service composition result table.

QWSC-K algorithm	DQWSC-K algorithm
GQoS=63	GQoS=63
GQoS=63	GQoS=63
GQoS=63	GQoS=63

5 Conclusion

This paper presents a Top-k QoS-optimal service composition algorithm under dynamic environment, which is based on the QWSC-K algorithm. This algorithm uses incremental adaptive algorithm to dynamically update the state of some affected services according to different service categories. The algorithm does not recalculate and search the entire service set space, which ensures the efficiency of the algorithm. The next step is to try to use the idea of distributed parallel or approximate computation to solve the Top-k QoS-optimal service combination problem in the dynamic service environment.

Acknowledgement. This work was partly supported by Open Research Fund from State Key Laboratory of Smart Grid Protection and Control, China, Rapid Support Project (61406190120) and the National Key R&D Program of China (2018YFC0830200).

References

1. Deng, S., Huang, L., Tan, W.: Top-k automatic service composition: a parallel method for large-scale service sets. IEEE Trans. Autom. Sci. Eng. **11**(3), 891–905 (2014)

2. Tan, W., Fan, Y., Zhou, M.: A petri net-based method for compatibility analysis and composition of web services in business process execution language. IEEE Trans. Autom. Sci. Eng. **6**(1), 94–106 (2009)
3. Benouaret, K., Benslimane, D., Hadjali, A., et al.: Top-k web service compositions using fuzzy dominance relationship. In: 2011 IEEE International Conference on Services Computing (SCC), pp. 144–151. IEEE, Washington (2011)
4. Almulla, M.. Almatori, K., Yahyaoui, H.: A QoS-based fuzzy model for ranking real world web services. In: 2011 IEEE International Conference on Web Services (ICWS), pp. 203–210. IEEE, Washington (2011)
5. Wang, X.L., Huang, S., Zhou, A.Y.: QoS-aware composite services retrieval. J. Comput. Sci. Technol. **21**(4), 547–558 (2006)
6. Jiang, W., Hu, S., Liu, Z.: Top k query for QoS-aware automatic service composition. IEEE Trans. Serv. Comput. **7**(4), 681–695 (2014)
7. Yan, Y., Poizat, P., Zhao, L.: Repair vs. recomposition for broken service compositions. In: Maglio, P.P., Weske, M., Yang, J., Fantinato, M. (eds.) ICSOC 2010. LNCS, vol. 6470, pp. 152–166. Springer, Heidelberg (2010). https://doi.org/10.1007/978-3-642-17358-5_11
8. Yan, Y., Poizat, P., Zhao, L.: Self-adaptive service composition through graphplan repair. In: 2010 IEEE International Conference on Web Services, pp. 624–627. IEEE, Miami (2010)
9. Kalasapur, S., Kumar, M., Shirazi, B.A.: Dynamic service composition in pervasive computing. IEEE Trans. Parallel Distrib. Syst. **18**(7), 907–918 (2007)
10. Wang, H., Wu, Q., Chen, X., et al.: Adaptive and dynamic service composition via multi-agent reinforcement learning. In: 2014 IEEE International Conference on Web Services, pp. 447–454. IEEE, Anchorage (2014)
11. Geyik, S.C., Szymanski, B.K., Zerfos, P.: Robust dynamic service composition in sensor networks. IEEE Trans. Serv. Comput. **6**(4), 560–572 (2013)
12. Feng, Y., Ngan, L.D., Kanagasabai, R.: Dynamic service composition with service-dependent QoS attributes. In: IEEE 20th International Conference on Web Services, pp. 10–17. IEEE Computer Society, Santa Clara (2013)
13. Groba, C., Clarke, S.: Opportunistic service composition in dynamic ad hoc environments. IEEE Trans. Serv. Comput. **7**(4), 642–653 (2014)
14. Lv, C., Jiang, W., Hu, S.: Adaptive method of composite service oriented to dynamic environment. Chin. J. Comput. **39**(2), 305–322 (2016)
15. Li, G., Wen, K., Wu, Y., Zhang, B.: Topk service composition algorithm based on optimal QoS. In: Sun, X., Pan, Z., Bertino, E. (eds.) Cloud Computing and Security, ICCC 2018, LNCS, vol. 11064, pp. 309–321. Springer, Cham (2018). https://doi.org/10.1007/978-3-030-00009-7_29
16. Yan, W., Hu, S., Muthusamy, V., et al.: Efficient event-based resource discovery. In: Proceedings of the Third ACM International Conference on Distributed Event-Based Systems, pp. 1–12. Association for Computing Machinery, New York (2009)

Big Data

Analysis on the Influencing Factors of Mooc Construction Based on SPSS Analysis

Chun Xu[1](✉) and Yuanbin Li[2]

[1] Shenzhen Polytechnic, Shenzhen 518000, Guangdong, China
[2] Information Engineering College, Sichuan Agriculture University, Ya'an 625014, Sichuan, China

Abstract. With the large-scale construction of MOOC, how to improve the construction quality of "MOOC" has become a question of interest for the course teaching team and MOOC platform managers. This paper mainly analyzes the relation between the open course and the number of learners for paid courses and class hours, course teaching forms, course nature, teachers, number of course evaluations, and course price on the MOOC platform, as well as the influencing factors and influence of MOOC course construction, by applying SPSS software.

Keywords: SPSS · Mooc · Factor

1 Research Background

In April 2015, *Opinions of Ministry of Education on Strengthening Open Online Course Construction, Application and Management of Higher Education Institutions* suggested that we should construct a batch of high-quality open online courses represented by open online courses which integrate course application and teaching services. In 2017 and 2018, the Ministry of Education identified 1,291 national superior open online courses, including 1,158 undergraduate courses and 133 junior college courses. With the large-scale construction of MOOC, how to improve the construction quality of "MOOC" has become a question of interest for the course teaching team and MOOC platform managers. Jordan [1] summarized the class ending rates of 39 MOOC courses in a study of 2014, and discovered that the class ending rates of the 39 MOOC courses were about 0.9%–36.1% (the class ending rates of most MOOC courses were about 5%). Meanwhile, Perna et al. [2] analyzed 16 MOOC courses of the University of Pennsylvania, and found that the class ending rates of these courses ranged from 3% to 4%. The highest-class ending rate of 6 MOOC courses introduced by Peking University on Coursera from September 2013 to January 2014 (open to the whole world) is 12.86%, the lowest rate is 9.64%, and the average value is 11.16% [3]. Wang Yu [4] classified learners of MOOC courses into four types: ineffective learner, resource sightseer, lost learner and finisher with poor performance. The study believed that the first two types occupied a proportion of more than 60%, but these two types of learners did not have a clear learning goal. Even if the courses were of high quality, they would not complete the courses, so they

X. Sun et al. (Eds.): ICAIS 2021, LNCS 12736, pp. 613–629, 2021.
https://doi.org/10.1007/978-3-030-78609-0_52

belonged to ineffective learners. The target population of course construction should be the last two types. Li Yazheng [5] considered that learners of paid courses had a clear learning goal and strong aspiration of completing the course. The author of this thesis analyzed the influence factors of MOOC construction and the influence degrees through exploring the relation between the number of learners for paid courses on the MOOC platform and class hours, course teaching forms, course nature, teachers, number of course evaluations, and course price.

On the MOOC platform of Chinese universities, there are 5,349 boutique open courses, 4500 undergraduate courses and 755 higher vocational courses. Thereinto, there are 820 national boutique open courses, taking up 63.5% of all national boutique open courses. Most courses on this platform are school-based courses recommended by various colleges and universities, and only a few are paid courses. The data of this research were taken from public data of this platform.

2 Data Analysis of Free Open Course

The course with the most learners on MOOC of Chinese universities is "linear algebra". Considering that course data of short curriculum time have a small size and involve distortion [6], the research data were taken from courses with a curriculum time of over 8 weeks on the platform. There were 46 MOOC course of "linear algebra" established for more than 8 weeks, thereinto, 11 were national boutique courses, and the total number of registered learners was 398009, please refer to Table 1.

2.1 Relation Between "National Boutique Course" and "Course of Famous Universities" and the Number of Learners

A correlation analysis was made on the number of learners and qualitative variables "National Boutique Open Course or Not" and "985/211 or Not" with SPSS software, and the results are shown in Table 2. The significance is greater than 0.05 in all cases, so there is no significant correlation, suggesting that "National Boutique Course" and "985/211 School Course" can not necessarily attract students to learn the course.

National Boutique Open Course or Not: No 0, Yes 1; 985/211 or Not: No 1, 211 2, 985 and 211 3.

2.2 Relation Between the Number of Learners and Quantitative Variables "number of Course Evaluations" and "number of Undergraduates"

A correlation analysis was made on the number of learners and quantitative variables "Number of Course Evaluations" and "Number of Undergraduates", and the results are shown in Table 3. Pearson's significance correlation of number of course registrants and "Number of Course Evaluations" is smaller than 0.01, and a significant correlation is presented. Besides, the correlation coefficient is 0.496, and a medium and low correlation is shown. Pearson's significance correlation of number of course registrants and "Number of Undergraduates" is greater than 0.05, and there is no correlation, indicating that schools with more undergraduates will not necessarily have more MOOC learners.

Table 1. Data of "linear algebra" on MOOC

Number of registrants	Number of course evaluations	National boutique open course or not	Number of undergraduates	985/211 or not
47780	323	0	28345	1
9790	445	1	22236	2
17921	67	0	40789	3
2685	4	0	24000	1
12499	75	0	10000	3
16048	203	0	36000	2
2922	15	0	18000	1
23053	676	0	20000	1
2630	201	1	16000	3
2898	30	1	37000	3
2197	6	0	20277	3
50552	882	1	40789	3
11141	40	0	15849	2
3224	7	0	21000	1
19625	215	1	16200	3
22904	121	0	18115	3
2088	254	0	15331	2
6674	48	0	29405	3
1992	30	0	19177	3
2758	58	0	20925	3
1546	37	1	20000	3
16881	699	0	18673	2
6106	1267	0	22236	2
2193	86	0	37000	3
5268	118	0	16500	1
994	21	0	30000	1
6182	91	1	14727	3
480	5	0	19000	1
10911	301	1	30059	3
2258	111	1	15675	3
4138	321	0	27435	1
371	7	0	13309	2

(*continued*)

Table 1. *(continued)*

Number of registrants	Number of course evaluations	National boutique open course or not	Number of undergraduates	985/211 or not
1114	8	0	14727	3
1500	105	0	16000	3
3110	45	0	20277	3
7829	37	0	11336	3
7575	97	0	34753	2
3596	177	1	19012	3
14091	78	0	1620	1
3545	85	1	20000	3
3616	42	0	16351	3
21524	290	0	20000	1
1279	36	0	30000	3
5480	323	0	28535	3
3928	4	0	17000	1
1113	12	0	28000	1

Table 2. Correlation analysis on qualitative variables

Chi-square test (number of learners and national boutique open course or not)				Chi-square test (number of learners and 985/211 school or not)			
	Value	Degree of freedom	Progressive significance (bilateral)		Value	Degree of freedom	Progressive Significance (bilateral)
Pearson's Chi-square	46.000[a]	45	0.431	Pearson's Chi-square	92.000	90	0.422
Likelihood ratio	50.607	45	0.262	Likelihood ratio	91.331	90	0.441
Linear association	0.341	1	0.559	Linear association	0.355	1	0.552
Number of effective cases	46			Number of effective cases	46		

a. The expected count of 92 table cells (100.0%) is smaller than 5. The minimum expected count is .24.

a. The expected count of 138 table cells (100.0%) is smaller than 5. The minimum expected count is .17.

Table 3. Correlation between the number of learners and quantitative variables "number of course evaluations" and "number of undergraduates"

		Number of registrants	Number of course evaluations	Number of undergraduates
Number of registrants	Pearson correlation	1	.496**	.263
	Sig. (two-tailed)		.000	.081
	Number of cases	46	46	45
Number of course evaluations	Pearson correlation	.496**	1	.172
	Sig. (two-tailed)	.000		.260
	Number of cases	46	46	45
Number of undergraduates	Pearson correlation	.263	.172	1
	Sig. (two-tailed)	.081	.260	
	Number of cases	45	45	45

** At the level of 0.01 (two-tailed), the correlation is significant.

2.3 SPSS Regression Analysis

The number of learners was set as the independent variable, and the number of course evaluations was set as the dependent variable, to conduct curvilinear regression analysis without constant. The results are shown in Table 4.

Table 4. Model summary and estimated value of parameter

Dependent variable: number of registrants								
Equation	Model summary					Estimated value of parameter		
	R^2	F	Degree of freedom 1	Degree of freedom 2	Significance	b1	b2	b3
Linear	.457	37.860	1	45	.000	30.315		
Quadratic	.616	35.297	2	44	.000	69.767	−.047	
Cubic	.623	23.725	3	43	.000	55.325	.002	−3.17E−5

The independent variable is the number of course evaluations.

All of the three models are tenable, but the degree of fitting is not good. The cubic function curve presents relatively good fitting. R2 is 0.623, and the fitted curve is shown in Fig. 1.

The fitted equation is:

$$y = 55.325x + 0.002x^2 - 3.077 \times 10^{-5}x^3$$

Reason analysis: Due to the interference of ineffective learners in the number of learners of free open course, fitting model cannot reflect the practical situations well. Therefore, we need to eliminate the impact of ineffective learners on the analysis result [7].

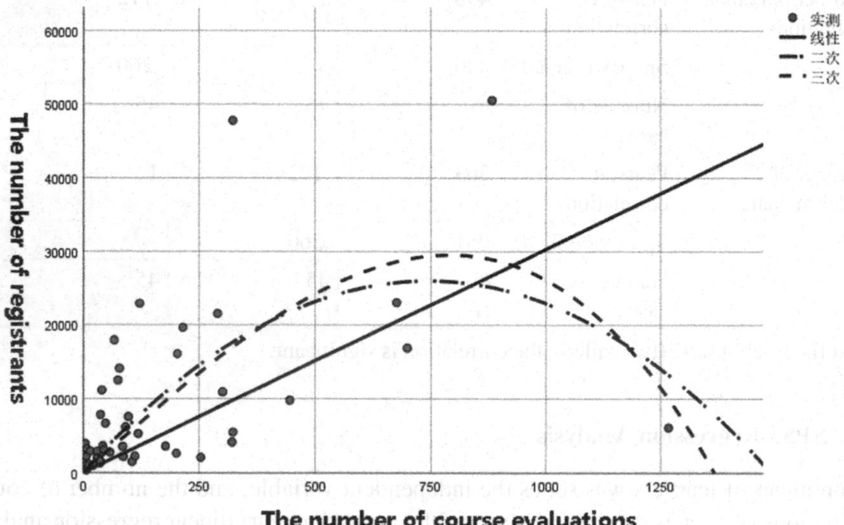

Fig. 1. Fitted curve chart

3 Data Analysis of Paid Course

Paid courses on MOOC platform of Chinese universities consist of five types, including success in final exam (basic courses), courses for obtaining certificates and employment, practical courses, courses for going abroad and training, and courses for civil servant exam. The last two kinds of courses are not relevant to school courses, so this research mainly focuses on the first three kinds of courses that are closely related to school teaching. The research data were mainly taken from the public data of paid courses with a curriculum time of over 8 weeks, and there were 53 courses in total, including quantitative data: number of learners, number of course evaluations, course price, and class hours; qualitative data: course teachers, course nature, and course teaching forms. The specific course data are presented in Table 5.

Table 5. Data about paid courses on MOOC platform of Chinese universities

Number of learners	Teacher	Class hour	Price	Course teaching form	Number of course evaluations	Course nature
30573	0	1	7.99	1	163	2
30530	0	1	7.99	1	176	2
5990	0	2	19.99	1	78	1
10300	0	2	29.99	1	204	1
108546	0	2	29.99	1	2056	1
112294	0	2	29.99	1	2195	1
32772	0	2	9.99	1	436	2
28099	0	3	29.99	1	416	1
77696	0	3	39.99	1	930	1
2517	0	3	39.99	1	17	3
57293	0	4	39.99	1	605	1
38566	0	4	40	1	1499	5
32759	0	4	39.99	1	352	2
23972	0	4	39.99	1	362	4
18779	0	4	39.99	1	292	4
13546	0	4	39.99	1	215	4
19202	0	4	39.99	1	462	4
2677	0	7	35.99	1	1	2
1842	0	9	70.38	1	1	6
1391	0	16	81.6	1	1	2
2446	0	7	64.26	1	1	6
4842	0	5	44.37	1	1	6
2628	0	4	38.25	1	1	6
1528	0	14	91.8	1	1	6
1265	0	18	111.5	1	1	6
1750	0	11	83.87	1	1	6
28487	0	20	78	1	580	1
7253	0	30	49.99	1	106	1
999	1	40	46	1	3	5
158	1	65	1999	1	12	5
90	1	65	1999	1	8	5

(*continued*)

Table 5. (*continued*)

Number of learners	Teacher	Class hour	Price	Course teaching form	Number of course evaluations	Course nature
15369	1	7	39.9	3	221	5
2580	1	75	199	2	33	5
2144	1	75	129	2	9	5
957	1	90	99	1	36	5
659	1	330	79	1	131	5
290	1	600	189	1	47	5
1822	1	1000	189	1	393	5
15478	1	191	498	2	1	7
3760	1	150	498	2	1	7
3453	1	306	998	5	1	7
975	1	243	948	5	1	7
183	1	152	358	5	1	7
2721	1	218	598	5	1	7
6791	1	138	348	5	1	7
2532	1	138	348	5	1	7
7964	1	60	99	4	35	8
4102	1	60	99	4	29	8
14639	1	40	49.9	4	116	8
7563	1	40	39.9	4	74	8
1098	1	60	899	1	102	9
1375	1	60	1199	1	73	9
330	1	60	1299	1	3	9

Teacher in the table: no lecturer introduction 0; lecturer introduction 1; Course Nature: Mathematics 1; Physics 2; Chemistry 3; Engineering 4; Computer 5; Combination 6; Postgraduate Entrance Exam 7; CET4 and CET6 8; Practical English 9; Course Teaching Form: 1 Recorded Broadcasting; 2 Recorded Broadcasting + Live Streaming; 3 Recorded Broadcasting + Mentoring; 4 90% Recorded Broadcasting + 10% Live Streaming; 5 Recorded Broadcasting + Live Streaming + Mentoring.

3.1 Impact of Course Price on the Number of Learners

One-factor analysis of variance was conducted with SPSS software, and Table 6 shows the variance analysis results. The significance is greater than 0.05, and the course price does not present a significant difference in number of learners, indicating that the course price does not have a big influence on students' learning interest when the price is not high.

Table 6. ANOVA

Number of learners			Quadratic sum	Degree of freedom	Mean square	F	Significance
Between groups	(Combination)		18533526203.118	34	545103711.856	.758	.763
	Linear term	Weighted	2494286353.046	1	2494286353.046	3.467	.079
		Deviation	16039239850.072	33	486037571.214	.676	.840
In groups			12948778365.750	18	719376575.875		
Total			31482304568.868	52			

3.2 Influence of Course Teaching Form on the Number of Learners

One-factor analysis of variance was conducted, and Table 7 shows the variance analysis results. The significance is greater than 0.05, so courses of different teaching forms do not have a significant difference in number of learners.

Table 7. ANOVA

Number of learners			Quadratic sum	Degree of freedom	Mean square	F	Significance
Between groups	(Combination)		1883049219.219	4	470762304.805	.763	.554
	Linearterm	Unweighted	665733745.265	1	665733745.265	1.080	.304
		Weighted	1559226311.341	1	1559226311.341	2.529	.118
		Deviaiton	323822907.878	3	107940969.293	.175	.913
In groups			29599255349.649	48	616651153.118		
Total			31482304568.868	52			

Teaching forms of paid courses on the MOOC platform of Chinese universities include recorded broadcasting, recorded broadcasting + live streaming, and recorded broadcasting + live streaming + mentoring. Meanwhile, only 18 free courses on the whole platform are imparted through partial live streaming, occupying 0.34% of all free courses. The other courses are imparted through recorded broadcasting. Studies on the differences in number of learners and course teaching forms indicate that students can accept the recorded broadcasting form of MOOC courses.

Shenzhen Polytechnic conducted questionnaire survey on the online courses in the school during the epidemic period [8], and collected 13,579 effective questionnaires. According to the survey results about teaching forms popular with students (Fig. 2), the online course teaching form popular with students is live streaming + mentoring, occupying a proportion of 52%; students choosing partial live streaming and online discussion take up 14%; students choosing live streaming account for 12%. Hence, the total proportion of the above three is 78%. Therefore, though the impact of course teaching form on the number of MOOC learners is not obvious, students prefer live

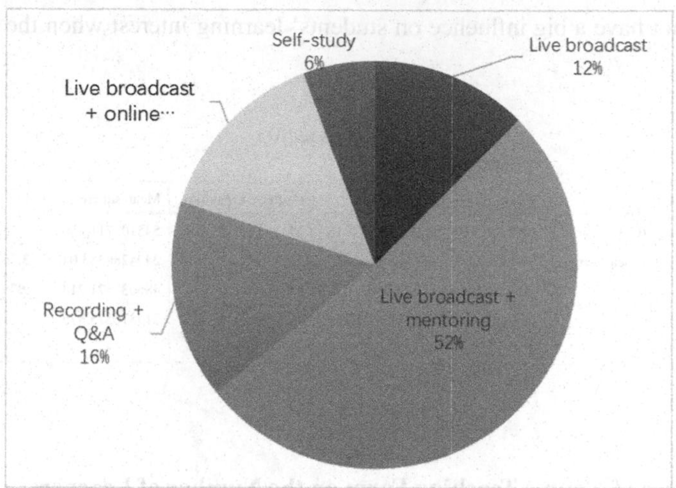

Fig. 2. Survey on teaching forms popular with students

streaming courses to recorded broadcasting, so in MOOC study, the course team can increase the teaching effect by arranging live streaming, mentoring or discussion for several times.

3.3 Influence of Hardware and Textbooks:

As for another question in the questionnaire, "What difficulties did you ever meet in the process of online learning? (multiple choice)" (see Fig. 3), 40% of the students chose "poor network", 53% of the students chose "internet lag affecting the learning effect", and 33% of the students chose "inconvenient operation". The above result shows that hardware is an important influence factor for MOOC construction, and that platform courses with easy operation, smooth video playing and less memory can help students put their heart into study better.

In the survey, most students considered that great difficulties were caused to learning and completion of assignments due to the lack of textbook. Second, too many APPs were installed in the mobile phone, leading to insufficient memory. Besides, students might suffer from eyestrain owing to long-time study. In allusion to the above problems, it is suggested that the MOOC course platform should develop a mini program at mobile terminal to replace the APP, that the MOOC course teaching team should develop electronic textbooks and upload them to the platform as appendixes, that online courses should be well-designed, and that the video of course should not be too long. In addition, many students in the survey expressed that they wanted to return to the classroom, so online and offline learning patterns are still students' favorite forms.

3.4 Influence of Course Nature on the Number of Learners:

The difference of course nature in number of learners was analyzed, and one-factor analysis of variance was conducted. The significance is smaller than 0.05, so the course

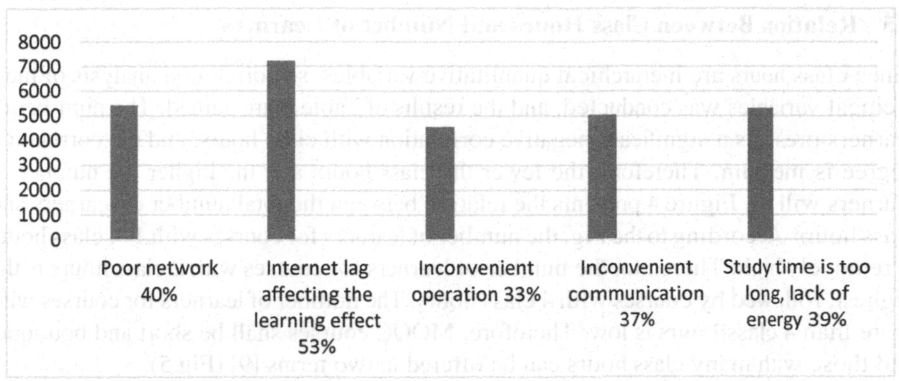

Fig. 3. Survey results about major difficulties encountered by students in online learning

nature presents a significant difference in number of learners. The analysis results are shown in Fig. 4.

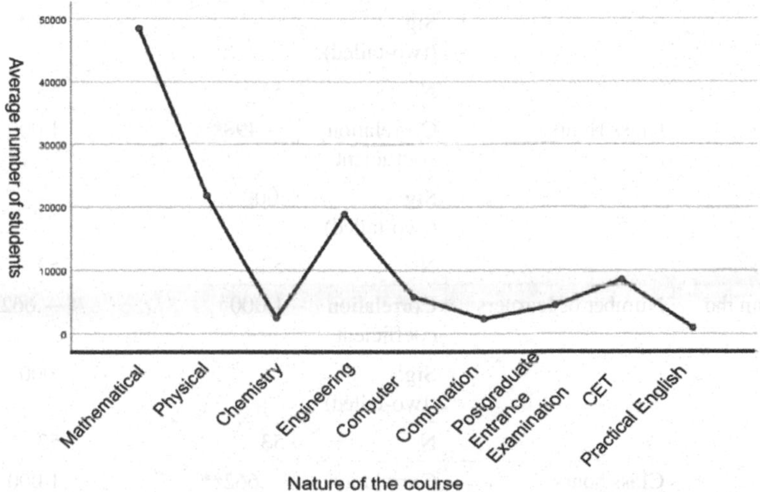

Fig. 4. Average value of number of learners for different course natures

According to the Fig, the number of learners for courses of success in the final exam is obviously higher than that for other types of courses. As for the first reason, mathematics and physics are elementary courses, and many college students need to take these courses. In terms of the second reason, theory courses are difficult. Therefore, though there are many corresponding free courses on the MOOC platform, and most of them are national boutique open courses or courses of 985 and 211 schools, not a few students are willing to pay to make up missed lessons, in order to get good marks or pass the exam.

3.5 Relation Between Class Hours and Number of Learners

Since class hours are hierarchical quantitative variables, so correlation analysis of hierarchical variables was conducted, and the results of Table 8 are gained. The num-ber of learners presents a significant negative correlation with class hours, and the correlation degree is medium. Therefore, the fewer the class hours are, the higher the number of learners will be. Figure 4 presents the relation between the total number of learners and class hours. According to the Fig, the number of learners for courses with 1–4 class hours is relatively high. Thereinto, the number of learners for courses with 2 class hours is the highest, followed by courses with 4 class hours. The number of learners for courses with more than 4 class hours is low. Therefore, MOOC courses shall be short and boutique, and those with many class hours can be offered in two terms [9] (Fig.5).

Table 8. Correlation

			Number of learners	Class hours
Kendall tau_b	Number of learners	Correlation coefficient	1.000	−.498**
		Sig. (two-tailed)		.000
		N	53	53
	Class Hours	Correlation coefficient	−.498**	1.000
		Sig. (two-tailed)	.000	
		N	53	53
Spearman rho	Number of learners	Correlation coefficient	1.000	−.662**
		Sig. (two-tailed)		.000
		N	53	53
	Class hours	Correlation coefficient	−.662**	1.000
		Sig. (two-tailed)	.000	
		N	53	53

** At the level of 0.01 (two-tailed), the correlation is significant.

3.6 Relation Between Number of Course Evaluations and Number of Learners

The number of course evaluations is a continuous quantitative variable, and the results in Table 9 can be obtained through correlation analysis of continuous variables. According

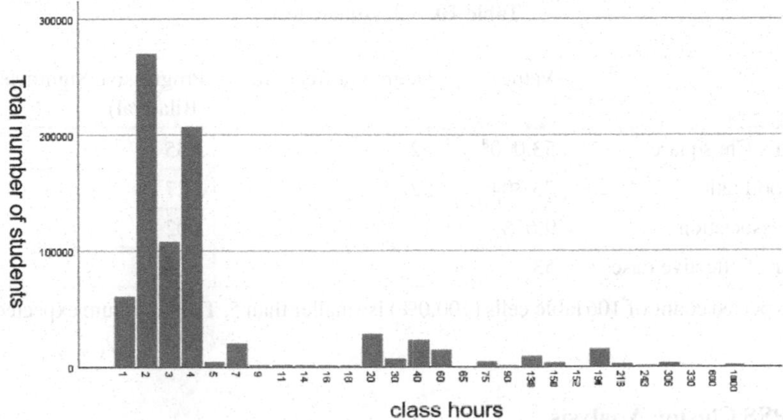

Fig. 5. Relation between total number of learners and class hours

to the data of Table 9, the number of course evaluations and number of learners show an obvious positive correlation, and the correlation degree is high. Hence, higher number of course evaluations can attract more students to join course learning.

Table 9. Correlation

		Number of learners	Number of Course evaluations
Number of learners	Pearson correlation	1	.920**
	Sig. (two-tailed)		.000
	Number of cases	53	53
Number of course evaluations	Pearson correlation	.920**	1
	Sig. (two-tailed)	.000	
	Number of cases	53	53

** At the level of 0.01 (two-tailed), the correlation is significant.

3.7 Relation Between Teachers and Number of Learners

The teacher is a qualitative variable, and the results in Table 10 can be obtained through correlation analysis of qualitative variables. According to Table 10, the progressive significance of Pearson's chi-square is greater than 0.05, and the correlation is not significant. However, the significance of likelihood ratio chi-square and linear correlation is smaller than 0.05, indicating that the correlation is significant. This study focused on 53 courses only, and adopted a small sample size. The likelihood ratio chi-square has comparatively high accuracy degree in small sample analysis. It is considered that teachers and number of learners have a correlation [10].

Table 10. Chi-square test

	Value	Degree of freedom	Progressive Significance (Bilateral)
Pearson's Chi-square	53.000[a]	52	.435
Likelihood ratio	73.304	52	.027
Linear association	9.678	1	.002
Number of effective cases	53		

a. The expected count of 106 table cells (100.0%) is smaller than 5. The minimum expected count is .47.

3.8 SPSS Cluster Analysis

Associated "number of learners", "number of course evaluations", "teachers", "course nature" and "class hours" were set as the classification variables, and cluster analysis was made on the courses. "Number of learners", "number of course evaluations" and "class hours" are quantitative variables; "teachers" and "course nature" are qualitative variables. Clustering was conducted with two-step cluster method, and all courses were divided into 2 categories (Fig 6). Thereinto, items 1–28 in Table 1 were clustered into 2 categories, as the basic courses, and items 29–53 were clustered into 1 category, as other courses for graduate school exam and certificate exam.

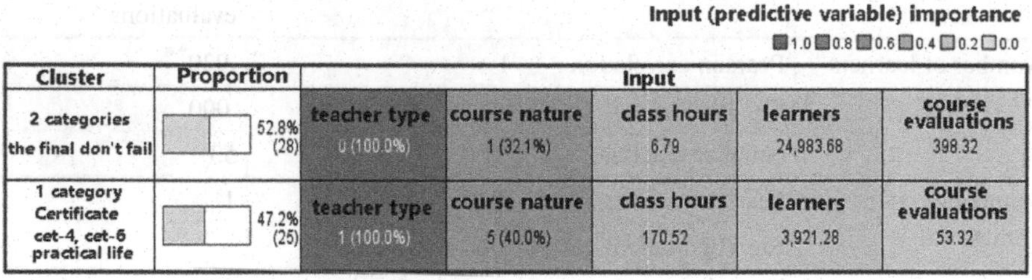

Input (predictive variable) importance

1.0 0.8 0.6 0.4 0.2 0.0

Cluster	Proportion	Input				
2 categories the final don't fail	52.8% (28)	teacher type 0 (100.0%)	course nature 1 (32.1%)	class hours 6.79	learners 24,983.68	course evaluations 398.32
1 category Certificate cet-4, cet-6 practical life	47.2% (25)	teacher type 1 (100.0%)	course nature 5 (40.0%)	class hours 170.52	learners 3,921.28	course evaluations 53.32

Fig. 6. Cluster analysis

3.9 SPSS Regression Analysis

According to the previous analysis, the number of learners for courses with 1–4 class hours is the highest. To remove the influence of class hours on regression effect, the number of learners per unit class hour was set as the dependent variable, the number of course evaluations per unit class hour was set as the independent variable, and the course teacher was set as the qualitative variable. The two characteristics were signified with 0 and 1. According to cluster analysis, the course nature was divided into success in the final exam and others, which were also signified with 0 and 1. The course teacher and course nature were adopted as virtual independent variables, and regression analysis

Table 11. Variables excluded [a]

Model		Input Beta	t	Significance	Partial correlation	Collinearity statistics
						Tolerance
1	Teacher	−.097[b]	−1.746	.087	−.240	.873
	Course nature	−.097[b]	−1.746	.087	−.240	.873

a. Dependent variable: Number of learners per unit class hour.
b. Predictive variable in the model: (Constant), number of course evaluations per unit class hour.

including virtual independent variables was conducted. The teacher and course nature were excluded due to the tolerance of collinearity statistics [11]. See Table 11.

The regression coefficient is shown in Table 12, and the significance of constant terms is greater than 0.05. The regression model without constant terms should be adopted.

Table 12. Coefficient [a]

Model		Unstandardized coefficient		Standardized coefficient	t	Significance
		B	Standard error	Beta		
1	(Constant)	1140.012	695.894		1.638	.108
	Number of course evaluations per unit class hour	53.647	3.085	.925	17.388	.000

a. Dependent variable: number of learners per unit class hour.

The number of learners per unit class hour was set as the dependent variable, and the number of course evaluations per unit class hour was adopted as the independent variable, to conduct curvilinear regression simulation. The results are presented in Table 13. The significance of primary, quadratic and cubic regression is less than 0.01, and it is significant. The curve fitting determination coefficients R2 of the three models are 0.874, 0.899 and 0.913 respectively, showing that the goodness of fit of the cubic function curve is the highest.

As for paid courses, the fitted curve is good, since the course completion rate is relatively high, meaning that most ineffective learners are removed. According to the coefficients in Table 12, the regression equation of cubic curve is gained: $y = 126.871x - 0.244x^2$, please refer to Fig. 7 for fitted curve, indicating that there will be about 130 extra learners when one course evaluation is added.

Table 13. Model summary and estimated value of parameter

Dependent variable: number of registrants								
Equation	Model summary					Estimated value of parameter		
	R^2	F	Degree of freedom 1	Degree of freedom 2	Significance	b1	b2	b3
Linear	.874	359.596	1	52	.000	55.465		
Quadratic	.899	228.126	2	51	.000	85.127	−.032	
Cubic	.913	175.603	3	50	.000	126.871	−.244	.000

The independent variable is the number of course evaluations per unit class hour.

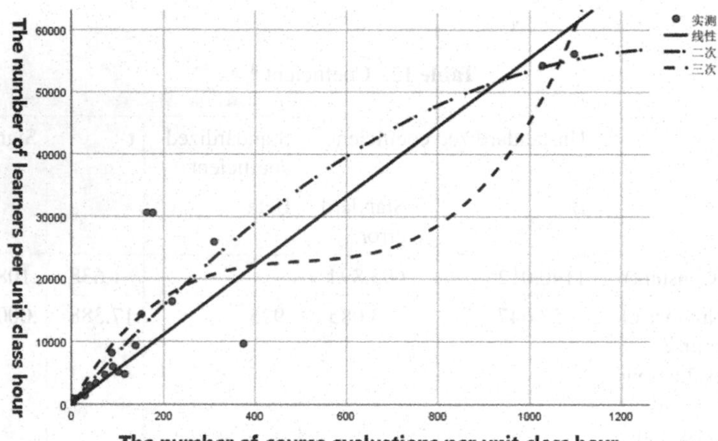

Fig. 7. Fitted curve chart

4 Suggestions and Reflections

1. Through studying the public courses on MOOC platform and related factors of paid courses, the following suggestions for the construction of MOOC courses are made:
2. The number of course evaluations is an important factor attracting students to join and finish the course, and the teaching team should pay high attention to this factor. Besides, the teaching team should maintain the courses in time, pick a proper issue, and increase the vitality of course discussion and communication.
3. The total duration of all videos for one MOOC course should be controlled within 4 class hours, and two class hours would be better. For courses with a lot of contents, teaching videos should be arranged in two semesters.
4. The course teaching team should elaborately design online classes, the teaching forms should be diversified, and each video should not be too long.

5. The videos can be in the form of recorded broadcasting, but it would be better to organize several live streaming or mentoring classes in each semester, to enhance exchange and interaction.
6. When the price is not high, whether the course is paid is not a major issue which course learners pay attention to.
7. Hardware construction is very important for the MOOC course platform, and a course platform of easy operation and smooth running is the basic guarantee for the sound development of MOOC courses.
8. The construction of MOOC open courses can be promoted through online and offline mixed classroom construction.

References

1. Jordan, K.: Initial trends in enrolment and completion of massive open online courses. Int. Rev. Res. Open Distrib. Learn. **15**(1), 133–160 (2014)
2. Perna, L.W., et al.: Moving through MOOCs: understanding the progression of users in massive open online courses. Educ. Res. **43**(9), 421–432 (2014)
3. Chen, H.: Research on WeChat mini program learning platform to improve MOOC class rate. Wirel. Interconn. Technol. **22**, 55–56 (2018)
4. Wang, Y.: The attribution and solution of MOOC's low completion rate. Mod. Educ. Technol. **9**, 80–84 (2018)
5. Li, Y.: Study on influence factors of online education platform users' continuance intention and willingness to pay for courses. University of Science and Technology of China, Anhui (2016)
6. Yang, Y., Zhou, D., Yang, X.: A multi-feature weighting based K-means algorithm for MOOC learner classification. Comput. Mater. Continua **59**(2), 625–633 (2019)
7. Fang, W., Zhang, F., Ding, Y., Sheng, J.: A new sequential image prediction method based on LSTM and DCGAN. Comput. Mater. Continua **64**(1), 217–231 (2020)
8. Zhang, M.: Survey report of Shenzhen Polytechnic. vol. 2020. Shenzhen Polytechnic, Shenzhen (2010)
9. Long, S., Long, Q.: The factor analysis of university English examination results based on the multilevel model. Intell. Auto Soft Comput. **26**(3), 585–595 (2020)
10. Fang, W., Pang, L., Yi, W.N.: Survey on the application of deep reinforcement learning in image processing. J. Artif. Intell. **2**(1), 39–58 (2020)
11. Yang, Y., Fu, P., Yang, X., Hong, H., Zhou, D.: MOOC learner's final grade prediction based on an improved random forests method. Comput. Mater. Continua **65**(3), 2413–2423 (2020)

A Copyright Protection Scheme of Visual Media in Big Data Environment

Shiqi Wang[1], Jiaohua Qin[1(✉)], Mingfang Jiang[2], and ZhiChen Gao[3]

[1] College of Computer Science and Information Technology, Central South University of Forestry and Technology, Changsha 410004, China

[2] Department of Information Science and Engineering, Hunan First Normal University, Changsha 410205, China

[3] Department of Applied Mathematics and Statistics, College of Engineering and Applied Sciences, Stony Brook University, Stony Brook, NY 11794, USA

Abstract. Rapid development and application of big data technology is speeding up the dissemination and utilization of visible media big data. The intensive application of visual media brings about some security issues. The building of copyright protection mechanism of visual media big data under Internet environment can provide safety guarantee for content services of visual media in a digital library, and enhance integrated serviceability of digital resources in the digital library. Firstly, sparse features are extracted by exploiting the data sparsity and perception sparsity of visual media, and then a sparse perception computing model for visual media big data is built. Then the design idea of visual media copyright encryption, copyright authentication, copyright notice, and audit trail scheme are given from the point of view of sparse feature computation of visual media. Finally, a copyright protection application scheme of visual media big data under the network environment is developed. Its application in the digital library validates the effectiveness of this copyright protection mechanism of visual media. It can safeguard the confidentiality, integrity, availability, and auditing of visual media big data in the digital library, and enhance content serviceability of visual media in the digital library under big data environment.

Keywords: Copyright protection · Visual media · Big data · Sparsity

1 Introduction

Vision is an important means for human beings to know the world, and 83% of the information received by people comes from vision. The visual media composed of image, video, digital geometry, and other media information has strong intuition and universality. Compared with other media, visual media is easier to store, communicate and transmit. With the continuous development of information technology and communication technology, the application of visual media is becoming more and more extensive, and gradually become an indispensable way of information acquisition, storage, display, and expression in people's life. In recent years, with the rapid development and

X. Sun et al. (Eds.): ICAIS 2021, LNCS 12736, pp. 630–642, 2021.
https://doi.org/10.1007/978-3-030-78609-0_53

popularization of mobile Internet and wireless network, the scale of Internet users has increased dramatically. At the same time, a large amount of visual media data has been produced, which accounts for more than 60% of Internet resources. The visual media data on the Internet has a wide variety, large volume, diverse data sources, low density, and sparse value of data. Users of visual media often need to get a quick response in a short time. Visual media has the characteristics of big data and has become an important information asset in modern society [1]. The emergence of network visual media has brought new opportunities and innovation for the library service model. The content service of visual media under big data environment is becoming a key form of visual media big data application, but at the same time, the disorder, uncontrollable, content authenticity and other security issues of visual media big data are increasingly urgent [2].

Due to the increasing volume of multimedia data, it is necessary to protect this data from external threats or malicious attacks. Therefore, to protect the copyright of visual media big data in the digital library, an effective security mechanism for visual media data is much needed. Kapil et al. [3] pointed out some current issues in multimedia big data and security approaches to these issues, and also discussed multimedia big data security and privacy. It analyzed possible directions to be taken while using multimedia along with security strategies. All the time data encryption and digital watermarking technology have always been used to protect the content security and copyright ownership of digital media [4–8]. Ting et al. [9] designed a provable copyright protection scheme for digital media by employing a digital watermarking technique and unpredictable signature-seeded pseudo-random bit sequence. This scheme can resolve the ownership dispute of the digital media data even though after adversarial watermark removal attacks. Kukreja proposed a copyright protection scheme using visual cryptography which produces meaningful shares to provide better security and handles false-positive cases efficiently [10]. The meaningful ownership share is generated based on the master share, both watermarks, and cover image, and the master share is overlapped with its corresponding ownership share to reveal the watermark. Experimental results show that the new scheme has good robustness against several image processing attacks and proves the copyright of the digital images. To protect the copyright of digital images on the internet, Roy et al. [11] developed an image watermarking scheme in the spatial domain. it embeds the watermark bits by adaptive LSB replacement approach and enhances watermark transparency by using a saliency map generation algorithm. Rani and Raman designed a digital image copyright protection scheme based on chaotic encryption and visual cryptography [12]. Hossaini et al. [13] designed a blind image watermarking algorithm by combining visual cryptography with directional controllable pyramid transform to protect image copyright. The use of visual cryptography makes the watermark embedded in the original image unchanged and has good robustness. Ahuja and Bedi embed a watermark by slightly adjusting some DCT coefficients to achieve a watermarking scheme suitable for MPEG-2 video and achieve copyright protection for digital video [14]. To protect the copyright of digital art images, Kamnardsiri [15] combines discrete cosine transform and discrete wavelet transform to design a robust image watermarking algorithm. However, the irrecoverability of original art image affects people's appreciation of art and reduces the artistic value of works. Hashmi et al. further combined visible watermarking and invisible watermarking technology to achieve real-time copyright protection of images and videos and designed a digital watermarking prototype system based on Android [16]. However, these copyright protection schemes do not take full advantage of the big data characteristics of the visual media in the network environment. They cannot provide effective copyright protection for visual media big data. While copyright protection of visual media big data is an unavoidable key technical problem in the application of visual media big data. The research results of copyright protection of visual media big data will greatly promote the innovation of library digital resource service model and achieve a healthy and sustainable visual media industry. This will certainly form new technological innovation and economic growth point. This paper aims to deeply analyze the characteristics of visual media big data and to fully exploit the value sparseness and visual perception sparseness of visual media big data, and then design new copyright protection strategies and methods of network visual media big data by exploiting sparse representation of visual media big data. Finally, we'll build a new application model of copyright protection of visual media.

2 Sparsity in Visual Media Data

In the network environment, the data volume of visual media is very large, data types are various, data sources are diversified, the data redundancy is very high, and the data processing speed is fast. To realize efficient real-time processing and copyright protection of visual media data in big data environment, it is necessary to fully exploit the inherent characteristics of visual media big data, especially the value sparsity and visual perception sparseness of visual media big data.

2.1 Value Sparsity

Low-value density is a typical feature of big data. In big data environment, visual media usually has multiple identical or similar copies. Although the volume of visual media is large, its value density is low. Visual media big data is massive and heterogeneous, and its sources are diversified, which often coexist with local density and global sparsity, large volume and low value, and availability and sparsity. Since not all the data in big data are valuable to users, some junk information even is harmful to the use of data. Effective information acquisition is like 'sourcing the sand in the waves'. How to effectively filter big data, remove the coarse and store the essence, remove the false and retain the true, and analyze and identify the sparse and useful information is the key to reflect the true value of big data.

2.2 Perceptual Sparsity

The sparsity of data is common in natural signals. Neurobiology studies have shown that the information processing mechanism of the human visual system is a highly complex nonlinear process, which has the characteristics of receptive field hierarchy, feedback mechanism, attention selection mechanism, feature selectivity, and so on. In the process of information processing, the human visual system does not treat information equally but shows the characteristics of selection. On the one hand, due to the limited capacity of the brain, it is difficult to process all the information in real-time. On the other hand, because the external information is not all of the important value, the brain only needs to respond to some important information. The high selectivity of the visual system to visual stimulus features is mainly reflected in orientation/direction selectivity, spatial frequency selectivity, speed selectivity, binocular disparity selectivity, color selectivity, and so on [17]. The feature selectivity of the human visual system and the perceptual sensitivity of color, intensity, texture, and temporal-spatial correlation in natural images and videos have shown that natural images, digital video, and other visual media are sparse signals, which can be expressed linearly with a small number of non-zero sparse coefficients under a set of over-complete bases, and the sparse representation of signals can obtain a good approximation of original signal.

Visual media data accounts for the overwhelming majority of big data on the internet. Data redundancy and value sparseness bring great challenges to network bandwidth and storage space. Besides, how to quickly complete data cleaning and data purification through efficient algorithms, and acquiring valuable information is an urgent problem to be solved in the application of big data. Developing the sparse representation model of visual media big data has important theoretical value and application significance for visual media content service and big data application.

3 Copyright Protection Scheme of Visual Media in Big Data Environment

Because the existing digital media copyright protection schemes do not make full use of the characteristics of visual media big data, it is difficult to provide real-time and effective copyright protection for visual media communication in big data environment. By fully exploiting the sparsity of big data of network visual media, this paper builds the application model of copyright protection of visual media in big data environment and protects the copyright of visual media big data by copyright encryption, copyright authentication, copyright notice, and violation tracking. It can provide theoretical and methodological support for the content service of visual media big data in the network environment. The visual media big data content service system is an organic system engineering that integrates the storage, analysis, utilization, and display of visual media big data. The design of the big data storage system model [18] and the OSI system of ISO (International Organization for Standardization) can provide a guide for the design of the copyright protection model integrated into the content service system of visual media big data. The ISO OSI model is divided into seven levels: the physical layer, data link layer, network layer, transport layer, session layer, presentation layer, and application layer. Therefore, according to the basic principle of the OSI reference model and the basic principle of 'data sinking, unified processing, and service improvement', the visual media copyright protection model in big data environment can be divided into five modules: resource layer, data analysis layer, function layer, interface layer, and presentation layer. Each module is interconnected with each other to form an organic system, as shown in Fig. 1.

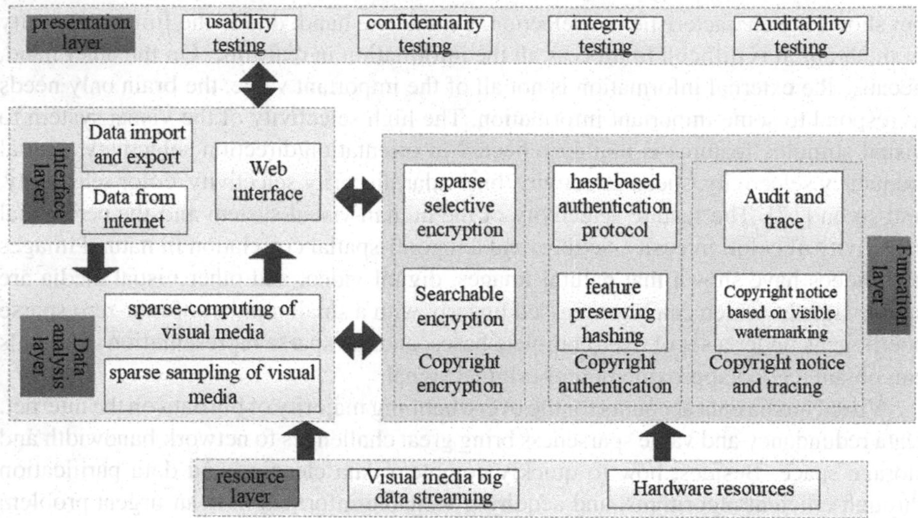

Fig. 1. Copyright protection model of visual media big data.

The basic idea of copyright protection model design of visual media big data is: starting from the sparsity of visual media big data, making full use of the value sparsity and visual sparsity of visual media big data, using sparse coding and statistical analysis to establish the sparse perception calculation model of visual media big data, take the sparse representation of visual media big data, extract the sparse features of visual media, and complete the redundancy removal Storage and data cleaning provide key technical support for real-time processing and content service of video media big data in the network environment. Through the design of visual media, big data selective encryption technology based on sparse characteristics and visual media big data searchable encryption scheme based on perceptual hash, the confidentiality, and availability of visual media are guaranteed. After that, we develop a visual media big data copyright authentication protocol based on Perceptual Hashing to maintain the content integrity of visual media big data. Through the combination of visible digital watermarking technology and robust perceptual hashing, the scheme of visual media big data copyright notice and piracy tracking is designed to ensure the audit ability of visual media content service, to realize the complete copyright protection model in the whole life cycle of visual media. The core technologies of visual media copyright protection model design in big data environment include the establishment of visual media big data perception computing model, visual media copyright encryption technology, visual media copyright authentication protocol, visual media big data copyright notice, and tracking scheme.

3.1 Visual Sparse Computing Model for Visual Media Big Data

In the network environment, visual media big data has the value sparsity and visual perception sparseness. Value sparseness refers to the large data scale and high data redundancy of the visual media in big data environment. To reduce the bandwidth and storage requirements and adapt to the real-time processing environment of big data streams, it is necessary to fully exploit the value sparsity of visual media big data to realize the sampling of large data of visual media. Taking digital image as an example, the image big data stream can be divided into fixed-size time slices, so the image big data can be expressed as a matrix, in which the image is an m-dimensional column vector, and n is the number of images in a certain time. In this way, low-rank optimization can be used to decompose the matrix M (expressed by Eq. 1), and reduce the dimension of image big data [19].

$$\begin{aligned} \min \quad & \|L\|_* + \lambda \|S\|_1 \\ s.t. \quad & L + S = M \end{aligned} \tag{1}$$

Where $\| \|_*$ and $\| \|_1$ represent kernel normal form and 1 normal form, respectively, which $\boldsymbol{\lambda}$ are non-negative regularization parameters. L is the low-rank component and S is the sparse component. Then the information entropy of the image can be calculated by the low-rank component L, and the sampled image (centroid media) can be determined according to the information entropy, and complete the sparse sampling of visual media

Figure 2 shows an example of low-rank decomposition. Taking the gray image 'Lena' as an example, the low-rank approximation and sparse component of the image matrix are illustrated in Fig. 2(a) and Fig. 2(b), respectively.

(a) low-rank component (b) sparse component

Fig. 2. Low-rank decomposition of Lena image.

Because of the visual sparsity of visual media, the sparse perception of centroid media is further analyzed according to the linear and nonlinear statistical characteristics of visual media, statistical characteristics in spatial and transform domain and the correlation of low dimensional and high-dimensional features. This will provide a theoretical basis for sparse sensing computing in real-time processing and copyright protection of visual media.

3.2 Copyright Encryption Technology for Visual Media Big Data

Encryption is an important method to protect the confidentiality of data, but for the massive heterogeneous, high redundancy visual media big data stream, the usual encryption algorithm cannot meet the real-time processing requirement in big data environment. One feasible solution to this issue is selective encryption technology where the sparsity of visual media big data will be fully exploited. The main steps of selective encryption are shown as follows.

Step1: Users send visual media streaming to remote servers.
Step2: Apply adaptive streaming sampling on visual media streaming by the use of the sparse sampling
Step3: The centroid media is selected according to the sparsity of visual media value
Step4: The low-rank component of the centroid visual media is selected to encrypt.

This selective encryption strategy for visual media big data can meet the real-time processing requirements of visual media big data.

The other scenario is privacy protection in the cloud computing environment. To maintain the security of user secret data, the visual media data must be first encrypted before uploading on the cloud server. But at the same time, people often need to retrieve the qualified visual media from the encrypted media data. To protect the privacy of the visual media data in the cloud, a privacy-preserving retrieval scheme is designed.

Step1: Apply low-rank decomposition to visual media data.
Step2: obtain the sparse representation of visual media and build a sparse computing model for visual media data.
Step3: Produce a perceptual hash of visual media.
Step4: Lossless data hiding is used to encrypt the visual media perceptual hash.
Step5: Public-key encryption is used to encrypt the keywords associated with perceptual hashes to generate keyword trapdoors.
Step6: During the user retrieval process, the server performs the retrieval according to the keyword trapdoor input
Step7: The cloud server returns the visual media ciphertext file containing the keyword corresponding to the trapdoor.
Step8: Finally, the user obtains the query results by decrypting the ciphertext of the visul media returned by the server with the user key.

An example of ‘Couple’ image encryption is illustrated in Fig. 3. Figure 3(a) and (b) show the plaintext and corresponding encrypted image, respectively. From Fig. 3(b), it can be found that one can hardly recognize meaningful information from the ciphertext generated by the proposed selective encryption method.

3.3 Copyright Authentication Protocol of Visual Media Big Data

In the network environment, the integrity authentication of visual media is very important, and the usual copyright authentication scheme based on digital watermark requires

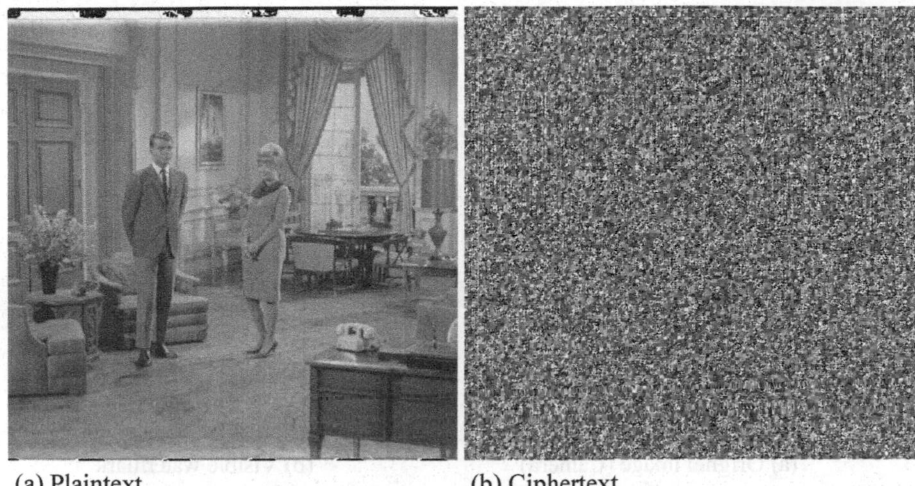

(a) Plaintext (b) Ciphertext

Fig. 3. Selective encryption of 'Couple' image

the user end to have the function of watermark embedding and detection. However, this is not realistic in the real-time processing environment. Therefore, we design a copyright authentication protocol for visual media big data based on the perceptual hash. The detailed procedure is as follows.

Step1: Read visual media data from the cloud server.
Step2: The visual sparse computing model is used to generate perceptual hash information.
Step3: To ensure the robustness and distinction of perceptual hash sequence, the value sparseness of visual media will be fully exploited to remove redundant information. High-level semantic features of visual media can be obtained by using visual sparsity,
Step4: User sends retrieval query to the remote server.
Step5: The server extracts the visual media perceptual hash and matching it with the registered hash code in the cloud authentication center.

3.4 Copyright Notice and Tracking Scheme of Visual Media Big Data

Compared with encryption and digital watermarking technology, visible watermarking technology can declare copyright without watermark detection. This is a more portable and fast copyright method and is more suitable for the application of visual media content services in big data environment. To protect copyright and realize audit trail, a copyright notice and tracking scheme is designed by using adaptive visible watermarking and robust hash. The algorithm is described below

Step1: Input a binary image as the visible watermark image.
Step2: Read a gray image as the original image need to be protected.

(a) Orignal image (Camera)

Visual
Media

(b) Visible watermark

(c) Watermarked image

(d) Watermark removal with correct key

(e) Watermark removal with wrong key

Fig. 4. Visible watermark insertion and removal

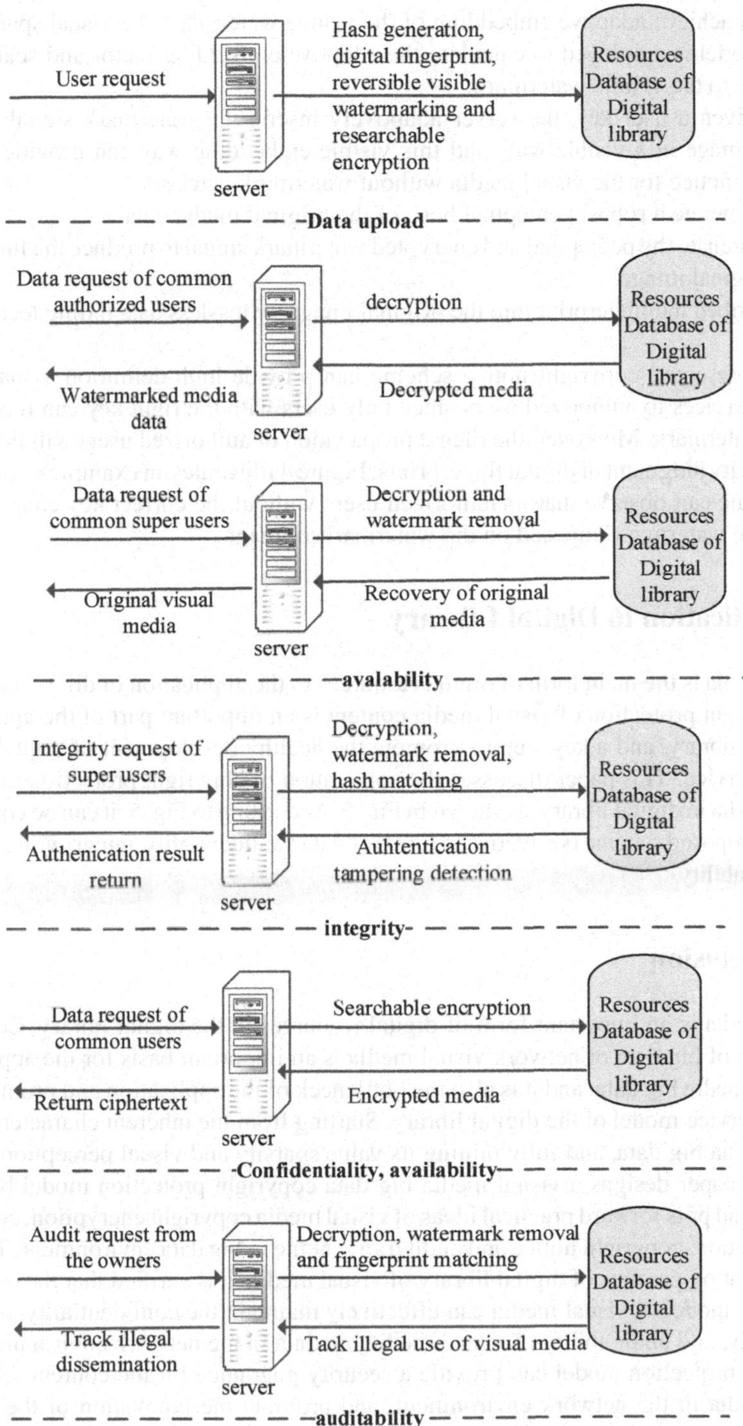

Fig. 5. An application scenario of copyright protection model for visual media in digital library

Step3: To achieve adaptive embedding of the visible watermark, the visual sparse computing model is employed to calculate the adaptive embedding factor and scale factor according to the visible watermark.
Step4: Given a user key, the server adaptively inserts the watermark signal into the original image in a visible way, and this visible embedding way can provide explicit copyright notice for the visual media without watermark detection.
Step5: Generate a robust perceptual hash of the original media data.
Step6: Catenate the perceptual and encrypted watermark signal to produce the fingerprint of the original image.
Step7: Embed the fingerprint into the original image by lossless data hiding technology.

The presented copyright notice scheme can provide high-definition visual media content services to authorized users since only users with the right key can remove the visible watermark. Moreover, the illegal propagation of authorized users will be tracked by similarity judgment of digital fingerprints. Figure 4 illustrates an example of copyright notice. One can observe that unauthorized users without the correct key cannot delete the visible watermark imposed on the watermarked image.

4 Application in Digital Library

Visual media is the main form of digital resources in the application of digital library, so the copyright protection of visual media content is an important part of the application of digital library, and a key step to promote the healthy development of digital library content service. This paper discusses the application of copyright protection model for visual media in digital library, as shown in Fig. 5. According to Fig. 5, it can be concluded that the proposed scheme is effective in terms of data confidentiality, integrity, availability and auditability.

5 Conclusion

Visual media is an important form of digital resources in the digital library. Copyright protection of big data of network visual media is an important basis for the application of visual media big data, and it is also the bottleneck of the application and promotion of content service model of the digital library. Starting from the inherent characteristics of visual media big data, and fully mining its value sparsity and visual perception sparseness, this paper designs a visual media big data copyright protection model based on sparsity, and puts forward practical ideas of visual media copyright encryption, copyright authentication, copyright notice and audit trail scheme in big data environment. Through the application practice of digital library of visual media, it is verified that the copyright protection model of visual media can effectively maintain the confidentiality, integrity, availability, and audit ability of visual media big data in the network environment. The copyright protection model can provide a security guarantee for the content service of visual media in the network environment, and promote the innovation of the content service model of the digital library.

Acknowledgements. This work was supported in component by the National Natural Science Foundation of China under Grant No. 61872408, the Natural Science Foundation of Hunan Province (2020JJ4238), the Social Science Fund of Hunan Province under Grant No. 16YBA102, and the Research Fund of Hunan Provincial Key Laboratory of informationization technology for basic education under Grant No. 2015TP1017.

References

1. Singh, A., Mahapatra, S.: Network-based applications of multimedia big data computing in IoT environment. In: Tanwar, S., Tyagi, S., Kumar, N. (eds.) Multimedia Big Data Computing for IoT Applications: Concepts, Paradigms and Solutions, vol. 163, pp. 435–452. Springer Singapore, Singapore (2020). https://doi.org/10.1007/978-981-13-8759-3_17
2. Ruoyu, R., Shulin, Y., Qi, Z.: Research on copyright protection of digital publishing in the era of big data. In: Proceedings of the 2019 2nd International Conference on Information Hiding and Image Processing, pp. 39–43. Association for Computing Machinery, London (2019)
3. Kapil, G., Ishrat, Z., Kumar, R., Agrawal, A., Khan, R.A.: Managing multimedia big data: security and privacy perspective. In: Tuba, M., Akashe, S., Joshi, A. (eds.) ICT Systems and Sustainability, vol. 1077, pp. 1–12. Springer Nature, Singapore (2020). https://doi.org/10.1007/978-981-15-0936-0_1
4. Liu, Y., Peng, H., Wang, J.: Verifiable diversity ranking search over encrypted outsourced data. Comput. Mater. Continua **55**, 037–057 (2018)
5. Wang, B., Kong, W., Li, W., Xiong, N.N.: A dual-chaining watermark scheme for data integrity protection in internet of things. Comput. Mater. Continua **58**, 679–695 (2019)
6. Yang, H., Yin, J., Yang, Y.: Robust image hashing scheme based on low-rank decomposition and path integral LBP. IEEE Access **7**, 51656–51664 (2019)
7. Xiang, L.Y., Yang, S.H., Liu, Y.H., Li, Q., Zhu, C.Z.: Novel linguistic steganography based on character-level text generation. Mathematics **8**, 1558 (2020)
8. Yang, Z., Zhang, S., Hu, Y., Hu, Z., Huang, Y.: VAE-Stega: Linguistic steganography based on variational auto-encoder. IEEE Trans. Inf. Forensics **16**, 880–895 (2021)
9. Ting, P., Huang, S., Wu, T., Lin, H.: A provable watermark-based copyright protection scheme. In: 2015 10th Asia Joint Conference on Information Security, pp. 124–129. IEEE, Kaohsiung (2015)
10. Kukreja, S., Kasana, G., Kasana, S.S.: Curvelet transform based robust copyright protection scheme for color images using extended visual cryptography. Multimed. Tools Appl. **79**, 26155–26179 (2020). https://doi.org/10.1007/s11042-020-09130-y
11. Sinha Roy, S., Basu, A., Chattopadhyay, A.: On the implementation of a copyright protection scheme using digital image watermarking. Multimed. Tools Appl. **79**, 13125–13138 (2020). https://doi.org/10.1007/s11042-020-08652-9
12. Rani, A., Raman, B.: An image copyright protection scheme by encrypting secret data with the host image. Multimed. Tools Appl. **75**(2), 1027–1042 (2014). https://doi.org/10.1007/s11042-014-2344-0
13. El Hossaini, A.E.A., Aroussi, M., Jamali, K., Mbarki, S., Wahbi, M.: A new robust blind copyright protection scheme based on visual cryptography and steerable pyramid. Int. J. Netw. Secur. **18**, 250–262 (2016)
14. Ahuja, R., Bedi, S.S.: Copyright protection using blind video watermarking algorithm based on MPEG-2 structure. In: International Conference on Computing, Communication & Automation, pp. 1048–1053. IEEE, Greater Noida (2015)

15. Kamnardsiri, T.: Digital art image copyright protection using combined DWT-DCT based watermarking technique. In: 1st International Conference on Digital Arts, Media and Technology (ICDAMT 2016), pp. 83–94. IEEE, Chiang Rai (2016)
16. Hashmi, M.F., Shukla, R.J., Keskar, A.G.: Real time copyright protection and implementation of image and video processing on android and embedded platforms. Proc. Comput. Sci. **46**, 1626–1634 (2015)
17. Mairal, J., Elad, M., Sapiro, G.: Sparse representation for color image restoration. IEEE Trans. Image Process. **17**, 53–69 (2007)
18. Chen, X., Wang, S., Dong, Y., Wang, X.: Big data storage architecture design in cloud computing. In: Chen, W., Yin, G., Zhao, G., Han, Q., Jing, W., Sun, G., Lu, Z. (eds.) BDTA 2015. CCIS, vol. 590, pp. 7–14. Springer, Singapore (2016). https://doi.org/10.1007/978-981-10-0457-5_2
19. Zhou, X., Yang, C., Zhao, H., Yu, W.: Low-rank modeling and its applications in image analysis. ACM Comput. Surv. **47**, 1–33 (2014)

A Fast Sound Ray Tracking Method for Ultra-short Baseline Positioning

Rong Zhang, Jian Li(✉), Jinxiang Zhang, and Zexi Wang

College of Internet of Things Engineering, Hohai University, Changzhou 213022, China
jian263@sina.com

Abstract. The basic principle of the ultra-short baseline (USBL) positioning system is to calculate the slant distance and azimuth between the underwater measurement target and the ultra-short baseline array through the different time delay between the underwater response signal and each receiving point, and finally calculate the position information of the target. When the number of vertical layers in the sound velocity profile is large, the calculation amount of using the equal gradient method is large. Based on the principle of equal gradient sound line tracking, this paper proposes a gradient difference based sound line adaptive layering method, which can eliminate the redundant layering points and the points whose sound velocity changes exceed the set threshold, simplify the sound velocity profile and improve the efficiency of sound line tracking. In this paper, the layered results under different thresholds are given through simulation experiments. By adjusting the threshold value, the calculation amount of this method can be reduced by 40% to 70%, and the deviation of slant distance is less than 1% compared with the equal gradient ray tracing method.

Keywords: Sound speed profile · Gradient difference · USBL

1 Introduction

The general method of underwater acoustic positioning is to measure the propagation time-delay between the launching point and the receiving point, and calculate the distance difference between the launching point and the receiving point according to the underwater acoustic velocity, so as to further calculate the location information of the target. The measurement and calculation process will inevitably lead to a variety of errors, such as time measurement errors, sound speed measurement errors, etc. [2]. Influenced by environmental factors such as water temperature, pressure and salinity, the sound speed in water is not constant, but varies with time and space. Because of the non-uniform distribution of sound speed in seawater, according to Snell's law, sound ray always bends in the direction of decreasing sound speed, so the propagation path of sound ray in seawater channel is curved. The faster the change of sound speed, the larger the bending radius of sound ray. In this case, if the constant speed of sound is used, a lot of calculation errors will be caused [3–5]. On the other hand, the bending of sound rays means that the propagation delay of sound signals from the transmitting point to the

X. Sun et al. (Eds.): ICAIS 2021, LNCS 12736, pp. 643–658, 2021.
https://doi.org/10.1007/978-3-030-78609-0_54

receiving point is longer than that of the straight line propagation of sound signals. The more bending the sound rays, the greater the difference of propagation delay [6]. If the slant distance is calculated directly by the time delay difference, it will result in larger error, so the sound ray needs to be corrected. The influence of SSP (SSP/SVP, Sound Speed/Velocity Profile) on sound ray propagation is illustrated in Fig. 1.

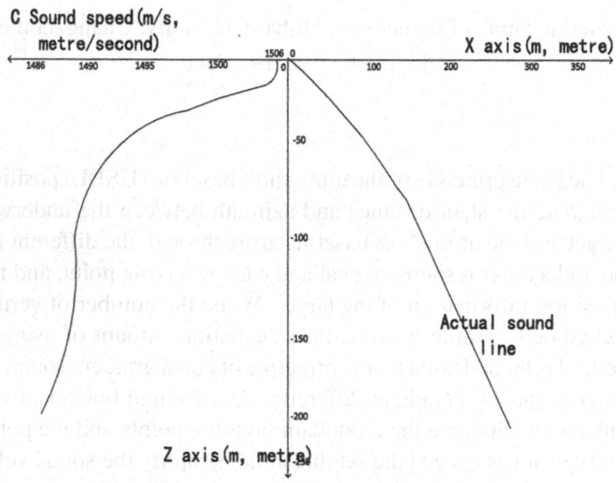

Fig. 1. Profile - sound ray tracing diagram

In the sound ray tracing method, the equal-gradient ray tracing method assumes that each sound speed layer in the underwater water has a constant sound speed gradient, and the sound speed on each layer is approximately linearly distributed. The equal gradient ray tracing method is consistent with the actual one, and the calculation accuracy is relatively high, but the calculation process is complicated and the calculation amount is large [8]. In order to reduce the calculation of sound ray tracing, based on the equal gradient layered ray tracing method, an adaptive layering method suitable for ultra-short baseline sound ray tracing is proposed, and its performance is analyzed and discussed through simulation.

2 Principle of USBL

2.1 Basic Theory of Ray Acoustics in Layered Media

The ray acoustic method is a common approximation method for studying the acoustic propagation characteristics in the sea under high frequency conditions [9]. The seawater medium has vertical stratification characteristics. In the layered medium, the sound ray propagation follows the Snell law [10], which is expressed as

$$\frac{\sin\theta_{\rm i}}{C_{\rm i}} = \frac{\sin\theta_{i+1}}{C_{i+1}} = \mathrm{P} \tag{1}$$

where $\theta_{\rm i}$ and $\theta_{\rm i+1}$ are the incident angles of sound ray at layer i and layer $i+1$ respectively, $C_{\rm i}$ and $C_{\rm i+1}$ are sound speed at layer i and layer $i+1$, respectively, p is the Snell constant [11].

2.2 Ultra-short Baseline Positioning Principle and Error Analysis

Different from long baseline positioning system and short baseline positioning system, the array length of ultra-short baseline positioning system generally varies from several centimeters to tens of centimeters. Ultra-short baseline array mounted on the bottom, at least, is made up of three hydrophone. Taking a hydrophone array composed of three basic elements as an example, the three elements of ultra-short baseline array are arranged on the X-axis and Y-axis according to equilateral triangle or right triangle. In Fig. 2, three hydrophones are placed in an isosceles right triangle. The length of the right Angle side is d, which is the baseline length. Usually take $d < \frac{1}{2}\lambda$, λ is the signal wavelength.

Figure 2 is the schematic diagram of ultra-short baseline positioning principle. S′ is the projection of S onto the plane of XOY. R is the distance from the origin to S prime. R is the distance from the origin to S.

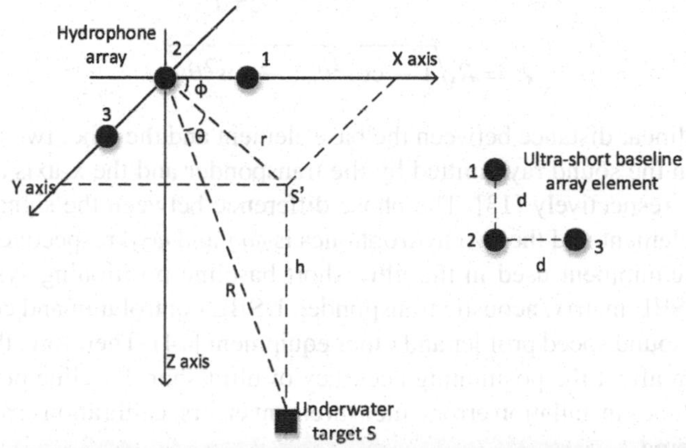

Fig. 2. Schematic diagram of ultra-short baseline positioning principle

The measuring array is placed in the XOY plane, and the X axis points to the brittle direction of the mother ship. The coordinates in Cartesian coordinate system are receiver 1 (d, 0, 0), receiver 2 (0, 0, 0), receiver 3 (0, d, 0) [12]. The distance between the three hydrophones is about a centimeter. In the process of USBL positioning, firstly, the transducer of the array transmits the interrogation signal, and then the transponder placed on the underwater target device sends out the response signal after receiving the interrogation signal. According to the time difference starting from the acoustic signal emitted by the transducer, then the transponder receives the sound signal and sends out the response signal, then the response signal emitted by the hydrophone receiver, and calculates the slant distance between the ultra-short baseline array and the underwater target by using the sound propagation velocity in the sea water. Then the azimuth angle of the underwater target to the ultra-short baseline array is calculated according to the time difference or phase difference of the acoustic wave arriving at each hydrophone. So the three-dimensional position coordinates of the underwater target relative to the sound source can be calculated by the geometric formula.

Since the size of the array is very small relative to the distance between the element and the transponder, it can be considered that the sound rays incident on all the elements are parallel to each other. When the signal frequency is f_0, i.e., the wavelength $\lambda = C/f_0$, As can be seen from Fig. 2, The relationship between the phase difference φ and incident angle of signal θ_m of the two hydrophones is as

$$\varphi = \frac{2\pi \mathrm{d}}{\lambda}\cos\theta_m \quad (2)$$

Then the position of transponder S in the header coordinate system is

$$X = R\cos\theta_{mx} = R\frac{\lambda\varphi_{12}}{2\pi \mathrm{d}} \quad (3)$$

$$Y = R\cos\theta_{my} = R\frac{\lambda\varphi_{23}}{2\pi \mathrm{d}} \quad (4)$$

$$Z = R\sqrt{1 - \cos^2\theta_{mx} - \cos^2\theta_{my}} \quad (5)$$

where d is the linear distance between the base element and the other two elements. The angles between the sound ray emitted by the transponder and the x-axis and y-axis are θ_{mx} and Bθ_{my}, respectively [13]. The phase difference between the signal received by the reference element and the two hydrophones is ϕ_{12} and ϕ_{23}, respectively.

The main equipment used in the ultra-short baseline positioning system includes ship's GPS, USBL matrix, acoustic transponder, USBL control unit and computer host, gyrocompass, sound speed profiler and other equipment [14]. Therefore, there are many factors that can affect the positioning accuracy of ultra-short baseline positioning systems. This includes installation errors, measurement errors, calibration errors, and errors in data processing.

3 Sound Ray Correction Method

The layered ray tracing method of sound ray correction is divided into Constant sound ray tracing method and Equal gradient ray tracing method [15]. The former has less calculation and low positioning accuracy. The latter has a large amount of calculation and high positioning accuracy.

3.1 Sound Speed Profile Layering Method

Since the temperature value remains substantially constant at the same depth in seawater, and the salinity and static pressure also have horizontal stratification and gradient changes in the depth direction [16], the sound speed in seawater also has the characteristics of horizontally stratified and gradient changes with depth [17]. Sound speed in sea water can be described by sound speed profile [18, 19]. The sound speed profile reflects the variation of sound speed along the depth direction [20]. The sound speed profile can be layered along depth. The layered result of sound speed profile also has some influence on the location result. Reasonable layered result can reduce the calculation amount of layered sound ray tracing without reducing the location accuracy.

The traditional layering method is to perform equal height stratification at the vertical target depth. The complex sound speed profile is approximately regarded as composed of multiple layers of sound speed with constant sound speed or constant sound speed gradient, and then the actual sound ray trajectory is approximated layer by layer [17].However, the traditional layering method has many layers [21], a large amount of calculation, low positioning accuracy and low positioning efficiency [22].

In order to solve the contradiction between calculation and positioning accuracy, Zhang et al. proposed an adaptive stratification method based on equivalent sound speed profile [23]. Li et al. proposed an adaptive stratification method for sound speed profile. Curvature radius is calculated by curve fitting, and part of the sound speed layer is merged according to curvature radius, which improves the positioning efficiency in deep-sea long baseline positioning [11]. Xiong et al. uses cubic spline interpolation to interpolate the corresponding sound speed at a fixed depth to reconstruct the sound speed profile. However, the equal gradient ray tracing method is not sensitive to the sampling interval variation of the sound speed profile, and the ability to reduce the computational amount when using the equal gradient ray tracing method is limited [24]. Gu et al. used the Douglas-Peucker algorithm to propose a method of maximum offset and applied it in ultra-short baseline positioning. According to a certain threshold, the point with the largest offset on the sound speed profile is selected as the layering point, which reduces the number of layers of the sound speed profile and reduces the calculation amount. The relative error of the slant range is controlled within 3% [25]. However, the Douglas-Peucker algorithm does not consider the characteristics of the bending of the feature points, so that the selected feature points can only macroscopically control the shape of the curve, and can not accurately distinguish the true feature points [26].

3.2 Equal Gradient Ray Tracing Method

The equal gradient ray tracing method assumes that sound waves experience N equal-gradient layers in water [27]. The gradient of the sound speed of each layer is constant, $\boldsymbol{Z}_i$, $\boldsymbol{C}_i$ and $\boldsymbol{\theta}_i$ are used to indicate the depth, speed of sound and angle of incidence of the sound ray of the i-th layer The sound speed gradient $\boldsymbol{g}_i$ in the i-th layer can be expressed by the following formula [28] as

$$\boldsymbol{g}_i = (\boldsymbol{C}_{i+1} - \boldsymbol{C}_i)/(\boldsymbol{Z}_{i+1} - \boldsymbol{Z}_i) \tag{6}$$

Since the propagation of sound waves satisfies the Snell's law, in the case of the sound speed gradient is constant, the actual propagation trajectory of the beam in the i-th layer is a continuous arc corresponding to a certain curvature radius $\boldsymbol{R}_i$ [8], and the expression of $\boldsymbol{R}_i$ is given as

$$\boldsymbol{R}_i = \left| 1/p\boldsymbol{g}_i \right| \tag{7}$$

The horizontal displacement [11] of sound ray in layer i is

$$\boldsymbol{x}_i = \boldsymbol{R}_i(\cos\boldsymbol{\theta}_{i+1} - \cos\boldsymbol{\theta}_i) = \frac{\cos\boldsymbol{\theta}_i - \cos\boldsymbol{\theta}_{i+1}}{p\boldsymbol{g}_i} \tag{8}$$

The length of the arc experienced by the beam at this layer is

$$S_i = R_i(\theta_i - \theta_{i+1}) \tag{9}$$

Then the time to go through the layer is

$$t_i = \frac{\arcsin[p(C_i + g\Delta Z_i)] - \arcsin(pC_i)}{pg_i^2 \Delta Z_i} \ln\left(1 + \frac{g_i \Delta Z_i}{C_i}\right) \tag{10}$$

Therefore, after calculating the horizontal and vertical displacement of each layer, if the entire water column is divided into N layers. Then the total horizontal distance X and vertical distance Z are equal to the superposition of (N−1) layers plus the horizontal Δx_r and vertical displacement of the last layer, that is

$$X = \sum_{i=1}^{N-1} \Delta x_i + \Delta x_r \tag{11}$$

The sound path traced by this method is consistent with the real sound ray, and the calculation accuracy is relatively high. However, when the number of data layers is large, the iteration time is consumed and the calculation amount is large.

3.3 Adaptive Stratification Method for Sound Speed Profile Based on Gradient Difference

In order to solve the problem of high precision positioning in the sea, an adaptive layering acoustic ray tracing fast positioning algorithm based on gradient difference is proposed. The idea of this method is that the gradient of sound speed reflects the speed of sound speed varying with depth, so the redundant data of sound speed profile are removed and the main feature points of sound speed profile are retained by gradient difference as a criterion. It can reduce the time-consuming of positioning under the premise of satisfying the requirement of positioning accuracy. The principle of adaptive stratification of sound speed profile is shown in Fig. 3.

Because the gradient reflects the degree of curvature of the curve, the two layers with similar gradient values on the sound speed profile are similar, so if the layers with similar gradient values can be merged into one layer, then perform iso-gradient sound ray tracing. It can reduce the amount of calculation in the process of sound ray tracing.

Selecting the appropriate threshold value can effectively extract the nodes of sound speed variation, discard the redundant layering points, and simplify the sound speed profile to improve the work efficiency. The simulation results show that the method can greatly reduce the computational complexity and ensure good positioning accuracy in the ultra-short baseline underwater positioning. Compared with Li's method, the principle of this method is simpler and the realization is more convenient.

Firstly, the sound speed gradient of each layer is calculated. Then the second layer is set as the current layer from the top layer, and the gradient difference between the current layer and the previous layer is calculated. If the gradient difference between the two layers is greater than the threshold value, the first layer is released, and the current

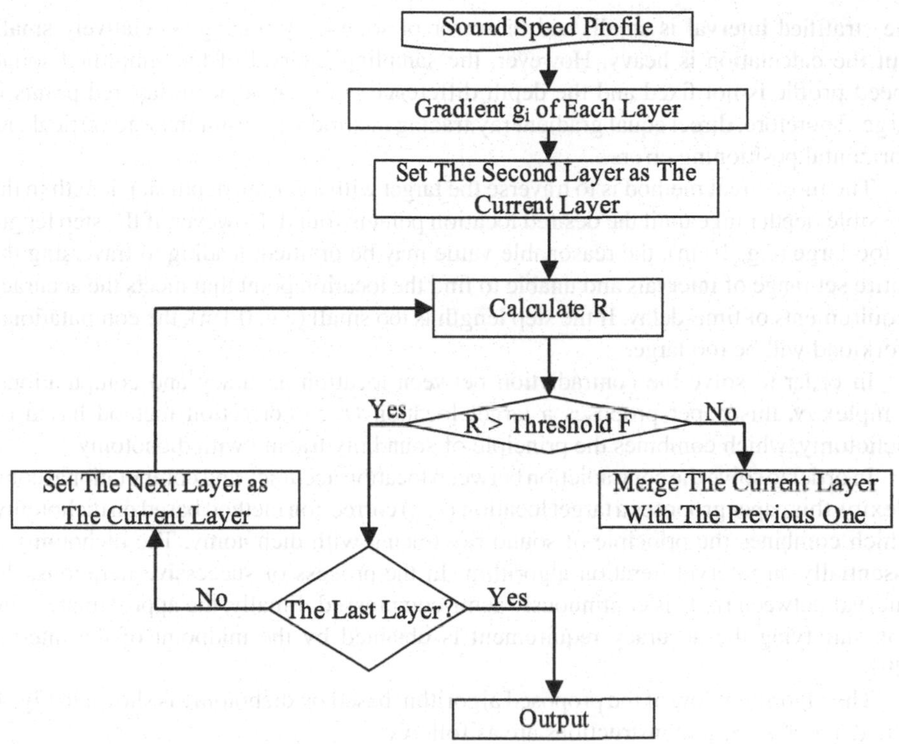

Fig. 3. Simplified algorithm for SSP based on gradient difference

layer is moved back one layer to continue to select two consecutive layers to calculate the gradient difference; if the gradient difference is less than the preset threshold, the two layers are merged into one layer. If the former layer is a merged new sonic layer during the merging process, only the gradient difference between the current layer and the former layer before merging is calculated. This method can effectively extract the nodes whose sound speed gradient varies greatly in the sound speed curve with slow gradient change, and judge whether to merge them according to their gradient difference. Until the whole sound speed profile is optimized. Through this method, the sound speed layer with little gradient change in the sound speed profile is filtered out, and the characteristic points of the sound speed profile are retained, thus reducing the computation of ray tracing.

3.4 Target Location Correction Method Based on Dichotomy

For ultra-short baseline and other gradient sound ray tracing, if the depth is known, the sound speed at the target depth can be calculated by interpolation. So the layered equal gradient ray tracing method is used. When the depth is unknown and the time-delay of sound propagation is known, the layered ray tracing calculation is usually carried out directly until the time T(n) of the ray tracing is greater than the time-delay ΔT. When the depth is unknown, the calculated target depth will only be at the stratified point of the sound speed profile. When the sound speed profile is sampled at a small interval, the stratified interval is small, and the error of sound ray tracing is relatively small. But the calculation is heavy. However, the sampling interval of the simplified sound speed profile is not fixed and the depth difference between adjacent layered points is large. Therefore, direct equal gradient ray tracing method will result in large vertical and horizontal positioning errors.

The most direct method is to traverse the target with a certain depth step length in the possible depth range until the desired location point is found. However, if the step length is too large (e.g. 10 m), the reasonable value may be omitted, leading to traversing the entire set range of intervals and unable to find the location point that meets the accuracy requirements of time-delay. If the step length is too small (e.g. 0.1m), the computational workload will be too large.

In order to solve the contradiction between location accuracy and computational complexity, this paper proposes a target location (r, z) correction method based on dichotomy, which combines the principle of sound ray tracing with dichotomy.

In order to solve the contradiction between location accuracy and computational complexity, this paper proposes a target location (r, z) correction method based on dichotomy, which combines the principle of sound ray tracing with dichotomy. The dichotomy is essentially an interval iteration algorithm. In the process of successive iterations, the interval between roots is continuously semi-compressed. Finally, the approximate solution satisfying the accuracy requirement is obtained by the midpoint of the interval [29].

The algorithm flow of the proposed algorithm based on dichotomy is shown in Fig. 4. The detailed steps and instructions are as follows:

(1) Calculate the equal gradient ray tracing method. Assuming that the location point is in the n + 1 layer, the total time T of the first n layer is obtained. ΔT is the time from the transmitter to the transponder, That is to say, layer N is the last layer where T is less than ΔT. Set the $n + 1$ layer as the current layer.
(2) Calculate the depth ΔZ of the current layer, and compare with the preset threshold b. If the threshold $b > \Delta$Z, enter the step 6, otherwise enter the next step.
(3) The midpoint of the current layer is taken as the stratification point, and the current layer is divided into two layers with the same depth, and then the former layer is taken as the current layer.
(4) Through the calculation of sound ray tracing of experience to the current layer time T, and compared with ΔT.
(5) When T < ΔT, set the next layer to the current layer and return to step 2. When T(n) >= ΔT, it returns directly to step 2.
(6) Calculate the location result to the current layer and output it.

The sound ray localization method based on the dichotomy can quickly find the depth interval where the target is located, and solves the problem that the inter-floor distance is too large due to the simplified stratification, and the direct use of the time delay positioning may cause a large error. But this method is also an approximate method. If the threshold is set too large, it will have a large error with the true value. If the threshold is set too small, the calculation amount will be further increased. Therefore, this paper

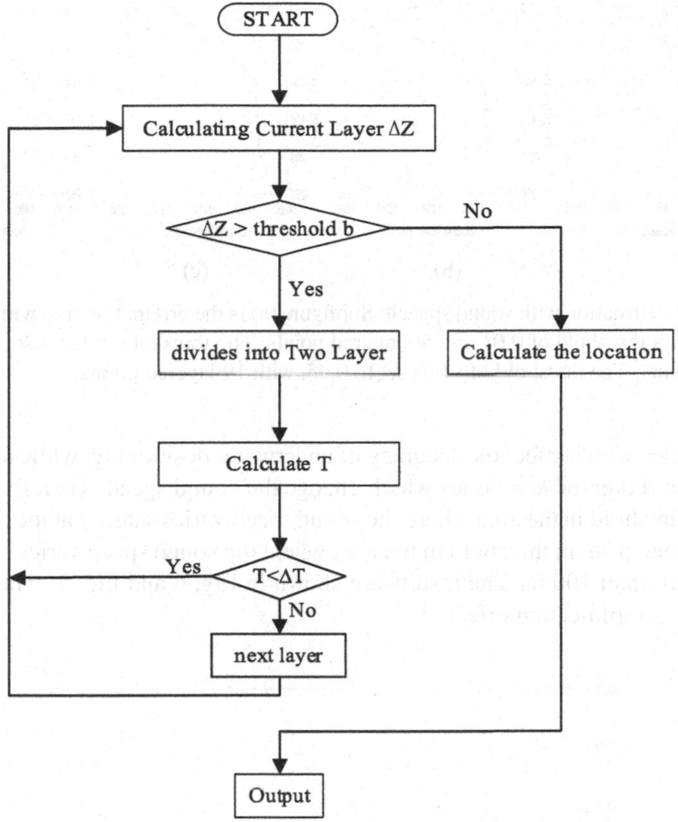

Fig. 4. Sound ray localization algorithm based on dichotomy

chooses a compromise threshold of 2 m, which will not cause large errors, nor will it increase the amount of calculation too much.

4 Simulation and Analysis

We select the measured sound speed profiles in a certain sea area and use different thresholds to stratify the sound speed profiles adaptively by gradient difference method. The results are shown in Fig. 5. From Fig. 5(b), (c) and (d), it can be seen that the sound speed profile between two nodes can be approximated to a straight line, so that the sound speed between two points can be expressed linearly.

From Fig. 6, it can be seen that the sound speed profile is bounded by 110 m depth. The sound speed gradient changes dramatically when the depth is less than 110 m, and slowly when the depth is greater than 110 m. Because in the region where the sound speed gradient varies sharply, selecting a larger threshold can remove some redundant jitter points on the curve while retaining the node of sound speed variation, so as to achieve better profile simplification effect. However, in the water layer where the sound speed gradient changes slowly, if we continue to select a larger threshold, we may abandon

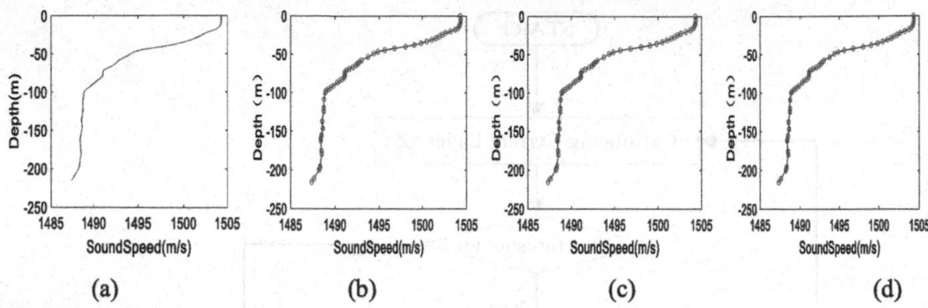

Fig. 5. Depth estimation with sound speech. Subfigure (a) is the original section with 98 stratified points, (b) has a threshold of 0.01 and 56 layered points. The threshold of (c) is set to 0.03, with 34 layered points. The threshold of (d) is set to 0.05, with 19 layered points.

some key nodes which affect the accuracy of underwater positioning, while using a small threshold can retain the key nodes which change the sound speed. Therefore, we try to use a large threshold in the area where the sound speed varies sharply at the depth of less than 100 m, and a small threshold in the area where the sound speed varies slowly at the depth of more than 100 m. The results are shown in Fig. 6 and Fig. 7, which achieves better profile simplification effect.

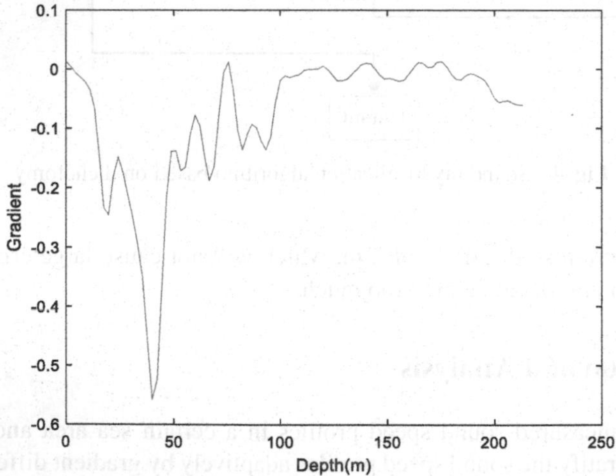

Fig. 6. Gradient diagram

The threshold in Fig. 7(a) is set to 0.05 at the point which is less than 100 m, a threshold of 0.02 at the point which is greater than 100 m and has 26 tiered points. The threshold in Fig. 7(b) is set to 0.07 at the point which is less than 100 m, a threshold of 0.03 at 100 m with 19 layering points.

Using the sound speed profile data of a certain sea area to calculate its simplification rate, the results are shown in Table 1 below. The original profile has 98 stratification points.

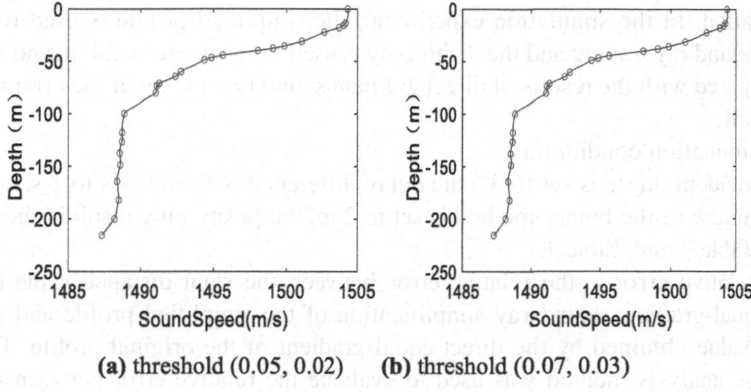

(a) threshold (0.05, 0.02) **(b)** threshold (0.07, 0.03)

Fig. 7. Sound speed profile processing results

From the Table 1, it can be found that as the threshold increases, the simplification rate of the sound speed profile also increases. When different thresholds are selected for different regions of the sound speed in a sound speed profile, the number of layers can be significantly reduced compared to the single threshold. And when the threshold is greater than 0.05, the simplification rate of the stratification point of the sound speed profile is more than 80%.

Table 1. Simplification rate table under different threshold

	Threshold	Number of layers	Reduced rate
Not layered	0.01	56	42.86%
	0.02	43	56.12%
	0.03	34	65.31%
	0.04	23	76.53%
	0.05	19	80.61%
	0.06	19	80.61%
	0.07	16	83.67%
	0.08	15	84.69%
	0.09	13	86.73%
	0.1	13	86.73%
Layered	0.05, 0.02	26	73.47%
	0.07, 0.03	19	80.61%

The sound speed profile is simplified by using different thresholds above. Next, the gradient difference based fast line tracking method is applied to the ultra-short baseline acoustic positioning, and the calculation efficiency and positioning accuracy are given by simulation. In the simulation experiment, the simplified profile is used for equal-gradient sound ray tracing and the dichotomy is used for accurate vocal line positioning. And compared with the results of direct gradient sound ray tracing of the original sound speed profile.

The simulation condition is:

The incident angle is set to 3°, the delay difference is from 0.4 s to 1 s, and when the threshold *b* of the binary method is set to 2 m, the positioning result is shown from Table 2, Table 3 and Table 4.

The relative error is the relative error between the slant distance value obtained by the equal-gradient sound ray simplification of the simplified profile and the slant distance value obtained by the direct equal-gradient of the original profile. The error percentage analysis method was used to evaluate the relative error between the slant distances obtained by the two methods.

The iteration amount is the number of iterations of the sound ray tracing experience, and each iteration is done with an equal gradient sound ray tracing calculation, and the calculation amount is the same each time. Therefore, the degree of reduction of the calculation amount can be observed by the degree of reduction of the iteration amount.

In order to measure the ability of the algorithm to select the preferred point on the sound speed profile, the simplification rate ξ is set to indicate the effect of preferential selection in the data of the sound speed profile by gradient difference method, and is defined by

$$\xi = \frac{|N_{pre} - N_{after}|}{N_{pre}} * 100\% \tag{12}$$

where N_{pre} represents the number of data nodes before the correction of the sound speed profile. N_{after} Indicates the number of nodes after the sound speed curve is corrected.

In this paper, the results of equal gradient sound ray tracing in the original section are used as a standard comparison Because the sound trajectory of the original sound speed profile directly undergoing equal gradient sound ray tracing is consistent with the real sound ray, and the calculation accuracy is relatively high, but the calculation amount is large. The positioning point coordinates are the coordinates of the positioning points in the plane composed of the azimuth angle and the z-axis when the azimuth angle is determined.

Table 2 shows the results of the equal-gradient sound speed traces of the original sound speed profile. It includes he slant distance and the coordinates of the underwater target. The accuracy is high, As a standard, it is compared with the results of equal gradient ray tracing of simplified Sound speed profile under different thresholds.

Among them, Td represents time delay, Ps represents simplified SSP points, Ds represents slant distance, Er represents relative error, Rr represents Reduction rate, Err represents positioning error.

As can be seen from Table 3, with the increase of time delay, the selection of key points decreases in the slow changing region of sound speed, and the simplification rate of calculation can be increased to 70%. Moreover, the relative error is less than 0.9%. The positioning point error is not more than 8 m.

Table 2. Positioning results under original SSP

Td	Ps	Ds (m)	(x, y) (m, m)
0.4	19	597	(596, 38)
0.5	27	749	(747, 57)
0.6	36	898	(895, 77)
0.7	46	1046	(1041, 99)
0.8	56	1196	(1189, 122)
0.9	67	1344	(1336, 144)
1.0	77	1492	(1482, 167)

Table 3. Positioning results with threshold 0.05

T_d	P_s	D_s (m)	E_r	R_r	(x, y) (m)	Err (m)
0.4	8	598	0.23%	57.89%	(597, 39)	1.42
0.5	14	749	0.01%	48.15%	(747, 57)	0.56
0.6	17	890	0.89%	52.78%	(887, 77)	8.02
0.7	20	1041	0.47%	56.52%	(1036, 99)	4.89
0.8	23	1191	0.34%	58.93%	(1185, 122)	4.09
0.9	23	1343	0.03%	65.67%	(1336, 145)	0.84
1.0	23	1494	0.17%	70.13%	(1485, 169)	2.81

From Table 4, it can be seen that with the increase of the delay difference, the simplification rate of calculation increases to 66%. Both of the two meters have the largest slant error and location error locations with a time delay of 0.6 s. Comparing the two tables, it can be seen that the calculation amount of Table 4 is equal to that of Table 3, and the positioning accuracy of Table 4 is higher than that of Table 3. It shows that this method can effectively improve the location efficiency by setting different thresholds in different regions.

Table 4. Positioning results with threshold 0.05 (lower SSP) and 0.02 (higher SSP)

T_d	P_s	D_s (m)	E_r	R_r	(x, y) (m, m)	Err (m)
0.4	3	291	0.23%	57.89%	(597, 39)	1.42
0.5	7	444	0.01%	48.15%	(747, 57)	0.56
0.6	8	598	0.89%	52.78%	(887, 77)	8.02
0.7	14	749	0.47%	56.52%	(1036, 99)	4.89
0.8	17	890	0.02%	62.50%	(1189, 122)	0.62
0.9	20	1041	0.15%	65.67%	(1334, 145)	2.09
1.0	21	1194	0.01%	66.23%	(1482, 168)	0.62

5 Conclusion

This paper focuses on the problem of sound ray correction in ultra-short baseline positioning system. In view of the problem that more layers of sound speed profile affect the calculation amount. In this paper, an adaptive stratification method of sound speed profile based on gradient difference is studied. By choosing key nodes, the sound speed profile is simplified to reduce the computational complexity. Aiming at the problem that the simplified sound speed profile has large layered spacing and it is difficult to calculate more accurate locating points by using time delay difference, this paper combines the principle of sound ray tracing with the principle of dichotomy to find locating points. The method studied in this paper not only reduces the time of iteration calculation, but also has the same accuracy as that of the original section calculation. Compared with the traditional method, it can obviously improve the positioning efficiency. When the appropriate threshold is selected, the method proposed in this paper has a slightly better positioning accuracy and a slightly lower positioning efficiency than the method in reference [25] under the same sound speed profile. At the same time, it should be noted that at present, the division of regions and the setting of thresholds are still selected manually in the selection of different thresholds in different regions, so the automatic selection method of thresholds needs further study.

Funding Statement. This work is supported by National Key R&D Program, China [2017YFC0306100] and National Natural Science Foundation of China under Grant No. 61671202

Conflicts of Interest. The authors declare that they have no conflicts of interest to report regarding the present study.

References

1. Wang, Y., Liang, G.L.: A method of sound ray correction for long baseline underwater acoustic positioning system. J. Harbin Eng. Univ. **05**, 32–34 (2002)
2. Su, L., Ma, L., Guo, S.M.: Influence of sound speed profile on source localization at different depths. J. Comput. Acoust. **25**(02), 1750026 (2017)

3. Yan, H., Wang, S., Liu, L., et al.: A reconstruction algorithm of temperature field taking into account the bending of sound wave paths. Shengxue Xuebao/Acta Acust. **39**(06), 705–713 (2014)
4. Zina, T.T.: Sound ray tracing technology in multi-beam strip bathymetry. J. Harbin Eng. Univ. **03**, 245–248 (2003)
5. Zhou, J., Zhou, Q., Lu, L., Chen, C., et al.: Discussion on correction of multi-beam sound speed profile. Marine Surv. Mapp. **34**(04), 62–68 (2014)
6. Liang, M.Z., Yu, Y., Wang, L.M.: A method of looking up table for sound ray correction. Acoust. Technol. **28**(04), 556–559 (2009)
7. Tang, J.F., Yang, S.E., Piao, S.C.: A method for calculating acoustic ray in unstratified ocean. J. Vibr. Shock **34**(04), 59–62 (2015)
8. Lu, X.X., Huang, M.: An improved method for calculating average sound speed in constant gradient sound ray tracing technology. Geomat. Inf. Sci. Wuhan Univ. **37**(05), 590–593 (2012)
9. He, L., Zhao, J., Zhang, H., Wang, X.: A precise multibeam sound ray tracking method taking into account the attitude angle. J. Harbin Eng. Univ. **36**(01), 46–50 (2015)
10. Liu, N.: Improved algorithm of sound ray tracing based on adaptive layering. In: Proceedings of Annual Conference of China Satellite Navigation (2019)
11. Li, S.X., Wang, Z.X., Nie, Z.X., Wang, Y., Wu, S.Y.: An adaptive layered ray tracing method for deep-sea long baseline positioning. Ocean Bulletin **34**(05), 491–498 (2015)
12. Cai, P., Liang, G.L., Hui, J.Y., Wang, Z.Y.: Ultra-short baseline underwater acoustic tracing system using adaptive phase meter. Appl. Acoust. **02**, 19–28 (1993)
13. Jin, B.N., Xu, X.S., Zhang, T., Sun, X.J.: Ultra-short baseline positioning technology and its application in marine engineering. Navig. Position. Timing **5**(04), 08–20 (2018)
14. Zhou, J., Xiao, B., Gong, H.C., Guo, Q.: Error analysis and treatment strategy of ultra-short baseline positioning system for submarine cable. Southern Energy Constr. **5**(02), 138–142 (2018)
15. Zhao, A.B., He, W.X., Dong, H.F., et al.: Positioning algorithm of deepwater USBL for random distributed velocity of sound. J. Syst. Simul. **21**(15), 4763–4767 (2009)
16. Cai, Y.H., Cheng, P.F.: Sound speed of sonar positioning in surface seawater. Remote Sens. Inf. **27**(06), 3–9 (2012)
17. Liu, B.S., Lei, J.Y.: Principles of Underwater Acoustics. Harbin Engineering University Press, Harbin (2017)
18. Zhang, W., Yang, S., Huang, Y., et al.: Inversion of sound speed profile in three-dimensional shallow water based on transmission time. Sci. Sinica Phys. Mech. Astron. **43**, 121–130 (2013)
19. Chen, C., Ma, Y., Liu, Y.: Reconstructing sound speed profiles worldwide with sea surface data. Aerosp. China **19**(04), 38–43 (2018)
20. Wang, Y.: Research on underwater high-precision positioning algorithm in petroleum exploration. China University of Petroleum (East China) (2014)
21. Zhao, D.N., Wu, Z.Y., Zhou, J.Q., et al.: Improved D-P algorithm and its evaluation for simplified calculation of sound speed profile. J. Surv. Mapp. **43**(07), 681–689 (2014)
22. Zhang, Z.W.Z., Wu, J.Y., Jin, S.: An adaptive layering method for multi-beam sounding line tracing. Marine Surv. Mapp. **38**(01) (2018)
23. Zhang, J.C., Zheng, C., Sun, D.J.: Adaptive layering method for sound ray tracing and location. J. Harbin Eng. Univ. **34**(12), 1497–1501 (2013)
24. Xiong, C., Jianjun, L.I., Yan, X., et al.: Optimal selection of sampling interval on multibeam bathymetry. Hydrogr. Surv. Chart. **37**(04), 47–50 (2017)
25. Li, J., Gu, Q.: Research on fast voice tracing algorithms in ultra-short baseline location. In: Proceedings of National Acoustic Congress (2018)
26. Zhang, D.H., Huang, L.N., Fei, L.F., Ren, X.N.: A curvature-based curve feature point selection method. Surv. Mapp. Sci. **38**(03), 151–153 (2013)

27. Li, J., Gu, Q., Chen, Y., et al.: A combined ray tracing method for improving the precision of the USBL positioning system in smart ocean. Sens. (Basel Switzerland) **18**(10), 3586 (2018)
28. Li, S.X.: Research on sound speed correction method in underwater acoustic location. China University of Petroleum (East China) (2015)
29. Gong, H.L., Chen, B., Wan, L.L., Jiang, N.: A binary iterative real-time sound ray correction algorithm. Acoust. Technol. **37**(04), 303–308 (2018)

Research on Auxiliary Target Extraction and Recognition Technology in Big Data Environment

Gui Liu(✉), Yongyong Dai, Haijiang Xu, Wei Xia, and Wei Zhou

Jiangnan Institute of Computing Technology, Wuxi, Jiangsu, China

Abstract. With the rapid development of global aviation industry, the flight volume is rising rapidly, and the aviation industry is also rapidly entering the era of big data. In this paper, the digital extraction of image information assisted target recognition technology is used to extract the route and waypoint information on the picture and make it into vector civil aviation route. Combined with the massive flight plan and target trajectory on the Internet, track feature matching is realized to assist users to quickly discover targets.

Keywords: Track feature matching · Track deviation

1 Introduction

With the rapid development of global aviation industry, the flight volume shows a rapid upward trend, and the aviation industry has rapidly entered the era of big data [1, 2]. In this paper, based on the massive vector civil aviation routes, combined with flight plan and target trajectory, track feature matching is realized, which provides a new way for users to quickly capture key targets and find targets.

2 Research Status at Home and Abroad

Using electronic map information query function, computer high-speed calculation and decision-making function to automatically generate planned route is a hot research topic in civil aviation field. There are many methods for automatic route generation, such as Dijkstra algorithm, heuristic search algorithm, fuzzy algorithm, neural network, and relatively new ant colony algorithm and genetic algorithm control [3–7].

Ant colony algorithm is easy to search, but it has a long time and slow convergence, and it is easy to stagnate and fall into local optimum; genetic algorithm has fast convergence and good optimization effect, but it is difficult to obtain the initial population and the coding is complex. With the development of digital information, a large number of map images with route and waypoint information can be obtained from the Internet. If the information of route and waypoint on the picture can be extracted digitally and made into an electronic map with vector civil aviation route, the track feature matching can be realized by combining the trajectory of aircraft flight target, which can assist users to quickly discover air targets.

X. Sun et al. (Eds.): ICAIS 2021, LNCS 12736, pp. 659–665, 2021.
https://doi.org/10.1007/978-3-030-78609-0_55

3 Digital Extraction of Image Information to Assist Target Recognition

3.1 Registration and Digital Extraction of Civil Aviation Routes

Traditional maps are passive for users, and they cannot choose the expression form of maps according to their requirements. Digital maps allow users to choose scale, projection data, symbols, colors, schemata, etc. according to their own design. The introduction of digital extraction technology of map data can solve the digital problems such as poor scaling effect and unclear of civil aviation route map, which is of great significance to improve user experience.

The registration of civil aviation route mainly includes two processes: selecting control point and obtaining coordinate information of control point. The representative aviation control points, such as large airports and route intersections, are selected as control points, and it is better to have more than three evenly distributed control points. The more accurate the coordinate is, the more accurate the vector information is obtained by reference map.

With the registration control points and coordinate information, a new ShapeFile file is established by using the map digitization extraction tool, and the ShapeFile file type is selected according to the point, line and surface attributes to be digitized. Setting appropriate projection and coordinate system parameters, the coordinate of civil aviation route map is CGCS2000 coordinate system. A new layer is created in the extraction tool, and the registration control point information and layer information are input, and the features to be digitized are selected, and then the digital extraction can be realized directly. In order to facilitate the use and management, different types of information need to be classified and digitized. For example, after the digital extraction of civil aviation route map, it is divided into three shapefiles: point element, point element buffer and route.

3.2 Target Recognition Based on Target Trajectory Feature Matching

The target trajectory can be used as an important basis for the research and judgment of the identity of the target. If the user can quickly judge the attribute of the target through the trajectory, he can quickly locate the important target, and further analyze and mine the deep-seated motion law. Generally, civil aviation must strictly follow the established route. When a certain target deviates from the center line of the route by a certain distance or obviously does not fly along the route, it can be regarded as an aircraft with unknown intention. Although some aircraft will generally follow the route when actual fly, they will not strictly follow the route when some waypoints and routes are changed. In this paper, based on vector civil aviation routes, combined with the flight plan of Internet traffic volume and target trajectory, track feature matching is realized, as shown in the figure below, which provides a new way for users to quickly capture key targets and find targets (Fig. 1).

Resampling of Track Pattern Based on Proximity Tracking. For an original target track sample, the initial feature points are sampled intensively, which is difficult to meet the requirements of subsequent track feature matching. Therefore, it is necessary to

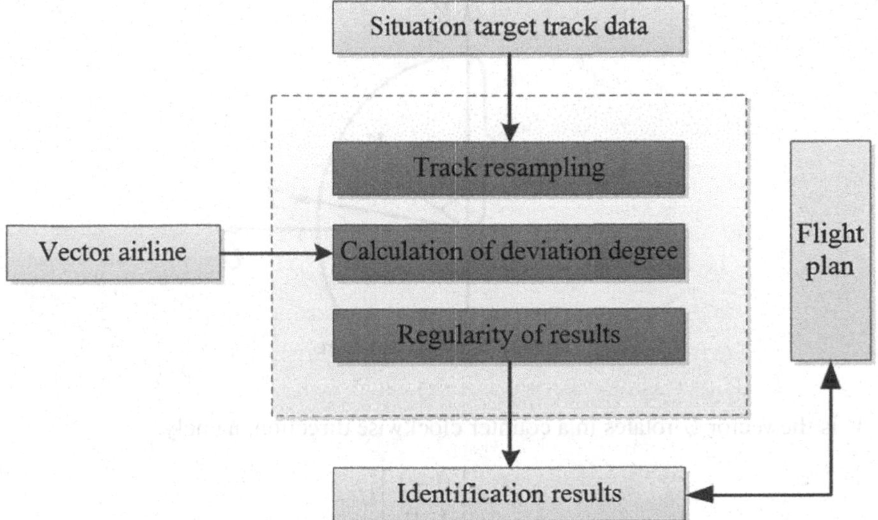

Fig. 1. Sketch map of digital extraction effect

resample the initial feature points. The resampling of track pattern based on proximity tracking not only improves the smoothness of the track, but also ensures the shape of the track and eliminates the undesirable twists and turns, thus ensuring a better track model quality.

The basic idea of neighborhood tracking resampling is: firstly, the spatial partition strategy is used to divide the initial graph data points to improve the efficiency of neighborhood search. Secondly, the optimal tracking idea is used to determine the initial point of the tracking point column by calculating the mean value of the data points contained in each partition area, and then the tracking direction and tracking step size are determined by the neighborhood search. The specific steps are as follows:

Firstly, the initial graph data points are obtained, and the minimum and maximum values of *X, Y, Z* coordinates are obtained, so that a square area parallel to the coordinate axis surrounding all feature points can be formed. According to the number and distribution of the original feature points, the square area is further divided into small cube grids.

Then, the initial points of the tracking point column are determined and the local coordinate system is established to determine the stereo grid with the most data points Q_0. If the mean value of the data points in the grid is taken as the initial point of the tracking point column, the tracking points can be listed as $\{Q_0, Q_1, \ldots\ldots Q_k\}$. For the current tracking point Q_k, it is assumed that they are two known adjacent points in the tracking point column Q_{k-1}, Q_k, as shown in the following Fig. 2:

Take the vector

$$U = (Q_k - Q_{k-1})/\| Q_k - Q_{k-1} \|$$

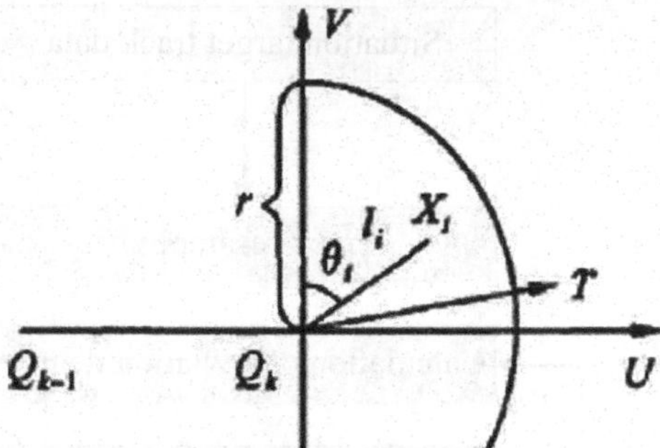

Fig. 2. Network structure

V is the vector U rotates in a counter clockwise direction, namely.

$$V = \begin{bmatrix} 0 & -1 \\ 1 & 0 \end{bmatrix} U$$

The local coordinate system is established with the tracking point Q_k as the origin and V and U as the coordinate axes.

Finally, the tracking step size and tracking direction are determined based on neighbor search. Assuming that $X = \{X_1, X_2, \ldots, X_n\}$ is the set of sampling points on the curve to be reconstructed, k nearest points are found in the stereo grid where the detection point X_i is located and among the *27(3 *3 *3)* small three-dimensional grids, i.e. up, down, left and right, front and back, which are recorded as S. Take point Q_k as the center of the circle and take the distance r of the farthest adjacent point as the radius to make a circle. All data points X_i in the circle with an angle less than 90° with U are investigated. Suppose θ_i is the angle between the vector $Q_k X_i$ and V, and $\overline{\theta_k}$ is the angle between the tracking direction T and V, and the tracking step length $l_i^2 = \| X_i - Q_i \|^2$. In order to make the constructed graph curve reflect the correct shape, the objective function is constructed.

$$I_1 = \sum_{X_i \in S} \left(\theta_i - \overline{\theta_k}\right)^2 l_i^2$$

Find the I_1 corresponding to the minimum of $\overline{\theta_k}$, and then determine the tracking party T.

$$\overline{\theta_k} = \frac{\sum_{X_i \in S} l_i^2 \theta_i}{\sum_{X_i \in S} l_i^2}$$

After determining the tracking direction T, we need to find Q_{k-1} along this direction to make it located in the center of S.

Constructor is:

$$I_2 = \sum_{X_i \in S} \left[l_i^2 + \overline{l_k^2} - 2 l_i \overline{l_k} \cos\left(\theta_i - \overline{\theta_k}\right) \right] \cos\left(\theta_i - \overline{\theta_k}\right)$$

Find the $\overline{l_k}$ that makes I_2 the smallest:

$$\overline{l_k} = \sum_{X_i \in S} \left[l_i \cos^2(\theta_i - \overline{\theta_k}) \right] \Big/ \sum_{X_i \in S} \cos(\theta_i - \overline{\theta_k})$$

Thus, a new tracking point is obtained:

$$Q_{k-1} = Q_k + \overline{l_k} \cdot T$$

The resampling of track feature points is completed.

Calculation of Track Deviation Degree Based on Maximum Distance. The system takes the digitized T_i of each given civil aviation route as the sample model, resamples the situation target track C to be matched, and then matches the target track C to be matched with all the established sample models T_i one by one, and calculates the distance d_i between the corresponding points of the graph C to be matched and the sample model T_i.

$$d_i = \frac{\sum_{k=1}^{N} \sqrt{(C[k]_x - T_i[k]_x)^2 + (C[k]_y - T_i[k]_y)^2}}{N}$$

When d_i is greater than a certain value set by the user, it means that the target obviously deviates from the center line of the route by a certain distance, or obviously does not fly along the established civil aviation route. It can be regarded as an aircraft with unknown intention. Using the maximum deviation distance, the unconventional changes of target track can be expressed intuitively and quickly.

Regularization of Recognition Results Combined with the Civil Aviation Flight Plan. For similar track shapes, there are great differences between the track points. We use seven track shape similarity indicators to measure from different angles, such as roundness, complexity, eccentricity, distance between center of mass and long axis, distance between center of mass and short axis, average distance between center of mass and distance between key points. Seven indexes of trajectory shape similarity are used to comprehensively evaluate the similarity between track shape and template track as the recognition result.

The integrity of the data obtained on the Internet is not necessarily the same, which also causes difficulties in the decision-making of trajectory shape similarity. However, the accuracy of the verification results can be greatly improved by combining with the flight plan. Using the information provided by the flight plan, we can know the target's estimated take-off time, flight number, aircraft type and take-off and landing airport, target updated estimated take-off time, flight number, aircraft type and take-off and landing airport information, accurate take-off time, flight number and transponder number of the target.Using this information, we can find out the correct target aircraft type according to the flight number Association and identify the target aircraft type, so as to achieve the purpose of aircraft identification.

Optimization Model Considering Data Noise. When building the model, it is assumed that the data is accurate, but the actual situation is not so, and the data noise needs to be considered. In the case of considering noise, the optimization of the model is mainly to solve the optimization problem by using the sequential minimum optimization algorithm, so as to provide effective parameter values for the aircraft identification model and obtain the optimal attribute classification recognizer.

$$\max_{\alpha} \quad \sum_{i=1}^{n} \alpha_i - \frac{1}{2} \sum_{i,j=1}^{n} \alpha_i \alpha_j y_i y_j K(x_i, x_j)$$

$$s.t. \quad 0 \leq \alpha_i \leq C, i = 1, \cdots, n, \sum_{i=1}^{n} \alpha_i y_i = 0$$

Where n is the number of flying targets in the training set, a_i is the i-th Lagrange operator, x_i is the eigenvector of the i-th flying target, y_i is the identity attribute of the i-th flying target, C is a preset constant, $K(x_i, x_j)$ is a kernel function, which can be any one of linear kernel function, polynomial kernel function, Gaussian kernel function and sigmoid function. The Lagrange operator $a_i(i = 1,\ldots)$ can be obtained by using the sequential minimal optimization (SMO) algorithm to solve the optimization problem Then, the optimal classifier is obtained.

Algorithm Flow of Aircraft Identification Based on SVM Model. The aircraft identification model based on SVM model is actually a process of information fusion on the input and output nodes. The model transforms the fuzzy nonlinear relationship between feature parameters and related attributes into the mapping relationship in the model.The algorithm flow is as follows:

Step 1: according to the requirements of the actual system, determine the number of input target characteristic parameters x, and establish the output and input relationship of model nodes;

Step 2: before learning and training, it is necessary to extract and normalize the aircraft feature parameter data, in order to provide SVM with appropriate recognition input and training samples; According to the original and indirect characteristics of the flying target, the input parameters can be generated:

$$x_{ij} = \mu_{ij} + \sigma_{ij} \times randn$$

Among them, randn is a random number which obeys the standard normal distribution.

Step 3: select the appropriate SVM model, and train a certain number of training samples with one to many classification (OAA) and one to one classification (OAO) to get the expected SVM;

Step 4: test the test data with the SVM model. If the accuracy of the system is satisfied, the model will be used as the target identification classifier model. Otherwise, go back to the third step again until the accuracy of the system is satisfied.

The process of aircraft identification attribute recognition based on SVM is the process of computing using SVM. With the increase of feature parameters, when the parameters reach a certain degree, SVM can achieve higher classification ability.

4 Concluding Remarks

In this paper, using the amount of civil aviation information on the Internet, track matching recognition and flight plan recognition are combined to regularize the recognition results, and consider how to optimize the model in the case of data noise, so as to improve the recognition accuracy to a great extent.

References

1. Chen, S., Huang, Y.H., Huang, W.Q.: Big data analytics on avaiation social media. In: The Case of China Southern Airlines on Sina Weibo IEEE Second International Conference on Big Data Computing Service and Applications, pp.152–155 (2016)
2. Sangaiah, A.K., Gaol, F.L., Mishra, K.K.: Guest editorial special section on big data & analytics architecture. Intell. Autom. Soft Comput. **26**(3), 515–517 (2020)
3. Alhroob, A., Alzyadat, W., Imam, A.T., Jaradat, G.M.: The genetic algorithm and binary search technique in the program path coverage for improving software testing using big data. Intell. Autom. Soft Comput. **26**(4), 725–733 (2020)
4. Zhou, S., Wang, J., Jin Y.: Route planning for unmanned aircraft based on ant colony optimization and voronoi diagram. In: Second International Conference on Intelligent System Design and Engineering Application, pp. 732–735. IEEE (2012)
5. Yakovlev, K.S., Makarov, D.A., Baskin, E.S.: Automatic path planning for an unmanned drone with constrained flight dynamics. Sci. Tech. Inf. Process. **42**(5), 347–358 (2015). https://doi.org/10.3103/S0147688215050093
6. Li, J., Meng, X., Dai, X.: Collision-free scheduling of multi-bridge machining systems: a colored traveling salesman problem-based approach. IEEE/CAA J. Autom. Sinica 1–9 (2018)
7. Liu, G., Xu, H., Yang, S.: Multi-stage replica consistency algorithm based on activity. In: Shen, J., Chang, Y.-C., Su, Y.-S., Ogata, H. (eds.) IC3 2019. CCIS, vol. 1227, pp. 96–104. Springer, Singapore (2020). https://doi.org/10.1007/978-981-15-6113-9_11

Analysis of Information Dissemination Orientation of New Media Police Microblog Platform

Leyao Chen, Lei Hong(✉), and Jiayin Liu

Jiangsu Police Institute, Nanjing 210000, China
honglei@jspi.edu.cn

Abstract. This article aims to analyze the microblog data released by a new social media platform for police in a certain province in China, and find out the characteristics of those microblogs which are more likely to be reposted from the perspective of modern police affairs. A new topic-based model is proposed in this article. In the first step, the LDA topic clustering algorithm is adopted to extract the topic categories with forwarding heat from the most-reposted microblogs, with a Naive Bayesian algorithm as followed to predict the topic categories. The pre-processed sample data is applied on the proposed method to predict the type of microblog reposting. The experimental results utilizing a large number of online microblog data demonstrate that the proposed method can accurately predict the reposting of microblogs with high precision and recall rate.

Keywords: Microblog prediction · LDA algorithm · Naive Bayesian algorithm · Data mining

1 Introduction

With the rapid development of network technology, new media is no longer a distant and unfamiliar concept. In particular, new media platform for public security and government affairs are gradually sprung up in recent years. As the "second battlefield" of public security, the new media for public security government plays a pivotal role in integrating new media technology with police work. In recent years, more and more attention has been attracted by local public security organs on the construction of new media. They have opened official microblog and WeChat public account to adapt to the new Internet era and the refreshing expectations of people. This makes the masses more and more aware of the work of public security. On the other hand, the development of the new media for the police also enables the public opinion database to be fully developed. Accordingly, the police can also make use of the social network behaviors of the masses (browse, like, repost, comment, etc.) and transmission range of the message to identify the social affairs and problems that the masses concern.

X. Sun et al. (Eds.): ICAIS 2021, LNCS 12736, pp. 666–675, 2021.
https://doi.org/10.1007/978-3-030-78609-0_56

2 The Status of Research

In recent years, there are numerous studies in the literature regarding different perspectives of microblog communication, including social influence of the accounts, the viewpoint features in microblog content, and the social characteristics of users' groups. However, the method based on BP (back propagation) neural network and the method of predicting the microblog reposting amount under the emergency event and using the SIM-LSTM model to predict the microblog reposting is too complicated and redundant [1, 3, 4, 6], and is not intuitive and interpretable enough. The disadvantages of other methods are also the same with above methods. Through the analysis of forwarding microblogs, we conclude that the highly reposted microblogs have certain thematic features. According to our proposed LDA-based naive Bayes algorithm, it is more intuitive and efficient to predict whether microblog will be reposted. At present, there is no research on the reposting forecasting of the microblog for public security police in China and current research on new media policing still focus on how to deal with public opinion. Hence, our research has the following advantages:

Fill in the current research gap, create a collection of methods that are exclusively targeted at public security microblogs, provide positive thoughts for public security work to guide public opinion, and enhance communication between groups of netizens.

This is a more accurate and intuitive algorithm. Comparing with the performance of the social network that has too much emphasis on reposting microblogs, the algorithm is more direct and easier to implement.

3 The Methods of Research

According to CNNIC's "Statistical Report on the Development of China's Internet Network", as of December 2018, the number of netizens nationwide reached 829 million. In the report of 2018 China Microblog User Scale and Usage, the data shows that the number of microblog users in China was 337 million in 2018, increasing by 34.56 million compared with the end of 2017. The proportion of microblog users among the total number of Internet users reached 42.3%. The increase in the number of user groups also implies that more and more problems and emergencies tend to appear during the communication process via microblog [2, 5, 7, 8]. However, the previous method is too complicated, and it is not easy to apply directly to the official microblog account of the public security. Therefore, we propose a method based on the LDA topic clustering model.

Firstly, we will introduce the model and research methods as followed:

3.1 Latent Dirichlet Allocation

Latent Dirichlet Allocation (LDA) is a probabilistic topic model, which assigns a probability distribution to the topic of each documents in the document set, and accordingly clusters or classifies topics by analyzing documents and extracting their potential topics. At the same time, it is also a typical word bag model, which views the document as composition of a group of words with no order between them.

The traditional way to measure the similarity between two documents is to calculate the number of words that appear in two documents simultaneously [9], such as TF-IDF. However, the semantic association behind the text and the polysemy of the word are not taken into account in this method. It is highly probable that there are few or no words in common between two documents, but they are very similar with closely related topic. LDA can handle this situation well by extracting the potential topics of the document and quantifying the existing probability of the relevant subject words.

The subject refers to a list of words that are semantically related to the topic and their weights, that is, the vector of the conditional probability of each word under the topic. The closer the relationship is between the subject and words, the greater the conditional probability, and vice versa. In the topic model, a topic represents a concept, or an aspect, representative by a series of related words, and is the conditional probability of these words. More specifically, the theme is a bucket of words with high probability of occurrence. These words have a strong correlation with this theme.

The model is built as follows:

Select a document d_i according to the prior probability $p^{(di)}$.
Extract the topic distribution θ_i of the generated sample document d_i from the α of the Dirichlet distribution,
Extract the subject $z_{(i,j)}$ of the j_{th} word from the polynomial distribution θ_i of the sample.
Extract the sample from the Dirichlet distribution β to generate the word distribution $\phi_{z(i,j)}$ corresponding to the topic $z_{(i,j)}$. The word distribution $\phi_{z(i,j)}$ is generated by the Dirichlet distribution with the parameter β.
Collect samples from the polynomial distribution $\phi z(i, j)$ of the word and finally generate the word $\omega(i, j)$ (Fig. 1).

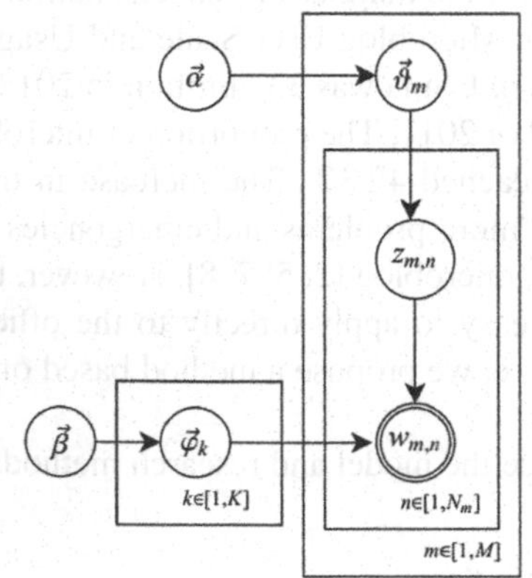

Fig. 1. LDA model generation flow chart

3.2 Naive Bayesian Algorithm

Bayesian classification is a general term for a class of classification algorithms. These algorithms are based on Bayes' theorem, so they are collectively called Bayesian classification. The Naive Bayes Classifier is a simple and easy-to-understand classification method that seems 'naïve' but works very well. The principle is Bayes' theorem, which obtains new information from the data and then updates the prior probability to obtain the posterior probability. Just like evaluating the quality of a good when you are shopping online. If you do a random guess, there will be 50% chance for this product to be an acceptable one. However, if you have the prior knowledge that the shop has a good reputation, then this information will increase the probability that this good will be an acceptable one. The advantage of Naive Bayes classification is that it will not be affected by "data impurities" or irrelevant variables. 'Naïve' means it assumes that features are independent with each other. A given item will be classified into the category that has the largest predictive probability.

The Bayesian formula is given below:

$$P(Bi|A) = \frac{P(A|Bi)P(Bi)}{\sum_{j=1}^{n} P(A|Bj)P(Bj)} \tag{1}$$

The Naive Bayes calculation formula (the expression under multiple features) is:

$$P(C = \mathrm{c}|A1 = a1...An = an) = \alpha P(C = c)\prod_{i=1}^{n} P(Ai|C = c) \tag{2}$$

In order to predict whether microblog will be reposted or not, we need to calculate the posterior probability of reposting. According to Bayesian inference, the adjustment factor is based on the probability that the event has occurred, the event may occur, and the ratio of the probability of detection. Adjusting the prior probability by this ratio can help us obtain the posterior probability, so as to make accurate prediction.

Through the screening of the acquired sample data, the frequently reposted sample microblogs are identified as the input data of the LDA model. The model aims to output the topic features of the frequently reposted text, and as the input of the naive Bayesian algorithm, the final prediction result is the output. The flow of our proposed research method is shown in the following Fig. 2:

First, we clean all the captured microblog sample data by removing those with repostnum equals to zero. Then, we perform the second-round data cleaning according to our proposed rule that reposting number is not less than 1.5 times of the average number. 22w+ strips of the full microblog sample are filtered into 10w+ strips data with high reposting number left to be further processed.

Next, input those frequently reposted data obtained in the first step into the LDA topic model, train the theme distribution of the text data through machine learning algorithm, set the number of displayed words for each topic, and leave the obtained subject as the simplest in the next link the subject classification feature of Bayesian.

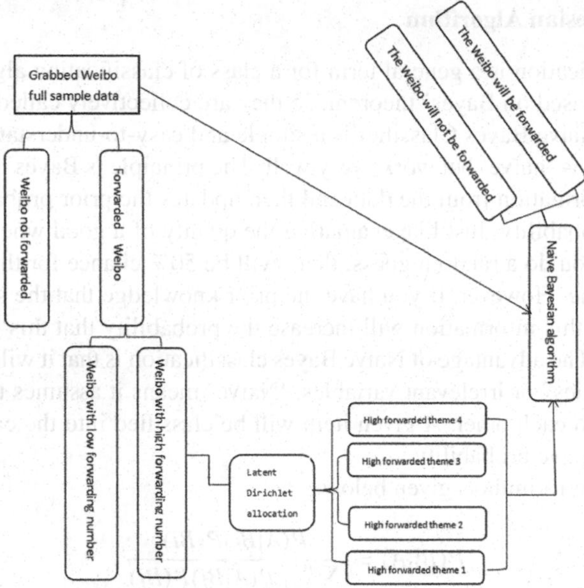

Fig. 2. Research method flow chart

The topics obtained in the second step are listed as the features for naive Bayesian algorithm, on which the training data are applied. In this step, we use the test data on the trained model to predict which microblogs will be reposted and which will not, waiting for the last step of verification.

In our last step, we write a verification script to check whether the predicted repost_num of the microblog is true by calculating the recall rate and the precision rate. Finally, 2 criteria are adopted to measure the prediction accuracy of our proposed algorithm.

4 The Experimental Process

4.1 Data Acquisition and Data Mining

Data Acquisition and Cleaning. First of all, we developed a crawler program based on the scrapy framework to capture the data needed for the experiment. Each official microblog account has a uniquely specified uid, so we can automatically complete the URL that will be crawled each time according to this rule. Use the URL query string to realize the automatic jumping from one page to another according to the URL rule. We chose to use cookies to keep each of the next sessions, and to bypass the anti-crawl mechanism by controlling the interval at which data was fetched. The crawler program adopts the principle of depth to climb down the historical records on each official microblog account in chronological order, and then inputs the microblog uid of thirteen fixed accounts into the queue program with loops to crawl the data. A total of 266,266 pieces of microblog information, 180,203 pieces of microblog comment data and related information such as the number of fans were obtained. For the storage of data, we use the non-relational mongodb database. Its light but abundant functions provide great help for the next step of text analysis. The crawled data is saved in the database in json format.

The first step of cleaning: use the json module in python to process the original data, converting the json format into a dictionary to operate further. We save the microblog data with the repost_num value greater than 1 to another file.

The second step of cleaning: through observation, we will study and analyze the content (microblog content) and repost_num (reposting number) in the acquired data. Here we first calculate the average number of reposting numbers in all the obtained microblog data. After calculating the full sample average, we empirically eliminate those samples with reposting number greater than the average but not less than the threshold, which is 1.5 times of the average number. On this basis, the first step of data processing is completed and a frequently-reposted microblog data sample is obtained. After calculation, the average sample size is 24, and the threshold is 36. Then, the statement is used to save the microblog data of repost_num not less than 36 to another file (Fig. 3).

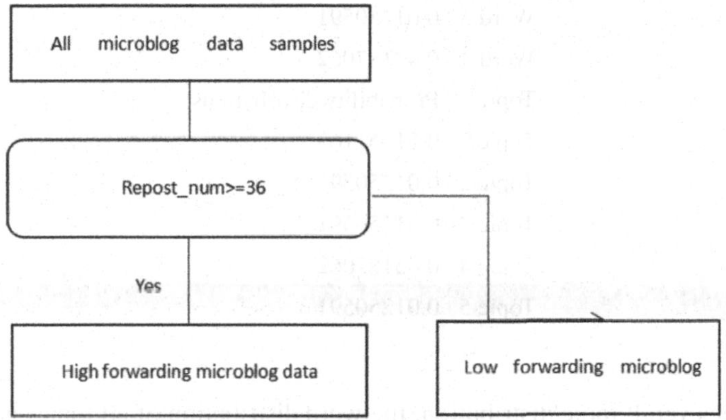

Fig. 3. Data cleaning diagram

4.2 Data Mining

In the LDA topic model processing procedure, the cleaned microblog text data is first processed by Jieba Chinese word segmentation to obtain the input corpus of the LDA model. At this point, the corpus should be cleaned again, and the special symbols (.[-9], -., ! ~ *) and the emojis that come with WeChat (such as [doge], [flowers], [microphones]) are removed. After reading the corpus data, the LDA model converts it into a dictionary, and calculates the text vector after counting the number of words. Then the document TF-IDF can be calculated to establish the LDA model and start our training procedure. After several times of trainings, the stop words are selected and included in the stop word library, and the model is imported to continue training. After the training process, we can identify the output theme and the keywords of each topic as needed. Since the microblog text is very short, it makes the topic classification more difficult and time-consuming to debug and find the right theme, the number of keywords, and the stop thesaurus. To achieve the balance between classification accuracy and interpretability closed to common-sense, we need to keep updating the parameters. The output of the LDA model is as follows:

In fact, we obtained the probability distribution of five topics in the experiment. Here is an example to illustrate the first topic probability distribution:

Top 5 topics in the 968th document (Table 1):

Table 1. Results of the experiment

Word	Word vector probability
Word 0	0.51061165
Word 1	0.01250591
Word 2	0.01250591
Word 3	0.01250591
Word 4	0.45187062
Topic	Probability distributions
Topic 1	0.51061165
Topic 2	0.01250591
Topic 3	0.01250591
Topic 4	0.45187062
Topic 5	0.01250591

From the overall topic distribution, the word distribution of all topics generated by the sample data is as follows (Table 2):

Table 2. Topics generated by the sample data

Topic	Word 1	Word 2	Word 3	Word 4	Word 5
Topic 1	High speed	Prevention	Means	Police	Internet
Topic 2	Remind	Prompt	Fraud	SMS	Mobile phone
Topic 3	Notice	Citywide	High temperature	Improve	Driver
Topic 4	College entrance examination	Candidate	Cheater	Remind	Receive
Topic 5	Peace	Police	Kids	110	Notice

After obtaining the frequently reposted theme through the LDA topic model, the features of the predicted category will be viewed as the input in the naive Bayesian algorithm of the next step. Here, the full sample data of the microblogs captured is divided into a training set and a test set according to a ratio of 6:4. We add an index "subject category +I" to each microblog in the algorithm (where i is a number, that is, an annotation). A microblog is the first item of this topic, and then based on the algorithm, we classify the microblog into the subject category it belongs to. More specifically, we carry out the training phase of machine learning algorithms based on the training set and then conduct the related tests on the test set to calculate whether the categories of these microblogs belong to the frequently reposted category. If they belong to that, they will be reposted, otherwise they will not be reposted. After all algorithm processing is performed, the output data is retained and left for verification.

The output data of Naive Bayes algorithm is presented as follows (Table 3):

Table 3. The output data of Naive Bayes algorithm

	Total	The number of microblog judged not to be forwarded	The number of microblog judged to be forwarded
Forward topic training set results	10000	90	9910
Forward topic test set results	4980	110	4870
Other topic training set results	10000	9960	40
Other topic test set results	4980	4930	50

The microblogs predicted to be reposted in the test set are extracted. Comparing with the truly reposted microblogs obtained by the first round of data cleaning, we can finally evaluate the accuracy of our proposed method using the criteria of the predicted and verified recall and precision.

5 Analysis of Verification Results

For the results obtained, we use precision and recall rate to measure the correctly predicted rate and accuracy of the above experimental model. The precision rate refers to the proportion of microblogs that are correctly predicted to be reposted among the items that are predicted positive. For example, the microblogs being reposted have an accuracy rate of $a/(a + c)$. The recall rate is the correctly predicted microblog among all relevant elements that are truly positive. The following results show that the model has a recall rate of 0.61 and a precision of 0.64.

It can be seen from the above table that the model has a high precision rate, and the microblog concerning safety warnings issued by the public security official microblog (pufa push, fraud prevention, security common sense push, etc.) tend to be easier to be reposted. It is reposted and shared by users, which is also a true reflection of the real life of the masses. The model can accurately predict those microblogs that are widely spread and more likely to cause sensation, which has a positive effect on guiding the public security departments to better build the microblog account of the police.

6 Summary

This paper first collects a large amount of online microblog data from microblog, simulating the real user environment on the Internet. Then through the data analysis with simple but efficient algorithm, it is found that the microblog text topic category is an important factor affecting its reposting rate. Based on this, we propose an experimental method to predict the reposting behavior of microblog. The method is based on the LDA model and adopts the Naïve Bayes algorithm for prediction. Experiments demonstrate that there are two themes related to popularity of the public security police microblog: social hotspot case notification and life safety. The final recall and precision of the model indicates the accurate prediction ability. Through the predictions of the model, the safety warning class (preventing fraud, etc.) is the most popular type of microblog that are frequently reposted by users. It can also be seen from the keywords of the displayed topic category that the users repost relevant contents most frequently before and after the college entrance examination.

It is the era of rapid development of the Internet, but this development is a double-edged sword. Once the technology is mastered by the outlaws, it is a tool for committing crime. Today, cybercrime intensifies, for example, telecom fraud is aggravated rapidly recently. The "Xu Yuyu" incident caused a sensation throughout the country, and the public opinion was unprecedented. The public's awareness of prevention cannot be built overnight. Public security organs should make good use of the favorable conditions for the development of new media policing, actively guide the masses to pay attention to their own property security issues, and inform the public about the relevant cases. We also hope that the new media of the public security microblog can make a good voice of public security, hold the "second battlefield" of public security work under the new era and new situation, make full use of data empowerment, be careful when releasing every microblog, and be considerate of everything the masses care about.

In order to achieve the full flexibility of the new media police platform, account operators should actively look for social hot issues. From the perspective of public security, they can edit the microblog daily with the help of some conclusion points in this paper. We should grasp the principle of timeliness of information, grasp the situation of malignant events in some regions where fans make replies and ask for help under the released microblog immediately, and effectively analyze the clues. We need to give this new media platform more interactivity and endow people more opportunities to express themselves, instead of simply instilling and transmitting rigid news to people.

Acknowledgement. Thanks to the teachers from the network security department of Jiangsu Police Institute for their guidance in the process of completing this article. This study is supported by Jiangsu Province University Students Practice Innovation and Entrepreneurship Training Program Project, Project Number: 201910329031Y, Project Name: Research on the influence of new media platform of Public Security Colleges under the background of big data. Many thanks to my classmates, they live and study with me, and help me a lot. At last, I will thank my parents, they are my best teacher, and I love them so much, nothing I can do without them.

Funding Statement. This study has been supported by Jiangsu Social Science Foundation Project (Grant No: 20TQC005). Philosophy Social Science Research Project Fund of Jiangsu University (Grant No: 2020SJA0500). The 13th Five-Year Plan Project of Educational Science in Jiangsu Province "Research on the reform and innovation of network public opinion teaching in public security colleges and universities from the perspective of overall national security" (Grant No: C-B/2020/01/27). Jiangsu Province modern education technology research project "Research on the innovation of public security network public opinion teaching mode based on modern information technology" (Grant No: 2017-R-59195). The key teaching reform project of Jiangsu Police Institute "Research on the reconstruction of online and offline hybrid" golden course "teaching system of Internet information" inspection course (Grant No: 2019A30).

Conflicts of Interest. The authors declare that they have no conflicts of interest to report regarding the present study.

References

1. Zhang, J., Yin, J., Hu, C.T.: Prediction of microblog forwarding based on active fan forwarding influence model. J. Jiangsu Police Officer Acad. **34**(1), 116–121 (2019)
2. Liu, W., He, M., Liu, Y., Shen, H.W., Cheng, X.Q.: Research on Weibo reposting prediction based on user behavior characteristics. J. Comput. **39**(10), 1992–2006 (2016)
3. Tian, L., Ren, G.H., Wang, W.: Prediction of Weibo user reposting behavior oriented to reading promotion. J. Inf. **36**(11), 1175–1182 (2017)
4. Deng, Q., Ma, Y.F., Liu, Y., Zhang, H.: Prediction of microblog forwarding based on BP neural network. J. Tsinghua Univ. (Sci. Technol.) **55**(12), 1342–1347 (2015)
5. Mu, S.K., Zhang, L.Q., Teng, C.F.: Prediction of microblog forwarding behavior based on recurrent neural network. Comput. Syst. **28**(8), 155–161 (2019)
6. Guan, P., Wang, Y.F., Fu, Z.: Analysis of the extraction of scientific literature subjects based on LDA topic model under different corpus. Libr. Inf. Serv. **60**(2), 112–121 (2016)
7. Zhao, H.D., Liu, G., Shi, C., Wu, B.: Prediction of microblog forwarding based on forward propagation process. Chin. J. Electron. **44**(12), 2989–2996 (2016)
8. Li, Y., Chen, Y.H., Liu, T.: A review of microblog information propagation prediction research. J. Softw. **27**(2), 247–263 (2016)
9. Hagen, L.: Content analysis of e-petitions with topic modeling: how to train and evaluate LDA models? Inf. Process. Manage. **54**(6), 1292–1307 (2018)

An Evaluation Method of Population Based on Geographic Raster and Logistic Regression

Yannan Qian[1,2], Yao Tang[3], and Jin Han[2](✉)

[1] Waterford Institute of Technology, Waterford X91 K0EK, Ireland
[2] Nanjing University of Information Science and Technology, Nanjing 210044, China
[3] Hunan Meteorological Disaster Prevention Technology Center, Hunan 410007, China

Abstract. Population estimation is of great significance for urban and rural planning, development policy-making, disaster early warning and loss assessment. However, current mainstream models are subject to administrative divisions and are difficult to conduct small-scale assessments, and closely rely on historical data. This paper introduces a new population estimation model that enables population assessment on geographic grids, which preprocesses the numbers of keywords crawled by the map keyword crawler and performs a weighted average calculation based on the proportion of the keyword data. Then, with the support of a small amount of data, this paper uses logistic regression fitting to assess the population of the specified area. Taking Hunan Province as an example, this paper evaluates the population of each county and city, and obtains good experimental results. The method described in this paper takes the number of keywords for evaluation and is not limited to specific administrative or natural divisions. It is more innovative compared to the current popular population evaluation methods.

Keywords: Population assessment · Keywords · Logistic regression · Hot crawler

1 Introduction

The variation of the population is closely connected to land usage, settlement form, economic status and social form. Therefore, making an evaluation of population at present time and predicting future population scientifically are conducive to the implementation of regional planning and policy formulation, and are also helpful for understanding scientificity, stability and continuity of the population policy of a country [1]. Since the regional population will also affect employment policy and market analysis of enterprises, population estimation will make a better contribution to the adjustment of business structure and the upgrade for the transformation of the economy [2]. Thus, population estimation is of great meaning no matter to the country, local government or enterprises.

Population estimation is commonly divided into population prediction, population forecasting and population projection. Population prediction depends on inherent law on developments of population, and population forecasting is a prediction of the change of population, based on some phenomena or events. Population projection is an extrapolation based on a certain assumption [3]. In terms of implementation methods, population

X. Sun et al. (Eds.): ICAIS 2021, LNCS 12736, pp. 676–688, 2021.
https://doi.org/10.1007/978-3-030-78609-0_57

projection and estimation can be divided into mathematical methods, statistical methods and demographical methods. The mathematical methods are usually adopted along with statistical methods and mainly divided into regression analysis, Grey theory, etc. Demographical methods are mainly based on the inner regularity of population development, and belong to population prediction, which requires more historical population data and horizontal data of other regions' population development.

Apart from this, there are approaches to make precise estimation such as censuses. However, censuses require much time and efforts, and the interval is too long to confirm the population distribution. So far, most population estimation methods are based on census using all the previous data to seek the regularity and make population prediction. This method, apart from the need for massive history data, divides by administrative division and is hard to divide by geographical features. For example, it is of large constraint to make population estimation by the range of natural disaster areas.

In this paper, a new model of population estimation is put forward without the need for historical data, using mathematical and statistical methods to make population estimation possible by geographical raster. Geographical rasters are divisions of geography area, which are usually made by longitude and latitude or distances. This paper takes Hunan Province as an example, the basic raster set as 1 km * 1 km, and makes statistics of the number of keywords among cities of Hunan Province, then makes logistic regression fitting of the statistics' weighted average and the population of training sample to estimate the population of each city. This method belongs to a population conducting method based on mathematics and statistics. It makes a promising result.

2 Related Works

In 1968, Keyfitz [4] put forward a basic mathematical method to solve population prediction problem. In 1982, vice professor Deng Julong put forward "Grey Theory", which can transform an unordered discrete sequence into an ordered one, and restore the original system's features better with a small number of data [5]. Jia Lingyun [6] applied this to the field of population prediction in 2006 and enormously decreased samples and history data needed for prediction. Mrios G et al. [7] conducted the population variation of Montreal in the future 20 years using logistic regression with the data of immigration and emigration.

The methods above are all based on the knowledge of history population data in a certain area to make predictions on future population. Under the circumstance of being unaware of history data, how to estimate population distribution is still a problem. Yue T X et al. [8] estimated population distribution on a small scale by surface modelling on population distribution. The result was relatively precise but required too much historical data. Vieira M R et al. [9] made population estimation based on the distribution data of the statistics of different base stations' phone call data, also got a considerable result. Based on this, Zhang Wenjuan [10] completed the estimation of the number of injury and death in an earthquake-affected area according to the variation of phone call data before and after the earthquake. Smart Mieka et al. [11] used an epidemiologic method to establish proportional samples, got a more accurate result in the cities with high vacancy and transient populations. Nevertheless, the methods above are all single cause analysis and do not consider the effect of multiple variations. Lin Wenqi et al. [12] made an overall estimation to the population distribution of Chao Yang district, Peking using geographical q-statics and Bayes-Gauss prediction model, with the records of taxi and several other data. This paper takes Hunan province as an example, extracts the distribution of 30 keywords in this province, and does a weighted average calculation on this, then uses logistic regression to make fitting analysis, makes it possible to estimate population with multiple causes, and gets a considerable result with only a few samples, without the need of the data of historical population distribution.

3 Evaluation Methods

The economic level between divisions, which is in the condition of the same or a similar magnitude, differs from each other because of their distinct industrial structure among divisions [13]. Concentration on service industry contributes to the development of economic. The increment of economic is influenced by Gross Trade Effect [14], so the divisions in rich areas are evaluated with more keywords per unit population which presents a nonlinear correspondence between population and counts of keywords. Therefore, logistic regression is used as the basic evaluation model in this paper.

The evaluation process is divided into the following steps: Data acquisition and processing, Logistic transformation, Regression analysis and parameter estimation, Population estimation, as are shown in the following Fig. 1:

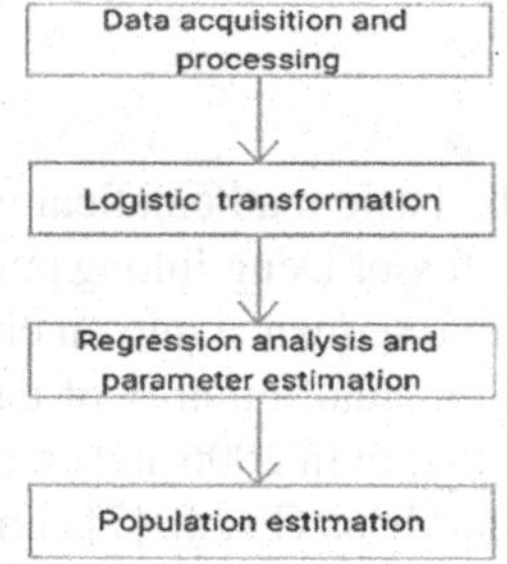

Fig. 1. Population estimation process

3.1 Data Acquisition and Processing

Firstly, this paper chooses a Geographic information system and then determines the sum of the regionalization range of the evaluation objects (Overall scope). In this system, nouns which represent the level of population or economics to some extent is called keywords, such as hotel, hospital, etc. And the result searched by one keyword in a certain extent of regionalization is called the number of the keyword.

Record k keywords in overall scope and the number of them is from m_1 to m_k. Then calculate the proportion of each number of these keywords in the total count as $p_1, p_2, \ldots$ p_k. The first, a small amount of one keyword may cause a large error by a few extreme values. The second, during the process of counting, this paper selects the same statistical method to get keywords, so the keyword which has a small amount may have some data recording errors that lead to low credibility.

And then, use each keyword's proportion as its weight, calculate:

$$m = \sum\nolimits_{i=1}^{k} p_i * m_i \quad (1)$$

In this equation, m_i represents the number of the ith keyword, p_i represents the proportion of the ith keyword.

3.2 Logistic Transformation

This paper considers that m as the average count of keywords in this area is related to this area's population in some way. And this paper supposes it is some specific function relation. The relation is consistent with Logistic regression:

$$y = \frac{K}{1 + ae^{-b(x-c)}} \quad (2)$$

In this equation, *K*, *a*, *b*, *c* are undetermined coefficients. The value of *K* means the limit could be reached by y in physics and usually can be concluded by observation. Select partial samples from the training set to determine the above parameters. For Eq. (2) deformation, get:

$$\ln\frac{K - y}{y} = -b * (x - c) + \ln a \quad (3)$$

Let

$$K' = -b,\ b' = \ln a, x' = x - c, y' = \ln\frac{K - y}{y} \quad (4)$$

Thus, (3) is transformed into

$$y' = k'x' + b' \quad (5)$$

Because $x' = x - c$ is linear, this paper selects the value of x to replace x' to get approximate values. And the error caused by this could be eliminated when this paper estimates the value of c afterwards.

3.3 Regression Analysis and Parameter Estimation

This paper selects the average number m of keywords from each data record in the training sets as x and selects population as y. This paper substitutes x, y into Eq. (5) and then uses the least square method to fit the parameter $k^{'}$ and $b^{'}$. The method is as follows:

Find certain acceptable values of $k^{'}$ and $b^{'}$ to make $\sum_{i=1}^{n}\left(y_i^{'}-y_{pi}^{'}\right)^2$ minimal. In this equation, n is the number of data records used for training and $y_{pi}^{'}$ is the ith value of population estimation.

Calculate partial derivative for $k^{'}$ and $b^{'}$ separately and make them equal to 0, get:

$$k^{'}=\frac{\sum_{i=1}^{n}\left(x_i^{'}-\overline{x^{'}}\right)\left(y_i^{'}-\overline{y^{'}}\right)}{\left(x_i^{'}-\overline{x^{'}}\right)^2} \tag{6}$$

$$b^{'}=\overline{y^{'}}-k^{'}\overline{x^{'}} \tag{7}$$

In this equation, $\overline{x^{'}}$ is the average number of $x^{'}$ and $\overline{y^{'}}$ is the average number of $y^{'}$. The mathematical meaning of $k^{'}$: The covariance between x and y divide by the variance of $x^{'}$.

Then, according to $k^{'}$, $b^{'}$ and Eq. (4), parameter a and b can be calculated. The analytic solution of c is hard to resolve. However, this paper can prove that the total error exists only one minimum value by adjusting the value of c and the minimum can be resolved by the computer. The proof is as follows:

Define total error as:

$$\sum_{i=1}^{n}\left|y_i-y_{pi}\right| \tag{8}$$

where y_i is the real population of the ith data, y_{pi} is its estimation value.

x_i is the average number of keywords in each group of data and has a one-to-one correspondence with y_i and y_{pi}. Draw point set (x_i, y_i) and fitting function $y(x)=\frac{K}{1+ae^{-b(x)}}$ in Plane Rectangular Coordinate System. The geometric meaning of Eq. (8) is the sum of vertical distances between point set (x_i, y_i) and $y(x)$. The geometric meaning of adjusting the value of c is left shift (negative values) or right shift (positive values). As is shown in the following Fig. 2:

Assume that $y(x)$ move Δx units along the positive direction of the x-axis, thus the distance from this point to $y(x+\Delta x)$ will change Δy. When Δx is infinite, $\Delta y/\Delta x$ is its derivative. The derivative of Logistic function increases at the first and then decreases and is always positive. This paper gets its maximum when $x = c$. So, to those points which are close to x_i, the changing value of c may cause a greater influence on the sum of vertical distances between point sets and $y(x)$. The logistic function is a monotone increasing function. During the change of c from $-\infty$ to $+\infty$, for any point (x_i, y_i), its vertical distance from $y(x)$ first gradually decreases from $+\infty$ to 0, and then gradually increases to $+\infty$. Since the point set (x_i, y_i) is given by the data set and has nothing to do with the value of c, the sum of the vertical distances between the point and the function must have a unique minimum value during the change of the value of c. That is, Eq. (6) has a unique minimum value.

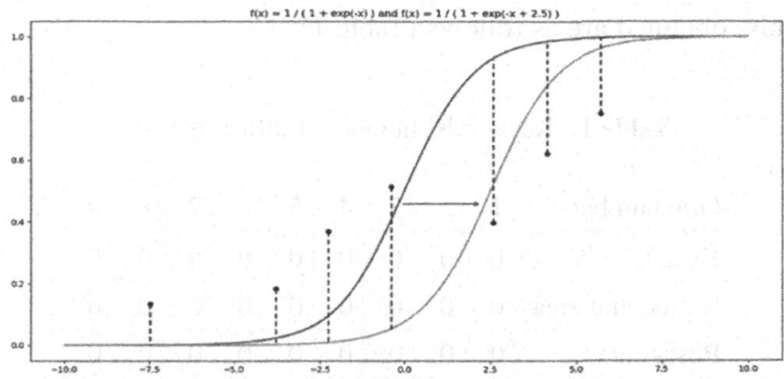

Fig. 2. The geometric meaning of *c*

According to the nature of the logistic function, the function increases monotonically and when $x = c$, $y(x) = K/2$. Since there are data with a population less than $K/2$ (e.g. 10000) in the data set, $c > 0$. Therefore, this paper sets the initial value of c as 0, substitutes the X value in each training data into Eq. (2) and records the obtained result y as y_p, which is the estimated value of the population. Compare the estimated population y_p of each region with its real value y and adjust the parameter c in Eq. (2) continuously in the positive direction at intervals of $K/100$ until the error is minimum to determine the c value. So far, all unknown parameters have been obtained.

3.4 Population Estimation

Substitute the obtained parameters k, a, b and c into Eq. (2) and substitute the average number m of keywords in each region as x, this paper can obtain the result y as y_p, which is the final estimation value of the population in this region.

4 Estimation Experiments

This paper adopts the above-mentioned population assessment method to carry out population assessment on counties and cities in Hunan Province. Firstly, according to the evaluation implementation process of this paper, a crawler program is developed, which uses the search interface of Baidu map keywords. This paper uses the crawler program and uses 1 km * 1 km as a single grid to search and query grid by grid.

In this paper, the keyword query statistics use a total of 30 keywords, respectively: Hospital, residential area, restaurant, university, school, shopping mall, Dining hall, express delivery, business hall, KTV, parking lot, ancestral hall, canteen, village, pond, hamlet, mountain, company, supermarket, Internet cafe, Internet bar, bus stop, police station, vegetable market, hotel, park, gas station, forest farm, public house, and tire repair.

Partial results obtained are as follows (Table 1):

Table 1. Keywords' number of different grids

Grid number	1	2	3	4	5	6	7	8	9
Hospital	0	0	0	0	0	0	0	0	0
Residential area	0	0	0	0	0	0	0	0	0
Restaurant	0	0	0	0	0	0	0	0	0
University	0	0	0	0	0	0	0	0	0
School	0	1	0	0	0	0	0	0	0
Shopping mall	0	0	0	0	0	0	0	0	0
Dining hall	0	0	0	0	0	0	0	0	0
Express delivery	0	0	0	0	0	0	0	0	0
Business hall	0	0	0	0	0	0	0	0	0
…	…	…	…	…	…	…	…	…	…

Add and count the obtained data according to the division scope. The divisions used in this experiment are county-level administrative divisions. Divide all grids into counties and add them up for statistics. Partial results are as follows (Table 2):

Table 2. Keywords' number of different counties

County	Anxiang	Dingcheng	Hanshou	Jinshi	Fengxian	Linfeng	Shimen
Hospital	21	126	38	13	60	21	30
Residential area	495	1511	424	219	1044	297	444
Restaurant	50	829	54	57	165	18	73
University	2	11	34	1	2	0	2
School	113	518	158	63	227	120	132
Shopping mall	2	19	26	0	8	3	3
Dining hall	495	1506	420	218	1036	297	443
Express delivery	24	133	94	17	80	30	36
Business hall	101	336	141	51	186	66	106
…	…	…	…	…	…	…	…

Preprocess the crawling data and analyze the partial differences and correlations among keywords. Ten representative keywords are finally selected as evaluation keywords: school, restaurant, parking lot, village, pond, village, mountain, company, supermarket and hotel.

Then take the population of each county and city in Hunan Province obtained from the yearbook of Hunan Province and the number of keywords in each county as a sample set. 30% of the data are randomly taken from the sample set as the training set and used to calculate each parameter in formula (2).

In the training set, the maximum population is 1.37 million people, and most of them are distributed around one million people. This paper considers that the population limit is close to 1.5 million people, so this paper makes $K = 150$. By least square fitting, this paper gets $k' = -0.001024$, $b' = 1.557287$. Thus $b = 0.001024$, $a = 4.745928$. Adjust $c = 175$. Substitute the keywords in each county to make an evaluation. The self-error in the training set is 25.14% and the remaining 70% data is taken as the test set, with an error of 39.87%. During the experiment, it is found that among the 10 keywords, more than two keywords are counting as zero in some districts or counties. So, the experimenter suggests that the keywords in this area are not collected accurately. According to the analysis of data sources, most of the districts or counties in the above situation have a population of less than 300,000 and are mostly located in mountainous areas. 87.5% of areas like that have this condition, while only 6.06% of districts or counties with a population of more than 300,000 have this condition. Therefore, in the subsequent comparison, the average error will be listed separately for comparison after excluding districts or counties with a real population of less than 300,000, to reduce the negative impact of the statistical error on the model. In this experiment, the error is 19.43% after removing those districts or counties with conditions above. If the assessment is carried out by municipal divisions, the error will be 15.06% (Fig. 3).

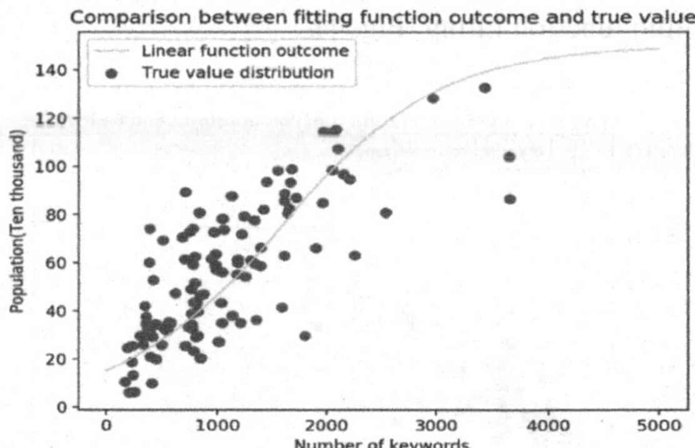

Fig. 3. Comparison between real values and fitting logistic function (Color figure online)

In the figure, the red curve is a curve-fitting logistic function and the blue point set is a real data point set. In order to eliminate the contingency of the experimental results, the training set was randomly selected again and several experiments were conducted. The results are as follows (Table 3):

Obviously that the average error of this method is about 37.47% and the error is 24.35% after removing the counties whose real population value is less than 300,000. This method has good accuracy for areas with the population not too small. At the same

Table 3. Logistic regression experiments and average errors

Experiment number	Average error (county)	Average error after removing counties with the real population less than 300,000 (county)	Average error (city)
1	39.87%	19.43%	15.06%
2	37.46%	25.18%	16.94%
3	35.19%	26.71%	18.06%
4	35.17%	27.92%	20.70%
5	39.67%	22.49%	15.18%

time, the average error of the city is about 17.19%, which shows that the method has better accuracy in a wider range.

5 Comparative Analysis and Discussion

Since all the relevant population estimation methods use historical population data and cannot change the zoning scope at will, it is not convenient to use them to compare with the method in this paper directly. As a result, the following will be compared with the other two commonly used fitting methods in the field of population estimation, linear fitting and logarithmic function fitting (Fig. 4).

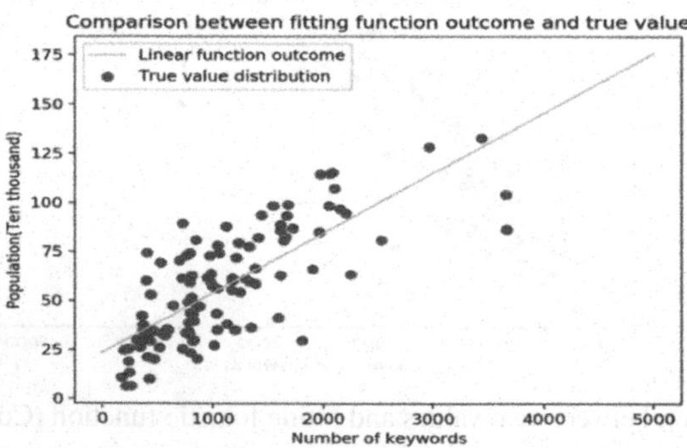

Fig. 4. Linear fitting function compared with real data (Color figure online)

In the figure, the red curve is a linear fitting function curve and the blue point set is a real data point set (Fig. 5).

In the figure, the red curve is a logarithmic fitting function curve and the blue point set is a real data point set.

Conduct five experiments respectively in the same way. The results are as follows (Tables 4, 5 and 6):

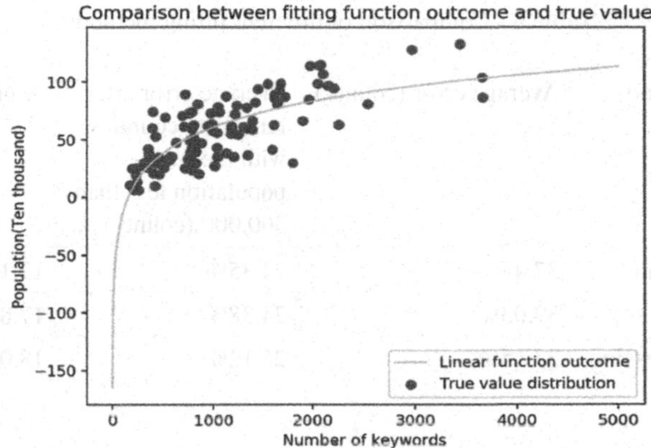

Fig. 5. Logarithmic fitting function compared with real data (Color figure online)

Table 4. Linear fitting result

Experiment number	Average error (county)	Average error after removing counties with the real population less than 300,000 (county)	Average error (city)
1	37.67%	22.01%	16.57%
2	43.38%	24.83%	19.93%
3	43.08%	24.72%	19.91%
4	34.00%	29.29%	15.81%
5	37.04%	21.06%	17.01%

Table 5. Logarithmic fitting result

Experiment number	Average error (county)	Average error after removing counties with the real population less than 300,000 (county)	Average error (city)
1	37.58%	25.52%	19.21%
2	38.81%	26.11%	18.30%
3	34.87%	23.72%	16.89%
4	39.04%	25.98%	19.40%
5	35.46%	24.26%	16.56%

Table 6. Comparison of different fitting methods

Experiment methods	Average error (county)	Average error after removing counties with the real population less than 300,000 (county)	Average error (city)
Logistic regression	37.47%	24.35%	17.19%
Linear regression	39.03%	24.38%	17.85%
Logarithmic regression	37.15%	25.12%	18.07%

This shows the advantage of logistic regression compared with linear regression in terms of average error after removing counties with the real population less than 300,000 (county).

In the following experiments, 10% of the samples are taken as the training sets (only 11 data at this time). This paper uses logistic regression fitting to conduct five experiments. The results are as follows (Table 7):

Table 7. Experiments with 10% sample

Experiment number	Average error (county)	Average error after removing counties with the real population less than 300,000 (county)	Average error (city)
1	31.65%	30.03%	14.15%
2	36.36%	26.97%	18.69%
3	39.81%	38.67%	33.27%
4	35.43%	25.07%	16.70%
5	33.50%	28.30%	19.39%

The average error (county) is about 35.35%. The average error is about 29.81% after removing counties with the real population less than 300,000. The average error (city) is about 20.44%. It is concluded that this method is of great accuracy with few training samples and on the other hand reflected that the model is accurate.

The conclusions are based on the fact that each division conducting population estimation has similar macro-scale. On this basis, due to the non-linear growth of keywords caused by different economic structures, logistic regression is a more effective evaluation method.

However, for cross-scale comparisons (e.g., mixed assessments among provinces, cities and counties), the impact of regional-scale size is stronger at this time. Because large-scale division is formed by merging several small-scale plans. In order to evaluate this, it should meet the following requirements:

$$g(A + B) = g(A) + g(B) \tag{9}$$

In this equation, *g(x)* is the estimation method, *A*, *B* are the numbers of keywords of two small-scale divisions.

This equation that requires that g(x) should be a linear function. Therefore, the linear model is more accurate under this condition.

As a result, it is more accurate to use logistic regression to make population estimation among divisions with similar macro-scales. When it comes to population estimation among divisions with large scale differences, linear regression is more accurate.

6 Conclusion

In the current mainstream population assessment methods, only administrative divisions can be used as separate assessments, and they are usually only effective for one specific division, lacking universality and the considerations for the impact of population migration. The method proposed in this paper can extract keywords in different self-defined divisions for evaluation, including cross-administrative divisions and natural-area divisions. This method only requires a small number of training samples to have good accuracy. Under the model based on mathematical derivation, the method has good interpretability and extensibility, indicating that the method is a population evaluation method of some practical value. In subsequent research, more efforts will be taken on how to collect higher quality keywords and take more reliable data preprocessing methods to improve the accuracy of the model.

In addition, this model makes it possible to evaluate the correspondence between the population and some specific keywords like infrastructures in different divisions, so as to conduct further research in the field of social resource allocation.

References

1. Liang, L., Zeng, J., Liu, B.: Future population trend prediction and policy suggestions in Xiongan new area. Contemp. Econ. Manage. (41), 59–67 (2019)
2. Du, W.: Floating population, sex ratio imbalance and industry development. Northwest Popul. J. (40), 25–37 (2019)
3. Woods, R.: Population Analysis in Geography, 1st edn, pp. 226–248. Longman, London (1979)
4. Keyfitz, N.: Introduction to the Mathematics of Population: with Revisions. Addison-Wesley Series in Behavioral Science: Quantitative Methods (1977)
5. Mi, R., Yang, X., Feng, F.: Population distribution projection in urban development zones and its planning value: taking Xi'an high-tech zone as an example. J. Northwest Univ. (Nat. Sci. Ed.) (49), 801–807 (2019)
6. Jia, L.: The increased grey model and its applications on population prediction. Ph.D. dissertation, Nanjing University of Information Science and Technology (2006)

7. Marios, G., Belanger, A.: Analyzing the impact of urban planning on population distribution in the montreal metropolitan area using a small-area microsimulation prediction model. Popul. Environ. **37**, 131–156 (2015)
8. Yue, T.X., Wang, Y.A., Chen, S.P., et al.: Numerical simulation of population distribution in China. Popul. Environ. (25), 141–163 (2003)
9. Vieira, M.R., Inez, V.F.I., Oliver, N., et al.: Characterizing dense urban areas from mobile phone-call data: discovery and social dynamics. In: Second International Conference on Social Computing 2010, Minneapolis, pp. 241–248. IEEE (2010)
10. Zhang, W.: Design of the population casualty acquisition and evaluation system in earthquake disaster areas based on mobile communication big data. China Earthq. Eng. J. (41), 1066–1071, 1097 (2019)
11. Mieka, S., Richard, S., Alan, H., Zachary, B., Amber, P., Furr-Holden, C.D.: The population randomization observation process (PROP) assessment method: using systematic habitation observations of street segments to establish household-level epidemiologic population samples. Int. J. Health Geogr. (18), article no. 24 (2019)
12. Lin, W., Chen, H., Xie, P., Li, Y., Chen, Q., Li, D.: Spatial-temporal variation evaluation and prediction of population in Chaoyang District of Beijing based on multisource data. J. Geo-inf. Sci. (20), 1467–1477 (2018)
13. Ren, B., He, M.: An analysis of spatial-temporal evolution of China's economic gap and its influencing mechanism. J. Xi'an Jiaotong Univ. (Soc. Sci.) (39), 47–57 (2019)
14. Wang, S., Wu, C.: Agglomeration of producer services and urban economic growth—based on the empirical analysis of 35 large and medium-sized cities. J. Tech. Econ. Manag. (12), 125–130 (2019)

Image Compression Algorithm Based on Time Series

Jie Chen[1], Zhanman Deng[2], Yue Wang[1], Xinglu Cheng[1], Yingshuang Ye[1], Xingyu Zhang[1], and Jin Han[1](✉)

[1] Nanjing University of Information Science and Technology, Nanjing 210044, China
[2] Hunan Meteorological Disaster Prevention Technology Center, Hunan 410007, China

Abstract. 21st century is a digital information age, different high technologies emerge in succession. Internet technology develops rapidly and is widely used in various industries and fields now. The popularity of 5G mobile communication technology, interactive multimedia, and remote sensing technology results in massive growth of image data. In recent years, image acquisition equipment has been widely used in production and life and the acquisition resolution has got continuous improvement as well. But how to store and transmit large numbers of image data has become big issues to production and life. How to efficiently compress, store and transmit images without destroying original information to be transmitted by the images is currently a major focus in the field of computer vision. The thesis mainly studies the methods of compressing images in time series. Firstly several basic image compression methods are introduced in details. Secondly traditional JEPG static image compression algorithm is fully analyzed. Thirdly time series are added on static image compression algorithm and groups of highly similar pictures are compressed in time series with video formats to eliminate redundant time for better efficiency optimization. Verifying through experiments and comparing with traditional compression algorithm, we get a conclusion that compressing images in time series can improve compression efficiency a lot.

Keywords: Image compression · JPEG · Time series · Eliminate redundancy · Video

1 Image Compression Algorithm Based on Time Series

With the new wireless communication era coming, people's demand for communication applications has changed from traditional data such as voices and texts to new multimedia applications such as images and videos in recent ten years. Images and videos contain a lot of information which cannot be replaced by words and languages and they gradually become indispensable modes for transmitting and receiving information in the daily life. And video applications such as mobile multimedia communication equipment, network streaming media and high-definition video surveillance are widely used, which leads to explosive growth of image information. Therefore, how to store image data efficiently becomes a hot issue in research [1]. How to compress the images efficiently and restore the images without distortion as much as possible has become the key issue of research excluding hard-ware factors.

X. Sun et al. (Eds.): ICAIS 2021, LNCS 12736, pp. 689–700, 2021.
https://doi.org/10.1007/978-3-030-78609-0_58

1.1 Development and Present Situation of Image Compression Algorithms

The research of image compression algorithm was originated from the classical data compression theory, which took the classical set theory as basis and described the information source with the model of statistical probability. The first stage of image compression algorithm began in the 1940s. Shannon, the founder of information theory, further put forward, deduced and expressed the information entropy by mathematical formula, making Shannon coding become a compression algorithm. The second stage began in 1990s when the defects and deficiencies of Huffman coding were gradually discovered by scientists and the efficiency of Huffman coding alone was not enough to meet the demand. Thus arithmetic coding came into being, which was closer to the entropy limit. The third stage which began in 1990s has made rapid progress in the field of image processing [2]. Wavelet transform, which has excellent decorrelation and high resolution, is one of the most popular research directions at present. And EZW algorithm has become one of the indispensable algorithms in practice because it's simple and could support multi-rate decoding.

At the same time, several video compression standards were worked out. MJPEG and H. 263 standards were first formulated in video compression. MJPEG was a standard for dynamic video compression. JPEG compression algorithm was dynamically called in video to compress video signal [3, 4], which was about 25–30 frames per second. Each picture was independent and had no connection with adjacent frames. Although the compressed picture quality was clear, it needed a lot of bandwidth and the compression ratio was not high. H. 263 standard was designed for moving images, which based on the predictive coding mentioned in the previous chapter. It used three different ways to store information in frames. There were three types of coded frames: I, B and P. In the P frame and B frame, the motion vectors obtained by motion estimation were entropy coded with reference to the coding table, and the final coding was stored in the frame. H. 263 picture clarity and color were not as good as MJPEG, but it had higher compression ratio, and its occupied bandwidth is determined by the amount of motion of each macro block in the moving image, which greatly fluctuated.

In 1990s, three compression standard formats, MPEG-1, MPEG-2 and MPEG-4, were born in succession [5]. When MPEG-1 transmitted moving video images, it could also transmit corresponding matched audios and the quality standards were mostly oriented to family rather than production requirements; MPEG-2 had higher image quality and better transmission rate, which was a standard for advanced industry. However, images quality was not significantly improved though there was a great leap in audio properties. MPEG-4 was the most widely used international standard, which combined the advantages of the former two. It had high compression efficiency and quality but didn't require high transmission rate. MPEG-4 tried to realize interactive AV service [6], which made the video interactive. Its occupied bandwidth could be manually controlled, which was proportional to the image definition, so it gained wide applicability [7].

1.2 The Purpose and Significance of the Research

The compression algorithm designed in this paper is mainly used in fixed image acquisition equipment, such as surveillance cameras, for the storage of captured images in actual production and life. Because generated pictures don't have obvious difference and contain redundant information, we consider to compress them based on time series. The coding idea of video compression coding is based on predictive coding. From the perspective of frame, it can be divided again by intra-frame and inter-frame. In inter-prediction coding, because the images of adjacent frames are usually highly similar, the moving images can be divided into several macroblocks and the position of each corresponding macroblock in the next frame can be found out [8]. The core idea of image video compression algorithm is to remove redundancy. Images in adjacent positions in time series are often extremely similar in content and have temporal redundancy.

2 Implementation of Image Compression Algorithm Based on Time Series

2.1 Experimental Framework and Flow Chart

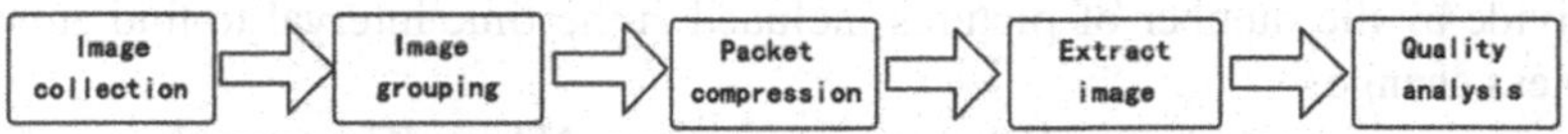

Fig. 1. Experimental framework

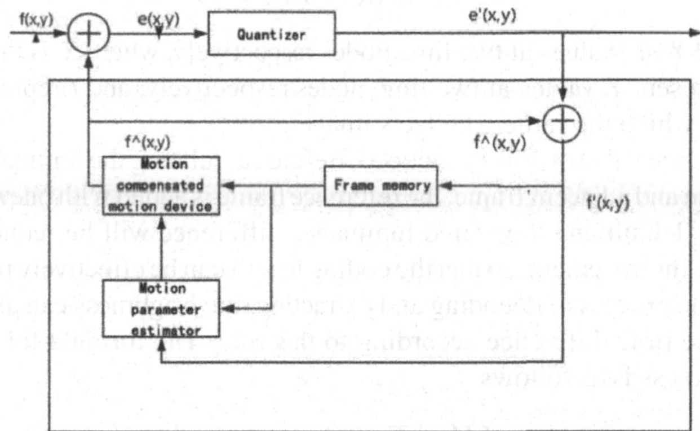

Fig. 2. P frame motion compensation flow chart

This experiment is mainly divided into five parts as shown in Fig. 1. Among the three frames used in this experiment, P frames account for the vast majority, while the flow of B frames is similar to P frames [9], so the flowchart of P frames motion compensation is given here, as shown in Fig. 2.

2.2 Algorithm Improvement Measures

Improvement of Compression Efficiency. The color space used in JPEG compression algorithm is not RGB but YUV color space. Y represents the brightness of the image, U and V represent the chroma and saturation of the images respectively. The conversion relationship between brightness Y and RGB color space is:

$$Y = 0.299R + 0.587G + 0.114B$$

All the images in this study are based on time series, and they are all fixed-point images. The same object between adjacent images is almost always still. However, the factor of light constantly changes in 24 h a day, so we can improve the compression process according to this natural law.

First of all, according to the change of seasons, we can design two nodes for the images collected every day and set two partitions for the storage space, one for the day and the other for the night. Take the equal time of day and night in the vernal equinox as an example and take the darkest time point and the highest brightness time point every day as nodes. For example, 4:00 and 16:00 every day are set as two time nodes. Pictures before 16:00 after 4:00 are stored in the day area of the storage space, and those after 16:00 and before 4:00 the next day are stored in the night area of the storage space. You can intercept the Y value at two time nodes, make a difference between them, and then divide by the number of pictures included in the time interval to find an average brightness change.

We can write down the predicted average value as N here. The formula is as follows:

$$N = \frac{a - b}{(X - Y)/t} \tag{1}$$

In which X and Y are values at two time nodes respectively, where X is the node behind Y. a and b represent Y values at two time nodes respectively, and t represents the time interval during which the camera collects images.

At this time, the value of N is introduced. Before calculating the luminance difference between P frame and adjacent frame, the reference frame is added with one n or subtracted with one N by default and the stored luminance difference will be reduced compared with that before improvement, so that the coding length can be effectively reduced. At the same time, in the process of decoding and extracting, the brightness can also be restored according to the time difference according to this rule. The formula for decoding and restoring brightness is as follows:

$$C = \left(\frac{M - T}{t} - 1\right) * N + D + Y \tag{2}$$

In above formula, C is the brightness value of the picture obtained after decoding. M is the current time, t is the nearest time node in the time series, and the difference between the two is the time difference from the time node to the present. T is the time interval for collecting images, N is the predicted average value obtained in Eq. (1), D is the initial brightness value, and Y is the brightness difference between the current P frame and the adjacent frame.

Improvement of Decoding Image Restoration Quality. In the process of extracting image frames from video to restore images, the image quality will have some loss more or less due to the influence of discrete cosine transform and quantization in JPEG image compression algorithm [10]. In this paper, an idea is proposed to improve the quality of decoded pictures as much as possible without changing the compression efficiency.

An inverse quantization process can be added to the restoration process. In the process of quantization, floating-point numbers are converted into binary numbers or integers and stored in the quantization table, and the number of bits occupied by pixels is saved by removing the decimal part after floating-point numbers. Therefore, we can introduce inverse quantization technology at the decoding end (Fig. 3).

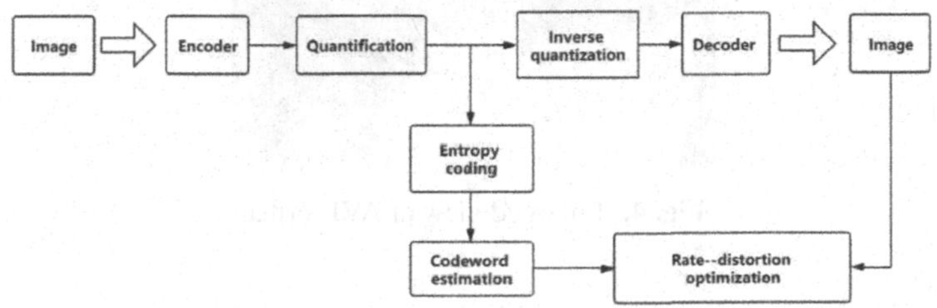

Fig. 3. Flow chart of optimization assumption

Before decoding by decoder, inverse quantization technology is used to restore the transformed feature data to floating-point numbers.

2.3 Comparison of Compression Test Results

Image compression based on time series has certain performance differences in different image formats and different compression coding methods [11]. This section mainly uses test pictures to test the performance of compression algorithms and tests the influence of different factors on compression efficiency by controlling variables. The experimental data came from three different cameras, which collected 182, 216 and 41 pictures respectively, totaling 439 pictures.

Efficiency Comparison of Different Video Coding Methods. The video formats tested in this paper are avi and mp4. The advantages and disadvantages of the two different coding methods are obtained by comparing the compression time and the size of the compressed video files (Table 1).

Table 1. Comparative experimental data of MP4 and AVI

	Picture file size	AVI compression time	AVI compression size	MP4 compression time	MP4 compressed size
Experiment 1	42.1 MB	4.496 s	15.30 MB	3.845 s	3.29 MB
Experiment 2	247 MB	33.533 s	136 MB	30.283 s	104 MB

We compare the compression quality mainly color clarity. And we change a set of test data and use the real pictures taken by the camera to test, so that we can get a more intuitive feeling by enlarging the local area. Let's look at a set of contrast pictures of two video clips with the same format. Compare the two pictures in partial enlargement.

Fig. 4. Enlarged view of AVI format

Fig. 5. Enlarged view of MP4 format

The above Fig. 4 and Fig. 5 are enlarged pictures in AVI and MP4 formats, and it's apparent that the definition of AVI format is better than that of MP4 format files. To sum up, the compression efficiency of MP4 format is better than that of AVI format, and the compression quality of AVI format is better than MP4 format. Both compression coding methods have their own advantages and disadvantages. In this paper, we mainly focus on the compression algorithm of data collected by cameras in time series. Because it only needs high-efficiency storage, and does not need high-quality video playback quality, it does not need to play, so it is more appropriate to adopt the video coding method of .mp4 format here.

Comparison Between Time Series Compression and Traditional JPEG Compression. In this paper, we will compare the performance of JPEG compression algorithm and compression algorithm based on time series, and compare the compression ratio of the two algorithms. In this comparative experiment, three groups of pictures were fixed-point shot by three groups of cameras. The content, size and total number of pictures in each group were different, and the original format was .png. The experi-mental results are as follows (Table 2):

Table 2. Data comparison between JPEG traditional algorithm and time series compression algorithm

	Original file size	JPEG compression size	Compression size based on time series
Experiment 1	1.8 GB	247 MB	103 MB
Experiment 2	916 MB	158 MB	50.4 MB
Experiment 3	255 MB	39.3 MB	19.6 MB

The experimental results show that the image compression algorithm based on time series can save a lot of production cost and storage management efficiency compared with JPEG loss compression alone.

Comparison Between the Compression Algorithm Improved by Brightness Compensation and the Original Algorithm. Based on video compression, this paper proposes an improved method according to the characteristics of this research object. On the basis of motion compensation, the improvement idea of this improved mode is to further reduce the difference coding length stored in B frame and P frame, and reduce the image difference between adjacent frames.

In this experiment, three groups of different test pictures collected and provided by State Grid cameras in three time series were used, and all the test pictures had undergone JPEG compression once.

Table 3. Data comparison between the improved brightness compensation compression algorithm and the original algorithm

	Original file size	Compression size of original algorithm	Compress size after brightness compensation
Experiment 1	247 MB	103 MB	86.6 MB
Experiment 2	158 MB	50.4 MB	43.3 MB
Experiment 3	39.3 MB	19.6 MB	17.2 MB

It can be seen from the experimental data in Table 3 that after brightness compensation, the length of compression code is reduced, the compression efficiency is significantly improved, and the performance of the original image compression based on time series is improved by about 15%.

3 Analysis and Evaluation of Algorithm Results

3.1 Performance Analysis of Image Compression Algorithm Based on Time Series

In order to study the effect of compression coding, the experimental objects in this chapter are the pictures before and after compression, and the pictures extracted by decoding. A set of 3840 * 2160 jpg format is used to test the pictures, and the compression ratio, compression time, decoding and extracting time and decoding picture quality are analyzed. The experimental platform is Intel Core (2.30 GHz CPU/8.00G memory) PC running Window 10 home Chinese version, and the program is written by Eclipse 2017.

Compression Ratio Analysis. Because this experiment is based on JPEG compression, the compression ratio of secondary compression is not as high as that of primary compression. According to the above calculation method, it can be calculated that the compression ratio of secondary compression is about 2.5, while the compression ratio of JPEG compression for other formats is generally about 10. Therefore, it can be concluded that the image compression algorithm based on time series can achieve a compression ratio of 25:1 for uncompressed pictures, and can save 2/3 of the actual storage space for loss compressed pictures again.

Compression Time and Compression Efficiency. Compression time is directly related to the efficiency of image data processing by compression coding. Generally speaking, compression time may be proportional to the amount of data in the image. Three groups of experiments were conducted here and the data were recorded in Table 4.

Table 4. Comparison of compression time with experimental data

	Number of pictures	Picture takes up space	Compression time
Experiment 1	182 pcs	158 MB	20.687 s
Experiment 2	216 pcs	247 MB	31.848 s
Experiment 3	41 pcs	39.3 MB	4.941 s

From the experimental data in Table 4, with the increase of the number of pictures and the occupied space of pictures, the compression time will increase, but whether the compression time is only related to the amount of image data still needs further calculation.

Firstly, we assume that there is only a correlation between compression time and data volume, and then calculate the average data volume processed per unit time in three groups of experiments in turn. Results: The results of data processing vary greatly. Obviously, the compression time is not only related to the data volume of pictures, but also affected by other factors. Then, we continue to calculate whether there is a fixed proportional relationship between compression time and image space. The experimental results of the three groups are almost similar and fluctuate slightly, which shows that the compression time tends to be proportional to the occupied space of pictures.

Because the MEMC (Motion Estimation and Motion Compensation) of the im-age is calculated in the process, the efficiency of the algorithm is not only affected by the amount of data, but also related to the file size, color mode and other factors. Generally speaking, the compression efficiency can process six to seven pictures per second. For image acquisition equipment with low acquisition frequency, this algorithm can save storage space greatly.

Decoding Time and Decoding Efficiency. In the previous group of experiments, three groups of picture data have been compressed into three groups of video files. To analyze the time of decoding and extracting pictures. Here, three decoding experiments of frames in different positions are carried out for three groups of experimental videos.

Table 5. Decoding time compared with experimental data

	Frame 1		Frame 2		Frame 3	
	Picture size	Decoding time	Picture size	Decoding time	Picture size	Decoding time
Experiment 1	296 KB	0.139 s	684 KB	0.143 s	1.32 MB	0.152 s
Experiment 2	596 KB	0.152 s	1.32 MB	0.165 s	1.28 MB	0.153 s
Experiment 3	704 KB	0.155 s	1.32 MB	0.155 s	1.18 MB	0.161 s

First, observe the data in Table 5 according to the row order. From the 20th frame experiment and 30th frame experiment of the third row data, it can be seen that although the picture size of the former is larger than that of the latter, the decodable time is shorter than that of the latter. Therefore, it can be concluded that the size of decoded pictures is not the decisive factor affecting the decoding time. To sum up, the decoding time is mainly affected by the number of extracted picture frames, and the later the picture frames are, the longer the extraction time will be. Judging from the growth rate, even if it is a video with 1,000 pictures or 1,000 frames, it should only take about 0.5 s to extract the last frame. In production practice, the working frequency of decoding is far less than that of compression coding. It may take hundreds of times of compression coding to use one decoding process, and decoding is not the main purpose, so the decoding efficiency can fully meet the demand.

Decoded Picture Quality. The above three points have analyzed the performance and results of the algorithm. In order to show the decoded picture effect more intuitively, the original Fig. 6 and the decompressed and restored Fig. 7 are directly compared together.

The decoded image quality is compared by overall comparison and local enlargement. The overall comparison shows that they are almost completely similar. After local enlargement, it is found that the decoded image color contrast is slightly worse than the original image.

Fig. 6. Original image

Fig. 7. Coded picture

3.2 Algorithm Evaluation

Image compression algorithm based on time series is suitable for correlation prediction and sorting on two-dimensional sequences at different scales, and can eliminate the correlation between pixels from two sequences in time and space. The specific advantages of this algorithm are mainly reflected in several aspects:

This algorithm is based on the traditional still image compression algorithm [12]. We can only calculate the time series, thus simplifying the coding process and further improving the coding efficiency.

After the image is compressed by this algorithm, it still retains the original time series, which provides indexing convenience for finding the designated decoding position, so the encoding and decoding process can be controlled according to actual needs.

The compressed file is in video format, so it is more convenient to observe the information of several pictures in the compressed file.

This algorithm belongs to lossless compression algorithm, which can meet our requirements for image restoration quality.

At the same time, in the actual compression coding process, the algorithm still has the following shortcomings:

First of all, the algorithm is applicable to pictures with a large number of similar pixels in time series, and the performance efficiency of the algorithm is directly related to the relevance of pixels at the same position in time series.

Secondly, the compression time of the image shows that the algorithm is not suitable for real-time compression or image acquisition equipment with too high acquisition frequency. Because if the generation speed of new pictures is higher than the re-encoding speed of pictures by the algorithm, some new files may be compressed too late and stored in the space in the original state, and the compression efficiency will be greatly affected.

If we want to improve the above shortcomings, we can store the image file by partition and block, and encode it in parallel with multiple compression programs. Picture format with higher compression ratio can be adopted, which can improve the speed of processing pictures by compression algorithm.

4 Summary

Most of the information people get from the outside world comes from vision, and the research on image analysis and video processing is the key research direction in the research field. The increase of image data means that more and more space is needed for the storage of digital images, and higher and higher bandwidth is needed for the transmission of image information. In recent years, the growth rate of image data is much higher than the development speed of storage hardware equipment and Internet transmission technology. It is obviously unrealistic to only increase hardware storage equipment and bandwidth. Therefore, we should start with the image itself and try our best to remove the redundant information of the image on the premise of ensuring that the image distortion is as small as possible, thus reducing the storage cost and consumption of storage and bandwidth.

Summarize the full text, mainly complete the following work:

Firstly, the background of image compression algorithm and the current demand for image compression algorithm are expounded and analyzed. Then, the development history and research status of image compression algorithm and several video compression coding standards are introduced.

In the module of explaining compression principle, the concept of redundancy is introduced, and the compression algorithm is designed around eliminating redundancy. Firstly, the basic principle of video coding is associated with the combination of motion compensation technology and prediction algorithm, so that the occupied space of compressed results is significantly reduced.

A comparative experiment was carried out to verify the feasibility of the pro-posed algorithm, find out the advantages and disadvantages of the algorithm, and adjust and improve it. Finally, the adopted video coding method was determined, and its coding and decoding efficiency was calculated. Combined with the practical application environment, the application method of the algorithm was put forward.

References

1. Wang, X.: A summary of research on image compression coding algorithms. J. Yantai Normal Univ. (Nat. Sci. Ed.) **17**(4), 288–295 (2001)
2. Chen, H., Wang, G., Yu, Y., et al.: Image compression algorithm based on DCT coefficient wavelet recombination. In: 12th National Annual Conference on Signal Processing (2005)
3. Zhang, Y., Liu, Y.: Research on still image compression algorithm based on JPEG standard. Electron. Des. Eng. (02), 84–86 (2010)
4. Yu, Y.X.: Research and optimization of text sentiment analysis based on machine learning. M.S. dissertation, Beijing University of Posts and Telecommunications, Beijing (2018)
5. Wang, M.: Overview of the development of image compression algorithms. Space Electronics Technology (2016)
6. Howard, P.G., Vitter, J.S.: Analysis of arithmetic coding for data compression. In: Data Compression Conference, DCC 1991 (1991)
7. Zhang, D.: Several Improved Fast Fractal Image Compression Algorithms. Dalian University of Technology, Dalian (2015)
8. Yan, X.: On the research and implementation of digital image compression algorithm. J. Chuzhou Vocat. Tech. Coll. **017**(002), 52–54 (2018)
9. Zhou, H.: Discussion on fast algorithm of motion compensation in image compression coding. Telev. Technol. (006), 7–10 (1995)
10. Yang, Y., Zhang, Y., Li, X.: An improved JPEG image compression coding algorithm. J. Yunnan Normal Univ. (Nat. Sci. Ed.) **036**(006), 32–39 (2016)
11. Li, A.: Research on hybrid compression coding algorithm of digital image. Xidian University (2008)
12. Lu, J., Zhao, T., Zhao, K., et al.: Improvement of still image encoding compression algorithm. Comput. Eng. **029**(004), 85–87 (2003)

A Resource-Saving Multi-layer Fault-Tolerant Low Orbit Satellite Network

Tianjiao Zhang[1], Fang Chen[1], Yan Sun[2], and Chao Guo[1(✉)]

[1] Department of Electronics and Communication Engineering, Beijing Electronic Science and Technology Institute, Beijing 100070, People's Republic of China

[2] China Industrial Control Systems Cyber Emergency Response Team, Beijing 100070, People's Republic of China

Abstract. Low-orbit satellites have the advantages of low latency, low cost, and flexible launching. They are the main direction for the development of next-generation satellite communications. Based on the STK analysis and simulation of the existing low-orbit satellite constellations, this article found that most of the current polar orbiting constellations can be seen at the same time near the equator, and the inclined orbits cannot cover the earth's poles. Therefore, a constellation with a polar orbit and an inclined orbit is designed to achieve global coverage under the conditions of reasonable number and cost of satellites and more optimized coverage performance. Lay the foundation for the network design of the future LEO satellite constellation.

Keywords: Low-orbit satellite · STK satellite network · Star chain

1 Introduction

Low-orbit satellites are low-earth orbit satellites, usually elliptical or circular orbits, with a height of less than 2,000 km. The regression cycle is roughly between 90 min and 2 h, with low latency, short development cycle, new technology, and low cost. The low-orbit satellite has a small coverage area, so it is necessary to configure a large number of satellites in the orbit. Low-orbit satellites basically perform space missions in the form of networks, can perform real-time information processing, and realize functions such as communication, remote sensing, and navigation.

At the end of the 20th century, the lack of sufficient financial support made these low-orbit satellite projects difficult to operate. With the development of technology and advancement in the field of communications, the cost of low-orbit satellites has been reduced, making it the most promising satellite mobile system. The system goal of LEO constellation is to provide continuous and stable services for demand [1].

China is still in its infancy in the field of low-orbit satellite communications. The low-orbit satellite constellations currently under planning mainly include the "Hongyun Project" and the "Hongyan Constellation". The foreign satellite constellations that emerged at the end of the 20th century mainly include Iridium and Global stars. Due to the pressure of technology and financing, Iridium and Globalstar both filed for bankruptcy

X. Sun et al. (Eds.): ICAIS 2021, LNCS 12736, pp. 701–713, 2021.
https://doi.org/10.1007/978-3-030-78609-0_59

protection shortly after starting operations. In recent years, technological advances in the communications field have reduced the operating costs of low-orbit satellites, and new rocket technology has greatly reduced launch costs, providing commercial support for the development of low-orbit satellites. LEO satellite constellations can overcome the shortcomings of other types of orbit satellite constellations. Therefore, companies in various countries around the world have started a new round of LEO satellite constellation plans, including Starlink Project and One Network Project. And most of them have entered the actual deployment stage.

For practical reasons, the constellation design in this subject considers more orbit and coverage factors, and less considers the design of system performance. There is still room for learning and improvement [2].

According to the above problems, in order to develop a more optimized low-orbit satellite constellation, this paper designs a global low-orbit satellite network based on STK. This article is divided into five parts. The first chapter introduces the general situation of low-orbit satellites. Section 2 briefly introduces the design and comparison of global low-orbit satellite constellations. The Sect. 3 carries on the simulation analysis of the low-orbit satellite, designs the new low-orbit satellite constellation, and uses STK software to carry on the simulation realization. Section 4 introduces the simulation results analysis of low-orbit satellites. Section 5 simulates and analyzes the designed constellation to verify its coverage performance. It is proved that it has better coverage performance.

2 Global Low-Orbit Satellite Constellation Design and Comparative Analysis

2.1 Iridium Constellation

The Iridium constellation system has 66 satellites distributed in 6 circular near-polar orbits, 11 satellites on each orbital plane, orbital height of 780 km, inclination of 86.4°, a single satellite provides 3840 channels, and the interstellar link rate is as high as 25 Mbps. Working in the L frequency band, the minimum elevation angle is 8.2°. The weight of a single satellite is 689 kg, the design life is 5–8 years, and about 6 replacement satellites need to be launched every year. The biggest feature of the Iridium constellation is the use of intra-system inter-satellite links (Inter-Satellite Link, ISL) [3]. Each satellite has 4 inter-satellite links, which are connected to the front and back two satellites in the same orbital plane and the left and right phases. The two nearest satellites in the adjacent orbital plane are connected to support real-time communication between users anywhere in the world, so that the information transmission in the system does not depend on the ground communication network.

Iridium is the first low-orbit satellite cellular system that can achieve global coverage. In addition to voice and data services, it also supports positioning services. Iridium constellation also has on-board processing and switching capabilities, which can improve the quality of communication links and efficiently use channel resources [4].

From the minimum elevation angle of the Iridium satellite system, the half-view angle of the satellite can be calculated. The simulation effect is shown in Fig. 1.

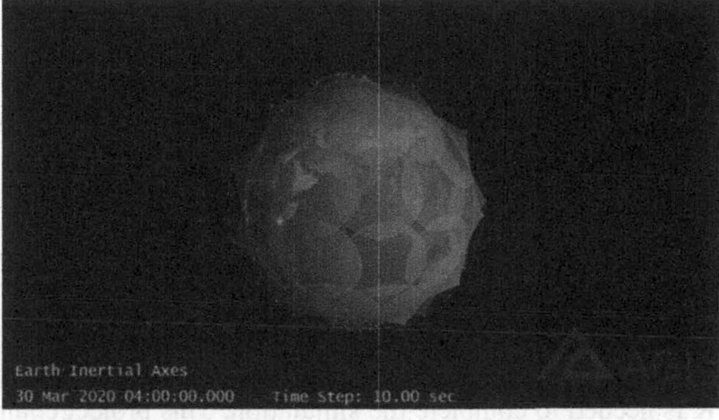

Fig. 1. Simulation effect of Iridium constellation

2.2 Global Constellations

There are 48 satellites in the global constellation system, distributed in 8 circular inclined orbits, 6 satellites on each orbital plane, and the parameters of the Walker constellation description are 48/8/1 orbital height 1414 km, inclination 52° each. The satellite provides 2,800 voice channels working in the L/S frequency band (uplink uses L frequency band, downlink uses L frequency band), the minimum elevation angle is 10°. The weight of a single satellite is 450 kg and the design life is 7.5 years [5]. The Global Star system does not use interplanetary links, nor does it have on-board processing and routing functions that need to be connected to the telecommunication network through a ground gateway. Information processing is carried out on the ground, and the cost is lower. The system needs to establish 150–200 customs stations around the world [6].

The Global Star system does not use interplanetary links, nor does it have on-board processing and routing functions that need to be connected to the telecommunication network through a ground gateway. Information processing is performed on the ground, and the cost is lower [7].

The constellation global star constellation is simulated, and the simulation effect is shown in Fig. 2.

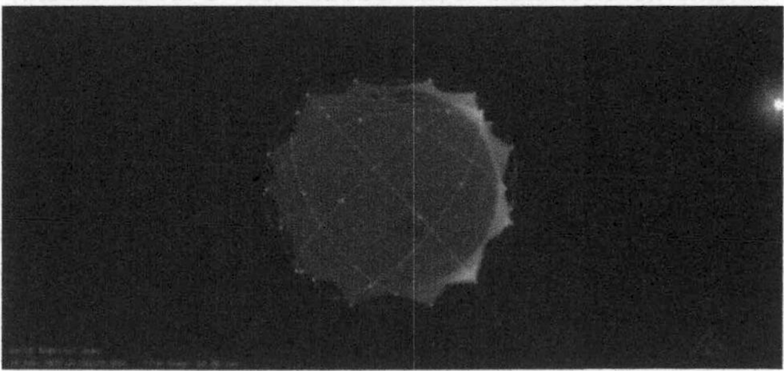

Fig. 2. Simulation results of global star constellations

2.3 Starlink Constellation

The Starlink constellation is divided into five layers, with a total of 4,409 satellites with 83 orbital planes. The orbital height of the first layer has been adjusted from the originally planned 1,150 km to 550 km, saving 16 satellites. The satellites will also have laser inter-satellite links, and the total throughput of each satellite is expected to reach 17–23 Gbit/s. The first layer satellite is 550 km from the ground, and 1,584 satellites are planned to be deployed; the second to fifth layer satellites are 1,110–1,325 km from the ground, and 2,825 satellites are planned to be deployed. This part of the satellite has a higher orbital height and can make the signal coverage wider [8].

The Starlink constellation has not been launched yet, and the Walker constellation designer in STK is needed to complete the simulation. This project completed the first phase of the simulation of 4,409 satellites, divided into five layers, with a total of 83 orbital surfaces. The color of each satellite is different. The simulation effect is shown in Fig. 3.

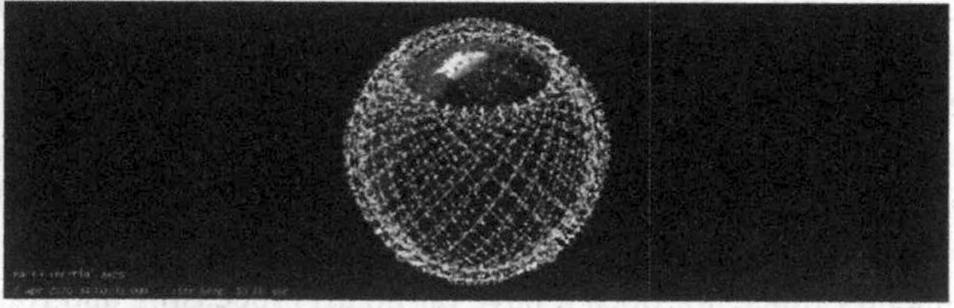

Fig. 3. Starlink constellation simulation effect

The purpose of the Starlink constellation is to develop low-cost, high-performance satellite buses and user ground transceivers to provide high-speed Internet access services covering the world. The Starlink constellation uses low-cost small satellites, a single satellite weighs about 227 kg, and can be mass-produced. The typical application scenarios and objects of Starlink satellites include. Civil aviation airliners and private jets, ocean-going vessels, islands, scientific investigations, rescues, and so on. After the Starlink constellation realizes communication services, it will not only solve the problem of surfing the Internet in remote areas, but also solve the time delay caused by the terrestrial optical fiber network during long-distance data transmission [9].

2.4 One Web Satellite Constellation

The satellites in the first phase of One Web are distributed in 18 circular orbit planes, with an orbit height of 1,200 km, an orbital inclination of 87°, and a single satellite weight of 147.7 kg. Each satellite can generate 16 Ku-band beams, which can achieve multiple beam coverage. Satellites can actively deorbit at the end of their life. The One Web constellation needs to deploy more than 50 gateways around the world to integrate and supplement the ground communication network [10].

The One Web constellation has not yet completed the networking, and the Walker constellation designer needs to be used to complete the simulation according to the published orbital parameters. The One Web constellation is different from the Iridium constellation. It finally did not adopt the inter-satellite link design. Instead, it deployed more than 50 gateways around the world to complement each other with the terrestrial communication network [11].

Due to the distance between the prograde orbit plane and the distance between the retrograde orbit plane, in the simulation, it is assumed that the constellation orbits are evenly distributed, and the orbit interval is 20°. The simulation effect is shown in Fig. 4.

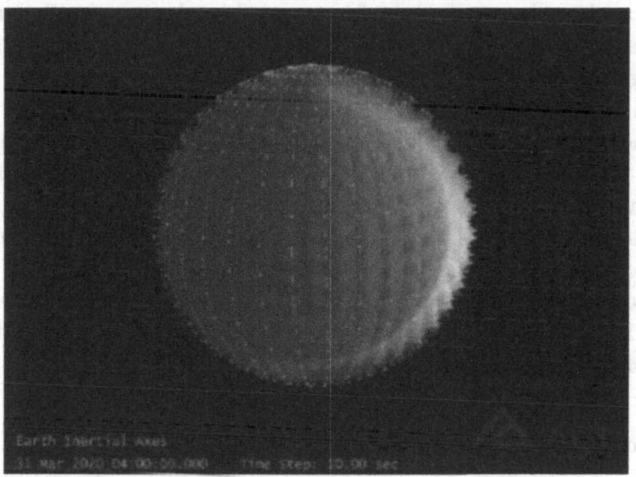

Fig. 4. One Web constellation simulation effect

2.5 Comparative Analysis of Global Satellite Constellations

Compared with Iridium and Global Star Systems, the main differences between One-Net constellation and Starlink constellation are.

- Realize global broadband access by LEO satellite constellation;
- One network constellation and star chain constellation are larger in number;
- Use more advanced digital communication payloads, advanced modulation schemes, multi-beam antennas and more complex frequency reuse schemes.

The star-link system and the one-network system use similar schemes in terms of frequency allocation. The satellite-to-user link uses the Ku band, and the satellite-to-ground station uses the Ka band. In addition, both systems use the Ka band as their feeder link. In terms of beam characteristics, the star-link system has individually shaped and controllable beams. The beams are circular, while the one-network system only has fixed beams and uses highly elliptical beams [12].

Among the constellations that have not yet been launched, only the One Net system and the Starlink system have disclosed their launch information, including the number of satellites launched each time and the total number of launches. The Starlink system uses the Falcon 9 launch vehicle to launch about 60 satellites each time. Yiwang plans to launch using Soyuz rockets, each carrying 34 to 36 satellites [13].

3 Satellite Network Orbit Design

3.1 Overview of Satellite Network Design

Compare and analyze the coverage performance of the above constellations through the reports generated by STK. The following conclusions can be drawn. The polar orbit constellation represented by the Iridium constellation can achieve global coverage, but the tilted orbit and Starlink first-layer satellites cannot cover the Polar Regions after the launch, and more tilted orbit small satellites are needed to supplement the network. However, the number of visible satellites in the Iridium constellation in low latitude areas with greater demand is only one third of that in the polar regions, while the Starlink constellation in low latitude areas has a higher number of visible satellites at the same time, and the change is smaller in higher latitude areas, and the coverage effect is obviously better. Inclined orbits and polar orbits have their own advantages and disadvantages, and currently fewer constellations have been launched and operated using polar orbits and inclined orbits [14].

3.2 Basic Considerations for Constellation Design

From the current point of view, the low-orbit satellite constellation takes a long time to complete the launch and network, and the cost is high. Therefore, the following points should be considered when designing this constellation.

(1) Realize coverage with as few satellites as possible
Achieving coverage with as few satellites as possible can improve the frequency utilization of the system. At the same time, the redundancy of the system should be considered. Compared with single-satellite coverage, multi-satellite coverage has a larger system margin;
(2) The user elevation angle is as large as possible
A larger user elevation angle can alleviate multipath and shadowing problems and improve the quality of communication links [15].
(3) The signal transmission delay is as low as possible.
Low delay is very important to the quality of communication services. Transmission delay will increase with the increase of distance. Therefore, low delay limits the altitude selection of the satellite system. At the same time, the impact of atmospheric resistance on the satellite must be considered.

3.3 The Basic Idea of Constellation Design

The direct realization of global coverage with polar orbit constellations requires higher orbital heights, smaller communication angles, and higher requirements for antennas. In this article, the role of the polar orbit constellation is to cover the Polar Regions, so the same small satellites as the first oblique orbit constellation can be used for networking, with lower cost and more stable system. When launching satellites, you can also consider adopting a multiple-satellite method similar to the Starlink constellation to reduce launch costs and shorten the networking cycle.

3.4 Determine Orbital Parameters

First, the initial design of the first-level LEO constellation orbit height is about 1,000 km, and the inclined orbit constellation is adopted to cover the area below the latitude 75°. The tilt angle of the satellite orbit is determined by the latitude range of the observation area and the field of view angle of the payload. As shown in Fig. 5, the load covers the ground with a field of view angle of 2α, and the coverage geocentric angle is 2θ. Is the half angle of view α, is the geocentric angle θ corresponding to the half angle of view, R_e is the earth's orbit radius, and h is the height of the satellite's equatorial ground. Covering the half-geocentric angle and orbital height, the relationship between the half-view angle is.

$$\theta = \arcsin\left(\frac{(h + R_e)\sin\alpha}{R_e}\right) - \alpha \tag{1}$$

For an orbit with an inclination angle of i, the range that the satellite can observe is north latitude $i + \theta$ ~ south latitude $i + \theta$, therefore, for a satellite whose observation range is $\pm N$, select to meet the observation requirements, take $h = 1{,}000$ km, $\alpha = 45°$, and calculate $\theta \approx 9.88°$, $i \geq 65.118°$.

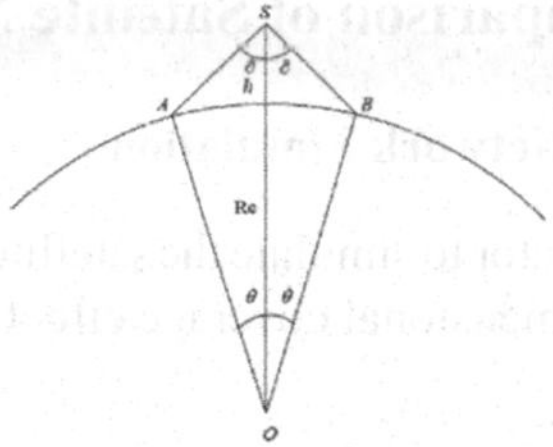

Fig. 5. Covered geocentric angle and half angle of view

Use polar orbit constellations to achieve polar cap coverage. Assuming that the lowest latitude of the polar cover area is φ, the width of the half-geocentric angle of the coverage zone is c, which is equal to the central angle of c' latitude on the equatorial plane. Then the constellation parameters should satisfy the equation when realizing continuous coverage.

$$(P - 1)\alpha + (P + 1)c = \pi\cos\varphi \tag{2}$$

$$(P - 1)\alpha + (P + 1)\arccos\left[\frac{\cos\alpha}{\cos(\pi/S)}\right] = \pi\cos\varphi \tag{3}$$

The number of orbital planes required can be solved when the orbital height and the number of satellites in the orbital plane are given [16].

The second layer of satellites supplement the network in the polar regions; the simulation and coverage analysis of the constellation composed of the first layer and the second layer of satellites shows that the coverage rate is low in the northern and southern hemispheres, and the third layer of satellites is used to supplement the network.

Constellation orbit parameters are shown in Table 1.

Table 1. LEO constellation parameters

Layers	Track height	Orbital inclination	Planes	Satellites/plane	Total number of satellites
Level one	1,000 km	66°	24	21	504
Level two	1,400 km	83°	3	18	54
Level three	1,350 km	75°	6	18	108

The vehicle load formula represents the number of cities traveled during the traversal process. In expressways, the speed limit of vehicles is 60–100 km/h, and in ordinary highways, the speed limit of vehicles is 40–60 km/h. In the formula design, the default speed is the lowest speed when the vehicle is empty and the vehicle is fully loaded. (30 t), the speed is the highest. The speed of the vehicle changes linearly with the load.

Two different types of styles can be used: In-line style, and Display style [17].

4 Realization and Comparison of Satellite Network Simulation

4.1 Realization of Satellite Network Simulation

Use Walker constellation generator to simulate the satellite network, the simulation effect is shown in Fig. 6. The two-dimensional coverage effect of the satellite constellation is shown in Fig. 7.

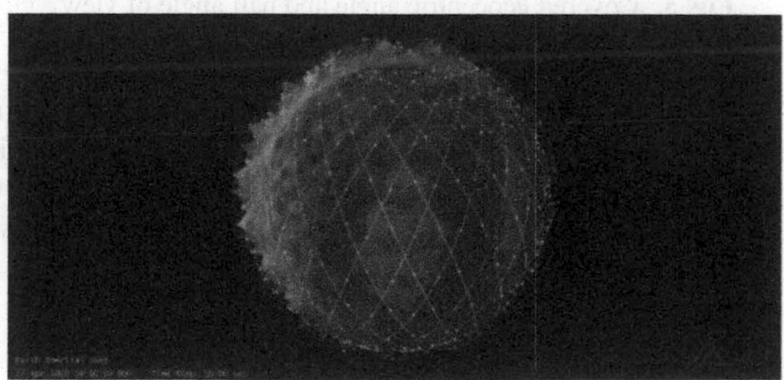

Fig. 6. Satellite constellation simulation effect

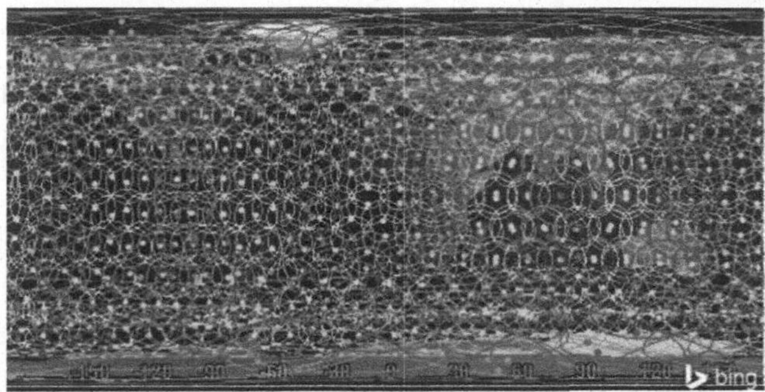

Fig. 7. Two-dimensional coverage map of constellation

It can be seen from the two-dimensional simulation diagram of the satellite constellation that the function of the first layer of inclined orbits is to provide coverage for more populous areas in the world. As can be seen from Fig. 8 and Fig. 9, the role of the second and third layer satellites is to cover high latitudes and Polar Regions.

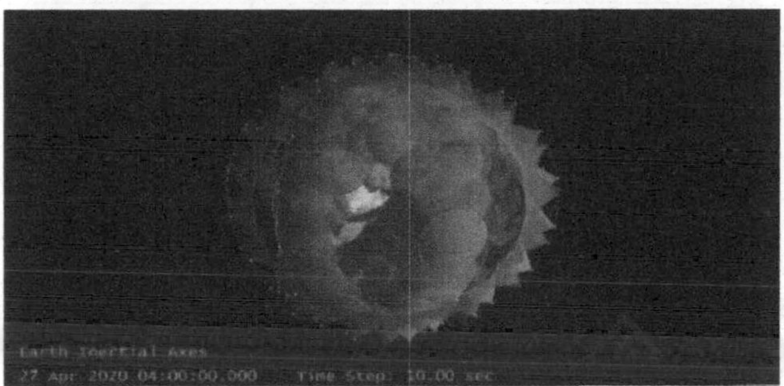

Fig. 8. The second and third layer satellite simulation diagram

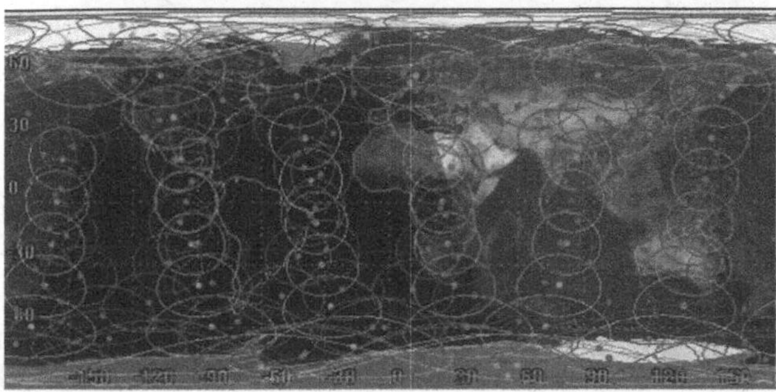

Fig. 9. Two-dimensional coverage map of the second and third layer satellites

4.2 Simulation Analysis of Constellation Design

Analyze the coverage performance of the constellation and generate an analysis report.

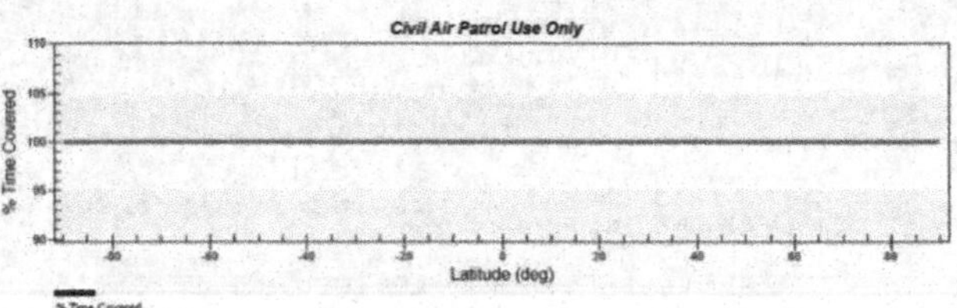

Fig. 10. Change of coverage time ratio with latitude

In Fig. 10, the horizontal axis represents latitude, and the vertical axis represents the coverage time ratio. It can be seen from the figure that this constellation can reach 100% of coverage time for all latitudes at any time.

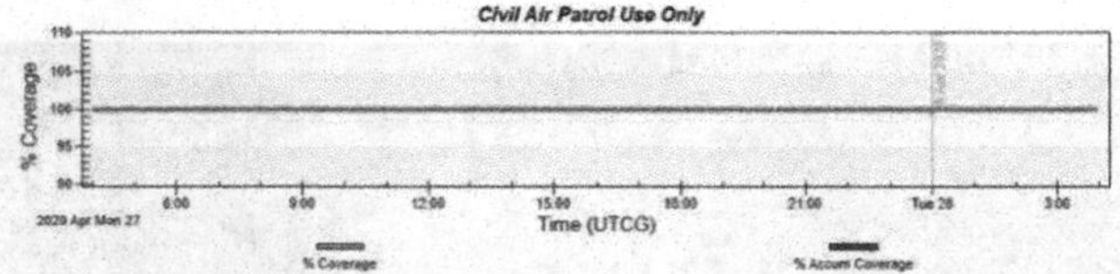

Fig. 11. Changes in coverage rate over time

In Fig. 11, the horizontal axis represents time and the vertical axis represents coverage. The figure shows that the constellation coverage can reach 100% at any time.

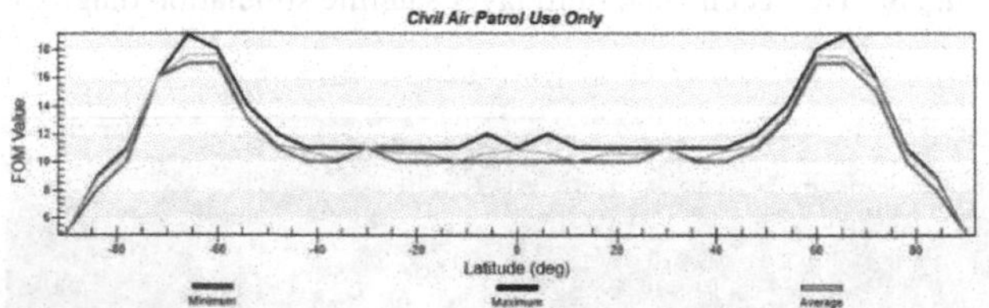

Fig. 12. The number of visible satellites varies with latitude

In Fig. 12, the horizontal axis represents latitude, and the vertical axis represents the number of simultaneously visible satellites. It can be seen from the figure that the number of simultaneously visible satellites in this constellation varies slightly with latitude, and the maximum value is 20. The number of satellites visible at the same time in the equatorial area is 10, and the number of satellites visible at the same time in the latitude 75° area is 15. Compared with the Polar Regions, the number of satellites visible at the same time in the equatorial region has dropped by about 1/3 [18] (Table 2).

Table 2. Comparison and analysis of constellation coverage performance

System	Coverage time ratio varies with latitude	Coverage changes over time	At the same time, the number of visible satellites varies with latitude
Iridium	100% in all latitudes	100% at any time	The equatorial region is 2/3 lower than the high latitude region
Global star	100% below 75° north-south latitude	99.7%	Compared with high latitude regions, the equatorial region has not changed much
Starlink	100% below 75° north-south latitude	96.5%	The equatorial region is down 2/5 compared to high latitude regions
OneWeb	100% in all latitudes	100% at any time	The equatorial region is 2/3 lower than the high latitude region
The subject design constellation	100% in all latitudes	100% at any time	The equatorial area is 1/3 lower than the high latitude area

It can be seen from the analysis results that the conclusion can be drawn through comparison. Compared with the Iridium constellation, the coverage performance curve of the constellation designed in this project is more stable and can better cover low-latitude areas. Compared with the global constellation, it can cover the Polar Regions. Compared with the Starlink constellation, the number of satellites used in this subject is smaller, and the time period and operating cost of the constellation network are smaller. At the same time, it can be seen that the number of satellites is mainly distributed in the area within the north-south latitude70°. Compared with a network constellation, the coverage resource distribution of the satellite constellation designed in this subject is more reasonable and the coverage efficiency is higher.

5 Constellation Design Summary

The satellite constellations studied in this article are quite different in system architecture and scale. Iridium, One-Net, Rainbow and Swan Goose all use polar orbit constellations to achieve global coverage; Global Star System and Starlink System Inclined orbits are mainly used, which is closely related to factors such as the satellite system coverage plan and the technology used. The Starlink system first solves the coverage problem in areas with large populations, and is expected to realize communications in North America this year. Other satellite constellations focus more on achieving global interconnection.

For practical reasons, the constellation design in this subject considers more orbit and coverage factors, and less considers the design of system performance. There is still room for learning and improvement.

Acknowledgement. We gratefully acknowledge anonymous reviewers who read drafts and made many helpful suggestions.

Funding Statement. This work is supported by Higher Education Department of the Ministry of Education Industry-university Cooperative Education Project.

Conflicts of Interest. The authors declare that they have no conflicts of interest to report regarding the present study.

References

1. Zhu, L., Wu, T., Zhuo, Y.: Introduction to Satellite Communication. Electronics Industry Press, Beijing (2015)
2. Li, Y.: Research on satellite-earth integrated Link16 low-orbit satellite data link. Radio Eng. **6**, 24–26 (2017)
3. Wei, X.: The deployment of the "Iridium" satellite constellation is complete. Int. Space **8**, 10–11 (1998)
4. Hou, X., Yan, J., Zhao, J.: Analysis and prospect of key technologies of satellite mobile communication system. Digit. Commun. World **07**, 52–54 (2011)
5. Li, B.: Analysis of SpaceX's launch of large-scale test satellite deployment. Int. Space **6**, 12–16 (2019)
6. Wang, M., Lu, Y.: STK and its application in satellite network simulation demonstration. China Radio **5**, 33–34 (2019)
7. Qin, D., Chen, X.: STK and its application in satellite network simulation demonstration. J. Acad. Command Technol. **4**, 66–69 (2001)
8. Ding, S., Zhang, B.: The Application of STK in Space Mission Simulation Analysis. National Defense Industry Press, Beijing (2011)
9. Hui, H., Zhou, C., Xu, S., Lin, F.: A novel secure data transmission scheme in industrial internet of things. China Commun. **17**, 73–88 (2020)
10. Zhang, D.: Beidou navigation satellite orbit simulation based on STK software. Eng. Survey. Mapp. **7**, 14-18+23 (2015)
11. Gong, C., Lin, F., Gong, X., Lu, Y.: Intelligent cooperative edge computing in internet of things. IEEE Internet Things J. **7**, 9372–9382 (2020)
12. Yang, B., Zhang, S., Fang, S.: Research and simulation analysis of satellite coverage model based on STK. Ship Electron. Warfare **1**, 66–71 (2016)
13. Hu, C., Wang, H., Hu, L.: STK software satellite visibility and coverage analysis. Global Position Syst. **4**, 43–46 (2007)
14. Li, W., Baoyintu, Jia, B., Wang, J., Watanabe, T.: An energy based dynamic AODV routing protocol in wireless ad hoc networks. Comput. Mater. Continua (CMC) **63**, 353–368 (2020)
15. Ke, Z., Yan, B.: Visibility simulation analysis of a new generation of Beidou navigation satellite based on STK. Electron. Des. Eng. **25**(15), 153–157 (2017)
16. del Portillo, I., Cameron, B.G., Shuaijun, L.: Technical comparison of the three global broadband low-orbit satellite constellation systems Telesat, One Web and Space X. Satell. Netw. **07**, 48–61 (2019)

17. Xiao, N., Liang, J., Zhang, J.: Design and planning of China's low-orbit satellite constellation network. Telecommun. Technol. **50**, 14–18 (2010)
18. Wei, Z., Wang, Q., Yao, J.: Design and optimization of low-orbit satellite inclined orbit. Shanghai Aerosp. **27**, 26–29 (2010)

Research on Business Travel Problem Based on Simulated Annealing and Tabu Search Algorithms

Jianan Chen[1], Fang Chen[1], Chao Guo[1](✉), and Yan Sun[2]

[1] Department of Electronics and Communication Engineering, Beijing Electronic Science and Technology Institute, Beijing 100070, People's Republic of China

[2] China Industrial Control Systems Cyber Emergency Response Team, Beijing 100070, People's Republic of China

Abstract. In logistics and transportation, it is usually necessary to take into account the distance, route, time, transportation cost, and human resources. In this paper, the coordinates of 31 cities are used as data storage, and the three parts of an ordinary distance, travel time, and high-speed cost between the two places are added with target weights to obtain the minimum comprehensive cost. In this paper, the shortest path at the core of the TSP is transformed into the minimum comprehensive cost, and each cost in transportation is weighted in proportion to the target. On the premise of finding the shortest path, to solve the logistics transportation planning problem in the business travel problem, it will simply find the minimum path Single objective function optimization is to add objective weights to achieve the objective function with the smallest comprehensive cost and optimize the algorithm. While comprehensively considering cost and time, it avoids the inoperability caused by the linear distance between two points, reduces logistics transportation costs, improves logistics timeliness, and improves customer satisfaction.

Keywords: Simulated annealing algorithm · Tabu search algorithm · Logistics transportation cost

1 Introduction

In today's economy and trade, the e-commerce industry has a strong momentum of development, and the overall development of "Internet+" is present [1, 2]. Since e-commerce and logistics are closely connected at present, how to reduce costs and how to plan more reasonable and efficient distribution routes to improve the efficiency of logistics and distribution are the primary issues that need to be considered to promote the development of e-commerce. In general, how to plan the most reasonable and efficient roads to reduce congestion; how to better plan logistics to reduce operating costs; how to set up nodes in the Internet environment to facilitate the flow of information, etc. [3]. To better solve this problem, based on the original traditional accurate solution algorithm, a heuristic algorithm is proposed for the TSP problem, which can better solve

X. Sun et al. (Eds.): ICAIS 2021, LNCS 12736, pp. 714–725, 2021.
https://doi.org/10.1007/978-3-030-78609-0_60

the limitations of time and space, and solve the complex problems in combinatorial optimization [4, 5]. It brings a more extensive update to the previous traditional methods based on mathematics that are not inspiring thinking.

TSP is one of the most widely studied combinatorial optimization problems. In TSP, the simpler idea is to use enumeration, but based on the existence of the optimal solution, the characteristics that can be found and the problems that can be solved are all small-scale problems. If the space complexity of the problem that needs to be realized and solved is increased in the form of exponential, and the solution method adopted is still a simple procedure, then it is indeed very difficult. The TSP problem is divided into symmetric TSP and asymmetric TSP according to the symmetry of the distance matrix formed by the distance between cities [6]. It is an NP difficult problem in terms of complexity. The TSP problem that this project mainly studies is one of the classic problems of combinatorial optimization. Explain the proposition of TSP: In n cities, the distance between cities is known. Travelers must depart from a specific city, pass only a few cities at a time, and eventually return to the city of departure. In n cities, as n increases, the calculation of the sum of various paths and distances increases, resulting in an "exponential explosion" phenomenon. Therefore, traditional enumeration algorithms are difficult to work, and other heuristic algorithms must be found.

2 Introduction to TSP Related Algorithms

2.1 Simulated Annealing Algorithm

Simulated annealing algorithm With the development of computers and the maturity of software and hardware conditions in the computer field, S. Kirkpatrick and others have successfully introduced annealing, a solution to solid metal cooling and annealing, into the field of combinatorial optimization [7]. It accepts the inferior solution through the probability of Metropolis acceptance criteria and jumps out of the local optimum. Through the iterative process of temperature and the de-temperature process of the function, it conducts a step-by-step search and then finds the global optimal solution. The simulated annealing algorithm starts from a certain higher initial temperature, with the constant decrease of the cooling rate determined in advance, combined with the sudden jump characteristic of the Metropolis criterion, and finally tends to the global optimum.

The simulated annealing algorithm is derived from the principle of metal solid annealing in real life. First, heat the solid to a sufficiently high temperature. At this time, the internal energy of the solid increases, and the internal particles are extremely active, showing a disordered state; then let it slowly cool down, and the internal particles gradually tend to be aligned at the current position. An orderly state and an equilibrium state is reached at every moment of cooling down. According to the physical knowledge learned in junior high school, the internal energy of a solid is the smallest among the three states. According to Metropolis' acceptance criteria, the probability of the internal particles of a solid tends to stabilize at a certain temperature.

The calculation process of the simulated annealing algorithm is shown in Fig. 1:

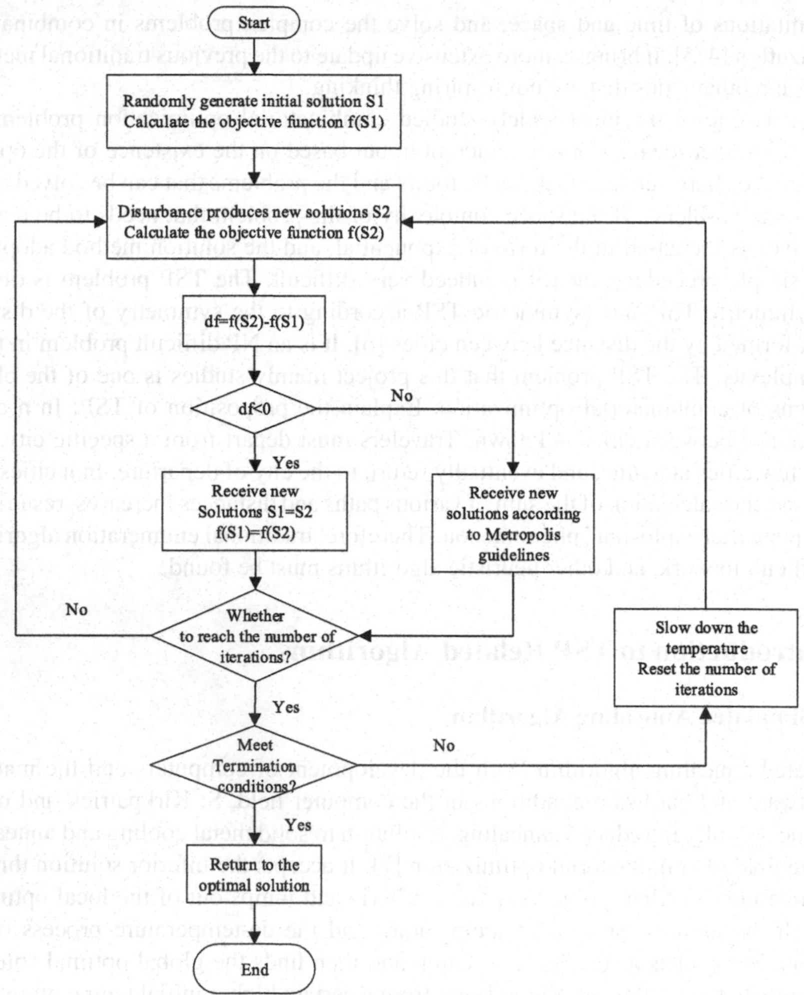

Fig. 1. Basic simulated annealing algorithm flow chart

To initialize the entire program, take the initial temperature T_0, sufficiently large, then set $T = T_0$, and calculate the objective function $f(S_1)$ after obtaining any initial solution according to the program.

(1) Determine the number of iterations required at each set T, which is the chain length L of Metropolis. And generate a new solution $f(S_2)$ for the current S_1 random disturbance, and calculate the objective function $f(S_2)$.
(2) Calculate the increment of S_2 $df = f(S_2) - f(S_1)$, where f is the cost function of S_1. (Loss function or cost function is a function that maps the value of a random event or related random variable to a non-negative real number to represent the "risk" or "loss" that the random event has to bear.)

(3) If df < 0, accept S_2 as the new current solution, is $S_1 = S_2$; otherwise, according to Metropolis criterion, accept the new solution with probability $\exp(-\frac{df}{T})$. See if the number of iterations is reached, if there is no continued disturbance, a new solution will be generated.

After the operation reaches the number of iterations, it is judged whether the termination condition has been met, and if it is satisfied, the current solution S_1 is output as the optimal solution, and the program ends. Otherwise, reduce the temperature and repeat the number of iterations and then perform disturbance, gradually reduce the control temperature, repeat the Metropolis process until the end criterion is met, and the optimal solution is obtained.

The advantage of the simulated annealing algorithm is that it can be used to solve nonlinear problems, and the algorithm has strong robustness, global convergence, implicit parallelism, and wide adaptability. It can also handle discrete, mixed, continuous, etc. Design variables do not require any auxiliary information, and there are no restrictions, and there are no requirements for objective functions and constraint functions. This is extremely competitive in optimization problems. The disadvantage is that the algorithm is based on randomness, so searching for solutions in the field is random, which makes it easy to miss good solutions.

2.2 Tabu Search Algorithm

Tabu search algorithm, also known as the "Tabu search algorithm", is a sub-heuristic search technology, first proposed in 1986 [8–10], is an approximate solution. The measure taken by the tabu search method is to first set an initial solution and then formulate the moving principle to approach the optimal solution of the taboo. The principle of the memory mechanism is to record the solutions that have been searched to avoid repeated searches. If a solution is found to be better than the current best solution, the new solution will replace the previous best solution.

The tabu search algorithm first determines that the initial solution is the current solution, and searches for candidate solutions in the current solution neighborhood; at this time, if a candidate solution corresponds to the target value that satisfies the contempt rule, it will choose to ignore its taboo characteristics and replace the current optimal solution with it Sum and determine that this candidate solution is the current global optimal solution, and then add the candidate solution to the taboo table, update the taboo table; determine whether the candidate solution meets the taboo attribute if not, select the most non-taboo object in the candidate solution [11, 12]. The best state is taken as the new optimal solution, and the new optimal solution is added to the taboo table; this is repeated until the iteration conditions are met, and then the program is terminated.

The implementation steps of the tabu search algorithm are shown in a flowchart as shown in Fig. 2:

Tabu search represents the process of local search and a greedy selection mechanism is introduced in the more advanced search process. The core content is to search the previous information sensitively to achieve a non-repetitive search. The advantages are obvious, local optimal solutions can be avoided, and the method is relatively simple

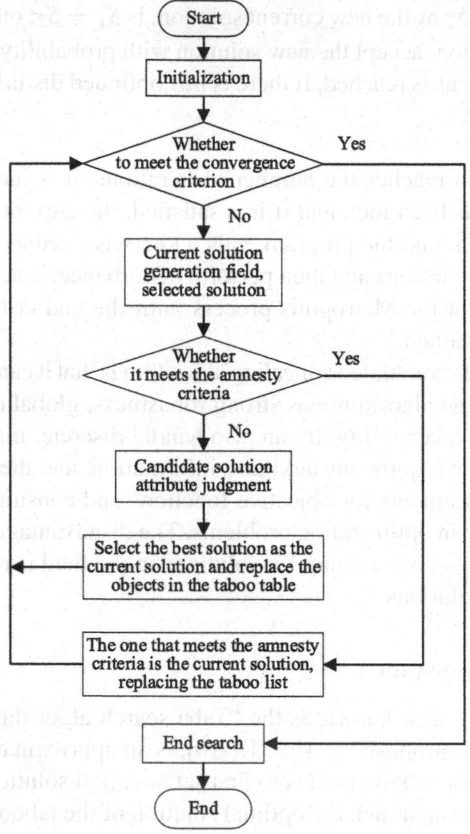

Fig. 2. Flow chart based on the tabu search algorithm

and universal; the disadvantage is that the efficiency depends on the initial solution. Therefore, the disadvantage of local search is that the search performance of the algorithm is relatively poor, which completely depends on the neighborhood structure and the setting of the initial solution, and cannot guarantee the global optimum.

3 System Design

Based on the actual logistics and transportation background, the shortest path at the core of TSP is transformed into the problem of minimum comprehensive cost, and the various costs in transportation are weighted in proportion to the target. Under the premise of finding the shortest path, the overall cost is minimized and business travel is solved. The logistics transportation planning problem in the problem, this kind of model can be applied to the logistics transportation industry. The scope of the established mathematical model is 31 municipalities and provincial capitals in mainland China, with a fixed value for the deadweight, with a total capacity of 30t. Every city unloads 1t of goods, and the unloaded volume is average. For the remaining three parts, the cost is ordinary distance.

The data of and high-speed charges are collected fixed values and the time spent is determined based on the collected high-speed distance and non-high-speed distance and the road speed limit and load. The three parts are summed and the weights are set to p_1, p_2, p_3, and $p_1 + p_2 + p_3 = 1$.

The scope of the solution space established is Beijing, Tianjin, Shanghai, Chongqing, Hohhot, Urumqi, Lhasa, Yinchuan, Nanning, Harbin, Changchun, Shenyang, Shijiazhuang, Zhengzhou, Jinan, Taiyuan, Lanzhou, 31 municipalities and provincial capital cities in Mainland China Xi'an, Xining, Chengdu, Wuhan, Hefei, Nanjing, Hangzhou, Fuzhou, Nanchang, Changsha, Guiyang, Kunming, Guangzhou, Haikou. Determine the latitude and longitude coordinates of 31 cities based on data collection. Serial number: 1 2 3 4 … n.

Collect the ordinary driving distance, high-speed driving distance, non-high-speed driving distance, and high-speed driving costs between 31 cities.

The core of TSP is to traverse the city to get the shortest path. The improvement plan of this topic is to add a single path element, by adding target weights, combining the ordinary distance, the time spent on ordinary roads and highways, and their driving on the highway. The final shortest path is obtained by comprehensively integrating the costs and costs in proportion. The time spent is determined by the distance between the ordinary road and the highway, and the driving speed is determined by the speed limit and load of the vehicle on the ordinary highway and the highway.

According to the load and road speed limit of vehicles, the defined formula is as follows:

Vehicle load:

$$C = 30 - \mathrm{i} \tag{1}$$

Highway speed:

$$\mathrm{V} = -\frac{4}{3} \times C + 100 \tag{2}$$

Non-highway speed:

$$\mathrm{V} = -\frac{2}{3} \times C + 60 \tag{3}$$

The vehicle load formula (1) represents the number of cities travelled during the traversal process. In expressways, the speed limit of vehicles is 60–100 km/h, and in ordinary highways, the speed limit of vehicles is 40–60 km/h. In the formula design, the default speed is the lowest speed when the vehicle is empty and the vehicle is fully loaded. (30t), the speed is the highest. The speed of the vehicle changes linearly with the load.

Two different types of styles can be used: In-line style, and Display style.

4 Realization of Real Problems

4.1 Realization of TSP Based on Simulated Annealing Algorithm

For the realization of the TSP problem through the simulated annealing algorithm, it is necessary to clarify the key factors and plan the steps reasonably. How to achieve it is divided into the following parts:

(1) Solution space
The solution space S starts from the initial city and traverses all the paths that visit each city exactly once. In the context of this algorithm, the initial solution can be expressed as {Beijing, Tianjin, Chongqing, …, Haikou}, where Beijing, Tianjin, Chongqing, …, Haikou is Beijing, Tianjin, Chongqing, …, Haikou is an arrangement of 1, 2, n, indicating that starting from Beijing, passing through, Tianjin, Chongqing, Haikou, and then returning to Beijing, The initial solution can be selected as (1, 2, 3, …, n).
(2) Objective function
The objective function is the total length of the path to visit all cities. The time spent visiting this route and the cost of visiting this route is the highway tolls.
(3) Neighborhood $N(x)$
For a solution: the neighborhood is the space formed by arbitrarily swapping the positions of two elements in the solution. Therefore, the method to generate a new solution is to randomly generate two different numbers between 1 and n, called 2-opt mapping. So the neighborhood size of any solution is $31 \times \frac{(31-1)}{2}$.
(4) Balance parameter L
According to the definition of neighborhood, if we want to make each solution $N(x)$ have a chance to be selected, we can make the balance parameter $L = 31 \times \frac{31-1}{2}$.
(5) Initial temperature T_0
The size of the initial temperature T_0 will affect the performance of SA, if it is too large, the annealing time will be longer, and of course, the quality of the solution may be improved; if it is too small, the speed will be faster and the quality of the solution may be poor. According to the experiment, the initial temperature of this article is 2000°.
(6) Cooling rate
The choice of cooling rate is one of the key technologies for the success of the simulated annealing algorithm. Considering the reason for convergence speed, the cooling rate is selected as $T_0 \to aT_0$ (a is a constant) and $a = 0.94$ can be made according to experience.
(7) Stop criteria
Due to the difficulty of NP-complete problems, in most cases, it is not difficult to obtain the optimal solution to the problem. In this case, it is necessary to introduce the key elements of the simulated annealing algorithm: the stopping criterion. The stop criterion selected this time is: set a maximum number of iteration steps or set the longest running time. During the running of the algorithm, if the maximum number of iterative steps or the maximum running time is exceeded, the algorithm will stop and the output will be in the iteration. The minimum value in the process is regarded as the optimal solution for this operation.

4.2 Implementation of TSP Based on the Tabu Search Algorithm

For the realization of the TSP problem through the tabu search algorithm, it is necessary to clarify the key factors and plan the steps reasonably. How to achieve it is divided into the following parts:

(1) Coding method
Regarding the characteristics of the TSP problem, the tabu search algorithm for the TSP problem with 31 cities in this article, this article expresses the solution as a sequence table of length 31, random arrangement of 31 numbers from 0 to 30 represents the traveling salesman Starting from the city numbered 0, visit each city in sequence $0 \to 7 \to 1 \to 6 \to 4 \to 3 \to 5 \to \ldots \to 8 \to 2$, and finally return to city 0 from the 2nd city.
(2) Neighborhood search
The neighborhood operation is performed by the interchange method, and the solution domain is mapped to 2-opt, that is, a fixed starting point city and every two cities after that are swapped. The number of elements in the neighborhood is $C_n^2 + 1$, and the number of fields in this article is $C_{31}^2 + 1$. The positions of the two points are randomly exchanged. The neighborhood solution of each state of this interchange method is $m \times \frac{(m-1)}{2}$ pieces.
(3) Determination of taboo objects
Put the optimal solution generated in each iteration as a taboo object into the taboo table to prevent the algorithm from falling into the local optimum. After an improved algorithm, the optimal solution generated by the iteration is the shortest path, which takes time and costs. The final comprehensive cost was obtained.
(4) Determination of taboo length and candidate solutions
The selected taboo length is 31. The selection range of candidate solutions is in the neighborhood of the current solution. The algorithm selects the best ones from the neighborhood of each state as candidate solutions and selects the best tabu length +1 elements from the neighborhood as the candidate set.
(5) Amnesty criteria
To improve the quality of the solution and prevent the phenomenon of infinite loops, the adopted amnesty criterion, also known as the contempt criterion, is a contempt criterion based on fitness value. If a candidate solution is taboo if its target value is better than the current one. If the optimal solution is obtained, the candidate will be released and the current optimal solution will be updated.
(6) Multi-initial point strategy
To increase the diversity and richness of the search space, each point in the 31 cities is used as the initial point, which can greatly optimize the probability of the optimal solution.
(7) Termination criteria
The termination criterion of this design selection is: set a maximum iteration period or longest running time. During the operation of the algorithm, if the maximum number of iteration steps or the maximum running time is exceeded, the algorithm will be stopped and the output will be in the iterative process. The minimum value obtained, is considered as the optimal solution for this run.

5 Algorithm Analysis and Simulation

The cities selected in this paper are the latitude and longitude coordinates of 31 municipalities and provincial capitals in Mainland China, and they are organized as shown in Table 1 below.

Table 1. City coordinates of China31 cities

$C_{1(Beijing)} = (116, 39)$	$C_{2(Tianjin)} = (117, 39)$	$C_{3(Shanghai)} = (121, 31)$
$C_{4(Chongqing)} = (106, 29)$	$C_{5(Hohhot)} = (111, 40)$	$C_{6(Urumqi)} = (87, 43)$
$C_{7(Lhasa)} = (90, 29)$	$C_{8(Yinchuan)} = (106, 38)$	$C_{9(Nanning)} = (108, 22)$
$C_{10(Harbin)} = (126, 45)$	$C_{11(Changchun)} = (125, 43)$	$C_{12(Shenyang)} = (123, 41)$
$C_{13(Shijiazhuang)} = (114, 38)$	$C_{14(Zhengzhou)} = (113, 34)$	$C_{15(Jinan)} = (117, 36)$
$C_{16(Taiyuan)} = (112, 37)$	$C_{17(Lanzhou)} = (103, 36)$	$C_{18(Xi'an)} = (108, 34)$
$C_{19(Xining)} = (101, 36)$	$C_{20(Chengdu)} = (104, 30)$	$C_{21(Wuhan)} = (114, 30)$
$C_{22(Hefei)} = (117, 31)$	$C_{23(Nanjing)} = (118, 32)$	$C_{24(Hangzhou)} = (120, 30)$
$C_{25(Fuzhou)} = (119, 26)$	$C_{26(Nanchang)} = (115, 28)$	$C_{27(Changsha)} = (113, 28)$
$C_{28(Guiyang)} = (106, 26)$	$C_{29(Kunming)} = (102, 25)$	$C_{30(Guangzhou)} = (113, 23)$
$C_{31(Haikou)} = (110, 20)$		

To verify the improvement and optimization of the algorithm, a simulation diagram is selected to show the optimization effect. In the unimproved algorithm, the number of cities is 70. The optimal solution only represents the optimal result of the path. The simulation diagram is as follows:

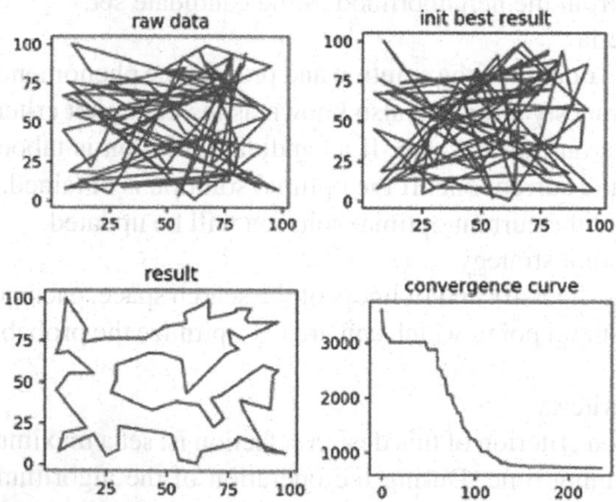

Fig. 3. Algorithm simulation diagram

Figure 3 shows the simulation diagram of the optimized algorithm obtained by combining the two algorithms. The connection of the original data is very messy, and the preprocessed data is also difficult to identify. After many iterations, the path length curve tends to be flat and no longer changes, and it can be determined that the optimal solution is reached at this time.

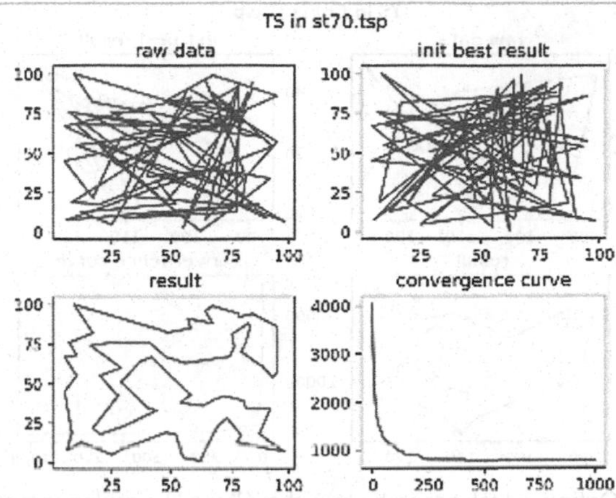

Fig. 4. Tabu search algorithm simulation diagram

For the simulation diagram of 70 cities when the tabu search algorithm is not optimized, as shown in Fig. 4, the initial data and the initial path are messy, the simulation diagram of the best path is a closed-loop, and the shortest path length finally obtained after multiple iterations. After that, it also flattened out.

The proportions of ordinary distance, time spent, and cost are different, and the shortest distance in the experiment is different. The characteristics of the two algorithms can be seen by comparing the simulation diagram.

As can be seen in the third small graphs in Fig. 5 and Fig. 6, the path difference between the simulated annealing algorithm and the tabu search algorithm is due to the characteristics of the two algorithms.

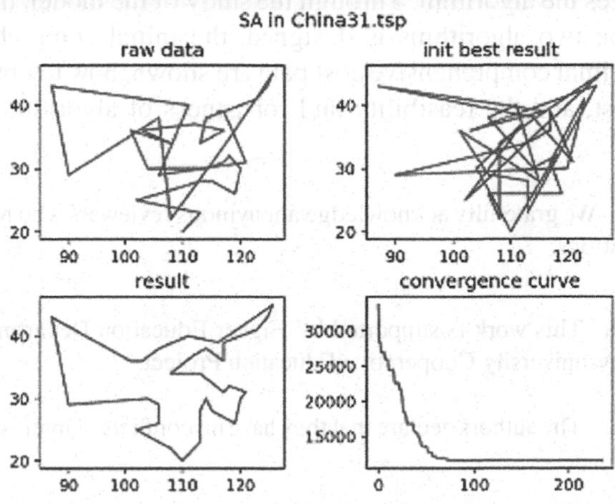

Fig. 5. Optimized simulated annealing algorithm China31 simulation diagram

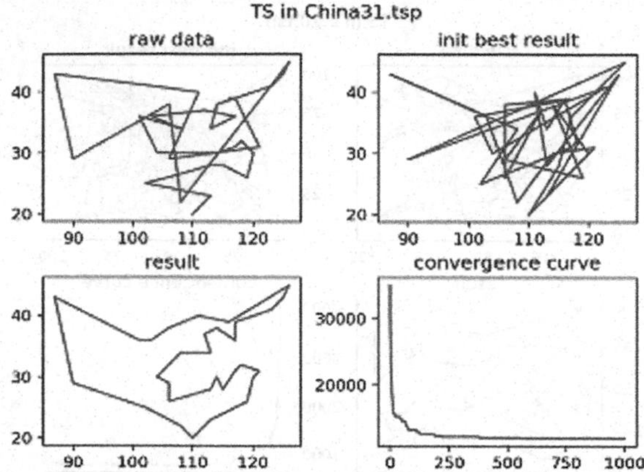

Fig. 6. Optimized tabu search algorithm China31 simulation diagram

After several weight adjustments, it is found that the simulation diagram has changed. In the simulation diagram, the meaning of the best comprehensive cost path diagram of the several diagrams is derived from the normal distance, the high-speed cost, and the time spent. Finally, when the ordinary distance addition ratio is 0.5, the cost is 0.2, and the time is 0.3, the setting ratio is appropriate. After many experiments and tests, the most suitable weight setting was finally determined.

6 Conclusion

Based on the study of the principles of simulated annealing and tabu search algorithms, this paper studies the significance of the two algorithms in solving the TSP problem for the TSP model in real life introduces the actual background to create a realistic model and optimizes the algorithm. Through the study of the model, the comprehensive optimization of the two algorithms is designed, the initial comprehensive cost path display and the optimal comprehensive cost path are shown, how to obtain the minimum comprehensive cost, and the feasibility and robustness of algorithm optimization are further determined.

Acknowledgement. We gratefully acknowledge anonymous reviewers who read drafts and made many helpful suggestions.

Funding Statement. This work is supported by Higher Education Department of the Ministry of Education Industry-university Cooperative Education Project.

Conflicts of Interest. The authors declare that they have no conflicts of interest to report regarding the present study.

References

1. Zhu, J.: A hybrid algorithm of simulated annealing algorithm and tabu search algorithm. Mod. Comput. (Prof. Ed.) **6**, 12–13+31 (2012)

2. Hui, H., Zhou, C., Xu, S., Lin, F.: A novel secure data transmission scheme in industrial internet of things. China Commun. **17**, 73–88 (2020)
3. Yan, L., Li, Z., Wei, J.: Research on a parameter setting method of simulated annealing algorithm. J. Syst. Simul. **20**, 245–247 (2008)
4. Gong, C., Lin, F., Gong, X., Lu, Y.: Intelligent cooperative edge computing in internet of things. IEEE Internet Things J. **7**, 9372–9382 (2020)
5. Yang, W., Zhao, Y.: Improved simulated annealing algorithm for solving TSP. Comput. Eng. Appl. **46**, 34–36 (2010)
6. Wang, S., Cheng, J.: Performance analysis of genetic algorithm and simulated annealing algorithm for TSP. Comput. Technol. Dev. **19**, 097–100 (2009)
7. Qiao, Y., Zhang, J.: TSP solution based on an improved genetic simulated annealing algorithm. Comput. Simul. **26**, 0205–0208 (2009)
8. Li, W., Baoyintu, Jia, B., Wang, J., Watanabe, T.: An energy based dynamic AODV routing protocol in wireless ad hoc networks. Comput. Mater. Continua **63**, 353–368 (2020)
9. She, Z., Zhuang, J., Zhai, X.: Research on path planning based on improved TSP model and simulated annealing algorithm. Ind. Control Comput. **31**, 56–57 (2018)
10. Tang, Y., Yang, Q.: Parameter design of ant colony optimization algorithm for solving traveling salesman problem. J. Dongguan Univ. Technol. **27**, 48–54 (2020)
11. Wang, X.L., Jiang, J.M., Zhao, S.J., Bai, I.: A fair blind signature scheme to revoke malicious vehicles in VANETs. CMC-Comput. Mater. Continua **58**, 249–262 (2019)
12. Chen, J., Wang, J., Qi, Z., et al.: A new simple solution to traveling salesman-style distribution problem. Logist. Eng. Manage. **41**, 93–95 (2019)

Intelligent Security Image Classification on Small Sample Learning

Zixian Chen, Xinrui Jia, Liguo Zhang(✉), and Guisheng Yin

School of Computer Science and Technology, Harbin Engineering University, Harbin 150001, China
{jiaxinrui,zhangliguo,yinguisheng}@hrbeu.edu.cn

Abstract. Image classification is an important task in the field of the intelligent security and deep learning methods represented by convolutional neural networks have achieved many great results in this field. Image classification based on deep learning usually performs well on large-scale datasets, but its performance is often greatly limited by the size of the data. When the dataset is not sufficient, the traditional deep learning method cannot perform well on the small-scale datasets and this situation often occurs in practical applications. To address the drawback, we propose a deep learning framework based on the combination of SoftMax classifier and Bayes learning for small-sample image classification. Within this framework, we utilize transfer learning to solve the problem of too few data, and it can also reduce model training time and space costs. At the same time, we make use of the combination of the above two classifiers to improve the effectiveness and accuracy of the model on different datasets. We empirically find that the model has higher classification accuracy and less training time than the general deep learning model on the datasets. The experiment results demonstrate that the proposed method generally has better classification accuracy on the small-scale datasets, compared with mainstream methods.

Keywords: Image classification · Small sample learning · Transfer learning · Bayes learning

1 Introduction

In recent years, deep learning has made significant progress, especially in the field of computer vision, where Convolutional Neural Network (CNN) has taken the lead. For example, the application of CNN to medical research can improve medical performance [1] and it effectively improves military reconnaissance and weapon guidance [2]. CNN related technologies have great application value in many aspects, such as intelligent security. CNN also has many applications in image classification involved in intelligent security, and it occupies an important part.

Despite the deep learning method in the field of computer vision has proven the most advanced machine learning technology is better than before, however,

X. Sun et al. (Eds.): ICAIS 2021, LNCS 12736, pp. 726–737, 2021.
https://doi.org/10.1007/978-3-030-78609-0_61

the unique characteristics of CNN learning ability makes it relies heavily on the existence of labeled datasets, the creation of such datasets requires a lot of resources, which will limit the application of CNN in some cases [3]. The image classification in intelligent security also has this problem. In some cases, their final performance is usually greatly reduced due to insufficient available data with labels. The current mainstream methods are mainly meta-learning, transfer learning and Bayes learning. Meta-learning has become an important research method for small-sample learning and has achieved good results, but it needs further improvement and development in the classification of complex image. Transfer learning can often greatly reduce the training cost of the target task, but it requires a strong correlation between the two tasks, which brings some constraints. Bayes learning is more similar to the way of human learning and more in line with the law of small sample learning, however, it requires more calculations.

In this paper, aiming at the difficulty of small sample learning in intelligent security, we raise a deep learning network framework with a combined classifier. The network can have less training cost and higher classification accuracy on small sample datasets. Compared with previous neural networks, our work has the following contributions: 1) We combine transfer learning with Bayes learning to reduce training time and improve classification accuracy. 2) The combined classifier not only maintains high classification accuracy, but also has high adaptability for classification on different databases.

2 Related Work

2.1 Meta Learning

Meta learning is also called learning to learn, and is mainly used to solve the problem of how the model learns. Its purpose is to enable the model to obtain a learning ability, which allows the model to automatically learn meta-knowledge. In small sample learning, meta learning refers to learning meta knowledge in a large number of prior tasks, and then use the prior knowledge to guide the model to learn better in small sample tasks. Long-Short Term Memory (LSTM) network has been proved to be applicable to meta learning in 2001 [4]. Based on this work, Memory-Augmented Neural Networks (MANN) [5] is proposed to solve single sample learning problems in 2016. The model takes neural truing machine as the basic model of MANN, which is a relatively successful attempt. Munkhdalai et al. [6] use convolutional neural networks to construct Meta Networks, which can use A neural network to predict some parameters of the target neural network, so it can speed up the learning rate of the network and reduce the calculation time. A large-scale lifelong memory method based on deep learning [7] is put forward, which can make neural networks show a high degree of meta learning ability, but there are still challenges on balance between efficiency and accuracy. Finn et al. [8] come up with a Model Agnostic Meta Learning (MAML). MAML is dedicated to finding parameters that are sensitive to each task in the neural network, and fine-tuning these parameters to make the model's loss function converge quickly, so that only training with fewer steps can see a better classification effect. In 2019, incremental learning and meta-learning is combined to propose the attention attractor networks (AAN) [9] model, which can use the knowledge learned from previous training to improve performance on new classes, making classification of the model more accurate. In the above-mentioned method based on meta-learning, meta learning needs to learn knowledge from multiple tasks, but the initial parameters of the model learned for different tasks are the same, ignoring the differences between different tasks, which is not rigorous. In addition, there is still a lot of room for improvement in the classification accuracy of more complex pictures.

2.2 Transfer Learning

Transfer learning is mainly based on that the learning between similar tasks have the same rules to follow. It reduces the training cost of the latter task (target task) by training the former task. Transfer learning is implemented in the feature extraction stage, and the key is to find the common features of the base data and the new data. Oquab et al. [10] make use of a model that has been trained on the ImageNet dataset, and on this basis, it extracts the features of the middle layer of the network to rebuild a new classification layer, thereby creating a new network model to classify the dataset. Wang et al. [11] propose a slightly different learning method in 2016. The main idea is to use the knowledge obtained when learning the model in a large sample set in order to identify new categories from a small number of samples. Global Prototype Learning (GPL) [12] is put forward, which builds a global prototype based on some examples. It has an activation function in the pre-classification layer of each new class. The model is also based on a CNN that has been trained with a large number of samples. The model, therefore, also depends on the performance of the CNN model. A novel method is raised to adapts the pre-trained neural network to novel categories by directly predicting the parameters of the fully connected layer [13]. There is a classification parameter predictor between the activation function and the classification layer of the model, which can better adjust the parameters of the classifier to make the image features and the classifier more matching. Qi et al. [14] came up with in 2018 to combine transfer learning and incremental learning to achieve small sample learning. The algorithm uses convolutional neural network as a feature extractor. After feature extraction of new samples, a classification weight vector is generated. It is expanded into the pre-trained classifier weights to achieve better results in the classification task of new samples. A new transfer learning method [15] is proposed to solve Cold start problem of vehicle model recognition under cross-scenario. This method uses relevant image information in common scenes to deal with the vehicle model recognition of rare scenes. The final performance of the target task in transfer learning depends on the latter task. How to effectively find the common features between the two task is also a key issue. In addition, how to effectively transfer features is also a problem to be solved.

2.3 Bayes Learning

Deep learning often requires a large amount of data for learning, so as to gain an understanding and generalization of some abstract concepts, and finally obtain a better classification effect. Its performance is closely related to the amount of data. However, for humans, even if there are not a large number of examples to learn, we can still imitate learning and obtain good results, and Bayes learning is exactly this kind of thinking. Bayes learning uses prior knowledge, which obtains the posterior distribution through small sample information, thereby directly obtaining the overall distribution. It uses probability to express the related uncertainty and realizes the process of learning and inference. Therefore, it is often not to obtain an optimal parameter value, but to set the distribution of the parameter (prior probability), after the conditional probability distribution is acquired with using the training data, the overall distribution of the whole sample is finally gained according to the bayes formula. Existing deep learning also introduces Bayes related knowledge, such as Bayes deep learning. The weight in the deep learning network is not a certain value but a distribution. Bayesian learning is proposed to solve fault detection [16] due to its effective logical reasoning. Lake et al. [17] propose Hierarchical Bayes Pro-gram Learning (HBPL) in 2013, which explains the structure of characters, and completes the classification and recognition of characters. The model introduces the concept of combination and causality, effectively solving small samples problem. After that, Lake et al. [18] raise a new Bayes learning framework in 2015, which can imitate human learning methods and separate basic components from existing characters. Then, the framework can create new characters based on these components, not just to classify and recognize characters. Bayes learning is more similar to human learning methods and is more suitable for small sample learning. However, because Bayes learning relies heavily on prior knowledge, it needs to combine background knowledge, prepared data and benchmark distributions to get estimates of prior knowledge. In addition, the computational complexity of Bayes learning in general is often high.

3 Methodology

3.1 Overview of the Framework

In this paper, the structure of our network is shown in Fig. 1. Since the lack of data in small sample learning is the greatest influence factor, so we can perform some basic data augmentation operations because CNN has the property of translation invariance. Therefore, the dataset can be expanded to prevent too little data. After completing data augmentation operations, we need to perform important feature extraction operations on the input images. This is a very critical step. In order to achieve good feature extraction results, we use pre-trained residual network (ResNet) as our basic network, and the pre-trained ResNet will save a lot of training time on datasets, which will bring great convenience. In this model, we use the feature vector obtained by ResNet as the final feature result, and then the model passes the feature vector to two classifiers, namely the SoftMax classifier and Bayes classifier. The final output of whole model will be adjusted according to the results of these two classifiers to get the best conclusion.

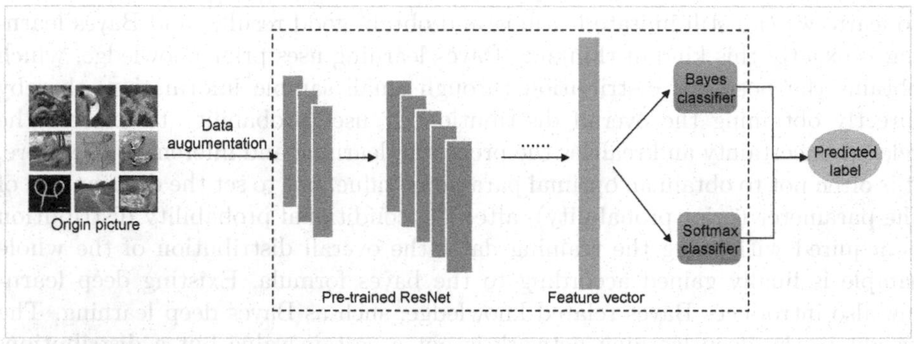

Fig. 1. The structure of our network.

3.2 How the Framework Resolves the Issue

In order to achieve better classification results, the basic model first need be determined. There are AlexNet, VGGNet, GoogLeNet and ResNet in CNNs [19]. The classification experiments show that the ResNet has the best classification capability [20] and the specific results are shown in the Table 1, Therefore, the ResNet network is decided as the basic network.

Table 1. The comparison of classification accuracy of CNNs on ImageNet dataset.

Model	Top-1 error	Top-5 error
VGG-16	28.07	9.33
GoogLeNet	–	9.15
ResNet-34	24.19	7.40
ResNet-50	22.85	6.71
ResNet-101	21.75	6.05
ResNet-152	21.43	5.71

In this model, the loss function is the cross entropy loss function. Through cross-entropy, we can determine the degree of similarity between the predicted data and the real data. When the cross-entropy is smaller, the predicted result is closer to the real result. It describes the distance between the actual output and the expected output. Assuming that the probability distribution p is the expected output, the probability distribution q is the actual output, and H is the cross-entropy, the cross-entropy calculation formula is as follows:

$$H(p,q) = -\sum_{i=1}^{n} p(x_i)log(q(x_i)) \tag{1}$$

This model deals with the calculation of cross entropy in image multi-classification. During the training period, the real label is y and prediction label is y'. The specific loss function calculation formula is as follows:

$$L(y, y') = -\frac{1}{n}\sum_{i=1}^{n} y_i \ln {y'}_i \tag{2}$$

In the process of model training, the optimization algorithm adopted by our model is Adam (Adaptive Moment Estimation) that can adjust the learning rates of different parameters adaptively. Its main advantage is that learning rates varies within a certain range in each iteration, which makes the parameters update more stable and efficient. After the model is trained, it can perform image classification. When the feature extraction is completed, the classifier will perform label prediction based on the image features. This model combines the classification results of two classifiers to predict, one is a classifier based on the naive bayes classification algorithm of Bernoulli distribution. The other is the SoftMax classifier.

Bernoulli naive Bayes classification assumes that each feature can be expressed by boolean variables, so the algorithm requires binary-valued feature vectors. After feature vector is processed, the classifier starts to classify the image. The decision rule for Bernoulli naive Bayes is as follows:

$$P(x_i|y) = P(x_i|y)x_i + (1 - P(x_i|y))(1 - x_i) \tag{3}$$

According to the decision rule formula, the algorithm calculates the probability that the label y has a feature x_i, and assumes that each feature is independently distributed, so the probability that different labels have the feature vector can be easily obtained. According to Bayes' fundamental theorem, the calculation formula of $P(y|x_i)$ is as follows:

$$P(y|x_i) = \frac{P(x_i|y)P(y)}{P(x_i)} \tag{4}$$

Combined with Bayes' fundamental theorem, it's easy to get $P(y|x_i)$ and the label y corresponding to the maximum $P(y|x_i)$ will be taken as the prediction result.

When the SoftMax classifier solves the multi-classification problem, assuming that the label y has a different k value, the determination formula of the SoftMax classifier is as follows:

$$f_\theta(x) = \begin{bmatrix} p(y=1|x;\theta) \\ p(y=2|x;\theta) \\ \vdots \\ p(y=k|x;\theta) \end{bmatrix} = \frac{1}{\sum_{i=1}^{k} e^{p(y^{(i)}|x;\theta)}} \begin{bmatrix} e^{p(y^{(i)}|x;\theta)} \\ e^{p(y^{(i)}|x;\theta)} \\ \vdots \\ e^{p(y^{(i)}|x;\theta)} \end{bmatrix} \tag{5}$$

In the above formula, θ, x and y represent parameters of the model, input data, and labels. The SoftMax classifier calculates the probability of each label and takes the label i that maximizes $e^{p(y^{(i)}|x;\theta)}$ as the final result.

For each input image, the above two classifiers will give two results. When the two results are the same, the model uses this result as the final result. When these two results are different, we found that based on experiments, the Bayes classifier performed better on simple images, while the SoftMax classifier performed better on complex images. Based on the above characteristics, we judge the complexity of the image according to the value of the feature vector, and determine the weight of the two classifiers accordingly, so that the classification result of the whole model is better. The definition formula of the combined classifier is as follows:

$$f(x_1, x_2) = \begin{cases} x_1, s \leq \text{threshold1} \\ \arg\max(P(x_i)), \text{threshold1} \leq s \leq \text{threshold2} \\ x_2, s \geq \text{threshold2} \end{cases} \tag{6}$$

In the above formula, x_1, x_2 are the prediction result of the Bayes classifier and the SoftMax classifier respectively, $P(x_i)$ is the probability of x_i $(i=1, 2)$ given by the classifier. By calculating the feature vector sum s and using the training data to calculate the relevant threshold, such as threshold1, threshold2 of the two classifiers. According to the feature vector sum of the input image, our model is able to make sure that one of the results is the final predicted result.

4 Experiment

4.1 Data and Evaluation Metrics

In this test, we used the public datasets Mini-ImageNet, CIFAR-FS and Omniglot for experiments. Mini-ImageNet dataset contains 100 classes color pictures, each of which has 600 samples. CIFAR-FS dataset contains 100 categories and there are 600 images in each class. Omniglot dataset contains 1623 different handwritten characters from 50 different letters. Each character was drawn online by 20 different people.

As shown in Fig. 2, most of the image components in the Mini-ImageNet dataset are very complex. There are some very similar classes in this database, and they have very similar characteristics. In addition, the background of the images in the database is usually very complicated, with lots of interference factors, such as plants, sky and water, etc. These factors will make the image classification of the Mini-ImageNet dataset more difficult. The image composition of the CIFAR-FS dataset is relatively simple. The database has a simple background, so there are no other interfering factors. There is usually only one object to be classified in an image, so the classification of this database is relatively easy. The images in the Omniglot database are handwritten characters from different regions. Compared with Mini-ImageNet and CIFAR-FS, this database requires the model to recognize text, but the number of recognizable classes is dozens of times that of the two databases.

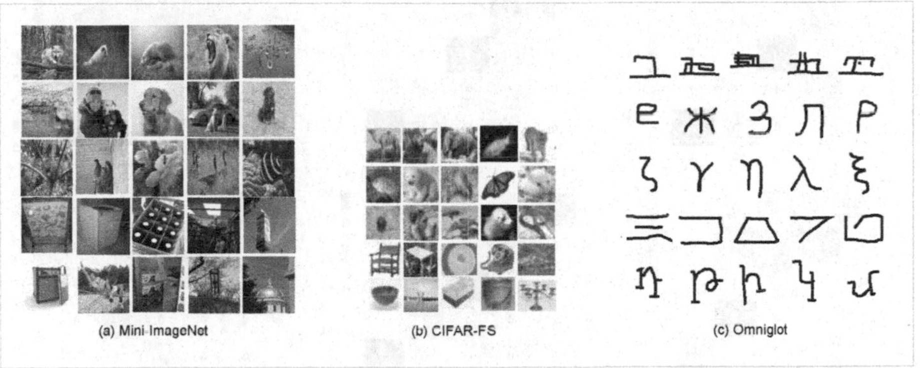

Fig. 2. The samples of the Mini-ImageNet, CIFAR-FS and Omniglot.

The evaluation criterion of small sample learning generally uses of N-way K-shot [21]. It means that N different categories of images will be randomly selected, and K samples of each class of image will be selected, then the model will use these $N \times K$ samples as training data, where $K \leq N$, and finally the accuracy of the model on the test set is used as the final evaluation metric. Here we use 5-way 5-shot as the evaluation metrics for this experiment. We repeat 20 sets of experiments on each dataset, and then calculate the mean and variance of classification accuracy.

4.2 Performance Results and Analysis

We take out one of the experimental results in the above three datasets and plot the confusion matrix of the experimental results. Figure 3 respectively display the results when our model separately makes use of SoftMax classifier, Bayes classifier and combined classifier on Mini-ImageNet, CIFAR-FS and Omniglot. We can find that the SoftMax classifier performs very well in the Mini-ImageNet database, while the Bayes classifier performs better in the Omniglot database, and there is little difference in performance in the CIFAR-FS database between them. Our combined classifier can combine the respective advantages of these two classifiers so that it can do well in the Mini-ImageNet database and the Omniglot database, and it can also have higher performance than these two classifiers in the CIFAR-FS database, which shows that our classifier is effective.

Fig. 3. The performances of different classifiers in the Mini-ImageNet, CIFAR-FS and Omniglot dataset.

Under the above conditions, we have compared with the result of other classic small sample learning methods such as MAML [8], TAML [22] and GNN [23], and the specific results are shown in the Table 2.

Table 2. The comparison of classification precision in few-shot learning methods.

Method/Dataset	Mini-ImageNet	CIFAR-FS	Omniglot
MAML	63.1 ± 0.92	66.8 ± 0.90	99.9 ± 0.10
TAML	66.0 ± 0.89	67.5 ± 0.86	99.8 ± 0.10
GNN	66.4 ± 0.63	68.2 ± 0.64	99.7 ± 0.06
Ours	95.0 ± 0.01	68.5 ± 0.01	78.0 ± 0.01

From the results of the Table 2, in the experiments on the Mini-ImageNet dataset, the accuracy of the pre-trained ResNet and our method is significantly higher than other small sample learning methods. In the experiments on the CIFAR-FS dataset, our method also performed better. In the experiments on the Omniglot dataset, meta-learning methods represented by MAML and TAML performed better. From the experiment results, we can find that our method performs better when the image data has more complex image components, and the meta learning method performs better when the image data has relatively simple components.

At the same time, we compare the classification effect of this method and a single classifier, and the specific results are shown in the Table 3.

Table 3. The comparison of classification precision in different classifier.

Method/Dataset	Mini-ImageNet	CIFAR-FS	Omniglot
ResNet + SoftMax classifier	94.5 ± 0.02	63.0 ± 0.01	56.5 ± 0.01
ResNet + Bayes classifier	68.5 ± 0.01	55.5 ± 0.01	81.0 ± 0.01
Ours	95.0 ± 0.01	68.5 ± 0.01	78.0 ± 0.01

Our method is based on the SoftMax classifier and Bayes classifier. SoftMax classifier is suitable for processing images with complex features, while Bayes classifier is suitable for processing images with simple features It can be seen that this method can effectively combine the advantages of the two classifiers, making the whole model have better classification effect. In short, the experimental results show that our combined classifier has better overall performance than a single classifier on different data sets, moreover, our method has certain advantages over existing advanced classification methods.

5 Conclusion

Deep learning techniques represented by CNN rely to large data, moreover, the labeled data available in the real world is usually not enough. In the image classification tasks of intelligent security, the performance of the neural network model will drop sharply if there are not enough samples for training. In this paper, we propose a method of combining classifiers based on transfer learning. The transfer learning makes our network embedded prior knowledge learned from other datasets into the current network to help reduce the number of samples required when training the network. In addition, the combined classifier we designed can make full use of the advantages of each classifier, which will further improve the classification performance of the model. The experiment results prove that our method can effectively improve the accuracy of image classification when the dataset is small. In the future research, we focus on how to further improve the classification accuracy. The reason why our method sometimes performs not as well as other methods is because of the deep network structure. Therefore, the number of network layers should be appropriately reduced to prevent overfitting. Besides, the classifiers and threshold parameters in the combined classifier are important factors that determine the performance of the classifier, different classifiers and threshold parameters should try to be adjusted in order to attain better performances.

Acknowledgement. We express our heartfelt thanks to google DeepMind team, Luca Bertinetto and Brenden M. Lake for providing the data.

Funding Information. Our research fund is funded by Fundamental Research Funds for the Central Universities (3072020CFQ0602, 3072020CF0604, 3072020CFP0601) and 2019 Industrial Internet Innovation and Development Engineering (KY1060020002, KY10600200008).

References

1. Shorfuzzaman, M., Masud, M.: On the detection of Covid-19 from chest X-ray images using CNN-based transfer learning. Comput. Mater. Continua **64**(3), 1359–1381 (2020)
2. Yang, Z., et al.: Deep transfer learning for military object recognition under small training set condition. Neural Comput. Appl. **31**(10), 6469–6478 (2018). https://doi.org/10.1007/s00521-018-3468-3
3. Song, C., Cheng, X., Gu, Y.X., Chen, B.J., Fu, Z.J.: A review of object detectors in deep learning. Comput. J. Artif. Intell. **2**(2), 59–77 (2020)
4. Hochreiter, S., Younger, A.S., Conwell, P.R.: Learning to learn using gradient descent. In: Dorffner, G., Bischof, H., Hornik, K. (eds.) ICANN 2001. LNCS, vol. 2130, pp. 87–94. Springer, Heidelberg (2001). https://doi.org/10.1007/3-540-44668-0_13
5. Santoro, A., Bartunov, S., Botvinick, M.: One-shot learning with memory-augmented neural networks. In: 33rd International Conference on Machine Learning, New York, NY, USA, pp. 1842–1850. JMLR.org (2016)
6. Munkhdalai, T., Yu, H.: Meta networks. In: International Conference on Machine Learning, Sydney, NSW, Australia, pp. 2554–2563 (2017)
7. Kaiser, L., Nachum, O., Roy, A.: Learning to remember rare events. In: International Conference on Learning Representations, Toulon, France, pp. 1–10 (2017)
8. Finn, C., Abbeel, P., Levine, S.: Model-agnostic meta-learning for fast adaptation of deep networks. In: International Conference on Machine Learning, Sydney, Australia, pp. 1126–1135 (2017)
9. Ren, M.Y., Liao, R.J., Fetaya, E.: Incremental few-shot learning with attention attractor networks. In: 33rd Conference on Neural Information Processing Systems, Vancouver, Canada, pp. 5275–5285 (2019)
10. Oquab, M., Bottou, L., Laptev, I.: Learning and transferring mid-level image representations using convolutional neural networks. In: IEEE Conference on Computer Vision and Pattern Recognition, Columbus, USA, pp. 1717–1724 (2014)
11. Wang, Y.-X., Hebert, M.: Learning to learn: model regression networks for easy small sample learning. In: Leibe, B., Matas, J., Sebe, N., Welling, M. (eds.) ECCV 2016. LNCS, vol. 9910, pp. 616–634. Springer, Cham (2016). https://doi.org/10.1007/978-3-319-46466-4_37
12. Athanasios, V., Nikolaos, D., Anastasios, D., Eftychios, P.: Few-shot learning in deep networks through global prototyping. Neural Netw. **94**, 159–172 (2017)
13. Qiao, S.Y., Liu, C.X., Shen, W.: Learning to learn: model regression networks for easy small sample learning. In: IEEE Conference on Computer Vision and Pattern Recognition, Salt Lake City, Utah, pp. 7229–7238 (2018)

14. Qi, H., Brown, M., Lowe, D.G.: Low-shot learning with imprinted weights. In: IEEE Conference on Computer Vision and Pattern Recognition, Salt Lake, UT, USA, pp. 5822–5830 (2018)
15. Wang, H., Xue, Q., Cui, T., Li, Y., Zeng, H.: Cold start problem of vehicle model recognition under cross-scenario based on transfer learning. Mater. Continua **63**(1), 337–351 (2020)
16. Maheswari, R.U., Umamaheswari, R.: Wind turbine drivetrain expert fault detection system: multivariate empirical mode decomposition based multi-sensor fusion with Bayesian learning classification. Intell. Autom. Soft Comput. **26**(3), 479–488 (2020)
17. Lake, B.M., Salakhutdinov, R., Tenenbaum, J.B.: One-shot learning by inverting a compositional causal process. In: 26th Conference on Neural Information Processing Systems, Lake Tahoe, Spain, pp. 2526–2534 (2013)
18. Lake, B.M., Salakhutdinov, R., Tenenbaum, J.B.: Human-level concept learning through probabilistic program induction. Science **350**(6266), 1332–1338 (2015)
19. Wu, H., Liu, Q., Liu, X.: A review on deep learning approaches to Image classification and object segmentation. Comput. Mater. Continua **60**(2), 575–597 (2019)
20. Sapijaszko, G., Mikhael, W.B.: An overview of recent convolutional neural network algorithms for image recognition. In: 2018 IEEE 61st International Midwest Symposium on Circuits and Systems, Windsor, ON, Canada, pp. 743–746 (2018)
21. Vinyals, O., Blundell, C., Lillicrap, T.: Matching networks for one shot learning. In: 30th International Conference on Neural Information Processing Systems, Barcelona, Spain, pp. 3630–3638 (2016)
22. Jamal, M.A., Qi, G.J.: Task agnostic meta-learning for few-shot learning. In: IEEE/CVF Conference on Computer Vision and Pattern Recognition, Long Beach, CA, USA, pp. 11711–11719 (2019)
23. Garcia, V., Bruna, J.: Few-shot learning with graph neural networks. In: International Conference on Learning Representations, Vancouver, Canada, pp. 1–13 (2016)

Intelligent Ecological Environment Control System Design

Juan Guo(✉) and Weize Xie

Guilin University of Electronic Technology, Vocational and Technical College, Beihai 536000, Guangxi, People's Republic of China

Abstract. According to the "863 Plan" of the People's Republic of China, the "intelligent ecological environment control system" is designed according to the use and specification of the corresponding rural facilities and its agricultural and forestry digital technology. The purpose is to liberate human resources, through the use of high and new technology to control a series of repetitive and cumbersome procedures that need human behavior regulation in the ecological environment, so as to realize the intensive production mode of low input, high yield and high efficiency, and realize the application and promotion of intelligent ecological environment control system, which can be widely used in agricultural greenhouses, house internal environment, home indoor garden, etc. In a series of complex and changeable environments. The main purpose of this design is to achieve high performance for ecological environment application, and to realize real-time CO_2 concentration measurement and control system. The performance index of the detector used in the ecological environment can largely determine the accuracy, stability and response time of the concentration adjustment of the detector. The temperature and humidity monitoring module selects DHT11 digital mode temperature and humidity composite sensor, and sends the measured data to the host STC89C52RC microcontroller regularly through weak current signal, so as to compare the predicted value to monitor whether the external environment is within the planning and design scope. If not, the central control single chip microcomputer chip will control the corresponding external equipment action to adjust the environment until the monitoring device is reached Stop when required by the condition.

Keywords: Single chip microcomputer system · STC89C52RC · SGP30 carbon dioxide monitoring · DHT11 temperature and humidity detection

1 Introduction

Please With the continuous development of social economy, the operation mode has changed from single to diversified, and the demand for cultural life and material life has increased sharply. In addition, China is a country with a large population, and the forestry area is constantly decreasing in the new scientific and technological life and social development.

X. Sun et al. (Eds.): ICAIS 2021, LNCS 12736, pp. 738–748, 2021.
https://doi.org/10.1007/978-3-030-78609-0_62

How to improve crop yield and maximize the utilization rate of field area is imminent. It is necessary for agricultural production to embark on the industrialization mode, that is, to make efficient use of resources, to integrate traditional knowledge, technology and experience, to introduce electronic information technology into modern automation equipment, and to maximize the realization of unmanned intelligent monitoring and optimal control of agricultural crops is one of the most basic conditions.

The nature under natural conditions is complex and changeable, which cannot fundamentally guarantee the development and harvest of agriculture. Through automatic control technology, we can create an optimal ecological environment suitable for the growth of crops, providing "one low and three high" services for flower and fruit vegetables, grain rice, endangered plants and ornamental potted plants, which are low input, high yield, high quality and high efficiency. Intelligent ecological environment control system has become a new research direction. It not only studies the living space environment of animals and plants, but also provides the feasibility data for the future research of human reproduction.

Since the industrial age, the wetland ecological environment has been deteriorating, and the underground mineral resources have been used for a long time in violation of the relevant national regulations. The main reason for the rapid deterioration is that the means of environmental protection are not strong enough. Industrial emissions, automobile exhaust, air conditioner and so on directly enter the atmosphere without meeting the emission standards, which results in a large number of harmful gases such as carbon dioxide, sulfur dioxide and carbon monoxide. Nowadays, the destruction of the ozone layer is becoming increasingly serious.

These gases not only do harm to human beings, but also have a completely irreversible impact on the living environment of animals and plants. Since 2010, China has grasped the rapid development trend of ecological environment destruction at the source, and has successfully built the first batch of ecological environment wetland nature reserves in response to the positive call of the state [1]. In the Wetland Nature Reserve, a number of composite sensors are applied to monitor the ecological environment indicators of the whole reserve. The temperature and humidity, oxygen content, carbon dioxide emission and other fixed-point and regular monitoring of specific animals and plants are carried out.

When the content of natural environment is not up to the standard, the system can automatically feedback, increase or decrease the corresponding parameters, so as to make the biological environment within the reasonable growth range. At present, most of the designs on the market are based on this design, such as agricultural irrigation greenhouse, family environment control, small-scale trial production test field, etc. the system has rich external expansion modules, which can provide external control equipment according to different environments and customer requirements, so as to meet the experimental requirements of the control objects.

The design of intelligent ecological environment control system is based on STC89C52RC microcontroller chip, and depends on peripheral devices such as SGP30 sensor, air atomizer, DHT11 sensor, motor set, etc. The control system includes LCD1602 display module, button module, alarm module, atomization module, motor fan module and power module.

The sensor monitor sends the data to the microcontroller chip STC89C52RC through the IO port for data analysis, and then sends the processed data to the LCD1602 LCD screen. According to the manual preset threshold and the test data, the corresponding motor control is executed.

Section 1 introduces the research background, research status at home and abroad, and systematically introduces the design ideas. Section 2 focuses on the block diagram of the system principle and the devices used, and provides reference for the following design. Section 3 introduces the principle of hardware circuit construction. Section 4 studies the programming of MCU algorithm and enforcement process. Section 5 analyzes the design and operation results through the physical display. Section 6 mainly summarizes and proposes ideas for the areas that need to be improved and explores future research directions.

2 System Principle Block Diagram

Compared with the more and more rapidly updated electronic hardware products in the market, the system adopts STC89C52RC single chip microcomputer chip with good price and performance [2]. The external module includes water molecule atomization module, sound alarm module and heat dissipation and humidity fan module. The whole system is driven by a 5 V regulated power supply module. The environmental monitoring sensor uses SGP30 sensor module and DHT11 temperature and humidity sensor module.

The display scheme is LCD1602 character LCD module, and the man-machine exchange mode is realized by button. The system schematic diagram is shown in Fig. 1.

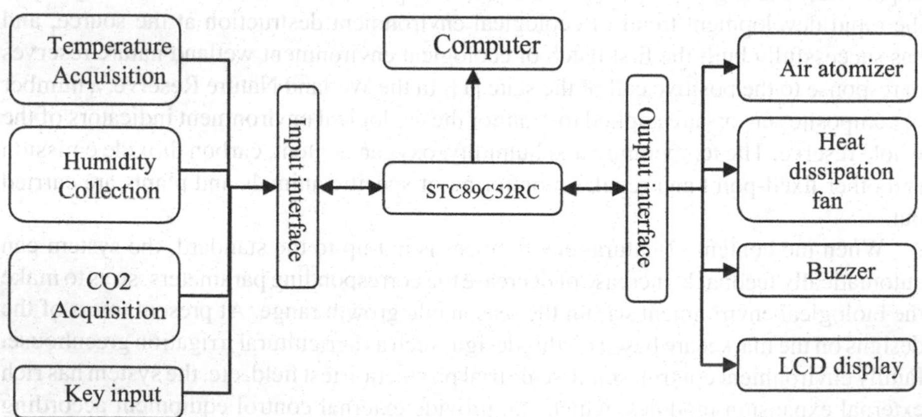

Fig. 1. System principle block diagram

2.1 STC89C52RC

This design uses modular thinking to build, A system employ a feedback control loop is table to tightly integrate sensing [3], with STC89C52RC chip as the control core. This MCU is a flash memory controller which is mainly suitable for medium and low-end flagship. It has 8K bytes memory system and users can freely modify the programming code [4]. The biggest reason is that the power consumption is low. It has 8 bits CMOS high-performance microcontroller, which can meet the storage requirements of SGP30, LCD1602 and other large capacity information devices. Compared with STC89C52 and AT89S52, the chip has more powerful processing capacity.

The system contains 8K bytes program storage space, 512 bytes data storage space and 4K bytes EEPROM memory space. It can fully ensure the smooth implementation of the design, and provide enough computing power and serial port output when new functions need to be developed in the later stage.

2.2 LCD1602 LCD Display

The design needs to achieve human-computer interaction, the corresponding key control is executed against the display screen. The display screen completely displays the changes of Arabic numerals, upper and lower case English and simple symbols, and adjustable brightness. Therefore, it can be normally and clearly displayed in day or night.

2.3 The Power Supply Module Adopts Dual Channel Power Supply Mode

The system is designed to carry more high-power equipment and consumes a lot of power, two power sources are used to separate them. One power supply ensures the basic operation of the single-chip microcomputer and the power supply for the use of LCD screen. The other power supply is used to ensure the use of motor and atomizer equipment.

2.4 DHT11 Temperature and Humidity Sensor

The sensor has a wide range of digital signal output for detailed sensor calibration. The resistance humidity sensing element and NTC temperature measuring element of the sensor are connected with high-performance chip through I/O port [5], and single bus communication is used to form obvious characteristics of strong anti-interference ability. It can realize small-scale space fixed-point test, and the test data fluctuates in the approximate range.

2.5 SGP30 Sensor

The design needs to monitor the concentration of carbon dioxide in the atmosphere in real time. SGP30 sensor is proposed. The other three metal oxide sensing elements are fused on the SGP30, which provides greater guarantee for accuracy. It is a sensitive air monitoring sensor in the atmospheric environment. It has multi pixel gas sensor.

The junction board provides all integrated MOX gas sensors [6]. It has IIC communication interface and fully calibrated output signal. The typical accuracy of measured value is about 14%, Science and technology management is faced with the problems of discontinuity of process and independence of relevant information system [7].

A single sensor on the market can only test one data value. Our system design needs to monitor multiple air values in the ecological environment, and different ecological environments require sensors with better comprehensive test performance, SGP30 can measure the content of carbon dioxide (CO_2) and volatile organic compounds (VOC) at the same time.

The response speed of SGP30 is faster and more intelligent than the old chip. The rapid development of Internet of things and smart home life benefits from this kind of composite sensor with better hardware performance. In terms of monitoring speed, it can better transmit the detected value to LCD screen in real time, which is convenient for later debugging.

3 Hardware Design

The minimum system MCU of single chip microcomputer is composed of STC89C52RC chip, reset RST circuit connected with reset terminal and clock circuit composed of two identical capacitors and crystal oscillator. The schematic diagram of STC89C52RC circuit is shown in Fig. 2.

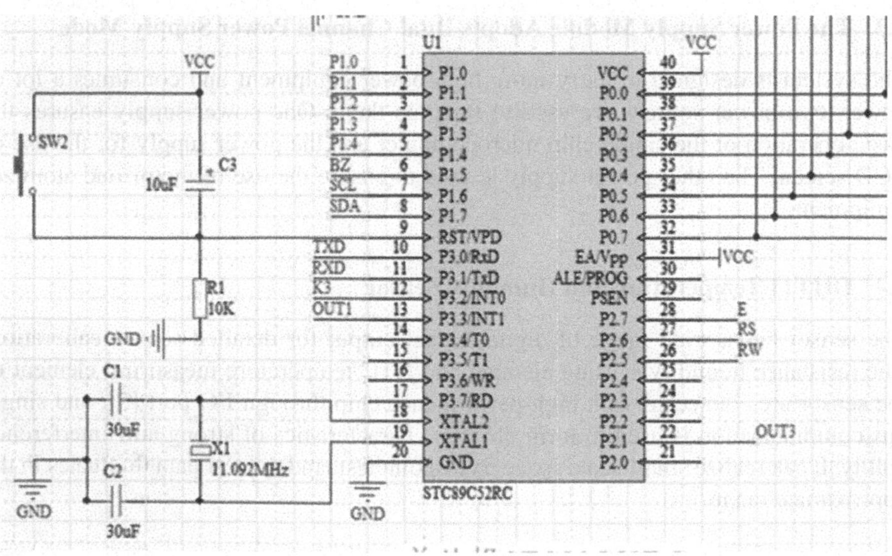

Fig. 2. Schematic diagram of STC89C52RC circuit

The working voltage of MCU is divided into two types, one is 5.5 V–3.3 V, the other is 3.8 V–2.0 V 3 V single-chip microcomputer. In this project, we use 5 V working voltage, connect VCC from the 40th pin for power supply, and connect GND ground wire at the 20th pin to form a closed circuit. In the above figure, port P0 is used as the output port of LCD. The reset circuit is connected to the RST of pin 9 and the xtal1 and xtal2 of clock circuit 19 and 20.

After the MCU is powered on or reset again, it provides a reverse voltage reset at the moment of power on through the reset circuit [8]. Using the principle that there is no sudden change between the capacitor and the voltage, the capacitor is not charged at the moment of power on, and the voltage at both ends is zero. At this time, a reset pulse signal is provided to charge the capacitor until the voltage at both ends of the capacitor is consistent with the voltage at both ends of the power supply, and the circuit enters into normal operation state, which completes the whole process of power on reset. With the same principle, in the process of operation and use of the equipment, the single-chip microcomputer will also appear logic errors, wrong use of keys, etc., the use of reset button can also make the microcontroller normal operation [9].

The crystal oscillator of single chip microcomputer is similar to the spring of clock. It is called crystal oscillator [10]. It is an ultra-high precision and super stable oscillator. A sine wave with stable frequency and peak value can be generated by a certain clock circuit, as shown in the figure above, including two 30 μF capacitors and an 11.0592 MHz crystal oscillator. The single-chip microcomputer needs pulse signal as the trigger signal to start, and crystal oscillator is the supplier of pulse signal, and this pulse is the working speed of single-chip microcomputer.

If the reset button has two high-level machine cycle outputs, it is the reset operation signal. As shown in the above figure, the reset button circuit uses manual reset button, connected with a 10 μF capacitor and a 10k resistance.

The hardware circuit is mainly built according to STC89C52RC single chip microcomputer chip. The external module includes water molecule atomization module, sound alarm module and heat dissipation and humidity fan module. The whole system is driven by 5 V regulated power supply module. The environmental monitoring sensor uses atmospheric carbon dioxide SGP30 sensor module and DHT11 temperature and humidity sensor module.

The display panel is LCD1602 character liquid Crystal module, man-machine exchange mode through the button module. The layout of power consumption is planned, and the high power consumption devices are preferentially arranged in the power supply accessories, which can ensure the sufficient operation of the subsequent power supply voltage. The stability and accuracy of the operation of the microcontroller chip can be ensured by using the external clock crystal oscillator.

In the design of the double-layer board, the current should be filtered by the filter capacitor before being used by the device. At the same time, the influence of the power supply noise generated by the device itself on the devices in the middle and lower reaches of the circuit should be fully considered. According to the design experience, the bus structure design is better, and the influence of the voltage drop caused by the long transmission distance on the device must be considered in the circuit design, the high power consumption module is placed and installed in the power interface accessory, which can achieve the highest efficiency. In order to reduce the interference between the signal and the external power amplifier, only the signal of GND is connected to the bottom of the analog circuit. There is no GND line connected, this difference is to pay more attention to avoid short circuit.

4 Analysis of System Program Structure

In this design, the code is written in the form of total score, and the main program is used to program the subprograms of SGP30 carbon dioxide sensor program, button program, alarm program, DHT11 temperature and humidity sensor program and other related subprograms, so as to realize the real-time monitoring and data display of wetland ecology [11].

The specific process is that the SGP30 carbon dioxide sensor detects the carbon dioxide data in the atmosphere and the temperature and humidity data detected by the temperature and humidity sensor, sets the corresponding threshold, compares the detected data with the set threshold, when the set threshold is exceeded, the alarm program is started, the corresponding motor module is run, and the unmanned dispatching system is realized, and three detection items are monitored in real time. The monitoring value is displayed on LCD1602.

After the microcontroller is powered on, the reset circuit will initialize first, then execute the main program function, pre scan once, and then wait for 1 min for sensor preheating, call the sub function to return the corresponding monitoring value, and compare with the preset value, it will scan and check whether the user presses the key module in each mechanical cycle, once the jitter is eliminated and confirmed, the preset value parameter setting will be executed.

In the fixed interface, if the real-time monitoring value exceeds the preset value, the alarm function will be entered, and the corresponding motor unit module will be executed to transmit the monitoring value to LCD1602 for display at the same time. The design flow of the main program is shown in Fig. 3.

The software is written in the form of total score and classified according to each module, which not only improves the efficiency of writing, but also shortens the debugging time. Because SGP30 sensor is a digital communication sensor, STC89C52RC needs to rely on IIC protocol to communicate with it. Therefore, in this system design, the writing of SGP30 sensor is separated separately, which ensures the logic and beauty.

The biggest advantage of writing the program into modules is that once a device has problems, it can find the corresponding module program directly, which simplifies the complexity of the main function, which is convenient for later rewriting and beautiful. At the same time, modular systems are more complete and logical, Provide more possibilities for product upgrade and subsequent function expansion. The system design software writing framework is shown in Fig. 4.

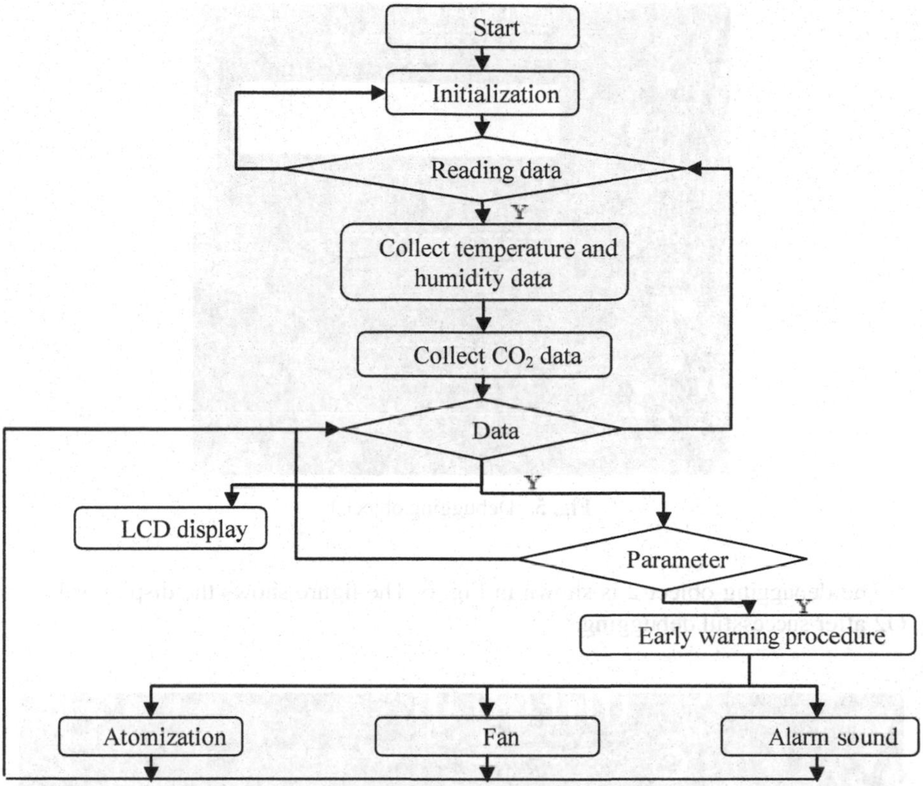

Start
Initialization
Reading data
Y
Collect temperature and humidity data
Collect CO_2 data
Data
Y
LCD display
Parameter
Y
Early warning procedure
Atomization
Fan
Alarm sound

Fig. 3. Flow chart of main program design

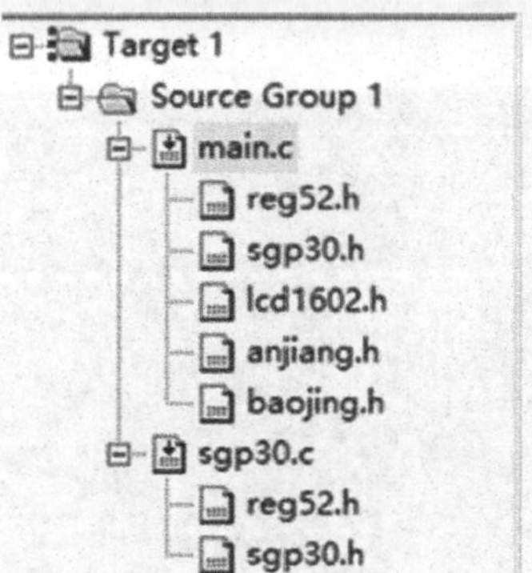

Fig. 4. Program framework

5 Achieved Purpose

The debugging object 1 is shown in Fig. 5. The figure shows the display value on LCD1602 after successful debugging.

Fig. 5. Debugging object 1

The debugging object 2 is shown in Fig. 6. The figure shows the display value on CO2 after successful debugging.

Fig. 6. Debugging object 2

The concentration of carbon dioxide will affect the living environment of animals and plants. The reaction of carbon dioxide concentration to human body is described in detail. The comparison table of CO_2 concentration in the air is shown in Table 1.

Table 1. Test table of CO_2 concentration in air

Category	CO_2 concentration value	Physiological response of human body
1	350–450 ppm	Same as general outdoor environment
2	350–1000 ppm	Fresh air and smooth breathing
3	1000–2000 ppm	Feel the air is cloudy and start to feel drowsy
4	2000–5000 ppm	Headache, fever, insomnia, boredom, maladjustment, tachycardia, nausea
5	>5000 ppm	It is easy to cause permanent brain injury, coma and death [12]

It can be found from Table 1 that when the concentration of carbon dioxide in the atmosphere is in the second category, and the concentration value is 350–1000 ppm, it is the most comfortable environment for human body. The high temperature alarm settings at 25°, and the low temperature alarm settings at 19°, the humidity alarm settings at 96% and 80%, the CO2 alarm settings at 500 ppm.

6 Conclusion

This design can detect the indoor temperature and humidity, detect the concentration of indoor carbon dioxide, in the case that the index is not up to standard or exceeds the standard, it can realize the functions of automatic heating, heat dissipation, humidification, exhaust gas discharge, etc. The improvement of these functions can greatly reduce the use of human resources and liberate the labor force, and it is undoubtedly better to replace human resources with machines in repetitive and monitoring work.

In this design, the SGP30 sensor is selected based on the consideration of monitoring transmission speed. To monitor the atmospheric change in a local range, the rapid response ability is required to control the growth needs of the experimental object in real time. Moreover, this sensor has excellent performance and strong reliability. In the long-term standby, it will not be due to the weather or temperature, as a result, frequent failures occur. At the same time, It saves the expense of daily maintenance of personnel and reduces the capital of frequent replacement of equipment.

The use of DHT11 sensor is to achieve integrated layout, this design also focuses on the development of the test performance of this sensor, in the high temperature and humidity environment can still maintain stable output work, It has the ability to work on standby for a long time, and the subsequent equipment is easy to replace, for this design provides a reliable guarantee.

For the sake of cost, the original oxygen concentration sensor is replaced by the carbon dioxide concentration sensor for indirect measurement of biological activity. If conditions permit, the oxygen concentration sensor can be directly designed to detect the biological environment more comprehensively, Ecosystem analysis will be more accurate, the output of more accurate feedback data, and the design will be more perfect.

In order to reflect the safety and reliability of the design system, the chip board of the core processing is packaged independently, which ensures that it works in a suitable temperature, humidity, shade and shade environment, and is isolated from the ecological environment. Remote control is carried out by sensors and motors, which is also convenient for visual maintenance and monitoring values of later personnel.

References

1. Kai, Z., et al.: Introduction to Ecological Environmental Supervision, vol. 463, pp. 1093–1110. China Environmental Science Press, 1 December 2003
2. Gong, X., et al.: Development of integrated training platform based on single chip microcomputer. J. Xi'an Aeronaut. Tech. Coll. (5), 80–81 (2012)
3. Zou, L., Wang, J., Jiang, L.Y.: A progressive output strategy for real-time feedback control systems. Intell. Autom. Soft Comput. **26**, 631–639 (2020)
4. Wang, T., et al.: Principle and Application of PLC. National Defence Industry Press, 1 June 2006
5. Zhou, J., et al.: Sensing Technology and Application. Central South University Press, 1 March 2005
6. Lai, Q.: Interface Between Sensor and Single Chip Microcomputer and Examples. Beijing University of Aeronautics and Astronautics Press, Beijing (2008)
7. Chen, N., Li, H., Fan, X.X., Kong, W.L., Xie, Y.H.: Research on intelligent technology management and service platform. J. Artif. Intell. **2**, 149–155 (2020)
8. Tan, S.: Design and Implementation of smoke alarm system based on single chip microcomputer. J. Daqing Normal Univ. (6), 40–41 (2018)
9. Yang, X.: Research on the design of dual controllable power supply drive circuit, pp. 24–25. Hebei University of Technology, Hebei (2006)
10. Zeng, L.: Analog electronics. Electronic Industry Press, Beijing (2009)
11. Liu, Y., Zhao, D.: Design of temperature and humidity detection system based on DSP and UCOS. Electron. Manuf. (1), 10–12 (2018)
12. Xu, X., et al.: New Progress in Modern Clinical Acute and Critical Illness. China Science and Technology Press, Beijing (1996)

Author Index

Printed in the United States
by Baker & Taylor Publisher Services

Printed in the United States
by Baker & Taylor Publisher Services